social PSYCHOLOGY 6e

Project Development Manager: Terri Beaudette

Project Development Assistant: Brandi Cornwell

Managing Editor: Joyce Bianchini

Production Manager: Della Brackett

Sales Manager: Robert Rappeport

Marketing Manager: Richard Schofield

Typesetting: Esther Scannell and Rhonda Minnema

Permissions Coordinator: Janai Bryand

Cover and Interior Design: Michael Myers

Photo Researcher: Michelle Hipkins

Text and Cover Printing: QuadGraphics

For information address BVT Publishing, LLC, P.O. Box 492831, Redding, CA 96049-2831

Some ancillaries, including electronic and print components, may not be available to customers outside the United States.

ISBN: 978-1-61882-033-4

Copyright © 2012 by BVT Publishing, LLC

PUBLISHING

The publisher of affordable textbooks

Dedication

To the women in my life:
Cheryl, Amelia, and Lillian;
to my parents, Lou and Joyce,
and to my brother and sister,
Randy and Susie–
together, and singly, they influence
the essential elements of my life.

About the Author

Stephen L. Franzoi is a professor of psychology at Marquette University in Milwaukee, Wisconsin. He received his BS in both psychology and sociology from Western Michigan University, his PhD in psychology from the University of California at Davis, and was a postdoctoral fellow in the NIMH-sponsored Self Program at Indiana University. At Marquette University, Professor Franzoi teaches both undergraduate and graduate courses in social psychology and has served as assistant editor of *Social Psychology Quarterly* and associate editor of *Social Problems*. His research has been published in a number of places, including *Journal of Personality and Social Psychology, Personality and Social Psychology Bulletin, Psychology of Women Quarterly, American Sociological Review, Journal of Research in Personality, Sex Roles,* and *Journal of Personality*. As an active researcher in the area of body esteem, Dr. Franzoi has discussed his work in such media outlets as the *New York Times, USA Today*, National Public Radio, and the *Oprah Winfrey Show*. Because of his desire to apply social psychological knowledge to real world problems, Dr. Franzoi provides gender equity and multicultural workshops to schools and organizations, including NAACP-sponsored programs. He and Cheryl Figg are the proud parents of Amelia and Lillian.

social
PSYCHOLOGY 6e

Stephen L. Franzoi

BRief •••• contents

Table of contents

Chapter 7
Social Influence 258

Chapter 8
Group Behavior 306

Chapter 9
Interpersonal Attraction 348

Chapter 11
Aggression 440

Chapter 12
Prosocial Behavior: Helping Others 484

Preface ● ● ● ●

The sixth edition of *Social Psychology* marks a new beginning for this textbook that I think both professors and students will appreciate. As anyone who teaches or takes college courses knows, textbook prices have "gone through the roof" in recent years, causing resentment throughout academia. In an attempt to resolve this problem, I have partnered with BVT Publishing to bring you this new edition at a substantially lower price than what was offered by my previous publisher. My ancillary team from past editions has joined me in this new endeavor and I am certain you will be very happy with our final product.

Regarding this course of study, one of the most important lessons I have learned as a teacher is that you should always have a good story to tell. Fortunately, social psychology is a dynamic science consisting of many fascinating stories. These "scientific stories" form the basis of this text, and my goal as an instructor and a textbook author is to emphasize the process of research in social psychology: to engage students in an exploration of how what we know about social psychology has evolved, to put students in the mind-set of the social psychologists who have left their mark on the field. Together, we explore the stories behind these classic and contemporary studies.

As a textbook author, I've learned that the text, too, must have its own story—one that resonates with students and instructors alike and helps tie all of the various theories and concepts together. In this sixth edition, I continue to emphasize a central theme—one that has worked well for me and my students—that I believe is essential to how we think about social psychology, and one that will encourage students to think about their own stories as they explore the concepts in this course.

THE SELF: AN INTEGRATED THEME

Social psychology is sometimes described as a scientific discipline consisting of loosely connected research topics with no "grand theory" to connect everything. Although we have no single theory that neatly packages social psychology for our students, I end the analysis of the topic areas in each chapter with a discussion of how these particular theories and studies "fit" into our overall understanding of social behavior. Throughout the text I emphasize a core concept in social psychology: the self. Social psychology is the study of how the individual, as a self, interacts with the social world. As selves we become active agents in our social world, not only defining reality but also anticipating the future and often changing our behavior to be in line with the anticipated reality. This essential fact of social living has always been at the heart of this book, and it reflects the orientation of social psychology in the twenty-first century.

To that end, the theme of the self is reflected in this text through the following:

- In Chapter 1, a section titled "The Self Is Shaped by—and Shapes—the Social Environment" introduces this central theme.
- The central theme of the self is integrated through the discussion of key concepts, including the following examples: Chapter 3's extensive examination of various self-related theories; Chapter 4's discussion of how self-esteem and self-regulation influence the hindsight bias and thought suppression; Chapter 5's look at the role of the self in attitude formation and persuasion; Chapter 6's analysis of reducing prejudice through self-regulation; Chapter 7's discussion of compliance and self-consistency; Chapter 8's coverage of reduced self-awareness and deindividuation; Chapter 9's research on gender differences in body esteem; Chapter 10's analysis of the self-inclusionary process of intimacy; Chapter 11's look at the self-regulation of aggressive thoughts; and Chapter 12's research on how giving and receiving help can affect self-esteem.
- Beginning with Chapter 3's analysis of the self, each chapter concludes with a "Big Picture" summary. These summaries discuss how we, as self-reflective creatures, can use the social psychological knowledge covered in the chapter to understand and actively shape our social world.

EMPHASIZING SOCIAL PSYCHOLOGY'S RESEARCH BASIS

Often I hear from instructors that students enter the course assuming that social psychology is "just plain common sense." It's a common goal among most social psychology instructors to emphasize that social psychology is research based and relies heavily on the experimental method.

With this common goal in mind, I emphasize research methods throughout the book in the following ways:

- Chapter 2, "Conducting Research in Social Psychology," expands on the introductory chapter's distinction between the scientific process and everyday thinking. This chapter explores the process of conducting research, diverse scientific methods and research strategies, emerging new scientific methodologies and measuring instruments, and includes comprehensive coverage of survey construction, meta-analysis, and ethical issues.
- Each chapter contains newly published research on social behavior and in-depth descriptions and critiques of selected studies.
- **Applications** sections at the end of Chapters 3–12 demonstrate how the theories and research in a particular area of social psychology can be applied to real-world settings and to your life.

TEXT ORGANIZATION CHAPTER BY CHAPTER

As with the fifth edition, the sixth edition of *Social Psychology* consists of twelve chapters. Chapter 1 introduces the discipline of social psychology, describes its history, and discusses its organizing principles. This chapter also makes a distinction between scientific analysis and everyday thinking. Chapter 2 expands on this discussion by describing the research process and the scientific methods that social psychologists employ. This chapter also examines ethical issues in conducting research and the effect of values on scientific inquiry and on the application of scientific knowledge. The purpose of these two chapters is to provide the background knowledge necessary for students to critically analyze the social psychological topics covered in the chapters that follow.

Chapter 3 analyzes how we attend to and understand a very important person in our lives, namely, ourselves. How does self-awareness influence our social behavior? How are we shaped by our surroundings? How do we balance our need to have positive self-beliefs with our need to have accurate self-beliefs? How do we present ourselves to others?

Chapter 4 explores how we interpret, analyze, remember, and use information about the social world. Are we careful or lazy social thinkers? What cognitive traps are we prone to fall into? Also, how do we form first impressions and how do we explain the causes of other people's behavior?

Chapter 5 examines the nature of attitudes and persuasion, including how attitudes are formed, how they predict behavior, and how they can be changed through persuasion. Can you have unconscious attitudes? Is cognitive consistency an important aspect of attitude formation and change? How does the source of a persuasive message, its content, the manner of transmission, and the nature of the audience determine whether it will be effective? We will examine persuasion not only from the "outside" but also from the "inside," meaning we will explore the cognitive processes of the "persuadee."

In Chapter 6, we will tackle an issue that has quite possibly plagued humankind since the dawn of our species, namely, prejudice and discrimination. How is stereotyping related to intergroup intolerance? What are the social causes of prejudice and discrimination? How do the victims of prejudice cope with and respond to stigmatization? Are there ways to combat these negative intergroup evaluations and behavior?

Chapter 7 examines how social power is used to influence our thoughts and behavior. How do personal, social, and cultural factors impact conformity? What happens to nonconformists or those who hold minority opinions in groups? How can we get others to comply with our requests? Furthermore, how susceptible are we to the destructive commands of authority figures?

Chapter 8 looks more closely at the psychology of the group. How does a collection of people become a group? How does the group shape the behavior of individual members? Do groups make more cautious or more risky decisions than individuals? How do leaders emerge in a group, and are there different types of leaders? Finally, what happens when group interests and individual interests conflict?

Chapter 9 examines our desire to seek out the company of others. Why do we seek affiliation? What characteristics of the situation and of others heighten our affiliation desires? Why are some of us more people oriented than others, and why are some of us chronically worried about everyday social life?

Chapter 10 investigates how this interpersonal process can progress to friendship and romance. Do our early childhood experiences shape how we view intimacy? Do men and women differ in their friendship patterns and romantic desires? How can we understand the social psychology of love? What strengthens and weakens romantic relationships?

Chapter 11 explores the difficult issue of how social interaction can sometimes erupt into aggressive outbursts. To what degree are aggressive actions driven by our biology? Should we act out our aggressive desires to "purge" ourselves of their influence, or is this a strategy doomed to backfire on us? Are there certain regions of the country where aggressive outbursts are more likely? What influence do television and pornography have on our aggressive tendencies?

Finally, in Chapter 12 we scrutinize the helping process by trying to answer five basic questions: Why do we help others? When do we help others? Who among us is most likely to help? Who are we likely to help? Are there hidden costs for receiving help? In pursuing these questions, we will explore how inherited genetic tendencies, gender socialization, parental modeling, and political orientation can shape our helping tendencies. We will also examine the decisions we make in deciding to help—or not help—others in need.

HALLMARKS AND NEW FEATURES OF THE SIXTH EDITION

Revising a textbook is like renovating a building. The goal is to retain those designs and features that are essential in maintaining the integrity and attractiveness of the original product, while enhancing and updating the contents so that it will continue to serve a useful function. Just as successful architects base their renovations on the feedback of those who actually live in the buildings being restored, I have substantially based my "renovations" of this sixth edition on the opinions expressed by professors and students who used the fifth edition. For those of you who "inhabited" previous editions, I think you will find many familiar features among the new additions. The primary goal of this updating process was to make the sixth edition of *Social Psychology* an even better structure for teaching and learning.

The sixth edition offers the following familiar features:

- **Critical thinking questions** encourage students to examine their own social surroundings while they simultaneously digest social psychological theories and research. These questions often invite students to guess a study's hypotheses, results, or alternative interpretation of findings. The questions, many of which are new, are either inserted in the captions of figures, tables, and photos, or are displayed in prominent critical thinking sidebars. Answers to the former can be found in the chapter; while the end-of-book appendix offers a possible answer to the latter.

- **Coverage of diversity and cultural analysis** is fully integrated in each chapter, rather than treated as a separate boxed insert or separate chapter. As in previous editions, I seek to foster a sense of inclusion for all readers. For example, in the discussion of social behavior in a cross-cultural context, the particular aspect of culture highlighted is individualism versus collectivism. Why? Throughout the history of American social psychology, the concept of individualism has been an influential, yet unexamined, force directing our analysis of social life. All too often American social psychologists have generalized their findings about social life in this country to all the inhabitants of the planet. Now, with the emerging influence of social psychology in Europe and in developing countries, some of the basic assumptions of the relationship of the individual to the group have been questioned. This text discusses how people from individualist and collectivist cultures respond to similar social situations, helping students to understand the richness and flexibility of social life.

- **The evolutionary perspective** illuminates how a universal pattern of social behavior might have developed. One of the benefits of cross-cultural research is that it allows us to not only identify those aspects of social behavior that vary from one culture to the next but also to identify social behaviors that are not culturally constrained. When a universal social behavior is identified, discussion turns to how this pattern of behavior may have evolved. Throughout the text I examine how evolutionary forces might have left us with certain behavioral capacities, while also recognizing that current social and environmental forces encourage or discourage the actual development and use of these capacities.

- **Social neuroscience** uses the latest cutting-edge technology to study the relationship between neural processes of the brain and social processes. This "window into the brain" provides another layer of knowledge in our understanding of social interaction.

- **More than twenty Self/Social Connection Exercises** contain self-report questionnaires currently being used by researchers, and the results of studies employing them are part of the text material. In these exercises, students are encouraged to consider how this text material relates to their own lives. Thus, as students learn about various social psychological theories and relevant research findings, they also learn something about themselves.

- **Bulleted end-of-section summaries** provide a concise presentation to better facilitate students' studying. The bulleted summaries in the fifth edition were well received and have been retained in the new edition.

Other new features of the sixth edition are as follows:

- Positive psychology investigates ways to enrich human experience and maximize human functioning. Throughout this text, information is presented about positive psychology topics, including morality, that relate to chapter material.

- Streamlined in depth description of scientific studies within the main body of each chapter rather than as single end-of-chapter featured studies.

- **Updated research and theories** are presented utilizing eight hundred new citations, studies, theories, and examples.

CHAPTER-BY-CHAPTER CHANGES

Chapter 1: Introducing Social Psychology

- New chapter-opening story
- New section covering how social psychology is studied in both psychology and sociology
- Expanded coverage on the history of social psychology and its European roots
- New section on positive psychology as a new perspective in social psychology
- New section on gender when introducing the sociocultural perspective

Chapter 2: Conducting Research in Social Psychology

- New section on the self-correcting nature of the scientific method
- Expanded coverage of meta-analysis as a research tool
- New section on why the study of actual behavior has declined in social psychology

Chapter 3: The Self

- New section on culture and self-awareness
- Expanded coverage of self-regulation
- New coverage of the multiple self-aspects framework
- New coverage of online self-presentation strategies

Chapter 4: Social Cognition and Person Perception

- New neuroscientific research on the social psychology of gossiping
- New section on the confirmation bias
- New research on gender and the fundamental attribution error

Chapter 5: Attitudes and Persuasion
- New section on immoral behavior and cognitive dissonance
- New research on the use of emotion in political ads

Chapter 6: Prejudice and Discrimination
- New chapter-opening story
- New research on the psychological impact of being stigmatized
- New research on why some White Americans fear multiculturalism
- New research on ambivalent sexism and reactions to female politicians
- Expanded coverage of sexual prejudice

Chapter 7: Social Influence
- New chapter-opening story
- New research on how peer pressure shapes expressions of prejudice
- New discussion on social influence and pluralistic ignorance
- New research on how the belief in a Supreme Being affects ostracism
- Expanded coverage of false confessions

Chapter 8: Group Behavior
- Expanded coverage of jury deliberations
- New research on how biculturalist thinking can affect groupthink tendencies

Chapter 9: Interpersonal Attraction
- New chapter-opening story
- New research on friends' effects on social anxiety
- New research on the contagiousness of loneliness

Chapter 10: Intimate Relationships
- New section on friendships and mate rivalry
- New section on "Friends With Benefits" relationships
- New section on long-distance friendships
- New research on online dating and speed dating
- New research on how romantic happiness is shaped by positive illusions versus accurate judgments

Chapter 11: Aggression
- New coverage of sarcastic humor as a form of hostile aggression
- New research on gender and perceptions of physical aggression
- New research on hormonal activity and physical aggression

Chapter 12: Prosocial Behavior: Helping Others
- New section on how political and social class differences shape willingness to help
- New research on the bystander effect

Supplements ● ● ● ●

A complete learning and teaching package, available at www.BVTlab.com, accompanies *Social Psychology, Sixth Edition.* Each component of this package has been thoroughly revised and expanded to support the sixth edition. **Student resources,** authored by David Jones at Westminster College, include chapter outlines, key term flashcards, and review questions. Password–protected instructor resources include an **Instructor's Manual, PowerPoint Slides** and a **Test Bank**, authored by Kris Vasquez at Alverno College.

Supplements for Instructors

Study Guide

A thorough and practical student study guide includes learning objectives, chapter outlines, questions, and ideas that help the student review the material presented in this text. Also included are student activities and projects designed to enhance the practical application of sociological concepts.

Instructor's Manual

A comprehensive manual provides a wealth of teaching suggestions, objectives and resources, outside activities stressing the importance of sociology to personal lives, suggested readings from short stories and novels, a guide to films, and much more.

Test Bank

An extensive test bank of approximately nine hundred questions is available to instructors in both hard copy and electronic forms. Each chapter consists of a variety of multiple choice, short answer and essay questions. Each question is referenced to the appropriate text page to make verification quick and easy.

Course Management Software

BVT's Course Management Software (Respondus) allows for the creation of randomly generated tests and quizzes that can be downloaded directly into a wide variety of course management environments, such as Blackboard, Web CT, Desire 2 Learn, Angel, E Learning and others.

Power Points

A set of PowerPoint slides is available to instructors who adopt this book. The set includes charts, tables, and graphs from the text, in addition to charts and graphs from other sources.

Customization

Customize This Book

If you have additional material that you would like to add (handouts, lecture notes, syllabus, etc) or simply rearrange and delete content, BVT Publishing's custom publishing division can help you modify this book's content to produce a book that satisfies your specific instructional needs. BVT Publishing has the only custom publishing division that puts your material exactly where you want it to go, easily and seamlessly. Please visit www.bvtpublishing.com or call us at 1-800-646- 7782 for more information on BVT Publishing's Custom Publishing Program.

BVTLab For Instructors

BVTLab is a simple, robust, online lab for college instructors and their students. It is an affordable option for students, with student lab fees costing only $19.99 for a full-semester course. Even if you do not use the lab as your online classroom, your students can still take advantage of the many free student resources.

Course Setup

BVTLab has an easy-to-use, intuitive interface that allows instructors to quickly set up their courses and grade books, and replicate them from section to section and semester to semester. Multiple choice and true/false questions can be delivered online as practice questions, homework assignments, quizzes, and tests—each of which draws from a separate bank of questions.

Homework, quizzes, and tests have assigned start and end times; and tests can be proctored in the computer lab or self-proctored for distance learners. Homework and quizzes offer optional hints and instructor tips. In addition, practice questions can be linked to fully worked solutions and multimedia tutorials. Instructors can preview and manually select questions assigned to students, or they can use the "quick-pick" feature in BVTLab to generate sets of questions.

Grade Book

Using an assigned passcode, students register themselves into the grade book. All homework, quizzes, and tests are automatically graded and recorded in the grade book. In addition, instructors can manually enter or modify scores, with provisions for extra credit, attendance, and participation grades.

Communications Tools

Instructors can post discussion threads to a class forum and then monitor and moderate student replies. Important notifications can also be sent directly to each student via email.

BVTLab For Students

BVTLab is a comprehensive online learning environment designed to help students succeed. It provides a complete online classroom, as well as the practice questions, learning aids, and communication tools that students need for success. For classes taught within the lab, students can view their grades for all completed work and also review prior homework and quizzes to identify areas that require additional study.

An online discussion forum allows students to interact with each other and the instructor to explore challenging concepts and share other resources, while providing an online community for distance learning.

Even if your instructor does not use the lab as a classroom, you are always welcome to visit as a guest and take advantage of the many free and premium resources, as described below.

Student Resources

Student resources, geared towards students needing additional assistance or those seeking complete mastery of the content, are available in BVTLab for this textbook. The following resources are available:

Practice Questions

Students work through hundreds of practice questions online. Questions are multiple choice or true/false format and are graded instantly for immediate feedback.

Flashcards

BVTLab includes sets of flashcards for each chapter that reinforce the key terms and concepts from the textbook.

Chapter Summaries

A convenient and concise chapter summary is available as a study aid for each chapter.

Study Guide

A thorough and practical student study guide includes learning objectives, chapter outlines, questions, and ideas that help the student review the material presented in this text. Also included are student activities and projects designed to enhance the practical application of sociological concepts. The study guide is available in physical and eBook format.

Shop Online ● ● ● ●

BVT Online Student Bookstore

For the student's convenience and pocketbook, students have the added option of purchasing this textbook and associated resources in the following formats at www. bvtlab.com:

- Full-color, hard-cover textbook
- Loose-leaf black & white textbook
- eBook subscription (six months)

- Study Guide – purchase or eBook subscription
- Premium student resources
- BVTLab

Direct Rental Program

BVT saves students even more money by offering a direct rental program. Textbooks can be rented for a full semester, with an economy shipping option under $5.00. Students may write pencil notes in the margins and highlight a modest amount of text. Two weeks of access to the eBook is made available while the rental textbook is being shipped. Return shipping is prepaid by BVT.

Student Resource Edition

This textbook is available as a Student Resource Edition, which includes the standard textbook plus the Student Resources package. Student Resource editions can be ordered through the campus bookstore or can be purchased or rented directly from BVT for additional student savings.

Acknowledgments ● ● ● ●

Many people have provided invaluable assistance and understanding while I was revising this text. I first want to thank my family, not only for supporting my writing efforts and forgiving my memory lapses during this time, but also providing me with wonderful examples of social psychological principles that I used throughout the text. Most importantly, I would like to thank my daughter, Lillian, who served as my research assistant during this revision process as she prepared for her own graduate studies in political science.

I also wish to thank the students in my social psychology courses at Marquette University, who are the first to be exposed to my new stories of the social psychological enterprise. In addition, I thank those students using my book at other colleges and universities who wrote me letters and e-mail concerning their reactions to what they read. The encouragement, enthusiasm, and criticism of all these students have made revising the book much easier.

My appreciation also goes to the many Internet-user members of the Society of Personality and Social Psychology (SPSP) who graciously responded to my requests for reprints and preprints of recent scientific articles describing recent advances in our understanding of social behavior. Their responses greatly aided me in preparing a sixth-edition Social Psychology that includes exciting new research and theoretical developments.Listed below are some of these individuals:

Andrea Abele-Brehm, University of Erlangen

Rainer Banse, Universität Bonn

Verónica Benet-Martínez, University of California, Davis

Amara Brook, Santa Clara University

Edward Burkley, Oklahoma State University

Kathy Carnelley, University of Southampton

Zeynep Cemalcilar, Koc University, Istanbul, Turkey

Jaime C. Confer, University of Texas

Ilan Dar-Nimrod, University of Rochester Medical Center

Martin Day, University of Waterloo

Joseph P. Forgas, University of South Wales

Bertram Gawronski, The University of Western Ontario

Michael J. Gill, Lehigh University

Sam Gosling, University of Texas at Austin

Gordon Hodson, Brock University

Yuen J. Huo, University of California, Los Angeles

Marc T. Kiviniemi, University at Buffalo , SUNY

Erika Koch, St. Francis Xavier University

Regina Krieglmeyer, University of Wuerzburg

Justin J. Lehmiller, Colorado State University

Edward Lemay, University of New Hampshire

Agostino Mazziotta, University of Jena

Allen R. McConnell, Miami University

Andrea L. Meltzer, University of Tennessee

Daniel Molden, Northwestern University

Nora A. Murphy, Loyola Marymount University

Debra Oswald, Marquette University

Susannah Paletz, University of Pittsburgh

Miles L. Patterson, University of Missouri-St. Louis

Carin Perilloux, University of Texas at Austin

John V. Petrocelli, Wake Forest University

Mariana A. Preciado, University of California, Los Angeles

Norbert Schwarz | University of Michigan

Phillip R. Shaver, University of California, Davis

James A. Shepperd, University of Florida, Gainesville

Donna Shestowsky, University of California, Davis

Steven J Stanton, Duke University

Weylin Sternglanz, Nova Southeastern University

Wolfgang Stroebe, Utrecht University

Jordan Troisi, University at Buffalo-SUNY

Michelle vanDellen, University of Georgia

Kathleen Vohs, University of Minnesota

T. Joel Wade, Bucknell University

Carol L. Wilson, Penn State Erie

Finally, I would like to thank Sales and Acquisitions Manager Robert Rappeport who provided unwavering support throughout this current revision. I was also extremely fortunate to work with Project Development Manager Terri Beaudette and Production Manager Della Brackett who kept everything on schedule. I had fun working with Managing Editor Joyce Bianchini, as well as Photo Researcher Michelle Hipkins. Designer Michael Myers made sure the book had the right "look" and that it would be pleasing to you, the reader's eye.

A Special Note to Instructors and Students ● ● ● ●

Whenever I teach a course in psychology, I learn a lot from my students and fellow instructors about how to make the course better. I would like to have a similar opportunity to learn from you how I can improve this textbook. Your feedback about what you like or do not like about the book is important to me. To make it easy for you to provide this feedback, my school address, telephone number, and e-mail address are listed below. I will personally respond to all comments and questions.

Professor Stephen L. Franzoi

Department of Psychology

Marquette University

P.O. Box 1881

Milwaukee, WI 53201-1881

Telephone: (414)288-1650

E-mail: Stephen.Franzoi@marquette.ed

1 Chapter 1
Introducing Social Psychology

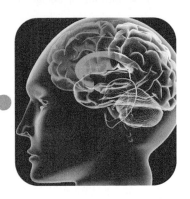

CHAPTER OUTLINE

INTRODUCTION

What Is Social Psychology?
Social psychology studies how we are influenced by others.
Social psychology is more than common sense.
Social psychology studies how social reality is created (and recreated).
Social psychology is studied in both psychology and sociology.
Social psychology has both European and American roots.

Organizing Concepts and Perspectives in Social Psychology
The *self* is shaped by—and shapes—the social environment.
Our social thinking can be automatic or deliberate.
Culture shapes social behavior.
Evolution shapes universal patterns of social behavior.
Brain activity affects and is affected by social behavior.
Positive psychology is an emerging perspective in social psychology.

WEB SITES

INTRODUCTION

It was a pleasant Saturday morning as Shazia, Catherine, and Leroy were ushered into a conference room at a local Milwaukee TV station. These three teenagers had been invited to audition for a reality news show on teenage life. The reporter for this upcoming show asked everyone to sit around a table and complete necessary paperwork before being interviewed on camera. One student in this audition session, Sam, arrived a bit later and, like the others, sat down to complete his paperwork.

When the reporter left the room to check on the next step in the audition process, the teens began conversing. Flashing a big smile, Sam announced that today was his birthday! Following a round of congratulations from the three others, Sam disclosed that he and his friends had been out all night long drinking and celebrating, and that was why he was late. Sam then chuckled and said, "I was so hung over this morning that I had a couple shots of alcohol before my friends dropped me off at the TV station. I'm still messed up!" Sam's self-disclosure led the assembled group into a spirited discussion regarding similar incidents in their past, but they abruptly ceased talking when the news editor for the show walked into the room. The editor informed the four teens that they were now all going to travel across town to a different location to complete some of the audition tapes. The editor, reporter, and camera crew were going to ride in one van while the teens followed in another vehicle. Then, producing a set of car keys, the editor announced, "I've been informed that it is Sam's birthday today, so Sam, you have the honor of driving Shazia, Catherine, and Leroy to the location where we will film!" After tossing the keys to Sam, the editor walked out, saying she would return shortly to escort them to their car.

How do you think Shazia, Catherine, and Leroy responded to the news that Sam was going to drive them across town? Would they voice the concerns they probably had about Sam's intoxicated state, or would they remain silent? What would you do if placed in such a situation?

In reality, Sam was not intoxicated; he was an actor playing the role of a drunken teen. The reporter and editor had set up this scenario, along with my guidance, to discover how the other three teens would respond. This entire event was being secretly filmed, with the permission of the teens' parents. I was in an adjacent room watching the scene unfold on a video screen. As a social psychologist at nearby Marquette University, I had been asked by the reporter and editor had asked me to offer my input on what might happen. Can you guess how the teens responded? Did the three teens confront Sam while the editor was out of the room? Did the three teens inform the editor about Sam's condition when she returned to escort them to their car? Did the three teens actually get into the car with Sam behind the wheel, despite believing that he was not fit to drive?

WHAT IS SOCIAL PSYCHOLOGY?

The reason I love social psychology is that it attempts to understand the social dynamics of everyday living, including our willingness to speak up and express our concerns when faced with a potentially dangerous situation. Here, perhaps more than in any other area of psychology, answers are sought to questions that we have pondered at different times in our lives. Thus, you, the new student in social psychology, will likely feel a natural affinity to this subject matter because it directly addresses aspects of your daily experience in the social world. Social psychology can provide some insight into why none of the teens at the TV station voiced any concerns about Sam's competence to drive—not when they were alone with Sam, not when the editor returned, and not even when Sam was about to drive the car with them sitting inside.

SOCIAL PSYCHOLOGY STUDIES HOW WE ARE INFLUENCED BY OTHERS.

social psychology

The scientific discipline that attempts to understand and explain how the thoughts, feelings, and behavior of individuals are influenced by the actual, imagined, or implied presence of others

Gordon Allport, one of the influential figures in social psychology, provided a definition of the field that captures its essence. He stated that **social psychology** is a discipline that uses scientific methods in "an attempt to understand and explain how the thoughts, feelings, and behavior of individuals are influenced by the actual, imagined, or implied presence of others" (Allport, 1985, p. 3).

To better understand this definition, let us consider a few examples. First, how might the actual presence of others influence someone's thoughts, feelings, and behavior? Consider how the presence of others influenced the teens' actions at the TV station. When the reporter asked Shazia, Catherine, and Leroy why they remained silent and put their lives in the hands of someone they thought was intoxicated, each stated that they were worried how the others might react to their speaking up. Instead of protecting their safety, they protected their social position in relation to their peers.

Why do people often fail to voice concerns when placed in a life-threatening situation, such as allowing an intoxicated person to drive? Pictured above is the *Jackass* star Ryan Dunn who was killed in a drunk driving accident June 20, 2011. Social psychology studies why people often fail to raise safety concerns during such life events.

Another example of how the presence of others can influence the individual occurs when basketball players prepare to shoot a free throw in a game. Fans from the opposing team often try to rattle players by making loud noises and gesturing wildly in the hope of diverting the player's attention from the task at hand.

In regarding how the imagined presence of others might influence thoughts, feelings, and behavior, think about past incidents when you were considering doing something that ran counter to your parents' wishes. Although they may not have actually been present, did their imagined presence influence your behavior? Imaginal figures can guide our actions by shaping our interpretation of events just as surely as do those who are physically present (Honeycutt, 2003; Shaw, 2003). Despite the fact that Shazia did not voice her concerns at the time about Sam driving the car, in a debriefing session held immediately after halting the staged event, Shazia disclosed that, faced with a similar situation, she would now act differently. Smiling sheepishly, Shazia explained, "The next time, I will listen better to the voice of my mother inside my head telling me to be smart and not get in the car!" With this statement, Shazia was articulating an important insight that social psychologists have documented in their research: In stressful situations, imagining the presence of others can lower your anxiety and provide you with an emotional security blanket (Andersen & Glassman, 1996; McGowan, 2002).

Finally, how can the implied presence of others influence an individual? Have you ever had the experience of driving on the freeway, going well beyond the speed limit, only to pass a sign with a little helicopter painted on it with the words "We're watching you" printed below? Did the implied presence of a police helicopter circling overhead influence your thoughts and feelings, as well as your pressure on the gas pedal? Similarly, fresh footprints on a deserted snowy path imply that others may be nearby, which may set in motion a series of thoughts in your mind: Who might this person be? Should I continue on my way or turn around, just to be safe?

Based on this discussion, you should better understand the type of topics we will analyze in this book. Although social psychology once was a relatively small field of scholars talking primarily to each other, there now are many opportunities to collaborate with the other sciences. Today, social psychology draws on the insights of sociology, anthropology, neurology, political science, economics, and biology to gain a better understanding of how the individual fits into the larger social system. Capitalizing on this movement toward an "integrative science," in this text we will periodically analyze how sociologists, neuroscientists, anthropologists, ethologists, and biologists explain various aspects of social behavior.

SOCIAL PSYCHOLOGY IS MORE THAN COMMON SENSE.

Occasionally when I meet new people and tell them that I am paid a salary to study how people interact with one another, a few brave souls will press the point and ask, "Isn't social psychology just warmed-over common sense?" One reason these persons may think of social psychology as simply rephrasing what we already know is because its subject matter is so personal and familiar: We all informally think about our own thoughts, feelings, and actions and those of others (Lilienfeld, 2011). Why would such naturally gained knowledge be any different from what social psychologists achieve through scientific observations? In many ways, this is true. For example, consider the following findings from social psychology that confirm what many of us already know:

• Attending to people's faces leads to the greatest success in detecting their lies. (Chapter 4)

• People who are paid a great deal of money to perform a boring task enjoy it more than those who are paid very little. (Chapter 5)

• Men express more hostile attitudes toward women than women do toward men. (Chapter 6)

• People think that physically attractive individuals are less intelligent than those who are physically unattractive. (Chapter 9)

• Playing violent video games or engaging in contact sports allows people to "blow off steam," making them less likely to behave aggressively in other areas of their lives. (Chapter 11)

• Accident victims are most likely to be helped when there are many bystanders nearby. (Chapter 12)

All these findings make sense, and you can probably think of examples from your own life that confirm them in your own mind. However, the problem is that I lied: Social psychological research actually informs us that all these statements are generally false—and the exact opposite is true. Of course, social psychology often confirms many commonsense notions about social behavior, but you will find many instances in this text where the scientific findings challenge your current social beliefs. You will also discover that by learning about the theories and research findings in social psychology you will have a greater ability to make intelligent life choices. In this case, knowledge really is power.

SOCIAL PSYCHOLOGY STUDIES HOW SOCIAL REALITY IS CREATED (AND RECREATED).

Do you realize that you play a vital role in creating your social world? If you'd like to personally experience the power you possess to actively shape your social reality, spend a few hours interacting with others while consciously smiling (make sure it's not a noticeably forced smile) and then spend another few hours wearing a frown or a scowl. I'm betting that the reactions of those around you—and your own mood—will be appreciably altered by these two different facial expressions (Frank et al., 2005).

The simple fact is that your social reality is not fixed and unchanging, but rather it is malleable and is in a constant state of flux. In 1948, sociologist Robert Merton introduced the concept of the **self-fulfilling prophecy** to describe how others' expectations about a person, group, or situation can actually lead to the fulfillment of those expectations. As Merton described it:

> The self-fulfilling prophecy is, in the beginning, a *false* definition of the situation evoking a new behavior, which makes the originally false conception come *true*. The specious validity of the self-fulfilling prophecy perpetuates a reign of error. For the prophet will cite the actual course of events as proof that he was right from the very beginning. (Merton, 1948, p. 195)

The self-fulfilling prophecy involves a three-step process (refer to Figure 1.1). First, the perceiver (the "prophet") forms an impression of the target person. Second, the perceiver acts toward the target person in a manner consistent with this first impression. In response, the target person's behavior changes to correspond to the perceiver's actions (Diekmann et al., 2003; Reich, 2004). Research indicates that behavior changes due to self-fulfilling prophecies can be remarkably long lasting (Smith et al., 1999).

The most famous empirical demonstration of the self-fulfilling prophecy was a study conducted by Robert Rosenthal and Lenore Jacobson (1968) in a South San Francisco elementary school. In this study, the researchers first gave IQ tests to children

"Not everyone's life is what they make it. Some people's life is what other people make it."

Alice Walker, American Author, born 1944.

self-fulfilling prophecy
The process by which someone's expectations about a person or group leads to the fulfillment of those expectations

"Imaginations which people have of one another are the solid facts of society."

Charles Horton Cooley, American sociologist, 1864–1929

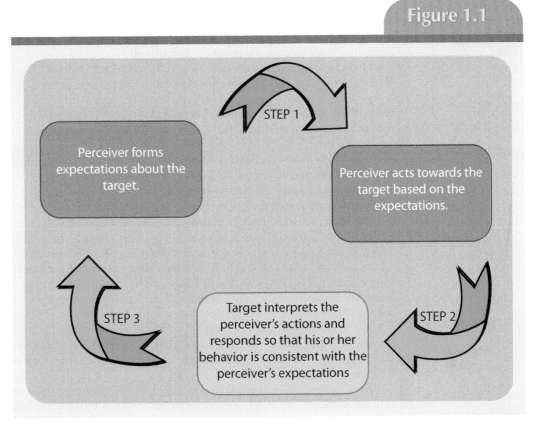

Figure 1.1

The Development of a Self-Fulfilling Prophecy

Self-fulfilling prophecies often develop as a three-step process. In step 1, the perceiver forms expectations about the target. In step 2, the perceiver behaves in a manner consistent with those expectations. In step 3, the target responds to the perceiver's actions in a manner that unwittingly confirms the perceiver's initial beliefs. The more interactions the target has with the perceiver, and the more this three-step process is repeated during those interactions, the more likely it is that the target will internalize the perceiver's expectations into his or her own self-concept. What personal qualities in a perceiver and in a target would make a self-fulfilling prophecy more or less likely?

> **"***If three people say you are an ass, put on a bridle.***"**
>
> ———————————
>
> Spanish proverb

and then met with their teachers to share the results. At these information sessions, teachers were told that the tests identified certain students in their classroom as potential "late bloomers" who should experience substantial IQ gains during the remaining school year. In reality, this information was false. The children identified as potential late bloomers had been randomly selected by the researchers and did not differ from their classmates. Although the potential late-blooming label was fabricated for these children (approximately 20 percent of the class), Rosenthal and Jacobson hypothesized that the teachers' subsequent expectations would be sufficient to enhance the academic performance of these students. Eight months later, when the students were again tested, this hypothesis was confirmed. The potential late bloomers not only exhibited improved schoolwork but also showed gains in their IQ scores that were not found among the non-labeled students (see Figure 1.2).

Follow-up studies indicated that teachers treat differently the students who are positively labeled in this manner (Jussim et al., 2009; Rosenthal, 2002). First, teachers create a warmer *socioemotional climate* for these students than for those who are perceived less positively. Second, they provide these gifted students with more *feedback* on their academic performance than they do to their average students. Third, they *challenge* these positively labeled students with more difficult material than the rest of the class. Finally, they provide these students with a *greater opportunity* to respond to presented material in class. The positively labeled students are likely to assume either that the teacher especially likes them and has good judgment or that the teacher is a likable person. Whichever attribution is made, it is likely that the positively labeled students will work harder and begin thinking about themselves as high achievers. Through this behavioral and self-concept change, the prophecy is fulfilled.

Unfortunately, not all self-fulfilling prophecies are positive. Teachers and fellow students often treat children who are negatively labeled as "troubled" or "disruptive" in a way that reinforces the negative label so that it is more likely to be internalized (Guyll et al., 2010; Rosenthal, 2003). To better understand this sort of negative self-concept change, Monica Harris and her colleagues (1992) studied the impact of *negative expectancies* on children's social interactions. In their research, sixty-eight pairs of unacquainted boys in third through sixth grade played together on two different tasks. The researchers designated one of the boys in the pairing as the *perceiver* and the other boy the *target*. Half the target boys had been previously diagnosed as being hyperactive, and the rest of the participants—the remaining targets and all the perceivers—had no history of behavioral problems. Prior to playing together, some perceivers were told—independently of their partner's actual behavior—that their partner had a special problem and may give them a hard time: He disrupted class a lot, talked when he shouldn't, didn't sit in his chair, and often acted silly. In contrast, other perceivers were not given this information. One of the activities the two boys mutually engaged in was an unstructured, cooperative task in which they planned and built a design with plastic blocks; the other task was more structured and competitive—separately coloring a dinosaur as quickly as possible using the same set of crayons. The boys' behavior on both tasks was videotaped and later rated by judges on a number of dimensions, such as friendliness, giving commands, and offering plans or suggestions. The boys also reported their own feelings and reactions to the tasks.

How do you think these different expectations shaped social reality? Consistent with the self-fulfilling prophecy, the target boys whose partners had been led to believe that they had a behavioral problem enjoyed the tasks less, rated their own performances as poorer, and took less credit for success than the boys whose partners were not expecting such problems. Likewise, the boys who held the negative expectancies about their partners enjoyed the tasks less themselves, worked less hard on them, talked less, and liked their partners less and were less friendly to them than those perceivers who were not provided with negative expectancies. These findings indicate that when people have negative expectations about others, they are more likely to treat these individuals in a negative manner, which often results in the targets of such negative treatment reacting

When a student is labeled as "troubled" his teachers and peers often treat him/her negatively. This reinforces the "troubled" label and may cause the student to act out more often, fulfilling the prophecy.

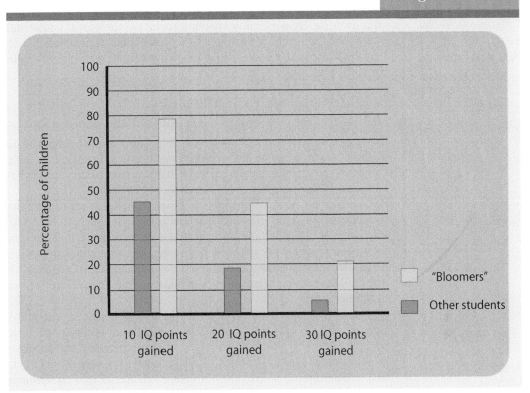

Percentage of Schoolchildren Whose IQ Test Scores Improved
over the Course of the School Year Due to the Self-Fulfilling Prophecy

Those first- and second-grade students who were identified as "potential bloomers" showed a significant improvement in their IQ test scores during the course of the school year. In actuality, these students were randomly chosen for the "potential blooming" category—they did not differ from the other students in any way. Yet, their teachers' expectations that they were "gifted" resulted in those students being challenged more in class, which caused the bloomers to try harder and to learn more. The same social psychological mechanisms that result in beneficial self-fulfilling prophecies can also operate in reverse, causing normally capable children to believe that they are intellectually inferior to others. What types of schoolchildren are most likely to be categorized in this negative manner?

Critical
THINKING

Do you think that a judge's beliefs about the guilt or innocence of a defendant in a criminal trial could create a self-fulfilling prophecy among the jury, even if the judge does not voice her opinions?

in kind, thus confirming the initial negative expectations. For half of the boys in this study, the negative expectations were groundless; however, this did not alter the outcome of the interaction. Unfortunately, this form of self-fulfilling prophecy is all too common, and over time it leads to negative self-beliefs and low self-esteem.

In thinking about these findings, how might they apply to your own life? Think of instances in your life where negative expectations of others may have created undesirable self-fulfilling prophecies. If you can identify someone whom you've viewed and treated in a negative fashion, try a little exercise to reverse this process. The next time you interact with that person put aside your negative expectations, and instead, treat him as if he were your best friend. Based on the research we have reviewed here, by redefining that person in your own eyes, you may create a new definition of social reality in his as well. People you thought were unfriendly, and even hostile, may respond to your redefinition by acting warm and friendly. If successful in redefining this particular social reality, you will have fulfilled one of my own prophecies of readers of this text—namely, that those who learn about social psychological principles will use this knowledge to improve the quality of their social relationships.

As a means of encouraging you to apply this knowledge of social psychology to your own daily living, I have included within the chapters of this text opportunities for you to learn how specific topics relate to yourself. Each of these *Self/Social Connection*

"*Self-knowledge is best learned, not by contemplation, but action.*"

— — — — — — — — —

Johann Wolfgang von Goethe, German author, 1749–1822

exercises consists of a self-report questionnaire or technique used by social psychologists in studying a particular area of social behavior. After personally completing and scoring the measure for yourself, you will gain insight into how this topic relates to your own life. By personally applying social psychological knowledge in this manner you are not only much more likely to absorb the content of this text (and thereby perform better in this course), you are also more likely to apply this knowledge outside the classroom.

SOCIAL PSYCHOLOGY IS STUDIED IN BOTH PSYCHOLOGY AND SOCIOLOGY.

You might be surprised to learn that there actually are two scientific disciplines known as social psychology, one in psychology and the other in sociology, with the larger of the two being the psychological branch. Both disciplines study social behavior, but they do so from different perspectives (Fiske & Molm, 2010).

The central focus of *psychological social psychology* tends to be individuals and how they respond to social stimuli. Variations in behavior are believed to be due to people's interpretation of social stimuli or differences in their personalities and temperament. Even when psychological social psychologists study group dynamics, they generally emphasize the processes that occur at the individual level (Quiñones-Vidal et al., 2004). The definition of social psychology in this text (and its focus) reflects the psychological perspective.

In contrast, *sociological social psychology* downplays the importance of individual differences and the effects of immediate social stimuli on behavior. Instead, the focus is on larger group or societal variables, such as people's socioeconomic status, their social roles, and cultural norms (Stryker, 1997). The role these larger group variables play in determining social behavior is of much keener interest to this discipline than to its psychological "cousin." Therefore, sociological social psychologists are more interested in providing explanations for such societal-based problems as poverty, crime, and deviance.

Although there have been calls to merge the two branches into a single field—and even a joint psychology-sociology doctoral program at the University of Michigan from 1946 to 1967—their different orientations make it doubtful that this will transpire in the foreseeable future. In the meantime, the two disciplines will continue to provide important, yet differing, perspectives on social behavior.

SOCIAL PSYCHOLOGY HAS BOTH EUROPEAN AND AMERICAN ROOTS.

As a scientific discipline, social psychology is less than 150 years old, with most of the growth occurring during the past six decades. By most standards, social psychology is a relatively young science (Franzoi, 2007).

Dawning of a Scientific Discipline: 1862–1894

German psychologist Wilhelm Wundt (1832–1921), who is widely regarded as the founder of psychology, had a hand in the early development of social psychology. Early in Wundt's career (1862), he predicted that there would be two branches of psychology: physiological psychology and social or folk psychology (*Völkerpsychologie*). His reasoning in dividing psychology into two branches was his belief that the type of individual psychology studied in the laboratory by physiological psychologists could not account for the more complex cognitive processes required for social interaction. Although social behavior consists of distinct individuals, Wundt argued that the product of this social interaction is more than the sum of the individuals' mental activities. Because of this distinction, Wundt asserted that while physiological psychology was part of the natural sciences and aligned with biology, social psychology was a "social science," with its parent discipline being philosophy. He further argued that while physiological psychologists should conduct experiments in studying their phenomena, social psychologists should employ nonexperimental methods because such an approach best captured the complexity of social interaction.

German psychologist Wilhelm Wundt (1832–1921), founder of psychology, provided some of the earliest scholarly work that provided the necessary inspiration for the development of social psychology.

Despite the fact that Wundt's ten volumes of writings on social psychology influenced scholars in Europe, his work remained largely unknown to American social scientists because it was not translated into English. Further hindering Wundt's ability to shape the ideas of young American scholars was the fact that these young scientists were much more interested in being identified with the natural sciences than with continuing an alliance with philosophy. Although Wundt's notion that social psychology was a social science was compatible with the nineteenth century conception of psychology as the "science of the mind" and was embraced by a number of European scholars, it was incompatible with the new behaviorist perspective in the United States that emerged during the early years of the twentieth century.

Underlying behaviorism was a philosophy known as *logical positivism*, which contended that knowledge should be expressed in terms that could be verified empirically or through direct observation. This new "science of behavior" had little use for Wundt's conception of social psychology and its reliance on nonexperimental methodology. An emerging American brand of social psychology defined itself both in terms of behaviorist principles and the experiment as its chosen research method. This was especially true for the social psychology developing in psychology, but less so for sociological social psychology. Psychological social psychology in America, which would become the intellectual core of the discipline, developed outside the influence of Wundt's writings. In contrast, American sociological social psychology was indirectly affected by Wundt's writings because one of its founders, George Herbert Mead, paid serious attention to the German scholar's work. Today Mead's symbolic interactionist perspective remains an active area of theory and research in American sociology.

Early Years: 1895–1935

Norman Triplett, an American psychologist at Indiana University, is credited with conducting the first social psychology experiment in 1895. Investigating how a person's performance of a task changes when other people are present, Triplett asked children to quickly wind line on a fishing reel either alone or in the presence of other children performing the same task. As predicted, the children wound the line faster when in the presence of other children. Published in 1897, this study formally introduced the experimental method into the social sciences. Eleven years later, in 1908, English psychologist William McDougall and American sociologist Edward Ross each published the first two textbooks in social psychology. Consistent with the contemporary perspective in psychological social psychology, McDougall's text identified the individual as

In 1924, Floyd Allport (1890–1978) published *Social Psychology,* a book that demonstrated how carefully conducted research could provide valuable insights into a wide range of social behaviors.

the principal unit of analysis, while Ross' text, true to the contemporary sociological social psychology perspective, highlighted groups and the structure of society.

Despite the inauguration of this new subfield within psychology and sociology, social psychology still lacked a distinct identity. How was it different from the other subdisciplines within the two larger disciplines? What were its methods of inquiry? In 1924 a third social psychology text, published by Floyd Allport (older brother of Gordon Allport), went a long way in answering these questions for psychological social psychology. Reading his words today, you can see the emerging perspective of psychological social psychology:

> I believe that only within the individual can we find the behavior mechanisms and consciousness which are fundamental in the interactions between individuals. … There is no psychology of groups which is not essentially and entirely a psychology of individuals. … Psychology in all its branches is a science of the individual. (Allport, 1924, p. 4)

Allport's conception of social psychology was proposed eleven years after John Watson ushered in the behaviorist era in American psychology. His brand of social psychology emphasized how the person responds to stimuli in the social environment, with the group merely being one of many such stimuli. Allport shaped the identity of American social psychology by emphasizing the experimental method in studying such topics as conformity, nonverbal communication, and social facilitation. His call for the pursuit of social psychological knowledge through carefully controlled experimental procedures contrasted with the more philosophical approach that both Ross and McDougall had taken sixteen years earlier.

Overseas, German social psychology was being shaped by *Gestalt* psychology, which emphasized that the mind actively organizes stimuli into meaningful wholes. Gestalt social psychologists contended that the social environment is made up not only of individuals but also of relations between individuals, and these relationships have important psychological implications. Thus, Gestalt social psychologists promoted an understanding of groups as real social entities, which directly led to the tradition of group processes and group dynamics that still exists today. These two schools of thought within psychological social psychology, one in America and the other in Germany that were developing independent of one another, would soon be thrust together due to events on the world scene.

Coming of Age: 1936–1945

During the first three decades of the twentieth century, Allport's conception of social psychology emphasized basic research, with little consideration given to addressing social problems. However, by the mid-1930s, the discipline was poised for further growth and expansion. The events that had the greatest impact on social psychology at this critical juncture in its history were the Great Depression in the United States and the social and political upheavals in Europe generated by the First and Second World Wars.

Following the stock market crash of 1929, many young psychologists were unable to find or hold jobs. Experiencing firsthand the impact of societal forces, many of them adopted the liberal ideals of the Roosevelt "New Dealers" or the more radical left-wing political views of the socialist and communist parties. In 1936 these social scientists formed an organization dedicated to the scientific study of important social issues and the support for progressive social action. This organization, the *Society for the Psychological Study of Social Issues* (SPSSI), contained many social psychologists that were interested in applying their theories and political activism to real-world problems. One of the important contributions of SPSSI to social psychology was, and continues to be, the infusion of ethics and values into the discussion of social life.

At the same time, the rise of fascism in Germany, Spain, and Italy created a strong anti-intellectual and anti-Semitic atmosphere in many of Europe's universities. To escape this persecution, many of Europe's leading social scientists—such as Fritz Heider, Gustav Ichheiser, Kurt Lewin, and Theodor Adorno—immigrated to America. When the United States entered the war, many social psychologists, both American and European, applied their knowledge of human behavior to wartime programs, including the selection of officers for the Office of Strategic Services (the forerunner of the Central Intelligence Agency) and the undermining of enemy morale (Hoffman, 1992). The constructive work resulting from this collaboration demonstrated the practical usefulness of social psychology.

During this time of global strife, one of the most influential social psychologists was Kurt Lewin, a Jewish refugee from Nazi Germany. Lewin was instrumental in founding SPSSI and served as its president in 1941. He firmly believed that social psychology did not have to make a choice between being either a pure science or an applied science. His oft-repeated maxim, "No research without action, and no action without research" continues to influence social psychologists interested in applying their knowledge to current social problems (Ash, 1992). By the time of his death in 1947 at the age of fifty-seven, Lewin had provided many of social psychology's defining characteristics and had trained many of the young American scholars who would become the leaders of contemporary social psychology (Pettigrew, 2010).

With the end of the war, prospects were bright for social psychology in North America. Based on their heightened scientific stature, social psychologists established new research facilities, secured government grants, and, most important, trained graduate students. Yet, while social psychology was flourishing in America, the devastating effects of the world war seriously hampered the discipline overseas, especially in Germany. In this postwar period, the United States emerged as a world power, and just as it exported its material goods to other countries, it exported its social psychology as well. Beyond the influence exerted by the liberal leanings of its members, this brand of social psychology also reflected the political ideology of American society and the social problems encountered within its boundaries (Farr, 1996).

Rapid Expansion: 1946–1969

With its infusion of European intellectuals and the recently trained young American social psychologists, the maturing science of social psychology expanded its theoretical and research base. To understand how a civilized society like Germany could fall under the influence of a ruthless dictator like Adolf Hitler, Theodor Adorno and his colleagues studied the *authoritarian personality*, which analyzed how personality factors emerging during childhood shape later adult obedience and intolerance of minorities. Some years later, Stanley Milgram extended this line of research in his now famous obedience experiments, which examined the situational factors that make people more likely to obey destructive authority figures. Social psychologists also focused their attention on the influence that the group had on the individual (Asch, 1956) and of the power of persuasive communication (Hovland et al., 1949). Arguably the most significant line of research and theorizing during this period was Leon Festinger's theory of cognitive dissonance (Festinger, 1957). This theory asserted that people's thoughts and actions were motivated by a desire to maintain cognitive consistency. The simplicity of the theory and its often-surprising findings generated interest and enthusiasm both inside and outside of social psychology for many years.

Social psychology's concern with societal prejudice continued to assert itself during the 1950s. For example, the 1954 United States Supreme Court decision to end the practice of racially segregated education was partly based on Kenneth Clark and Mamie

Kenneth and Mamie Phipps Clark conducted groundbreaking research on the self-concept of Black children. In 1971, Kenneth Clark became the first African American to be elected president of the American Psychological Association.

Phipps Clark's research indicating that segregation negatively affected the self-concept of Black children. In that same year, Gordon Allport provided a theoretical outline for how desegregation might reduce racial prejudice, the contact hypothesis.

The decade of the 1960s was a time of social turmoil in the United States, with the country caught in the grip of political assassinations, urban violence, social protests, and the Vietnam War. People were searching for constructive ways to change society for the better. Following this lead, social psychologists devoted more research to such topics as aggression, helping, attraction, and love. As the federal government expanded its attempts to cure societal ills with the guidance of social scientists, the number of social psychologists rose dramatically. Among these new social scientists were an increasing number of women and, to a lesser degree, minority members. Whole new lines of inquiry into social behavior commenced, with an increasing interest in the interaction of the social situation with personality factors.

Crisis and Reassessment: 1970–1984

The explosion of research in the 1960s played a part in another explosion of sorts in the area of research ethics because a few controversial studies appeared to put participants at risk for psychological harm. The most controversial of these studies was the previously mentioned obedience experiments conducted by Milgram, in which volunteers were ordered to deliver seemingly painful electric shocks to another person as part of a "learning experiment." In reality, no shocks were ever delivered—the victim was a confederate and only pretended to be in pain—but the stress experienced by the participants was indeed real. Although this study and others of its kind asked important questions about social behavior, serious concerns were raised about whether the significance of the research justified exposing participants to potentially harmful psychological consequences. Spurred by the debate surrounding these issues, in 1974 the U.S. government developed regulations requiring all institutions seeking federal funding to establish institutional review boards that would ensure the health and safety of human participants.

At the same time that concerns were being raised about the ethical treatment of human participants in research, social psychologists were questioning the validity of their scientific methods and asking themselves whether their discipline was a relevant and useful science. When social psychology first emerged from World War II and embarked on its rapid expansion, expectations were high that social psychologists could work hand-in-hand with various organizations to solve many social problems. By the 1970s, when these problems were still unsolved, a "crisis of confidence" emerged. When this disappointment and criticism of social psychology was followed by accusations from women and minorities that past research and theory reflected the biases of a White, male-dominated view of reality, many began to reassess the field's basic premises. Fortunately, out of this crisis emerged a more vital and inclusive field of social psychology, one employing more diverse scientific methods while also having more diversity within its membership.

One final important development during this time period was the importing of ideas from cognitive psychology in explaining social behavior. This "cognitive revolution" (see p. 17) greatly enhanced theory and research in all areas of social psychology, and its impact persists today.

Expanding Global and Interdisciplinary View: 1985–Present

By the 1970s, both European and Latin American social psychological associations had been founded, and in 1995 the Asian Association of Social Psychology was formed. The social psychology that developed overseas placed more emphasis on intergroup and societal variables in explaining social behavior than did its American cousin. By the mid-1980s, the growing influence of social psychology beyond the borders of the United States was well on its way in reshaping the discipline as scholars throughout the world actively exchanged ideas and collaborated on multinational studies. One of the principal questions generated by this exchange of information concerns which aspects of human behavior are *culture specific*—due to conditions existing within a particular culture—and which ones are due to our shared *evolutionary* heritage. Although social psychology's "professional center of gravity" still resides in the United States, social psychology in other world regions offers the entire field opportunities to escape what some consider the limitations of this "gravitational pull" to perceive new worlds of social reality (Krisztian, 2009; Ross et al., 2010; Shinha, 2003; Tam et al., 2003). This multicultural perspective will continue to guide research in the coming years.

Contemporary social psychologists have also continued the legacy of Kurt Lewin and SPSSI by applying their knowledge to a wide arena of everyday life, such as law, health, education, politics, sports, and business. In commenting on the goals of a social psychology graduate program, Morton Deutsch captures what many in the discipline still see as the ideal: "I wanted to create tough-minded but tender-hearted students. Science is very important. But science without a heart can be destructive. And a heart without a mind is not very valuable." This interest in applying the principles and findings of social psychology is a natural outgrowth of the search for understanding.

Some of the milestones of the social psychology are listed in the timeline on pp. 29–30. If the life of a science is similar to a person's life, then contemporary social psychology is best thought of as a "young adult" in the social sciences. Compared to more established sciences, social psychology is "barely dry behind the ears." Yet it is a discipline where new and innovative ideas are unusually welcome, and where new theoretical approaches and scientific methods from other scientific disciplines are regularly incorporated into the study of social thinking and behavior. Let us now examine some of the organizing concepts and perspectives in this discipline.

SECTION SUMMARY

- Social psychology uses scientific methods to study how the thoughts, feelings, and behavior of individuals are influenced by the actual, imagined, or implied presence of others.

- Social reality is changeable, with people's expectations about a person, group, or situation often leading to the fulfillment of those expectations.

- Social psychology has both psychological and sociological branches.

- Although social psychology has a distinct American imprint, its focus is becoming increasingly international.

ORGANIZING CONCEPTS AND PERSPECTIVES IN SOCIAL PSYCHOLOGY

If you surveyed social psychologists, you would discover that there is no agreement on a single theoretical perspective that unifies the field. Despite the fact that social psychology has no grand theory that explains all aspects of social behavior, there are some important organizing concepts and perspectives.

THE SELF IS SHAPED BY
—AND SHAPES—THE SOCIAL ENVIRONMENT.

Throughout most of the past century, the behaviorist perspective in psychology, with its focus on studying only observable actions, effectively prevented the concept of the self from becoming a focus of research in social psychology. During that time, most social psychologists explained people's behavior simply by examining the social cues in the situation, without considering how each person's life experiences and self-evaluations might also shape their responses. Fortunately, some social psychologists argued against such a narrow focus. For example, Gordon Allport's 1943 presidential address to the American Psychological Association presented the following appeal:

> One of the oddest events in the history of modern psychology is the manner in which the self became sidetracked and lost to view. I say it is odd, because the existence of one's self is the one fact of which every mortal person—every psychologist included—is perfectly convinced. An onlooker might say, "Psychologists are funny fellows. They have before them, at the heart of their science, a fact of perfect certainty, and yet they pay no attention to it. Why don't they begin with their own ego, or with our egos—with something we all know about? If they did so we might understand them better. And what is more, they might understand us better." (Allport, 1943, p. 451)

Despite Allport's call to action, it wasn't until the early 1970s that an increasing number of social psychologists, led by their empirical studies and a growing interest in human cognition, backed into a focus on the self (Greenwald & Ronis, 1978; Pepitone, 1968). Today, in contemporary social psychology, the self and self-related concepts are important explanatory tools of the discipline. Yet what is the self?

The **self** is both a simple and a complex concept. It is not something located inside your head—it is you, a social being with the ability to engage in symbolic communication and self-awareness. The reason I use *social being* to define the self is because selves do not develop in isolation, but do so only within a social context (Hardin, 2004; Harter, 2006). Likewise, the reason the cognitive processes of *symbol usage* and *self-awareness* are so important in this definition is that both are essential for us to engage in planned, coordinated activities in which we can regulate our behavior and anticipate the actions of others (Bandura, 2005; Heatherton, 2011). For example, suppose Jack has been working long hours at the office and, as a result, has ignored his wife and children. One day, it dawns on Jack that if he continues in this pattern of "all work and no play," he will not only be dull, but also divorced and depressed. Based on this anticipation, he revises his work schedule to enjoy the company of his family. In other words, Jack consciously changes his behavior to avoid what he perceives to be a host of unpleasant future consequences. This ability to analyze surroundings, our possible future realities, and ourselves allows us to actively create and re-create our social world and ourselves.

Self-awareness and symbol usage—and thus, the self—may have evolved in our ancestors as a means to better deal with an increasingly complex social environment (Oda, 2001; Sedikides & Skowronski, 1997). For instance, self-awareness not only provided our ancestors with knowledge about their own behavior, but they could also use this inner experience to anticipate how rivals might behave in the future—perhaps in war or in social bargaining—thus giving them an advantage in these activities. Similarly, the development of language not only allowed our ancestors to better coordinate group activities but also to use this symbolic communication to discuss things not physically present, such as a herd of antelope or a band of hostile warriors (Dunbar, 1993; Shaffer, 2005). These two defining features of the self became the means by which our ancestors developed an adaptive advantage in their environment, thus increasing their chances of surviving and reproducing.

Selfhood also allowed our ancestors to ponder their existence and mortality: Why are we here? What happens when we die? The artwork and elaborate burial sites created by our ancestors during the Upper Paleolithic period forty thousand years ago provide compelling evidence that the modern human mind—and the self—was emerging (Mellars, 1996; Rossano, 2003). Social psychologist M. Brewster Smith (2002), among others, contends that this new search for ultimate meaning led to the development of myth,

self
A symbol-using social being who can reflect on his or her own behavior

"The Self is the honey of all beings, and all beings are the honey of this Self."

The Upanishads sacred texts of Hinduism, 800–500 BC.

ritual, and religion, which affirmed to each social group its value as "The People." As you will discover throughout this text, this search for meaning and value in our groups profoundly shapes social interactions.

Beyond seeking meaning and value of group life, our ancestors also used self-awareness to size up and understand themselves. The way we think of ourselves (our *self-concept*) influences our social behavior and how we respond to social events (Baumeister, 1998). This influence is often dramatically illustrated in situations in which our own performance results in either success or failure. In such situations, many people tend to take credit for positive behaviors or outcomes—but to blame negative behaviors or outcomes on external causes (Campbell & Sedikides, 1999; McCall & Nattrass, 2001). For example, when students receive a good grade on an exam, they are likely to attribute it either to their intelligence, their strong work ethic, or a combination of the two. However, if they receive a poor grade on the exam, they tend to believe their failure is due to an unreasonable professor or pure bad luck. This tendency to take credit for positive outcomes but deny responsibility for negative outcomes in our lives is known as the **self-serving bias**.

self-serving bias

The tendency to take credit for positive outcomes but deny responsibility for negative outcomes in our lives

The most agreed-upon explanation for the self-serving bias is that it allows us to enhance and protect our self-worth. If we feel personally responsible for successes or positive events in our lives but do not feel blameworthy for failures or other negative events, our self-worth is likely to be bolstered. This self-enhancement explanation emphasizes the role of motivation in our self-serving biases. Although the self-serving bias may provide us with a less-than-accurate view of ourselves, it may be "functionally efficient" because it often boosts our self-confidence. For example, explaining any current successes as being caused by enduring personality characteristics creates a personal expectation of future success in related tasks, increasing the likelihood that we will attempt new challenges (Taylor & Brown, 1988). Similarly, explaining repeated failures to bad luck or unfortunate situations may well serve to maintain an optimistic belief in the possibility of future success, resulting in our not giving up. Wilmar Schaufeli (1988), for instance, has found that unemployed workers seeking reemployment have more success if they exhibit the self-serving bias in their job search (that is, convincing themselves that not being hired for a particular job is due to external factors and not to internal ones such as incompetence).

Although there appears to be tangible benefits to explaining away negative events, the self-serving bias can create problems if it allows us to repeatedly overlook our own shortcomings in situations where a more realistic appraisal would generate useful corrective steps (Kruger & Dunning, 1999; Robins & Beer, 2001). Further, in group settings, the tendency to take credit for success and deny blame for failure can quickly lead to conflict and dissension among members. For example, the more the members of groups overestimate their individual contributions to group accomplishments, the less they want to work with each other in the future (Banaji et al., 2003; Caruso et al., 2004).

As you see, the self plays an important role in how we think and behave as social creatures. Social psychology's emphasis on the self represents an affirmation of Kurt Lewin's belief that both person and situational factors influence social behavior. Lewin's perspective, later called **interactionism** (Blass, 1984; Seeman, 1997), combines personality psychology (which stresses differences among people) with traditional social psychology (which stresses differences among situations). In keeping with Lewin's legacy,

How might self-serving explanations for personal setbacks be beneficial to people's self-confidence and future success?

interactionism
....

An important perspective in social psychology that emphasizes the combined effects of both the person and the situation on human behavior

❝*General laws and individual differences are merely two aspects of one problem; they are mutually dependent on each other and the study of the one cannot proceed without the study of the other.* ❞

⸺⸺⸺⸺⸺⸺

Kurt Lewin, German-born social psychologist, 1890–1947

social cognition
....

The ways in which we interpret, analyze, remember, and use information about our social world

throughout this text we will examine how these two factors contribute to the social interaction equation, and we will use the self as the primary "person" variable. The previously mentioned *Self/Social Connection Exercises* will further reinforce the idea that social behavior is best understood as resulting from the interaction of person and situational factors.

OUR SOCIAL THINKING CAN BE AUTOMATIC OR DELIBERATE.

Throughout the history of social psychology there has been a running debate concerning the nature of human behavior. One perspective is that people are moved to act due to their needs, desires, and emotions (also known as *affect*). Social psychologists subscribing to this "hot" approach argue that heated, impulsive action that fulfills desires is more influential than cool, calculated planning of behavior (Zajonc, 1984). The alternative viewpoint is that people's actions are principally influenced by the rational analysis of choices facing them in particular situations. Followers of this "cold" approach assert that how people think will ultimately determine what they want and how they feel (Lazarus, 1984).

In the 1950s and 1960s, the hot perspective was most influential, but by the 1980s the cold perspective dominated the thinking within social psychology. One reason for this shift was the advent of the computer age, which resulted in people's everyday lives being saturated with the terminology and thinking of this new "technoscience." Reflecting this new view of reality, many social psychologists borrowed concepts from cognitive psychology and developed theories of **social cognition** that provided numerous insights into how we interpret, analyze, remember, and use information about our social world (De Jaegher et al., 2010; Rendel et al., 2011). Like a computer, these theories often describe people methodically processing information in a fixed sequence, or *serially* working on only one stream of data at a time. The sequential computer model of thinking is useful in explaining many aspects of human cognition, especially how we execute certain mental operations or follow certain rules of logic when making some decisions. For instance, if a normally sociable person acts irritable just before taking his midterms, you may logically consider the available information and conclude that his irritability is caused by situational factors.

Despite its usefulness, the computer model is less helpful in explaining other ways of thinking because the human brain is much more complex than a computer and performs many mental operations simultaneously, "in parallel" (Gabrieli, 1999). For example, why might a former soldier experience a panic attack while at a fireworks display? Here, a more useful model of cognition might conceive of information in memory being in a web-like network of connections among thousands of interacting "processing units"—all active at once. For the former soldier, memories of war and loud explosions are stored in a neural network: Activating one part of the network simultaneously activates the rest of the network.

Even though many social psychologists have embraced the social cognitive perspective, others argued that it dehumanizes social psychology to think of motives and affect as merely end products in a central processing system. In response to such criticism, cognitively oriented social psychologists have established a more balanced view of human nature by blending the traditional hot and cold perspectives into what some have termed the *warm look* (Sorrentino, 2003; Sorrentino & Higgins, 1986).

Reflecting this warm perspective, most contemporary social cognitive theories discuss how people use multiple cognitive strategies based on their current goals, motives, and needs (Dunning, 1999; Strack & Deutsch, in

dual-process theories
....
Theories of social cognition that describe two basic ways of thinking about social stimuli, one involving automatic, effortless thinking and the other involving more deliberate, effortful thinking
....

press). In such discussions, theorists typically propose **dual-process theories** of social cognition, meaning that our social thinking and behavior is determined by two different ways of understanding and responding to social stimuli (Kruglanski & Orehek, 2007; Petty, 2004). One mode of information processing—related to the cold perspective legacy in social psychology—is based on effortful, reflective thinking, in which no action is taken until its potential consequences are properly weighed and evaluated. The alternative mode of processing information—related to the hot perspective legacy in social psychology—is based on minimal cognitive effort, in which behavior is often impulsively and automatically activated by emotions, habits, or biological drives. Which of the two avenues of information processing people take at any given time is the subject of ongoing research that we will examine throughout this text. The essential assumption to keep in mind regarding dual-process theories is that many aspects of human behavior result from automatic processes that may occur spontaneously and outside our awareness (Moors & De Houwer, 2006).

Some dual-process theories rely on the computer model of serial information processing, which assumes that people can engage in only one form of thinking at a time. According to this perspective, in human cognition there often is a conflict between an initial, automatic evaluation and a more deliberate, rational assessment (Gilovich & Savitsky, 2002) The only way you can resolve this conflict is by engaging in either effortful thinking or relatively effortless thinking. You can switch back and forth between the two forms of thinking, but you cannot do both simultaneously. In contrast to this sequential "either-or" way of describing human thought, other dual-process theories rely on the neural network model of parallel information processing, and describe two mental systems that operate simultaneously, or parallel to one another (Kahneman & Frederick, 2002).

explicit cognition
....
Deliberate judgments or decisions of which we are consciously aware
....

Social scientists who assume parallel-processing systems often make a distinction between *explicit cognition and implicit cognition.* **Explicit cognition** involves deliberate judgments or decisions of which we are consciously aware. Although this type of cognition is intentional, it can sometimes be relatively effortless when the task is easy. However, a good deal of explicit thinking consumes considerable cognitive resources. The upside is that it is flexible and can deal with new problems. Trying to understand this definition of explicit cognition is literally an example of this very thought process. In contrast, **implicit cognition** involves judgments or decisions that are under the control of automatically activated evaluations occurring without our awareness (Dorfman et al., 1996). This type of thinking is unintentional, it uses few cognitive resources, and it operates quickly; however, it is inflexible and often cannot deal with new problems. The unintentional and automatic qualities of implicit cognition are demonstrated by the fact that you cannot stop yourself from reading the words on this page when you see them. Your reading skills are automatically and effortlessly activated.

implicit cognition
....
Judgments or decisions that are under the control of automatically activated evaluations occurring without our awareness
....

How might implicit cognition affect social interaction? Feeling uneasy and irritable around a new acquaintance because she unconsciously reminds you of a disagreeable person from your past is an example of how unconscious, automatically activated evaluations can shape your social judgments. For many years, social psychologists primarily studied and discussed the conscious decision making that shapes social interaction, but recently there has been a great deal of interest in how thinking below the "radar" of conscious awareness can influence social judgments and behavior (Karpinski, 2004). Throughout the text, we will discuss how both explicit and implicit cognitive processes shape our social world.

❝*In fact, I cannot totally grasp all that I am. Thus, the mind is not large enough to contain itself; but where can that part of it be which it does not contain?***❞**

– – – – – – – – – –

St. Augustine, Christian theologian, AD 354–434

CULTURE SHAPES SOCIAL BEHAVIOR.

To what extent do you agree with the following statements?

I think I am a unique person.
I enjoy being the center of attention.
I should be able to live my life anyway I want to.
If I could make the laws, the world would be a better place.

Over the past thirty years, surveys of sixteen thousand American college students indicate that if you were born after 1980 you are more likely to agree with these statements than if you were born before that year. Why might this be so?

culture

The total lifestyle of a people, including all the ideas, symbols, preferences, and material objects that they share

The answer is cultural experience. In trying to understand how people interpret and respond to social reality, we must remember that people view the world through cultural lenses. By **culture**, I mean the total lifestyle of a people, including all the ideas, symbols, preferences, and material objects that they share. This cultural experience shapes people's view of reality and of themselves, and thus, significantly influences their social behavior (Sieck et al., 2011).

The Social World of "Generation Next"

Most of you reading these words are members of what social commentators are calling "Generation Y" or "Generation Next," young adults born between the 1980s and the 1990s. The "Y" and "Next" labels are meant to distinguish you from the somewhat older "Generation X" adults born between 1966 and 1980. Lumped together, these two age groups are the children of the "Baby Boom" generation that was born after World War II. Your cultural upbringing is very different from that of your parents. You grew up with personal computers, the Internet, and cell phones. For many of you, your childhood was chronicled by your parents' video cameras, and it is quite possible that you were treated like a "shining star" and told, "You can be anything you want to be."

A recent national survey conducted by the Pew Research Center (2007) found that more than two-thirds of GenNexters see their generation as unique and distinct. Illustrating this generational self-view, today many young adults publicly proclaim their individuality by posting personal profiles on social networking sites such as Facebook and MySpace. GenNexters' desire for individual expression is also witnessed by the fact that about half either have a tattoo, a body piercing, or have dyed their hair a nontraditional color. The value this generation places on their own individuality also extends to accepting differences in others. GenNexters are the most tolerant of any generation in stating that homosexuality and interracial dating should be accepted and not discouraged. Although more socially tolerant than previous generations, most GenNexters believe that their generation is more interested in focusing on themselves than in helping others. When asked to identify important life goals of those in their age group, most GenNexters named fortune and fame. About 80 percent stated that "getting rich" is either the most important or second most important life goal for their peers, with half stating that "becoming famous" is also highly valued. In contrast, less than one-third of young adults identified "helping people who need help" as an important goal of their generation.

If there is some truth in this snapshot of young Americans' perceptions of their generation, you might be wondering how your generation became so self-focused in comparison to your parents' generation. Actually, the difference between the two generations is simply a matter of degree. Americans are generally a self-focused people; GenNexters are simply the best current example of the particular way in which our culture shapes people's thoughts, feelings, and actions.

The Cultural Belief Systems of Individualism and Collectivism.

individualism

A philosophy of life stressing the priority of individual needs over group needs, a preference for loosely knit social relationships, and a desire to be relatively autonomous of others' influence

Directly related to our understanding of both these survey findings and social behavior in general are the cultural belief systems concerning how individuals relate to their group, namely individualism and collectivism (Adamopoulos, 1999; Miller & Prentice, 1994). **Individualism** is a preference for a loosely knit social framework in society in which individuals are supposed to take care of themselves and their immediate families only. This belief system asserts that society is a collection of unique individuals who pursue their own goals and interests and strive to be relatively free from the influence of others (Bhargava, 1992).

As a philosophy of life, traces of individualism can be seen in early Greek and Roman writings and in the values and ideas of the medieval Anglo-Saxon poets of England (Harbus, 2002). However, it did not make a significant appearance on the world stage until the sixteenth century, when people became more geographically mobile and, thus, more regularly interacted with others from radically different cultures (Kim, 1994). Exposed to different social norms and practices, people began entertaining the possibility of having goals separate

"Generation Next's" desire for self-expression has led many of them to get tattoos and or body piercings.

from those of their group (Kashima & Foddy, 2002). In the arts, characters in novels and plays were increasingly portrayed as having individual states of emotion and as struggling with conflicts between their true self and the social roles assigned to them by their family and community (Stone, 1977). During the late 1800s and early 1900s—the age of industrialization and urbanization in Western societies—social roles became increasingly complex and compartmentalized. Now it was common practice to "find" or "create" one's own personal identity rather than being given an identity by one's group. This belief also holds true today in our contemporary society. Self-discipline, self-sufficiency, personal accountability, and autonomy are highly valued characteristics in a person (Kagitçibasi, 1994; Oishi et al., 2007).

Many observers of American culture contend that the history of voluntary settlement in the frontier greatly contributed to individualism developing in the United States (de Tocqueville, 1862/1969; Turner, 1920). Examples of this individualist orientation can be seen throughout U.S. history. In the 1700s, Thomas Jefferson's penning of the Declaration of Independence was essentially a bold assertion that individual rights were more important than group rights. In the 1800s, poet/philosopher Ralph Waldo Emerson believed that individualism was the route that, if truly traveled, would result in a spontaneous social order of self-determined, self-reliant, and fully developed citizens. In contemporary America, one can see the influence of individualism in everyday activities. For example, an analysis of popular American songs finds many more self-focused words compared to other-focused words in the lyrics, significantly more than even a generation ago (DeWall et al., 2011). Similarly, American parents' tendency over the past twenty years to increasingly give their children unusual names reflects the individualist desire to "stand out" from others and be unique (Twenge & Campbell, 2010).

In contrast to individualism, there is an alternative perspective known as **collectivism**, which represents a preference for a tightly knit social framework in which individuals can expect relatives or other members of their social group to look after them in exchange for unquestioning loyalty. This cultural belief system asserts that people become human only when they are integrated into a group, not isolated from it. Although individualists give priority to personal goals, collectivists often make no distinctions between personal and group goals. When they do make such distinctions, collectivists subordinate their personal goals to the collective good (Abrams et al., 1998; Oyserman et al., 2002). Due to the greater importance given to group aspirations over individual desires, collectivist cultures tend to

"*The union is only perfect when all the individuals are isolated.***"**

Ralph Waldo Emerson, U.S. philosopher/poet, 1803–1882

collectivism

A philosophy of life stressing the priority of group needs over individual needs, a preference for tightly knit social relationships, and a willingness to submit to the influence of one's group value similarity and conformity, rather than uniqueness and independence. (See Chapter 7 for a more detailed discussion.)

> *Human beings draw close to one another by their common nature, but habits and customs keep them apart.*
>
> Confucius, Chinese sage, 551–479 BC

How does this different perspective on the relationship between the individual and the group influence thought and behavior? Consider a modern, industrialized society with a collectivist orientation: Japan. The Japanese, like other people living in a collectivist society, view group inclusion and allegiance to be one of the primary goals in life. Indeed, in Japan the expression for individualist, *kojin-shugi*, is considered a socially undesirable characteristic, suggesting selfishness rather than personal responsibility (Ishii-Kuntz, 1989). Persons who defy the group's wishes, often considered heroes in an individualist culture, would bring shame upon themselves and their families (and their ancestors) in Japan. In North American society, to stand above the crowd, to be recognized as unique and special, is highly valued. In Japan, such attention detracts from the group. The different perspectives these cultures have about the individual standing out from the group is illustrated in contrasting proverbs or mottos. In North America, "The squeaky wheel gets the grease" and "Do your own thing" are commonly heard phrases, while the Japanese credo is "The nail that sticks up shall be hammered down."

It may surprise you to know that approximately 70 percent of the world's population lives in cultures with a collectivist orientation (Singelis et al., 1995). Indeed, the collectivist perspective is a much older view of the relationship between the individual and the group than is the individualist orientation. For most of human history, the group was the basic unit of society. Whether you were born into a clan or a tribe, you would generally live in one geographic region your entire life and would, upon maturing, assume the same social role as your parents. You did not have to "search" for your identity; your group gave it to you. Political scientist Ronald Inglehart and social psychologist Daphna Oyserman contend that collectivism is the older of the two philosophies because it focuses on the type of thinking and behavior that affords the most protection for people who live in threatening environments where survival needs are extremely salient. This is exactly the type of environment that has historically confronted all human groups until

Table 1.1

Differences between Collectivist and Individualist Cultures

COLLECTIVIST INDIVIDUALIST	INDIVIDUALIST
Identity is based in the social system and given by one's group	Identity is based in the individual and achieved by one's own striving.
People are socialized to be emotionally dependent on organizations and institutions.	People are socialized to be emotionally independent of organizations and institutions.
Personal and group goals are generally consistent, and when inconsistent, group goals get priority.	Personal and group goals are often inconsistent, and when inconsistent, personal goals get priority.
People explain others' social behavior as being more determined by social norms and roles than by personal attitudes.	People explain others' social behavior as being more determined by personal attitudes than by social norms and roles.
Emphasis is on belonging to organizations, and memberships is the ideal.	Emphasis is on individual initiative, individual achievement, and leadership is the ideal.
Trust is placed in group decisions.	Trust is placed in individual decisions.

fairly recently. In contrast, individualism is a much more recent philosophy of life because it develops among people who inhabit relatively safe environments where their survival is less dependent on maintaining strong group ties. This liberation from immediate physical threats reduces the importance of survival-focused values and gives higher priority to freedom of choice (Inglehart & Oyserman, 2004).

Table 1.1 lists some of the differences between these two cultural ideologies. Currently, individualism and collectivism are considered by the majority of cross-cultural researchers to be two ends of a continuum, with the United States, Canada, Australia, and Western European societies located more toward the individualist end, and Asian, African, and Latin and South American nations situated near the collectivist end. Within both individualist and collectivist cultures, individualist tendencies tend to be stronger in large urban or remote frontier settings—where people are less dependent on group ties—while collectivist tendencies are more pronounced in small regional cities and rural settings—where social relationships are more interdependent (Kashima et al., 2004; Kitayama, 2007).

Which perspective is better? Your answer depends on what values you have internalized (Sampson, 1988). As previously mentioned, although individualism and collectivism are seen by many theorists as two ends of a continuum, this doesn't mean that individualist tendencies do not influence people living in collectivist cultures, nor that collectivist yearnings do not shape individualists (Göregenli, 1997). Indeed, social scientists commonly think of these differing ideologies as reflecting two seemingly universal and common human needs: the *need for autonomy and the need for communion* (Hornsey & Jetten, 2004; Schwartz, 2003). Thus, although all humans have a need for both autonomy and communion, individualist cultures place greater value on autonomy, while collectivist cultures place greater value on communion. Because one of the goals of social psychology is to understand how the past experiences and present conditions of others influence their interpretation of social reality, these two contrasting cultural perspectives will regularly figure in our chapter discussions. Spend a few minutes completing *Self/Social Connection Exercise 1.1* to better understand the relative importance of these two cultural orientations in your own life.

A few additional points bear mentioning regarding these two cultural orientations. As already suggested, individualism and collectivism are not permanent, unchanging

> *"The American cultural ideal of the self-made man, of everyone standing on his own feet, is as tragic a picture as the initiative—destroying dependence on a benevolent despot. We all need each other. This type of interdependence is the greatest challenge to the maturity of individual and group functioning.*"
>
> — — — — — — — — —
>
> Kurt Lewin, German-born social psychologist, 1890–1947

Individualist and collectivist strivings can and do coexist within a person. The conflict that can often result from striving for personal goals that hinder group health and harmony is often depicted in popular movies. For example, in the 1946 classic Christmas movie, *It's a Wonderful Life,* Jimmy Stewart's character, George Bailey, is continually faced with life decisions that pit his own personal desires against his feelings of community obligation. This movie has a clear collectivist message: The self is affirmed by fulfilling the needs of the group. Why do you think this movie's message is so warmly received in North America's individualist culture? Do all societies need their share of George Baileys in order to thrive and prosper?

Self/Social Connections Exercise 1.1

To What Degree Do You Value Individualist and Collectivist Strivings?

Individualist-Collectivist Values Hierarchy

Directions

Listed below are twelve values. Please rank them in their order of importance to you with "1" being the "most important" and "12" being the "least important."

Pleasure (Gratification of Desires)
Honor of Parents and Elders (Showing Respect)
Creativity (Uniqueness, Imagination)
Social Order (Stability of Society)
A Varied Life (Filled with Challenge, Novelty, and Change)
National Security (Protection of My Nation from Enemies)
Being Daring (Seeking Adventure, Risk)
Self-discipline (Self-restraint, Resistance to Temptation)
Freedom (Freedom of Action and Thought)
Politeness (Courtesy, Good Manners)
Independence (Self-reliance, Choice of Own Goals)
Obedience (Fulfilling Duties, Meeting Obligations)

Scoring

The individualist and collectivist values are listed in alternating order, with the first (Pleasure) being an individualist value and the second (Honor of Parents and Elders) being a collectivist value. People from individualist cultures such as the United States, Canada, England, or Australia tend to have more individualist values than collectivist values in the upper half of their values hierarchy. This order tends to be reversed for those from collectivist cultures such as Mexico, Japan, Korea, or China. Which of the two cultural belief systems is predominant in your own values hierarchy? If you know someone from another culture, how do they rank these values?

"An individual has not started living until he can rise above the narrow confines of his individualistic concerns to the broader concerns of all humanity."

Martin Luther King, Jr., U.S. civil rights leader, 1929-1968.

characteristics of given societies (Park et al., 2003). Individualism is closely linked with socioeconomic development (Welzel et al., 2003). When collectivist cultures become industrialized and experience economic development, they often also develop some of the thinking associated with individualism. This is at least partly so because the increased prosperity brought on by economic development minimizes the type of concerns for survival that prompt people to strongly identify with—and unquestionably submit to—their social group (Inglehart & Baker, 2000; Oyserman et al., 2002). When economic conditions shift in this manner, many collectivists begin developing an interest in individual freedom-focused rights and privileges. The transition to democracy, which stresses individual rights over the rights of the state, is currently taking place in such collectivist countries as Egypt, China, Jordan, Turkey, the Philippines, South Africa, Taiwan, and Slovenia.

EVOLUTION SHAPES UNIVERSAL PATTERNS OF SOCIAL BEHAVIOR.

One of the added benefits of cross-cultural research is that it not only allows us to identify those aspects of social behavior that vary from one culture to the next, but it also allows us to identify social behaviors that are common to all cultures. When a universal social behavior is identified, discussion naturally turns to how this pattern of behavior may have evolved. **Evolutionary psychology** may provide useful insights here (Barrett et al., 2002; Kenrick & Maner, 2004).

The evolutionary perspective is partly based on the writings of biologist Charles Darwin (1809–1882), who theorized that genetic changes in the population of a species occur over many generations due to the interaction of environmental and biological variables. **Genes** are the biochemical units of inheritance for all living organisms, and the human species has about thirty thousand different genes. According to Darwin (1859, 1871), all living organisms struggle for survival, and within each species a great deal of competition and genetic variation occurs between individuals. Those members of a species with genetic traits best adapted for survival in their present environment will produce more offspring, and, as a result, their numbers will increase in the population. As the environment changes, however, other members within the species possessing traits better suited to the new conditions will flourish, a process called **natural selection**. In this way, the environment selects which genes of a species will be passed onto future generations. As this process of natural selection continues, and as the features best suited for survival change, the result is **evolution**, a term that refers to the gradual genetic changes that occur in a species over generations. *Reproduction* is central to the natural selection process, and the essence of natural selection is that the characteristics of some individuals allow them to produce more offspring than others.

An example of social behavior from another species that may be the product of natural selection is water splashing by male gorillas. Males regularly create massive water plumes by leaping into pools or by slapping the water with their powerful hands. Why is it that female gorillas do not engage in this behavior nearly to the same degree, and what precipitates male splashing? Evolutionary theorists hypothesized that male gorillas engage in water splashing to intimidate other males and keep them away from their females. To test this hypothesis, researchers observed the splashing displays of lowland gorillas in the Congo over a three-year period (Parnell & Buchanan-Smith, 2001). They found that more than 70 percent of the splashing was carried out by dominant males in the presence of males not from their social group, with more than half the displays occurring when no females were present. These findings suggested to the researchers that the splashing was being directed at strange males who might challenge the dominant male's control of his group. They speculated that over the course of gorilla evolution, males who engaged in intimidating behavior like water splashing were more successful in preventing strange males from stealing females from their group than those who did not water splash. Thus, acting tough by literally making a big splash when other males were present resulted in greater reproductive success, and that is why this social behavior persists in the male gorilla population today.

Social psychologists who adopt the evolutionary approach apply a similar type of logic to understanding humans. Many social behaviors extensively studied by social psychologists, such as aggression, helping, interpersonal attraction, romantic love, and stereotyping, are thought to be shaped by inherited traits (Buss & Kenrick, 1998; Gangestad & Simpson, 2007). If this is true, then attempts to understand human social behavior should consider how these inherited traits might have given our ancestors a reproductive advantage in their environment, thus maximizing their ability to survive and reproduce.

There are two important points to keep in mind when considering the process of evolution. First, individual organisms don't evolve—populations evolve. The role that individuals play in evolution is their interaction with the environment and their genes being screened by natural selection. Thus, individuals contribute to a change in their species' population by their own successes or failures in reproducing. Over many generations, the accumulated effects of literally thousands or even millions of individuals'

evolutionary psychology
....
An approach to psychology based on the principle of natural selection

genes
....
The biochemical units of inheritance for all living organisms

natural selection
....
The process by which organisms with inherited traits best suited to the environment reproduce more successfully than less well-adapted organisms over a number of generations, and a process which leads to evolutionary changes.

evolution
....
The genetic changes that occur in a species over generations due to natural selection.

❝*It may metaphorically be said that natural selection is daily and hourly scrutinizing ... the slightest variations; rejecting those that are bad, preserving and adding up all that are good ... We see nothing of these slow changes in progress, ... we see only that the forms of life are now different from what they formerly were.*❞

From Darwin (1859)

reproductive successes and failures led to evolution of the species. The second point to remember is that evolution does not necessarily result in species being transformed into more complex forms of life (Smith & Szathmáry, 1995). Instead, the key feature of the evolutionary process has to do with the degree to which an organism's inborn genetic traits help it adapt to its current environment. Thus, just as a trait that was once highly adaptive can become maladaptive if the environmental conditions change, the reverse is also true: a maladaptive trait can become extremely adaptive.

Cautions in Applying Evolutionary Principles to Humans' Social Behavior

Despite the importance of adding the evolutionary perspective to our explanation of social behavior, many social scientists are cautious in applying these principles to contemporary human behavior (Conway &, 2002; Scher & Rauscher, 2003). The grounds for such caution rest on the fact that when biologists study an animal, they tend to examine it in terms of how it has adapted to its environment so that it can reproduce and pass on its genes. However, as British ethologists Mark Ridley and Richard Dawkins (1981) point out, when a species changes environments—or when its environment changes—an unavoidable period of time exists in which its biological makeup is not in tune with its surroundings. They contend that all species are probably slightly "behind" their environment, but this is especially so for human beings. We are the youngest primate species on earth, but our brains and bodies are biologically no different than they were one hundred fifty thousand years ago when our ancestors lived on the Pleistocene plains of East Africa. How we behave today in the modern world of city congestion and space-age technology may bear some relation to the roles for which our brains and bodies were originally selected, but the connection is probably weaker than we might think and needs to be interpreted with a great deal of care. In this text, we will approach evolutionary explanations with this sort of justifiable caution—that is, acknowledging that ancient evolutionary forces may have left us with capacities (such as the capacity to behave helpfully), but recognizing that current social and environmental forces encourage or discourage the actual development and use of those capacities (Tomasello, 2011).

What Is the Difference between Sex and Gender?

Throughout this text when comparisons are made between women's and men's decision-making and social behavior, contrasting interpretations regarding any group-based differences will be offered from both the evolutionary and the sociocultural perspectives. In these analyses, it is important to understand the difference between the terms sex and gender (Lippa, 2005). **Sex** refers to the biological status of being female or male, while **gender** refers to the meanings that societies and individuals attach to being female and male. Put simply, sex is a matter of genetic construction, and gender is a matter of cultural construction. Sex is something we are, whereas gender is something we do with the help and encouragement of others.

People are often confused about the distinction between sex and gender because the two concepts are generally thought of as going together—that is, female = feminine, and male = masculine. Yet behaviors or interests considered masculine in one culture may be defined as feminine in others. For instance, in certain North African societies, decorating and beautifying the face and body is a sign of masculinity, not femininity. Similarly, within cultures, beliefs about gender transform over time. For instance, in contemporary North American culture, it is now acceptable—even encouraged—for girls to participate in sports that were previously designated only for boys. Among adults, women are now much more actively involved in careers outside the household (a masculine domain), and men are more involved in child care (a feminine domain) than in previous generations. Gender is not fixed—it is constantly changing and being redefined.

Because sex is biologically based and gender is culturally based, when research finds that men and women actually behave differently, we often ask whether this difference is due to sex (biology) or to gender (culture). This is not an idle question. If someone labels the behavior in question a sex difference, the implication is that the cause of

sex
....
The biological status of being female or male

gender
....
The meanings that societies and individuals attach to being female and male

the difference is rooted in human biology rather than in social or cultural factors. In contrast, when people talk about gender differences, the implication is that these differences do not stem from biology but, rather, that they develop in the course of socialization as boys and girls learn about appropriate gender-based attitudes, roles, and behaviors (Rudman & Glick, 2008).

Men and women differ biologically in a number of ways. The most basic sex difference is that males carry the chromosomal pattern XY, and females carry the pattern XX. This important difference at the chromosomal level produces differences in female and male anatomy and physical appearance. For instance, a newborn male has a penis and testicles, while a newborn female has a vagina and ovaries. At puberty, a male develops a prominent Adam's apple, while a female's breasts enlarge. Although the changes associated with puberty occur well after birth, no one would seriously argue that boys have been taught how to grow an Adam's apple or that girls learn how to grow breasts. These particular differences are due to biological factors—that is, they are a sex difference and are not due to cultural experience.

Beyond these identifiable biological differences in chromosome pattern and anatomy, it is extremely difficult, if not impossible, to presently conclude that differences in the way women and men think, feel, and act are clearly due to sex or gender (Wood & Eagly, 2010). Social psychologists with a biological or evolutionary orientation emphasize biological factors in explaining such differences, whereas those with a sociocultural orientation weigh in with cultural explanations. Yet as already mentioned, when discussing genetics, even in those instances when genetics influences behavioral differences between two groups, such as men and women, these biologically based differences can be greatly increased or decreased due to social forces.

How great are the differences between women and men in their psychological functioning? This is an issue we will address throughout this text. As a preliminary answer, I can tell you that research conducted over the past twenty years indicates there are many more similarities than differences (Hyde, 2005). Across a wide variety of cognitive skills, psychological motives, and social behaviors, men and women do not differ from one another. Thus, despite cultural stereotypes to the contrary, women and men are remarkably alike in much of their psychological functioning. Reflecting these scientific findings, in this text I do not use the misleading term *opposite sex* when comparing one sex with the other but instead use the more appropriate term *other sex*.

BRAIN ACTIVITY AFFECTS AND IS AFFECTED BY SOCIAL BEHAVIOR.

Beyond the organizing principles currently shaping theory and research, social psychologists are constantly exploring new connections with other disciplines, both within and outside the social and behavioral sciences. Like the evolutionary perspective, one new connection that comes from the field of biology is the subfield of **social neuroscience**, which studies the relationship between neural processes of the brain and social processes (Cacioppo et al., 2007; Smith-Lovin & Winkielman, 2010). This analysis emphasizes not only how the brain influences social interaction, but also how social interaction can influence the brain.

social neuroscience
·····················
The study of the relationship between neural processes of the brain and social processes

The increased collaboration between social psychology and neuroscience is largely due to the development of more accurate measures of physiological changes, especially those involving *brain-imaging techniques* that provide pictures—or scans—of this body organ (Cacioppo et al., 2004). These techniques generate "maps" of the brains of living people by examining their electrical activity, structure, blood flow, and chemistry (Cunningham et al., 2003; Ito & Urland, 2003). For example, *functional magnetic resonance imaging (fMRI) measures* the brain's metabolic activity in different regions, revealing which parts of the brain are most active in such social tasks as talking or listening to others, watching social interactions, and thinking about oneself (Iacoboni et al., 2004; Lieberman & Pfeifer, 2005). Researchers using fMRI technology have found that when love-struck research participants look at photos of their romantic partners, specific brain regions (the *caudate nucleus*) that play key roles in motivation and rewards—including feelings of elation and passion—exhibit heightened activation (Fisher, 2004).

cerebral cortex
....
The wrinkled-looking outer layer of the brain that coordinates and integrates all other brain areas into a fully functioning unit, that is the brain's "thinking" center, and that is much larger in humans than in other animals

frontal lobe
....
The region of the cerebral cortex situated just behind the forehead that is involved in the coordination of movement and higher mental processes, such as planning, social skills, and abstract thinking. This is the area of the brain that is the originator of self processes

Similarly, neuroscientists have discovered areas in the *frontal lobe* of the cerebral cortex that are of particular importance in understanding self-related processes (Devue & Bredart, 2011; Heatherton, 2011). As depicted in Figure 1.3, the **cerebral cortex** is the wrinkled-looking outer layer of brain tissue that coordinates and integrates all other brain areas into a fully functioning unit. About 90 percent of our cerebral cortex is of relatively recent evolution, and the frontal lobe is its largest region. The **frontal lobe** is involved in the coordination of movement and higher mental processes, such as planning, social skills, and abstract thinking (Poldrack & Wagner, 2004; Rochat, 2011). Recent brain-imaging studies indicate that a region in the frontal lobe of the cerebral cortex, called the *anterior cingulate cortex*, is especially active when people are self-aware (Lieberman & Eisenberger, 2005; Vanhaudenhuyse et al., 2011). The anterior cingulate cortex contains a special type of brain cells or neurons, called *spindle neurons*, which are much larger than other neurons in the brain. These spindle neurons collect waves of neural signals from one region of the brain and send them on to other regions. It appears that the anterior cingulate cortex with its spindle neurons acts as an executive attention system that facilitates self-awareness (Stuphorn et al., 2003; Weissman et al., 2003). Humans are one of only a few species of animals that possess spindle neurons. Additional research indicates that when people are trying to exert self-control over their own thinking and behavior, the anterior cingulate cortex is also actively working in concert with areas in the prefrontal lobe regions (*dorsolateral prefrontal cortex* and *orbitofrontal cortex*).

Figure 1.3

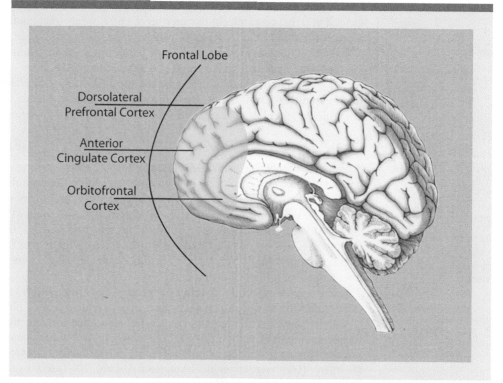

Brain Regions in the Frontal Lobe Associated with Self Processes

The primary neural source for self-awareness is the frontal lobe of the cerebral cortex, which is the wrinkled-looking front outer layer of the brain. The frontal lobe is involved in the coordination of movement and higher mental processes, such as planning, social skills, and abstract thinking. A region in the frontal lobe, the anterior cingulate cortex, is especially active when people are self-aware.

A natural question for you to ask at this point in my discussion of social neuroscience is why such knowledge is important in gaining insight into social interaction. The importance of social neuroscience for social psychology is not that research in this area will reveal the location in the brain of the self, romantic love, or any other topic in social psychology. Instead, its potential power is that it might help social psychologists understand which cognitive processes and motivational states play a role in specific social behaviors. That sort of knowledge is vitally important because the topics in social psychology are often very complex, with competing theories trying to adequately explain the complexity. If social neuroscience's "window into the brain" can identify what type of neural activity is associated with specific types of social thinking and behavior, it will be that much easier to rule out competing explanations. In this way, the neuroscientific perspective provides another layer of knowledge in our understanding of social interaction (Haxby, 2011; Zaki, J. & K. Ochsner, 2011).

Reflecting this hope and possibility, the U.S. federal government's National Institute of Mental Health—which has an annual budget of 1.3 billion dollars—has begun giving priority to research grants that combine social psychology and neuroscience (Willingham & Dunn, 2003). In this text, we discuss some of the findings in this new area of research. For example, when discussing self-awareness and self-regulation (Chapter 3), we examine how the anterior cingulate cortex facilitates the monitoring and controlling of intentional behavior and focused problem solving. Similarly, when discussing attitude formation and change (Chapter 5), we analyze how one brain region engages in an immediate primitive "good-bad" emotional assessment that may be followed by higher-order processing conducted in the brain's cerebral cortex.

POSITIVE PSYCHOLOGY IS AN EMERGING PERSPECTIVE IN SOCIAL PSYCHOLOGY.

positive psychology
....
An approach to psychology that studies ways to enrich human experience and maximize human functioning.

Another psychological perspective that has become increasingly influential within social psychology and the larger discipline of psychology is **positive psychology**, which studies ways to enrich human experience and maximize human functioning (Seligman, 2011). Social psychologists who identify themselves as proponents of positive psychology are currently studying what makes people happy and optimistic in their daily living, as well as what social conditions contribute to healthy interaction (Sheldon & Ryan, 2011; Sherman, 2011). For example, when does an optimistic view of life help people overcome hurdles to success, and when does it cause people to overlook impending failure? Teaching people to avoid harmful self-deceptions while still maintaining a sense of realistic optimism about life is one of the goals of positive psychology (Mauss et al., 2011; Snyder, 2000).

An increasingly important area of social psychological study related to positive psychology is *morality*, which involves standards of right and wrong conduct (Haidt & Kesebir, 2011; Jordan et al., 2011). In studying morality, social psychologists are trying to better understand how moral judgments help or hinder social living by regulating not only fair and just social relations but also personal behaviors that reflect self-interest and self-indulgence. Periodically in this text, information will be presented about positive psychology topics, including morality, that relate to chapter material.

The remaining chapters in this text will provide you with some fascinating insights into your social world and yourself. That is the beauty of social psychology. The more you learn about the psychology of social interaction, the more you will learn about how you can more effectively fit into—and actively shape—your own social surroundings. Let us now begin that inquiry.

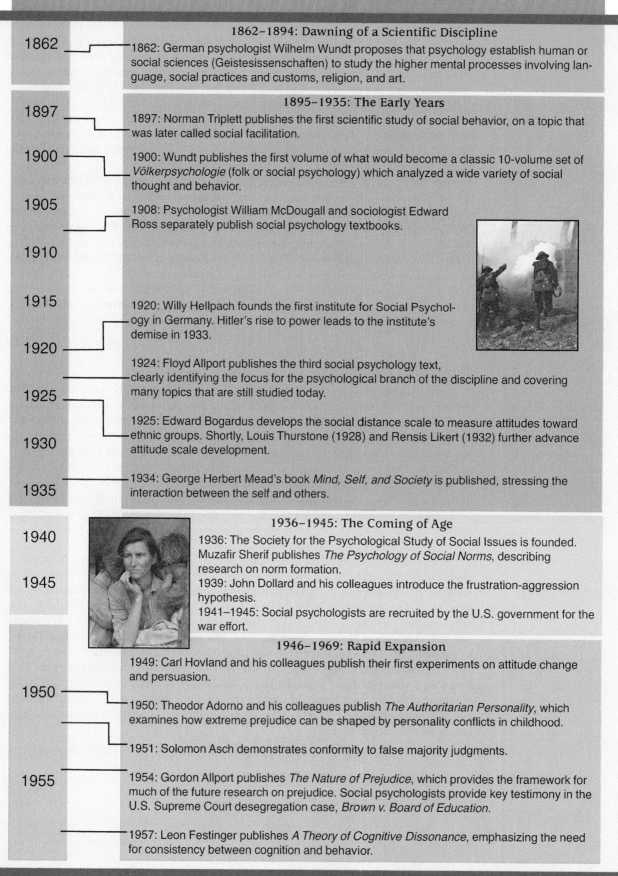

SOME MILESTONES IN THE FIELD OF SOCIAL PSYCHOLOGY

1862 ———

1862–1894: Dawning of a Scientific Discipline

1862: German psychologist Wilhelm Wundt proposes that psychology establish human or social sciences (Geistesissenschaften) to study the higher mental processes involving language, social practices and customs, religion, and art.

1897 ———

1895–1935: The Early Years

1897: Norman Triplett publishes the first scientific study of social behavior, on a topic that was later called social facilitation.

1900 ———

1900: Wundt publishes the first volume of what would become a classic 10-volume set of *Völkerpsychologie* (folk or social psychology) which analyzed a wide variety of social thought and behavior.

1905 ———

1908: Psychologist William McDougall and sociologist Edward Ross separately publish social psychology textbooks.

1910

1915

1920 ———

1920: Willy Hellpach founds the first institute for Social Psychology in Germany. Hitler's rise to power leads to the institute's demise in 1933.

1924: Floyd Allport publishes the third social psychology text, clearly identifying the focus for the psychological branch of the discipline and covering many topics that are still studied today.

1925 ———

1925: Edward Bogardus develops the social distance scale to measure attitudes toward ethnic groups. Shortly, Louis Thurstone (1928) and Rensis Likert (1932) further advance attitude scale development.

1930

1934: George Herbert Mead's book *Mind, Self, and Society* is published, stressing the interaction between the self and others.

1935

1940

1936–1945: The Coming of Age

1936: The Society for the Psychological Study of Social Issues is founded. Muzafir Sherif publishes *The Psychology of Social Norms*, describing research on norm formation.

1945

1939: John Dollard and his colleagues introduce the frustration-aggression hypothesis.

1941–1945: Social psychologists are recruited by the U.S. government for the war effort.

1946–1969: Rapid Expansion

1949: Carl Hovland and his colleagues publish their first experiments on attitude change and persuasion.

1950 ———

1950: Theodor Adorno and his colleagues publish *The Authoritarian Personality*, which examines how extreme prejudice can be shaped by personality conflicts in childhood.

1951: Solomon Asch demonstrates conformity to false majority judgments.

1955

1954: Gordon Allport publishes *The Nature of Prejudice*, which provides the framework for much of the future research on prejudice. Social psychologists provide key testimony in the U.S. Supreme Court desegregation case, *Brown v. Board of Education*.

1957: Leon Festinger publishes *A Theory of Cognitive Dissonance*, emphasizing the need for consistency between cognition and behavior.

SOME MILESTONES IN THE FIELD OF SOCIAL PSYCHOLOGY continued

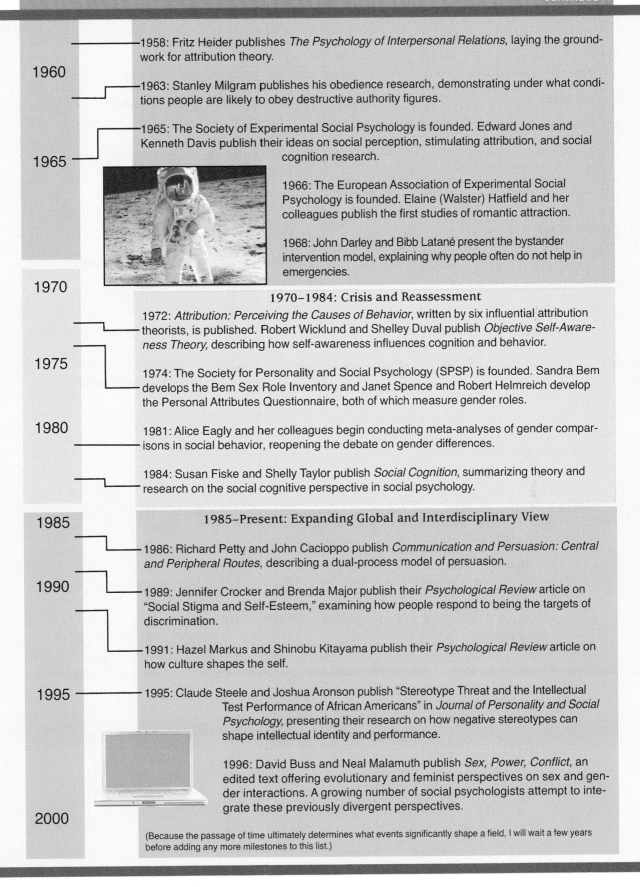

1960

1965

1958: Fritz Heider publishes *The Psychology of Interpersonal Relations*, laying the groundwork for attribution theory.

1963: Stanley Milgram publishes his obedience research, demonstrating under what conditions people are likely to obey destructive authority figures.

1965: The Society of Experimental Social Psychology is founded. Edward Jones and Kenneth Davis publish their ideas on social perception, stimulating attribution, and social cognition research.

1966: The European Association of Experimental Social Psychology is founded. Elaine (Walster) Hatfield and her colleagues publish the first studies of romantic attraction.

1968: John Darley and Bibb Latané present the bystander intervention model, explaining why people often do not help in emergencies.

1970

1970–1984: Crisis and Reassessment

1972: *Attribution: Perceiving the Causes of Behavior*, written by six influential attribution theorists, is published. Robert Wicklund and Shelley Duval publish *Objective Self-Awareness Theory*, describing how self-awareness influences cognition and behavior.

1975

1974: The Society for Personality and Social Psychology (SPSP) is founded. Sandra Bem develops the Bem Sex Role Inventory and Janet Spence and Robert Helmreich develop the Personal Attributes Questionnaire, both of which measure gender roles.

1980

1981: Alice Eagly and her colleagues begin conducting meta-analyses of gender comparisons in social behavior, reopening the debate on gender differences.

1984: Susan Fiske and Shelly Taylor publish *Social Cognition*, summarizing theory and research on the social cognitive perspective in social psychology.

1985

1985–Present: Expanding Global and Interdisciplinary View

1986: Richard Petty and John Cacioppo publish *Communication and Persuasion: Central and Peripheral Routes*, describing a dual-process model of persuasion.

1990

1989: Jennifer Crocker and Brenda Major publish their *Psychological Review* article on "Social Stigma and Self-Esteem," examining how people respond to being the targets of discrimination.

1991: Hazel Markus and Shinobu Kitayama publish their *Psychological Review* article on how culture shapes the self.

1995

1995: Claude Steele and Joshua Aronson publish "Stereotype Threat and the Intellectual Test Performance of African Americans" in *Journal of Personality and Social Psychology*, presenting their research on how negative stereotypes can shape intellectual identity and performance.

1996: David Buss and Neal Malamuth publish *Sex, Power, Conflict*, an edited text offering evolutionary and feminist perspectives on sex and gender interactions. A growing number of social psychologists attempt to integrate these previously divergent perspectives.

2000

(Because the passage of time ultimately determines what events significantly shape a field, I will wait a few years before adding any more milestones to this list.)

SECTION SUMMARY

- The self is a central and organizing concept in social psychology.

- Interactionism studies the combined effects of both the situation and the person on human behavior.

- Many contemporary social cognitive theories attempt to reconcile the "hot" and the "cold" perspectives of human nature into a more inclusive "warm look."

- Social psychologists have become more attentive to cultural influences on social behavior.

- The cultural variables of individualism and collectivism are particularly helpful in understanding cultural differences

- Evolutionary theory is increasingly used to explain social behavior.

- In explaining any male-female differences in social behavior, the evolutionary perspective emphasizes biological factors and the sociocultural perspective emphasizes cultural factors.

- Integrating ideas from neuroscience and social psychology are becoming more a part of social psychological research and theory.

- Understanding how life can be enriched is one goal of positive psychology, en emerging perspective in social psychology.

▶ Check out our web site

www.BVT*Lab*.com

for chapter-by-chapter flashcards, summaries, and practice quizzes.

WEB SITES

ACCESSED THROUGH www.BVTLab.com/sop6

SOCIAL PSYCHOLOGY NETWORK
This is the largest social psychology database on the Internet, with more than five thousand links to psychology-related resources.

SOCIETY FOR PERSONALITY AND SOCIAL PSYCHOLOGY HOME PAGE
This is the web site for the largest organization of social and personality psychologists in the world. This organization was founded in 1974.

PEW RESEARCH CENTER
This is the web site link for the national survey results of the 2007 report *How young people view their lives, future, and politics: A portrait of Generation Next.*

EVOLUTIONARY PSYCHOLOGY FOR THE COMMON PERSON
This web site provides an introduction to evolutionary psychology and provides links to other related web resources.

2 Chapter 2
Conducting Research in Social Psychology

CHAPTER OUTLINE

INTRODUCTION

The Goals and Process of Research
Two research goals focus on acquiring and applying knowledge.
The research process involves a series of steps.
Meta-analysis examines the outcomes of many studies.
One strength of the scientific method is its self-correcting nature.

Common Scientific Methods
Description is the goal of observational research.
Correlational research assesses the direction and strength of the relationship between variables.
Experimental research can determine cause-effect relationships.

The Promise and Caution in Using Emerging Technologies
Social psychologists are increasingly using new technologies.
The study of actual behavior is declining in social psychology.

WEB SITES

INTRODUCTION

In the early 1960s, Leonard Eron was conducting research at an elementary school in the hope of gaining a better understanding of aggression in children. One aspect of the study involved administering a survey to parents, asking them a series of questions about their eight-year-old children. Included in the survey were a few items covering children's TV-viewing habits. Eron inserted these queries solely as interesting "icebreakers," hoping to provide parents with a brief diversion from the central research questions. However, when he analyzed his data, Eron was surprised by what he found. The one thing that was most associated with children's aggression was how much violent television they watched. "What is going on here?" wondered Eron.

Bullying is a common occurrence in most schools around the world. There have been many studies conducted in an effort to find out more about childhood aggression.

Scientific discovery is essentially a form of human problem solving (Klahr & Simon, 1999). The type of problem solving that occurs in scientific enterprises is highly valued because it enhances our ability to understand, predict, and control the forces that shape our physical and social world. The question that Eron asked, after analyzing his initial aggression study, set him on a scientific exploration that spanned three decades. His work also inspired other social scientists to conduct their own studies of TV violence. Together, their findings have prompted concerned parents, educators, and politicians to lobby the television industry to modify the content of its programs. In this chapter we examine the scientific methods that social psychologists use in their research, and in so doing, we review some of the influential studies that examined the relationship between TV violence and aggression.

THE GOALS AND PROCESS OF RESEARCH

scientific method

A set of procedures used to gather, analyze, and interpret information in a way that reduces error and leads to dependable generalizations

The **scientific method** consists of a set of procedures used to gather, analyze, and interpret information in a way that reduces error and leads to dependable generalizations. This method has been practiced in some form across various disciplines for at least one thousand years. In comparison to other sciences, social psychology is very young, with just a little over a century of experience using scientific methods. Yet, social psychology shares with its sister sciences the same underlying goals in conducting research and it follows the same basic process in executing its scientific methods.

TWO RESEARCH GOALS FOCUS ON ACQUIRING AND APPLYING KNOWLEDGE.

basic research

Research designed to increase knowledge about social behavior

applied research

Research designed to increase the understanding of and solutions to real-world problems by using current social psychological knowledge

Social psychologists conduct both *basic* and *applied research*. The goal in **basic research** is to simply increase knowledge about social behavior, knowledge for knowledge's sake (Fiske, 2004). No attempt is made to solve a specific social or psychological problem. In contrast, **applied research** is designed to increase the understanding of and solutions to real-world problems by using current social psychological knowledge (Barton et al., 2009; Maruyama, 2004).

Although many social psychologists label themselves as either basic or applied researchers, the efforts of one group often influence those of the other. As in other sciences, the knowledge gained through the work of basic researchers provides applied researchers with a better understanding of how to solve specific social problems. Likewise, when applied researchers cannot solve problems by employing basic research findings, such failure often suggests to basic researchers that they need to refine their theories to better reflect how the social world operates.

One important ethical question surrounding applied research is whether there should be any limits on the use of social psychological knowledge. For example, as you will see in Chapters 5 and 7, basic research has taught us a great deal about the conditions under which people become susceptible to persuasion and influence. Social influence theories could be utilized to help the tobacco industry persuade consumers to purchase their products, which are known to cause serious, long-term health problems. These same theories could also be used to design television, radio, and magazine ads to convince people not to use tobacco products. Although most of us would have few qualms about social psychological theory being used to prevent people from consuming products known to cause serious health problems, there would be grave reservations expressed about using these theories to encourage such consumption.

These very concerns have stirred considerable debate about the proper role that social psychologists should play in applying their knowledge in the world (Unger, 2011). One point of view is that the discoveries of any science should be used for whatever purposes interested parties consider important. In such endeavors, scientists should be neutral truth seekers and should not be concerned about how their discoveries are utilized. Followers of this *value-free* perspective believe that social psychologists that use the facts of their science to influence social policy decisions undermine the scientific basis of the discipline (Hammond, 2004). A second point of view, first proposed by Kurt Lewin in the 1940s, is that social science and social action should not be separated. Contemporary followers of this *value-laden* perspective believe that merely studying society and its problems without a commitment to changing society for the better is irresponsible (Álvarez, 2001).

A commonly accepted belief within the philosophy of science today is that no science is untouched by values and the politics of the culture in which it is practiced (Harris, 1999). In social psychology, the things studied matter a great deal to people, including those who do the investigating. Social psychologists are human beings, and their own values often determine what sort of research and application they are most interested in undertaking, as well as influencing the theories they develop to explain the social facts (Redding, 2001). Yet when there is a clash of social psychological theories based on different value orientations, science does not grind to a halt. Instead, scientific inquiry persists, studies are conducted and published, and new social facts are discovered. In some instances, the adversaries in a scientific dispute even work together to resolve their differences (Mellers et al., 2001). By relying upon the scientific method, social psychology will continue to contribute to our understanding of human behavior, and many of those within the discipline will also use this knowledge to make changes in their social world (refer to Table 2.1).

Our discussion in each chapter of this text will begin with an analysis of the findings of basic research; for as Kurt Lewin (1951) argued, it is essential to have a good understanding of psychological processes *before* trying to solve difficult social problems. Yet, in keeping with Lewin's maxim of "No research without action, and no action without research," throughout the text we will also examine how basic research is applied to important social problems. In addition, each chapter (beginning with Chapter 3) will conclude with an application section in which you can learn how the content of that chapter sheds light on a specific social or personal issue.

THE RESEARCH PROCESS INVOLVES A SERIES OF STEPS.

For social psychologists to effectively study social behavior—be it basic or applied research—they must carefully plan and execute their research projects (Sansone et al., 2004). This entire process of scientific inquiry unfolds in six basic steps, which are summarized in Table 2.2.

Table 2.1

Values and Social Commitment in the Field of Social Psychology

Social psychologist Dalmas Taylor, past president of the Society for the Scientific Study of Social Issues, expressed the problem faced by social psychologists that study aspects of social behavior directly related to contemporary social issues:

The problem is that when you are involved in studying something, it requires a certain amount of objectivity and detachment. When you are involved in pursuing a remedy, there is less objectivity and a great deal of attachment. So you essentially end up wearing two hats, playing two different roles. I think that can be done, but it's very difficult. So occasionally I have advocated that the practitioners of social psychology not be the same people who generate the data or the findings. But I've modified that over the years, consistent with the discipline itself recognizing that the very selection of hypotheses and the paradigms that we use contain values either covertly or overtly, and at any point along the line there's a certain amount of subjectivity. What we have is a series of methodological strategies that mitigate against our biases, and I think they perform a sufficient check and balance to let us play this dual role with less concern and less error. (Aron & Aron 1986, pp. 125–126).

Step 1: Select a Topic and Review Past Research.

Research ideas do not develop in a vacuum. In selecting a topic to study, inspiration could come from someone else's research, from an incident in the daily news, or from some personal experience in the researcher's own life. It is not a coincidence that the research topics chosen by American social psychologists have the greatest meaning to Americans. Social psychologists generally investigate topics that have relevance to their own lives and culture.

Once a topic has been chosen, the researcher must search the scientific literature to determine whether prior investigations of the topic exist. The findings from these previous studies generally shape the course of the current investigation. Today, literature searches are greatly accelerated by using a number of computer-based searching programs that catalog even the most recently published studies. In addition, social psychologists can quickly obtain unpublished articles from researchers at other universities through the Internet. This means that access to the scholarly contributions of others' is often literally at one's fingertips.

Step 2: Develop a Theory, Generate Hypotheses, and Select a Scientific Method.

As previously noted, the basic motivation underlying research is the desire to answer questions. The questions of interest usually revolve around whether some phenomenon can be explained by a particular principle or theory. A **theory** is an organized system of ideas that seeks to explain why two or more events are related. Put simply, a theory provides a particular picture of reality concerning some phenomenon. What makes a good theory depends on a number of factors, some of which are listed in Table 2.3 (Higgins, 2004; Nowak, 2004).

The most important factor to the working scientist is the *predictive accuracy* of the theory: can it reliably predict behavior? A second necessary factor is *internal coherence*— there should not be any logical inconsistencies or unexplained coincidences among any of the theoretical ideas. A third characteristic of a good theory is that it should be *economical*, meaning that it contains only the principles or concepts necessary to explain the phenomenon in question and no more (Taylor, 2007a). Finally, a fourth and very important quality in a good theory is *fertility*—the ability to fire the imagination of other

---

Critical THINKING

Prior to conducting research, what precautions do you think social psychologists should take to ensure that the people who participate in their research will not be harmed? Should social psychologists be allowed to study people without their consent?

theory
- - - - - - - - - - - - - - - - -
An organized system of ideas that seeks to explain why two or more events are related

“*There is nothing so practical as a good theory.*”

Kurt Lewin, German-born social psychologist, 1890–1947

Table 2.2

Steps in the Process of Social Psychological Research

Step 1: Select a topic and review past research. *Ideas come from a variety of sources, including existing theories, past research, current social events, and personal experiences. Social psychologists must also become knowledgeable about past research findings in their area of interest and keep abreast of recently published studies and those reported at scientific meetings.*

Step 2: Develop a theory, generate hypotheses, and select a scientific method. *Once the research literature has been digested, a theory must be developed that can be empirically tested using hypotheses that logically flow from the theory. A scientific method must also be selected that allows the hypotheses to be tested in a way that minimizes error and leads to dependable generalizations. Research can be conducted in the laboratory or in the field, and the social psychologist can either employ observational, correlational, or experimental methodology.*

Step 3: Obtain approval to conduct the study. *Prior to conducting research, all proposed studies must be submitted for approval to institutional review boards (IRBs). IRBs follow guidelines based on the risk/benefit ratio, which weighs the potential risks to those participating in a study against the benefits that the study may have for advancing knowledge about humanity.*

Step 4: Collect the data. *Social psychologists use both qualitative and quantitative data. The three basic techniques of data collection are self-reports, direct observations, and archival information.*

Step 5: Analyze the data and reevaluate the theory. *Data can be analyzed using either descriptive or inferential statistics, with the latter mathematical analysis being the more valuable because it allows researchers to generalize their findings to the population of interest. If the results from these analyses do not support the study's hypotheses, the theory from which the hypotheses were derived needs to be reconsidered and perhaps revised.*

Step 6: Report the results. *Just because a social psychologist conducts a study does not mean it will be published and make its way into the social psychological literature. In most cases, a scientific journal will not publish a submitted article if there are problems with the hypotheses or methods, or flaws in the data analysis. In addition, articles are often rejected for publication because reviewers decide the research isn't very important. Due to these factors, the top journals in social psychology (Journal of Personality and Social Psychology, Personality and Social Psychology Bulletin) regularly publish less than 10 percent of the submitted research articles.*

Table 2.3

What Makes a Good Theory?

Predictive Accuracy: Can it reliably predict behavior?

Internal Coherence: Are there any logical inconsistencies between any of the theoretical ideas?

Economy: Does it only contain what is necessary to explain the phenomenon in question?

Fertility: Does it generate research, and can it be used to explain a wide variety of social behavior?

Children who watch more violent television are believed to be more aggressive as adults than children who do not watch violent television.

hypothesis

An educated guess or prediction about the nature of things based upon a theory

scientists so that the ideas in the theory are tested and extended to a wide variety of social behavior.

The way that scientists determine the predictive accuracy of a theory is by formulating hypotheses. A **hypothesis** is an educated guess or prediction about the nature of things based upon a theory—it is a logical implication of the theory. The researcher asks, "If the theory is true, what observations would we expect to make in our investigation?" For example, during the course of his work, Leonard Eron developed the idea that exposure to a lot of TV violence was detrimental to children's social development. This theory led him to formulate the hypothesis that individuals who watch a great deal of TV violence during childhood will be more physically aggressive in adulthood than individuals who watch little TV violence.

After developing a theory and hypotheses, researchers must next select a scientific method that allows the hypotheses to be tested in a way that minimizes error and leads to dependable generalizations. The three primary scientific methods used by social psychologists are *observational, correlational,* and *experimental.* Whereas observational research describes behavior, the correlational and experimental methods study the relationships among variables. Of the three, experimentation is much more widely used by social psychologists in psychology; observational studies are more often conducted by sociological social psychologists; and correlational methods enjoy roughly equal popularity in both disciplines (Morrill & Fine, 1997; Sherman et al., 1999). We will discuss these three methods in the next section of the chapter.

variables

Factors in scientific research that can be measured and that are capable of changing (or varying).

operational definition

A very clear description of how a variable in a study has been measured

In all scientific methods, social psychologists seek to determine the nature of the relationship between two or more factors, called **variables** because they are things that can be measured and that are capable of changing. When scientists describe their variables, they do so by using *operational definitions*. An **operational definition** is a very clear description of how a variable in a study has been measured. For example, social psychologists studying TV violence and aggression among children may operationally define aggression as any behavior that appears to have the goal of causing physical harm or physical discomfort to another person. This concrete definition of aggression would help other social psychologists know what was measured in the study, and it would also allow them to repeat the study if they desired.

Step 3: Obtain Approval to Conduct the Study.

Although careful attention to a study's methodology is essential in any scientific investigation, even more important is the safety and psychological security of the research participants (Kimmel, 2004; Nagy, 2011). In the 1960s and 1970s, the issue of research ethics was uppermost in the minds of social psychologists because of a few controversial studies that appeared to put participants at risk for psychological harm (Milgram, 1963; Zimbardo, 1972). The most controversial of these studies were Stanley Milgram's obedience experiments, in which volunteers agreed to act as teachers in a learning experiment that in actuality was a study of obedience. During the course of the experiment, teachers were ordered to deliver seemingly painful electrical shocks to a person merely because he was not performing well on a memory task. Even when the victim screamed in agony and demanded to be released, the experimenter insisted that the teacher continue delivering the shocks. In reality, no shocks were ever delivered—the victim only pretended to be in pain—but the stress experienced by the participants in their role as teacher/torturer was indeed real. Although this study and others of its kind asked important questions about social behavior that remain relevant today (Dutton & Tetreault, 2009), serious concerns were raised about whether the significance of the research topics justified exposing participants to potentially harmful psychological consequences (Baumrind, 1964; Savin, 1973).

The psychological harm that could occur in such studies may take many forms. For example, to conduct his obedience studies Milgram had to use **deception**, a methodological technique in which the researcher misinforms participants about the true nature of what they are experiencing in a study (Ortmann & Hertwig, 1997). The reason for using deception is to increase the likelihood that the responses of participants are as close as possible to the responses of people in real-world settings where the topic of study naturally occurs.

There are two main forms of deception in research. One form of deception involves not fully disclosing the true nature of the study until it is over. For example, participants in Milgram's study were told they were involved in a learning experiment, but later discovered that the study was actually investigating obedience. If Milgram's participants had been fully informed about the study's purpose, this knowledge very likely would have caused them to act differently. A second form of deception involves exposing participants to a trained member of the research team, called a **confederate**, who follows a script designed to create a specific impression on the participants. In the obedience study, the person who was supposedly receiving the electrical shocks was the confederate. By their nature, confederates misinform participants about the true nature of what they are experiencing.

Researcher should use deception cautiously because it could lead to a loss of trust in social scientists by those participating, if they believe the researcher had abused them in the course of the investigation. Beyond the possible loss of trust, placing participants in situations where they are encouraged or coerced to engage in antisocial activity may induce feelings of guilt, shame, or inferiority. Although this type of reaction is possible, little empirical evidence indicates this is the case. In Milgram's (1963) obedience research, for example, only 1.3 percent of those who participated reported any negative feelings about their experiences, and 84 percent were glad to have participated.

Other studies employing deception have found that the vast majority of participants are not bothered by subterfuge (Epley & Huff, 1998; Smith & Berard, 1982). Yet, even though the incidence of negative consequences due to research participation appears to be quite low, social psychologists must be sensitive to the effects such studies may have on individuals' views of themselves and the discipline of social psychology. Ignoring these potentially negative effects may lead to a "participant beware" atmosphere surrounding social psychological research, a development harmful to all concerned (Elms, 1994).

Spurred by the debate surrounding these issues, in 1974 the U.S. government developed regulations requiring all institutions seeking federal funding to establish **institutional review boards (IRBs)** for research involving human participants (there are comparable IRBs for studies using nonhuman subjects). These reviewing bodies, which are composed of scientists, medical professionals, clergy, and other community members, make sure that the welfare of human participants is protected (Wolf, 2010). In 1982, the American Psychological Association attempted to facilitate this review process by publishing detailed guidelines on the conduct of research with human participants (American Psychological Association 1982). These guidelines focus on the *risk/benefit ratio*, which weighs the potential risks to those participating in a study against

---

deception
. . . .
A methodological technique in which the researcher misinforms participants about the true nature of what they are experiencing in a study

confederate
. . . .
A trained member of the research team who follows a script designed to create a specific impression on the research participant

Critical
THINKING
. . . .
If you were a member of your college's institutional review board and a research proposal similar to the Milgram obedience study was submitted for approval, what questions would you ask to determine its risk/benefit ratio? Based on your assessment, would you approve the study?

institutional review boards (IRBs)
. . . .
A panel of scientists and nonscientists who ensure the protection and welfare of research participants by formally reviewing researchers' methodologies and procedures prior to data collection

the benefits that the study may have for advancing knowledge about humanity. In assessing proposed studies, priority is always given to the welfare of the participants over any potential benefits of the research (Swartz, 2011). However, unlike risks in medical research, which are often clear and quantifiable, the risks in psychological studies are often not apparent (Follette et al., 2003). This ambiguity results in more guesswork by IRBs in assessing the risks involved in psychological studies.

In addition to assessing risks and benefits, the guidelines for conducting research with human participants also urge scientists to do the following:

informed consent

A procedure by which people freely choose to participate in a study only after they are told about the activities they will perform

1. Provide adequate information about the research to potential participants, so they can freely decide whether they want to take part. This procedure is known as **informed consent**.
2. Be truthful whenever possible. Deception should be used only when absolutely necessary and when adequate debriefing is provided.
3. Allow participants the *right to decline* to be a part of the study or to discontinue their participation at any point without this decision resulting in any negative consequences (for example, not receiving full payment for their participation).
4. *Protect participants* from both physical and psychological harm.
5. Ensure that any information provided by individual participants is kept *confidential*.

debriefing

A procedure at the conclusion of a research session in which participants are given full information about the nature and hypotheses of the study

6. **Debriefing** individuals after they complete their participation is very important. Explain all aspects of the research, attempt to answer all questions, and resolve any negative feelings. Make sure they realize that their participation contributes to better scientific understanding.
7. Provide participants information on the results of the research if they request it.

As it now stands, participating in social psychological research is a very low-risk activity, despite the fact that deception often is incorporated into research designs (Kemmelmeier et al., 2003). When treated with respect and dignity, individuals generally come away from the research experience feeling enriched, even if they were initially deceived about its true nature (Christensen, 1988).

Step 4: Collect the Data.

sample

A group of people who are selected to participate in a research study.

When the IRB has granted approval, it is time to collect data from your sample. A **sample** is a relatively small group of people who are selected to participate in a given study. The people who are selected to participate in the study come from a **population**, which consists of all the members of an identifiable group from which a sample is drawn. In Eron's study of childhood aggression, his population was eight-year-old children in the United States, but his sample was much smaller. It consisted of only 856 eight-year-olds attending school in Columbia County, New York. The more similar a sample is to a population, the greater confidence researchers have in generalizing their findings from the sample to the population.

population

All the members of an identifiable group from which a sample is drawn

Regarding the data collected from your sample of participants, there are two broad categories: *qualitative* and *quantitative*. Qualitative data exists in a nonnumeric form, such as a scientist's narrative report of a conversation between two people. In contrast, quantitative data is numerical. A scientist collecting this type of data, when studying the same two people conversing, might rate each person's level of physical attractiveness with a numerical scale in which "1" indicates "very unattractive" and "5" indicates "very attractive." As this example suggests, researchers often collect both qualitative and quantitative data in the same study.

Besides data categories, there are three basic techniques of data collection: (1) *self-reports*, (2) *direct observations*, and (3) *archival information*. Collecting data using self-reports allows researchers to measure important subjective states, such as people's perceptions, emotions, or attitudes. *Self/Social Connection Exercise 2.1* provides an example of a commonly used self-report scale in social psychology. The disadvantage of self-report data, however, is that it relies on people accurately describing these internal states—something they are not always willing or able to do (Mathie & Wakeling, 2011; Schwarz, 2003). Because of this drawback, many researchers prefer to directly observe people's behavior, recording its quantity and direction of change over time. This technique is widely employed in observational

Self/Social Connection Exercise 2.1

How is Self-Esteem Measured Using a Self-Report Format?

The Rosenberg Self-Esteem Scale (Rosenberg, 1965) is the most widely used self-reporting measure of self-esteem and it has been translated into many different languages.

Instructions

Read each item below and then indicate the degree to which you agree or disagree with how well each statement describes you using the following response scale:

1 strongly disagree   3 agree
2 disagree   4 strongly agree

1. On the whole, I am satisfied with myself.
2. At times I think I am no good at all.*
3. I feel that I have a number of good qualities.
4. I am able to do things as well as most other people.
5. I feel I do not have much to be proud of.*
6. I certainly feel useless at times.*
7. I feel that I'm a person of worth, at least on an equal plane with others.
8. I wish I could have more respect for myself.*
9. All in all, I am inclined to feel that I am a failure.*
10. I take a positive attitude toward myself.

Directions for Scoring

Half of the self-esteem items are reverse-scored; that is, for these items a lower rating actually indicates a higher level of self-esteem. Before summing all ten items to find out your total self-esteem score, recode those with an asterisk ("*") so that 1 = 4, 2 = 3, 3 = 2, and 4 = 1. Your total self-esteem score can range from 10 to 40, with a higher score indicating a higher level of self-esteem. Scores greater than 25 indicate generally positive attitudes toward the self; those below 25 indicate generally negative self-attitudes.

and experimental studies. Finally, researchers sometimes examine existing documents, or archives, to gather information. These accumulated records come from a wide variety of sources (for example, census information, court records, and newspaper articles) and can provide researchers with a great deal of valuable information (Simonton, 1998). These three ways of collecting information are not always mutually exclusive. For example, the personal memoirs of historical figures represent both self-report and archived data.

Step 5: Analyze the Data and Reevaluate the Theory.

Once the data have been collected, the first part of the fifth step is to conduct data analysis, which usually requires extensive knowledge of statistical procedures and computer software packages. The two basic kinds of statistics are descriptive and inferential. *Descriptive statistics* merely summarize and describe the behavior or characteristics of particular sample of participants in a study, whereas *inferential statistics* move beyond mere description to make generalizations about the larger population from which the sample was drawn. Inferential statistics are used to estimate the likelihood that a difference found in the people studied would also be found if everyone in the population participated in the study. Social psychologists generally accept a difference as *statistically significant* if the likelihood of it having occurred by mere chance is less than one in twenty; that is, a probability of less than 5 percent (McGrath, 2011). Because one of the main objectives of social psychological research is to generalize research findings to the population of interest, inferential statistics are the more valued type of statistic in the discipline.

After data analysis determines whether the hypotheses successfully predicted the outcome of the study, researchers next reevaluate the theory. Were the research hypotheses supported by the data, which thereby supports the validity of the theory? If the data do not support the study's hypotheses, or if only some of the hypotheses are supported, the theory probably needs revising.

Step 6: Report the Results.

As in any scholarly pursuit, for advancements to be made researchers must share their knowledge with others in the field. Researchers disseminate their findings by either publishing articles in scientific journals, making presentations at professional meetings, or by personally informing other researchers. Through the dissemination of these findings, researchers build upon and refine one another's work, and our understanding of social behavior is enriched.

This final step in the research process is a very important one for the advancement of the discipline. However, others do not uncritically accept these findings. At scientific conventions, where research is often first reported, all steps in the research process are scrutinized and the study's strengths and weaknesses are illuminated.

When a written report of the study is later submitted to a scientific journal, it is reviewed to determine whether it should be published. So throughout this process of scientific inquiry, there are numerous checks and balances that ultimately determine whether a research project will make its way into the discipline's body of knowledge. One of the most important factors in this determination is a study's scientific procedure for collecting, analyzing, and interpreting information. The next chapter section will examine the primary scientific methods employed by social psychologists.

META-ANALYSIS EXAMINES THE OUTCOMES OF MANY STUDIES.

The findings from a single study are far less convincing than the findings from a series of related studies. This is why researchers are so interested in **replication**, which involves repeating a study's scientific procedures using different participants in an attempt to duplicate the findings. The issue often faced in replications is that of contradictory findings from one study to the next. If, for example, seven studies find that boys are more aggressive than girls and three studies find no differences, what conclusions should be drawn? In the past, researchers used the "majority rules" approach to resolve such controversies. That is, they merely counted up the number of studies that found or did not find a particular effect and then concluded that the effect existed if it occurred in the majority of studies.

To rely on more sophisticated comparison procedures when dealing with contradictory findings from replication studies, researchers now use techniques called meta-analysis (Hall & Brannick, 2002). **Meta-analysis** is the use of statistical techniques to summarize results from similar studies on a specific topic to estimate the reliability and overall size of the effect (Kastrin, 2008; Rothstein et al., 2002). The term meta-analysis literally means "analyses of analyses." Because many studies may find small differences between groups that do not reach statistical levels of significance, meta-analysis can determine whether these small effects are indeed "real" or merely measurement error. Meta-analyses can also examine whether studies using different research methods, such as experimental versus correlational designs, lead to different results.

replication
Repeating a study's scientific procedures using different participants in an attempt to duplicate the findings

meta-analysis
The use of statistical techniques to sumarize results from similar studies on a specific topic to estimate the reliability and overall size of the effect.

Researchers may also be interested in examining whether there are different effect sizes for published versus unpublished studies on a given topic. This sort of meta-analysis is of interest because scientific journals may be more likely to publish studies with results that support research hypotheses than they are to publish studies that have nonsignificant findings. This sort of publication bias is often referred to as the *file-drawer effect* because the unpublished results are tucked away in researchers' file cabinets. The possibility of a publication bias can be tested using meta-analytic procedures that estimate the number of nonsignificant studies necessary to change a significant effect size to being nonsignificant (Rosenthal & Rubin, 1982). If the number is large, researchers are more confident that there is no publication bias. Throughout this text, you will see how meta-analysis helps us better understand social psychological findings.

ONE STRENGTH OF THE SCIENTIFIC METHOD IS ITS SELF-CORRECTING NATURE.

Truth in science is never final. Scientific theories are explanations of how things in the world are related to one another and how they operate. Theories are logically constructed and reconfigured from careful observations and testable hypotheses. You can have such overwhelming data supporting your theory that you have very strong confidence that it accurately explains the phenomena in question. Yet, at the core of the scientific journey of discovery is the assumption that any theory can be modified or completely discarded tomorrow if new evidence calls into question its validity. In other words, all theories in science are fundamentally tentative. Thus, if you seek to understand the human mind using the scientific method, it is a mistake to believe that any theory can achieve a "final truth."

A recent example of why theories should always be considered tentative explanations, subject to disconfirmation and alteration, involves research on *implicit egotism*, which is a nonconscious attraction to people and things that we associate with ourselves. For example, laboratory studies have found reliable evidence that people evaluate the letters contained within their name more favorably than other letters in the alphabet (Nuttin, 1985; Hoorens & Nuttin, 1993). So, for instance, Wendy is more likely to express positive attitudes toward the letters W, E, N, D, and Y than other letters. Laboratory studies also find that people express more liking of products with brand names resembling their own names (Brendl et al., 2005). Over the past decade, a number of social psychologists attempted to generalize these laboratory findings on implicit egotism to explain how it might influence important life decisions. They proposed that because people form positive associations with the sight and sound of their own names they are more likely to choose spouses, places to live, places to work, and occupations with names similar to their own (Pelham et al., 2002). In a series of provocative studies, these researchers found evidence supporting this *Name Letter Effect* (e.g., Anseel & Duyck, 2008; Jones et al., 2004; Pelham et al., 2005) Their studies suggested, for instance, that there are more Andrews married to someone named Andrea, there are more Smiths living in

Although research in the past fifteen years suggested that we are more likely to marry someone who has a name similar to our own, recent studies challenge these findings and call into question the validity of the theory upon which the original research is based.

Smithville, there are more Freds at Ford Motor Company, and there are more lawyers named Laura than you would expect by chance. These findings were very intriguing because they suggested that who you pick as a life companion, where you choose to live, and what occupation you pursue may be partly influenced by the letters in your name!

As you might guess, this theory and the accompanying research findings created considerable interest among social psychologists, generated a good deal of media coverage, and was widely reported in many social psychology textbooks. However, a recent series of studies conducted by Uri Simonsohn challenges the Name Letter Effect, stating that the findings supporting this theory are likely due to the researchers failing to control certain factors in their analyses. For example, when Simonsohn (in press) examined the finding that a higher than expected number of workers and their employers share the same initials in their names, his preliminary analyses confirmed the original study's findings (Anseel & Duyck, 2008): more than two and a half times as many people as would be expected worked for a company that shared their initials. However, more in-depth analysis revealed that this significant effect was caused by those cases in the data where the first three letters of a person's last name and the name of their employer matched up, while the effect disappeared altogether for cases where only the first initials matched. The pattern of these results strongly suggested to Simonsohn that the reason past research found an association between workers' and employers' initials was simply because many people work for companies that they started themselves or that were started by their family members. Similarly, Simonsohn (2011) found evidence that one factor explaining why people tend to marry someone with a similar sounding name is because certain names, such as Andrew

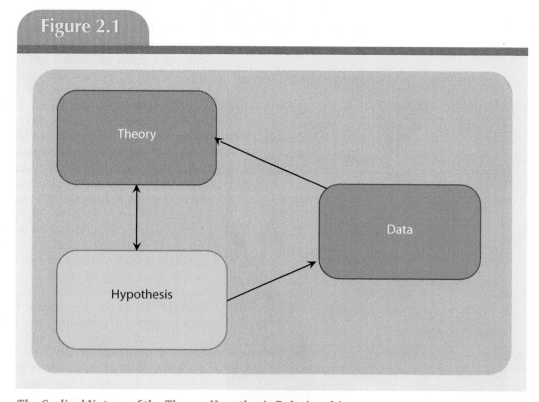

Figure 2.1

The Cyclical Nature of the Theory-Hypothesis Relationship

The data from a study provides the evidence to support or disconfirm the hypothesis. If the hypothesis is supported, the validity of the theory is also supported, generating new hypotheses to test in future research. If the hypothesis is not supported, the validity of the theory is questioned, prompting researchers to revise the theory to reflect the insights gained from their investigation. This revised theory is then used to develop new hypotheses that are then tested in another round of research. Research results that disconfirm a study's hypotheses not only reveal flaws in a scientist's theory but also provide clues to greater scientific truths. Scientists who can think "outside the box" of their own theories and regularly entertain explanations for their hypotheses are best equipped to advance scientific knowledge.

and Andrea or Susan and Stephen, were popular baby names during the same decade, and thus, similar name marital pairings were statistically more likely when these children reached adulthood. Simonsohn's research and his reinterpretation of previous findings does not mean that implicit egotism is not a real psychological phenomenon, but it does call into question the theory that people base crucial life decisions on an unconscious attraction to a letter. It is still possible that we are attracted to things that have names with the same initials as our own names, but this attraction is likely so small that it only influences decisions in a laboratory setting or decisions in the real world that do not matter much to us, such as perhaps buying soda X over soda Y.

The lesson here is that one of the key strengths of the scientific method is that it is self-correcting. When results from scientific studies do not support stated hypotheses, the researchers who conduct these studies are often understandably disappointed because the findings undermine their confidence in the theories on which their hypotheses were generated. However, many researchers also realize that great discoveries often follow such disappointment. In this regard, social psychologist William McGuire (1999) asserts that the task of science is "not the dull and easy job of showing that a fixed hypothesis is right or wrong in a given context. . . . Science has the more exciting task of discovering in what senses the hypotheses and its theoretical explanations are true and in what senses false" (p. 407). From this perspective, failure to find support for a research hypothesis provides the opportunity for future discovery (Banaji, 2004; McGuire, 2004). Figure 2.1 illustrates the cyclical nature of the relationship between a theory and a testable hypothesis.

SECTION SUMMARY

- Social psychologists conduct both basic and applied research.

- The research process unfolds in sequential steps involving theory building and theory testing.

- Meta-analysis is a statistical technique to determine whether specific variables have important effects across many studies.

- Scientific theories cannot be proven, and it is a mistake to believe that they can achieve a "final truth."

COMMON SCIENTIFIC METHODS

observational research
....
A scientific method involving systematic qualitative and/or quantitative descriptions of behavior

naturalistic observation
....
A descriptive scientific method that investigates behavior in its natural environment.

Social psychologists can choose among a variety of scientific methods. The three most prominent research approaches used in social psychology are observational, correlational, and experimental designs.

DESCRIPTION IS THE GOAL OF OBSERVATIONAL RESEARCH.

To understand behavior so that it can be predicted, controlled, or explained, a scientist must first describe it accurately. **Observational research** is a scientific method involving systematic qualitative and/or quantitative descriptions of behavior. In collecting this data, the scientific observer would not try to manipulate (that is, change) the behavior under study but would simply record it. Description is the primary goal here. Three common types of observational methods employed by social psychologists are *naturalistic observation, participant observation*, and *archival research.*

Naturalistic Observation

Naturalistic observation is a type of descriptive method that investigates behavior in its natural environment (Lofland & Lofland, 1995). This observation and recording of behavior sometimes occurs over a prolonged period. Settings for such social psychological research could take place at sporting events, where the interactions between opposing fans might be recorded, or in neighborhood shopping malls, where the courtship behavior of adolescents might be documented. In studying childhood aggression in playgroups, researchers might carefully document students' activities on school playgrounds during recess periods. In such naturalistic settings, observers usually remain as unobtrusive as possible, so that their presence does not influence the behavior under study. In some studies, researchers are not present at all during data collection—hidden video cameras record the events. Later, researchers analyze the behaviors being investigated (Pomerantz et al., 2004). Besides employing naturalistic observation as a primary scientific method, researchers often use it during the initial stages of a project to generate ideas and to gather descriptive data.

One example of a naturalistic observation study was Robert Levine and Ara Norenzayan's (1999) analysis of the pace of everyday life in thirty-one cultures. Some of the data they collected were measurements of people's average walking speed on city sidewalks, the speed at which postal clerks responded to a simple request, and the accuracy of clocks in public settings. Notice that these measurements simply involved the researchers observing how people behaved in their natural surroundings. Their findings indicated that the pace of life was faster in colder and more economically productive cultures (such as Switzerland and Japan) than in those that were hotter and less economically energetic (such as Mexico and Indonesia). Based on these observations, the researchers suggested that the difficulty working in hot temperatures might explain the slower paced life in certain cultures around the world.

Participant Observation

participant observation

A descriptive scientific method where a group is studied from within by a researcher who records behavior as it occurs in its usual natural environment

Another type of observational method is **participant observation**. Here, as in naturalistic observation, a researcher records behavior as it occurs in its natural environment but does so as a participant of the group being studied (Rutherford et al., 2011; Winchatz, 2010). One of the chief benefits of this research strategy is that it allows investigators to get closer to what they are studying than any other method.

A classic example of participant observation research in social psychology was Leon Festinger's study of a Chicago-based doomsday cult in the 1950s (Festinger et al., 1956). The leader of the cult, Mrs. Keech, claimed she was in contact with aliens from outer space who had told her the world was going to end on a specific date, December 21. She told reporters that the only survivors of this catastrophe would be members of her group. When Festinger and his coworkers learned of Mrs. Keech, they became interested in documenting how the cult members would react when the doomsday passed with the world still intact. Acting quickly, these researchers infiltrated the cult

Robert Levine and Ara Norenzayan analyzed the pace of everyday life of thirty-one cultures. They collected data on many different things, including the measurement of peoples' walking speed on the sidewalk.

as participant observers and described the interactions of the members and its leader. This descriptive study was one of the first tests of Festinger's (1957) *cognitive dissonance theory* (see Chapter 5, pp. 171–178). The rich narrative accounts emerging from this participant observation method proved invaluable in demonstrating how some of the basic principles of cognitive dissonance operate in a specific—albeit unusual—situation.

Listed below are four advantages of both naturalistic and participant observation research (Hong & Duff, 2002; Weick, 1985):

1. Allow researchers the opportunity to watch behavior in its "wholeness," providing the full context in which to understand it.
2. Provide researchers the opportunity to record rare events that may never occur in a controlled laboratory environment.
3. Allow researchers the opportunity to systematically record events that were previously seen only by nonscientists.
4. Allow researchers to observe events that would be too risky, dangerous, or unethical to create in the laboratory.

Despite numerous benefits in using naturalistic and participant observation methods, some problems also bear mentioning. First, due to the absence of control that researchers have in such studies, conclusions must be drawn very cautiously. For example, if you observe that shoppers are more likely to donate money after walking out of a store rather than when walking in, do you know for certain what is causing this difference in behavior? Perhaps shoppers have more spare change after making purchases, or perhaps something in the store puts them in a giving mood. Because observational research does not manipulate events to determine their effect on outcomes, researchers must be careful in concluding how events are related to one another.

A second problem is **observer bias**, which occurs when scientists' preconceived ideas about what they are studying affect the nature of their observations. For instance, if you are investigating aggression and believe ahead of time that men are more aggressive than women, you might more likely perceive an ambiguous shove as a nonaggressive nudge when delivered by a woman rather than by a man. Such biasing can be minimized if the behaviors observed are carefully defined and more than one observer is trained in identifying them. If these trained observers, working independently, exhibit a high level of agreement in identifying the behaviors, you have high *interobserver reliability*. With modern technology, researchers often videotape events for later reliability checks.

A third potential problem facing you in naturalistic and participant observation research is that your presence can significantly alter the behavior of those being studied and thus taint the data. For example, in studying children's behavior in a playground setting, the presence of researchers may alter the children's actions. Seeing an older person nearby may cause a few children not to fight one another because they fear being punished. The danger of researchers altering participants' behavior due to their presence is especially troublesome in participant observation research, because the researchers are often actively involved in the observed events (Palmer & Thompson, 2011). Although observational researchers assume that after a period of time those who are being observed will become accustomed to their presence, it is difficult to evaluate to what degree this actually occurs.

Finally, one last problem posed by these types of observational methods is that, more than any other scientific method, they pose the most ethical problems involving invasion of others' privacy. This is especially true in the small minority of studies where informal consent is not feasible.

Archival Research

The third observational method that we will discuss is **archival research**, which examines the already-existing records of an individual, group, or culture. Examples of archival material include diaries, music lyrics, television programs, census information, novels, and newspapers. Archival research is often employed as one component in a larger

observer bias
....
Occurs when preconceived ideas held by the researcher affect the nature of the observations made

❝*Every journey into the past is complicated by delusions, false memories, false namings of real events.*❞
━━━━━━━━━
Adrienne Rich, U.S. poet, born 1929

archival research
....
A descriptive scientific method in which already-existing records are examined

Archival research looks at existing records of an individual, group, or culture.

research effort that includes other scientific methods. For example, in studying friendship networks in high school, a researcher might use information found in the yearbook to evaluate students' physical attractiveness and involvement in school activities. This archival information might be combined with self-reports from students and teachers using survey research and then analyzed together.

Social scientists regularly use the archival method to examine cultural beliefs and norms, such as beauty standards. For example, Gayle Bessenoff and her colleagues (2007) examined the images of female models in magazines, recording their approximate age, body size, and the degree to which they were clothed. Their analyses found that older women are under-represented in magazines, and that younger women are depicted as thinner and as less clothed than older women. Based on these findings, the researchers suggested that one reason younger women have more negative body esteem than older women in American culture is partly because younger women are exposed to more media images of similarly aged models who are very thin than are older women.

Bessenhoff's archival study of magazine images analyzed the photos of female models using *content analysis*, a technique in which two or more people (called judges), working independently, count images, words, sentences, ideas, or whatever other category of information is of interest. As with all scientific inquiry, it is important to clearly define the research variables before beginning a content analysis. It is also important that the judges are carefully trained so that they consistently follow the same guidelines when coding information (Hoyt, 2000). If each category of information is clearly defined and if the judges are adequately trained, *interjudge reliability*— which means the same thing as interobserver reliability—should be sufficiently high to ensure that the observations are not the result of observer bias.

As mentioned in the chapter-opening story, television has been identified as a potentially powerful socializing agent, and TV violence has been the subject of social psychological study for decades. From 1994 to 1997, over eighty researchers at four universities assessed television violence as part of the National Television Violence Study, with one component of their work involving archival research (Federman, 1998). Each year, these researchers conducted content analysis of about 2,700 randomly selected programs broadcast between 6:00 AM and 11:00 PM, representing more than 2,000 hours of television. Their analysis covered many areas, including how characters reacted when violence occurred, how violence was presented in the context of the overall program, and whether violent interactions showed pain, realistic injury, and long-term negative consequences. For the study, violence was defined as any depiction of physical force, or the credible threat of such force, intended to harm an animate being or group of beings.

Their results indicated that violence was a popular theme in TV programs over the three-year period of the study. More than 60 percent of all TV shows contained some violence, with premium cable channels having the highest rate (85 percent) and public broadcasting having the lowest (18 percent). Regarding how violence was depicted, most incidents were sanitized—they showed no pain and little harm for victims, and there were seldom any long-term negative effects. Only 4 percent of violent programs emphasized an antiviolence theme. Instead, violence was often glamorized. More than one of every three violent incidents involved attractive perpetrators, who were likely role models for children, using violence to solve problems. Equally alarming were the findings that children's programs were the least likely to show the long-term negative effects of violence, and they frequently portrayed violence in a humorous context (67 percent of the time). The researchers contended that the message conveyed to young viewers in these programs is that violence is a successful and an appropriate method for good people to solve problems, and that it rarely results in any serious harm to victims or their families.

As this study illustrates, archival research can provide us with valuable information about a culture. The high level of violence in television programming, and the manner in which it is portrayed, suggests that many people enjoy this form of entertainment (Hamilton, 1998). Does watching violent programs cause people to become more violent themselves? Or does observing such violent events have a purging effect on viewers, reducing their aggressive impulses? Archival research cannot answer these questions. Given the purely descriptive nature of all observational research, we must look to other scientific methods to answer questions about how variables are related to one another.

CORRELATIONAL RESEARCH ASSESSES THE DIRECTION AND STRENGTH OF THE RELATIONSHIP BETWEEN VARIABLES.

correlational research
....
Research designed to examine the nature of the relationship between two or more naturally occurring variables

Besides describing behavior, social psychologists are also interested in learning whether two or more variables are related, and if so, how strongly. When changes in one variable relate to changes in another variable, we *say* that they *correlate*. **Correlational research** assesses the nature of the relationship between two or more variables that are not controlled by the researcher. In studying the relationship between children's TV viewing habits and their aggressive behavior, researchers using the correlational method do not try to influence how much time any of the children in the study actually spend viewing violent shows. Instead, they merely gather information on the amount of time the children spend watching such programs and their degree of aggressive behavior, and then determine how these two variables correlate.

Surveys

surveys
....
Structured sets of questions or statements given to a group of people to measure their attitudes, beliefs, values, or behavioral tendencies

Studying the relationships among variables can be done by directly observing behavior or examining archived information, but it is often accomplished by asking people carefully constructed questions. **Surveys** are structured sets of questions or statements given to a group of people to measure their attitudes, beliefs, values, or behavioral tendencies (Lavrakas, 1993; Schuman, 2002).

The four major survey techniques are *face-to-face surveys, written surveys, phone surveys,* and *computer surveys*. The face-to-face format provides highly detailed information and allows researchers the best opportunity to clarify any unclear questions. However, it is costly and there is always the possibility that people's responses might be influenced by the interviewer's presence. Written, phone, and computer surveys eliminate such interviewer bias and are much less expensive. Although obtaining information using surveys is generally relatively easy, the main disadvantage in all three techniques is that they rely on self-report data. As previously mentioned, self-reports suffer from respondents' faulty memories, wishful thinking, and outright deception.

An important consideration in constructing surveys involves how questions are asked. Survey questions usually are either open ended or closed ended. An *open-ended question* requires a response that must have more than just a yes or no answer—research participants provide a narrative response. A *closed-ended question*, in contrast, is answered with a yes or no, or by choosing a single response from several alternatives. To illustrate this difference, consider how the following two formats might be used to study people's TV-viewing preferences:

Closed-ended: Do you enjoy watching violent TV shows?

Response: Yes_____ No_____

Open-ended: Why do you enjoy (or not enjoy) watching violent TV shows?

Response: _____

Each question format has advantages and disadvantages. Closed-ended questions are the quickest and easiest to score. In contrast, open-ended questions may provide information from respondents that might be missed with closed-ended questions. However, open-ended responses require coding by carefully trained judges (see previous discussion of interjudge reliability, p. 49), and this is a time-consuming process.

Attempting to capitalize on the strengths of both types of questions, survey researchers sometimes provide a set of response alternatives and then invite participants to write down a response of their own choosing if they wish. Despite the increased freedom of this type of response format, most respondents are reluctant to go outside the frame of reference provided by the fixed answers. For example, in one study examining this blended format, Howard Schuman and Jacqueline Scott (1987) asked a national sample of Americans to name the most important problem facing the country. From these responses, they identified four problems that had been mentioned by fewer than 3 percent of the respondents. Next, Schuman and Scott asked a second sample of Americans a parallel question, but provided as choices the four infrequently chosen problems identified in the previous sample. The question also invited participants to substitute a different problem of their own choosing if they desired (see Table 2.4). Despite this invitation, the majority of the respondents (60 percent) picked one of the rare problems. Were these respondents too cognitively lazy to sift through their own beliefs about the nation's problems? Did the listing of the four problems elevate their importance in the respondents' minds? Whatever the reason, these results suggest that the form of a question often conveys the "rules of the game" for respondents; researchers must keep this in mind when interpreting survey findings (Schuman, 2002). Most of the surveys that you will be asked to complete in this textbook include closed-ended questions (for example, see p. 42).

As previously noted, one of the most important considerations in conducting surveys—as well as when using other methods—is getting responses from people who represent the population as a whole. This *representative sample* is often obtained through **random selection**, which is a procedure in which everyone in the population has an equal chance of being selected for the sample. As long as a sample is selected randomly, you are reasonably assured that the data will represent the overall population. However, when samples are not randomly selected, drawing conclusions from the data can lead to serious errors. For example, in 1936, a large survey conducted by the magazine *Literary Digest* indicated that Republican Alf Landon would soundly defeat then-President Franklin Roosevelt in the upcoming election. In fact, Roosevelt won by a landslide. The problem with the magazine's survey was that it did not randomly select voters from the population—the sample was obtained from telephone books and automobile registration listings. Because telephones and cars were luxury items during the Depression of the 1930s, most of the people in the sample were affluent Republicans who represented a minority of eligible voters.

Today, major polling organizations typically are very careful in securing representative samples in order to avoid errors in generalizing their findings to the population. However, many surveys that you find in popular magazines or on the Internet

random selection
....
A procedure for selecting a sample of people to study in which everyone in the population has an equal chance of being chosen

Table 2.4

Does Adding an Open-Ended Response Choice Correct the Problem with Closed-Ended Survey Questions?

OPEN-ENDED QUESTION	CLOSED-ENDED QUESTION

What do you think is the most important problem facing this country today?	Which of the following do you think is the most important problem facing this country today? If you prefer, you may name a different problem as most important.
	  1. Energy shortage
	  2. Quality of public schools
	  3. Legalized abortion
	  4. Pollution
	  5. _____

When a national sample of Americans were asked to identify the most important problem facing the country, fewer than 3 percent named the energy shortage, the quality of public schools, legalized abortion, or pollution. However, when these infrequently chosen problems were placed on a second questionnaire and given to another national sample of Americans, 60 percent of the respondents picked one of these items as the most important national problem, despite being told that they could write in a different problem of their own choosing (Schuman & Scott 1987). What do these findings suggest about the effects of adding an open-ended response format to a closed-format question?

Adapted from Schuman, H., & Scott, J. (May 22, 1987). Problems in the use of survey questions to measure public opinion. Science, 236, 957–959.

asking you to report your opinions on various personal and social issues have limited generalizability. Why? Because the results are based only on those people who read the magazine or go to the Web site and are sufficiently motivated to send in their opinions. The results of such nonrepresentative surveys may not provide an accurate portrayal of societal opinions.

Finally, one last problem in conducting survey research is **social desirability bias**, which occurs when people respond to survey questions by trying to portray themselves in a favorable light rather than responding in an accurate and truthful manner. Over the years, researchers have discovered that people exaggerate their tendency to engage in such socially desirable behaviors as attending religious services and voting, while underreporting their socially undesirable actions, such as taking illegal drugs or evading taxes (Hadaway et al., 1993; Krosnick, 1999). On the more positive side, it is heartening to know that even when survey participants desire to "look good" in the researchers' eyes, they also often have a concern with the accuracy of their responses (Holtgraves, 2004). In the final analysis, as with all research methods, the results of survey research have to be interpreted with its strengths and weaknesses in mind; increased confidence in its conclusions will occur when other methods provide converging results.

social desirability bias
....
A type of response bias in surveys in which people respond to a question by trying to portray themselves in a favorable light rather than responding in an accurate and truthful manner

The Correlation Coefficient

Whether information for studying the relationships among variables is obtained from surveys or some other data-gathering procedure, the primary benefit of conducting correlational research is *prediction*. This method allows researchers to predict a change in one

**correlation
coefficient**

· ·

A statistical measure of the
direction and strength of the
linear relationship between
two variables, which can
range from −1.00 to +1.00

variable by knowing the value of another variable. More specifically, it provides information on the *direction* and *strength* of the relationship between variables. The direction of the relationship between variable A and variable B tells *how* they are related (positively or negatively). The strength of the relationship can be thought of as the degree of accuracy with which you can predict the value of one variable by knowing the value of the other variable. The direction and strength of the relationship between two variables are described by the statistical measure known as the **correlation coefficient** *(r)*. This correlation coefficient can range from −1.00 to +1.00.

Returning to the previous example of television viewing and aggression, a correlation at or very near zero indicates the absence of a *linear relationship* between these two variables. This zero correlation may mean one of two things: (1) viewing television violence has no association with children's aggressive behavior, or (2) there is a *curvilinear relationship* between television viewing and aggression. One can easily determine the meaning of a zero correlation by plotting the pairing of these two variables on a graph, as is illustrated in Figure 2.2. A correlation close to "0.00" would have dots scattered all around the graph, while a correlation near +1.00 would have dots lining up on an imaginary straight line running between the X and Y axes of the graph. The farther the dots on the graph fall from the imaginary straight line the lower is the correlation.

In marked contrast to a zero correlation, one that is near −1.00 would suggest that children who watch a lot of violent television are less aggressive than those who watch little violence on television. In contrast, a correlation near +1.00 indicates that children who watch a lot of violent television are more aggressive than those who watch little violence.

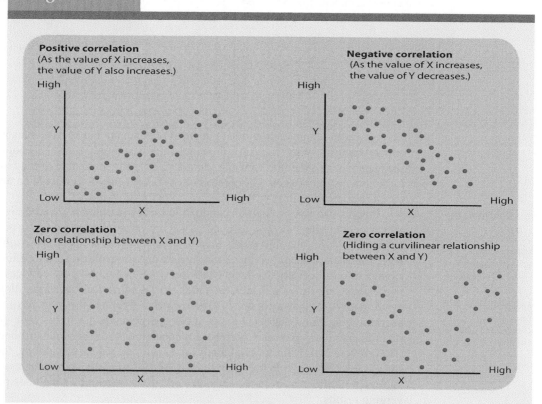

Figure 2.2

Plotting the Relationship Between Variable X and Variable Y on a Graph

Each point on the graphs represents a pairing of variable X with variable Y for each participant in the study. Examine the curvilinear relationship graph. The zero correlation is hiding a meaningful relationship, where both high and low levels of X are associated with high levels of Y, but moderate levels of X are associated with low levels of Y. What sort of social variables might have a curvilinear relationship?

Regarding the strength of a relationship, researchers seldom find a perfect or near perfect ($r = -1.00$ or $r = +1.00$) correlation between variables. In Leonard Eron's (1963) initial study, he examined the relationship between the viewing of violent television shows by eight- and nine-year-old children and their aggressiveness (as rated by their classmates and teachers). For boys, he found a correlation of +.21 between viewing television violence and aggression, whereas for girls, the correlation was +.02. Thus in this sample, if you knew that a particular boy watched a lot of violent television, you would predict that he may be rather aggressive (due to the direction of the relationship); however, you would not be confident in your prediction (due to its low strength). For girls, because the correlation is virtually nonexistent, you would be wise not to make any predictions.

Although the boys' correlation of +.21 might seem small, social science correlations rarely exceed .60. The reason for this is that many factors determine human behavior. What variables besides television viewing might influence aggression in children? Personality, mood, social class, and parental attitudes certainly influence aggressive tendencies. Furthermore, even if we could identify all relevant variables influencing aggression, because of the nature of our subject—humans with self-reflective abilities and minds of their own—we would not be able to perfectly predict people's actions.

The major disadvantage of the correlational study is that it cannot definitively determine the *cause* of the relationship between two variables. That is, besides knowing the strength and direction of a relationship, it is extremely valuable to know which variable caused a change in the other. Does watching violent shows make boys more aggressive, or are aggressive boys more likely to watch violent shows? This methodological disadvantage can result in the *reverse-causality problem*, which occurs whenever either of the two variables correlated with each other could just as plausibly be the cause or the effect. Thus, you might falsely conclude that watching violence on television causes increased aggressiveness in boys when, in fact, aggressive boys are simply more likely to choose to watch violent television shows.

Sometimes when you have a significant correlation between two variables, there is only one possible causal direction. For example, a number of studies have found a strong correlation between being the victim of physical abuse as a child and being the perpetrator of family violence as an adult (Straus et al., 1980; Widom, 1989). Because a past event cannot be caused by a future event, researchers conducting these studies were more confident in asserting that the physical abuse suffered in childhood was a likely cause of the victimization of others in adulthood.

Another way to address the problem of reverse causality is to measure your variables twice. In such a *cross-lagged panel correlation study*, the two variables are measured at two different times, and correlations between the variables across time are examined. For example, in Eron's study of the relationship between childhood television-viewing preferences and aggressive behavior, he recontacted the children ten years later and obtained new information on these two variables (Eron et al., 1972). As you can see in Figure 2.3, when the across-time correlations were examined, the researchers found that the amount of violent television the males had watched as children was positively correlated ($r = +.31$) with their current aggressive behavior at age nineteen. On the other hand, no relationship was found between their childhood aggression and their current preferences for violent television shows ($r = +.01$). Again, as before, no relationship was found for females. Based on these findings, the researchers felt more confident in concluding that the single most plausible causal hypothesis was that a preference for watching violent television during childhood contributes to the aggressive habits in males.

A second problem resulting from the inability to confidently determine causality is that it is possible that a third, unspecified variable causes differences in both variables under study. This is known as the *third-variable problem*. In the Eron study, the positive correlation between television violence and boys' aggression may be due to a third variable not measured by the researcher. Therefore, what looks like an actual relationship between these two variables is really an illusion. The third variable could be the beliefs that the children's parents have about the use of violence both in childrearing and in society. That is, parents who use physical punishment in discipline may also prefer violent television shows because they seem more realistic and familiar. As a result of this mind-set toward violence, these children are taught to be

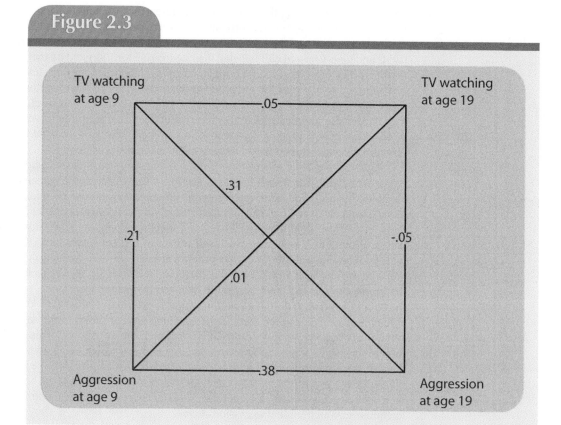

Figure 2.3

A Cross-Lagged Panel Correlation Study of Violent TV and Male Aggression

The important correlations in Eron et al.'s (1972) cross-lagged panel correlation study are on the diagonals. The correlation between the amount of TV violence watched by the male children at age nine, and aggression measured ten years later was much larger than the correlation between male aggression at age nine and TV watching measured ten years later. What do these different correlations suggest about which variable is causing a change in the other? Although this study's findings make us more confident that TV violence causes increased aggression in boys, strictly speaking, we can never definitely infer causality from correlational data.

aggressive and are also exposed to many violent television programs through their parents' own viewing habits. Can you think of other possible variables that might also explain the relationship between TV violence and children's aggression?

experimental method
∙∙∙∙∙∙∙∙∙∙∙∙∙∙∙∙∙∙∙∙∙∙
Research designed to test cause-effect relationships between variables.

independent variable
∙∙∙∙∙∙∙∙∙∙∙∙∙∙∙∙∙∙∙∙∙∙
The experimental variable that the researcher manipulates

dependent variable
∙∙∙∙∙∙∙∙∙∙∙∙∙∙∙∙∙∙∙∙∙∙
The experimental variable that is measured because it is believed to depend on the manipulated changes in the independent variable

EXPERIMENTAL RESEARCH CAN DETERMINE CAUSE-EFFECT RELATIONSHIPS.

Because correlational studies cannot definitively tell us why variables are related to one another, social psychologists use the **experimental method** to examine cause-effect relationships (Hoyle, 2005). In an experiment, the scientist manipulates one variable by exposing research participants to it at contrasting levels (for example, high, medium, low, no exposure), and then observes what effect this manipulation has on the other variable that has not been manipulated.

The variable that is manipulated is called the **independent variable**, and it is the one the experimenter is testing as the possible cause of any changes that might occur in the other variable. The variable whose changes are considered to be the effect of the manipulated changes in the independent variable is called the **dependent variable**. The dependent variable is the response measure of an experiment that is *dependent* on the participant's response to the experimenter's manipulation of the setting (the independent variable). Once the participants in the study have been exposed to the independent

The film *Bonnie and Clyde* was used in a study exposing young boys to violent films.

variable, their behavior is carefully monitored to determine whether it varies in the predicted fashion with different levels of the independent variable. If it does, the experimenter can tentatively conclude that the independent variable is the cause of the changes in the dependent variable.

Let's return to the question of whether watching violent entertainment programs leads to increased aggressiveness in children. A number of experimental studies have explored this topic. For example, Jacques-Philippe Leyens and his colleagues (1975) conducted an experiment in a Belgian private institution for secondary-school boys. The independent variable in this study was exposure to violent films. In two cottages at the school, boys were shown a violent film every night for one week (for example, *Bonnie and Clyde, The Dirty Dozen*). The boys in two other cottages were shown the same number of nonviolent films during the same period of time (for example, *Lily, Daddy's Fiancée*). Thus, the experimenters created two levels of the independent variable—one group of boys (the *treatment group*) were exposed to the phenomenon believed to cause aggressiveness (violent films); the other group of boys (the *control group*) was not exposed to it. The experimenters then observed and recorded the children's aggressive behavior (the dependent variable) outside of the film-viewing settings. Significant differences were found between the two groups of boys, with the treatment group exhibiting higher levels of aggression both toward other boys and toward inanimate objects. Based on these findings, the social psychologists concluded that exposure to violent films had indeed caused increased aggressiveness.

Field Experiments

The study just described is a special type of experiment called a *field experiment*, which is similar to the more common *laboratory experiment*, except that it is run in a natural setting, and participants often do not realize they are being studied (Reis & Gosling, 2010). Because of this more natural atmosphere, participants tend to be less suspicious of what they are experiencing than in laboratory studies; thus, their responses tend to be more spontaneous. This greater realism increases the study's **external validity**, which is the extent to which its findings can be generalized to people beyond those in the study itself (Wilson et al., 2010).

Unfortunately, one drawback to field experiments is that researchers have less control over what is happening to each participant during the study because they are in a setting where many variables are uncontrollable (such as boys being called away

external validity
. . . .
The extent to which a study's findings can be generalized to people beyond those in the study itself

from their cottages during a movie by a phone call from their parents). Another draw-back is that experimenters have less control over precisely measuring the dependent variable because participants often move outside an area of easy observation (such as boys fighting in the bathroom or during "lights out"). These problems of control decrease the study's **internal validity**, which is the extent to which cause-and-effect conclusions can validly be made (Cook & Shadish, 1994). There is often a trade-off between internal and external validity, meaning that if you strengthen one you tend to weaken the other. By conducting his experiment in the children's normal social environment, Leyens was maximizing his external validity, making him reasonably confident that his findings would provide insights into how similar children respond to media violence. But did the "realness" of the research setting seriously compromise the study's internal validity? That is the risk often taken in field experiments.

internal validity

The extent to which cause-and-effect conclusions can validly be made in a study

Laboratory Experiments

By far, most social psychology experiments are conducted in laboratories. As an illustration, consider the following experiment investigating the effects that two independent variables, television violence and anger, have on boys' aggressive behavior. In this study, Donald Hartmann (1969) randomly assigned teenage boys to different levels of the two independent variables. At the beginning of the experiment, the boys' anger was manipulated by either having a confederate—who was posing as a fellow participant—insult him or treat him in a neutral fashion. Following the anger manipulation, the boys were assigned to one of three film conditions lasting two minutes. The first minute of each film showed two boys shooting baskets on a basketball court. For the remaining minute, the boys in the control group film merely played basketball, while in the two treatment-group films one of the boys began beating the other following an argument. In one of these violent films, the camera focused on the pain experienced by the boy who was being beaten. In the other, the camera focused on the aggressor's actions and facial expressions during the beating.

After viewing the film, each boy participated in a seemingly unrelated learning study. As the "teacher" in the study, the participant was instructed to administer an electrical shock to a "learner" whenever the learner made a mistake on the learning task. The learner was the confederate who had either insulted the participant or treated him neutrally. The intensity of the shock chosen by the boys was the dependent variable. In reality, no shocks were ever delivered, but the boys were not aware of this until the end of the experiment. As predicted, boys exposed to a violent film and boys previously angered tried to deliver stronger shocks to the learner than did boys in the control conditions. Further, boys who had been both angered and exposed to a violent film chose the strongest shock levels of the six groups of boys. No significant differences were found, however, between the two types of aggressive films. Thus, the combination of being exposed to a violent film while angry caused the greatest amount of aggression. This latter finding, in which the combined effects of the two independent variables have different effects on the dependent variable than when alone, is known as an **interaction effect**.

As previously mentioned, the main advantage of a lab experiment like Hartmann's is that variables can be well controlled, thus increasing internal validity. An important component of this control is that participants can be randomly assigned to the different levels of the independent variable. In **random assignment**, the experimenter, by some random procedure, decides which participants are exposed to which level of the independent variable. Due to this random assignment, the experimenter can be reasonably confident that there are no preexisting average differences between the participants who are in the different experimental conditions. Often in a field study, groupings of participants already exist (as in the Belgian aggression study). In such cases, the researcher must collect additional data to determine if any preexisting differences between the groups might account for different variations of the dependent variable. If such assurances can be obtained, or preexisting conditions can be controlled when the data are analyzed, then failure to obtain random assignment is less of a threat to the study's internal validity.

interaction effect

An experimental result that occurs when two independent variables in combination have different effects on the dependent variable than when alone

random assignment

Placement of research participants into experimental conditions in a manner that guarantees that all have an equal chance of being exposed to each level of the independent variable

Critical THINKING

What are some similarities and some differences between "random assignment" and "random selection"?

Unfortunately, because of the researcher's desire to control as much of the experimental situation as possible in order to properly assign causality, an air of artificiality may exist in the lab (Gosling, 2004; Rozin, 2001). In the Hartmann lab study, for instance, because the boys believed that delivering shocks was part of a learning study, they may have believed that their "aggression" was socially acceptable. Further, because there was no possibility of retaliation or punishment surrounding this experimental aggression, some social psychologists have argued that it is difficult to generalize these types of findings to real-world aggression (Freedman, 1984). Despite the potential problem of external validity in some lab experiments, an analysis of many aggression studies conducted inside and outside the laboratory found that the results in both types of settings were very similar (Anderson & Bushman, 1997). These findings suggest that lab experiments on aggression have adequate external validity, and that field experiments have adequate internal validity.

SECTION SUMMARY

- *Observational* research involves systematic qualitative and/or quantitative descriptions of behavior.

    Primary advantage: Provide opportunity to study behavior in its wholeness

    Primary disadvantage: Cannot determine how variables are related to one another

- *Correlational research* provides information on the direction and strength of the relationship between variables.

    Primary advantage: Prediction

    Primary disadvantage: Cannot establish causality

- *Experimental research* manipulates one or more variables to determine what effect this has on nonmanipulated variables.

    Primary advantage: Can determine causality

    Primary disadvantage: High control can make generalizability difficult.

THE PROMISE AND CAUTION IN USING EMERGING TECHNOLOGIES

Beyond the scientific methods already discussed, social psychologists also rely on a number of other procedures and techniques in science to better understand social behavior. Let us briefly examine three sophisticated technologies that are providing social psychologists with new avenues for data collection. While these emerging technologies provide the means for important new discoveries, some scientists are concerned that these new technologies will have the effect of moving research further away from studying actual social behavior.

SOCIAL PSYCHOLOGISTS ARE INCREASINGLY USING NEW TECHNOLOGIES.

In addition to using more powerful statistical techniques, social psychologists are increasingly employing new technologies in their research. Four prominent cutting-edge technologies currently being used are virtual environment devices, the Internet, implicit measures, and brain-imaging techniques.

Virtual Environment Technology

As previously discussed, the high degree of control that a researcher can obtain in laboratory experiments often has a price: the danger of artificiality. In contrast, the researcher having less control over variables that may markedly influence participants'

Researchers are turning to virtual reality for some of their experiments. The military also uses virtual reality in their training.

thoughts and actions accompanies the realism in a field experiment. Some social psychologists believe they have found a possible remedy to the dilemma of choosing between greater control and greater realism in experiments (Blascovich, 2003). They recommend using *virtual environment technology*, in which they create a virtual research environment using a computer. Once this simulated reality is created, participants wearing virtual reality equipment are "immersed" in the setting. A commonly used piece of virtual reality equipment is a head-mounted or binocular-style device that allows an individual to view 3-D images and "walk" through the virtual environment. Despite the fact that this type of simulated environment is completely controlled by the experimenter—even more than the traditional laboratory setting—it has a very "real-world" feel to it, similar to that of a field experiment.

Research suggests that participants behave relatively naturally in virtual environment settings (Blascovich, 2002; Waller et al., 2002). Although still in its infancy, virtual environment technology is currently being used to study such topics as conformity, eyewitness testimony, and violent video games. As this technology improves, psychologists hope to involve senses beyond sight and hearing, as well as to improve the ways people can interact with the virtual creations they encounter. This technology is not meant to replace traditional field and laboratory studies but, instead, to provide another research vehicle that social psychologists can use in their work.

The Internet

The Internet is a relatively new medium for communication, and many social psychologists are employing it as an avenue to collect data (Reis & Gosling, 2010). One of the biggest advantages in using the Internet is that researchers can recruit participants from the entire world and test them remotely (Birnbaum, 2004; Lohrke & Frownfelter-Lohrke, 2011). This technology has greatly facilitated the ability of social psychologists to conduct cross-cultural research. For example, in a series of Internet experiments on social exclusion, Kipling Williams and his colleagues (2000) collected data from more than 1,500 participants from over sixty countries. Other advantages of the Internet as a data collection site are that studies can be run without the presence of a researcher, without the need for large laboratories, without expensive equipment (except access to a computer and an Internet connection), and without limitations on the time of day in which the data are collected. These advantages can yield huge data sets. Over a four-year period, one research team studying attitudes collected a data set of over 1.5 million completed responses (Nosek et al., 2002)! The advantages of Internet research do not end with merely obtaining participants and collecting data. Once researchers have programmed the computer, data can be automatically coded and stored by an Internet server, saving researchers great amounts of tedious labor. Together, these advantages add up to low-cost studies with large sample sizes, and the ability to do in weeks what previously took months or years to accomplish.

Web-based studies are not without limitations (Heiervang & Goodman, 2011). In the United States, Internet users are more likely to be White, to be young, and to have children than the general population (U.S. Department of Commerce 2002). Thus, obtaining a representative sample is one of the primary concerns with Internet studies. Further, even when researchers intentionally target certain groups on the Internet, they cannot control completely the nature of the sample obtained. For example, if researchers use the Internet to survey young adults about their alcohol use, web masters who manage web sites for self-help groups for alcoholics may establish links for their web users to the study's web site. The consequence of this link between the self-help sites and the study site could be that the survey results are not an accurate representation of alcohol use among young adults. Currently, there is no effective way in which Internet researchers can guarantee obtaining a representative sample (Kraut et al., 2003).

Another limitation of the Internet is that researchers cannot guarantee that someone hasn't sent multiple copies of the same data to them masquerading as different participants. Although such multiple submissions would jeopardize the validity of a study's findings, studies that have examined the possibility of such abuse by respondents suggest that it does not appear to be a serious problem (Musch & Reips, 2000). Because of the advantages of using the Internet for research, it is highly likely that web-based social psychological studies will dramatically increase in the coming years.

Implicit or Unconscious Measures

For many years social psychologists have realized that research participants are often unwilling or unable to accurately assess their thoughts and feelings using standard self-report measures. Sometimes this inaccuracy is caused by people being unwilling to admit that they have socially undesirable thoughts and feelings, such as negative stereotypes and racist attitudes. At other times, inaccurate self-reporting may be caused by people being honestly unaware that they have unconscious thoughts and feelings shaping their conscious perceptions and actions. As a means of overcoming such self-report problems, social psychologists have developed computer programs that are designed to tap into participants' unconscious thoughts and feelings (Payne et al., 2004; von Hippel et al., 2008).

Implicit Association Test (IAT)

. . . .

A technique for measuring implicit attitudes and beliefs based on the idea that people will give faster responses to presented concepts that are more strongly associated in memory

The most popular of these implicit or unconscious measures is the **Implicit Association Test (IAT)**, which is a computer-assisted evaluation, developed by Anthony Greenwald and his coworkers (1998). The IAT is designed to measure the strength of automatic associations between different concepts in memory (Cvencek et al., 2011). For example, an implicit or unconscious race bias toward African Americans might be measured by first comparing how quickly participants can press computer keys to categorize pleasant words (such as *gentle* and *kind*) as "good" when these words appear on a computer screen next to Black faces rather than White faces. Next, this task is reversed with participants quickly categorizing unpleasant words (such as *rough* and *mean*) as "bad" while these words are presented next to either Black or White faces. If participants take longer to categorize pleasant words as "good" when they are paired with Black rather than White faces, while also taking longer to categorize unpleasant words as "bad" when they are paired with White rather than Black faces, this indicates an implicit race bias.

A number of studies suggest that the IAT is a better predictor of some forms of behavior, such as discrimination, than traditional self-report methods and it is less vulnerable to faking; yet some studies question the IAT's validity in measuring self-esteem (Buhrmester et al., 2011; Nosek et al., 2007). Currently, the IAT is being used in research all over the world, and we will discuss many of these studies in various chapters in this text.

Brain-Imaging Techniques

In the last decade, new technologies have permitted us to peer deep into the living brain, providing researchers with a unique opportunity to understand how social thinking and

One of the most commonly used brain scanning techniques is the electroencephalograph (EEG).

behavior are associated with neural activity. The most commonly used brain-imaging techniques are the *electroencephalograph (EEG), computerized axial tomography (CAT), magnetic resonance imaging (MRI), positron-emission tomography (PET),* and *functional magnetic resonance imaging (fMRI).*

The EEG records "waves" of electrical activity in the brain using many metal electrodes placed on a person's scalp. In contrast, CAT and MRI scans document the brain's structure. The CAT scan accomplishes this task by taking thousands of X-ray photos of the brain, while the MRI produces three-dimensional images of the brain's soft tissues by detecting magnetic activity from nuclear particles in brain molecules (Senior et al., 2002). Instead of recording the brain's electrical activity or mapping its structure, the PET scan and fMRI measure the brain's metabolic activity in different regions. The PET scan accomplishes this by showing each region's consumption of glucose, the sugar that is the brain's chemical fuel (Nyberg et al., 2002). The disadvantage of this technique is that the pictures of brain activity that PET scans provide are an average of the activity that occurs over several minutes. Another disadvantage is that it exposes people to small amounts of radioactivity, making extensive scanning somewhat risky. The newer technology of fMRI does not have these drawbacks (Thompson, 2011). First, fMRI can produce a picture of neural activity averaged over seconds, not minutes. Second, like a standard MRI, it uses magnetism to measure fluctuations in naturally occurring blood oxygen levels, not fluctuations in ingested radioactive glucose. The images produced by fMRI scans are also much sharper, and thus they can be used to identify much smaller brain structures than those of PET scans.

Brain-imaging techniques are becoming so good at detecting the ebb and flow of neural activity that it is not far-fetched to predict that this technology will one day be able to literally "read" people's minds, determining such things as their degree of racial prejudice or their truthfulness when answering specific questions (Cacioppo et al., 2004). For example, research by Tatia Lee and her colleagues (2002) indicates that certain areas of the brain are more active when people lie. These researchers are now trying to determine whether this knowledge can be used to produce an effective lie detector that would outperform the conventional polygraph machine.

Such possibilities raise ethical concerns among many scientists and are becoming an important topic of discussion in the new field of *neuroethics* (Illes & Raffin, 2002; Kulynych, 2002). "If you were to ask me what the ethical hot potato of this coming century is," remarked Arthur Caplan, director of the University of Pennsylvania's Center for Bioethics, "I'd say it's new knowledge of the brain, its structure and function" (Goldberg, 2003).

THE STUDY OF ACTUAL BEHAVIOR IS DECLINING IN SOCIAL PSYCHOLOGY.

Although emerging technologies provide new avenues by which scientists can study the social behavior of everyday life, some social psychologists are concerned that these technologies are part of a larger trend within the discipline to study social behavior through a cognitive lens that seldom measures actual behavior (Hebl & Dovidio, 2005; Patterson, in press). For example, content analysis of scientific studies published over the past five decades in two of the top social psychology journals, *Journal of Personality and Social Psychology* and *Personality and Social Psychology Bulletin*, found that studies with either the independent or dependent variables being actual behavioral measures dropped from about 75 percent in the 1970s to about 20 percent during the past two decades (Baumeister et al., 2007; Patterson, 2008). Today, instead of studying how people behave by directly observing their actions in various social settings, researchers are more likely to either ask people how they think they behave in those settings or measure their cognitions after showing them stimuli that often are present in those social settings. While self-reports and cognitive reactions can be extremely useful in understanding the psychology of social behavior, most social psychologists would agree that these measurement techniques should not completely replace the actual measurement of behavior. Further, while brain-imaging technology can provide further insight into the complexity of social behavior, it is most likely to do so when studies involve research participants who are immersed in genuine social interactions rather than simply responding to stimuli while laying inside an fMRI scanner in a laboratory (Rilling, 2011).

In summary, the take-away message of this chapter is that there is no one best scientific method or data collection technique for all research settings. In each investigation, social psychologists must decide not only how to best measure their variables of interest but also what scientific method provides the best opportunity of meeting the study's goals. Given the ability of the observational method to capture the richness of social behavior as it happens, many social psychologists believe that this approach is best suited for *theory building* (Fine & Elsbach, 2000). In contrast, because the experimental method can determine the cause of events, it is generally considered the method best suited for *theory testing*. The best overall strategy in developing theories of social behavior that are valid and useful is to take a *multimethod* approach—employing different methods to study the same topic and thereby capitalizing on each method's strengths and controlling for their weaknesses.

SECTION SUMMARY

- Virtual environment technology creates a virtual research environment using a computer.

- The Internet allows researchers to conduct low-cost studies with many participants from the entire world and test them remotely.

- Implicit measures determine the strength of automatic associations in memory.

- Brain-imaging techniques provide researchers with measures of participants' neural activity while they engage in various tasks.

- Actual behavior is less likely measured in social psychology studies today than in past decades.

- A multi-method approach capitalizes on each method's strengths while controlling for its weaknesses.

WEB SITES

ACCESSED THROUGH www.BVTLab.com/sop6
Web sites for this chapter contain the main scientific journals in both psychological and sociological social psychology, information on recent theory and research, as well as a web page containing social psychological studies currently being conducted on the Web, many of which you can participate in.

JOURNAL OF PERSONALITY AND SOCIAL PSYCHOLOGY WEB SITE
Check out the web site for the main scientific journal in psychological social psychology. Here you will find current abstracts of journal articles. The journal publishes theoretical and empirical papers on attitudes and social cognition, interpersonal relations and group processes, and personality processes and individual differences.

SOCIAL PSYCHOLOGY QUARTERLY WEB SITE
Explore the web site for the main scientific journal in sociological social psychology, where you will find information on current journal articles. The journal publishes theoretical and empirical papers on the link between the individual and society.

INTERNATIONAL ASSOCIATION FOR CROSS-CULTURAL PSYCHOLOGY
This is the web site for an organization devoted to facilitating communication among persons interested in a diverse range of issues involving the intersection of culture and psychology.

WESLEYAN'S SOCIAL PSYCHOLOGY NETWORK
This web site contains social psychological studies that are currently being conducted on the Internet, many of which you can participate in.

PSYCHOLOGICAL TESTS FOR STUDENT USE
This web site at Atkinson College of York University in Canada contains psychological tests and measures that are used by social psychologists in their research, including the Attitudes Toward Women Scale, Authoritarianism-Rebellion Scale, Body Esteem Scale, and Personal Attributes Questionnaire.

▶ Check out our web site
www.BVTLab.com
for chapter-by-chapter flashcards, summaries, and practice quizzes.

3

Chapter 3
The Self

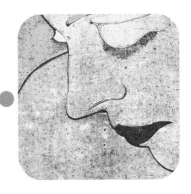

CHAPTER OUTLINE

INTRODUCTION

The Self as Both Active Agent and Object of Attention

Contemporary self theories are based on the insights of James and Mead.
Self-awareness is reflective thinking.
Self-regulation is the self's most important function.

The Self as a Knowledge Structure

Self-concept involves a network of self-aspects.
Cultural beliefs about self-group relationships shape self-concept.
Cultural beliefs about gender shape self-concept.
Social identities establish the "what" and "where" we are as social beings.

Presenting the Self to Others

Self-presentations are either consciously or automatically constructed.
Self-presentation strategies differ in their goals.

Evaluating the Self

Self-esteem influences how we approach and respond to life challenges.
Self-enhancement and self-verification motives conflict in low self-esteem persons.
There is a dark side to high self-esteem.
In social relationships, self-esteem is maintained through social reflection and social comparison.

APPLICATIONS

Do You Engage in Binge Drinking or Eating to Escape from Yourself?

PREVIEW   Binge drinking and eating are self-destructive behaviors that are common problems on college campuses. How can you use the knowledge in this chapter to better regulate and control your behavior?

THE BIG PICTURE

WEB SITES

INTRODUCTION

At the pivotal age of sixteen, I was ready to surmount one of the most important adolescent hurdles: the driver's test. My mother had driven me to the license bureau, but I was sure I would be driving home. The small testing room was filled with would-be drivers. After a thirty-minute wait, the "testing" man motioned me to come behind the counter. As I complied, he first pointed to an eye chart, then pointed at a line on the floor some twenty feet from the chart, and said, "touch your toes to the line."

For some reason, I placed the most significance on the first three words in this sentence—"Touch your toes"—and guessed this was a coordination test before the eye and driving exams. So I placed the tips of my shoes on the line. Then, with stiffened knees, I bent down and touched my toes. Because his instructions mentioned nothing about the duration of this "coordination test," I remained in this contorted position and awaited further instructions. As the blood rushed to my head, I happened to glance at my mother sitting on the other side of the room and noticed her surprised expression as she tried to fathom what her son was doing making a spectacle of himself in front of a room full of strangers. Now realizing that something was amiss, I suddenly understood the true meaning of the tester's words and stood bolt upright. Even though my head was no longer south of my knees, the blood now seemed to be rushing to my face ten times faster. The tester and the other exam-takers didn't laugh at me outright, but I was so flustered by my social gaffe that I actually failed the eye exam!

I'm sure you can relate to the embarrassment I felt on that day so long ago. Yet, why do we often become red-faced when our social behavior is out of step with the situation? Why do we sometimes misinterpret the meaning of others' words and gestures? Why does success and failure mean so much to us? For an answer to these questions, we must examine a central concept in social psychology: the self (Lent et al., 2011; Swann & Bosson, 2010).

self

· · · · · · · · · · · · · · · · · ·

A symbol-using social being who can reflect on his/her own behavior

self-concept

· · · · · · · · · · · · · · · · · ·

The sum total of a person's thoughts and feelings that defines the self as an object

THE SELF AS BOTH ACTIVE AGENT AND OBJECT OF ATTENTION

As defined in Chapter 1, the **self** is a symbol-using social being who can reflect on his or her own behavior. In studying the self, social psychologists typically make a distinction between the self as "subject" of awareness and the self as "object" of awareness.

CONTEMPORARY SELF THEORIES ARE BASED ON THE INSIGHTS OF JAMES AND MEAD.

Two of the most influential early contributors to our understanding of the self were psychologist William James (1890) and sociologist George Herbert Mead (1934). Both James and Mead described the self as having two separate aspects, the self as subject of awareness (the *I*), and the self as object of awareness (the *me*). The "I" is the aspect of your self that is actively perceiving, thinking, and behaving in your world, while the "me" is the aspect of your self that the "I" is sometimes perceiving and thinking about. In other words, as a self, "I" am conscious of many things in my world, and sometimes "I" focus my consciousness on myself ("me"). Contemporary social psychologists refer to the "me" as **self-concept**, which is the sum total of a person's thoughts and feelings that defines the self as an object (Snodgrass & Thompson, 1997). Knowing yourself, or at least believing that you know yourself, is critically important in having a purpose and meaning in life (Schlegel et al., 2011). Self-concept also consists of numerous evaluations of self as being good, bad, or mediocre. This evaluative aspect of self-concept is called **self-esteem** (Swann et al., 2007; Watson et al., 2002). As you will discover in this chapter, seeking self-knowledge and seeking self-esteem are often important motivating forces in daily living.

According to James, things become part of your self-concept through your emotional identification with them. Thus, your parents, siblings, friends, and lovers are most likely very important components of your self-concept. Indeed, your clothes, your iPod, your major area of study in college, and perhaps even your fuzzy little teddy bear could be elements in your "me." In this regard, your self-concept includes not just that which is inside your body but also anything that symbolizes and affirms who and what you are (Burris & Rempel, 2004; Lewandowski et al., 2006). James's idea that the self in the form of the "me" can extend beyond your physical body is important because it challenges the belief that we are separate, encapsulated egos. His notion of the self-identification process also highlights the ever-changing nature of the self. That is, because who and what you identify with often changes over time, the way you define yourself is not stable like a diamond, but rather, it is constantly changing. Your self of today is different, even if only subtly, from your self of yesterday.

While James described how emotional identification shapes self-concept, Mead described how the self develops in infancy and how people, as selves, actively shape their social reality. He asserted that a human infant is not born a self but rather that a self *emerges* through social interaction. According to Mead (1925), the self develops as children acquire language and start taking the role of other people in their play activities. An example of role taking would be a child adopting the perspective of "Daddy" and reprimanding himself for disobeying a family rule. Through the symbolic interaction of language and role taking, children develop beliefs about themselves, which are largely a reflection of how they believe others perceive them. By internalizing the beliefs and expectations commonly held by the larger society—what Mead called the *generalized other*—the person becomes a fully mature self.

Both James's and Mead's theories have profoundly influenced social psychology, with James's writings reflecting the affective or "hot" perspective on the nature of human behavior and Mead's writings reflecting the cognitive or "cold" approach (see Chapter 1, p. 17). Their initial ideas on how we define ourselves and how we consciously strive to become what we desire involve two essential human characteristics: *self-awareness* and *self-regulation*. Let us now examine how contemporary social psychologists study the interplay between these two complementary psychological processes.

SELF-AWARENESS IS REFLECTIVE THINKING.

Stop for a moment and think about your current mood. If you followed my suggestion, you just engaged in **self-awareness**, which is a psychological state in which you focus attention on yourself (Lewis, 2011). Another way to describe self-awareness is that it is a temporary state of mind where you psychologically "step outside yourself" and examine your thoughts, feelings, motives, behavior, or appearance. This "stepping outside one's self" is what Mead considered necessary for the self to develop; children adopt the perspective (or role) of others to examine their own behavior. To have a self-concept, you must be able to engage in self-awareness. As discussed in Chapter 1 (p. 27, Figure 1.3), a region in the frontal lobe of the cerebral cortex, called the anterior cingulate cortex, is especially active when people are self-aware. The *anterior cingulate cortex* contains *spindle neurons* that are special types of neurons that collect waves of neural information from one region of the brain and send it on to other regions. The anterior cingulate cortex with its spindle neurons acts as an executive attention system, facilitating self-awareness and other intelligent behavior.

Self-Awareness Development

You might be surprised to know that we are not born with self-awareness ability but rather that we develop it. Psychologists discovered this fact by placing a spot of rouge on

---

self-esteem

A person's evaluation of his or her self-concept.

❝ *The Self is the honey of all beings, and all beings are the honey of this Self.* ❞

The Upanishads, sacred texts of Hinduism, 800–500 BC

❝ *Nothing is greater than one's self.* ❞

Walt Whitman, U.S. poet 1819–1982

self-awareness

A psychological state in which one takes oneself as an object of attention babies' noses and then placing them in front of a mirror (Lewis & Brooks, 1978). They reasoned that in order for the infants to recognize their mirror image as their own they must have an internalized identity that permits them to recognize this external representation of themselves. Infants between the ages of nine and twelve months treated their mirror image as if it were another child, showing no interest in the unusual rouge spot; they literally were not able to take themselves as an object of awareness. Yet those around eighteen months of age exhibited self-recognition—and thus, self-awareness ability—by staring in the mirror and touching the mysterious spot on their noses. Recognizing the image in the mirror as their own, they realized that they looked different. Based on such studies, it appears that self-awareness develops at about eighteen months of age (Amsterdam, 1972; Butterworth, 1992), which is the same age that Mead stated that the self develops. Perhaps not coincidentally, the development of self-awareness occurs at the same time as children's brains are experiencing a rapid growth of spindle neurons—which are not present at birth—in the frontal lobe of the cerebral cortex (Allman & Hasenstaub, 1999).

Self-Awareness in Other Animals

The only other animals known to have spindle neurons in the brain are the great apes, our closest genetic relatives, and certain species of whales and dolphins (Hayashi, 2006; Hof & Van der Gucht, 2006). Do these animals also possess self-awareness? In a study investigating chimpanzee self-awareness, comparative psychologist Gordon Gallup (1977) painted an odorless red dye on one eyebrow and one ear of anesthetized chimps. When the chimps later looked into a mirror, they immediately began to touch the red dye marks on their bodies, indicating that they recognized the mirror image as their own. Subsequent research further supported the hypothesis that our great ape cousins (chimpanzees, bonobos, orangutans, and gorillas) do indeed possess self-awareness (Boysen & Himes, 1999; Hyatt & Hopkins, 1994; Patterson & Cohen, 1994). What about other mammals? There is evidence that whales and dolphins, along with elephants, may also possess self-awareness (Hart & Whitlow, 1995; Plotnik et al., 2006). Do these findings further suggest that these self-aware animals also possess self-concepts? As yet, we do not know; however, contrary to previous scientific beliefs, humans may not have a monopoly on self-concept.

Disengaging Self-Awareness

Of course, we are not always self-aware. Selfhood is most apparent when we have the luxury of time for contemplation. When we need to focus on difficult tasks requiring

Babies around eighteen months of age start to exhitbit self recognition.

quick decisions, neuroimaging studies indicate that self-awareness temporarily disappears as our brains divert cognitive resources toward the task at hand. In one such study, Ilan Goldberg and his colleagues (2006) conducted functional magnetic resonance imaging (fMRI) scans of participants' brains as they identified animals depicted in pictures and also reported their emotional responses. Pictures were either presented slowly or quickly. When pictures were shown slowly, heightened neural activity was observed in the anterior cingulate cortex, but not when pictures were shown quickly. In contrast, speed of picture presentation did not change the amount of neural activity in brain regions that process and make sense of sensory information. In other words, when circumstances require the brain to divert most of its cognitive resources to carry out a difficult task, neural activity in the anterior cingulate cortex is inhibited, which "switches off" self-awareness.

Disengaging self-awareness in this manner makes sense from an evolutionary perspective (Vince, 2006). When encountering sudden danger, such as stumbling upon a deadly predator, it is not helpful to spend critical seconds wondering how you feel about the situation. Instead, quick action is much more likely to insure your safety and survival. However, one additional consequence of the fluctuating nature of self-awareness is that, while it may be an adaptive response, disengaging self-awareness may also result in less "humane" responses. That is, in situations requiring quick and difficult choices, we are less likely to consider our personal values or societal standards before responding. As you will see in other chapters, disengaging self-awareness when responding quickly to social events can have profound consequences for our likelihood of acting contrary to our personal values (Chapters 5 and 8), stereotyping and discriminating against others (Chapter 6), flaunting social norms (Chapter 7), lashing out in anger (Chapter 11), and helping those in need (Chapter 12).

Private and Public Self-Awareness

Social scientists have long debated whether personal or social standards are more important in determining people's behavior. Some theorists have assumed that people are motivated primarily by a desire to meet personal goals and are responsive largely to their own attitudes and feelings (Maslow, 1970; Rogers, 1947). Others have argued that we are largely a reflected image of our social group, and that before acting we consider how others will judge us (Cooley, 1902; Mead, 1934). Self-awareness research indicates that whether behavior is more influenced by personal or social standards is partially determined by whether self-awareness is focused on private or public self-aspects (Silvia & O'Brien, 2004).

Private self-awareness is the temporary state of being aware of hidden, private aspects of the self, such as your personal attitudes and beliefs, as well as your current mood. Feeling sad or content, seeing your face in a small mirror, or feeling the hunger pangs of your stomach will likely cause you to become privately self-aware. Two effects of private self-awareness are that you become more aware of the discrepancy between your behavior and your personal standards, and you also are more likely to behave in line with those standards (Froming et al., 1998; Goukens et al., 2009). Private self-awareness also makes you more aware of and responsive to your current moods (Lyubomirsky et al., 1998; Scheier & Carver, 1977). Thus, if you are happy and become privately self-aware, your happiness is intensified. Likewise, if angered, private self-awareness causes more anger.

In contrast to private self-awareness, *public self-awareness* is the temporary state of being aware of public self-aspects, such as your physical appearance and the way you talk and behave in public settings. Being watched by others, having your picture taken, or seeing yourself in a full-length mirror could induce public self-awareness (Buss, 1980; Green & Sedikides, 1999). One effect of public self-awareness is *greater adherence to social standards of behavior*, meaning a heightened degree of conformity (Duval & Wicklund, 1972). This increased conformity when publicly self-aware is often preceded by concerns about being negatively evaluated by others (Culos-Reed et al., 2002; Mesagno et al., 2009).

As adults, we all have the ability to engage in either private or public self-awareness. However, when some stimulus induces self-awareness, that focus is only temporary. Yet

"*Self-awareness is, then, one of the most fundamental, possibly the most fundamental, characteristic of the human species. ... Self-awareness has, however, brought in its train somber companions—fear, anxiety, and death-awareness. ... A being who knows that he will die arose from ancestors who did not know.*"

Theodosius Dobzhansky, Russian-born geneticist, 1900–1975

"*There are three things extremely hard: steel, a diamond, and to know one's self.*"

Benjamin Franklin, U.S. statesman and scientist, 1706–1790

researchers have also determined that some people spend more time self-reflecting than others. This habitual tendency to engage in self-awareness is known as the personality trait of **self-consciousness**. Just as there are two types of self-awareness, there are also two types of self-consciousness. *Private self-consciousness* is the tendency to be aware of the private aspects of the self, while *public self-consciousness* is the tendency to be aware of publicly displayed self-aspects. These traits are two distinct tendencies; therefore, a person could either be very attentive to both sides of the self, attentive to one but inattentive to another, or relatively inattentive to both. Before reading further, spend a few minutes completing the items in *Self/Social Connection Exercise 3.1* to learn more about your own levels of private and public self-consciousness.

Many private self-awareness effects are the same whether they result from the psychological state of private self-awareness or the personality trait of private self-consciousness (Kemmelmeier, 2001; Scheier & Carver, 1980). Individuals high in private self-consciousness are more aware of and behave more in line with their personal standards, and react more strongly to their current moods, than do their less self-conscious counterparts. Because they are more attentive to their personal attitudes, values, and motives, high private self-conscious people tend to have self-concepts that are more complex than those low in private self-consciousness (Davies, 1994). However, habitual attention to private self-aspects can contribute to depression and chronic unhappiness (Ingram, 1990; Trapnell & Campbell, 1999). Why might this be so? One possibility is that greater attention to private self-aspects intensifies current emotions. When people's experiences fall short of their expectations, prolonging private self-awareness heightens their disappointment. Thus, the *trait* of private self-consciousness or the state of private self-awareness might encourage destructive self-critical analysis (Silvia & O'Brien, 2004; Ward et al., 2003). A number of studies suggest that reducing self-awareness by engaging in distracting activities that shift attention away from the self—such as watching television—can improve well-being among depressed individuals (Moskalenko & Heine, 2003; Nix et al., 1995). Taking all these studies into account, it appears that attending to our private self has both benefits and drawbacks. The insights gained from this research can perhaps help you gauge how your own life might benefit from or be harmed by the amount of attention you devote to your private self.

What about public self-consciousness? As with situationally induced public self-awareness, persons high in public self-consciousness are more concerned about how others judge them (Fenigstein & Vanable, 1992; MacDonald & Nail, 2005). As a result, they are more conforming to group norms (Chang et al., 2001) and are more likely to withdraw from embarrassing situations (Froming et al., 1990) than those low in this trait. This tendency to comply with external standards encompasses physical appearance as well. High public self-conscious individuals are more concerned about their physical appearance and are more likely to judge others based on their looks (Ryckman et al., 1991; Striegel-Moore et al., 1993).

How do these two traits of private and public self-consciousness collectively influence a person's behavior in public settings? As you might expect, people high in private self-consciousness and low in public self-consciousness are the ones most likely to act according to their true attitudes. On the other hand, people high in public self-consciousness, regardless of their level of private self-consciousness, are much less likely to publicly act according to their true attitudes (Scheier, 1980). Therefore, even when people have an accurate understanding of their own attitudes as a result of their habitual private self-focus, being simultaneously high in public self-consciousness can lead to behavior that runs counter to those attitudes.

CULTURE AND SELF-AWARENESS

Virtually all the self-awareness research discussed thus far was conducted in the United States, an individualist culture. However, as stated in Chapter 1, most of the world's population resides in collectivist cultures. Is there any evidence that people in individualist and collectivist cultures differ in their self-awareness tendencies? Perhaps. A number of studies, for example, have documented how collectivist-oriented East Asians attend more to the perspective of others than do individualist-oriented Westerners, meaning they are more likely than people from Western cultures to habitually view themselves through the eyes of other people (Cohen & Gunz, 2002; Cohen, Hoshino-Browne, & Leung, 2007). Viewing

self-consciousness

The habitual tendency to engage in self-awareness

❝*Know thyself? If I knew myself, I'd run away.***❞**

Johann Wolfgang von Goethe, German intellectual, writer, and composer, 1749–1832

What Are Your Levels of Private and Public Self-Consciousness?

Self-awareness researchers contend that your levels of private and public self-consciousness predict the degree to which your thinking and behavior are shaped by your "private self" or your "public self," respectively. Private and public self-consciousness are measured by items on the Self-Consciousness Scale (SCS: Fenigstein, et al. 1975). To take the SCS, read each item below, and then indicate how well each statement describes you using the following scale:

    0 extremely uncharacteristic (not at all like me)
    1 uncharacteristic (somewhat unlike me)
    2 neither characteristic nor uncharacteristic
    3 characteristic (somewhat like me)
    4 extremely characteristic (very much like me)

1. I'm always trying to figure myself out.
2. I'm concerned about my style of doing things.
3. Generally, I'm not very aware of myself.*
4. I reflect about myself a lot.
5. I'm concerned about the way I present myself.
6. I'm often the subject of my own fantasies.
7. I never scrutinize myself.*
8. I'm self-conscious about the way I look.
9. I'm generally attentive to my inner feelings.
10. I usually worry about making a good impression.
11. I'm constantly examining my motives.
12. One of the last things I do before I leave my house is look in the mirror.
13. I sometimes have the feeling that I'm off somewhere watching myself.
14. I'm concerned about what other people think of me.
15. I'm alert to changes in my mood.
16. I'm usually aware of my appearance.
17. I'm aware of the way my mind works when I work through a problem.

Directions for Scoring

Several of the SCS items are reverse-scored; that is, for these items a lower rating actually indicates a higher level of self-consciousness. Before summing the items, recode those with an asterisk (*) so that 0 = 4, 1 = 3, 3 = 1, and 4 = 0.

Private self-consciousness. To calculate your private self-consciousness score, add up your responses to the following items: 1, 3*, 4, 6, 7*, 9, 11, 13, 15, and 17.

Public self-consciousness. To calculate your public self-consciousness score, add up your responses to the following items: 2, 5, 8, 10, 12, 14, and 16.

When Fenigstein, Scheier, and Buss developed the SCS, the mean college score for college students on private self-consciousness was about 26, whereas the average score of public self-consciousness was about 19. The higher your score is above one of these values, the more of this type of self-consciousness you probably possess. The lower your score is below one of these values, the less of this type of self-consciousness you probably possess. In reading the research findings regarding private

Self/Social Connections Exercise 3.1 *Continued*

and public self-consciousness, consider how your own thinking and behavior might be shaped by the degree to which you are habitually aware of your "private self" and your "public self." Does it provide insight into the degree to which you:

(a) are interested in understanding what "makes you tick"? ⟶ private self-consciousness effect

(b) follow your own personal standards in daily decisions? ⟶ private self-consciousness effect

(c) "stew in your own juices" when someone irritates you? ⟶ private self-consciousness effect

(d) pay a lot of attention to how you look? ⟶ public self-consciousness effect

(e) feel pressure to conform to others' opinions and expectations? ⟶ public self-consciousness effect

(f) feel anxious when the public spotlight is cast your way? ⟶ public self-consciousness effect

> *"The one self-knowledge worth having is to know one's own mind."*
>
> F. H. Bradley, English philosopher, 1846–1924

> *"He who knows others is clever; He who knows himself has discernment."*
>
> Lao-Tzu, Chinese philosopher and founder of Taoism, sixth century BC

yourself from the perspective of others is another way of saying that you are engaging in self-awareness.

As already noted, seeing your face in a small mirror induces private self-awareness, which results in you being more aware of the discrepancy between your behavior and your personal standards. Based on these past research findings, Steven Heine and his colleagues (2008) asked college students at a Japanese university and an American university to rate how much a series of twenty positive statements, such as "I am extremely considerate," described them. Next the participants rated how much they wished each of these same statements described them. The discrepancy between these "actual versus ideal" judgments measured how much the participants thought that they fell short of their ideal selves. Half of the participants completed this task while sitting in front of a small mirror, while half did not.

As depicted in Figure 3.1, the American college students noticed a significantly bigger discrepancy between their actual versus ideal selves when completing the task in front of a mirror than when completing this task outside the presence of a mirror. Another way to describe these findings was that the American participants were more self-critical when they were situationally induced into private self-awareness. In contrast, the Japanese students' actual versus ideal judgments were unaffected by whether a mirror was present or not; they noticed a fair amount of actual versus ideal self-discrepancies in both the mirror and non-mirror conditions. Heine and his colleagues argued that these results provide evidence that the Japanese tendency to be self-critical is at least partly caused by them being chronically self-aware; they act as if they have mirrors in their heads. These results raise the possibility that people from East Asian cultures are more self-reflective than Americans.

SELF-REGULATION IS THE SELF'S MOST IMPORTANT FUNCTION.

Have you ever driven your car somewhere and been so absorbed in your thoughts that you barely noticed your surroundings? You obeyed all traffic rules, negotiated all turns, and maintained a safe distance from nearby cars while thinking about other matters. During the course of our everyday life, there are countless activities that are so well learned that we carry them out automatically, without conscious thought. These habits are very beneficial because they allow us to perform actions without expending much cognitive effort (Bargh & Chartrand, 1999). However, there are other times when we must consciously control and

Figure 3.1

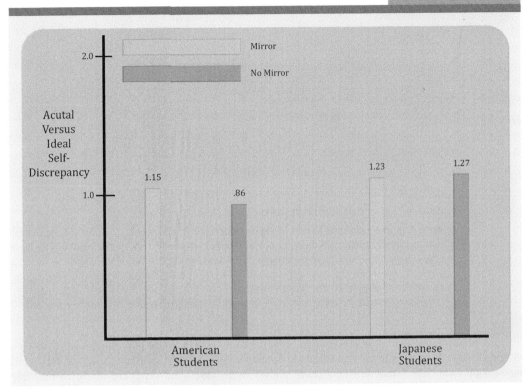

Effects of Mirror on American and Japanese College Students' Self-Assessments

American college students who judged their actual versus ideal selves in front of a mirror noticed more discrepancies than American college students who made these same judgments in a room without a mirror. The presence of a mirror had no impact on the self-discrepancies of Japanese college students.)

self-regulation
....
The ways in which people control and direct their own actions

direct our behavior, often expending a great deal of cognitive effort in the process (Rudasill, 2011). How is this process of **self-regulation** related to self-awareness?

Simply put, you must be self-aware to engage in self-regulation (Baumeister & Vohs, 2002; Lieberman & Eisenberger, 2005). Indeed, self-regulation involves activation of the same brain region—the anterior cingulate cortex—as in self-awareness, as well as activation of areas in the prefrontal lobe regions (refer back to Figure 1.3 in Chapter 1) associated with selecting and initiating actions (*dorsolateral prefrontal cortex*) and planning and coordinating behavior designed to achieve goals (*orbitofrontal cortex*). Brain-imaging studies find significant activation of these brain regions when people are perform-ing difficult tasks requiring considerable cognitive effort and attention, but not during simple memory recall tasks (Amodio et al., 2004b; Schacter & Buckner, 1998). Case studies of people with brain damage in these areas find that while they have intact intelligence and comprehension, they have great difficulty maintaining interest and focus on tasks (Damasio & Anderson, 2003; Knight & Grabowecky, 1995).

One of the important functions of self-regulation is that it provides us with the capacity to forgo the immediate gratification of small rewards to later attain larger rewards (Mischel et al., 1996). Anyone who has ever turned down a party invitation to study for an exam understands this particular benefit of the self-regulatory process. People who learn how to delay gratification early in childhood are better adjusted later in life—academically and socially—than low self-regulators (Oyserman et al., 2004; Shoda et al., 1990). However, not all self-regulation is beneficial. Brain-imaging research suggests that obsessive-compulsive disorder, which is characterized by unhealthy levels of self-regulation, typically involves abnormal functioning of the anterior cingulate cortex (Ursu et al., 2003).

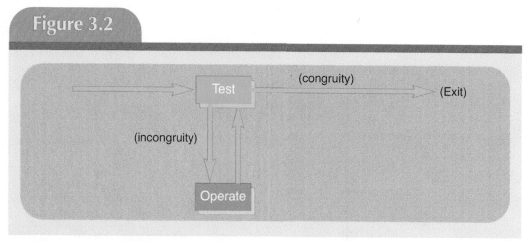

Control Theory of Self-Regulation

According to the control theory of self-regulation, self-awareness provides the means by which we assess how successful we are in meeting our standards. When we become self-aware, we enter the first "test" phase. If we notice a difference between our actual behavior and our standards, we next enter the "operate" phase in which we try to change our behavior to match the standard. Soon, we again self-reflect—the second "test" phase—to discover whether we have reduced or eliminated the discrepancy. When there is no longer a difference between our behavior and the standard, we exit this control process.

**control theory
of self-regulation**
....
A theory contending that, through self-awareness, people compare their behavior to a standard, and if there is a discrepancy, they work to reduce it

What specific role does self-awareness play in exerting self-control? Charles Carver and Michael Scheier's (1981, 1998) **control theory of self-regulation** proposes that self-awareness allows us to assess how we are doing in meeting our goals and ideals. The core idea in control theory is a cognitive feedback loop (see Figure 3.2), summarized by the acronym TOTE, which stands for the steps taken in self-regulation: Test-Operate-Test-Exit. In self-regulation, engaging in self-awareness allows us to compare how we are doing against some standard. This is the first test phase. When privately self-aware, we compare ourselves against a *private* standard (for example, our own values); however, when publicly self-aware we compare ourselves against a *public* standard (for example, our beliefs about what other people value). In the test phase, if we discover that we are falling short of the standard (for example, not studying enough), then we operate to change ourselves (we study harder). Soon, we self-reflect again—the second test phase—to see whether we are closer to reaching our standard. This test and operate cycle repeats itself until there is no difference between our behavior and the standard. When we meet the standard, the control process ends, we feel happy, and we exit the feedback loop. If repeated attempts to move closer to the standard fail, we feel bad and eventually exit the loop (Silvia & Duval, 2001a).

self-discrepancies
....
Discrepancies between our self-concept and how we would ideally like to be (ideal self) or believe others think we should be (ought self)

What happens to us emotionally when self-regulation does not lead to us meeting our standards? That is, how do we react when a discrepancy exists between our self-concept and how we would ideally like to be or believe others think we should be? Tory Higgins (1987) suggests that these **self-discrepancies** produce strong emotions. When we realize there is a discrepancy between our actual self and our *ideal self* (for example, "I wish I was more physically attractive"), we experience *dejection-related emotions*, such as disappointment, frustration, and depression. On the other hand, when we notice a discrepancy between our actual self and what we think we ought to possess (*ought self*) to meet our obligations and responsibilities (for example, "I should be helping my family out more financially"), we are vulnerable to *agitation-related emotions*, such as anxiety and guilt (Keltner & Beer, 2005). A number of studies have found that people with considerable self-discrepancies not only experience negative self-focused emotions but also are often indecisive in their behavior, have unclear self-concepts, and evaluate themselves negatively (Dana et al., 1997; Phillips & Silvia, 2005). The more important these self-discrepant attributes are to the self-concept, the greater are the negative emotions experienced (Boldero & Francis, 2000).

In most instances, negative emotions hinder the type of self-regulation necessary for achieving longer-term goals (Tice et al., 2001). When people become upset, they tend to give

in to their immediate impulses to make themselves feel better. For example, if you are trying to stop smoking, you are likely to grab for a cigarette after having an argument with someone. This "weakness" on your part amounts to giving short-term emotion regulation priority over your longer-term self-regulatory goal of being smoke-free.

Although a high capacity for self-regulation appears to improve your chances for success in life, self-regulating on one task often makes it harder to immediately self-regulate on unrelated tasks (Baumeister & Alquist, 2009; Schmeichel et al., 2006). For example, Mark Muraven and his colleagues (1998) instructed some research participants to exercise self-control by suppressing their emotional reactions to an upsetting movie on environmental disasters. In contrast, other participants were either given no emotional control instructions or were told to increase their emotional responses by "really getting into the film." In this study, self-regulation was measured by determining how long participants would persist at a difficult physical task, namely squeezing a hand grip as long as possible. Such squeezing requires self-control to resist giving up and releasing the grip. Participants squeezed the grip both before (*pretest*) and after (*posttest*) watching the movie, and the difference between the pre and posttest was the dependent measure of self-regulation depletion. Consistent with the hypothesis that self-regulation strength is weakened following the exercise of self-control, those who were told to control their emotions while watching the upsetting film exhibited self-regulation depletion as measured by the hand-grip test. No such depletion was found in the other participants. Because complex tasks require greater self-regulation than simple tasks, prior self-regulation is most likely to harm people's subsequent activities when these later activities require higher-order cognitive processing (Fujita et al., 2006; Wheeler et al., 2008).

In explaining such findings, Roy Baumeister and his coworkers (1994) propose that controlling or regulating our behavior is best understood in terms of the following principles from a strength model of self-regulation:

1. At any given time, we have only a limited amount of energy available to self-regulate.
2. Each exercise of self-regulation depletes this limited resource for a period of time.
3. Right after exercising self-regulation in one activity, we will find it harder to regulate our behavior in an unrelated activity.

According to this self-regulation model, if Tameeka is cramming for final exams and forces herself to study instead of going to a party (self-regulation success), she should be less able to control her anger later that evening (self-regulation failure) when her freeloading roommate eats the dessert that Tameeka was saving for a late-night snack. Consistent with the model, numerous studies have found that exertion of self-control causes a subsequent decline in self-control performance on other tasks, especially when people feel pressured to engage in the first act of self-control (Moller et al., 2006; Segerstrom & Nes, 2007). Thus, Tameeka is more likely to lose her temper if she is studying primarily due to external pressures rather than genuine interest in the course material.

What happens in the brain to cause this deficit in self-regulation? For many years neuroscientists have known that glucose from the bloodstream provides the chemical fuel for neurons to fire impulses so that specific brain regions can function effectively (Laughlin, 2004). However, when the brain consumes glucose faster than it can be replenished, cerebral functioning is disrupted, producing cognitive deficits. Although nearly all brain functions rely primarily on glucose for fuel, some cognitive activities are more sensitive than others to changes in glucose. In a series of studies, Matthew Gailliot and his colleagues (2007) found evidence that self-regulation is especially sensitive to glucose fluctuations. First, the researchers found that participants' blood glucose levels dropped significantly after they engaged in acts of self-control. Second, they found that participants who had low glucose levels after engaging in acts of self-control exhibited less self-regulation ability on a subsequent task. Third, after exerting self-control on a task, participants who then consumed a glucose drink showed significantly less self-regulatory deficits on a later task than did those who had consumed a similarly tasting placebo drink. These and other findings suggest that depleting the available supply of glucose more severely impairs brain functions associated with self-control than more basic and simple cognitive abilities because self-control is a relatively advanced human capacity (Gailliot & Baumeister, 2007; Inzlicht & Gutsell, 2007). The Applications section at the end of the chapter discusses some social problems associated with self-regulation failure.

Short of simply sleeping or resting, how can people recover from self-regulation depletion and once again engage in effective self-control? Diane Tice and her coworkers (2007) explored this question by hypothesizing that positive emotion or mood can counteract self-regulation depletion. Their reasoning was that previous studies had found that positive emotion facilitates creativity, which is a cognitive process that requires considerable self-regulation. Further, because emotions are associated with general bodily arousal, they reasoned that positive emotions' arousing potential might counteract the tired feeling that people often experience due to self-regulation depletion.

In one study testing this hypothesis, participants were told that they would take part in two separate studies, one a cognitive thought-listing study and the other a health study. First, participants listed all their thoughts for a five-minute period. For those participants in the *thought suppression* (depletion) condition, they were also instructed to avoid thinking about a white bear during the task and to indicate on their sheet whenever the thought of a white bear occurred. Past research has found that actively trying not to think about something is cognitively taxing and leads to self-regulatory depletion. In the *control* (no depletion) condition, participants were told that those in other conditions had to restrict various specific thoughts (like a white bear) but they were free to think about anything. When this phase of the study was completed, the experimenter returned to the room and gave participants something. In the *mood induction* condition participants were given a small bag of candy as a gift, while in the *neutral mood* condition participants did not receive candy. Then participants were ushered into a different room for what they thought was the second experiment, which was administered by a different person. Here participants were told that they were to drink as much of a "healthful" beverage (actually, unsweetened Kool-Aid mixed with vinegar water) as they could, but they were also informed that it tasted bad. The amount of beverage consumed was the measure of participants' ability to self-regulate.

Results indicated that while positive mood did not increase drinking in general, there was a significant interaction effect between mood and experimental condition; participants in the thought suppression/pleasant mood condition consumed as much beverage as participants who were not required to suppress their thoughts. Thus, as hypothesized, happy mood eliminated the self-regulation impairment that was produced by the initial act of self-control. Similar results were obtained in three additional studies in this research, each using either different self-regulation exercises or different mood inductions.

What do these results tell us? As already discussed, past research indicates that acts of self-regulation appear to temporarily deplete self-regulatory resources, making later self-control more difficult. The findings from this study indicate that positive mood or emotion can counteract self-regulation depletion. These findings are potentially very important because losing self-control can make people more susceptible to a variety of maladaptive behaviors, such as drug abuse and aggression. The current findings suggest that inducing positive affect in people somehow helps restore their capacity and/or willingness to self-regulate. At present it is unclear whether positive mood actually is able to influence the blood glucose levels which provide the brain with its necessary nutrients or whether positive mood merely makes people more willing or motivated to continue self-regulating despite their depleted state of mind. Future research needs to further explore these possibilities.

SECTION SUMMARY

- Both William James and George Herbert Mead identified the *self* as having two separate aspects: the self as subject of awareness (the "*I*") and the self as object of awareness (the "*me*" or *self-concept*).

- *Self-concept* is our theory of our personal behavior, abilities, and social relationship constructed with the help of others.

- Self-awareness is necessary for self-concept development.

- The anterior cingulate cortex, located in the frontal lobe of the cerebral cortex, is especially important in self-awareness.

- Humans develop self-awareness at around eighteen months of age.

- The great apes and a few other species appear to have self-awareness ability.

- Private self-awareness is a temporary state of being aware of hidden, private self-aspects.

Effects: affect intensification, knowledge clarification, and adherence to personal standards.

- Public self-awareness is a temporary state of being aware of observable, public self-aspects.

Effects: social uneasiness, temporary self-esteem loss, adherence to social standards

- The tendencies to habitually engage in private and public self-awareness are known as the personality traits of private self-consciousness and public self-consciousness.

- Self-regulation involves the ways in which we control and direct our actions.

- The control theory of self-regulation contends that we compare our behavior to a standard; and if there is a discrepancy, we try to reduce it.

- Exerting self-control depletes self-regulatory resources.

THE SELF AS A KNOWLEDGE STRUCTURE

Thus far we have learned that self-awareness allows us to analyze our thoughts and feelings, as well as anticipate how others might respond to us interpersonally. Through self-awareness, we develop a self-concept, which helps us regulate our behavior and adapt to our surroundings (Higgins, 1996). Yet how is this self-information organized in memory and what social forces shape this self-knowledge?

SELF-CONCEPT INVOLVES A NETWORK OF SELF-ASPECTS.

Social psychologists have expended considerable effort to better understand how information about the self is stored and categorized in memory. In describing this process, the computer has often been used as a metaphor: the subjective self (the "I") consists of program components, and the objective self (the self-concept or the "me") is the data aspect of the computer (Greenwald & Pratkanis, 1984). To describe *how* self-knowledge is stored in memory, a number of theorists have proposed that self-related information is

Figure 3.3

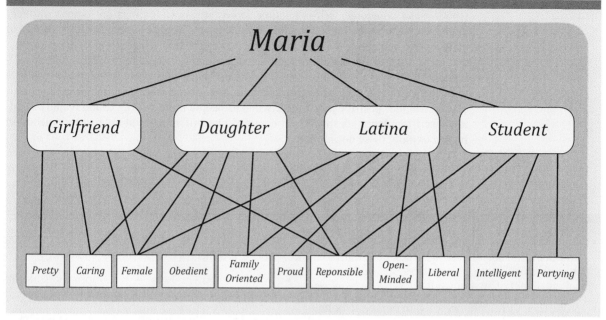

Multiple Self-Aspects Framework

This is a simplified representation of the multiple self-aspects framework which describes self-concept as a collection of numerous self-aspects, each associated with certain personal attributes. Shaded attributes are those associated with more than one self-aspect. Here, Maria's "girlfriend" self-aspect shares attributes with her "daughter," "Latina," and" student" self-aspects. What types of social situations are likely to activate Maria's various self-aspects?

multiple self-aspects framework

A theory that describes self-concept as a collection of multiple self-aspects that organize and guide a person's behavior when they are activated in specific situations

❝*What you think of yourself is much more important than what others think of you.*❞

Seneca, Roman playwright, 4 BC–AD 64

organized in a complex network of associations (e.g., Collins & Loftus, 1975; Markus, 1977). Recently, Allen McConnell (2011) combined these theoretical insights in his **multiple self-aspects framework**, which describes self-concept as a collection of multiple self-aspects that organize and guide a person's behavior when they are activated in specific situations.

Figure 3.3 depicts an example of a simplified, multiple self-aspects framework. In this framework of Maria's self-concept, four of her self-aspects are shown, each associated with certain personal qualities or attributes. At any given moment, the activation in memory of a particular self-aspect or a particular attribute can make other self-aspects or attributes more accessible in memory (Brown & McConnell, 2009). Whenever a self-aspect or attribute is activated, it has the potential to shape the person's thinking and behavior. For Maria, walking on campus to attend her first class of the day may activate her student self-aspect that, in turn, makes more accessible, from memory, Maria's student-associated attributes: responsible, open-minded, liberal, intelligent, and partying. Further, when Maria thinks of her student attribute of being responsible, this thought may activate her "girlfriend" and/or "daughter" self-aspects because they also share the "responsible" attribute.

Certain social contexts are more likely to activate certain self-aspects and attributes than are other social contexts (Aquino et al., 2009; McGuire et al., 1978). Thus, Maria's behavior is more likely to be organized and guided by her student self-aspect when she is in class or studying at the library than when she is at her boyfriend's apartment watching television or at home visiting her parents. Likewise, when someone compliments Maria on being open-minded, her student or Latina self-aspects are more likely to become accessible from memory than are her girlfriend or daughter self-aspects. This is so because the student and Latina self-aspects both are associated with the open-minded attribute, while the other self-aspects share no such association. Research suggests that when one aspect of self-concept is spontaneously activated, potentially conflicting or irrelevant self-aspects are more likely to be inhibited from being simultaneously activated (Hugenberg & Bodenhausen, 2004).

Whether or not a specific attribute or self-aspect becomes a defining feature of one's self-concept and is chronically activated from memory often depends on the degree to which it "stands out" in everyday interactions. This is often the experience of people who have attributes or self-aspects that run counter to the stereotype of their social group. For example, White Americans are stereotypically perceived to be inferior to African Americans in athletic endeavors, while African Americans are typically perceived to be inferior to White Americans in academic pursuits (see Chapter 6). Research by William von Hippel and his colleagues (2001) suggests that when members of one of these groups behave counter to these stereotypes, their performances are more likely to be noticed and commented upon than are the stereotype-consistent performances of the other group members. Such unexpected behaviors not only grab other people's attention, the performers themselves are more likely to begin thinking of their behaviors as distinctive, also. As a result, they are more likely to develop attributes and/or self-aspects around these abilities than are members of the other group who perform at the same level but for whom the performances are not considered unusual for their group.

The multiple self-aspects framework proposes that self-concept structure plays an important role in people's daily moods and self-esteem (McConnell et al., 2009). Positive and negative social feedback regarding attributes and self-aspects that are regularly activated from memory will have a larger impact on daily moods and self-esteem than social feedback regarding less activated attributes and self-aspects. For Maria, when she is home with her family, feedback regarding her daughter self-aspect is more likely to affect her daily mood and self-esteem than feedback regarding the other self-aspects, simply because Maria is most likely to think of herself as a daughter when home. Further, positive and negative feedback about one self-aspect will influence evaluations of other self-aspects that share greater attribute associations. Thus, if Maria's boyfriend treats her in such a way to make Maria feel very positive about her "girlfriend" self-aspect, it will more likely also increase her evaluations of her "daughter" self-aspect than about her "student" or "Latina" self-aspects.

CULTURAL BELIEFS ABOUT SELF-GROUP RELATIONSHIPS SHAPE SELF-CONCEPT.

In Chapter 1 we examined how the cultural experiences of young adults born between 1966 and the 1990s shaped their views of reality and of themselves. To explore how your cultural upbringing influences your self-beliefs, spend a few minutes completing *Self/Social Connection Exercise 3.2.* You will not only discover something about the psychology of self-development, you may also learn something fascinating about yourself.

Individualist-Collectivist Comparisons

When social psychologists have examined how people describe themselves using the Twenty Statements Test (TST), they find some interesting cross-cultural differences (Cross & Gore, 2002; Markus & Kitayama, 1991). In general, American, Canadian, and European self-concepts are composed of predominantly attributive self-descriptions, indicating that these individualist cultures foster the development of an **independent self** for their members. GenNexters (see p. 19) are the generation of Americans who most clearly embody the independent self. In contrast, people from collectivist cultures such as China, Mexico, Japan, India, and Kenya have more social self-descriptions, indicating a fostering of an **interdependent self** (Kanagawa et al., 2001; Ma & Schoeneman, 1997). Within the United States, European Americans, African Americans, and Latino Americans tend to have highly independent selves, despite the latter two ethnic groups having collectivist heritages (Oyserman et al., 2002). Latino Americans with interdependent selves are much more likely to be recent immigrants to the country than those with independent selves (Castro, 2003).

This differing view of the individual due to a culture's collectivist or individualist orientation begins to influence children from birth so that their culturally based thinking becomes habitual and automatic (Kashima, 2009; Kitayama et al., 2009). Collectivist and individualist beliefs and values are reinforced in daily living. They not only shape

---

"*Who in the world am I? Ah, that's the great puzzle!***"**

━ ━ ━ ━ ━ ━ ━ ━

Lewis Carroll, British author, 1832–1898, *Alice in Wonderland*

"*I have a very valuable parrot,"* declared the pet store owner. *"It speaks both Spanish and English! If you pull the left leg, he speaks English, and if you pull the right leg he speaks Spanish."* *"What happens if you pull both legs at once?"* asked the customer. *"Will he speak TexMex?"* *"Noooo,"* answered the parrot. *"I will fall on my ass.***"**

━ ━ ━ ━ ━ ━ ━ ━

Mexican American folk tale, adapted from West (1988)

---

independent self
· · · · · · · · · · · · · · · · · · · ·
A way of conceiving the self in terms of unique, personal attributes and as a being that is separate and autonomous from the group

interdependent self
· · · · · · · · · · · · · · · · · · · ·
A way of conceiving the self in terms of social roles and as a being that is embedded in and dependent on the group

Self/Social Connections Exercise 3.2

Who Are You?

Directions

In 1954 sociologists Manford Kuhn and Thomas McPartland devised the Twenty Statements Test (TST) to measure self-concept. Spend a few minutes describing yourself by answering the question *"Who am I?"* when completing the following twenty "I am ..." statements. Respond as if you were giving the answers to yourself, not to someone else.

1. I am	_____.		11. I am	_____.
2. I am	_____.		12. I am	_____.
3. I am	_____.		13. I am	_____.
4. I am	_____.		14. I am	_____.
5. I am	_____.		15. I am	_____.
6. I am	_____.		16. I am	_____.
7. I am	_____.		17. I am	_____.
8. I am	_____.		18. I am	_____.
9. I am	_____.		19. I am	_____.
10. I am	_____.		20. I am	_____.

Scoring

Examine your TST responses and code each into one of the following four categories (see Hartley, 1970)

Physical self-description—identifies yourself in terms of physical qualities that do not imply social interaction ("*I am a male*"; "*I am a brunette*"; "*I am overweight*")

Social self-descriptions—identifies yourself in terms of social roles, institutional memberships, or other socially defined statuses ("*I am a student*"; "*I am a daughter*"; "*I am a Jew*")

Attributive self-descriptions—identifies yourself in terms of psychological or physiological states or traits ("*I am intelligent*"; "*I am assertive*"; "*I am tired*")

Global self-descriptions—identifies yourself so comprehensively or vaguely that it does not distinguish one from any other person ("*I am a human being*"; "*I am alive*"; "*I am me*").

Which category occurs most frequently for you? Using this classification scheme, Louis Zurcher (1977) found that while American college students in the 1950s and early 1960s tended to describe themselves in terms of social roles, college students in the 1970s identified themselves in terms of psychological attributes. This self-concept trend has continued (Trafimow, et al. 1991) and coincides with a rise in individualist attitudes among Americans (Roberts & Helson 1997). Do your own self-responses fit this pattern?

the structure of self-concept, they also determine beliefs about how self-development should proceed (Hashimoto, 2011; Zou et al., 2009). Within collectivist societies, child-drearing practices emphasize conformity, cooperation, dependence, and knowing one's proper place, whereas within more individualist societies, independence, self-reliance,

and personal success are stressed. In a series of studies, Qi Wang (2006) documented this difference in childrearing when mothers from the United States and China shared memories with their three-year-old children in a semi-structured interview setting. When discussing past events with their children, American mothers' conversations made their child the focus of attention, often referring to the child's likes and dislikes. In contrast, Chinese mothers' conversations frequently referred to social norms and group expectations.

One consequence of these differing socialization practices is that in an individualist society, people develop a belief in their own uniqueness and diversity (Miller, 1988). This sense of individuality is nurtured and fostered within the educational system, and its manifestation is considered a sign of maturity (Pratt, 1991). On the other hand, in a collectivist society, uniqueness and individual differences are often seen as impediments to proper self-growth (Kim & Choi, 1994). Instead, the self becomes most meaningful and complete when it is closely identified with—not independent of—the group (DeVos, 1985). Heejun Kim and Hazel Markus (1999) provided a simple demonstration of how these two cultural belief systems influence people's judgments when they asked Americans and East Asians to choose one of five pens like those depicted in Figure 3.4. They found that 77 percent of the Americans, but only 31 percent of the East Asians, chose the pen with the uncommon color. These results suggest cultural differences in uniqueness versus conformity needs. Figure 3.5 outlines how cultural differences regarding individualism-collectivism influence the structure of self-concept.

Figure 3.4

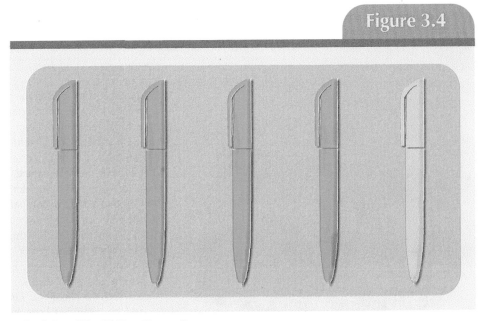

Which Pen Would You Choose?

When asked to choose one pen from an array of pens like those here, 77 percent of Americans, but only 31 percent of East Asians, chose the pen with the uncommon color (Kim & Markus, 1999). How does this finding relate to individualist and collectivist beliefs?

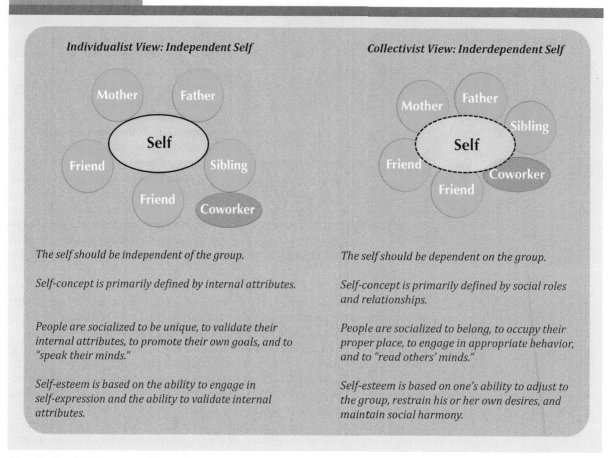

Figure 3.5

Individualist View: Independent Self

Mother | Father
Self
Friend | Sibling
Friend
Coworker

The self should be independent of the group.

Self-concept is primarily defined by internal attributes.

People are socialized to be unique, to validate their internal attributes, to promote their own goals, and to "speak their minds."

Self-esteem is based on the ability to engage in self-expression and the ability to validate internal attributes.

Collectivist View: Inderdependent Self

Mother | Father
Self | Sibling
Friend | Coworker
Friend

The self should be dependent on the group.

Self-concept is primarily defined by social roles and relationships.

People are socialized to belong, to occupy their proper place, to engage in appropriate behavior, and to "read others' minds."

Self-esteem is based on one's ability to adjust to the group, restrain his or her own desires, and maintain social harmony.

How Is the Self Construed in Collectivist and Individualist Cultures?

Individualist cultures foster the development of the independent self—characterized by independence, uniqueness, self-expression, and the validation of internal attributes. In contrast, collectivist cultures foster the development of the interdependent self—characterized by dependence, conformity, and adjustment of one's social roles to accommodate group goals. How might these two different views of the self lead to personal conflicts between individualists and collectivists when they interact with one another?

As you see, conceiving the self as either independent or interdependent has important implications for how people think, feel, and interact in their social world. The ideas and activities of a culture promote a way of life that provides a constant reminder to its members of what type of self is valued. Immersed within these social environments, the dominant mode of thinking will be that which is compatible with either an independent self or an interdependent self (Wu & Keysar, 2007). However, within these cultures there will be times when people enter settings that trigger the alternative sense of self. For example, people who live in an individualist culture may watch the movie *It's a Wonderful Life* (see Chapter 1, p. 22) and be reminded how their own lives are deeply intertwined with their family, friends, and community. This setting triggers a spontaneous interdependent self, increasing the likelihood that people will at least temporarily set aside selfish interests, act cooperatively, and attend to others' needs (Gardner et al., 1999). In other words, cultures do not create people with rigidly independent or interdependent selves. Situational factors can trigger spontaneous self-concepts in people that run counter to the independent self or interdependent self fostered by their culture (Kühnen et al., 2001; Kühnen & Oyserman, 2002).

What About Biculturalists?

Although cultures can be characterized as being more oriented toward individualism or collectivism, not everyone living within a particular culture will have the same individualist-collectivist leanings; individuals differ in the degree to which they identify with individualist and collectivists beliefs and values (Ayyash-Abdo, 2001). For example, if you are a Native American, Mexican American, Indian American, or Asian American, your cultural heritage may encourage you to seek collectivist goals (Gaines, 1995). The same is true of Jews and Arabs who live in Israel, where a Western individualist ideological system often conflicts with traditional Arab and Jewish collectivist beliefs and values. Numerous studies indicate that individuals with such a *bicultural* background view themselves and the world through both individualist and collectivist lenses, which can cause internal conflict as they attempt to reconcile individualist strivings with collectivist yearnings (Hong et al., 2001; Rattan, 2011; Sussman, 2000).

How is this conflict best resolved? Based on studies of Pueblo, Navajo, Latino, Iranian American, Indian American, and Asia American/Canadian children and adults, neither abandoning one's ancestral collectivist culture nor isolating oneself from the dominant individualist culture is good for mental health and social inclusion (Benet-Martínez & Karakitapoglu-Aygun, 2003; Rutland et al., 2011). Instead, successful biculturalism entails retaining ancestral values and practices while incorporating new values and practices from the dominant culture (see pp. 86–87). This acknowledgment and acceptance that the two cultural identities are not fully compatible or overlapping results in a self-concept that is both more inclusive and more complex (Benet-Martínz et al., 2006; Roccas & Brewer, 2002). People who possess dual cultural identities engage in **cultural frame switching**, in which they move between the two different cultural belief systems in response to situational cues and demands (Haritatos & Benet-Martínez, 2002; Sui et al., 2007). As one Native American woman explained how she successfully attained her PhD while still maintaining her strong tribal ties:

> My family and I talked about the "I" and the "we," all the pressure there was when I was going to school to be this "I," to climb the old ladder, claw your way up to success. … I'm part of a "we" and I've never lost sight of that. … Because of the "we," this community and my family, I can do all of this. … (Stratham & Rhoades, 2001)

By accessing their two different cultural belief systems, biculturalists can engage in culturally appropriate behaviors depending on the social context (Pouliasi & Verkuyten, 2007). Among families who have recently emigrated to a new culture, children and younger adults within the family tend to have an easier time than older adults in successfully engaging in cultural frame switching (Cheung et al., 2011). In other words, people are better able to identify with a new culture if their exposure to it occurs when they are relatively young. The melding of the collectivist and individualist orientations not only benefits the health of biculturalists but can also provide long-term benefits to society, by infusing it with individuals who deeply understand the value of both autonomy and social obligation (Chiu & Hong, 2005; Oyserman et al., 1998).

cultural frame switching
....
The process by which biculturalists switch between different culturally appropriate behaviors depending on the context

Critical
THINKING

If you were to tell someone to "just be yourself," what would that mean to them depending on whether they were from an individualist or a collectivist culture?

CULTURAL BELIEFS ABOUT GENDER SHAPE SELF-CONCEPT.

Gender beliefs and expectations can also have a profound impact on how we define ourselves. For example, one evening as we ate dinner, Amelia, who was three-years-old at the time, surveyed the table, and then looked at me and announced, "Daddy? I'm a girl, and Mommy's a girl, and Lillian's a girl, but you're not a girl. You're a boy." Then, glancing at our dog, Yocker, who was sleeping on the floor near my feet, she added, "and Yocker's a boy, too." Ignoring the possibility that my daughter had recognized some characteristics other than sex that helped her in categorizing me with the family dog (perhaps a tendency to stare off in space or to pant at the sight of food), I complimented Amelia on her ability to distinguish males from females.

gender identity
....
The identification of oneself
as a male or a female

This "Amelia story" describes an identification process that all children experience at approximately this age, namely, **gender identity**, which is the identification of oneself as a male or a female. Knowing that "I am a girl" or "I am a boy" is one of the core building blocks in a child's developing self-theory (Denny & Pittman, 2007). When children develop gender identity they strive to act in ways consistent with this identity (Le Maner-Idrissi & Renault, 2006; Maccoby, 1990). What Amelia demonstrated at the dinner table was that she was trying to act in line with her emerging gender identity and her understanding of gender issues.

One important gender distinction that girls and boys often learn in North American culture involves the degree to which they should define the self in terms of close relationships (Cross & Gore, 2004). Numerous studies indicate that girls are more likely than boys to be raised to think, act, and define themselves in ways that emphasize their emotional connectedness to other people (Gore & Cross, 2006; Maccoby, 1998). Susan Cross contends that this difference in gender socialization results in girls developing cooperative relationships with others and valuing intimate friendships, while boys are more likely to develop competitive and less nurturing social relationships (Cross et al., 2011; Cross & Madson, 1997). According to Cross, these gender differences persist into adulthood, fostering the construction of a *relational* self-concept among women and an *independent* self-concept among men. Individuals that construct a relational self-concept place high value on having warm, close relationships; those who construct an independent self-concept express less interest in cultivating emotional relationships (Cross & Gore, 2002; Cross & Morris, 2003). In Chapter 10 (pp. 403–407), we will examine more closely how these differences in gender socialization shape the nature and quality of friendships and romantic relationships.

To what degree are these gender differences in self-concept similar to the cross-cultural differences we previously reviewed? That is, are American women's self-concepts similar to the self-concepts of people from collectivist cultures? Actually, it appears that the similarities are more superficial than substantive. A five-culture study by Yoshihisa Kashima and his colleagues (1995) indicates that American and Australian women's self-concepts are not like Asians' self-concepts. Instead, these researchers found that while individualist-collectivist cultural differences are captured mostly by the extent to which people see themselves as acting as independent agents in relation to the group, gender differences are best summarized by the extent to which people regard themselves as *emotionally related* to other individuals. This suggests that gender socialization has much more to do with encouraging girls to pay attention to the emotional "pulse" of their social relationships while discouraging boys from doing so, than it does in encouraging boys to be independent of the group and girls to be dependent on the group. In other words, individualist-collectivist socialization has decidedly different effects on the nature of self-concept than male-female socialization.

> **"**A race of people is like an individual man—until it uses its own talent, takes pride in its own history, expresses its own culture, affirms its own selfhood, it can never fulfill itself.**"**
>
> Malcolm X, U.S. Muslim and Black Nationalist, 1925–1965

SOCIAL IDENTITIES ESTABLISH "WHAT" AND "WHERE" WE ARE AS SOCIAL BEINGS.

social identities
....
Aspects of a person's self-
concept based on his or her
group memberships

Cultural identities and relational self-concepts both involve including others into our self-concepts. Similarly, following the terrorist attacks of September 11, 2001, millions of Americans experienced a renewed sense of national unity and patriotism, most clearly expressed by the sharp increase in the displaying of the American flag (Skitka, 2006). In explaining this process of group identification, Henri Tajfel (1982) and John Turner (1985) have taken William James's notion of the social "me" and developed it into the concept of social identity. **Social identities** are those aspects of our self-concepts based on

Ethnic identity is an individual's sense of personal identification with a particular ethnic group.

our group memberships (Hogg & Abrams, 1988). They establish *what* and *where* we are in social terms (Ellemers et al., 2002; Mussweiler & Bodenhausen 2002).

One of the consequences of group identification is an internalization of the group's view of social reality. Social identities provide members with a shared set of values, beliefs, and goals about themselves and their social world. As Mead might describe it, to have a social identity is to internalize the group within the individual, which in turn serves to regulate and coordinate the attitudes and behavior of the separate group members. However, if social identities are a representation of the group within the mind of the individual, what happens when we live in a society where our group is devalued by the larger culture? Don't we run the risk of falling victim to a negative self-fulfilling prophecy?

This is the dilemma faced by members of social groups who have been subjected to prejudice, discrimination, and negative stereotypes (Crocker et al., 1994). Sometimes the negativity is subtle and not necessarily intentional, such as being regularly mistaken as a foreigner in one's own country, which is a common occurrence among Americans of Asian, Muslim, and Hispanic descent (Huynh et al., 2011). One way that ethnic minority groups have coped with intolerance and nonacceptance is by rediscovering their own ethnic heritage and actively rejecting the negative stereotypes in the larger culture (Joseph & Hunter, 2011; Kelman, 1998). **Ethnic identity**, which is a type of social identity, is an individual's sense of personal identification with a particular ethnic group (Yip, 2005).

In describing ethnic identity formation, most theories propose an age-related progression from the unawareness of ethnic membership to the habitual use of an ethnic category to describe the self (Castro, 2003). For example, Jean Phinney (1991, 1993) has proposed a three-stage model (see Table 3.1). In stage 1, the *unexamined ethnic identity stage*, individuals often have not personally examined ethnic identity issues and may have incorporated negative stereotypes from the dominant culture into their own self-concepts, resulting in feelings of inadequacy (Clark & Clark, 1939; Phinney & Kohatsu, 1997). Other people in stage 1 may have been exposed to positive ethnic attitudes from others but have simply not incorporated them into their self-concepts.

In stage 2, *ethnic identity search*, people have an experience that temporarily dislodges their old worldview, making them receptive to exploring their own ethnicity. In many cases, the catalyst for this exploration is a personal experience with prejudice (Sanders Thompson, 1991). This stage often entails an intense period of searching, in which people passionately consume ethnic literature and participate in cultural events. During stage 2, some individuals may also develop an *oppositional identity*, in which they actively reject values of the dominant culture. While in this oppositional stance,

ethnic identity
An individual's sense of personal identification with a particular ethnic group

Critical THINKING

If your ethnic heritage is relevant to who you think you are, what stage are you at in Phinney's model? Is this model an accurate portrayal of your own ethnic identity development?

Table 3.1

Stages in Ethnic Identity Formation

Stage 1: Unexamined ethnic identity   Lack of exploration of ethnicity, due to lack of interest or due to having merely adopted other people's opinions of ethnicity

Stage 2: Ethnic identity search   Involvement in exploring and seeking to understand the meaning of ethnicity for oneself, often sparked by some incident that focused attention on one's minority status in the dominant culture

Stage 3: Achieved ethnic identity   Clear and confident sense of one's own ethnicity; able to identify and internalize those aspects of the dominant culture that are acceptable and stand against those that are oppressive

> "*Born into the skin of yellow women we are born into the armor of warriors.*"
>
> Kitty Tsui, Chinese American poet, 1989

anything associated with the dominant group is typically devalued, whereas anything associated with one's own ethnic group is declared superior and highly valued (Carter, 2003; Cross, 1991).

The third stage and culmination of this process is a deeper understanding and appreciation of one's ethnicity—what Phinney labels *achieved ethnic* identity. Confidence and security in a newfound ethnic identity allow people to feel ethnic pride along with a new understanding of their own place within the dominant culture. They are able to internalize those aspects of the dominant culture that are acceptable (for example, financial security, independence, pursuit of academics) and stand against those that are oppressive (for example, racism and sexism).

A number of studies support Phinney's view of the mental health benefits of ethnic identity development, among them being high self-esteem and having a stable self-concept (Bailey & Bradbury-Bailey, 2010; Phinney et al., 1997). These findings suggest that when our commitment and attitudes toward our ethnic group are strongly positive, they can serve as buffers to the negative stereotypes in the larger society. This process of social identity development in oppressed ethnic groups has parallels in other social groups that have historically been discriminated against, such as women, lesbians and gay men, and the disabled. Although such positive social identities can short-circuit the negative effects that prejudice can inflict on self-esteem (Branscombe et al., 1999), they are not always effective (Major et al., 2007). In Chapter 6 we will examine in greater detail some of these negative effects (see pp. 230–233).

SECTION SUMMARY

- *Self-related information is organized in a complex network of associations.*

- The *interdependent self* identifies with societal institutions and is more common in collectivist cultures.

- The *independent self* identifies with personal attributes and is more common in individualist cultures.

- *Gender identity* is our identification as being female or male.

- In North-American culture, women have a greater sense of relational interdependence than men, and this difference is reflected in how women and men define themselves.

- *Social identities* situate us within clearly defined groups.

- *Ethnic identities* insulate us from the negative effects of derogatory stereotypes.

PRESENTING THE SELF TO OTHERS

Whenever we interact with others, we often try to manage their impressions of us by carefully constructing and monitoring our presented selves (Lampel & Bhalla, 2007; Schlenker & Wowra, 2003). Indeed, sociologist Erving Goffman (1959) suggests that social interaction is like a theatrical performance, with the interactants being the actors on stage playing prescribed roles. While "on stage," people act out "lines" and attempt to maintain competent and appropriately presented selves. In observing this performance, the audience generally accepts the presented selves at face value and treats them accordingly. The acceptance may not be genuine, but Goffman asserts that people have learned to keep their private opinions to themselves, unless the performers prove wholly incompetent. To do otherwise would disrupt the smooth flow of social interaction. Let us examine in more detail these everyday performances.

SELF-PRESENTATIONS ARE EITHER CONSCIOUSLY OR AUTOMATICALLY CONSTRUCTED.

strategic self-presentation
••••••••••••••••
Conscious and deliberate efforts to shape other people's impressions in order to gain power, influence, sympathy, or approval

The process of constructing and presenting the self in order to shape other people's impressions and achieve ulterior goals is known as **strategic self-presentation** (Fine, 2006; Jones & Pittman, 1982; Nezlek & Leary, 2002). Such impression management can be stressful and is associated with increases in heart rate and blood pressure (Hartley et al., 1999; Heffner et al., 2002). It can also require considerable self-regulation (see pp. 73–78), and as the self-presentation demands increase people sometimes lose control of their performance (van den Bos et al., 2011; Vohs et al., 2005). For example, you could go into a job interview intending to convey intelligence and social skill, only to spill coffee all over yourself. Or you could act like an idiot while taking your driver's exam. Perhaps you can relate to the following account of a woman's ill-fated attempt to impress the parents of her fiancé (Knapp et al., 1986):

> I was invited to my fiancé's home for a special dinner. It was the first time I had met everyone and I was trying to impress them. As we sat down to eat, his father turned to me and said, "I hope you'll say grace." I was so unsettled by this request that I immediately bowed my head and said, "Now I lay me down to sleep … " (p. 40)

Making social blunders and not being able to project an appropriate presented self often causes embarrassment (Sabini et al., 2001). College students report being embarrassed at least once a week, while younger teenagers become embarrassed even more often (R. Miller, 1995). Embarrassment is accompanied by an activation of the sympathetic nervous system, which is that part of our nervous system that prepares us to deal with threatening situations. The blushing, sweating, and heart pounding we experience during embarrassing incidents is our body's way of harnessing its energy to respond to the perceived threat (Gerlach et al., 2003). The good news about embarrassment is that onlookers generally judge us less harshly for our social gaffes than we think they do (Savitsky et al., 2001). Further, embarrassing situations are also often unpleasant for onlookers, and thus, they typically help us recover our self-presentations (Marcus et al., 1996; Miller, 1987). Because friends and loved ones are part of our self-concepts, we can also experience embarrassment when their self-presentations are discredited (Thornton, 2003). However, we might also laugh until we cry when those close to us commit social blunders, which was exactly my mother's reaction when we left the license bureau after my failed "coordination test."

The more skilled we become in particular self-presentations, the more likely they are automatically activated and guided without conscious monitoring. Such automatic self-presentations are efficient because they conserve cognitive resources that can then be devoted to other tasks (Pontari & Schlenker, 2000). This idea that self-presentation involves both automatic and deliberate cognitive processes reflects the *dual-process* approach to social cognition first introduced in Chapter 1 (p. 18). According to this perspective, human beings employ two broad cognitive strategies to interact in their social world—one involving effortless thinking and the other involving effortful thinking.

Although we are most aware of employing strategic self-presentations when interacting with strangers or casual acquaintances (Leary et al., 1994; Tice et al., 1995), these self-presentations also play important roles in our intimate relationships. Two common differences between most of the self-presentations we construct in non-intimate and intimate relationships involve *evaluation concerns* and *cognitive effort.* When socializing with friends and loved ones, we are typically both less anxious about how we are being evaluated and more skilled with the self-presentations we typically employ. As a result, our intimate self-presentations are likely activated and guided with less conscious monitoring than when we are with strangers and casual acquaintances (Gosnell et al., 2011; Schlenker & Wowra, 2003). In other words, they are operating below our level of awareness (implicit cognition), much like a computer program runs in the background without any obvious visual detection on the screen to remind us that it is active. Because these self-presentations are being activated and monitored nonconsciously, we think of them as "more genuine" than those that are more deliberately executed. However, we will consciously attend to and regulate our self-presentations on those occasions when our friends and family "get the wrong impression" of us.

One relatively new and extremely popular avenue by which people consciously present themselves to others is on online social networking sites such as Facebook and MySpace. In fact, more than 700 million people worldwide have profiles on such online sites. One important difference between the manner in which online and offline selves are presented is in the degree of control people have over their self-presentations; people have much greater control in consciously constructing and presenting themselves online compared to normal everyday self-presentations (Schack, 2010). Because of the high degree of control that people have over their online-presented selves, is there any evidence that people exercise this control to construct overly idealized versions of themselves in their profiles?

Content analysis of social networking sites suggests that at least some people engage in shameless embellishment of their personalities when they create a public self to present to others (Manago et al., 2008). Yet other research suggests that the ability of "friends" to post comments about people's profiles may cause most online self-presenters to monitor and control the construction of unrealistically idealized public selves. In one such study that investigated profiles on the most popular social networking sites in the United States (Facebook) and Germany (StudiVZ, SchuelerVZ), Mitja Back and his colleagues (2010) obtained the online social network profiles of research participants before asking them to describe their ideal selves and having four friends

Are the self-presentations that people post on their Facebook profiles an accurate representation of their actual selves, or are they more likely reflections of their idealized selves?

Critical
THINKING

Do you think that people raised in collectivist cultures might sometimes have different self-presentation concerns than persons raised in individualist cultures?

"*The world's a stage, and most of us are desperately unrehearsed.***"**

—————————

Sean O'Casey, Irish playwright, 1880–1964

describe their actual selves. Comparison of their online profiles with their ideal self-descriptions and their friends' description of their actual selves found little evidence that participants presented themselves in an idealized manner online. Taken together, the findings from these separate studies suggest that while some people may present themselves in an idealized manner in their online profiles, most people construct fairly accurate self-presentations, perhaps partly due to the fact that they realize that their friends will likely provide them with corrective feedback if they stray too far from their actual selves.

SELF-PRESENTATION STRATEGI ES DIFFER IN THEIR GOALS.

As a self-presenter, do you think it is generally better to be modest or to promote yourself? Should you ever be deceptive in your dealings with others? Have there been circumstances when you have consciously presented yourself as being helpless or, in contrast, threatening to others? The process of self-presentation often conjures up images of social gamesmanship and deception. Yet there is nothing necessarily unsavory about strategic self-presentations—we all employ them. When John Nezlek and his coworkers (2007) studied college students' self-presentations, they found that being socially accepted is a powerful motive. While trying to manage others' impressions, students were more concerned about appearing friendly, likable, and honest than about appearing competent and intelligent. Additional research finds that when people engage in these positive self-presentations, they tend to feel happy afterward, often happier than they anticipated they would be prior to the interaction (Dunn et al., 2007). What self-presentation strategies are associated with this valued acceptance and heightened mood?

The most commonly employed self-presentation strategy to gain acceptance is *ingratiation*, in which others' impressions are shaped through flattery (Varma et al., 2006). Because flattery increases recipients' self-esteem, and hence, increases their liking for the flatterer, Edward Jones (1990) calls ingratiation the most fundamental of all strategies—"a pinch or two of ingratiation helps to leaven the other self-presentation strategies as well." A testament to the power of ingratiation is the finding from one study that business managers who regularly used this self-presentation strategy received the greatest salary increases and the most promotions over a five-year period (Orpen, 1996). Similarly, a field experiment found that waitresses who complimented customers on their dinner selections received significantly larger tips than servers who did not give compliments (Seiter, 2007). Despite such potential rewards, ingratiation requires social skill, and it is a double-edged sword (Treadway et al., 2007). A meta-analysis of sixty-nine ingratiation studies found that while the recipient of ingratiation is positively affected by flattery, bystanders who observe the ingratiating self-presentation are more likely to question the motives of the flatterer (Gordon, 1996). These findings suggest that such disparaging terms as *brownnoser* and *apple polisher* are more likely to be used by observers of ingratiation than by recipients.

Another strategy that is often used to gain acceptance is *modesty*. Being modest means underrepresenting your positive traits, contributions, or accomplishments. Modesty can be extremely effective in increasing your likability, even while it preserves high levels of perceived competence and honesty (Baumeister & Ilko, 1995; Draelants & Darchy-Koechlin, 2011). Modesty is considered a more feminine response following achievement (Miller et al., 1992). Thus, it is not surprising that women are not only more likely than men to employ it but that they also are more successful in using it (Wosinska et al., 1996). Despite the generally favorable response to modesty, you should use it only when others are aware of your successes and can recognize that an underrepresentation is taking place (Miller & Schlenker, 1985). For example, modesty will not be an effective strategy for talented students to employ when trying to secure strong letters of recommendation from professors who are unaware of their many accomplishments.

In situations where competency is highly valued, people often rely upon *self-promotion*, which strives to convey positive information about the self either through one's behavior or by telling others about one's positive assets and accomplishments. People who use *self-promotion* want to be respected for their intelligence and competence, and thus this strategy is commonly employed during work-related interactions (Ellis et al., 2002; Stevens & Kristof, 1995). In contrast to modesty, self-promotion is considered to be a more masculine response following achievement, and thus it is not surprising that men are more likely than women to employ self-promotion (Miller et al., 1992). Although often effective in conveying a positive social image, self-promotion does not always result in desired consequences. This is because in addition to evaluating competence, perceivers also judge such interpersonal dimensions as likability and humility. Therefore, while self-promoters may be seen as competent, they also may be judged as less likable because they are perceived to be bragging (Godfrey et al., 1986; Inman et al., 2004). To counter this social danger, astute self-promoters often acknowledge possessing certain minor flaws or shortcomings along with their many competencies, or enlist others to extol their virtues (Baumeister & Jones, 1978; Pfeffer et al., 2006).

A strategy that has much in common with self-promotion is exemplification, which is a self-presentation designed to elicit perceptions of integrity and moral worthiness, at the same time that it arouses guilt and emulation in others (Leary, 1996). Exemplifiers often come across as being absorbed by devotion to some cause and suffering for the welfare of others. Workers who encourage fellow employees to go home while they sacrifice personal time for the "good of the company," religious leaders who profess to "walk with the Lord," or politicians who tell their constituents that they will be a "moral beacon" in government—all are displaying this form of strategic self-presentation. The danger of taking on the saint-like role is that one runs the risk of being perceived as hypocritical if actions deviate from this moral high ground (Stone et al., 1997). Exemplifiers also run the risk of being socially shunned because some people experience guilt and shame while in the presence of exemplifiers due to being reminded of their own shortcomings. Although there are dangers in using this strategy, skillful execution does bring benefits. Leaders who embody exemplification in their presented selves foster strong loyalty and group cohesion among their followers (Rozell & Gunderson, 2003).

When people want to coerce others into doing something, they might use *intimidation*, a self-presentation tactic of arousing fear and gaining power by convincing others that they are powerful and/or dangerous (Christopher et al., 2005). This self-presentation strategy is the hallmark of schoolyard bullies and is also employed by athletes in such aggressive sports as football, hockey, and boxing (Jeffrey et al., 2001). Drivers who tailgate you on the highway are using this strategy to get what they want—a speedy unencumbered path (Bassett et al., 2002). In its more subtle forms, parents also use intimidation. A frown combined with a lowered tone of voice and a pointed index finger is often sufficient in securing compliance from a child.

What if people lack the skills necessary for the preceding strategies? Under such circumstances, they may rely on *supplication*. In this technique, people advertise their weaknesses or their dependence on others, hoping to solicit help or sympathy out of a sense of social obligation (Harris et al., 2007). For example, a homeless person asking passersby for spare change relies on societal norms of empathy for those who are less fortunate (Dordick, 1997). A less extreme example is a student who repeatedly seeks help in completing class assignments, professing an inability to understand the material. This technique, while effective in many circumstances, is loaded with psychological land mines. One danger is that people tend to "blame the victim" (Lerner, 1980), often believing their suffering is self-inflicted. Another danger is that even though supplicators often receive help and support, they are privately judged as poorly functioning individuals (Powers & Zuroff, 1988). Not surprisingly, the final toll of advertising one's incompetence is often a loss of self-esteem (Osborne, 2002).

Perhaps the most interesting of all self-presentation strategies is **self-handicapping**, a strategy in which a person creates obstacles to his or her own performance either to provide an excuse for failure or to enhance success (Lotar & Kamenov, 2006; Maddison & Prapavessis, 2007). For example, the night before an important exam, Barry may go to a party instead of studying. By choosing to socialize, he is greatly decreasing his likelihood of success. An observer of Barry's actions might conclude that his decision not to study was self-defeating. However, someone versed in social psychological theory might sug-

Critical THINKING

Of the different self-presentation strategies that you employed today, under what circumstances and with whom were they used? Which ones achieved the desired effect? Was there one strategy that you frequently employed? If you didn't use any, why was this the case?

"*Humility is something I've always prided myself on.*"
—————————
Bernie Kosar, former NFL quarterback

self-handicapping
....
Actions that people take to sabotage their performance and enhance their opportunity to excuse anticipated failure.

gest that his actions serve a second purpose: to protect his self-esteem. Putting barriers in the way of your success not only provides you with an excuse for failure, it also enhances your self-esteem if success is secured despite the handicap. Thus, creating obstacles to success cannot only *protect* self-esteem, it can also *enhance* it. These are the two primary motives underlying self-handicapping. People are more likely to use this strategy when they are being evaluated on skills or attributes central to their self-concepts rather than on unimportant characteristics (Ferrari & Tice, 2000).

Of the two motives underlying self-handicapping, which is dominant? A series of studies by Diane Tice (1991) indicates that it depends on a person's level of self-esteem. She found evidence that individuals with high self-esteem handicap themselves to enhance their success, and they are largely unconcerned about protecting themselves against failure. In contrast, low self-esteem persons self-handicap to protect themselves from the negative implications of failure. Thus, the desire to further enhance self-esteem appears to motivate high self-esteem people to self-handicap, but it is the desire to protect self-esteem that appears to motivate those low in self-esteem.

When people engage in self-handicapping, they use two different forms. The milder form is *self-reported handicapping*, which simply involves people complaining about illness or stress-induced ailments before performing a task (Hirt et al., 1991). The beauty of self-reported handicapping is that it provides an excuse for failure without actually hampering performance. Further, employing self-reported handicapping can actually enhance performance! By providing plausible excuses for inadequate performance *prior* to actually performing the task, self-reported handicappers may sufficiently reduce their anxiety so that they perform better than they would normally (Sanna & Mark, 1995). However, it is also likely that preparing excuses for failure in advance will result in people exerting less effort on the task: why work hard if you think you are likely to fail? In contrast to self-reported self-handicapping, the more active and damaging form is *behavioral self-handicapping*, which involves people handicapping themselves either by not adequately preparing for a task or by using drugs or alcohol beforehand to inhibit their performance (Higgins & Harris, 1988). Although both women and men equally use self-reported handicaps, numerous studies indicate that men are more likely to behaviorally self-handicap, especially when they are publicly self-aware (Hirt et al., 2000; McCrea et al., 2008). Why might this be the case?

One possible explanation is that men are generally more competitive and driven by public standards in performance situations than women (Travis et al., 1988). When experiencing this heightened performance pressure and feeling uncertain concerning their own ability to succeed, men may seize upon behavioral self-handicapping as the best way for them to avoid self-esteem loss if they fail. However, when people behaviorally self-handicap they run the risk of being perceived as lazy and unmotivated (Luginbuhl & Palme, 1991). Thus, the form of self-handicapping that men use more than women is more likely to guarantee failure, and it is also more likely to generate negative evaluations from observers. A series of studies conducted by Edward Hirt and his coworkers (2003) found that men are consistently less critical of behavioral self-handicappers than women. They are much less likely than women to question the motives of self-handicappers, and they are much less likely to perceive them as lazy. These results suggest that the people most likely to engage in behavioral self-handicapping (men) are also the people who are less likely to judge self-handicappers harshly. Table 3.2 summarizes the self-presentation strategies discussed in this section.

High Self-Monitors Are Social Chameleons.

We all use self-presentation strategies, but some of us are more likely than others to construct self-presentations that best fit whatever social situations we encounter. According to Mark Snyder (1987), these differences are related to a personality trait called **self-monitoring**, which is the tendency to use cues from other people's self-presentations in controlling our own self-presentations. Individuals high in self-monitoring are extroverted social actors who spend considerable time learning about other people and emphasize impression management in their social relationships (John et al., 1996; Peluchette et al., 2006). In 1974, Snyder developed a self-monitoring scale to measure this personality

self-monitoring
. . . .
The tendency to use cues from other people's self-presentations in controlling one's own self-presentations

Table 3.2

Common Self-Presentation Strategies

	Attributions Sought	Negative Attributions Risked	Emotions to Be Aroused	Typical Actions
Ingratiation	Likable	Brownnoser	Affection	Compliments and favors
Modesty	Likable and competent	Nonassertive	Affection and respect	Understatement of achievements
Self-promotion	Competent	Conceited	Respect	Performance claims
Exemplification	Worthy	Hypocrite	Guilt	Self-denial
Intimidation	Dangerous	Blowhard	Fear	Threats
Supplication	Helpless	Stigmatized	Nurturance	Self-deprecation
Self-handicapping	Competent	Incompetent	Respect	Obstacle creation

trait, and it has been studied extensively since that time. To get an idea about your own level of self-monitoring, spend a few minutes completing the items in *Self/Social Connection Exercise 3.3*.

High self-monitoring persons are skilled impression managers who experience significantly less physiological arousal due to social encounters than low self-monitoring persons, even while striving to perform whatever behavior projects a positive self-image (Blakely et al., 2003; Hofmann, 2006). Due to their greater attention to social cues, those high in self-monitoring are better able to communicate and discern the meaning of emotions and other nonverbal behaviors and often spontaneously mimic others' behavior—for example, laughing when others laugh or yawning when they yawn (Estow et al., 2007). When trying to initiate a dating relationship, high self-monitoring men and women behave in a chameleon-like fashion, strategically and often deceptively changing their self-presentations in an attempt to appear more desirable (Leck & Simpson, 1999; Rowatt et al., 1998). In contrast, individuals low in self-monitoring are less attentive to situational cues, and their behavior is guided more by inner attitudes and beliefs. As a result, their behavior is more consistent across situations.

When high self-monitors employ impression management strategies, they favor those that are positive. They are particularly adept at using ingratiation, self-promotion, and exemplification to achieve favorable impressions (Bolino & Turnley, 2003; Turnley & Bolino, 2001). On the negative side, people high in self-monitoring have less intimate and committed social relationships (Snyder & Simpson, 1984), and they tend to judge people more on superficial characteristics, such as physical appearance and social activities, rather than their attitudes and values (Jamieson et al., 1987). Perhaps because of these social skills, high self-monitors are more likely to become leaders than those low in self-monitoring (Day et al., 2002).

Noting the differences between high and low self-monitoring, which orientation do you prefer? Perhaps you see high self-monitoring as being more socially adaptive because it allows you to better negotiate in an ever-changing and complicated social world. Or maybe you view the chameleon-like nature of the high self-monitor as indicating a distasteful shallowness and instead prefer the principled consistency of someone low in self-

Self/Social Connections Exercise 3.3

The Self-Monitoring Scale

The personality trait of self-monitoring is measured by items on the Self-Monitoring Scale (Snyder, 1974; Gangestad & Snyder 2000). To discover your level of self-monitoring, read each item below and then indicate whether each statement is true or false for you.

1. I find it hard to imitate the behavior of other people.
2. At parties and social gatherings, I do not attempt to do or say things that others will like.
3. I can only argue for ideas that I already believe.
4. I can make impromptu speeches, even on topics about which I have almost no information.
5. I guess I put on a show to impress or entertain others.
6. I would probably make a good actor.
7. In a group of people, I am rarely the center of attention.
8. In different situations and with different people, I often act like very different persons.
9. I am not particularly good at making other people like me.
10. I'm not always the person I appear to be.
11. I would not change my opinions (or the way I do things) to please others or win their favor.
12. I have considered being an entertainer.
13. I have never been good at games like charades or improvisational acting.
14. I have trouble changing my behavior to suit different people and different situations.
15. At a party I let others keep the jokes and stories going.
16. I feel a bit awkward in company and do not show up quite as well as I should.
17. I can look anyone in the eye and tell a lie with a straight face (if for a right end).
18. I may deceive people by being friendly when I really dislike them.

Directions for Scoring

Give yourself one point for answering "True" to each of the following items: 4, 5, 6, 8, 10, 12, 17, and 18. Also give yourself one point for answering "False" to each of the following items: 1, 2, 3, 7, 9, 11, 13, 14, 15, and 16. Next, add up your total number of points for your Self-Monitoring score. The average self-monitoring score for North American college students is about 10 or 11. The higher your score is above these values, the more of this personality trait you probably possess. The lower your score is below these values, the less of this trait you probably possess.

monitoring. Yet what you see as principled consistency, others may interpret as inflexibility. The safest and perhaps wisest conclusion to draw is that neither high nor low self-monitoring is necessarily undesirable unless it is carried to the extreme. Fortunately, pure high and low self-monitoring is rare—most of us fall somewhere on a continuum of these two extremes (Miller & Thayer, 1989).

At this point, you may be wondering how self-monitoring differs from the personality trait of public self-consciousness (p. 71). Both personality traits have to do with a concern about and awareness of how others react to the self. They differ in that high self-monitoring, but not high public self-consciousness, describes individuals who are actively and effectively changing their behavior to adjust to the reactions and expectations of others. Individuals high in public self-consciousness may be aware of and concerned about themselves as social objects, but they are not sufficiently attentive to social cues to structure their self-presentations in such a way as to manage the impressions others have of them (Vrij et al., 2001). In addition, although people high in public self-consciousness are motivated more by a concern to avoid presenting themselves negatively, high self-monitors strive to achieve a favorable self-presentation in others' minds.

> *It is not whether you really cry. It's whether the audience thinks you are crying.*

Ingrid Bergman, Swedish actress, 1915–1982

SECTION SUMMARY

- Self-presentations manage the impression we make on others.

- Self-presentations involve both automatic and deliberate thinking, with well-learned self-presentations often operating on "autopilot".

- Common strategic self-presentations include ingratiation, modesty, self-promotion, exemplification, intimidation, supplication, and self-handicapping.

- High self-monitors are highly attuned to social cues and readily alter their self-presentations to match the current situation.

- Low self-monitors are relatively inattentive to social cues, and their behavior is guided more by their attitudes and beliefs.

EVALUATING THE SELF

self-esteem

A person's evaluation of his or her self-concept

As previously noted, **self-esteem** is your evaluation of your self-concept. Mark Leary and his colleagues (1995) assert that during the course of human evolution, self-esteem emerged as an internal "meter" (a *sociometer*) of our sense of group inclusion. That is, individuals were much more likely to survive and reproduce when firmly embedded within a social group rather than being forced to survive on their own (Leary, 2005; Leary & Guadagno, 2011). Consistent with the sociometer model of self-esteem, when people behave in ways that decrease the likelihood they will be rejected or when others socially embrace them, their self-esteem increases (Lemay & Ashmore, 2006; Stinson et al., 2010).

SELF-ESTEEM INFLUENCES HOW WE APPROACH AND RESPOND TO LIFE CHALLENGES.

Most people regard themselves more positively than they regard their peers (Bonanno et al., 2005; Moore & Small, 2007). Longitudinal research suggests that this *better-than-average effect* offers people protection against social stress and fosters better mental health (Zuckerman & O'Loughlin, 2006). Consistent with this tendency, a multinational study of self-esteem indicates that the vast majority of people who are identified as having low self-esteem do not see themselves as worthless, incompetent losers (Schmitt & Allik, 2005). Instead, they are people who evaluate themselves more *neutrally* than either very positively or very negatively. In most cases, it is only in comparison to the very positive evaluations of people with high self-esteem that these individuals can be

I'm Kind of a
BIG Deal

described as having "low" self-esteem. The good news here is that most of us do not have very negative self-views; instead, we judge our personalities rather positively (Twenge & Campbell, 2008; vanDellen et al., 2010a). Yet what about those individuals who do hold themselves in low regard? What are the consequences?

A wealth of research indicates that individuals with low self-esteem are generally more unhappy and pessimistic (DeNeve & Cooper, 1998; Shepperd et al., 1996), more needful of social acceptance (Anthony et al., 2006), less willing to take risks to benefit themselves (McElroy et al., 2006), more likely to encounter academic and financial problems (Crocker & Luhtanen, 2003), less likely to have successful careers (Judge & Bono, 2001), and less likely to be physically healthy (Vingilis et al., 1998) than high self-esteem individuals. Cross-cultural research in fifty-three countries involving about seventeen thousand participants indicates that people around the world have relatively high levels of self-esteem (Schmitt & Allik, 2005). Collectivist cultures tend to have lower levels of self-esteem than individualist cultures, which may be partly due to the fact that people from collectivist cultures are socialized to be more self-critical than people from individualist cultures (Falk et al., 2009; Hamamura & Heine, 2008). Underlying this self-critical tendency among collectivists is a greater desire for self-improvement compared to individualists (Heine & Ranieri, 2009).

Although most people are motivated to feel good and to create and maintain pleasant or positive states of mind (Larsen, 2000), there is evidence that those who differ in self-esteem also differ in their emotional reactions to positive and negative daily events. When experiencing positive emotions following some desirable outcome, high self-esteem individuals tend to savor their feelings, while low self-esteem individuals tend to dampen these emotions and may even become anxious (Wood et al., 2003, 2005). In contrast, while negative events generally dampen people's daily moods regardless of their level of self-esteem, low self-esteem people are more adversely affected (Richter & Ridout, 2011).

For example, in a ten-week study of college students' daily moods, John Nezlek and Rebecca Plesko (2003) found that individual differences in self-esteem had a significant impact on emotional reactions to daily events. Twice a week, these students reported their daily experiences, including how positive they felt about themselves that day. Results indicated that daily fluctuations in feelings of self-worth were affected by positive and negative events, but that negative events were much more damaging to the daily feelings of self-worth among the low self-esteem students than among those with high self-esteem.

These findings are consistent with other studies indicating that low self-esteem people are more adversely affected by hassles and personal setbacks in their everyday lives than high self-esteem people (Brown & Dutton, 1995). It appears that high self-esteem people self-regulate in a manner that helps to sustain their highly positive self-regard, whereas low self-esteem people regulate their emotions in a way that maintains their relatively low self-regard.

What is it about the emotional self-regulation of high and low self-esteem people that contributes to these differences? Studies suggest that low self-esteem persons are more adversely affected by negative events because they appear to be less motivated to repair their negative moods (Heimpel et al., 2002). One reason for this lack of motivation to engage in self-regulation may be that low self-esteem people are simply more accustomed to negative moods, and hence they come to accept them more readily than high self-esteem persons. Another possibility is that for low self-esteem persons, negative emotions are accompanied by two experiences that are especially harmful to their motivation to self-regulate. First, the negative event depletes their self-regulatory resources (see pp. 76–78). Second, this depletion may be particularly harmful to them because their engaging in mood regulation may require more energy than it does for high self-esteem persons, who have more experience with positive moods. This greater experience requires high self-esteem persons to expend less energy to repair their negative moods. Thus, a "double whammy" exists for low self-esteem persons, which has the effect of undermining their motivation to take any action to repair negative moods.

SELF-ENHANCEMENT AND SELF-VERIFICATION MOTIVES CONFLICT IN LOW SELF-ESTEEM PERSONS.

self-enhancement
. . . .
The process of seeking out and interpreting situations so as to attain a positive view of oneself

self-verification
. . . .
The process of seeking out and interpreting situations so as to confirm one's self-concept

❝*Self-esteem and self-contempt have specific odors; they can be smelled.*❞
— — — — — — — — —
Eric Hoffer, U.S. social philosopher, 1902–1983

The greater difficulty that low self-esteem people have in experiencing positive feelings may also be partly caused by conflicting self-enhancement and self-verification motives. Over the years there has been an ongoing debate regarding self-evaluation and self-concept that is related to the hot and cold perspectives discussed in Chapter 1. The **self-enhancement** perspective embodies the emotional, or hot, viewpoint of human nature and is based on the notion that people are primarily motivated to maintain high self-esteem (Beach & Tesser, 2000; Dunning et al., 1995). According to this view, the need for self-enhancement will increase as one's negative self-evaluations increase. In contrast, the **self-verification** perspective reflects the cognitive, or cold, viewpoint. According to this view, people are motivated to maintain consistent beliefs about themselves, even when these self-beliefs are negative (Swann, 1997; Swann et al., 2004). By verifying firmly held self-beliefs, people feel more secure that their social world is predictable and controllable.

For those with high self-esteem, there is often no conflict between these two motives because receiving positive feedback verifies positive self-beliefs. However, for low self-esteem persons these two motives often conflict: the need for self-enhancement causes those with low self-esteem to seek positive feedback and that action conflicts with their desire to verify existing negative self-beliefs (Brown, 1993). Self-enhancement theorists contend that people with low self-esteem will seek out positive social feedback because it will bolster their self-esteem. In contrast, self-verification theorists argue that this positive feedback will create the fear in people with low self-esteem that they may not know themselves after all; and therefore, they will reject it. Which of these perspectives is correct?

Research suggests that *both* the need for self-enhancement and the need for self-verification operate simultaneously, but the first operates in response to a person's feelings, while the second operates in response to a person's thoughts (Jussim et al., 1995; Shrauger, 1975; Swann et al., 1987). That is, when judging social feedback about themselves, people's emotional reactions ("Do I like it?") are based on whether the feedback bolsters their self-esteem (self-enhancement need), and their cognitive reactions ("Is it correct?") are based on whether it is consistent with their self-concepts (self-verification need). Thus, negative feedback that is expected will be considered more accurate, but self-enhancing feedback will be more satisfying. In these studies, people were presented with either favorable or unfavorable feedback about themselves. Although they typically felt better after receiving positive feedback than after receiving negative feedback (as predicted by the self-enhancement view), people accepted more responsibility for feedback consistent with their self-concepts than inconsistent feedback (as predicted by the self-verification view).

So which of these motives is the strongest, the need for self-enhancement or the need for self-verification? Based on a host of studies, self-enhancement appears to be the automatic response to favorable feedback (Sedikides & Strube, 1997); however, self-verification is the slower, more deliberate, and more lasting response (Brooks et al., 2011). As depicted in Figure 3.6, when people first receive favorable evaluations, or when they are distracted or aroused, they tend to automatically self-enhance (Paulhus & Levitt, 1987); but when they have time to critically analyze the feedback, or are instructed to do so, they tend to self-verify (Krueger, 1998; Swann, 1990). To the casual observer who witnesses the person's initial delight in receiving praise from others, the need to self-enhance may seem the stronger of the two motives. However, later, once the warm emotional glow of the praise wears off, extra cognitive processing often results in self-verification overriding self-enhancement. For example, if you have low self-esteem and someone says you are absolutely wonderful, your initial reaction may be to accept this positive feedback and thereby increase your self-esteem. However, if you engage in more complex cognitive analysis, you may realize that internalizing this positive feedback will require a major

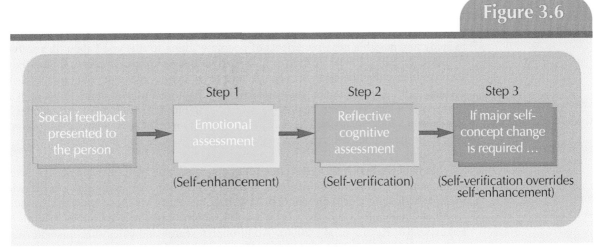

Figure 3.6

Step 1	Step 2	Step 3
Social feedback presented to the person	Emotional assessment	Reflective cognitive assessment	If major self-concept change is required …
	(Self-enhancement)	(Self-verification)	(Self-verification overrides self-enhancement)

The Interplay Between Self-Enhancement and Self-Verification Motives

What happens when people with low self-esteem receive positive feedback? Do they accept it and enhance their self-esteem, or do they reject it because it doesn't verify their self-concept? Research suggests that people follow a three-step process in resolving this conflict (Swann, 1990). In step 1, the initial reaction is to self-enhance. However, with more time to think about the feedback (step 2), self-verification dominates thinking. In step 3, if accepting this positive feedback requires a major reassessment of their self-concept, people will reject the feedback. Why wouldn't people with high self-esteem have this same dilemma?

Critical THINKING

If low self-esteem people are likely to reject your attempts to increase their feelings of self-worth, what strategy might you use to feed their self-enhancement needs without triggering their need for self-verification?

reassessment of your self-concept, a task you may feel ill-equipped to accomplish. Faced with the possible upheaval caused by such a major self-reconstruction, you are likely to abandon self-enhancement and instead seek self-verification. Therefore, you reject the feedback and retain your original self-concept. A recent meta-analysis of the findings from more than one hundred studies that examined reactions to self-esteem threat found that self-verification is the strongest motive for both high and low self-esteem individuals (vanDellen et al., 2011).

One final thing to understand when considering the importance of self-enhancement versus self-verification motives is that the studies that have been discussed were conducted in individualist cultures. The findings should not be generalized to collectivist cultures. Why? Steven Heine and Takeshi Hamamura (2007) conducted a meta-analysis of numerous cross-cultural studies involving more than thirty-three thousand participants and found pronounced differences between people from collectivist and individualist cultures in their self-enhancement tendencies. While individualists clearly self-enhance when it doesn't sharply conflict with self-verification, collectivists are much less likely to do so (Heine, 2011). Thus, while self-verification may be a universal human motive, the self-enhancement motive appears to be shaped more by cultural factors. This finding makes sense viewed in the context of Heine's research (p. 73) indicating that people from collectivist cultures are more chronically privately self-aware than people from individualist cultures. Because past research indicates that private self-awareness leads to more accurate self-knowledge, collectivists' greater self-reflective tendencies should result in them being less self-enhancing and more self-critical than individualists.

THERE IS A DARK SIDE TO HIGH SELF-ESTEEM.

Thus far we have discussed research that generally extols the virtues of high self-esteem. However, are there instances where high self-esteem is problematic? We have learned that people with high self-esteem can effectively defend themselves against negative social feedback, but it is also true that rejecting feedback that is inconsistent with favorable self-beliefs may prevent high self-esteem people from acknowledging weaknesses or faults.

Based on Heine and Hamamura's (2007) cross-cultural comparisons of self-enhancement tendencies, it appears that individualist cultures are much more likely than collectivist cultures to believe that high self-esteem is essential for mental health and life satisfaction (Oishi et al., 1999; Spencer-Rodgers et al., 2004; Twenge & Campbell, 2001). Perhaps due to this cultural belief, American social psychologists have been slow to study any possible negative effects of people wanting to feel good about themselves (Crocker & Park, 2004). Fortunately, that trend has reversed. Several studies have found evidence that there can be a hidden cost to trying to achieve or maintain high self-esteem: Certain individuals with superficially high self-esteem tend to react with aggression when someone challenges their favorable self-assessments (Bushman & Baumeister, 2002; Campbell et al., 2004). The source of this aggressive response appears to be a defensive reaction to avoid having to make any downward revision of self-esteem.

Michael Kernis (2003) asserts that it is the *stability* of high self-esteem that determines whether threats to self-esteem lead to aggression. He states that people with *unstable* high self-esteem are the ones who become angry and hostile when their self-worth is challenged, and they have trouble controlling these emotions (Kernis & Lakey, 2010; Kernis et al., 2000). Additional research indicates that unstable high self-esteem is associated with *narcissism*, a personality trait characterized by insecurity and the need for constant reassurance (Konrath et al., 2006; Thomaes & Bushman, 2011). Those with unstable high self-esteem lack confidence of their own self-worth, and thus, they are much more dependent on having it regularly validated by others. When such validation is denied by social criticism, these unstable high self-esteem people exhibit poor self-regulation and react by attacking their critics (Lambird & Mann, 2006; Stucke & Sporer, 2002). In contrast, *stable* high self-esteem individuals may not enjoy being criticized, but they can control their emotions and are no more aggressive in such circumstances than low self-esteem people. Their general desire to enhance self-esteem is not fed by a narcissistic defensiveness but instead is a sign of mental health (Taylor et al., 2003).

explicit self-esteem

A person's conscious and deliberate evaluation of his or her self-concept

implicit self-esteem

A person's unintentional, and perhaps unconscious, evaluation of his or her self-concept

It appears that underlying the unstable high self-esteem of narcissists are actually two conflicting types of self-esteem. Their **explicit self-esteem**, which is their conscious and deliberate self-evaluation, is quite high, whereas their **implicit self-esteem**, which is their unintentional and perhaps unconscious self-evaluation, is conflicted and quite low in certain areas (Campbell et al., 2007; McGregor et al., 2005). Explicit self-esteem is what people report when they are asked directly how they feel about themselves on self-report measures. How do we measure implicit self-esteem?

Implicit self-esteem is typically assessed using Implicit Association Test (IAT) measures discussed in Chapter 2 (p. 60). One version of this test measures the automatic

People with unstable high self-esteem can become angry and hostile when their self-worth is challenged.

"One must not be a name-dropper, as Her Majesty remarked to me at luncheon yesterday."

‒‒‒‒‒‒‒‒‒

Norman St. John-Stevas, member of British Parliament, born 1929

"... We have the paradox of a man shamed to death because he is only the second pugilist or the second oarsman in the world.... Yonder puny fellow, however, whom everyone can beat, suffers no chagrin, for he has long ago abandoned the attempt to "carry that line."

‒‒‒‒‒‒‒‒‒

William James, American psychologist and philosopher, 1842–1910

self-evaluation maintenance model
·····················
A theory predicting under what conditions people are likely to react to the success of others with either pride or jealousy

associations between a person's self-concept and positive and negative affect (Karpinski, 2004; Nosek et al., 2007). In one measurement stage, participants categorize pleasant words and self-related words on the same computer key, and unpleasant and other-related words on another computer key (self + pleasant/other + unpleasant). In a later stage, the tasks are reversed, and participants categorize unpleasant words and self-related words and other-related words on another computer key (self + unpleasant/other + pleasant). An overall IAT score is computed by taking the difference between the average response times to the two test stages. The assumption is that participants with high implicit self-esteem have many positive associations and few negative associations with the self. As a result, the self + pleasant task will be very easy for them, and they will have fast response times; but the self + unpleasant task will be more difficult, and they will have slow response times. In contrast, it is assumed that participants with low implicit self-esteem have many negative associations and few positive associations with the self. Therefore, they will have faster response times for self + unpleasant associations than self + pleasant associations. If you would like to take an implicit self-esteem test, check out the web site at the end of the chapter.

In a series of studies, Christian Jordan and his coworkers (2003) have found support for the hypothesis that unstable high self-esteem individuals have two conflicting types of self-esteem, one consciously positive and the other unconsciously negative. Their results indicate that among individuals with high explicit self-esteem, those with relatively low implicit self-esteem have feelings of self-worth that depend more on others' social approval, their physical appearance, and how well they perform on competitive tasks. Further, after failing at a task, these individuals are likely to quit, while the high explicit/high implicit self-esteem persons often persist in the face of failure. Finally, and of particular interest, the researchers found that, while high explicit/low implicit self-esteem individuals score very high on narcissism, high explicit self-esteem persons who also have high implicit self-esteem score very low on narcissism (see Figure 3.7).

In viewing this research from a cultural perspective, it may be that the emphasis in individualist cultures on feeling good about oneself has resulted in some people consciously fabricating a high sense of self-worth that is inconsistent with their life experiences. The result is they have two conflicting types of self-esteem, with the consciously positive form requiring constant bolstering and defense in order for it to survive. When others do not comply with this need and, instead, threaten their self-esteem through social criticism, these unstable high self-esteem people are likely to respond by engaging in antisocial self-enhancement strategies. This is the dark side of high self-esteem.

IN SOCIAL RELATIONSHIPS, SELF-ESTEEM IS MAINTAINED THROUGH SOCIAL REFLECTION AND SOCIAL COMPARISON.

If one of our most important motives is the desire to perceive ourselves positively, how might this influence our relationships with others? The link between the quest for self-esteem and social relationships has been elaborated in Abraham Tesser's (1988) **self-evaluation maintenance model**. This theory primarily explains how we draw closer to or draw away from successful people due to our desire to maintain or enhance self-esteem.

According to Tesser, in personal relationships, self-esteem is maintained through two processes: *social reflection* and *social comparison*. In social reflection, identifying ourselves with the outstanding accomplishments of others reinforces self-esteem. In daily conversations, we hear this reflection process when people tell us proudly about "My son, the banker" or "My best friend, who was on the David Letterman Show. ..." Similarly, basking in the reflected glory of our sports teams' victories is an example of social reflection (Cialdini et al., 1976; End et al., 2004). Social comparison, on the other hand, is a process in which we evaluate our accomplishments by comparing them with others. Our self-esteem suffers when we are outperformed, but it increases when we surpass them (Festinger 1954; Mussweiler & Rüter, 2003). As you can see, reflection and comparison produce opposite self-esteem results when others excel at some task: self-esteem increases with reflection, but it decreases with comparison (Tyler & Feldman,

Figure 3.7

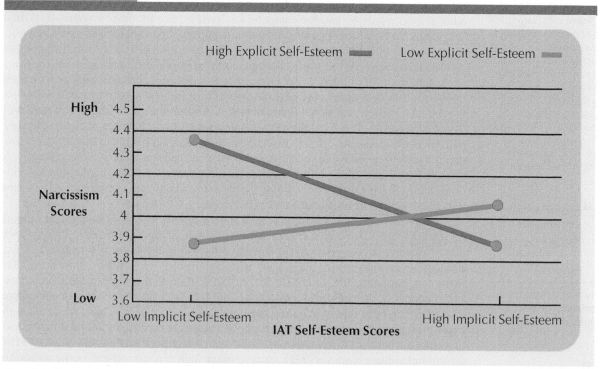

Narcissism as a Function of Implicit Self-Esteem and Explicit Self-Esteem

Narcissism is a personality trait characterized by insecurity, the need for constant reassurance, and the tendency to respond to negative feedback with anger and aggression. Jordan and his colleagues (2003) found that explicit self-esteem interacts with implicit self-esteem to create either high or low levels of narcissism. People who are high in explicit self-esteem but low in implicit self-esteem show the highest levels of narcissism. In contrast, those high in both explicit and implicit self-esteem show levels of narcissism no higher than people who are low in both implicit and explicit self-esteem. Why might this unstable form of self-esteem (high explicit/low implicit) be more prevalent in individualist cultures than in collectivist cultures?

> **❝***All knowledge may be reduced to comparison and contrast.***❞**
>
> ---------------------
>
> I. F. Stone, U.S. journalist and newspaper publisher, 1907–1989

2005). The stronger the emotional bond between you and the successful person, the stronger the self-esteem effects for both reflection and comparison (Zuckerman & Jost, 2001). Thus, you gain (or lose) more self-esteem if your best friend accomplishes some great task than if your former third-grade classmate does. Research further indicates that being outperformed by a close friend threatens your self-esteem, and it negatively affects your mental health (Kamide & Daibo, 2009).

What determines whether you engage in reflection or comparison following someone else's success? One important factor is the *relevance* of the task to your self-concept (Morf & Rhodewalt, 1993). If your sister wins first prize in the state chess tournament, your self-esteem may increase due to reflection, but only if chess is not highly relevant to your own self-concept. If you also entered the contest and did poorly, it's likely that your sister's success will lower your self-esteem because it makes you look that much worse by comparison. The implication of Tesser's theory is that the people who make you feel good about yourself are either individuals who are (1) less competent than you in domains that are relevant to your self-concept (social comparison) or (2) very talented in domains that are irrelevant to your self-concept (social reflection).

In a study testing these two hypotheses, Tesser and his colleagues (1984) asked fifth and sixth-grade students to identify their closest friends and evaluate these best buddies in comparison to themselves. The researchers also obtained teacher ratings of the students. Consistent with the social comparison process, they found that students perceived their best friends as being less competent than themselves in self-defining activities. Further, consistent with the social reflection process, students perceived their best friends as having at least equal ability to themselves in activities that were not self-relevant. For example, if a student was avidly interested in math but only minimally interested in music, her closest friends were unlikely to be as good at math but they could easily be highly skilled in music.

In those instances when social comparison in a self-relevant domain makes you look bad, how can you recover lost self-esteem? One way is to exaggerate the ability of those who outperform you (Alicke et al., 1996). By seeing your victor as truly outstanding, you can still perceive yourself as well above average. A second way to reduce self-esteem threat is to reduce your closeness to the better performing person (O'Mahen et al., 2000; Pleban & Tesser, 1981). Salvaging self-esteem through such emotional distancing, however, usually exacts a high price on the relationship—it often ends. A third method of protecting self-esteem—and one that also preserves your relationship—is to change your beliefs so that the task is no longer important to your self-concept (Pilkington & Smith, 2000). Now, instead of comparing yourself with this superior person, you simply bask in his or her reflected glory. This sort of emotional "disidentification" with the task is precisely the psychological process outlined by William James more than one hundred years ago (refer back to p. 85). Let's return to your hypothetical sister, the budding chess master. Instead of her accomplishments making you feel bad and straining your relationship, by making chess a less defining aspect of your self-concept you can (through reflection) elevate your self-esteem. In this way, a decidedly different outcome is achieved: Family ties and self-esteem prevail.

Despite the negative effect that comparing ourselves to superior others can have on our self-esteem, we sometimes consciously and repeatedly engage in these upward comparisons. Can you guess under what circumstances we are likely to do so? Often, when striving to improve ourselves in some important area of our lives, we compare our performance with others who are doing much better (Collins, 1996). For example, an aspiring high-school golfer may try to improve her game by carefully studying the golf swing of superstar Tiger Woods. Although such upward comparison may temporarily lower self-esteem ("I'm terrible compared to him!"), it can also motivate the less accomplished golfer to reduce the discrepancy between her current performance level and that of her role model (Tiger Woods). However, it is also possible that this aspiring golfer's self-esteem can be enhanced if she focuses on her social identity as a "Tiger Woods" fan (Wänke et al., 2001). By engaging in social reflection toward her role model, she can bask in reflected glory whenever Tiger Woods wins a tournament. Thus, role models may be in a unique position to temporarily both diminish our self-esteem through social comparison and heighten it through social reflection.

Critical THINKING

Our self-esteem will often be threatened when we compare ourselves with those superior to us on some task. However, a review of the literature indicates that upward comparison can sometimes lead to higher self-esteem (Collins 1996). How do you think this particular self-enhancement effect might occur?

SECTION SUMMARY

- Self-esteem is positively associated with happiness and physical health.

- Self-verification may be a universal motive.

- Self-enhancement is a stronger motive in individualist cultures.

- Unstable high self-esteem persons become angry and hostile when their self-worth is challenged.

- *Self-evaluation maintenance model* contends self-esteem is maintained by *social reflection* and *social comparison*.

    In social reflection, self-esteem is enhanced by association with others' successes.

    In social comparison, self-esteem is enhanced by outperforming comparison to others.

- In Table 3.3, review how the self terms are related to one another.

Table 3.3

Self Terms and Their Relation to One Another

The "I"

SELF-AWARENESS

This is awareness directed toward oneself, and it can be focused on private self-aspects (e.g., emotions, motives, personal standards) or public self-aspects (e.g., physical appearance, self-presentations). The tendency to engage in this self-aware state is known as self-consciousness, and it too is described in private and public terms.

SELF-REGULATION

These are the ways in which we control and direct our own actions. You must be self-aware to engage in self-regulation.

The "Me"

SELF-CONCEPT

Due to self-awareness, we develop a theory about ourselves.

*Gender identity: the knowledge that one is a male or a female

*Self-aspect: the aspect of the self-concept that is salient and activated in a particular setting

*Social identities: the aspects of the self-concept based on group membership

SELF-ESTEEM

We not only develop a theory of ourselves, but we also develop an evaluation of this theory. The need to enhance self-esteem is a primary motive but may not be as strong as the need to verify the self-concept. In social relationships, we can enhance self-esteem by basking in others' reflected glory or by comparing ourselves with those we outperform. High self-esteem people are generally happier and healthier and can regulate their moods better than those with low self-esteem.

APPLICATIONS

DO YOU ENGAGE IN BINGE DRINKING OR EATING TO ESCAPE FROM YOURSELF?

As you have learned from reading this chapter, we all have the ability to engage in self-awareness. When we experience failure or a significant personal loss, we generally spend some time afterward in focused self-awareness as a means to better understand what happened. Although this self-focused answer seeking can be quite helpful, most of us soon disengage from intense introspection and return to our normal states of awareness. However, what happens when our failure or loss is very great, such that we can find no ready solution? In such instances, we may become depressed, which increases self-focus, which increases depression, and so forth (Pyszczynski & Greenberg, 1992). Thus, intense self-awareness can be thought of as both resulting from depression as well as contributing to it.

Unfortunately, one way depressed individuals sometimes try to break out of this negative self-aware state is by engaging in self-destructive behaviors that have the side benefit of temporarily reducing self-awareness, thereby temporarily reducing depression (Neighbors et al., 2004). Binge eating and drinking are two activities that can be motivated by a desire to escape from self-awareness.

They also are two of the most serious social problems faced by college students today (Keller et al., 2007; Vandereycken, 1994).

Regarding alcohol abuse, Jay Hull (1981) not only found evidence that alcohol reduces self-awareness but also that individuals high in private self-consciousness are more likely to use it to deal with negative information about themselves. In one study, undergraduate participants were given intelligence-related tests and were then randomly given either success or failure feedback (Hull & Young, 1983). Immediately following this feedback, they participated in a seemingly unrelated wine-tasting study. Although the amount of wine consumed by those low in private self-consciousness was not influenced by their previous success or failure, those high in private self-consciousness drank more wine after receiving failure feedback than after success feedback. In effect, consuming alcohol following failure temporarily caused the high private self-conscious individuals to act like low private self-conscious individuals—their degree of self-awareness was reduced, and they were then not as attentive to their failure. Similar results have been found in adolescent alcohol abuse. Following academic failure, high private self-conscious students drink more than low self-conscious students (Hull et al., 1986). These studies suggest that some people—especially high private self-conscious individuals—may use alcohol as a "psychological crutch" to avoid the chronic attention to their own private thoughts and feelings that causes emotional pain.

While alcohol seems to reduce self-awareness by physically interfering with cognitive functioning, other techniques can accomplish the same result by simply focusing attention narrowly on concrete, unemotional stimuli. By paying attention to simple, here-and-now movements and sensations, a person can divert attention away from troubling self-aspects (Steele & Josephs, 1990). This shift from self-awareness to "other-awareness" effectively allows the person to avoid the type of self-reflective activities that evoke unpleasant emotion (Baumeister, 1991). *Binge eating*, which involves episodes of huge amounts of food consumption, may serve this function for some people. Indeed, difficulties regulating emotions has been found to be a significant triggering mechanism for binge eating (Abramson et al., 2006; Whiteside et al., 2007). By redirecting attentional focus from the self to the simple acts of chewing, tasting, and swallowing, binge eaters may temporarily find relief from depression (Heatherton & Baumeister, 1991). As one binger expressed it, "Eating can help me bury my emotions when I don't want to feel them" (Smith et al., 1989).

Ironically, although some people may engage in binge behavior to escape negative self-awareness, self-regulation theory contends that they must actually consciously engage in self-awareness if they desire to gain control over their self-destructive actions. The following four suggestions, derived from self-regulation theory, indicate how binge drinkers and eaters can work to change their behavior by employing self-reflective thought and a special kind of behavioral intention:

1. *Focus your awareness beyond the immediate situation.* An important mechanism in effective self-regulation of negative behavior is keeping attention focused beyond the immediate situation to more distant, long-range goals (Baumeister & Heatherton, 1996). This sort of situational *transcendence* is clearly an important factor in effective food or alcohol management because it requires you to forgo the temporary relief of binging so that you will achieve your long-term goal of learning to eat and drink responsibly. By focusing on your long-range goal, the more-immediate goal of bingeing on cheesecake or beer becomes cognitively *reframed*: it becomes an obstacle to your long-term goal rather than an appealing treat.

2. *Pay attention to cues that trigger undesirable behavior.* Certain stimuli in your social environment can serve as signals that you may be "sliding" down a path that leads to your undesirable behavior. The sooner you identify signals of impending undesirable behavior, the better chance you have of controlling your impulse to engage in that behavior (Wegner 1994). Thus, if you know that arguments with family members have triggered binge behavior in the past, pay attention to your feelings when conversing with these people and try to defuse arguments before they get out of hand.

3. *Recognize when your resolve is weak.* As suggested by the *strength model of self-regulation* (p. 76), at any given time, you have only a limited amount of energy available to self-regulate. With this knowledge, be aware that you are going to find it hardest to keep yourself from binging with food or alcohol right after exercising a great deal of control in some other unrelated activity.

4. When you realize that your past self-control has been weak, or if you expect to have a limited amount of energy available to self-regulate in a particular situation, a number of studies indicate that establishing an *implementation intention* is effective in steering yourself away from the problematic

behavior (Sheeran, 2002; Schoenmakers et al., 2007). Implementation intentions are statements to yourself that as soon as a particular situation occurs you will automatically initiate goal-directed behavior. For example, if you wanted to avoid engaging in binge drinking at a party you might make the following implementation intention beforehand: "As soon as people start drinking shots of liquor, I will switch to drinking soda." It appears that forming implementation intentions can cognitively bypass the need for normal self-control (Webb & Sheeran, 2003). In effect, by specifying ahead of time when and how you will act, this strategy passes control of behavior to anticipated environmental cues (Gollwitzer & Schaal, 1998). Evidence suggests that implementation intentions are particularly beneficial for people with low motivation (Brandstätter et al., 2001).

THE BIG PICTURE

As stated previously, the self is not something "inside" you. Rather, it is you—a social being with the ability to communicate with others, analyze your past actions, regulate your present behavior, and anticipate the actions of others. In other words, being a self allows you to actively create and recreate your social world.

Your culture and the groups to which you belong significantly shape your self-concept. Further, your social behavior is influenced by what aspect of your self-concept is most salient in a given situation. When you are attentive to your private self-aspects, you behave more in line with personal standards, while public standards exert greater influence when you are aware of your public self-aspects.

As a self, you sometimes struggle with conflicting desires. Should you seek out and interpret information to attain a more positive view of yourself, even if it contradicts your self-concept? There certainly are benefits to high self-esteem, especially in an individualist culture. However, the valuing of self-esteem is sometimes so strong that people with uncertain high self-regard react aggressively when others challenge it. This desire to maintain appropriately high levels of self-esteem also influences whether you react to the successes of those close to you with pride or jealousy. As social beings, we try to maintain competent and appropriate presented selves, and we often consciously try to manipulate people's impressions of us. Throughout the remaining chapters, you will see how interpretations of social events are filtered through self-beliefs and self-desires.

WEB SITES

Check out our web site
www.BVTLab.com
for chapter-by-chapter flashcards, summaries, and practice quizzes.

ACCESSED THROUGH www.BVTLab.com/sop6
Web sites for this chapter focus on the self, including cross-cultural research, an international society devoted to the study of the self, and information on the history of the self-concept in the social sciences.

SOCIETY FOR CROSS-CULTURAL PSYCHOLOGY
This is the web site for an organization pursuing cross-cultural research from a multidisciplinary perspective.

INTERNATIONAL SOCIETY FOR SELF AND IDENTITY

This is the web site for an interdisciplinary association of social and behavioral scientists dedicated to promoting the scientific study of the self. Users can find abstracts of unpublished articles and recent books.

OVERVIEW OF SELF-CONCEPT THEORIES

This web page investigates the history of the self-concept in the social sciences. It also includes ideas for people who aspire to be counselors.

AMERICAN PSYCHOLOGICAL ASSOCIATION

The web site for the American Psychological Association contains a web page that discusses the possibility that high self-esteem narcissists tend to be aggressive when criticized.

PROJECT IMPLICIT

The web site provides you with the opportunity to assess your conscious and unconscious preferences for over ninety topics, including self-esteem. At the same time, you will be assisting psychological research.

4

Chapter 4
Social Cognition and Person Perception

CHAPTER OUTLINE

INTRODUCTION

Reporter Stephen Glass was an ambitious young man. He exuded integrity, intelligence, and supreme confidence. In the mid-1990s, while serving as executive editor for the University of Pennsylvania's student-run newspaper, Glass wrote, "The role of *The Daily Pennsylvanian* is not to make allies and not to make enemies—it is to report the truth." As leader of the school's paper, Stephen was both charming and demanding. Holding court with fellow reporters, he enthralled them with vivid stories of his journalistic adventures, while simultaneously admonishing these budding journalists to check their facts before filing a story. One of those reporters recalled, "While fact-checking my writing, he once admonished me for inverting a quotation I had taken from a politician's speech. I had not changed the meaning of the speaker's words, but Steve insisted I quote the words in the order in which the speaker actually spoke them. At the time, I was impressed that Steve could be creative and also hold himself to such strict ethical standards" (Brus, 1998).

Following graduation, this likable, talented, and high-minded reporter soon became associate editor of *The New Republic* and, at the age of twenty-five, was a rising star in the world of journalism with his freelance reporting for such high-profile magazines as *George, Rolling Stone,* and *Harper's Magazine.* His articles about fundamentalist Christian nudists, the Union of Concerned Santas and Easter Bunnies, and his stint as a professional phone psychic were bold and goofy snapshots of contemporary American culture. Readers and fellow reporters loved his stories because they were so vivid and contained such lively quotes. But *The New Republic* readers were also drawn to Glass's stories because the people about whom he wrote conformed to cultural stereotypes: conservative Republicans who were secret sex maniacs, Wall Street brokers who were such workaholics that they kept deskside urinals, young African-American men who were too lazy to drive a cab but not too lazy to rob the cab driver.

Then something happened. In May 1998, Glass wrote a story for *The New Republic* about a fifteen-year-old computer hacker who broke into the database of a software company and posted the salaries of its executives on its web site. Instead of prosecuting this wayward computer whiz, the executives wanted to hire him! During his salary negotiations, Glass reported that the teenager shouted at the executives, "Show me the money!" One of the differences between this story and most of Glass's other stories was that he published the full name of the story's principal character and identified the company and its web site address. When a reporter at another magazine became curious and tried to contact the teenager, he could not locate him. In fact, the reporter could not confirm any of the facts in the Glass article. Soon everyone realized that the reason Stephen Glass's stories were so vivid and compelling was that he was fabricating almost all of the characters, quotes, and scenarios! As you might guess, Glass was fired and all his freelance employers dropped their contracts with him.

How was Stephen Glass able to fool so many people for so long? In 2003, Glass's escapades were depicted in the Hollywood movie *Shattered Glass.* Actor Peter Sarsgaard, who plays Glass's editor in the movie, offers the following opinion:

> I think what made all of this possible for him has more to do with the public than it does him. It's more interesting to think about why people believe people like that than why they lie. (Rowe, 2003)

social cognition

· ·

The way in which we interpret, analyze, remember, and use information about the social world

The Stephen Glass incident is unusual because it was played out on the national stage. Yet it is similar to events we face on a daily basis, and it illustrates several important aspects of **social cognition**, which is the way in which we interpret, analyze, remember, and use information about our social world. As discussed in Chapter 1 (pp. 17–18), we interpret events in our world and make sense of them by using two types of thinking: automatic and relatively effortless thinking or deliberate and relatively effortful thinking. In this chapter we will examine how people use this dual-process thinking to organize their knowledge about the social world, form impressions of others, and make sense of people's actions. Let us begin by examining some of the basic principles of social thought.

HOW DOES AUTOMATIC THINKING HELP US MAKE SENSE OF SOCIAL INFORMATION?

As the Stephen Glass story illustrates, life is often complicated and difficult to understand. Faced with such complexity and thrust into the world as both actors and observers, we rely on two different ways of thinking (Kruglanski & Orehek, 2007). As previously defined in Chapter 1 (p. 18), *explicit cognition* involves deliberate judgments or decisions of which we are consciously aware, while *implicit cognition* involves judgments or decisions that are under the control of automatically activated evaluations occurring without our awareness. Being unintentional and consuming few cognitive resources, implicit cognition operates quickly, while explicit cognition is generally a slower process. As you will see, the fast and automatic operation of implicit cognition sets the stage for all social judgments.

WE ARE CATEGORIZING CREATURES.

A mental grouping of objects, ideas, or events that share common properties is called a *category*. For example, *insect* stands for a category of animals that have three body divisions (head, thorax, abdomen), six legs, an external skeleton, and a rapid reproductive cycle. Categories are the building blocks of cognition (Markman, 1999; Woll, 2002). Like the heart that pumps life-giving blood throughout the body, or the lungs that replenish oxygen to this blood, the scientific consensus is that humans could not survive without automatically categorizing things. Imagine, for example, how lost and bewildered you would be if you attended a college class without an appreciation of some key categories such as professor, student, lecture, chairs, or notes.

This automatic tendency to perceive and understand the world in categorical terms is an implicit cognitive process that greatly expands our ability to deal with the huge amount of information constantly presented to us (Dijksterhuis, 2010). Categorization allows us to generalize from one experience to another, making it possible to assign meaning to novel stimuli. Thus, if someone tells you to meet at the student union by the magnolia tree, you probably know what to look for even if you have never seen a magnolia tree. By understanding the general properties of the category *tree*, you will probably seek out an object that is taller than yourself, with branches and leaves that provide shade from the sun. By relating new stimuli to familiar categories, you are much more efficient in understanding and making decisions in your environment.

We also naturally form categories about people based upon their common attributes. This process is called **social categorization** (Hampson, 1988). When categorizing people, we tend to initially rely on readily apparent physical features, such as sex and race (Klauer et al., 2003; Quinn & Macrae, 2005). Because categorizing others by physical features is done so frequently, it becomes habitual and automatic, occurring without conscious thought or effort (Fiske & Neuberg, 1990; Schneider, 2004). In fact, such categorization is so automatic that it probably is impossible to inhibit. Under normal circumstances can you meet someone and not notice whether the person is a she or he? Wouldn't it seem strange not to remember whether the person was young or old?

Exactly how do we mentally group things, including people, into categories? Consider classifying someone based on race. How would you classify someone who has a combination of Caucasian and Afrocentric facial features? Do all Africans or all Caucasians have the same skin color? Research suggests that categorizing has less to do with the features that define *all* members of a category and has more to do with the features that characterize the *typical* member (McGarty, 2004). The most representative member of a category is known as a **prototype**; it is our mental model that stands for or symbolizes the category (Barsalou, 1991; Zimmerman & Sieverding, 2011). Because a prototype is the member of a category that best represents it for you, members of that category will vary in how closely they match the prototype. Thus, although patrol officers and

social categorization

The process of forming categories of people based on their common attributes

prototype

The most representative member of a category

undercover officers both fit into our category of police officer, for most of us, patrol officers are more "cop-like." Not surprisingly, we can more quickly categorize prototypical members than those who less closely match the prototype (Olson et al., 2004; Rosch & Mervis, 1975). Failing to correctly categorize people because they do not resemble the prototype often leads to errors in decision-making. This is why female doctors are more often mistaken for nurses than are male doctors, while male nurses are more likely than female nurses to be miscategorized as doctors. In both cases, the mistaken judgments are due to our culturally derived prototypes for these two professions.

Generally, the more experience we have with a particular category, the more accurate we are in noticing similarities and differences between members of that category. Thus, a birdwatcher will more quickly and accurately identify different types of birds and recognize individual birds based on subtle markings than will someone with limited bird watching experience. The fact that it is more difficult to notice subtle differences between members of a category with which you have limited exposure helps explain why you may think that members of another ethnic group have faces that "all look the same" to you. While this *other-race effect* can be embarrassing when you misidentify someone of another race during everyday interaction, the consequences can be life changing and extremely negative in cases of eyewitness misidentification (Brigham et al., 2007; Michel et al., 2009).

SCHEMAS AFFECT WHAT INFORMATION WE NOTICE AND LATER REMEMBER.

Implicit cognition allows us to group objects, ideas, or events into categories and also to develop theories about those categories. The theories we have about categories are called schemas. A **schema** is an organized structure of knowledge about a stimulus that is built up from experience and that contains causal relations; it is a theory about how the social world operates (Chen, 2001; Kunda, 1999). The stimulus could be a person, an object, a social group, a social role, or a common event. A student who observes her psychology professor conducting research will have a schema for the professor role, a schema for the research process, and schemas for various other relevant concepts that this particular professor fits (for example, female, middle aged, and Pakistani). Without these schemas, the student would have great difficulty making sense of the professor and her actions. However, with these schemas, the student can not only understand what is happening in the situation but also can go beyond the presented information and anticipate the next set of events that might occur in this setting. Thus, schemas enrich our understanding of the world. Because they provide a theory about the category of interest, schemas also hasten the processing of information, and hence, decision-making.

Some of our schemas are not well developed. For example, my computer schema is very limited. Sure, I can identify some major parts of the computer (I can proudly point to the central processing unit), but I lack the knowledge to accurately explain how the components work together to create the images that appear on the computer screen. People with well-developed schemas about some domain are often experts about that domain. A computer repairperson would have a highly developed computer schema and thus would be much more accurate than me in predicting how a computer will perform specific functions. We also have schemas about ourselves, *self-schemas*, which are the personal attributes with which we identify. These self-schemas are the ingredients in the multiple self-aspects that together constitute our self-concepts (see Chapter 3, pp. 78–80).

Culture shapes many schemas, such as **gender schema**, which is a cognitive structure for processing information based on its perceived female or male qualities. People with a well-developed gender schema habitually organize things in their minds according to gender categories. When information is filtered through a gender schema, social perceptions and judgments typically adhere to cultural gender standards. Thus, for example, if George and Laura have strong gender schemas, they may perceive such things as dogs, football, sports cars, math, assertiveness, meat and potatoes, and action movies as "guy-like," while labeling as "girl-like" things such as cats, aerobics, hybrid cars, the fine arts, empathy, salads, and romance movies. For George and Laura, their

schema
....
A schema is an organized structure of knowledge about a stimulus that is built up from experience and that contains causal relations; it is a theory about how the social world operates.

gender schema
....
A cognitive structure for processing information based on its perceived female or male qualities

We use different scripts for different occasions in our lives.

gender schemas help them organize and make sense of their lives. If Laura's gender schema causes her to perceive math ability as a male quality, regardless of any inborn potential, Laura is now less likely to identify skill in math as an important personal quality (Nosek et al., 2002). Due to this disidentification, she is unlikely to spend time developing her math skills, and she is unlikely to choose careers that emphasize math. In contrast, perceiving this same math = male association, George may develop positive attitudes toward math activities and may ultimately choose a career in a math-oriented occupation. This is just one example of how schemas can shape our social perceptions and thereby shape our own self-perceptions.

script

A schema that describes how a series of events is likely to occur in a well-known situation and which is used as a guide for behavior and problem solving

We also have schemas about common events. A **script** describes how a series of events is likely to occur in a well-known situation (Woll, 2002). The script is used as a guide for behavior and problem solving in the situation. We have numerous scripts, including those for attending class, eating dinner at a restaurant, going to the dentist, interacting with hired help, asking someone out on a date, and even breaking off a romantic relationship (Battaglia et al., 1998; Lan, 2003). Learning scripts is an important part of the socialization process, and children as young as three years of age have well-developed preconceptions about familiar routine events in their lives, such as having lunch at the day-care center or getting ready for bed at night (Nelson, 1986). Scripts often help us clear up ambiguities in social situations. For example, if you go over to someone's house for dinner and are later asked to "spend the night," your interpretation of this question will be shaped by the script that you have in mind. If a platonic friend asks this question, you are likely following a different script than if the questioner is a much-desired romantic partner. Embarrassment is likely if your host has a very different script in mind from your own.

Two types of schemas applied to people are implicit personality theories (see p. 135) and *stereotypes* (Banaji, in press; McGarty et al., 2002). Like other types of schemas, stereotypes influence how we process and interpret information, even when we are not consciously aware the schema has been activated from memory (Kawakami et al., 2002; Schubert & Häfner, 2003). Once a stereotype is activated, we tend to see people within that social category as possessing the traits or characteristics associated with the stereotyped group (Krueger et al., 2003). For example, if a personnel director thinks of elderly people as being frail, forgetful, and slow to grasp new skills, she may spend little time reviewing the employment histories of job applicants over a certain age. Likewise, her positive stereotypes of graduates from Ivy League schools may cause her to overlook glaring blemishes in another applicant's job history who is an Ivy Leaguer. In Chapter 6 we will examine in detail how stereotypes are related to prejudice and discrimination.

❝*Labels are devices for saving talkative persons the trouble of thinking.*❞

John Morley, English statesman and author, 1838–1923

As you can see, once schemas are formed they can have a profound effect on our social thinking and behavior. Schemas will often determine what information in our surroundings we pay attention to and how quickly we process it, what information we form memories about, and what information we later recall when making decisions. In general, we tend to have better memories of past events and people when this information was originally processed through well-formed schemas (Hirt, 1990), but schemas can also cause us to "misremember" information. Why is this so?

Regarding attention and processing, a schema acts as a cognitive filter, often screening out information that is inconsistent with it (Dijksterhuis & Knippenberg, 1996; Sherman et al., 1998). How might this screening of information affect our impressions of people?

As an example, imagine seeing someone assisting a handicapped person across the street. While watching this situation unfold, you would typically assume that the person is empathic and helpful. However, what if this individual is a skinhead? Because empathy and helpfulness are qualities inconsistent with most people's skinhead schema, research indicates that in this situation you are much less likely to make the typical spontaneous social judgment of helplessness (Wigboldus et al., 2003). Instead, in this situation you may automatically dismiss this behavioral information as not being useful in making inferences about the skinhead's personality; however, you may engage in more effortful, non-schematic-based thinking and consider what situational factors may be causing him to behave this way (perhaps this is a ploy to rob the handicapped person).

Sometimes, however, information is so sharply inconsistent with an existing schema that we take great notice of it and store—or *encode*—it into a new, separate schema (Stangor & McMillan, 1992). With our skinhead, imagine that you learn that he volunteers at a homeless shelter and an AIDS center, and that he strongly believes in social justice and civil rights for all groups. This information may be so inconsistent with your skinhead schema that you spend time thinking about how he could have become a skinhead in the first place. This effortful thinking may result in you forming a new schema for "socially progressive skinheads," while still retaining your more general skinhead schema.

Schemas also play an important role in what we remember. However, unlike photographs that freeze exact images of past events, scientific studies indicate that our memories are often sketchy reconstructions of the past. English psychologist Sir Frederic Bartlett (1932) was the first theorist to characterize memory in this manner. When testing people's memories of stories they had read, Bartlett found that accurate recollections by his participants were rare. Instead, participants seemed to reconstruct the material they had learned, shortening and lengthening different aspects, and changing details overall to better fit their own preexisting schemas. These memory distortions became more pronounced over time, yet Bartlett's participants were largely unaware that they had reconstructed the past. In fact, the reconstructed memories were often those aspects of the story that they most adamantly claimed to be true!

Linda Carli (1999) conducted a more recent experiment demonstrating similar effects. In this study, college students read a story about a woman named Barbara and a man named Jack who had been dating awhile before going to a ski lodge for the weekend. In one condition of the experiment, Jack proposed marriage to Barbara at the end of the story, whereas in the other condition the story ended with Jack raping Barbara in their lodge room. Two weeks after reading their Jack-Barbara story, participants read several details about the two characters and were asked whether this information appeared in the original story or not. As depicted in Figure 4.1, Carli found that in both conditions participants tended to misremember details that were consistent with their original schema for the Barbara and Jack event. Those in the *proposal* condition were likely to falsely remember that "Jack wanted Barbara to meet his parents" and "Jack gave Barbara a dozen roses." Similarly, participants in the *rape* condition were likely to misremember that "Jack was unpopular with women" and "Jack liked to drink."

Critical THINKING

How is the spontaneously activated self-concept discussed in Chapter 3 related to schemas and priming effects?

SCHEMAS CAN BE SITUATIONALLY OR CHRONICALLY ACTIVATED.

Schemas help us make sense out of our world, but what activates a schema from memory? The process by which recent exposure to certain stimuli or events increases the accessibility

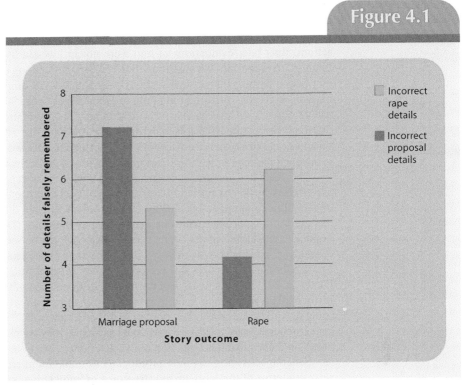

Figure 4.1

Schemas and Misremembering the Past

Linda Carli (1999) found evidence that people's schemas about a past event shaped their later recall of the event in a way that led them to falsely remember details that never occurred. Those who had read a story about a man raping his girlfriend were more likely to falsely remember details that were consistent with their rape schema, while those who read a story about a man proposing to his girlfriend were more likely to falsely remember details that were consistent with their proposal schema. What implications does this research have for the validity of witnesses' testimony in criminal trials?

priming
....
The process by which recent exposure to certain stimuli or events increases the accessibility of certain memories, categories, or schemas

of certain memories, categories, or schemas is known as **priming**. More than a century ago, psychologist William James described priming as the "wakening of associations." As an example of this memory process, answer the following two questions as quickly as possible: How do you pronounce the word spelled p-o-k-e, and what do you call the white of an egg? If you answered "yolk" to the second question, you've demonstrated priming, Priming is a good example of automatic thinking because it occurs spontaneously and unconsciously (Custers & Aarts, 2007).

In one priming experiment, Tory Higgins and his colleagues (1977) informed college student volunteers they would be participating in two different and unrelated studies. In the first "perception" study, the participants were asked to identify different colors while simultaneously memorizing a list of words. Some participants in the treatment condition were shown words designed to prime the positive schema of *adventurousness* (such as "brave" or "self-confident") while others were shown words designed to prime the negative schema of *recklessness* (such as "foolish" or "careless"). In the second "reading comprehension" study, the students read a story about a man named Donald who climbed mountains, shot rapids, piloted a jet-powered boat, and drove in a demolition derby. Donald was now planning on trying skydiving or crossing the Atlantic Ocean in a sailboat. What sort of impressions did the participants form of Donald? This was the dependent measure in the study.

Results indicated that it depended on what schemas had been primed. Those who previously memorized words associated with the schema of adventurousness tended to evaluate Donald positively, perceiving him as a likable person who enjoyed challenges. In contrast, those who had memorized words related to the schema of recklessness tended to evaluate Donald negatively, viewing him as a conceited person who took needless risks. In control conditions, when the researchers asked participants in the "perception" study to memorize positive or negative words that were not descriptive of Donald's actions, their later evaluations of him were not influenced by these words. These latter findings are important because they indicate that evaluations of Donald were not shaped by whether participants were first shown words that were simply positive or negative. To have an effect the words had to apply to Donald's actions. Stated differently, the words had to activate a schema that was related to the information about to be presented. Together, the results from this experiment demonstrate that situational cues can activate schemas, and these activated schemas will influence how we perceive new information in our surroundings if that information is relevant to the activated schemas.

The fact that certain situations can activate certain schemas goes a long way in explaining why both women and men are more or less likely to think of themselves in terms of masculine or feminine personality traits based on whether they are engaged in activities that are more associated with one gender versus the other (Deaux & Major, 1987). For example, competitive sports contexts tend to activate the masculine dimension of the gender schema, causing both women and men to be more aware of and responsive to their masculine rather than their feminine personality traits in these situations (Clément-Guillotin & Fontayne, 2011). The activation of the masculine dimension of the gender schema also may partly explain why people tend to perceive women who excel in competitive athletics as being less feminine than other women (Sage & Loudermilk 1979). The activation of the gender schema in competitive sports contexts shapes how we perceive ourselves, as well as others, in those situations (Harrison & Lynch, 2005).

Schema activation not only prompts us to think about and evaluate others and ourselves in terms of these organized structures of knowledge, schemas can also prompt us to physically behave in ways consistent with them. For example, in one experiment, John Bargh and his coworkers (1996) asked participants to work on unscrambling word puzzles similar to the one depicted in Figure 4.2. For some participants, the puzzles con-

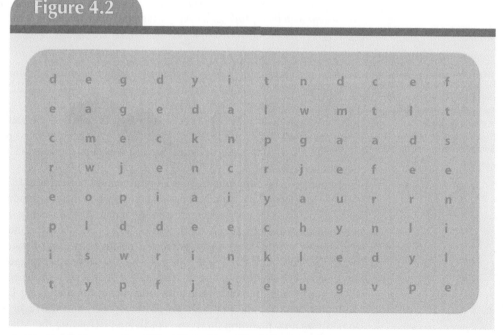

Figure 4.2

Activated Schemas Can Affect Behavior: The Word Puzzle Study

How many words can you find in this word puzzle? When John Bargh and his colleagues (1996) asked people to engage in a similar word puzzle task, those who worked on puzzles with embedded aging-related words later walked more slowly down a hallway than people who worked on puzzles containing neutral words. How do these findings support the hypothesis that an aging schema was activated in those who saw the aging-related words?

tained words related to the schema for *aging* (such as "elderly" and "slow"), while for others the puzzles included neutral words unrelated to the aging schema (such as "classroom" and "corn"). The researchers hypothesized that for those participants who worked on puzzles with embedded age-related cues, their culturally learned aging schema—a stereotype—would be automatically primed in such a way that it would shape their immediate behavior. Consistent with this prediction, when leaving the experiment, participants whose elderly schema had been primed walked more slowly down a hallway than those who had not been similarly primed.

In the studies discussed thus far, schemas were activated after people consciously focused their attention for a period of time on specific situational cues. Do you think we could activate schemas even if people do not consciously notice the relevant situational cues? What if the situational cue is presented *subliminally*, meaning that it is presented so fast or so faintly that it is just below the absolute threshold for conscious awareness? In another "Donald" experiment, Bargh and Paula Pietromonaco (1982) asked people to read a brief story on a computer screen about a salesman knocking on Donald's door and Donald responding by refusing to let the salesman in. The question of interest was how people would interpret Donald's behavior. Was this a hostile response or not? In the treatment group, hostile words such as "unkind" and "hostile" were subliminally flashed on the computer screen just prior to participants reading the story. In the control group, neutral words such as "water" and "between" were used as subliminal primes.

Consistent with the findings from the first "Donald" study, results indicated that participants who were presented with hostile words evaluated Donald as more hostile than those who were presented with neutral words—even though they did not know they had seen the words! These findings not only support the hypothesis that priming is an automatic, unconscious process, they also raise the possibility that our social judgments can be unconsciously manipulated. In Chapter 5 we will examine in more detail the feasibility of using subliminal messages to substantially alter people's attitudes and behavior.

Thus far we have discussed how schemas can be situationally activated. Yet there are many examples in life where schemas are chronically accessible due to past experiences. For example, imagine observing a parent and child engaged in an animated and loud verbal exchange in a public setting. If you suffered from physical abuse as a child, you may habitually perceive such emotionally ambiguous scenes as signs of impending violence. However, if you grew up in a household where family members regularly expressed themselves in a raucous but loving manner, you may expect such situations to end with hugs and smiles. The Applications section at the end of the chapter discusses how people with optimistic versus pessimistic outlooks on life habitually respond in different ways to similar life events. Their contrasting interpretations of positive and negative outcomes can be understood in terms of them having markedly different schemas chronically accessible.

HEURISTICS ARE TIME-SAVING MENTAL SHORTCUTS.

Our social world is literally saturated with information. However, at any given moment, we are capable of processing only a limited amount of this information. Faced with such limitations, we employ various mental strategies that "stretch" our cognitive resources so that we can sift through some of this information with less effort. For example, imagine that you wanted to phone your friend John Smith but did not know his number. You could pull out the phone book and systematically dial every one of the thirty-seven John Smiths until you found the right one. This problem-solving strategy employs an *algorithm*, which involves following a specific step-by-step procedure until you inevitably produce the correct solution. In the dual-process approach to understanding cognition, employing algorithms is an example of high-intensity work. However, you could try solving this problem by relying on a simple rule: John is a student, and most students live near campus and have a "288" phone prefix. You have just used a *heuristic* to reduce the number of John Smiths to seven. **Heuristics** are timesaving mental shortcuts that reduce complex judgments to simple rules (Tversky & Kahneman, 1974).

heuristics
. . . .
Time-saving mental shortcuts that reduce complex judgments to simple rules

In dual-process thinking, heuristics require very little thought; people merely take the shortcut and make the judgment. The downside of using heuristics, however, is that they may not work. What if your John Smith lives far away from campus or uses an unlisted cell phone? Thus, to be useful, heuristics must satisfy two requirements: (1) They must allow us to make quick social judgments. (2) They must be reasonably accurate. Unfortunately, satisfying the first requirement often works against judgment accuracy (Ajzen, 1996; Higgins, 2000). That is, you can make a quick judgment by ignoring a great deal of potentially relevant information in your environment, but what cost does this have on the accuracy of your judgment? Yet keep in mind that the second requirement of heuristics involves "reasonable" accuracy, not "high" accuracy. With that in mind, let us consider some commonly used mental shortcuts that social psychologists have identified and studied over the years.

The Representativeness Heuristic

During my first few years as a professor, people often mistook me for a student. Why was this so? Well, to them I did not fit their image of what a university professor looked like. This judgment is an example of the **representativeness heuristic**, which is the tendency to judge the category membership of things based on how closely they match the prototype of that category (Gilovich & Savitsky, 2002; Kahneman & Tversky, 1973). Because I looked younger than my age, and because I dressed more casually than most professors, people guessed I was a student.

The representativeness heuristic helps people to quickly decide in what categories to place others. It is essentially stereotyping operating in reverse. That is, when we stereotype someone, we first place them in a particular social category and then infer that they possess the personal attributes associated with people in that category. When we rely on the representativeness heuristic, we merely reverse this cognitive process: because a person possesses attributes we associate with a particular social category, we infer that he/she must be a member of that category. The old saying "If it looks like a duck and if it quacks like a duck, then it probably is a duck" is an example of the representativeness heuristic. Although this cognitive shortcut is a rapid method of identifying people, it does not consider other important qualifying information. The most important information relates to *base rates*—the frequency with which some event or pattern occurs in the general population.

The tendency to overlook base-rate information was demonstrated in a study by Tversky and Kahneman (1973). Research participants were told that an imaginary person named Jack had been selected from a group of a hundred men. Some were told that thirty of the men were engineers (a base rate for engineers of 30 percent), and others were told that seventy were engineers (a base rate of 70 percent). Half the participants were given no other information, but the other half were given a description of Jack that either fit the common stereotype of engineers (for example, practical, likes to work with numbers) or did not. They were then asked to guess the probability that Jack was an engineer. Results indicated that when participants received only information related to base rates, they were more likely to guess that Jack was an engineer when the base rate was 70 percent than when it was 30 percent. However, when they received information about Jack's personality and behavior, they tended to ignore the base-rate information and, instead, focus on whether Jack fit their image of an engineer. The tendency to ignore or underuse useful base-rate information and overuse personal descriptors of the individual being judged has been called the *base-rate* fallacy.

The Availability Heuristic

I have a friend who was planning to purchase a new car, and I asked her if she was considering a particular brand that had received excellent reliability ratings in *Consumer Reports*. Her reply was no because she had just spoken to someone who had that type of car and was not satisfied with its reliability. In nixing this car from her list, my friend was basing her judgment on the content of this fresh memory. The **availability heuristic** is the tendency to judge the frequency or probability of an event in terms of how easy it

representativeness heuristic
....
The tendency to judge the category membership of things based on how closely they match the "typical" or "average" member of that category

Critical THINKING
If the representativeness heuristic is stereotyping operating in reverse, does that mean that stereotyping is also a heuristic?

availability heuristic
....
The tendency to judge the frequency or probability of an event in terms of how easy it is to think of examples of that event

is to think of examples of that event (Kunda, 1999; Tversky & Kahneman, 1973). Thus, in estimating the likelihood of car problems with this particular model, my friend relied on the easy accessibility in her memory of this one person's negative experiences. If the information she accessed from memory had been reasonably representative of the actual reliability of these cars, relying on the availability heuristic would have resulted in an accurate assessment. Unfortunately, this was not the case here.

In the use of the availability heuristic, the most important factor for people is not the content of their memory recall but the ease with which this *content* comes to mind (Higgins, 2000; Schwarz & Vaughn, 2002). For example, Norbert Schwarz and his colleagues (1991b) found that participants who were asked to recall twelve examples of their own assertive behaviors (a difficult cognitive task) subsequently rated themselves as less assertive than participants who were asked to recall only six examples (an easy cognitive task). Similar results were obtained for participants who were asked to recall examples of their unassertive behaviors. The implication here is that people pay attention to how easy or difficult it is for them to recall examples of a particular event or behavior in making attributions. They rely only on the content of their recall (for example, assertive behavior) if its implications are not called into question by the difficulty they experience in bringing the relevant material to mind. Thus, individuals would conclude that they must not be assertive if it is difficult to recall personal examples of assertive behavior in their past.

The availability heuristic provides insight into a number of faulty social judgments (Gana et al., 2011), including why White Americans often overestimate the frequency with which minority group members are represented in popular media. In one study, Donnel Briley and his coworkers (2007) found that while African Americans' estimates of the number of times they encounter Blacks in TV ads are fairly accurate, White Americans overestimate the frequency of Black representation. It appears that the greater accuracy of African-American viewers is due to the fact that they place higher importance on Black representation in the media, and thus engage in more effortful thinking by keeping a subjective tally of the number of times they encounter Blacks in TV ads. In contrast, White Americans are relatively uninterested in the number of Blacks in the media, and thus do not keep a subjective tally. Nevertheless, White Americans are more likely to notice and later more easily recall that a Black actor appeared in a TV ad compared to a White actor. Thus, White Americans' overestimations of Black representation in the media is based on the ease with which these past specific instances of Black actors appearing in ads can be recalled.

Despite these examples of social judgment errors, availability is a fairly valid cue for the judgment of frequency because frequent events are more likely than infrequent events to be stored in memory and later recalled. If a doctor is seeing patients during the height of the flu season, the fact that he can easily bring the flu virus to mind will influence how many patients he diagnoses with this ailment. A busy doctor may quickly diagnose ailments as normal influenza and make correct judgments 99.9 percent of the time; but with "the flu" on his mind, he is also more likely to misdiagnose a far more serious ailment as simple influenza (Weber et al., 1993).

The Anchoring and Adjustment Heuristic

anchoring and adjustment heuristic
····················
A tendency to be biased toward the starting value or anchor in making quantitative judgments

Do you think the population of Cincinnati, Ohio, is more than one hundred thousand? Yes is the correct answer. Now estimate Cincinnati's actual population, and then check on p. 119 for the correct answer. If instead of asking whether Cincinnati's population is *more than one hundred thousand*, I had asked whether it is *less than one million*, your answer probably would have been higher. The reason this effect often happens is because we want to be correct in our judgments. In trying to meet this goal, our quantitative judgments are often biased toward an initial anchor point—in our example, this was the one hundred thousand figure. Later when making our estimate, we use this anchor as our starting point and, thus, usually insufficiently adjust toward the correct answer. This mental bias is known as the **anchoring and adjustment heuristic** (Epley & Gilovich, 2001; Tversky & Kahneman, 1974).

As demonstrated in a survey study Scott Plous (1989) conducted, the anchoring and adjustment heuristic can affect our social judgments. Respondents were first asked

Cincinnati has a population of 332,000.

whether they thought there was greater than 1 percent chance of a nuclear war occurring soon. Other respondents were asked whether nuclear war had less than a 90 percent chance of occurring soon. All respondents were then asked to estimate the likelihood of such a war occurring soon. Those who started from the 1 percent anchor guessed at a 10 percent risk factor, while those who started from the 90 percent anchor estimated the risk of nuclear war to be 25 percent.

Like other heuristics, anchoring and adjustment can help us make correct judgments. For example, imagine that you inherit an old painting from a distant relative and are trying to determine its value for resale. You notice that a local antique store is selling a similar old painting for $400, and that painting is in slightly better condition than your piece. In estimating a value for your painting you might start with that price, and then adjust downward slightly. In many instances, this would probably provide you with a quick and fairly accurate way to judge the painting's value. However, there are instances when people greatly overvalue their antiques because they think their pieces are similar to something they saw on Public Television's *Antiques Road Show* that was judged to be a masterpiece.

Why do arbitrary numbers influence us? In making a judgment, when we are given a number or value as a starting point, we appear to selectively recall information from memory that is consistent with this anchor (Chapman & Johnson, 1999; Mussweiler & Strack, 2000). Thus, after starting with the modest price of the antique store painting as the anchor value, you are likely to remember instances when other people sold antiques at a similar modest price. However, if your painting's anchor is the high price from the *Antiques Road Show*, you are likely to recall from memory stories of people discovering they had inherited masterpieces worth millions. In a very real sense, the anchor becomes a situational cue that triggers relevant memories, just as priming people with words can activate relevant schemas (refer back to the "Donald" experiments, pp. 114–116). In both instances, people's automatic, effortless thinking has an effect on the way they make judgments (Chapman & Johnson, 2002).

Is Heuristic Thinking "Stupid" Thinking?

Examining the research on heuristics may lead you to conclude that we are irrational decision makers, with distortions and errors being the most common end products of social thinking. In fact, John Kihlstrom (2004) half-jokingly suggests that social psychology has informally developed a new school of thought that he calls the "People Are Stupid" perspective. Similarly, other social psychologists assert that many experts within the field are too quick to conclude that our demonstrated cognitive biases reveal a fundamental flaw in social cognition (Krueger & Funder, 2004). Instead, they insist that although basing decisions on heuristics may lead to errors and may be motivated by lazy thinking, relying on them can actually be adaptive under conditions where we do not have the luxury of systematically analyzing all our options (Haselton & Nettle, 2006). For example, reacting quickly in an emergency based only on information that is most accessible from memory (the availability heuristic) may often be the difference between life and death. Sure, heuristics can lead to sloppy decision-making., but their timesaving quality may sometimes be a lifesaver.

From an evolutionary perspective, human beings can be thought of as having evolved a large number of mental strategies to adapt to their surroundings. In this regard, heuristics and other effortless thinking have been very helpful to us because they yield reasonably accurate and adaptive results under most environmental conditions (Figueredo et al., 2004). If these biased reasoning strategies were eliminated from human decision making, social judgment accuracy would get much worse, not better.

If the use of heuristics is considered to more often be a part of "useful thinking" rather than "stupid thinking," with what frequency do we pull these mental shortcuts out of our cognitive toolbox when making social judgments? Are we constantly cutting corners, or is it a rare occurrence? Common experience and social psychologists' best reasoned analysis suggest that we do not always rely on heuristics. Often we systematically analyze a

Critical THINKING

In the days and weeks following the suicide attacks at the Pentagon and World Trade Center by Arab terrorists, FBI offices around the country were flooded with calls from citizens reporting possible leads and suspects. Virtually every person who was perceived as being suspicious was of Arab descent. What cognitive heuristic was being used in making these social judgments? Why do you think people were relying on this heuristic?

situation using a variety of information. Research has identified the following conditions that are most likely to lead to the use of heuristics rather than more careful decision-making (Macrae et al., 1993; Ruder & Bless, 2003):

1. We simply do not have *time* to engage in systematic analysis.
2. We are *overloaded with information* so that it is impossible to process all that is meaningful and relevant.
3. We consider the issues in question to be *not very important.*
4. We have *little other knowledge* or information to use in making a decision.
5. Something about the situation calls to mind a given heuristic, making it *cognitively available* (priming).
6. We are in a *positive mood*, signaling to us that everything is fine and no effortful thinking is necessary.

SECTION SUMMARY

- Social categorization entails classifying people into groups based on common attributes.

- Schemas are organized knowledge structures that:

    provide theories about how the social world operates,

    hasten information processing and decision making, and

    influence what information is remembered and later recalled.

- Priming makes memories, categories, and schemas more accessible.

- Heuristics allow quick judgments with minimal cognitive effort but can cause biased and inaccurate judgments.

    The representativeness heuristic *involves* judging the category membership of things based on how closely they match the prototype for that category.

    The availability heuristic involves judging the probability of an event in terms of how easy it is to think of examples of it.

    The anchoring and adjustment heuristic involves being biased toward the starting value or anchor in making quantitative judgments.

HOW DOES DELIBERATE THINKING HELP US MAKE SENSE OF PAST EVENTS?

In Chapters 1 and 3 we discussed how imagining future events can help us construct effective self-presentations and how imagining our future self can motivate current behavior. Yet what about past events? We spend a lot of time "thinking about the past." For example, I discovered that this phrase yields 3,160,000 hits on the Internet. How do we employ effortful thinking to make sense of past events?

THE HINDSIGHT BIAS IS FUELED BY OUR DESIRE FOR SENSE MAKING.

When recalling past events we often believe that we "knew all along" how things would turn out. After learning that your friend's lover has been unfaithful, you might think, "I could see this coming for some time." Or after your favorite sports team defeats its archrival for the first time in years you exclaim, "All week long I could tell that my team would win!" In such instances, this after-the-fact overestimation of our ability to have foreseen the outcome is known as the **hindsight bias** (Blank et al., 2003; Hawkins & Hastie, 1990).

Cross-cultural studies indicate that the hindsight bias occurs throughout the world (Pohl et al., 2002). This bias develops by age three and is more pronounced among

hindsight bias

• • • • • • • • • • • • • • • • • •

The tendency, once an event has occurred, to overestimate our ability to have foreseen the outcome preschoolers and elderly adults due to enhanced memory problems at these ages (Bernstein et al., 2011). The most commonly accepted explanation for the hindsight bias is that it is fueled by our desire for *sense making*, and we are most likely to rewrite our memory of a past event when the outcome is initially surprising (Erdfelder et al., 2007; Pezzo & Pezzo, 2007). When thinking about a past event that had a surprising outcome, we appear to selectively recall information in constructing a plausible story that is consistent with the now-known outcome (Muller & Stahlberg, 2007). This "rewriting" of how events occurred allows us to insert the missing causal connections so that the story makes sense given the outcome. Claiming hindsight reassures us that we understand—and can anticipate—events in our world.

Hindsight biasing can and does occur right after an event's outcome is known, but it tends to gain strength over time as we increasingly forget our earlier beliefs about what we thought would happen (Bryant & Guilbault, 2002). However, not all unexpected events produce the hindsight bias. It does not occur for events that are so unusual that you simply cannot think of any good reasons for why they would occur (Pezzo, 2003). For instance, few people showed much hindsight bias for the September 11, 2001, terrorist attacks or the 2000 Bush-Gore election results. These events were so bizarre that people could not easily reconstruct their memory of the prior events in a way that would allow them to think that they foresaw the final outcomes. The hindsight bias is also unlikely to occur if the sense making threatens self-esteem. For example, if you were among a group of employees laid off at work, do you think you would be more or less likely to claim that "there were many warning signals" than if you were merely an unaffected observer of these layoffs?

In one study that explored this question, people living near a factory were surveyed about their beliefs and opinions about recent factory layoffs (Mark & Mellor, 1991). Results indicated that townspeople who did not work at the factory and were not personally affected by the layoffs were most likely to claim that they knew the layoffs were coming (high hindsight bias). People who worked at the factory but kept their jobs were less likely to claim hindsight. Those who expressed the greatest surprise (no hindsight bias) were the workers who lost their jobs. These results and the findings from other studies suggest that, although we often engage in the hindsight bias when explaining past events, we are less likely to do so when those events affect us personally *and* are negative (Hoelzl et al., 2002; Mark et al., 2003). That is, we are less likely to claim hindsight for negative outcomes because claiming ignorance allows us to avoid blaming ourselves: "If I could not foresee being laid off, I cannot be blamed for not working harder or changing jobs."

COUNTERFACTUAL THINKING LIKELY FOLLOWS NEGATIVE AND UNEXPECTED EVENTS.

Our social judgments and current moods are also affected by the ease with which we can imagine alternative versions and outcomes of past events. For example, imagine the following day at the ski slopes:

> Hector loves to ski but is cautious and never goes down the expert slope. Yesterday, however, he tried it and broke his leg. Martina also loves to ski and frequently goes down the expert slope. Yesterday she broke her leg going down this slope.

Research suggests that the majority of us believe that Hector will feel the greatest regret following his injury, and most of us will also express greater sympathy toward him than toward Martina (Roese et al., 1999). The reason for these different judgments is that we engage in **counterfactual thinking**, which is the tendency to evaluate events by imagining alternative versions or outcomes (Kahneman, 1995; Segura & McCloy, 2003). We are most likely to engage in counterfactual thinking following negative and unexpected events, and the thoughts that are generated usually deal with how the negative outcome might have been prevented (Mandel & Lehman, 1996; Sanna & Turley, 1996). Regarding Hector and Martina, it is easier for us to imagine that Hector would be uninjured if he had not deviated from his normal cautious skiing style than it is to imagine this altered outcome for Martina, given her tendency to take greater risks on the

---

" *I just knew I should have picked door number two.* **"**

Let's Make a Deal TV-show contestant

" *Oh God! That it were possible, To undo things done, to call back yesterday! That Time could turn up his swift sandy glass, To untell the days, and to redeem these hours.* **"**

Thomas Heywood, English dramatist, 1574–1641

Critical **THINKING**

Why might a neuroscientist argue that the hindsight bias is triggered by some of the same neurological activity that creates the storyline of dreams?

counterfactual thinking
. . . .
The tendency to evaluate events by imagining alternative versions or outcomes to what actually happened

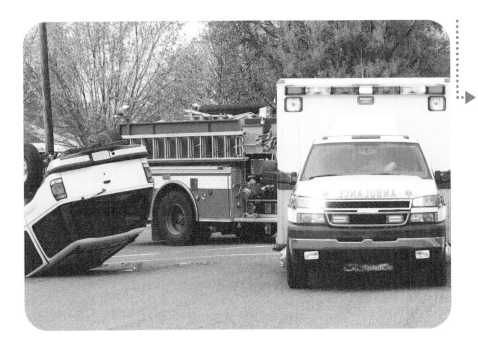

When we engage in counterfactual thinking we are constantly asking, "What if ...?" For example, when in a car accident we may think, "What if I had only gone down a different street?"

slopes. Because it is easier to undo Hector's broken leg through counterfactual thinking ("If only he had stuck to his usual routine ..."), we are more likely to feel sympathy for him. When our skiers engage in this same "What if ...?" thinking, Hector will experience greater regret over his injury than Martina, for the same reasons as we do.

Why do we engage in counterfactual thinking? Neal Roese (1997) suggests two possible functions served by these "What if ...?" thoughts. First, they may simply help us feel better following a negative outcome. Following a traffic accident in which your car is damaged, you may think, "At least I didn't get hurt." By imagining an even worse outcome, your accident seems less negative by contrast (Sanna et al., 2001). Besides helping us emotionally cope in the present, a second function of counterfactual thoughts may be to better prepare us for the future. By considering alternatives to past actions, we can better understand our mistakes and thereby improve our chances for future success (Galinsky & Moskowitz, 2000). For example, after doing poorly on an exam, you may mentally imagine alternative study strategies that you could have used, such as memorizing key terms or working through the study guide. If you implement these new strategies in preparing for your next exam, you may improve your grade.

Summarizing these two functions, then, we can say that imagining alternative versions or outcomes to what actually happened may not only help us emotionally cope with negative events, but it may also help us to achieve success in the future. Unfortunately, as discussed in Chapter 3 (p. 75), the sustaining of negative affect is often necessary to motivate behavioral change. When counterfactual thinking is used to emotionally cope with a negative event, our improved mood can reduce our motivation to take corrective steps to avoid similar negative events in the future (McMullen & Markman, 2000).

Sometimes counterfactual thinking is not only ineffective in emotionally coping with negative events, it is downright counterproductive. This is most likely following traumatic life events when the reality is already the worst-case scenario. For instance, Christopher Davis and his coworkers (1995) interviewed people who had lost a spouse or a child in an accident. The more they imagined how the tragedy could have been averted by mentally undoing events preceding it, the more distress and guilt they felt. This tendency to engage in counterfactual thinking following traumatic life events also helps to explain why crime victims often blame themselves for their victimization (C. Davis et al., 1996). In trying to understand how their plight could have been avoided, victims tend to focus on trivial aspects of their own behavior rather than on the causally more significant behavior of the perpetrator. If they can imagine some plausible way in which they *could* have prevented the crime, they may come to believe that they *should* have prevented it. Although crime victims who engage in such counter-factual thinking may not blame themselves for being the cause of their injuries, they may blame themselves for not avoiding the situation that was the cause (Mandel, 2003; Miller & Turnbull, 1990). Recent studies suggest that psychological therapies that challenge such harmful counterfactual thinking can help people effectively deal with these life tragedies (Petrocelli et al., 2011)

SUPPRESSING THOUGHTS CAN SOMETIMES BACKFIRE.

thought suppression
. . . .
The attempt to prevent certain thoughts from entering consciousness

In counterfactual thinking, mentally reconfiguring past events and imagining alternative outcomes often occurs spontaneously without people intending on rehashing these experiences. If such thoughts are unwelcome, people often try to consciously suppress them. Such **thought suppression** is a good example of explicit and implicit cognition working in tandem to prevent unwelcome thoughts from entering consciousness. When studying for an exam, you engage in thought suppression by trying not to think about things that would distract you from learning the course material. Likewise, when dieting you avoid thinking about your favorite foods. As these examples suggest, thought suppression plays an important role in self-regulation, which was a topic of discussion in Chapter 3 (pp. 73–78).

Keeping undesired thoughts out of consciousness requires two different cognitive processes, one that is relatively automatic and the other that is more deliberate (Wegner, 1994). First, the automatic *monitoring process* of implicit cognition acts like an "early warning system" by searching for evidence that the undesired thoughts are about to intrude into consciousness. When such evidence is found, the more controlled *operating process* of explicit cognition is activated. This second cognitive process acts like an active prevention system, consciously distracting attention away from the unwanted thoughts by finding something else to think about.

When you are well rested and highly motivated, these two cognitive processes work pretty well together to keep unwanted thoughts from intruding into consciousness. However, as you know from personal experience, when you become tired or lose focus, your ability to suppress these thoughts declines rapidly. When studying for that test, you may find yourself thinking about your friends having fun at a party, despite your best efforts at concentration. When dieting, you may discover that the more you try not to consume your favorite foods, the more they seem to consume your thoughts ("They're calling to me!"). What appears to be happening here is that the automatic monitoring process continues its identification of unwanted thoughts, but the more controlled operating process no longer has sufficient cognitive resources to direct conscious awareness away from these thoughts. Faced with this breakdown, the unwanted thoughts come flooding into consciousness in what is called the *rebound effect or ironic reversal* (Wegner & Schneider, 2003). Additional research suggests that people in a negative mood are better able to suppress unwanted thoughts than those in a positive mood (Wyland & Forgas, 2007). This is so because negative moods promote just the kind of attentive, detail-oriented information processing required for successful thought suppression. The downside of this greater success, however, is that thought suppressors who are in a negative mood later experience larger rebound effects.

Studies examining the neural correlates of thought suppression using functional magnetic resonance imaging (*f*MRI) have found a certain brain region more active when people are trying to suppress a particular thought than when they are thinking freely about any thought (Mitchell et al., 2007). This region, the *anterior cingulate*, is in the frontal lobes of the cerebral cortex. As you recall from Chapter 3 (pp. 68 and 69), this same brain region plays a critical role in self-awareness and the general process of self-regulation. Neuroscientists believe that psychological disorders involving recurring, intrusive thoughts, such as anxiety disorders (for example, phobias, obsessive-compulsive disorders, and posttraumatic stress disorder), may involve an underactive anterior cingulate.

Although thought suppression often plays a critical role in keeping us focused so that we can accomplish goals, there can be physical and emotional costs to this aspect of self-regulation (Hooper et al., 2010; Purdon et al., 2007). For instance, in one study, medical students were asked to write about a personal topic once a day for three days (Petrie et al., 1998). In the experimental condition, students were told to suppress all thoughts about what they had just written for five minutes, while in the control condition no such instructions were given. Results indicated that the students who engaged in thought suppression experienced a significant decrease in immune system functioning compared with those who had not suppressed thoughts. Similarly, Richard Wenzlaff and David Luxton (2003) identified people who had low levels of negative thoughts and depression but who differed in their habitual tendencies to engage in thought suppression. Ten weeks later, they found that high suppressors who had experienced relatively high levels of stress reported the greatest increase in negative thoughts and unhappiness compared with all other participants. Together, these studies suggest that thought suppression can take both a physical and mental toll on our health, especially during times of stress.

SECTION SUMMARY

- The hindsight bias involves overestimating our ability to have foreseen the outcome of an event

- Counterfactual thinking involves evaluating events by imagining alternative versions or outcomes.

- Thought suppression involves both an automatic "early warning" monitoring process for unwanted thoughts and a conscious "active prevention" operating process to distract attention away from the unwanted thoughts.

PERSON PERCEPTION

When Stephen Glass's story about the teenaged computer hacker began generating skeptical queries from another magazine, his coworkers initially strongly defended their colleague's honesty and integrity. As observers of Glass's past self-presentations, they had formed an impression of him that resulted in their rejecting this new unflattering information because it was so inconsistent with their existing beliefs. The process by which we try to detect other people's temporary states—such as their emotions, intentions, and desires—and their enduring dispositions—such as their beliefs, traits, and abilities—is known as **person perception** (Gilbert, 1998). This aspect of social cognition is often not a single, instantaneous event but rather comprises a number of ongoing processes, as illustrated in the Stephen Glass scandal.

person perception

The process by which we try to detect other people's temporary states and enduring dispositions (also called social perception)

The process of forming impressions of others is viewed by social psychologists as a dynamic one, involving both explicit and implicit cognition, with judgments being continually updated in response to new information (Freeman & Ambady, 2011; Todorov, 2011). It is analogous to building a "working model" of a person and then using this as a guideline in our actions toward him or her (Ickes, 2003). Person perception is also integrative, meaning that each bit of information about a person is interpreted within the context of all the other information we have about her or him. As you will discover, however, not all bits of information are created equal (Kenny, 2004).

NONVERBAL BEHAVIORS OF OTHERS SHAPE OUR IMPRESSIONS OF THEM.

nonverbal communication

Communicating feelings and intentions without words.

First impressions—the first phase of person perception—are often based on **nonverbal communication**, which is the sending and receiving of information using gestures, expressions, vocal cues, and body movements rather than words (Ambady & Weisbuch, 2010). Whether a person smiles when greeted by another, whether a person's walk is "bouncy" or "purposeful," or whether one's gestures are expansive or constricted can provide important information in developing a working model of those we meet on a daily basis. Two of the more important nonverbal channels of communication are facial expressions and body movements.

Facial Expressions and Emotions

The face is a critical stimulus in person perception (Ito, 2011; Macrae et al., 2005). More than two thousand years ago, the Roman orator Marcus Cicero wrote that the "face is the image of the soul." Centuries later, Charles Darwin (1872) proposed that *facial expressions* play an important role in communication, and that certain emotional expressions are also inborn and thus are understood throughout the world. Studies conducted during the past thirty years generally support Darwin's assertions: there is substantial cross-cultural agreement in both the experience and expression of emotions although certain emotions are easier to distinguish than others (Ekman, 1994; Izard, 1994; Elfenbein & Ambady, 2002). For example, people from all cultures can easily tell the difference between happiness and anger, but it is harder for them to distinguish adoration from desire. The upshot of these findings is that most researchers have concluded that certain emotions are more basic, or *primary*, than others. Primary emotions are similar to primary colors in perception. Like primary colors, by combining primary emotions and altering their intensity, the full variety of other emotions can be derived. Most classification lists include the following seven primary emotions: *anger, disgust, fear, happiness, surprise, sadness* and *contempt* (although some dispute that contempt is a primary emotion). These primary emotions are also the ones people around the world can accurately "read" by examining facial expressions.

Facial expressions signaling specific emotions tend to be brief, lasting between one and five seconds; and they are hard to produce voluntarily (Keltner & Lerner, 2010). There is a noticeable difference, for example, between a genuine smile of pleasure and a forced smile, but most people cannot reliably tell the difference. When a smile is genuine, the eyes crease up and the end of the eyebrows dip slightly (Ekman et al., 1988).

When Darwin proposed that certain emotional expressions are universally understood, it was within the context of introducing evolutionary theory to the sciences. He believed that this ability to recognize emotion from the observation of facial expressions was genetically programmed into our species and had survival value for us. How might this ability aid survival? One possibility is that being able to read the emotions of others by attending to facial expressions allows us to not only better predict their behavioral intentions ("Do they mean to harm me?") but also to understand how others are interpreting the world ("Why are they afraid? Are we all in danger in this situation?"). This "survival value" hypothesis would

Happiness is a primary emotion easily recognized in people's facial expressions.

predict that we do not attend equally to all facial expressions, but rather exhibit the most sensitivity to those that would give us the best chances of survival. In other words, we should be most attentive to facial expressions that signal potential danger.

Research supports the survival value hypothesis. For instance, a number of studies have shown people pictures of crowds of faces to determine what facial expressions were most recognizable in such a clustered setting. As Darwin would have predicted, people spotted threatening faces (anger first, fear second) faster and more accurately than nonthreatening faces, even when the nonthreatening faces depicted negative emotions such as sadness (Hansen & Hansen 1988; Öhman et al., 2001). The threatening faces appeared to "pop out of the crowd," while the nonthreatening faces were often overlooked. Apparently, the threatening facial expressions function as general danger cues, evoking anxiety and preparing people for self-protective action. Interestingly, people's current psychological needs can sensitize them to specific facial expressions. In one study, when researchers induced a fear of social rejection and loneliness in participants, they were quicker to notice faces in a crowd with friendly, welcoming expressions (DeWall et al., 2009).

Body Movements and Nonconscious Mimicry

Besides facial cues, the body as a whole can convey a wealth of information (Keating, 2006). For example, people who walk with a good deal of hip sway, knee bending, loose jointedness, and body bounce are perceived to be younger and more powerful than those who walk with less pronounced gaits (Montepare & Zebrowitz-McArthur, 1988). Numerous studies indicate that observers often infer other people's underlying emotional states by reading their body movements during social interaction. For example, body movements that are fast, energetic, and spatially expansive signal to observers that the person displaying these movements is angry or elated, rather than sad or bored (Macrae & Quadflieg, 2010).

In a creative analysis of dance characters in classical ballet, Joel Aronoff and his colleagues (1992) found that the body and arm displays of the angry and threatening characters were more *diagonal* or *angular*, while those of the warm and welcoming characters were more *rounded* (refer to Figure 4.3). Subsequent studies with college students found that, when asked to evaluate various geometric shapes, participants judged those with diagonal shapes to be worse, powerful, and active than those that were rounded. It appears from these findings that people analyze the shape of large-scale body movements to better determine another person's behavioral intentions. Additional cross-cultural research revealed that diagonal and angled geometric patterns appear to be universally identified with angry emotions, while rounded geometric patterns seem to convey happy emotions (Aronoff, 2006). Together, this research suggests that body movements, in addition to facial gestures, convey a wide variety of information to others that may well have a significant impact on our perceptions of them. Yet although there are commonly shared meanings of many physical gestures, it is also true that people from different cultures often assign different meanings to the same physical movements. *Self/Social Connection Exercise 4.1* provides a brief sketch of how certain nonverbal cues are interpreted differently around the world and a suggestion for a nonverbal exercise to try yourself.

Beyond interpreting the meaning of specific nonverbal gestures, our perception of others is also shaped by **nonconscious mimicry**, which is the tendency to adopt the behaviors, postures, or mannerisms of interaction partners without conscious awareness or intention (Chartrand et al., 2002). What are some examples of nonconscious mimicry? When conversing with others, we tend to mimic their speech tendencies and accents, we laugh and yawn when they do, and we adopt their body postures and gestures (DePaulo & Friedman, 1998; Yoon & Tennie, 2010). Mimicking others' facial expressions appears to be so inborn that one-month-old infants have been shown to smile, stick out their tongues, and open their mouths when they see someone else doing the same (Meltzoff & Moore, 1989).

Evidence that mimicry is often nonconscious and unintentional comes from a number of studies (Lakin & Chartrand, 2003; van Baaren et al., 2003b), including an experiment by Tanya Chartrand and John Bargh (1999) where participants interacted with two

----

"Your face, my thane, is as a book where men may read strange matters."

Shakespeare, English poet and playwright, 1564–1616, from *Macbeth*, Act 1, Scene 5

"You know about a person who deeply interests you more than you can be told. A look, a gesture, an act—which to everybody else is insignificant—tells you more about that one than words can."

Henry David Thoreau, philosopher, author, naturalist, 1817–1862

----

nonconscious mimicry

The tendency to adopt the behaviors, postures, or mannerisms of interaction partners without conscious awareness or intention

Figure 4.3

Rounded, Diagonal, and Angular Body Displays

Based on an analysis of classical ballet dance movement and people's judgments of simple geo-metric shapes, Aronoff and his colleagues (1992) contend that rounded body postures convey warmth and friendliness to an observer, while diagonal and angled body postures imply threat and danger. Using this information, try a little experiment on your friends. Act out some diago-nal and angled body displays for them, as well as some that are rounded. In this variation of "charades," what sort of emotions do they believe underlie each of these body displays?

unknown confederates. For half the participants, the first confederate rubbed her face and the second confederate shook her foot throughout their interaction. For the other participants, the confederates reversed roles. Results revealed that participants mim-icked the gestures of the confederates—they rubbed their face more when they were with the face-rubber than the foot-shaker, and they shook their foot more when they were with the foot-shaker than the face-rubber. When the experiment was over and par-ticipants were asked about the gestures of the confederates and about their own ges-tures, they did not report noticing either.

Insight into the biological basis for nonconscious mimicry comes from PET scans and EEG recordings of people's brains while they observe another person performing an action: Similar neural circuits are firing in the observers' brains as they are firing in the brains of those who are carrying out the action (Iacoboni, 2007). These specialized neural circuits located in the premotor cortex are called *mirror neurons* (Gallese et al., 2007; Oberman et al., 2007). The firing of these mirror neurons probably does not directly cause imitative behavior, but they may serve as the basis of imitation learning, which is closely associated with mimicry.

Self/Social Connections Exercise 4.1

What Are a Few Cultural Differences in Nonverbal Behavior?

Although a number of facial gestures and body movements appear to convey universal meaning, here are some nonverbal behaviors that are more culture-specific. To avoid misunderstandings when traveling overseas, or when hosting an international visitor, North Americans should duly note that everyday gestures and accepted interaction patterns in this culture are not universally shared.

Eye contact: Most North Americans and Arabs are taught to look others directly in the eye when conversing. Avoiding eye contact is considered to be a sign of shyness, disinterest, or weakness. In Japan, Nigeria, Puerto Rico, Thailand and Korea, people are taught to avert the eyes and avoid direct eye contact. There, engaging in eye contact is considered intimidating, disrespectful, or perhaps a signal of sexual interest.

Nodding the head: When North Americans nod their heads up and down, this means "yes," while shaking their heads from side to side means "no." The opposite meaning holds true in some areas of India and Africa. In Korea, shaking the head means "I don't know."

Shaking hands: North Americans are taught to shake hands as a friendly sign of greeting. A firm, solid grip is thought to convey confidence and good character. Japanese prefer greeting one another by bowing, Southeast Asians press their own palms together in a praying motion, and when Middle Easterners and many Asians shake hands, they prefer a gentle grip, because a firm grip suggests aggressiveness.

Touching: North Americans and Japanese are generally not very touch oriented, and hugging is almost never done among casual acquaintances, especially among men. In contrast, Latin Americans, Koreans, and those in the Middle East often embrace and hold hands as a sign of friendship.

Personal Space: North Americans and northern Europeans generally maintain a distance of about thirty inches during normal social interaction. Asians tend to stand farther apart, and Latin Americans, Middle Easterners, and southern Europeans stand very close, often brushing up against one another. In those cultures where space relationships are small, moving away is interpreted as a sign of unfriendliness.

Spend some time breaking each of the above nonverbal social norms for your culture. For example, if you are a North American, when conversing with others, avoid eye contact, reverse your head nodding when voicing agreement and disagreement, press your palms together when greeting others, purposefully touch people, and invade their personal space. What sort of reactions does your norm breaking elicit from your social targets? Ask these individuals whether they noticed your norm breaking and inquire about their cognitive and emotional reactions.

How does mimicking affect the person perception process? In a follow-up experiment to their face-rubbing/foot-shaking study, Chartrand and Bargh (1999) found evidence that mimicry increases liking for the imitator. The researchers instructed confederates to subtly imitate the mannerisms of people they were interacting with in a "get acquainted" session (for example, rubbing their face or tapping their foot when their partner did so). Their findings indicated that people whose gestures had been mimicked liked the confederates more than those who had not been mimicked. Similarly, in a field experiment (van Baaren et al., 2003a), waitresses who verbally mimicked their customers by repeating their orders were given bigger tips than those who replied to orders

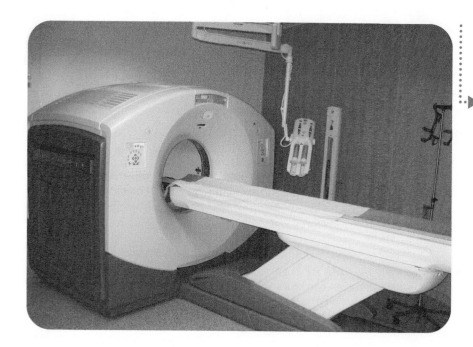

PET scans give us insight into the basis of nonconscious mimicry.

by saying "okay!" or "coming up!" Additional research indicates that as people interact with one another and establish rapport, they exhibit an increase in mimicking each other's gestures (Jefferis et al., 2003; van Baaren et al., 2006). This mimicry not only increases their prosocial behavior toward one another, but the targets of mimickers also become more prosocial to others in the immediate vicinity (van Baaren et al., 2004). Together, these studies suggest that mimicry triggers positive reactions in people that lead to benefits to those who are present.

Why do we have this fascinating tendency to mimic? What function does it serve? As previously discussed in Chapter 1 (p. 24), throughout human evolution, individual survival and success at reproduction depended on our ancestors having successful social interactions. Individuals who were able to cooperate with others and maintain harmonious social ties were more likely included in group activities, thereby giving them an adaptive advantage over those who were ostracized from the group. Due to this process of natural selection, behaviors that fostered group cohesion eventually became widespread throughout the human population (Caporael, 2001). Over time, many of these behaviors became automatically activated without awareness. A number of social scientists believe that nonconscious mimicry is an example of this form of automatically activated behavior that creates affiliation and rapport among people, and thereby fosters safety in groups (Chartrand et al., 2005; de Waal, 2002).

CULTURE AND GENDER INFLUENCE THE EXPRESSION OF NONVERBAL CUES.

Recognizing the important role that nonverbal behavior plays in person perception, people often consciously employ nonverbal cues in their self-presentation strategies (Matsumoto & Willingham, 2006; Mendoza-Denton, 2008). For example, have you ever forced yourself to smile at someone you did not like? Have you ever deliberately fixed someone with a cold, angry stare to convey your displeasure or your feeling of social dominance?

Given the important role that emotions play in human interactions, it makes abundant sense that cultures would develop social rules for when and how different emotions are expressed (Mesquita & Frijda, 1992). For example, the cultural belief systems of individualism and collectivism have shaped norms related to acting in ways that might threaten group harmony. That is, collectivists are much more likely than individualists to monitor their behavior so that it does not disrupt the smooth functioning of the group. Regarding emotions, although people from collectivist and individualist cultures do not generally differ in publicly displaying positive emotions, collectivists are much more uncomfortable about publicly expressing negative emotions (Matsumoto et al., 2002; Stephan et al., 1996).

Whether you tend to use the forced smile over the cold stare may also be associated with your gender socialization and the resulting social roles you learned (Brody, 1999). A **social role** is a cluster of socially defined expectations that individuals in a given situation are expected to fulfill. According to Alice Eagly's (1987, 1996) **social role theory**, the different social roles occupied by women and men lead to differences in the perception of their behavior. In other words, because the two sexes typically operate in different domains within most societies—for example, women in the home and men in the world of paid employment—they engage in different patterns of behavior to properly play their roles. Social role theorists contend that the two sexes do not differ in their ability to experience an array of emotions, but they do differ in monitoring which emotions they publicly express. In a meta-analysis of about 110,000 participants in 162 studies, Marianne LaFrance and her colleagues (2003) found that women and adolescent girls smile more than men and adolescent boys. Further, this gender difference is stronger during same-sex interactions (male-male or female-female) than during other-sex encounters (male-female). LaFrance contends that the likely reason females smile the most when with other females and males smile the least when with other males is because gender norms for smiling are most in effect when people are interacting with those of their same sex.

A key factor underlying these gender norms is the exercise of social power and dominance within society. For women, the most acceptable emotional style to publicly display is *extravagant expressiveness*, which is an open style of experiencing and communicating emotion associated with nurturing and intimate relationships (Shields, 2002, 2007). For men, the most acceptable emotional style is *manly emotion*, which telegraphs intense emotion under control. The underlying message of manly emotion is that the person is independent and powerful: "I can control my emotion (and thereby, my *self*), and I can harness it to control the situation." In contrast, the underlying message of extravagant expressiveness involves nurturance and service: "My emotion (and thereby, my *self*) is at your service and I am not seeking power." Research indicates that boys are encouraged to express emotions—such as anger, contempt, and pride—that reflect a sense of entitlement to power in society and are discouraged from displaying vulnerable emotions. In contrast, this same research suggests that girls are encouraged to express emotions associated with satisfaction, powerlessness, and service to others, such as happiness, fear, and empathy (Buck, 1977; Saarni, 1999). Consistent with this encouragement, women are not only better nonverbal communicators of happiness than men, but they are also better at masking disappointment

social role

A cluster of socially defined expectations that individuals in a given situation are expected to fulfill

social role theory

The theory that virtually all of the documented behavioral differences between males and females can be accounted for in terms of cultural stereotypes about gender and the resulting social roles that are taught to the young.

Research has shown that women tend to smile more when with other women than men do when with other men.

Critical
THINKING

How might an evolutionary theorist explain the gender differences in decoding nonverbal communication? That is, from an evolutionary perspective, why would it be more beneficial for females than males to have good nonverbal skills?

with a positive expression (Davis, 1995). In thinking about your own upbringing, are your skills at constructing fixed stares and forced smiles consistent with these gender socialization patterns?

Beyond the gender differences in using specific nonverbal cues, meta-analytic studies indicate that females are significantly more adept than males in *decoding* nonverbal communication. For example, in a review of seventy-five studies testing the ability of men and women to decode nonverbal behavior, Judith Hall (1978) found that 68 percent of the investigations reported superior female performance. Later meta-analyses found that this gender difference is greatest for decoding facial expressions, next largest for body cues, and smallest for correctly interpreting voice tone (Hall, 1984). The studies further suggest that this gender difference is not isolated in adult samples but can also be found in adolescents and children. Although these gender differences vary in size from study to study, females appear to be consistently better than males at decoding nonverbal cues (Brody & Hall, 1993).

As with emotional expression, social psychologists principally explain these gender differences in reading nonverbal cues by examining the different social roles played by females and males. Because the social roles played by women tend to have lower status relative to male roles, it is more important for women to learn to be accommodating and polite (Mast & Hall, 2004). Thus, by being more skilled at nonverbal communication, females are better able to understand people's feelings and thus increase their interpersonal comfort. This explanation is consistent with research indicating that regardless of gender, those who have less powerful social roles are more sensitive to the feelings of their superiors than vice versa (Hecht & LaFrance, 1998). Beyond gender and status considerations, research also finds that intimacy fosters more accurate decoding of subdued facial expressions. People involved in close friendships are more accurate at reading their friends' subtle facial expressions compared to reading the subtle expressions of those who are less close to them (Zhang & Parmley, 2011).

OUR BRAINS ARE WIRED FOR GOSSIP.

As already discussed, we more quickly recognize faces that convey anger and fear compared to other emotions. Evolutionary theorists contend that this heightened attentiveness to negative emotions in others is adaptive because these facial expressions signal potential danger; and therefore, quickly recognizing such emotions better prepares us for self-protective actions (Rozin & Royzman, 2001). These findings are consistent with research indicating that, when forming impressions of others, we give more weight to negative information than positive information (Lupfer et al., 2000; Peeters, 2003). The common explanation for this *negativity effect* is that negative information about someone is more unusual and therefore more distinctive. The automatic nature of attending more to negative information has been repeatedly demonstrated in brain imaging studies and provides further evidence that evolution favored brain mechanisms that facilitate a rapid and intense response to aversive events (Carretie et al., 2003; Smith et al., 2003).

One commonly used avenue to convey negative information about others is gossip (Foster & Rosnow, 2006). In a recent brain imaging study, Eric Anderson and his coworkers (2011) found evidence that gossiping may have become such a popular pastime for human beings not simply because we enjoy learning about the personal flaws of others but also because gaining such information through gossiping increased our ancestors' ability to survive and reproduce. In this study, the researchers first showed participants photos of individuals with neutral facial expressions paired with negative, positive, or neutral gossip about them (see Figure 4.4). An example of negative gossip was "threw a chair at his classmate," an example of positive gossip was "helped an elderly woman with her groceries," and an example of neutral gossip was "passed a man on the street." Next, while their brain activity was being measured, participants were presented with different visual images to their two eyes, an image of a human face and a nonhuman image, such as a house. The human faces presented to the participants were those that were previously associated with negative, neutral, or positive gossip. Because the brain can only process one visual image at a time, when competing images are presented to the two different eyes, the brain tends to focus on

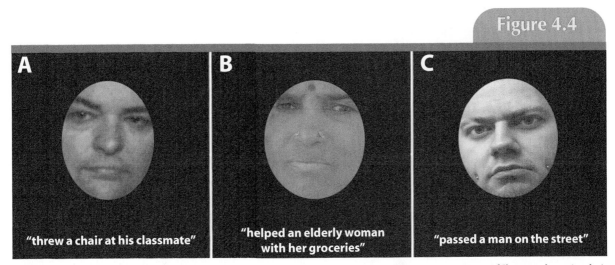

When participants were shown a neutral face paired with (A) negative gossip, (B) positive gossip, or (C) neutral gossip, their brains were later more likely to fix on the faces associated with negative gossip. How do these findings relate to the negativity effect in impression formation?

the image it considers more important. Results indicated that participants' brains were most likely to focus on faces associated with negative gossip.

Based on these findings, Anderson and his coworkers concluded that our brains appear to be hardwired to pay more attention to people if we've been told they are dangerous or dishonest or unpleasant. From this perspective, you could argue that interest in gossip is not necessarily a character flaw—it simply may be a basic human trait that exists for good evolutionary reasons. In other words, even when primitive humans lived in small groups, they needed to know who in their group might be a threat to them and who couldn't be trusted. One shortcut in obtaining such important information would have been gossip. Our ancestors who had an interest in gossip gained a competitive advantage over those in their group who did not engage in gossiping. Perhaps this is why people throughout the world, both women and men equally, devote anywhere from a fifth to two-thirds or more of their daily conversation to gossip (Dunbar, 1996). Of course, this does not mean that all gossip is good for a group and that all gossipers are viewed positively. Studies find that self-serving gossip is frowned upon and can actually harm a group because it poses a threat to healthy group functioning and productivity (Kniffin & Wilson, 2005). Further, people who are known to be high-frequency gossipers tend to be viewed negatively, especially if their gossiping emphasizes negative information about others (Farley, 2011).

MOST OF US ARE POOR DECEPTION DETECTORS.

In the 2009 movie *The Invention of Lying*, the main character—played by actor Ricky Gervais—lives in a world where no one has ever lied, until he seizes the opportunity for personal gain. The humor in this movie is based on how absolutely gullible everyone is to the main character's outrageous lies. How common is lying in everyday life, and how gullible are we to others' deceptions?

Research informs us that while we are not born liars by about four or five years of age we have the ability to effectively tell strategic lies, and this ability increases in sophistication as we mature (Evans et al., 2011). During an average week, we lie to about one-third of those with whom we interact, and we also often lie during job interviews (Griffith et al., 2007; Weiss & Feldman, 2006)? On average, we tell about ten lies per week, with the greatest lying committed by those of us who are more sociable, manipulative, and concerned about creating favorable self-presentations (DePaulo et al., 1996; Kashy & DePaulo, 1996). Although lying is a fact of life, it is a risky and often costly self-presentation strategy. We dislike those who frequently deceive us and tend to reciprocate with lies of our own (Tyler et al., 2006).

In the film *The Invention of Lying,* Ricky Gervais' character lives in a world where everyone tells the truth and no one has any notion of lying. Have you ever lied for personal gain? If you answered "no" to that question, you are almost certainly lying.

Given that others may try to conceal their true feelings and intentions from us, how do we—as person perceivers—respond to the possibility of such subterfuge? Erving Goffman (1959) contended that when we judge other people's self-presentations, we pay attention to two different types of social stimuli, which he called *expressions*. First, there are expressions that people freely "give" to others in what is typically thought of as their traditional communication patterns. These *given expressions* consist of the words and gestures that people are consciously trying to transmit to others. Besides these strategic gestures, there are also expressions that people "give off," which are mostly nonverbal in nature. *Expressions given off*, also known as *nonverbal leakage*, cover a wide range of behavior unintentionally transmitted and of which people are much less aware. The lack of gusto when chewing a host's poorly prepared meal and the tortured look on your face are examples of expressions given off.

Of the two types of expressions, those unintentionally "given off" by self-presenters are better indicators of possible deception than those consciously "given" (Ekman & O'Sullivan, 1991). Unfortunately, in those situations where detecting lies is most important to us, we tend to give more weight to messages that people consciously convey to us. James Forrest and Robert Feldman (2000) found that when people were highly involved in a discussion topic, they paid more attention to speakers' words, and thus, were more easily deceived than less involved people, who attended more to nonverbal behavior.

Although attending to nonverbal behavior can improve our ability to reveal the lie in others' self-presentations, not all nonverbal cues are equally instructive. One mistake we often make is placing too much importance on the face to reveal deception. We tend to believe that others do not smile when they lie, when in fact, smiling is a common device used by deceivers to hide their true feelings (Ekman et al., 1988). We also tend to believe that liars won't look us in the eye (Wyland & Forgas, 2010), which experienced deceivers use to their advantage. We are also often fooled by the *structure* of people's faces, falsely assuming that babyfaced individuals (large eyes and symmetrical facial features) and physically attractive persons are more honest than those with mature-looking and less attractive faces (Zebrowitz & Montepare, 1992; Zebrowitz et al., 1996).

It is sometimes possible to detect deception by attending to certain changes in people's speech patterns—what is known as *paralanguage*—and by analyzing the quality of their stories (see Table 4.1). Several studies indicate that when people lie, they give shorter answers, their stories make less sense, their voices sound tense, and their pitch rises slightly (DePaulo et al., 2003). Liars' speech is also slower and filled with many pauses ("ahs" and "uhms") and other sentence hesitations. Experts believe that the less complexity, logic, and fluidity of liars' stories, combined with the heightened voice tension, reflect the additional cognitive burden of their attempt to deceive. Liars also tend to use fewer first-person singular pronouns (*I, me, my*) and sound less involved in their storytelling, which is thought to reflect their attempt to dissociate themselves from the lie (Newman et al., 2003). Finally, liars also use negative emotion words at a higher rate than truth tellers, which may be caused by their feeling of guilt, triggering negative emotions (Newman et al., 2003; Vrij, 2000). These cues to deception are more likely to be revealed when people are lying about something very important rather than for more trivial matters (DePaulo & Morris, 2004).

However, despite such cues, meta-analysis of more than two hundred experiments finds that people are just slightly better than chance—54 percent—at distinguishing truths from lies (Bond & DePaulo, 2006). This is, also, the accuracy level of those who make these judgments for a living, such as judges, police officers, CIA polygraphers, and customs inspectors. Indeed, the best of the professional deception detectors, namely Secret Service

Table 4.1

What Are Some Possible Verbal Symptoms of Lying?

SYMPTOMS	LIKELY CAUSES
Shorter answers to questions Stories make less sense. Slower speech filled with pauses and other sentence hesitations	The cognitive burden of concealing the truth interferes with the generation of smooth conversation.
Slight rise in voice pitch and vocal tension	Activation of the sympathetic nervous system
Less use of first-person singular pronouns Sounds less involved in what they are saying	Psychological attempt to dissociate oneself from the lie
More use of negative emotion words	Feelings of guilt trigger negative emotions.

agents, are successful only about 70 percent of the time (Ekman & O'Sullivan, 1991). People are particularly bad at detecting deception from strangers (Anderson et al., 1999). One important reason for this low level of accuracy among the unacquainted is that people often individually behave in distinctive ways when lying. However, when interacting with strangers we have no knowledge of their distinctive "lying signals." Fortunately, we do appear to gain insight into people's telltale lying signals the longer we know them. In a longitudinal study of friendship development, researchers found that friends become more accurate in detecting each other's deception as their relationship progresses, improving from 47 percent accuracy early in the friendship to 61 percent accuracy after five months (Anderson et al., 2002). Of course, this accuracy level is still not up to the standards of Secret Service agents (who still have a 30 percent failure rate!), but it does provide some hope that we can improve our deception detection skills in important areas of our lives. The key ingredient in increasing your ability to detect deception is having relevant information. The more relevant information you have about people who might be deceiving you and the more relevant information you have about the social context in which the possible deception occurs, the greater your ability to identify lies from truths (Blair et al., 2010; Levine, et al., 2010).

Taken as a whole, the research suggests that deceivers often succeed in duping us regardless of our sex, race, cultural background, socioeconomic status, or educational level; and they are most successful when we do not know them well and the issue is important to us (Geary & DePaulo, 2007). However, it is also true that liars are most likely to reveal deception cues when the issue is important to them. Perhaps the primary reason why we so often fail to detect deception is that, by and large, we tend to believe that others are basically honest (Zuckerman et al., 1981). Yet one thing that works to our advantage when dealing with habitual liars is that while we may not detect their deception the first few times, we are more likely to do so as we observe them over time and become more familiar with their self-presentation strategies (Yamagishi et al., 2003).

WE DEVELOP IMPLICIT PERSONALITY THEORIES BASED ON CENTRAL TRAITS.

The initial phase of person perception often involves little cognitive effort and is based on easily recognizable physical characteristics, such as sex, age, and race, as well as nonverbal actions presented by the target persons (Fiske & Neuberg, 1990; Park, 1986). If the individuals are of no interest or the interaction is very brief, we will not bother to analyze them further and may judge them based on cultural stereotypes. However, if we are motivated to learn more about these people as individuals, our thinking becomes more deliberate and effortful, resulting in our impressions becoming more abstract and less tied to superficial physical qualities (Sherman & Klein, 1994; Van Overwalle et al., 1999). Some of these more descriptive characteristics are *traits*, which are stable personal qualities such as "intelligent," "kind," and "unscrupulous." Because personality traits are commonly used in forming impressions (Fiske & Cox, 1979), one of the first questions asked by social psychologists was how traits are combined to form a meaningful picture of a person.

In the 1940s, Solomon Asch worked within the German tradition of *Gestalt psychology*, which studied how the mind actively organizes stimuli into a coherent whole, or *gestalt*. In person perception, Asch hypothesized that our overall impression of others is not simply determined by adding up all their personality traits. Instead, certain traits exert greater influence than do others on people's overall impressions, literally changing the meaning of other traits. In other words, not all traits are equally important in person perception: the whole is more than the sum of its parts. He called the dominant traits **central traits**.

In testing this hypothesis, Asch (1946) asked participants to examine a list of discrete traits that belonged to a particular person and then form an impression based on this information. For some participants, the following traits were presented: intelligent, skillful, industrious, warm, determined, practical, and cautious. For other participants, the trait *warm* was replaced with the trait *cold*, but otherwise everything else was identical. Those who had been told that the hypothetical person was warm rated him as significantly more generous, humorous, sociable, and popular than those who had been told that he was cold. In contrast to the effect of switching these two central traits, when Asch switched the traits *polite* and *blunt* from a similar list that people rated, the resulting impressions differed very little from one another. These less important traits Asch called *peripheral traits*.

Asch's (1946) groundbreaking study was later replicated in real-life settings (Judd et al., 2005; Kelley, 1950). However, additional research indicated that the importance of specific traits varies depending on the social context in which we make evaluations (Singh & Teoh, 2000). For example, the traits *intelligent* and *humorous* may generally have equal value in forming impressions of people, but *intelligent* would carry more weight for a psychology department's graduate school admissions committee when evaluating applicants, while *humorous* would have more of an impact on the owner of a comedy nightclub when looking for a new act.

Inspired by Asch's ideas about central traits, social cognitive theorists proposed that our knowledge about specific *types* of individuals is structured by assumptions or naive belief systems that we develop after learning something about their central traits. These **implicit personality theories** are a type of schema (Bruner & Taguiri, 1954; Norenzayan et al., 2002). Like many other schemas, implicit personality theories are shaped by both personal experiences and cultural beliefs, and they are often passed from generation to generation (Chiu et al., 2000). Thus, for example, many people within American culture have similar implicit personality theories about honest people and dishonest people. In these personality assumptions, we tend to assume that all good things occur together in persons and that all bad things do so as well, with little overlap between the two. In other words, there appears to be operating a principle of *evaluative consistency*, which is a tendency to view others in a way that is internally consistent (Hosoda et al., 2003; Leyens, 1991). When contradictory information is made available, we are reluctant to abandon our existing implicit theory, often distorting or explaining away the contradictions (Plaks et al., 2005). Thus, when Stephen Glass was accused of fabricating his news stories, almost everybody who knew him or knew of him was shocked. Glass was the epitome of the young, hardworking, honest, ambitious journalist. He just didn't seem like *the kind of person* who would do such a thing. These people's implicit personality theory of Stephen Glass caused them to initially believe that a respected, high-profile reporter could not possibly be making up his urban stories. This conclusion was arrived at because the alternative judgment ("Glass is a liar") was inconsistent with their assumptions about the relationships among traits and behaviors (Cook et al., 2003).

Although implicit personality theories are commonly employed in making social judgments, some people rely on them more than others (Gervey et al., 1999). In studies conducted in both individualist and collectivist cultures, it appears that implicit theories are used more often by people who believe that personality consists of fixed, static traits than by those who believe that personality is dynamic and changing (Church et al., 2003; Werth

central traits

·····················

Traits that exert a disproportionate influence on people's overall impressions, causing them to assume the presence of other traits

implicit personality theories

·····················

A type of schema people use to organize and make sense of which personality traits and behaviors go together.

& Foerster, 2002). These findings are important because they suggest that although implicit personality theories may be used by people around the world, there is a good deal of *individual* variation in the extent to which they are used. Additionally, findings by Chi-yue Chiu and his colleagues (1997) point toward a possible *cultural* variation in the use of implicit personality theories. They found that more Americans than Chinese believe in fixed personality traits, which suggests that Americans use implicit personality theories more often.

WE OFTEN SEEK INFORMATION TO CONFIRM OUR FIRST IMPRESSIONS.

Our tendency to view others in a way that is internally consistent causes us to also selectively seek information about them. The tendency to seek information that supports our beliefs while ignoring disconfirming information is know as the **confirmation bias** (Hart et al., 2009). In one experiment testing the confirmation bias during first encounters, Mark Snyder and William Swann (1978) asked research participants to find out whether the person with whom they were about to interact was an introvert or an extravert, depending on the experimental condition. Consistent with the confirmation bias, the questions that participants asked their interaction partners were biased in the direction of the original question. For instance, if they had been asked to find out whether the person was an introvert, they asked questions such as, "What do you dislike about loud parties?" or "In what situations do you wish you could be more outgoing?" However, in the extravert condition, they asked questions such as, "How do you liven things up at a party?" or "What kind of situations help you to meet new people?" Because most people can recall both introverted and extraverted incidents from their past, the interaction partners' answers provided confirmatory evidence for either personality trait. Experiments like this indicate that one barrier to accurate social judgments can be our tendency to search for information that will confirm our beliefs more energetically than we pursue information that might refute them (Edwards & Smith, 1996).

We are more likely to engage in the confirmation bias when the situation we are analyzing is one in which we are personally invested and the possible solution is agreeable to us rather than threatening (Dawson et al., 2002). Faced with an agreeable possible solution we are motivated to confirm it and ask ourselves, "*Can* I believe this?" In such situations, our standards of judgment are rather permissive, paving the way for the confirmation bias. On the other hand, when the possible solution is threatening or disagreeable we adopt a more stringent standard of judgment, and instead ask, "*Must* I believe this?" This latter question prompts more critical analysis, increasing the likelihood that any flaws or limitations in the available evidence will be discovered (Ditto et al., 1998). Such confirmation seeking not only leads to mistakes about individuals but also perpetuates incorrect stereotypes about social groups (Yzerbyt et al., 1996).

confirmation bias

The tendency to seek information that supports our beliefs while ignoring disconfirming information.

"For a man always believes more readily that which he prefers."

Francis Bacon, English Renaissance author, 1561–1626

"When you look for the bad in mankind expecting to find it, you surely will."

Abraham Lincoln, sixteenth U.S. president, 1809–1865

SECTION SUMMARY

- First impressions are often based on nonverbal behavior.

- We reliably identify seven primary emotions: anger, disgust, fear, happiness, surprise, contempt, and sadness.

- Nonconscious mimicry is automatically activated, and it fosters affiliation and rapport.

- Women and men differ in expressing and detecting emotional states.

- When forming impressions, we give more weight to negative information than positive information.

- Detecting deception in others is very difficult, but there are some useful cues.

- Central traits exert more influence in personality impressions than peripheral traits.

- Implicit personality theories operate on the principle of evaluative consistency.

- Confirmation bias occurs when we seek information that verifies our beliefs.

MAKING ATTRIBUTIONS

A few years ago after a snowstorm, I arrived home from work and noticed that our garbage had not been collected. When I phoned the company, an exasperated woman replied to my query by sarcastically stating, "Well sir, with all the snow we had yesterday I would have thought people wouldn't have been stupid enough to put out their garbage today." Now, despite the public perception of psychologists as detached observers, constantly analyzing other people's behavior and motivation, this psychologist's response was not quite so analytical. Later, however, I wondered what caused her to act so rudely. Was she simply an insensitive person, or was it just a bad day for her?

About a year later, my garbage was not picked up again and I had to contact this woman a second time. Now there was no snowstorm. As I dialed, I wondered if I was about to be chastised again for yet another mental failing. To my relief, she was very cordial and apologetic. Based on this second conversation, I concluded that her previous behavior was most likely not due to some stable personality trait such as rudeness but rather to an external, uncontrollable, and unstable event—the situational stress she experienced on that snowy winter day. How did I arrive at this judgment, and how do people in general assign causal explanations for events?

WE RELY UPON PARTICULAR INFORMATION WHEN EXPLAINING PEOPLE'S ACTIONS.

Everybody has a general theory of human behavior—what Fritz Heider (1958) called a *naive psychology*—and we use it to search for explanations of social events. In searching for understanding, we focus not only on people's personalities but also consider the situational context. Our desire to understand and explain social events is strongest when the events are the actions of other people and are unexpected, unusual, or distressing (Kanazawa, 1992). The process by which we use such information to make inferences about the causes of behavior or events is called **attribution** (Heider, 1958; Ichheiser, 1934, 1943).

In seeking attributions, Heider believed people are motivated by two primary needs: the need to form a coherent view of the world, and the need to gain control of the environment. Being able to predict how people are going to behave goes a long way in satisfying both of these needs. If we can adequately explain and predict the actions of others, we will be much more likely to view the world as coherent and controllable than if we have no clue to their intentions and dispositions. In satisfying these two needs, Heider asserted that we try to act like *naive scientists*, rationally and logically testing our hypotheses about the behavior of others.

Locus of Causality

In making causal attributions, by far the most important judgment concerns the *locus of causality*. According to Heider, people broadly attribute a given action either to internal states or external factors. An **internal attribution** (also called *person attribution*) consists of any explanation that locates the cause as being internal to the person, such as personality traits, moods, attitudes, abilities, or effort. An **external attribution** (also called *situation attribution*) consists of any explanation that locates the cause as being external to the person under scrutiny, such as the actions of others, the nature of the situation, or luck. In my "garbage" example, I ultimately made an external attribution about the woman's actions, explaining it due to the stress of the job brought on by adverse weather. For Heider and other attribution theorists, whether my explanation is correct or not is not the issue. Their task is not to determine the *true* cause of events but rather to explain how people *perceive* the causes.

Stability and Controllability of Causality

Besides making internal or external distinctions, people also attempt to determine whether causes are *stable* (Weiner, 1986). Stable causes are permanent and lasting, while

---

attribution

The process by which people use information to make inferences about the causes of behavior or events

internal attribution

An attribution that locates the cause of an event to factors internal to the person, such as personality traits, moods, attitudes, abilities, or effort

external attribution

An attribution that locates the cause of an event to factors external to the person, such as luck, or other people, or the situation

Table 4.2

Possible Causes of Academic Achievement Due to Locus, Stability, and Controllability

Controllability	Internal		External	
	Stable	**Unstable**	**Stable**	**Unstable**
Controllable	Typical effort	Temporary effort exerted for a particular exam	Some forms of teacher bias	Unusual help from others
Uncontrollable	Exerted ability	Mood	Exam difficulty	Luck

unstable causes are temporary and fluctuating. This stable/unstable dimension is independent of the direction of causality. Some causes, called *dispositional*, are both internal and stable ("She insulted me because she is rude"). Other causes are considered to be internal but unstable ("She insulted me because she has a cold"). Likewise, some causes are seen as external and stable ("She insulted me because I, the external factor, rub people the wrong way"), while others are perceived as external and unstable ("She insulted me because the weather conditions that day made her job very difficult").

Although judgments of the locus and stability of causes are the most important in making attributions, a third dimension we often consider is whether causes are *controllable*. We think of some causes as being within people's control and others as being outside their control; this controllable/uncontrollable dimension is independent of either locus or stability. Weather is a good example of an uncontrollable factor.

Table 4.2 illustrates how these three dimensions might interact with one another in assigning causality to academic performance. For example, how much you generally study for exams would be considered an internal, stable, and controllable factor, while how much you *choose* to study for any particular exam would be an internal, unstable, and controllable factor. Sometimes a controllable factor like effort will get you only so far in academic achievement. Then we must consider internal factors that are seen as uncontrollable, such as innate intellectual ability (stable) and one's mood during exam time (unstable). External factors that are considered controllable might be rather stable, such as knowing that your teacher looks for specific definitions of terms and use of examples in test answers, or they might also be unstable, such as others deciding to help you prepare for an exam (this help is presumably under their control). Finally, the difficulty of tests given by the teacher would be perceived as being external, stable, and uncontrollable, while luck is an external, unstable factor typically perceived as uncontrollable.

The locus, stability, and controllability of causal attributions appear to be the primary dimensions employed when people explain events (Meyer & Koebl, 1982). For example, people use these three dimensions to help them interpret requests for help and how to view those who have stigmatizing diseases such as cancer and AIDS (Schmidt & Weiner, 1988). Cross-cultural studies have also demonstrated that these dimensions are not only employed in individualist countries but in collectivist ones as well (Hau & Salili, 1991; Schuster et al., 1989).

Following these initial formulations, other social psychologists expanded on their insights and developed formal attribution theories. The following pages focus on theories that have had the most influence on the field and also discuss recent refinements in our understanding of the attribution process.

CORRESPONDENT INFERENCE THEORY ASSUMES THAT PEOPLE PREFER MAKING DISPOSITIONAL ATTRIBUTIONS.

When we observe others, we not only attend to their behavior, but we also are aware of the consequences of the behavior. In developing correspondent inference theory, Edward Jones and Keith Davis (1965) were particularly interested in how people infer the cause of a single instance of behavior (For example, why did the garbage woman act rudely?). According to them, people try to *infer* from an overt action whether it *corresponds* to a stable personal characteristic of the actor. (*Note*: Social psychologists refer to "actors" as the persons whose behavior we are attempting to understand.) Thus, a **correspondent inference** is an inference to which the actor's action corresponds, or is indicative of a stable personal characteristic. For example, if Jane acts compassionately toward Bob, his correspondent inference would be that Jane is a compassionate person. But will Bob actually make a correspondent inference? Not always. If there are several plausible reasons why someone may have performed a certain act, correspondence is low; therefore, you cannot be confident about the cause of the act. However, if there is only one plausible reason to explain the act, correspondence is high and you will be confident in your attribution.

In explaining social events, Jones and Davis argued that people have a preference for making dispositional attributions (that is, those that are internal and stable), and that external attributions are merely default options, made only when internal causes cannot be found. The reason for this preference is the belief that knowing the dispositional attributes of others will enable one to better understand and predict their behavior. The problem in confidently making these attributions, however, is that social behavior is often ambiguous and the causes are not always readily apparent to the observer. Therefore, to guide them in their attempts to infer personal characteristics from behavior, Jones and Davis stated that people use several logical rules of thumb.

One such rule deals with the *social desirability* of the behavior. That is, people are much more likely to make dispositional attributions about behavior that is socially undesirable than about behavior that is desirable. This is the case because socially desirable behavior is thought to tell us more about the cultural norms of the group than about the personality of the individuals within that group. Yet when people are willing to break from these norms to act in a certain way, such unexpected behavior demands an explanation. When such action is taken, people realize that the social costs incurred by the actor may be great, and they are much more confident that the behavior reflects a stable and internal disposition (Jones et al., 1961).

Imagine that you are watching several candidates for political office addressing a meeting of Mothers Against Drunk Drivers (MADD). Every candidate voices support for tougher laws against those who drive while intoxicated. How confident would you be in concluding that the candidates' words truly reflect an underlying personal conviction? Now let's imagine that one of the speakers stands up and denounces the actions of MADD as an infringement on a citizen's pursuit of happiness. It is likely that you would be more confident that this candidate's words reflect his or her true convictions because they run so counter to prevailing societal norms.

Another rule people consider is the actor's degree of *choice*. Actions freely chosen are considered to be more indicative of an actor's true personal characteristics than those that are coerced. Support for the freedom of choice factor comes from a study in which college students read a speech, supposedly written by a fellow student who either supported or opposed Fidel Castro, the former communist leader of Cuba (Jones & Harris, 1967). Some students were told that the student speechwriter had freely chosen her or his position, while others were told that the student was assigned the stated position by a professor. When asked to estimate what the student speechwriter's true attitudes were toward Castro, those who believed that the speechwriter had freely chosen her or his position were more likely to assume there was a correspondence between the student's essay (behavior) and her or his true attitudes.

correspondent inference

· ·

An inference that the action of an actor corresponds to, or is indicative of, a stable personal characteristic

Critical THINKING

Health experts have grown increasingly alarmed about AIDS among young adults because most of this population are not practicing safe sex by using condoms (Langer et al., 2001). How might young adults' implicit personality theories about safe-sex partners be shaping their decisions not to use condoms?

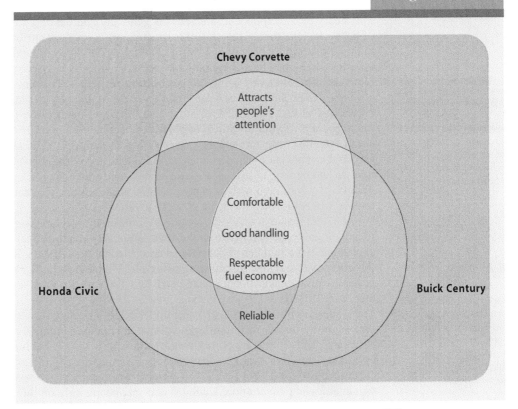

Figure 4.5

Why Did Zoua Buy the Chevy Corvette? Looking for Noncommon Effects

When there are a number of common effects for a given action, it is difficult to tell why people do what they do. However, when people engage in a behavior that has a noncommon effect—as is the case with Zoua's decision to buy the Chevy Corvette—it is much easier to make a correspondent inference: Zoua is an attention seeker.

According to Jones and Davis, we not only observe the social desirability of behaviors and the degree of choice of the actors, but we also analyze the actor's chosen behavior in the context of other potential behaviors. We then ask, "Is there some effect or outcome unique to the chosen behavior?" By comparing the consequences of the chosen behavior with the consequences of other actions not taken, people can often infer the strength of the underlying intention by looking for unique or "noncommon" consequences. Thus, this third rule of inference has to do with actions that produce *noncommon effects*—outcomes that could not be produced by any other action.

Research indicates that behaviors with unique noncommon effects result in stronger inferences about an actor's dispositions than behaviors with common effects (Ajzen & Holmes, 1976). For example, let's imagine Zoua is looking to buy a used car. She is considering a 2002 Honda Civic, a 2004 Buick Century, and a 2000 Chevy Corvette. As illustrated in Figure 4.5, some effects are common to any of these cars (comfortable ride, good road handling, and respectable fuel economy). However, only one of these cars will attract a lot of attention to whoever is driving it. If Zoua chooses the Corvette as her new car, observers may likely conclude that she is an attention seeker. In drawing this conclusion, they are using the unique noncommon effect of Zoua's behavioral decision to infer her personality traits.

Taking these three rules into account, according to Jones and Davis's theory, people are most likely to conclude that other people's actions reflect underlying dispositional traits (that is, they are likely to make correspondent inferences) when the actions are perceived to (1) be low in social desirability, (2) be freely chosen, and (3) result in unique, noncommon effects.

Critical
THINKING

Why might someone argue that correspondent inference theory would not have been developed in a collectivist culture? Put another way, what individualist assumption is at the core of this theory?

THE COVARIATION MODEL EXPLAINS ATTRIBUTIONS DERIVED FROM MULTIPLE OBSERVATION POINTS.

The theory of correspondent inferences is generally applied only to single observations of behavior. One theory that specifically attempts to explain attributions derived from multiple observational points is Harold Kelley's (1967) covariation model, which also assumes that human beings are rational and logical observers. According to Kelley, people make attributions by using the **covariation principle**. This principle states that for something to be the cause of a particular behavior, it must be present when the behavior occurs and absent when it does not occur—the presumed cause and observed effect must "covary." If your boyfriend or girlfriend becomes cold and irritable only when you spend extended time with others, that is high covariation. If he or she is only occasionally cold and irritable when you spend extended time with others, that is low covariation. In attempting to assign a cause to the cold and irritable behavior, you would observe its covariation with as many potential causes as possible and attribute the effect to the cause with which it has the greatest covariance.

Our confidence in assigning a cause to some effect will be lowered if we cannot distinguish significant differences in the covariation between the effect we are interested in explaining and a number of possible causes (Fiedler et al., 1999). Kelley (1972) called this cognitive "fact" the **discounting principle**. Whenever a particular event has several possible causal explanations, we are much less likely to attribute the effect to any particular cause (Morris & Larrick, 1995).

In describing the locus of causality, Kelley elaborated on the internal/external dimension by further distinguishing external attributions in terms of the *entity* and *circumstances*. The *entity* is the object toward which the actor's behavior is directed and can be another person or a thing. *Circumstances* are simply the conditions in which actions or events occur.

In assessing covariation, Kelley stated that people rely on three kinds of information. *Consensus* information deals with the extent to which others react the same way to some stimulus or entity as the person whose actions we are attempting to explain. *Consistency* information concerns the extent to which the person reacts to this stimulus or entity in the same way on other occasions. Finally, *distinctiveness* information refers to the extent to which the person reacts the same way to other, different stimuli or entities. Kelley's theory predicts that people are most likely to attribute another person's behavior to internal and stable (dispositional) causes when consensus and distinctiveness are low but consistency is high. On the other hand, circumstance attributions are most likely when consensus and consistency are low and distinctiveness is high. When all three kinds of information are high, people are likely to make entity attributions.

How might the covariation model explain people's process of making attributions in the Stephen Glass scandal? In May of 1998 when another reporter could not verify Glass's *New Republic* story about a fifteen-year-old computer hacker, many journalists began wondering why this story contained so many unverified sources. Did Glass make some uncharacteristically bad decisions due to deadline pressures (circumstance attribution)? Was Glass a lying and deceitful reporter (dispositional attribution)? Was there something about the social norms and management style at *The New Republic* that caused bad reporting (entity attribution)?

Table 4.3 outlines how Kelley's theory might predict specific attributions about this behavior. The covariation model predicts that people would seek an attribution by gathering consensus, consistency, and distinctiveness information. For consensus, they would look at the behavior of journalists at *The New Republic*: Are other journalists having problems with fact checking? For consistency, they would examine Glass's past *New Republic* stories. Did any of his previous *New Republic* stories contain unverified sources? For distinctiveness, they would gather information about Glass's stories for other magazines. Did he write any stories for other magazines that contained unverified sources?

For a dispositional attribution (Condition 1: Stephen Glass is a lying and deceitful reporter), there must be evidence for low consensus and distinctiveness and high consistency. This would be likely if none of the other *New Republic* reporters are found to

---

covariation principle

A principle of attribution theory stating that for something to be the cause of a particular behavior, it must be present when the behavior occurs and absent when it does not occur

discounting principle

A principle of attribution theory stating that whenever there are several possible causal explanations for a particular event, people tend to be much less likely to attribute the effect to any particular cause

Table 4.3

Why Did Stephen Glass's Story Contain Unverified Sources?

Available Information

Condition	Consensus	Consistency	Distinctiveness	Most Common Attribution
1	Low—No other journalists at *The New Republic* are having problems with unverified sources.	High—A number of Stephen Glass's previous *New Republic* stories also contain unverified sources.	Low—Stephen Glass's stories for other magazines also contain unverified sources.	Dispositional: Stephen is a lying and deceitful reporter.
2	High—Many journalists at *The New Republic* have problems with unverified sources.	High—A number of Stephen Glass's previous *New Republic* stories also contain unverified sources.	High—Stephen Glass's stories for other magazines do not contain unverified sources.	Entity: There is something about *The New Republic* management that causes bad reporting.
3	Low—No other journalists at *The New Republic* have problems with unverified sources.	Low—None of Stephen Glass's previous *New Republic* stories contain unverified sources.	High—Stephen Glass's stories for other magazines do not contain unverified sources.	Circumstance: Due to deadline pressures, or illness, Stephen Glass was unable to verify all the facts in his story.

have problems with fact checking, many other Glass articles for *The New Republic* are found to contain unverified sources, and it is discovered that Glass's stories for other magazines display a similar problem with fact checking. For an entity attribution (Condition 2: There is something about *The New Republic* management that causes bad reporting), there must be evidence of high consensus, distinctiveness, and consistency. This attribution is likely if many *New Republic* reporters are found to have fact-checking problems, and none of Glass's stories for other magazines contain unverified sources, even though many of his other *New Republic* stories do. A circumstance attribution is likely if consensus and consistency are low but distinctiveness is high (Condition 3). So if no one else at *The New Republic* is having problems with fact checking and Glass never had any problems before with any of his stories at *The New Republic* or elsewhere, some unusual circumstance must have caused this incident. Perhaps Glass was simply unable to check all his facts because of deadline pressure or because he was not feeling well. In the Glass scandal, the available information resulted in almost all observers making a dispositional attribution, concluding that Stephen Glass was a lying and deceitful reporter.

How accurate is the covariation model in explaining the attribution process? Empirical studies generally support its basic assumptions (Chen et al., 1988; Windschitl &

Wells, 1997). However, when making dispositional attributions about an actor's actions we appear to primarily focus on information that can be obtained by attending to the actor (Was his or her behavior distinctive or consistent?). In contrast, our external attributions are more influenced by consensus information.

THERE ARE BIASES IN THE ATTRIBUTION PROCESS.

Correspondent inference theory and the covariation model have significantly advanced our understanding of how we make inferences about the causes of behavior. Both theories assume that the attribution process is highly rational. Yet if people do follow logical principles in assigning causality to events, this cognitive process—likened by some to a computer program—has a few interesting and all-too-illogical human "bugs."

In Chapter 1 we discussed the *self-serving bias*, which involves assigning an internal locus of causality for our positive outcomes and an external locus for our negative outcomes. A desire to enhance or protect self-esteem is the most agreed-upon explanation for this particular attributional bias. Given our discussion in Chapter 3 concerning the high value placed on self-esteem in individualist cultures, it should not be surprising to learn that individualists are more likely to exhibit the self-serving bias than collectivists (Boven et al., 2003; Heine & Lehman, 1999). What are some other biases that occur when making attributions?

The Fundamental Attribution Error

As discussed in Chapter 1, behavior is generally caused by an interaction of an individual's internal characteristics and external factors. However, in explaining other people's actions, we tend to locate the cause in terms of their dispositional characteristics rather than to what might be more appropriate situational factors. Lee Ross (1977) named this tendency to overestimate the impact of dispositional causes and underestimate the impact of situational causes on other people's behavior the **fundamental attribution error** (also known as the *correspondence bias*).

In one of the more important studies to investigate this cognitive bias, Ross and his colleagues (1977a) devised a simulated TV quiz game in which students were randomly assigned to serve the role of "quizmaster" or "contestant." The quizmasters were told to think up ten challenging but fair questions, and the contestants were told to answer as many as possible. Under such conditions, the quizmasters were able to devise some rather tough questions; and on average, the contestants answered only four of the ten questions correctly. Despite the fact that the quizmaster role gave students playing that part a decided advantage, the contestants failed to discount or take this external factor into account in assigning a causal explanation for the quiz show's results. As you can see in Figure 4.6, contestants saw the quizmasters as far more knowledgeable than themselves. Observers who watched the game, but were not directly involved in the outcome, also rated the quizmasters as more knowledgeable than the contestants.

Why do we engage in this sort of systematic bias? One possibility was already mentioned when discussing correspondent inference theory (see p. 139). We prefer making dispositional attributions because locating the cause of people's behavior in their attitudes and personalities gives us greater confidence that we can accurately predict their future behavior. Thus, our desire for predictability may make us more susceptible to the fundamental attribution error. A second possibility has to do with what is most noticeable to us as social perceivers. When we observe a person in a social setting, what is often most *perceptually salient* is that particular person: their dynamic movements, their distinctive voice, and their overall physical presence. In comparison, the relatively static situational forces that may actually cause those behaviors are often less salient, and therefore less likely to be factored into the attribution equation.

Shelley Taylor and Susan Fiske (1975) tested this hypothesis by varying the seating arrangements of six people who observed two actors engaging in a carefully staged, five-minute conversation. In each session, observers were seated so they faced actor A,

**fundamental
attribution error**
· · · · · · · · · · · · · · · · · ·
The tendency to overestimate the impact of dispositional causes and underestimate the impact of situational causes on other people's behavior

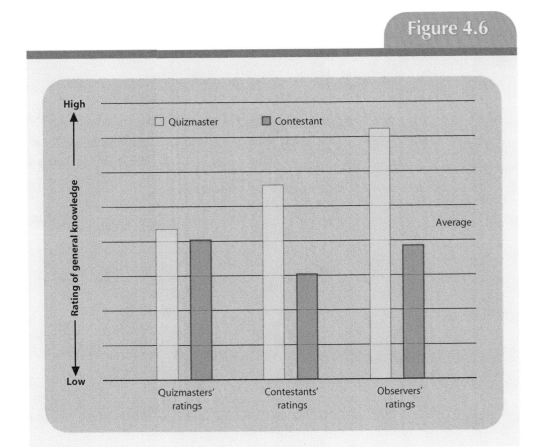

Figure 4.6

Fundamental Attribution Error and the TV Quiz Game

Even though students playing the role of quizmaster held a decided advantage over contestants, the contestants failed to discount or take this external factor into account in assigning a causal explanation for the quiz show's results. Like the observers, the contestants judged the quizmasters as more knowledgeable than themselves. What might explain this fundamental attribution error?

actor B, or both. This seating arrangement is illustrated in Figure 4.7. Following the conversation, the observers were asked questions about the two actors to determine whom they thought had the most impact on the conversation. Results indicated that whichever actor they faced was the one the observers judged as the more dominant member of the dyad. Further research has confirmed perceptual salience as a contributing factor to the fundamental attribution error (Krull & Dill, 1996; Lassiter et al., 2002).

For many years, social psychologists believed that people throughout the world exhibited the fundamental attribution error equally. Yet, as more research was conducted in non-Western cultures, it became clear that this particular attribution error was less common in collectivist cultures than in those that were individualist (Norenzayan & Nisbett, 2000). For example, Joan Miller (1984) found that South Asian Indians made more situational attributions when explaining people's everyday behavior, whereas North Americans were much more likely to make dispositional attributions. Faced with such findings, social psychologists began wondering *why* culture affects the fundamental attribution error. Is it because collectivists are less attentive than individualists to how attitudes and personality traits (dispositions) can shape behavior? Or is it due to individualists being less attentive than collectivists to how situational forces can influence behavior?

Subsequent research found that collectivists are just as likely as individualists to take into account people's dispositions when explaining their behavior (Krull et al., 1999; Miyamoto & Kitayama, 2002). Where they differ is in their awareness of the situation's power. Collectivists are more attentive to how situational factors may influence

Figure 4.7

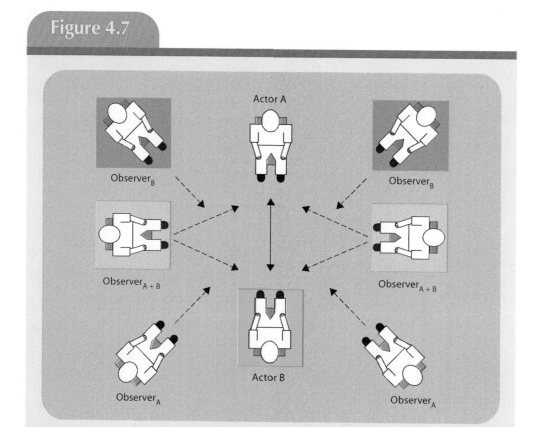

Perceptual Salience and the Fundamental Attribution Error

This is the seating arrangement for the two actors and six observers in the perceptual salience study. Taylor and Fiske found that observers rated the actor they could see most clearly as being the dominant contributor to the conversation. How do these findings help explain the fundamental attribution error?

people's behavior, and that is apparently why they are less susceptible to the fundamental attribution error (Choi et al., 1999). This cultural difference in person perception is rooted in different views of the self (Chua et al., 2005). As stated in Chapter 3, individualists view the self as internally driven and relatively uninfluenced by situational forces (the independent self). In contrast, collectivists view the self as dependent on the group and strongly influenced by social obligations (the interdependent self). It appears that the interdependent self fosters a greater appreciation of how personal and situational factors interact in shaping behavior, which is essentially how social psychology understands social behavior. Based on these findings, some social psychologists suggest that the type of naive psychology that members of collectivist cultures develop leads to more accurate attributions than that typically developed in individualist cultures (Lieberman et al., 2005).

However, as you recall from our discussion in Chapter 3 (p. 83), cultures do not create people with rigidly independent or interdependent selves. Situational factors can trigger spontaneous self-concepts in people that run counter to the independent self or interdependent self fostered by their culture (Kühnen & Oyserman, 2002). When this occurs in people whose typical self-views are independent, their situationally induced interdependent self will likely foster a greater awareness of how the interaction of dispositional and situational factors influences others' behaviors. Likewise, when collectivists' thoughts are temporarily shifted to an independent self-view, their social judgments are more likely to suffer from the fundamental attribution error (Hong et al., 2000, 2003).

Whether perceptual salience, individualism, or a combination of these and other factors explain the fundamental attribution error, this particular bias can have significant social consequences. Attributing the behavior of others to internal factors allows social perceivers to block actors' attempts to deny responsibility for negative events with which they are associated (Inman et al., 1993). For example, the tendency to disregard situational forces in explaining the plight of victims within our society (rape victims, street people, disadvantaged minorities, etc.) can result in less sympathy because we hold these people responsible for their condition due to "bad" dispositions.

Even if our response is one of sympathetic caring for unfortunate others, the assignment of dispositional blame will influence the type of solutions we as a society implement for these people (Leung & Chan, 1999). That is, if we attribute the difficulties of unfortunate others to personal defects rather than to their circumstances, treatment programs will likely focus on changing individuals and not on improving their social environment. Yet if many of the individuals in these programs are members of social groups whose difficulties often stem from societal discrimination rather than personal defects (like ethnic minorities and women), our attempted interventions may prove to be psychologically damaging.

In concluding our analysis of the fundamental attribution error, it is worth mentioning one final study that suggests that cultural stereotypes may also account for this attributional bias, at least in certain social contexts. Lisa Barrett and Eliza Bliss-Moreau (2009) found evidence that people are more likely to commit the fundamental attribution error when inferring the cause of women's versus men's emotions. In their research, Barrett and Bliss-Moreau showed participants the photos of faces expressing the negative emotions of anger, sadness, fear, and disgust, paired with a situational explanation for why that emotion was experienced (for example, "argued with a coworker" or "was pushed and fell to the ground"). These faces were morphed to either look male or female in appearance. Following exposure to the faces and the situational explanations for the expressed emotions, participants were then shown only the faces and told to make a snap judgment on whether the person in the photo was either "emotional" or "having a bad day." Results indicated that participants more frequently judged the female-looking target photos as emotional, whereas they more frequently judged the male-looking target photos as having a bad day. The researchers contend that this difference in assigning causality is caused by the widely held cultural belief that women are the more emotional sex. For example, when a woman has an emotionally angry outburst, people are likely to infer that she is an emotionally responsive person because this is consistent with their belief that women are emotional creatures. Yet when a man rages in the same manner, people are more likely to infer that he is "simply having a bad day" because this is also consistent with their gender stereotype that men are less defined by their emotions. Thus, regardless of whether women are objectively more emotionally expressive, people attribute their emotional behaviors to a more emotional nature, whereas this happens less for expressions made by men.

Actor-Observer Effect

When explaining the actions of others we are likely to give more weight to internal (dispositional) factors, but when explaining our own behavior we tend to give more weight to external (or situational) factors. This tendency to attribute our own behavior to external causes but that of others to internal factors is known as the **actor-observer effect** (Jones & Nisbett, 1972; Karasawa, 1995). For example, if Charisse is talking with an attractive male stranger and her boyfriend, Singh, sees them from a distance, they may well arrive at different explanations for this social interaction. Although Charisse may attribute it to an external factor (the stranger was asking for directions), Singh may assign an internal cause (Charisse is infatuated with this guy).

Michael Storms (1973) created such conversational setups (minus the jealousy component) to test for the actor-observer effect. Employing a design similar to the previously discussed Taylor and Fiske (1975) study, Storms had four unacquainted research participants—two playing the role of observers and two playing the role of conversational actors—arranged in a seating pattern similar to the one shown in Figure 4.8. The

actor-observer effect
. . . .
The tendency for people to attribute their own behavior to external causes but that of others to internal factors

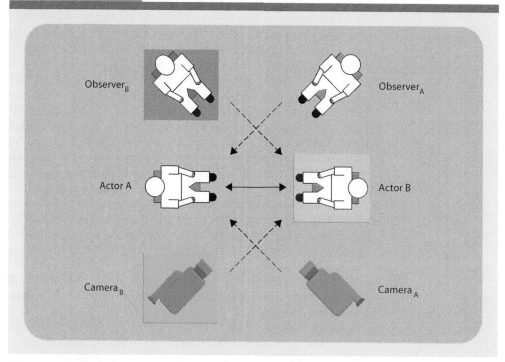

Perceptual Salience and the Actor-Observer Effect

This is the seating arrangement for the two actors and two observers in Storm's (1973) perceptual salience study. Why would two actors who watched themselves on videotape following the coversation with the other actor make more dispositional attribution about each other's behavior?

two actors were instructed to engage in a five-minute conversation, and the two observers were told to focus their attention on the actor they were facing. Two video cameras also separately recorded the facial expressions of the actors as they conversed. Immediately afterward, both the actors and the observers rated the actors' behavior along a number of dimensions, and then they were asked to indicate the degree to which the actors' behavior was determined by their personal characteristics and by the situation. Consistent with the actor-observer effect, the observers placed greater importance on *dispositional factors* when explaining the actions of the actor they were watching, whereas the actors emphasized *situational factors* when explaining their own behavior.

Why does the actor-observer effect occur? As with the fundamental attribution error, a likely possibility is perceptual salience. While engaged in a particular activity, the actor's attention is typically turned outward toward the situation, but the observer's attention is likely focused on the actor. Thus, what is salient for the actor (the situation) and what is salient for the observer (the actor) differs due to their perspectives in viewing the event.

If perceptual salience is important, what would happen if you manipulated this salience *after* the event had transpired but *prior* to observers and actors making any formal attributions? In another condition of Storms's study, he showed the videotapes to the participants before they made their attributions. Instead of seeing on tape what they had experienced live, however, some of them watched the *opposite* visual perspective. Thus, actors A and B saw their own faces, observer A saw actor B, and observer B saw actor A.

In contrast to participants who saw on tape what they had experienced live, *reversed-perspective* viewers no longer exhibited the typical actor-observer effect. Instead, the actors who had seen themselves made more dispositional attributions, and the observers made more situational attributions about the actor they had previously faced. These findings, along with others, not only demonstrate the power of perceptual salience in the attribution process but also demonstrate that if we manipulate the attention of the actors

Critical THINKING

Based on your understanding of correspondent inference theory, why do you think the fundamental attribution error is also known as the correspondence bias?

so that they become *self-aware*, they tend to place more importance on internal factors when explaining their own actions; the actor-observer effect disappears (Fejfar & Hoyle, 2000). In a very real psychological sense, when the actors engaged in self-awareness, they became observers of their own actions.

Although the actor-observer effect is a well-documented attributional phenomenon (Krueger et al., 1996), it appears to operate most often when people are explaining recent events in their lives. When explaining events that took place long ago or when predicting events that will occur in the distant future, actors generally make dispositional attributions, just like observers (Pronin & Ross, 2006). In such circumstances, situational factors are less salient and even less available in memory or the imagination than is the "self as actor." In other words, people generally adopt an observer perspective rather than an actor perspective when explaining distant events in their lives.

What are some possible implications of this finding? First, it suggests that people are more likely to accept personal responsibility for events that occurred years ago than for events that just occurred. Second, it suggests that when imagining and planning their futures, people are likely to assume that their personal traits will override any situational factors, a mindset that results in people being overly optimistic in their planning and expectations (Newby-Clark & Ross, 2003).

MAKING ATTRIBUTIONS INVOLVES BOTH AUTOMATIC AND DELIBERATE THINKING.

So where are we in understanding the process of making attributions about people's behavior? The early attribution theorists conceived of human beings as *naive scientists*, who are highly rational and logical information processors, heavily relying on explicit cognition. Early attribution theories reflect the classic "cold" perspective in social psychology (see Chapter 1, p. 17). Those who developed correspondent inference theory and the covariation model assumed that people survey all the evidence and then consciously decide on either an internal or an external attribution. However, many social psychologists now contend that **dual-process models of attribution** involving both explicit cognition and implicit cognition best explain the attribution process. The dual-process model reflects the "warm look" of social cognition in social psychology (again, see p. 17).

dual-process models of attribution
. . . .
Theories of attribution that propose that people initially engage in a relatively automatic and simple attributional assessment but then later consciously correct this attribution with more deliberate and effortful thinking

According to this dual-process model, automatic and simple attributional assessments typically occur first and are then sometimes followed by more deliberate and effortful analysis (Newman, 2001; Krull, 2001). On the individual level, adjustments of initial judgments are most likely to occur among people who doubt their ability to understand the reasons for others' actions (Weary et al., 2006). On the cultural level, whether first assessments focus on dispositional or situational factors is often determined by whether social perceivers are from individualist or collectivist cultures (Lieberman et al., 2005). When people from individualist cultures observe others perform some action, they may first characterize this behavior as having a dispositional cause and then later may correct this initial judgment with situational information (Gilbert et al., 1988). In contrast, people from collectivist cultures are more likely to initially form attributions based on situational information. Regardless of culture, the initial step in the social judgment process involves spontaneous and relatively effortless thinking (Van Hiel et al., 2008), while the second step involves a deliberate and often more effortful adjustment of the first judgment.

As an example of how this process works, let's return to my "garbage lady" incident in which she responded to my phone inquiry about tardy garbage pickup by stating, "Well sir, with all the snow we had yesterday I would have thought people wouldn't have been stupid enough to put out their garbage today." What explains her behavior toward me? As depicted in Figure 4.9, in the first stage of my attributional thinking, I would spontaneously categorize the garbage lady's behavior ("Whoa! That sounds like an insult directed at me!"). In the second stage, I would make an initial dispositional inference ("I think she is a rude person!"). While the first and second stages in this process are automatic and relatively effortless, the third stage is much more deliberate and requires a good deal of cognitive effort. In stage 3, I consciously hesitate in going

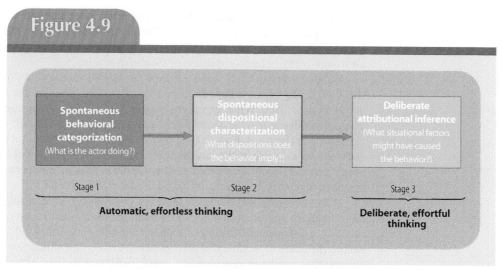

Figure 4.9

A Dual-Process Model of Attribution

Many contemporary attribution theorists contend that when trying to explain others' behaviors, people from individualist cultures often initially automatically focus on dispositional factors and then later consciously correct this attribution to better account for situational factors. What might short-circuit this more deliberate judgmental phase of the attribution process? How does this attribution process proceed for people in collectivist cultures?

with my initial snap judgment and, instead, consider possible situational factors that might explain the garbage lady's response: "Maybe the weather stressed her out." "Maybe my tone of voice sounded accusatory and this irritated her." "Maybe this is the fiftieth call she received today, and she's fed up." When we are distracted, too busy, or unmotivated, we may not engage in this second judgmental process because correcting the initial, spontaneous dispositional characterization of other people's behavior is cognitively demanding. In individualist cultures, when we don't engage in deliberate attributional inference our explanations of other people's actions are likely to fall prey to the fundamental attribution error (Uleman, 1999). However, the tendency to commit this error is greatly reduced when we take the time to engage in more effortful thinking (Deutsch et al., 2006; Riggs & Gumbrecht, 2005; Yost & Weary, 1996).

SECTION SUMMARY

- Locus of causality (internal or external) is the most important judgment in making attributions.

- Correspondent inference theory states we use rules when inferring whether a target person's action corresponds to a stable personal characteristic.

  Rules: social desirability, choice, noncommon effects

- The covariation model explains attributions derived from multiple observations.

- The information used in assessing covariation involves consensus, consistency, and distinctiveness.

- The attribution process is characterized by cognitive biases that cause judgmental errors.

  The fundamental attribution error is the tendency to make internal versus external attributions and is more common in individualist cultures that in collectivist cultures.

  The actor-observer effect is the tendency to make external attributions for our own behavior but internal attributions for others.

- The attribution process involves both automatic and deliberate thinking, and the more deliberate and effortful thinking may correct for some of our attributional biases.

HOW DO YOU EXPLAIN NEGATIVE EVENTS IN YOUR LIFE?

According to Lyn Abramson and her colleagues (1978), people differ in their attributional style, which can affect how they respond to uncontrollable life events. As previously discussed, reactions to uncontrollable events are determined by three types of attributions: *internal versus external, stable versus unstable,* and *global versus specific* (that is, whether the event extends to many spheres of life or is confined to one sphere). Those who make *internal* attributions for uncontrollable events tend to experience more negative self-esteem. Individuals who make *stable* and *global* attributions for uncontrollable events are more likely to feel helpless in future events. When all three types of negative attributions are habitually used to explain stressful events in one's life, this attributional tendency is called the **pessimistic explanatory style**; and people from cultures around the world who fit this pattern have been found to be at greater risk for depression (Cole et al., 2008; Nolen-Hoeksma et al., 1992). For them, an unfortunate event has an internal cause ("It's my fault"), a stable cause ("It will always be this way"), and a global cause ("It's this way in many different situations"). In contrast, when something positive happens to them, people with a pessimistic explanatory style tend to make external, unstable, and specific attributions.

pessimistic explanatory style
. . . .
A habitual tendency to attribute negative events to internal, stable, and global causes, and positive events to external, unstable, and specific causes.

optimistic explanatory style
. . . .
A habitual tendency to attribute negative events to external, unstable, and specific causes, and positive events to internal, stable, and global causes

An attributional style that contrasts sharply to the pessimistic style is the **optimistic explanatory style**. Optimists tend to explain negative events in terms of an external cause ("It's someone else's fault"), an unstable cause ("It won't happen again"), and a specific cause ("It's just in this one area"). On the other hand, when faced with positive events, optimists explain them by making internal, stable, and global attributions (Peterson & Park, 2007; Seligman, 1991). Do you think you tend to have an optimistic or a pessimistic explanatory style of explaining the causes of good and bad events? Spend a few minutes answering the questions in *Self/Social Connection Exercise 4.2.*

Christopher Peterson and Martin Seligman conducted a series of studies to better understand the relationship between explanatory style and illness. In one of their first studies, the researchers measured college students' attributional style and asked them to list all illnesses they had experienced during the previous month (Peterson & Seligman, 1987). Students also completed this illness measure one year after the initial testing. Results indicated that even after controlling for the number of illnesses reported at the first session, students with an optimistic explanatory style reported fewer illnesses and fewer visits to a physician for diagnosis or treatment of an illness than did those with a pessimistic style.

❝The optimist sees the rose and not its thorns; the pessimist stares at the thorns, oblivious to the rose.**❞**

━ ━ ━ ━ ━ ━ ━ ━

Kahlil Gibran, Lebanese-American poet, 1883–1931

In an archival investigation, the researchers used the responses that ninety-nine male college graduates gave in 1946 to an open-ended questionnaire about their wartime experiences to classify them in terms of their degree of pessimistic explanatory style (Peterson et al., 1988). Although style did not predict health in young adulthood—when nearly all the men were healthy—there was a link between explanatory style and illness by the age forty-five, when health became more variable. After this age, the men who had a pessimistic explanatory style in their youth tended to have more health problems than those who had a more optimistic outlook. In a second archival study, Peterson and Seligman (1987) investigated the deceased members of the Baseball Hall of Fame who played between 1900 and 1950. First, they searched the sports pages of old newspapers for the explanations these players gave of their successful and unsuccessful performances. Next, they had independent judges rate these quotes for internality, stability, and globality. Finally, they recorded the age at which each baseball player had died. Results indicated that players that made internal, stable, and global explanations for bad events died at a younger age; those who explained positive events as being due to external, unstable, and specific factors died at a younger age.

One final archival study conducted by the researchers found that globality was a better predictor of early death than internality and stability (Peterson et al., 1998). When people habitually believed that a bad event in one specific life area would undermine everything else in their life, they were more likely to die at an early age. Globality was also a significantly better predictor of deaths by accident or violence than deaths by cardiovascular disease or cancer. The fact that globality best predicted deaths by accident

Self/Social Connections Exercise 4.2

Do You Have a Pessimistic or an Optimistic Explanatory Style?

To gain insight into how you tend to explain events in life that personally happen to you imagine yourself in the two situations described below. Recognizing that events often have many causes, if these situations happened to you, what do you think would be the primary cause of each? Answer questions a to c about each situation by circling a number from 1 to 5 for each question.

Situation 1:

While eating at a restaurant, your dinner companion appears bored.

a. Is this outcome caused by you or by the other person or the circumstances?
Completely caused by other   **1   2   3   4   5**   *Completely caused by me*
people or circumstances

b. Will this cause be present in the future?
Will never be present again   **1   2   3   4   5**   *Will always be present*

c. Is this cause unique to this situation, or does it also affect other areas of your life?
Affects just this situation   **1   2   3   4   5**   *Affects all situations in my life*

Situation 2:

You receive an award for a university or community project.

a. Is this outcome caused by you or by the other people or the circumstances?
Completely caused by other   **1   2   3   4   5**   *Completely caused by me*
people or circumstances

b. Will this cause be present in the future?
Will never be present again   **1   2   3   4   5**   *Will always be present*

c. Is this cause unique to this situation, or does it also affect other areas of your life?
Affects just this situation   **1   2   3   4   5**   *Affects all situations in my life*

Scoring

For the negative outcome situation 1, high scores (4, 5) on questions a to c describe an internal, stable, and global attribution (pessimistic explanatory style). Low scores (1, 2) on these same questions describe an external, unstable, and specific attribution (optimistic explanatory style). For the positive outcome situation 2, high scores on questions a to c again describe an internal, stable, and global attribution, but now this indicates an optimistic explanatory style. Low scores indicate a pessimistic explanatory style.

or violence suggests that expecting bad events to spread throughout one's life may lead to poor problem solving and risky decision making by pessimists.

Regarding deaths by disease, additional research indicates that optimists may have better immune systems than pessimists, making them less susceptible to diseases. For example, one study found that optimists have higher numbers of helper T-cells that mediate immune reactions to infection than pessimists (Segerstrom et al., 1998). Combined with the previous results from the college sample and the first archival study, these findings suggest that pessimists may be more stress-prone than optimists (Bennett & Elliott, 2005). A central feature in this susceptibility to stress appears to be the beliefs that people develop about why both positive and negative events occur in their lives.

Fortunately, people with a pessimistic explanatory style can be taught to change their self-attributions through cognitive therapy (Goldwurm et al., 2006; Meevissen et al., 2011). Typically, this therapy involves keeping a diary of daily successes and failures, and identifying how you contributed to your successes and how external factors caused your failures. Essentially, it trains people to do what most of us do naturally: engage in the self-serving bias (see Chapter 1, p. 16) and imagine better possible selves. In one such intervention program among children in mainland China, David Yu and Martin Seligman (2002) found that children with a pessimistic explanatory style who were placed in an "optimistic child" intervention program showed significantly fewer depressive symptoms six months later compared with children in the control group. Because people in collectivist cultures are less likely to engage in the self-serving bias than are individualists, it is possible that these "optimistic" intervention programs might be particularly effective in such cultures. However, it is also possible that intervention programs to increase optimistic explanatory style may be short-lived in cultures where the overall approach to the self does not encourage the sort of self-esteem enhancement associated with self-optimism. The lesson to be learned from this research on explanatory style is one of the basic truths of social psychology: those around you will shape your interpretation of events, and your subsequent social thinking will profoundly influence your emotions and actions.

THE BIG PICTURE

Whether it is in first impressions, attributions, or how we generally try to make sense of our social world, problems can arise at many points in the social judgment process. Adding to this complexity is the fact that sometimes our judgments are under the control of automatically activated evaluation without our awareness. Because of these and other considerations, rational models are often inadequate in reliably describing the social judgmental process. Sometimes judgments must be made very quickly and do not allow for careful observation and logical analysis. At other times, information in our social world is so unreliable, biased, and incomplete that a rational analysis is not possible. In such situations, we typically rely on heuristics and other mental shortcuts as a means to judge our world.

You may be wondering how we survive in a complex and ever-changing world, given that we are predisposed to make such a wide variety of errors. One thing to keep in mind is that our social world is much more flexible and dynamic than the static and artificial laboratory conditions that often characterize social psychological research (Schliemann et al., 1997). In a laboratory study, once a research participant makes a judgmental error, it becomes a data point, frozen in time. However, in the course of everyday life, people are constantly revising their social assessments due to feedback from the environment. As a result of this flexibility, many of the social judgment errors committed in the "real world" are corrected through normal interaction with others (Fiske & Haslam, 1996). For example, you may meet someone and, based on that limited encounter, form a certain impression. Another person, upon hearing of that impression, may provide new meaningful information that redefines your initial impression. This evolution of social reality is ongoing and can be extremely forgiving of individual judgmental errors, so that you can arrive at an "efficient definition" of others that can be used in the social world.

A second thing to keep in mind is how social cognitive theorists conceive of us as social thinkers. What motivates us in a given situation often determines whether we make careful and rational decisions or quick and sloppy ones. Unlike computers, we have an investment in our self-beliefs and our beliefs about others (Ames, 2004). This psychological fact makes motivational biases likely in social thinking. Through such biases, we often can justify our self-concepts and our worldviews, making it possible for us to more confidently engage in social interaction and meet daily challenges.

Anthony Greenwald (1980), in an analysis of how the self figures into the social cognition equation, makes this very point. He argues that cognitive biases serve very useful and self-protective functions.

Likening the self to a totalitarian government, Greenwald states that both are designed to manage (and distort) information so as to maintain a stable and efficiently functioning system. The distortion of reality is functional for both the self and the dictatorship. If this biasing did not occur, the system—either self or governmental—would likely collapse.

In the final analysis, our social judgments should not be expected to be any more accurate or efficient than our self-judgments. Just as we have a need for consistency when assessing our self-beliefs, we also express that need in our social judgments. When we are faced with contradictory information, our inclination is to distort or explain away the contradictions. As proposed by Greenwald (1980), these distortions may well have functional value, allowing us to maintain a set of beliefs and perceptions of the world that have proven useful and efficient in making everyday decisions. Just as there are individual differences in accuracy of self-assessments, there are variations in people's ability to judge their social surroundings. In the final analysis, perhaps a key factor in increasing accuracy both about the self and about others is *curiosity* (Hartung & Renner, 2011). When analyzing the complex and changing nature of both the self and the surrounding social world, being both eager for new information and willing to learn from others will greatly increase your likelihood of making smart personal and social judgments.

Check out our web site

www.BVTLab.com

for chapter-by-chapter flashcards, summaries, and practice quizzes.

WEB SITES

ACCESSED THROUGH www.BVTLab.com/sop6

Web sites for this chapter focus on social cognition and person perception topics, including social categorization, stereotyping, counterfactual thinking nonverbal communication and the history of attribution theory.

SOCIAL COGNITION PAPER ARCHIVE AND INFORMATION CENTER

This web page maintained at Purdue University archives various abstracts of social cognition articles in such areas as judgment and decision-making, social categorization, stereotyping, and person memory.

COUNTERFACTUAL RESEARCH NEWS

How might your life have unfolded differently? This web site contains a bibliography of counter-factual publications, in press articles, and cartoons.

NONVERBAL COMMUNICATION WEB PAGE

Dane Archer's web page will introduce you to the topic of nonverbal communication and give you a chance to try to guess the meaning of some real nonverbal communication.

FACIAL ANALYSIS WEB SITE

This Web site highlights the work of many past and present researchers, including deBoulogne, Darwin, Ermiane, and Ekman.

Chapter 5
Attitudes and Persuasion

Chapter Outline

Introduction

The Nature of Attitudes
Attitudes are positive or negative evaluations of objects.
Implicit attitudes may underlie explicit attitudes.
Reference groups shape social and political attitudes.

How Does Automatic Thinking Shape Attitudes and Behavior?
Mere exposure can lead to positive attitudes.
Attitudes can form through classical conditioning.
Reinforcement and punishment can shape attitudes.
Attitudes are influenced by changes in facial expression, head movement, and body posture.

How Does Deliberate Thinking Shape Attitudes and Behavior?
Cognitive dissonance theory asserts that rationalization shapes attitudes.
Cognitive consistency is not a universal motive.
Self-perception theory contends that behavior causes attitudes.
The theory of planned behavior explains "thought-through" actions.

The Nature of Persuasion
Persuasion can occur through both effortful and effortless thinking.
Persuader credibility and attractiveness can affect persuasion.
Rapid speech encourages peripheral-route persuasion while hindering central-route processing.
Emotions motivate, enhance, and hinder persuasion.
Two-sided messages inoculate audiences against opposing views.
We can develop attitude certainty by actively trying to counterargue.

APPLICATIONS
Can You Be Persuaded by Subliminal Messages?

PREVIEW Most people believe that subliminal messages can shape thinking and behavior, but is there scientific research to back up this belief? What is the history of subliminal persuasion research and how have social psychologists studied this phenomenon?

THE BIG PICTURE

WEB SITES

INTRODUCTION

Alcohol is a key ingredient at most college parties. It is also the key contributing factor to an array of antisocial behaviors on college campuses, including fights, vandalism, rape, and drunk-driving accidents (Ciesla, et al., 2011). A survey of students at 119 U.S. college campuses found that almost 50 percent of the men and 40 percent of the women were binge drinkers, meaning that they consumed five or more drinks per episode (Wechsler, et al., 2002). An extensive three-year investigation by the Task Force on College Drinking, commissioned by the National Institute on Alcohol Abuse and Alcoholism, found that every year approximately fourteen hundred college students die from alcohol-related causes and another one hundred fifty thousand students develop a health problem related to alcohol (NIAAA, 2002). In addition, each year more than six hundred thousand students are assaulted by other students who have been drinking. This pattern of binge drinking among college students has remained stable over the past decade (Beets, et al., 2009).

Imagine for a minute that you are a college administrator trying to figure out how to deal with the problem of excess alcohol consumption on your campus. Further imagine that within the past year you have had the heartbreaking task of informing a mother and a father that their son had died of alcohol poisoning, and you regularly work with campus security and local law enforcement officials on incidents involving physical and sexual assaults in which alcohol was a contributing factor. How do you think these experiences would influence your attitude toward campus drinking? Do you think you would try to persuade students to change their own attitudes toward alcohol and excess drinking? If so, would you promote "Just Say No" or "Think Before You Drink" ad campaigns to convince students to drink less? Could social psychological theory and research help you develop an effective program to lower students' health and safety risks involving alcohol? This chapter will address these and other questions by examining the social psychological dynamics of attitude formation and change, as well as the factors that promote and hinder persuasion.

THE NATURE OF ATTITUDES

In 1935, in the *Handbook of Social Psychology*, Gordon Allport declared that attitude was social psychology's most indispensable concept:

Binge drinking is a serious problem on college campuses. What might influence students' attitudes toward excess alcohol consumption?

Without guiding attitudes the individual is confused and baffled. Some kind of preparation is essential before he can make a satisfactory observation, pass suitable judgment, or make any but the most primitive reflex type of response. Attitudes determine for each individual what he will see and hear, what he will think and what he will do. To borrow a phrase from William James, they "engender meaning upon the world"; they draw lines about and segregate an otherwise chaotic environment; they are our methods for finding our way about in an ambiguous universe. (Allport, 1935, p. 806)

The principal reason the attitude concept has been so popular in social psychology is that attitudes are supposed to influence behavior (Friedkin, 2010). Any concept that is believed to have such power is bound to come under serious scrutiny by those who desire to unlock the mysteries of human functioning. Social psychologists are not alone in recognizing the importance of attitudes as a key to behavioral change. Most people believe that if they can influence people's attitudes, their behavior will follow.

ATTITUDES ARE POSITIVE OR NEGATIVE EVALUATIONS OF OBJECTS.

Prior to the 1990s, attitudes were often defined in terms of three distinct components: cognitive, affective, and behavioral (Breckler, 1984). According to this multidimensional, or *tricomponent* view, attitudes are made up of our beliefs about an object, our feelings about the object, and our behavior toward the object. Although this definition is appealing because it so neatly carves up the attitude concept into three distinct categories, research indicates that not all three of these components need be in place for an attitude to exist (Huskinson & Haddock, 2004). For example, you could develop a positive attitude toward a product you see on television without developing any beliefs about it or ever engaging in any behavior relevant to the product. As you will learn (see pp. 163-165), simply by repeatedly being exposed to the product, you can develop a positive attitude toward it.

Because the three aspects of the tricomponent definition are not always present in an attitude, many social psychologists have moved away from this elegant multidimensional view to an earlier, more basic unidimensional, or *single component*, definition in which *evaluation* is central. Here, **attitude** is simply defined as a positive or negative evaluation of an object (Schuman, 1995). "Objects" include people, things, events, and issues. When people use such words as *like, dislike, love, hate, good,* and *bad,* they are usually describing their attitudes. Social psychologists also use specialized terms to describe certain classes of attitudes. For example, an attitude toward the self is called *self-esteem* (Chapter 3), certain attitudes toward groups are referred to as *prejudice* (Chapter 6), and attitudes toward individuals are referred to as *interpersonal attraction* (Chapter 9), *friendship,* and *love* (Chapter 10). The movement away from the tricomponent attitude definition does not mean that social psychologists no longer consider beliefs, feelings, and behavior important in explaining attitudes. Instead, as illustrated in Figure 5.1, these three sources of evaluative judgment—beliefs, feelings, and past behavior—are thought of as determining attitudes singly or in combination.

attitude
···················
A positive or negative evaluation of an object

As attitudes holders, we appear to be automatic evaluators (Ferguson, 2007). Brain-imaging studies suggest that when encountering people, things, and events, the *amygdala* in the brain's limbic system engages in an immediate primitive "good-bad" emotional assessment that may be followed by higher-order processing in the cerebral cortex (Banaji & Heiphetz, 2010). Greater amygdala activity occurs for initial negative assessments than for those that are positive, with much of this evaluative processing being unconscious. The importance of the amygdala in making such "good-bad" assessments is so great that damage to this brain area severely limits the ability to acquire classically conditioned preferences (see pp. 166–167). Once the amygdala makes this automatic evaluation, it is the job of the cerebral cortex to analyze and interpret this initial

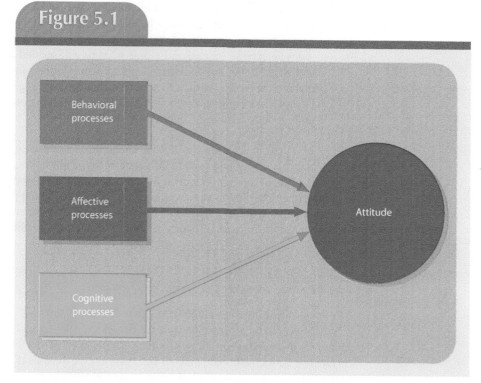

Figure 5.1

Three Different Types of Attitude Antecedents

Attitudes are believed to be formed through affective, behavioral, and cognitive processes. The assumption that attitudes are formed on the basis of affective or emotional experiences is reflected in classical conditioning principles and the mere exposure hypothesis. The idea that evaluations are based on behavioral responses is reflected in operant conditioning principles, self-perception theory, and the facial feedback hypothesis. Finally, the claim that attitudes derive from a process of cognitive learning can be seen in a host of theories, including the theory of planned behavior and cognitive dissonance theory.

assessment into the subjective experience of various emotions, which often leads to consciously held positive or negative attitudes (Le-Doux, 1998).

Just because we can evaluate with ease does not necessarily mean that we all place equal importance on the evaluative process; we differ in our need to evaluate (Jarvis & Petty, 1996; Tuten & Bosnjak, 2002). Spend a few minutes completing *Self/Social Connection Exercise 5.1*, which measures individual differences in the tendency to evaluate.

IMPLICIT ATTITUDES MAY UNDERLIE EXPLICIT ATTITUDES.

implicit attitude
. . . .
An attitude that is activated automatically from memory, often without the person's awareness that she or he possesses it

The Need to Evaluate Scale measures individual differences in the desire to engage in conscious evaluation. Besides such deliberate evaluation, an increasing number of social psychologists and other social scientists are studying attitude evaluations resulting from implicit cognitive processes (Di Conza et al., 2010; Perez, 2010). As discussed in Chapter 4, *implicit cognition* involves judgments or decisions that occur automatically without our awareness. Being a product of implicit cognition, an **implicit attitude** is an attitude that is activated automatically from memory, often without the person's awareness that she or he even possesses it (McConnell et al., 2008). Feeling uneasy and irritable around a new acquaintance because you unconsciously associate him with a disagreeable man from your past is an example of an implicit attitude. Likewise, feeling more comfortable around women than men because you unconsciously associate women with your mother and other women who raised you during childhood is also an example of an implicit attitude (Rudman & Goodwin, 2004). Implicit attitudes are

How Strong Is Your Need to Evaluate?

The extent to which people chronically engage in evaluation is measured by items on the Need to Evaluate Scale (NES: Jarvis & Petty, 1996). To take the NES, read each item below and then indicate how well each statement describes you using the following scale:

1 = extremely uncharacteristic (very much unlike me)
2 = somewhat uncharacteristic (somewhat unlike me)
3 = uncertain
4 = somewhat characteristic (somewhat like me)
5 = extremely characteristic (very much like me)

1. I form opinions about everything.
2. I prefer to avoid taking extreme positions.*
3. It is very important to me to hold strong opinions.
4. I want to know exactly what is good and bad about everything.
5. I often prefer to remain neutral about complex issues.*
6. If something does not affect me, I do not usually determine if it is good or bad.*
7. I enjoy strongly liking and disliking new things.
8. There are many things for which I do not have a preference.*
9. It bothers me to remain neutral.
10. I like to have strong opinions even when I am not personally involved.
11. I have many more opinions than the average person.
12. I would rather have a strong opinion than no opinion at all.
13. I pay a lot of attention to whether things are good or bad.
14. I only form strong opinions when I have to.*
15. I like to decide that new things are really good or really bad.
16. I am pretty much indifferent to many important issues.*

Directions for Scoring

Several of the NTE items are reverse-scored; that is, for these items a lower rating actually indicates a higher level of evaluation need. Before summing the items, recode those with an asterisk (*) so that 1 = 5, 2 = 4, 4 = 2, and 5 = 1. To calculate your need to evaluate score, add up your responses to the sixteen items. When Jarvis and Petty developed the NTE in 1996, the mean score for college students was about 52. The higher your score is above this value, the greater is your motivation to evaluate objects and events. The lower your score is below this value, the less of this need to evaluate you probably possess.

Interpretation of Scores   How do individuals with a high versus a low need to evaluate differ from one another? People with a high need to evaluate are more likely to hold attitudes toward issues they have previously encountered and are more likely to describe daily events in evaluative terms than those with a low need to evaluate (Jarvis & Petty 1996). Further, the attitudes of high need to evaluate individuals are more accessible from memory and more extreme than those of low need to evaluate persons (Federico 2004; Hermans, et al. 2001). Individual differences in the need to evaluate are hypothesized to affect people's response to both positive and negative life events. For example, the impact that romantic or academic successes and failures might have on your self-esteem or overall happiness could be influenced by the degree to which you chronically evaluate these events.

simple gut-level evaluations, and whether they will be positive or negative depends on whether the associations activated in memory are pleasant or unpleasant (Gawronski & Bodenhausen, 2006). In contrast, an **explicit attitude** is consciously held, and it is a much more thoughtful and deliberate evaluation. If you consider once again the tricomponent view of attitudes (p. 158), implicit attitudes are simply produced by the affective component, but explicit attitudes are typically a joint product of affective, cognitive, and behavioral components.

The idea that you can have two attitudes toward someone or something—one explicit and the other implicit—raises an intriguing question. What happens when a person's explicit and implicit attitudes are evaluatively opposite? This simultaneous possession of contradictory implicit and explicit attitudes toward the same object is known as **dual attitudes** (Wilson et al., 2000). In M. Kierstead's (1981) short story, "The Shetland Pony," a woman realizes while reminiscing about her beloved childhood pony—which regularly bit her—that she actually had an unconscious hatred of it as a child:

> It wasn't until Blake said it [that he hated the pony] that Kate realized that she, too, had always hated Topper. For years they had been conned into loving him, because children love their pony, and their dog, and their parents, and picnics, and the ocean, and the lovely chocolate cake. (Kierstead, 1981, p. 48)

This literary example illustrates the idea that contradictory explicit and implicit attitudes can develop simultaneously, due to different situational factors, with implicit attitudes developing first (Rudman et al., 2007). For Kate, her positive explicit attitude toward Topper was shaped by other people's expectations that children should love their pets, while her earlier negative implicit attitude developed because of Topper's unpleasant behavior. Here, the later developed explicit attitude overrode the earlier developed implicit attitude in young Kate's conscious evaluation of Topper.

In Chapter 2 we discussed the most common means of measuring explicit attitudes, namely, self-reporting. In contrast to this relatively straightforward approach in measuring consciously held attitudes, determining a person's implicit attitudes requires less direct methods. Implicit attitude researchers believe that monitoring attitude holders' nonverbal behavior and physiological responses can reveal the existence of implicit attitudes that contradict explicit attitudes (Cunningham et al., 2001; Mahaffey et al., 2005). In our pony example, young Kate's tendency to flinch and frown when near Topper was a telltale sign that she possessed a negative implicit attitude toward her pet. Similarly, the dilation of your pupils and elevated blood pressure that occur whenever you are near your best friend's boyfriend or girlfriend may signify that you have an implicit romantic attitude of which you may be unaware.

Although implicit attitudes can be measured by attending to nonverbal responses and physiological arousal, the most popular technique employed by researchers is the Implicit Association Test (IAT), which was described in Chapter 3 (p. 99). In assessing implicit attitudes, the IAT measures differences in memory associations between target categories (for example, *dog* or *cat*) and evaluative categories (such as *like* or *dislike*). This is accomplished by relying on a response *latency indicator* obtained by pairing target and evaluative categories. Using a computer, participants are asked to respond quickly with a right-hand key press to items representing one target category and one evaluative category (*dog* and *like*), and with a left-hand key press to items from the remaining two categories (*cat* and *dislike*). Participants then perform a second task in which the key assignment for one of the pairs is switched (*dog* and *dislike* share a response, likewise *cat* and *like*). If a person repeatedly responds to one of these pairings (for example, *dog* and *like*) faster than to the other pairing (for example, *dog* and *dislike*), this is interpreted as indicating that the person has a stronger tendency to automatically associate the category dog with positive evaluations.

Research suggests that dual attitudes will most likely develop for issues that are socially sensitive, such as people's attitudes toward pornography, racial and ethnic groups, or their friends' romantic partners (Neumann et al., 2005; Yoo et al., 2010). Although much more research is needed before we understand how implicit attitudes operate and influence behavior, and whether they are truly unconscious (Gawronski et al., 2007), when describing traditional attitude theories in this chapter we will discuss how they might account for both explicit and implicit attitudes.

REFERENCE GROUPS SHAPE SOCIAL AND POLITICAL ATTITUDES.

Have you ever observed pleasant dinner conversation change into bitter accusations due to one person discovering that another held different attitudes about some political or social issue? Have you yourself been one of these dinner combatants?

reference group
. . . .
A group to which people orient themselves, using its standards to judge themselves and the world

The groups to which we belong or with which we identify often determine our attitudes. A **reference group** is a group to which people orient themselves, using its standards to judge themselves and the world. An important defining characteristic of a reference group is that people have an *emotional attachment* to it and refer to it for guidance, even if they are not actual members. Reference groups can be large and inclusive, such as an entire nation or religion, but they can also be much smaller, such as one's family or friends.

One of the first and best studies investigating reference group influence on attitudes was the research of Theodore Newcomb in the 1930s documenting college students' shift from social and political conservatism when they entered college to liberalism when they graduated. Newcomb's research began in 1934 when he was hired as a young faculty member at the recently established Bennington College for women in Vermont. This new college was very exclusive, with almost all students coming from upper class, politically conservative New England families. In contrast, Newcomb and most of the other young faculty were very liberal in their social views. Thus, the first-year entering students were moving from one social context—a conservative family and social life—into a new context in which the authority figures and role models held exactly opposite social views.

Due to its small size (three hundred students and faculty) and its location in a relatively isolated area of rural Vermont, Bennington fostered a great deal of interaction between the faculty and the female student body. This unique convergence of circumstances prompted Newcomb to test a belief that he had about how people's attitudes are influenced by changes in their reference groups. To accomplish this task, Newcomb (1943) tested the social and political attitudes of the arriving first-year students, and he remeasured their attitudes each year until they graduated.

What did Newcomb find? Each passing semester, the students' social and political attitudes became increasingly liberal. As one student explained her shift in attitudes over the course of time, "I'm easily influenced by people whom I respect, and the people who rescued me when I was down and out, intellectually, gave me a radical intellectual approach" (Newcomb, 1958, p. 273). Newcomb believed that this attitude change was due to the students' disengagement from their conservative hometown reference group and their integration into a new, more liberal reference group at Bennington. Those students who maintained their conservative political perspective throughout their college years were those who spent their vacations with their parents and frequently traveled home on weekends and therefore did not blend into the Bennington culture.

In two separate follow-up studies of the Bennington College women, Newcomb and his colleagues (1967) demonstrated the importance of reference groups in maintaining attitudes even when the person is no longer immersed within the group. The first follow-up interviews were conducted in the 1960s, twenty-five years after the original study. These Bennington alumnae were now in their 40s and 50s and were also in the top 1 percent of the population in socioeconomic status. Comparing them with non-Bennington-educated women of comparable wealth, age, religion, and geographic region, Newcomb found that the Bennington women's political attitudes and behavior were much more liberal. In addition, the Bennington women's selection of a spouse and friends was partly based on their liberal political preferences.

In the 1980s, the Bennington women, who were now in their 60s and 70s, were recontacted. It was discovered that these women's liberal reference groups, forged during their college days a half century ago, still significantly influenced their lives (Alwin et al., 1991). When compared with other college-educated women in their same age group, the Bennington graduates consistently preferred the more liberal candidate in each presidential election from 1952 to 1984. Despite the fact that college-educated women of the 1930s generation were much more likely than noncollege-educated women to align themselves with the more conservative Republican Party throughout their lives, this was not the case for the Bennington women. In fact, their social and political attitudes were even more intensely liberal than most women of their generation (Cohen & Alwin, 1993).

Other studies, testing different social groups, have replicated Newcomb's overall findings (Marwell et al., 1987; Verkuyten & Yildiz, 2007). For example, female college students who enroll in women's studies courses develop stronger feminist attitudes and beliefs than women who are interested, but do not enroll, in these courses (Henderson-King & Stewart, 1999). Together, these findings illustrate the important role that reference groups play in shaping and maintaining social and political attitudes, as well as the role that these attitudes play in shaping the life course of those who hold them (Arendt, 2010; Carey, et al., 2006). To a substantial degree, when you select a college or a university to attend following high school graduation, you may also be inadvertently choosing a new social and political perspective. Sometimes, these newly adopted political and social attitudes become the "little surprises" young adults spring upon their parents around the dinner table during semester breaks and summer holidays. If you have had such conversations with your parents, or believe you will have some in the not-too-distant future, now you can also describe the social psychological dynamics of your political transformation as well. Pleasant dining!

SECTION SUMMARY

- Attitudes are positive or negative evaluations of objects.

- Attitudes are determined by a number of factors, including past behavior, emotions, and cognitions.

- Explicit attitudes are consciously held.

- Implicit attitudes are activated automatically outside of conscious awareness and may conflict with explicit attitudes.

- Reference groups shape and maintain our social and political attitudes, as well as our life choices.

HOW DOES AUTOMATIC THINKING SHAPE ATTITUDES AND BEHAVIOR?

As already mentioned, attitudes can develop from your beliefs, your feelings, and your behavior, singly or in combination. In this section of the chapter, we examine theories that explain how attitudes often develop through relatively effortless thinking. Some of these theories are largely feeling or *affect-based* explanations (*mere exposure* and *classical conditioning*), while others involve more behavioral sources (*operant conditioning*).

MERE EXPOSURE CAN LEAD TO POSITIVE ATTITUDES.

One day while walking on campus I noticed a young man walking toward me. As we drew closer I noticed that my mood had brightened upon seeing him, but that also confused me. Why was I happy to see this perfect stranger? I smiled as we passed each other, but my mind was in overdrive trying to understand this spontaneous positive response. Then it hit me. This young man sat in a glass booth in my campus parking garage, monitoring daily traffic flow. Each time I parked my car, I passed by his booth, but we had never had an occasion to actually meet or converse. I knew absolutely nothing about this young man, yet seeing him had elevated my mood. I liked him! But why?

My positive attitude is best explained by a theory Robert Zajonc (pronounced like "science") first developed in 1968. Zajonc proposed that simply exposing people repeatedly to a particular object (such as a person in a booth) causes them to develop a more positive attitude toward the object. This phenomenon, which he called the **mere exposure effect**, does not require any action toward the object, nor does it require the development of any beliefs about the object.

Zajonc (1968) conducted several experiments in which increased exposure resulted in greater liking for previously neutral objects. In one study, college students were told that they were participating in an experiment on how people learn a foreign language. They were then shown ten Chinese-like characters for two seconds at a time, with instructions to pay close attention as they appeared on the screen. Two of the characters were presented only once, two others twice, two others five times, two others ten times, and a final two were presented twenty-five times. Besides these ten characters, Zajonc had two others that the participants did not see at all. Once the exposure trials were completed, participants were told that the characters were Chinese adjectives and they were now going to guess their meaning. The experimenter hastened to add that he realized it would be virtually impossible for them to guess the exact adjective; therefore, they should merely indicate whether each character meant something good or bad in Chinese. Participants then rated the characters—including the two they had not seen—using a seven-point good-bad scale. The results, shown in Figure 5.2, indicated

mere exposure effect

The tendency to develop more positive feelings toward objects and individuals the more we are exposed to them

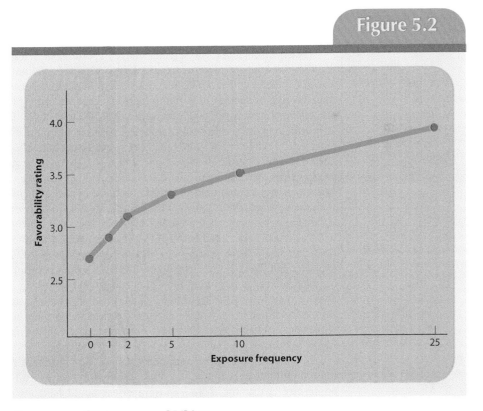

Figure 5.2

Frequency of Exposure and Liking

Research participants' attitudes toward Chinese-like characters became more positive as the frequency of their exposure to these stimuli increased. Can you think of how the mere exposure effect has influenced your own attitudes?

Source: Data from R.B. Zajonc, "Attitudinal Effects of Mere Exposure." *Journal of Personality and Social Psychology Monograph Supplement*, 9 (2, part 2), pp 1–27. American Psychological Association, 1968.

that the more often a character was repeated, the more favorable participants estimated its meaning. Zajonc obtained similar findings by using nonsense syllables and facial photographs taken from a college yearbook. Consistent with Zajonc's findings, more than two hundred experiments confirm that the mere exposure effect leads to greater liking (Bornstein, 1989).

Theodore Mita and his coworkers (1977) conducted one of the more interesting mere exposure studies. They reasoned that people are more exposed to their mirrored facial images than they are to their true facial images, and thus, they should have more positive attitudes toward the former than the latter. To test this hypothesis, they photographed women students on campus and later showed each one her picture along with a mirror image print of it. When asked to indicate which of the two prints they "liked better," two-thirds of the women preferred the mirror print, while 61 percent of their close friends preferred the actual picture, a significant difference in preference. What is impressive about these findings is that the mirrored and true facial photographs were almost indistinguishable from one another, and no one suspected they were looking at altered images.

Overall, the significance of the mere exposure effect regarding our understanding of attitudes is that it illustrates how affect can become associated with an object independent of any knowledge about it (Dechene et al., 2009; Murphy, 2001). These feeling-based attitudes develop outside the realm of rational thoughts and represent a very basic and powerful form of evaluation (Petty et al., 2001). In addition, many attitudes developed by mere exposure are implicit attitudes; they come into existence without the attitude holders' awareness and are automatically activated from memory (Hansen & Wanke, 2009; Kawakami & Yoshida, 2010). This unconscious process explains my surprise at noticing my positive feelings toward the young garage attendant. Before seeing him on campus that day I was unaware that I had formed an implicit positive attitude toward him due to my repeated exposures. Research further suggests that when an attitude formed by mere exposure is consciously held, the attitude holder is often unaware *why* they hold this attitude. In my encounter, I had to engage in some effortful thinking before piecing together why I had a positive attitude toward this unknown—yet strangely familiar—young man.

On a neurological level, scientists have hypothesized that different brain areas account for different kinds of mere exposure effects. This speculation is based on many years of research indicating that the right hemisphere of the brain tends to be superior to the left in spatial activities such as identifying faces, and the left hemisphere is superior at language processing (Gazzaniga, 2000; McAuliffe & Knowlton, 2001). In a recent series of studies, Rebecca Compton and her colleagues (2002) asked participants to stare at a dot on a computer screen while either words or faces were flashed quickly across their visual field. In one condition the stimuli were presented to the left visual field of each eye (which is processed by the right hemisphere), while in another condition the stimuli were presented to the eyes' right visual field (which is processed by the left hemisphere). Later, participants were asked to rate their liking for the stimuli. Results indicated that faces were liked better if they had previously been presented to the left visual field (right hemisphere processing), whereas words were liked better if they had previously been presented to the right visual field (left hemisphere processing). These findings suggest that the relationship between exposure and liking is primarily controlled by the right hemisphere for faces, while the left hemisphere shapes our liking for words and language. Taking these findings to a personal level, it may be that the right hemisphere of your brain played a larger role than the left hemisphere in shaping your preference for the face you see in the mirror each morning, while your left hemisphere may have been more active in shaping your positive response to seeing or hearing your name.

Beyond exploring the neurological basis for the mere exposure effect, perhaps a more important question is *why* does repeated exposure lead to positive attitudes? One possibility is that the mere exposure effect could have its roots in an evolutionarily adaptive tendency to be attracted toward those things that are familiar, because they are unlikely to pose a danger to our safety and health. That is, we may have evolved to view unfamiliar objects or situations with caution, hesitation, and even fear (Bornstein, 1989). Such caution in the presence of the unfamiliar enhances our biological fitness because we are better prepared for danger. Only through repeated exposure to that which is unfamiliar does our caution and hesitation subside—the unfamiliar and potentially dangerous becomes familiar and safe, and thus, our positive feelings increase.

ATTITUDES CAN FORM THROUGH CLASSICAL CONDITIONING.

Now let's consider another life situation. Andrew and Coretta are two young siblings who have developed extremely negative attitudes toward Muslims and Jews despite having no direct contact with anybody from these religions. How did they develop these hostile attitudes? Their hatred may have developed from listening to their parents and other adults use negatively evaluated words such as *greedy, dangerous, dishonest,* and *dirty* in referring to Muslims and Jews. Through such **classical conditioning**, a previously neutral attitude object (the conditioned stimulus) can come to evoke an attitude response (the conditioned response) simply by being paired with some other object (the unconditioned stimulus) that naturally evokes the attitude response (the unconditioned response).

classical conditioning

Learning through association, when a neutral stimulus (conditioned stimulus) is paired with a stimulus (unconditioned stimulus) that naturally produces an emotional response

Arthur and Carolyn Staats were two of the first researchers to investigate the classical conditioning of attitudes. In one study (Staats et al., 1962), they repeatedly presented participants with meaningful words (for example, *large*) paired with aversive unconditioned stimuli (shocks or loud noises). Later, the conditioned words were presented alone and the participants were asked to evaluate them on a seven-point unpleasant-pleasant scale. As they completed this task, the participants' physiological arousal was measured by monitoring their galvanic skin response. Consistent with the classical conditioning hypothesis, participants showed increased arousal in response to the presentation of the conditioned words, but little arousal in response to control words. Additionally, in comparison to a control group who had not undergone the experimental treatment, the participants also expressed more extreme negative attitudes toward the classically conditioned words.

If classical conditioning resulted only in people disliking certain words, this research would have limited importance. Yet the Staatses demonstrated that people could also be conditioned to develop negative attitudes toward specific social groups. In another experiment (Staats & Staats, 1958), they asked participants to remember words paired with various nationality names, such as "German-table," "French-with," "Dutch-gift," and "Swedish-failure." For one group of participants, the target nationality "Dutch" was always followed by a word with a positive meaning, and the target nationality "Swedish" was always paired with negative words. This evaluative pairing was reversed for a second group of participants: "Dutch" was paired with negative words, and "Swedish" was followed by positive words. At the end of the experiment, participants rated how they actually felt about the various nationality groups using a seven-point pleasant-unpleasant scale. As Figure 5.3 shows, the group that heard favorable word pairings with "Dutch" and negative pairings with "Swedish" had more positive attitudes toward the Dutch and less positive attitudes toward the Swedes. These ratings were reversed for the group that had opposite word pairings. Although the attitude shifts were not extreme (participants did not leave the lab hating one nationality and loving the other), the fact that these mild emotional stimuli produced significant attitude shifts caused attitude researchers to sit up and take notice. Classical conditioning could play a role in establishing some of the emotional components of attitudes and prejudice (Cacioppo & Berntson, 2001).

The Staatses' research and other studies conditioned attitudes to familiar English words (Zanna et al., 1970). However, this effect is even stronger when the words are unfamiliar. John Cacioppo and his colleagues (1992) found stronger conditioning effects when electric shock was paired with unfamiliar nonsense words (for example, *tasmer*) as compared with meaningful words (for example, *finger*). This study suggests that classical conditioning is a more powerful determinant of attitude formation when people possess little knowledge about the attitude object.

Having reviewed research on the conditioning of attitudes, let's return to our children, Andrew and Coretta. How might they have acquired negative attitudes toward Muslims and Jews by simply hearing their parents use a number of negative adjectives (dirty, dishonest, dangerous, greedy) in referring to these groups? As we have seen, the novel religious labels (like Muslims or Jews) were initially neutral stimuli to the children because they had not previously been associated with either positive or negative adjectives. However, once the negative adjectives were introduced, repeated pairings of the religious labels with these negative adjectives caused Andrew and Coretta to acquire negative attitudes toward these people. They may never have met a Muslim or a Jew, but this attitude conditioning played a significant role in their aversion and hostility nonetheless.

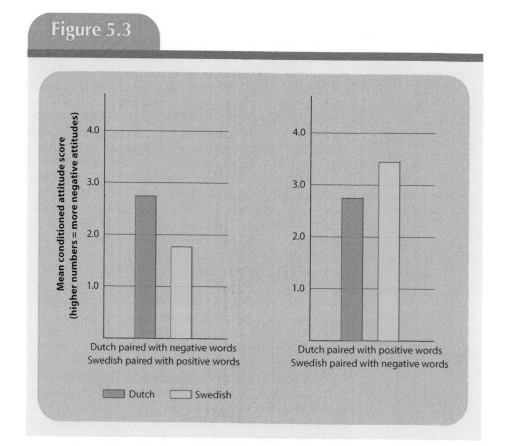

Classical Conditioning of Attitudes to Nationality Names

Research by Staats and Staats (1958) demonstrated that classical conditioning could play a role in establishing some of the emotional components of attitudes and prejudice. Participants who heard favorable word pairings with "Dutch" and negative pairings with "Swedish" subsequently had more positive attitudes toward the Dutch and less positive attitudes toward the Swedes. Those individuals who had opposite word pairings later had more favorable attitudes toward the Swedes. Can you think of instances in your own life in which certain attitudes toward other social groups have been similarly classically conditioned?

subliminal conditioning
....
Classical conditioning that occurs in the absence of conscious awareness of the stimuli involved

Additional studies indicate that classical conditioning of attitudes can occur below the level of conscious awareness, a process known as **subliminal conditioning**. In one such study, Jon Krosnick and his coworkers (1992) showed college students slide photos of a stranger going about her daily activities. These slides were preceded by very brief (13/1000 of a second) subliminal presentations of photos known to induce either positive emotions (for example, a bridal couple, people laughing, kittens) or negative emotions (for example, a skull, a werewolf, open-heart surgery). These pleasant and unpleasant photos were presented so quickly that the students did not consciously perceive them. However, despite not consciously perceiving these photos, they did affect the students' later attitudes toward the stranger. Those exposed to the positive photos reported more positive attitudes toward this unknown person than did those exposed to the negative photos. These findings and other studies suggest that attitudes can be formed through subliminal conditioning (Veltkamp et al., 2011).

operant conditioning
....
A type of learning in which behavior is strengthened if followed by reinforcement and weakened if followed by punishment

REINFORCEMENT AND PUNISHMENT CAN SHAPE ATTITUDES.

Because classical conditioning and mere exposure influence emotions, they contribute most directly to shaping the affective component of attitudes (Petty et al., 2001). Yet one of the most powerful ways in which the *behavioral* component can shape attitudes is through **operant conditioning**, a form of learning extensively studied by such behavioral psychologists as Edward Thorndike (1911) and B. F. Skinner (1938). According to operant conditioning principles, when an action toward an object is rewarded or reinforced, it will probably be repeated in the future. On the other hand, if behavior is not rewarded or is punished, similar future actions are less likely. Learning theorists who study attitudes contend that accompanying this increase or decrease of behavior will be an attitude consistent with the behavior. For example, if a child's parents and teachers praise her for doing well in math, she may redouble her efforts and develop a positive attitude toward mathematics in general. However, if her academic accomplishments go unrewarded, her interest in math may diminish and eventually extinguish. She probably will also develop a negative attitude toward the subject matter.

Although attitudes can develop by being directly rewarded and punished when interacting with the attitude object, they can also develop through the indirect means of *observational learning* (Bandura, 1986). In such instances, attitudes are shaped after observing other people being reinforced or punished when interacting with the attitude object (Chen et al., 2011). Thus, for example, you might develop a dislike for rock climbing after a friend is injured during her first attempt to learn this sport. Although your friend's newly formed dislike for rock climbing is due to operant conditioning, your negative attitude is a result of observational learning. In forming attitudes through observational learning, the people whom we observe and imitate are called *role models*, because they teach us how to play social roles. People in our reference groups (see p. 162) are often role models for us. Observing these role models helps us as children learn how to behave in our families and in the larger culture, and it also help us as adults learn the attitudes and skills necessary for career success (Buunk & van der Laan, 2002; Rogoff et al., 2003).

Observational learning can also foster positive attitudes toward unhealthy behaviors, such as smoking. A number of survey studies have found that adolescents who had never smoked were much more likely to later take up the habit if they had watched many Hollywood movies packed with smoking scenes (Dalton et al., 2003). Experimental studies indicated that as exposure to such movies increases attitudes toward smoking and smokers become more favorable (Gibson & Maurer, 2000). Teens who identify with movie stars who smoke on screen are those most likely to start smoking (Tickle et al., 2006). Cognitively, what appears to be happening is that observing actors smoking creates implicit associations in memory of smoking with desirability. In turn, these implicit associations later influence personal smoking attitudes and intentions (Dal Cin et al., 2007).

ATTITUDES ARE INFLUENCED BY CHANGES IN FACIAL EXPRESSION, HEAD MOVEMENT, AND BODY POSTURE.

One of the earliest uses of the term *attitude* came from the theater and dates back to the 1800s, where it described a physical posture or body position. An actor onstage would assume a certain body posture (for example, drooping shoulders and head), to signify the mental state of the character (dejection or sadness). Would it surprise you to learn that attitude researchers have since discovered that your emotions—and thus your attitudes—can be manipulated by changing your facial expressions, body posture, or other motor responses?

In an innovative experiment, German psychologist Fritz Strack and his colleagues (1988) asked college students to hold a pen in their mouths while they were shown a series of amusing cartoons. Participants in the *lips condition* were instructed to hold the pen tightly with their lips, while those in the *teeth condition* were told to hold the pen with their front teeth (see photographs on p. 169). In a control condition, participants were told to hold the pen in their nondominant hand. After reading the cartoons, all students rated how funny they were using a ten-point scale. Results indicated that participants who held the pen between their teeth found the cartoons to be the most amusing, followed by those who held it in their hand. Students who held the pen in their lips gave the cartoons the lowest ratings of amusement. Why do you think this was the case?

You can tell by looking at the photographs that holding a pen with the teeth causes a person to smile, while holding it with the lips prevents smiling. Could the participants have inferred their attitudes toward the cartoons based on their facial muscle movements? This is a possibility, referred to as the *facial feedback hypothesis*: People are aware of their

The facial feature hypothesis states that changes in facial expression can lead to corresponding changes in emotion. If this hypothesis is correct, what contrasting emotions might be elicited by holding a pen between one's teeth versus between one's lips?

facial expressions and infer that they must have attitudes consistent with their expressions (Dimberg & Soderkvist, 2011).

Not satisfied with this explanation, other researchers suggested that facial expressions produce physiological changes in the brain, which, in turn, spark specific emotion. For example, Robert Zajonc (1993) suggested that smiling causes facial muscles to increase the flow of air-cooled blood to the brain, which, in turn, produces a pleasant mood by lowering brain temperature. In contrast, frowning decreases blood flow, causing heightened brain temperature and an unpleasant mood. In support of this *vascular theory of emotion*, Zajonc and his coworkers (1989) found that simply having people repeat a series of vowel sounds twenty times each was sufficient to change their forehead temperature and their mood: sounds such as *ah* and *e*, which caused the speakers to mimic smiling, decreased temperature and elevated mood, whereas the *u* and the Germanic *ü* sound, which mimic frowning, had the opposite effect. Regardless of whether these findings are due to increased blood flow to the brain, this study is important because it indicates that even when people are not aware they are wearing a particular expression, movement of facial muscles can alter their mood. In other words, consciously recognized self-perception processes may not be necessary for facial feedback to work.

Besides facial expressions, other expressive behaviors also appear to influence feelings. For instance, have you ever watched passersby and guessed their emotional states based on their body postures? If you see individuals walking in an erect and upright posture, you might assume they are proud and confident, while you might guess that others are feeling dejected because they have a slumping posture. Does posture actually affect mood? In one study examining this possibility, Sabine Stepper and Strack (1993) manipulated people's posture to determine what effect it would have on their feelings of pride following success on an achievement test. Posture was manipulated by having participants take a test and then learn about their results while either sitting upright at a normal-height table or sitting slumped over at a short-legged table. Those who sat upright felt prouder after succeeding than those who were slumped over. Similarly, Gary Wells and Richard Petty (1980) asked students to "test the sound quality of headphones" by moving their heads either vertically up and down (nodding) or horizontally side to side (shaking) while listening to a taped editorial. The head nodders later expressed more positive attitudes toward the editorial than did the head shakers. Finally, John Cacioppo and his colleagues (Cacioppo et al., 1993; Priester et al., 1996) found that when research participants were presented with neutral or meaningless words and symbols while gently pressing their arms upward against a table (mimicking an inviting "approach" gesture), they expressed greater liking for the words and symbols than participants who gently pressed their arms downward on a table (mimicking a rejecting "avoidance" gesture).

Because participants in all these studies did not perceive a connection between their motor responses and their attitudes, this suggests that these findings cannot be explained by self-perception. Likewise, Zajonc's vascular theory cannot account for these findings. Instead, what may best explain these effects is classical conditioning (refer back to pp. 166–167), where an upright posture, head nodding, and "approach" arm movements have become associated with and facilitate the generation of favorable thoughts, while the reverse is true for a slumped posture, head shaking, and "avoidant" arm movements (Alluisi & Warm, 1990; Förster & Strack, 1996).

Although classical conditioning may provide an adequate explanation for how these attitudes are formed, recent studies suggest that nonverbal actions can also shape people's attitudes by influencing their *confidence* in the thoughts they are having about the attitude object. In these studies, Pablo Briñol and Richard Petty (2003) induced people to either nod or to shake their heads while listening to persuasive messages. When the arguments in the persuasive messages were strong, thereby generating mostly favorable thoughts in listeners, head nodding produced more confidence in participants, resulting in more positive attitudes than head shaking. However, when the arguments were weak and generated mostly negative thoughts, participants' head shaking produced more confidence in the resulting negative attitudes than head nodding. These findings suggest that when people are already having positive or negative thoughts about an attitude object, their head movements can increase their confidence in these thoughts if they match the underlying feelings. Briñol and Petty contend that these findings are consistent with a *social validation* explanation, meaning that head nodding (or shaking) validates people's positive (or negative) thoughts and thereby increases their confidence in the attitudes they are forming. Even here, however, classical conditioning is relevant because we learn through conditioning to associate head nodding with approval and head shaking with disapproval.

Regardless of the ultimate explanation for how body movements affect attitudes, all these studies suggest that performing actions associated with happiness cause us not only to feel happier but also to perceive other objects in our environment more favorably. Similarly, performing actions associated with sadness cause us to feel sadder and to perceive our world less favorably. So, smile and be happy!

Critical THINKING

Is there any wisdom in parents admonishing their children to straighten their posture and avoid slouching? How might the manner in which parents try to correct slouching destroy these possible benefits?

"*Without doubt, it is a delightful harmony when doing and saying go together.*"

Michel de Montaigne, French writer, 1533–1592

SECTION SUMMARY

- Some attitudes form through simple emotional mechanisms.

- In the mere exposure effect, we develop more positive feelings toward objects the more frequently we are exposed to them.

- In classical conditioning, an attitude forms when a previously neutral attitude object (the conditioned stimulus) evokes an attitude response (the conditioned response) by being paired with some other object (the unconditioned stimulus) that naturally evokes the attitude response (the unconditioned response).

- Some attitudes form through performing behaviors.

- In operant conditioning and observational learning, we develop attitudes consistent with reinforced and punished behavior.

- Attitudes can be influenced by our facial expressions, body posture, or other motor responses.

HOW DOES DELIBERATE THINKING SHAPE ATTITUDES AND BEHAVIOR?

Although attitudes sometimes develop automatically and with little cognitive effort, they are also often created and maintained through a conscious and deliberate thinking process. What are some of the psychological routes we travel in forming these more effortful attitudes?

One of the most influential approaches in social psychology, especially in the study of explicit attitudes, has been the notion that people are motivated to keep their own explicit cognitions (beliefs, attitudes, self-perceptions) organized in a consistent and tension-free manner (refer to Chapter 3, p. 97). This principle of **cognitive consistency** was first introduced by Fritz Heider (1946) and has its roots in the Gestalt belief that human beings not only expect and prefer their perceptions to be coherent and harmonious but are also motivated to make them so (Koffka, 1935; Köhler, 1929). How might this desire for consistency influence both people's attitudes and their behavior?

cognitive consistency

The tendency to seek consistency in one's cognitions

COGNITIVE DISSONANCE THEORY ASSERTS THAT RATIONALIZATION SHAPES ATTITUDES.

Over fifty years ago Leon Festinger (1957) developed the most influential consistency theory of attitudes. His *cognitive dissonance theory* proposed that although we may appear logical in our thinking and behavior, we often engage in seemingly irrational behavior to maintain cognitive consistency. It also describes and predicts how we spend much of our time *rationalizing* our behavior rather than actually engaging in rational action.

Insufficient Justification and Dissonance

Imagine that you volunteer to participate in an experiment and, upon arriving at the lab, are asked to perform two 30-minute tasks. The first task consists of emptying and refilling a tray with spools, and the second consists of repeatedly turning forty-eight wooden pegs on a board. As you work on these tasks, you silently curse their monotony. Finally, when your hour of boredom ends, the experimenter tells you that the real purpose of the study is to determine if a person's performance is influenced by whether he is told beforehand that it will be "very enjoyable" and "fun," or, like yourself, is told nothing. Then he tells you that his assistant has not shown up and will not be able to help him with the next participant who will be in the "favorable information condition." The experimenter then asks if you would tell the participant that you had just completed the task—a true statement—and that you found it to be extremely enjoyable—a lie. You agree to become the assistant and tell your lie to the waiting participant. When the participant completes the tasks and departs, the experimenter sends you to an office where an interviewer asks how fun and interesting you in fact found the tasks to be. Do you think your attitude toward these tasks would be influenced by whether the experimenter had promised you $1 versus $20 to tell your lie? If yes, which sum of money would lead to the greatest attitude shift?

This is the scenario of a classic cognitive dissonance experiment conducted by Festinger and J. Merrill Carlsmith (1959). As depicted in Figure 5.4, participants who, for $1, told others (who were actually confederates) that the task was "very enjoyable" and "fun" came to believe that it was enjoyable to a far greater degree than those who said so for $20. These $1 liars also expressed greater enthusiasm for the task than a control group who were not asked to lie. Do these findings surprise you? They certainly surprised a lot of attitude researchers because it contradicted reinforcement theories, which predicted that participants who were paid more to lie would exhibit greater attitude change than those who were paid less (see p. 168). Although these findings seemed surprising to many, they are consistent

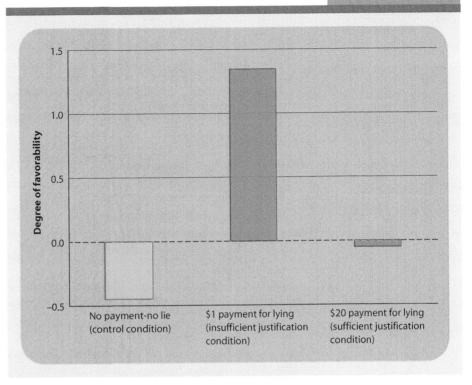

Effects of Payment on Attitudes Toward a Dull Task

Festinger and Carlsmith (1959) predicted that participants who were given insufficient mone-tary justification for lying (the $1 liars) would experience greater cognitive dissonance and, thus, would express more liking for the dull task than those who received sufficient monetary justification (the $20 liars). Why would insufficient justification create greater dissonance?

with cognitive dissonance theory. The theory states that if you simultaneously hold two cognitions that are incon-sistent ("This was a boring task" and "I told someone it was very enjoyable"), you will experience a feeling of discomfort known as **cognitive dissonance**. Fes-tinger believed dissonance was analogous to hunger in its aversiveness; that is, people are nat-urally motivated to reduce or eliminate the dis-sonance. How is this cognitive dissonance eliminated or reduced? Table 5.1 lists some ways to reduce dissonance.

In the Festinger and Carlsmith study, only two dissonance-reducing outlets were available to the liars: (1) They could add a third cognition to make their attitude-behavior inconsistency less inconsistent, or (2) they could change their attitude about the task. The reason the "$1 partici-pants" showed more attitude change toward the boring task than the "$20 participants" was that they experienced a greater *amount* of cognitive dissonance. Festinger and Carl-smith reasoned that the $20 participants would not need to change their attitudes because they could justify their actions and, thus, reduce dissonance by adding a third cognition that makes the original cognition less inconsistent: Their high payment was *sufficient justification* for their counterattitudinal behavior. Thus, the $20 participants had a reasonable justification for lying. The same could not be said for the $1 participants. They were given only $1 for their lie. This amount of payment provided *insufficient jus-tification* for their counterattitudinal behavior. According to Festinger, when people

cognitive dissonance
• •
A feeling of discomfort caused by performing an action that is inconsistent with one's attitudes

Table 5.1

Ways to Reduce Cognitive Dissonance

There are a number of ways to reduce dissonance. For example, consider college students who have decided to quit consuming alcohol in excessive amounts but then resume binge drinking. How might they reduce the dissonance aroused by the discrepancy between their attitude ("I don't like binge drinking") and their behavior ("I'm drinking excessively again")?

COMMON STRATEGIES

Changing attitudes: People can simply change their attitudes to make them consistent with discrepant attitudes or prior behaviors. ("I don't really need to quit. I like getting drunk with my friends.")

Adding cognitions: If two discrepant thoughts cause dissonance, people can add more consonant thoughts. ("Getting drunk relaxes me and makes me happy, which is good for my mental health while in college.")

Altering the importance of the discrepancy: People can alter the importance of the discrepant thoughts or actions. ("It's more important to stay relaxed and to 'fit in' with my friends than to worry about the health effects of alcohol.")

Reducing perceived choice: People can convince themselves that they are not freely choosing to engage in the discrepant behavior. ("I have no choice but to drink. I have so much stress in my life now that getting drunk is one of the only ways to blow off steam.")

Making self-affirmations: People can remind themselves of cherished aspects of their self-concept that are unrelated to the current dissonance, thus restoring their feelings of overall integrity. ("I have so many other positive qualities and accomplishments in other areas of my life, so it's all right that I have 'fallen short' in this one small area.")

Changing behavior: People can change their behavior so it no longer conflicts with their attitudes. ("I'm going to stop getting drunk again.")

"Inconsistencies of opinion, arising from changes of circumstances, are often justifiable.**"**

––––––––––

Daniel Webster, American statesman, 1782–1852

engage in a counterattitudinal behavior without receiving a sufficient reward, they should experience cognitive dissonance. Faced with this dissonance, the $1 group strove to reduce the negative drive state. They could not deny that they lied, so instead they changed their attitude about the task: It was not so boring after all.

Just as the offer of a small reward is insufficient justification for engaging in counterattitudinal behavior, the threat of mild punishment is insufficient justification for *not* engaging in some desired action. In an experiment demonstrating this effect, four-year-old children were prohibited by an adult from playing with a toy in a playroom (Aronson & Carlsmith, 1963). In one condition, the prohibition was induced by a severe threat ("I don't want you to play with the toy on the table. If you play with it, I will be very angry. I will have to take all of my toys and go home!"). In another condition the threat was mild ("I don't want you to play with the toy on the table. If you play with it, I will be annoyed."). Even though all the children had previously stated that they liked this toy, all obeyed the adult's command.

Before reading further, based on your understanding of cognitive dissonance, how should these two groups of children have differed in their attitudes toward this toy after not playing with it? Remember, for both the mildly and severely threatened children, the attitude that "I like the toy on the table" was inconsistent with the realization that "I didn't play with the toy." Yet, for the children who received the severe threat, this was sufficient external justification for not engaging in the desired behavior, and therefore they should not have experienced much dissonance. However, the mildly threatened children had insufficient justification for not playing with the desired toy, and therefore they should have experienced greater dissonance. The only way for them to reduce their dissonance was to devalue the forbidden toy. This is exactly what they did. No similar attitude change was found in the severely threatened group, or in a control group of children who received no threats. Forty-five days after the initial testing, the children who had been mildly threatened still had more negative attitudes toward this toy than did those who had been severely threatened. A replication of this study found that the tendency to shun the highly attractive toy persisted up to nine weeks after the presentation of the mild threat (Freedman, 1965).

This notion of insufficient justification is so important in understanding how cognitive dissonance operates that it bears reviewing. As Festinger stated, if the reasons for engaging in counterattitudinal behavior are strong (for example, "I was paid $20 to lie" or "I was severely threatened not to play with the toy"), little or no dissonance will be generated. However, if these reasons are weak ("I was paid only $1 to lie" or "I was only mildly threatened"), then people are confronted with the dissonance-producing thought that they had no strong or clear basis for acting inconsistently with their attitudes. In other words, cognitive dissonance theory demonstrates that the weaker the reasons for acting inconsistently with one's attitudes, the *greater* the pressures to change the attitudes in question.

Freedom of Choice and Dissonance

Another factor that can create cognitive dissonance is freely choosing to engage in a counterattitudinal behavior. For example, let's suppose young Jack tells his grade-school friends that he hates girls, but later they see him sitting next to Betty Lou on the bus. If the bus driver forced Jack to sit next to Betty Lou, he can legitimately explain his close proximity to her as being beyond his control. According to dissonance theory, due to Jack's lack of choice, he is unlikely to feel responsible for his actions; therefore he will not experience cognitive dissonance. However, if no one forced Jack to sit next to Betty Lou, then his behavior would be seen as freely chosen; therefore, he should experience discomfort due to his dissonant thoughts ("I hate girls, but I sat next to a girl").

Darwyn Linder and his colleagues (1967) conducted an experiment that demonstrated the role that choice plays in dissonance arousal. College students were asked to write essays in favor of a law barring controversial individuals from speaking on campus. This law, in fact, was actually being discussed in the state legislature, and almost all students opposed its passage. Students were offered either $.50 or $2.50 for their essays. In the "free-choice" condition, the experimenter stressed the students' freedom to refuse to write the essay, while in the "no-choice" condition, no mention was made about the students' right to refuse. Instead, the experimenter acted as if by volunteering to participate in the study, the students had committed themselves to its requirements.

As predicted by cognitive dissonance theory, when students' free choice was stressed, the group that was paid $.50 changed their attitude toward the law so that it was more in line with the essay content, but the attitudes of the group paid $2.50 did not shift. In the "no-choice" condition, the exact opposite effects occurred: The larger amount of money produced greater attitude change (see Figure 5.5). The attitude change in the "no-choice" condition does not conform to dissonance theory, but instead follows the principles of operant conditioning, in which external incentives shape attitudes. Thus, to experience dissonance, people must feel that they *freely chose* to behave in a counterattitudinal manner.

Justification of Effort and Dissonance

Although we have seen that using negative incentives—in the form of mild threats—can induce cognitive dissonance, which, in turn, results in less liking for the attitude object, negative incentives can also lead to *increased liking*. Recall the discussion in Chapter 2 of Leon Festinger's study of doomsday cult members (Festinger et al., 1956). Here, people had given up their worldly possessions and had left loved ones to await the arrival of space aliens. As the evidence mounted that their leader's prophecy was false, many of the cult members increased their psychological commitment to the cult. Were they

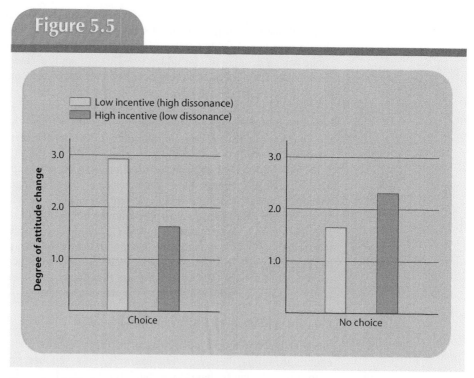

Figure 5.5

Perceived Choice, Incentive, and Attitude Change

Linder, Cooper, and Jones (1967) manipulated participants' freedom of choice and incentive. Consistent with cognitive dissonance theory, in the "free-choice" condition, low-incentive students expressed greater attitude change than high-incentive students. However, in the "no-choice" condition, reward or incentive effects occurred: Low-incentive students showed less attitude change than high-incentive students. What do these results tell you about the role that perceived freedom of choice plays in attitude change?

insane? Not according to cognitive dissonance theory. What about romantic decisions? Have you ever tried to convince yourself that a longstanding romantic relationship was "good for you" or worthwhile simply because you had invested a good deal of time and effort into it? Dissonance theorists argue that when people have a bad experience with some group or relationship they have freely chosen to join, there is a natural tendency for them to try to transform the bad experience into a good one to reduce cognitive dissonance. In addition, the greater the sacrifice or hardship associated with the choice, the greater the level of dissonance people experience (Cooper et al., 2005).

To better understand the actions of those who incur large costs in questionable ventures, let's look at an experiment carried out by Elliot Aronson and Judson Mills (1959) on the effects of the *severity of initiation* on liking for a group. Participants were college women who volunteered to take part in discussions of the psychology of sex. It was their false understanding that these discussions would be analyzed to better understand group dynamics. Prior to being admitted into the discussion group, each woman, except those in the control condition, was told that she would have to take an "Embarrassment Test" to assure the researchers that she could talk frankly and freely about this intimate topic. The real purpose of this test was to make the participants pay a different "price" to get into the group. Those women in the *severe initiation* condition were required to read aloud to the male experimenter a list of obscene words, as well as some extremely graphic sexual scenes from contemporary novels. (Keep in mind that this was the 1950s, when uttering obscene and sexually graphic words to a university psychologist would make most undergraduates extremely uncomfortable.) In the *mild initiation* condition, women were asked to read aloud such mildly sex-related words as *prostitute, virgin,* and *petting.* This group, then, paid a lower initiation "price" than the severe group. Regardless of how embarrassed the women were or how haltingly they read the words in either condition, all were told they had passed the test and could join the group. The women were then given earphones and instructed to listen in on the group they would soon be joining. What they heard was a discussion that Aronson and Mills described in the following manner:

> The participants spoke dryly and haltingly on secondary sex behavior in the lower animals, contradicted themselves and one another, mumbled several non sequiturs, started sentences that they never finished, hemmed, hawed, and in general conducted one of the most worthless and uninteresting discussions imaginable. (Aronson & Mills, 1959)

After listening to this discussion, the women were asked to rate both the discussion and the group members on such evaluative scales as "dull-interesting" and "intelligent-unintelligent." According to dissonance theory, the women in the severe initiation group should have experienced a pair of dissonant thoughts: "I willingly went through a very embarrassing initiation in order to join this sex discussion group"; "These group discussions are dull and worthless." To reduce cognitive dissonance, these women had to alter one of these thoughts. Because they could not deny that they willingly paid a high price to join the group, the only thought they could reasonably alter was their group evaluation. In contrast, the women in the "mild" and "no initiation" groups had invested little, if anything, to join, and thus should not have experienced much dissonance. Consistent with this reasoning, the severe initiation group gave significantly more positive evaluations of the discussion than those who were in either the mild initiation or the control groups (see Figure 5.6).

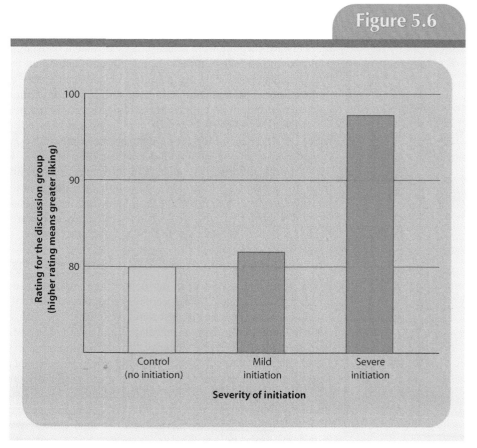

Figure 5.6

Cognitive Dissonance and the Effects of Initiations

Participants' attitudes toward the quality of the discussion in the Aronson and Mills (1959) experiment were significantly influenced by the "price" they had to pay to join the group. Based on cognitive dissonance theory, why did those women in the severe initiation condition express greater liking for the quality of the discussion?

"_That which costs little is less valued._**"**

Miguel de Cervantes, Spanish writer, 1547–1616

"_Those who have free seats at a play hiss first._**"**

Chinese proverb

Replications of this experiment have demonstrated that this effect is strong: The more you pay for something, the more you like it (Axsom, 1989; Gerard & Mathewson, 1966). Is it any wonder that many of the members of Festinger's doomsday cult increased their allegiance when those outside the group were calling it a fraud and a sham? Agreeing with this judgment would have called into question all that they had suffered. Faced with such a choice, they justified to themselves not only the actions of their group but their own actions as well.

Immoral Behavior and Dissonance

One area of life where cognitive dissonance often plays a decisive role is in moral reasoning. People care about being moral and behaving ethically (Aquino & Reed, 2002). Despite our motivation to act morally, everyday experience informs us that most of us are sometimes capable of behaving counter to our own values and moral standards if it benefits us in some way. For example, have you ever cheated on a test despite believing that cheating is wrong? Have you ever stolen something despite believing that stealing is wrong? Have you ever lied to a friend despite believing that lying is wrong? If you have engaged in such counterattitudinal actions—which is highly likely—did you revise your self-concept accordingly and think of yourself as a cheater, a thief, and a liar? Probably not. Most likely, you justified your questionable actions in some way. _Moral hypocrisy_ is the motivation to appear moral while avoiding the cost of being moral.

In a study examining how students' attitudes toward cheating are affected by their own act of cheating, Judson Mills (1958) first measured sixth graders' attitudes toward cheating and then had them take an exam in which those who scored the highest would win prizes. The exam was designed so that it was almost impossible for students to perform well without cheating. Mills also created the illusion that any cheating could not be detected. Not surprisingly, some of the students cheated. The following day students' attitudes toward cheating were remeasured. Consistent with cognitive dissonance theory, the students who had cheated now expressed more lenient attitudes toward cheating, while those who had resisted the temptation to cheat became more critical of such behavior.

Additional research suggests that, for most people, moral codes are not fixed and unchanging, but operate more like sliding scales. When people engage in actions that violate their sense of right and wrong, they often reduce the resulting cognitive dissonance by strategically forgetting their previous moral "set points" and becoming more lenient and accepting of immoral conduct (Shu et al., 2011; Tenbrunsel & Messick, 2004). In other words, they engage in self-deception and justify their immoral actions. Such moral disengagement can send people on a downward spiral of having ever more lenient ethics and ever more unethical behavior; we read about these people in the news every day when their unethical actions are finally discovered. Yet, our difference from them in moral hypocrisy may be simply a matter of degree.

Postdecision Dissonance and Altered Perceptions

A few years ago, a student in our department applied to several graduate programs in social psychology and was accepted into three of his top choices. Following a long process of weighing the strengths and weaknesses of each school, he made his choice. Shortly thereafter, I saw him on campus and asked if he had any regrets. "No, Dr. Franzoi," he said with genuine sincerity. "Since making my decision, I'm even more certain I made the right choice." Then, being the bright student that he was, he smiled and said, "Now I really understand the concept of postdecision dissonance."

What this aspiring social psychologist meant by this statement was that making a decision often arouses cognitive dissonance. As Festinger explained, whenever we must decide between attractive alternatives, the final choice is to some extent inconsistent with some of our beliefs. That is, as soon as we _commit_ ourselves to a particular course of action, the attractive aspects of the unchosen alternatives and the unattractive aspects of our choice are inconsistent with our decision. As the difficulty or importance of the decision increases, the amount of postdecision dissonance increases. Because of our tendency to react to decisions in this manner, we often try to reduce dissonance by _altering our perceptions_ of the choices we had entertained prior to making our final choice. We do this by improving our evaluation of the chosen alternative and lowering our evaluations of the unchosen alternatives (Frenkl & Doob, 1976).

Such after-the-fact, altered perceptions have been found in the behavior of consumers following product choices (Gilovich et al., 1995; Murphy & Miller, 1997), voters on election day (Regan & Kilduff, 1988), and even bettors at a racetrack (Brownstein et al., 2004; Knox & Inkster, 1968). Because votes, bets, and many product purchases cannot be changed once a decision has been made, once we commit ourselves we experience "buyers' remorse" and are motivated to reduce postdecision dissonance. Under these circumstances, the only way for us to accomplish this task is to convince ourselves that we made the right choice.

COGNITIVE CONSISTENCY IS NOT A UNIVERSAL MOTIVE.

In Festinger's theory, he assumed that everyone has an equal desire to engage in cognitively consistent actions. However, cross-cultural research later found that this desire is more descriptive of individualist cultures than those with a collectivist orientation (Heine & Lehman, 1997; Hoshino-Browne et al., 2005). Based on these findings, many cross-cultural researchers argued that the need for consistency is based on the premise that the person is an independent entity unaffected by the social context. Although this is the way people in individualist cultures are generally taught to think, people in collectivist cultures are socialized to develop interdependent selves, which are defined in relation to others, and thus tend to be more flexible. This more flexible conception of the self encourages people from collectivist cultures to think in more holistic ways than individualists, making them more comfortable with contradiction and inconsistency (Choi & Nisbett, 2000; Kitayama et al., 2006).

An illustration of the weaker attitude-behavior consistency need can be seen in the Japanese notion of the self. In traditional Japanese culture, there are two important aspects to the self: "Omote" (front) is presented to the public as a socially acceptable aspect of the self, whereas "ura" (back) is that aspect of the self that is hidden from the public (Bachnik, 1992). The Japanese value both self-aspects and teach their young how to appropriately use them. Thus, when presenting omote, not acting according to one's true attitudes is perfectly acceptable and would not cause dissonance. For example, in one study, Japanese and American students read episodes in which hypothetical characters had to choose between honestly expressing their attitudes and not doing so to maintain social appropriateness (Iwao, 1989). As expected, American students more likely favored attitude-consistent choices than their Japanese counterparts. For instance, in one hypothetical situation, a father privately disapproved of his daughter marrying someone of another race. Almost half of the American students (49 percent) stated that it would be wrong for the father to think to himself that he would never allow the marriage yet tell the couple that he favored it. On the contrary, less than 7 percent of the Japanese felt this sort of attitude-discrepant behavior was inappropriate. In summary, then, what many North Americans and other individualists consider to be discrepant and psychologically aversive—namely, believing one thing but saying something else—may not be as troubling to collectivists. However, it is important to note that there are exceptions to this Japanese-American dissonance distinction. Japanese citizens living on Hokkaido, the country's northern island with a frontier tradition and a spirit of independence, exhibit cognitive dissonance similar to that of North Americans and unlike Japanese in other areas (Kitayama et al., 2006 ; Takemura & Arimoto, 2008).

If you are from an individualist culture, you might be thinking, "I don't often get upset with acting differently from my attitudes. What gives?" Beyond cultural considerations, research indicates that some people tolerate cognitive inconsistencies better than others. Spend a few minutes completing the *Preference for Consistency Scale* in *Self/Social Connection Exercise 5.2*. Robert Cialdini and his colleagues (1995) have found that people who score high on this scale are highly motivated to keep their behavior consistent with their attitudes, as predicted by cognitive dissonance theory. In contrast, those who score low on this preference scale are much less bothered by inconsistent actions, and instead, appear open and oriented to flexibility in their behavior. Given these diverging motivational patterns, it is not surprising that those with a high preference for consistency are more likely to experience cognitive dissonance than those with a low consistency preference (Newby-Clark et al., 2002).

"Consistency, madam, is the first of Christian duties."

Charlotte Brontë, British author, 1816–1855

"The only completely consistent people are the dead."

Aldous Huxley, British novelist, 1894–1963

Critical THINKING

Can you think of instances in your own life in which you convinced yourself that a bad experience was really a good and worthwhile one?

Self/Social Connections Exercise 5.2

The Preference for Consistency Scale

Instructions

The extent to which people have a preference for consistency is measured by items on the Preference for Consistency Scale (PCS: Cialdini, et al. 1995). To take the PCS, read each item below and then indicate how well each statement describes you using the following response formats:

> 1 = Strongly disagree
> 2 = Disagree
> 3 = Somewhat disagree
> 4 = Slightly disagree
> 5 = Neither agree nor disagree
> 6 = Slightly agree
> 7 = Somewhat agree
> 8 = Agree
> 9 = Strongly agree

1. It is important to me that those who know me can predict what I will do.
2. I want to be described by others as a stable, predictable person.
3. The appearance of consistency is an important part of the image I present to the world.
4. An important requirement for any friend of mine is personal consistency.
5. I typically prefer to do things the same way.
6. I want my close friends to be predictable.
7. It is important to me that others view me as a stable person.
8. I make an effort to appear consistent to others.
9. It doesn't bother me much if my actions are inconsistent.

Directions for Scoring

The last PCS item (#9) is reverse-scored; that is, for this item a lower rating actually indicates a higher level of consistency preference. Before summing the items, recode item 9 so that 1 = 9, 2 = 8, 3 = 7, 4 = 6, 6 = 4, 7 = 3, 8 = 2, 9 = 1. To calculate your preference for consistency score, add up your responses to the nine items.

Interpretation of Scores   When Cialdini and his colleagues developed the PCS in 1995, the mean score for college students was about 48. The higher your score is above this value, the greater is your preference for consistency. The lower your score is below this value, the less of this preference you probably possess.

When we consider the universality of the cognitive consistency motive, it appears that at least two factors can derail expected cognitive dissonance effects when otherwise they should be aroused: A person's cultural upbringing may make attitude-discrepant behavior an appropriate and valued option, and a person's underlying psychological needs may reduce the aversiveness of attitude-discrepant acts.

In closing our discussion, it should be noted that cognitive dissonance theory is an excellent example of a "fertile" theory (see Chapter 2) that continues to generate novel ways of understanding attitudes (McMillan et al., 2011; Pugh et al., 2011). We now know that cognitive dissonance does not always result when we act in a counterattitudinal manner. Whether or not dissonance is aroused depends not only on how central the need for cognitive consistency is in our thinking but also on whether the attitude-behavior discrepancy is important to the self and is substantial (Cooper, 2007).

SELF-PERCEPTION THEORY CONTENDS THAT BEHAVIOR CAUSES ATTITUDES.

A few years ago, I was asked to teach a research methods course in our department. I taught the course without developing a clear liking or disliking for it. Then later, while discussing with my colleagues how best to teach research methods, I suddenly realized that I was dominating the conversation. Why was I so enthusiastic about a course I had never placed high on my preferred teaching list? As I contemplated both my current behavior and my past actions in the course—involving numerous class projects—I thought, "Wow, maybe I like teaching research methods!"

Was my newly formed positive attitude about teaching research methods caused by my experiencing cognitive dissonance? Did I feel a need to reduce the psychological discomfort of doing something that was counter to my teaching preferences? Not according to Daryl Bem's (1965, 1972) **self-perception theory**. Instead, at that moment, Bem would contend that I had simply formed an attitude by observing my behavior toward the attitude object. There was no personal conflict.

self-perception theory
• • • • • • • • • • • • • • •
The theory that we often infer our internal states, such as our attitudes, by observing our behavior

Influenced by Skinner's behaviorist perspective, Bem's self-perception theory posed the first serious challenge to cognitive dissonance theory. This explanation of the development of attitudes downplays the importance of introspection and self-awareness in the process. Instead, Bem argues that we often do not know what our attitudes are and, instead, infer them from our behavior and the situation in which the behavior occurs. Self-perception theory is a radical explanation of the attitude concept because it contends that, instead of attitudes causing behavior, it is behavior that causes attitudes.

The process of inferring attitudes based on observing behavior should sound familiar because it describes the attribution principles introduced in Chapter 4. Self-perception theory contends that when we form attitudes, we function like an observer, closely observing our past actions and then attributing them to either external (the situation) or internal (atti-

tude) sources. Comparable to the *discounting principle* in Kelley's covariation model of attribution (p. 141), Bem argued that we are more likely to make attitude inferences when our behavior is *freely chosen* rather than coerced. In my personal example, Bem would assert that the reason I did not initially infer an attitude about teaching research methods was because I felt mildly coerced into teaching the course. I wasn't teaching research methods because I liked doing so (an internal attribution), but rather because I was yielding to someone's influence (an external attribution). At our faculty discussion, however, no one was forcing me to talk about this course; thus my enthusiasm could not be easily attributed to an external source.

Shelly Chaiken and Mark Baldwin (1981) conducted an interesting empirical demonstration of how the self-perception process influences attitudes. First, they separated participants into two groups: those who held strong, consistent, proenvironmental attitudes and those who had weak, inconsistent attitudes on this issue. They then induced participants to endorse either relatively proenvironment or relatively antienvironment behavioral statements on a questionnaire. They were able to secure the desired behavioral endorsements by inserting either the word *frequently* or *occasionally* into the questions. For example, participants who were asked "Do you occasionally carpool?" were more likely to answer "Yes" and perceive themselves as proenvironment. In contrast,

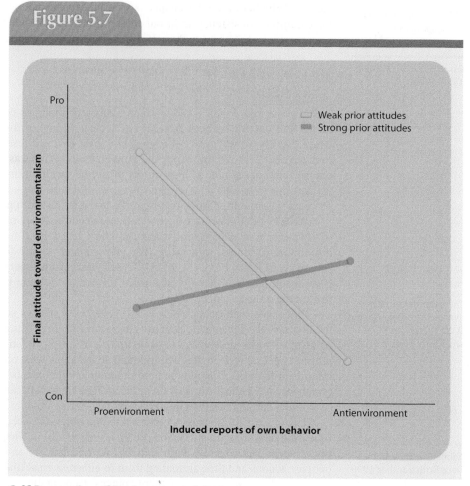

Figure 5.7

Self-Perception of Environmental Attitudes

In a study of environmental attitudes, Chaiken and Baldwin (1981) found that when people were induced into reporting past personal behavior that was either proenvironment or antienvironment, they came to view themselves in ways consistent with this behavior, but only if their prior environmental attitudes were weak and vaguely defined. What limits does this suggest about the self-perception process in attitude formation?

those asked "Do you frequently carpool?" were more likely to answer "No" and feel somewhat antienvironment. Figure 5.7 shows that participants who were induced into reporting proenvironmental behaviors later rated their attitude as more proenvironmental than those who were induced into reporting antienvironmental behaviors—but only if their initial environmental attitudes were weak and inconsistent. Among the participants whose prior attitudes were strong and consistently proenvironment, the manipulation of self-reported environmentalist behaviors had no significant impact on their attitudes.

Based on a number of such studies, it appears that when we behave in ways that are significantly at odds with well-defined attitudes, we are likely to experience cognitive dissonance and change our attitudes to rationalize our behavior. However, consistent with self-perception theory, when we act in ways that are only slightly out of line with our attitudes, we may experience no dissonance, and simply change our attitudes by making inferences from our behavior. Research suggests that this self-perception process is most likely to operate when we have little prior experience with an attitude object or our attitudes are vaguely defined (Schnall et al., 2002).

In closing our examination of self-perception theory, allow me to suggest that this theory may also provide an explanation for how implicit attitudes become explicit attitudes. That is, we may have an implicit attitude that is influencing our behavior, prompting us to consistently behave toward a target object in a particular way. This implicit

Critical THINKING

How do implicit and explicit attitudes relate to the self-perception process?

attitude is influencing our actions but we have not yet formed an explicit attitude toward the target object. Then something happens that causes us to consider what our explicit attitude is toward this target object. We examine our past behavior, infer that we have an attitude that is consistent with our past actions, and articulate to ourselves an explicit attitude that is consistent with our already existing and long-operating implicit attitude. To date, no research has specifically tested this possible extension of self-perception theory, so it remains a speculative hunch.

THE THEORY OF PLANNED BEHAVIOR EXPLAINS "THOUGHT-THROUGH" ACTIONS.

While both cognitive dissonance theory and self-perception theory predict how our attitudes are shaped by a desire to justify or explain our past actions, another important theory outlines how attitudes predict behaviors that are planned and deliberate. This theory was initially developed by Martin Fishbein and Icek Ajzen (1975) and called the *theory of reasoned action*, but was later renamed the **theory of planned behavior** (Ajzen, 1991, 2001). By using the term *reasoned action* in the original theory and *planned behavior* in the updated version, Ajzen and Fishbein convey their belief that people rationally think about the consequences of their behavior prior to acting.

theory of planned behavior
. . . .
The theory that people's conscious decisions to engage in specific actions are determined by their attitudes toward the behavior in question, the relevant subjective norms, and their perceived behavioral control

According to this theory, the reason attitudes are often not better predictors of behavior is because people contemplate more than just their attitudes prior to deciding whether to initiate an action (Fishbein & Ajzen, 2009). As you can see in Figure 5.8, the theory of planned behavior contends that our behavior is guided by three kinds of considerations: our *attitudes* toward performing the behavior, our perceptions about whether other people will approve of the behavior (*subjective norms*), and our beliefs about how easy or difficult it is to perform the behavior (*perceived behavioral control*). These three factors jointly determine whether we form a behavioral intention, which is a conscious decision to carry out a specific action (Sheeran et al., 1999). The importance that each of

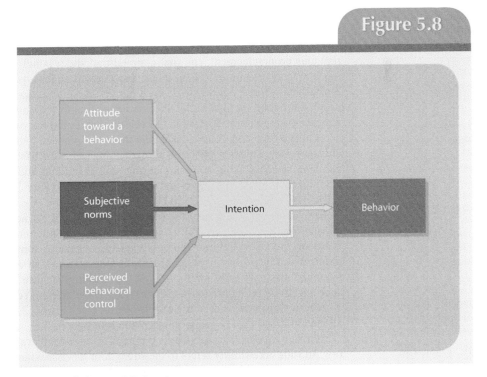

Figure 5.8

Theory of Planned Behavior

The theory of planned behavior hypothesizes that the most immediate cause of behavior is not attitudes, but rather, behavioral intentions. According to this theory, what factors combine with attitudes to determine these intentions?

these three factors has in determining a person's behavioral intention can vary depending upon the behavior.

The theory of planned behavior states that our behavioral intentions are influenced less by general attitudes than by attitudes toward performing the specific behavior in question. Consider again our chapter-opening story of college binge drinking. Fishbein and Ajzen believe that students' general attitudes about alcohol consumption are less likely to predict their intentions to engage in binge drinking than are their specific attitudes about binge drinking.

What about subjective norms? Subjective norms are shaped by the perceived expectations of significant others, and the person's motivation to conform to those expectations. Thus, college students' subjective norms about binge drinking are determined both by the beliefs that significant others have about binge drinking ("My roommates think that pounding down beer proves your toughness." "My parents think my binge drinking is immature."), and their motivation to conform to these expectations ("I want to fit in with my roommates." "My parents' views are outdated.").

In many instances, attitudes and subjective norms are adequate determinants of behavioral intention (Armitage & Conner, 1999; Corby et al., 1996). Yet when people have low perceived behavioral control because they believe they lack ability or resources, then their behavioral intentions will be low regardless of their attitudes or subjective norms (Kaiser et al., 2010). For example, suppose that Lyle desires to quit his thirty-year smoking habit (positive attitude toward quitting smoking). In addition, he knows that his family and doctor approve of him quitting and he would like to please them (subjective norm). Over time, however, after realizing how ingrained this habit is in his everyday activities, Lyle may lose confidence in his ability to become a nonsmoker (low perceived behavioral control). Thus, despite the proper attitude and subjective norm, Lyle is likely to change his intention to quit smoking.

My daughter Lillian, when she was three years old, demonstrated another example of perceived control thwarting intention. We had been trying to get her to stop sucking her thumb, and one day she said to me, "Dad, do you know … do you know … do you know why I don't like sucking my thumb anymore? Because … because … because I want to get big." I was pleased. Our little talks were finally paying off: She understood and wanted to conform to our household's "no thumb sucking" norm. Later that night, however, I saw Lillian vigorously sucking her thumb. When I reminded her about her previous pronouncement, she first claimed that she was not sucking it, but merely giving it a "good cleaning." Then, in the exasperated anger typical of three-year-olds, she blurted out, "But I *have* to suck my thumb!" Despite Lillian's attitude and subjective norm, both pointing toward the termination of thumb sucking, at the end of a hard day's play she just did not feel capable of keeping that thumb out of her mouth.

Quite a few studies have tested the theory of planned behavior, and the general conclusion is that it does a good job of explaining behavior based on rational thinking and planning, such as using condoms during sex, exercising and eating healthier to reduce heart disease, or purchasing valued consumer products (Kim & Chung, 2011; McLachlan & Hagger, 2011; Molla et al., 2007). The more "mindful" people are when making decisions on their future actions, the more likely they will act according to their intentions (Chatzisarantis & Hagger, 2007). However, by placing intention after attitudes and before behavior, the theory ignores the possibility that attitudes sometimes result in impulsive, *unintentional* behavior (Friese et al., 2007). For example, an employee who strongly dislikes his boss may fully intend to hide his loathing because he realizes that expressing such negativity is inconsistent with workplace social norms. Yet when stressed, the harried employee may experience a loss of self-control (see Chapter 3, p. 73–78) and unintentionally tell his boss what he really thinks about him.

Often such impulsive actions are triggered by attitudes that are highly accessible in memory. **Attitude accessibility** refers to the strength of the association between an object and an evaluation of it, which is typically measured by the speed with which people can *access* the evaluation from memory (Fazio, 1995; Vonofakou et al., 2007). This notion of attitude accessibility is similar to the concept of the *availability heuristic* discussed in Chapter 4 (p. 117). Recall that the availability heuristic is the tendency to judge the frequency or probability of an event in terms of how easy it is to recall examples of the event. In both instances, the more

---

"The ancestor of every action is a thought."

Ralph Waldo Emerson, American philosopher/poet, 1803–1882

---

attitude accessibility
....
The strength of the association between an object and an evaluation of it, typically measured by the speed with which people can access the evaluation from memory

readily information is activated in memory, the greater impact it will have on subsequent behavior (Holland et al., 2003; Wänke et al., 1996). Further, these more accessible attitudes can be spontaneously and automatically activated, triggering actions that are unplanned.

Another class of behaviors that the planned behavior model cannot explain is well-established *habits* (de Bruijn et al., 2007). With habits, there is no assessment of attitudes and norms prior to behaving. There is no real planning or conscious intention. Instead, the behavior is performed in a relatively unthinking fashion, with little self-regulation (Ajzen, 2001). Research indicates that habits shape many different kinds of behavior, including donating blood, attending college classes, and voting for a particular political party (Bagozzi, 1981; Echabe et al., 1988). At one time, all of these behaviors were exclusively under conscious, self-regulatory control. However, through repetition, they may have slipped into a rather automatic mode and thus are now less influenced by conscious intentions. Under these circumstances, this relatively *mindless behavior* limits the likelihood that we will act deliberately. Ask anyone who has ever tried to break a bad habit, such as eating fatty foods or tailgating fellow motorists on the highway. They will attest to the power that habitual behavior can have in overriding rational action.

SECTION SUMMARY

- Cognitive consistency is an important motive in many people's attitudes and behavior.

- Cognitive dissonance theory contends that if people hold inconsistent cognitions, they experience an unpleasant emotion (cognitive dissonance), which they try to reduce.

- Cognitive dissonance is most likely when the attitude is important to the self and the inconsistency is substantial.

- The need for cognitive consistency appears to be less in collectivist cultures.

- According to self-perception theory, we infer our attitudes based on observing our past behavior.

- The theory of planned behavior contends that behavioral intentions are shaped by attitudes, subjective norms, and perceived behavioral control.

- The theory of planned behavior is based on explicit attitudes and cannot explain unintentional or habitual behavior.

THE NATURE OF PERSUASION

persuasion

The process of consciously attempting to change attitudes through the transmission of some message

Having examined how attitudes are formed and how they influence behavior, let us now turn our attention to **persuasion**, which is the process of consciously attempting to change attitudes through the transmission of some message (Albarracín & Vargas, 2010). Social psychologists' interest in understanding persuasion began in earnest during World War II. The resulting research and theory over the next twenty years is credited with providing a good deal of insight into *when* and *how* persuasion occurs. In the 1970s, the increasing popularity of the social-cognitive perspective resulted in social psychologists focusing their attention on understanding *why* people change their attitudes in response to persuasive messages (Chaiken, 1980; Petty & Cacioppo, 1986). The assumption in this social-cognitive approach is that the thoughts that people generate in response to a message are believed to be the end result of information-processing activity (Chaiken & Trope, 1999). In this section we will examine the insights from both the early persuasion researchers and contemporary social psychologists.

PERSUASION CAN OCCUR THROUGH BOTH EFFORTFUL AND EFFORTLESS THINKING.

A number of theories have been developed to explain how people respond to persuasive messages. Generally these theories propose that people either attempt to carefully and

People attempt to carefully judge the truth of a persuasive message. Juries do this everyday in a courtroom.

elaboration likelihood model

A theory that persuasive messages can cause attitude change in two ways, each differing in the amount of cognitive effort or elaboration it requires

central route to persuasion

Persuasion that occurs when people think carefully about a communication and are influenced by the strength of its arguments

peripheral route to persuasion

Persuasion that occurs when people do not think carefully about a communication and instead are influenced by cues that are irrelevant to the content or quality of the communication

intentionally judge the truth of a persuasive message or use simple decision rules to spontaneously and automatically estimate the validity of a persuasive message (Tormala & Petty, 2007). Arguably the most influential theory in the past twenty-five years has been Richard Petty and John Cacioppo's (1986) **elaboration likelihood model** (ELM), which assumes that people want to be correct in their attitudes. The term *elaboration likelihood* refers to the probability that the target of a persuasive message will elaborate (that is, carefully analyze and attempt to comprehend) the information contained in the message. According to the model, we either engage in high or low elaboration when attending to and processing persuasive messages (Petty et al., 2009).

When motivated and able to think carefully about the content of a message (high elaboration), we are influenced by the strength and quality of the arguments: Petty and Cacioppo say we have taken the **central route to persuasion**. Whether central-route processing leads to attitude change or not is determined by the proportion of thoughts we generate that are consistent with or counter to the persuasive message. If our elaboration of the message yields more thoughts consistent with the message arguments we are likely to be persuaded, but no attitude change occurs when we generate many counterarguments.

In contrast to this critical thinking, when unable or unwilling to analyze message content we take the **peripheral route to persuasion**. In peripheral-route processing, we pay attention to cues that are irrelevant to the content or quality of the communication (low elaboration), such as the attractiveness of the communicator or the sheer amount of information presented (San Martin et al., 2011). By attending to these peripheral cues, we evaluate a message without extensively thinking about the actual issues under consideration. This means that it is not necessary for a person who takes the peripheral route to comprehend the content of a message: Attitude change can occur without comprehension. Figure 5.9 depicts these two different persuasion routes.

Do these two different types of cognitive processes sound familiar? Think back to our discussion of social cognition in Chapter 4. As flexible social thinkers, we sometimes carefully analyze all relevant factors and behave in a systematic and rational fashion, but at other times we rely upon a quick analysis by taking mental shortcuts. This "effortful" versus "effortless" way of thinking is essentially what comprises the two routes to persuasion. When elaboration is high, central-route processing dominates thinking; but when elaboration is low, peripheral-route processing is dominant (Petty et al., 2004a; Wegener et al., 2004). Under conditions of moderate elaboration, a combination of central and peripheral-route processing determines whether persuasion occurs.

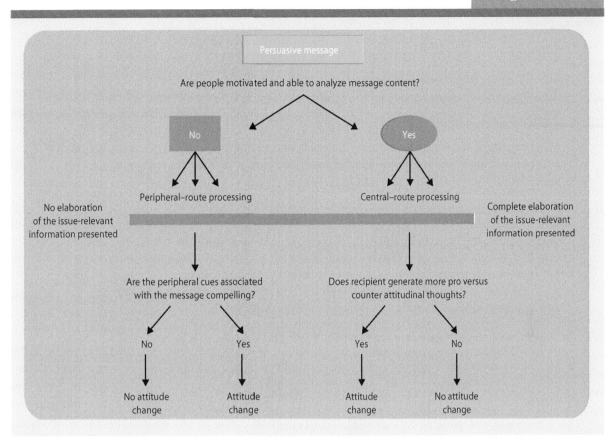

Figure 5.9

Two Routes to Persuasion

The elaboration likelihood model describes how people evaluate persuasive messages based on their ability and motivation to analyze its content. As the likelihood of thinking about the persuasive message increases, the processes specified by the central route become more likely determinants of attitudes, and those specified by the peripheral route become less likely determinants. This process is reversed as the likelihood of thinking about the persuasive message decreases. In central-route processing, message content is carefully scrutinized, and attitude change is likely if the message recipient generates a greater proportion of thoughts that are consistent with the message rather than counter to the message. However, in peripheral-route processing, evaluation of the message is based on a shallow analysis of incidental cues, such as the communicator's credibility, status, or likability. If these peripheral cues are compelling, the recipient's attitudes will change in line with the persuasive message, even if the recipient doesn't comprehend the message arguments. Of the two routes to persuasion, which do you think secures the most enduring attitude change?

❝*Profound thoughts arise only in debate, with a possibility of counterargument, only when there is a possibility of expressing not only correct ideas, but also dubious ideas.***❞**

——————————

Andrei Sakharov, Russian scientist and social critic, 1921–1989

Although attitude change can occur through either the effortful mode of central processing or the effortless mode of peripheral processing, attitudes formed by means of the effortless route are weaker, less resistant to counterarguments, and less predictive of actual behavior than those formed through the more effortful route (Petty et al., 1995). An analogy might be that if attitudes are like houses, then attitudes formed by the peripheral route are like houses made from straw or sticks. They require little effort to develop and are extremely vulnerable to destruction. In contrast, attitudes formed by the central route are like houses made of bricks. They take a good deal of effort to construct and are strong and durable. As we know from both childhood fairy tales and our own life experiences, well-built houses and highly elaborated attitudes are the best insurance against the huffing and puffing of someone with either a strong set of lungs or a strong set of counterarguments. Before reading further, spend a few minutes with *Self/Social Connection Exercise 5.3*, which provides some interesting information on our individual preferences for engaging in effortful cognitive activities.

Self/Social Connections Exercise 5.3

To What Degree Do You Have a Need for Cognition?

Although almost everybody is capable of critically analyzing many persuasive messages they receive, some people are more interested and motivated to do so than are others. This individual preference for and tendency to engage in effortful cognitive activities is called the **need for cognition**. John Cacioppo and Richard Petty (1982) have designed a personality scale to measure individual differences in this need for cognition (NFC). Below are listed some of the items from this scale.

Directions and Scoring

Read the following eight items. If you agree with items 1, 3, 5, and 7 and disagree with items 2, 4, 6, and 8, you exhibit behaviors that are indicative of a person high in the need for cognition. If your responses to these items are exactly in the opposite direction, you may be low in the need for cognition. Based on your responses, which route to persuasion do you think you tend to take? [Items taken from Cacioppo & Petty 1982]

1. I really enjoy a task that involves coming up with new solutions to problems.
2. Thinking is not my idea of fun.
3. The notion of thinking abstractly is appealing to me.
4. I like tasks that require little thought once I've learned them.
5. I usually end up deliberating about issues even when they do not affect me personally.
6. It's enough for me that something gets the job done; I don't care how or why it works.
7. I prefer my life to be filled with puzzles that I must solve.
8. I only think as hard as I have to.

Interpretation   High-NFC persons are much more likely than low-NFC persons to actively seek out and persist in difficult cognitive tasks (Fleischhauer, et al. 2010; Petty, et al. 2009). High-NFC persons tend to take the central route to persuasion and are more influenced by fact-based messages, while low-NFC individuals are more likely to take the peripheral route and are more influenced by emotion-based persuasive messages (Cacioppo, et al. 1996; Lin, et al. 2011). As a result, the attitudes of low NFCs are easier to change than those of high NFCs (Shestowsky, et al. 1998).

PERSUADER CREDIBILITY AND ATTRACTIVENESS CAN AFFECT PERSUASION.

> "Man is but a reed, the weakest in nature, but he is a thinking reed."
>
> Blaise Pascal, French scientist, 1625–1662

An important component in persuasion is the way in which audiences often perceive persuaders differently. Although a persuader is a peripheral cue to the actual content of the message, the persuader as the message source is nonetheless vitally important in determining whether the message will be effective in producing attitude change (Jones et al., 2003). This is especially true when the recipient lacks the motivation to think about the message arguments carefully. Two factors that affect persuader effectiveness are credibility and attractiveness (Hovland et al., 1949; McGuire, 1999).

Persuader Credibility

People listening to the source of a persuasive message pay a good deal of attention to his or her *credibility* or believability (Cecil et al., 1996; Lee & Cheng, 2010). Persuader credibility is

sleeper effect
• • • • • • • • • • • • • • • • •
The delayed effectiveness of a persuasive message from a noncredible source

based on perceptions of expertise and trustworthiness. Expert persuaders are those who appear to have extensive knowledge regarding the topic of the persuasive message. Trustworthy persuaders are those who seem to lack hidden motives and instead express honest opinions based on the information they possess. Persuaders who are perceived as both expert and trustworthy have high credibility, but expert credibility is seriously undermined if their opinions are perceived to be biased. Thus, if you were a college administrator developing an ad campaign to change students' attitudes toward binge drinking, it might be a mistake to use as persuaders governmental scientists who study alcohol abuse (Johnston et al., 2003). Research suggests that teenagers and young adults often perceive anti-drinking campaigns from governmental agencies as lacking credibility due to low trustworthiness ("They're adults who don't want us partying and having fun!"). As noted by social psychologist Lloyd Johnston, who tracks drug use trends among this age group, "I'm worried putting that tagline [a governmental affiliation] causes kids to dismiss the message they've just consumed because they're not sure they like who is giving it to them."

Numerous studies have found that a source's low credibility is a *discounting cue* that results in the audience rejecting the message (Lev-Ari & Keysar, 2010; Zhu et al., 2010). For example, Hovland and Walter Weiss (1951) asked American college students to read an article proposing that nuclear-powered submarines were both feasible and safe (at the time, no such submarines had yet been built). Some of those reading the article were told that the author was J. Robert Oppenheimer, the American physicist who supervised the construction of the atomic bomb. Others were told that the source was the Soviet newspaper *Pravda*. The researchers assumed that during the height of the cold war, the average American would perceive Oppenheimer as a highly credible source (expert and trustworthy) and would consider *Pravda* a low-credibility source. True to expectations, readers who believed the highly credible Oppenheimer wrote the article were more persuaded by its message immediately after reading it than those who believed they were reading a Soviet article.

If this was all there was to learn about source credibility, we might conclude that persuasion seems pretty straightforward and uncomplicated. Yet four weeks after the initial reading of the submarine article, Hovland and Weiss again measured their participants' attitudes toward nuclear-powered submarines and found a surprise. As you can see in Figure 5.10, the highly credible Oppenheimer had lost some of his persuasive power, whereas *Pravda* had actually gained in persuasiveness. Similar studies revealed the same delayed effects; highly credible sources are more persuasive immediately after the message presentation than less credible sources, but over time the credibility gap weakens. The researchers called this enhanced, delayed effect that the low-credible source has on attitude change the **sleeper effect**.

What could explain the sleeper effect? Herbert Kelman and Hovland (1953) believed it occurs because people who receive a message from a low-credibility source eventually forget where they heard it and then are influenced by the message content alone. If true, this would also explain why the highly credible Oppenheimer lost some of his persuasive power over time—the credible source became disassociated from the message. To test this hypothesis, the researchers extended the Hovland and Weiss (1951) design by adding a condition in which participants were reminded of the source's identity before their attitudes were reassessed. If the sleeper effect occurred because people forgot that the persuasive message came from a low-credible source, then it could be eliminated by reestablishing this link. This is exactly what happened. Participants who were not reminded of the source showed the expected sleeper effect, but those who were reminded did not.

A meta-analysis of over seventy different sleeper effect studies found that the magnitude of this effect depends on the strength of the discounting cue (Kumkale & Albarracín, 2004). The more effective the discounting cue in suppressing the immediate impact of the persuasive message, the larger the sleeper effect. Not surprisingly, the meta-analysis also found that when the discounting cue is ineffective, there is no delayed increase in persuasion (that is, no sleeper effect). This meta-analysis and one other (Pratkanis et al., 1988) indicate that the sleeper effect most likely occurs under the following conditions:

1. The message must be convincing enough by itself to lead to persuasion.
2. People are sufficiently able and motivated to elaborate on the message arguments prior to receiving the discounting cue.

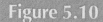

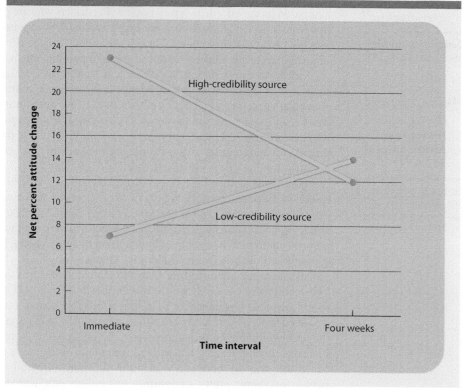

The Sleeper Effect

Immediately following the reception of a message, people are more likely to be persuaded by a highly credible source than one of low credibility. However, as Hovland and Weiss (1951) found, over time, the message becomes disassociated from its source, resulting in less agreement with the highly credible source and more agreement with the source having lower credibility. What is a possible explanation for this effect?

3. People are given information discounting the credibility of the source following the persuasive message, not before.
4. The impact of the discounting cue (the low-credibility information) decays in memory faster than the persuasive message.

Persuader Attractiveness

During the 1920s, when feminists were demonstrating against women's inequality, Edward Bernays, the nephew of Sigmund Freud, was a public relations executive for the cigarette industry. In trying to persuade women to smoke cigarettes, Bernays thought that cigarettes could serve as a "torch of freedom" symbol for women if he could photograph attractive and "liberated" women using the product. Bernays arranged to have a group of attractive, cigarette-smoking women marching in Manhattan's 1929 Easter Parade; and when photographs of this event appeared in the nation's newspapers, many women took up the "torch of freedom" habit (Greaves, 1996). Since Bernays's time, research has demonstrated that a communicator's attractiveness can be based on several factors, including *likability, similarity to the audience,* and *physical attractiveness.*

Regarding likability, merely saying nice things is often enough to get people to like you and thereby increase your ability to persuade (Eagly & Chaiken, 1993). In fact,

Roger Ailes, a well-known public relations adviser to Republican presidents, believes likability is a persuader's most important quality:

> If you could master one element of personal communication that is more powerful than anything, it is the quality of being likable. I call it the magic bullet, because if your audience likes you, they'll forgive just about everything else you do wrong. If they don't like you, you can hit every rule right on target and it doesn't matter. (Ailes, 1988, p. 81)

"To please people is the greatest step toward persuading them."

— — — — — — — — — —

Philip Dormer Stanhope, Earl of Chesterfield, 1694–1773

We are also attracted to those who are similar to us, and this attraction often results in us being influenced by similar others (Bohm et al., 2010). Communicators can be similar to their audience in a number of ways, including sharing attitudes and values ("Are his politics and morals like mine?"), having similar backgrounds ("Is he from my hometown?"), and having a similar appearance ("Does he look like me?"). Of the different ways in which people can be similar, perceived similarity in attitudes and values appears to be the most important in enhancing persuasion (Simons et al., 1970). This is why politicians try to present themselves as having attitudes and values in step with the majority. This is also why effective campaigns to reduce binge drinking on college campuses use fellow students to deliver the persuasive messages; compared with nonstudents, student communicators are more likely perceived by the message recipients as sharing their attitudes, values, and interests (Johnston & White, 2003).

Finally, beautiful people are highly attractive to most of us, and thus, they are effective persuaders (Petty et al., 1997; Shavitt et al., 1994). For example, in one study by Shelly Chaiken (1979), university undergraduates attempted to persuade fellow students to sign a petition to get the university to stop serving meat during breakfast and lunch. Although less attractive persuaders only secured signatures 32 percent of the time, the more attractive students convinced 41 percent of the students they approached to sign the petition. Other persuasion studies have found that good looks can sometimes even overcome a poor presentation style (Pallak, 1983).

When advertisers associate their products with attractive persons, do you think they are trying to induce central-route or peripheral-route processing in their target audience? Have you noticed how many beer commercials feature young, attractive women in skimpy clothing? These women are peripheral cues, consciously placed in commercials to induce positive feelings in male viewers, which then become associated with the beer through classical conditioning (see p. 166). This is attitude change without much thought—peripheral-route processing. Putting on your hypothetical college administrator hat again, if you were developing an ad campaign to change students' attitudes toward binge drinking, how could you use the powerful peripheral cue of attractiveness to enhance your message?

Beautiful people are very attractive to most people and are effective persuaders.

RAPID SPEECH ENCOURAGES PERIPHERAL-ROUTE PERSUASION WHILE HINDERING CENTRAL-ROUTE PROCESSING.

Another quality of persuaders that affects persuasion is their speaking pace. Research indicates that people who speak rapidly are generally more persuasive than those who speak more slowly because fast talkers convey the *impression* that they are more credible (Miller et al., 1976). Certain marketing studies also report this benefit of rapid speech—people seem to be more favorably

Critical
THINKING

Why is it that when radio lottery advertisers are trying to persuade you to spend your money, they speak at a normal rate of speed, yet when they convey the odds of winning, their speech rate dramatically increases? Are they simply trying to save money by cutting down the length of the commercial, or is there an equally important reason for this shift to fast-paced speech?

disposed toward advertisements and the products advertised when the product spokesperson talks at a faster-than-normal rate of speech (LaBarbera & MacLachlan, 1979; Street & Brady, 1982). Is fast talking, however, always beneficial to persuasion?

According to the elaboration likelihood model, fast talking will be beneficial to the persuasive communicator only when the audience's initial attitudinal position is *opposite* to that of the communicator (Petty & Wegener, 1998). Because the audience's counterarguing is "short-circuited" by the sheer speed at which the opposing viewpoints are presented, audience members are more likely to be persuaded by the message than if they had more time to scrutinize it. Put another way, the difficulty in processing rapid speech prompts the audience to abandon the central route; instead, they take the peripheral route to persuasion. In contrast to the hypothesized benefits of rapid speech when the audience opposes the communicator, the elaboration likelihood model further predicts that fast talking will hurt the persuasive power of the message when it is presented to an audience that favors the communicator's point of view. Why? Because the arguments are presented so quickly, the audience cannot adequately process them and incorporate them into their existing belief system to further bolster their current attitudes on the issue.

Stephen Smith and David Shaffer (1991) found support for this explanation in a study in which college students listened to persuasive messages arguing for or against raising the legal drinking age. A survey conducted prior to the study revealed that the overwhelming majority of undergraduates on campus opposed such a law. Students heard the persuasive arguments either at a slow, normal, or rapid rate of speech. Consistent with the elaboration likelihood hypothesis, when students listened to arguments counter to their perspective, rapid speech suppressed the tendency to rebut the counterattitudinal message, and hence, listeners were more susceptible to persuasion. However, when students listened to arguments consistent with their own attitudes toward the drinking-age law, rapid speech inhibited favorable elaboration of the proattitudinal message, thus undermining its persuasive impact. These findings suggest that rapid speech may either promote or inhibit persuasion through its impact on message elaboration.

EMOTIONS MOTIVATE, ENHANCE, AND HINDER PERSUASION.

For many years social scientists made predictions about elections under the assumption that voters made their decisions based on deliberate, rational thought (Kinder, 1998). More recently, this approach has changed to take into account the role that emotions play in the voting process (Lakoff, 2004). Drew Westen (2007) contends that research findings strongly suggest that when political decisions evoke strong emotional reactions in voters, reason plays virtually no role in the decision making of the average citizen. Based on his analysis of controversial political issues and how the two major political parties in the United States have crafted their persuasive messages, Westen concludes that the Republican Party has a much better understanding than does the Democratic Party of how emotions shape voter decision making. Put simply, Democrats emphasize the crafting of strong arguments to shift voters' attitudes, while Republicans emphasize strong emotional appeals.

Why do emotions play such a pivotal role in many persuasion attempts? Early research indicated that people who are in a positive mood are more susceptible to persuasion than the average person. For example, Irving Janis and his colleagues (1965) had some people read persuasive messages while they ate a snack and drank soda, while others simply read the messages without the accompanying treats. Greater attitude change occurred among the "munchers" than among the "food-free" group. Similar effects were also found among people listening to pleasant music (Milliman, 1986).

Why do you think these effects might occur? Many social psychologists consider emotions as having an indirect influence on persuasion and other behaviors rather than playing a direct role (Baumeister et al., 2007; Briñol et al., 2010). The *feelings-as-information* explanation suggests that positive moods signal to people that everything is fine in their environment and no effortful thought is necessary (Isbell, 2004; Schwarz, 1990). As a result, happy people are likely to be influenced by poor arguments because they are unlikely to engage in extensive processing of the presented message (Cesario et al., 2006; Ruder & Bless, 2003). What about people in negative moods? Their moods signal that something is wrong and

"There are two levers for moving man— interest and fear."

–––––––––––––

Napoleon Bonaparte, French general and emperor, 1769–1821

"People react to fear, not love— they don't teach that in Sunday school, but it's true."

–––––––––––––

Richard M. Nixon, U.S. president, 1913–1994

that some action is necessary. Unhappy people adopt a problem-solving mode and central-route processing is associated with problem solving.

While the feelings-as-information view contends that happy people are more susceptible to persuasion than unhappy people because they engage in less effortful thinking, there is evidence that people in positive moods sometimes engage in effortful thinking. The *hedonic-contingency* view asserts that happy people will engage in cognitive tasks that allow them to remain happy and will avoid tasks that lower their mood (Wegener & Petty, 1994). Consistent with this view, research indicates that those in positive moods will engage in central-route processing if the message is expected to advocate something pleasant (Wegener et al., 1995). Thus, counter to the feelings-as-information view, it appears that happy people do not always process information less than neutral or sad people. Overall, the research suggests that happy people are generally more susceptible to persuasion than neutral or sad people. However, when a persuasive message does not threaten happy people's moods, they may carefully scrutinize it and, thus, be less persuaded than neutral or sad individuals.

Fear Appeals

> *"No passion so effectually robs the mind of all its powers of acting and reasoning as fear."*
>
> Edmund Burke, Irish philosopher, 1729–1797

Beyond inducing generally positive or negative moods, would-be persuaders sometimes try to evoke the negative emotion of fear in order to persuade. An antismoking ad tells you how your nicotine habit will shorten life expectancy. An antidrinking ad depicts the negative consequences of drunk driving. An antigambling ad warns against the dangers of compulsive gambling (Munoz et al., 2010).

A number of studies have found that high fear appeals sometimes induce so much anxiety that the audience is unable to efficiently process later information in the appeal about how to avoid the danger (de Hoog et al., 2005; Sengrupta & Johar, 2001). For example, Christopher Jepson and Shelley Chaiken (1990) measured participants' anxieties about cancer and then asked them to read and evaluate an article advocating regular checkups for cancer. Following this exercise, participants were asked to list all their thoughts about the article and as many of the arguments contained in the article. Those who were highly anxious about cancer listed fewer thoughts, remembered fewer arguments, and were ultimately less persuaded than those who were less anxious. This study and others suggest that if a fear-inducing message immobilizes its audience with anxiety, they may be unable to carefully process the message content concerning how to avoid the danger. Instead of promoting healthy change, the message may instead induce a feeling of helplessness. Although this is certainly an undesirable consequence of fear appeals, existing research indicates that if fear appeals are combined with information that one can do something about the danger, important behavioral changes can and do occur (Morrison, 2005; Mulilis et al., 2001). Does this notion of being personally capable of changing one's own behavior sound familiar? It should, because it bears a striking similarity to the concept of *perceived behavioral control* in the theory of planned behavior (see p. 182).

Unfortunately, when feeling highly vulnerable to some threat, we often do not critically analyze the recommended actions others offer us to avoid the danger (Das & de Wit, 2003; de Hoog et al., 2007). Our desire to perceive the recommended actions as effective causes us to ignore information that might cast doubt on the persuaders' message. This strong "desire to believe" that a highly threatening situation can be

Fear appeals capture people's attention, but they also often induce anxiety and helpless feelings. What can persuaders do to short circuit helpless reactions in the target audience?

avoided places a great deal of power in the hands of those who are offering solutions (Landau et al., 2004). Many individuals with life-threatening illnesses fall victim to medical and religious charlatans who promise renewed health if their highly questionable remedies are followed. Similarly, many voters fail to critically analyze highly questionable social policies because they are accompanied by fear-based appeals.

Humor Appeals

Would-be persuaders also use the positive emotion of humor to prompt attitude change, which is why about 40 percent of all advertisements employ humor (Unger, 1996). Public relations consultants also believe that humor is an effective persuader, and they regularly recommend that their clients punch up their persuasive speeches with humorous anecdotes (Weinberger & Campbell, 1991). Even some recent student-designed ad campaigns to increase alcohol awareness on college campuses have employed humor to change students' attitude on drinking (Saltzman, 2002). Are they correct in their beliefs?

Critical
THINKING

In addition to using humor, the anti-binge drinking SMU ad also provides information on how much alcohol the typical SMU student consumes. Why might this information be effective in reducing binge drinking at SMU? When would reporting such normative information possibly promote—rather than reduce—binge drinking?

Research clearly shows that using humor in persuasive messages does increase people's *attention* to the message more than serious-sounding communication attempts (Duncan & Nelson, 1985; Nabi et al., 2007). People are simply more likely to listen to persuaders who are trying to make them laugh, or at least smile. However, one of the problems with using humor is that it may interfere with the listener's *comprehension* of the message, by directing attention away from the persuasive content (Cantor & Venus, 1983). That is, the jokes may be so funny that people remember only them and not the persuasive information. Thus, if a persuader merely wants to get people to notice the message, humor may be useful in this regard. However, with no message elaboration, any attitude change is likely to be extremely vulnerable to a counterpersuasive attack (Haugtvedt & Petty, 1992).

A study conducted by Stephen Smith and his coworkers (1994) found that whether humor either promotes message processing or disrupts it is determined by the *relevance* of the humor to the message content. When humor is relevant, people appear to be more motivated to take a central route to persuasion and process the message arguments. However, when humor is irrelevant to the message content, people are likely to take a peripheral route and base their evaluation of the message merely on cues such as source credibility.

Given our previous discussion of fear and persuasion, it is interesting to note that humor may be effective in persuading certain individuals to take protective steps when facing potential health threats. In studies of persuasive appeals involving health issues such as the responsible consumption of alcohol, sunscreen use to avoid skin cancer, and condom use to prevent AIDS, humorous messages appear to be more effective than non-humorous messages for men and women high in psychological masculinity (Conway & Dubé, 2002). *Psychological masculinity* consists of an assertive, task-oriented approach to life, reflected in such personality characteristics as being independent, forceful, and dominant. Although men are, on average, higher than women in masculinity, these gender differences are shrinking (Twenge, 1997).

Why might people high in psychological masculinity respond more favorably to humorous appeals related to health threats? As discussed in Chapter 4 (p. 130-131), masculinity is associated with *manly emotion*, in which people exert control over their emotions, just as they try to exert control over other aspects of their lives (Shields, 2002). Persuasive messages that induce fear can hinder message elaboration if the perceived threat is high. For people who place a high value on controlling their emotions— that is, those high in masculinity—humor in the context of a fear-inducing message may be very much appreciated because it helps them manage their fear, which then allows them to more effectively process the message.

TWO-SIDED MESSAGES INOCULATE AUDIENCES AGAINST OPPOSING VIEWS.

Beyond who is presenting the message and the emotions of the recipient, another factor in determining whether a message will persuade is whether it is "one-sided" or "two-sided." *One-sided messages* are those in which persuaders try to convince others by presenting only

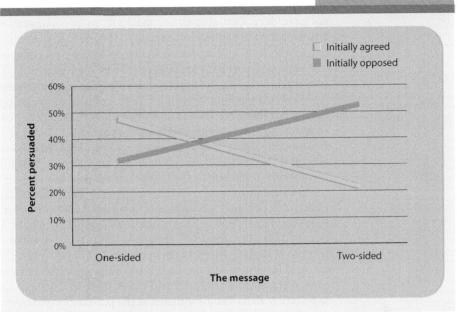

One-Sided Versus Two-Sided Appeals

Following Germany's defeat in World War II, American soldiers who initially agreed with a message that Japan was strong and that the war in the Pacific would last a long time were more persuaded by a one-sided appeal. In contrast, soldiers skeptical of this message were more persuaded by a two-sided appeal.

Source: Data from C. I. Hovland et al., *Experiments on Mass Communications* (Princeton University Press, 1949).

their arguments. In contrast, *two-sided messages* involve acknowledging the opposing arguments and then refuting them.

Hovland and his colleagues (1949), in a study conducted during World War II, attempted to determine whether one-sided or two-sided messages were more effective audience persuaders. Working in the Army's Information and Education Division immediately after the surrender of Nazi Germany, their objective was to convince American soldiers that the war was far from over and that the armed conflict against Japan would last at least two more years. Some soldiers heard a one-sided message that did not bring up opposing viewpoints, and other soldiers heard a two-sided message that also mentioned and then refuted the opposing viewpoints. As illustrated in Figure 5.11, the effectiveness of the appeal depended on who was listening. A one-sided appeal was most effective with those who already believed that the war would be long, while a two-sided appeal worked better with those who initially believed that the war would be over soon.

Later research found that two-sided messages are more effective in persuading not only those who initially disagree but also people who are either well informed on the topic or are going to be exposed to opposing viewpoints in the future (Crowley & Hoyer, 1994; Lumsdaine & Janis, 1953). In such circumstances, mentioning the opposition's arguments suggests that you are being an objective, fair-minded person, thereby increasing your trustworthiness and, thus, your effectiveness at persuasion (Bohner et al., 2003).

Besides increasing communicator trustworthiness, another important factor is operating in two-sided messages. For those who are soon going to hear the opposition state its case, raising and then refuting its arguments can *inoculate* these people against it, making it harder for them to be persuaded. William McGuire developed this inoculation explanation during the 1950s in partial response to Cold War fears about Americans' susceptibility to communist propaganda from the Soviet Union. McGuire reasoned that people become vulnerable to propaganda when they are raised in a society that overprotects them from hearing things that attack culturally shared beliefs. Using a biological analogy, he stated that people who are raised in such a "germ-free" environment would not have developed appropriate mechanisms to adequately defend themselves against attacking viruses (outside propaganda). However, just as administering a small dose of a dangerous virus will stimulate the body to develop defenses to fight off the disease, McGuire asserted that exposing people to a weakened dose of the attacking material would also stimulate the development of resistance-promoting counterarguments.

Research supports some of the basic elements of inoculation theory, and its principles have been effectively applied in many realms, including commercial advertising, political campaigning, and health-intervention programs (Goldberg et al., 2006; McGuire & Papageorgis, 1961). However, as the application of inoculation theory spread, it became clear that the inoculation effect does not only protect people from "dangerous" political perspectives, it can also be used to manipulate people's attitudes and beliefs on any topic.

Besides inoculation effects, another possible reason that two-sided messages are effective in persuading an audience involves the rules of everyday communication. Eric Igou and Herbert Bless (2003) propose that people generally expect that persuaders will present their most important arguments first. This presentation format is most efficient because it allows recipients the opportunity to rapidly develop a mental framework, or schema, for processing the presented information (see Chapter 4, pp. 111–116). However, when presented with a two-sided argument, people quickly develop a different expectation about the information in the persuasive message. They now assume that the arguments the communicator favors are presented at the end of the message, and they therefore give these arguments a special weight in their final judgments.

WE CAN DEVELOP ATTITUDE CERTAINTY BY ACTIVELY TRYING TO COUNTERARGUE.

What happens when people successfully resist persuasion? The typical assumption has been that if persuasion is resisted, people's attitudes remain unchanged. Is this true?

Richard Petty and his colleagues (2002) question this widespread assumption and suggest instead that when people resist persuasion, they often become more confident in the attitude that was targeted. Successful resistance increases confidence in the attitude because people infer that their resistance was due to the validity of the attitude. The researchers further hypothesize that people will experience the greatest increase in attitude confidence after resisting messages they perceive as being very strong. In contrast, when people successfully defend their attitude against a weak attack, their confidence in the attitude should not increase because they cannot be certain that the attitude would have survived a strong challenge.

In a test of these hypotheses, Zakary Tormala and Petty (2002) conducted a study in which college students were presented with a proposal supposedly from the University's Board of Trustees to implement a new policy in two years requiring graduating seniors to pass a comprehensive exam in their major field of study (sound familiar?). As justification for the experiment, students were led to believe that the trustees wanted to assess students' reactions. In order to induce resistance to persuasion, participants in the experimental conditions—but not those in the control condition—next received the following instructions:

> The University's Board of Trustees would also like to gather all possible arguments that students can raise against the issue. After you read the proposal, we would like you to list your arguments *against* the exam policy.

Following these instructions, all participants were exposed to a persuasive message that contained two weak and two strong arguments on the issue. An example of a weak argument was that implementing the exams would allow the university to take part in a national trend. An example of a strong argument was that implementing the exams would increase the average starting salary of graduates. Participants in the *perceived strong arguments* condition were told that they were given only the strongest of all the arguments raised in favor of the exam policy, while those in the *perceived weak arguments* condition were informed that they were given only the weakest of all the arguments in favor of the policy.

After receiving the persuasive message, participants in the two experimental conditions—but not those in the control condition—were told to generate a list of as many counterarguments as they could. All participants then completed measures to assess their attitudes and attitude certainty toward the comprehensive exam proposal. Results found no group differences in attitude toward the exam proposal. However, as expected, the groups did differ in their later attitude confidence. When participants resisted what was described as a strong message, their attitude confidence increased compared with those who thought they received a weak message from the no-message control group. Subsequent studies in this same series found that successful resistance to persuasion not only enhances people's confidence in their initial attitude but also renders the attitude more resistant to subsequent attacks—and increases the likelihood that people will later behave in a manner consistent with the attitude (Tormala & Petty, 2002).

These studies demonstrate how counterarguing can produce successful and sustained resistance to persuasion. But what happens if the persuasive arguments are so strong that people cannot generate convincing counterarguments? Derek Rucker and Petty (2004) predicted that if people try to find fault in a persuasive message and fail, the new attitude resulting from this successful persuasion attempt will be held with more conviction and certainty. In testing this hypothesis, the researchers used the ever-popular scenario of telling students about a new proposal to require graduating seniors to pass a comprehensive exam. However, in this study, students in the two experimental conditions received very strong message arguments that were designed to be difficult to counterargue. An example of one of these hard-to-refute arguments was:

> Universities that implement senior comprehensive exams are given additional funding by a new government program that rewards performance-based education. For students, this means that at least a 5 percent tuition decrease would accompany the passing of the exam proposal. In addition to an immediate 5 percent tuition decrease, the government program provides funds to ensure that students' tuition will not be raised for a period of at least five years.

Before receiving the message arguments, participants in the experimental conditions were instructed to either focus on their thoughts while the message was presented (*thought condition*) or generate counterarguments to the message (*counter-argument condition*). Students in the control condition did not receive any persuasive message. All participants then completed measures to assess their attitudes and attitude certainty toward the comprehensive exam proposal.

The researchers found that students in the two experimental conditions—those who received the persuasive message—had more favorable attitudes toward the comprehensive exam proposal than students in the no-message control group. This suggests that the persuasive message was successful in securing attitude change. More important, these new attitudes were held with greater certainty in the *counterargument condition* than in the *thought condition*. In other words, when students were told to generate counterarguments toward a strong persuasive message, their failure to refute the message caused them to adopt a new attitude that was stronger than students who did not try to find fault with the message. Being impressed with how hard it was to counterargue, the active resisters became more confident in their new attitudes than did people who simply thought about the persuasive message without engaging in active resistance.

Considering these findings from the persuaders' point of view, when you are trying to persuade others and are convinced that you have very strong arguments that cannot be refuted, you might consider going against intuition and encourage your audience to try to find fault in your message. When audience members fail to find fault, they may say to themselves, "I changed my attitude even though I tried to fight the persuasive attempt. I now know that I have few negative thoughts about the message and my new attitude is a good one." In essence, this is a form of self-generated persuasion (Darke & Chaiken, 2005).

Thus far, we have examined the conditions under which we may become impressed with our ability or our inability to counterargue a persuasive message. As demonstrated

"*It is true that you may fool all the people some of the time; you can even fool some of the people all the time; but you can't fool all of the people all the time.***"**

Abraham Lincoln, U.S. president, 1809–1865

in these studies, being impressed with our resistance can lead to increased confidence in our initial attitude, but being impressed with our failure to resist can lead to increased confidence in our new attitude. But what if we are not so impressed with either our resistance or our lack of resistance?

In such instances, we should have less confidence in our attitudes. Consider first the case in which we are able to counterargue and resist persuasion, but we believe that our resistance was difficult or lacking in some way. Even though we do not change our attitude, we may now be less confident in the attitude, rendering it more susceptible to future persuasion attempts. In the case of failing to resist persuasion, if we believe that our changed attitude occurred because we did not try very hard to resist or that there were many distractions that prevented us from mounting a good defense, we may have less confidence in our new attitude. Figure 5.12 presents a summary of the key ideas developed by Petty and his colleagues (2004b) regarding the process of counterarguing and the conditions under which various outcomes are likely. Table 5.2 reviews some of the factors that influence central versus peripheral processing.

"You can fool all the people all the time if the advertising is right and the budget is big enough."

Joseph E. Levine, U.S. Film Producer, 1984

Figure 5.12

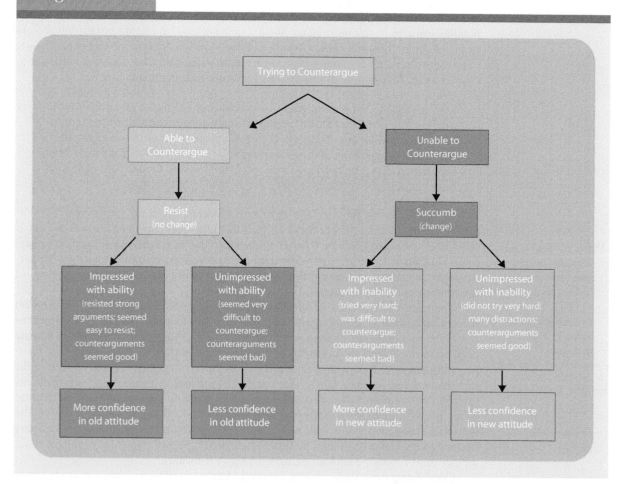

A Model of Attempted Resistance to Persuasion

Richard Petty and his colleagues (2004b) have outlined how attempts at counterarguing a persuasive message can either succeed or fail. Being impressed or unimpressed with one's ability to resist or not resist a persuasive message will either increase or decrease one's confidence in the new or old attitude.

Source: R. E. Petty et al., "Resisting Persuasion by Counterarguing: An Attitude Strength Perspective." In *Perspectivism in Social Psychology: The Yin and Yang of Scientific Progress*, ed. J. T. Jost, M. R. Banaji, & D. A. Prentice. Washington, D.C.: American Psychological Association, 2004b.

Table 5.2

Central Versus Peripheral Processing of Persuasive Messages

Route to Persuasion	Most Likely to Occur When	Effect on Attitudes
Central Route		
The person carefully scrutinizes all the available information in the persuasion environment in an attempt to determine the merits of the presented arguments.	People find the message personally relevant and involving. People are high in need for cognition. People are in a neutral or mildly negative mood. The communicator speaks at a normal rate of speed.	Attitudes tend to be strong, resistant to counterarguments, and predictive of behavior.
Peripheral Route		
Instead of actively thinking about the attitude object, the person relies on incidental cues and simple rules of thumb, such as the attractiveness of the communicator or the length of the message.	People find the message to be irrelevant and noninvolving. People are low in need for cognition. People are in a positive mood. The communicator speaks rapidly.	Attitudes tend to be weak, susceptible to counterarguments, and not predictive of behavior.

SECTION SUMMARY

- Persuasion involves conscious attempts to change attitudes through the transmission of some message.

- The elaboration likelihood model contends that people engage in either high or low cognitive elaboration when attending to persuasive messages.

    central-route processing: high elaboration of message content by focusing on information central to message

    peripheral-route processing: low elaboration of message content by focusing on information not central to message

- Highly credible sources are more persuasive, at least initially, than less credible sources.

- Attractive sources are more persuasive than unattractive sources.

- Rapid speech can increase or decrease persuasiveness, depending on the audience's initial position and the message strength.

- Positive moods generally induce more persuasion than neutral or somber moods.

- Fear can persuade, yet it can also immobilize an audience with anxiety.

- Humor increases message attention, but it can interfere with message comprehension.

- Two-sided messages are effective in persuading those who initially disagree are well informed are going to be exposed to opposing viewpoints.

- Encouraging people to actively counterargue a message can strengthen or weaken either an existing attitude or a new attitude.

APPLICATIONS

CAN YOU BE PERSUADED BY SUBLIMINAL MESSAGES?

In the summer of 1957, advertising executive James Vicary claimed that he had induced customers at a New Jersey theater to dramatically increase their popcorn and coke purchases by secretly splicing the words *EAT POPCORN* and *DRINK COKE* into the Hollywood movie *Picnic* and flashing it before their eyes for a fraction of a second. These messages were *subliminal*, meaning that they were presented so fast or so faintly that they were just below the absolute threshold for conscious aware-

subliminal perception
....
The processing of information that is below one's threshold of conscious awareness

ness. **Subliminal perception** is the processing of such information. Vicary's "study" created a sensation with the public, and it is credited with being partially responsi-ble for subliminal advertising being legally banned in the United States, Great Britain, and Australia (Key, 1989). What most people don't realize is that James Vicary never spliced those words into the movie reel. He fabricated the entire inci-dent in an attempt to attract customers to his failing marketing business!

A likely reason why Vicary's surprising claims were so uncritically accepted may be that they fit popular assumptions about the powers that new communica-tion technologies can have over the attitudes and behavior of viewers (Wartella & Reeves, 1985). Indeed, almost 70 percent of people who have some knowledge of subliminal advertising believe that it can influ-ence consumer buying habits (Zanot et al., 1983), and millions of people buy subliminal self-help tapes to help them lose weight, improve their memory, or increase their self-esteem (Pratkanis & Aronson, 1992). Yet is there any real scientific evidence that these efforts to subliminally persuade are effective?

Let us examine one representative study investigating subliminal persuasion and consumer purchasing. A few years after the popcorn/Coke results were reported, researchers conducted a field study of subliminal advertising effects with the help of an Indianapolis television station and a local grocery store chain (DeFleur & Petranoff, 1959). Over a period of several weeks, the television station ran a series of subliminal commercials for a food product. During the first week, the station ran a subliminal ad for the product, while during the second week this subliminal message was embedded in an ordinary advertisement for the prod-uct. Alone, the subliminal ad produced an unimpressive 1 percent increase in normal sales. However, when the subliminal message was coupled with the ordinary commercial, sales increased by a whopping 282 percent! Before you draw any hasty conclusions from this seemingly impressive sales figure, let's com-pare this increase with the sales figures for other products in the grocery store that had received consumer exposure through normal advertising during the same period of time. Ordinary advertisements without any subliminal messages increased sales, on average, by 2,509 percent! Although this study demonstrated the importance of control groups in experimental research, it did not provide any evidence whatsoever that subliminal messages have the slightest effect in persuading people to increase their product purchasing. Similar studies investigating subliminal advertising have also yielded nonsignificant effects (Trappey, 1996).

Although there is no evidence that subliminal persuasion influences consumer behavior, what about those people who have used subliminal tapes and swear that their lives have been changed? Isn't this evi-dence that subliminal persuasion can be effective at least some of the time? This was the question that Anthony Pratkanis and his colleagues (1994) were interested in answering when they conducted a study of such self-help tapes. Participants were first pretested for their level of self-esteem and memory recall ability and then given an audiotape containing various pieces of classical music. The tape manufacturers claimed that embedded within these self-help tapes were subliminal messages designed either to increase self-esteem (e.g., "I have high self-worth and high self-esteem") or to increase one's memory (e.g., "My ability to remember and recall is increasing daily."). However, the researchers purposely misla-beled half of the tapes, leading participants who received them to believe they had a memory tape when they really had a self-esteem tape, or vice versa. The remaining participants received the rest of the tapes, with correct labels. During the next five weeks, these volunteers listened daily to their tapes at home. After this exposure period, they were again given self-esteem and memory tests, and they were also asked whether they believed the tapes had been effective. Was there any evidence that the participants experienced subliminal persuasion?

Pratkanis and his coworkers found no self-esteem or memory increases; the subliminal tapes were utterly ineffective. These null findings, however, stood in sharp contrast to the participants' beliefs about the tapes. Those who thought they had received the self-esteem tape tended to believe their self-esteem had increased, and those who thought they had been given the memory tape were more likely to believe that their memory had improved. This was true even if they had received a mislabeled tape! According to the researchers, these findings indicate that users of self-help audiotapes expect self-improvement through their use, and actually convince themselves that the improvement has taken place, when, in fact, it has not. Combined with the findings from other subliminal tape studies (Merikle & Skanes, 1992; Moore, 1995), this research suggests that whatever benefits people derive from such self-help products have little to do with the content of the subliminal messages. Instead, people's expectations and their desire to reduce cognitive dissonance ("I invested a lot of time and money in this tape, it must be good!") appear to be the sole means of influence operating here. When all is said and done, what very likely explains attitude and behavior change in those who use subliminal self-help products are good old-fashioned persuasion principles.

Before dismissing the possibility that subliminal persuasion can influence people's everyday attitudes and behavior, it must be kept in mind that subliminal perception does indeed exist. Numerous psychological studies indicate that perception without awareness can take place (Eimer & Schlaghecken, 2002). More important, some of these studies, conducted under carefully controlled laboratory conditions, have been able to manipulate people's attitudes and behavior using subliminal stimuli. For example, in a series of experiments, Robert Bornstein and his colleagues (1987) found evidence for a *subliminal mere exposure effect*. Participants who were repeatedly exposed to subliminal stimuli (abstract geometric figures or people's faces) later expressed greater liking for those stimuli. Similarly, John Bargh and Tanya Chartrand (1999) found that participants who were subliminally exposed to achievement-oriented words (*strive, succeed, master*) while completing a "word search" puzzle were more likely to continue working on the puzzle task (57 percent) when signaled to stop than those in the control group (22 percent). These findings, along with others (Krosnick et al., 1992; Weisbuch et al., 2003), suggest that subliminally embedded messages may be able to energize—or at least sustain—a person's actions, perhaps even their desire to purchase products.

One study that explored this possibility was conducted by Erin Strahan and her colleagues (2002). These researchers enlisted college students to participate in what was described as a "marketing study" in which they performed a "taste test" on two different types of cookies. Next, thirst was manipulated by telling half the participants to "cleanse their palate" by drinking as much water as they desired, while the other participants received no water. Then, as part of a test administered by computer, the researchers subliminally exposed some participants to neutral words (pirate, won) and others to thirst-related words (thirst, dry). Following this computer test, all participants performed a second taste test in which they judged two different types of Kool-Aid beverages. Participants were left alone in the room and told they could drink as much of the beverages as they desired. Results indicated that the subliminal thirst primes had little impact on participants whose thirst had just been quenched, but they significantly increased consumption among those who were already thirsty (see Figure 5.13). In other words, the subliminal thirst primes did not appear to generate a desire in people to begin drinking beverages, but they did appear to strengthen or sustain the desire for thirsty people to drink greater quantities of beverages. This study suggests that when people are already motivated to behave in a certain manner (for example, consume liquids), subliminal messages may have the power to cause them to behave more vigorously than they would without exposure to the subliminal messages. Additional laboratory studies have also supported this hypothesis (Jaskowski et al., 2003).

In examining these recent studies it must be mentioned that it is unclear how long such subliminal priming effects last. In many of the laboratory studies, the subliminal effects appear to be very short, perhaps lasting only a few seconds. Only one study has found evidence that people exposed to subliminal stimuli in the laboratory showed any noticeable effects seven days following exposure (Sohlberg & Birgegard, 2003). If subliminal effects last only a short time, they are unlikely to influence product purchases unless the subliminal messages are presented to people in stores while they are shopping. However, if this finding of longer duration effects can be replicated in future research, it is not beyond the realm of possibility that practitioners of persuasion could sometime in the future develop clever subliminal techniques that influence the thinking and behavior of the general public over longer periods of time.

The findings from a few studies suggest that advertisers in the not-too-distant future may be able to subliminally persuade people who are already motivated to actually purchase specific products over others. Johan Karremans and his coworkers (2006) found that thirsty people who were subliminally exposed to a brand name drink were much more likely to choose that drink for consumption than were either thirsty people who were not subliminally primed or nonthirsty people who were subliminally primed. This research suggests that movie goers who are already thirsty may be induced to buy a Coke, rather than a Pepsi or a Sprite, after being exposed to subliminal "Buy Coke" messages while standing in line at the movie theater food counter. However, if this same subliminal prime is presented to these same thirsty individuals while at home, it is as yet unknown whether it would later influence what they order to drink at the movie theater. Future research will determine the actual potential use—and abuse—of subliminal procedures in persuasion (Strahan et al., 2005).0

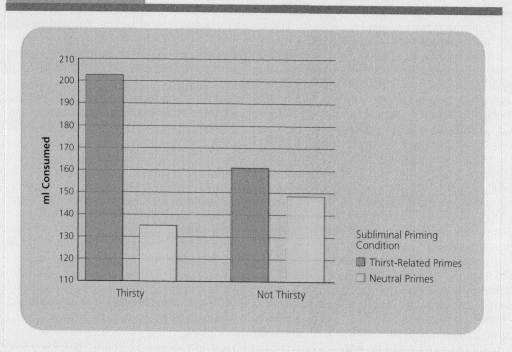

Amount of Liquid Consumed as a Function of Thirst and Subliminal Priming

Source, E. J. Strahan et al., "Subliminal Priming and Persuasion: Striking While the Iron Is Hot." *Journal of Experimental Social Psychology*, 38, (2002), pp. 556–8.

THE BIG PICTURE

Attitudes and persuasion are more than textbook topics. With the information learned in this chapter, do you now have a better understanding of how your own attitudes guide your behavior and why some persuasion attempts are more effective than others? As attitude holders, we differ in our need to evaluate the world, just as we differ in the need to keep our attitudes consistent with our behavior. We are sometimes active and at other times relatively passive in this process of attitude formation and change. One of the more important issues attitude researchers are now exploring involves the conditions under which explicit versus implicit attitudes predict behavior.

Regarding persuasion, when receiving persuasive messages we either critically analyzing the content or attend to incidental cues surrounding the message. Celebrity product endorsers and physically attractive spokespersons are there as peripheral cues to enhance your receptivity to their messages. Fast-talking and wisecracking salespersons also use persuasion strategies that have ties to chapter material. First, they hope that their humor grabs our attention and increases our liking for them. Second, they count on their rapid speech serving as a peripheral cue of their expertise, while simultaneously rendering us less able to fully comprehend what they actually say. And what about our own persuasion attempts? Do you first try to induce a good mood in those you hope to persuade, banking on their happiness lowering their resistance to what you have to say? Perhaps this is a mistake if your message is complex and in need of an audience ready to expend a great deal of cognitive effort. These examples illustrate the essential *message* of this chapter, which is that we are flexible social thinkers who rely on different cognitive strategies when evaluating information designed to shape and change our attitudes and behavior.

ACCESSED THROUGH www.BVTLab.com/sop6

Web sites for this chapter focus on attitudes and persuasion, including the use of consistency theories to increase retail sales, an analysis of propaganda, and recent research employing the elaboration likelihood model.

THEORIES OF COGNITIVE CONSISTENCY

This web page analyzes cognitive consistency theories and explores the question of whether cognitive consistency needs can be used to increase retail sales.

STEVE'S PRIMER OF PRACTICAL PERSUASION AND INFLUENCE

This web page discusses the elements of attitude theory, including vivid examples that demonstrate how attitudes function in daily living.

PROPAGANDA ANALYSIS HOME PAGE

This web page contains an analysis of common propaganda techniques, historical examples, and a bibliography of relevant publications.

JOHN CACIOPPO'S HOME PAGE

John Cacioppo, cocreator of the elaboration likelihood model, has a home page where you can learn more about his recent research and ideas.

Check out our web site
www.BVTLab.com
for chapter-by-chapter
flashcards, summaries,
and practice quizzes.

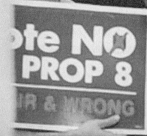

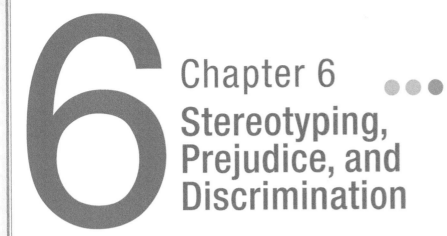

Chapter 6
Stereotyping, Prejudice, and Discrimination

CHAPTER OUTLINE

INTRODUCTION

Cognitive, Affective, and Behavioral Components of Intergroup Conflict
Stereotypes are beliefs about social groups.
Prejudice is an attitude and discrimination is an action.
There are three basic forms of prejudice.

Common Targets of Intolerance in Contemporary Society
Race-based appearance cues can trigger discrimination.
Modern-day racism is more ambivalent than openly hostile.
Sexism has both a hostile and a benevolent component.
Intolerance based on weight and sexual orientation is often accepted.
Stigmatized groups can experience stereotype threat.

What Motives and Social Factors Shape Prejudice and Discrimination?
Ingroup members are favored over outgroup members.
Intergroup competition can lead to prejudice.
Prejudice can serve as a justification for oppression.
Authoritarianism is associated with hostility toward outgroups.

Can We Reduce Intergroup Bias and Intolerance?
Prejudice and discrimination can be reduced by monitoring stereotyped thinking.
Targets of prejudice can become positive social change agents.
The contact hypothesis identifies social conditions that reduce intergroup conflict.

APPLICATIONS
How Can Our Schools Be Positive Institutions of Social Change?

PREVIEW   Over the years, prejudice research has examined both the social conditions that support and weaken intergroup intolerance, as well as the impact that such intolerance has on those who are its targets. How have social psychologists applied this knowledge to promote diversity acceptance and academic achievement in the schools?

THE BIG PICTURE

WEB SITES

INTRODUCTION

"Give me your tired, your poor,
Your huddled masses, yearning to breathe free,
The wretched refuse of your teeming shore,
Send these, the homeless, tempest tossed to me,
I lift my lamp beside the golden door!"

This passage from Emma Lazarus' poem is inscribed on a tablet within the pedestal of the Statue of Liberty that stands on Ellis Island in New York Harbor, greeting immigrants to the United States of America. Despite the welcoming sentiment expressed in this famous poem, immigrants are not always treated fairly when they arrive on this country's shores. For example, during the 1800s and early twentieth century, Jews and Italian immigrants were perceived as non-Anglo and non-White; and they experienced extreme prejudice, discrimination, and even violence. Next to African Americans, Italian Americans were the second most likely ethnic group to be lynched during this time period.

Anti-immigrant bias in this country persists in the twenty-first century, especially toward people from Latin America and those of Arab descent. Prejudice toward immigrants can be fueled by a number of factors, including a fear by Americans that these newcomers will take their jobs, threaten their safety, deplete social welfare services, and destroy the American way of life by refusing to adopt mainstream cultural values and practices.

Hostility toward immigrants is not limited to America's shores. In 2011 German Chancellor Angela Merkel declared the death of multiculturalism in her country, claiming that it had "failed utterly." She stated that it had been foolhardy to think that Germans and foreign workers could "live happily side-by-side." Similar anti-immigration sentiments are expressed in other European countries such as Great Britain, France, Austria, Italy, Sweden, Switzerland, Holland, Hungary, and Spain. The factors underlying this anti-immigrant tide in these countries are similar to those in America: fear of job loss, fear of crime, fear of social welfare depletion, and fear of national identity loss.

In all these countries, resentment toward immigrants has been strongly fueled by the worldwide economic crisis and rising unemployment. Yet Dartmouth Business Professor Vijay Govindarajan (2010) contends that the reasoning underlying the resentment that foreign immigrants take jobs from a country's existing citizens is often both flawed and short-sighted. Govindarajan states that many immigrants have skills and capabilities that are unique and not readily available among most current residents of a country. Further, these talented immigrants regularly create innovation that builds new industries and thereby create more jobs in their host countries. For example, in the United States, Govindarajan notes that the founders or cofounders of the following recently created high-tech companies were all recent immigrants: Google, Sun Microsystems, eBay, Juniper Networks, YouTube,

Anti-immigrant sentiment is not new to the United States. For example, in the 1920s, Italian immigrants Ferdinando Sacco and Bartolomeo Vanzetti were labor activists executed for the murder of two men, despite controversial evidence. Many historians contend that anti-immigrant prejudices led to a miscarriage of justice in this case.

Yahoo!, and Intel. These new companies, in which highly skilled immigrants played a lead role in creating, have generated hundreds of thousands of new jobs for Americans. Despite evidence that immigrants can strengthen and help to rejuvenate their host countries, hostility toward these people persists; for many citizens in countries around the world, immigrants are "those people" who threaten "us" and "our way of life."

When you think of a recent immigrant to this country what is the most typical image that comes to mind for you? Mexican migrant workers and Chinese high-tech entrepreneurs often elicit very different stereotypes among Americans, but both immigrant groups are targets of prejudice and discrimination.

In this chapter, we examine the social psychology of intergroup bias and intolerance, including the type of prejudice and discrimination experienced by immigrants around the world, as well as the intergroup intolerance based on other social identities. We also analyze the many social, cognitive, and developmental causes of prejudice and discrimination, and the consequences that this bias and intolerance have for those who are targeted. Finally, we explore research and theory concerning possible remedies.

The three most important social psychological terms associated with the bias and conflict that occurs between members of different social groups are *stereotyping, prejudice,* and *discrimination*. These three terms are closely tied yet distinct. Very few of us view these terms positively, but they are a part of all human cultures. We generally go to great lengths to avoid being accused of stereotyping, being prejudiced, or discriminating against others; and most of us realize that being the target of prejudice and discrimination is almost never a good thing. Yet what is prejudice? How is prejudice different from discrimination? Is stereotyping sometimes a good thing, or is it always wrong? Can you be prejudiced without knowing it? What causes prejudice, both at the intergroup level and at the interpersonal level? Can you fix a prejudiced mind? These and other important questions will be addressed in this chapter.

COGNITIVE, AFFECTIVE, AND BEHAVIORIAL COMPONENTS OF INTERGROUP CONFLICT

Chapter 5 examined how attitudes and beliefs are related to behavior. In this chapter we examine how some specific types of attitudes and beliefs about members of other social groups are related to specific types of antisocial behaviors. On the most basic level, stereotypes involve beliefs about specific groups; prejudice involves attitudes toward those groups; and discrimination involves actions toward those groups. Thus, in understanding intergroup conflict and intolerance, stereotyping is the cognitive component, prejudice is the affective component, and discrimination is the behavioral component.

STEREOTYPES ARE BELIEFS ABOUT SOCIAL GROUPS.

As you recall from Chapter 4 (pp. 110–111), we naturally and automatically develop social categories based on people's shared characteristics. Once categorized, we begin to perceive people differently. Often the nature of these different perceptions is determined by whether the individuals are ingroup members or outgroup members (Deaux, 1996). An **ingroup** is a group to which we belong and that forms a part of our social identity, while an **outgroup** is any group with which we do not share membership.

Outgroup Homogeneity Effect

How many times have you heard a woman say, "Well, you know men … They're all alike and they all want the same thing!" Likewise, how often have you heard men describing women in similar terms? This tendency to see members within a given outgroup as being more alike than members of one's ingroup is found in children as well as in adults (Guinote et al., 2007). Research has shown that merely assigning people to different social groups can create this **outgroup homogeneity effect**, but it is stronger when directed toward well-established groups (Boldry et al., 2007). Bernadette Park and Charles Judd found that on college campuses, sorority members, business majors, and engineering students all tend to perceive students in other campus social groups (those in other sororities or those with other majors) as more alike than those in their ingroup (Judd et al., 1991; Park & Rothbart, 1982). Perhaps you have witnessed some of your own college professors making homogeneous assumptions about certain minority groups by asking minority students in their classrooms to represent their group's attitudes and beliefs. Do you think those students—perhaps you were one of those students—might have felt uncomfortable and even stigmatized by this signaling out?

Brain-imaging studies indicate that this tendency to notice differences among ingroup members while perceiving outgroup members as being more alike is due to the

ingroup
····················
A group to which we belong and that forms a part of our social identity

outgroup
····················
Any group with which we do not share membership.

outgroup homogeneity effect
····················
Perception of outgroup members as being more similar to one another than are members of one's ingroup

fact that we engage in less thorough neural processing when attending to outgroup members (Ambady & Adams, 2011; Van Bavel et al., 2008). In other words, we invest less cognitive effort when attending to outgroup members compared to ingroup members, relying more on group-based stereotypes when making social judgments (Amodio, 2011). What factors influence our tendency to see outgroups as uniform? Research indicates that this illusion of outgroup homogeneity is more likely to occur between competing than noncompeting groups (Rothberger, 1997), and more likely for negative group characteristics than for positive group characteristics (Kosic et al., 2002). It is also more likely when relatively few outgroup members are being judged (Mullen & Hu, 1989).

Although we tend to perceive outgroups as being fairly uniform, our view of ingroup members is generally that they are relatively *distinct* and *complex*. For example, young adults tend to perceive others of their age as having more complex personalities than the elderly, whereas older adults hold exactly opposite beliefs (Brewer & Lui, 1984). Interestingly, the outgroup homogeneity effect actually reverses and becomes an "ingroup homogeneity effect" when members of *small groups* or *minority groups* compare their own group with the majority outgroup on attributes central to their social identity (Castano & Yzerbyt, 1998). This reversal is especially likely to occur when the ingroup members strongly identify with one another (Simon et al., 1995). In such instances, by emphasizing their similarities with fellow ingroup members, minority group members affirm their social identity and perceive themselves as a unified, and therefore, similar group in comparison to the larger and seemingly more diverse comparison group.

Our tendency to perceive outgroup members as similar to one another sets the stage for developing beliefs about their personalities, abilities, and motives. These social beliefs, which are typically learned from others and maintained through regular social interaction, are **stereotypes** (Schneider, 2004). Stereotypes are a type of *schema*, which is an organized structure of knowledge about a stimulus that is built up from experience and contains causal relations; it is a theory about how the social world operates (see Chapter 4, pp. 111–113 for a review).

As with other areas of social thinking, stereotyping can involve both deliberate and automatic cognitive processing (Wegener et al., 2006). Like other types of schemas, stereotypes significantly influence how we process and interpret social information—even when we are not consciously aware that they have been activated from memory (Kiefer & Sekaquaptewa, 2007). When activated in this manner, stereotypes can nonconsciously influence our thoughts and actions. These *implicit stereotypes* can be activated by various stimuli. Once a stereotype is activated, we tend to see people within that social category as possessing the traits or characteristics associated with the stereotyped group.

The Purpose of Stereotyping

In studying stereotyping, social psychologists have pondered what purpose it serves as a cognitive process. As previously discussed in Chapter 4 (p. 116), the quickness of stereotyped thinking is one of its most apparent qualities: being *fast*, it gives us a basis for immediate action in uncertain circumstances. In a very real sense, stereotypes are "shortcuts to thinking" that provide us with rich and distinctive information about individuals we do not personally know (Dijker & Koomen, 1996; Gilbert & Hixon, 1991). Not only do stereotypes provide us with a fast basis for social judgments, but stereotyping also appears to "free up" cognition for other tasks (Florack et al., 2001; Macrae et al., 1994). Thus, a second function of stereotyped thinking is that it is *efficient* and allows people to cognitively engage in other necessary activities. Daniel Gilbert (1989) suggests that this resource-preserving effect has an evolutionary basis. That is, expending cognitive resources as cheaply as possible enables perceivers to redirect their energy to more pressing concerns. This speed and efficiency of stereotype-based information apparently motivates people to rely on it over the more time-consuming method of getting to know a person as an individual (Pendry & Macrae, 1994).

One of the important reasons the activation of stereotypes often results in fast social judgments is that filtering social perceptions through a stereotype causes people to ignore information that is relevant but inconsistent with the stereotype (Dijksterhuis & Knippenberg, 1996). For example, Harriet might believe that Jews are more deceptive

stereotypes
• • • • • • • • • • • • • • • •
Beliefs about the personalities, abilities, and motives of a social group that doesn't allow for individual variation

Critical
THINKING

Test your knowledge of racial and ethnic group stereotypes by writing down what you think are some of the positive and negative characteristics typically associated with the following social groups in North American culture: Anglo-Whites, Asians, Blacks, Jews, and Latinos. Once you have listed characteristics for each group, compare them with the research findings summarized in the Appendix. Does your knowledge of group stereotypes tell us anything about your degree of prejudice toward these racial and ethnic groups?

in their business dealings than non-Jews. When asked why she holds this belief, Harriet might recall a set of pertinent cases of either business deception or honesty from her own personal experiences or from the experience of others. In recalling these instances, Harriet remembers those few cases that conform to her stereotype of Jews, but she forgets or explains away all those that clash with it. Based on this selective recall of past cases, Harriet concludes that there is an association between Jews and deception even though the correlation is no greater than it is for non-Jews. This example illustrates the power of an **illusory correlation**, which is the belief that two variables are associated with each other when no actual association exists.

At least two factors can produce an illusory correlation. The first is *associative meaning*, in which two variables are associated with each other because of the perceiver's preexisting beliefs. Because Harriet expects Jews to be more deceptive, she is not only more likely to notice possible instances of deception in her business dealings with Jews than in those with non-Jews, but she is also more likely to interpret ambiguous actions by Jews as reflecting sinister intentions. Numerous studies have found that people's preexisting attitudes and beliefs can predispose them to perceive associations that are truly illusory (Berndsen et al., 2002). Once the stereotype is activated, the person engages in biased processing of social information by attending to information consistent with the stereotype and ignoring contradictory information.

A second factor contributing to the development of illusory correlations is *shared distinctiveness*, in which two variables are associated because they share some unusual feature. According to this view, Harriet should develop an illusory correlation about Jews and dishonesty because both the minority group and the unfavorable trait are "infrequent" or "distinct" variables in the population. These two distinct variables are more likely associated in Harriet's memory simply because of their shared distinctiveness.

In an experiment demonstrating this effect, David Hamilton and Robert Gifford (1976) asked participants to read information about people from two different groups, "Group A" and "Group B." Twice as much information was provided about Group A than about Group B, making Group B the smaller or "minority group" in the study. In addition, twice as much of the information given about both groups involved desirable behaviors rather than undesirable actions. Desirable information included statements such as, "John, a member of Group A, visited a sick friend in the hospital." An example of an undesirable statement was, "Bob, a member of Group B, dropped litter in the subway station." Even though there was no correlation between group membership and the proportion of positive and negative information, participants perceived a correlation. As Figure 6.1 shows, participants overestimated the frequency with which Group B, the "minority group," behaved undesirably. In this study, the members of the "minority group" (who were described only half as much as the "majority group") and the undesirable actions (which occurred only half as much as the desirable behaviors) were both distinctive aspects of participants' social perceptions. This shared distinctiveness resulted in their illusory correlation, a finding replicated in later studies (Mullen & Johnson, 1995). Together, these studies indicate that although stereotyping may be beneficial because it allows us to redirect our energies to other pressing cognitive activities, the cost appears to be that we run the risk of making faulty social judgments about whomever we stereotype. Such biased information-processing often occurs unconsciously (Payne et al., 2004).

Stereotype Content and Intergroup Relations

Although research has traditionally focused on the inaccuracy of stereotypes, Lee Jussim and his coworkers (2009) contend that their review of studies examining stereotype accuracy strongly suggests that it is false to characterize stereotypes as inherently inaccurate. The truth is that stereotypes can lead to accurate social judgments (Ashton & Esses, 1999; Ryan, 2003). However, because stereotypes develop in a social environment in which groups are often regularly interacting with one another, each group's beliefs about the other are shaped and distorted by the interaction. For example, the negative stereotypes that African Americans and White Americans have about each other's group have been shaped by the history of their intergroup relations and the resulting mutually shared feelings of threat (Stephan et al., 2002). While many African Americans perceive White Americans as powerful, dominating,

illusory correlation
The belief that two variables are associated with each other when in fact there is little or no actual association

Critical
THINKING
One of the important functions of stereotyping is that it saves cognitive effort. Thus, when we are tired, we may be more likely to base our impressions of others on stereotypes. If this is true, during what times of the day are people likely to rely on stereotypes when judging others?

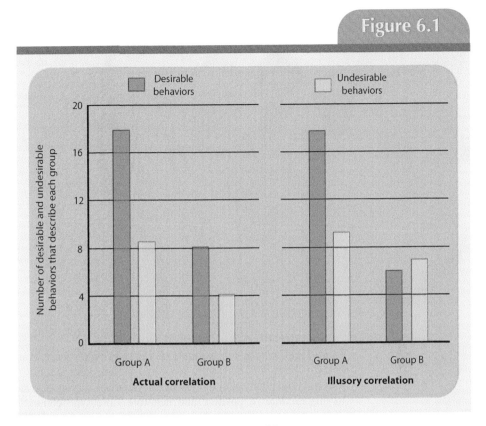

Figure 6.1

Illusory Correlations and the Persistence of Stereotypes

In Hamilton and Gifford's (1976) study of illusory correlations, participants read sentences in which a person from Group A or Group B was associated with either a desirable or an undesirable behavior. As you can see in the actual correlation graph, both groups were described with the same proportion of desirable and undesirable behaviors, but only one-third of the provided information was about Group B members, making them the "minority group." The illusory correlation graph indicates that participants later overestimated the number of undesirable behaviors in the minority group (Group B), which suggests that people tend to perceive an illusory correlation between variables that stand out because they are unusual or deviant.

threatening, and intentionally oppressive, many White Americans perceive African Americans as irrational, hostile, destructive, and out of control (Alexander et al., 2005). These findings illustrate how stereotypes often reveal a good deal more about the nature of the relationship between groups than they reveal about the groups themselves.

As we will discuss in more detail later (pp. 213–215), within a society the stereotypes that are commonly held about a particular group of people are shaped by the group's social status (low or high) and whether it is perceived to have a competitive or cooperative relationship with mainstream society. Doctors, for example, are generally perceived as a high-status, cooperative group because they possess valuable skills that are used to maintain and improve the lives of other people in society. As a result, most people view them with respect and even admiration, and doctors are often stereotyped as being intelligent, hardworking, and caring, although perhaps sometimes arrogant. In contrast, high-status groups that are perceived to have a competitive relationship with many mainstream groups within society are stereotyped as being highly competent but also as having sinister or selfish motives. The stereotype of Jews being clever, good with money, but devious in their financial dealings with other members of society is an example of this envious-based stereotyping. Recent immigrants from such countries as India and China are similarly labeled with envious-based stereotypes.

Stereotypes surrounding low-status groups often have an air of condescension, but they can include positive qualities for groups that are perceived as offering benefits to

Critical
THINKING

Recently in the United States, media commentators have increasingly used the terms "red" and "blue" to refer to perceived cultural differences in America and American politics. Why might the increased use of these terms increase prejudice and conflict between political groups in America?

Within our society there are many different positive and negative stereotypes associated with various groups. Doctors, for example, are favorably perceived as a high status, cooperative group.

mainstream society. For example, sexist men might view women as being nurturing and "pure of heart" but inherently weak and incompetent, while sexist women might think of men as being likable and fun loving but hopelessly immature and irresponsible. In contrast to this mixture of positive and negative stereotype content, stereotypes of low-status groups who are perceived as taking valuable resources from mainstream society are almost exclusively negative, such as the characteristics associated with homeless people, welfare recipients, obese individuals, and low-skilled immigrants. The negative stereotypes directed toward low-skilled immigrants—including those who are illegal immigrants—are largely shaped by perceptions that this particular social group is taking jobs from American citizens, draining the resources of social welfare agencies, and threatening the national identity of the United States with its cultural practices (Huntington, 2004).

PREJUDICE IS AN ATTITUDE AND DISCRIMINATION IS AN ACTION.

The type of shared social beliefs that some Americans have toward immigrants can create a psychological climate that leads to prejudice and discrimination (Jackson, 2011). Yet what is prejudice, and how is it different from discrimination? The traditional definition of prejudice is that it is a *negative* attitude toward members of a specific group. This conventional view assumes that prejudice can be represented as a simple continuum of one emotion that varies in intensity from mild dislike to burning hatred. However, many forms of prejudice involve complex and contradictory emotions, combining negative attitudes toward group members on some dimensions with positive attitudes on other dimensions. As an example, consider the following hypothetical statement made by a man about women:

> I adore women. I love the way they look, the way they cook. I put women on a pedestal and worship them. But if a woman begins thinking she can "lord it over" a man, then she's a problem and is no good for anything.

Is this statement an expression of prejudice? Using the traditional definition as a guide, we would probably conclude that the first three sentences don't conform to the definition of prejudice, but the last sentence does. However, an increasing number of social scientists contend that it is misleading and overly simplistic to define prejudice solely in terms of varying degrees of dislike. These critics of the traditional definition would argue that underlying the first three sentences' seemingly positive evaluations is an underlying judgment that women are somehow undeserving of having a social status equal to men.

"The whole world is festering with unhappy souls: The French hate the Germans, the Germans hate the Poles; Italians hate Yugoslavs, South Africans hate the Dutch; And I don't like anybody very much!"

Sheldon Harnick, American songwriter, born 1924. From *The Merry Little Minuet.*

prejudice
....
Attitudes toward members of
specific groups that directly
or indirectly suggest they
deserve an inferior social
status

Due to these concerns with the traditional definition, in this chapter **prejudice** is defined as attitudes toward members of specific groups that directly or indirectly suggest they deserve an inferior social status (Glick & Hilt, 2000). This definition has the advantage of being able to account for seemingly positive attitudes that prejudiced individuals often express toward other social groups that simultaneously justifies placing these groups into a lower social status. By allowing for the possibility of both positive and negative evaluations, this definition includes prejudices that are sometimes described as "ambivalent." This definition can also account for "upward-directed" prejudices, meaning prejudice expressed by members of lower-status groups toward groups that have higher status but are seen as undeserving of their higher rank. The prejudice expressed by some members of minority groups, some women's prejudice toward men, and some working-class resentment and envy of the upper social classes—all are examples of this upward-directed prejudice.

Beyond recognizing prejudice in others, is it possible to harbor prejudice toward another group without being aware of it? The overwhelming scientific opinion is that it is indeed possible (Amodio et al., 2004a; Brendl et al., 2001; Levy & Banaji, 2002). In other words, prejudice can be either explicit or implicit. **Explicit prejudice** involves consciously held prejudicial attitudes toward a group, while **implicit prejudice** involves unconsciously held prejudicial attitudes. This perspective on prejudice mirrors similar developments in attitude research in general (see Chapter 5, pp. 159–162). People with low explicit prejudice but high implicit prejudice toward a particular outgroup may not be aware of their negative bias. Therefore, while responding in negative ways toward members of outgroups, these low explicit/high implicit prejudice individuals might honestly believe that they are nonprejudiced. In general, research suggests that implicit prejudice is more stable, enduring, and difficult to change than explicit prejudice (Dasgupta & Greenwald, 2001; Kim, 2003).

explicit prejudice
....
Prejudicial attitudes that are
consciously held, even if they
are not publicly expressed

implicit prejudice
....
Unconsciously held
prejudicial attitudes

Despite the hidden nature of implicit prejudice, scientists study its process using various techniques, including the Implicit Association Test and brain-imaging technology (see Chapter 2, p. 60). Researchers often employ both techniques in one study: using the Implicit Association Test to identify White individuals with high implicit racial prejudice and then using functional magnetic resonance imaging (fMRI) to scan their brains while they look at photos of familiar and unfamiliar Black and White faces (Amodio & Lieberman, 2009; Phelps et al., 2000). As depicted in Figure 6.2, these studies find that the unfamiliar Black faces are much more likely than the unfamiliar White faces to activate the *amygdala* in both the right and left cerebral hemispheres and the *anterior cingulate* in the frontal lobes. These brain structures are involved in arousal and emotional learning and play a crucial role in detecting threat and triggering fear (Phelps et al., 2000). No heightened amygdala and cingulate activity occurs when these high implicit/low explicit prejudiced participants view familiar black faces. These findings suggest that, despite not consciously reporting any negative racial attitudes toward African Americans, implicitly prejudiced Whites, perhaps unknowingly, experience heightened arousal associated with some level of anxiety and negativity toward Blacks. Similar findings have also been obtained from African-American students when they viewed photos of White faces (Hart et al., 2000).

discrimination
....
A negative and/or
patronizing action toward
members of specific groups.

In contrast to prejudice, there is relative consensus in social psychology when defining discrimination. For our purposes, we define **discrimination** as a negative and/or patronizing action toward members of specific groups (Brewer & Brown, 1998). Disliking, disrespecting, and/or resenting people because of their group membership are examples of prejudice. Both physically attacking or failing to hire them for jobs because of their group membership are examples of discrimination. As we learned in Chapter 5, behavior does not always follow attitude. Similarly, discrimination is not an inevitable result of prejudice. For example, a storeowner who is prejudiced against Blacks might not act on this negative attitude because most of his customers are Black and he needs their business. In this case, the subjective norm (see Chapter 5, p. 182) dictates against the storeowner acting on his prejudice.

It is also true that discrimination can occur without prejudice. Sometimes people who are not prejudiced engage in *institutional discrimination* by carrying out the discriminatory guidelines of institutions. For instance, due to new state immigration laws, police

Figure 6.2

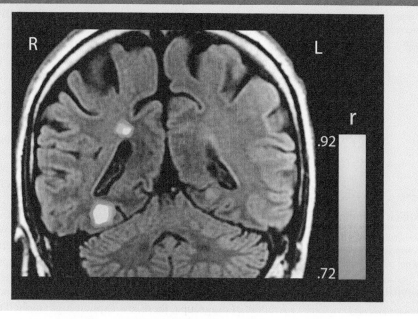

Measuring Implicit Prejudice Using Brain Scans
*When White research participants with high scores on an implicit measure of racial prejudice
(but low explicit prejudice scores) were shown photos of familiar and unfamiliar Black and
White faces, the unfamiliar Black faces were much more likely than the unfamiliar White faces
to activate the amygdala in both the right and left cerebral hemispheres of the brain, as well as
the anterior cingulate in the frontal lobes (Phelps et al., 2000). These brain regions are associated with arousal and emotional responses and the brain's "alarm" system for threat, pain, and
danger. What implications does the existence of implicit prejudice have for attempts at reducing intergroup hostility?*

Source: Phelps, et al., (2000). Performance on indirect measures of race evaluation predicts amygdala
activation. *Journal of Cognitive Neuroscience, 12,* 729–738.

officers in Georgia can demand at traffic stops that people of Hispanic descent show doc-
umentation of their citizenship while not making similar demands of drivers whose facial
features fit the European-American prototype. Similarly, real-estate agents in large urban
settings may show African American clients only houses located in Black or racially
mixed neighborhoods even though they have no animosity toward African Americans
(and may be Black themselves). They carry out this institutional practice, known as
redlining, because they are following the guidelines of their superiors, who believe that
integration will lower property values.

THERE ARE THREE BASIC FORMS OF PREJUDICE.

Consistent with the updated conception of prejudice and our previous discussion of
stereotypes, Peter Glick and Susan Fiske (2001) propose that there are three basic forms
of prejudice that account for the different ways in which groups are perceived and
treated. According to these theorists, the form of prejudice that is directed toward a particular group is determined by two social factors.

The first social factor is whether the target group is perceived as having a competitive
or cooperative relationship with mainstream society. A group has a *competitive relationship*
if they are perceived as intentionally grabbing resources for themselves at the expense of
other groups. Examples of competitive groups would be rich and poor people, who are
often perceived as unfairly taking or receiving societal resources. In contrast, a group has
a *cooperative relationship* with mainstream society if they are perceived as undemanding

Table 6.1

Three Forms of Prejudice Based on a Social Group's Relative Status and Its Relationship with Mainstream Society

GROUP'S RELATIONSHIP WITH MAINSTREAM SOCIETY

Group's Relative Social Status	Cooperative	Competitive
High	*No Prejudice*	*Envious Prejudice*
Negative Emotions	None	Envy, fear, resentment, hostility
Positive Emotions	Respect, admiration, affection	Grudging admiration of abilities
Behavior	Defer	Avoid, exclude, segregate, exterminate
Common Targets	Dominant groups perceived as generous, allies	Jews, Asian Americans, feminists, rich people, Black professionals
Low	*Paternalistic Prejudice*	*Contemptuous Prejudice*
Negative Emotions	Disrespect, condescension	Disrespect, resentment, hostility
Positive Emotions	Patronizing affection, pity, liking	None
Behavior	Personal intimacy, but role segregation	Avoid, exclude, segregate, exterminate
Common Targets	The elderly, the disabled, housewives, women in general, adolescents, and young adults	Poor Whites, poor Blacks, homeless people, obese persons, welfare recipients lesbians and gay men, illegal immigrants

Adapted from: Glick, P. (2002). Sacrificial lambs dressed in wolves' clothing: Envious prejudice, ideology, and the scapegoating of Jews. In L. S. Newman & R. Erber (Eds.), *Understanding Genocide: The Social Psychology of the Holocaust.* Oxford: Oxford University Press, pp. 113–142.

(such as self-sufficient elderly people), contributing (such as homemakers raising children), or as needing help through no fault of their own (such as the disabled).

The second social factor is whether the target group is of relatively low or high social status within mainstream society. Examples of relatively *low-status* groups in the United States are poor people, women in general, homeless people, working-class people, obese individuals, gay men and lesbians, Blacks, Hispanics, Muslims, the disabled, housewives, and the elderly. Examples of relatively *high-status* groups are rich people, men in general, Whites in general, heterosexuals, middle-class Whites, highly educated people, Christians, Jews, Asians, and career women.

As depicted in Table 6.1, if a group has relatively low social status and is perceived as having a competitive relationship with mainstream society, it is likely to become the target of *contemptuous prejudice*, characterized by exclusively negative attitudes of disrespect, resentment, and hostility. Contemptuous prejudice is most people's prototype for prejudice because it is characterized by uniformly negative emotions and attitudes; it most closely fits the traditional definition of prejudice (Cottrell & Neuberg, 2005). The blatant prejudices often expressed toward poor Whites, poor Blacks, homeless people, obese individuals, welfare recipients, lesbians and gay men, and low-skilled immigrants are examples of contemptuous prejudice. The contempt and disrespect that obese individuals often experience on a daily basis are also examples of this form of prejudice (Maranto & Stenoien, 2000).

In contrast to this easily recognized intergroup hostility, the other two forms of prejudice each represent a type of *ambivalent prejudice*, because they consist of both negative and positive attitudes. For instance, if a high-status group has a competitive relationship with mainstream society, it may become the target of *envious prejudice*, in which feelings of resentment and hostility are mixed with fear and envy, as well as with the positive emotions of respect and admiration. So-called model minorities—such as Jews and Asian Americans—are often targets of envious prejudice (Lin et al., 2005). Similarly, the mixed evaluations of feminists, Black professionals, and people in the upper classes of society are often rooted in envious prejudice. When a high-status outgroup is perceived as highly competent and threatening, the resulting envious prejudice can sometimes generate "hot" discrimination, in which the outgroup becomes a convenient target for high levels of frustration-fed aggression (Duckitt, 2001).

Finally, a low-status group that has a cooperative or noncompetitive relationship with mainstream society may become the target of *paternalistic prejudice*. Paternalism is the care or control of subordinates in a manner suggesting a father's relationship with his children. The ambivalent attitudes expressed in this form of prejudice might involve patronizing affection and pity, mixed with condescension and disrespect. Sociologist Mary Jackman (1994) refers to paternalistic prejudice as the "velvet glove" approach to dominance, because dominant groups emphasize rewards rather than punishments in maintaining their control over subordinate groups. Although paternalism in intergroup relations often conjures up the nineteenth-century ideology of the "White man's burden," Jackman contends that it is still an identifiable and influential form of prejudice. The elderly, the disabled, housewives, women in general, and adolescents and young adults are often the targets of paternalistic prejudice (Chrisler, 2003; Viki et al., 2003).

SECTION SUMMARY

- The outgroup homogeneity effect is the tendency to perceive people in outgroups as more similar to one another than ingroup members.

- Stereotypes are social beliefs typically learned from others and maintained through regular social interaction.

- Two qualities of stereotyped thinking are that it is fast and efficient, but often faulty.

- Prejudice involves attitudes toward members of specific groups that directly or indirectly suggest that they deserve an inferior social status.

- Explicit prejudices are consciously held, while implicit prejudices are unconsciously held.

- Discrimination is a negative and/or patronizing action toward members of specific groups.

- The form of prejudice directed toward a group is determined by two social factors:

  whether the target group is perceived as having a competitive or cooperative relationship with mainstream society

  whether the target group is of low or high social status within mainstream society

- Contemptuous prejudice occurs when the target group has a competitive relationship with mainstream society and has low social status.

- Envious prejudice occurs when the target group has a competitive relationship with mainstream society and has high social status.

- Paternalistic prejudice occurs when the target group has a cooperative relationship with mainstream society and has low social status.

COMMON TARGETS OF INTOLERANCE IN CONTEMPORARY SOCIETY

stigma

....

An attribute that serves to discredit a person in the eyes of others

In all societies, some social groups are valued while other groups are stigmatized. A **stigma** is an attribute that discredits a person or a social group in the eyes of others (Shana & van Laar, 2006; Ullah, 2011). Stigmatized persons are not simply different from others, but society judges their difference to be discrediting. Individual members of society may vary in how they personally respond to a particular stigma, but everyone shares the knowledge that the characteristic in question, the "mark," is negatively valued and having it "spoils" the person's full humanity (Herek et al., 2005; Major & O'Brien, 2005). Being marginalized because of a stigma induces feelings of threat and a loss of social power; the stigma engulfs the person's entire identity (Oswald, 2007). It becomes the central trait for that person (see Chapter 4, p. 135), shaping the meaning of all other traits.

In his classic monograph, *Stigma: Notes on the Management of Spoiled Identity*, Erving Goffman (1963) distinguished the following three different categories of stigma:

1. *Tribal identities*: race, sex, ethnicity, religion, and national origin
2. *Blemishes of individual character:* mental disorders, addictions, homosexuality, and criminality
3. *Abominations of the body:* physical deformities, physical disabilities, diseases, and obesity

The concept of stigma is related to prejudice and discrimination because people who are stigmatized are almost always the targets of intolerance, which can be either subtle or blatant. While anyone can be stereotyped, research indicates that members of stigmatized groups are more frequently stereotyped than members of nonstigmatized groups (Adams et al., 2006). In one such investigation, Jonathan Cook and his colleagues (2011) conducted a seven-day experiential-sampling study in which they measured stigmatized and nonstigmatized individuals' reactions to being stereotyped while they engaged in normal daily activities. Some of the participants were members of stigmatized groups in American society (African Americans, gay men, and lesbians), while other participants were members of the dominant group in the country (heterosexual Caucasian Americans). As expected, participants who were members of stigmatized groups reported more frequent stereotyping than did nonstigmatized participants. For members of all groups, being stereotyped was associated with feeling more socially anxious and inhibited in "being oneself," as well as feeling low in social power. In essence, rather than feeling in control of the situation, stereotyped people felt like they were controlled by the situation and by the stereotyped role they had been cast into.

Although many societal groups fall into one of the stigma categories, let us examine examples of these three different categories that are of particular importance in contemporary society. First we will examine intergroup intolerance associated with race-based and sex-based tribal identity stigmas, then we will analyze intolerance based on perceived blemishes of individual character (homosexuality/bisexuality), and then we will explore perceived abominations of the body (obesity).

Do you have an attribute that discredits you in the eyes of others? Members of stigmatized groups face social challenges that nonstigmatized individuals do not encounter.

RACE-BASED APPEARANCE CUES CAN TRIGGER DISCRIMINATION.

Prejudice and discrimination based on a person's racial background is called **racism**. Blatantly negative stereotypes based on beliefs in the racial superiority of one's own group, coupled with open opposition to racial equality, characterize *old-fashioned racism* (McConahay, 1986). Old-fashioned racism involves contemptuous prejudice and often leads to movement against the despised group, including physical violence.

Although old-fashioned racism is far less common in contemporary American society than a generation ago, racial stereotypes continue to provide fuel for volatile expressions of prejudice and discrimination. Due to socialization about what constitutes different racial categories, a person's skin color and facial characteristics (such as shape of eyes, nose, and lips) are physical features that often automatically activate racial stereotypes among people of many different ethnicities in the United States, as well as in a number of countries around the world (Maddox, 2004). When such race-based stereotype activation occurs, people generally associate more positive personality traits to those with lighter skin and Eurocentric facial features than those with darker skin and Afrocentric features (Blair et al., 2002; Livingston & Brewer, 2002). Furthermore, the more Afrocentric the features of the target person in these studies, the more she or he is assumed to have the traits that are stereotypically associated with African Americans. Research suggests that when a person of any race makes a judgment on the basis of physical appearance, the target person's race-related features may influence social judgments in two ways (Blair et al., 2004; Judd et al., 2004). First, those features provide the basis for racial categorization, which then activates the relevant stereotypes. Second, those features may directly activate race-associated stereotypes even for a person who is not a member of the relevant race. Thus, a man with curly hair and/or a darker complexion who identifies himself as "White" and is also categorized by others as "White" may still be nonconsciously perceived by others as having characteristics stereotypically associated with Black males.

This tendency to negatively stereotype those with darker skin and Afrocentric facial features is found even among African Americans (Clark & Clark, 1939, 1947). For example, when African American teenagers were surveyed about their skin tone preferences (Anderson & Cromwell, 1977), they associated very light-brown skin with positive characteristics (the prettiest skin, the smartest girl, the children fathers like best) and black skin with more negative traits (the dumbest person, the person one would not like to marry, the color one would prefer not to be). Further, when African American children were read stories in which Black characters were portrayed in either stereotype-consistent or stereotype-inconsistent ways, they were more likely to remember stories when light-skinned Blacks were associated with positive traits and high-status occupations, or when dark-skinned Blacks were associated with negative traits and low-status occupations (Averhart & Bigler, 1997). These findings are consistent with the general observation that lighter-skinned Blacks attain higher status in society than darker-skinned Blacks (Hughes & Hertel, 1990). In fact, some social scientists contend that the social status gap between light and dark-skinned Blacks in the United States is as large as the gap between Whites and Blacks (Hunter, 1998). Similar social status gaps are also found among lighter-skinned and darker-skinned Mexican Americans (Arce et al., 1987; Telles & Marguia, 1990).

The mistaken shooting of Amadou Diallo by New York City police officers is widely considered an example of the sometimes deadly consequences of racial profiling. Was his killing caused by implicit racism?

The negative effects of automatically stereotyping people with Afrocentric facial features can have real-world life-and-death consequences. For example, around midnight on February 4, 1999, four White New York City police officers were looking for a rape suspect in the Bronx when they saw twenty-two-year-old Amadou Diallo, a West African immigrant, standing in his apartment building doorway. Stopping their car, they told Diallo to "freeze," but then they saw him reach into his pants' pocket. Fearing that this suspicious-looking man was reaching for a weapon, the officers drew their pistols and opened fire. Within five seconds they fired a total of forty-one shots at the unarmed Diallo, nineteen of which found their mark, killing him. The object that Diallo was reaching for was his wallet, which contained his ID. The officers were tried for murder but were acquitted of all charges on the grounds that although they made a mistake, their actions were justified (Fritsch, 2000).

Motivated by this high-profile case and the resulting charges of racism and racial profiling by law enforcement officers, Keith Payne (2001) conducted a series of studies to understand how the mere presence of a Black face could cause people to misidentify harmless objects as weapons. In his research, Payne showed pictures of guns or tools to White participants and asked them to classify the objects as quickly as possible. Just prior to seeing an object, participants were primed by a brief presentation of either a White or a Black face (see Figure 6.3). Results indicated that when a Black face immediately preceded a tool, the tool was significantly more likely mistaken for a handgun compared with conditions in which this same tool was preceded with a White face. This stereotype difference emerged mainly when participants were required to react quickly, a condition that mimics the time pressure involved in real-world police confrontations like the Diallo shooting.

As you recall from our previous discussion of implicit prejudice (p. 212), when Whites with high implicit but low explicit race prejudice see an unfamiliar Black face, brain regions that trigger fear and threat responses are activated. Combined with the present

Figure 6.3

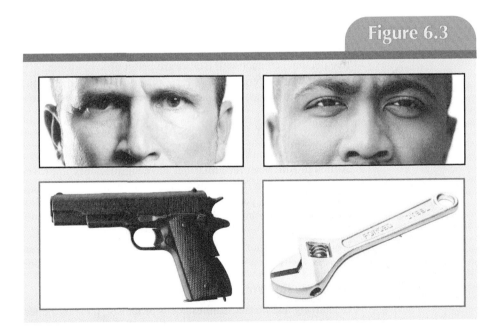

Race and the Misperception of Weapons
After being primed by Black or White faces, White participants were shown pictures of guns or tools and asked to classify the objects (Payne, 2001). When participants were required to react quickly, they were more likely to misidentify tools as guns after being primed with Black faces rather than with White faces. How does this research provide insight into police shootings of unarmed suspects in real-world confrontations?

Source: Payne, B. K. (2001). Prejudice and perception: The role of automatic and controlled processes in misperceiving a weapon. *Journal of Personality and Social Psychology, 81*, 181–192.

results, this research suggests that, due to racial stereotypes, simply seeing a Black man may automatically and nonconsciously trigger a fear response in police officers. Further, under conditions that require quick and decisive action, this race-based reaction may result in police officers misperceiving harmless objects as weapons. This perceptual bias does not seem to simply reflect explicit prejudice toward African Americans. Instead, this effect appears to be caused by the racial stereotypes that exist in our culture (Judd et al., 2004).

Subsequent studies using computer-simulated "shooter/nonshooter" scenarios have verified these findings and have also found evidence suggesting that if a criminal suspect is Black versus White, people generally require less certainty that he is, in fact, holding a gun before they decide to shoot him (Greenwald et al., 2003; Ito et al., 2006). Importantly, this race-based bias was found between both African American and White participants (Correll et al., 2002). Thus, African American police officers may be as likely as White officers to misperceive that a Black man is holding a weapon and respond by shooting in self-defense. These studies also suggest that such race-based bias is very difficult to control because it is operating below a person's level of conscious awareness. However, results also indicate that when given ample time, people make few stereotypical misidentifications of weapons because their automatic, reflexive response is controlled and altered by more deliberate cognitive analysis. Of course, the problem here is that urging a police officer to react slowly during a confrontation with a potentially armed suspect can be extremely dangerous for the officer.

In considering the implications of these studies, it must be kept in mind that participants were not actual members of a police force. Is it possible that police training reduces or eliminates this race-based shooter bias by teaching officers to focus on the presence of a weapon during confrontations rather than fixating on the target's race? Joshua Correll and his coworkers (2007) tested this possibility in a series of studies comparing police officers to similarly matched community members. Results indicated that the police officers were significantly faster in correctly identifying the presence of a weapon and were less "trigger-happy" when the target was a Black than other community members would be. However, the police officers still manifested racial bias in the speed with which they made shoot/don't shoot decisions: they were much faster in accurately responding when the targets were armed Blacks or unarmed Whites than when the targets were unarmed Blacks or armed Whites. Additional research indicates that officers who have had positive personal contact with Blacks are better able to eliminate the shooter bias with simulation training (Peruche & Plant, 2006). Together, these studies inform us that police training does reduce race-based shooter bias, but it does not eliminate it.

MODERN-DAY RACISM IS MORE AMBIVALENT THAN OPENLY HOSTILE.

Although American race relations have significantly improved over the past fifty years, surveys of African Americans find that more than half still report having at least thirteen racial hassles per year (Kessler et al., 1999; Sellers & Shelton, 2003). Most racial hassles involve brief interactions with strangers in which respondents were ignored, overlooked, not given service, treated rudely, or perceived as a threat. Other minorities in the United States report comparable prejudice experiences (Park et al., 2009). What are some of the underlying causes of this more subtle form of racism?

Aversive Racism

In studying less blatant manifestations of racism, most of the research during the past thirty years has examined White Americans' racial attitudes (Pearson et al., 2009). Researchers such as Samuel Gaertner and John Dovidio (2000) and Irwin Katz and R. Glen Hass (1988) assert that the fundamental nature of White Americans' current attitudes toward many racial groups, but especially toward African Americans, is complex and conflicted. They contend that on the one hand, the majority of Whites hold to egalitarian values that stress equal treatment of all people and a sympathy for social groups who have been mistreated in the past. Therefore, they sympathize with the victims of racial prejudice and tend to support public policies that promote racial equality. On the other hand, because of exposure to unflattering stereotypes and media images depicting African Americans as lazy, unmotivated, and violent, and due to simple ingroup-outgroup biases, these researchers believe that many Whites come to possess negative feelings and beliefs about Blacks that directly contradict their egalitarian values. The American individualist value of the Protestant work ethic, which emphasizes self-reliance and individual initiative in pursuing life goals, reinforces these negative social perceptions about Blacks. Given their own relative lack of personal experience with the negative impact of racial prejudice, many Whites tend to believe that anyone who works hard has a good chance of succeeding in life. Therefore, many of them conclude that at least part of the source of continued racial inequality is what they perceive as a low level of motivation and effort on the part of Blacks and other disadvantaged groups, such as American Indians and Latinos (Adams et al., 2008; Biernat et al., 1996).

According to this perspective on contemporary racism, the negative feelings engendered by Whites' perceptions of disadvantaged racial groups do not encompass anger or contempt, as in old-fashioned racism; however, they do include uneasiness and even fear. As you recall, these are the precise emotions activated when Whites with high implicit and low explicit racial prejudice see an unfamiliar black face (refer back to pp. 217–219). Due to the fact that an egalitarian value system plays an important role in their self-concepts, this perspective assumes that many White Americans typically do not even acknowledge to themselves, much less to others, that they have these negative feelings. Because interacting with members of these other racial groups tends to make Whites aware of their negative—though not fully understood—racial feelings and beliefs, they avoid such interactions and, thus, avoid confronting their hidden prejudice (Nail et al., 2003). This is why the combination of both positive and negative beliefs and feelings about a particular racial group is called **aversive racism**. Interracial encounters make salient the attitudinal conflict, and this awareness threatens one's self-concept as a fair-minded person.

aversive racism

Attitudes toward members of a racial group that incorporate both egalitarian social values and negative emotions, causing one to avoid interaction with members of the group

One study, conducted by Katz and Hass (1988), suggests that many White Americans may indeed have conflicting attitudes regarding African Americans. In this research, White college students first completed a questionnaire that either contained items measuring adherence to the individualist Protestant ethic of self-reliance, initiative, and hard work or contained egalitarian and humanitarian items stressing equal treatment of all people and empathy for those who are less fortunate (see Table 6.2).

Table 6.2

Conflicting American Values Related to Racial Ambivalence

People with a strong Protestant ethic would agree with the sample items from the first scale, while those with a strong humanitarianism-egalitarianism value orientation would agree with the sample items from the scale bearing its name. If a White American believes in both of these value orientations, according to Katz and Hass (1988), what sort of attitudinal conflict might this create in their overall perceptions of African Americans or American Indians?

THE PROTESTANT ETHIC (Sample Items from Katz & Hass, 1988)	HUMANITARIANISM-EGALITARIANISM (Sample Items from Katz & Hass, 1988)
1. Most people who don't succeed in life are just plain lazy.	1. One should find ways to help others less fortunate than oneself.
2. Anyone who is willing to work hard has a good chance of succeeding.	2. There should be equality for everyone—because we are all human beings.
3. If people work hard enough they are to make a good life for themselves.	3. Everyone should have an equal chance and an equal say in most things.
4. Most people spend too much time in unprofitable amusements.	4. Acting to protect the rights and interests of other members of the community is a major obligation for all persons.

When participants completed the questionnaire, the researchers administered a second questionnaire that measured their explicit prejudice toward Blacks. Because Katz and Hass believed that both sets of values were part of the participants' worldview, they predicted that their *explicit prejudice* would be influenced by whichever of these two values was made salient. Consistent with their hypothesis, when Whites were first primed by egalitarian statements, their subsequent prejudice scores went down. When they were primed by individualist work ethic statements, their prejudice scores went up. This is what one would expect if the participants held both value orientations. In any given situation, whichever one is made salient will exert the most influence over attitudes and behavior.

Katz and Hass believe that another consequence of Whites having ambivalent attitudes toward minority groups is that it can cause them to act in a more extreme manner toward minority members than they would to other Whites (Katz et al., 1986). This tendency for responses to become more extreme when one holds ambivalent attitudes is called *response amplification*; and it can occur in either a favorable or an unfavorable direction, depending on the social context (Hass et al., 1991). Thus, Whites with ambivalent attitudes toward Blacks may act overfriendly and solicitous when being introduced to African Americans whom they perceive to be competent and ambitious. This is because such encounters discredit the negative components of their ambivalent attitudes. Likewise, they may react with great annoyance and anger when interacting with Blacks that they judge to be incompetent and lazy because the encounter discredits the positive component of their ambivalent attitudes. When either one of these components has been discredited in a given situation, the person's evaluative response is likely to be exaggerated in the opposing direction.

As you might guess, when aversive racists cannot easily avoid interacting with African Americans or with members of other minority groups for whom they hold similarly ambivalent attitudes, the resulting exchanges are often uncomfortable for both parties (Dovidio, 2001). During such interactions, aversive racists—who generally sincerely believe that they are not prejudiced—consciously focus on their egalitarian attitudes and actively monitor and regulate their self-presentations to convey warmth and friendliness. Simultaneously, they try to ignore their feelings of discomfort that are induced by their implicit prejudice. In contrast, based on past interactions with aversive racists, many minority group members have learned not just to attend to White individuals' consciously constructed self-presentations but also to note their nonverbal behavior for evidence of implicit prejudice. Nonverbal behavior related to negative arousal and tension in face-to-face interactions includes such things as excessive blinking, gaze aversion, and forced smiles. When minority group members detect these behaviors, they feel more uncomfortable and less satisfied with the interaction than the aversive racists (Vorauer & Kumhyr, 2001). In other words, the research evidence suggests that because aversive racists pay most attention to their consciously held egalitarian attitudes and overtly friendly self-presentations, whereas their minority partners pay most attention to aversive racists' less consciously controlled—and less friendly—nonverbal behaviors, these two conversational partners often have different reactions to their interracial exchange (Devine et al., 1996; Dovidio et al., 2002). While aversive racists often walk away feeling relieved that things "went well" and comforted by the belief that they indeed are nonprejudiced, minorities often walk away feeling angry and certain that they have just encountered another prejudiced White person (Penner et al., 2010).

What About Racial Prejudice Among Minority Group Members?

Because minorities are much more likely to be targets of racial discrimination than Whites, minority race bias is often over-looked in the larger culture (Shelton, 2000). One important finding is that just as Whites' racial attitudes vary from positive to negative, so too do the racial attitudes of minorities. Despite being the target of prejudice from Whites, not all Blacks, Asians, Latinos, and American Indians are prejudiced against Whites (Shelton, 2000). Studies also suggest that although many Whites' negative attitudes toward Blacks are related to their perceptions that Blacks are not living up to cherished values such as industriousness and perseverance, many Blacks' racial attitudes originate primarily from perceptions of threat or conflict and their reaction to White racism (Monteith & Spicer, 2000). Other minority groups' prejudicial attitudes toward Whites have similar origins.

Just as Whites often have ambivalent attitudes toward various minority groups, there is evidence that minority groups have ambivalent attitudes toward Whites (Livingston, 2002). Minority group ambivalence may be caused by resenting the social power given to Whites in society, while simultaneously depending on this power to gain social status and financial rewards, or respecting Whites for certain positive traits associated with their group (Shelton, 2000). This represents a form of envious prejudice.

Another reason that minority groups' racial perceptions and attitudes might differ from that of Whites is that, because of their history of being the targets of oppression, people of color are much more likely to consider their race and ethnicity as an important aspect of their self-concepts. For example, when Black and White Americans are questioned about their perceptions and attitudes toward each race, differences in the ways in which these two groups are socialized to think about race appears to increase the likelihood of misunderstandings and conflicts (Judd et al., 1995; Ryan et al., 2007). Young Whites are generally socialized to avoid thinking about racial differences and stereotypes because such thinking is considered the source of prejudice and discrimination. In contrast, young Blacks are typically socialized to emphasize their ethnic identity and to recognize the differences between themselves and Whites because such thinking is considered to help them better deal with ongoing prejudice and discrimination.

Both of these perspectives have psychological merit: Stereotyping and recognizing group differences can lead to prejudice, and developing an ethnic identity can insulate one from many of the negative effects of prejudice. The former view emphasizes eliminating known causes of prejudice, while the latter perspective emphasizes protecting oneself from existing prejudice. To a certain extent, White Americans' racial views contend that an ideal society should be a "melting pot" or "color-blind," in which everyone is judged equally regardless of their race or ethnicity. In contrast, Black Americans tend to believe that eliminating their racial identity in a cultural melting pot would strip them of their most important defense against racism. Instead, their perspective on race contends that society is a "patchwork quilt" in which their group's unique strengths and qualities buffer them from ongoing racism. These two contrasting views on the wisdom of recognizing race in one's life and using it as a basis for making social judgments may partly explain why many Blacks and Whites hold different opinions about social issues such as affirmative action (Crosby et al., 2006). Whereas Whites may believe that such programs create unhealthy racial divisions and emphasize group differences, Blacks may believe that these programs serve to correct the continuing unfair treatment of minorities in society. Here, once again, we see how differences in our definitions of social reality lead to sharply contrasting social judgments.

Despite the potential merits in both viewpoints, research indicates that the "patchwork quilt" perspective is more effective in reducing implicit racial bias in the United States than the "melting pot" perspective (Norton et al., 2006; Richeson & Nussbaum, 2004). Indeed, research suggests that underlying the "melting-pot" perspective is a fear by some White Americans that multiculturalism is a threat to their dominant group's core values and societal power. White Americans who are most likely to react negatively to multiculturalism are those who identify strongly with their ethnicity and have a strong desire to maintain their group's social dominance (Morrison et al., 2010). Similar sentiments against multiculturalism have been expressed throughout Europe (see German Chancellor Merkel's comments in our chapter-opening story) during the past decades. For many Americans expressing such views, the "melting-pot" perspective is driven less by a valuing of color blindness and more by a valuing of ingroup dominance. Given the fact that racial and ethnic minorities now comprise more than half of the total population in California, Hawaii, New Mexico, and Texas, and given the prediction that individuals of non-White descent will likely become the "new majority" in the United States somewhere between 2040 and 2050 (Burnstein, 2005; Ortman & Guarneri, 2009), it appears that multiculturalism is here to stay. Facing this reality, the more that

Research suggests that the "patchwork quilt" perspective on ethnic diversity reduces prejudices more than the "melting pot" perspective.

White Americans think of their ethnicity as being "one of many" ethnicities in a multicultural society rather than being *the* ethnicity by which all others are judged, the more likely they will embrace multiculturalism (Plaut et al., 2009; Wolsko et al., 2006).

SEXISM HAS BOTH A HOSTILE AND A BENEVOLENT COMPONENT.

Another destructive form of intergroup intolerance is based on a person's sex, namely **sexism** (Swim & Hyers, 2009). Much as racism in Western societies is mostly discussed in terms of White hostility toward racial minority groups, sexism around the globe primarily focuses on the prejudice and discrimination that males direct at females. This is so because virtually all societies in the world are *patriarchal*, meaning that the social organization is such that males dominate females (Neely, 2008). Evolutionary theorists propose that the social dominance of men over women is probably due to the biology of human sexual reproduction, in which the competition between males for sexual access to females eventually resulted in men being more aggressive and having a stronger social dominance orientation than women. As outlined by social dominance theory (see p.240), the patriarchal systems that resulted from males' greater dominance seeking eventually led to the development of a sexist ideology to justify control over females (Krefting, 2003; Sidanius et al., 1995). The basic storyline of this ideology is that women are inferior and irrational creatures who need to be controlled by men. This patriarchal belief system underlying *old-fashioned sexism* justifies continued oppression and has many psychological similarities to old-fashioned racism.

Ambivalent Sexism

Unlike most dominant-subordinate relationships, in male-female relationships there is a great deal of intimacy: Men are dependent on women as mothers, wives, and sexual/romantic partners. Historically, this intimacy has resulted in many sexist men idealizing women in traditional feminine roles: They cherish these women and want to protect them because these traditional relationships fulfill their dual desires for social dominance and intimacy. However, these same sexist men are hostile toward women in nontraditional gender roles, such

sexism
....
Any attitude, action, or institutional structure that subordinates a person because of her or his sex

ambivalent sexism
....
Sexism directed against women based on both positive and negative attitudes (hostility and benevolence) rather than uniform dislike.

as career women and feminists. In other words, these men view women as "wonderful" provided they do not step out of traditional gender roles and compete with men for the more socially valued and powerful social roles historically associated with men (Rudman, 2005). Peter Glick and Susan Fiske (1996) contend that this orientation toward women, which is based on both positive and negative attitudes (benevolence and hostility) rather than uniform dislike, constitutes **ambivalent sexism**.

A field experiment tested Glick and Fiske's theory by having female confederates pose as either job applicants or customers at retail stores while wearing or not wearing padding that made them appear pregnant (Hebl et al., 2007). How people responded to the confederates was predicted by whether they conformed to traditional gender roles. Store employees behaved more rudely toward the female job applicants when they looked pregnant versus not pregnant, but employees were friendlier toward the female customers when they looked pregnant versus not pregnant. Further, the "pregnant" confederates encountered greater hostility from both men and women when applying for masculine as compared with feminine jobs. A similar set of experimental studies examined the effect of power-seeking intentions on backlash toward women in political office (Okimoto & Brescoll, 2010). Results indicated that both men and women were less likely to vote for a female politician if they believed that she had aspirations for power. No similar negative effects were for found for male politicians who sought power. These results suggest that a female politician's career progress may be hindered by the belief that she seeks power, because such desire violates the feminine gender role, and thus, elicits interpersonal penalties. Together, these findings of benevolent responses toward women who conform to traditional gender roles and hostility toward those who seek nontraditional roles demonstrate how sexist beliefs foster and maintain sexual inequality in the workforce.

The degree to which ambivalent sexist views are held varies from culture to culture and is related to cultural differences in gender equality (Glick et al., 2004; Sakalli-Ugurlu & Glick, 2003). As demonstrated in the "pregnant-nonpregnant" field experiment, although benevolent sexist beliefs lead people to express many positive attitudes about women, they share common assumptions with hostile sexism, namely, that women belong in restricted domestic roles and are the "weaker" sex. Both beliefs serve to justify male social dominance (Feather, 2004). For example, in Turkey, Brazil, and Japan, men and women who endorse hostile and benevolent sexist beliefs toward women justify and also minimize domestic violence against women; and they are also more likely to blame women for triggering the violence against them (Glick et al., 2002; Yamawaki et al., 2009). Spend a few minutes completing the Ambivalent Sexism Inventory in *Self/Social Connection Exercise 6.1.*

How might some Americans' negative reactions to Hillary Clinton as a politician be explained by ambivalent sexism and the belief that she has a desire for power?

Self/Social Connections Exercise 6.1

What Is Your Degree of Ambivalent Sexism Toward Women?

The Ambivalent Sexism Inventory

Instructions

Below is a series of statements concerning men and women and their relationships in contemporary society. Please indicate the degree to which you agree or disagree with each statement using the following scale:

0 = Disagree strongly   3 = Agree slightly
1 = Disagree somewhat   4 = Agree somewhat
2 = Disagree slightly   5 = Agree strongly

1. No matter how accomplished he is, a man is not truly complete as a person unless he has the love of a woman.
2. Many women are actually seeking special favors, such as hiring policies that favor them over men, under the guise of asking for "equality."
3. In a disaster, women ought not necessarily be rescued before men.*
4. Most women interpret innocent remarks as being sexist.
5. Women are too easily offended.
6. People are often truly happy in life without being romantically involved with a member of the other sex.*
7. Feminists are not seeking for women to have more power than men.*
8. Many women have a quality of purity that few men possess.
9. Women should be cherished and protected by men.
10. Most women fail to appreciate fully all that men do for them.
11. Women seek to gain power by getting control over men.
12. Every man ought to have a woman whom he adores.
13. Men are complete without women.*
14. Women exaggerate problems they have at work.
15. Once a woman gets a man to commit to her, she usually tries to put him on a tight leash.
16. When women lose to men in a fair competition, they typically complain about being discriminated against.
17. A good woman should be set on a pedestal by her man.
18. There are actually very few women who get a kick out of teasing men by seeming sexually available and then refusing male advances.*
19. Women, compared with men, tend to have a superior moral sensibility.
20. Men should be willing to sacrifice their own well being in order to provide financially for the women in their lives.
21. Feminists are making entirely reasonable demands of men.*
22. Women, as compared with men, tend to have a more refined sense of culture and good taste.

Scoring Instructions

Before summing either scale, first reverse the scores for the "*" items:

0 = 5, 1 = 4, 2 = 3, 3 = 2, 4 = 1, 5 = 0.

Exercise 6.1 *Continued*

Hostile Sexism Scale Score: Add items 2, 4, 5, 7, 10, 11, 14, 15, 16, 18, 21

The average score for men is about 29, while the average score for women is about 20.

Higher scores indicate greater degrees of hostile sexism.

Benevolent Sexism Scale Score: Add items 1, 3, 6, 8, 9, 12, 13, 17, 19, 20, 22

The average score for men is about 28, while the average score for women is about 24.

Higher scores indicate greater degrees of benevolent sexism.

Total Ambivalent Sexism Inventory Score: Sum the Hostile Sexism Scale score and the Benevolent Sexism Scale score.

The average score for men is about 57, while the average score for women is about 44.

Higher scores indicate greater degrees of ambivalent sexism.

> *We have mistresses for our enjoyment, concubines to serve our person, and wives for the bearing of legitimate offspring.*
>
> Demosthenes, Ancient Greek orator, 385–322 BC

> *The prejudice against color, of which we hear so much, is no stronger than that against sex. It is produced by the same cause, and manifested very much in the same way. The Negro's skin and the woman's sex are both prima facie evidence that they were intended to be in subjection to the white Saxon man.*
>
> Elizabeth Cady Stanton, U.S. feminist and abolitionist, 1815–1902

Based on your understanding of cognitive dissonance theory (Chapter 5, pp. 171–178), you might be wondering how ambivalent sexists avoid feeling conflicted about their positive and negative beliefs and attitudes toward women. Shouldn't people experience considerable dissonance if they simultaneously believe that women are inferior, ungrateful, sexual teasers who are also refined, morally superior goddesses?

In two separate studies investigating this apparent internal contradiction, Glick and his colleagues (1997) asked men and women to spontaneously list the different categories they use to classify women. Men who scored high and low on the Ambivalent Sexism Inventory (ASI) generated many of the same subcategories, but ambivalent sexists evaluated their traditional and nontraditional female subcategories in a much more polarized fashion than did the nonsexists. Ambivalent sexist men's negative feelings (fear, envy, competitiveness, intimidation) toward career women were predicted by their degree of hostile sexism, not by their degree of benevolent sexism. Similarly, these men's positive feelings (warmth, respect, trust, happiness) toward homemakers were predicted by their degree of benevolent sexism, not by their degree of hostile sexism. These findings suggest that, among ambivalent sexist men, specific categories of women activate either hostility or benevolence, but not both. Apparently, reserving negative attitudes for nontraditional women (the "bad" women) and positive attitudes for those who are traditional (the "good" women) allows sexist men to simultaneously hold contradictory views of women in general.

What about women who hold sexist attitudes toward other women? Do they also evaluate traditional and nontraditional women in a similar polarized benevolent-hostile manner? Apparently not. When female participants completed this same task, although sexist—as compared with nonsexist—women also evaluated career women less favorably and reported more positive feelings for homemakers, their degree of benevolent sexism was not significantly correlated with evaluations of these two categories of women. These findings suggest that the sexism of women against other women is not of the polarized variety seen in sexist men, but instead, simply constitutes an expression of hostility toward women who have not adopted traditional feminine roles.

What About Sexism Expressed by Women Against Men?

Similar to the greater acceptability of racial prejudice expressed by minority groups toward Whites, it is generally more acceptable in American society for women to express sexist attitudes toward men than vice versa. This is so because in an egalitarian society, higher-status groups—such as men and Whites—are more likely to be considered fair game for criticism. In contrast, because low-status groups—such as women and minorities—have historically been the targets of discrimination by the higher-status

"Our nation has had a long and unfortunate history of sex discrimination ... rationalized by an attitude of "romantic paternalism" which, in practical effect, put women not on a pedestal but in a cage."

— William J. Brennan, Jr., U.S. Supreme Court judge, 1906–1998

"But how can a man respect his wife when he has a contemptible opinion of her and her sex, when from his own elevation he looks down on them as void of understanding, full of ignorance and passion, so that folly and a woman are equivalent terms with him?."

— Mary Astell, English pamphleteer, 1666–1731

groups, criticism of them is much more likely to call into question the critics' egalitarian credentials. What do social scientists know about the often overlooked expression of sexism by women against men?

One important finding is that just as men's sexism can be described as ambivalent, women also appear to simultaneously hold positive and negative attitudes about men (Glick & Fiske, 1999; Jackson et al., 2001). In childhood, girls exhibit signs of intergender hostility even before boys. Their anti-boy attitudes may develop because of the frustration they often experience when interacting with boys, whose dominant play style of grabbing what they want and not taking turns clashes with girls' more polite style of asking for things and sharing play opportunities (Maccoby, 1990). Regardless of whether these conflicting play styles are due to biology, gender socialization, or some combination of the two, the greater power that boys exert in these cross-gender interactions creates resentment of that power among girls. Peter Glick and Lori Hilt (2000) suggest that this hostility represents an early-childhood version of many women's later resentment of patriarchy. Thus, just as patriarchal systems foster the expression of hostile sexism by men, they also create a similar intergender hostility in women.

During adolescence, as heterosexual teenagers grow increasingly interested in members of the other sex as romantic partners, the resulting emotional ties foster the development of benevolent attitudes (Glick & Fiske, 1996). The fact that male power in society can sometimes be used to protect and provide for women's welfare also contributes to the development of benevolent attitudes in both women and men. However, although both men and women develop benevolent attitudes toward the other sex, research suggests that women express much less benevolence than men (Glick & Fiske, 1999). Indeed, women's overall sexist attitudes toward men appear to be more hostile than benevolent, while men's overall sexist attitudes toward women are more clearly ambivalent, with levels of hostility and benevolence being fairly equal. The greater hostility expressed by women, as compared with men, may reflect the more negative experiences that women tend to have during intergender exchanges throughout their lives. This greater negativity is likely caused both by the frustration that women often experience due to men's more dominant interaction style, and by the fact that women are more likely than men to be the targets of sexual harassment and everyday sexism (Seta & Garren, 2011; Swim et al., 2001).

Like racism, sexism is a complex social problem. Although both men and women hold sexist attitudes and engage in sexist behavior, the ambivalent attitudes constituting male-initiated and female-initiated sexism are different. Current social psychological research suggests that these gender differences in expressing benevolence and hostility toward the other sex are best understood in terms of the respective historical roles that men and women have played as oppressors and oppressed. As a contemporary "actor" in this ongoing gender drama, you now have a better understanding of the social psychological dynamics surrounding sexism. With this knowledge, you are better equipped to redefine gender relations in your own life so that sexism is less problematic for you and for future generations.

INTOLERANCE BASED ON WEIGHT AND SEXUAL ORIENTATION IS OFTEN ACCEPTED.

Aversive racism and ambivalent sexism involve the expression of both positive and negative attitudes toward the target group. Yet there are other social groups within society that arouse little positive feelings in those who are biased toward them. Instead, these groups are more likely to arouse the emotions of revulsion and contempt. Two examples of such contemptuous prejudice involve weight and sexual orientation.

Weight Prejudice

Perhaps more so than facially unattractive individuals (see Chapter 9, p. 363), obese people in the United States are subjected to disdain and discrimination in their daily lives (Crandall et al., 2009; Puhl et al., 2008b). Such prejudice is substantially due to the fact that most people view obesity as a condition that is controllable (Blaine et al., 2002). Thus, heavy individuals, unlike those who are facially unattractive, also are viewed as weak willed, lazy, and self-indulgent (Puhl & Brownell, 2006). In this sense, their stigma involves not only an "abomination of the body" but also a "blemish of individual character." Anti-fat prejudice is more pronounced in individualist cultures like the United States and Australia compared with collectivist cultures like Mexico and India, partly because individualists are more likely than collectivists to hold people accountable for personal outcomes (Crandall et al., 2001).

The prejudice and discrimination faced by obese people permeates both their personal and professional lives, and also negatively affects their physical and mental health (Miller & Downey, 1999; Schafer & Ferraro, 2011). They are less likely to be chosen as friends and romantic partners than normal weight persons, and they are treated in a less friendly manner by health care workers (Harvey & Hill, 2001; Hebl et al., 2003). The stigma of obesity is especially strong for women. One study even found that heavier college women were less likely than normal weight women to receive financial assistance from their own parents (Crandall, 1994).

In the job market, obese individuals are discriminated against at every stage of employment, beginning with the hiring process and ending with the firing process (Muennig, 2008). Obesity is such a strong stigmatizing characteristic in our culture that it even affects how people evaluate individuals who are seen with obese persons. Michelle Hebl and Laura Mannix (2003) found that an average-weight male job applicant was rated more negatively when seen with an overweight woman prior to a job interview than when seen with a woman of normal weight. Weight prejudice is so pervasive in our society that even children evaluate normal-weight peers more negatively when they are seen with an obese child (Penny & Haddock, 2007). This tendency for individuals who are associated with stigmatized people to face negative evaluations from others is known as **courtesy stigma** (Goffman, 1963). This threat of negative evaluation causes many nonstigmatized people to avoid those who are stigmatized (Swim et al., 1999).

In the United States and Canada, anti-fat attitudes are stronger among men, Whites, and people with traditional gender roles compared with women, Blacks, and individuals with nontraditional gender roles (Hebl & Turchin, 2005; Puhl et al., 2008a). One explanation for these differences is that weight issues and the female thinness standard in North American culture is most closely associated with White, heterosexual beauty ideals that are closely aligned with traditional gender roles (see Chapter 9, pp. 365–370). A series of studies have found strong implicit anti-fat prejudice even among people with few explicit anti-fat attitudes and even among individuals who were overweight themselves (Schwartz et al., 2006; Wang et al., 2004). This automatic and unconscious negative reaction is very resistant to change. For example, Bethany Teachman and her coworkers (2003) found that even after informing research participants that obesity is mainly due to genetic factors, there was no significant reduction in implicit prejudice toward obese individuals. When participants read stories of discrimination against obese persons to evoke empathy, diminished implicit bias was observed only among overweight participants. This last finding may be important, given that self-blame and internalizing negative social messages are common in obese individuals. Reminding obese persons about anti-fat discrimination may promote ingroup support and help them develop a positive social identity (Saguy & Ward, 2011).

courtesy stigma

The tendency for individuals who are associated with stigmatized people to face negative evaluations from others

"Though your tissues gel, And you rot in hell, Don't feel gloomy, friend—It will never end. Happy Death, Faggot Fool."

From "Death Threat Christmas Cards" sent to gay students by a hate group at the University of Chicago

Sexual Prejudice

In 2010 Marquette University, a private Catholic university in Milwaukee, Wisconsin, received national attention when the university's president, Father Robert Wild, terminated a just-signed job contract with a professor he had chosen as the new Dean of the College of Arts and Sciences. The reason for this decision reversal was not because Father Wild, a Jesuit priest, believed that the faculty committee who had conducted an eight-month nation-wide search had chosen an incompetent person for the deanship. Instead, his decision was based on second thoughts about hiring an openly lesbian professor for this high-profile job. Despite rigorous scientific studies finding no evidence of an association between homosexuality and psychopathology, many conservative religious and political organizations persist in stigmatizing lesbians, gay men, and bisexual individuals as sexually deviant and mentally disturbed, and therefore less deserving of the same civil rights as heterosexual individuals (Herek & Garnets, 2007; Minton, 2002). In the vast majority of states and municipalities, gay relationships have no legal status, and lesbians and gay men often lose the custody of their children when their homosexuality becomes known. This societal reaction is an example of stigma based on "blemishes of individual character," with homosexual and bisexual individuals being targets of a type of contemptuous prejudice (refer back to p. 214) called **sexual prejudice**. Sexual prejudice refers to all negative attitudes based on sexual orientation, whether the target is homosexual, bisexual, or heterosexual (Herek, 2009).

Social scientists often explain sexual prejudice as being caused and fueled by **heterosexism**, which is a system of cultural beliefs, values, and customs that exalts heterosexuality and denies, denigrates, and stigmatizes any nonheterosexual form of behavior or identity (Fernald, 1995; Herek, 2004). Calling another person a "faggot" or a "dyke," are certainly examples of heterosexism, but this cultural belief system also operates on a more subtle level. Like the fish that doesn't realize it's wet, most people are so used to defining heterosexual behaviors as normal and natural that they cease to think of them as being a manifestation of sexuality. For instance, heterosexual individuals who don't look twice at a man and woman holding hands, hugging, or even kissing in public, often react very differently if the couple is of the same sex. Gay couples expressing affection in public are typically criticized for flaunting their sexuality. Even when not victims of openly blatant discrimination, gay men, lesbians, bisexual and transgendered individuals often experience *interpersonal discrimination*, where they are treated in a less friendly manner and made to feel unwelcome or "invisible" in various social settings (Hebl et al., 2002).

Although many cultures can be characterized as heterosexist, people in those cultures who hold extremely negative attitudes toward gay men and lesbians are those who conform most strongly to socially conservative—and even racist and sexist—value systems. In contrast to less-prejudiced individuals, people who express antigay attitudes tend to have the following characteristics:

1. Be male rather than female (Herek, 2002; Ratcliff et al., 2006)
2. Be racially prejudiced, sexist, and authoritarian (Case et al., 2008)
3. Have membership in conservative religious organizations (Herek, 1987; Herek & Gonzalez, 2006)
4. Hold traditional attitudes toward gender roles (Kite & Whitley, 1996)
5. Have friends and family who hold similarly negative attitudes (Franklin, 2000; Lehmiller et al., 2010)
6. Have had less personal contact with gay men or lesbians (Sakalli-Ugurlu, 2002; Vonofakou et al., 2007)

Why do heterosexual men have more negative attitudes than heterosexual women? Social scientists contend that this gender difference exists because many cultures emphasize the importance of heterosexuality in the male gender role (Jellison et al., 2004). A defining characteristic of this *heterosexual masculinity* is to reject men who violate the heterosexual norm, namely, gay men. This is also why heterosexual men express more negative attitudes toward gay men than toward lesbians. They perceive a male transgression of the heterosexual norm to be a more serious violation than that of a female transgression. As we will discuss in Chapter 10 (p. 406), concern for not straying from the narrowly defined boundaries of heterosexual masculinity is also believed to be the main reason heterosexual male same-sex friendships are often lacking in emotional tenderness. This is especially true for men with strongly antigay attitudes (Devlin & Cowan, 1985).

sexual prejudice
· · · · · · · · · · · · · · · · · ·
Negative attitudes based on sexual orientation, whether the target is homosexual, bisexual, or heterosexual

heterosexism
· · · · · · · · · · · · · · · · · ·
A system of cultural beliefs, values, and customs that exalts heterosexuality and denies, denigrates, and stigmatizes any nonheterosexual form of behavior or identity

"*I just thought, "Oh God, what if they pick up that I'm gay?" It was that fear and shame. ... I watched the whole Gay Pride march in Washington in 1993, and I wept when I saw that. I mean I cried so hard, thinking "I wish I could be there," because I never felt like I belonged anywhere.***"**

Ellen DeGeneres, comedian and actor, 1996

> **"***It wasn't easy telling my parents that I'm gay. I made my carefully worded announcement at Thanksgiving. I said, "Mom, would you please pass the gravy to a homosexual." Then my Aunt Lorraine piped in, "Bob, you're gay. Are you seeing a psychiatrist?" I said, "No, I'm seeing a lieutenant in the Navy.***"***

———————————
Comedian Bob Smith, 2001

stereotype threat
· · · · · · · · · · · · · · · · ·
The apprehension people feel when performing a task in which their group is stereotyped to lack ability

The fact that people who hold strongly antigay attitudes also have friends who hold similar opinions is consistent with our previous discussion in Chapter 5 (pp. 162–163) about the important role that reference groups play in the formation of attitudes. Research indicates that perceiving social support is very important in encouraging men, but not women, to express antigay attitudes (Herek, 1988). This gender difference suggests that expressing antigay attitudes helps some heterosexual males, especially those who are adolescents, to identify themselves as "real men" and be accepted into heterosexual friendship cliques.

Although sexual prejudice is typically targeted at sexual minorities, heterosexual individuals are also at risk. Friends, family members, and "allies" who take a public stand against sexual prejudice often experience courtesy stigma. Heterosexual individuals can also become victims of sexual prejudice because of "mistaken identity." That is, due to the fact that sexual orientation is concealable, inferences are often made about people's sexual orientation based on the degree to which they deviate from traditional gender roles or gendered behavior (Majied, 2010; Poteat et al., 2007). Thus, for example, when heterosexual men hug other men in public outside the confines of a sporting event, they run the risk of being labeled "gay" and targeted for verbal and/or physical assault.

STIGMATIZED GROUPS CAN EXPERIENCE STEREOTYPE THREAT.

A common belief about women is that they are not as good at math as men. Is it possible that when competing against male students in a college math course that female students might feel intimidated by the nagging possibility that in their performance they might confirm this negative stereotype?. Similarly, Black students enrolled in largely White schools and colleges sometimes feel that they carry the burden of "representing their race" in academic pursuits. Accompanying this concern is the added social stigma associated with the minority label, which often implies a suspicion of intellectual inferiority (Shapiro, 2011). Because these negative stereotypes are widely known throughout society, as the target of such stereotyping, both women and Black students are susceptible to developing what Claude Steele (1997) identifies as **stereotype threat**. Stereotype threat is the apprehension people feel when performing a task in which their group is stereotyped to lack ability (Steele & Aronson, 1995; Steele et al., 2002). People experience this apprehension because they are concerned that if they perform poorly, others—and perhaps even themselves—are more likely to believe the negative stereotype (Shapiro & Neuberg, 2007).

Physiological measures of people experiencing stereotype threat indicate that this uncomfortable psychological state triggers arousal, and this arousal can hinder task performance in at least two different ways. First, when the task involves complex cognitive skills, the arousal creates an extra cognitive burden that reduces individuals' working memory capacity (Ben-Zeev et al., 2005; Bonnot & Croizet, 2007). People experiencing such stereotype threat have a more difficult time concentrating on the task and quickly remembering relevant information. Second, when the task requires the execution of well-learned skills that do not rely heavily on working memory, the arousal triggered by stereotype threat induces too much attention to how the task is being executed (Beilock et al., 2006). In such instances, instead of allowing their actions to "flow" unimpeded, people begin second-guessing well-learned responses and their performance suffers. Regardless of whether arousal disrupts working memory or well-learned motor skills, the disruption can occur even without the person consciously experiencing any anxiety (Blascovich et al., 2001b; Bosson et al., 2004).

The first evidence for the stereotype threat effect among African American college students came from a series of experiments conducted by Steele and Joshua Aronson (1995). In one of these studies, Black and White student volunteers were given a difficult English test. In the *stereotype threat condition*, the test was described as a measure of intellectual ability—while in the *nonstereotype threat condition,* it was described as a laboratory problem-solving task that did not measure intelligence. Because cultural stereotypes depict Blacks as intellectually inferior to Whites, the researchers presumed that describing the test as an intellectual measure would make this negative stereotype relevant to the Black students' performance. They also expected that making this stereotype

Figure 6.4

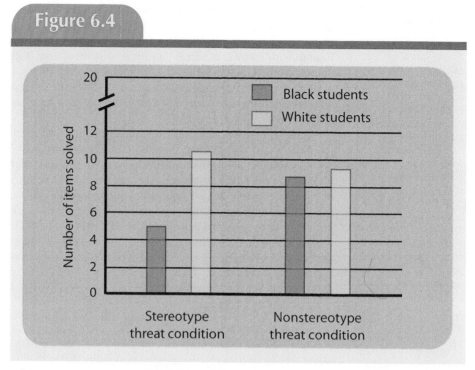

African-American Intellectual Test Performance and Stereotype Threat

Steele and Aronson (1995) administered a difficult English test to Black and White college students. When the test was described as a measure of intellectual ability (stereotype threat condition), Blacks performed worse than Whites. However, when it was not associated with ability (nonstereotype threat condition), no racial differences were found. How are these findings consistent with the stereotype threat hypothesis?

relevant would induce concern in the Black students that they might confirm the stereotype ("If I do poorly, my performance will reflect badly on my race and on me"). Steele and Aronson hypothesized that the self-evaluation apprehension created by such thinking would interfere with the Black students' performance. In contrast, when the task was described as not measuring intelligence, researchers assumed that this would make the negative racial stereotype about ability *irrelevant* to the Black students' performance and, therefore, not arouse stereotype threat. As you can see in Figure 6.4, consistent with the stereotype threat hypothesis, when the test was presented as a measure of ability, Blacks performed worse than Whites. However, when it was not associated with ability, no significant racial differences were found.

Stereotype threat has also been found among women in math classes (Gunderson et al., 2011; Steffens & Jelenec, 2010). In one of the first studies documenting this effect, Steven Spencer and his colleagues (1999) gave male and female college students a difficult math test but divided it into two halves and presented it as two distinct tests. Half of the students were told that the first test was one on which men outperformed women, and that the second test was one on which there were no gender differences. The other students were told the opposite—test 1 was described as exhibiting no gender differences, but men outperformed women on test 2. As you can see in Figure 6.5, consistent with the stereotype threat hypothesis, when told that the test yielded gender differences, women greatly underperformed in relation to men. However, when the test was described as not exhibiting any gender differences, women's underperformance disappeared. This dramatic change occurred even though the two tests were the same!

Subsequent research has found that merely placing women in a room where men outnumber them is sometimes sufficient to induce stereotype threat and lower math performance (Inzlicht & Ben-Zeev, 2003). However, additional research suggests that women are less susceptible to stereotype threat in math performance when they have consistently had

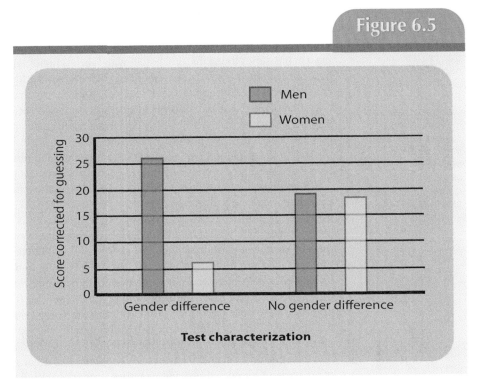

Figure 6.5

Stereotype Threat and Women's Math Performance

Spencer and his colleagues (1999) found that when a difficult math test was described as exhibiting gender differences (men outperforming women), women did indeed underperform. However, when the test was described as exhibiting no gender differences, women's underperformance disappeared. How do these results support the stereotype threat hypothesis?

positive math experiences in school and also have parents and teachers who encouraged and intentionally sheltered them from negative gender stereotypes (Oswald & Harvey, 2003). These high-achieving women not only have strong confidence in their math abilities, they also have little awareness of negative gender stereotypes in the area of math. Other studies find that women who become immersed and successful in academic math environments appear to insulate themselves from stereotype threat by *disidentifying* with feminine characteristics and behavior seen as incompatible with math success (such as being flirtatious or wearing a lot of makeup) but not with those feminine characteristics (such as being sensitive, nurturing, and having good fashion sense) perceived as unlikely to hinder such success (Pronin et al., 2004). Other ways that women can insulate themselves from stereotype threat is by consciously developing positive math attitudes, avoiding social comparisons to men, and developing a social identity (for example, math major or psychology research assistant) that has positive stereotypes for math performance (Forbes & Schamder, 2010; Rydell & Boucher, 2010; von Hippel et al., 2011). Overall, this and other research suggests that one effective way to reduce the negative effects of stereotype threat among women regarding their performance in traditional masculine domains is to discourage them from internalizing cultural gender beliefs related to *benevolent sexism* (Dardenne et al., 2007).

What happens when you are not as fortunate as these women and repeatedly experience stereotype threat? One likely consequence is that you will avoid and *disidentify* with whatever task is associated with the threatening scrutiny (Davies et al., 2005). For example, if the stereotype threat involves intellectual performance, you may change your self-concept so that academic achievement is no longer very important to your self-esteem. This sort of academic disidentification is much more common among African American students than among White American students, and it often begins in the lower elementary grades (Ambady et al., 2001; Osborne, 1995).

In one experiment investigating disidentification, Brenda Major and her coworkers (1998) manipulated success and failure feedback on a supposed test of intelligence. White

Critical THINKING

Can you think of a negative stereotype about Whites relative to Blacks that might cause White individuals to experience stereotype threat in a particular area of pursuit, thereby motivating them to disidentify with this activity?

students reacted with higher self-esteem after success than after failure, but Black students' self-esteem was unaffected. These findings are consistent with the hypothesis that Black students tend to disengage their self-esteem from academic performance. A second experiment in this series found that, consistent with Steele's notion of stereotype threat, academic disidentification among African American students is most likely to occur when negative racial stereotypes concerning Black intellectual inferiority are salient in an academic setting. Stereotype threat and academic disidentification also occur among American Indians, Hispanic Americans, lower-class Whites, and female students in male-dominated majors (Croizet & Claire, 1998; Inzlicht & Ben-Zeev, 2000). Although such disidentification protects self-esteem and is a coping response to prejudice and discrimination, it also is one of the psychological factors that undermines school achievement (Aronson et al., 2002).

Stereotype threat is most noticeable and problematic among social groups that have been historically disadvantaged, (Nadler, & Clark, 2011), but it also occurs among members of privileged groups, such as White middle-class men. For example, in one study, White male undergraduates who were proficient in math performed poorly on a difficult math test when they were told beforehand that the test was one on which Asians outperformed Whites (Aronson et al., 1999). The lesson to be learned here is that negative stereotypes can create damaging self-fulfilling prophecies among members of many different social groups by inducing stereotype threat. The findings from all the studies discussed here raise the further possibility that stereotype threat may explain a substantial amount of the racial differences found in intelligence testing and the gender differences found in advanced math testing (Wicherts et al., 2005).

Recent studies suggest that stereotype threat, like other stressors, can spill over into other areas of people's lives and negatively affect their judgment and decision making (Inzlicht & Kang, 2010). For example, when a Black student discovers that she is the only person of color in her most challenging university course, she may experience stereotype threat and begin monitoring what she says and how she says it in this course, while simultaneously trying to suppress and deny her emotions so that others will not think less of her. All this constant self-regulation may eventually deplete her self-regulatory resources, causing problems even when she leaves the threatening environment of this course. She may begin overeating at meals, become overly sensitive to helpful criticism and generally begin making less sound daily decisions. In the Applications section at the end of the chapter, we discuss possible ways to reduce the effects of stereotype threat in academic settings.

SECTION SUMMARY

- There are three different categories of stigma:
  tribal identities,
  blemishes of individual character, and
  abominations of the body.

- Race-based cues automatically activate threat responses and negative stereotypes, which may contribute to shooter bias among law enforcement officers.

- Old-fashioned racism has declined and been largely replaced by *aversive racism*, which is a combination of both positive and negative beliefs and feelings about a racial group.

- Blacks' and other minority groups' racial attitudes toward Whites originate primarily from perceptions of threat or conflict and their reaction to White racism.

- Sexism is best conceptualized as involving *ambivalence*, based on both hostility and benevolence.

- Obesity is an example of both a "blemish of individual character" stigma and an "abomination of the body" stigma, and it results in weight prejudice and discrimination.

- Homosexuality is an example of a "blemish of individual character" stigma, and it is related to the cultural ideology of heterosexism.

- Stigmatized groups can respond to negative stereotypes by experiencing stereotype threat.

WHAT MOTIVES AND SOCIAL FACTORS SHAPE PREJUDICE AND DISCRIMINATION?

Beyond the role that negative stereotypes and other cultural beliefs and values play in both the causes and effects of prejudice and discrimination, additional powerful motivational and social variables also exert a significant influence in the creation of intergroup intolerance (Gerstenfeld, 2002). In this section of the chapter we examine some of these causes, beginning with how group membership creates ingroup bias.

INGROUP MEMBERS ARE FAVORED OVER OUTGROUP MEMBERS.

Have you ever gone to a campus social event and felt that students who were members of different campus groups than your own were evaluating you less positively simply because you were not "one of them?" Have you yourself ever engaged in this sort of biased evaluation of other students? We have already discussed how social categorization sets the stage for perceiving members of other groups as having similar characteristics and how such stereotyping can lead to intergroup intolerance. However, research by Henri Tajfel and his colleagues (1971) demonstrated that the simple act of categorizing people as ingroup or outgroup members affects how we evaluate and compare them, independent of stereotyping. To test their hypothesis that group membership is often sufficient to foster ingroup favoritism, these researchers created what they called *minimal groups*, which are groups selected from a larger collection of people using some trivial criterion such as eye color, a random number table, or the flip of a coin. The people comprising these newly created groups were strangers to one another and were never given the opportunity to get acquainted. In some studies, participants were individually taken into a room with the experimenter and asked how much money two other participants should be paid for a subsequent task. These two people were identified only by code numbers, indicating to the participant that one came from his or her own group and the other was a member of the other group. Although participants knew only the others' membership status, they proceeded to reward the ingroup person more than the outgroup person (Tajfel et al., 1971).

ingroup bias

The tendency to give more favorable evaluations and greater rewards to ingroup members than to outgroup members

Subsequent research on minimal groups replicated these findings, indicating that people often habitually engage in **ingroup bias** when evaluating others. That is, if they observe two people performing the same task, one of whom is a member of their ingroup, their evaluations of the two people's performance will be biased in favor of the ingroup member. This ingroup favoritism may manifest itself by people selectively remembering ingroup persons' good behaviors and outgroup members' bad behaviors, or by selectively forgetting or trivializing ingroup members' bad behaviors and outgroup members' good behaviors (Dovidio & Gaertner, 2010). Such selective information processing causes an overestimation of ingroup performance relative to outgroup performance. Because of this ingroup biasing, ingroup members are consistently rewarded more than outgroup members (Crisp et al., 2001; Reynolds et al., 2000).

Ingroup preference tends to be so automatically activated that simply using ingroup pronouns is often sufficient to arouse positive emotions,

Have you ever gone to a social event and felt that others were evaluating you less positively simply because you were not part of their ingroup?

while using pronouns signifying outgroups can trigger negative emotions. Evidence for this effect comes from a series of studies conducted by Charles Perdue and his coworkers (1990), in which college students saw 108 seemingly randomly paired letter strings on a computer screen. Each pair of letter strings consisted of a nonsense syllable (*xeh, yof, laj*) presented with either an ingroup-designating pronoun (*we, us, ours*), an outgroup-designating pronoun (*they, them, theirs*), or, on the control trials, some other pronoun (*he, she, his, hers*). Students were told to quickly decide which letter string in each pair was a real word (*we-xeh, they-yof*). Unbeknownst to the students, one nonsense syllable was consistently paired with ingroup pronouns and another with outgroup pronouns. After the trials, students were asked to rate each of the nonsense syllables in terms of its degree of pleasantness-unpleasantness. As you can see from Figure 6.6, students evaluated the nonsense words that had previously been paired with the ingroup pronouns as more pleasant than those paired with either outgroup pronouns or with the control pronouns. These results suggest that merely associating a previously neutral stimulus to words that designate either ingroup or outgroup affiliations is sufficient to create biased emotional responses. As you might guess, ingroup biasing is often subtle and not recognized as being unfair by either the target or the perpetrator.

Not only do people evaluate ingroup members more positively than outgroup members, studies show that they are more likely to be "sensitive" to ingroup members' emotions and

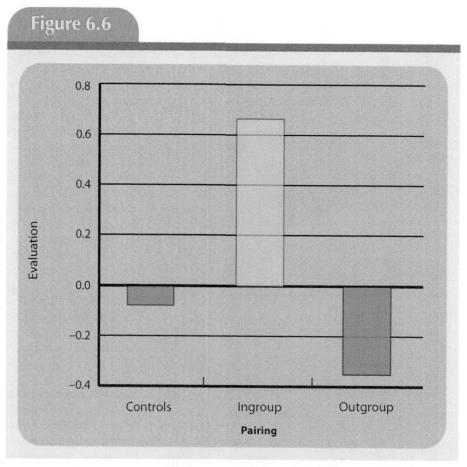

Figure 6.6

Us and Them: Ingroup Biasing

How pervasive is ingroup biasing? Perdue and colleagues (1990) found that nonsense words that had previously been paired with ingroup pronouns (e.g., us) were evaluated as more "pleasant" than nonsense words that had been paired with either outgroup pronouns (e.g., them) or control pronouns (e.g., hers). This study suggests that the ingroup-outgroup distinction has such emotional meaning to people that it can even shape their evaluation of unfamiliar words.

feelings than to those of outgroup members (Chambon et al., 2008). Further, ingroup members also tend to spontaneously prefer other ingroup members who are openly biased toward their ingroup, even when doing so violates egalitarian values (Castelli et al., 2008). Overall, people's desire to place their ingroup higher than a comparison outgroup results in them evaluating more positively other ingroup members who enable the ingroup to be perceived as better than other groups (Castelli & Carraro, 2010).

Tajfel and John Turner, in their **social identity theory** (Tajfel & Turner 1979; Turner 1987), offered one of the most popular explanations for why ingroup biasing occurs. As you recall from Chapter 3 (p. 85), besides our personal identity, another important aspect of our self-concept is our social identity, which derives from the groups to which we belong. Our social identity establishes *what* and *where* we are in social terms. Because our social identity forms a central aspect of our own self-definition, our self-esteem is partly determined by the social esteem of our ingroups. When our ingroups are successful, or even when members of our ingroups achieve some level of personal success, we can bask in their reflected glory. Consistent with several self-concept theories discussed in Chapter 3, social identity theory asserts that we are motivated to achieve or maintain a high level of self-esteem. Therefore, when the social esteem of our ingroup is threatened, we attempt to maintain a positive social identity by engaging in ingroup biasing, perceiving our ingroup as being better than other groups (Lwin et al., 2010; Vanhoomissen & Overwalle, 2010).

Research generally supports social identity theory, although there are some interesting exceptions to who may engage in more extreme forms of ingroup bias to heighten feelings of self-worth (Gramzow & Gaertner, 2005; Rowatt et al., 2005). A number of studies indicate that people who engage in ingroup biasing experience an increase in self-esteem compared with those who are not given the opportunity to express this bias (Rubin & Hewstone, 1998). Also as expected, members of lower-status groups—whose social esteem, by definition, is perpetually low—tend to engage in more ingroup biasing than members of higher-status groups (Ellemers et al., 1997). Further, people who exhibit great pride in their ingroups and believe these groups are a central component of their own self-concept are more likely to engage in ingroup biasing than those who do not identify so strongly with their ingroups (Mohr & Fassinger, 2006; Verkuyten et al., 1999). These findings are consistent with social identity theory, but additional research suggests that the people who are most likely to engage in prejudiced thinking as a means of enhancing or protecting self-esteem are those with defensive high self-esteem. As discussed in Chapter 3 (p. 99), individuals with high explicit self-esteem but low implicit self-esteem often lash out at others who threaten their fragile feelings of self-worth. Similarly, these same individuals are the ones who are particularly likely to engage in discrimination toward outgroups as a means of protecting threatened self-esteem (Jordan et al., 2005). Thus, social identity theory may best explain the prejudiced thinking of individuals who have relatively fragile feelings of high self-worth.

INTERGROUP COMPETITION CAN LEAD TO PREJUDICE.

If social identity theory has merit, what happens when we take this tendency to perceive our ingroups as being better than other groups and mix it with "hot" intergroup competition, where one group's successes become the other group's failures? Hostility and violence are common results. Numerous studies and real-world events inform us that when two groups compete for a limited number of scarce resources such as jobs, housing, consumer sales, or even food, tensions dramatically increase and create a breeding ground for prejudice (Duckitt & Mphuthing, 1998; Quillian, 1995).

Realistic Group Conflict Theory

Examining the competitive roots for intergroup intolerance is exactly the perspective taken by **realistic group conflict theory** (Levine & Campbell, 1972). It argues that groups become prejudiced toward one another because they are in conflict over competition for scarce resources. The group conflict is considered "rational" or "realistic" because it is based on real competition. Contemptuous prejudice and envious prejudice are often fed by the intergroup competition examined by this theory. According to realistic group

social identity theory
A theory suggesting that people seek to enhance their self-esteem by identifying with specific social groups and perceiving these groups as being better than other groups

Critical THINKING
How would social identity theory explain the relationship between "pride" and "prejudice"?

realistic group conflict theory
The theory that intergroup conflict develops from competition for limited resources

conflict theory, some Americans' hostility toward immigrants is escalating because of the perception that many immigrants are taking jobs away from American citizens and draining resources from various social service agencies. Likewise, African Americans' hostility toward Asian Americans may increase if they believe that Asian shopkeepers in their neighborhoods are taking business opportunities away from them. Similarly, White Americans' prejudice toward African Americans may increase if Blacks are hired ahead of Whites due to affirmative-action programs. On the international scene, Americans' anti-Arab attitudes have substantially increased following the September 11th terrorist attacks (Oswald, 2005).

ethnocentrism

· · · · · · · · · · · · · · · · · · · ·

A pattern of increased hostility toward outgroups accompanied by increased loyalty to one's ingroup

Realistic group conflict theory contends that when groups are in conflict, two important changes occur in each group. The first change involves increased hostility toward the opposing outgroup, and the second change involves an intensification of ingroup loyalty. This pattern of behavior is referred to as **ethnocentrism** (Cunningham et al., 2004; Sumner, 1906). In an archival study of ethnocentrism, Taya Cohen and her colleagues (2006) analyzed data from 186 preindustrialized societies between 1850 and 1950 and found that as people's loyalty to their local communities increased, people valued outgroup violence more than ingroup violence, engaged in more external than internal warfare, and placed a higher value on external warfare. To better understand how ethnocentrism can develop due to conflict, let's examine a classic field experiment investigating this psychological phenomenon.

The Robbers Cave Experiment

What happens if you randomly place people into one of two groups and manipulate circumstances to promote intergroup competition? This was the central question surrounding a classic field experiment designed by Muzafer Sherif and his colleagues (Sherif et al., 1961; Sherif & Sherif, 1956). They conducted the study in the summer of 1954 at a densely forested and hilly two hundred-acre camp that the researchers had created at Robbers Cave State Park, which is 150 miles southeast of Oklahoma City. Participants were twenty White, middle-class, well-adjusted, eleven- and twelve-year-old boys who had never met one another before. In advance, the researchers divided the boys into two groups, with one group leaving by bus for the camp a day before the other. Upon arrival, each group was assigned a separate cabin out of sight of the other, and thus, neither knew of the other's existence. The camp counselors were actually researchers who unobtrusively observed and recorded day-to-day camp events as the study progressed.

The study had three phases. The first phase was devoted to *creating ingroups*, the second was devoted to *instilling inter-group competition*, and the third phase involved *encouraging intergroup cooperation*. During the first week of ingroup creation, each group separately engaged in cooperative activities such as hiking, hunting for hidden treasures, making meals, and pitching tents. As the week progressed, each group developed its own leader and unique social identity. One group named itself the "Rattlers," established a tough-guy group norm, and spent a good deal of time cursing and swearing. The other group called itself the "Eagles," and they instituted a group norm forbidding profanity. As the first week drew to a close, each group became aware of the other's existence. How do you think they responded? By making clear and undeniable ingroup-outgroup statements: "*They* better not be in *our* swimming hole!" "*Those* guys are using *our* baseball diamond again!"

During the second phase of the study, Sherif tested his main hypothesis that intergroup competition would cause prejudice. To do this, he created a weeklong tournament between the two groups, consisting of ten athletic events such as baseball, football, and tug-of-war. The winner of each event received points, and at the end of the week the group with the most points received highly prized medals and impressive four-bladed pocketknives. True to Sherif's expectations, the intergroup conflict transformed these normal, well-adjusted boys into what a naive observer would have thought were "wicked, disturbed, and vicious" youngsters (Sherif, 1966, p. 58).

During this phase, the counselors heard a sharp increase in the number of unflattering names used to refer to outgroup members (for example, "pig" and "cheater").

Sherif and his colleagues (1961) created intergroup hostility between two groups of boys (the "Eagles" and the "Rattlers") at a summer camp by having them complete against one another. In the top photo shown here, the Eagles grab and burn the Rattlers' group flag after losing a tug-of-war contest. Later (bottom photo), the Rattlers hang from a pole an Eagles pair of jeans upon which they have painted, "The Last of the Eagles." Can you recall incidents from your own life where competition with another group resulted ih the development of prejudicial attitudes and discriminatory behavior?

The boys also rated their own group as being "brave," "tough," and "friendly," while those in the outgroup were "sneaky," "smart alecks," and "stinkers." This ingroup favoritism was also manifested in the boys' friendship preferences. Sherif, playing the role of camp handyman, asked the boys to tell him who their friends were at camp. The sharp division between the two groups was reflected in the fact that 93 percent of the friendship preferences were of the ingroup variety. If negative attitudes previously existed between ingroup members, they were now redirected against the outgroup. These findings indicate that one by-product of intergroup hostility is an increase in ingroup solidarity.

As the two groups competed in the various games, intergroup hostility quickly escalated from name-calling to acts of physical aggression. For example, at the end of the first tug-of-war contest, the losing Eagles demonstrated their outgroup attitudes by seizing and burning the Rattlers' group flag. Not to be outdone, the Rattlers raided the Eagles' cabin, overturning cots, ripping mosquito netting, and carrying off one of the Eagles' blue jeans as booty. The next day, armed with bats and sticks, the Eagles returned the favor. Then they retreated to their cabin, proceeded to stuff rocks in their socks, and waited for the next wave of Rattler reprisals.

Who ultimately won the valued prizes for which they were competing? The Eagles. Not surprisingly, the Rattlers thought they had been cheated. While the victors were taking a celebratory swim, the Rattlers stole their medals and knives. When the Eagles returned to find their prizes gone, the Rattlers admitted to the deed and told the incensed Eagles they could have them back … if they got down on their bellies and crawled for them! These are only a few of the incidents that occurred between the Eagles and the Rattlers. Intergroup hostility became so intense that members of the opposing groups held their noses whenever they passed by one another in camp.

This second phase of the study illustrates how easily hostility can develop between groups when they are brought into competition. The third phase of the experiment was designed to reverse the hostility, a task that proved to be much more difficult to accomplish. First, the researchers sought to determine whether simple noncompetitive contact between the groups would ease tensions. They tested this hypothesis during the first two days of phase three by bringing the groups together for some pleasant activity, such as a meal or a movie. The results were not encouraging. Both groups used each interaction as an opportunity to merely increase their mutual animosity for one another. During mealtimes, for example, food was more likely to be thrown at opposing group members than eaten.

This failure of simple contact to reduce hostility did not surprise Sherif and his colleagues. They hypothesized that to reduce intergroup conflict, they needed to introduce what they called a **superordinate goal**, which is a mutually shared goal that can be achieved only through intergroup cooperation. To test this hypothesis, the researchers arranged for a series of problem situations to develop over the course of the next six days. Each problem was urgent and involved both groups. The first problem was the "failure" of the camp's water supply. The groups initially responded to this emergency by trying to solve it on their own, without the other group's assistance. However, after converging on the source of the water problem, the camp water tank's plugged faucet, they cooperated in fixing it. A few days later, the camp truck "broke down" while the two groups were on an overnight camping excursion; all the boys had to work together to pull it up a steep hill. Following this incident of cooperation, name-calling and negative outgroup stereotypes declined. Sherif, still in his guise as the camp handyman, again asked the boys who their friends were. Now, outgroup friendships had grown from a measly 7 percent average at the end of phase one to a rather robust 30 percent average, a significant increase in outgroup liking. In keeping with this newfound outgroup appreciation, at their final campfire the two groups decided to put on a joint entertainment program, consisting of skits and songs. When departing from camp the following day, the two groups insisted on traveling home on the same bus. On the way home, the Rattlers used money they had won in their previous competitions with the Eagles to buy milkshakes for everyone.

Taken as a whole, the Robbers Cave experiment is an excellent example of how ethnocentrism can develop when two groups compete for scarce resources. It also demonstrates that having a superordinate goal can lead to peaceful coexistence between previously antagonistic groups. Although this study used children as participants, similar results have also been obtained with adult samples (Jackson, 1993).

Despite the fact that the original theory assumed that prejudice develops due to real, tangible conflict between groups, later work demonstrated that the mere *perception* of conflict is often sufficient to fuel intolerance (Esses et al., 1998). For example, Michael Zárate and his colleagues (2004) found that when American research participants were led to believe that Mexican immigrants had similar skills and attributes as themselves, their sense of job security was threatened, which led to more negative attitudes toward immigrants. These findings suggest that when members of two groups share some important job-related skills, they may begin to view the other group as their rival, even where no actual rivalry exists. This is an important extension of realistic group conflict theory; and it also illustrates how attributing positive characteristics to a group—Americans who perceive Mexican immigrants as having useful skills—can trigger intergroup prejudice.

superordinate goal
....
A mutually shared goal that can be achieved only through intergroup cooperation

PREJUDICE CAN SERVE AS A JUSTIFICATION FOR OPPRESSION.

What if two groups come in contact with one another, but one group is much more powerful than the other? In laboratory experiments, when groups are given different amounts of social power, members of high power groups discriminate more against outgroups than members of low power groups (Sachdev & Bourhis, 1987, 1991). Additional research suggests that having social power increases automatic negative evaluations of stigmatized groups and increases the experience of negative affect when encountering stigmatized group members (Guinote et al., 2010). What sort of beliefs might foster and justify these automatically activated negative feelings that often lead to discrimination?

Social Dominance Theory

social dominance theory
· ·
A theory contending that societal groups can be organized in a power hierarchy in which the dominant groups enjoy a disproportionate share of the society's assets and the subordinate groups receive most of its liabilities

Social dominance theory proposes that in all societies, groups can be organized in a hierarchy of power with at least one group being dominant over all others (Pratto, 1996). Dominant groups enjoy a lopsided share of the society's assets, such as wealth, prestige, education, and health. In contrast, subordinate groups receive most of the society's liabilities, such as poverty, social stigma, illiteracy, poor health, and high levels of criminal punishment. History teaches us that the negative stereotypes and prejudicial attitudes that dominant groups develop about those they oppress serve to justify their continued oppression (Frederico & Sidanius, 2002; Rosenthal & Levy, 2010). Contemptuous prejudice and paternalistic prejudice are the two forms of intolerance expressed by the oppressor group, while the prejudice that subordinate groups express toward those who oppress them is of the envious form.

A good deal of the prejudice in the history of the United States rests on social dominance. Europeans who founded this country did not arrive on uninhabited shores in the "New World." These settlers used their superior weapons to dominate and conquer the indigenous people of North America. At the same time that Europeans were colonizing North America, they were also capturing and buying Africans and transporting them to the colonies as slaves. They justified the inhuman exploitation that took place by stigmatizing both Native Americans and Africans as inferior races who needed civilizing.

❝_The Whites told only one side. Told it to please themselves. Told much that is not true. Only his own best deeds, only the worst deeds of the Indians, has the White man told._**❞**
▬ ▬ ▬ ▬ ▬ ▬ ▬ ▬ ▬
Yellow Wolf of the Nez Perce Indians, 1940

Consistent with social dominance theory, research indicates that people develop less egalitarian beliefs toward outgroups as the social status of their own group increases in comparison to the target outgroups (Levin, 2004; Schmitt et al., 2003). A number of experimental studies have also demonstrated that developing prejudicial and stigmatizing attitudes toward the victims of one's own harmful actions is a common response (Georgesen & Harris, 2000; Rodriguez-Bailon et al., 2000). For example,

▶ The European settlers used their superior weapons to conquer the indigenous people of North America. How does social dominance theory explain the Europeans' subsequent treatment of Native American tribes?

Stephen Worchel and Virginia Mathie Andreoli (1978) found that when instructed to deliver electric shocks to a man when he responded incorrectly on a learning task, college students were more likely to dehumanize him than were students who were instructed to reward the man for correct answers. By dehumanizing and derogating their own victims, powerful exploiters can not only avoid thinking of themselves as villains but can also justify further exploitation (Quist & Resendez, 2002).

Old American textbooks illustrate the racist attitudes generated from such exploitation. For example, Figure 6.7 is an excerpt from a popular high school geography book published in 1880 devoted to the "Races of Man" around the globe. The five listed races are classified in a descending order of capacity for civilization—the *Caucasian* races, the *Yellow* race, the *Negro* type, the Malays, and the *Indians*. Can you guess the race of the author of this civilized hierarchy? Particularly interesting about this section is how the White American author describes the two races that his social group had the most contact with, and whom they had historically treated so harshly. African tribes are described as living in a "savage or barbarous state," while the descendants of native Africans had "been Christianized and civilized" by Whites. What about the representatives of the native races of America, whose land had been taken by the same European descendants as the author of the text? According to the author, American Indians "have always shown but little capacity for civilization" (Swinton, 1880, p. 17). In these characterizations, we see how an oppressor group justifies its exploitation of less powerful groups by denigrating them.

Of course, not all members of dominant groups denigrate those below them in the status hierarchy. People differ in the degree to which they perceive their social world as a competitive jungle with "haves" and "have-nots" fighting to gain or maintain supremacy over the other. Individuals with a strong *social dominance orientation* desire and support the organization of societal groups in a status hierarchy, with designated "inferior" groups being dominated by designated "superior" groups (Bassett, 2010; Costello, & Hodson, 2011). Research suggests that this motivation to view the world in terms of a status hierarchy dominated by the powerful causes people to adopt belief systems and to seek out membership in groups that promote prejudice and social inequality (Dambrun et al., 2002; Guimond et al., 2003).

System Justification Theory

How do members of disadvantaged groups respond to this unequal distribution of societal resources? A number of studies find that while members of disadvantaged groups readily acknowledge that their group is frequently targeted for prejudice and discrimination, they tend to minimize the extent to which they have personally experienced discrimination in their jobs and daily lives. This tendency for members of disadvantaged groups to minimize personal discrimination in their own lives is known as the **personal-group discrimination discrepancy** (Taylor et al., 1990).

Why might people often fail to appreciate the degree to which they are the victims of discrimination? One reason is that admitting that you have been the victim of discrimination would challenge your belief that you have control over your life, which would in turn weaken your confidence that you can obtain your personal goals (Sechrist et al., 2004). Thus, denying personal discrimination allows you to maintain the belief that you personally control what happens to you. A second reason for denying personal discrimination is that you may want to distance yourself from the negative attributes stereotypically assigned to your fellow ingroup members (Hodson & Esses, 2002). Underlying this type of thinking is an acknowledgment that there is at least some legitimacy to the discrimination directed at your ingroup but at the same time denying that you personally possess the objectionable attributes.

One of the consequences of failing to realize that you have been the victim of discrimination is that such denial increases the likelihood that the existing unfair status hierarchy in society will remain intact. **System justification theory** contends that members of disadvantaged groups often endorse the group status hierarchy in society as being legitimate and fair. Unfortunately, this endorsement of the existing status quo often serves as a stumbling block to disadvantaged individuals' own personal and social advancement (Jost et al., 2007; Tyler & Jost, 2007).

> **"** *We first crush people to the earth, and then claim the right of trampling on them forever, because they are prostrate.* **"**
>
> Lydia Maria Child, U.S. author and abolitionist, 1802–1880

personal-group discrimination discrepancy

The tendency for members of disadvantaged groups to minimize personal discrimination in their own lives

system justification theory

A theory proposing that members of disadvantaged groups often adopt beliefs endorsing the legitimacy and fairness of the unequal group status hierarchy in society

Figure 6.7

RACES OF MEN.   17

SECTION III.—POLITICAL GEOGRAPHY.

TOPIC I.
RACES OF MEN.

I. ORAL OUTLINE.

1. Have you ever seen an Indian? Can you always tell an Indian from a white man? You can; then it must be because the Indian has some natural marks that distinguish him from a white man. What is one of these marks? Red or copper complexion. Yes. Another? Long, straight black hair. Yes. Another? Another? These natural marks are called *physical characteristics*.

2. Have you ever seen a Chinaman?—a Japanese? What was his complexion? Hence we may call the Chinese and Japanese the Yellow Race. They are also called Mongolians. Many peoples of Asia belong to this race. How do the eyes of a Mongolian differ from those of an American? Do the Chinese wear beards? Now give a connected statement of the physical characteristics of the Mongolian race. [In like manner let the teacher draw from the pupils what they know about the other races.]

II. FOR RECITATION.

1. **The races are classified** according to five types,—the Caucasian, Mongolian, Negro or African, Malay, and Indian types.

2. **The Caucasian Races** are represented by the peoples of Europe and their descendants in America and elsewhere. To this type belong also the Arabs and Hindoos. The Caucasians have generally a fair complexion (though some representatives are swarthy), regular features, soft flowing hair, and full beards. They are the leaders in the world's civilization.

3. **The Yellow Race** is spread over Central and Eastern Asia (*examples*: China, Japan, Tartary), and includes the sparse population of the Arctic regions on both continents. The Mongolians have an olive-yellow complexion, straight black hair, broad countenance, high cheek-bones, and eyes set obliquely. In civilization they rank next to the Caucasians.

4. **The Negro Type** is spread over most of Africa, where it is represented by various tribes. These differ in many respects, but are all alike in having a dark or black complexion, short crisp

woolly hair, broad flat nose, and thick lips. Most of the African tribes are in a savage or barbarous state. Several millions of colored people in the United States (descendants of native Africans) have been Christianized and civilized.

5. **The Malays** are found in the Malayan Peninsula, and in many of the islands of the Pacific Ocean. They have a brown complexion and features considerably resembling those of the Chinese, but they have generally straight-set eyes.

6. **The Indians** are the representatives of the native races of America. They have a copper-colored complexion, rather regular features, straight black hair, and scanty beard. They have always shown but little capacity for civilization.

REFERENCE TABLE OF RACES.

Race.	Physical Characteristics.	Representative Types.	Numbers.
Caucasian.	COLOR: white to swarthy. FEATURES: regular. HAIR: waving or curling. BEARD: heavy.	Leading European peoples — descendants of European colonists — Hindoos, Arabs.	600 millions.
Mongolian	COLOR: olive yellow. FEATURES: face broad and flat, with high cheek-bones, and small, black, obliquely set eyes. HAIR: coarse and stiff. BEARD: scanty.	Chinese — Japanese — Tartars — Turks — Esquimaux.	550 millions.
African	COLOR: brown to black. FEATURES: flat nose, retreating forehead, prominent jaws. HAIR: short and crisp. BEARD: scanty.	Tribes of Central Africa — their descendants in America.	180 millions.
Malay	COLOR: brown. FEATURES: much like Mongolians, but with horizontally set eyes.	Inhabitants of Malacca, of East India Islands, and most of the isles of the Pacific.	60 millions.
Indian	COLOR: red, or copper-hue. FEATURES: high cheek-bones, prominent nose, and black eyes. HAIR: straight and black. BEARD: scanty.	Indian tribes in North and South America.	10 millions.

An Example of Racist Attitudes in an Old American Textbook

The characterization of the various races in Swinton's text conveys the ingroup biases of the author. In comparing our own beliefs against the beliefs of this author of the nineteenth century, before we smugly assume a superior attitude of intergroup tolerance, we must ask ourselves how our current attitudes and beliefs toward different social groups will be judged by future generations. What sort of overlooked ingroup prejudices and biases permeate the text you are reading at this very moment? As the author of this social psychology book, I am sure my ingroup biases have occasionally made their way into my writing. Later, when discussing ways to monitor stereotypical thinking, we will examine how becoming aware of our current prejudices can steer us toward nonprejudiced thinking.

Societal stereotypes play an important role in system justification because they justify the positive outcomes of dominant groups, the negative outcomes of subordinate groups, and the exploitation of subordinate groups by dominant groups (Jost et al., 2005). For example, women are often rewarded and encouraged to conform to the feminine gender role by presenting themselves as "nice, but weak" (Rudman, 2005). Women who adopt this benevolently sexist self-presentation style receive positive reinforcement for being warm and nurturing, but they also are perceived as being less competent and powerful (Jackman, 1994). Despite these negative consequences, by focusing on the rewards of this subordinate role women tend to develop an automatic preference for male over female authority, which perpetuates the existing status quo and short-circuits any collective action to reduce gender inequality (Becker & Wright, 2011).

Similar system justification is observed among the social classes in society. Throughout literature, film, and popular culture, poor people are often stereotyped as being happier and more honest than rich people, and also as being more likely to be rewarded in the afterlife. According to system justification theory, by reinforcing the idea that the material advantages of the rich are offset by the nonmaterial advantages of the poor, an illusory belief is maintained that overall benefits in society balance out, and therefore, the status hierarchy is fair and justifiable. In support of this hypothesis, Aaron Kay and John Jost (2003) found that when people read stories about characters who matched societal rich and poor stereotypes they later were more likely than those not exposed to such stereotyped characters to believe that the status hierarchy in society is fair and equitable. Although believing that existing social arrangements are generally desirable may reduce personal distress and lead to greater satisfaction among those at the lower end of the status hierarchy, it also breeds inaction (Kay et al., 2007). If moral outrage is one of the primary motivators of social reform and efforts to help the disadvantaged, then system justification effectively defuses the emotional component triggering such social action (Wakslak et al., 2007).

AUTHORITARIANISM IS ASSOCIATED WITH HOSTILITY TOWARD OUTGROUPS.

One of the early inquiries into prejudice-prone personalities was the work of Theodor Adorno and Else Frenkel-Brunswik, two social scientists who fled Nazi Germany during World War II. Motivated by their desire to explain the psychology underlying the mass genocide of millions of Jews and other "undesirables" by the Nazi regime, Adorno and Frenkel-Brunswik set out to discover how people with certain personality characteristics might be prone to intergroup hostility.

authoritarian personality

A personality trait characterized by submissiveness to authority, rigid adherence to conventional values, and prejudice toward outgroups

Along with their colleagues at the University of California at Berkeley, Adorno and Frenkel-Brunswik believed that the cause of extreme prejudice could be traced to personality conflicts developed during childhood (Adorno et al., 1950). Operating from a psychoanalytic perspective, and using survey, case study, and interview methods, they identified what they called the **authoritarian personality**. Based on their studies, the researchers concluded that authoritarians are submissive to authority figures and intolerant of those who are weak or different. The intergroup hostility they express toward lower status groups generally takes the form of contemptuous prejudice. Authoritarians also conform rigidly to cultural values and believe that morality is a matter of clear right and wrong choices.

The Berkeley researchers believed that authoritarian personalities resulted from harsh childrearing practices that taught children to *repress* their hostility toward authority and, instead, to redirect or *displace* it onto less powerful targets who could not retaliate. Although this original theory is acknowledged as an important attempt to understand prejudice in terms of personality conflict and childrearing practices, questions about how people actually become authoritarians and criticisms of the Berkeley scientists' research methods resulted in this approach losing credibility by the late 1960s (Hiel et al., 2004).

In the 1980s, interest in the authoritarian personality was revived when Bob Altemeyer (1981, 1988) suggested that its origins have nothing to do with personality conflicts from childhood and instead are caused by children learning a prejudicial style of thinking from their parents and other important people in their lives. Operating from a social learning perspective, Altemeyer contended that children who are socialized by authoritarian and strict disciplinarians develop similar tendencies because they model and reinforce this intolerant worldview. He further asserted that most of this social learning occurs during adolescence, with the principal modelers being parents and peers. Socialized to view their world as a dangerous and threatening place, and isolated from personal contact with nonconventional people or minorities, adolescents in authoritarian environments learn that it is acceptable and even encouraged to express hostility toward various outgroups.

A number of studies conducted over the past twenty years support Altemeyer's social learning view over the earlier psychoanalytic perspective (Duckitt & Fisher, 2003; Feldman & Stenner, 1997). What appears to motivate the prejudice of the authoritarian personality is not repressed parental conflict, but rather, a strong desire to identify with and conform to the existing social order, coupled with a learned sense of fearfulness and insecurity about the social world and a perception that other groups pose a threat to one's ingroup (Altemeyer, 2004; Jost et al., 2003). Individuals growing up in authoritarian households are most likely to adopt authoritarian attitudes and beliefs when they have strong needs for social order and conformity.

In many different societies, people with authoritarian personalities not only express greater antipathy toward threatening outgroups than the average person but are also more likely to act on their hostility (Lippa & Arad, 1999; Verkuyten & Hagendoorn, 1998). Authoritarians also tend to generalize their outgroup prejudices. For example, if they hate Blacks, they are also likely to express hostility toward Jews, feminists, gay men and lesbians, the homeless, and people with AIDS (Pek & Leong, 2003; Whitley, 1999). Authoritarians' distaste for threatening outgroups is also reflected in greater support for their government's military actions against other countries during times of international tension. They not only support such actions, but they are also more likely to excuse atrocities committed by their own military forces during these interventions (Doty et al., 1997; Unger, 2002).

Besides identifying individual variations in authoritarianism, social scientists have also examined how it might vary on a societal level over time. An important catalyst for the manifestation of societal authoritarianism is *perceived social threat* (Burris & Rempel, 2004; Doty et al., 1991). That is, when societies undergo economic hardships and social upheaval, mildly authoritarian individuals may become motivated to join social, political, or religious organizations that express dogmatic and rigid social attitudes and preach intolerance of outgroups who are perceived as threats to the social order (Hunsberger, 1995; McCann, 1999). For example, in a series of archival studies of church membership patterns in the United States, Stuart McCann (1999) found that people were

The widespread abuse of Iraqi detainees by U.S. occupying forces in Abu Grahib prison was widely condemned. What type of person is more likely to excuse such prisoner abuse, an individual with an authoritarian personality or someone with a high social dominance orientation?

Critical
THINKING

The terrorist attacks in the United States in 2001 greatly increased Americans' perceived social threat. Based on authoritarianism research, what type of social consequences might we see in this country due to this heightened threat? Further, how might this same research explain the mind-set and behavior of the terrorists?

most attracted to intolerant religious teachings and authoritarian churches when the country was experiencing heightened social and economic threat. Similarly, longitudinal studies of South Koreans' social values between 1982 and 1996 found that as economic and military threats diminished, endorsement of authoritarian beliefs also diminished among the young and the educated portions of the population (Lee, 2003).

A Dual-Process Model of Personality-Influenced Prejudice

One of the more recent developments in the search for personality-influenced explanations of prejudice is John Duckitt's (2001, 2005) contention that the individual difference characteristics of authoritarianism and social dominance orientation are more correctly identified as social attitudes and that they account for different types of outgroup prejudice. In explaining how these two social attitudes shape people's social-world beliefs and perceptions of outgroups, Duckitt developed a *dual-process model* in which he asserts that underlying authoritarianism and social dominance orientation are two different personality traits: social conformity and tough-mindedness.

As depicted in Figure 6.8, in explaining the origins of the authoritarian personality, Duckitt asserts that individuals who are socialized by strict and punitive disciplinarians develop a strong need to conform to authority figures and social conventions. Because this desire for conformity is associated with the existing social order, these individuals develop a sensitivity to anything that might threaten this order. Thus, they tend to view

Figure 6.8

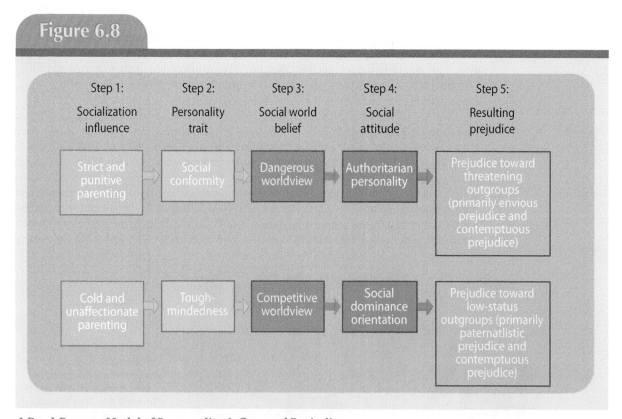

A Dual-Process Model of Personality-Influenced Prejudice

John Duckitt (2005) proposes that authoritarianism and social dominance orientation are shaped by different socialization and personality forces, resulting in different expressions of prejudice. Children raised by strict and punitive parents (step 1) develop a strong need for social conformity (step 2), and this sensitivity to authority and social conventions causes them to perceive their diverse social world as a threatening place (step 3). Their resulting authoritarian social attitudes (step 4) lead them to develop prejudice toward out groups perceived as threatening their social order (step 5). In contrast, children raised in a cold and unaffectionate household (step 1) develop a tough-minded personality (step 2), which leads them to develop beliefs that their social world is ruthless and competitive (step 3). This worldview activates a desire for group power and social dominance (step 4), which causes them to develop prejudice toward low social status outgroups (step 5).

the diversity in their social world as being dangerous and threatening. Motivated by social conformity and having threatening worldview beliefs, strong authoritarians develop prejudice toward outgroups they perceive as threatening their existing social order.

Regarding the development of a strong social dominance orientation, Duckitt proposes that people who are socialized in a cold and unaffectionate manner develop a tough-minded personality, in which they view the world as a ruthlessly competitive jungle where the strong win and the weak lose. In turn, this worldview activates a desire for group power, dominance, and superiority over others and a disdain for those who are weak or of low social status. The prejudices of people with a strong social dominance orientation are not triggered by perceptions that outgroups threaten social conventions and norms, but instead by perceptions that outgroups are weak or pose a threat to their own group's social status.

A number of studies support this dual-process model of personality-based prejudices (Dru, 2007; Roccato & Ricolfi, 2005; Sibley et al., 2007). For example, in a study of disliked groups, Duckitt and Chris Sibley (2007) found that prejudicial attitudes toward groups perceived as dangerous are related only to authoritarianism, while prejudicial attitudes toward groups perceived as inferior were related only to social dominance orientation (Duckitt & Sibley, 2007). Similarly, a survey study of Americans' support for the Iraq War one week before the 2003 invasion found that individual differences in authoritarianism and social dominance predicted different sets of beliefs about the war (McFarland, 2005). High authoritarianism but not social dominance orientation intensified Americans' belief that Iraq posed a threat to the United States, while high social dominance orientation but not authoritarianism intensified support for the attack by reducing concern for the loss of life that the war would almost certainly produce. Together, these findings support the dual-process model's hypothesis that high authoritarians' tendency to perceive the world as a threatening place triggers outgroup hostility, while high social dominance individuals' callousness and lack of empathy underlies their prejudice toward outgroups. Thus, by emphasizing different socialization and personality forces in the shaping of different forms of prejudice, this dual-process model provides a broader and more comprehensive understanding of the causes and dynamics of intergroup intolerance.

> "It's always a simple matter to drag the people along whether it's a democracy, a fascist dictatorship, a parliament, or a communist dictatorship. All you have to do is tell them they are being attacked, and denounce the pacifists for lack of patriotism, and exposing the country to great danger."
>
> Herman Goring, Hitler's Commander of Nazi Storm Troopers, 1893–1946

SECTION SUMMARY

- People appear to be automatically biased toward ingroup members.

- Social identity theory asserts that prejudice and discrimination can result from people trying to increase or maintain self-esteem.

- Realistic group conflict theory argues that groups become prejudiced toward one another because they are in conflict over competition for scarce resources.

- Social dominance theory explains how dominant groups develop stereotypes and prejudicial attitudes to justify their oppression of others.

- System justification theory explains how disadvantaged groups endorse oppressive societal beliefs.

- Research on authoritarianism suggests that some forms of prejudice can be traced to personality and socialization factors.

CAN WE REDUCE INTERGROUP BIAS AND INTOLERANCE?

Having analyzed the psychological and social mechanisms underlying intergroup bias and intolerance, let us now explore the prospects for reducing prejudice and discrimination. First, we examine whether changing people's thinking can reduce prejudice (an *individual-based approach*), and then we outline situational factors necessary to reduce intergroup intolerance (a *group-based approach*). Finally, the chapter ends with a brief look at social psychological attempts to remedy some of the negative consequences of prejudice and discrimination in our educational system.

PREJUDICE AND DISCRIMINATION CAN BE REDUCED BY MONITORING STEREOTYPED THINKING.

Although thinking in terms of stereotypes may often be an automatic process, and while it also is often socially beneficial, these advantages can, at times, be outweighed by the negative consequences of unmonitored stereotypical thinking. As we have already discussed, many stereotypes about various outgroups contain unflattering and demeaning characteristics. When they become activated, they can result in harmful biasing effects toward outgroup members who possess none of the objectionable qualities ascribed to their group. Given the fact that stereotypes are resistant to change, how can motivated individuals avoid judging others in this manner?

Patricia Devine and Margo Monteith contend that people can circumvent stereotypical thinking if they make a conscious effort to use more rational, inductive strategies (Devine & Sharp, 2009; Monteith & Mark, 2009). That is, even though individuals may have *knowledge* of a stereotype and may have relied on it in the past to make social judgments, their current *personal beliefs* may no longer be in agreement with the stereotype. Due to this change in circumstances, instead of making judgments based on the stereotype, they may now consciously decide to rely on their own personal beliefs (Monteith, 1993; Monteith et al., 1998).

For example, imagine that Clayton has grown up being taught that women are intellectually inferior to men. However, during the course of his life, Clayton has been exposed to people who do not fit this gender stereotype. Because of these experiences, as well as his desire to perceive himself as nonsexist, Clayton may begin to adopt a more egalitarian view of women. Although Clayton no longer accepts this stereotype, he has not eliminated it from his memory. Quite the contrary. During his relearning process, this stereotype remains a well-organized, frequently activated cognitive structure, and it is more accessible than his newly adopted personal beliefs. In fact, Clayton's unwanted stereotype will be most on his mind precisely when he is with women and feeling most anxious about saying the wrong thing (Lambert et al., 2003). In a very real sense, for a person like Clayton, censoring the negative stereotype and guarding against ingroup biasing takes conscious and deliberate attention—like trying to break a bad habit. As you may recall from Chapter 5 (p. 184), habits involve a good deal of automatic and unthinking responses, and because of this, they are often difficult to break. In addition, as discussed in Chapter 4 (pp. 123–124), attempting to suppress particular thoughts—such as stereotypes—can actually cause these thoughts to flood our consciousness, which is referred to as the *rebound effect* (Follenfant & Ric, 2010).

For people like Clayton, although the unwanted stereotype will likely be automatically activated as soon as he encounters a woman, the good news is that this stereotype is likely to become deactivated the longer the interaction continues (Kunda et al., 2002). This suggests that cognitively guarding against unwanted stereotypes is most important during the initial phases of an encounter with a person from the stereotyped group. Additional research further suggests that the likelihood of rebound effects due to stereotype suppression is much lower among people who are relatively unprejudiced compared to high prejudiced individuals who suppress in order to avoid social disapproval (Wyer, 2007).

Figure 6.9 outlines how self-awareness and self-regulation (see chapter 3) may play a role in reducing prejudiced responses. Continuing with our example, whenever Clayton encounters a woman, the gender stereotype is involuntarily activated. If he does not consciously monitor his thoughts, he may automatically slip back into acting as though women were the intellectual inferiors of men (a *discrepant response*). Becoming aware of this discrepancy in his actions, Clayton will experience *discrepancy-associated consequences*. These include feelings of guilt and self-criticism that will in turn motivate him to heighten his self-awareness and search for situational cues that may have spontaneously triggered this prejudiced response (Hing et al., 2002; Zuwerink et al., 1996). Through such attentiveness to prejudice-triggering cues, Clayton will slowly build up self-regulatory mechanisms that should produce more controlled and careful responses on future occasions (Kawakami et al., 2000; Monteith et al., 2002).

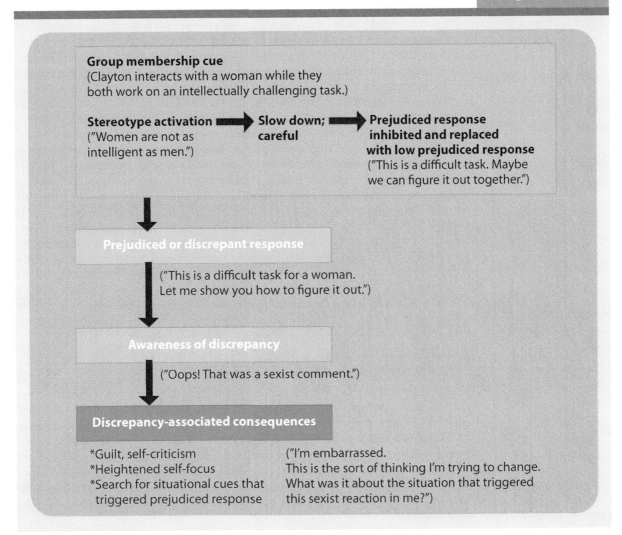

Reducing Prejudiced Responding Through Self-Regulation

According to Devine and Monteith, when low prejudiced persons first begin to try to respond in a nonprejudiced manner toward previously denigrated outgroup members, stereotype activation often spontaneously triggers a discrepant (i.e., prejudiced) response, which subsequently triggers a series of discrepancy-associated consequences. This cognitive process is depicted by the arrows running vertically from top to bottom in the left side of the figure. Over time, through careful self-regulation of one's thoughts and attention to one's nonprejudiced standards, low prejudiced people break the "prejudice habit" and respond as depicted by the horizontal arrows at the top of the figure. If this model accurately describes how prejudiced behavior can be eliminated, what would be the first step you would need to take to reduce your own prejudiced responding?

The importance of Devine and Monteith's perspective for reducing prejudice and discrimination is that it does not assume that prejudice is an inevitable consequence of the natural process of social categorization. People can avoid prejudiced responding (that is, discrimination) if low-prejudiced standards are central to their self-concept *and* they bring these standards to mind before acting. Thus, although automatic stereotype activation makes nonprejudiced responding difficult, research indicates that people can inhibit such intolerance through conscious and deliberate selfregulation (Gordijn et al., 2004; Legault et al., 2007). However, the biggest stumbling block in unlearning prejudicial responding is that, as we discovered in Chapter 3 (pp. 70–71), many people do not spontaneously engage in the self-awareness necessary to think about their own personal nonprejudiced standards (Monteith, 1996). If they do not think about these standards, there will be no guilt and internal conflict when they respond in a prejudicial manner. Yet if people do engage in self-awareness, they can learn to avoid using stereotypes in their social judgments (Kawakami et al., 2000).

A further implication of Devine and Monteith's perspective is that it draws some necessary boundaries around the pervasiveness of aversive racism among White Americans (refer back to pp. 219–221); not all Whites are desperately trying to hide their racial prejudices from themselves and others. Indeed, this perspective contends that many people, regardless of their race, sex, or sexual orientation, are motivated and consciously attempt to develop nonprejudicial thinking. Although it is not easy, and although it will undoubtedly induce instances of guilt and self-criticism, with conscious effort, prejudicial thinking can be reduced if you internalize egalitarian values and norms into your self-concept.

This perspective also holds out hope for reducing prejudice even among aversive racists. However, the cognitive hurdle here is that, unlike people who recognize that they sometimes engage in prejudiced thinking, aversive racists are convinced they are nonprejudiced, so they believe there is no need to monitor their thoughts for bias. How can their prejudiced thinking be reduced without them engaging in careful self-regulation? The answer is that someone else must point out to aversive racists the inconsistencies between their explicit and implicit attitudes, at least initially. Research by Leanne Son Hing and her coworkers (2002) indicates that when aversive racists are confronted with evidence exposing their hidden biases they tend to experience guilt and make conscious efforts to behave in a nonprejudiced manner. In essence, other people are playing the self-regulatory role for aversive racists, raising their consciousness and prompting them to reduce their prejudicial thinking and behavior.

TARGETS OF PREJUDICE CAN BECOME POSITIVE SOCIAL CHANGE AGENTS.

Thus far our discussion has focused on how prejudiced individuals can reduce their own biased thinking and responding, but those who are the targets of prejudice and discrimination can become powerful social change agents themselves. For example, imagine that you are the only African-American student in a college class and the non-Black students around you act awkward when the professor instructs everyone to break into small groups to do a project. It appears that they don't want you in their group. What would you do? Or imagine that you are a lesbian student in a class and someone blurts out "That's so gay!" to express a negative opinion about another student's comments. What would you do?

A number of studies find that individuals who are the targets of negative stereotyping and prejudice report that they often want to respond by assertively communicating their displeasure to the perpetrator, but they do not always act on this desire (Swim et al., 1998). This strategy of "breaking the silence" is consistent with current activist norms that have replaced oldfashioned norms of social deference in the United States (Feagin & Sikes, 1994; Swim et al., 2003). One important social benefit of assertively responding is that it provides the opportunity to educate perpetrators by raising their awareness and hopefully reducing their prejudice (Zitek & Hebl, 2007). An additional personal benefit is that an assertive response often reduces negative feelings aroused by the perpetrators' comments (Hyers, 2007).

While assertively responding may be beneficial on both personal and social levels, survey studies find that targets of negative stereotyping and prejudice sometimes decide to remain silent (Foster, 1999; Wright et al., 1990). The most common reason for not assertively responding to others' biased thinking is a concern about being judged negatively (Dodd et al., 2001). Assertive confrontations risk confirming stereotypes that your group is "difficult," "aggressive," or "oversensitive" when interacting with outgroup members (Latting, 1993). A related reason for not assertively responding is a desire to avoid conflict (Gutek & Koss, 1993). Yet one negative personal consequence of not assertively responding to prejudice is that targets report that they carry negative feelings with them afterward (Hyers, 2007).

In reviewing this research, it must be acknowledged that the types of positive social change necessary to reduce intergroup intolerance cannot occur through face-to-face

"If we accept and acquiesce in the face of discrimination, we accept the responsibility ourselves and allow those responsible to salve their conscience by believing that they have our acceptance and concurrence. ... We should therefore, protest openly everything ... that smacks of discrimination."

Mary McLeod Bethune, U.S. educator and civil rights activist, 1875–1955 confrontations alone. Yet when the targets of prejudice actively try to redefine their social world through these interpersonal confrontations, they are planting the seeds of social change that might otherwise lie dormant.

THE CONTACT HYPOTHESIS IDENTIFIES SOCIAL CONDITIONS THAT REDUCE INTERGROUP CONFLICT.

contact hypothesis

The theory that under certain conditions, direct contact between antagonistic groups will reduce prejudice

At the time of the original U.S. Supreme Court *Brown v. Board of Education* decision on school desegregation, Gordon Allport (1954) outlined how desegregation might reduce racial prejudice. Later, other social psychologists also contributed to what came to be known as the **contact hypothesis** (Amir, 1969; Hewstone, 1996). The contact hypothesis can be thought of as a blueprint for reducing hostility between groups that have had a history of conflict by manipulating situational variables. According to this perspective, intergroup contact will decrease hostility when specific situational conditions are met (refer to Table 6.3).

Equal Social Status

The first necessary condition is that the groups interacting must be roughly *equal in social status*. When this condition is not met and traditional status imbalances are maintained, long-standing stereotypes that are largely based on status discrepancies are generally not revised (Gaertner & Dovidio, 2000). However, research indicates that when equal-status people from different racial and ethnic groups interact, such as soldiers in the U.S. Armed Services, racial stereotyping and prejudices decline (Pettigrew, 1969).

Sustained Close Contact

The second condition is that the two groups must have *sustained close contact*. Several public-housing studies conducted in the 1940s and 1950s demonstrated the importance of this

---

Table 6.3

Reducing Prejudice Through Social Contact

Now that you have learned how to develop an individual program to reduce your own prejudice (refer back to Figure 6.9), let's set to work on reducing prejudice on a group level. According to the contact hypothesis, intergroup prejudice can be reduced if the four conditions listed below are met. Think about intergroup hostilities on your own college campus or in your local community. Perhaps this conflict involves men and women, gays and heterosexuals, or people from different racial groups. How could you develop a "Tolerance Campaign" utilizing these four principal conditions? Does research indicate that all four conditions are essential for prejudice reduction to occur?

Four Situational Conditions

1. *Equal Social Status:* Members of groups in conflict should interact in settings where everyone has roughly equal status.
2. *Sustained Close Contact:* Interaction between members of different groups should be one-on-one and should be maintained over an extended period of time.
3. *Intergroup Cooperation:* Members of different groups should engage in joint activities to achieve superordinate goals.
4. *Social Norms Favoring Equality:* There must be a clear social perception, largely fostered by group authority figures, that prejudice and discrimination are not condoned.

Fifth Condition in the Reformulated Model

Friendship Potential: Developing friendships with outgroup members precipitates initial reductions in intergroup tensions and fosters emotional ties that are important in reducing prejudice over time.

condition in reducing prejudice. Reflecting on these social experiments in racial integration, Stuart Cook stated:

> One of the clearest findings of studies on the relation between intergroup contact and attitude change is that, while individuals rather quickly come to accept and even approve of association with members of another social group in situations of the type where they have experienced such association, this approval is not likely to be generalized to other situations unless the individuals have quite close personal relationships with members of the other group. (Cook, 1964, pp. 41–42)

❝Only equals can be friends.**❞**

———————————
Ethiopian proverb

❝You cannot judge another person until you have walked a mile in his moccasins.**❞**

———————————
American Indian proverb

Similarly, survey studies and field experiments in France, Chile, Great Britain, Germany, Finland, and the Netherlands confirm that intergroup friendships significantly reduce both subtle and blatant explicit prejudice, as well as reducing implicit prejudice (e.g., Brown et al., 2007; Gonzalez et al., 2010). The sustained close contact necessary to reduce prejudice does not even have to be something that one directly experiences; simply knowing that some of your ingroup members have outgroup friends is often sufficient to reduce prejudice toward that outgroup (Wright et al., 1997).

One likely reason school desegregation has not produced a significant reduction in racial prejudice is that students of different races generally avoid interacting with one another. That is, even though the school building is integrated, students segregate themselves on the bus and playground, and in the cafeteria and classroom. School officials often magnify the problem by separating students based on academic achievement, which results in advantaged White students and disadvantaged minority students having very little classroom contact (Epstein, 1985). One type of school activity that is fairly effective in reducing racial prejudice is team sports. When sports teams have a high percentage of minority athletes, there is a decrease in intergroup intolerance among the participants (Brown et al.; 2003).

Intergroup Cooperation

A third necessary condition in reducing hostility is *intergroup cooperation*. As the Robbers Cave experiment demonstrated, animosity between the Rattlers and the Eagles subsided when they engaged in a joint activity to achieve mutually shared goals (*superordinate goals*). Similar results have been obtained in a variety of experimental and field settings, including school, work, and the armed forces (Desforges et al., 1997). One possible reason why cooperation reduces intergroup bias and hostility is that cooperating members of different

When individuals from various ethnic groups join the armed services, situational conditions often reduce previously learned ethnic prejudices. In school settings, what type of activity is likely to also have these same situational conditions?

social groups appear to cognitively *recategorize* one another into a new ingroup (Gaertner & Dovidio, 2009).

Social Norms Favoring Equality

The fourth condition for successful conflict reduction is that there must be in place *social norms favoring equality* (Monteith et al., 1996). As demonstrated in Chapter 6, social norms have a significant effect on determining people's behavioral intentions. Here is where authority figures and group leaders play a pivotal role. If they publicly state support for equality and actively oppose intolerance, others are likely to follow their lead (Bahns & Branscombe, 2011). If they oppose intergroup contact, prejudice reduction is unlikely (Crandall et al., 2002; Nesdale & Dalton, 2011). The lack of institutional tolerance of homosexuality was the principal reason the "Don't Ask, Don't Tell" policy instituted by the U.S. Congress in 1993 led to increased discrimination against lesbians and gay men in the armed services rather than reduced intolerance. At that time, many officers up the chain of command consistently expressed intolerance for homosexual enlisted personnel (Herek, 2003). By 2010, social attitudes had significantly changed and most of the top military leaders now supported repealing the policy, which President Obama did in December of that year. Now, with the support of the top military authorities, anti-gay prejudice in the military is likely to decrease.

Are All Four Conditions Necessary?

Thomas Pettigrew and Linda Tropp (2006) conducted a meta-analysis of 713 separate studies that tested Allport's contact hypothesis and its assumption that these four conditions are necessary for successful reductions in intergroup conflict. Their results indicated that intergroup contact does indeed have a substantial effect in reducing prejudice toward outgroups. However, while the greatest reductions in prejudice tended to occur when all four conditions in Allport's model were present, significant reductions emerged even when some conditions were absent. Thus, counter to Allport's initial thinking, while these four conditions do facilitate prejudice reduction, all four conditions are not necessary for reductions to occur.

Beyond the four conditions outlined in the original theory, Pettigrew (1998) has offered a reformulated version of the contact hypothesis, in which he adds a fifth situational factor that facilitates prejudice reduction, namely, *friendship potential*. Pettigrew argued that developing friendships with outgroup members is not only important in precipitating the initial reduction in intergroup tensions, but fostering these emotional ties becomes increasingly important in reducing prejudice over time. These cross-group friendships are most effective in reducing prejudice when individuals live in segregated neighborhoods and have had only few, or no, previous contact with outgroup members (Baum, 2010; Christ et al., 2010).

intergroup anxiety
. . . .
Anxiety due to anticipating negative consequences when interacting with an outgroup member

Beyond the Contact Hypothesis

One criticism of the contact hypothesis has been its overemphasis on changing the dominant group's prejudicial attitudes, while ignoring the attitudes of minority group members (Devine et al., 1996). To more effectively promote intergroup harmony, social scientists must also consider (1) the attitudes and beliefs of minority group members, and (2) the beliefs and anxieties of everyone involved in intergroup contact. For example, according to this perspective, during intergroup contact, minority group members may feel anxious because they fear being victimized and negatively evaluated (refer back to the *stereotype threat* discussion, pp. 230–233), while dominant group members may be anxious from fear of saying or doing something that might be interpreted as a sign of prejudice (Blascovich et al., 2001a; Shelton et al., 2005). Compounding this anxiety is the concern by both parties that their interest in contact and interaction will not be reciprocated (Shelton & Richeson, 2005). The combined effect of this **intergroup anxiety** often creates difficulties in such social encounters, even in the absence of any real prejudicial attitudes (Ashburn-Nardo & Smith, 2008; Littleford et al., 2005). Among low prejudiced individuals, those who have had very limited contact with the outgroup are the ones most likely to experience intergroup anxiety (Blair et al., 2003; Brown et al., 2001).

When people experience this anxiety during intergroup exchanges, they often adopt a *protective self-presentation style*, in which they focus on trying not to make a bad impression, rather than trying to make a good one. Thus, they might talk less and generally act more cautiously than less anxious individuals. This strategy often backfires, however, because their outgroup partners tend to interpret their reticence as hostility (Plant & Butz, 2006). The good news is that if people place themselves in intergroup situations and do so with an open mind, their intergroup anxiety will likely decrease (Flynn, 2005; Phills et al., 2011).

In the final analysis, no single strategy eliminates prejudice and discrimination from the vocabulary of intergroup relations (Aboud & Levy, 2000; Walsh, 2011). Because of the manner in which we as a species process information from our social world, and because of the importance we place on our group affiliations, we will always need to be attentive to the way we judge others. Although there is nothing inherently wrong with social stereotyping, it can easily diminish our ability to see the shared humanity in those who fall outside the favored category of "we."

SECTION SUMMARY

- Stereotypical and prejudicial thinking can be reduced through self-regulation.

- The contact hypothesis identifies four conditions to reduce prejudice:

    equal status interaction

    intergroup cooperation

    sustained close contact

    social norms favoring equality

- A reformulated version of the contact hypothesis adds a fifth condition: friendship potential.

- Intergroup anxiety hinders the development of greater understanding between conflicted social groups.

APPLICATIONS

HOW CAN OUR SCHOOLS BE POSITIVE INSTITUTIONS OF SOCIAL CHANGE?

In 1971, Elliot Aronson was asked by the superintendent of the Austin, Texas schools to devise a plan to reduce interracial tensions in the recently desegregated classrooms. After observing student interaction, Aronson realized that the social dynamics were strikingly similar to those described by Sherif in the Robbers Cave field experiment (refer back to pp. 237–239). Using that study and the contact hypothesis as guides, he and his colleagues developed a cooperative learning technique that came to be called the **jigsaw classroom** (Aronson et al., 1978; Aronson & Thibodeau, 1992). The technique was so named because students had to cooperate in "piecing together" their daily lessons, much the way a jigsaw puzzle is assembled. Ten fifth-grade classrooms were ntroduced to this technique, and three additional classes served as control groups.

jigsaw classroom
....
A cooperative group-learning technique designed to reduce prejudice and raise self-esteem

In the jigsaw classroom, students were placed in six-person racially and academically mixed learning groups. The day's lesson was divided into six subtopics, and each student was responsible for learning one piece of this lesson and then teaching it to the other group members. With the lesson divided up in this manner, cooperation was essential for success. In contrast to traditional classroom learning, in which students compete against one another, the jigsaw classroom promoted superordinate goals. It also promoted racial harmony. Compared with students in the control classrooms in which traditional learning techniques were employed, students in the jigsaw groups showed a decrease in prejudice and an increase in liking for one another. This change in students' attitudes toward one another was due to them recategorizing previous outgroup members as new ingroup members—"we" versus "us against them." Their liking for school also improved, as did their level of self-esteem. The cooperative learning also improved minority students' academic test scores, while White students' scores remained the same.

Since these studies were first conducted and reported meta-analysis of the results from similar cooperative classroom settings have found that the jigsaw method offers a promising way to improve race relations in desegregated schools by breaking down the "outgroup" barriers that drive a cognitive and emotional wedge between students (Miller & Davidson-Podgorny, 1987).

Another common social problem in academic settings is the failure of many minority students to perform up to their intellectual potential. For example, African-American college students tend to underachieve academically, even when their college equivalency scores are equal to those of White students (Neisser et al., 1996). Based on our previous discussion of stereo-type threat, this underachievement may be partly caused by two factors. First, the anxiety and/or extra cognitive burden associated with stereotype threat may directly impair Black students' academic achievement (Blascovich et al., 2001b). Second, following repeated instances of this anxiety-induced underperformance, many students may disidentify with academic achievement so that it is no longer important to their self-esteem.

To counteract these two negative effects of stereotype threat, social psychologists have been instrumental in developing a new—and still evolving—educational approach, often referred to as "wise" schooling. An important component in wise schooling is to provide students with critical feedback concerning their academic progress in a manner that does not induce stereotype threat (Steele, 2010). Thus, instead of offering students stigmatizing remedial help, which often only reinforces doubts they may have about their intelligence and academic ability, wise schooling invites minority students to participate in a racially integrated and intellectually challenging learning program. Often working cooperatively, students receive the message that regardless of their current skill level, they have the ability to reach their academic potential. This message is another important component in wise schooling: Intelligence is not fixed and unchanging, but rather, through hard work it is expandable (Aronson et al., 2002).

Beyond reducing stereotype threat, one impediment to improving the academic performance of members of historically stigmatized groups is convincing them that critical feedback regarding their academic efforts is not motivated by prejudice (Steele et al., 2002). African-American students who enter college with high expectations of race-based rejection are more likely to perceive themselves as targets of discrimination on campus (Mendoza-Denton et al., 2002). How do such perceptions of race-based bias affect these students' academic motivation? In one study investigating this question, Black and White students at Stanford University were given the same critical feedback by a White evaluator about an essay they had written about their favorite teacher (Cohen et al., 1999). Compared with White students, Black students saw the feedback from the White critic as more biased. Seeing it that way, the Black students were less motivated to improve their essays for possible publication in a teaching journal than the White students. These Black students were talented writers, but their incorrect perception of racial prejudice caused them to not take the helpful feedback to heart.

If you consider the perspective of these students, how would you know whether criticism of your academic performance is based on prejudice or not? This is a question White students typically never have to ask. Is there any way over this academic hurdle? Perhaps. In this same study, researchers found that there was one form of academic feedback that bridged this racial divide: telling students that the academic activity they were engaged in had very high standards and that after evaluating their performance the instructor believed that the student could meet those standards with *hard work*. Receiving this form of feed-back, Black students perceived no bias and were highly motivated to improve their work. Apparently, this feedback conveyed to the Black students that they were not being judged by negative stereotypes about their group's intellectual abilities.

Research on wise schooling programs among low-income, minority, and female students indicate that, compared with control groups who receive conventional schooling, wise schooling fosters greater enjoyment of the academic process, greater identification with academic achievement and college-based careers, and higher grade point averages among stigmatized groups who are most likely to experience stereotype threat (Good et al., 2003). In a very real sense, like stereotype threat, wise schooling is another example of the self-fulfilling prophecy. Yet now, instead of teachers expecting little from their minority students and ultimately having their expectations confirmed when these students fail and drop out of school, teachers in wise schooling programs begin with high expectations and act on that conviction.

THE BIG PICTURE

John Dovidio (2001) suggests that there have been three "waves" of scholarship in the study of prejudice. The first wave developed after World War II and conceived of prejudice as a form of personal psychopathology. The authoritarian personality is this wave's most identifiable theory. The second wave began in the 1950s and approached prejudice as more of a social problem, much like a social cancer that spread from person to person. A number of theories developed from this social perspective, including realistic group conflict theory, the social contact hypothesis, and social identity theory. This second wave, which peaked during the early 1990s, did not consider prejudice to be a manifestation of mental illness. Instead, it was conceptualized as an outgrowth of socialization, normal cognitive processes, and the natural desire to receive rewards and raise self-esteem. Now we are in the third wave of research on prejudice. Here, more attention is paid to understanding unconsciously held prejudicial attitudes, as well as how the targets of intergroup intolerance adapt to and cope with stigmatization. Examples of recent work in this third wave include implicit prejudice, stereotype threat, and ambivalent sexism. Together, these three research waves have deepened our understanding of how prejudice develops, spreads, and diminishes, as well as what consequences it has for both its targets and perpetrators.

We are far from being a nonprejudiced species. Our natural inclination to categorize people can set the stage for prejudice. It is also true that competition, ingroup loyalties, and social ideologies fan the flames of this tendency to see people as "them" rather than "us" (Lanning, 2002). However, as has been demonstrated throughout this text, our ability to reflect on our actions, our desire to act in ways consistent with our internalized personal beliefs, and our ability to reshape social reality means that prejudice can be reduced. If self-concept is truly a process of identification, what we need to do on an individual level is expand our ingroup identification to include humanity as a whole (Gaertner & Dovidio, 2009). In doing so, we will be able to see ourselves in those who were previously thought of as merely inferior "others." This is by no means an insignificant cognitive shift. As you will discover in Chapter 10, when we include others in our self-concept, our resources become theirs to share, and their successes and failures become our own. Therefore, the first step in achieving a community with a low level of prejudice is to monitor our own thinking and action. The second step is to work collectively to change the perceptions of others. The question to ask yourself is whether you are ready to take that first step.

WEB SITES

Check out our web site
www.BVTLab.com
for chapter-by-chapter flashcards, summaries, and practice quizzes.

ACCESSED THROUGH
www.BVTLab.com/sop6
Web sites for this chapter focus on the nature of prejudice, including an analysis of ethnic stereotypes, sexual harassment, anti-gay prejudice, the history and psychology of hate crimes, and how to break prejudicial habits.

AMERICAN PSYCHOLOGICAL ASSOCIATION
The American Psychological Association has web pages that explore a number of issues related to prejudice and discrimination. For example, one web page analyzes whether all of us have some degree of prejudice, as well as the possibility that we can break our prejudicial habits. Another web page explores the history of hate crimes, including its prevalence, perpetrators, and emotional effects.

AMERICAN ASSOCIATION OF UNIVERSITY WOMEN

This web site of the American Association of University Women has separate sites devoted to sexual harassment (Hostile Hallways: The AAUW Survey on Sexual Harassment in America's Schools) and gender discrimination in education ("Gender Gaps: Where Schools Still Fail Our Children").

SEXUAL ORIENTATION: SCIENCE, EDUCATION, AND POLICY

This web site features the work of Dr. Gregory Herek, a noted authority on anti-gay prejudice, and his Northern California Community Research Group. A number of the studies conducted by Herek and this group are cited in the present chapter.

7

Chapter 7
Social Influence

CHAPTER OUTLINE

INTRODUCTION

The 2011 Egyptian revolution against President Hosni Mubarak gained international attention on January 25 of that year, but its roots were embedded in years of grievances against the president's thirty-year reign. Egyptians' anger at Mubarak focused on political corruption, police brutality, unfair elections, lack of civil rights, high unemployment, food price inflation, and low minimum wages. One incident that served as a catalyst for wide-scale protests against Mubarak's government was the June 2010 murder of twenty-eight-year-old Khaled Said. Said was beaten to death by two policemen on a public street, allegedly for posting a video on the Internet about police corruption. "All of us are Khaled Said, because all of us might face the same destiny at any point in time," said one man who was a key organizer of the protests that later swept through Cairo, Egypt's capital. Images of Khaled's beaten body, posted on Facebook just days after his death, sparked a cyber campaign that spread outrage among Egypt's youth.

Within a few months, the nation was in the grips of large-scale protests not seen since the 1970s. In a series of demonstrations, marches, acts of civil disobedience, and labor strikes, millions of protesters from a variety of educational, social class, and religious backgrounds demanded sweeping social and political changes. The government responded by characterizing the protestors as troublemakers and criminals, and by blocking Twitter and Facebook. Simultaneously, the much-hated riot police took to the

President of Egypt Hosni Mubarak received international attention when the Egyptians' anger with his thirty-year reign turned into a revolution.

Sometimes when people dissent from the majority, they are dealt with in the harshest of terms. Yet sometimes, the majority responds favorably to the dissent, as was the case in Egypt in 2011 when citizens rose up to oppose President Hosni Mubarak's government.

streets, attacking and arresting protestors in an attempt to crush the reform movement. There were up to 840 deaths reported, and over 6,000 people were injured. Finally, after more than two weeks of nonstop protests and clashes, Mubarak lost the support of the army and was forced to resign from office, ending his rule and the influence of those he had placed in key positions of power. The "People's Revolution" provided a new sense of hope for many Egyptians, particularly the nation's youth; and it's success in toppling a corrupt government inspired similar social reform movements in other Arab countries including Yemen, Bahrain, Jordan, Syria, and Libya.

A very different illustration of social influence occurred in China as the government prepared to mark the 90th anniversary of its Communist Party on July 1, 2011. At the height of nostalgia for the late Chairman Mao Zedong, founder of the Chinese Communist Party, an elderly reform-minded economist, Mao Yushi (no relation to the former leader), publicly criticized the founder of the People's Republic of China by writing an online essay arguing that the Chairman should not continue to be held up as a hero in the nation. In an interview with National Public Radio, Yushi stated, "The three biggest murderers of the twentieth century are Hitler, Stalin and Mao Zedong. That's commonly accepted among historians outside China, and Mao killed the most people. They're seen as representatives of evil. However, in China, Mao's portrait is still in Tiananmen Square. If China wants to develop further, it needs to distinguish between basic right and wrong."

Yushi's opinion stood in sharp contrast to the official government view of Chairman Mao, best illustrated by a star-studded blockbuster 2011 movie, *The Beginning of the Great Revival*, depicting Mao as the nation's revered Founding Father. In response to Yushi's essay, Fan Jinggang, founder of the website Utopia, collected fifty thousand signatures in a campaign calling for the economist to be prosecuted for libel. The petition was then sent on to China's parliament, the National People's Congress. In explaining his actions, Jinggang stated that this reform-minded economist had gone too far: "What he published smashed the baseline of free speech. In any country, you can't just insult the country's leader and people's beliefs, and oppose the regime." Responding to the petition calling for his prosecution, Yushi stated, "Of course, I never thought it would cause such a strong backlash. I'm a scholar. I write what I think, without really thinking about the consequences." Besides the threat of prosecution, Yushi has also received threatening phone calls, making his wife worry about their safety. Yet Jinggang, the Utopia founder, viewed such threats positively: "If there were no such threats, that would mean China no longer has any patriots."

WHAT IS SOCIAL INFLUENCE?

social influence

The exercise of social power by a person or group to change the attitudes or behavior of others in a particular direction

Social influence involves the exercise of social power by a person or group to change the attitudes or behavior of others in a particular direction (Cialdini & Goldstein, 2004). Our chapter-opening stories represent social influence on both the individual and group level. In Egypt, Khaled Said and the other protestors were trying to influence majority opinion concerning the legitimacy of President Hosni Mubarak's government through their actions in the streets and on the Internet. Similarly, President Mubarak and his followers tried to influence majority opinion by characterizing the protestors as criminals, curtailing the flow of information regarding events in the country, and by resorting to sheer physical force. In China, the reform-minded dissenter, Mao Yushi, attempted to sway majority opinion against the prevailing view that the late Chairman Mao Zedong was a national hero, while Fan Jinggang was equally determined to suppress Yushi's opinions.

As these notable historical events demonstrate, social influence moves both up and down—and across—the social hierarchy of society. Those who can wield the power of societal institutions typically have much more influence than those outside the power structure (see social dominance theory in Chapter 6, p. 240). In this chapter we examine the social psychology of influence in its various forms. Let's begin by identifying and defining the behavioral consequences of social influence.

CONFORMITY, COMPLIANCE, AND OBEDIENCE ARE DIFFERENT TYPES OF SOCIAL INFLUENCE.

conformity

A yielding to perceived group pressure by copying the behavior and beliefs of others

Social psychologists typically identify three main behavioral consequences of social influence. The first consequence that we will examine is **conformity**, which is a yielding to perceived group pressure by copying the behavior and beliefs of others. To what degree do you conform to others' social influence? Consider the clothing you wear, the food you eat, the music you prefer, the religion you practice, and so on. How are these areas of your life influenced by the social standards of your friends, family, and larger culture? How about when you yawn after seeing someone else do so? Is this imitative response an example of conformity? What about when you actively defy a particular group's influence, such as when the Egyptian protestors denounced their government's policies or Mao Yushi publicly criticized the founder of the People's Republic of China? Are you and they acting independently, or are these acts simply instances of conforming to different reference group standards?

independence

Not being subject to control by others

Sometimes it's difficult, if not impossible, to distinguish conformity from independence. Even though the former is a yielding to group standards and **independence** is being free of others' control, they often result in the same behavioral outcomes. We discuss this issue and many others in more detail later in the chapter.

compliance

Publicly acting in accord with a direct request

The second behavioral consequence of social influence is **compliance**, which is publicly acting in accord with a direct request. In compliance, people responding to a direct request may privately agree or disagree with the action in which they are engaging, or they may have no opinion about their behavior. Complying with a request upon which you have no personal attitude is not uncommon. Do you really think about what passing the salt to a dinner companion implies about your relationship with this person or your own values? Probably not. You simply comply out of habit. Now, consider for a moment a cultural ritual that you have probably engaged in on numerous occasions, namely, singing your country's national anthem. Being asked to stand and sing the national anthem during public ceremonies and before sporting events illustrates compliance. Prior to the terrorist attacks on September 11, 2001, many Americans stood and sang the "The Star-Spangled Banner" without considering the meaning of their actions. To them, it was a ritual with which they habitually complied before all sporting events, and they did so in a mindless fashion (Langer, 1989). Following September 11, however, many Americans' previous mindless compliance to singing this song became decidedly mindful.

Have you ever granted a friend's request to copy your homework even though you believed it was the wrong thing to do? This *external compliance*—acting in accord with a direct request despite privately disagreeing with it—occurs because we are concerned how others might respond if we refuse them (Deutsch & Gerard, 1955; Tyler, 1997). On the other hand, we often comply with a request because we have a personal allegiance to the values and principles associated with it. Such *internal compliance* (or *internalization*) involves both acting and believing in accord with a request (Kelman, 1958, 2006). Agreeing to donate money to a social cause consistent with your own values is an instance of internal compliance. Expressing your patriotism by singing the national anthem or saying the Pledge of Allegiance are also manifestations of the internalization process.

What happens when you do not respond by complying with others' requests? Well, they may simply shrug their shoulders and forget about it, or they may conclude that you're a jerk and resolve to return your noncompliance at an opportune future date. However, another possible response to noncompliance is to up the ante by trying to secure the third behavioral consequence of social influence—namely, obedience. **Obedience** is the performance of an action in response to a direct order, usually from a person of high status or authority. Because most of us are taught from childhood to respect and obey authority figures (parents, teachers, police officers), obedience to those of higher status is common and is often perceived as a sign of maturity. However, all things being equal, most people prefer being "asked" to do something (compliance) rather than being "ordered" (obedience). Obedient behavior is more likely than compliant behavior to imply a loss of personal freedom, which is a valued commodity by most people, especially in individualist cultures.

obedience

The performance of an action in response to a direct order

PEOPLE WITH SOCIAL POWER ARE MORE LIKELY TO INITIATE ACTION.

How powerful are you? I'm not referring to your physical strength, but to your social strength. Do you exercise power or do you shrink from possessing it? There is a famous saying: "Power corrupts, and absolute power corrupts absolutely." Is there any truth to this assertion?

As previously defined, social influence is the exercise of social power to change people's attitudes or behavior in a particular direction. **Social power** refers to the force available to the influencer in motivating this change (Cook et al., 2006). This power can originate from having access to certain resources (for example, rewards, punishments, information) due to one's social position in society, or from being liked and admired by others (Jetten et al., 2006; Raven, 2001). In most instances, those who are the targets of influence resent the use of social power when they perceive it as coercive and heavy-handed, but they often respond positively to "soft" power usage based on accepted social norms, expertise, and likability (Elias & Mace, 2004; Schwarzwald et al., 2004).

social power

The force available to the influencer to motivate attitude or behavior change

The findings from a number of empirical studies support the commonly held belief that possessing social power increases people's tendencies to take action, whereas powerlessness activates a general tendency to inhibit action (Anderson & Berdahl, 2002; Keltner et al., 2003). For example, when research participants are randomly assigned to experimental conditions with high or low social power, those given high power are more likely than those with low power to take action to achieve goals, even when their social power has nothing to do with the task at hand (Galinsky et al., 2003). This suggests that the possession of power in one context can lead to action in an unrelated context.

Why might people with social power be more likely to initiate action compared with those with low power? One reason is that having power makes people less dependent on others; they feel better equipped to act on their own without having to consider how others might impede or obstruct their actions. Because social power allows them to ignore or pay less attention to other people's viewpoints, powerful people tend to act more quickly, with less deliberation than those with low power (Greenspan et al., 2003; Smith & Trope, 2006). In essence, possessing power allows people to loosen the grip that social norms and standards typically exert on their behavior. With power, people can more easily and quickly exert their influence on the situation, including influencing those individuals in the situation. In fact, one avenue by which quick action is taken by the powerful is stereotyping: they judge the less powerful people around them based on stereotypes (Fiske, 1993). As discussed in Chapter 6 (p. 208), although stereotyping often leads to errors in judgment, it does allow for quick decision making and action.

Critical
THINKING
How might an individual's personality and behavior change as they gain or lose social power?

The fact that people with social power tend to be less concerned about the social consequences of their actions creates a paradox. The decisions made and the actions taken by those with high social power are much more likely to affect other people's lives than are the decisions and actions of those with little power. Thus, the people who have the biggest influence on others' lives are the very people who often seem to care less about the social consequences of their actions. Do you see a potential danger here for those with less power?

SECTION SUMMARY

- Social influence is the exercise of social power by a person or group to change the attitudes or behavior of others in a particular direction.

- Conformity, compliance, and obedience represent the three main behavioral consequences of social influence:

  Conformity: yielding to perceived group pressure

Compliance: publicly acting in accord with a direct request

Obedience: performance of an action in response to a direct order

- Social power increases people's tendencies to take action, perhaps because power gives them more freedom from social constraints.

CLASSIC AND CONTEMPORARY CONFORMITY RESEARCH

To better understand social influence, let's begin by analyzing three classic conformity studies conducted more than forty years ago: Muzafir Sherif's work on norm development, Solomon Asch's work on group pressure, and Stanley Schachter's work on how people react to nonconformists. Analysis of each of these classic studies is followed by discussion of more recent studies that provide additional insight into the psychology of conformity.

SHERIF ANALYZED CONFORMITY TO AN AMBIGUOUS REALITY.

The first widely recognized conformity study was that of Turkish-born Muzafir Sherif, who in 1935 published his research on the development of social norms. Sherif's research was partly spurred by his disagreement with the prevailing individualist view of social psychology that a group was merely a collection of individuals and that no new group qualities arise when individuals form into a collective entity. Sherif countered that a group was more than the sum of its individuals' nongroup thinking, and he set out to test this hypothesis by studying how social norms develop in a group (Sherif, 1936).

In his study, Sherif enlisted college students into what was described as a visual perception experiment. Participants were individually placed in a small, totally darkened laboratory where, fifteen feet in front of them, a small dot of light appeared. They were told that after a short time the light would move, and their task would be to judge how far it moved. In all cases the light was left on for two seconds after the participants indicated the beginning of movement. Each participant made one hundred light movement judgments. Although they did not realize it, the experimenter never actually moved the dot of light. What the participants perceived as light movement was really an optical illusion known as the autokinetic effect. The *autokinetic effect* refers to the fact that when someone stares at a stationary point of light in a darkened room where there is no frame of reference, it appears to move in various directions.

In this highly ambiguous situation, each participant's first few guesses were generally quite different from one another. However, after a few more trials, they settled on a consistent range of light movement. Thus, even though this was an optical illusion, participants assigned some order to the visual chaos, zeroing in on a stable estimate as if they were actually mastering this perceptual task. Yet because the light movement was illusory, there was not much consistency between those making their isolated judgments. One person would settle on a stable range of about two inches, while another would make an estimate of six inches. During the experiment's second phase, Sherif placed these same individuals together in groups of two and three and asked them to publicly announce their estimates after each trial. What ensued was not a free-for-all bickering of light movement experts. Instead, all participants tended to gradually change their estimates to be more similar to the others. Moving from their individual standards, they converged on an expected standard established and enforced by the group, known as a **social norm** (Figure 7.1).

social norm

An expected standard of behavior and belief established and enforced by a group

This demonstration of the process by which social norms develop is also an illustration of the more general process of social influence (Bar-Tal 2000). Participants were in a fluid and ambiguous situation, and they looked to the group to help them define reality. They all conformed to an emerging social norm that was different from their individually developed standards. Interestingly, even though the data clearly indicated such social influence occurred, most of Sherif's participants denied that the others had influenced their own judgments. Sherif also found that the more uncertain participants were about the reality of the situation, the more they were influenced by others' opinions. For example, in a variation of the original experiment, Sherif had participants experience the autokinetic effect for the first time in a group setting rather than alone, and thus, they had not established

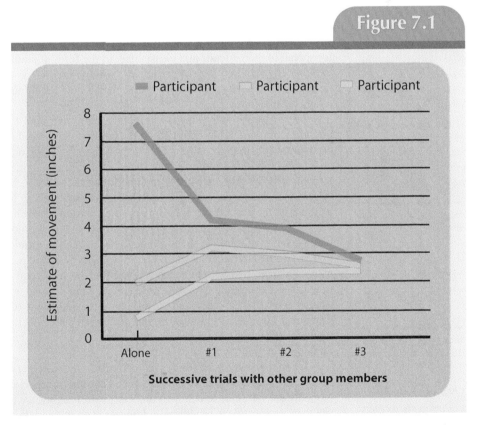

Figure 7.1

Norm Development

In Sherif's autokinetic experiments, when participants in three-person groups announced their individual judgments of light movement to one another, their initial divergent norms gradually converged over the course of the trials. In other words, in an ambiguous reality, the individuals established an expected standard (a social norm) of light movement. Can you think of instances in your own life where you and others established social norms to guide your own behavior and beliefs?

their own individual norms. Under such circumstances, participants were even more influenced by others' view of reality, and convergence toward a common social norm occurred much faster than in the original group condition.

The Power of Confidence in Shaping Norm Development

A third finding of Sherif's study was that when participants were uncertain about how to define reality, they were highly influenced by others who appeared confident. The basis for these findings came by placing a participant in the lab with a confederate who had been instructed to make all of his judgments within a predetermined range. As expected, the participant quickly adopted the confederate's range of judgments, and later used this social norm when placed in the autokinetic situation alone. In essence, faced with a confusing situation, people conformed to those who appeared confident in dealing with their surroundings, and they continued to be influenced by these opinions even in their absence.

The expression of intergroup attitudes is an area of life where one person's confident declaration of a social norm often shapes other people's thinking and behavior. A number of studies find that people express more tolerance of prejudiced speech following a peer's expression of prejudiced views, and less tolerance after a peer condemns such speech (Blanchard et al., 1994; Ford & Ferguson, 2004). Capitalizing on the power that confident individuals have on influencing others, Elizabeth Paluck (2011) recently designed an antiprejudice intervention program at five different high schools in which "peer trainers" were trained how to confront expressions of intergroup prejudice. Suggested actions given to the peer trainers included speaking directly to the perpetrator as the incident unfolded or afterwards, making their disapproval known to other students, calling an adult to intervene, and offering support to the target of prejudice following the incident. All these actions conveyed assertiveness and confidence on the part of the peer tutors. Consistent with Sherif's norm development findings, over a five-month period the peer tutors' behavior spread to their friends and classmates, in the form of students becoming more willing to publically stand up against prejudice. Through their consistent and confident reactions to intolerant behavior, peer tutors established a new social norm at their high school that other students followed.

Robert Jacobs and Donald Campbell (1961) explored the extent of the power that confident others can have over the less confident, and the durability of the social norms established in such a situation. They exposed a single person to the autokinetic effect in the company of three confederates who made extreme judgments (light movement of sixteen inches). Even though these judgments were twelve inches larger than what people typically made, the participants strongly conformed, making judgments nearly as extreme as those of the confederates. Following the creation of the light movement norm in this "extreme" group, the researchers created successive generations of four-person groups to judge a series of thirty light movements, but in each generation they removed one of the extreme confederates and replaced him with a naive participant. By the fourth generation all confederates had been replaced, and the four-person group consisted of four actual participants. Although the extreme confederates were no longer in the group, their extreme group-derived norm continued to influence the judgment of successive generations of groups for quite some time. Jacobs and Campbell's study demonstrates, experimentally, a regularly occurring social phenomena—the views of past generations largely shape the thinking of current and future generations.

Taken together, these studies indicate that when faced with uncertainty about how to interpret or judge events, we are influenced by others, especially if they appear confident. Not only are we likely to conform to their view of reality, we are also likely to continue to use their perspective in rendering judgments even in their absence (Nye & Brower, 1996). This conformity forms the bedrock of the socialization process in all societies. First, we learn and practice common ways of conduct that are characteristic for our social group. Through rehearsal, we develop mental representations, or *schemas* (see Chapter 4, p. 111), of how to behave according to these social norms. Our social environment—parents, friends, teachers, and popular culture—regularly communicate and enforce beliefs concerning which social norms should be used as guidelines for behavior in different situations. This socialization process helps us develop cognitive scripts for a wide variety of social situations. As discussed in Chapter 4 (p. 112), these scripts—which contain perceptions of relevant social norms—guide our behavior and problem solving in the situation. Without this script learning, coordinated social interaction would be very difficult.

In understanding conformity to social norms and also conformity in general, there is one important social psychological process to keep in mind. When we are uncertain about how to understand an event, we often misperceive what others are thinking. We think that everyone else is interpreting a situation in a certain way, when in fact they are not. This state of mind is known as **pluralistic ignorance**, and it plays a role in a wide range of social mishaps. For example, imagine sitting in a large class listening to a professor lecture and being very confused. Your confusion could be due to the complexity of the topic, the poor lecture style of the professor, or some combination of these two factors. After several minutes the professor pauses and asks if there are any questions. You certainly have questions that need answering; yet before raising your hand, you look around the room. No hands are raised. Are you the only student who is completely lost? You interpret the other students' passive response as a sign that they understand the lecture and have no questions. However, your conclusion is almost certainly incorrect; there are most likely numerous students who are equally as confused as you, yet are similarly under the impression that they are the only ones lost. Pluralistic ignorance is driven by conformity to social norms; in this instance, conforming to normative expectations that students will comprehend the professor's lecture and will not question the professor's competence. Do you recall the story in Chapter 1 of the three teenagers who did not speak up even though they believed that the person who was about to drive them in a car was intoxicated? By no one speaking up, they all assumed they were alone in their concerns. Pluralistic ignorance plays a similar role in people often failing to intervene in emergencies due to falsely believing that their fellow bystanders' inaction means that no emergency is occurring (see Chapter 12, pp. 500–508).

pluralistic ignorance

The tendency to think that everyone else is interpreting a situation in a certain way, when in fact they are not

SPECIFIC SITUATIONS CAN AUTOMATICALLY ACTIVATE SPECIFIC SOCIAL NORMS.

Over time and with experience and practice, social norms become associated with specific settings, so that the situation itself can activate mental representations of normative behaviors automatically. This idea that situations automatically activate social norms from memory is consistent with research discussed in Chapters 4 and 6, showing that specific social groups often automatically activate stereotypes from memory (Dijksterhuis & Bargh, 2001). Both stereotype activation and norm activation illustrate how social stimuli can spontaneously trigger well-learned thoughts and responses.

In a series of experiments testing the ability of specific social environments to automatically activate situational norms, Dutch social psychologists Henk Aarts and Ap Dijksterhuis (2003) asked college students to perform two seemingly unconnected tasks on a computer. In the first "Picture Task," a photo either of the inside of an empty library or an empty platform at a railway station was shown on the computer screen for thirty seconds. Participants were told to examine the photo because they would answer questions about it later. Two-thirds of the students were also told that they would visit the depicted environment after the experiment. In one version of this experiment, upon completion of the first task, participants performed a "Word Recognition Task." They were told that when a word flashed on the computer screen, they were to decide as quickly as possible whether it was a meaningful word or a nonsense word. Four of the twelve meaningful words presented to participants represented normative behavior for a library setting (*silent, quiet, still, whisper*). The speed of their response was measured by how quickly they pressed "yes" or "no" keys indicating whether the word was meaningful or not. In a second version of this experiment, the word recognition task was replaced with a "Word Pronunciation Task," in which participants read aloud ten words that were presented on the computer screen. The intensity level of each spoken word was measured, although participants were not informed about this measurement until the end of their session.

What results were obtained in these two separate experiments? In the first experiment, Aarts and Dijksterhuis found that participants in the word recognition task were quicker at identifying library-related "quiet" words as meaningful if they had previously been exposed

The anticipation of entering a specific situation often automatically—and nonconsciously—activates the relevant social norms for that situation, which then directly shapes people's behavior. Approaching a library is likely to cause you to act more subdued.

to the photo of the library rather than the train station photo. This finding suggests that the words related to the "silent" library norm were more readily accessible in memory, meaning that this situational social norm had been primed. As discussed in Chapter 4 (p. 114), *priming* is the process by which recent exposure to certain stimuli or events increases the accessibility of certain memories, categories, or schemas. Priming is a good example of automatic thinking because it occurs spontaneously and unconsciously. Similar results were found in the second experiment. These participants pronounced words in a quieter voice if they had previously been exposed to the library photo rather than the picture of the train station. Again, this finding suggests that the behavior of speaking softly occurred because the "silent" library norm had been primed. It should be added that in neither of these experiments did the participants make a conscious connection between looking at the photo of the library in the first task and responding to the word meanings or speaking the words in the second task. However, most important, in both studies these effects occurred only when participants thought they were later going to visit the library. Those participants who had been shown the library photo but were not told that they would later visit the location showed neither of these effects.

This and other research suggests that the *anticipation* of entering a specific situation automatically heightens the accessibility of the relevant social norms for that situation from memory, which then can have a direct effect on subsequent behavior (Cesario et al., 2006). In other words, when preparing to visit the library, the social norm of being quiet while in the library automatically becomes more accessible in your memory, which may result in your behavior becoming more subdued before you even open the library door. Do you see how these findings challenge a basic assumption of the theory of planned behavior, which is discussed in Chapter 5 (pp. 182–184)? The theory of planned behavior contends that our perception of the social norms in a given situation *indirectly* influence our behavior by shaping our behavioral intentions. The present findings by Aarts and Dijksterhuis suggest that situational norms are able to guide social behavior *directly*. In essence, we have conformed to these situational norms so often that our norm-consistent behavior in the situation becomes a *habit* that occurs without conscious attention or monitoring.

Does this then mean that *all* situational norms guide social behavior directly? Of course not. Additional research by Aarts and Dijksterhuis (2003) suggest that only well-learned situational norms have the ability to directly guide social behavior. If situational norms are not well learned, they are not readily accessible in memory and norm-consistent behavior is not spontaneously expressed. Further, even when situational norms are well learned, there are many instances in which we consciously consider how to match our behavior to these norms; and there are also many situations in which we consciously consider whether we should flout the relevant norms. However, norm-consistent automatic behavior is fairly common; and the cognitive resources we save by acting on automatic pilot allows us to consciously think about other matters, which can increase our overall social efficiency. After all, don't you enjoy an elegant meal better when you don't have to spend time thinking about which of the five utensils in front of you is the correct one to use when eating the next course? Or maybe you are like me and are still trying to master this particular situational norm.

ASCH ANALYZED CONFORMITY TO A UNANIMOUS MAJORITY.

In the spring of 1992, Los Angeles was rocked by its worst race riot in twenty-five years following a jury trial in which four White Los Angeles police officers were acquitted of using excessive force in the beating of Rodney King, a Black man. The actual beating was captured on videotape, and most who viewed the tape believed that Mr. King was a victim of police brutality. One of the jurors, Virginia Loya, stated shortly after the trial that she initially favored a guilty verdict. Yet when the jury deliberated, the strength of her convictions waned as other jurors argued that King deserved the beating he received. In reflecting on her fellow jurors' thinking, Loya said, "The tape was the big evidence to me. They couldn't see. To me, they were people who were blind and couldn't get their glasses clean. If anything, I wish these people weren't so blind." Despite her belief that the other jurors were incorrectly assigning blame, Loya conformed to their judgment and changed her vote from guilty to not guilty on all counts but one. Why did she accept what she believed to be an incorrect judgment by the rest of the jurors? To understand her actions, we might be tempted to search for character flaws or an all-too-compliant personality structure. Yet in doing so, we would be overlooking the power of social influence and how group pressure can cause us to go against what our eyes tell us about social reality.

This account of an important jury trial bears a striking resemblance to the experience of participants in a classic study of conformity conducted by Solomon Asch (1951, 1952, 1956) fifty years ago. In a series of experiments, college students volunteered for what was described as a visual perception experiment. Upon arriving at the lab, they discovered that six other students would also be participating in the study. All six were confederates who were given prior instructions by Asch to behave a certain way. After the assembled students were seated around a table, Asch placed a card on an easel and pointed to a vertical line on the card that he said was the standard line. On this same card were three more vertical lines labeled "a," "b," and "c" (see Figure 7.2). Asch explained that the students' task was to call

The videotaped beating of Rodney King by Los Angeles police officers was shown at the officers' assault trial, but they were judged "not guilty." Do you think you would have acted differently than Virginia Loya, a juror who changed her vote from guilty to not guilty due to social pressure from fellow jurors?

In Asch's conformity experiments, individuals in seven-person groups publicly announced their judgements of which comparison line matched the standard line. Person 6, the only naive participant, appears perplexed and uneasy after the five people before him all choose the incorrect line. If you were in his place, would you have picked the correct line or conformed to the groups incorrect judgement?

out the letter corresponding to the line that was the same length as the standard line. Participants made a total of eighteen different line judgments and were seated so that five of the six confederates stated their judgments before the actual participant gave an opinion.

Undoubtedly, all participants in this study must have initially thought that their task would be simple, for it was obvious that "c" was the correct answer. For the first two trials, confederates picked the correct line; but thereafter, on a prearranged basis, they unanimously chose a clearly incorrect line in twelve of the remaining sixteen problems. What would the second-to-last student—the only "real" participant—do when faced with this dilemma? Would he conform to the judgment of others, or would he stick with what his eyes told him?

Although participants did differ in their degree of conformity, overall they conformed by naming the same incorrect line as the confederates on over one-third (37 percent) of the critical trials. Further, a large majority (76 percent) conformed to the incorrect judgments on at least one of the critical trials (see Figure 7.3). In contrast, when other participants in a control condition made their judgments privately, less than 1 percent made errors (Asch, 1951). Similar to juror Virginia Loya, Asch's research participants demonstrated that many people could be induced to forgo what their own eyes tell them, and instead conform to the incorrect judgment of others. These findings are consistent with later research indicating that people often find it easier to conform rather than challenge the unanimous opinions of others (Tanford & Penrod, 1984).

As discussed in previous chapters, many people prefer their attitudes, beliefs, and actions to fit into a consistent pattern. Research also finds that people see others as more conforming than themselves (Pronin et al., 2007). Given these preferences and beliefs, how do people typically react to the reality of their own conforming behavior, especially when it seems to run counter to their private views? Research suggests that when faced with the choice of admitting that one has arbitrarily conformed to a group standard versus convincing oneself that the facts forced one's agreement with that standard, almost everyone attempts to reconstruct the facts (Buehler & Griffin, 1994). This sort of *postconformity change-of-meaning* allows conformers to justify their behavior and maintain cognitive consistency. Postconformity change-of-meaning likely explains a statement made by one of the teenagers in the Chapter 1 story about intoxicated driving. When asked why he allowed himself to be driven by someone whom he thought was drunk, Leroy claimed that he did so because he did not believe that the driver was actually drunk, but was just bragging. While this may explain Leroy's actions, it is much more likely that this claim is a postconformity change-of-meaning.

Although the Asch findings demonstrate the strength of social influence even when the group's judgment seems clearly misguided, they do not imply that we are merely slaves to others' judgments. As illustrated in Figure 7.3, 24 percent of Asch's participants never followed

"Once conform, once do what other people do because they do it, and a lethargy steals over all the finer nerves and faculties of the soul. She becomes all outer show and inward emptiness; dull, callous, and indifferent."

Virginia Woolf, British novelist, 1882–1941

Figure 7.2

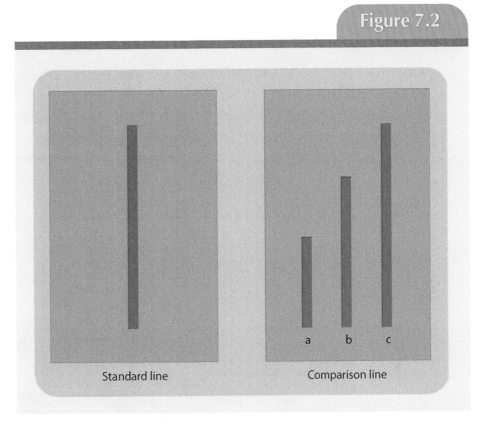

Standard line   Comparison line

Asch's Line Judgment Task

This is an example of the stimulus lines used in Asch's classic conformity experiments. Participants were asked to judge which of the three comparison lines was equal in length to the standard line.

the group on a single trial, and less than one-third conformed on more than half the trials. Likewise, in explaining why she dissented from the majority of the jurors on one count against one of the police officers after conforming to their not guilty judgment on all other counts, juror Loya stated, "They couldn't make me change my mind on guilty for [that officer]. I wasn't going to give in." As heartening as this act of independence may appear, the fact that people often are willing to go along with erroneous group judgments, or are willing to accept the judgments of others when they feel uncertain how to define their surrounding reality, suggests there are compelling social forces in need of further inquiry.

NORMATIVE AND INFORMATIONAL INFLUENCE SHAPE CONFORMITY.

Let's explore a bit further the differing dilemmas that participants faced in the Sherif and Asch experiments. First, Sherif's participants found themselves in an ambiguous reality in which they undoubtedly felt less than confident about their own abilities to judge the movement of this fluctuating point of light. They could stumble along doing the best they could under the circumstances, or they could seek the guidance of others. Did the participants in the Asch experiments face a similar ambiguous reality? Hardly. In fact, in one form of the experiment, Asch (1952) tested sixteen naive participants and instructed a lone confederate to answer incorrectly, like the majority had in the original experiment. How did the naive participants respond when the confederate repeatedly picked the wrong lines? At first they were stunned, but soon they were laughing uproariously at each of his judgments! Clearly, there was no ambiguity here. The dilemma faced by Asch's original participants was deciding whether to maintain their own judgments and thereby stick out like a sore thumb, or go along with the group and thus avoid the uncomfortable stares and

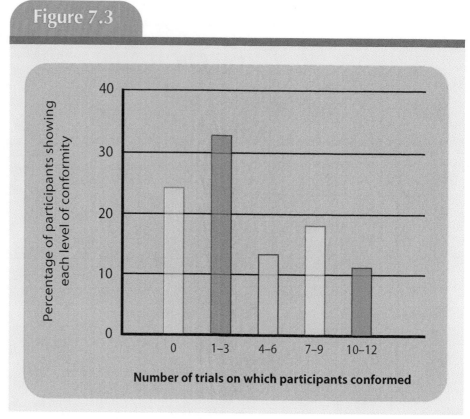

Figure 7.3

Number of trials on which participants conformed

Degree of Conformity in Asch's Research

In judging line length, when faced with a group of people who picked incorrect lines, participants conformed to their false judgments on 33 percent of the trials. Although less than one-third conformed on more than half the judgmental trials, 76 percent conformed on at least one occasion. What type of social influence likely accounts for these effects?

raised eyebrows of others. In the Asch study, by publicly adopting the opinions of others, participants demonstrated that "fitting in" was of greater concern to them than giving the correct answer. In the Sherif study, however, adopting the opinions of others was the avenue participants followed in their search for the correct answer.

In explaining the different social pressures in these two studies, Morton Deutsch and Henry Gerard (1955) suggested that group pressure derives from two sources: normative and informational influence. **Normative influence** occurs when a person conforms in order to gain rewards or avoid punishment from another person or group (Stewart-Knox et al., 2011). If Asch's participants changed their judgments because they were afraid others might laugh at them or evaluate them negatively, they were responding to normative pressure. However, if they modified their answers because they thought the unanimously responding confederates might have a more accurate view of the lines, then they were responding to informational pressure. **Informational influence** occurs when the individual conforms due to the belief that others may have more accurate information. We often look to groups for information, especially if we doubt our own judgment (Baron et al., 1996). Because it is unlikely that very many participants in the Asch studies actually believed that the group was correct in its line judgments, we are probably safe in concluding that their conformity was principally due to normative influence rather than informational influence. In the Sherif study, on the other hand, the conformity exhibited was more likely due to informational influence because light movement was extremely ambiguous. If you would like to try creating a situation that induces informational influence, check out *Self/Social Connection Exercise 7.1.*

These two different types of social influence reflect two different types of social dependence. Informational influence reflects a form of social dependence called *information*

normative influence

• •

Conformity, compliance, or obedience based on a desire to gain rewards or avoid punishments (outcome dependence).

informational influence

• •

Conformity based on the belief that others may have more accurate information

What's Up?

We often conform to other people's actions, even in subtle and trivial ways. For example, in the 1960s, Stanley Milgram and his colleagues conducted an interesting field study that demonstrated this social psychological process. These social psychologists instructed a group of confederates to gather together on a busy New York City sidewalk and simultaneously gaze up at nothing in the sky. When one confederate looked up at nothing, only 4 percent of passersby imitated this behavior. When five people stood on the sidewalk looking up at nothing, 18 percent of passersby imitated their upward gazing. When a group of fifteen confederates gazed skyward, 40 percent of passersby joined in this action, nearly stopping surrounding traffic.

Do you think you could replicate this study yourself? Enlist a group of your friends and classmates in this exercise. Have your confederates stand together in a public setting looking up in the air. Tell them to simply tilt their heads up and look skyward. Do not have them point skyward with their arms. Watch passersby from a short distance. Do they look up?

First try this exercise with only one confederate looking up in the air and then add more skyward-gazing confederates with each trial. Does adding these confederates increase conformity? How long do bystanders look up and how long do they linger in the vicinity? How would you describe their facial expressions? Do they look confused? Do they ask your confederates any questions? Why is their behavior an example of conformity and not compliance or obedience? Is their behavior more related to normative influence or informational influence? Why?

Approach some of the individuals who look up and try to engage them in conversation. Ask why they looked up. Also ask them if they think their behavior is an example of conformity. How do they respond? If they allow you to ask them more questions, ask them whether they think that conformity is a good or a bad thing? How might this type of conformity have survival value for the human species? How do your results compare to Milgram's findings?

> **❝***The fish dies because he opens his mouth.***❞**
> ————————
> Spanish proverb

dependence, which is dependence on others for information about the world that reduces uncertainty. Underlying normative influence is the dependence on others for positive outcomes or rewards, which is called *outcome dependence* (also known as *normative dependence*). Therefore, the need to reduce uncertainty in a given situation leads to information dependence, while the need to gain acceptance or approval results in outcome dependence. Although in some cases these two mechanisms of influence operate separately, in many others they function simultaneously (Baron et al., 1996; Insko et al., 1985). This is likely what occurred as Virginia Loya deliberated with her fellow jurors in the Rodney King case. Faced with fellow jurors who pressured her to accept defense claims that the videotape did not tell the entire story (normative influence), the strength of her convictions weakened and she may well have begun to more seriously consider their interpretation of events (informational influence).

SCHACHTER INVESTIGATED THE REJECTION OF THE NONCONFORMIST.

Thus far we have discussed the forces brought to bear on us so that we conform to the group's judgment. What about those of us who do not knuckle under to this influence, but instead, openly oppose the majority? How does a group typically respond to the nonconformist who never offers anything resembling consensus with their views?

About the same time that Asch was conducting his group conformity research, Stanley Schachter (1951) provided an excellent experimental analysis of the consequences of not conforming to majority opinion. Schachter arranged for groups of eight to ten volunteers to form a "case study club" to discuss the case of a juvenile delinquent, Johnny Rocco, and then make a recommendation of what the authorities should do with Johnny. In making their recommendations, participants used a seven-point love-punishment rating scale ranging from a position 1 "loving" treatment of Johnny to a position 7 "punishment" treatment. Unknown to the participants, each group contained three confederates instructed to take a particular position in the discussion of Johnny. Expecting that the participants would select a position closer to the "loving" end of the scale, Schachter instructed his confederates to take differing positions. The "deviate" argued for position 7 throughout the discussion, acting unswayed by contrary opinions; the "slider" began at position 7 but slid toward the majority position of the group, while the "mode" held the group's most agreed upon position throughout the discussion.

How do you think the participants reacted to these three different positions during discussion, and how do you think they dealt with the deviate at the end, when their best efforts at persuasion failed to secure conformity? At first, participants communicated a great deal with the deviate and the slider in an attempt to convince them to change their minds about Johnny. During this same time period, very little attention was paid to the right-thinking mode. Once participants concluded that the deviate was not going to alter his judgment, and once the slider adopted the group's position, communication toward them dropped sharply. If you think of this communication as an indicator of social pressure, these findings suggest that those who hold minority opinions become the focus of influence attempts until they either conform or convince the group that such attempts are fruitless. This direct persuasive communication is a form of normative influence.

At the end of group discussion, Schachter informed everyone that the group was simply too large for their next discussion and that he wanted them to decide whom to retain in the group. Participants' responses provided the answer to how groups respond to nonconformists—the deviate was excluded from future discussions. A more recent meta-analysis of twenty-three Schachter-like "deviant" studies found that rejection by the group is most likely when there are only one or two nonconformists rather than a more substantial number (Tata et al., 1996). Additional research suggests that group members are least likely to tolerate dissension when it involves an important group value and the dissent is expressed in an intergroup context (Matheson et al., 2003). "Airing the group's dirty laundry" is perceived as the ultimate sign of disloyalty to the group and leads to very harsh judgments by the majority. Together, these studies provide compelling evidence that social rejection is the final, and perhaps most powerful, form of normative influence directed toward nonconformists (James & Olson, 2000). It is believed to be one of the primary causes of depression (Nolan et al., 2003).

In high school and in college, many teenagers and young adults conform to their friends' alcohol and drug use to gain acceptance (Reifman et al., 2006). For other students with different group standards, acceptance entails forgoing these forms of harmful indulgences. In both instances, nonconformists are often banished from the group (Williams & Zadro, 2001). *Ostracism* is used as a social control mechanism at all age levels, and it is such a powerful tactic of social influence that it is even effective when used over the Internet (Williams, 2007; Zadro et al., 2004).

Brain-imaging studies indicate that the social pain we experience following rejection is neurologically similar to physical pain, with both originating in the brain's anterior cingulate cortex (Eisenberger, 2011; Onoda, 2010). Why might social and physical pain have similar neural origins? Due to the fact that social bonds promote survival in most species of mammals, it is possible that during the course of human evolution our social attachment "alarm" system came under the control of the same brain area that already controlled the physical pain system. Because pain is the most primitive signal that "something is wrong," piggybacking the social attachment system onto the physical pain system would have kept young human children near their caregivers, thus increasing their chances of survival (MacDonald et al., 2005; MacDonald & Leary, 2005).

The greater neural activity in the anterior cingulate caused by social rejection may be associated with another consequence of being excluded by others: impairment in reasoning and logic. Studies suggest that when people believe they are going to be excluded by others, their reasoning and complex thinking skills suffer (Baumeister et al., 2005; Baumeister et al., 2002). Because the anterior cingulate plays a role in both the social attachment alarm system and in the process of self-regulation (see Chapter 3, pp. 68–74), the threat of social exclusion disrupts self-regulation (Salvy et al., 2011). Interestingly, excluded people don't actually lose the cognitive ability to self-regulate; instead, they become unwilling to do so. Facing social rejection, excluded people lose their desire to put forth the effort or make the sacrifices that self-regulation often requires. Part of this lack of desire to self-regulate is undoubtedly due to the fact that effective self-regulation requires self-awareness (see Chapter 3, p. 75). Yet self-awareness is problematic when facing social rejection because this state heightens the negative emotions induced by rejection (Twenge et al., 2003). People can diminish these negative emotions by avoiding self-awareness, but the cost is diminished self-regulation. Although being ostracized is a powerful experience for individuals in all age groups, research suggests that adolescents and emerging adults may be the most sensitive of the age groups to such rejection (Pharo et al., 2011).

Although the research discussed thus far highlights the costs incurred by those who are socially rejected, recent studies suggest that one possible benefit of being ostracized is an increased appreciation for religion and communion with a Supreme Being. That is, experiencing social exclusion can motivate some people to develop a greater appreciation for God and a heightened level of religious affiliation (Epley et al., 2008). Further, this increased religious identification often has the effect of reducing loneliness and the stress caused by social rejection (Aydin et al., 2010). In other words, at least for some individuals, developing a close relationship with God can provide a suitable substitute for the social and emotional bonds that are lost due to ingroup rejection. A challenge for future research is to determine under what conditions are ostracized individuals likely to seek positive alternative relationships versus spiraling into a state of negativity after being rejected by their ingroup.

Having considered some of the effects of social exclusion on the targets of this social process, let us now consider how ostracism affects the perpetrators. When people use their social power to ostracize someone, it typically comes at a psychological price (Kerr et al., 2008). For example, in a series of studies, Natalie Ciarocco and her coworkers (2001) found that ostracizing someone temporarily depletes the self's resources, making it more difficult to engage in self-regulation on other tasks. In other words, just as being shunned has a negative impact on our ability to think clearly, shunning someone takes substantial cognitive effort; and the stress is likely to make you less effective in other areas of your life. Thus, although ostracism is an effective way to "straighten out" nonconformers, those who use it are also likely to suffer from these strains of silence.

> "*I could never divide myself from any man upon the difference of an opinion, or be angry with his judgment for not agreeing with me in that from which perhaps within a few days I should dissent myself.*"
>
> Sir Thomas Browne, English physician, 1605–1682

SECTION SUMMARY

- Sherif's norm development research demonstrated that we look to others when defining social reality and are most influenced by people who appear confident.

- Informational influence is social influence that derives its power from people's desire for accurate information.

- Asch's line judgment experiments demonstrated that we often conform out of concern for "fitting in."

- Normative influence is social influence that derives its power from people's desire to gain rewards or avoid punishments.

- Schachter's "Johnny Rocco" study demonstrated that cohesive groups react to nonconformers by first trying to persuade them, and then rejecting nonconformists if persuasion is unsuccessful.

WHAT FACTORS INFLUENCE CONFORMITY?

Thus far, we have learned that people sometimes mindlessly conform due to the automatic activation of situational norms. We have also learned that people are likely to conform when they are uncertain about their own ability to make accurate judgments and others are confident, or when they are concerned about being negatively evaluated by others. What social and personal factors foster this uncertainty and concern?

SITUATIONAL FACTORS IMPACT CONFORMITY.

In attempting to understand the conditions that facilitate conformity, social psychologists have paid particular attention to the social setting. The assumption is that these situational factors exert a social force on individuals that can cause uniform behavior.

Group Size

One situational factor contributing to conformity is the size of the influencing group. When Asch (1955) varied the number of unanimous confederates from one to fifteen, he found that conformity increased as group size increased, but only up to a certain size (Figure 7.4). Conformity was near its peak level when the number of confederates was between three and four, and then actually tapered off so that there was no greater conformity with a group of fifteen confederates than with a group of three.

Other research suggests that group size will only be a predictor of conformity levels in certain situations. Jennifer Campbell and Patricia Fairey (1989) found that group size is important when the social reality is clear (judgments are easy), but that the size of the

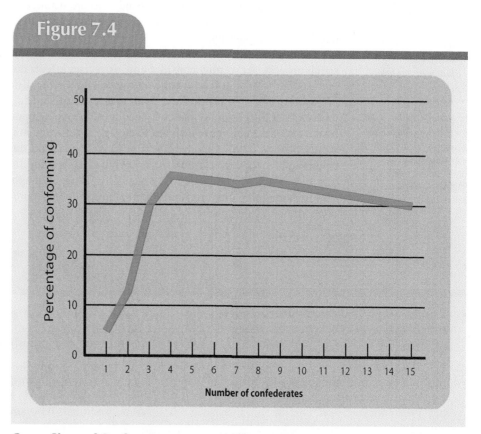

Figure 7.4

Group Size and Conformity

In Asch's (1955) conformity research, when the number of unanimous confederates was varied from one to fifteen, conformity approached its maximum level when the number of confederates was between three and four. Why do you think group size effects leveled off in this manner?

group is relatively unimportant when the social reality is ambiguous (judgments are difficult). The explanation for this interaction effect has to do with what type of social influence is most potent in an ambiguous or clear reality. As previously discussed, when the reality is clear, whether or not you conform depends on the amount of normative influence the group can exert. Adding more people to the group (up to four or so) will increase normative influence, and thus, increase conformity. On the other hand, if the reality is ambiguous, informational influence is more of a factor than normative influence. In this state of information dependence, one or two people may influence you just as well as three, four, or twenty-four.

Group Cohesiveness and Topic Relevance

A group is termed cohesive when its members are highly attracted to one another. In general, cohesive groups engender more conformity than noncohesive groups (Christensen et al., 2004; Hogg, 1992). For example, in other conditions of Schachter's (1951) deviant study, he varied the cohesiveness of the group as well as the relevance of the contested discussion topic. When the group was highly cohesive and the topic was also highly relevant, the group exerted its greatest pressure on deviates and was most likely to reject nonconformists. These findings indicate that if groups with a strong sense of togetherness are discussing important topics, they will tend to be intolerant of those who hold differing opinions. The best examples of cohesive groups influencing members come from our own friendship networks. We are much more likely to accept their influence than that of others because of our respect for their opinions, our desire to please them, and our fear of rejection (Crandall, 1988).

Social Support

In Asch's study, what sort of effect do you think a single confederate picking the correct line would have on the conformity levels of the participants? Actually, Asch (1956) found that when one of the confederates picked the correct line, conformity dropped dramatically, to one-fourth the original levels. Research by Vernon Allen and John Levine (1969) indicates that a social supporter reduces conformity by diminishing the group's normative influence. In one of their studies, participants worked with four confederates on a visual perception task. Three of the confederates had previously been instructed to consistently agree on incorrect judgments. The fourth confederate went along with the other confederates, agreed with the participant, or made a different incorrect judgment. Conformity was not only reduced when the fourth confederate agreed

Why do friendship networks typically exert greater influence over us than other social relationships?

with the participant but also when this confederate merely disagreed with all opinions, including the participants' opinions. In a second experiment (Allen & Levine, 1971), conformity was reduced even when the social supporter wore thick glasses and complained about not being able to see the visual displays!

These findings suggest that almost any dissent from the majority can diminish normative influence and thereby reduce conformity. Although breaking social consensus appears to be the crucial factor here, receiving social support early is more effective than receiving such support after normative pressures have already built up (Morris et al., 1977). Unfortunately, if this support is later removed, normative influence again is exerted. In one of Asch's studies, when the confederate who had previously agreed with the participant switched and began to conform to the majority opinion, the participants' own level of conformity returned to near the levels observed in the original experiments (Asch, 1955). Thus, to promote nonconformity in others, one should voice dissent, and do so early and consistently. Remember this bit of advice, for it will be important when we later discuss how minorities can exert influence in not only resisting majority opinion but also in actually changing it.

PERSONAL FACTORS INFLUENCE CONFORMITY.

The consensus is that situational forces are most important in determining whether we conform or not. Yet we are not machines who respond identically to these situational factors. Although specific personality traits related to conformity have been difficult to identify (McGuire, 1968), research does suggest that conforming to group pressure is related to our *values* and *self-concept*.

Self-Awareness

As noted in Chapter 3, whether behavior is more influenced by personal or social standards is at least partially determined by what aspect of the self is salient (private or public). When people are privately self-aware, they tend to act in line with their own personal standards; however, social standards are more influential when people are publicly self-aware (Froming et al., 1982; Kallgren et al., 2000). Thus, being privately self-aware reduces conformity, while being publicly self-aware increases conformity.

Self-Presentation

The irony of yielding to social influence out of concern for how others might evaluate you is that in many cultures it is not desirable to be recognized as a conformist. Robert Cialdini and his coworkers (1974), for example, found that American college students generally perceived people as more intelligent if they do not yield to social influence—unless, of course, they were the ones trying to get others to conform! Further research found that often underlying the conformity and independence responses of people are calculated assessments of the impressions they are making on those present (Collins & Brief, 1995; Santee & Maslach, 1982). Conformity is most likely to occur when self-presenters are alone with those trying to influence them and when the conformity will be viewed as indicating intelligence or open-mindedness. On the other hand, open defiance of influence attempts is most likely under two conditions (Baumeister, 1982): (1) when others not involved in the influence attempt are present and (2) when the attitude of those exerting the influence makes any subsequent yielding seem like weak-kneed surrender rather than intelligent decision making. Under such conditions, it would be difficult to conform and still maintain a public image of independence and autonomy.

The Desire for Personal Control

Although self-presentation concerns may sometimes explain conformity and nonconformity, on other occasions we may resist social influence simply to feel that we personally control our own actions. Jack Brehm (Brehm, 1966; Brehm & Brehm, 1981) has proposed a **theory of psychological reactance**, which states that people believe they possess specific behavioral freedoms and that they will react against and resist attempts to limit this sense of freedom. For example, if parents demand that their daughter not date a

certain boy, she might defy the parents as a way to restore a feeling of personal control over her own behavior. When reactance is aroused, the forbidden behavior (dating the disapproved boy) becomes more desirable. Similarly, if the daughter believes her parents are trying to coerce her into dating some other boy, reactance results in this boy becoming a much less desirable date than the forbidden boy.

Jerry Burger (1987) found evidence indicating that individual differences in desire for personal control may partly explain susceptibility to social influence. In his study, he asked college students to rate the humor in a series of newspaper cartoons using a scale from 1 ("very unfunny") to 100 ("very funny"). In one condition, participants rated the cartoons alone; in another condition, they rated them after hearing two other students' evaluations. These other students, being confederates, had been instructed to rate the cartoons as being relatively funny (averaging 70 on the 100-point scale), even though Burger had specifically chosen cartoons that had previously been judged to be quite dull (average humor rating of only 25). Prior to rating the cartoons, participants' desire for personal control (DPC) had been measured by a paper-and-pencil questionnaire. Results indicated that DPC did not predict how students rated the cartoons when they were alone (both groups rated them as not very funny), but high DPC participants were less likely to agree with confederates' favorable ratings than were low DPCs. Although the high DPCs certainly were not immune to the confederates' influence, they did appear to be better equipped to resist conformity than those who had a low desire for control.

Individuals may not conform to social pressures due to their desire for personal control, but this does not mean that they are necessarily acting independently. There are two different types of nonconformity responses. One is *independence*, which was previously defined as not being subject to others' control. The person who dates someone not because her parents approve or disapprove but because she genuinely likes her dating partner is demonstrating independence; psychological reactance does not play a factor in her behavioral choices. On the other hand, opposition to social influence on all occasions characterizes **anticonformity**; psychological reactance often explains these behavioral choices (Nail et al., 2000). The anticonformist would date people whom her parents disapproved and would not date those whom they approved. Thus, the actions of two people may be identical but may be motivated by very different desires. A person who has a strong desire for personal control could express this either through independence or anticonformity. Some people "take the road less traveled," not because they disagree with the group's direction, but by disagreeing they can satisfy their need for personal control.

" *I wouldn't have turned out the way I was if I didn't have all those old-fashioned values to rebel against.* **"**

Madonna, American rock singer, 1990

anticonformity
. . . .
Opposition to social influence on all occasions, often caused by psychological reactance

Gender and Conformity

Early social influence research found a slight tendency for women to conform more than men, but later studies found little, if any, gender differences in overall conformity (Eagly, 1987). Where small gender differences sometimes occur is in face-to-face encounters in which a person must openly disagree with others (Becker, 1986). Whatever small gender differences exist in susceptibility to influence appears to be due to the social roles that men and women have traditionally been socialized to assume in our culture, and to their concerns about self-presentation. That is, when people believe they are being observed, women tend to conform more and men tend to conform less than they do in more private settings (Eagly & Chravala, 1986). It is likely that in attempting to create a favorable impression when questions of conformity arise, people tend to fall back on well-learned patterns of behavior that are considered socially acceptable for their sex.

This gender difference is observed most clearly when women and men are in mixed-sex settings and seeking romantic partners. In such competitive mating situations, men often behave in a nonconforming manner as a way to appear unique and assertive, while women often act more conforming as a way to appear agreeable and foster group cohesion (Griskevicius et al., 2006). If this gender difference is primarily the result of gender socialization, you would expect that as men and women adopt less traditional gender roles such self-presentation concerns will diminish in importance; and whatever conformity differences there are will similarly diminish, if not disappear entirely.

CULTURES DIFFER IN THEIR CONFORMITY PATTERNS.

Does knowing a person's cultural background give you any insight into how he or she might respond to social influence? The guiding principle of individualism is that individual interests are more important than those of the group. In decided contrast, collectivism asserts that group interests should guide the thinking and behavior of individual members (Ho & Chiu, 1994). According to Harry Triandis, people from collectivist cultures are more concerned than individualists with maintaining group harmony and gaining the approval of their group (Triandis, 1989; Wall et al., 2010). A person from an individualist culture, on the other hand, has a higher need for autonomy from the group and a desire to feel unique. Because of these different orientations, people from collectivist cultures tend to be more conforming to their own group than individualists (Cialdini et al., 2001; Morling & Kitayama, 2008). This yielding to the group by collectivists is not considered to be a sign of weakness, as it is often perceived in our individualist culture, but rather it is believed to indicate self-control, flexibility, and maturity (White & LeVine, 1986). Because people from collectivist cultures are much less likely than those from individualist cultures to view conformity as a sign of weakness, they are also less likely than individualists to engage in psychological reactance when their individual freedom is threatened (Jonas et al., 2009).

Although these cultural differences suggest that conformity is generally more likely in a collectivist culture, this does not mean that collectivists submit to any and all group influence attempts. To understand social influence in such a culture, it is important to distinguish *ingroups* from *outgroups*. As described in Chapter 3, an ingroup is a group to which you belong and which forms a part of your social identity, whereas an outgroup is any group with which you do not share membership. Research suggests that people from collectivist cultures perceive ingroup norms as universally valid and feel obligated to obey ingroup authorities. On the other hand, collectivists tend to distrust outgroup norms and, as a result, often are unwilling to yield to their influence (Triandis, 1972; Wosinska et al., 2001).

Most of the nonconformity that occurs in a collectivist culture is to the social norms of outgroups, not ingroups. This difference in the perceived validity of ingroup norms is one of the reasons that collectivist cultures tend to breed more conformity than individualist cultures. Therefore, a person from a collectivist culture such as traditional Greece might be very yielding to his family's and his village's influence attempts (his ingroup), yet be staunchly defiant of any pressure exerted by the distant national authorities (a perceived outgroup). When we consider those who belong to an individualist culture, although they too tend to trust ingroup norms more than outgroup norms, they are more

The young always have the same problem—how to rebel and conform at the same time. They have now solved this by defying their parents and copying one another.

Quentin Crisp, British author, 1908–1999

I'm not gonna change the way I look or the way I feel to conform to anything. I've always been a freak. So I've been a freak all my life and I have to live with that, you know. I'm one of those people.

John Lennon, English rock musician, 1940–1980

The man who never submitted to anything will soon submit to a burial mat.

Nigerian proverb

likely than collectivists to question ingroup norms as well, especially when they run counter to their self-interests or when adherence to these social norms makes them feel average or ordinary (that is, nonunique).

THE MINORITY CAN INFLUENCE THE MAJORITY.

History is filled with stories of lone individuals or small, relatively powerless groups expressing unpopular views and enduring abuse from the majority until their views are eventually adopted. Our chapter-opening stories of Egyptian protestors' success in overthrowing their government and Mao Yusjhi's attempt in China to reshape his countrymen's understanding of their founder are examples of dissenters whose minority opinions were aimed at majority group members. The process by which dissenters produce change within a group is called **minority influence**.

minority influence

The process by which dissenters produce change within a group

Commenting on what it takes to exert minority influence, nineteenth-century feminist Susan B. Anthony said, "Cautious, careful people always casting about to preserve their reputation and social standing never can bring about a reform. Those who are really in earnest must be willing to be anything or nothing in the world's estimation." Social research bears out Ms. Anthony's pronouncement. Those who dissent from the majority, although generally perceived as competent, often are heartily disliked (Bassili & Provencal, 1988). Indeed, during the 1960s civil rights movement in this country, dissenters such as Medgar Evers, Malcolm X, and Martin Luther King, Jr. were so heartily despised by some people that they were murdered to eliminate their nonconforming voices, just as the police silenced Khaled Said in Egypt in 2010. One consequence of the social isolation experienced by those in the minority is a hesitation in voicing their opinions. This tendency of those who hold a minority opinion to express that opinion less quickly than people who hold the majority opinion is called the **minority slowness effect**. People with a minority opinion are particularly slow in stating their views when they perceive the majority opinion to be widely held (Bassili, 2003). As articulated by Ms. Anthony, championing the minority viewpoint is not for the weak of heart.

minority slowness effect

The tendency of those who hold a minority opinion to express that opinion less quickly than people who hold the majority opinion

When minority influence is expressed, how exactly does it operate? As previously discussed, movement to the majority position is often due to the common belief that there is truth in numbers (informational influence) and due to the concern for being accepted by those numbers (normative influence). Underlying this social influence is a generally positive judgment of and an attraction toward the majority by those being influenced (Wood et al., 1994). This favorable view of the majority often results in people adopting the majority opinion without much critical analysis (Martin et al., 2007). However, unlike the majority group, minority groups tend to be viewed negatively by others; and therefore, their viewpoints are subject to more critical analysis, and thus, need greater time to register with group members (Martin et al., 2003; Mugny & Perez, 1991). The good news for minority persuaders is that if their views are eventually adopted by the majority, these new attitudes and beliefs tend to be more resistant to change than those adopted from majority persuaders (Martin et al., 2008). Do you know why? As discussed in Chapter 5, attitudes changed through critical analysis (*central-route processing*) are stronger and more resistant to change than attitudes changed through lazy thinking (*peripheral-route processing*).

Martin Luther King, Jr. and Malcom X were two powerful influence agents during the 1960s' civil rights movement. Which one of these individuals' actions most closely demonstrated effective minority influence principles?

French social psychologist Serge Moscovici (1980) contended that the most important factor in determining the effectiveness of minority group influence is the *style of behavior* used in presenting nonconforming views. For minorities to exert influence on majority members, they must consistently and confidently state their dissenting opinions (Moscovici & Mugny 1983). In a demonstration of the importance of consistency in minority group influence, Moscovici and his colleagues (1969) asked groups of individuals to judge whether the color of projected blue slides was blue or green. Each group consisted of four participants and two confederates. In the *inconsistent minority condition*, the confederates randomly varied calling the blue slide green and blue, while in the *consistent minority condition* they always claimed that it was green.

Figure 7.5 shows that when the confederates were inconsistent in labeling the blue slide green, their ability to influence the majority's opinion was negligible (1.25 percent).

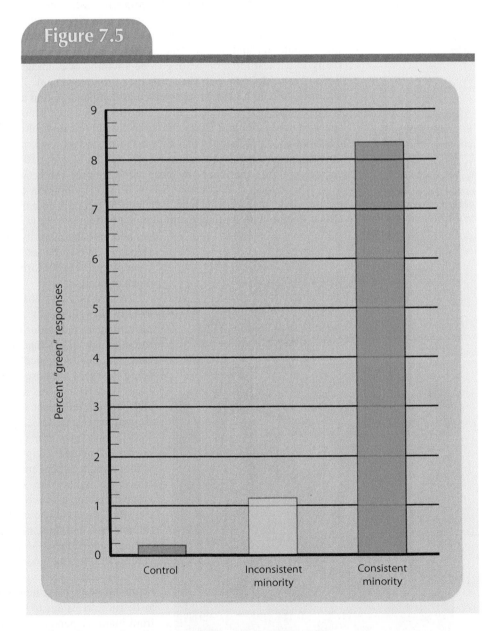

Figure 7.5

Conformity to a Consistent and Inconsistent Minority

Moscovici et al., (1969) found that the degree to which participants labeled a blue slide "green" was partly determined by whether they were tested alone (control condition), with a minority saying "green" inconsistently (inconsistent condition), or with a minority saying "green" consistently (consistent condition). Why is consistency so important for minority group influence?

However, when the confederates were consistent, more than 8 percent of the time participants conformed to this minority point of view. In addition, after the color trials, those who were exposed to the consistent minority shifted the point on the blue-green color spectrum where they identified a color green instead of blue; now they called more stimuli "green" and fewer "blue." These findings not only suggest that a consistent minority can affect overt responses in the majority but also suggest that a unified minority can cause majority members to alter their private beliefs as well.

Although this research indicates that those sharing minority opinions must appear confident in consistently stating their views, other research indicates that minorities must walk a fine line in presenting their nonconforming opinions. They cannot appear dogmatic or rigid, for that will also reduce their influence (Nemeth et al., 1974). Therefore, for majority members to consider their perspective in the first place, the minority must come across as consistent and confident, and also flexible and open-minded. Nelson Mandela, a longtime opponent of the former apartheid government of South Africa, is an excellent example of a minority group leader (a minority in power but not in numbers) whose consistent, unwavering call for Black equality was combined with a nondogmatic approach to reform that won over many White South Africans. In 1994, he became the first president of a nonapartheid South Africa.

One other factor that also affects the ability of the minority to influence the majority is the *degree of difference* between the minority and the majority. *Single minorities* are individuals who differ from the majority only in terms of their beliefs, while *double minorities* are those who differ from the majority in terms of both beliefs and group membership (Martin, 1988). An example of a single minority is a heterosexual arguing for equal rights for gay people to the heterosexual majority. A gay person advocating such rights is a double minority. Research indicates that single minorities are more likely to exert influence over the majority than are double minorities (Alvaro & Crano, 1997). For example, in one study (Maass et al., 1982), conservative male participants engaged in a discussion of abortion with either a single (male confederate) or double (female confederate) minority. In these discussions, the minority consistently defended a liberal position rather than the conservative viewpoint of the male participants. Results indicated that the male participants perceived the double minorities (the liberal females) as having a stronger self-interest in the discussion, and they were less influenced by them than they were by the single minorities (the liberal males). By perceiving self-interest in the position of a double minority, it appears that people can more easily discount their arguments. Nelson Mandela recognized this tendency to discount double

" *Whenever you find yourself on the side of the majority, it is time to pause and reflect.* "

Mark Twain, American author and satirist, 1835–1910

" *Every society honors its live conformists and its dead troublemakers.* "

Mignon McLaughlin, U.S. author, 1913–1983

In 1977, Harvey Milk became the first openly gay politician elected to public office in California. Championing gay rights, Milk was a "double minority" influencer. Milk was assassinated on November 27, 1978, by another politician. He was posthumously awarded the Presidential Medal of Freedom in 2009.

minorities in the struggle to put Black South Africans on an equal footing with their White counterparts. Some of the most effective influencers of White public opinion were fellow Whites who expressed antiapartheid beliefs.

Finally, minorities have the strongest influence when they take positions in the same direction as evolving cultural norms, but they are relatively ineffective when they argue against these emerging norms (Kiesler & Pallack, 1975). For example, during the early stages of the civil rights movement in the United States, Martin Luther King, Jr., and other civil rights activists espoused beliefs about equality and human justice that were in line with the emerging liberalism within the nation as a whole. A similar cultural shift is currently underway regarding support for gay rights, largely fueled by more accepting attitudes among young Americans. Same-sex marriages are now legal in six states, with another eight states approving civil unions (Crary, 2011). The importance of social movements being aligned with emerging norms was powerfully demonstrated in various Middle Eastern countries in 2011. Dissidents' calls for social reform and democracy gained traction in certain countries but failed to do so in others partly based on how aligned each social movement was with its country's emerging human rights norms. In China, economist, Mao Yushi's condemnation of Chairman Mao was itself roundly condemned because there is as yet no emerging norm among the people of China to reassess the past actions of their country's founding father.

Overall, minorities are most successful in exerting influence on the majority when arguing for positions that are not too far from the prevailing majority position, and when they show a *consistent behavioral style* that the majority interprets as indicating *certainty* and *confidence*. On the other hand, minority influence will surely fail if the minority group *argues against evolving social norms* and exhibits a *rigid* style of negotiation with *inconsistently held beliefs*. In explaining why this is the case, Moscovici and Charlan Nemeth (1974) draw from the insights of Harold Kelley's attribution theory. As you remember from Chapter 4, we tend to infer that the behavior of others is due to internal causes when (1) consensus is low (few others are behaving this way), (2) consistency is high (these people have behaved the same way over time), and (3) distinctiveness is low (they act this way in other situations). These conditions describe the behavior of strongly committed minorities. Not only are few others taking the belief position of the minority, but they consistently maintain this position over time and voice it in many varied situations. The logical conclusion that majority group members draw from all this information is that the voicing of such beliefs can only be due to deep and abiding personal convictions—convictions that perhaps should be seriously considered and scrutinized.

Even if minority groups follow a consistent avenue of persuasion, this does not mean that those holding majority beliefs will necessarily change. Remember, majority groups can impose sanctions and withdraw rewards from their members if they begin to espouse minority viewpoints, and this often is enough to maintain public compliance with majority opinions. Further, people's social identities generally consist of majority-held values and beliefs, and those aspects of the self-concept are resistant to change. However, although overt change toward minority positions may not readily take place, when majority members engage in critical analysis of these positions, it often stimulates *divergent thinking*, a cognitive process in which one considers a problem from varying perspectives (Gruenfeld & Preston, 2000). What appears to initially motivate this enhanced scrutiny of the minority message is simply that it is different and unexpected (Baker & Petty, 1994). The benefit for the minority persuader is that this increased scrutiny often causes people to consider a wider variety of possible explanations or novel solutions to problems (Peterson & Nemeth, 1996).

Interestingly, when majority opinions eventually change due to the impact of the minority viewpoint, people often forget where they first heard their newly adopted views (refer to the *sleeper effect*, Chapter 5, p. 188). In other words, the efforts of those who first propose minority positions often are not acknowledged when their influence attempts finally succeed. Such is the thankless job of the dissenter.

> "The power of a movement lies in the fact that it can indeed change the habits of people. This change is not the result of force but of dedication, of moral persuasion."
>
> Steve Biko, South African political leader, 1946–1977

CONFORMITY IS SOMETIMES AUTOMATICALLY ACTIVATED.

Of the three behavioral consequences of social influence discussed in this chapter, conformity is the one that you are most likely to engage in with minimal thought. We have already discussed how simply thinking about entering a social setting can cause us to automatically conform to the setting's social norms (see pp. 266–268). Yet conformity can be automatically activated in ways having nothing to do with social norms (Dimberg et al., 2000; Epley & Gilovich, 1999). For example, I'm sure that you have had the experience of yawning after seeing someone else yawn or laughing when seeing others laugh. This *nonconscious mimicry* represents a type of conformity that we engage in within days of birth (Meltzoff & Moore, 1989). Make a happy, sad, or surprised face to a newborn, and he or she will likely imitate the facial expression.

As discussed in Chapter 4 (p. 129), evolutionary psychologists believe that this innate tendency to automatically imitate others' expressions is a survival reflex (Izard et al., 1995). For newborns, mimicking their mothers' gestures—especially facial gestures—helps establish an emotional bond between the two, making it more likely that the newborn will be nurtured and protected. In adulthood, mimicking others' expressions fosters positive feelings in those who are mimicked, even when they do not consciously notice the mimicry (van Baaren et al., 2004). Thus, nonconscious mimicry appears to create affiliation and rapport among people, and thereby fosters safety in groups.

SECTION SUMMARY

- Situational forces that influence conformity:

    the *size* of the influencing group

    the *cohesiveness* of the influencing group

    whether there is any *social support* for contrary positions

- Personal factors that influence conformity:

    private and public self-awareness

    self-presentational concerns

    desire for *personal control*

gender differences are small and likely due to social roles

- *Collectivists* engage in more ingroup conforming than *individualists*.

- *Minority group influence* is most likely when the minority group consistently and confidently states its dissenting views presents itself as flexible and open-minded.

- Automatic imitation of others' gestures represents a type of unconscious conformity.

COMPLIANCE

In trying to "get our way" with others, sometimes we forget the most direct route—simply asking them to do what we desire. However, because compliance involves a direct request, it generally induces more thinking and critical analysis by the target of social influence than conformity. As a compliance seeker, what strategies can you employ to increase the likelihood that others will grant your requests?

MANIPULATING MOODS AND INVOKING NORMS FOSTER COMPLIANCE.

When people are roughly equal in social status, establishing the correct atmosphere or mood is especially important to increase compliance. Three factors that help create the proper atmosphere are to make people feel good, to do something for them, and to give them reasons for compliance. As you will discover, these factors also often reduce the likelihood that people will critically analyze the request.

Positive Mood

In the course of making requests, people soon discover that others are more likely to comply when they are in a good mood, especially if the requests are prosocial, such as helping others (Forgas, 1998). One reason for this is that people who are in good moods are simply more likely to be active and, thus, are more likely to engage in a range of behaviors, including granting requests (Batson et al., 1979). A second reason is that pleasant moods activate pleasant thoughts and memories, which likely makes people feel more favorable toward those making requests (Carlson et al., 1988). A third reason is that people in a happy mood are often less likely to critically analyze events, including requests, and thus, are more likely to grant them (Bless et al., 1996).

Because of this general awareness that good moods help create compliance, we often try to "butter someone up" before making a request. As discussed in Chapter 4, this self-presentation strategy of *ingratiation* is designed to get others to view us favorably (Liden & Mitchell, 1988). Although people may be suspicious of ingratiators' motives after receiving their requests, the preceding flattery is still often effective in securing compliance (Kacmar et al., 1992), yet subtlety is the best strategy. A recent survey study of managers and chief executive officers at Forbes 500 companies found that managers and directors were more successful in having their requests for board appointments at other firms granted when they employed relatively subtle forms of flattery and opinion conformity rather than blatant ingratiation (Stern & Westphal, 2010).

Reciprocity

reciprocity norm

. . . .

The expectation that one should return a favor or a good deed

How often have strangers offered you small gifts, such as flowers, pencils, or flags, and then asked you to donate money to their organization? If so, they were hoping that the token would lower your resistance to their request. The hope rested on a powerful social norm that people in all cultures follow, namely the **reciprocity norm**. Although this unwritten social norm helps to maintain fairness in social relationships by prescribing that favors or good deeds should be reciprocated, it can also be used to increase compliance (Uehara, 1995).

Research clearly demonstrates that giving someone a small gift or doing him/her a favor can easily lead to reciprocal compliance, especially if you seek compliance shortly after doing the good turn (Chartrand et al., 1999). For example, Dennis Regan (1971) had a college student work on a task with another student (a confederate) who acted in either a friendly or an unfriendly manner. During a break, the confederate left and returned a few minutes later either with a soft drink for the student participant or with nothing. Shortly afterward, the confederate asked the student to buy twenty-five-cent raffle tickets. Those given the soft drink "gift" bought an average of two tickets, whereas those not given a soft drink bought only one. The effect of reciprocity was so strong that the students returned the favor even when the confederate had previously acted in an unlikable manner.

Everyday experience tells us that reciprocity is commonly used as a strategy in making sales (Howard, 1995). Grocery stores provide free product samples. Insurance agents give away free pens or calendars. Car salespeople give potential customers new twenty-five-cent key rings—just right to hold the key to that new $25,000 automobile. In offering these "gifts," salespeople are often counting on the salience of the reciprocity norm overriding customers' careful consideration of the consequences of purchasing these products.

However, it is not just professional salespeople who employ such tactics. Those who habitually use reciprocity to secure compliance are called *creditors*, because they try to keep others in their debt so they can cash in when necessary. People who are creditors tend to agree with statements such as "If someone does me a favor, it's a good idea to repay that person with a greater favor." Creditors know the power of indebtedness, and they work hard to make sure they are on the influential side of the reciprocity equation (Eisenberger et al., 1987). They know all too well the wisdom of the proverb, "Beware of strangers bearing gifts."

Giving Reasons

In granting someone's request, we often require a reason for complying. For instance, if you are in line at a grocery store with a small number of food items, and someone with only one item asks to go ahead because his sick grandmother is waiting for her cold medicine, you are likely to grant the request. The explanation given for his request strikes a responsive chord within you—it is "reasonable." Ellen Langer (1978) and her colleagues found evidence for the power of reason giving in gaining compliance when they had confederates try to cut in line ahead of others at a photocopying machine. In one condition the confederates gave no reason, merely asking, "May I use the photocopying machine to make five copies?" Sixty percent of those waiting complied with this "no reason" request. In another condition, when the confederates gave an explanation for their request ("May I use the photocopying machine to make five copies because I'm in a hurry?"), compliance increased to 94 percent, a significant difference. What Langer was interested in determining at this point was whether the actual content of the reason was important or whether any reason at all would suffice. To test this, she had her confederates try a third version of the request, where the reason given for cutting in line was really no explanation at all; it was merely a restatement of their desire to make copies ("May I use the photocopying machine to make five copies because I have to make copies?"). Surprisingly, this mere reiteration of a desire to make copies resulted in 94 percent compliance, identical to when an actual explanation was given ("I'm in a hurry").

Why does merely giving a reason—any reason—result in greater compliance? Giving reasons may be important because of our habitual desire to explain others' actions and our use of cognitive heuristics or "mental shortcuts" in arriving at these explanations (refer to Chapter 4). We are especially likely to seek an explanation for behavior when it runs counter to the standard social norms (for example, cutting in front of someone in a line). We have also learned through experience that there are exceptions to these social norms; and when people ask to be granted an exception, it is expected that they will provide a reason why the exception should be granted. Because we believe that others are as concerned about acting appropriately as we are, we tend to assume that when someone gives us a reason for doing something, it must be worthy of an exception. As a result, we may often mindlessly grant a request accompanied by a reason because we assume the requester would not ask if the request was illegitimate. When my daughter Lillian was two years old, she had already learned the importance of giving reasons when seeking compliance from her parents. In asking to go outside she would say, "Can I go outside and play? Because I have to go outside and play." Based on Langer's findings, when it comes to securing compliance, Lillian had already developed sufficient social skills to do quite nicely in the adult world.

> ❝A fair request should be followed by the deed in silence.❞
> ------------
> Dante Alighieri, Italian poet, 1265–1321

In summarizing this analysis of factors that affect compliance, additional insight is provided by the *elaboration likelihood model* of persuasion discussed in Chapter 5 (pp. 185–191). As you recall, according to this model, persuasion can occur through either the thoughtful mode of central processing or the lazy mode of peripheral processing (Petty & Cacciopo, 1986; Petty et al., 1995). Regarding compliance, the research discussed here suggests that positive moods, making the reciprocity norm salient, or providing reasons for why one should grant a request are all likely to foster compliance by inducing lazy peripheral processing of the requester's message. In other words, whenever any of these factors are present, the resulting compliance is less likely to be based on thoughtful consideration of the request.

TWO-STEP STRATEGIES ARE EFFECTIVE COMPLIANCE TRAPS.

Earlier, we discussed how "creditors" secure compliance by keeping tabs on others' debts to them. Professional creditors, such as insurance agents, car dealers, or door-to-door salespersons, rely on more than just indebtedness to secure compliance to their sales requests. In making sales, they realize that it often takes more than a single plea to win over a potential customer. Social psychologists have studied how two requests, employed in different ways, can result in some very effective compliance techniques. The first request sets the trap, while the second request captures the prey.

Foot-in-the-Door

foot-in-the-door technique
. . . .
A two-step compliance technique in which the influencer secures compliance to a small request, and then later follows this with a larger, less desirable request

In Chapter 5, we saw that many people feel pressure to remain consistent in their beliefs. Salespersons, recognizing this need for consistency, often employ a two-step compliance strategy known as the **foot-in-the-door technique**. In this strategy, the person secures compliance with a small request and then follows it up later with a larger, less desirable request. For example, imagine that a young woman knocks on your door and tells you she is gathering signatures on a petition supporting environmental protection. Would you be willing to sign? This question represents the first small request. Being proenvironment, you readily agree. After signing, the woman says she is also seeking money for her organization to better fight for the environment, and would you be willing to make a contribution? This is the second, larger request. Chances are, if you signed the petition you will also contribute some money. Joseph Schwarzwald and his coworkers (1983) found that, using a very similar scenario, they were able to produce a 75 percent increase in donations over a comparison request strategy involving no prior petition signing. Similar results have also been obtained in fund-raising efforts on the Internet (Gueguen & Jacob, 2001).

Meta-analyses of studies using the foot-in-the-door technique indicate that it is fairly reliable in securing compliance (Beaman et al., 1983; Cialdini & Trost, 1998). However, if people reject the small request, they are even less likely to comply with the larger request than those who were not approached with the small request (Snyder & Cunningham, 1975). Can you guess why? It appears that the foot-in-the-door effect causes a change in self-perception (Burger & Caldwell, 2003; Fointiat, 2006). In not granting the small first request, people may decide that they are not the type of person who grants those kinds of requests. Therefore, because of this new self-image, they are more likely to later reject the larger request. The same self-perception process operates for those who do grant the small request. They perceive themselves as cooperative, and therefore, later comply to the second, larger request in order to be consistent with their cooperative self-image. For this technique to work, the initial request must be large enough to cause people to think about the implications of their behavior, and they must believe they are freely complying (Gorassini & Olson, 1995).

Additional cross-cultural studies indicate that people from individualist cultures are more susceptible to the foot-in-the-door technique than people from collectivist cultures (Petrova et al., 2007). Why? As discussed in Chapter 5 individualists have a higher need to behave consistently than collectivists, and this results in higher compliance to the second larger request in this strategy.

Door-in-the-Face

A second compliance technique that also uses multiple requests is in some sense the reverse of the foot-in-the-door strategy. In the **door-in-the-face technique**, the person seeking compliance starts by asking for a very large favor—one the recipient is almost certain to reject. When the rejection occurs, the request is changed to a much less costly request. Securing this second request was the objective of the influencer from the start. The first rejection is the door in the face, and it is presumed that the second request stands a better chance of being accepted if it is preceded by this rejection (Cialdini & Trost, 1998). Phone solicitors for charities and other nonprofit organizations typically employ this technique by first asking people for a large donation and then reducing their request when the large request is refused. Likewise, teenagers have been known to ask their parents whether they could go on an unsupervised weekend trip with their friends (a fabrication), and then respond to the inevitable refusal by asking whether they could at least join their friends at a local party (their actual goal).

A study by Robert Cialdini and his colleagues (1975) illustrates the effectiveness of this compliance strategy. College students were approached by teams of confederates who asked them to volunteer to spend two hours a week over the next year as "big brothers" or "big sisters" to juveniles in need of older role models. Not surprisingly, no one agreed to this request, which is exactly what Cialdini expected. Then the confederates followed this rejection with a second request: Would the students be willing to spend two hours just once taking the same kids to the zoo? Fifty percent agreed to this request. In a control condition, when this smaller request had been presented without being preceded by the large request, less than 17 percent of the students agreed to comply.

For the door-in-the-face effect to occur, three conditions must be met. First, the initial request must be very large so that when people refuse they make no negative inferences about themselves (for example, "I'm not a very generous person"). Second, the interval between the first and second requests must be relatively short so that the feeling

door-in-the-face technique
....
A two-step compliance technique in which, after having a large request refused, the influencer counteroffers with a much smaller request

❝*He that does not ask will never get a bargain.*❞
— — — — — — — — — —
French proverb

of obligation is still salient. In contrast, a longer interval (weeks or even months) between the two requests can still be effective for the foot-in-the-door technique. Finally, the third condition is that the same person who made the first large request must make the subsequent smaller request. People perceive this second request as a concession by the requester that the first request was too large. Once this perceived concession occurs, due to the reciprocity norm, people feel pressure to reciprocate with a concession of their own—agree to the second request. Of the two sequential compliance techniques discussed thus far, the "face" approach has been shown to be more effective than the "foot" technique (Harari et al., 1980; Rodafinos et al., 2005).

The door-in-the-face strategy is often used by both parties in negotiating contracts for such things as houses, cars, and salaries. Both parties begin with an economic position that is extremely favorable to themselves but very unfavorable to the other side. Following the initial proposal rejections, one or both of them might make concessions that are actually closer to what they really hope to obtain from the other. Often, those who make less reciprocal concessions and who are also less concerned with appearing unreasonable are the ones who secure the best deals (Pendleton & Batson, 1979).

That's Not All

that's-not-all technique
· · · · · · · · · · · · · · ·
A two-step compliance technique in which the influencer makes a large request, then immediately offers a discount or bonus before the initial request is refused

Closely related to the door-in-the-face technique is the **that's-not-all technique**, which involves the influencer making a large request, but then immediately offering a discount or bonus that makes the request more reasonable. Unlike the door-in-the-face technique, however, the person is not given the opportunity to reject the large request before it is reduced or "sweetened." The lowered price tags on store merchandise and the ads for "Buy One, Get One Free" deals are examples of this two-step compliance strategy.

Jerry Burger (1986) demonstrated the effectiveness of this tactic when he conducted a bake sale at Santa Clara University. On the table where the sale was taking place were a number of cupcakes with no indicated price. In one condition, when potential buyers asked how much one cupcake cost, they were given a high price. Then, before they could respond, they were also told that this price included a "bonus" bag of cookies. In a control condition, potential buyers were immediately shown the bag of cookies and told that they were included in the total price. Results indicated that 73 percent of those who experienced the that's-not-all tactic bought the sweets, versus only 40 percent of those who were offered everything up front.

In a second cupcake study, instead of the request being "sweetened" by a bonus, it was reduced in size. In the that's-not-all condition, people were told that the cupcakes

How could you use the "That's Not All" technique to increase your cupcake sales?

cost $1.25 but that they would be sold to the buyer at $1.00, because the booth would be closing soon. In the control condition, people were merely told that the cupcakes cost $1.00. As shown in Figure 7.6, the that's-not-all strategy was again more effective in selling cupcakes; 55 percent of those in this condition bought cupcakes, versus only 20 percent in the control condition.

Burger was also interested in determining whether the that's-not-all effect occurred only because the offered items were now a bargain, and so he created a third condition. In this *bargain* condition, the seller stated to the potential buyer that the cupcakes were now priced at $1.00, although formerly they were $1.25. The bargain condition resulted in only a 25 percent purchase rate (see Figure 7.6). This finding suggests that the that's-not-all strategy is not just effective because it offers a bargain to the influence target, but there also appears to be a psychological potency created by the influencer personally sweetening the deal that lowers people's resistance to the request.

How exactly does the that's-not-all technique lower resistance? One possibility is that when the salesperson's request is reduced or sweetened, the customer may perceive this as a concession that the original request was unreasonable. Following the norm of reciprocity, the customer may now feel an increased obligation to reciprocate this act by agreeing to the better price (as in the door-in-the-face effect). Another possible way in which the that's-not-all technique may lower resistance is by altering the customer's "anchor point" against which the purchase decision is made (see Chapter 4 discussion of the *anchoring and adjustment heuristic*, p. 118). That is, if customers are contemplating the purchase of a product for which they themselves don't have a fixed price in mind (such

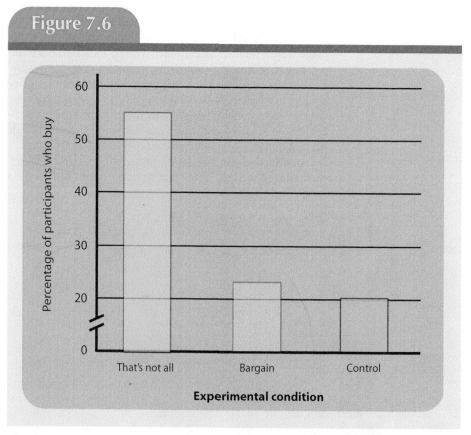

Figure 7.6

That's Not All!

The effectiveness of the "that's-not-all" compliance technique was demonstrated in a campus bake sale. By far, the highest percentage of potential customers purchased cupcakes when the deal was "sweetened" by first stating one price and then lowering it before the customer could respond. When customers were told that the price had already been lowered (bargain) or when they were merely given the low price right away (control), purchases were much less likely.

as cupcakes at a bake sale), the salesperson's costly first request sets the price standard, or anchor. When the second cheaper price immediately follows the costly price, it alters the anchor point and creates the impression that the product is a bargain.

Although the that's-not-all technique is effective, success appears to depend on targets responding rather mindlessly to the request (Pollock et al., 1998). For example, one recent study found that compliance occurs only when the initial request is within reason (Burger, 1999). If you first ask people to buy cupcakes for the extremely high price of $3.00 apiece, lowering your price to $1.00 is unlikely to induce compliance because the initial request appears ridiculous, and it places potential customers on guard. Now, instead of engaging in the type of "lazy" thinking discussed in Chapter 4 (*heuristics*) and Chapter 5 (*peripheral route processing*), the target is motivated to more critically analyze the offer. Under this greater scrutiny, compliance decreases.

Low-Balling

A few years ago I went shopping for a new car to replace my badly rusted "old reliable." After test-driving one car, I made an offer that included my car as a trade-in for $700. The salesperson said we had a deal; he just had to get the manager's OK. After ten minutes, however, the salesperson returned looking forlorn, saying the manager would take my trade-in for only $300. Then with a big smile he declared, "And that means you can have your new car for only $400 more!"

low-ball technique
....
A two-step compliance strategy in which the influencer secures agreement with a request by understating its true cost

I had been "low-balled." The **low-ball technique** is a strategy in which an influencer secures agreement with a request by understating its true cost. When the size of the request is increased by revealing the hidden costs, most people often stick to their initial commitment and proceed with the new arrangement, even though they are disappointed and even angry that the deal has been made less desirable, (Gueguen et al., 2002). Fortunately, I was aware of the research on low-balling and recognized the scam.

In one low-balling study, psychology students were phoned and asked to participate in an experiment (Cialdini et al., 1978). Some students were told before answering the request that the experiment would begin at the undesirable time of 7 A.M. Other students were first asked if they would agree to participate, and only after they had agreed were they told that the experiment began at such an early hour (the low ball). As testament to the power of low-balling, more than half of the students in the low-ball condition agreed to participate, while fewer than one-third of the control condition students did so. Furthermore, more than half of the low-balled students actually kept their 7 a.m. appointment, as opposed to less than one-quarter of the control condition students.

Why does the low-ball procedure work? One important factor is the psychology of commitment. Once people make a decision, they tend to justify it to themselves by thinking of its positive aspects. As they become increasingly committed to their course of action, they grow more resistant to changing their minds. This is why car dealers will let you, the prospective buyer, sit in the showroom for a while before telling you that they require more money. During that time, they count on you fantasizing about "your new car" so that later you will pay the extra money to drive it off the lot. Yet, if you spend that time reviewing what you have learned here, you stand a better chance of leaving the showroom with a deal to your liking. In this case, knowledge truly is power—social influence power.

SECTION SUMMARY

- Factors that foster compliance:

  positive moods

  reciprocity norm

  providing reasons

- Compliance techniques that utilize multiple requests:

  foot-in-the-door

  door-in-the-face

  that's-not-all

  low-balling

OBEDIENCE

"*Obedience to the law is demanded as a right, not asked as a favor.***"**

▬ ▬ ▬ ▬ ▬ ▬ ▬

Theodore Roosevelt, U.S. president, 1858–1919

As you can see from our overview of both conformity processes and compliance strategies, many social influence pressures are relatively hidden and subtly employed. In this respect, obedience differs from these other types of influence because it is overt and easily recognized as an exercise of power.

When authority figures order people to obey their commands, you might expect that people's need for personal control would trigger disobedience. If the order involved possibly causing serious health risks to others, you might predict that wide-scale disobedience would occur. Would it? What would you do under such circumstances? Let's explore the most discussed social psychological study ever conducted that examined this very issue (Blass, 2000).

MILGRAM'S RESEARCH SUGGESTS THAT DESTRUCTIVE OBEDIENCE IS FAIRLY COMMON.

Imagine that you have volunteered to participate in an experiment on learning. Upon arriving at the laboratory, you find that a fifty-year-old man is also taking part in the study. The experimenter explains that the study will investigate the effects of punishment on the learning of word pairs. The punishment will be electrical shock. One of you will be the "teacher," and the other will be the "learner." A drawing of names determines that you will be the teacher. When the learner discovers that he will be receiving shocks, he tells the experimenter that he has a mild heart condition ("Nothing serious, but since electricity is being used I thought I should tell you"). The experimenter replies that while the shocks may be painful, they will not cause permanent tissue damage. The learner is then taken to an adjacent room where he is strapped into a chair and electrodes are attached to his arms. As this is being done, the experimenter explains that your task is to teach the learner a list of word pairs, to then test him on the list, and to administer punishment whenever he makes a mistake. In front of you is a shock generator, which has a row of thirty switches ranging from 15 to 450 volts. You are instructed to start at the lowest intensity level and to increase the shock by one switch (15 volts) for each subsequent learner error. To give you some idea of what the shock feels like, the experimenter gives you a 45-volt shock—and it hurts. You are a bit nervous now, but you do not say anything.

Once the study begins, the learner makes many mistakes, and you respond by flipping the shock switches. Starting at 75 volts, you hear through the intercom system the learner grunting and moaning in pain whenever you deliver the shocks. At 150 volts he demands to be released, shouting, "Experimenter! That's all! Get me out of here. My heart's starting to bother me now. I refuse to go on!" Now your nervousness becomes nail-biting anxiety. At 180 volts he shouts that he can no longer stand the pain. At 300 volts he says that he absolutely refuses to provide any more answers. Responding to this attempt by the learner to halt the study, the experimenter instructs you to treat the absence of a response as equivalent to an error and to deliver the appropriate level of shock. Even though the learner no longer gives answers, he continues to scream in agony whenever your finger flips the shock generator switch. When you surpass the 330-volt switch, the learner not only does not give any answers, he falls silent, not to be heard from again. As you continue to increase the shock intensity, the labels under the switches now read, "Danger—Severe Shock" and you realize you are getting closer to the last switch, the 450-volt switch, which is simply labeled "XXX." You desperately want to stop, but when you hesitate, the experimenter first tells you, "Please continue," then "The experiment requires that you continue," then "It is absolutely essential that you go on," and finally, "You have no other choice, you must go on!"

"*... far more, and far more hideous, crimes have been committed in the name of obedience than have ever been committed in the name of rebellion.***"**

▬ ▬ ▬ ▬ ▬ ▬ ▬

C. P. Snow, English novelist, 1905–1980

What would you do? Would you disobey the experimenter's commands? When would you stop obeying? Is it possible that you would continue to deliver all the shocks, including the dangerous 450 volts, despite the learner's protests? How many of your friends do you think would obey the experimenter's orders if they were the teachers?

I'm guessing that your prediction is that you and your friends would disobey the experimenter's authority and refuse to continue the learning experiment well before the 450-volt limit. If this is your prediction, you are in good company, for widespread

(Top) Stanley Milgram and the "shock generator," which he used in his obedience experiments. (Bottom) In this replication of the obedience experiment, the teacher (participant) had to force the learner's (confederate's) hand onto a shock plate. Less than one-third obeyed the experimenter under these conditions.

"Oh God, let's stop it."
A reluctant but obedient participant in the Milgram experiments, Milgram, 1963, p. 377

❝In schools all over the world, little boys learn that their country is the greatest in the world, and the highest honor that could befall them would be to defend it heroically someday. The fact that empathy has traditionally been conditioned out of boys facilitates their obedience to leaders who order them to kill strangers.**❞**

Myriam Miedzian, U.S. author, 1991

disobedience is exactly what was predicted by college students, middle-class adults, and psychiatrists who were presented with this hypothetical scenario (Milgram, 1963). People in all three groups guessed that they would disobey by about 135 volts, and none thought they would go beyond 300 volts. The psychiatrists, when asked about other people's level of obedience, predicted that less than one-tenth of 1 percent of participants—one person out of one thousand—would obey the experimenter completely.

To determine the actual level of obedience, Milgram conducted this study at Yale University, using forty adult males who ranged in age from twenty to fifty years and who came from all walks of life. The drawing was rigged so that the participant always became the teacher. The learner was a confederate and received no actual shocks. Even his screams of protest and pain were prerecorded so that all participants heard exactly the same thing. To Milgram's surprise, 65 percent of the participants (twenty-six out of forty) obeyed the experimenter completely, despite these convincing cries of agony from the learner. In fact, all participants who reached 450 volts obeyed the experimenter's command to continue with the procedure using the 450-volt switch until the experiment was halted a short time later. Those who disobeyed often did so at the 150-volt level, when the learner demanded his release, claiming that his heart was bothering him.

The simplest interpretation of the high obedience levels in this study is that Milgram inadvertently recruited closet sadists who were more than willing to inflict pain on the hapless learner. However soothing this explanation would be to our collective psyches, it does not stand up to the available evidence (Darley, 1995). Milgram's participants were not suffering from any personality disorders that would cause them to enjoy their destructive obedience. In fact, their actions caused them a great deal of stress (Elms, 1995; Elms & Milgram, 1966). Participants were observed sweating, trembling, stuttering, biting their lips, and groaning as they struggled through the experimental procedure.

Some sense of their state of mind can be gleaned from remarks made by one of the fully obedient individuals in Milgram's fifth study who began his participation calmly but became increasingly tense as the learner protested the shocks being delivered:

150 volts delivered: "You want me to keep going?"

165 volts delivered: "That guy is hollering in there. There's a lot of them here. He's liable to have heart condition. You want me to go?"

180 volts delivered: "He can't stand it! I'm not going to kill that man in there! You hear him hollering? He's hollering. He can't stand it. What if something happens to him? ... I'm not going to get that man sick in there. He's hollering in there. You know what I mean? I mean I refuse to take the responsibility. He's getting hurt in there. He's in there hollering. Too many left here. Geez, if he gets them wrong. There's too many of them left. I mean who is going to take responsibility if anything happens to that gentleman?"

[The experimenter accepts responsibility]: "All right."

195 volts delivered: "You see he's hollering. Hear that. Gee, I don't know."

[The experimenter says, "The experiment requires that you go on"]: "I know it does, sir, but I mean—ugh—he don't know what he's in for. He's up to 195 volts."

210 volts delivered.

225 volts delivered.

240 volts delivered: "Aw no. You mean I've got to keep going up with the scale? No sir. I'm not going to kill that man! I'm not going to give him 450 volts!"

[The experimenter says, "The experiment requires that you go on."]: "I know it does, but that man is hollering there, sir ...."

Because the findings were so unexpected, Milgram carried out a number of variations of his experiment to better understand the conditions under which obedience and disobedience would be most likely. When college students and women served as participants, the same level of destructive obedience was found (Milgram, 1974). Different researchers also obtained similar results in several other countries, suggesting that these high levels of obedience were not solely an American phenomenon. Australia had a 68 percent obedience level (Kilham & Mann, 1974), Jordan was at 63 percent (Shanab & Yahya, 1977), and Germany was the highest at 85 percent (Mantell, 1971).

Some critics initially suggested that the high obedience was due to the prestige of Yale University and participants' presumed belief that no one at Yale would allow harm to come to anyone in the study (Baumrind, 1964; Orne, 1962). To test this possibility, Milgram (1965) moved the experimental site to a run-down office building in Bridgeport, Connecticut, with no noticeable affiliations with Yale. Although obedience decreased slightly, the difference was not significant—48 percent of the participants delivered the maximum shock level. Switching locations from a prestigious to a nonprestigious institution also did not significantly reduce obedience; however, when the experimenter was replaced with an ordinary person (actually a confederate), obedience dropped to 20 percent. These findings suggest that the social role of "scientist" or "researcher" has sufficient prestige and authority to secure obedience, regardless of the social context (see Blass, 1996).

Although an authority figure is much more likely to be obeyed than a nonauthority, situational factors strengthen or weaken this influence. In a follow-up study, Milgram varied the proximity of the experimenter to the teacher. In one condition, the experimenter sat a few feet from the teacher as he delivered the electrical shocks to the learner. In a second condition, after giving initial instructions, the experimenter left the room and gave his orders by phone. In a third condition, the teacher received his instructions

" ... Obedience, bane of all genius, virtue, freedom, truth, makes slaves of men, and, of the human frame, a mechanized automaton."

Percy Bysshe Shelley, English poet, 1792–1822

"The doctrine of blind obedience and unqualified submission to any human power, whether civil or ecclesiastical, is the doctrine of despotism."

Angelina Grimke, U.S. abolitionist and feminist, 1805–1879

on a tape recorder and never actually met the experimenter. Findings from these three conditions indicated that obedience decreased as the distance to the experimenter increased. In fact, when the experimenter was absent, several participants administered shocks of a lower voltage than the experimenter called for.

In another series of experiments, the proximity of the learner to the teacher was varied (Milgram, 1974). In one condition, the learner and teacher were located in separate rooms without access to intercom systems, and thus, the teacher could not hear the learner's cries of protest and pain. The teacher's only knowledge of the victim's reaction was that he pounded on the adjoining wall at 300 volts and subsequently stopped responding to the word pairs. In another condition, the learner was seated in the same room only a few feet from the teacher. In a third condition, the learner sat right next to the teacher, resting his hand on a metal plate in order to receive the shock. At 350 volts, the learner refused to put his hand on the plate to receive the shock, and the experimenter then ordered the teacher to force the learner's hand onto the shock plate. In all of these studies, results indicated that the closer the teacher was to the learner, the lower the level of obedience.

In addition to testing for proximity and site effects, Milgram also investigated how group pressure might influence obedience. In one study, three teachers (two of them confederates) split up the duties previously assigned to one. The naive participant was always assigned the role of actually delivering the electrical shock, while the confederate-teachers read the word pairs and told the learner if his answers were correct. In one condition, the confederate-teachers simply followed the experimenter's commands and did not express any sympathy for the learner. In another condition, the confederates were openly rebellious—one refused to continue after 150 volts and the other quit at the 210-volt level. The first condition only slightly increased obedience (72 percent) above the original study's level, but the second condition resulted in complete obedience in only 10 percent of the participants.

The likely explanation for this sharp drop in obedience is that the open defiance of the confederates broke the social consensus of the situation and reduced the strength of the experimenter's social power. Did the participants in this study recognize the liberating effect that the rebellious confederate-teachers had on their own willingness to disobey the orders of the authority figure? No. Three-fourths of the participants who disobeyed believed that they would have stopped even without the other teachers' examples. Yet the previous studies strongly argue against this belief, suggesting that people seriously underestimate the impact that others have on their own behavior. Figure 7.7 summarizes the findings of some of these studies and identifies factors that foster and inhibit obedience.

RECENT STUDIES PROVIDE FURTHER INSIGHTS INTO MILGRAM'S ORIGINAL FINDINGS.

Four decades after Milgram's research, two separate investigations have reanalyzed his data, revealing additional insights. First, François Rochot and his coworkers (2000) analyzed the audio recordings of one of Milgram's obedience studies to better understand how participants behaved over the course of the experiment. Seeking similar answers, Dominic Packer (2008) recently conducted a meta-analysis of data from eight of Milgram's studies involving 320 participants.

Both investigations found that a crucial factor in resisting the destructive commands of authority figures is an early and firm statement of opposition to what is transpiring. As you recall, all participants were initially cooperative toward the experimenter, but this changed at the 150-volt level as the learner began complaining and made his first demand for release. This was the point of no return for many participants regarding obedience (Gilbert, 1989). Rochot's analysis of the audio recordings revealed that those who firmly verbally opposed the experimenter by 150 volts all ended up defying his authority by disobeying. In contrast, if participants began their verbal challenges after 150 volts, only about half of them ever disobeyed.

Packer's (2008) meta-analysis similarly found that participants who did not disobey when the learner first demanded his release at the 150 volt level were generally

"Obedience is the mother of success, and the wife of security."

Aeschylus, Greek dramatist, 525–456 BC

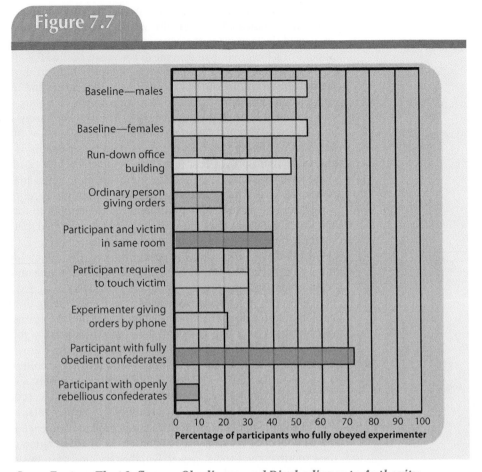

Figure 7.7

Some Factors That Influence Obedience and Disobedience to Authority

To determine what factors increase or decrease obedience beyond the baseline 65 percent level, Milgram varied the location of the experiment, the participant's proximity to the victim and the experimenter, and the presence of obedient or disobedient confederates. As you can see, all of these factors influenced obedience levels.

nonresponsive to his escalating expressions of pain as the session proceeded. As noted by Packer, the 150 volt level marked the first point in the study where participants realized that there was a conflict between the experimenter's orders and the desires of the learner. The experimenter's quick dismissal of the learner's demand for release signaled to participants that in the experimenter's mind the learner's pain and his freedom of choice were irrelevant issues in this setting. For the obedient participants, after accepting the experimenter's definition of the situation at the 150-volt level, the learner's apparent agony no longer exerted much influence over their willingness to obey the experimenter's commands.

What about the disobedient participants? The crucial factor in them disobeying was an early and firm questioning of the experimenter's authority to disregard the rights of the learner. These participants' verbal questioning signaled their refusal to passively accept the experimenter's definition of reality in this emotionally charged and conflicted situation.

When people learn about Milgram's findings, they often speculate whether similar results would be obtained today. Of course, ethical concerns prevent a definitive answer to this question, but Jerry Burger (2009) recently conducted a partial replication of the Milgram procedure based on the fact that the 150-volt level was largely a point of no return in the original studies. Nearly four out of five participants who obeyed the experimenter's instructions at the 150-point level continued to obey his commands all the way to 450 volts. Burger reasoned that knowing how Milgram's participants responded up to and including the 150-volt level allows us to reasonably estimate what they would do if allowed to complete the entire study. Stopping the study immediately after participants decide what to do at the 150-volt level also avoids exposing them to the extreme stress often experienced in the original studies.

In partially replicating Milgram's most well-known study (Experiment 5), Burger found that seventy percent of his forty participants obeyed up to and at the 150-volt level, and were prepared to read the next item of the test when the experimenter stopped the study. This obedience rate was slightly lower than the percentage that continued beyond this point in Milgram's study (82.5 percent), but the difference was not statistically significant. There were also no gender, age, or ethnicity differences in willingness to obey. The Milgram obedience scenario was also repeated as part of both a 2009 British and a 2010 French television documentary with very similar results. While Burger's partial replication and the findings from these two documentary-based studies are not definitive tests of the durability of Milgram's findings, a reasonable conclusion to draw from their results is that there is little to no evidence that contemporary authority figures' ability to secure obedience has diminished in the past fifty years (Dambrun & Valentine, 2010; Martin & Bull, 2010).

In the past few years, Milgram's findings have been regularly discussed by journalists and other social commentators when trying to make sense of the mistreatment of prisoners of war and suspected terrorists by American military personnel in Iraq, Afghanistan, and Cuba (Dutton & Tetreault, 2009). While discussing the meaning of his obedience experiments, Milgram made the following remarks that are as relevant today as they were in his time:

> The behavior revealed in the experiments reported here is normal human behavior but revealed under conditions that show with particular clarity the danger to human survival inherent in our make-up. And what is it we have seen? Not aggression, for there is no anger, vindictiveness, or hatred in those who shocked the victim. Men do become angry; they do act hatefully and explode in rage against others. But not here. Something far more dangerous is revealed: the capacity for man to abandon his humanity, indeed, the inevitability that he does so, as he merges his unique personality into larger institutional structures. This is a fatal flaw nature has designed into us, and which in the long run gives our species only a modest chance of survival. (1974, p. 188)

OBSERVING OTHERS DEFY AUTHORITY GREATLY REDUCES OBEDIENCE.

Milgram's commentary on his own obedience research paints a bleak picture of humankind's ability to resist destructive authoritarian pressure. Yet is the abandonment of our humanity as inevitable as he suggests? Perhaps the depth of Milgram's pessimism is partly due to the special circumstances created in his research design. In most of the obedience studies discussed thus far, a lone individual engages in destructive behavior after being placed in a situation in which he or she receives orders from an authority figure. What would happen if antisocial orders are delivered not to a lone individual but, rather, to an entire group of people? Would this collective be as malleable as the lone individual?

William Gamson and his colleagues (1982) explored this question when they recruited groups of people to participate in a purported discussion of community standards. Participants, scheduled in groups of nine, arrived at a local motel for the discussion and were greeted by the "coordinator." This coordinator told them that the proceedings would be videotaped for a large oil company that was being sued by a former manager of one of its local gas stations. This former employee was fired after the company learned he was living with a woman to whom he was not married. The company justified its actions by stating that its representatives must be beyond moral reproach. Despite this explanation by the coordinator, participants soon learned some additional information that cast a different light on the firing—the manager was fired after appearing on local TV, where he spoke out against higher gas prices.

Shortly after discussion began about whether the manager's lifestyle was morally offensive to those in the community, the coordinator interrupted and told three group members to argue on camera as if they were offended by the manager's lifestyle. A short time later, he again interrupted and told three more members to also act offended. Soon

> *"I hold it that a little rebellion now and then, is a good thing, and as necessary in the political world as storms in the physical. ... It is a medicine for the sound health of government."*
>
> Thomas Jefferson, U.S. president, 1743–1826

"*Disobedience when it is not criminally—but morally, religiously, or politically—motivated is always a collective act, and it is justified by the values of the collectivity and the mutual engagements of its members.***"**

Social historian Michael Walzer, 1970

"*One who breaks an unjust law that conscience tells him is unjust, and who willingly accepts the penalty of imprisonment in order to arouse the consciousness of the community over its injustice, is in reality expressing the highest respect for the law.***"**

Martin Luther King, Jr., U.S. civil rights leader, 1929–1968

the coordinator had instructed all members to act offended on camera concerning the manager's lifestyle and to state that they would not do business at his gas station. Then he told them there was an affidavit to be signed and notarized that gave the oil company the right to introduce the videotapes as evidence in court, editing them as they saw fit.

As originally designed, some discussion groups were to include a confederate member who would either take a more or less active role in mobilizing rebellion against the oil company's actions. However, as the malicious intent of the videotaped discussion began to dawn on the actual group participants, they began to rebel on their own. One participant, when told to act offended before the videocamera, expressed his defiance by adopting a mocking, twangy accent and stating, "Next to ma waaf, ma car is my favritt thing, an ah ain't sending neither of 'em tuh that gas stoishen." Some groups became so outraged at the company's attempts to use them to discredit the former employee that they threatened to forcibly confiscate the videotapes and expose the company to the local news media. Confronted by one outraged group after another, the researchers were forced to terminate the experiment due to fears that it was causing too much stress on the participants.

Why did this experiment result in such open disobedience when Milgram's research produced such widespread obedience? In both studies there were agents of authority, the experimenter and the coordinator. In both studies the original intention of participants was to obey the instructions of these authorities. In both studies the authorities over-stepped the proper moral boundaries and began to demand unjust actions by the participants. The possibility that people generally became less prone to obedience over the twenty years separating these studies is not supported by an analysis of other obedience studies conducted during this time period (Blass, 1999). Instead the basic difference between these studies is that Milgram's participants were alone, whereas Gamson's were in groups. Because eight or nine of Gamson's group members were naive participants, the possibility of collective action always existed. Milgram's design, on the other hand, has never been tried with more than one naive participant in the teacher role, and so the possibility of collective action here has never been studied.

Although the Milgram design never tested more than one participant at a time, in one of his experiments he did use two confederates who posed as coteachers along with the actual participant. As discussed previously (see p. 294), when the participant observed others openly defying the destructive commands of the authority figure, he became much more willing to disobey as well. In a very real psychological sense, the rebellious confederates served as models for the participant's own disobedience. Similar findings were also obtained in Asch's conformity studies; social support allowed others to more easily express their own opinions.

SECTION SUMMARY

- Obedience research indicates that almost two-thirds of Milgram's participants obeyed the destructive commands of an authority figure and social support helps people follow their own beliefs when confronted by powerful others.

- A recent partial replication of Milgram's original study finds no evidence that obedience levels have diminished in the past forty years.

TOWARD A UNIFIED UNDERSTANDING OF SOCIAL INFLUENCE

Although different factors are involved in the various forms of social influence discussed in this chapter, the task of social scientists is to discover common principles operating in the exercise of social power. In this section, we examine one theory that attempts to predict when influence attempts are most likely to succeed.

SOCIAL IMPACT THEORY EXPLAINS INFLUENCE STRENGTH.

social impact theory
· ·
The theory that the amount of social influence others have depends on their number, strength, and immediacy to those they are trying to influence

As developed by Bibb Latané (1981), **social impact theory** states that the amount of influence others have in a given situation (their social impact) is a function of three factors: their *number, strength,* and *immediacy.* This social impact operates like physical impact. For example, the amount of light falling on a surface depends not only on how many lights are turned on but also on the strength or power of the bulbs and how close they are to the surface. Similarly, as illustrated in Figure 7.8, Box A, a person will be more influenced by others when there are more of them, when they are stronger sources of influence, and when they are physically closer (Pederson et al., 2008).

Although social impact theory predicts that people become more influential as their numbers increase, what about the "leveling off " effect found in the Asch (1956) conformity research? In that study, adding more confederates beyond three or four had little impact on conformity. Latané contends that this is due to another principle of social impact theory, which states that as the number of influencing persons increases, their individual impact decreases. Returning to the lightbulb analogy, when you turn on a second light in a room that previously had only one bulb illuminating it, the increased impact that the second light has on your sight is quite perceptible. Yet the impact of adding a fifteenth bulb to a room illuminated by fourteen lights is hardly seen at all. Latané claims that the same is true with individuals and their social impact on others: the second person has less impact than the first, and the nth person has less effect than the $(n-1)$th.

Figure 7.8

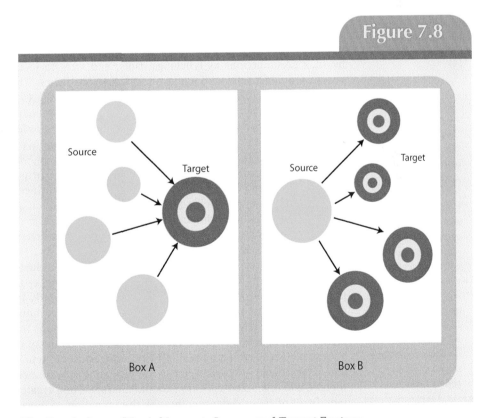

Box A

Box B

The Psychology of Social Impact: Source and Target Factors

According to social impact theory, the impact of other people on the target person depends on (a) the number of people present (number of source circles), the strength or importance of these people (size of the source circles), and their immediacy to the target person (nearness of the source circles to the target). Social impact increases as source factors increase. In addition, the total impact of other people on target persons depends on (b) the number of target persons (number of target circles), the strength of these targets (size of target circles), and their immediacy (nearness to one another). Social impact decreases as target factors increase.

Latané states that the strength of would-be influencers depends on their status, expertise, and power. For example, in most circumstances, a police officer will have greater social impact than a mail carrier. Similarly, in the Milgram studies, the experimenter was more successful in securing obedience than an ordinary person. Finally, the immediacy of others is determined by their closeness to the individual in time or space. In other words, others will have greater social impact on you if they are actually present than if they are watching you on a monitor in another location or watching a videotape of your actions at a later date (Latané et al., 1995). In the obedience studies, people were more likely to obey the experimenter when he was physically present rather than when he gave orders over the phone.

Social impact theory can explain the social influence exerted in the Asch and Milgram studies, but how would it explain the *disobedience* in Gamson's oil company research? As you can see in Figure 7.8, Box B, social impact theory also predicts that people are more likely to *resist* others' influence attempts when the social impact is dispersed among many strong and closely situated targets. In the oil company study, the social impact of the authority figure was divided among nine participants, not one, making disobedience easier. Similar disobedience occurred in the Milgram study when participants were in the presence of confederates who actively resisted the authority's orders. These findings indicate that when a group of individuals is confronted with the dictates of an immoral authority, there is always the possibility that the group will collectively redefine social reality and draw individual strength and conviction from the assembled others. With this group-originated conviction, they can more easily defy the social power of the authority. This same strength is simply not available to the lone individual, and therefore it is not surprising that obedience is more common here.

Having made the argument that groups can resist destructive obedience more effectively than the individual, I must also note that groups can often trigger destruction as well. You need only consider for a moment the death and suffering that has been caused by such group actions as lynchings, riots, and wars to recognize that groups do not always provide a safeguard against destructive obedience. The power of groups can be used for either constructive or destructive purposes (see Chapter 8). However, when prosocial values are made salient within a group setting, individual members can draw strength from those in their midst, enabling them to resist orders they consider immoral.

Over the years, social impact theory has been useful in predicting when other people will exert influence over someone's actions. Latané (2000) has also expanded the theory to explain how ordinary communication between people can create what he calls *dynamic social impact*, in which targets of social influence can, in turn, influence those who are exerting their social power. In a series of studies, he and his coworkers have found that people who are physically closer and/or in regular direct contact with one another become more similar in their attitudes and beliefs than those separated by greater distances and infrequent contact (Huguet et al., 1998; Latané & L'Herrou, 1996). In essence, the social impact that these individuals regularly exert on one another appears to increase their similarity. Latané believes that this tendency for people to create like-minded *social clusters* when they regularly interact helps explain how regional differences may come to exist within a country, how minority viewpoints can survive within a larger culture, and why majority opinions in a culture tend to increase in size over time and reshape the opinions of the majority (Ramirez & Latan, 2001). This same process of reciprocal influence also is useful in understanding how scattered and unorganized protests against the Egyptian government quickly became more focused and organized as demonstrators interacted and created like-minded social clusters. In all of these instances, through the operation of dynamic social impact, people become organized into social clusters where they collectively reinforce one another's similarly held attitudes, values, and worldviews (Latané, 1997; Latané & Bourgeois, 1996). Latané also speculates that with the sharp increase of Internet use by people around the world, physical proximity will be a relatively unimportant factor in determining the strength of web-based social influence attempts.

College students' attitudes toward alcohol and their drinking tendencies are an example of how dynamic social impact can create like-minded social clusters. Campus surveys indicate that students who live in the same dormitory have more similar

" *We must not confuse dissent with disloyalty.* "

———————————

Edward Murrow, news commentator, 1908–1965, commenting on Senator Joseph McCarthy's campaign to fire and/or imprison all governmental employees who ever had any associations with socialist or communist political organizations (March 7, 1954)

" *We must dare to think "unthinkable" thoughts. We must learn to explore all the options and possibilities that confront us in a complex and rapidly changing world. We must learn to welcome and not to fear the voices of dissent. We must dare to think about "unthinkable things" because when things become unthinkable, thinking stops and action becomes mindless.* "

———————————

Senator J. William Fulbright, 1905–1995, speech in the Senate, March 27, 1964

drinking patterns than students who live in different dorms (Bourgeois & Bowen, 2001). The social influence that dorm residents exert on one another in the course of their daily activities creates campus dormitories with distinct "personalities" regarding alcohol consumption. Residents in one building might identify themselves as the "party dorm," while students in another residence hall may have more restrictive attitudes and beliefs concerning excess drinking. Distinct social clusters can develop even on different floors of the same residence hall. One of the most noticeable effects of these distinct campus social clusters is that they tend to foster a misperception of campus drinking norms (Pederson et al., 2008; Wechsler & Kuo, 2000). Further, because excess drinking is more likely to be noticed than moderate drinking, college students tend to overestimate how much alcohol their peers regularly consume, which by itself may encourage excess drinking (Lewis & Neighbors, 2004). The good news is that, upon graduation, these same individuals develop new social clusters in their new work settings and new places of residence, which generally results in them adopting drinking norms more in line with full-time employment and adult role responsibilities (Bartholow et al., 2003b).

SECTION SUMMARY

- *Social impact theory* contends that the amount of influence people have is a function of three factors:

  their number
  their strength
  their immediacy

- Dynamic social impact can create social clusters of individuals who become more similar to each other as they interact.

APPLICATIONS

COULD YOU BE PRESSURED TO FALSELY CONFESS TO A CRIME?

In 1986 following a brutal murder of a woman in Clearwater, Florida, police invited Thomas Sawyer, a neighbor of the victim, to assist them in the investigation. They first flattered Sawyer by asking him to provide his own theory on how the murder occurred, and then used leading questions to shape his responses so that they fit the actual crime. When he was first accused of committing the crime, Sawyer vehemently denied the charge. To support their claim, the police lied to Sawyer about having "a lot of evidence" that implicated him in the murder. After hours of this sort of interrogation, Sawyer began to doubt his innocence, saying, "I honestly believe that I didn't do it. … I don't remember doing it. … You almost got me convinced I did, but. …" Finally, after sixteen hours of interrogation, Sawyer confessed to a crime he did not commit, stating, "I guess all the evidence is in, I guess I must have done it."

Sawyer's nightmare is an excellent example of how unusual influence can sometimes cause *internal compliance* (see p. 262). Internal compliance occurs when police interrogators' influence techniques are so effective that innocent suspects not only confess but also actually come to believe that they are indeed guilty (Johnson & Drucker, 2009). The influence operating here, namely informational, was observed in Sherif's autokinetic studies on group norm formation described earlier in this chapter. In contrast, false confessions can also occur through *external compliance* (see p. 261), where innocent suspects admit to crimes they know they did not commit in order to avoid further aversive interrogation. This form of normative influence was illustrated in Asch's conformity studies. Do you think you could fall prey to either one of these influence processes if you were a suspect in a crime you didn't commit?

In one representative investigation of false confessions, Saul Kassin and Katherine Klechel (1996) tested the following two hypotheses: (1) False evidence can lead people who are in a heightened state of uncertainty to confess to an act they did not commit. (2) These "false confessors" will internalize the confession and create details in memory consistent with this new guilt. In this study, college students who thought they were participating in a reaction time study were randomly assigned to one of four experimental conditions: either involving high or low vulnerability, and either the presence or absence of a false incriminating witness. In each session, two people worked together on a computer "reaction" task. One of these people (a female confederate) read aloud a list of letters while the participant typed them on the computer keyboard. Before the session began, the participant was specifically warned not to press the "ALT" key because doing so would cause the program to crash and data to be lost. However, one minute after beginning work on the task, the computer ceased to function, and a highly agitated experimenter accused the participant of having pressed the forbidden key. In reality, the computer was rigged to stop functioning through no fault of the participant. When first accused, all participants denied responsibility for the computer damage. However, in the *false-witness* condition, the confederate disputed the participant's denial, testifying that she saw the participant press the forbidden key. In the *no-witness* condition, the confederate did not challenge the participant's denial, but simply stated that she did not see the key pressed. The participant's vulnerability was manipulated by varying the pace of the task. In the *high vulnerability* condition the confederate—following the beat of a metronome—read the letters at a frenzied pace of sixty-seven letters per minute, while in the *low vulnerability* condition the pace was set at a leisurely forty-three letters per minute.

The dependent measures involved three forms of social influence. To measure *external compliance*, the experimenter asked participants to sign a handwritten confession stating that they had hit the ALT key and caused the program to crash. To assess *internal compliance*, participants' private descriptions of what happened—told to a second confederate waiting outside the lab—were recorded and later coded for whether they unambiguously internalized guilt for what happened. To measure the *creation of memories*, the experimenter also asked participants to "recall" specific details of how they caused the computer program to crash.

Results indicated no gender differences in susceptibility to influence. Overall, 69 percent of the participants signed the confession, 28 percent exhibited internalization, and 9 percent created memories to support their false beliefs. As expected, participants in the high vulnerability condition were most susceptible to all three forms of social influence following the false accusation. In addition, regardless of the vulnerability condition, participants in the false witness conditions not only were more likely to sign a confession prepared by the experimenter but also were more likely to later admit their guilt to the second confederate. Finally, participants in the low vulnerability/no-witness condition were the least susceptible to these effects, while those in the high vulnerability/witness condition were the most susceptible. Although the false confessions coerced out of participants in this study are much less dramatic than many of the false confessions squeezed out of suspects in criminal cases, they do demonstrate that people can be induced to erroneously confess to crimes, and to believe in their own guilt, following the presentation of false evidence.

In actual criminal cases, suspects generally make false confessions due to external compliance in exchange for penalty reductions. Here, their perceptions of the strength of the evidence against them—which police interrogators may highly exaggerate—significantly determines whether they will confess (Gudjonsson, 2003). Of course, many suspects will not falsely confess to a crime regardless of how strong the evidence appears. What distinguishes them from those who do? Not surprisingly, "resisters" are less susceptible to normative influence in general than are "confessors" (Gudjonsson, 1991).

By far, the most psychologically interesting confession is the one in which innocent defendants—anxious, confused, and desperately trying to make sense out of their current situation—actually come to believe that they committed the crime (Gudjonsson, 2001). As demonstrated in the Kassin and Klechel (1996) study, this internalization of guilt is closely related to the creation of false memories (Ost et al., 2001; Read, 1996). In one interesting study, Elizabeth Loftus and James Coan (1995) successfully implanted false memories of being lost as a child in five research participants ranging in age from 8 to 42. Following the researchers' instructions, trusted family members told these five individuals that, at age five, they had been lost in a shopping mall for an extended time before being rescued by an elderly man. This information had the effect of convincing all participants that they indeed had been lost! Such studies demonstrate that false memories can be implanted into the minds of both children and adults (Ceci & Bruck, 1993; Kassin, 1997). In fact, research indicates that simply repeating imaginary events to people causes them to become more confident that they actually experienced these events (Zaragoza & Mitchell, 1996). Once constructed, these false memories may feel as real as—or even more real than—genuine memories (Brainerd et al., 1995). Susceptibility to such false memory construction is especially likely when people have been deprived of sleep, which is often the state of mind of crime suspects who are interrogated late at night (Blagrove, 1996).

How often do false confessions lead to miscarriages of justice? Based on a review of more than four hundred cases in which innocent people were convicted of murder in the United States, Michael Radelet and his colleagues (1992) found that 14 percent (or fifty-six cases) were caused by false confessions. Similar percentages have been obtained in other countries (Sigurdsson & Gudjonsson, 1996). Additional research suggests that while most jurors in criminal cases believe that police use coercive interrogation tactics to elicit confessions from guilty suspects, they tend to believe that innocent suspects won't falsely confess to a crime (Blandon-Gitlin et al., 2011). Although these facts are alarming, other research indicates that confessions, in general, are less important in securing a guilty verdict than is independent evidence. Few convictions are sustained on confession evidence alone, and it is estimated that a defendant's confession is pivotal in only 5 percent of cases (McConville, 1993).

Fortunately, few of you reading this text will ever be falsely accused of murder. However, all of you have been—and will continue to be—falsely accused of less serious transgressions. When facing your accusers, you will stand a better chance of successfully professing your innocence if you keep in mind the lessons of this chapter.

THE BIG PICTURE

Earlier, when describing the situation confronting participants in Milgram's research, I asked whether you would have fully obeyed the experimenter's commands. This is a question I have asked myself over the years. Most people emphatically believe that they would resist the destructive commands and openly rebel. They further believe that those who would obey fully must be more aggressive, cold, and unappealing than the average person (Miller et al., 1973). This harsh judgment is consistent with the belief that those who are susceptible to influence are weak-minded (Douglas et al., 2010). How do we reconcile these beliefs with the actual experimental findings?

To answer this question, let me return to information presented in Chapter 4. There is a widely held assumption—more common in individualist than in collectivist cultures—that people's actions are caused by internal dispositions rather than by external forces. This *fundamental attribution error* often results in a gross underestimation of the inherent power of the situation to shape behavior (Haney & Zimbardo, 2009; Masters, 2009). The likely source for this belief in the power of the individual to act independent of situational forces resides in the desire of many people to believe that they have control over their own lives. This need to believe that the self is relatively uninfluenced by outside forces fosters a misrepresentation of how the social world actually operates.

Gunter Bierbrauer (1979) attempted to eliminate this misperception by having college students either observe a vivid reenactment of the Milgram experiment or play the role of obedient teachers themselves. Despite being exposed to the power that situational factors had in causing high levels of obedience, students still predicted that their friends would be only minimally obedient if they participated in Milgram's study. Even after being confronted by the social psychological facts, these students still essentially believed that only bad people do bad deeds, and good people do only good deeds. The danger in such a view of the social world is that it leaves us wide open to being manipulated by the very social forces we underestimate. Previous chapters have documented how the self and self-beliefs shape our interpretation and response to our social surroundings. In the matter of social influence, it is our *misinterpretation* of how the social world is constituted that helps to explain how we are so often easily manipulated. If our self-beliefs were not so firmly based on our power to remain uninfluenced by the wishes, desires, and dictates of others, we might be better able to recognize when we are in danger of falling prey to such social manipulation.

In closing this chapter on social influence, I'd like to introduce you to an excerpt from a humorous poem by Russell Edson (1976), in which a man awakens one morning to find strings coming through his window attached to his hands and feet.

> *It may be that we are puppets—puppets controlled by the strings of society. But at least we are puppets with perception, with awareness. And perhaps our awareness is the first step to our liberation.*

Stanley Milgram, social
psychologist, 1933–1984

… I'm not a marionette, he says, his voice rising with the question, am I? Am I a marionette?
One of the strings loosens and jerks as he scratches his head.
… Hmmm, he says, I just wonder if I am a marionette?
And then all the strings pull and jerk and he is jumping out of bed.
Now that he's up he'll just go to the window and see who's doing tricks with him when he's half asleep …
He follows the strings up into the sky with his eyes and sees a giant hand sticking through a cloud, holding a crossbar to which the strings are attached …
Hmmm, he says, that's funny, I never saw that crossbar before … I guess I am a marionette …

Based on your own newfound knowledge of the social influence process, you are undoubtedly more aware of the social strings to which you too are attached. The "anchor" for these social strings may well be based in an evolutionary past, predisposing you to be naturally receptive to others' influence. However, as Stanley Milgram's quote here in the margin reminds us, the difference between you and a marionette (and many other animal species) is that you can reflect on your own actions, and you can analyze the strings that bind you to your social world. Through such analysis, you can become less a puppet of other people's desires and more a coactor in a rich and interlocking web of social intercourse.

 # WEB SITES

> ▶ Check out our web site
> **www.BVTLab.com**
> for chapter-by-chapter flashcards, summaries, and practice quizzes.

ACCESSED THROUGH www.BVTLab.com/sop6
Web sites for this chapter focus on the social influence
process, including the ordinary and extraordinary varieties.

SOCIAL INFLUENCE WEB SITE
This web site is devoted to the psychological study of social influence, examining everyday and interpersonal influence, mindful versus mindless behavior, and the influence tactics used by cults.

AFF CULT GROUP INFORMATION
This web site contains information about cults, mind control, and psychological manipulation. The recruitment and socialization practices of known cults are discussed, and former cult members tell their personal stories.

SOCIAL PSYCHOLOGY NETWORK
Among other things, this large social psychology database offers links to other web sites dealing with social influence, including those that discuss marketing and sales techniques, social influence countermeasures, and relevant research.

STANLEY MILGRAM WEB SITE
The purpose of this web site is to be a source of accurate information about the life and work of social psychologist Stanley Milgram.

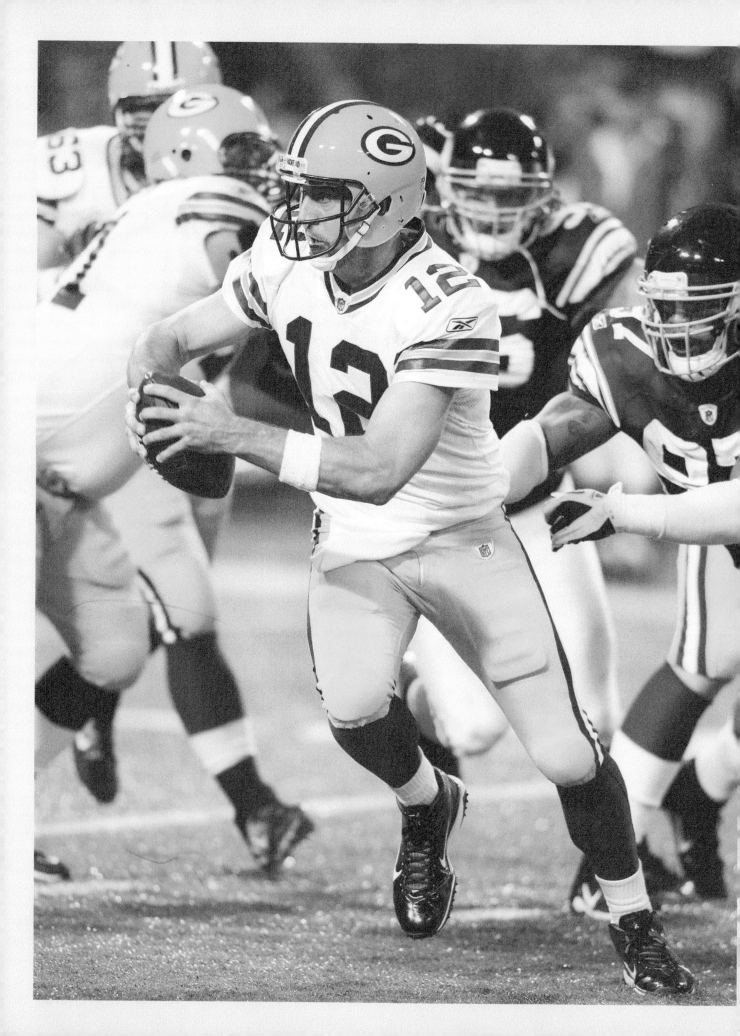

8 Chapter 8
Group Behavior

Chapter Outline

INTRODUCTION
The Nature of Groups

Group Success Fosters Social Identification.
Groups differ in their social cohesiveness.
Groups accomplish instrumental tasks and satisfy socioemotional needs.
Group structure develops quickly and changes slowly.
There are five phases to group membership.

Group Influence on Individual Behavior
The presence of others can energize us.
The presence of others can hide us.
Being both energized and hidden can lower our inhibitions.

Decision Making in Groups
Group decision making occurs in stages and follows various rules.
Group discussion enhances majority opinions.
Consensus seeking overrides critical analysis in groupthink.

Leadership
A leader is an influence agent.
Transformational leaders inspire followers.
The contingency model is an interactionist view of leadership.
Gender and culture can influence leadership style.

Group Interests Versus Individual Interests
Social dilemmas occur when short-term and long-term interests conflict.
Cooperation is necessary to resolve social dilemmas.

Applications
How Do Juries Make Decisions?

PREVIEW   The decision-making process of juries demonstrates the social psychology of small-group behavior, except for the fact that dissenters cannot be expelled. Yet how do jury size and rules concerning conviction influence the deliberation process?

THE BIG PICTURE

WEB SITES

INTRODUCTION

Summer jobs in college are interesting. You try to fit in with coworkers who know that your group membership has an August expiration date. One summer I worked for the U.S. Postal Service in my hometown and was assigned tasks wherever extra help was needed. My more seasoned and permanent coworkers referred to me as the "college kid," a label that designated me as residing at the very bottom rung of the post office status hierarchy.

Although the postmaster was the official leader at work, I quickly noticed that most of the regular employees followed the lead of Joe, a coworker who had different ideas from the postmaster about "worker productivity." Joe's most important unwritten rule was to "take your time" in completing tasks. For example, during my first day delivering mail to neighborhood houses, I was so excited about driving a mail truck and being a postal carrier that I finished my deliveries 90 minutes before any of the regular mail carriers. Early the next morning, Joe pulled me aside and told me that I was making the other carriers look bad. In explaining the situation, Joe said, "If the postmaster sees you coming in early, he'll want all the carriers to finish early, and then we're all stuck sorting mail for the last hour and a half of our shift!" Joe suggested that I take more breaks so that I finished my deliveries just before the end of my shift. Lesson learned.

In looking back at my three-month stint as a member of the U.S. Postal Service, I realize that we were a very efficient work group, despite—or perhaps because of—Joe's unwritten work rules. If we had spent less time conversing and joking around we might have completed more tasks, but at what cost to group morale?

What is important for a group's health and longevity? How do a collection of individuals like those at my hometown post office come to perceive themselves as a group? How does leadership style influence group performance? The essential message of social psychology is that humans are social animals. Through the process of natural selection and evolutionary adaptation, we have inherited specialized skills from our ancestors that help us efficiently perform tasks that are essential for survival. Because our ancestors lived together in small groups, it makes evolutionary sense that many of these specialized skills relate to group behavior. In this chapter, we examine how specific social skills operate in a group context. First, let's start with the most basic of questions: What is a group?

THE NATURE OF GROUPS

group

Several interdependent people who have emotional ties and interact on a regular basis

There is little agreement about how to precisely define a **group**, but one common definition is that it consists of several interdependent people who have emotional ties and who interact on a regular basis (Kessler & Hollbach, 2005; McGrath et al., 2000). By *interdependence*, I not only mean that members depend on one another to achieve group goals, but events that affect one member affect others as well. At my local post office, coworkers not only relied on one another to deliver the mail five days a week, but they each were influenced by fellow members' personal joys and sorrows. Their lives were intertwined.

GROUP SUCCESS FOSTERS SOCIAL IDENTIFICATION

❝All things being equal, you root for your own sex, your own culture, your own locality. ... Whoever you root for represents you. And when he or she wins, you win.**❞**

Isaac Asimov, science fiction writer, 1920–1992

As first discussed in Chapter 6 (p. 207), an *ingroup* is a group to which we belong and which forms a part of our social identity. Identifying with an ingroup is associated with a variety of positive consequences, including health and well-being (Amiot & Sansfacon, 2011; Haslam et al., 2009). For example, among a sample of workers at a highly demanding and stress-inducing call center, those who identified with their organization had fewer burnout symptoms and greater job satisfaction than those with low ingroup identity (Wegge et al., 2006).

One factor that encourages ingroup identification is being associated with a successful group. When our group achieves success or when individual ingroup members are

We treat our favorite sports team's successes as if they are our own, and we suffer their defeats as well. What are the two psychological terms for how we often respond to our team's successes and failures?

singled out for praise or awards, we tend to respond with pride and satisfaction, even if we had nothing to do with the achievement. This identification with and embracing of ingroup success is known as *basking in reflected glory (BIRGing)* and it is common in a variety of social arenas (Cialdini et al., 1976; Stelzl et al., 2008). Examples are the joy expressed by citizens following their nation's military and political successes, fan reaction to their sports teams' victories, and the pride ethnic group members have for other members' accomplishments. When such successes occur, group members often describe the success as "our victory." This process of reflected glory enhances members' personal self-esteem because their group identity constitutes an integral part of their self-concept (Boen et al., 2002; End et al., 2004; Smith & Henry, 1996).

Although we often readily share our group's and individual members' successes, what happens following failure? The common reaction is to make excuses ("Our group was treated unfairly!"), while devaluing the qualities in the successful outgroup that led to our defeat ("I'm glad our group isn't that vicious!"). If we strongly identify with our group, we tend to be more angry than sad following defeat, while the reverse is true if our ingroup identity is not strong (Crisp et al., 2007). For strong ingroup identifiers, defending the ingroup and angrily blasting the competition, indirectly defends self-esteem (Hastorf & Cantril, 1954; Schmader & Major, 1999).

What happens when our group is repeatedly outperformed by other groups? To protect self-esteem, we may psychologically distance ourselves from the group, a process called *cutting off reflected failure (CORFing)*. Both the embracing of success and psychological distancing from failure—which is exactly the type of identification that William James contended was typical of the self—plays an important role in attracting or repelling new members and in enhancing or diminishing strong ingroup emotional bonds. In the arena of sports competition, where there are clear winners and losers, fair-weather fans often engage in CORFing (Bernache-Assollant et al., 2010). Yet what about sports fans whose teams truly are an integral part of their self-concepts? Research by Edward Hirt and his coworkers (1992) suggests that a team's poor performance can significantly lower fans' own self-evaluations. In one of their studies, college students who were avid fans of their school's men's basketball team watched live televised games in which their team either won or lost. Not only were the moods of these zealous fans lower following defeat, but their immediate self-esteem and feelings of competence were also depressed. These and other studies suggest that forming a strong allegiance to a team is a risky venture (Bristow & Sebastian, 2001; Dalakas et al., 2004). Because true fans generally do not CORF, each season they subject themselves to an emotional roller coaster that must be ridden out, regardless of how exhilarating or nauseating the ride. CORFing or adopting a more successful team would certainly make life easier for a fan. However, true fans could no sooner change teams than they could change their names—for better or worse, their team affiliation is an important social identity.

> "Three stinking cobblers with their wits combined can equal the wisest philosopher."
>
> Chinese folk saying

GROUPS DIFFER IN THEIR SOCIAL COHESIVENESS.

Group success and failure are affected by—and influence—*social cohesiveness,* or "groupiness" (Goncalo et al., 2010; Sherman & Johnson, 2003). As social cohesion increases, people think, feel, and act more like group members and less like isolated individuals (Sani et al., 2005).

They are more likely to highly value the social identity they have and are more willing to sacrifice for the good of the group than those in low cohesive groups (Gomez et al., 2011; Swann et al., 2010). In turn, high cohesiveness allows the group to exert more influence on members, which often leads to greater productivity (Gammage et al., 2001; Langfred, 1998). Beyond group success and failure influencing group cohesion, additional factors that affect groupiness are *group size, member similarity and diversity,* and *perceived subversion of the group's identity.*

Group Size

Although the size of the group in which animals live in a given habitat is partly determined by existing resources and other environmental limitations, comparative studies of various species indicate that the upper limit of group size is set by each species' cognitive abilities. Based on his analysis of humans and various nonhuman primate species (New and Old World monkeys and apes), Robin Dunbar (1993, 2002) concluded that the average size of a species' social group is directly related to what percentage of the species' brain is devoted to higher cognitive functions (the *neocortex* ratio). The group size identified by this relationship refers to the maximum number of individuals with whom an animal can maintain social relationships by personal contact. Subsequent research indicated that this relationship between group size and neocortex size involves the areas of the frontal lobes of the cerebral cortex, which are crucial for social cognition (Stuss et al., 2001). According to Dunbar (2000, 2003), animals cannot maintain the cohesion and integrity of groups larger than a size set by the information-processing capacity of their frontal lobes.

What is the upper limit of group size for which human brains are best adapted? As depicted in Figure 8.1, Dunbar's calculations suggest that the relevant group size for modern humans is about 150 individuals, which approximates quite closely the observed sizes of clan-like groupings in contemporary and early human hunter-gatherer cultures. In contrast, the average group size among chimpanzees is about fifty individuals. Given that human brain size has remained unchanged over the past two hundred fifty thousand years, we can assume that our current brain size is more a product of the evolutionary pressures of hunter-gatherer groups rather than the environmental demands we now face in our technologically advanced cultures (Barrett et al., 2003). Dunbar contends that if this assumption is correct, then it is possible that our current brains are not well adapted to the very large social groupings sometimes found in modern societies.

Even in modern societies, most groups contain less than four persons (Mullen & Copper, 1994). As a group grows and as it reaches or exceeds the upper limit of our brain's capacity to process information on the individual members, there is a tendency for member participation to decline, power to become concentrated in the hands of a few, conflicts to increase, and cooperation to decrease (Hill & Dunbar, 2003; Wagner, 1995). Large groups make it harder for members to control what happens to them (Lawler, 1992), and as group size increases, members become more selfish and less group-focused because they perceive the impact of their own behavior on group success or failure being weaker and less identifiable (see *social loafing,* pp. 319–320).

Member Similarity and Diversity

Within groups, members tend to be more similar than different (Jackson et al., 1991). One reason for this similarity characteristic is that membership in most groups involves the performance of specific activities (for example, all members of an aerobics class exercise), and thus, people are drawn toward a specific group because they mutually share an interest in that group's activities. Another reason for within-group similarity is socialization. That is, in the process of socializing new members, attempts are made to mold them to the group's way of thinking and acting (see p. 314). As discussed in Chapter 5 (p. 190), similarity is often the "glue" of affiliation and liking. Thus, it is no surprise that when group members are dissimilar rather than similar, conflict and turnover are more likely (Ely & Thomas, 2001; Paletz et al., 2003).

Although member dissimilarity can be dangerous to groups, it can also provide benefits. As group tasks change and become more complex, and as the group's social environment changes, diversity among members gives the group more flexibility in adapting

Figure 8.1

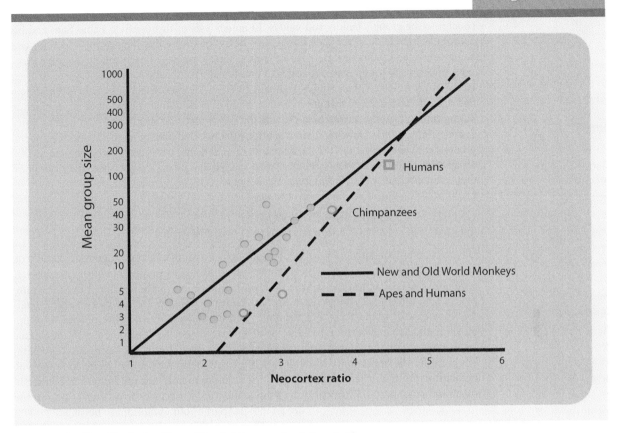

Does Brain Size Limit the Size of Social Groups in Primates?

When Robin Dunbar (1993) plotted the average group size in different primate species against the percentage of the species'
brain devoted to higher cognitive functions (the neocortex ratio), he found a positive linear relationship. In other words, as
the neocortex size of monkeys' and apes' brains increased relative to other brain areas, the average size of a primate species'
social group also increased. The relevant group size for modern humans is about 150 individuals, which closely approxi-
mates the observed sizes of contemporary hunter-gatherer groups. If these findings are correct, do they have any implica-
tions for the type of social problems typically found in large metropolitan settings?

to these changes and may provide more accurate decision making over the long term
(Paletz & Schunn, 2010; Sommers, 2006). For example, as North American culture has
become more diverse and complex, many successful businesses have recognized the
need to increase the diversity of their employees to better meet the challenges in the
marketplace. Thus, although similarity tends to promote group cohesion, diversity can
promote flexibility in group functioning.

What is the best strategy for capitalizing on the value of diversity? Recent studies
suggest that groups become the most creative in solving problems when they celebrate
and embrace the diversity of their members rather than minimizing these differences
(Swann et al., 2003). This highlighting of diversity creates a social environment where
members' distinct personal and social qualities are verified and validated by the group.
Receiving such self-verification promotes satisfaction and commitment among members (Swann et al., 2000, 2002).

Perceived Subversion of Group Identity

Members' emotional identification with the group is vitally important to group cohesiveness.
However, when members believe that a current or proposed group norm strongly deviates
from the group's identity, this cohesiveness and emotional connection is seriously threatened
(Sani & Todman, 2002). For example, in 1992 more than seven hundred male clergy in the

Church of England left the group in protest when church leaders decided to ordain women priests. By the year 2000, there were about one thousand congregations in the Church of England who refused to accept the authority of women priests because they believed it was counter to the group's beliefs and values. In an analysis of this conflict, Fabio Sani and his colleagues found that when church members began believing that their group's identity was being subverted by this new norm of ordaining female priests, their resulting negative emotions undermined group cohesiveness and emotional identification with the Church of England (Sani & Reicher, 2000; Sani & Todman, 2002). Additional research by Sani (2005) found that one effective strategy that group leaders often employ to manage member dissatisfaction during times of group change is to provide the opportunity for displeased members to voice dissent (Sani, 2005). Allowing dissent is often effective in maintaining dissatisfied members' group identification, but only if the dissent is moderate and not radical. When members of a group who hold radical views about change realize that others do not share their opinions, they often disidentify with their group (Becker et al., 2011).

GROUPS ACCOMPLISH INSTRUMENTAL TASKS AND SATISFY SOCIOEMOTIONAL NEEDS.

Have you ever wondered why people join groups? Existing evidence suggests that they do so for several reasons, all of which can be traced to the accomplishment of *instrumental* tasks and the satisfaction of *socioemotional* or affiliation needs (Schachter, 1959). Put simply, people often join groups because they desire to achieve certain task-oriented goals that they cannot attain alone. For example, you will have a much better chance of extinguishing the fire in a burning building or of finding shelter for the homeless if you pursue these tasks within the supportive network of a group. In addition, becoming a group member provides the opportunity to satisfy such affiliative motives as the desire for approval, belonging, prestige, friendship, and even love. These mutual desires for task accomplishment and emotional fulfillment in a group setting are observed across many species and are an integral part of our evolutionary heritage.

The work of Robert Bales, which began in the late 1940s, suggests that *accomplishing tasks* and *dealing with emotional and social relationships* are indeed the two principal functions of groups (Bales, 1970; Bales & Slater, 1955). Some groups are primarily task-oriented, while others are principally constituted to foster social relationships (Johnson et al., 2006; Sherman et al., 2002). Examples of *task-oriented* groups are work groups, such as a surgical team operating on a patient or postal workers delivering the mail. Examples of *socioemotional* groups are friendship and family groups nurturing and emotionally supporting fellow members or neighbors organizing a summer block party.

Although some groups can be identified as more oriented toward one function than the other, almost all groups engage in at least some degree of both task and socioemotional activity. Indeed, Bales contends that this continual oscillation between task and socioemotional activities is what characterizes group process. As a group engages in task-oriented activities, members' feelings tend to be neglected, and this inattention creates group tension in the socioemotional area. However, when the group attempts to reduce these socioemotional tensions by paying more attention to members' feelings, task goals become temporarily sidetracked and this, in turn, creates task tension. According to Bales, groups constantly strive to strike a proper balance between their attention to task and socioemotional concerns so that they can keep group

▶ Socioemotional groups can range from friendships to family members to neighbors.

tension to a minimum. During my first week of postal work, my coworkers placed very high demands on the "college kid." Sensing my growing resentment, at the end of the week they invited me to join them for some after-work socializing. I happily accepted and all was well.

GROUP STRUCTURE DEVELOPS QUICKLY AND CHANGES SLOWLY.

One characteristic upon which groups differ is _structure_, the regular, stable patterns of behavior between members (Wilke, 1996). These group behavior patterns generally develop quickly and change slowly. Most major corporations are highly structured with clearly defined social roles for employees and clearly designated status hierarchies. For at least a few years, one notable exception to this rule was Ben & Jerry's Homemade ice cream business. When Ben Cohen and Jerry Greenfield ran this multimillion dollar business, monthly board meetings were occasionally held in Ben's swimming pool and the lines of authority within the company were only vaguely defined. At one point, the company's search for a new corporate executive officer became a national "Yo! I Want to Be CEO!" contest with applicants instructed to send in 100-word applications.

In analyzing the structure of groups, social psychologists from different theoretical perspectives have identified a number of common elements (Poole et al., 2004). Three of the more important ones are social norms, social roles, and status systems.

Social Norms

As defined in Chapter 7 (p. 264), _social norms_ are expected standards of behavior and beliefs established and enforced by a group. Some groups have norms for personal appearance (for example, shaved heads for Marine recruits), others have norms for opinions (for example, liberal views in environmental organizations), and most have norms for behavior (for example, profanity is forbidden in school classrooms). Sometimes, these norms are formally conveyed to group members in written guidelines. However, as illustrated by my own postal work experience, most often these norms are learned through everyday conversations or observing other members (Miller & Prentice, 1996). As demonstrated by Sherif's classic studies (see Chapter 7), once norms are established, they tend to be stable over time, despite changes in group membership. Although social norms certainly increase conformity and reduce deviancy within groups, they also can enhance performance when structured in such a way as to reward effort, efficiency, and quality (Taggar & Ellis, 2007).

Social Roles

As defined in Chapter 4 (p. 130), _social roles_ are clusters of socially defined expectations that individuals in a given situation are expected to fulfill. In a group, roles often define the division of labor, and well-defined roles improve group dynamics and performance (Barley & Bechky, 1994). In some cases social roles _evolve_ during group interaction, while in other cases people _import_ a role into their new group that they enjoyed playing in previous groups (Rose, 1994). For instance, if you were known as a "good listener" in your high school friendship groups, you may import this role into your college friendships. Likewise, others may try to shape their "comedian" friendship role into the "class clown" role at school.

Status Systems

The third aspect of group structure is its _status system_, which reflects the distribution of power among members (Kaplan & Martin, 1999; Robinson & Balkwell, 1995). Status is a valued commodity in a group. Even in groups that do not have formal status systems, such as friendship cliques, members often differ in their prestige and authority. You can tell who has higher status in a group by paying attention to verbal and nonverbal behavior: higher-status members maintain greater eye contact, stand more erect; are more likely to criticize, command, or interrupt others; and not only speak more often but are also spoken to more often than those of lower status (Fournier et al., 2002; Leffler et al., 1982). Although status can be _achieved_ by helping a group reach its goals, it is often _ascribed_ rather than earned: people are given higher status simply because of who or what they are (Anderson et al., 2001; Ridgeway, 1991).

How exactly are these status differences created in the first place? According to **expectation states theory**, when group members first meet, they form expectations about each

When joining a new group, you may import social roles you played in previous groups. Can you identify roles that you have imported from your high school friendships into your college friendships?

other's probable contributions to the achievement of group goals (Berger & Webster, 2006; Kalkhoff & Thye, 2006). These expectations are not only based on members' *task-relevant characteristics*, such as social skills and past experience, but also on *diffuse-status characteristics*, such as race, sex, age, and wealth (Correll & Ridgeway, 2003; Wittenbaum, 1998). Those members whose characteristics produce higher expectations in fellow members are assigned higher status in the group. Thus, for example, White, middle-aged, wealthy men might be perceived as better potential leaders by other group members than young, poor, Hispanic women. Although these initial status assignments can be later modified based on actual performance, members who are unfairly given an initially low status will have trouble proving their worth to the group (Ridgeway, 1982). Because women have lower ascribed status than men in many groups, they report more dissatisfaction with their group status and must work harder to gain influence with other members (Burke et al., 2007; Ridgeway, 2001).

As this brief overview suggests, there are many advantages to having high status in a group. Higher-status individuals have higher self-esteem, are better liked by other group members, and are more satisfied with their group relations than lower-status persons (Lovaglia & Houser, 1996). Further, when high-status individuals make decisions that lead to minor negative consequences for the group, they are more likely than lower-status members to be forgiven. However, when the bad decisions cause major negative group consequences, high-status persons are judged more severely than those with low or medium status (Wiggins et al., 1965). This is one instance where high-status members can be treated very harshly by the group.

THERE ARE FIVE PHASES TO GROUP MEMBERSHIP.

An important characteristic of group membership is that it is a *temporal* process, meaning that change occurs over time, involving different *phases* (Arrow et al., 2005). Richard Moreland and John Levine's (1988, 2002) **temporal model of group membership** examines not only how people are changed through their membership in a group, but also how the group is changed by members' ideas and actions. Three psychological processes that propel people into and out of groups are the *ongoing evaluations* the individual and the group make of one another, the *feelings of commitment* that follow these evaluations, and the *role transitions* that result from these changes in commitment (Levine et al., 1998; Van Vugt & Hart, 2004). The two faces of evaluation that occur during the course of group membership involve (1) the degree to which the individual meets the needs of the group, and (2) the degree to which the group meets the needs of the individual.

Critical THINKING

In Chapter 6 you learned how ingroup biases can lead to prejudice and discrimination. How might this knowledge help you better understand the process by which the diffuse status characteristics of group members might significantly determine their power in the group?

---

temporal model of group membership
••••••••••••••••••••••
A theory of group membership describing the changes that occur over time in members and in the group due to their mutual influence and interdependence

Figure 8.2

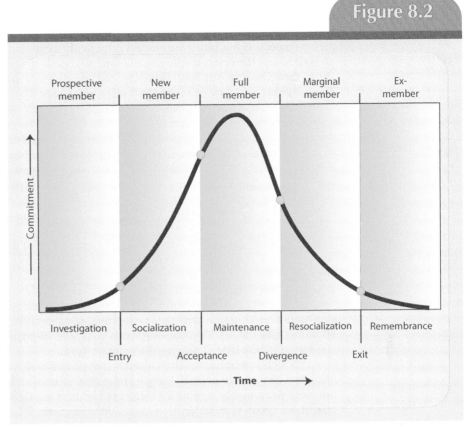

A Temporal Model of Group Membership

Based on Moreland and Levine's (1982) model of the phases of group membership, in what phase is commitment the greatest?

According to Moreland and Levine, the temporal passage of the individual through the group generally occurs in five phases, with each phase associated with a different social role played by the individual. The movement from one membership phase to the next represents a role transition. In Figure 8.2, the line of the bell-shaped curve represents the personal history of someone passing through all five phases of group membership. As people move up the line, their commitment to the group and the group's commitment to them strengthens, while as they move down the line, this mutual commitment weakens. Commitment is most likely to weaken during times of change within the group (Prislin & Christensen, 2005).

In the *investigation phase*, the group seeks people who seem likely to attain group goals, and prospective members seek groups that provide the opportunity to satisfy personal needs. If both the individual's and the group's commitment levels are sufficiently strong, a prospective member enters the group. Although many groups have low entrance criteria and continually admit new members, other groups establish strict criteria and only periodically allow others to join. Although many factors influence a group's tendency to be relatively open or closed to new members, groups that are unsuccessful or understaffed at key positions tend to be more accepting of new members than those that are successful or overstaffed (Cini et al., 1993).

In the *socialization phase*, the group tries to shape the new members' thinking and behavior so that they can and will make the maximum contribution to the group (Moreland & Levine, 2001; Ryan et al., 2004). Groups accomplish this task through formal and informal indoctrination sessions and through "coaches" who model the appropriate thinking and behaviors (Keating et al., 2005). While this socialization process is taking place new members often try to change the group so that it will accommodate their needs (Swann et al., 2000). The socialization phase ends when the individual's and the group's commitment levels increase so that the individual becomes a full member of the group.

> **"** *I don't care to belong to any club that will have me as a member.* **"**
>
> Groucho Marx, U.S. comedian, 1875–1977

During the *maintenance phase*, the group attempts to define specialized roles for full members that maximize their contributions to the group's goals (Levine et al., 2005). In contrast, the full members often try to define their roles in the group to maximize personal needs. If this influence process is mutually satisfying, commitment is increased on both sides. However, if role negotiation fails, both the member and the group will regard the relationship as less rewarding, and commitment to one another will decrease. The individual will now be viewed as a marginal member.

When relabeled as marginal, group members enter the *resocialization phase*, in which both parties once again try to persuade the other to meet their expectations. If the group or the individual succeeds in convincing the other to accept their role expectations, or if a mutually agreeable compromise can be struck, the marginal member once again becomes a full member. As Figure 8.2 shows, this means that the person moves backward on the curve toward a higher commitment level. If, however, no agreement is reached, the individual's and the group's commitment levels fall even further, prompting the individual to exit the group. In the resulting *remembrance phase*, the group develops a consensus concerning the ex-member's contributions to the group's goals, and similarly, the ex-member reminisces about the benefits and costs of being a member of the group.

How does this model fit your experiences with various groups in your own life? A number of the social psychological processes that unfold in the different phases of group membership, such as majority and minority influence, have been discussed in Chapter 7. Perhaps some of you have also noticed that the dynamics of group membership bears a striking similarity to the dynamics of romantic relationships, which we will discuss in Chapter 10. The reason for this is simple: Romantic relationships are often considered to be a type of group—the intimate dyad.

Although research generally indicates that people with high group commitment are much less likely to voluntarily leave a group than those with low commitment, there are instances when highly committed members exit because they think their departure will benefit the group (Levine & Moreland, 2002; Zdaniuk & Levine, 2001). This type of scenario often occurs when highly committed members conclude that they are no longer adequately contributing to the group. Instead of "taking up space" that could be better filled by more productive individuals, these loyal members exit the group. Many employee retirements fall into this category.

The idea that members might place the welfare of the group ahead of their own is generally an exception to the rule in this model. In this sense, Moreland and Levine's depiction of the phases of group membership has an individualist bent to it. That is, they assume that members' personal goals often diverge from group goals. In a collectivist culture, phases of group membership are less affected by individual-group tensions (Abrams et al., 1998; Markus & Kitayama, 1994).

SECTION SUMMARY

- A group consists of several interdependent people who have emotional ties and interact on a regular basis.

- We often bask in the reflected glory of our ingroup members' successes.

- Factors that affect group cohesion include the following:
    group size
    member similarity and diversity
    perceived subversion of group identity

- There are two main functions of groups:
    accomplish instrumental tasks
    satisfy socioemotional needs

- Every group has a *structure*, consisting of
    social norms   social roles   status systems.

- There are five phases to group membership, each with an associated social role:
    investigation phase—prospective member
    socialization phase—new member
    maintenance phase—full member
    resocialization phase—marginal member
    remembrance phase—ex-member

GROUP INFLUENCE ON INDIVIDUAL BEHAVIOR

If one of the main functions of groups is to perform tasks, what factors influence the ability of people to successfully engage in task activities? In this section, we examine how the presence of others affects a person's work performance. The two types of situations investigated are (1) an individual performing an activity in the presence of an audience (*social facilitation*), and (2) an individual performing an activity as part of a larger group of performers (*social loafing*). We also examine how both being aroused and being hidden in the group can loosen one's behavioral inhibitions.

THE PRESENCE OF OTHERS CAN ENERGIZE US.

During my first week's work at the post office, I found it difficult and stressful to quickly place outgoing letters into the correct slots in the mail-sorting room. Having a coworker sorting next to me increased both my anxiety and my mistakes. However, by the second week, I mastered this task and performed it faster with a colleague nearby rather than when alone. What might explain these work experiences?

In 1895 Norman Triplett was pondering a similar question: "How does a person's performance of a task change when other people are present?" The question was prompted by Triplett noticing that a bicycle racer's speed was faster when the biker was paced by other cyclists than when racing alone. Desiring to learn what caused these different race times, he devised the first social scientific experiment by having children quickly wind line on a fishing reel either alone or in the presence of other competing children. As he had predicted, the children wound the line faster when in the presence of other children (Triplett, 1897). Subsequent experiments during the first quarter of the twentieth century found that the presence of others enhances the speed with which people perform relatively simple tasks but inhibits task efficiency in more complex activities (Allport, 1920; Travis, 1925). This *social facilitation* effect, as it came to be called, was also found in other animals, such as dogs, rats, birds, fish, and even ants and cockroaches (Chen, 1937; Gates & Allee, 1933). Although researchers extensively documented these divergent effects through the 1930s and 1940s, no one could explain why the presence of others would sometimes enhance and sometimes hinder individual performance. This explanatory conundrum ultimately led to a loss of interest in social facilitation as a research topic.

The Mere-Presence Explanation

In the mid-1960s, Robert Zajonc (1965) renewed the field's interest in social facilitation by proposing a theory to reconcile the contradictory findings. His social facilitation theory involved three basic propositions or steps (see Figure 8.3). First, he argued that all animals (including humans) are genetically predisposed to become physiologically aroused when around *conspecifics* (members of one's own species). This is so, he believed, because animals receive most of their rewards and punishments in life from conspecifics, and through the process of evolution have developed an innate arousal response due to their *mere presence*. Second, resurrecting an old behaviorist principle of learning (Hull, 1943), Zajonc stated that this physiological arousal enhances the performance of whatever response tendency is dominant (that is, well learned) in an animal. Third, and last, he contended that for well-learned tasks the correct responses are also the dominant responses, but for novel, unlearned tasks the dominant responses are the incorrect ones. What this means is that the presence of others will enhance correct execution of well-learned tasks at the same time that it will interfere with or inhibit correct performance of novel, unlearned tasks.

Zajonc argued that when we perform a simple task like hand clapping, the mere presence of an audience increases our arousal, eliciting the dominant response, and we clap more vigorously than when we are alone and not aroused. Now, if instead, we calculated difficult math problems in front of others, our increased arousal would inhibit execution of this task because the correct answers are not dominant responses. They would be dominant responses only if we had them memorized. Taken together, these two different effects due to the presence of others—enhancement of correct performance on easy tasks and inhibition of correct performance on difficult tasks—are known

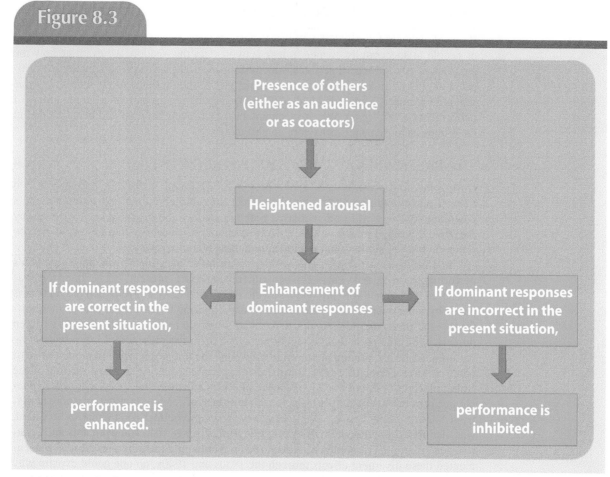

Figure 8.3

Zajonc's Drive Theory of Social Facilitation

According to Zajonc (1965), the presence of other people increases arousal, which, in turn, enhances the performance of dominant responses. If the dominant responses are correct, performance will also be enhanced. However, if the dominant responses are incorrect, performance will be inhibited. Can you think of instances from your own life in which the presence of others had these two contrasting effects on your performance of different types of tasks?

social facilitation

The enhancement of dominant responses due to the presence of others

as **social facilitation**. The reason the same term is used for both effects is that on both easy and difficult tasks, the performance of the dominant response is *facilitated* in others' presence. For easy tasks the correct response is dominant, and thus, the person's performance is enhanced. Yet for difficult tasks the correct response is not dominant, hence the decline in performance efficiency.

The Evaluation-Apprehension Explanation

Numerous studies either specifically tested Zajonc's theory or more generally examined social facilitation. Two separate meta-analyses of more than three hundred experiments involving more than twenty-five thousand participants indicates that social facilitation does indeed exist (Bond & Titus, 1983; Guerin, 1986), but there is a considerable debate concerning the nature of this arousal. Some contend that rather than being due to the mere presence of others, arousal is a result of *evaluation apprehension*—concern over being judged by others (Aiello & Douthitt, 2001; Strauss, 2002).

In one study supporting this explanation, participants worked on a task either alone, in the presence of confederates who were also working on the task, or in the presence of blindfolded confederates who supposedly were preparing for a perception experiment (Cottrell et al., 1968). Participants working on the task in the company of "seeing" confederates exhibited social facilitation effects when compared with those working alone.

Both the evaluation-apprehension and the mere-presence explanations would predict this outcome. However, in the presence of blindfolded confederates, there was no evidence for social facilitation. Participants' dominant responses did not differ from those who were alone. Because the blindfolded confederates were physically present but could not evaluate the peformance of participants, these findings support the evaluation-apprehension explanation at the same time they contradict the mere-presence explanation. Similar effects were found in other studies in which observers were present but not evaluating an individual's performance (Worringham & Messick, 1983). According to the evaluation-apprehension perspective, if people are present but not attending to another person's task performance, their presence is unlikely to produce social facilitation effects. A recent meta-analysis of past studies also suggests that the people who are most adversely affected by evaluation apprehension when performing tasks in others' presence are those with low self-esteem (Uziel, 2007).

The Distraction-Conflict Explanation

As appealing as the evaluation-apprehension explanation is, there are social facilitation effects it cannot explain. Recall that social facilitation has been observed in such animals as ants and cockroaches. Does this mean that insects "worry" about other insects evaluating them? Because this possibility is unlikely, other social scientists contend that heightened arousal is simply caused by a conflict between two tendencies (Baron, 1986). This *distraction-conflict theory* states that when an animal (human or other) is working on a task in the presence of other conspecifics, it experiences conflict regarding whether to attend to its companions or the task at hand. Distraction-conflict theorists contend that it is this conflict, and this conflict alone, that induces heightened arousal. Because conflict is a well-documented source of arousal, this perspective can explain both human and nonhuman social facilitation effects. In addition to social stimuli (that is, conspecifics) causing conflict, and thus arousal, the distraction-conflict theory hypothesizes that nonsocial objects that distract a performer can also induce conflict. True to this contention, loud noises and flashing lights have been found to produce the same enhancement/impairment effects produced by the presence of others (Pessin, 1933; Sanders & Baron, 1975; Wanshaffe, 2002). Research has also found that people perform simple tasks better and complex tasks worse in the presence of a picture of a favorite TV character, but not when in the presence of a nonfavorite TV character (Park & Catrambone, 2007). In this instance, favorite TV characters were apparently more distracting than nonfavorite TV characters. Taken together, the one advantage that the distraction-conflict theory has over the other two explanations is that it can explain task enhancement both in social and nonsocial settings (see Figure 8.4).

Given the research discussed with the three theories of social facilitation, can we declare that one of them is clearly the best explanation of this phenomenon? Joshua Feinberg and John Aiello (2006) recently tested the effects of evaluation apprehension, distraction, and physical presence in a single study and found that physical presence may be sufficient, but it is not necessary to produce social-facilitation effects for either simple or complex tasks. On simple tasks, evaluation apprehension had a larger enhancing effect than distraction. On complex tasks, there was evidence of stronger impairment effects when participants were being simultaneously evaluated and distracted rather than being only evaluated or distracted. These findings suggest that both evaluation-apprehension and distraction-conflict explanations are necessary to understand social facilitation. On a practical level, this research further suggests that when working on a complex task, you should be equally attentive to how your performance might be undermined both by others evaluating you and by distractors in your surroundings. However, when working on a simple task, your performance is likely to be raised to its highest level simply by having others evaluate you.

THE PRESENCE OF OTHERS CAN HIDE US.

Social facilitation research identifies the conditions under which the presence of others can motivate individuals to enhance their performance. Usually this enhancement occurs when a person's efforts can be individually evaluated. Yet, what if the performers' efforts

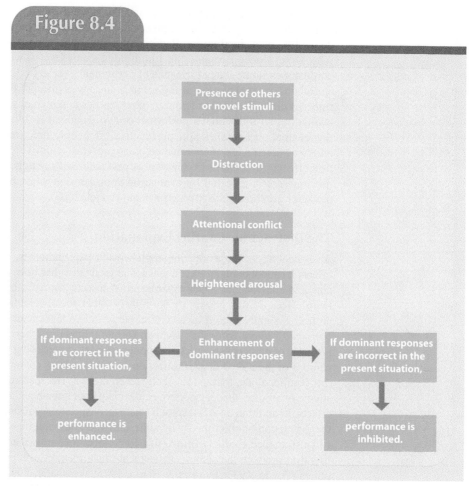

Distraction-Conflict Theory

According to the distraction-conflict theory, when one is working on a task, the presence of others or the presence of novel stimuli is distracting. This distraction produces a conflict between paying attention to the task and paying attention to these stimuli. This conflict causes arousal to increase, which leads to the social facilitation effects previously discussed.

are *pooled* so that individually judging them is difficult or even impossible? Do you know what often happens? If you guessed that individuals work less hard under these conditions than when performing alone, you are correct. This group-induced reduction in individual output is known as **social loafing** (Karau & Williams, 1995).

French agricultural engineer Max Ringelman (1913) conducted the first empirical study suggesting such an effect in the 1880s. He found that people's efforts pulling on a rope or pushing a cart were less when they worked in a group than when they performed these tasks alone. More recently, social loafing has been documented in a host of behaviors. For example, Bibb Latané and his associates (1979) had six blindfolded college students sit in a semi-circle and wear headphones that blasted sounds of people shouting into their ears. The students' task was to shout as loud as possible while listening to the headphone noise. On some trials, they believed that the five other students were also shouting, while on other trials they believed they were either shouting alone or with only one other person. In actuality, on all these trials only one student was performing. Consistent with what you would expect due to social loafing, when students thought one other person was yelling, they shouted 82 percent as intensely as when alone, and when they believed everyone was yelling, they shouted 75 percent as intensely.

Social loafing is not restricted to simple motor tasks like rope pulling or cheering; it also takes place when people perform cognitive tasks (Price et al., 2006). In addition, cross-cultural research indicates that social loafing occurs in both individualist and

social loafing
· · · · · · · · · · · · · · · · · · · ·
Group-induced reduction in individual output when performers' efforts are pooled and, thus, cannot be individually judged

collectivist societies, although the effect is not as strong in the latter (Gabrenya et al., 1985; Karau & Williams, 1993).

What might explain social loafing? A likely explanation is that when people work in a group, they realize that their individual output will be "lost in the crowd." As a result, they feel less personally responsible for the outcome, and their performance effort declines (Comer, 1995). The cognitive process that group performers go through in feeling less personally responsible for task outcomes is known as the **diffusion of responsibility**, and in Chapter 12 (pp. 505–508) we will examine how it causes a variation of social loafing, namely, bystanders to an emergency failing to aid victims.

diffusion of responsibility
. . . .
The belief that the presence of other people in a situation makes one less personally responsible for the events that occur in that situation

Reducing Social Loafing

If social loafing is truly caused by a diffusion of responsibility, then it is also true that social loafing is not an inevitable consequence of people working together in groups. That is, if people's individual efforts can be judged while they work on a group task, they should not lose personal responsibility for their actions, and there should be no social loafing. This is exactly what was found in a variation of the cheering study (Williams et al., 1981). Here, as before, participants shouted alone or in groups. In some conditions, shouters were led to believe that their individual performance was being monitored; in other conditions they believed their output was never identifiable. Results indicated that if participants believed their individual shouting was being monitored, no performance drop off occurred in a group context. This study suggests that when group performers cannot conceal minimal effort from observers, social loafing is unlikely.

The fact that social loafing is greatly reduced when individual effort can be identified and evaluated suggests that evaluation apprehension can curtail minimal effort. However, what if performers in a group are made aware of their own individual efforts or those of the group in comparison with a social standard without others being privy to this information? Would this private information still reduce social loafing on their part? There is ample evidence that people tend to overestimate their individual contributions to group efforts (Savitsky et al., 2005). This being so, perhaps receiving private feedback that one is underperforming might be sufficient to reduce social loafing. Research indicates that receiving such feedback does increase individual effort (Harkins & Szymanski, 1989). Thus, providing the potential for *evaluation*—even if it is only private self-evaluation—seems essential in reducing the loss of individual output on a group task.

Although informing group members of the potential for evaluation may generally reduce loafing, how should habitual social loafers be handled? Short of physically rejecting lazy workers from the group, one common technique to increase their output is to socially shun them until they conform to the group productivity norm. Yet is such *ostracism* effective? Singling out group members for deliberate disrespect runs the risk of alienating them, but it could also motivate these targeted members to increase their work efforts and win back the group's respect (Branscombe et al., 2002; Sleebos et al., 2006). Kipling Williams and Kristin Sommer (1997) found that the effectiveness of this technique was different for female and male loafers. The women loafers reacted to ostracism by socially acknowledging their feelings of rejection and openly questioning their own attractiveness and abilities. When given a chance to get back into the good graces of the group, the women worked hard to do so. In contrast, the men appeared to cope with ostracism by redirecting their interests toward nontask objects in their surroundings. Also, their concern for impression management caused the men to hide their emotions and to reinterpret the situation; they tended to perceive their separation from the group as being due to their own personal choice rather than something imposed on them. By engaging in these face-saving coping strategies, the men now had a lower need to seek the group's approval, and hence, they were more likely to continue loafing. Williams and Sommer speculate that these gender differences are due to most societies socializing women to be emotionally expressive and men to be nonexpressive. That is, women's learned response of attending to and expressing their emotions enhances the effectiveness of ostracism as a control technique. For men, however, their learned response of directing their attention away from their emotions to other environmental stimuli dilutes the effectiveness of ostracism. These findings suggest that, although ostracism may be an effective control strategy for social loafing in people who regularly attend to and publicly express their emotions, it may be ineffective for those who are psychologically invested in controlling any such public displays.

Are Group Performance Settings Always Demotivating?

So far, we've assumed that there is something about group settings that lowers people's motivation to perform. Yet research suggests that there are circumstances in which group performance triggers higher motivation among people than does individual performance. The individuals who are most likely to become highly motivated during group performance are members who have either high or low competence on the task at hand (Kerr et al., 2007). Highly competent group members often increase their efforts on collective tasks to compensate for the expected poor performance of other members (Hart et al., 2001; Todd et al., 2006). In sports, these are the superstar athletes who "carry" their lower-performing team members to victory with their superb play. Such heightened motivation, however, typically occurs only when success at the group task is highly valued. Exhibition games don't motivate highly skilled athletes nearly as much as championship games.

What about group members who have relatively low skills? In performance settings where group success hinges on the performance of the least competent members, the motivation level of these poor performers tends to be significantly higher than when they are performing solely for themselves (Hertel et al., 2000; Kozlowski & Bell, 2003). In sports, these are the bench athletes who are periodically given the opportunity to compete side-by-side with their more highly skilled teammates. In such settings, these lower-skilled members typically exert great effort in trying to match others' performance levels. Unlike their highly skilled group members, it appears that the motivation of low-skilled performers is less adversely affected by the value that the group places on task success. Even when success isn't that important to the group, low-skilled group members work hard to do as well or better than their more highly skilled group members.

BEING BOTH ENERGIZED AND HIDDEN CAN LOWER OUR INHIBITIONS.

One Halloween night a few years ago, I heard a noise outside my house. Looking out the window, I saw a group of teenagers in masks and costumes carrying pumpkins—my pumpkins. I quickly went to the front porch and noticed that my lamppost light had been shattered by one of the pumpkins being thrown against it. Although I was barefoot and dressed in pajamas, I gave chase after these "hooligans." As I sprinted toward them, they took off running. They ran faster than I sprinted and I abruptly gave up the chase. As I ended my pursuit they stopped, too, and turned back to check me out. Standing there in the cold and the dark, it suddenly dawned on me that I was their "old geezer"—the feeble, angry man who chases pranksters on Halloween night. At that moment, memories of my own youthful Halloween escapades came back to haunt me. Just like me years ago, these "hooligans" were normally well-behaved adolescents who had been caught up in a one-night antisocial neighborhood romp. What caused them—and me, at that age—to act this way? Have you ever been in a similar situation and later wondered why you behaved so contrary to acceptable standards?

Group-Induced Lowering of Inhibitions

Social facilitation research demonstrates that groups can arouse us. Social loafing studies indicate that groups can also diffuse responsibility and lower evaluation apprehension. What happens when groups diffuse responsibility and lower evaluation apprehension at the same time that they arouse us? In such circumstances, our normal inhibitions may diminish, and we may engage in behaviors we normally avoid. This state of mind has come to be called **deindividuation**.

Deindividuation not only helps to explain the vandalism of many Halloween pranksters but also provides insight into other forms of collective antisocial behavior. Philip Zimbardo (1969, 2007) outlined the antecedents and consequences of a deindividuated state, noting that important contributing factors are *arousal, anonymity,* and

---

Critical THINKING

Imagine that you have been hired to design a training course to teach company employees how to efficiently use a complex computer program. How can you use the findings of social loafing research to design a training course that not only facilitates quick learning, but also encourages high productivity following learning?

---

deindividuation
. . . .
The loss of a sense of individual identity and a loosening of normal inhibitions against engaging in behavior that is inconsistent with internal standards

How does the state of mind known as deindividuation explain why normally law-abiding individuals occasionally behave counter to social norms?

diffused responsibility. Zimbardo argued that when people become deindividuated by a combination of these factors, their inhibitions will be lowered and they will be much more likely to impulsively engage in such antisocial behavior as vandalism, aggression, and rioting. Steven Prentice-Dunn and Ronald Rogers (1980) believe that *accountability cues*, such as anonymity, tell people how far they can go without being held responsible for their actions. These cues loosen restraints against deviant behavior by altering a person's *cost-reward calculations*. For example, during a riot, people often think they won't be caught and punished for engaging in illegal activities, and this reassessment of the costs and rewards lowers their inhibitions. Although early investigators believed that deindividuation occurred only in groups, later research demonstrated that it could also be induced outside of a collective (Chiou, 2006; Festinger et al., 1952).

One example of deindividuation causing antisocial consequences is when onlookers goad people who are threatening suicide. For example, while writing this chapter, I read a newspaper account of a distraught truck driver who committed suicide in his truck after passing motorists used citizens band radios to egg him on when they learned he was threatening to shoot himself. Similarly, in an analysis of newspaper accounts of people witnessing someone threatening suicide by jumping from a building or bridge, Leon Mann (1981) found that when a crowd of onlookers was large or masked by darkness (that is, deindividuated) they often jeered and encouraged the person to jump. Although large crowds and darkness facilitated the antisocial actions of onlookers during suicide attempts, when people were more easily identifiable—small crowds exposed by daylight—Mann found that they generally did not jeer the would-be jumper.

The perceived anonymity of the Internet causes some people to experience diffused responsibility while interacting in "chat rooms" or accessing pornographic material on various web sites. Does this diffused responsibility loosen people's normal inhibitions? In one study investigating Internet-induced deindividuation, Christina Demetriou and Andrew Silke (2003) established a Web site to determine whether people who visited it to gain access to legal material would also try to access illegal and/or pornographic material at the site when they discovered it was available (no such material was actually available). Over a three-month period, a majority of the more than eight hundred visitors who entered the site to view the advertised legal materials also tried to access the illegal and/or pornographic material. Like actual groups, it appears that the "virtual" groups created on Internet sites have the capacity to induce deindividuation.

Because Halloween festivities tend to deindividuate celebrants, it is not surprising that researchers have used this annual event to investigate this process. In one such study,

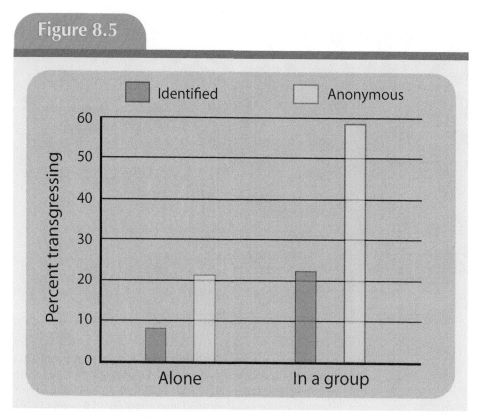

Figure 8.5

Effects of Deindividuation on Stealing Among Halloween Trick-or-Treaters

When trick-or-treating in a group or when anonymous, children were more likely to take extra Halloween candy. However, when both of these factors were present (group immersion and anonymity), candy stealing arose dramatically. What do these results tell us about the effects that deindividuation have on people's normal inhibitions?

Ed Diener and his colleagues (1976) set up testing sites in twenty-seven homes throughout Seattle and waited for young trick-or-treaters to come calling. Some children arrived alone, and others came in groups. On some trials, the experimenter asked the children their names and where they lived, and on other trials the children remained anonymous. Then, the experimenter showed the children a bowl of candy and told them to "take *one* of the candies." Then the children were left alone with the candy bowl while hidden observers recorded how much candy the children actually took. The researchers discovered that, compared to those who were alone, children in a group were more than twice as likely to take extra candy. In addition, compared with children who identified themselves, those who remained anonymous were also more than twice as likely to take more than one piece of candy. As you can see in Figure 8.5, the greatest candy stealing occurred when children were in a group and remained anonymous.

Deindividuation and Reduced Self-Awareness

In explaining deindividuation, Diener (1980) argued that the crucial cognitive factor is a lack of self-awareness. Without such self-awareness, the deindividuated do not think of themselves as separate individuals and do not attend to their own inner values and behavioral standards (see Chapter 3 for a discussion of self-awareness effects). To test this hypothesis, he and his coworkers conducted a second Halloween study in which, as before, experimenters waited for young trick-or-treaters to arrive to request candy (Beaman et al., 1979). After the children were asked to give their names, they were told to take only one candy each and were then left alone by the candy bowl. On some trials, a mirror was placed behind the bowl so that when the children reached for the candy they saw their own image in the mirror. On other trials, no mirror was present. As you may recall from Chapter 3, a mirror induces self-awareness, a psychological state in which one is aware of oneself as an object of attention and is also more attentive to behavioral standards. In such a state, one is not deindividuated. Not surprisingly, in the *mirror present* condition, only 12 percent of the children took extra candy, yet when the mirror was absent, candy stealing increased to 34 percent. These results, and those of other investigations, suggest that *reduced self-awareness* is a component of deindividuation (Diener & Wallbom, 1976; Prentice-Dunn & Rogers, 1982); the deindividuated lose their sense of personal identity in a group by not engaging in self-awareness. Here, as in other aspects of social behavior discussed throughout the text, people abdicate their personal standards of conduct and fall prey to the influence of the immediate situation when they fail to take themselves as objects of attention.

Can Social Identity Activation Explain Deindividuation?

How could you use your knowledge of deindividuation when designing social environments to reduce crime?

Throughout the past forty some years of deindividuation research, the prevailing view has been that it is an expression of antinormative and disinhibited behavior caused by a loss of personal identity. However, Dutch social psychologists Tom Postmes and Russell Spears (1998) propose that what we call antinormative and disinhibited behavior in such situations may actually be a behavioral expression of *conformity* to group norms specific to the situation. Arguing from a social identity perspective (see Chapter 3), Postmes and Spears assert that deindividuating settings do not lead to a loss of personal identity and an acting on impulse; instead, deindividuating settings facilitates a transition from a personal to a more social identity. The so-called antinormative behavior is really an expression of whatever group norm is salient in the situation. Whether they are taking extra candy and stealing pumpkins as Halloween pranksters or touching and hugging strangers in a pitch-black room, the deindividuated are simply conforming to the prevailing group norm of the moment.

Which of these two explanations is correct? Does deindividuation involve a loss of self-awareness and personal identity, or does it involve a shift from a personal identity to a social identity? Postmes and Spears's counterexplanation has received some empirical support (Klein et al., 2007; Kugihara, 2001), but a study conducted by Brian Mullen and his coworkers (2003) suggests a possible resolution of this controversy. These researchers asked European-American college students who had parents belonging to the same ethnic group (for example, Irish or Italian-American) to answer a questionnaire concerning themselves and that aspect of their social identity related to ethnicity. There were three experimental conditions and one control condition in this study. Participants in the *mirror condition* completed the questionnaire while seated at a table in front of a small mirror. Participants in the *mask condition* were asked to wear a featureless, transparent mask while answering the questions, while those in the *family tree condition* were told to write the name of their ethnic group into the three boxes of a small family tree labeled "Father," "Mother," and "You," and to keep the family tree in front of them while completing the questionnaire. A control group simply completed the questionnaire with no manipulations of the testing setting. The questionnaire measured participants' current degree of self-awareness and their current degree of identification with their ethnic group. The researchers reasoned that if the conventional view of deindividuation is correct, participants in the mask condition would exhibit a decrease in both self-awareness and ethnic identity awareness (which is a form of social identity awareness). However, if the social identity explanation is correct, Mullen and his colleagues reasoned that the mask condition would cause an increase in ethnic identity awareness.

As expected, the mirror condition caused an increase in self-awareness and a decrease in ethnic identity awareness in participants, and the family tree condition caused a decrease in self-awareness and an increase in ethnic identity awareness. However, more important, the mask condition caused a decrease in both self-awareness and ethnic identity awareness, which is consistent with the conventional view of deindividuation, but inconsistent with the social identity explanation. As such, this study suggests that deindividuation involves different psychological processes from social identity awareness. This does not mean that certain crowd behavior is not sometimes caused by the activation of a common social identity among crowd members. However, it does suggest that deindividuation is a distinct psychological state, separate from social identification. The deindividuated mindset of being "lost in the crowd" involves a psychological shifting of awareness away from the self; it does not appear to involve a shift from a personal identity to a social identity.

SECTION SUMMARY

- *Social facilitation* involves the enhancement of dominant responses due to the presence of others.

- In social facilitation, others affect our performance:

  by their mere presence,

  as evaluators, and

  by distracting us.

- *Social loafing* occurs when the presence of coperformers reduces individual output because coperformers allow diffusion of task outcome responsibility.

- Group members will work hard on a task when it is highly involving for them, they believe that success depends on their efforts, and their efforts can be judged.

- *Deindividuation* occurs when people's normal inhibitions are diminished due to a loss of individual identity, triggered by anonymity and reduced self-awareness.

DECISION MAKING IN GROUPS

> **❝**I am the people—the mob—the crowd—the mass. Do you know that all the great work of the world is done through me?**❞**
>
> ----------
>
> Carl Sandburg, U.S. poet and historian, 1878–1967

Due to the fact that groups sometimes influence people to behave in ways that are antisocial, some social scientists have suggested that this is evidence that people in groups think and behave more irrationally than they would alone. Although this belief in the inferiority of group thinking and action may be partly a function of the individualist bias of these scientists (Markus & Kitayama, 1994), it is not a new view in the social sciences, nor is it unique to North American scholars. Over a century ago, French sociologists Gustave LeBon (1903) and Gabriel Tarde (1903) described people being magnetically drawn toward crowds, where they then develop a "collective mind." Although the research already discussed in this chapter indicates that people in groups can sometimes act in an inferior and impulsive manner (due to social loafing and deindividuation, respectively), you have learned in previous chapters that individuals acting alone can exhibit similar undesirable actions. Thus, group processes, like individual processes, are amply designed to foster both positive and negative outcomes (Kerr & Tindale, 2004; Luhan et al., 2009). In this chapter section, we examine the decision-making process of groups and the conditions under which group decision making meets with success or failure.

GROUP DECISION MAKING OCCURS IN STAGES AND FOLLOWS VARIOUS RULES.

In making decisions, groups typically move through four distinct stages (Forsyth, 1990). As depicted in Figure 8.6, the *orientation stage* involves the group identifying the task it is trying to accomplish and the strategy it will use to solve it. As you will shortly discover, the type of task presented to the group generally determines the strategy it chooses. In the *discussion stage*, the group gathers information, identifies possible solutions, and evaluates them. Members' influence attempts—either normative or informational—are most apparent in this second stage and in the following *decision stage*. In making decisions, the group relies on either implicit or explicit decision rules (see the section "Group Decision Rules"). Finally, in the *implementation stage*, the group first carries out the decision and then evaluates its effectiveness.

Beyond the stages in group decision making, *how* a group makes a decision depends on what *kind* of decision it is making. Many of the issues on which groups make

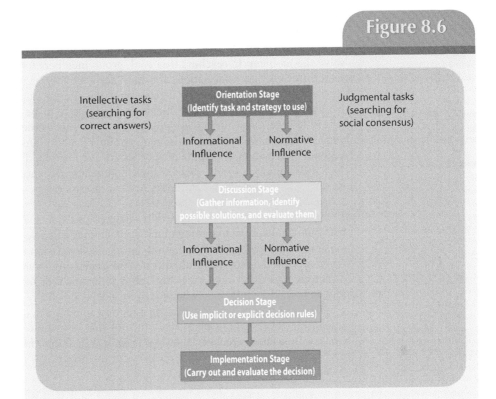

Figure 8.6

Intellective tasks (searching for correct answers)

Orientation Stage
(Identify task and strategy to use)

Judgmental tasks (searching for social consensus)

Informational Influence

Normative Influence

Discussion Stage
(Gather information, identify possible solutions, and evaluate them)

Informational Influence

Normative Influence

Decision Stage
(Use implicit or explicit decision rules)

Implementation Stage
(Carry out and evaluate the decision)

The Stages of Group Decision Making

Group decision making typically moves through four distinct stages: orientation, discussion, decision, and implementation. In what two stages are members' social influence attempts—either normative or informational—most apparent?

decisions can be located on a continuum (Laughlin, 1996). At one end of the continuum are *intellective* issues for which there are demonstrably correct solutions. Here, the group's task is to discover the "true" or "correct" answer. Scientists searching for a cure for AIDS or campers trying to determine how to put together a tent are both examples of groups struggling with an intellective task. In contrast, at the other end of the continuum are *judgmental* issues involving behavioral, ethical, or aesthetic judgments for which there are no demonstrably correct answers. Examples of judgmental tasks are members of an arts council deciding which artists are most worthy of receiving monetary awards, or corporate executives deciding how to market their products. In these types of cases, although the groups' decisions often involve weighing facts, the ultimate decision is principally based on the appeal to social norms and group consensus.

The type of social influence that shapes group decision making often depends on what type of issue a group is addressing (Green, 1998). As you recall from Chapter 7 (pp. 270–272), there are two principal types of social influence: *informational influence* and normative influence. Informational influence occurs when a person accepts others' logical arguments and factual information in defining reality; *normative influence* involves accepting

A scientist trying to find the cure for AIDS and campers trying to put together a tent are all struggling with an intellective task.

others' definition of reality based on the desire to win approval or avoid criticism. Informational influence is most likely to shape the discussion and decision stages when groups work on intellective tasks. The goal is to find and use any information that helps solve the problem. In reaching this goal, group members tend to engage in a thorough search for relevant information, and they are generally eager to share what they find with other members during the discussion stage. On the other hand, when working on judgmental tasks, normative influence is most likely to be used. Because there is no purely "correct" answer, the decision goal is to persuade other group members to accept your judgment. In reaching this goal, group members are less diligent in trying to uncover information, and some members may even withhold information during discussion if divulging it would weaken their arguments. Because of this different strategy, groups working on judgmental tasks tend to discuss only enough information to reach consensus (Wittenbaum & Stasser, 1996).

Informational influence generally dictates decision making on intellective tasks, but when groups have to make a quick decision they often do not have the luxury of systematically searching for information during the discussion stage and instead must rely on more superficial or heuristic information processing (Karau & Kelly, 1992). In such instances, regardless of whether the task is judgmental or intellective, members tend to rely on normative influence when reaching a decision (Kelly et al., 1997).

Because group decision making requires some level of agreement or consensus among members, groups also develop rules that determine when a sufficient level of consensus has been reached. A *group decision rule* is simply the required number of group members that must agree with a position for the group as a whole to adopt it. Common decision rules include the following:

> *Unanimity rule*: All group members must agree on the same position before a decision is finalized.
>
> *Majority-wins rule*: A group opts for whatever position is held by more than 50 percent of its members.
>
> *Plurality-wins rule*: When there is no clear majority, the group opts for the position that has the most support.

Decision rules may be explicit and formal, as is the case with the instructions given a jury to return a unanimous verdict, or they may be implicit and informal, such as a chairperson's intuitive assessment that the group sufficiently agrees on a previously disputed topic to consider it settled (Kaplan & Miller, 1983). Groups that use the unanimity rule are not only more thorough in discussing the issues than groups that employ the majority or plurality decision rules, but they also are more likely to use compromise in reaching a decision, which, not surprisingly, results in greater satisfaction with the final decision (Miller, 1989).

The importance of the group decision rule in shaping the group's final decision has been demonstrated in jury trials (Kaplan & Miller, 1987). The two decision rules employed in the civil jury system in the United States are the unanimity rule and the majority-wins rule. Because the unanimity rule gives every jury member veto power over the group's decision, Yuhsuke Ohtsubo and his coworkers (2004) hypothesized that jury decisions under that rule would be more influenced by extreme member opinions than jury decisions under the majority rule. To test this hypothesis, participants were placed in six-person groups and randomly assigned to either a unanimity rule or a majority rule condition. The defendant in the civil case they analyzed was a hospital whose allegedly negligent treatment left a newborn child with incurable disabilities. Pilot testing indicated that this case would likely produce an initial distribution of juror preferences containing at least one or two opinions that recommended high punitive damages. After reading the case, but before discussing it with fellow jurors, participants were asked to individually indicate their opinion about the appropriate level of punitive damages. Next each group was given twenty minutes to deliberate the case and make a group decision on the punitive damages. In the majority rule condition, participants were told that to reach a group decision, at least four members had to agree on the level of damages (if any) to be awarded. All groups were successful in reaching a decision within the time frame. Consistent with predictions, the correlation between the group decision and the initial preference of the most extreme group member was significant in the unanimity rule condition ($r = .58$), but not in the majority rule condition ($r = .01$), with the difference between these correlations also significant. This finding indicates that group decisions took into account the preferences of the extreme members more under the unanimity rule than under the majority rule. In other words, when the initial preferences of one or two jury members were for high punitive damages, jury decisions were influenced more by those jurors under the unanimity rule than when juries worked under the majority rule. Because assigning the unanimity rule to civil juries appears to increase the influence of jurors with extreme opinions, some might consider the use of that rule undesirable compared with the use of the majority rules. However, the end-of-chapter Applications section discusses research indicating that there are some real benefits in the greater consideration given minority opinions under the unanimity rule as compared with the majority rule in civil jury trials.

GROUP DISCUSSION ENHANCES MAJORITY OPINIONS.

Imagine that you are on the board of directors of a computer company that strives to act in a socially responsible manner. Tomorrow the board will be voting on whether to buy a key component for your new line of laptop computers from supplier A, which is a traditional business, or get them for the same price from supplier B, which employs handicapped workers and does wonderful things in its community. At first, the choice seems clear, because giving business to supplier B fulfills your company's goal of social responsibility. Upon closer inspection, however, you discover that the traditional supplier has years of experience producing both high-volume and high-quality components, but the nontraditional supplier has never produced these components in such huge quantities. In choosing supplier B, you run the risk that your own product could be compromised if the supplier cannot meet your high-volume, high-quality requirements. In making a decision, what would be the *lowest* probabilities or odds of supplier B meeting your requirements you would consider acceptable? A five in ten chance? Seven in ten? Nine in ten? Would it surprise you to know that the level of risk you would settle on would likely be different if you made it on your own versus as part of the board?

Are Group Decisions More or Less Cautious?

Using hypothetical situations like the preceding one, James Stoner (1961) set out to test the commonly held belief that decision making by groups is more cautious than that made by individuals. To accomplish this task, Stoner asked management students to individually respond to twelve hypothetical dilemmas. When done, he brought them together in groups with instructions to discuss each of the problems until they reached a unanimous decision as to what odds they would accept as a group. His findings indicated that the final group decisions were actually *riskier* than the initial individual decisions. For a time this effect was called the risky *shift* (Cartwright, 1971; Pruitt, 1971). However, as more studies were conducted, researchers realized that some group decisions became reliably *more* cautious after discussion, not more risky (Fraser et al., 1971; Knox & Safford, 1976).

How could group discussion produce both greater risk taking and greater conservativism? In time, researchers understood that what was occurring in these group discussions was not a consistent shift toward risk or caution but, rather, a tendency for discussion to *enhance* the initial attitudes of people who already agree (Myers & Lamm, 1976). This group-produced enhancement or exaggeration of members' initial attitudes through discussion was called **group polarization**, and its basic nature is outlined in Figure 8.7. In many respects, group polarization is psychologically similar to what Bibb Latané refers to as *dynamic social impact* in which people become organized into social clusters where they collectively reinforce one another's similarly held attitudes, values, and worldviews (see Chapter 7, p. 299). Political talk shows on the radio and television with either conservative or liberal leanings are good examples of how the group polarization process pushes listeners and viewers to more extreme partisan positions.

group polarization
Group-produced enhancement or exaggeration of members' initial attitudes through discussion

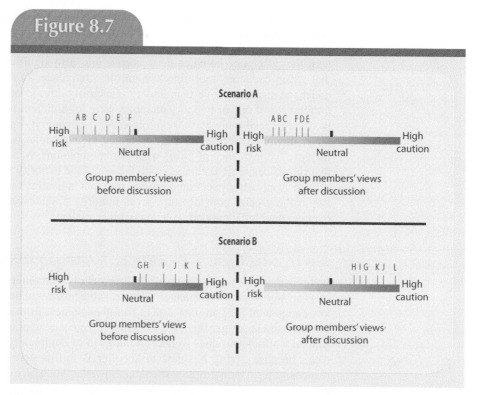

The Process of Group Polarization

In group polarization, discussion by group members enhances the initial attitudes or views of those who already agree, regardless of whether those views reflect caution or risk. Thus, in scenario A, prior to discussion, all members (A, B, C, D, E, and F) have varying degrees of support for engaging in a particular course of action, reflecting their willingness to take somewhat of a risk. Member "A" is most willing to take a risk and member "F" is least willing. Following discussion, the average opinion of the group members has shifted to being strongly in favor of the proposed group action (a shift to greater risk). Similarly, in scenario B, before discussing the issue, all members (G, H, I, J, K, and L) have varying degrees of opposition to the proposed course of action, with member "L" being most cautious and member "G" being least cautious. After discussion, the average opinion of the group members has shifted to being strongly opposed to the group action (a shift to greater caution).

Research indicates that group polarization is more likely to occur on important issues rather than on trivial ones (Kerr, 1992). For example, based on high school students' responses to a racial attitudes questionnaire, David Myers and George Bishop (1970) classified them as high, medium, and low on prejudice. Groups of like-minded students then met to discuss racial issues. The researchers found that students who were initially low in prejudice were even *less* so after the group discussion. In contrast, those who were moderately or highly prejudiced became even *more* prejudiced. Similar strengthening of initial attitudes is also found in many other group settings. In juries, for instance, group discussion tends to lead individual members to more extreme opinions about a defendant's guilt or innocence than they initially held (Myers & Kaplan, 1976).

Even terrorist groups' actions appear to be shaped by group polarization effects. An analysis of terrorist organizations around the world found that these groups typically become more extreme only gradually over time (McCauley & Segal, 1987). Being relatively isolated from those who hold more moderate views, terrorists become more extreme as they interact with one another. The result is increased violence, something the individual members may never have initially endorsed. In response to the September 11, 2001 terrorist attacks, social scientists have analyzed the socialization process in terrorist organizations and found that it typically involves isolating recruits from other belief systems, dehumanizing potential targets, and demanding complete obedience (McCauley,

2002; Moghaddam, 2005). To varying degrees, a similar socialization process occurs in many countries' armed service units during times of war. In that process, group polarization contributes to the escalating calls for retribution and violence among the soldiers who are actively engaged in battle (Kunovich & Deitelbaum, 2004).

Critical
THINKING

Based on social influence research, what type of individuals might be more susceptible to group polarization effects when working on judgmental tasks?

What Produces Group Polarization?

Several different explanations have been offered for the group polarization effect, but the two receiving the most attention and support are the *social comparison* and *persuasive arguments* perspectives (Chen et al., 2002). The social comparison view stresses the role of normative influence in the polarization process, while the persuasive arguments view focuses more exclusively on informational influence.

As you may recall from Chapter 3 (p. 100), the social comparison perspective contends that we are motivated to self-evaluate, a process that we accomplish primarily by comparing ourselves with others (Festinger, 1954). Accordingly, during group discussion, members are concerned with how their positions on relevant issues compare with those of other group members (Goethals & Zanna, 1979). Most assume that they hold better views (more extreme in the valued direction) than others. However, through social comparison, individual members discover that they are not nearly as extreme in the socially valued direction as they initially thought. Because they want others to evaluate them positively (normative influence), discussants begin to shift toward even more extreme positions. Ultimately, this one-upmanship drives the group toward a decision that is either more conservative or more risky than individual members would otherwise have chosen (McGarty et al., 1992).

In contrast to this view, the persuasive arguments position states that group polarization involves *mutual persuasion*. According to this perspective, group discussion is not driven by the desire to be evaluated positively by oneself and others but by the desire to arrive at the correct or true solution. Here, the sheer strength of the arguments offered for certain decision choices is relevant (informational influence). Put simply, when people hear arguments from others, they learn new information. If even a slight majority of group members supports a particular position, most of the arguments presented will favor this view. With more arguments presented in favor of their own position rather than against it, and hearing new supportive arguments that they had not initially considered, members gradually adopt more extreme positions (Brauer et al., 1995).

Daniel Isenberg's (1986) meta-analysis of twenty-one different group polarization studies indicates that social comparison and persuasive argumentation often occur in combination to produce extreme group decisions. In an attempt to explain how these two forces could both produce group polarization, Martin Kaplan (1987) suggests that they may operate in different situations. That is, when the issue involves intellective tasks in which facts are weighed, group members will be primarily concerned with the information presented in people's arguments. In such a scenario, the persuasiveness of the arguments is what pushes their position toward extremity. However, when the issue involves judgmental tasks for which there are clearly no objectively right or wrong solutions, people are more likely to compare their views with those of others. Here, social comparison is more important in group polarization effects.

CONSENSUS SEEKING OVERRIDES
CRITICAL ANALYSIS IN GROUPTHINK.

On March 19, 2003, President George W. Bush ordered the invasion of Iraq with the objective of overthrowing the dictatorial government of Saddam Hussein. The Central Intelligence Agency provided evidence indicating that Iraq had weapons of mass destruction and that Hussein's government was planning terrorist attacks with Osama bin Laden's al-Qaeda organization. Citing this evidence, President Bush launched a preemptive military strike and believed that his forces would achieve a quick and decisive victory, the Iraqi people would welcome the invading force, and America would become a beacon of hope for people in the Middle East.

Many social commentators used the term groupthink to characterize the group dynamics of President George W. Bush and his cabinet during their decision to invade Iraq in 2003. To best prevent groupthink, what stage in group decision making should be principally targeted?

Nothing could have been further from the truth. Sixteen months following the invasion of Iraq, with American soldiers being killed daily, the U.S. Senate Select Committee on Intelligence issued a highly critical report on the decision making leading up to the war, charging that CIA analysts withheld information from Congress that did not support a military strike. Individual members of the committee also accused the Bush administration of actively orchestrating this distortion of information so that it could win public support for the war. In assessing the war's effects on the nation's security and prestige, Senate Committee member John Rockefeller stated, "Our credibility is diminished. Our standing in the world has never been lower. We have fostered a deep hatred of Americans in the Muslim world, and that will grow. As a direct consequence, our nation is more vulnerable today than ever before."

How could otherwise intelligent and competent people make such poor decisions? After analyzing an equally disastrous 1961 decision by the Kennedy administration to invade Cuba, Irving Janis (1982, 1996) contended that groups are sometimes susceptible to an extreme form of group polarization, which he called **groupthink**. This condition refers to a deterioration of mental efficiency, reality testing, and moral judgment in groups that have an excessive desire to reach consensus. According to Janis, groupthink emerges when maintaining a pleasant social atmosphere becomes more important than making the best decision.

Janis hypothesized that three major factors contribute to groupthink. The first factor is *high group cohesiveness*. Although a high level of cohesiveness among group members would seem to be a very positive group characteristic, it also is associated with increased conformity. That is, when people are strongly attracted to a group and want badly to be accepted by it, they are more likely to allow group members to influence their thinking and actions (t'Hart et al., 1993). Janis believed that when high cohesiveness is combined with the other two factors, namely a *threatening situational context* and *structural and procedural faults*, groups become more susceptible to groupthink. Regarding the situational context, Janis contended that groups faced with a threatening or stressful situation may value speed of decision making over accuracy. In addition, as we will discuss in Chapter 9 (pp. 357–359), during times of stress people become more dependent on the reassuring support of others, which should increase the group's influence on individual members. According to Janis, structural and procedural faults that contribute to groupthink are a lack of systematic procedures for making and reviewing decisions, the isolation of the group from others, and a strong, directive leader who lets other members know what his or her inclinations are regarding the group's final decision.

groupthink

A deterioration of mental efficiency, reality testing, and moral judgment in a group that results from an excessive desire to reach consensus

Symptoms of Groupthink

Janis believed that there are three symptoms indicating that a group is suffering from groupthink. These are as follows:

1. *An overestimation of one's ingroup* Members develop an illusion of invulnerability and an unquestioned belief in the ingroup's own morality. During the Iraq War decision-making process, the Bush ingroup uncritically accepted the CIA's flawed information on Iraq's alleged weapons of mass destruction and their ties to al-Qaeda. They also falsely assumed that the U.S. military could simultaneously crush armed opposition and win the "hearts and minds" of the Iraqi people (Rodrigues et al., 2005).

2. *Close-mindedness* Members rationalize the correctness of their decisions and develop a stereotyped view of their opponents. "It was all about finding a way to do it. That was the tone of it," said Paul O'Neill, Bush's Treasury secretary. "The President saying, 'Go find me a way to do this' " (Mackay, 2004). Because Bush and his advisers were convinced that Iraq had a program to develop weapons of mass destruction, they ignored evidence that disconfirmed their beliefs and instead emphasized information provided by discredited Iraqi defectors. Later, Secretary of State Colin Powell stated that after the September 11th terrorist attacks, Deputy Defense Secretary Paul Wolfowitz "was always of the view that Iraq was a problem that had to be dealt with … And he saw this as one way of using this event" (Smith, 2004).

3. *Increased conformity pressure* Members reject those who raise doubts about the group's assumptions and decisions, and they censor their own misgivings in what becomes a "spiral of silence." With all this conformity pressure, members develop an illusion that everyone is in agreement, which serves to confirm the group's ill-chosen decisions. "Groupthink is more likely to arise when there is a strong premium on loyalty and when there is not a lot of intellectual range or diversity within a decision-making body," says political scientist Stephen Walt. "The Bush administration has been an unusually secretive group of like-minded people where a high premium is placed on loyalty" (Kemper, 2004).

" *That is no use at all. What I want is men who will support me when I am in the wrong.* **"**

————————

Lord Melbourne, British prime minister, 1779–1848, in reply to a politician's pledge: "I will support you as long as you are in the right."

Research on Groupthink

Besides the Iraq War and the invasion of Cuba, groupthink tendencies have been identified in various tragedies, political blunders, and national conflicts, such as the decision to launch the space shuttle *Challenger* on its doomed mission in January of 1986 (Moorhead et al., 1991), the long-lasting Northern Ireland conflict (Hergovich & Olbrich, 2003), the 1994 genocide of ethnic Tutsis during the Rwandan Civil War (Dutton, 2007), and the Bush Administration's policies that endorsed torture at Abu Ghraib Prison during the Iraq War (Post & Panis, 2011). However, in the years since the theory's creation, research called into question some of its proposed causes (Turner et al., 2007).

In a comprehensive test of Janis's theory, Philip Tetlock and his colleagues (1992) conducted a content analysis of the factual accounts of ten historic decisions that potentially involved groupthink. Consistent with the theory, historic events involving disastrous decisions exhibited significantly more groupthink characteristics than those that led to successful decisions. Some of these groupthink characteristics were suspicion of outsiders, restriction of information exchange, and punishment of group dissenters. Further, as groups became more concerned with maintaining consensus, they exhibited more groupthink symptoms, which in turn caused more defective decision making. However, contrary to Janis's theory, this study did not find any evidence that group cohesiveness or situational threat were predictors of groupthink symptoms. Later research indicates that cohesiveness can increase the risk of groupthink when it is accompanied by other risk factors, such as high stress or directive leaders who promote their own agenda rather than encouraging alternative viewpoints (Chapman, 2006; Hornsey & Imani, 2004). These and other findings suggest that groupthink does exist, but it does not appear to function in the exact manner first proposed by Janis (Henningsen et al., 2006; Straus et al., 2011).

Due to the potential harm groupthink processes generate, what can groups do to prevent it? Based on the available evidence, the most important recommendation is to improve decision-making structures and procedures during the group's orientation stage (Schafer & Crichlow, 1996). Doing so will increase the likelihood that alternative perspectives will be fully weighed and considered during the discussion and decision stages. To facilitate this process, group leaders should encourage criticism and skepticism of all ideas, and once a decision has been reached, the group should return to the discussion stage so that members can express any lingering doubts (Kowert, 2002; Nemeth et al., 2001).

At the individual level, recent studies have provided additional insights into the characteristics of group members that make them more or less willing to express unpopular opinions that can short circuit groupthink. Dominic Packer (2009 found that strongly identified group members are more attentive to group decision making and are often more willing than those who are weakly identified to express dissenting opinions about a group problem they believed is collectively harmful . As a result, groups with strongly identified members may be less likely to fall prey to groupthink than groups that have less involved members. There is also evidence that a group with diversity in its membership is less likely to fall prey to groupthink than a group with a more homogenized membership. The key contribution that group diversity appears to provide is an increased resistance to group consensus. In a study of bicultural individuals' actions during group decision making, Aurelia Mok and Michael Morris (2011) found that bicultural individuals with conflicted cultural identities were more likely to challenge bad group decisions than were bicultural individuals with highly integrated cultural identities. Mok and Morris contend that the conflict that some bicultural individuals experience between their cultural identities provides them with a contrarian mindset that makes it easier for them to play the "devil's advocate" in challenging faulty group decision making. Combining Packer's findings with those of Mok and Morris, it appears that groups will be more resistant to groupthink to the extent that their membership is strongly identified with the group and has the type of diversity that encourages contrarian thinking.

SECTION SUMMARY

- Most group decisions involve intellective or judgmental issues:

  Intellective decisions are generally reached through informational influence.

  Judgmental decisions typically rely on normative influence.

- Group decisions are also influenced by formal and informal rules.

- Group polarization occurs when group discussion enhances the initial positions of members.

- Groupthink is an extreme form of group polarization, which refers to a deterioration of mental efficiency, reality testing, and moral judgment resulting from an excess desire to reach consensus.

LEADERSHIP

As previously mentioned, members of a group accept influence from others whom they believe have greater ability. In this chapter section, we examine these high-status individuals and the nature of their relationship with those who have lower status.

leader
• • • • • • • • • • • • • • • • •
The person who exerts the most influence and provides direction and energy to the group

A LEADER IS AN INFLUENCE AGENT.

The person who exerts the most influence and provides direction and energy to the group is the **leader** (Riggio & Conger, 2007). This is the person who initiates action, gives orders, doles out rewards and punishments, settles disputes between fellow members, and pushes and pulls the group toward its goals. Many groups have only one leader; other groups have two or more individuals with equally high levels of influence. Generally, groups tend to have multiple leaders as their tasks become more diverse and complex (Fletcher & Käufer, 2003).

In their position of social influence, leaders are called on to perform two basic types of activities. *Task leadership* consists of accomplishing the goals of the group, and *socioemotional leadership* involves an attention to the emotional and inter-personal aspects of group interaction (Bales, 1970; Hare & Kent, 1994). The necessary qualities for effective task leadership are efficiency, directiveness, and knowledge about the relevant group task. Task leaders tend to have a directive style, giving orders and being rather impersonal in their dealings with group members. In contrast, friendliness, empathy, and an ability to mediate conflicts are important qualities for effective socioemotional leadership. A socioemotional leader's style is more democratic, with greater emphasis on delegating authority and inviting input from others (Fiedler, 1987).

In some groups, one person is the task leader and another person is the socioemotional leader (*see the contingency model,* pp. 336–337). In other groups, one leader performs both functions. In such instances, the leader must know when to be the taskmaster and when to be the supportive confidant—a difficult feat because the two leadership styles often conflict. Research indicates that individuals with a *flexible* leadership style know when to focus on task production and when to show concern for interpersonal relations. They also tend to receive the highest leadership ratings by other group members (Kirkpatrick & Locke, 1991).

One of the earliest approaches to understanding leadership was to search for personality traits that caused some people and not others to become leaders. Unfortunately, few leader characteristics have been identified (Northouse, 2001). Research conducted primarily in the United States finds that leaders tend to be slightly more intelligent and taller than nonleaders, are more confident and adaptable, and, not surprisingly, are harder working, more ambitious, and have a higher desire for power (Ottati & Deiger, 2002; Simonton, 1994). A social identity perspective on leadership is that people become leaders when they best reflect group members' identity (Haslam et al., 2011; Hogg, 2010). From this social identity perspective, the reason leaders in the United States are taller, smarter, more confident, adaptable, and ambitious than the average person is because that is how Americans like to think of their collective selves, their national identity. Of course, picking leaders who best reflect our collective identity can have unfortunate consequences when we base our judgments more on image than on substance. This may partially explain why women, for example, are so underrepresented as leaders in American business and government; they don't fit most people's leader prototype (see p. 339).

" *I am a leader by default, only because nature does not allow a vacuum.* **"**

Archbishop Desmond Tutu, Nobel Peace-Prize winner and primate of the Anglican Church in South Africa, b. 1931

TRANSFORMATIONAL LEADERS INSPIRE FOLLOWERS.

transformational leaders
∙∙∙∙∙∙∙∙∙∙∙∙∙∙∙∙∙
Leaders who change (transform) the outlook and behavior of followers so that they move beyond their self-interests for the good of the group or society

Besides representing the group's identity, another important quality that many effective leaders possess is charisma, a quality that has prompted a number of researchers to analyze the psychological dynamics of *charismatic* or **transformational leaders** (Halevy et al., 2011; Rowold & Heinitz, 2007). A transformational leader changes—or transforms—the outlook and behavior of followers, which allows them to move beyond their self-interests for the good of the group or society (Bass, 2008; Conger et al., 2000). The great leaders of the twentieth century—Mahatma Gandhi and Jawaharlal Nehru in India, Franklin Roosevelt and Martin Luther King, Jr., in the United States, Nelson Mandela in South Africa, and even Adolf Hitler in Germany—all inspired tremendous changes in their respective societies by making supporters believe that anything was possible if they collectively worked toward a common good (as defined by the leader). Transformational leaders are most effective when the vision they offer fits the group's current norms and values. The general view of transformational leaders is that they are "natural born" influence agents who inspire high devotion, motivation, and productivity in group members (Lowe et al., 1996). Because transformational leaders often use unconventional strategies that put them at risk, it is not uncommon for them to face severe physical hard-

One of the great transformational leaders of the twentieth century was Franklin D. Roosevelt, 32nd president of the United States. Can you identify three components of transformational leadership?

ships—and even death—in moving the group to its goals.

Survey, interview, and experimental studies suggest there are at least the following three core components to transformational leadership (Goethals, 2005; Kirkpatrick & Locke, 1996):

1. *Demonstrating a charismatic communication style:* Transformational leaders have a captivating communication style, in which they make direct eye contact, exhibit animated facial expressions, and use powerful speech and nonverbal tactics.

2. *Communicating a vision:* A vision, which is a future ideal state embodying shared group values, is the main technique that transformational leaders use to inspire followers. In communicating a vision, leaders convey the expectation of high performance among followers and a confidence that they have the ability to reach the vision.

3. *Implement a vision:* Transformational leaders use a variety of techniques to implement a vision, such as clarifying how task goals are to be accomplished, serving as a role model, providing individualized support, and recognizing accomplishments.

The concept of transformational leadership has stimulated renewed interest in the trait approach to understanding leader influence, but it explains only a small percentage of leaders. Further, even theorists studying these charismatic types admit that they are most likely to emerge during times of change, growth, and crisis (Barbuto, 1997; Nemanich & Keller, 2007). What about times of relative stability, and what about the majority of leaders who do not have these special qualities?

> **"** *Without a shepherd sheep are not a flock.* **"**
>
> Russian proverb

> **"** *The charismatic leader gains and maintains authority solely by proving his strength in life.* **"**
>
> Max Weber, German sociologist, 1864–1920

> **"** *An army of sheep led by a lion would defeat an army of lions led by a sheep.* **"**
>
> Arab proverb

THE CONTINGENCY MODEL IS AN INTERACTIONIST VIEW OF LEADERSHIP.

Instead of simply attending to special personality characteristics, an alternative approach to understanding leadership—which draws inspiration from Kurt Lewin's notion of *interactionism* (see Chapter 1, p. 16)—is to view it as a combination of personal and situational factors. Fred Fiedler's (1967, 1993) **contingency model of leadership** contends that people do not become effective leaders because they possess a particular set of personality traits but, rather, because their particular personality matches the circumstances of a particular group. In other words, the traits that make a leader effective are *contingent* on the circumstances the leader encounters. Fiedler's model has four basic components, the first dealing with leadership style and the remaining three encompassing the characteristics of the situation.

Leadership Style

Consistent with earlier research, Fiedler argued that there are two basic types of leaders. A *task-oriented leader* is one who gives highest priority to getting the work of the group accomplished and is much less concerned with the relations among group members. In contrast, a *relationship-oriented leader* assigns highest priority to group relations, with task accomplishment being of secondary concern. Vince Lombardi, who coached the Green Bay Packers football team in the 1960s, was a task-oriented leader. In describing his focus

contingency model of leadership
....

The theory that leadership effectiveness depends both on whether leaders are task oriented or relationship oriented and on the degree to which they have situational control

of concern as a leader, he stated, "Winning isn't everything, it's the *only* thing." Although Lombardi's leadership style was instrumental in the Packers winning five championships in nine years, his style would be ill-suited for a children's team, where coaches must attend to players' feelings. Instead, this situation requires a relationship-oriented leader who would place priority on fostering positive social relationships first ("Having fun is more important than winning or losing"). Fiedler believed that these contrasting leadership styles were a product of enduring personality traits, and thus, would be difficult or impossible to change.

To identify these two leadership styles, Fiedler developed the *Least Preferred Coworker Scale*, which asks leaders to evaluate the person in the group they like least. Fiedler found that leaders who evaluated their least preferred coworker (LPC) very negatively were primarily motivated to attain successful task performance and only secondarily motivated to seek good interpersonal relations among group members. These low LPC leaders fit the mold of the task-oriented leader. In contrast, Fiedler found that leaders who evaluated their LPCs positively were primarily motivated toward achieving satisfactory interpersonal relationships among the group members and only secondarily motivated to successfully complete group tasks. These high LPC leaders fit the mold of the relationship-oriented leader. Spend a few minutes completing *Self/Social Connection Exercise 8.1* to gain some insight into your own leadership style.

Self/Social Connections Exercise 8.1

Who is Your Least Preferred Coworker?

Directions

To learn more about your own leadership style, think of all the individuals with whom you have ever worked, in school organizations, sports teams, jobs, or whatever. Now, think of the one person with whom you could work least well, meaning the person with whom you had the most difficulty completing a task. This is the person with whom you would least want to work. Describe this person using the following scale, circling numbers between each of the following opposing adjectives:

Unfriendly	1	2	3	4	5	6	7	8	Friendly
Uncooperative	1	2	3	4	5	6	7	8	Cooperative
Unsupportive	1	2	3	4	5	6	7	8	Supportive
Unpleasant	1	2	3	4	5	6	7	8	Pleasant
Closed	1	2	3	4	5	6	7	8	Open
Depressing	1	2	3	4	5	6	7	8	Cheerful
Disloyal	1	2	3	4	5	6	7	8	Loyal
Gloomy	1	2	3	4	5	6	7	8	Jovial
Negative	1	2	3	4	5	6	7	8	Positive

Scoring

Determine your total score by adding all nine circled numbers. If your score is 36 or above, this indicates you tend to have a "relationship-oriented" leadership style. If your score is 32 or below, this indicates you tend to have a "task-oriented" leadership style. If your score is 33 to 35, you may have a mixture of both.

Source: Adapted from Fiedler & Garcia (1987).

Situational Control

According to Fiedler, the favorability of the situation for task-oriented (low-LPC) and relationship-oriented (high-LPC) leaders will depend on the degree to which the situation allows them to exert influence over group members. This *situational control* depends on three factors:

1. *The leader's relations with the group* The leader's personal relations with group members can range from very good to very poor and are similar to the previously discussed idiosyncrasy credits. Fiedler believes that leader/member relations is the most important factor determining the leader's influence on followers (Fiedler, 1967).
2. *Task structure* How clearly defined are the goals and the tasks of the group? The amount of structure can vary a great deal, from clear to unclear.
3. *The leader's position power* This factor includes the power and authority inherent in the leadership position. Does the organization back the leader? Does the leader have the power to reward and punish followers? The leader's position power can vary from strong to weak.

Taking these three situational factors into consideration, a leader has high situational control when the leader/member relations are good, there is clear task structure, and the leader has strong position power. In contrast, poor leader/member relations, an unstructured task, and weak position power indicate low situational control.

Predicting Leader Effectiveness

As Figure 8.8 shows, Fiedler hypothesizes that task-oriented (low-LPC) leaders are the most effective in situations in which they have either high or low situational control. In contrast, relationship-oriented (high-LPC) leaders should be associated with better group performance when they have only a moderate degree of control.

As Fiedler explains, under difficult conditions of low situational control, groups need considerable guidance to be productive, and thus they benefit from leaders who have this as their primary motivating goal. This challenging situation plays to the strengths of the task-oriented leader. In contrast, a relationship-oriented leader's more democratic style offers too little guidance in these low-control situations. When the situation in the group is very favorable, task-oriented leaders realize that their goal of task accomplishment is likely to be met and relationship-oriented leaders realize that they already enjoy good relations with their followers. With both leaders' primary motivating goals already achieved, they switch to achieving their respective secondary motives. For task-oriented leaders, their subsequent adoption of a more relaxed style increases group productivity, but the more directive style adopted by relationship-oriented leaders harms group performance because members perceive it as needless meddling. The only situation in which relationship-oriented leaders are more effective than task-oriented leaders is when they have only moderate situational control, such as when the task is unclear or the leader has little power. In such circumstances, a considerate, open-minded management approach should be best at rallying group support and fostering creative solutions to problems.

In support of the contingency model, both field and laboratory studies find that no one style of leadership is effective in all situations (Peters et al., 1985; Schriesheim et al., 1994). Effective leadership requires a good fit between the leader's personal style and the demands of the situation. When the fit is not good, group productivity suffers (Ayman, 2004). When a leader's style does not properly fit the situation, this mismatch also causes increased job stress and stress-related illnesses in the leader (Fiedler & Garcia, 1987; Graen & Hui, 2001)—a bad situation for all concerned. One limitation of this theory is that it assumes leaders can have only one style, yet some leaders can adapt their style to meet the needs of the situation (Huczynski & Buchanan, 1996).

GENDER AND CULTURE CAN INFLUENCE LEADERSHIP STYLE.

Women are assuming larger leadership positions in many countries around the world at the same time that the general public believes that the sexes substantially differ in their

> **❝***There is no such thing as a perfect leader either in the past or present, in China or elsewhere. If there is one, he is only pretending, like a pig inserting scallions into its nose in an effort to look like an elephant.***❞**
>
> Liu Shao-chíi, founding member of the Chinese Communist Party, 1898–1969

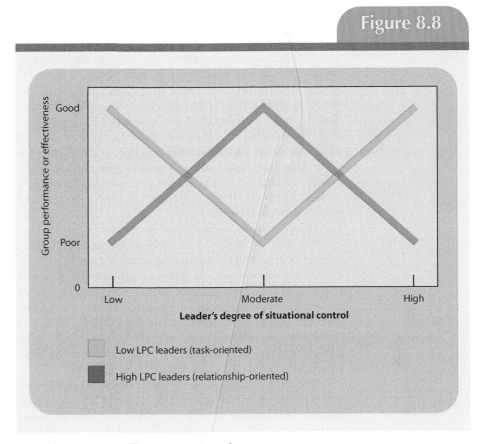

Figure 8.8

Predicting Group Effectiveness Based on Leadership Style and Situational Control

Based on your understanding of Fiedler's contingency theory of leadership and your reading of the figure, when are high LPC (relationship-oriented) leaders most effective in encouraging group productivity? How about low LPC (task-oriented) leaders?

style or approach to leadership. Although there appear to be some gender differences in leadership, research indicates that there are more similarities than differences (Eagly & Johannesen-Schmidt, 2001). In a meta-analysis of more than 150 studies of leadership in which men and women were compared, Alice Eagly and Blair Johnson (1990) found that in organizational settings, female leaders are as task oriented as their male counterparts. Where they differ from males is in their tendency to adopt a more democratic or participative leadership style. That is, women are more likely than men to invite subordinates to participate in the decision-making process. In contrast, male leaders tend to have an autocratic or directive style, in which orders are given rather than suggestions solicited. A more recent meta-analysis of leadership styles found similar results, including that women are somewhat more likely than men to acknowledge and reward subordinates for good performance (Eagly et al., 2003).

These leader differences, while relatively small, are consistent with findings indicating that women tend to be friendlier and agree more in group discussions than men, and men tend to have higher rates of counterarguments (Johnson et al., 1996). Overall, it appears that male leaders tend to be more pure task-oriented types, while female leaders blend in a bit more of the interpersonal concerns typical of relationship-oriented leaders (Eagly et al., 1995; Helgesen, 1990). In explaining these small, yet significant, gender differences, various social psychologists suggest that they may exist because women are more socialized to develop stronger empathic and interpersonal skills than men, while men are more socialized to seek dominance in their social relationships (Foels & Pappas, 2004; Wilson & Liu, 2003). The greater superiority that women appear to have in attending to others' concerns and feelings may allow them to more easily adopt a leadership style employing considerable give-and-take with subordinates that can facilitate group productivity (Bartone et al., 2002; Peterson, 2003).

One potential impediment to some women assuming leadership positions in mixed-sex groups is gender stereotypes. In many cultures around the world, the leader prototype is more closely associated with male stereotypes (Eagly & Karau, 2002). This masculinization of the leader role often leads to the perception that women are less qualified for elite leadership positions than men (Becker et al., 2002). Indeed, there is evidence that people—including women—react more negatively to women than men who adopt a directive leadership style (Eagly et al., 1992; Garcia-Retamero & Lopez-Zafra, 2006). However, there is also evidence suggesting that women who are highly confident in their leadership abilities are not negatively affected by the "women are not natural leaders" stereotype (Hoyt & Blascovich, 2007). Success in leadership by these highly confident women positions will chip away at the traditional gender-based leader stereotype (Singh & Vinnicombe, 2006).

Moving from gender to cultural considerations, how might leadership style operate differently in individualist and collectivist cultures? A growing body of research suggests that the ideal leader may be different in these two cultures (Teagarden, 2007). Collectivists' concerns about group needs and interpersonal relations appear to foster a social climate in which nurturing, relationship-oriented leaders are highly desired by group members (Smith et al., 1990; Walumbwa et al., 2007). In contrast, individualists are socialized to work alone, to concentrate on the task, and to emphasize achievement over socializing (Sanchez-Burks et al., 2000). This training appears to make individualists somewhat more responsive to task-oriented leaders.

One possible implication of these findings is that the previously discussed contingency model of leadership—which proposes that task-oriented leaders exhibit greater effectiveness in more varied situations than relationship-oriented leaders—may be better suited to explain leadership in individualist cultures than in those that are collectivist. Further, what about people living in multicultural societies like the United States and Canada who are also members of collectivist-oriented ethnic groups within these predominantly individualist societies? If you are a member of one of these ethnic groups, does your collectivist heritage cause you to respond to leaders somewhat differently than the typical individualist? It's possible. Jeffrey Sanchez-Burks and his coworkers (2000) found that Mexican Americans tend to be more responsive to relationship-oriented work groups than are Anglo Americans. These findings raise the possibility that even within an individualist society like the United States, how we respond to task-oriented versus relationship-oriented leaders may be partly determined by whether our ethnic heritage has individualist or collectivist roots.

SECTION SUMMARY

- A leader is the person who exerts the most influence and provides direction and energy to the group.

- Transformational leaders are those who dramatically change the outlook and behavior of followers. Their attributes include the ability to engage in charismatic communication and communicate and implement a vision.

- In the contingency model of leadership, leader effectiveness is determined by the interaction of the personal factor of *leadership style* (task-oriented and relationship-oriented) and three situational factors that provide the leader with situational control:

  leader's relations with the group

  task structure

  leader's position power

- Although female leaders are as task oriented as male leaders, women tend to have a more democratic leadership style.

- In collectivist cultures, relationship-oriented leaders may be more effective than they are in individualist cultures.

GROUP INTERESTS
VERSUS INDIVIDUAL INTERESTS

The idea that followers' responsiveness to certain types of leaders may partly depend on whether they are individualists or collectivists has relevance to the final topic in this chapter. Whenever individuals are involved in group activities, the possibility always exists that they will be faced with a situation in which their own immediate interests diverge from those of the group. How individuals resolve this conflict has been the subject of considerable attention by social psychologists over the years.

SOCIAL DILEMMAS OCCUR WHEN
SHORT-TERM AND LONG-TERM INTERESTS CONFLICT.

social dilemma

Any situation in which the most rewarding short-term choice for an individual will ultimately cause negative consequences for the group as a whole

A **social dilemma** is any situation in which the most rewarding short-term choice for an individual will ultimately cause negative consequences for the group as a whole (de Kwaadsteniet et al., 2010). A classic example of a social dilemma concerning how two or more people share a limited resource is the "tragedy of the commons" described by ecologist Garret Hardin (1968). Imagine a small town with a communal piece of land—the commons—available to all the townspeople's cattle. For many years the commons has been able to grow enough grass to support fifty cattle, one for each farmer. Now suppose that one farmer selfishly adds another cow to the commons to increase his milk production. Other farmers, noticing this addition, also add more cattle. Soon the farmers reap the results of their selfishness and competitiveness—the commons dies and all the cattle perish. By pursuing short-term individual gains, the farmers orchestrated a collective disaster. This type of social dilemma is known as a *resource dilemma* (Kortenkamp & Moore, 2006).

We read about numerous examples of resource dilemmas in the newspapers or confront them in our daily lives. The depletion of the South American rain forests brings timber companies short-term profits, but it poses a serious long-term threat to our environment. Even closer to home is the tendency for people to regularly use or benefit from certain public services—such as schools, libraries, parks, roads, public radio, and consumer groups—at the same time that they fail to contribute to their continued existence. If users do not contribute, the services will no longer be available. This willingness to use a public good, coupled with an unwillingness to contribute to it, has been called the *free-rider problem*.

In all social dilemmas, people are in a situation of *mixed motives* in which it is to their advantage both to cooperate and to act selfishly. Their short-term interests will be advanced if they act selfishly, but their long-term interests and those of the group will be advanced if they cooperate. Although you might expect that people would cooperate when such cooperation will enhance their long-term interests, this is often not the case. For example, in a study of resource dilemmas, Julian Edney (1979) had college students play a game in which ten metal nuts were placed into a bowl. They were told that the goal of the game was for each student to gather as many nuts as possible. They were further told that they could remove as many nuts from the bowl as they wished, and every ten seconds the number of nuts remaining in the bowl would be doubled. Despite the fact that the most rational choice for individual players was to leave the nuts in the bowl for a period of time so that they would multiply in numbers, this was not the typical strategy game players adopted. Instead, when the game started, most players simply grabbed as many nuts as they could snatch from the grasp of others. Sixty-five percent of Edney's groups did not even make it past the first ten-second replacement period!

Have you noticed a psychological similarity between resource dilemmas and the phenomenon of social loafing examined earlier? In resource dilemmas, individuals deplete the group resource by taking from it more than their fair share, and in social loafing, individuals deplete group productivity (a group resource) by taking some of their own effort out of the collective effort. In both instances, being "lost in the crowd"—or deindividuated—allows members the protection necessary to behave selfishly (Williams et al., 1995). Although there are these similarities, research indicates that, unlike social loafing, fear and greed are two primary motives driving social dilemma decisions (Bruins et al., 1989; Simpson, 2006). When people notice that others are taking a free ride or depleting collective resources, they abandon a socially responsible strategy and grab what they can (Kerr, 1983).

Social dilemmas are not limited to conflicts involving limited resources. Another type of dilemma, the *prisoner's dilemma*, derives its name from the research paradigm employed by social psychologists to study it. In its original format, the prisoner's dilemma involves a situation in which two men suspected of a crime are arrested by the police and placed into separate interrogation rooms (Luce & Raiffa, 1957). The district attorney is confident that the two together committed the crime but she does not have sufficient evidence to convict them. She approaches each suspect individually and tells him he has two alternatives: to confess to the crime the police are certain they both committed or not to confess. If they both do not confess, the district attorney states that she will charge them on some minor offense and each will get one year in prison. If both confess, they will be prosecuted, but the district attorney will recommend less than the most severe sentence; both will get eight years in prison. However, if one confesses and the other does not, then the one who confesses will receive a very lenient sentence of only six months for testifying against the other, but the one who holds out will get the maximum penalty of twenty years in prison.

The essentials of the prisoner's dilemma are presented in Figure 8.9, representing what will happen to each prisoner in the four possible combinations of confessing and not confessing. Each prisoner knows that the other has the same options and knowledge as himself.

> *I have labored to procure the good of every individual everywhere, so far as this did not conflict with the good of the whole.*
>
> ------------
>
> Catherine II, Empress of Russia, 1729–1796

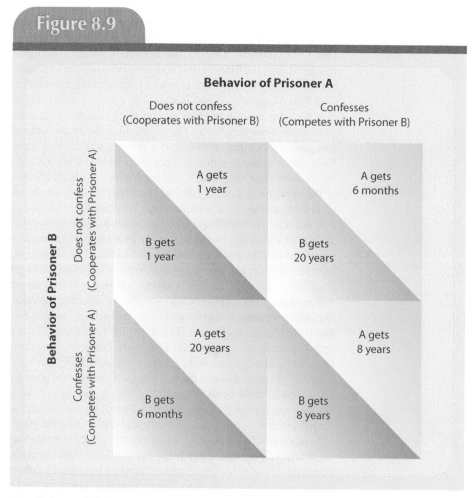

Figure 8.9

The Prisoner's Dilemma

In this form of social dilemma, two suspected criminals are interrogated separately and are given a choice: to confess or not to confess. If both cooperate with each other by staying silent, both get off with fairly light sentences (upper left). If both compete with each other by confessing, both receive moderate sentences (lower right). But if one confesses while the other stays silent, the confessor gets a very light sentence and the nonconfessor spends a long time in prison (lower left and upper right).

Mutual nonconfession would produce a reasonably agreeable outcome for both; it would be their second choice of the four outcomes. However, the outcome most advantageous for one prisoner (getting six months) is the outcome that the other prisoner would least prefer (getting twenty years). Both prisoners would select mutual confession as their third choice among the outcomes. What would you do in this situation?

Numerous studies have used variations of the prisoner's dilemma to identify the factors that tip the balance toward cooperation or competition (Liberman et al., 2004). Frequently, the game is played over a series of trials so that players can alter their choices based on how their partner/competitor previously behaves. One variation entails two countries involved in an arms race, with each trial involving decision makers from each country choosing between competing (by building missiles) or cooperating (by building factories) with the other country. Initially in these multiple-trial games, competition typically occurs in the early trials, but then people begin to cooperate as they experience the negative consequences of competition and try to reduce them (Insko et al., 2001; Nowak & Sigmund, 1993). The findings from prisoner's dilemma studies and those involving resource dilemmas suggest that many factors play a role in promoting cooperation versus competition in mixed-motives situations. Let us now turn our attention to those factors.

COOPERATION IS NECESSARY TO RESOLVE SOCIAL DILEMMAS.

The basic problem in resolving many social dilemmas is that it requires the cooperative efforts of numerous people (Stouten et al., 2006). Yet all too often, people are unwilling to give up their short-term gain strategies until the social dilemma becomes quite serious or they sustain many competitive losses (Yamagishi, 1988). Resolving social dilemmas is not easy under such conditions, but research reveals several ways to promote cooperation.

Sanctioning Cooperative Behavior

"He who acts with a constant view to his own advantage will be much murmured against."

Confucius, Chinese philosopher, 554–479 BC

Without a sanctioning system in place to regulate people's short-term interest strategies, cooperative group members are often taken advantage of by their more competitive neighbors (Koole et al., 2001). One way to increase the cooperation of selfish individuals is to threaten them with punishment. Often this is accomplished by establishing an authority that will set up guidelines of conduct that are consistent with the collective welfare of the group (Van Vugt & De Cremer, 1999). Interestingly, people who tend to be less cooperative and less trusting of others' behavior are more willing to contribute money to establish such an authority (Yamagishi, 1986). A sanctioning system that intermittently punishes noncooperators increases cooperation among those not punished (Loukopoulos et al., 2006). Is punishment the only effective sanctioning system to increase cooperation? A recent meta-analysis of 187 studies found that offering incentives for cooperation is as effective as doling out punishment in resolving social dilemmas (Balliet et al., 2011).

Education

A second way to solve a social dilemma is to educate group members. For example, in one study using a laboratory simulation of a water shortage, participants were told that they could draw water from a hypothetical lake, which would then renew itself by a small amount, much as rain replenishes a real lake (Allison & Messick, 1985). Those who understood the consequences of their actions behaved in a more socially responsible manner. Similarly, other studies have found that after receiving training in cooperation, even habitual competitors tend to become more cooperative and sustain this prosocial behavior over extended periods of time (Sheldon, 1999).

Group Identification

"We are all members of one another."

James Baldwin, African-American author, 1924–1987

Solutions to social dilemmas also may be achieved by encouraging the adoption of a meaningful group identity (Simpson, 2006; Swann et al., 2010). For example, in resource dilemmas, people are more likely to cooperate if they think of the other users of limited resources as being a part of their ingroup rather than as mere competitors. In support of this hypothesis, research has found that when situational cues prime people's group identity or their interdependent selves, they are more likely to exercise personal restraint in their use of an endangered resource (Brewer & Kramer, 1986; Liu & Li, 2009). Similarly, when participants play the prisoner's dilemma game, they are more likely to cooperate rather than compete when exposed to situational cues that prime their interdependent selves (Wong & Hong, 2005). These findings suggest that if groups can develop a "sense of community" in their members, they may call on this group identification when it is crucial that individuals put collective needs ahead of immediate self-interest.

Promoting a Cooperative Orientation

"Who see Me in all, And sees all in Me, For him I am not lost, And he is not lost for Me."

— — — — — — — — —

Bhagavad Gita ("The Lord's Song"), a sacred writing of Hinduism

As we have already seen, not everyone automatically places cooperation ahead of competition when confronted with a social dilemma. This is because people differ in their *social value orientation*, which is a person's rules specifying how outcomes or resources should be divided between oneself and others (Van Lange, 1999). Those with a *cooperative orientation* seek to maximize joint gains; those with an *individualistic orientation* try to maximize their own well-being regardless of what happens to others; and those with a *competitive orientation* strive to outdo others by as much as possible. Cooperators see the long-term value of sustained mutual cooperation, and they focus on how the future can be better from the past (Parks et al., 2003). Not surprisingly, it is far easier to solve a social dilemma when you are dealing with cooperators rather than individualists or competitors (De Dreu & McCusker, 1997; Joireman et al., 2001). Recognizing this simple truth, and further realizing that a cooperative value system should be internalized early in life, educational programs have been established to teach children how to think and behave cooperatively rather than competitively in social interaction (Van Lange et al., 1997). In addition to instilling cooperation as an important self-defining value, research indicates that social value orientations become better predictors of behavior when situational cues activate them from memory (Sagiv et al., 2011). Thus, while instilling a cooperative orientation is a crucial first step in promoting cooperative solutions to social dilemmas, priming this positive social value orientation within the actual situation where cooperation is needed is also important.

Promoting Group Discussion

"It is our task in our time and in our generation to hand down undiminished to those who come after us, as was handed down to us by those who went before, the natural wealth and beauty which is ours."

— — — — — — — — —

John F. Kennedy, 35th U.S. president, 1917–1963

One final way to reduce the free-rider problem is simply to give people the opportunity to discuss the dilemma among themselves (Bicchieri & Lev-On, 2007). Studies indicate that groups allowed to talk about the dilemma cooperate more than 95 percent of the time (van de Kragt et al., 1986). Why is discussion so effective? The most likely explanation appears to be that group discussion allows members to make explicit promises as to how they will behave, and these promises act as a binding social contract (Kiesler et al., 1996). If individual members hesitate to go along with this commitment to cooperate, group pressure is often sufficient to eventually secure compliance (Orbell et al., 1988).

Taking these strategies together, we can escape the destructive consequences of social dilemmas by (1) establishing guidelines and sanctions against self-serving behavior, (2) getting people to understand how their actions help or hurt everyone's long-term welfare, (3) encouraging people to develop a group identity, (4) fostering the internalization of social values that encourage cooperation rather than competition, and (5) promoting group discussion that leads to cooperation commitments.

SECTION SUMMARY

- Social dilemmas occur when people's most rewarding short-term choices ultimately cause negative consequences for the group.

- Several factors help resolve social dilemmas:

  sanctioning cooperative behavior

  education

  group identification

  promoting a cooperative orientation

  promoting group discussion

HOW DO JURIES MAKE DECISIONS?

In the Applications section of Chapter 7, you learned how people can be coerced into confessing to a crime they did not commit. In this section, let's examine how juries weigh the evidence presented by both prosecution and defense attorneys. What goes on behind those closed doors once the jury has gone into seclusion to deliberate? Unfortunately for those interested in better understanding the social psychological dynamics of this process, federal and virtually all state laws forbid eavesdropping on jury deliberations. Ironically, the catalyst for these laws was the public outrage that ensued when a judge in the 1950s allowed University of Chicago researchers to tape-record the deliberations of five juries (Ferguson, 1955).

Due to the inaccessibility of real juries, social scientists have resorted to alternative means of gaining insight into the inner workings of this group. Some of these are (1) interviewing jurors once a verdict has been reached, (2) analyzing court records, and (3) simulating the jury deliberation process by staging simulated trials using mock juries. What do these studies tell us about the jury as a decision-making group?

THE DELIBERATION PROCESS

As in most groups, juries move through distinct stages in making their decisions (see p. 325). During the orientation stage, jurors pick a foreperson, set an agenda, and begin to get to know one another. Next, in the discussion stage, they tackle the task of reviewing the evidence. This review process and the following decision stage can generate considerable tension because jurors often actively disagree with one another. Post-trial interviews with jurors in criminal cases indicate that the deliberation process typically involves remarkably high levels of competent and critical analysis (Gastil et al., 2007). As jurors move toward a decision in stage 3, the majority exerts pressure on dissenters to fall in line so that a unanimous verdict can be reached. Once consensus is within reach, the group tries to resolve the remaining differences and conflicts so that a verdict can be rendered. When no such consensus is reached, however, a jury does not have the option open to most other groups—rejecting nonconforming members. Instead, jurors who hold the majority opinion must continue to search for consensus with their minority counterparts. If after exhaustive and fruitless discussion, the jury proclaims itself hung and, if the judge agrees that further deliberation would be fruitless, a mistrial is declared.

As important as the deliberation process is to our legal system, in most cases the verdict is actually determined before the jurors even begin discussing the case. Harry Kalven and Hans Zeisel (1966) found that in 97 percent of the court cases they reviewed, the jury's final decision was the same as the one a majority of the jurors favored on the initial vote before deliberation commenced. Similar results have been obtained in other studies (Sandys & Dillehay, 1995), suggesting that by the time the first vote is taken, the jury has generally already decided about the defendant's guilt. It appears that the initial majority opinion wins over the entire group due to the greater informational influence and normative influence that majority members have at their disposal. That is, jury discussion is more likely to focus on majority-held opinions rather than opinions shared by the minority, and those sharing the majority opinion exert greater pressure to conform than do those who hold minority positions (Wittenbaum et al., 1999).

Does this then mean that group discussion of the facts does not significantly influence individual juror opinions? Maybe not. When jurors on fifty randomly selected felony cases were contacted by researchers and interviewed regarding their jury experience, they revealed that even when first-ballot votes were taken before formal discussion of the evidence, some informal discussion almost always took place among individual jurors (Sandys & Dillehay, 1995). In such cases, it's possible that jurors were indeed influenced by the other jurors' opinions. In only 11 percent of these trials did the first ballot occur before any discussion or deliberation took place at all. These trials, then, represent individual juror first-ballot verdicts with the least amount of influence from other jurors. Did these individual first-ballot verdicts predict the jury's subsequent final verdicts? Interestingly, they did not; thus, these findings suggest that the deliberation process may play a more significant role in shaping the verdicts of juries than was previously thought to be the case.

Although jurors holding minority viewpoints have little chance of dramatically shifting majority opinion, the research on minority influence described in Chapter 7 suggests that jurors may be persuasive when their positions are not too far away from the prevailing majority position. Support for this hypothesis comes from a mock jury study that Nancy Pennington and Reid Hastie (1990) conducted, in which they found that a minority on a jury was often able to change the majority's minds on the degree of guilt of a defendant. This suggests that if ten out of twelve jurors believe a defendant is guilty of first-degree murder, even though there is virtually no chance that the two dissenting jurors will be able to convince the majority that the defendant is innocent, the ten might be able to convince the other two to change their verdict to second-degree murder. Based on minority influence research, jurors holding minority positions would be most persuasive when they consistently and confidently state their dissenting views and, at the same time, come across as flexible and open-minded.

THE CONSEQUENCES OF SMALL JURIES

In the 1970 case of *Williams v. Florida*, the U.S. Supreme Court heard the appeal of a defendant who was convicted of armed robbery by a six-person jury instead of the traditional twelve-person jury. In their arguments, his lawyers contended that a six-person jury was biased against defendants because the possibility of juror dissent was greatly reduced with such a small group. The Supreme Court justices disagreed, ruling that in civil cases and state criminal cases not involving the death penalty, courts could use six-person juries instead of the traditional twelve. In making their rulings, the justices stated that there is no reason to believe that smaller juries will arrive at different decisions than the traditional jury. Is this true?

Although research indicates that jury size does not appear to affect rates of convictions or acquittals, a meta-analysis of studies involving fifteen thousand mock jurors who deliberated in over two thousand six-person or twelve-person juries found that smaller juries spend less time deliberating, recall less of the evidence, and are less likely to represent minority segments of the population (Saks & Marti, 1997). In addition, other studies have found that six-person juries are only half as likely to become hung than twelve-person juries (Kerr & MacCoun, 1985). Because trials resulting in hung juries often do so because of legitimate disagreements, it may be that smaller juries weaken a necessary safeguard in our legal system (Davis et al., 1997). One likely reason twelve-person juries are more likely to become deadlocked is that with more people in a group, there is a greater likelihood that more than one person will be dissenting from the majority. As Asch's (1956) conformity research suggests (see Chapter 7, p. 276), when someone has a social supporter he or she is much more likely to resist majority pressure to conform.

THE CONSEQUENCES OF NONUNANIMOUS VERDICTS

In 1972, the U.S. Supreme Court ruled in a split 5-4 decision that courts could accept verdicts based on less-than-unanimous majorities. The majority of the justices stated that a nonunanimous decision rule (for example, a guilty verdict by a 9 to 3 margin) would not adversely affect the jury; however, four justices disagreed, arguing that it would reduce the intensity of deliberations and negatively affect the potential for minority influence. Was this Supreme Court decision consistent with the findings from scientific studies of juries? Based on your own understanding of group influence, do you think that people on a jury that needs only a 9-to-3 majority would engage in a different type of deliberation process than juries that require a unanimous decision?

Reid Hastie and his colleagues (1983) studied the deliberations of more than eight hundred people in sixty-nine different mock jury trials and found that juries with rules requiring less-than-unanimous verdicts behaved very differently from juries requiring unanimous verdicts. Their results indicated that majority-wins-rule juries (10-to-2 or 8-to-4 margins) are not only less likely to end up hung than unanimity-rule juries (12-to-0 margin) but are also likely to render harsher verdicts—and do so in a relatively short period of time using a bullying persuasive style rather than relying on carefully reasoned arguments. Jurors who participate in these nonunanimous juries also emerge rating themselves as less informed, feeling less confident about their final decision, and perceiving their peers as more close-minded than jurors in the unanimous-rule groups (Nemeth, 1977). These findings clearly suggest that allowing nonunanimous verdicts is very likely to decrease the robustness of the arguments heard in deliberation. This, in turn, may well hinder the minority's ability to persuade the majority.

Today, only two states permit nonunanimous verdicts in criminal trials, but thirty-three states permit such verdicts in civil cases. Most civil cases today also employ six-member juries. Based on the research conducted since the Supreme Court loosened the restraints on jury size and unanimity, it appears that these changes result in faster and harsher trials by encouraging close-mindedness in jurors. The question we must ask ourselves is whether this is what we want to call "justice under the law" (Brigham, 2006).

THE BIG PICTURE

What I hope you understand by this time is that, although you are a unique individual in your own right, you are also a creature of the group (Miller & Prentice, 1994). In a psychological sense, you are not fully mature until you have internalized the group into your everyday thinking. As already discussed in Chapter 7, an important aspect of group living is the process of social influence. There is nothing inherently wrong with such influence—in fact, it is the social "stitching" that organizes the fabric of everyday life. Yet, in our individualist culture, the group has often been viewed with distrust and even condescension. It is true that you can sometimes act in an inferior and impulsive manner when in a group (due to *social loafing* and *deindividuation*, respectively), but you can also exhibit similar undesirable actions when acting alone. Thus, group processes, like individual processes, are amply designed to foster both positive and negative outcomes.

Whenever you become involved in a group, the possibility always exists that your own personal, self-focused interests will diverge from those of the collective. In such *social dilemmas*, your short-term interests will be advanced if you act selfishly, but your long-term interests and those of the group will be advanced if you cooperate. Resolving social dilemmas—and maintaining group membership itself—may be harder for individualists than collectivists (Chen et al., 2007). Based on your responses to the "Values Hierarchy Exercise" in Chapter 1 (p. 23), do you think it would be difficult or easy for you to work to resolve social dilemmas when they arise in your own groups?

In summarizing the content of this chapter, contemporary social science confirms that the group fabric of human nature is strong. Yet, within the fabric of the group, you will find the creative weaving of the many interconnected selves. This unique blending of the self with others powers group dynamics. When you interact with group members, you are actively creating and recreating your social reality—yet you are often unaware of the situational forces that shape this reality. Despite the fact that you may think of yourself as being a relatively autonomous creature, your current understanding of group processes should tell you that much of this self-perceived independence is illusory. Regardless of your culture of origin, you are influenced by others, both singly and collectively. One of the most important goals of social psychology as a discipline is to increase knowledge of how the person—as a self—helps to weave the fabric of group life and how the paths of these individual life threads are influenced by one another. The better you understand the complex nature and influence of the group fabric, the better you will be able to weave your own unique, yet group-influenced, patterns.

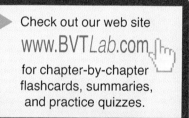

Check out our web site
www.BVTLab.com
for chapter-by-chapter flashcards, summaries, and practice quizzes.

WEB SITES

ACCESSED THROUGH www.BVTLab.com/sop6

Web sites for this chapter focus on why we form into groups, what needs and functions they serve, as well as the psychology of collective behavior and social institutions.

WHY SO SOCIAL AN ANIMAL?

This web site by Donelson Forsyth presents a thorough analysis of why we form into groups, what needs they satisfy, and what functions they perform.

CENTER FOR LEADERSHIP STUDIES

This web site for the Center for Leadership Studies contains the findings of recent studies on the social psychological dynamics of leaders as instruments of change within a group.

SELF-DIRECTED WORK TEAMS

This web site analyzes self-directed work teams, discussing research on group work and how to improve teamwork.

Chapter 9
Interpersonal Attraction

CHAPTER OUTLINE

INTRODUCTION

Affiliation Needs
Two reasons for affiliation are comparison and exchange.
Our evolutionary heritage and biology influence our affiliation desires.
Socialization shapes our inborn affiliation tendencies.

Characteristics of the Situation and Attraction
Close proximity fosters liking.
Our affiliation desires increase with anxiety.

Characteristics of Others and Attraction
We are drawn toward the physically attractive.
There are gender-based attractiveness standards.
Gender-based attractiveness standards shape body esteem.
Social comparison influences attractiveness judgments.
Birds of a feather really do flock together.
We like those who like us.

When Social Interaction Becomes Problematic
Social anxiety can keep us isolated from others.
Loneliness is the consequence of social isolation.

APPLICATIONS
How Can Social Skills Training Improve Your Life?

PREVIEW People who are comfortable and successful in social settings possess important social skills. What makes one person socially skilled and another socially inept? How can you use social psychological knowledge to have more satisfying social interactions?

THE BIG PICTURE

WEB SITES

INTRODUCTION

"Short men! Short men! What do you think of them? Some people say that short men are deceitful; that they're always sneakin' around causin' trouble; that they are insecure and always out to put other people down because of their insecurity, especially women. ... Well, today I'm going to talk to short men who have felt insecure about their height at different times in their lives. ... And we will also talk to a social psychologist who studies the effect of height on a man's self-esteem."

This was Oprah Winfrey's introduction for an episode on her widely popular television talk show about short men. The three diminutive men who were Oprah's guests for this episode—all ranging in height from 4' 10" to 5' 2"—were outgoing, seemingly well-adjusted adults who had been shunned, taunted, and discriminated against throughout their adolescent and adult lives due to their short stature. I was the fourth guest who was there to provide a scientific perspective on why these men face obstacles in their daily lives. What was the motivation for the severe judgments these men often received because of their physical appearance? At one point I mentioned that there is a "male-taller norm" in heterosexual dating relationships, meaning that women prefer to date men who are about four inches taller than themselves. I further explained that this unwritten social norm is shaped by cultural beliefs concerning proper gender roles. After my comments, Oprah responded, "There's a psychological feeling of protection when the guy is taller. ... We admit it; it's a terrible thing. But if I date a shorter guy I feel like I'm his mother!" A female audience member agreed and disclosed that, "I like to hug 'up' rather than hug 'down.' Short guys make me feel bigger than I am, and they're like a little boy that I'm dragging along with me." These comments were sharply challenged by another woman who defended short men by stating, "I can't believe the insensitivity of the women in the audience toward those men! My husband is short and I love him. He is a great man and he has a great personality. I just cannot believe that they would act like these men are second-class citizens because they're short. ... It doesn't matter how tall you are!"

As you will soon discover, the comments made by Oprah and her audience members are directly related to the subject matter of this chapter, interpersonal attraction. You may not know what it feels like to be the target of the type of ridicule that these short men experience in their lives, yet many of us have been shunned or rejected by others because one or more of our personal qualities does not measure up to others' standards of acceptability. Interpersonal attraction is the desire to approach other people.

Besides physical appearance, what qualities influence your need to seek out others for interaction? What situational factors shape your desire to approach or avoid others? As a way to help you ponder these questions, try the following exercise. Think about your best friend. How did you first meet? On paper, list up to ten reasons why you were initially attracted to this person. These reasons could be profound or mundane. Now think about a casual friend. In addition to listing factors that initially attracted you, also identify reasons why you think this relationship hasn't come close to achieving the level of "best friend." Finally, think about someone you dislike. List the factors that shaped the course of this bad relationship. Now compare the three lists. How are they different? How are they similar? Can you develop any hypotheses about the nature of interpersonal attraction based on any patterns you observe?

▶ Issues related to interpersonal attraction, such as people's physical appearance, are popular topics on television talk shows. Why is physical appearance so important to interpersonal attraction?

interpersonal attraction
....
The desire to approach other people

As we study the "chemistry" of **interpersonal attraction** in this chapter, keep these lists handy and remember the obstacles faced by the short men in our chapter-opening story, for we will refer to them on more than one occasion. Following a discussion of two basic reasons why people affiliate, we examine how personal characteristics of the individual, situational factors, and characteristics of others influence the attraction process. Then we analyze how social interaction can be chronically problematic for some people and end by discussing ways to improve the interpersonal skills of the socially anxious and lonely. Then, in Chapter 10, we will investigate how this interpersonal process can progress—and sometimes deteriorate—in close friendships and romantic relationships.

AFFILIATION NEEDS

Have you ever wondered why your need to be around other people often changes due to your daily experiences? Have you ever questioned why your need to socialize is different from that of some of your friends and acquaintances? I'm guessing that the answer to both of these questions is yes. In this first section you can explore how closely your personal musings on affiliation match the insights of social scientific theory and research.

TWO REASONS FOR AFFILIATION ARE COMPARISON AND EXCHANGE.

Two factors that shape affiliation involve the desire to gain knowledge about ourselves and the world through *social comparison*, and the desire to secure psychological and material rewards through *social exchange*. These two reasons for seeking out others relate to our dependence on others for information (information dependence) and our dependence on others for positive outcomes (outcome dependence) that we first discussed in Chapter 7. Can you guess which of these two factors is associated with the "cold" perspective of human nature, and which is associated with the "hot" perspective?

Social Comparison

social comparison theory
....
The theory that proposes that we evaluate our thoughts and actions by comparing them with those of others

According to Leon Festinger's (1954) **social comparison theory**, we possess a strong need to have accurate views, both about our social world and about ourselves. As you may recall from our discussion in Chapter 3, one way to know ourselves and better understand our place in the social environment is to compare ourselves with others (Locke, 2007). The information that such social comparison provides is used to evaluate the self. According to Festinger, social comparison is most likely when we are in a state of *uncertainty* concerning a relevant self-aspect. He further hypothesized that we generally prefer to compare ourselves with *similar* others. Why? Because the more similar people are to us, the more likely we will be to use the information gained through social comparison in better understanding ourselves and our future actions.

For example, imagine trying to decide whether to take a particular course next semester. You know three people who were previously enrolled in the course: Juan, who is always the top student in every course; Vanessa, who usually receives grades similar to yours; or Sarah, who is always on academic probation. According to social comparison theory, you should go to Vanessa for information about the course because of her academic similarity to you. Her opinions and her actual final grade will be much more useful in predicting your own performance than information learned from Juan and Sarah.

We use social comparison, not only to judge—and improve—ourselves, but also to judge our emotions and choose our friends (Buunk et al., 2007; Wood, 1996). Today, our understanding of social comparison processes is more complex than originally formulated by Festinger, but it still conforms to the general principles outlined here. This knowledge-based motive for affiliation reflects the "cold" perspective of human nature.

Social Exchange

Although the desire to evaluate ourselves through social comparison is one reason for affiliation, a second theory explaining affiliation focuses more closely on the *interactions* between

social exchange theory

The theory that proposes that we seek out and maintain those relationships in which the rewards exceed the costs

"Almost all of our relationships begin, and most of them continue, as forms of mutual exploitation, a mental or physical barter, to be terminated when one or both parties run out of goods."

—————————————

W. H. Auden, English poet, 1907–1973

people. According to **social exchange theory,** people seek out and maintain those relationships in which rewards exceed costs, and they avoid or terminate relationships when costs are greater than rewards (Erdoga350n & Enders, 2007; van de Rijt & Macy, 2006). The assumption underlying this "hot" perspective on affiliation is that people are basically *hedonists*—they seek to maximize pleasure and minimize pain, and to do so at minimal cost. Operating from this assumption, the theory also states that people will be attracted to those who best reward them.

One of the earliest versions of social exchange theory was presented by George Homans (1958), who stated that all social relationships are like economic bargains in which each party places a value on the goods they exchange with one another. The "goods" exchanged could be either material (for example, money, flowers, food) or nonmaterial (for example, social influence, information, affection). For instance, teachers instruct students in various subjects (a nonmaterial good) in exchange for a certain amount of money from their school districts (a material good). Similarly, a husband may do the grocery shopping, daily food preparation, and weekly yard work; in exchange, his wife may do the laundry, dinner cleanup, and weekly vacuuming and dusting. Social exchange theory assumes that people keep track of the goods they exchange, and on some level they know whether their rewards are exceeding their costs.

John Thibaut and Harold Kelley (1959) stated that, when people are deciding whether to remain in a relationship, they will not consider the rewards and costs in isolation. Instead, the level of costs and rewards accruing in the current relationship will be compared with the possible rewards and costs available in alternative relationships. If no alternative relationships are available, or none appear appreciably more rewarding than the current one, the person will make no changes. This is one reason why some people remain in dissatisfying or even harmful relationships—they would rather receive some rewards than run the risk of receiving none at all (Rusbult & Martz, 1995)

These two explanations for why we affiliate—the desire for social comparison and the desire for social exchange—do not exhaust the explanatory powers of current social psychological theories. Instead, they provide an anchoring point for the discussion that follows. With this in mind, let us now explore more specific aspects of interpersonal attraction.

OUR EVOLUTIONARY HERITAGE AND BIOLOGY INFLUENCE OUR AFFILIATION DESIRES.

Our *need to belong* is a powerful, fundamental, and extremely pervasive motivation (Baumeister & Leary, 1995; Gere & MacDonald, 2010). When this need is unfulfilled due to social exclusion or rejection, we react in a variety of negative ways, including increased stress, anxiety, and self-defeating thinking and behavior, which are often followed by decreased physical health (Buckley et al., 2004; DeWall & Baumeister, 2006). As discussed in Chapter 7 (p. 273), human brain-imaging studies indicate that the social pain we experience following rejection is neurologically similar to the affective distress associated with physical pain, with both originating in the brain's anterior cingulate cortex in the frontal lobes (Eisenberger, 2011). Evolutionary psychologists suggest that during the course of primate evolution the social attachment "alarm" system came under the control of the same brain area involved in pain detection because this promoted the goal of social connectedness. In other words, our tendency to seek out others, to make friends, and to form enduring close relationships seems to be an inherited trait that has helped us survive and reproduce (Bugental, 2000).

Affiliation desires are also associated with central nervous system arousability and brain activity related to the experience of positive and negative emotions. *Arousability* is the habitual degree to which stimulation produces arousal of the central nervous system (Stelmack & Geen, 1992). Research inspired by Hans Eysenck's (1990) work on introversion and extroversion suggests that introverts have inherited a nervous system that operates at a higher level of arousal than extroverts. For example, brain-imaging studies suggest that the anterior cingulate cortex—the brain's danger and pain alarm system—is more active among introverts than extroverts (Johnson et al., 1999). Because of this higher arousability, introverts avoid a great deal of social interaction and situational change in order to keep their arousal from reaching uncomfortable levels. Similar patterns of hypersensitivity to

Our affiliation desires are associated with heightened central nervous system activity. Do introverts and extraverts respond differently to such heightened arousal?

stimuli and overstimulation are also associated with shyness, a personality characteristic related to introversion (Aron et al., 2001). Extroverts have the opposite problem. Because their nervous system normally operates at a relatively low level of arousal, they seek out situations that stimulate them (Depue et al., 1994). For instance, while extroverted students prefer studying in relatively noisy settings where they can socialize with others, introverted students prefer studying in quiet, socially isolated settings (Campbell & Hawley, 1982). Socially active extroverts not only choose to perform tasks in noisy settings but actually perform better in such settings (Beauducel et al., 2006; Geen, 1996).

Beyond arousability, extroverts appear to experience greater activation of dopamine pathways in the brain associated with reward and positive affect than introverts (Depue & Collins, 1999; Lucas et al., 2000). Further, when introverts and extroverts are shown positive images (for example, puppies, a happy couple, or sunsets), extroverts experience greater activation of brain areas that control emotion, such as the frontal cortex and the amygdala (Canli et al., 2001). This research suggests that introversion and extroversion are associated with distinct patterns of brain activity, and that the experience of positive affect may be a primary feature of extroversion. Overall, it appears that each of us is born with a nervous system that causes us to have varying degrees of tolerance for the stimulation resulting from social interaction, which may influence the emotions we experience in such settings. It is this biological difference that significantly shapes our affiliation desires.

SOCIALIZATION SHAPES OUR INBORN AFFILIATION TENDENCIES.

Although we have inborn affiliation tendencies, our cultural experiences further shape and direct these tendencies. For instance, Geert Hofstede's (1980) study of twenty-two countries found a positive relationship ($r = .46$) between a culture's degree of individualism and its citizens' affiliation needs; the more individualist cultures had higher needs for affiliation. In explaining this finding, Hofstede stated that in individualist cultures, people are generally expected to individually develop their own relationships and to do so in many varied social settings. Because they develop social ties with people in various social groups, their relationships may be numerous, but they are not particularly intimate.

This affiliative, yet relatively nonintimate, approach to social relationships typifies our own culture. Individualist Americans have numerous relationships that are marked by friendliness and informality, but relatively few develop into deep and lasting friendships (Bellah et al., 1985; Stewart & Bennett, 1991). Whereas many Americans tend to

"*I'll do my thing and you do yours. If two people find each other—it's beautiful. If not, it can't be helped.*"

An individualist "prayer" by Fritz Perls, psychotherapist, 1893–1970 restrict friendship to an area of common interest, collectivist Russians expect to form deep bonds with their friends and to have these intimate friendships extend over many years (Glenn, 1966). As Harry Triandis observed in his analysis of these possible cross-cultural affiliation differences:

> People in individualist cultures often have greater skills in entering and leaving new social groups. They make "friends" easily, but by "friends" they mean nonintimate acquaintances. People in collectivist cultures have fewer skills in making new "friends" but "friend" in their case implies a life-long intimate relationship with many obligations. So the quality of the friendships is different. This difference in quality may complicate our understanding of the construct of collectivism, since people in individualistic cultures are likely to *appear* more sociable, while intimacy is not a readily observable attribute. (Triandis et al., 1988, p. 325)

Although individualists' social relationships tend to be less intimate than those of collectivists, some individualists cultivate more intimacy than others (Chen et al., 2006). In North America, members of many ethnic and religious groups are taught to think of themselves as *interdependent* with close others and as defined by their social relationships (Oved, 1988).

In terms of gender, girls are also more likely than boys to be raised to think, act, and define themselves in ways that emphasize their emotional connectedness to other individuals (Cross & Madson, 1997). This more socially connected *relational self* can be contrasted with the more solitary *independent* self typically taught to boys, which conceives of the person as independent and less interested in cultivating emotional relationships (see Chapter 3, pp. 84–85).

A number of studies find that people with a relational self-concept are more committed to and involved in their social relationships, self-disclose more personal information to friends, and are more likely to consider the needs of others when making decisions than those who have a more independent self-concept (Gore & Cross, 2006; Gore et al., 2006). Susan Cross and her coworkers (2002) have also found that people who primarily define themselves in terms of close personal relationships (high RISCs) have a much richer network of cognitive associations in memory for relationship-oriented terms than people who are less likely to think of themselves in this manner. One consequence of this different way of defining the self is that high relational individuals have better memories for relational events than low relational persons. This might explain why women are more likely than men to remember birthdays, anniversaries, who said what during important conversations

Women tend to remember events, important conversations, and even what casual acquaintances look like more than men. What does this suggest about women's and men's emotional connectedness to others?

with friends or loved ones, and even what casual acquaintances sound and look like (Schmid Mast & Hall, 2006; Ross & Holmberg, 1993). Before reading further, complete *Self/Social Connection Exercise 9.1*, which contains the *Relational-Interdependent Self-Construal (RISC) Scale* developed by Cross and her colleagues (2000).

Self/Social Connection Exercise 9.1

How Important Are Your Close Relationships in Defining You?

The Relational-Interdependent Self-Construal (RISC) Scale

To what degree do you define yourself in terms of your close relationships with others? In other words, to what degree are your friendships and other close relationships an important aspect of your self-concept? The Relational-Interdependent Self-Construal Scale (Cross et al., 2000) measures your *relational interdependence*.

Instructions

Below is a series of statements concerning men and women and their relationships in contemporary society. Please indicate the extent to which you agree or disagree with each of these statements using the following scale:

Strongly disagree   1   2   3   4   5   6   7   Strongly agree

1. My close relationships are an important reflection of who I am.
2. When I feel very close to someone, it often feels to me like that person is an important part of who I am.
3. I usually feel a strong sense of pride when someone close to me has an important accomplishment.
4. I think one of the most important parts of who I am can be captured by looking at my close friends and understanding who they are.
5. When I think of myself, I often think of my close friends or family also.
6. If a person hurts someone close to me, I feel personally hurt as well.
7. In general, my close relationships are an important part of my self-image.
8. Overall, my close relationships have very little to do with how I feel about myself.*
9. My close relationships are unimportant to my sense of what kind of person I am.*
10. My sense of pride comes from knowing who I have as close friends.
11. When I establish a close friendship with someone, I usually develop a strong sense of identification with that person.

Directions for Scoring

Two of the Relational-Interdependent Self-Construal (RISC) Scale items are reverse-scored; that is, for these items a lower rating actually indicates a higher level of relational-interdependence. Before summing the items for a total score, recode those with an asterisk ("*") so that 1 = 7, 2 = 6, 3 = 5, 5 = 3, 6 = 2, and 7 = 1

When Cross and her colleagues (2000) developed the RISC, the mean score for 2,330 female college students was about 57, whereas the average score for 1,819 male college students was about 53, indicating significant differences between women and men. Higher scores indicate greater interest in developing close, committed social relationships.

Exercise 9.1 *Continued*

One important thing to keep in mind in interpreting these findings and your own RISC score is that your sex does not necessarily determine your gender beliefs and expectations (Hyde 2005). There are many men who score considerably higher on the RISC than the average woman, and likewise, there are many women who score considerably lower than the average man. In other words, many men construct a relational self-concept and many women develop an independent self-concept. However, despite this qualifier, there are differences in the way women and men define themselves, with women generally having a greater sense of relational interdependence than men.

Based on this brief overview of possible influences on affiliation needs, we can tentatively conclude that the desire for affiliation is an important defining characteristic of our species; yet individuals differ in the expression of this need. For some, our optimal arousal level is fairly high, and we seek a great deal of social and nonsocial stimulation. For others, our optimal arousal level is relatively low, and we live our lives in a more socially introverted fashion. Within our pursuit of social relationships, we also differ in the degree of emotional connectedness we seek; and our culture substantially shapes this individual difference in seeking interdependence.

SECTION SUMMARY

- Two basic reasons for interpersonal attraction are social comparison and social exchange:

  In social comparison, we seek out similar others for comparison purposes due to our need to have an accurate self and worldview.

  In social exchange, we seek out others because of the social rewards exchanged in such interactions, and we maintain the relationships if the rewards exceed the costs.

- Affiliation desires are influenced by the following:

  evolutionary heritage

  biological arousability and other neural activity

  culture and gender

CHARACTERISTICS OF THE SITUATION AND ATTRACTION

Individual differences can foster social contact or withdrawal, but a number of situational factors also can trigger affiliation needs and interpersonal attraction. In the following sections, we consider two of the more important situational factors: proximity and anxiety.

CLOSE PROXIMITY FOSTERS LIKING.

One of the most powerful factors in determining whether you become friends with other people is their sheer *proximity* to you (Back et al., 2008). Is this one of the reasons why you were initially attracted to your best friend? Chances are, most of your friends live in close proximity to you, or at least did so in the past.

We often grow to like our neighbors. How might the mere exposure effect explain why proximity fosters liking?

Leon Festinger, Stanley Schachter, and Kurt Back (1950) conducted one of the earlier and better studies of how proximity influences social relationships when they investigated the development of friendships in married graduate student housing at the Massachusetts Institute of Technology. Following World War II, the university had randomly assigned these student families to available apartments in seventeen different buildings; therefore, virtually none of the residents knew one another prior to moving in. When residents were asked to name their three closest friends in the housing units, physical proximity was the single most important determinant of friendship choices. Not only did about two-thirds of the listed friends reside in the same building as those who nominated them, about two-thirds also lived on the same floor. Further, 41 percent of next-door neighbors were chosen compared with only 22 percent of those living two doors away and 10 percent of those at the end of the hall (see Figure 9.1). Similar proximity effects have been found in urban housing projects for the elderly (Nahemow & Lawton, 1975), in freshmen college dormitories (Priest & Sawyer, 1967), in office work environments (Conrath, 1973), and even in classroom settings (Segal, 1974). In the latter study, police academy trainees who were assigned classroom seats based on the alphabetical order of their last names made friends with those who sat adjacent to them.

For you romantics, there is even evidence that proximity can affect intimate relationships. In an early sociological study, James Bossard (1932) plotted the residences of each applicant on five thousand marriage licenses in Philadelphia and found a clear relation between proximity and love. Couples were more likely to get married the closer they lived to each other. This finding was replicated in later research as well (Ramsoy, 1966).

At least part of the reason close proximity fosters liking is that it often leads to more frequent exposure and increased familiarity (Reis et al., 2011). As discussed in Chapter 5, Robert Zajonc's (1968) *mere exposure hypothesis* proposes that repeated exposure to something or someone is sufficient, by itself, to increase attraction. The mere exposure effect also helps in explaining why you can become attracted to someone through the Internet's electronic proximity (Bargh & McKenna, 2004). The increased use of electronic mail and Internet chat rooms provides people with the opportunity to be "virtually close" to others without ever physically meeting.

Based on the studies discussed in this section, you might think we have stumbled on a solution to the anger and violence in our world; move enemies next door to one another and soon they will be friends! Before you act on this newfound belief, let's consider one last study. Ebbe Ebbesen and his colleagues (1976) found that residents in a California condominium complex not only established most of their friendships with people who lived in the same housing units but also developed most of their enemies close by as well. Was proximity one of the contributing factors in the development of your own "bad relationship" listed earlier? Ebbesen explains this effect by stating that those who live closer to you are better able than those living farther away to spoil your happiness and peace of mind by having loud parties late at night, throwing trash on your lawn, and just generally getting on your nerves. Thus, although proximity typically leads to liking, the lamb lying down next to the lion is not likely to develop anything that could be called a friendship.

Figure 9.1

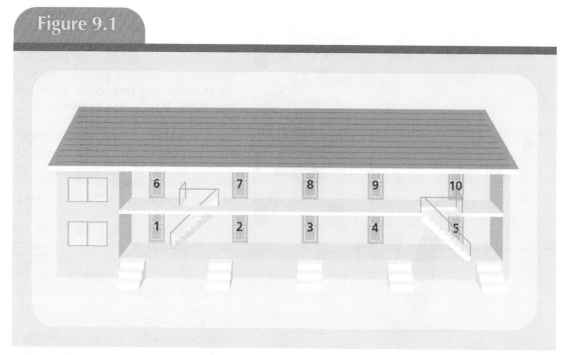

Proximity and Friendship Development

This schematic diagram of an apartment building in the Festinger et al. (1950) study shows the two floors contain-ing five apartments each, connected by two staircases. Within each floor, people were more likely to be nominated as close friends if they lived in the middle apartments on their floors (apartments 3 and 8) rather than in the end apartments. Further, those who lived in the first-floor apartments near the staircases (apartments 1 and 5) tended to be nominated more than those living farther away from the stairs. The reason for this effect was that the resi-dents living near the staircase had less "functional distance" from others in the building; people were more likely to bump into them as they came and went during the day. If you live—or have lived in an apartment complex—does this pattern of results mirror your own friendship patterns?

OUR AFFILIATION DESIRES INCREASE WITH ANXIETY.

Although individuals differ in their habitual desire for affiliation, external events can also motivate people to seek out others. For example, do you recall what you did when you first learned about the terrorist attacks on New York City and Washington, D.C., on Sep-tember 11, 2001? If you are like most people, during that time of anxiety, grief, and uncertainty, you sought the companionship of others who were similarly affected by this tragedy. How can social psychological research and theory help us understand our need for others during such times of anxiety and crisis? Does misery love company?

Schachter's Anxiety Research

In the late 1950s, Stanley Schachter attempted to answer this question by bringing female college students into the laboratory and creating a stressful event. In his initial study, Schachter (1959) introduced himself to the women as "Dr. Gregor Zilstein" of the Neurology and Psychiatry Department. He told them that they would receive a series of electrical shocks as part of an experiment on their physiological effects. In the "high-anxiety" condition, participants were told that the shocks would be quite painful but would cause no permanent damage. In the "low-anxiety" condition, they were led to believe that the shocks were virtually painless, no worse than a little tickle. In actuality, no shocks were ever delivered—the intent was merely to cause participants to believe that they soon would be receiving these shocks.

After hearing this information, the women were told there would be a ten-minute delay while the equipment was set up. They could spend this time waiting either in a room alone or in a room with another participant in the study. Their stated preference

Figure 9.2

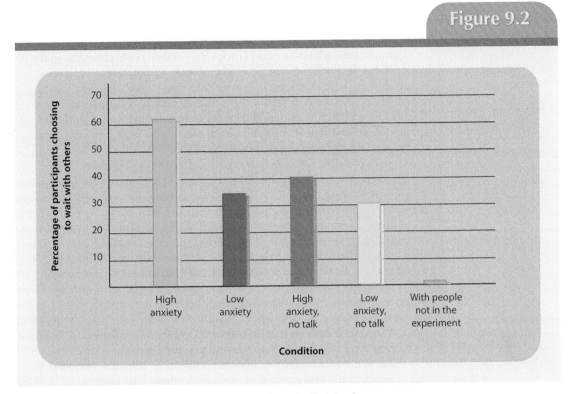

Desire to Affiliate Among High and Low Anxious Individuals

Schachter (1959) found that research participants' desire to be with others depended on their level of anxiety and the similarity of their potential "waiting mates." His findings indicated that when anxious or fearful, people desire to affiliate with others who are also experiencing similar feelings. Based on these findings, how would you amend the old folk saying "Misery loves company" to better reflect how we react to anxious situations?

Source: Data from S. Schachter, *The Psychology of Affiliation*, Stanford University Press, 1959.

was the dependent variable. As soon as participants stated their preference, they were told the true purpose of the study. As Figure 9.2 shows, 63 percent of those in the high-anxiety condition chose to wait with others, while only 33 percent of the women in the low-anxiety condition did so. Thus, it appears that high anxiety caused people to seek out others. Misery does indeed appear to love company.

Yet why did they desire affiliation? Perhaps others serve as a *social distraction* to anxious individuals, temporarily taking their minds off their anxiety. If this were the case, then anyone would be an acceptable "waiting mate" for these anxious individuals. To test this hypothesis, Schachter (1959) conducted a follow-up study identical to the first experiment except for one important variation: some of the high-anxiety participants were told they could either wait alone or with other students who weren't in the experiment but were in the building to see their advisers. If anxious people merely want to be around others, regardless of who they are, then these nonanxious students would be acceptable "waiting mates."

Results did not support this reasoning: high-anxiety participants overwhelmingly wanted to wait with others undergoing the same stress, and they were not interested in waiting with students who were not in the experiment (see Figure 9.2). Schachter somewhat facetiously asserted that these findings added a new wrinkle to the old "Misery loves company" proverb—misery appears to love only *miserable* company. Put another way, when anxious or fearful, people desire to affiliate with others who are also experiencing similar feelings. Why?

As you might have guessed, Schachter (1959) conducted a third experiment to determine whether anxious participants were motivated to seek out similarly anxious others to share their thoughts about the impending event, or whether there was something more basic about this affiliation desire. If they sought out others to verbally discuss and compare information, then they shouldn't bother seeking out this company if it was made clear that such information exchange wasn't allowed. Schachter created such a scenario by having "Dr. Zilstein" inform certain high-anxiety participants that they could choose to wait with other participants, but they would not be allowed to discuss the upcoming experiment while in their presence. Even with these restrictions on information exchange, high-anxiety participants exhibited a greater desire to wait with others experiencing the same anxiety-producing event than did those in the low-anxiety condition (again, refer to Figure 9.2). Thus, in addition to a specific desire to discuss their anxiety with others who were similarly anxious, these findings suggest that the *mere* presence of others also motivates the affiliative need. Of what possible benefit could their mere presence be to the anxious individuals?

Based on his previous work with Festinger, Schachter believed that *social comparison* was the motivating factor in these affiliation needs. Specifically, he believed that the high-anxiety participants wanted to wait with similarly threatened others, not necessarily to talk to them, but rather to compare the others' *emotional reactions* to the stressful event with their own. This social comparison process could occur even if they were not allowed to actually speak about their thoughts and feelings—observing similar others would suffice. As discussed in Chapter 4, we tend to believe that we can gather a great deal of information about other people's state of mind by watching their nonverbal behavior. This was exactly what Schachter believed the anxious women in the "no-talking" condition were seeking when they chose to wait with other experimental participants. They could better evaluate their own emotional reactions to this experiment by comparing them with those of similarly distressed people.

Have you noticed that the information-seeking behavior exhibited by Schachter's research participants bears a striking similarity to those who participated in Sherif's autokinetic experiments, discussed in Chapter 7 (p. 263)? In Sherif's experiments, when faced with uncertainty about how to interpret events ("How far did the dot of light move?"), people became dependent on others for information. Likewise, in Schachter's research, when people faced an uncertain future ("How worried should I be about the impending painful electrical shocks?"), they too looked toward those who might help them evaluate their circumstances. Although Sherif's research demonstrated that *information dependence* makes us more susceptible to others' influence, Schachter's work indicates that it also causes us to be drawn toward others in the first place to gather the necessary information to hopefully make sound social judgments. In this regard, Schachter's anxiety research marked the first major extension of social comparison theory. Subsequent research has largely supported Schachter's general conclusion that stress increases the desire to affiliate (Rofé, 1984; Taylor et al., 2003).

> **"**Common danger makes common friends.**"**
>
> Zora Neale Hurston, U.S. author, 1903–1960

Limitations and Wrinkles in the Anxiety-Affiliation Effect

One limitation to this stress-induced affiliation response has to do with people who are faced with an upcoming embarrassing event. When college students were told that they would soon be expected to suck on large nipples and baby pacifiers in the presence of an experimenter, as part of a study related to Freud's "oral stage of psychosexual development," most preferred to wait alone for the start of this embarrassing event (Sarnoff & Zimbardo, 1961). Further, if they did choose to affiliate, they preferred to do so with people who were not going to be in the same embarrassing experiment (Firestone et al., 1973). Under these circumstances, the type of social dependence most likely influencing participants' behavior was not information dependence but outcome dependence. Participants avoided social contact because they did not want anyone to know that they were about to engage in a series of infantile acts. For these individuals, affiliation was expected to increase, not decrease, the negative impact of the stressful situation. They chose to affiliate only when others had no knowledge of their impending embarrassment.

Besides this limitation to the anxiety-affiliation effect, there also is a "wrinkle" involved in this social comparison process. Although Schachter believed that anxious people affiliate with others who are similarly anxious in order to compare emotional states, this is not always so. Sometimes when anticipating a fearful event, people prefer not to be around those who are also fearful. Instead, they prefer someone who has already experienced the fearful event and who can tell them something about it. In such instances, people are seeking *cognitive clarity*—a desire to obtain information from others regarding the nature and dangerousness of the threat (Shaver & Klinnert, 1982). For example, a field study (Kulik & Mahler, 1989) found that the vast majority of hospital patients about to undergo coronary bypass surgery preferred to room with someone who had already undergone the procedure rather than with someone like them who had not yet had surgery (78 percent versus 22 percent). Subsequent research suggests that the cognitive clarity gained from having a postoperative heart patient as a roommate not only does the best job lowering anxiety but also results in faster recovery from surgery (Kulik et al., 1996). These findings and others like it suggest that our desire to affiliate when anxious is not only based on a need to compare our emotional state with others but also is fueled by our need to appraise the stressful situation itself so that we have better cognitive clarity—and this cognitive clarity provides us with both psychological and physical benefits (Kulik et al., 1994; Van der Zee et al., 1998).

Affiliation Following a National Disaster

In Schachter's study, participants were introduced to a stressful scenario while alone and were then given the option to be with another person. In the real world, however, people are often actively interacting with others when stressful events occur. In such circumstances, the resulting stress and anxiety might cause a *change* rather than an increase in affiliation. Matthias Mehl and James Pennebaker (2003) observed this very pattern of affiliation in the aftermath of the September 11 terrorist attacks. The two social psychologists had just begun studying how adults cope with personal traumas when the terrorists struck, so they quickly shifted their study's focus onto how their participants interacted with others during this time of national crisis. Using small digital voice recorders that could be attached to clothing, participants' conversations were randomly recorded between 10:00 AM and 4:00 PM from September 10 to September 21.

Did this real-world anxiety-inducing event cause an increase in people's affiliation desires? Yes, but not in the exact manner documented by Schachter. As depicted in Figure 9.3, immediately after the terrorist attacks participants spent a good deal of time talking about the disaster, but discussions significantly decreased during the course of the week. For instance, during the forty-eight-hour period following the attacks, 28 percent of people's total conversations involved the event. By the fifth and sixth days this percentage had fallen below 20 percent, and by the ninth and tenth days only 3 percent of people's total conversations were about September 11. During this time, people did not change their overall amount of interaction with others, but their interaction did

When anxious or fearful, we seek out others who are also experiencing similar feelings. Such affiliation needs were dramatically demonstrated following the terrorist attacks on September 11, 2001. What sort of social dependence is likely operating in these cases? What sort of interaction appears to be the most beneficial—group or dyadic—in coping with the stress surrounding such tragedies?

Figure 9.3

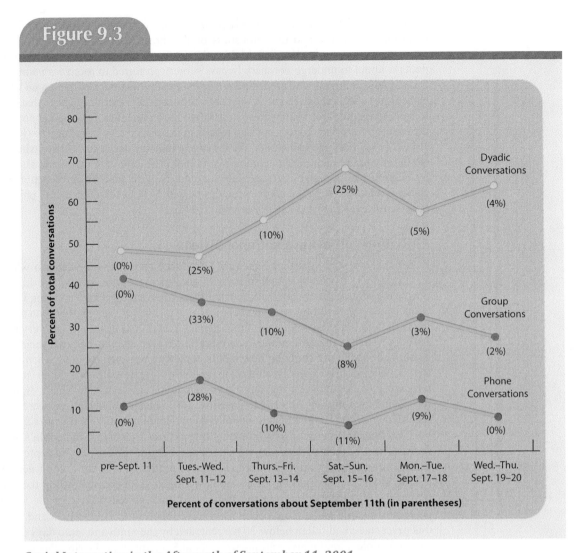

Social Interaction in the Aftermath of September 11, 2001

Following the terrorist attacks of September 11, 2001, people's amount of interaction with others did not significantly increase, but their interaction did shift from group and telephone conversations to in-person dyadic encounters. The percentage of dyadic, group, and phone conversations that involved the September 11th terrorist attacks during each two-day period are listed in parentheses. People who seemed to best cope with the stress caused by the disaster were those whose interactions shifted from group discussions to one-on-one personal dialogues. How do these findings provide further insight into the relationship between anxiety and affiliation?

Adapted from data in Mehl, M.R., & Pennebaker, J. W. (2003). The social dynamics of a cultural upheaval: Social interactions surrounding September 11, 2001. *Psychological Science, 14,* 579–585.

shift from group and telephone conversations to in-person dyadic encounters. For instance, whereas less than 10 percent of total group conversations involved the attacks by days five and six, one-on-one in-person conversations about the event were still at 25 percent. Mehl and Pennebaker believe that the initial group-focused interactions may have most efficiently satisfied people's information dependence, while the gradual shift to more one-on-one interactions best helped them psychologically cope with the event. These one-on-one conversations about the tragedy seemed to have a beneficial effect; people who best dealt with their stress were those who shifted from group discussions to one-on-one personal dialogues. Many Americans' cultural worldviews were challenged due to September 11, and these one-on-one encounters may have provided the necessary intimacy and social support for people to reaffirm their shaken worldviews and reevaluate their beliefs and opinions (Davis & Macdonald, 2004).

What about less direct forms of affiliation? The Internet also provides an outlet for affiliation during times of national trauma. In an attempt to understand how such anxiety affects electronic affiliation tendencies, Mehl and Pennebaker, along with Michael Cohn, analyzed the online diaries (known as web logs or "blogs") of 1,084 Americans during the two months prior to and after the September 11 attacks (Cohn et al., 2004). Using computerized text analysis, the researchers developed measures of Internet users' degree of cognitive processing and social orientation. The cognitive-processing measure counted how often Internet users typed words such as *think, question,* and *because.* Previous research indicates that such words are associated with a desire to comprehend an issue or event (Davis & Nolen-Hoeksema, 2001). The social-orientation measure counted how often such words as *talk, share,* or *friends* were typed because such words reflect a desire for affiliation or social bonding. Results indicated a significant increase in cognitive processing and social orientation during the confusion and speculation following the attacks, with a gradual return to pre-attack levels within two weeks. These findings are similar to those of the face-to-face communication study previously described, and suggest that Internet users' online behavior immediately following the attacks was similarly motivated by an increased need for both cognitive clarity and affiliation.

Overall, the results from these two studies support Schachter's finding that stressful events heighten people's information dependence, and thereby, increase the likelihood of affiliation. However, the "wrinkle" provided by these studies is that it demonstrates that when stressful events trigger anxiety in people, they are often already embedded in an existing social network, not socially isolated like the participants in Schachter's study. The present findings further suggest that in the aftermath of a national disaster, the affiliation desires triggered by anxiety may be most successfully satisfied in dyadic interactions rather than large-group gatherings.

Critical THINKING

Immediately following the New York and Washington terrorist attacks on 9/11, people around the country were highly anxious and uncertain about what was happening. How do you think information dependence and outcome dependence shaped their thoughts, feelings, and behavior during this time?

SECTION SUMMARY

- Two situational factors that influence interpersonal attraction:

    Proximity: We form emotional bonds with those who are physically (or virtually) close to us.

    Anxiety-inducing events: The desire for social comparison attracts us to similarly anxious others.

- Affiliation provides opportunities for cognitive clarity.

- Dyadic interactions satisfy affiliation desires more than large-group gatherings.

CHARACTERISTICS OF OTHERS AND ATTRACTION

In fourth grade, my classmates and I began rating each other's "interpersonal appeal." I distinctly recall Colleen McCash walking up to me one morning and telling me that she liked Walter first, Chuckie second, John third, and me fourth. Wow! I was number four on Colleen McCash's boyfriend chart! I immediately moved her up two notches on my own chart, from fourth to second, just behind Jane Hauserman. I didn't listen very attentively that morning as our teacher talked about the colonization of America or the rotation of the earth on its axis. No, as the Europeans sailed and as the world turned, I wondered what Colleen would do when I told her she was now "number two" with me.

Today, looking back on my first systematic attempt to evaluate why others appealed to me, I can identify a number of factors that determine peer-group popularity (Dijkstra et al., 2010). First there was the girl's physical appearance—was she "cute"? Then, there was the matter of her personality—was she a "nice" person? Did we have similar interests? Finally, there was the consideration of her opinion of me—where did I fall on her "liking chart"? As outlined in the following sections, some of these factors are easily perceived, while others require time to determine their presence or absence.

WE ARE DRAWN TOWARD THE PHYSICALLY ATTRACTIVE.

Do you recall the negative comments made about short men in our chapter-opening story? Despite the frequently quoted folk saying that "you can't judge a book by its cover," people tend to believe that they know a good deal about others based on their "external packaging." Unfortunately for short men, in many cultures their physical appeal is much less than that of tall men (Brewer & Riley, 2009). An example of the warm glow that tall men have received over the centuries compared to the cold shoulder that short men often experience is the first century judgment by the Roman historian Tacitus that male height not only indicated physical strength but also moral virtue. In this chapter section we will review research indicating that physical qualities associated with physical attractiveness provide advantages to those who possess them. Another way to describe this appeal is that we have a very favorable *implicit personality theory* for physical attractiveness (see Chapter 4, p. 135). The appeal of physical attractiveness can even be observed in brain-scan studies where those who are shown photos of attractive faces have greater activation in brain areas associated with more positive emotions compared to when they are shown photos of unattractive faces (Principe & Langlois, 2011).

What Is Beautiful Is Good.

**physical attractive-
ness stereotype**
....
The belief that physically attractive individuals possess socially desirable personality traits and lead happier lives than less attractive persons

In one of the first studies of the **physical attractiveness stereotype**, Karen Dion, Ellen Berscheid, and Elaine [Walster] Hatfield (1972) asked college students to look at pictures of men and women who either were good-looking, average, or homely—and and to then evaluate their personalities. Results indicated that students tended to assume that physically attractive persons possessed a host of socially desirable personality traits relative to those who were unattractive. This beauty-goodness effect has also been documented in Hollywood movies. Steven Smith and his coworkers (1999) asked people to watch the one hundred most popular movies between 1940 and 1990 and to evaluate the movies' main characters. Consistent with the physical attractiveness stereotype, beautiful and handsome characters were significantly more likely to be portrayed as virtuous, romantically active, and successful than their less attractive counterparts. A similar beauty-goodness effect has been documented in animated Disney movies, where, for example, the heroic prince and virtuous princess are attractive but the wicked witch and evil giant are ugly (Bazzini et al., 2010). Over the past thirty-five years, many researchers have examined this stereotype; and two separate meta-analyses of these studies reveal that physically attractive people are perceived to be more sociable, successful, happy, dominant, sexually warm, mentally healthy, intelligent, and socially skilled than those who are unattractive (Eagly et al., 1991; Feingold 1992b).

Although these findings are based solely on samples from individualist cultures, the physical attractiveness stereotype also occurs in collectivist cultures; however, its content is a bit different (Chen et al., 1997b). For example, Ladd Wheeler and Youngmee Kim (1997) found that, as in individualist cultures, physically attractive Koreans are perceived to be more sexually warm, mentally healthy, intelligent, and socially skilled than unattractive Koreans. However, consistent with the greater emphasis on harmonious relationships in collectivist cultures, physically attractive Koreans are also assumed to have higher integrity and to be more concerned for others than those who are physically unattractive. These findings suggest that although the physical attractiveness stereotype appears to be universal, its actual content is shaped by cultural values.

The positive glow generated by physical attractiveness is not reserved solely for adults, however. Adults perceive attractive infants as more likable, sociable, competent, and easy to care for than unattractive babies (Casey & Ritter, 1996; Karraker & Stern, 1990). In elementary school, cute children are more popular with their peers than unattractive children (Vaughn &

Langlois, 1983), and there even is evidence that physical appearance may influence parents' and teachers' expectations (Martinek, 1981). For example, in one study by Dion (1972), female college students who were studying to become teachers read a negative evaluation of a child given by her teacher after the child had allegedly been caught throwing stones at a cat. Attached to each evaluation was a photo of either an attractive or unattractive child. When the child was attractive, the would-be teachers tended to excuse the negative behavior as being atypical, and they did not recommend punishment. However, the unattractive child was generally not given the benefit of the doubt—her negative behavior was more likely to be attributed to her personality. In a typical reaction to the attractive child's transgression, one of the college students remarked:

> She appears to be a perfectly charming little girl, well-mannered, basically unselfish. It seems that she can adapt well among children her age and make a good impression. ... She plays well with everyone, but like anyone else, a bad day can occur. Her cruelty ... need not be taken too seriously. (p. 211)

In contrast, the typical reaction to the unattractive child's negative behavior was captured in the following remark:

> ... think the child would be quite bratty and would be a problem to teachers. ... She would probably try to pick a fight with other children her own age. ... She would be a brat at home. ... All in all, she would be a real problem. (p. 211)

Can your degree of physical attractiveness have an impact on your earning potential and career success as an adult? Field and laboratory studies conducted in both individualist and collectivist cultures indicate that physical attractiveness does have a moderate impact on a variety of job-related outcomes, including hiring, salary, and promotion decisions (Chiu & Babcock, 2002; Collins & Ziebrowitz, 1995; Hosoda et al., 2003; Marlowe et al., 1996). In one representative study, Irene Frieze and her coworkers (1991) obtained information on the career success of more than seven hundred former MBA graduates of the 1973 to 1982 classes at the University of Pittsburgh. They also judged former students' facial attractiveness based on photos taken during their final year in school. Results indicated that there was about a $2,200 difference between the starting salaries of good-looking men and those with below-average faces. For women, facial attractiveness did not influence their starting salaries, but it did substantially impact their later salaries. Once hired, women who were above average in facial attractiveness typically earned $4,200 more per year than women who were below average in attractiveness. For attractive and unattractive men, this difference in earning power per year was $5,200. Further, although neither height nor weight affected a woman's starting salary, being 20 percent or more overweight reduced a man's starting salary by more than $2,000. Overall, the research literature informs us that physical appearance does indeed influence success on the job.

"Beauty is power."

Arab proverb

Is the Attractiveness Stereotype Accurate?

Based on our analysis thus far, it is clear that we tend to give beautiful people high marks on many socially desirable personality traits and, as a result, give them high social exchange value. But do the beautiful really have more desirable personalities? Overall, the answer is clearly no. Alan Feingold (1992b) conducted a meta-analysis of more than ninety studies that investigated whether physically attractive and physically unattractive people actually differed in their basic personality traits. His analysis indicated no significant relationships between physical attractiveness and such traits as intelligence, dominance, self-esteem, and mental health. Thus, even though we think good-looking people are more intelligent, dominant, happy, and mentally healthy than unattractive people, this is not really the case. Feingold did discover, however, that good-looking people do tend to be less socially anxious, more socially skilled, and less lonesome than those who are unattractive, which has been confirmed in other studies (Meier et al., 2010). One likely reason good-looking individuals are more at ease socially is that people generally seek out their company and respond favorably to them. As a result of this history of rewarding social encounters, the physically attractive have an increased sense of personal control when interacting with others (Diener et al., 1995).

Mark Snyder and his coworkers (1977) conducted an experimental demonstration of how such positive feedback can bolster social poise and confidence. They first gave college men information about a woman with whom they soon would converse on the telephone. Included in their information package was a photograph of the woman. Some of the men were given a photo of an attractive woman, while others saw an unattractive photo. Based on the research we have already discussed, Snyder and his colleagues assumed that the men would believe that the attractive woman would be more warm, likable, interesting, and outgoing than the unattractive woman. In reality, the women they talked to were not the women in either photo. As predicted, independent judges, who later listened to tape recordings of the phone conversations, rated the men who thought they were talking to an attractive woman as being more outgoing and sociable than those who believed they were conversing with an unattractive woman. Even more interesting was the response of the women on the other end of the line. Judges rated the women whose male partner thought they were attractive as being more warm, confident, animated, and attractive than the women whose partners thought they were unattractive. The same results were obtained in a related study when the roles were reversed and women were led to believe they were conversing with either an attractive or an unattractive man (Anderson & Bem, 1981).

Together, these findings suggest that there is a self-fulfilling prophecy involved in the physical attractiveness stereotype. As discussed in Chapter 1 (pp. 5–9), the self-fulfilling prophecy is the process by which someone's beliefs about another person can cause that person to behave in a manner that confirms those expectations. The apparent reason physically attractive people tend to be socially poised and confident is that those who interact with them convey the clear impression that they truly are very interesting and sociable individuals.

THERE ARE GENDER-BASED ATTRACTIVENESS STANDARDS.

Our examination of the research evidence thus far suggests that we are drawn to physically attractive people like bees to honey. Yet, what makes a person physically attractive? Is there a universal standard that can be identified and measured?

Cross-cultural studies indicate that physical attractiveness—however defined—is generally more important for women than for men (Ford & Beach, 1951; Townsend & Wasserman, 1997). Curiously, however, this relation between the importance of physical attractiveness and gender is reversed for homosexual partners. Physical attractiveness is an important quality for gay men, yet it is a less important feature for lesbians (Fawkner & McMurray, 2002; Harrison & Saeed, 1977). This suggests that men, regardless of their sexual orientation, place greater value on the physical appearance of a potential romantic partner than do either lesbians or heterosexual women. However, this gender difference is much stronger when people are contemplating long-term romantic relationships rather than casual short-term sexual encounters or when first meeting someone. In initial encounters or when considering a one-night stand, Women, like men, tend to place a high value on physical attractiveness (Bryan et al., 2011; Luo & Zhang, 2009).

Although culture does have an impact on who is judged physically appealing (Langlois et al., 2000; Marcus & Miller, 2003), cross-cultural studies have found some interesting universal gender-based attractiveness standards. For example, men worldwide are generally attracted to women who have a lower waist-to-hip ratio, meaning that the circumference of their waist is smaller than that of their hips (Furnham et al., 2003; Singh, 1993). The most desirable waist-to-hip ratio appears to be 0.7, so that a desirable woman with a waist of 25 inches would have a 35-inch hip size, or a desirable woman with a 35-inch waist would have 50-inch hips (Streeter & McBurney, 2003). Consistent with these findings are brain-scan studies indicating that men show the most activation in brain reward centers when they are shown naked female bodies with waist-to-hip ratios of 0.7 compared to when they are shown thinner or larger female body shapes (Platek & Singh,

2010). Evolutionary psychologists contend that this 0.7 waist-to-hip ratio is universally perceived as attractive because it is a biologically accurate indicator that the woman is young, fertile, but currently not pregnant—and therefore sexually available (Crandall et al., 2001; Furnham et al., 2002). According to this argument, over the course of human evolution, those men who mated with women with a waist-to-hip ratio of about 0.70 were more likely to successfully conceive an offspring. Consistent with this reasoning, research findings indicate that deviations from the 0.7 ratio are associated with decreases in fertility (Van Hooff et al., 2000).

The 0.7 waist-to-hip ratio may be the generally preferred female body type, but additional cross-cultural research indicates that this preference is sensitive to the reliability of a culture's food supply (Marlowe & Wetsman, 2001). For example, as depicted in Figure 9.4, Judith Anderson and her colleagues' (1992) analysis of fifty-four societies found that heavy women were strongly favored in cultures where the availability of food was highly unpredictable (71 percent preference), but their popularity decreased in cultures with moderately or very reliable food supplies (40 percent preference). In contrast, slender

> **"***Besides being young, a desirable sex partner—especially a woman—should also be fat.***"**
>
> Observations of the semi-nomadic Siriono Indians of Bolivia, 1946

Figure 9.4

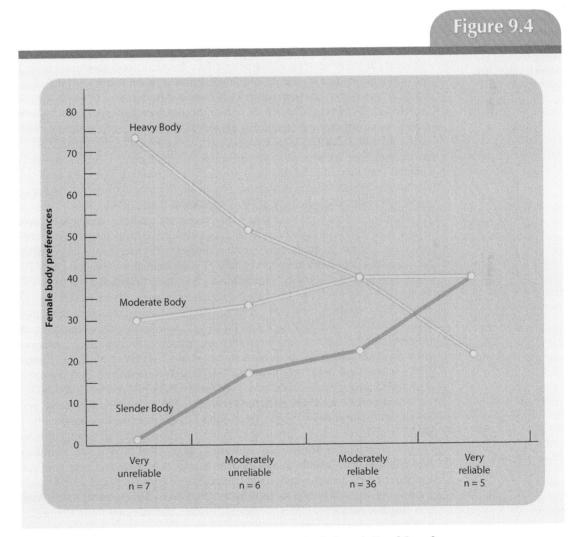

Female Body Preferences Due to the Reliability of a Culture's Food Supply

Women with heavy bodies have relatively high waist-to-hip ratios, while women with slender bodies have relatively low waist-to-hip ratios. Cross-cultural research indicates that heavy women are considered more attractive in societies with highly unreliable food supplies. Evolutionary theorists believe this preference for heavy women over slender ones in environments with frequent food shortages has an evolutionary basis and has fostered our species survival. In environments with more reliable food supplies, why might men's preferences increase for women with lower waist-to-hip ratios?

women were not at all popular in cultures with unreliable food supplies, but their popularity increased to match heavy women when the culture's food supply was very reliable. The researchers believe that in environments that have periods of acute food shortages, male preference for heavy women is evolutionarily adaptive because fat represents stored calories. Put simply, heavy women carry a built-in food supply that helps them to not only survive food shortages but also be fertile and produce offspring. Thus, in cultures where the food supply is unreliable, the extra fat associated with a higher waist-to-hip ratio overrides the typical evolutionary advantage of choosing women with a lower ratio.

This male preference for women with larger waist-to-hip ratios during "hard times" has even been found in the United States. Terry Pettijohn and Brian Jungeberg (2004) conducted an analysis of *Playboy* magazine *Playmates of the Year* between 1960 and 2000, and found that when social and economic conditions were difficult, *Playmates* had larger waists and larger waist-to-hip ratios. As social and economic conditions improved, lighter and smaller-waisted playmates were more prevalent in the men's magazine. In general, survey studies in the major world regions find that heavier female body types are preferred in poor countries while slender body types are preferred in more prosperous countries (Swami et al., 2010).

Taking into consideration all the cross-cultural research we have reviewed here, it appears that—all things being equal—men prefer women with relatively low waist-to-hip ratios because this body type signifies youth, fertility, and current nonpregnancy. However, in environments where people face frequent food shortages, male preference shifts to a higher female waist-to-hip ratio because this body type signifies greater ability to both produce and nurse offspring when food is scarce.

Beyond body type, there is also evidence that there are universal standards of *facial attractiveness*. For example, a number of studies indicate that we prefer faces in which the right and left sides are well matched, or *symmetrical* (Burris et al., 2011; Danel & Pawlowski, 2007). What is so appealing about symmetry? Evolutionary psychologists contend that we prefer facial symmetry because symmetry generally indicates physical health and the lack of genetic defects, which are important attributes for a sexual partner to possess (Henderson & Anglin, 2003; Ozener & Fink, 2010).

Besides symmetry influencing attractiveness, studies of people's perceptions of young men and women's individual faces and composite faces (computer-generated "averages" of all the individual faces) indicate that what people judge most attractive are faces that represent the average face in the population (Baudouina & Tiberghienb, 2004; Langlois et al., 1994). This tendency to define physical attractiveness according to the "average rule" has been found in many cultures (Jones & Hill, 1993; Pollard, 1995). Why might we perceive average faces as more attractive than more unusual faces? Drawing upon the insights of the *mere exposure effect*, Carol Langlois and her colleagues maintain that average faces are more attractive because they are more prototypically facelike and, thus, seem more familiar to us (Hoss et al., 2005; Langlois et al., 1994). Consistent with this hypothesis is research indicating that we are also more attracted to average dogs, fish, birds, and wristwatches (Halberstadt & Rhodes, 2003).

Evolutionary psychologists further contend that, besides symmetry and averageness, youthfulness and maturity figure into facial attractiveness judgments. For example, David Buss (1989) found that in thirty-seven cultures around the world, men express a preference for women who are younger than themselves, and women prefer men slightly older (except in Spain). This gender difference has been confirmed in both a large-scale national sample in the United States (Sprecher et al., 1994) and in a meta-analysis of forty different attractiveness studies including both North American and non-North American samples (Feingold, 1992a). In analyzing these findings (see Figure 9.5), social scientists conclude that they reflect a *looks-for-status exchange* in mating relationships (Fletcher et al., 2004; Li et al., 2011). Men are attracted to young women because female youth signifies beauty, and women are attracted to older men because male maturity signifies higher social status.

In terms of facial features, a number of studies have found that possessing youthful or slightly *immature* facial features (large eyes and thin eyebrows, full lips, small nose and chin) enhances female attractiveness, while possessing *mature* facial characteristics related to social dominance (small eyes, broad forehead, thick eyebrows, thin lips, large

> **"** *No woman can be too slim ...* **"**
> ------------
> Wallis Simpson, the Duchess of Windsor, 1896–1986

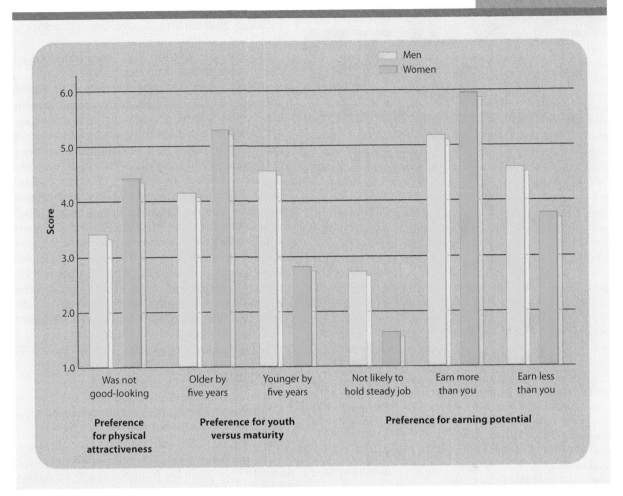

Gender Differences in Mate Selection Preferences

Sprecher, Sullivan, and Hatfield (1994) asked more than 1,300 English-speaking and Spanish-speaking Americans who were single and under the age of 35 to consider some possible assets and liabilities in a marriage partner and to indicate their willingness to marry someone possessing each of these characteristics. A score of "1" indicated "not at all," while a score of "7" indicated "very willing." All of the gender comparisons listed above are significant. What do these findings tell us about gender differences in heterosexual mate preferences?

Source: Data from S. Sprecher et al., "Mate Selection Preferences: Gender Differences Examined in a National Sample" in *Journal of Personality and Social Psychology*, 66: 1074–1080, American Psychological Association, 1994.

jaw) increases the attractiveness of males (Cunningham, 1986; Johnston & Franklin, 1993; Keating, 1985). Although additional studies indicate that heterosexual women are also attracted to men with large eyes (an immature feature) and heterosexual men show a preference for women with high cheekbones (a mature feature), male preferences for youthfulness and female preferences for slightly more maturity appear to be the norm (Cunningham et al., 1990a; Valenzano et al., 2006).

What are the attributions people make of those with immature facial features? Based on their studies of infant faces, Leslie Zebrowitz and her colleagues contend that immature features signal to people that the observed individual is dependent and help-less—like an infant (Andreoletti et al., 2001; Zebrowitz, 1997). Accompanying these perceptions are attributions that adults with immature features are weaker, less compe-tent, less dominant, and less intelligent than the average adult (Poutvaara et al., 2009). In the workplace, these attributions result in baby-faced applicants being recommended for lower-status jobs than applicants with mature-looking faces (Zebrowitz et al., 1991).

Actors Cary Grant and Marilyn Monroe were cast as potential romantic partners in the 1952 movie *Monkey Business*, despite Grant being 22 years older than Monroe. How do different theories explain this common heterosexual romantic age mismatch?

Taken as a whole, these findings suggest a double bind that women face in their social lives. When they try to match physical attractiveness standards by using cosmetics to enlarge the appearance of their eyes and lips and make their eyebrows thin, others may perceive them as more beautiful, but also as more weak and helpless.

Do you think this looks-for-status effect is more influenced by biology or social conditions? The evolutionary perspective contends that what will be valued as desirable and attractive in men and women is that which increases their probability of producing offspring who will carry their genes to the next generation (Kenrick & Trost, 1987). Given the biological fact that women have a shorter time span to reproduce than do men, evolutionary psychologists assume that evolution predisposes men to perceive women who look *young* as being more desirable (that is, more physically attractive) because youth implies high reproductive potential (Alley & Cunningham, 1991). Using this same logic, evolutionary theorists also assume that women will instead favor male traits signifying an ability to provide and protect resources for them and their offspring. Thus, instead of valuing youth in men, women should place more importance on status, ambition, and other signs of *social dominance* (Kenrick & Luce, 2000).

In contrast to this evolutionary explanation, sociocultural theorists maintain that men seek beauty in a woman and women seek power in a man because of the widely different social statuses they have historically held in society (Howard et al., 1987). This social-exchange explanation argues that women have historically been excluded from power and are viewed by men as objects of exchange in the social marketplace. Men place a premium on the quality or the beauty of this exchange object, and that is why physical attractiveness is sought in a woman. Because of their historically low status and their restricted ability to socially advance based on their own individual skills, women have been forced to tie their social advancement with the status of their mate. Thus, women seek men who are socially dominant and can be "good providers" (Bernard, 1981).

Which of these perspectives provides the best explanation is currently a hotly debated topic (Rasmussen et al., 1998). If the sociocultural perspective is correct, recent social advances made by many women in North American and European countries (higher pay and increased social status) may cause shifts in the attractiveness preferences of both women and men (see Eagly & Wood, 1999). Women may look for more "beauty" in men, and men may look for more "economic status" in women. A handful of recent studies suggest that such changes may be taking place. In Spain, a content analysis of personal ads in newspapers found that although the overall preferences in what men and women seek in a mate are consistent with predictions from evolutionary theory, there is an age difference among women in their preferences that is consistent with the sociocultural perspective (Gil-Burmann et al., 2002). Unlike older women, those younger than the age of forty seek mainly physical attractiveness in men, not socioeconomic status. These changes in mate preferences among the younger women may be at least partly caused by the newfound financial independence they are enjoying due to Spain's current economic prosperity. Similarly, Donald Strassberg and Stephen Holty (2003) examined male mate preferences by posting four "female seeking male" personal ads on two large Internet bulletin boards, but varied the ads slightly to highlight different characteristics in the imaginary women. Their analysis of over five hundred e-mail responses found that the most popular ad was one in which the woman described herself as "financially independent . . . successful [and] ambitious." This ad generated over 50 percent more responses than the next most popular ad, which described a woman who was "lovely ... very attractive and slim." If future studies provide additional evidence that mate preferences are indeed changing, this would not necessarily mean that evolutionary forces don't shape perceptions of attractiveness. It may simply mean that, in this instance, these inherited tendencies have been overridden by more powerful cultural forces.

GENDER-BASED ATTRACTIVENESS STANDARDS SHAPE BODY ESTEEM.

Our culture, like many around the world, places a premium on physically attractive women; as a result, women frequently express concerns about being rejected based on their appearance (Park, 2007). Starting at a very young age, from the Barbie dolls and toy makeup cases with which girls are encouraged to play, to the close attention given to clothing fashion and other bodily adornments, females are taught that their body as an *object* is a significant factor in how others will judge their overall value. The pervasiveness of this attention is seen in the message conveyed in television commercials and magazine advertisements, where difficult-to-attain standards of female beauty are established, especially relating to weight (Bessenoff & Del Priore, 2007; Posavac & Posavac, 1998). One consequence of this greater attention to the female form is that women of all age groups are more aware of and influenced by attractiveness standards than are men, and this heightened focus has a lasting negative impact on their body attitudes, or **body esteem** (Cordero, 2011; Franzoi & Klaiber, 2007). Beginning in late childhood and early adolescence, girls not only experience more dissatisfaction with their bodies than boys, they also experience a steady increase in this dissatisfaction over time (Feingold & Mazzella, 1998). By adulthood, negative affect is a pervasive quality of female body esteem, and women are more likely to habitually experience what researchers identify as *social physique anxiety*—anxiety about others observing or evaluating their bodies (Szymanski & Henning, 2007). Curiously, women's evaluations of their own bodies tends to be more negative than their perceptions of how others' evaluate their bodies—women are their own harshest critics (Dijkstra & Barelds, 2011; Franzoi et al., 2012). The women most likely caught in this hypercritical "beauty trap" are those who are most attentive to cultural beauty standards (Strahan et al., 2008; Vartanian & Hopkinson, 2010).

body esteem
....
A person's attitudes toward his or her body

Although women generally express greater dissatisfaction toward their bodies than do men, evidence shows that minority women and lesbians feel less pressure to conform to the unrealistic standard of thinness in the larger culture than White heterosexual women (Franzoi & Chang, 2002; Lakkis et al., 1999). As a result, they are less concerned about dieting and weight loss, although the differences are not large (Grabe & Hyde, 2006). For example, although survey studies find that most women prefer a curvaceous body shape, more Caucasian-American women prefer this ideal to be slender with medium breasts whereas more African-American women prefer this ideal to be curvier with medium breasts and large buttocks (Overstreet et al., 2010). These somewhat different body shape and size preferences appear to be partly due to a greater valuing of larger body sizes in minority and lesbian cultures, but it also may be a by-product of a more general tendency to reject White and heterosexual cultural standards, respectively (Share & Mintz, 2002; Webb et al., 2004). Yet, despite the fact that minority heterosexual women appear to have greater body satisfaction than White heterosexual women, this does not mean they are unconcerned about weight issues (Stephens & Few, 2007). In general, they are still more dissatisfied with their bodies—particularly their weight—than are heterosexual minority men (Harris, 1995; Mintz & Kashubeck, 1999). Young adult lesbians experienced similar ambivalent feelings regarding the importance of weight and overall physical appearance (Beren et al., 1997). These findings suggest that although lesbians and minority women may adhere less to the dominant White heterosexual standard of female thinness, they are not immune to this beauty norm.

In contrast to the way that most females are socialized, males are taught to view their bodies as dynamic instruments of action, and they are judged more positively if they engage in physical activities (Shields et al., 2007). For boys, their ability to adeptly move their bodies through physical space is an important contributor to their overall self-esteem (Langlois & Downs, 1980). In adulthood, power and function are important criteria for evaluating the male physical self, and women judge the male body-as-object more positively if it is muscular (Parent & Moradi, 2011). Because greater importance is placed on the body as a functioning unit in the daily experiences of males, they are more likely than women to judge their bodies as a unified whole and less as a collection of parts (Franzoi, 1995). Accompanying this more unified view of the body is a higher level of body esteem than typically found among women (Frederick et al., 2006). One notable exception to this general finding is gay men. Like many heterosexual women, many gay men experience considerable pressure to conform to attractiveness standards that are difficult to attain (Wiseman & Moradi, 2010). This heightened scrutiny of the body as a beauty object undoubtedly accounts for the lower levels of body esteem found in this population (Martins et al., 2007).

Although men generally have more positive body esteem than women, their negative body attitudes are often linked to the large and muscular male body standard (Spitzer et al., 1999). A survey of American college students found that over 90 percent wanted to be more muscular (Frederick et al., 2007). This desire for muscles is not a new phenomenon, but heightened media and cultural attention to this masculine body ideal is playing a role in the increasing trend of male body dissatisfaction (Leit et al., 2001; Neumark-Sztainer et al., 1999). For example, male action toys marketed for boys and male models in print and television advertisements have become substantially more muscular over the last thirty years (Pope et al., 1999, 2001). In an attempt to match this hypermuscular male standard, an increasing number of teenage boys and young men are taking anabolic steroids and untested dietary supplements, which can cause a variety of health problems (Moradi & Huang, 2008). Before reading further, spend a few minutes completing *Self/Social Connection Exercise 9.2* to gain additional insight into your own body esteem.

SOCIAL COMPARISON INFLUENCES ATTRACTIVENESS JUDGMENTS.

Sometimes factors other than one's actual appearance influence physical attractiveness judgments. In fact, sometimes it is the attractiveness of others that determines how we ourselves are judged. For example, people of average attractiveness tend to be judged more attractive when they are with a same-sex person who is very good-looking, but they are thought of as less attractive when with someone who is unattractive (Geiselman et al., 1984). This physical appearance *radiation effect* occurs when two people are observed simultaneously.

What happens when individuals are observed separately, one after the other? Interestingly, instead of sequential observations resulting in a radiation effect, they often lead to a *contrast effect*. People are generally judged more attractive after others have seen an unattractive same-sex person and less attractive when others have just seen someone who is very good-looking (Wedell et al., 1987). Consistent with earlier findings that men are more attentive to the physical attractiveness of potential and actual romantic partners, the contrast effect appears stronger in male than in female viewers (Kenrick et al., 1989).

Thus far we have considered only other people's judgments of our physical attractiveness. What about how we perceive our own physical appearance? In research that Jonathan Brown and his colleagues (1992) conducted, female undergraduates evaluated their own physical attractiveness after being exposed to either an attractive or an unattractive man or woman. Consistent with the contrast effect, participants' perceptions of their own beauty were greater after they were exposed to unattractive female targets than after they were exposed to attractive female targets (refer to Figure 9.6). Male targets did not influence the women's self-perceptions. These findings have been replicated in a number of studies and indicate that social comparison does indeed influence self-perceptions of attractiveness (Evans, 2003; Little & Mannion, 2006). Put simply, we feel prettier or more handsome after seeing same-sex persons who fall well below conventional beauty standards and less attractive after seeing "perfect 10s." Not surprisingly, this

"The pursuit of beauty is much more dangerous nonsense than the pursuit of truth or goodness, because it affords a stronger temptation to the ego."

Northrop Frye, Canadian literary critic, 1912–1991

"First man: 'How's your wife?' Second man: 'Compared to what?'"

Vaudeville joke

"To like and dislike the same things, that is indeed true friendship."

Gaius Crispus, Roman historian & politician, 86–34 BC

The Body Esteem Scale

Instructions

Below are listed a number of body parts and functions. Please read each item and indicate how you feel about this part or function of your own body, using the following scale:

1 = Have strong negative feelings
2 = Have moderate negative feelings
3 = Have no feeling one way or the other
4 = Have moderate positive feelings
5 = Have strong positive feelings

1.	body scent	19.	arms
2.	appetite	20.	chest or breasts
3.	nose	21.	appearance of eyes
4.	physical stamina	22.	cheeks/cheekbones
5.	reflexes	23.	hips
6.	lips	24.	legs
7.	muscular strength	25.	figure or physique
8.	waist	26.	sex drive
9.	energy level	27.	feet
10.	thighs	28.	sex organs
11.	ears	29.	appearance of stomach
12.	biceps	30.	health
13.	chin	31.	sex activities
14.	body build	32.	body hair
15.	physical coordination	33.	physical condition
16.	buttocks	34.	face
17.	agility	35.	weight
18.	width of shoulders		

Scoring Instructions and Standards

In 1984, Stephanie Shields and I developed the Body Esteem Scale (BES) that measures three different body esteem dimensions in men and women. For men, the dimensions are physical attractiveness, upper body strength, and physical condition; for women they are sexual attractiveness, weight concern, and physical condition. To determine your score for each of the subscales for your sex, simply add up your responses for the items corresponding to each body esteem dimension. For example, for women, to determine self-judgments for the weight concern dimension of body esteem, add up the responses to the ten items comprising this subscale. For men, the items of "physical coordination" and "figure or physique" are on both the upper body strength and the physical condition dimensions. The subscale items—plus the means and standard deviations for 964 college men and women (Franzoi & Shields 1984)—are listed below. How do you suppose your own body esteem has been influenced by your culture's physical attractiveness standards?

Exercise 9.2 *Continued*

Women

Sexual attractiveness: *body scent, nose, lips, ears, chin, chest or breasts, appearance of eyes, cheeks/cheekbones, sex drive, sex organs, sex activities, body hair, face* (Mean = 46.9, S = 6.3)

Weight concern: *appetite, waist, thighs, body build, buttocks, hips, legs, figure or physique, appearance of stomach, weight* (Mean = 29.9, SD = 8.2)

Physical condition: *physical stamina, reflexes, muscular strength, energy level, biceps, physical coordination, agility, health, physical condition* (Mean = 33.3, SD = 5.7)

Men

Physical attractiveness: *nose, lips, ears, chin, buttocks, appearance of eyes, cheeks/cheekbones, hips, feet, sex organs, face* (Mean = 39.1, SD = 5.7)

Upper body strength: *muscular strength, biceps, body build, physical coordination, width of shoulders, arms, chest or breasts, figure or physique, sex drive* (Mean = 34.0, SD = 6.1)

Physical condition: *appetite, physical stamina, reflexes, waist, energy level, thighs, physical coordination, agility, figure or physique, appearance of stomach, health, physical condition, weight* (Mean = 50.2, SD = 7.7)

social comparison process has more of an effect on the self-evaluations of those of us who place a high importance on our physical appearance (Patrick et al., 2004).

BIRDS OF A FEATHER REALLY DO FLOCK TOGETHER.

Imagine the following scene. It is the beginning of the fall semester in Ria's first year in college, and she has just checked into her dormitory room and will soon meet her new roommate. As she unpacks, Ria wonders what her roommate will be like. What is her race and ethnic background? What sort of music does she like? What are her politics? Does she like to party, or will she spend all her time studying? Abruptly, Ria's thoughts are interrupted by her new roommate entering. "Hi! I'm Kate," the tall, dark-haired woman exclaims as she smiles and extends her hand in greeting. "I guess we're roomies!"

This scene probably resonates with similar experiences you have had in your own life. In new surroundings, what sort of people do you typically seek out? Social psychological research generally indicates that we are attracted to those who are similar to us in particular characteristics, a tendency known as the **matching hypothesis** (Lee et al., 2009; Selfhout et al., 2009). Matching characteristics is a common practice in forming many different types of social relationships. For example, when seeking romantic partners on a popular online dating site, people often seek to match themselves with others based on self-worth, physical attractiveness, and popularity (Taylor et al., 2011).

In one of the first tests of the matching hypothesis, Theodore Newcomb (1961) conducted a longitudinal study of friendship development in an all-male boardinghouse. He found that the residents tended to like other residents who were similar to them in age and family background, as well as in social attitudes. In later laboratory studies, Donn Byrne and his colleagues accelerated the getting-acquainted process by having participants complete attitude questionnaires and later "introducing" them to another person by having them read his or her responses to a similar questionnaire (Byrne & Nelson,

matching hypothesis
....
The proposition that people are attracted to others who are similar to them in particular characteristics

Figure 9.6

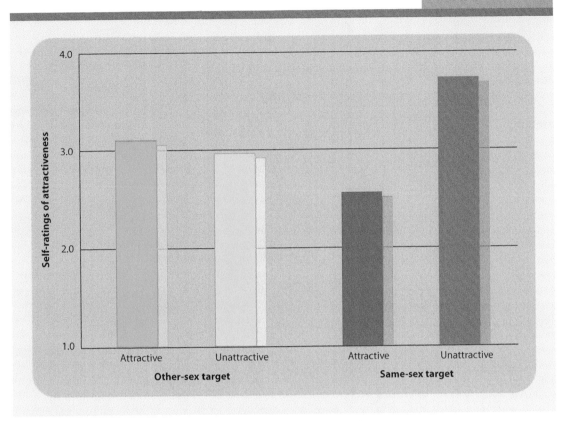

*Self-Ratings of Attractiveness Following Exposure to Attractive
and Unattractive Same-Sex and Other-Sex Individuals*

When women evaluated their own physical attractiveness after being exposed to either an attractive or unattractive man or woman, their perceptions of their own beauty were greater after they were exposed to unattractive female targets than after they were exposed to attractive female targets. Male targets' attractiveness did not influence the women's self-perceptions. What do these findings tell us about how social comparison influences self-perceptions of attractiveness?

1965; Schoneman et al., 1977). As you might have already guessed, the researchers had actually filled out the questionnaire so that the answers were either similar or dissimilar to the participants' own attitudinal responses. As you can see from Figure 9.7, participants expressed much stronger liking when they thought they shared a greater percentage of similar attitudes with the individual. This finding is important, for it suggests that the *proportion* of similar attitudes is more important than the actual *number* of similar attitudes. Thus, we should be more attracted to someone who agrees with us on four of six topics (66 percent similarity) than one with whom we share similar opinions on ten of twenty-five topics (40 percent similarity).

Why are similar others so interpersonally attractive? One reason is our desire for social comparison. As Schachter's anxiety experiments demonstrated, when we are uncertain about how to define social reality, we are drawn to those with whom we can best compare ourselves. Meeting others who share our views on important issues makes us feel better because it reassures us that essential aspects of our self-concept have social validity. According to this social comparison perspective, when others validate our own self-beliefs through agreement, we should develop positive attitudes toward them. In contrast, when others disagree with us, this questioning of our judgment may raise doubts in our own minds about our self-concept and worldview. The negative feelings created by such nonagreement should cause us to avoid these people in the future.

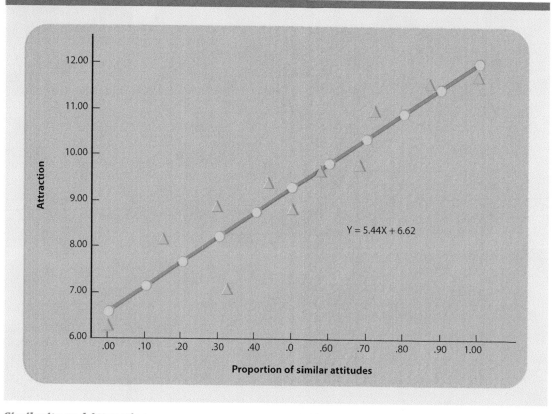

Y = 5.44X + 6.62

Attraction (vertical axis)

Proportion of similar attitudes

Similarity and Attraction

Donn Byrne and his colleagues found that the greater the proportion of similar attitudes held by people, the greater their attraction to one another. Does this type of relationship between attitude similarity and attraction help explain why you are attracted to or repelled by certain people in your own life?

A second possible explanation is that our affinity for similar others is part of our evolutionary heritage. That is, our ancestors may have used similarity cues (physical and attitudinal) to detect those who were genetically similar to them. John Rushton (1989), for example, has found that friends tend to be more similar to one another on certain genetically determined characteristics than one would expect by chance. It's possible that humans have unconsciously been attracted to similar others because they share many of the same genes. If we become friends with these people and provide them with help when they are in need, as friends often do, we are increasing the probability that genes like our own will find their way to succeeding generations. It is this biological predisposition that may cause us to respond positively to those who appear to have "a bit of us in them."

Another reason why we may be attracted to similar others is that we like that which is familiar. As we have already discussed (p. 356), it may have been evolutionarily adaptive to perceive unfamiliar others with caution and distrust because of the dangers inherent in dealing with the unfamiliar (Bornstein, 1989). Due to this biological predisposition, we may perceive similar others as attractive because they *mimic* familiarity. That is, their similarity to us makes them seemingly familiar creatures! Thus, similarity may lead to liking because the similar appear familiar.

The attractive power of similar attitudes has been demonstrated not only in mixed and same-sex dyads but also in various cultures throughout the world (Byrne, 1997; Byrne et al., 1971). Indeed, as we learned in the "Johnny Rocco" study of Chapter 7 (pp. 272–274), our desire for attitudinal similarity is so sufficiently strong that we will actively eject members from our groups if they refuse to share our attitudes on important issues. In fact, research indicates that the similarity of people's attitudes is more important in determining their attraction toward one another than the similarity of their personalities (Clore & Baldridge, 1968; Montoya & Horton, 2004). It is not surprising, then, that when trying to match up people into new friendship groups, we pay particular attention to their shared attitudinal characteristics (Chapdelaine et al., 1994).

While similar attitudes are important in attracting people into both friendships and romantic relationships, satisfaction over time in these relationships is more influenced by personality similarity rather than attitudinal similarity. For example, in a study of recently married couples, Shanhong Luo and Eva Klohnen (2005) found that men and women were attracted to their partners due to sharing similar attitudes, values, and religious beliefs, and not because they shared similar personality traits. In other words, attitudinal similarity played a crucial role in triggering initial attraction and in fostering relationship development and commitment. However, Luo and Klohnen also found that both partner's satisfaction with the relationship after one year of marriage was strongly influenced by the similarity of their personalities, but not by the similarity of their attitudes. Subsequent research has also found that personality similarity predicts relationship satisfaction among college-age dating partners (Gonzaga et al., 2007). Overall, these findings suggest that we are attracted to others who share our attitudes, values, and beliefs; and we may even enter into committed relationships with these individuals based on this similarity (Crandall et al., 2007). Yet once having committed ourselves to these relationships, people with similar personalities may be better able than those with different personalities to coordinate their daily activities and thereby avoid the friction and conflict that lowers relationship satisfaction.

WE LIKE THOSE WHO LIKE US.

So far, we have discussed how attraction can be based on a number of personal and situational factors. Yet one very simple reason why people might make it on our "liking chart" is that we discover they like us. Research has shown that we like people who like us and say nice things about us (Berscheid & Reis, 1998, Luo & Zhang, 2009). For example, after viewing the Facebook profiles of male college students who they believed had previously seen their own profiles, female college students were more attracted to the men who they were told liked them a lot compared to the men who they thought liked them only an average amount (Whitchurch et al., 2011).

In an interesting study, Rebecca Curtis and Kim Miller (1986) examined how people's interaction style changes once they believe that another likes or dislikes them. Upon arriving at the lab, participants were paired up, asked to spend five minutes getting to know one another, and then were separated. One half of this interaction pair was assigned to the target group and told that their partners (the perceivers) either liked or disliked them based on false information the experimenter provided. The experimenter stressed to the target person that she was interested in determining how the perceivers would act now that they had been given this false information about the targets. In actuality, the perceivers were never given any information at all. The experimenter's real goal was to manipulate the targets' perceptions, not the perceivers'. After this manipulation, the targets were asked to act as naturally as possible when they interacted again with the perceivers during a ten-minute discussion of current events.

Because this study is similar to the previously discussed phone experiments involving the physical attractiveness stereotype (Anderson & Bem, 1981; Snyder et al., 1977), it is not surprising that these false perceptions about the perceivers not only influenced the targets' behavior but also influenced the perceivers' beliefs about their partner. Those targets that believed the other person liked them disclosed more, had a more pleasant tone of voice and general attitude, and disagreed less with the perceiver than those who thought the perceiver disliked them. How did the perceivers evaluate their partners? They liked better those targets that had been led to believe they were liked more than those who thought they were disliked. These findings suggest there is a *self-fulfilling prophecy* of liking, just as there is for the physical attractiveness stereotype. If we think others like us, we tend to act in ways that increase the likelihood that they will, indeed, like us. However, if we think they dislike us, our subsequent interaction style may fulfill the negative prophecy even if it is based on false information.

"Live with wolves, howl like a wolf."

Russian proverb

Critical THINKING

How has the similarity effect influenced your own personal relationships? Consider your best friends and your more casual friends. With whom do you share more similarities? Do these similarities fall into a particular category, such as shared values versus shared preferences?

SECTION SUMMARY

- We are attracted to beautiful people.

- Regarding the physical attractiveness stereotype, beautiful people are perceived to have better personalities and to lead healthier and happier lives; this stereotype is untrue, except that beautiful people are less socially anxious.

- Cross-cultural studies find some universal beauty standards:

  Men place a higher value on a physically attractive partner than do women.

  Women are judged more attractive if they have immature and dependent-looking facial features.

  Men are judged more attractive if they have mature facial characteristics related to social dominance.

- Greater focus on the female body as a thin beauty object causes lower body esteem, especially among women with feminine gender roles.

- Negative body esteem in men is often linked to the large and muscular male body standard.

- We are attracted to those similar to us.

  Attitudinal similarity is more important than personality similarity for relationship attraction.

  Personality similarity is more important than attitudinal similarity for longer-term relationship satisfaction.

- We are attracted to those who like us.

WHEN SOCIAL INTERACTION BECOMES PROBLEMATIC

> "*The only way to have a friend is to be one.*"
>
> ---------------
>
> Ralph Waldo Emerson, U.S. poet, 1803–1882

Throughout this chapter we have examined factors that prompt us to seek out others. However, whenever we approach others, we risk rejection. Even if others do accept our social overtures, there is the further possibility that we may commit a social blunder that will cause them to form a negative impression of us. How do we respond to these social "land mines"?

SOCIAL ANXIETY CAN KEEP US ISOLATED FROM OTHERS.

social anxiety
....
The unpleasant emotion people experience due to their concern with interpersonal evaluation

Social anxiety is the unpleasant emotion we experience due to our concern with interpersonal evaluation and the loss of social status (Weeks et al., 2011). This anxiety is what causes us to occasionally (or frequently) avoid social interaction, even when it involves virtual interaction on the Internet (Valkenburg & Peter, 2007). When socially anxious, we are less likely to initiate interactions, and when in an interaction, we talk less, sometimes stammer and stutter when we do speak, disclose less about ourselves, and occasionally even withdraw from the anxiety-producing situation altogether (Daly et al., 1997; McCroskey, 1997). This tendency to socially withdraw is not an effect characteristic of anxiety per se. As you have already discovered (see pp. 357–359), when we are anxious due to nonsocial factors, we often affiliate more, not less (Schachter, 1959). Therefore, avoiding affiliation generally occurs only when the source of the anxiety involves other people, either real or imagined.

The Self-Fulfilling Prophecy of Social Anxiety.

When people are thrust unexpectedly into the social spotlight they often overestimate the extent to which onlookers notice their thoughts, feelings, and emotions, a reaction known as the *illusion of transparency* (Savitsky & Gilovich, 2003). Although almost everyone occasionally thinks that others can "see right through them" more than is actually the case, people that experience chronic social anxiety, or *social anxiousness*, are more susceptible to the illusion that others notice their nervousness. In this uncomfortable state of mind, socially anxious individuals come to expect, readily

Individuals high in social anxiousness often withdraw from social situations, and such behavior on their part is sometimes interpreted as unfriendliness. How can nonanxious friends help socially anxious individuals overcome their social anxiety?

perceive, and intensely react to rejection cues in their surroundings (Downey et al., 2004). For example, they are more attentive to faces with negative expressions than they are to those with positive or neutral expressions (Pishyar et al., 2004). It is not surprising then to find that individuals with high social anxiety often evaluate their performance in social settings more unfavorably than others judge them. Their attentional bias in noticing negative social feedback results in highly anxious persons often acting in ways—avoiding eye contact, appearing nervous and jittery—that fulfill the self-prophecy more in their own minds than in others (Pozo et al. ,1991).

Friends' Effects on Social Anxiety.

When researchers have used experience-sampling methodology to randomly sample participants' feelings and experiences while they go about their daily activities, they have found that social anxiety does not always cause people to avoid affiliation. When participants became socially anxious while conversing with others, they wanted to end the interaction more when they were with less familiar and trusted individuals than when they were with close friends (Brown et al., 2007; Kashdan & Steger, 2006). These findings suggest that trusted friends can help us effectively deal with social anxiety, yet it is also true that there are times when friends can make matters worse. A recent study indicates that socially anxious adolescents tend to choose friends who are similarly socially anxious, and over time they influenced each other into becoming more socially anxious (Van Zalk et al., 2011). The disheartening insight here is that friends who have socially anxious tendencies can, through their ordinary daily interactions, socialize and strengthen each other's social anxiety.

On the positive side, there also is evidence that friends who do not suffer from debilitating social anxiety can help pull their socially anxious peers out of self-defeating behavior patterns. In a study that examined this possibility, Beth Pontari (2009) had people who were either high or low in social anxiety interact with a stranger either in the presence of a close friend or alone. Although the presence of friends had no effect on the social performance or anxiety of the participants who were low in social anxiety, a friend's presence was beneficial to the socially anxious participants. They appeared more socially competent and experienced less negative self-focused thoughts when their friend was present than when they were alone with the stranger. Further analyses revealed that high socially anxious participants seemed to benefit from their friend's subtle prompting during the interaction with the stranger. There was a typical pattern in which socially anxious participants would hesitate for a moment during their introductions and the friend would respond by briefly reminding them of something to share. Pontari contends that these small suggestions helped the socially anxious participants avoid resorting to some of their "safe" self-presentation tactics that signal social awkwardness and nervousness. Instead, the friend's prompts helped the socially anxious participant to engage in more assertive self-presentation strategies. Results also indicated that socially anxious participants appreciated, rather than resented, their friend's presence and support. Friends in return did not seem to mind supporting their anxious comrades, responding positively to their role as social facilitator.

In summary, the findings of friends' effects on social anxiety suggests that while similarly anxious friends can strengthen each other's anxiety around others, the subtle but helpful behavior of non-anxious friends can encourage socially anxious individuals to put aside their protective yet socially awkward self-presentation strategies in favor of more assertive strategies that convey social competence. Over time and with continued practice with their friends' assistance, these self-presentation strategies will begin to be automatically activated so that socially anxious individuals are not only less dependent on their friends' presence but are also less likely to define themselves as being socially anxious.

LONELINESS IS THE CONSEQUENCE OF SOCIAL ISOLATION.

Although the anticipation of evaluation can make us anxious, how do you think you would react to being cut off from meaningful interaction with others? Because of our need for others, the loss of meaningful social exchange is literally detrimental to our health. Feeling socially isolated significantly increases our risk for depression, obesity, elevated blood pressure, sleep problems, and diminished immunity to various diseases, including heart disease and Alzheimer's disease (Caspi et al.,2006; Wilson et al., 2007).

Defining and Measuring Loneliness

Loneliness is defined as having a smaller or less satisfying network of social and intimate relationships than we desire (Green et al., 2001; Rokach, 2007). In understanding loneliness, keep in mind that this is a subjective experience, reflecting what we feel and think about our interpersonal life, and, as such, is not the same thing as solitude or being alone. We can spend long periods of time alone without feeling lonely, and we can also feel terribly lonely in a crowd. In fact, research has shown that lonely and nonlonely people do not differ in the *quantity* of their social interaction, but rather in the *quality* of such exchanges. Chronically lonely individuals tend not to trust other people, partly explaining why they spend more time with strangers and acquaintances and less time with friends and family than those who are not lonely (Jones et al., 1985; Rotenburg et al., 2010). As we will explore more fully in Chapter 10, feelings of trust are a critical component of intimate relationships during all stages of life (see pp. 394–399).

Similar to social anxiety, we can experience loneliness as both a short-lived *state* and a chronic, long-term *trait*. For example, when you first arrived on campus in your freshman year, you may have experienced a temporary sense of loneliness until you became integrated into the college community. In contrast, some people suffer from chronic loneliness, regardless of the length of time they spend becoming acclimated to new social settings.

Although almost everyone experiences loneliness, adoption and twin studies indicate that some people are more likely to experience loneliness due to inherited traits (Bartels et al., 2008). While genetics plays an important role in susceptibility to loneliness, our recovery from it often depends on how we interpret and react to its perceived causes (Anderson et al., 1994). In an examination of the duration of loneliness experienced by first-year college students, Carolyn Cutrona (1982) found that it lasted longer among those who initially blamed themselves for their social isolation. That is, the chronically lonely made significantly more *internal, stable attributions* for their loneliness (for example, "I'm too shy" or "I don't know how to start a new relationship") than those who overcame their sense of isolation. Unfortunately, as can be seen in Table 9.1, this sort of self-blaming can discourage people from seeking out others and can perpetuate their dissatisfaction with social relationships. On the other hand, Cutrona found that those who thought of loneliness as being caused by a combination of personal and external factors (for example, "I'm lonely because I don't know anyone here.

"I turn pale at the outset of a speech and quake in every limb and in all my soul.**"**

Marcus Tullius Cicero, Roman philosopher and politician, 106–43 BC

loneliness
Having a smaller or less satisfactory network of social and intimate relationships than one desires

"To whom can I speak today? I am heavy-laden with trouble through lack of an intimate friend.**"**

The Man Who Was Tired of Life, 1990 BC

Table 9.1

Causal Attributions for Loneliness

STABILITY	LOCUS OF CAUSALITY	
	Internal	**External**
Stable	"I'm too shy." "I don't know how to start new relationships."	"Other people don't try to make friends."
Unstable	"I'm lonely because I haven't tried hard enough to meet others. I can change that by letting others know I'm fun to be around."	"I'm lonely because I don't know anyone here. Things will get better as I meet others."

Things will get better as I meet others") seemed to be more hopeful that they could make things change for the better. True to what would be expected from attribution theory (refer to Chapter 4), *these external, unstable attributions* resulted in relatively short-lived loneliness for most of these students.

Age, Gender, Culture, and Loneliness

Beyond genetic predisposing tendencies, who suffers the most from loneliness? Contrary to popular stereotypes, it is not the elderly. Numerous studies have identified the young—adolescents and young adults—as the loneliest age groups (Peplau et al., 1982). As people

Studies have shown that adolescents and young adults are the loneliest age groups.

" *I felt so lonesome I most wished I was dead.* **"**

––––––––––––––

Huck Finn in *The Adventures of Huckleberry Finn,* by Mark Twain

mature and move beyond the young adult years, their loneliness tends to decrease until relatively late in life, when factors such as poor health and the death of loved ones increase social isolation (Fung et al., 2008). One reason why adolescents and young adults may be lonelier than older individuals is that young people face many more social transitions, such as annually entering increasingly challenging academic settings, falling in and out of love for the first time, leaving family and friends, and training and searching for a full-time job—all of which can cause loneliness (Benner, 2011). Another reason for this decrease in loneliness with age is that as we mature, we often become more motivated to develop meaningful, long-term, romantic relationships where the accompanying emotional bonds contribute to mental health and happiness (Luong et al., 2010).

There are clear age differences in loneliness, but gender differences are not as clear-cut. Some studies have found a slight tendency for women to report greater loneliness than men, yet other studies fail to find any differences at all (Archibald et al., 1995; Brage et al., 1993). Despite any firm evidence for gender differences in the *degree* of loneliness, there does appear to be evidence that men and women feel lonely for different reasons. Men tend to feel lonely when deprived of group interaction; women are more likely to feel lonely when they lack one-to-one emotional sharing (Stokes & Levin, 1986). This different pattern of loneliness reflects a difference in the friendship patterns of women and men that we will discuss in Chapter 10 (pp. 403–406).

Regarding cultural differences, research suggests that loneliness shares common features across cultures, yet culture also shapes loneliness (van Staden & Coetzee, 2010). For example, a survey of people living in Canada, Turkey, and Argentina conducted by Ami Rokach and Hasan Bacanli (2001) found that the individualist Canadians not only experienced higher levels of loneliness than the collectivist Turks and Argentineans, they also had different perceptions of what caused their loneliness. Canadians were much more likely to explain their loneliness as being caused by personal inadequacies than the Argentineans and Turks.

" *I see loneliness ooze damply from people's bodies, trail after them, trickling, widening, running deep, flowing on and on forever.* **"**

––––––––––––––

Kaneka Mitsuharu, 1977, Japanese poet

These cultural differences in loneliness are most likely due to the expectations that individualists and collectivists have about social relationships and the degree of help they receive in establishing social ties. While individualists are socialized to develop loosely knit relationships, and to do so by relying on their own social skills and initiative, collectivists are taught to develop tightly knit relationships within their existing group, and to do so with the assistance and supervision of ingroup members (Miller & Prentice, 1994; Tower et al., 1997). In a very real sense, the social world constructed by individualists is more likely to create loneliness in its members than the social world created by collectivists. Further, when loneliness is experienced, individualists are more likely than collectivists to explain it in terms of internal, stable factors ("I'm lonely because I'm personally inadequate"). As we have just learned, this type of self-blaming creates a mind-set that discourages lonely people from seeking out others. Overall, Rokach and Bacanli's findings suggest that the social world created in an individualist culture is not only more likely to cause loneliness but is also more likely to perpetuate it. The take-away message here is that the more that you conceive of yourself as being embedded in a network of social relationships—being an interdependent self—the less likely you will feel lonely, even during the latter stages of life when many important social bonds are broken through death (Zhang et al., 2011).

Is Loneliness Contagious?

Although it is only natural to think of loneliness as a uniquely individualistic experience, like social anxiety, a recent study suggests that one person's loneliness can influence another person's loneliness. Using data from a large-scale longitudinal study begun in 1948, John Cacioppo and his coworkers (2009) examined the life experiences of more than five thousand people for sixty years. The researchers found that loneliness occurred in clusters and that as people who experienced loneliness got older, they tended to spread their loneliness among others, often by pushing people away. Instead of engaging with and supporting one another, lonely people gradually, over time, became more isolated from others. Further, nonlonely individuals who were around lonely individuals tended to become lonelier over time. As Cacioppo and his colleagues describe this process, like the fraying of a sweater, lonely people make others around them feel lonely; and the social fabric that knits people together starts to unravel.

This study also found that the social contagion of loneliness was more likely to spread among women's social networks than among men's networks. This gender difference may be partly due to the fact that women are more likely than men to express and share their emotions and are more attentive to the emotions of others (Hatfield et al., 1994). There is also a stigma associated with loneliness, particularly among men. As such, women might be more willing than men to engage in intimate self-disclosure about their lonely feelings, which may hasten the spread of loneliness among women compared to men.

How did members of a social network respond to loneliness in their midst? Interestingly, nonlonely people tended to distance themselves from lonely people, avoiding or rejecting them. In explaining this distancing effect by nonlonely people, Cacioppo and his coworkers stated that if loneliness is contagious, social distancing might be an attempt to keep the contagion in check. That is, because loneliness spreads through a network and reduces the social ties among its members, isolating lonely people may be an attempt by the larger group to protect the health and structure of their social network. Knowing that loneliness is associated with a variety of mental and physical diseases that can shorten life, Cacioppo and his colleagues contend that if loneliness does indeed function like a contagious disease, it is important to identify loneliness in a social network as early as possible and prevent it from spreading.

Social Skills Deficits and Loneliness

One important factor that contributes to lonely people being likely targets for social rejection is that they often think and behave in ways that reduce their likelihood of establishing new, rewarding relationships. Studies conducted with college students illustrate some of these self-defeating patterns of behavior. Typically, in these investigations, students who are strangers to one another are asked to briefly interact in either pairs or groups, after which they rate themselves and their partners on such interpersonal dimensions as friendliness, honesty, and openness. Compared with nonlonely individuals, lonely college students rate themselves negatively following such laboratory interactions. They perceive themselves as having been less friendly, less honest and open, and less warm (Christensen & Kashy, 1998; Jones et al., 1983). They also expect those who interact with them to perceive them in this negative manner. This expectation of failure in social interaction appears all the more hopeless to the chronically lonely because they believe that improving their social life is beyond their control (Duck et al., 1994).

If chronically lonely people were merely misperceiving their effect on others, you might expect that other people's positive feedback concerning their social competence would break down their misperceptions. The problem, however, is that the chronically lonely tend to lack social skills and, as a result, receive little positive reinforcement from others concerning their interaction style. Indeed, they are generally disliked or ignored by others, who see them as weak, unattractive, and insincere (Rotenberg et al., 1997).

What sort of social skills deficits do chronically lonely persons exhibit in their daily interactions? When conversing with another, the chronically lonely spend more time talking about themselves and take less interest in what their partner has to say than do nonlonely people (Jones et al., 1982). Consistent with the interaction style of those with low self-esteem, they also tend to perceive others in a negative light (Rotenberg & Kmill, 1992). When meeting such a person, new acquaintances often come away with negative impressions (Jones et al., 1983).

Are lonely individuals' lack of social skills due to their inattentiveness to social cues that would help them interact smoothly with others? That does not appear to be the case. Research by Wendi Gardner and her colleagues found no evidence that lonely people have deficiencies in noticing social cues that are important in maintaining smooth social interaction (Gardner et al., 2005; Pickett et al., 2004). In fact, lonely people appear to be especially attentive to others and are more accurate than other people in reading social signs of whether they are being socially included or excluded. Such hypervigilance may, in fact, induce social anxiety in lonely people, especially in awkward social situations.

Confronted with negative social judgments resulting from their inept social style, lonely individuals often immerse themselves in their occupations, withdraw into wish-fulfilling fantasies, or engage in self-destructive activities such as alcohol and drug abuse. Not surprisingly, lonely people often use the television, computer, and radio as substitutes for interpersonal relationships (Greenwood & Long, 2011). Unfortunately, the content of a good deal of mass media programming focuses on failed relationships and sadness, which actually can deepen one's sense of social isolation (Davis & Kraus, 1989). One type of nonsocial activity that appears to raise the spirits of those suffering from loneliness is the consumption of "comfort food." Research suggests that because certain foods are typically initially eaten with intimate family members and friends, the experience of eating those foods is encoded into long-term memory along with the emotion of social comfort. Later, eating this food when feeling lonely and depressed automatically activates the experience of psychological comfort that was initially encoded along with the food (Troisi & Gabriel, 2011). Similar comforting effects can be achieved by literally embracing objects—such as your favorite childhood stuffed animal—that are associated with previous nurturing life experiences (Harlow & Harlow, 1962). The take-home lesson here is that a move away from home, a fight with a close friend, and many other instances when you feel socially isolated can be temporarily remedied by "embracing" a familiar food or object that is associated with previous nurturing relationships.

> **“** *... Sitting down to one plate, that loneliest of all positions.* **”**
>
> ——————————
> Caroline Gilman, U.S. author and educator, 1794–1888

SECTION SUMMARY

- Social anxiety can cause people to avoid interaction, and chronic social anxiety can lead to increasingly unpleasant social exchanges.

  - Socially anxious individuals are attracted to one another and can heighten each other's anxiety.

  - Non-anxious friends can reduce socially anxious individuals' awkwardness by prompting them during social exchanges.

- Loneliness is an unpleasant subjective state in which a person has a smaller or less satisfying network of social and intimate relationships than desired.

  - Adolescents and young adults are the loneliest age groups.

  - As people mature, loneliness decreases until relatively late in life.

  - Loneliness tends to cluster in social networks and spread through them.

  - The chronically lonely often lack social skills.

APPLICATIONS

How Can Social Skills Training Improve Your Life?

While eating your favorite food and hugging a teddy bear may temporarily relieve feelings of loneliness, these activities are not long-term remedies for social isolation. One of the most important obstacles that chronically lonely people must overcome is their lack of social skills (Solano & Koester, 1989). The same statement could also be made of those who experience high levels of social anxiousness, for they do not make good first impressions and often experience loneliness (Curran, 1977). This social deficiency is likely one of the more important causes of the low self-esteem of lonely and socially anxious individuals. It can also lead to a feeling of hopelessness and increased social withdrawal (Page, 1991). On the other hand, those who have well-developed social skills find it easy to talk to strangers, are perceived by others as friendly, are not easily angered, and possess high self-esteem.

What makes a person socially skilled? One of the most important factors determining social skill is the *amount of personal attention given to one's partner* in interaction (Kupke et al., 1979). People who are judged to be socially skilled direct more questions toward their conversational partners and make more positive personal statements about them. On the other hand, the unskilled are more self-focused and less responsive when conversing. Some social scientists suggest that this sort of "conversational narcissism," in which people habitually turn conversational topics to themselves without showing interest in their partners' topics, may be more prevalent in individualist cultures than in those with collectivist orientations (Vangelisti et al., 1990). These conversational narcissists have taken the individualist notion that personal needs are more important than group needs to the point where they ignore the interaction needs of others. The all-too-common price for such narcissism is social rejection.

A second factor related to social effectiveness is the *ability to recognize and conform to social norms.* People who have social skills problems often engage in situationally improper behavior. For example, they may make new acquaintances uncomfortable by disclosing very personal details about their lives. Although this sort of self-disclosure is important and valuable in intimate relationships, it is considered inappropriate when interacting with strangers and new acquaintances. Such norm violations generally discourage future encounters.

A third factor associated with social skill is *regulating one's mood prior to commencing social interaction.* Research indicates that people who are socially skilled monitor and impose constraints on their emotions prior to interacting with others (Lopes et al., 2004; Tamir & Mauss, 2011). Such mood regulation is especially necessary when interacting with strangers, due to the importance of first impressions. In general, when people anticipate interacting with a stranger, they try to regulate their mood in the direction of *neutrality,* regardless of whether their current mood is positive or negative (Erber et al., 1996). This self-imposed mood neutrality is sought because being perceived by new acquaintances as "cool" and "calm" is a socially desirable goal for most people, and a neutral mood is most consistent with attaining that goal. Further, during first encounters, one's arriving with a preexisting positive or negative mood might be interpreted by a new interaction partner as an attempt to impose one's own mood on her or him, which could lead to negative evaluations. The only times the socially skilled do not seek mood neutrality is when they know beforehand that the person they are about to meet shares their current mood, or when people are happy and they know that the person they are about to meet is depressed. In the latter instance, the failure to neutralize a happy mood might be a self-protective strategy employed by happy people. That is, they may not neutralize their positive emotions because they may believe that they will soon need their positive mood to buffer themselves against the contagious sadness of their interaction partner.

Finally, a fourth factor in fostering effective social interaction is *realizing that others do generally not notice another's nervousness.* As previously mentioned (p. 377), the belief that one's thoughts, feelings, and emotions are more transparent to others than is actually the case is known as the illusion of transparency. This illusion derives from the difficulty people have in getting beyond their own subjective experience when trying to figure out how they appear to others. As a result, they exaggerate the degree to which their internal states "leak out" and overestimate the degree to which others can detect their private thoughts and feelings. Research indicates that when socially anxious individuals are educated about the illusion of transparency and realize that their nervousness is not as apparent as they think, this knowledge not only reduces their anxiety, it improves their ability to speak in a public setting (Savitsky & Gilovich, 2003). These findings lend support to the idea that "the truth can set you free" regarding the social psychology of everyday socializing.

One fairly risk-free way to practice this newfound knowledge of effective social interaction is to "converse" with others online. In a survey of almost eight hundred adolescents, Patti Valkenburg and Jochen Peter (2007) found that socially anxious individuals perceived the Internet as a valuable social arena for them to develop friendships, possibly because online communication induced less anxiety and allowed more time to formulate conversational responses. The relative anonymity possible during online conversations appears to play a key role in reducing anxiety.

In a study of Internet use and shyness, Paul Brunet and Louis Schmidt (2007) asked female college students to engage in a ten-minute online free-chat conversation with and without a live webcam. Analysis of these conversations found that shy women disclosed less personal information than non-shy women only when their visual image was being transmitted. When the Web cam was not present, the shy women's conversations were no different in quality from those of the nonshy women. Additional research finds that Internet sites such as Facebook help shy people to become better acquainted with others and makes them feel more comfortable socially (Baker & Oswald, 2010). Together, these studies suggest that the Internet, under the proper conditions, can provide individuals who lack confidence in their social skills with a relatively safe social arena to practice the art of social interaction.

social skills training
....
A behavioral training program designed to improve interpersonal skills through observation, modeling, role-playing, and behavioral rehearsal

Besides simply encouraging people to enhance their social skills through practice, considerable research has been devoted to developing **social skills training** programs to promote greater relationship satisfaction (Margie, 2006). These programs employ various learning techniques, including the observation and modeling of socially skilled trainers, role-playing various problematic social encounters, and observing one's own social interactions on videotape. The social skills taught in these training sessions cover such areas as initiating conversations, speaking fluently on the telephone, giving and receiving compliments, handling period, (Brackett et al., 2007).

Training is usually conducted in groups. In a typical session, the instructor might show a videotape of a model starting a conversation inappropriately or failing to respond to someone's compliment. The group might then discuss ways in which the model could have acted more appropriately. Following this discussion, another videotape might be shown in which the model performs more effectively. Each person in the training group might then role-play a conversation while others observe and then provide feedback. This role-playing might even be videotaped so that group members can see exactly how they had interacted. The session might end with a homework assignment for group members to start a conversation with a stranger during the following week.

A growing body of research indicates that those who participate in such training exercises show improvements in their social skills and an increased level of social satisfaction (Hennessey, 2007). In one intervention study, Warren Jones and his colleagues (1982) taught lonely college men to increase their personal attention shown to female strangers during a series of dyadic interactions. They were first given information on the importance of paying attention to others in conversation, and then they interacted individually with four women in successive five-minute, taped conversations. Following these four dyadic interactions, the lonely men were next instructed how to ask questions of their conversational partners, how to refer to their partners while talking to them, and how to discuss topics of interest with their partners. Training consisted of modeling, practice interaction, and feedback. Compared with two control groups of lonely men who did not receive instruction in personal attention, the trained students subsequently reported feeling less lonely, less self-conscious, and less shy.

The particular skills emphasized in many training programs appear best suited to facilitate the initiation of social relationships. Although this is a necessary starting point, it is also important for people to learn skills for "deepening" relationships and overcoming interpersonal conflict.

One study that attempted to train such skills was conducted by Robin Cappe and Lynn Alden (1986). They recruited twenty-six men and twenty-six women who were at least moderately socially impaired and exposed them to different types of training programs. Some recruits were instructed on four human relations skills necessary in developing and strengthening friendships: *active listening, empathic responding, communicating respect, and self-disclosure.* The instructors discussed and modeled each skill. Participants then practiced their own problematic social situations and incorporated these new skills into each situation. In addition to learning these social skills, participants also learned how to relax when feeling anxious. A second group of recruits was not given any social skills training, but merely learned how to relax in anxiety-producing situations. Finally, a third group received no training at all. Results indicated that the shy, socially avoidant individuals who received a combination of social skills training and relaxation instruction reported significantly greater improvements in their social functioning in the community than those who either received only relaxation training or no instruction at all. In addition, those who were given training in social skills were judged by independent observers to be more comfortable and skillful in social interactions than those in the other groups. A three-month follow-up assessment indicated that a greater proportion of those who had received the social skills training reported having made significant social changes in their lives. These events varied in social impact from minor ("I was able to join a club") to major ("I was able to date and am now engaged").

Taken together, these studies suggest that social skills training programs can, in a fairly short time, teach socially anxious and lonely people how to interact more effectively with others. The resulting interpersonal successes they experience can not only reduce their feeling of social isolation but can also boost their sense of social competence and their overall level of self-esteem.

THE BIG PICTURE

In studying social psychology, have you noticed a recurring set of psychological principles that appear to shape people's thoughts and actions? These two psychological cousins are the general desire to be liked and accepted by others and the general desire to have an accurate view of things. They correspond to the "hot" and "cold" perspectives on the nature of human behavior first mentioned in Chapter 1. You can see these two principles operating in your self-enhancement and self-verification motives, in your social judgments, and in your ability to exert and be susceptible to social influence. These principles also shape your attraction to others. According to *social exchange theory,* you seek out and maintain those relationships that make you feel good about yourself and bring you more rewards than costs. According to *social comparison theory,* you seek out similar others for accurate comparison so that you can judge and improve yourself.

What you have learned about the psychology of relationships should prove useful in the coming years. As you seek the company of others, remember that a self-fulfilling prophecy is associated with the "desire to be liked" principle. If you approach new social settings thinking that others will like you, you will probably act in ways that fulfill this prophecy. However, if you expect rejection, your subsequent interaction style may fulfill the negative prophecy, even if it is based on false information.

Also keep in mind that although almost everyone experiences loneliness, your recovery often depends on how you interpret and react to its perceived causes. People who make *internal, stable attributions* for their loneliness ("I just don't know how to make new friends") tend to be chronically lonely, while those who make *external, unstable attributions* ("I'm lonely because I don't know anyone here") are generally only temporarily lonely. The advice to be gleaned from this research is that you should be careful what you think you are, for you will likely behave consistent with those self-beliefs. Here again is an example of how the self is an active participant in creating its social reality.

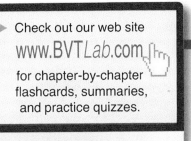

Check out our web site
www.BVTLab.com
for chapter-by-chapter flashcards, summaries, and practice quizzes.

WEB SITES

ACCESSED THROUGH www.BVTLab.com/sop6
Web sites for this chapter focus on research and theory on interpersonal relationships, as well as an analysis of shyness, social anxiety, and loneliness.

INTERNATIONAL SOCIETY FOR THE STUDY OF PERSONAL RELATIONSHIPS
This web site for the International Society for the Study of Personal Relationships lists information about interpersonal relationship publications and conferences, as well as links to other relevant sites.

SHYNESS INSTITUTE
This web page is a gathering of network resources for people seeking information and services for shyness and social anxiety.

AMERICAN PSYCHOLOGICAL ASSOCIATION
The American Psychological Association web site contains a web page that discusses research indicating that the Internet increases social isolation among users.

Chapter 10

Intimate Relationships

Chapter Outline

INTRODUCTION

What Is Intimacy?
Intimacy involves including another in your self-concept.

Parent-Child Attachment and Later Adult Relationships
Attachment is an inborn adaptive response.
Attachment styles influence romantic relationships.

Friendship
Self-disclosure shapes friendship development and maintenance.
Gender differences exist in heterosexual friendships.
Cross-sex heterosexual friendships gravitate to an "intimacy mean."
"Friends-with-benefits" relationships pose unique challenges and dangers.
Gender differences disappear in same-sex homosexual friendships.
Important barriers to long-distance friendships are falling.

Romantic Relationships
Culture shapes how we think about romantic love.
Online romance and speed dating follow similar rules as face-to-face romance.
Passionate love can be triggered by excitation transfer.
Companionate love is more stable and enduring than passionate love.
Women and men may differ in their experience of love.

Will Love Endure?
Social disapproval of one's partner harms relationship stability.
People are happiest with romantic equity.
Self-esteem can both facilitate and undermine romantic love.
Romantic happiness is based on both positive illusions and accurate judgments.
Social support predicts relationship satisfaction.
We are meaner to those we love than we are to strangers.
People use different strategies to cope with a troubled relationship.
Romantic breakups often cause emotional distress.

APPLICATIONS
What Causes Jealousy and How Can You Cope with It?

PREVIEW   Jealousy can cause irreparable harm to romantic relationships. What are some of the short-term and long-term strategies that you can use to constructively resolve jealousy?

THE BIG PICTURE

WEB SITES

Introduction

In Robert Munsch's (1986) children's book *Love You Forever*, he tells a movingly offbeat story about a mother-son relationship. It begins with the mother holding her new baby and slowly rocking him back and forth while singing the following verse:

> I'll love you forever,
> I'll like you for always,
> As long as I'm living
> my baby you'll be.

As the child grows, he gets into all sorts of messes and squabbles and does a nice job aging the mother. Despite these hassles of childrearing, each night as he sleeps, his mother looks into his room, crawls across the floor, and peers up over the side of the bed. If he is truly asleep, she carefully picks him up, slowly rocks him back and forth, and sings her song to him.

When he grows up and moves across town, sometimes the mother straps a ladder to her car late at night, drives to her son's house, climbs into his room, and crawls to the foot of his bed. If he is truly asleep, she carefully picks up this full-grown man and slowly rocks him back and forth, singing her song as she gazes into his peaceful face.

Well, one day when the mother is old and feeble, she phones her son and tells him to come over quickly because she is very sick. When he arrives, the mother tries to sing her song but can not finish. Instead then, the grown-up son carefully picks up his mother, holds her in his arms, and begins to slowly rock her back and forth. As he rocks her, he sings the following verse:

> I'll love you forever,
> I'll like you for always,
> As long as I'm living
> my Mommy you'll be.

Later, when he returns to his own home, he goes to his newborn daughter's room where she peacefully sleeps. Reaching down, he gently picks her up in his arms, holds her close, and slowly begins to rock her back and forth. As he rocks her, he sings:

> I'll love you forever,
> I'll like you for always,
> As long as I'm living
> my baby you'll be.

The deeply tender and nurturing feelings expressed in Robert Munsch's verse mirror the story that psychologists tell about intimate relationships: children learn about intimacy and love during the first few years of life, and this forms the basis for how they will interact with others in later years. In Chapter 9, you learned that people differ in their affiliation needs, and that women are more likely than men to seek an emotional connectedness to other individuals (see p. 353). Now, you will continue this analysis by examining the intimacy experienced in friendships and romantic relationships, each of which offers its own unique contributions to people's health and welfare (Perlman, 2007). This is a journey you have traveled before. Yet now, instead of trying to understand friendship and love simply by immersing yourself in the experience, you will survey the social psychological literature to better understand how scientists explain the communion of selves. Your social psychological journey begins with a discussion of what is encompassed in the term *intimacy*.

WHAT IS INTIMACY?

intimacy
....
Sharing that which is inmost with others

Imagine that you overhear another person make a disparaging remark about someone you love. How would you feel, and how might you respond? Now imagine that the one you care about has succeeded (or failed) on an important task. How would their success and failure influence your moods? If you are like most people, you would *share* with that person the emotional highs and lows accompanying these events. **Intimacy** refers to sharing that which is inmost with others (McAdams, 1988). The word itself is derived from the Latin *intimus*, which means "inner" or "inmost." Because we share that which is most important to us with our loved ones it is not surprising that we seek from them verification of who we think we are; their opinions matter and this self-verification need is automatically activated when thinking of those most close to us (Kraus & Chen, 2009).

INTIMACY INVOLVES INCLUDING ANOTHER IN YOUR SELF-CONCEPT.

"*A friend is, as it were, a second self.*"

Marcus Tullius Cicero, Roman statesman, 106–43 BC

"*We are molded and remolded by those who have loved us; and, though the love may pass, we are nevertheless their work, for good or ill.*"

François Mauriac, French novelist, 1885–1970

As you recall from Chapter 3, William James conceived of the "self as object" (or self-concept) as being a process of identification, expanding and contracting to include that which one values. Arthur Aron and Elaine Aron (1986, 1997) employ James's notion of *self-expansion* in their analysis of intimacy. They contend that in intimate relationships, we seek to psychologically expand ourselves by acting as if some or all aspects of our partner are part of our own selves (Aron et al., 2001). The degree to which our partner is included in our self-concept is an indicator of our level of relationship intimacy (Lewandowski et al., 2010). Figure 10.1 provides a schematic illustration of different levels of intimacy through this self-expansion process.

This removal of psychological boundaries between people so that one experiences another as part of him or herself is often identified as the most important distinguishing feature of intimacy (Cross & Gore, 2002; Rempel & Burris, 2006). Yet if intimacy is really an inclusionary experience, can researchers detect it by studying the structure and the process of the self? A number of social psychologists respond with an affirmative yes to this question. They contend that in memory this inclusion of the other in the self is represented by a direct link between the self and the close other, so that activating either memories of the self or the close other will automatically activate memories of both persons and their associated traits (Mashek et al., 2003). Neurologically, scientists have observed this inclusion of the other in the self in terms of how the brain processes names. This research indicates that recognizing our own names and the names of our loved ones involves a similar pattern of brain activity that is different from the neural patterns occurring when we recognize the names of people in general (Tacikowski et al., 2001). The implication of these studies as a whole is that we will think about and respond to intimate others very similarly to the way we think about and respond to ourselves. Let us examine other studies where evidence for this inclusionary process has been found.

Figure 10.1

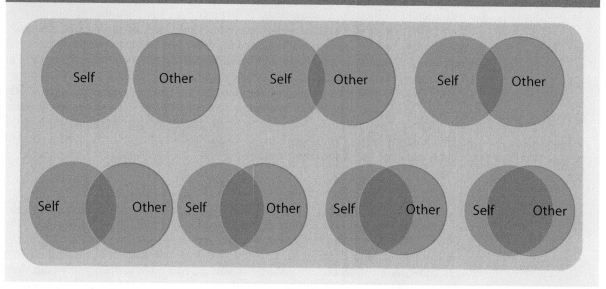

Inclusion of Other in the Self

This is a schematic illustration of seven different degrees of self-other relatedness, from no inclusion of the other in the self to an immersion of the other in one's self. Which of the pictures best describes different intimate relationships in your own life?

Self-Schemas

One way in which intimate relationships reflect the inclusion of the other in the self-concept is in what constitutes self-concept ingredients, or *self-schemas*. As discussed in Chapter 3, traits that we identify as being important in our self-concepts are recognized as being self-descriptive more quickly than traits that are not relevant to our self-concepts (Markus, 1977). Research comparing the self-schemas of strangers, friends, and married couples has found that as the intimacy bond deepens between two people, they begin to incorporate some of the other's self-schemas into their own self-concepts. As a result of this cognitive blurring of the self-other distinction, people involved in intimate relationships need less time to recognize self-descriptive traits if the traits are also shared with their partner (Aron et al., 1991; E. Smith et al., 1999). For example, imagine that Ann and Stephanie are involved in an intimate relationship. Ann has self-schemas consisting of such traits as independent, tidy, and industrious. Stephanie sees herself as independent, industrious, and athletic. The speed at which they can individually process and recall self-descriptive traits will be faster for traits they share (independent, industrious) rather than those upon which they differ. Even though Ann has a self-schema for "tidy" and Stephanie has a self-schema for "athletic," because the intimate other does not share this trait, it takes them longer to identify it as being self-descriptive. Given that we include our intimate others in our self-concepts, the loss of such relationships have significant impacts on how we conceive ourselves. For example, after a romantic breakup, individuals' self-concepts typically become both less clear and smaller, with these effects being stronger the more emotionally committed people are to the relationship (Slotter & Gardner, 2009; Slotter et al., 2010).

The Attribution Process

As discussed in Chapter 4, when we make attributions about events, the perspective we have of our own versus others' behavior results in the *actor-observer effect*—we attribute our own behavior to external causes but that of others to internal factors (McCall et al., 2000). This self-other discrepancy has been found to be much less pronounced when the "other" is more intimate with the self (Nisbett et al., 1973). In other words, when explaining the actions of someone for whom we care a great deal, the attributions we infer are more similar to those we would have for our own actions versus those of the average person on the street (Gardner et al., 2002; Lavin, 1987).

What are five ways in which people often demonstrate the inclusion of intimate others in their self-concepts?

Resource Allocation

Resource allocation is another way we include others within our self-concept. People in an intimate relationship make less of a distinction between self and other when allocating resources than do those who are less intimate (Aron et al., 1991). This is so because if another is included in your self-concept, your resources are also her or his resources. Imagine two couples going out to dinner together, one pair deeply in love, the other on their first date. During the course of the meal, the two lovers eat from each other's plate, reaching for morsels of food without asking permission. If, in a similar manner, one person from the nonintimate pair reached for the other's food, it would likely be interpreted as very bad manners—an encroachment on the other's personal resources.

Communal Versus Exchange Relationships

The different disbursement of resources to an intimate other naturally leads to another quality indicative of the "self-inclusion of other" perspective. As discussed in Chapter 9 (p. 351), most of our everyday relationships operate on the principle of *social exchange* in which we carefully tally our costs and balance those against our rewards to determine whether we should maintain the relationship. However, a number of studies demonstrate that when we are involved in intimate relationships, we often do not think about our rewards and costs as if we were balancing our bank accounts (Mills & Clark, 2001). Instead, these *communal relationships* are organized according to the principle that people should be given what they need, with little concern for what we will receive in return (Medvene et al., 2000). Thus, in intimate relationships, we treat our loved ones' needs as if they were our own, with little to no tallying of costs. Because these intimate others are important elements in our own self-concept, our needs and their needs are intertwined and often indistinguishable; when our friends, family members, or romantic partners need help we freely lend a hand. Establishing a communal relationship in a budding romance or friendship is so important to many people that the relationship can be destroyed if one partner maintains an exchange orientation by regularly trying to balance costs and rewards (Clark & Mills, 2004). Table 10.1 summarizes the differences between these two different types of relationships.

Transactive Memory

One final way that the self-inclusion of the other is manifested is in the use of *transactive memory*. Daniel Wegner and his colleagues (1991) found that people in intimate relationships have a shared memory system for encoding, storing, and retrieving information that is

"If I have no love, I am nothing. ... Love is patient; love is kind and envies no one. Love is never boastful, nor conceited, nor rude; never selfish, not quick to take offence. Love keeps no score of wrongs; does not gloat over other men's sins, but delights in the truth. ... Love will never come to an end."

I Corinthians 13

Table 10.1

Exchange Versus Communal Relationships

EXCHANGE RELATIONSHIPS (Governed by concern for equity)	**COMMUNAL RELATIONSHIPS** (Governed by responsiveness to the other's needs)
1. Person motivated by a desire to have a "fair" relationship	1. Person motivated by a desire to please the other person
2. Person desires to be immediately repaid for favors	2. Person dislikes being immediately repaid for favors
3. Person feels exploited when favors are not returned	3. Person does not feel exploited when favors are not returned
4. Person keeps track of who is contributing what to the relationship	4. Person does not keep track of who is contributing what to the relationship
5. Helping one's partner doesn't elevate one's mood	5. Helping one's partner elevates one's mood

> *"Knowledge is of two kinds. We know a subject ourselves or we know where we can find information about it."*
>
> Samuel Johnson, English author, 1709–1784

greater than either of their individual memories. In this transactive memory, each partner enjoys the benefits of the pair's memory by taking responsibility for remembering just those items that fall clearly to her or him (Andersson & Rönnberg, 1997; Hollingshead, 2001). For a romantic couple living together, this may involve one person remembering the proper place for all the workroom tools, while the other remembers where the special dinnerware and napkins are stored. If each person learns in a general way what the other knows in detail, the two can share the detailed memories enjoyed by both. Through updating one another on what is in each other's knowledge area, the partners further embellish their transactive memory (Engestrom et al., 1990).

In summary, these studies illustrate the utility of viewing close relationships as including the other in the self-concept. Partners who are high in intimacy are concerned about the other's welfare and happiness, often even more than their own (Cross et al., 2000). The rewards shared by intimates go far beyond "warm fuzzies." Cross-cultural studies find that having successful intimate relationships is among our most important life goals and aspirations, and it is the only factor that consistently predicts happiness in every country studied (Diener et al., 1999; Reis & Gable, 2003). Let us now examine the foundation for these intimacy beliefs.

SECTION SUMMARY

- Intimacy is an inclusion of others in one's self-concept, and manifests itself in

    self-schemas

    attribution processes

    resource allocation

    communal relationships

    transactive memory

PARENT-CHILD ATTACHMENT
AND LATER ADULT RELATIONSHIPS

When a national sample of American teenagers and young adults were asked in 2007 to identify what makes them happy and who were their heroes in life, spending time with family was the top answer for happiness, and nearly half of the respondents listed one or both of their parents on their list of heroes (Noveck & Tompson, 2007). These findings suggest that the majority of young people in America have a healthy emotional attachment to their families. Psychologists define **attachment** as the strong emotional bond that develops between infants and their caregivers; it is considered the cornerstone for all other relationships in a child's life (Cummings & Cummings, 2002). This bond is not unique to humans but is found in most species of birds and mammals (Graves & Hennesy, 2000; Mason, 1997).

attachment

The strong emotional bond between an infant and a caregiver

ATTACHMENT IS AN INBORN ADAPTIVE RESPONSE.

As with affiliation tendencies discussed in Chapter 9 (p. 351), the emotional bond of attachment is sparked by biological processes and genetic tendencies. Human infants have an inborn attachment response that is observable within minutes of birth, beginning with attempts to suckle their mother's breasts (the *rooting instinct*) and the ability to grasp and hold fast when startled (the *Moro reflex*). Within days, newborns recognize and prefer the face, voice, and smell of their mother to those of unfamiliar people, and they spontaneously imitate their caretakers' facial expressions (Jones, 2007; Maestripieri, 2001). New mothers are similarly predisposed to bond with their infants. During labor and later when breast-feeding their children, mothers produce *oxytocin*, a hormone that also acts as a neurotransmitter in the brain and has a positive influence on parenting behavior. Both human and animal studies indicate that individuals—both females and males—with higher levels of oxytocin more strongly desire companionship, have higher levels of trust, and take better care of their young than those with lower levels (Kosfeld et al., 2005; Taylor & Gonzaga, 2007). The positive effects that oxytocin has on intimate emotions and behavior has led some scientists to call it the "love hormone" (Lawrence, 2004).

British psychiatrist John Bowlby (1969) was one of the first social scientists to systematically study the attachment process. Based on his analysis of human infants and the young of other species, Bowlby proposed that attachment is part of many species' genetic heritage, with its evolutionary function being the protection of immature, highly vulnerable animals. Infants who cling or remain close to their parents are better

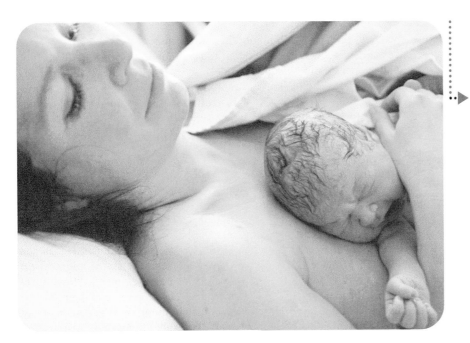

The affection of mothers for their offspring is at least partly based on the hormones present during the birth process and later during nursing. Whether children develop a secure versus an insecure attachment style is significantly determined by the parenting style of the primary caregiver.

protected from predators and thus stand a better chance of surviving to adulthood than those who wander away from parental care.

In his evolutionary analysis of attachment, Bowlby proposed a standard pattern of three responses produced by infants of many species when they become separated from their primary caregivers: protest, despair, and detachment. *Protest* is the first strategy employed following parental separation, and it is characterized by infants creating a ruckus. Infants who wail and scream are likely to draw their parents near, thus increasing the likelihood that they will be protected and fed. However, if this protest strategy does not succeed, Bowlby reasoned that the next best survival strategy is for infants to remain quiet (*despair*), thus reducing the likelihood of attracting the attention of predators. Finally, if left unattended for long periods, infants will develop emotional *detachment* and begin to behave independently.

One of Bowlby's associates, Mary Ainsworth (1989), took his basic ideas about attachment and studied how human infants develop different *attachment styles*. Ainsworth reasoned that although our biological heritage may propel us toward caregivers, the basic principles of reinforcement theory suggest that the caregiver's response will influence the strength of this desire to establish such proximity. Subsequent research on parent-child attachment indicated that as infants interact with their parents they develop either optimistic or pessimistic beliefs about human relationships (Meins, 1999; Moss et al., 2004). Children with parents who are nurturing and sensitively responsive to their needs develop a *secure attachment* style characterized by a belief that they are worthy of others' love and that people can be trusted. In marked contrast, children with parents who are inattentive to their needs develop an *insecure attachment* style characterized by a belief that they are unworthy love objects and that others cannot be relied upon (Huth-Bocks et al., 2004). Not surprisingly, people who are insecurely attached are much less likely than those who are securely attached to experience positive emotions associated with safety and contentment (Gilbert et al., 2008).

From a social cognitive perspective, one way to understand attachment styles is that they consist of people's cognitive representations of what constitutes love and intimacy (Dykas & Cassidy, 2011). In essence, individuals with different attachment styles have different *prototypes* for intimate relationships (Vicary & Fraley, 2007). As you recall from Chapter 4 (p. 110), a prototype is the most representative member of a category. If people behave in a warm and affectionate manner towards them, securely attached persons quickly recognize this as an overture for intimacy; but those with insecure attachment will be less likely to do so because the behavior does not match their "intimate relationship" prototype. This difficulty in associating signals of intimacy with the cognitive category of "intimate relationships" causes trouble in the social world of the insecurely attached (Knee & Canevello, 2006).

Generally speaking, throughout childhood insecurely attached children exhibit less social competence and lower levels of self-esteem and self-concept complexity than children with secure attachment (Schulman et al., 1994). Insecurely attached children often exhibit contradictory social behavior, sometimes initiating social contact, but then unexpectedly spurning others' social advances. This vacillating pattern of approach-avoidance invites social rejection from peers, which then serves to confirm the child's original sense of insecurity and distrust.

ATTACHMENT STYLES INFLUENCE ROMANTIC RELATIONSHIPS.

Up until the mid-1980s, all research on attachment styles focused on children and adolescents' social relationships. Then, in 1987, social psychologists Cindy Hazan and Philip Shaver developed self-report measures of secure and insecure attachment styles derived from the work of Ainsworth and other developmental psychologists. Hazan and Shaver were interested in determining whether these attachment styles might affect adult romantic relationships. Inserting their attachment measures into a "love quiz" printed in a local newspaper, they asked respondents questions about their current romantic relationships. The results of this pioneering study found that the percentage of adults who endorsed each attachment style were similar to the figures obtained in studies of infant-parent attachment (Fraley, 2002). Hazan and Shaver also found that securely attached adults reported more positive relationships with their parents than did adults with insecure attachment styles.

After the publication of this research, many social psychologists began exploring how attachment styles influenced the nature and quality of adult social relationships and found that they were consistent with the findings for children (Mikulincer & Shaver, 2006; Powers et al., 2006). Although questions persist regarding the degree of overlap between childhood and adulthood measures of attachment (see Roisman et al., 2007), a number of infant and adult studies suggest that attachment styles are best thought of as being determined by two basic attitudes: (1) the extent to which one's self-esteem is positive or negative, and (2) the extent to which one perceives others as trustworthy (a positive attitude) or untrustworthy (a negative attitude). In turn, these two basic attitudes cause different reactions whenever intimacy becomes an issue; low self-esteem triggers anxiety and low interpersonal trust triggers avoidance (Mikulincer & Shaver, 2003; Scharf et al., 2004). As depicted in Figure 10.2, this new conception of attachment—which is still consistent with Ainsworth's original research—yields four kinds of attachment style (Brennan et al., 1998; Fraley & Spieker, 2003).

Individuals with a **secure attachment style** have positive self-esteem and believe that people are basically loving and trustworthy; therefore, they experience low anxiety and low avoidance in their social relationships. Securely attached adults easily become close to others, expect intimate relationships to endure, and handle relationship conflict constructively by discussing problems and forgiving occasional transgressions (Creasey & Ladd, 2005; Lawler-Row et al., 2011). In college, securely attached first-year students adjust better to university life and have higher achievement aspirations than students with other attachment styles (Elliot & Reis, 2003; Kanemasa, 2007).

Although persons with a **preoccupied attachment style** have positive expectations that people will be loving and trustworthy, they have a negative view of themselves as not being worthy of others' love. Thus, they are low on avoidance but high on anxiety. They desperately seek out intimate relationships, but they tend to be obsessed and preoccupied with their friends and romantic partners; and they fear that their friendship and love will not be reciprocated. Preoccupied individuals' often judge their self-worth in terms of their physical attractiveness, and their orientation toward sexual activity is strongly shaped by their insecurity and strong intimacy needs (D. Davis et al. 2004; Park et al., 2004). They tend to have sex as a way to feel valued by their partners or as a means to induce their partners to love them more (Schachner & Shaver, 2004).

In contrast to the belief by secure and preoccupied people that others are basically loving and trustworthy, people with a **dismissing-avoidant attachment style** have little faith in other people, and thus, they avoid intimacy. They find it hard to trust others, have difficulty even recognizing expressions of warmth and empathy from others, and often withdraw from relationships when conflicts arise (Schindler et al., 2010). Due to their positive self-esteem and lack of self-insight, dismissing-avoidant individuals typically experience little interpersonal anxiety (Gjerde et al., 2004). In fact, they are generally confident—even arrogant—but because they do not trust others they exhibit a compulsive self-reliance. Unlike preoccupied individuals who are motivated to engage in sexual activity to reduce insecurity and foster intense intimacy, dismissives are likely to have sex simply because they enjoy it or because they can then brag about it and increase their status with their social group (Schachner & Shaver, 2004). This pattern of behavior might suggest that dismissive-avoidant individuals have a low need to belong (see Chapter 9, p. 351). However, a recent series of studies indicate that individuals with a dismissive-avoidant style experience higher than average levels of positive affect and heightened self-esteem after being accepted by others (Carvallo & Gabrel, 2006; MacDonald & Borsook, 2010). This research suggests that dismissive avoidants do indeed desire social inclusion, even though they avoid intimacy, and it provides further evidence that a strong and basic need for affiliation and acceptance is present in all humans.

Finally, similar to dismissives, persons with a **fearful-avoidant attachment style** do not trust others; however, unlike dismissives, they also have a low opinion of themselves and therefore experience a great deal of anxiety in interpersonal settings. Fearful-avoidant individuals expect to be rejected by others, and they have a heightened

---

secure attachment style

....

An expectation about social relationships characterized by trust, a lack of concern with being abandoned, and a feeling of being valued and well liked

preoccupied attachment style

....

An expectation about social relationships characterized by trust but combined with a feeling of being unworthy of others' love and a fear of abandonment

dismissing-avoidant attachment style

....

An expectation about social relationships characterized by low trust and avoidance of intimacy, combined with high self-esteem and compulsive self-reliance

fearful-avoidant attachment style

....

An expectation about social relationships characterized by low trust and avoidance of intimacy, combined with a feeling of being unworthy of others' love and a fear of rejection

Figure 10.2

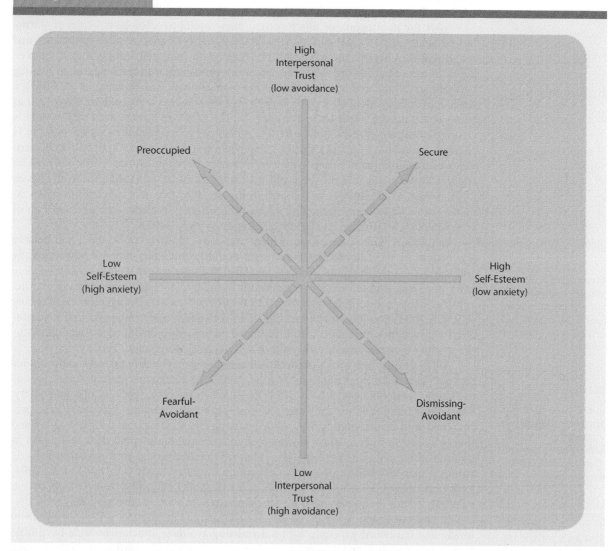

Four Attachment Styles Based on Perceptions of Self-Worth and Others' Trustworthiness

Derived from Bowlby's cross-species analysis of attachment and Ainsworth's research on child-parent attachment styles, the current perspective on attachment style is that it is shaped by two basic attitudes: (1) the degree to which one's self-esteem is positive or negative, and (2) the degree to which one perceives others as trustworthy or untrustworthy. High self-esteem persons experience low anxiety whereas persons with low self-esteem experience high anxiety whenever intimacy becomes an issue. Further, persons with high interpersonal trust respond with little or no avoidance during intimate encounters, but those with low interpersonal trust respond with avoidance. Together, these two dimensions of self-esteem and interpersonal trust identify four adult attachment styles: secure, preoccupied, dismissing-avoidant, and fearful-avoidant. Which attachment style is associated with the most successful intimate relationships?

attentiveness and reaction to angry and sad facial expressions (Niedenthal et al., 2003). Like preoccupied individuals, fearful avoidants base their self-worth on their physical level of attractiveness (Park et al., 2004). As you might guess, this attachment style is associated with negative interpersonal experiences and the abuse of alcohol to reduce anxiety in social settings (McNally et al., 2003). Fearful avoidants often have a history of psychological, physical, or sexual abuse (Bartholomew, 1990; Bartholomew et al., 2001). To better understand how social psychologists identify these four different attachment styles in adults using self-report questionnaires, spend a few minutes completing the Relationship Questionnaire in *Self/Social Connection Exercise 10.1*.

What Is Your Adult Attachment Style?

The Relationship Questionnaire

Directions

Following are four general relationship styles that people often report. Read each description and indicate the degree to which each style describes you using the following 7 point scale.

Disagree Strongly   1   2   3   4   5   6   7   Agree Strongly

_____ A.   It is easy for me to become emotionally close to others. I am comfortable depending on them and having them depend on me. I don't worry about being alone or having others not accept me.

_____ B.   I am uncomfortable getting close to others. I want emotionally close relationships, but I find it difficult to trust others completely, or to depend on them. I worry that I will be hurt if I allow myself to become too close to others.

_____ C.   I want to be completely emotionally intimate with others, but I often find that others are reluctant to get as close as I would like. I am uncomfortable being without close relationships, but I sometimes worry that others don't value me as much as I value them.

_____ D.   I am comfortable without close emotional relationships. It is very important to me to feel independent and self-sufficient, and I prefer not to depend on others or have others depend on me.

Scoring

Based on your own evaluations, which of these relationship styles best fits you?

Style A = Secure Attachment Style   Style B = Fearful-Avoidant Style

Style C = Preoccupied Style   Style D = Dismissing-Avoidant Style

Source: Bartholomew, K. & Horowitz, L. M. (1991). Attachment styles among young adults: A test of a four-category model. *Journal of Personality and Social Psychology*, 61, 226–244.

"What is love? Ask him who lives, what is life. Ask him who adores, what is God ... [Love] is that powerful attraction towards all that we conceive, or fear, or hope beyond ourselves, when we find within our own thoughts the chasm of an insufficient void, and seek to awaken in all things that are, a community with what we experience within ourselves."

Percy Bysshe Shelley, English poet, 1792–1824

Research that has examined the childhood experiences of adults who differ in attachment styles finds that the securely attached report positive family relationships when young, while the insecurely attached rate their childhood family environments as emotionally cold and openly conflicted (Klohnen & Bera, 1998; Orina et al., 2011). These findings suggest that securely attached people have learned how to foster intimacy while adults with one of the three insecure attachment styles have unwittingly learned how to destroy it. The dismissing-avoidant lover tends to starve intimacy by being emotionally distant and aloof, while the preoccupied lover smothers intimacy by being overly possessive, jealous, and emotionally demanding. Finally, fearful-avoidant lovers perhaps have the worst dilemma because they want approval, but not only do they not feel worthy of receiving it, they also do not believe others can be trusted. So they avoid intimacy in relationships, thinking it is safer to fantasize about a relationship instead of actually trying to establish one.

Is it surprising to you that securely attached lovers are the most desired partners by the vast majority of adults, regardless of their own attachment style (Chappell & Davis, 1998)? Does it further surprise you that the two least desirable attachment styles in romantic relationships are the dismissing avoidants and the fearful avoidants (Pietromonaco & Carnelley, 1994)? What about securely attached people makes them so desirable? Given the warmth

Critical
THINKING

The self-sufficient cowboy who keeps to himself and doesn't engage in idle chitchat is one of the great icons of the American West. Hollywood actors John Wayne, Gary Cooper, and Clint Eastwood personified this extreme form of individualism in many of their film roles. Today, Hollywood uses this same rugged, individualist personality in creating the lead male role in action adventure films (Matt Damon, George Clooney, Will Smith). What attachment style would you say these film characters most often represent? Is this an attachment style we should be placing in our male cultural role models?

and openness that securely attached people bring to romantic relationships, plus their willingness to forgive others for transgressions, it is not surprising that securely attached adults are attracted to each other and are the happiest couples (Holmes & Johnson, 2009). For other securely attached people, a secure partner confirms their expectations of love; they each share the same intimate relationship prototype (Hepper, & Carnelley, in press).

Warmth and openness are such desirable qualities in a potential romantic partner that insecurely attached individuals often present themselves as warm and open when communicating with potential romantic partners (Brumbaugh & Fraley, 2010). This engaging interaction style may be successful in attracting a securely attached individual, but what happens as the romantic relationship progresses? When securely attached people become romantically involved with insecure partners, there is prototype mismatch; however secure types can buffer the negative effects that their partners bring to the relationship, providing the emotional stability necessary to disconfirm negative expectations (Feeney, 2003). If the secure partner consistently encourages openness, trust, and acceptance, the insecure partner may gradually change her or his beliefs about intimacy and/or her or his own feelings of self-worth. This involves the adoption of a new prototype of the category "intimate relationship" that conforms to the secure attachment style.

The idea that attachment styles can change is a relatively new one (Davila & Sargent, 2003). Studies suggest that although childhood attachment style does predict adulthood attachment style with reasonable accuracy, changes can occur (Waters et al., 2000; Weinfield et al., 2000). Yet the change may not always be for the better. Just as parental divorce or physical abuse can cause a child to slip from a secure to an insecure style, a romantic couple containing at least one insecure partner or a relationship fraught with conflict can destroy a person's secure attachment style. In one study investigating married couples expecting their first child, women became more insecure in their attachment style when they received less support and more anger from their husbands (Simpson et al., 2003). It appears that people are most likely to undergo attachment style changes when they grapple with stressful, life-altering events that expose them to experiences that challenge their existing attachment beliefs. These stressful events could be either positive or negative in nature. Upon evaluation and reflection, if they change one or both of the basic attitudes underlying their current attachment style, their orientation toward intimate relationships will either become more optimistic or more pessimistic. This ability to significantly revise core attitudes and beliefs is another example of the dynamic nature of the self.

SECTION SUMMARY

- Attachment evolved to keep the young close to adults where they are better protected from predators.

- Parent-child attachment patterns influence later childhood peer relations and intimate adult relationships.

- Attachment style is shaped by two basic attitudes: (1) the degree to which one's self-esteem is positive or negative, and (2) the degree to which one perceives others as trustworthy or untrustworthy.

- Four adult attachment styles:

    Secure attachment style: high self-esteem and high trustworthiness

    Preoccupied attachment style: low self-esteem and high trustworthiness

    Dismissing-avoidant attachment style: high self-esteem and low trustworthiness

    Fearful-avoidant attachment style: low self-esteem and low trustworthiness

- People with a secure attachment style have more successful intimate relationships later in life than those who are insecurely attached.

FRIENDSHIP

As we mature, we not only form emotional ties with our family members, we also form friendships outside the home. Although intimacy is expressed in both social arenas, friendships often satisfy different needs than do family relationships. While relationships with relatives are based on largely nonvoluntary forces, relationships based on friendship are primarily voluntary and mutually satisfying. The distinction between friends and family is summed up in the old saying, "you can pick your friends, but not your family."

SELF-DISCLOSURE SHAPES FRIENDSHIP DEVELOPMENT AND MAINTENANCE.

self-disclosure
....
The revealing of personal information about oneself to other people

social penetration theory
....
A theory that describes the development of close relationships in terms of increasing self-disclosure.

One of the prime avenues for creating close friendships is through **self-disclosure**, which is the revealing of personal information about oneself to other people (Derlega et al., 2011). Disclosing emotional and private information about oneself conveys a sense of trust, and thus, this type of *emotional self-disclosure* is most important in developing intimate relationships (Kashdan & Roberts, 2006). Individuals who do not avail themselves of emotional self-disclosure tend to have dysfunctional relationships and experience greater loneliness than those who reveal their important private self-aspects to friends and lovers (Brunell et al., 2007; Stokes, 1987).

Irving Altman and Dalmas Taylor (1973) sought to explain the self-disclosure process in their **social penetration theory**. According to Altman and Taylor, the development of a relationship is associated with communication moving gradually from a discussion of superficial topics to more intimate exchanges. During the first initial interactions, people are likely to discuss such impersonal topics as the weather, sports events, or popular culture. If this superficial discussion is rewarding, they may broaden and deepen the social exchange by covering a wider range of topics and choosing to divulge more personal and sensitive information. As you can see in Figure 10.3, when discussion topics move from the very narrow and shallow range to a broader and deeper scope, the intimacy level also increases (Gibbs et al., 2006; Laurenceau et al., 1998). In a very real sense, the process of relationship development involves the proper "pacing" of self-disclosure so that one avoids negative reactions if personal revelations are too large or too small.

During first meetings, new acquaintances usually follow the norm of *self-disclosure reciprocity*—they match each other's level of self-disclosure, revealing more when the

As we mature we form friendships outside of the family.

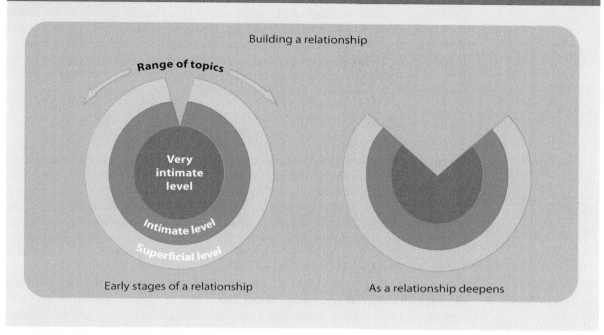

Figure 10.3

The Theory of Social Penetration

According to Altman and Taylor's (1973) theory of social penetration, the amount of information people disclose early in a relationship is rather narrow and shallow; yet as the relationship progresses, self-disclosure becomes broader (covering a wider range of topics) and deeper (revealing more personal information).

> **❝** *Fondness is a poor substitute for friendship.* **❞**
>
> ‒ ‒ ‒ ‒ ‒ ‒ ‒ ‒ ‒ ‒
>
> Anna Green Winslow, Canadian poet, 1759–1780

other person does so, and decreasing personal revelations if the other person becomes reticent (Omarzu, 2000). In most first encounters, self-disclosure reciprocity is useful in building a mutually satisfying level of information exchange that benefits relationship development. However, if one person ignores this gradual self-disclosure process and instead reveals a great deal of personal information, there is a good chance the recipient will feel threatened with this premature rush to intimacy and will evaluate the discloser negatively (Kaplan et al., 1974; Lips-Wiersma & Mills, 2002). Once the relationship progresses beyond the "getting acquainted" stage and intimacy barriers have been lowered, this tit-for-tat exchange of personal information is not as important and occurs much less frequently (Altman, 1973). In fact, in an intimate relationship, instead of reciprocating with self-disclosure, a partner may simply offer support and understanding (Archer, 1979).

What happens to self-disclosure in troubled friendships? In their theory, Altman and Taylor also discuss the dynamics of what they called *depenetration*, which is the disengagement from an intimate relationship. When intimate relationships are in trouble, some people emotionally withdraw by engaging in less breadth and depth in their personal revelations (Baxter, 1987). Other people reduce the number of topics they discuss but increase the depth of their self-disclosure (Tolstedt & Stokes, 1984). The deeply personal feelings and beliefs that are disclosed are usually negative and are designed to accuse and hurt the other person. Thus, just as self-disclosure can build a relationship and provide it with a solid emotional foundation, it can also serve to weaken and tear it down.

> **❝** *Each friend represents a world in us, a world possibly not born until they arrive, and it is only by this meeting that a new world is born.* **❞**
>
> ‒ ‒ ‒ ‒ ‒ ‒ ‒ ‒ ‒ ‒
>
> Anaïs Nin, U.S. novelist, 1903–1977

Although social penetration theory's description of a gradual and orderly pattern of increasing self-disclosure fits most developing friendships and romantic relationships (Collins & Miller, 1994), not all intimate relationships progress in this fashion. In some, the type of intimate self-disclosure normally seen in long-term relationships develops almost immediately. For example, in studies of friends, roommates, and dating partners, John Berg found that some relationships just "click" right from the start

In troubled intimate relationships, depenetration refers to reducing the range and depth of self-disclosure, signifying disengagement from the relationship.

rather than gradually becoming close over time (Berg, 1984; Berg & Clark, 1986). Berg explained that this early exchange of highly personal information occurs because the respective partners make quick judgments that the other person fits their prototype of the ideal friend or romantic partner. In situations in which people immediately become best friends or lovers, self-disclosure does not serve to deepen the relationship in the same way that it does in the more common and gradually developing relationships described by social penetration theory. Instead, when the partners recognize that this is an intimate relationship, the highly personal self-disclosure begins to flow.

Cultural Differences in Self-Disclosure

Despite the importance of self-disclosure in friendship development and maintenance, research indicates that there are cultural differences in self-disclosure tendencies (Adams & Anderson, 2004). North Americans tend to disclose more about themselves in a wider variety of social settings than people from collectivist cultures such as China, Japan, and the West African nation of Ghana (Chen, 1995; Kito, 2005). These differences do not mean that Americans have more intimate relationships than people from China or Japan (refer to Chapter 9, pp. 352–355), but they may be rooted in their respective individualist and collectivist orientations. For example, in Chapter 3 (p. 82), we discussed research indicating that many individualist Americans have a need to feel unique or distinct from others (Pratt, 1991; Triandis, 1989). Perhaps the willingness to reveal private self-aspects through self-disclosure provides individualists with the opportunity to identify and share their uniqueness.

"*He who has nothing has no friends.*"

— Greek proverb

These self-disclosure differences may also be partly due to preferred communication channels within the respective cultures. In many Western societies, social expressiveness tends to be a sign of social competence and is valued as an avenue to intimacy, yet in Eastern cultures such as Japan, China, and Korea, oral communication skills are not as highly valued. In fact, being socially *nonexpressive* is often interpreted as an indication of emotional strength and trustworthiness (Kim & Sherman, 2007; Russell & Yik, 1996). Although great value is not placed on social expressiveness in these collectivist cultures, it is considered virtuous to be able to quickly and accurately interpret and respond to others' vaguely expressed feelings and desires before they have to be clearly articulated (Barnlund, 1989). In this kind of cultural context, self-disclosing one's desires or fears may be considered inappropriate, because others are expected to "read" them through indirect means.

GENDER DIFFERENCES EXIST IN HETEROSEXUAL FRIENDSHIPS.

Both men and women value friendship throughout their lives, but research suggests certain gender differences in heterosexual friendship patterns from childhood through adulthood (Johnson et al., 2007; Zarbatany et al., 2007).

Intimacy

One notable gender difference involves the level of emotional expressiveness within same-sex friendships. Put simply, women's friendships tend to be more intimate and involve more emotional sharing than men's friendships (Fehr, 2004; Thomas & Daubman, 2001). This specific gender difference is part of a larger pattern of gender-based behavior found in same-sex friendships. That is, when men and women interact with same-sex friends, they are more likely to conform to gender stereotypes than when interacting with other-sex friends; men are more dominant and women are more agreeable and nurturing (Suh et al., 2004). Women are much more likely than men to treat their friends like "family" (Ackerman et al., 2007).

Initially, research conducted in the 1970s and 1980s suggested that in contrast to the friendships of women, men's friendships are more likely to revolve around shared activities. This seemingly different orientation toward friendship was characterized as *face-to-face* versus *side-by-side*: women spend a good deal of time together talking about personal and intimate matters, and men spend the majority of their time together working or playing, with considerably less personal self-disclosure. Even though these contrasting descriptions of men's and women's friendships have an appealing simplicity, later studies found that they were just that—too simplistic. Research by Steve Duck and Paul Wright (1993) found that both women *and* men meet most often just to talk. They also discovered that although women are indeed more emotionally expressive than men in their friendships, they are just as likely as men to engage in shared activities. Therefore, it is misleading to describe men's friendships as being exclusively side-by-side encounters and women's friendships as being exclusively face-to-face interactions.

One important point to keep in mind is that even though women tend to have more intimate friendships than men, this does not mean that *all* men's friendships are less emotionally expressive than the average women's friendships. In all such comparisons, we are discussing *group averages*. The general consensus among social scientists is that although some aspects of these intimacy differences between men and women may be weakly rooted in biology, they are primarily caused by gender socialization. Indeed, Dorie Williams (1985) has found that both men and women who possess personality traits associated with psychological femininity report being more intimate in their same-sex friendships than men and women who exhibit few feminine traits. Perhaps because women's same-sex friendships are generally more intimate, they also regard them more favorably than do men (Wright & Scanlon, 1991). This greater intimacy in female friendships is expressed in a number of ways.

Self-Disclosure

In a meta-analysis of 205 studies, Kathryn Dindia and Mike Allen (1992) found that women generally self-disclose more than men, especially in intimate relationships. Their analysis indicates that women self-disclose more than men to their same-sex friends and other-sex romantic partners, but men and women do not differ in their disclosure to male friends. They also found that these gender differences, although not as great as once thought, have shown no evidence of reduction during the past thirty years. More recent studies confirm these findings; women emphasize self-disclosure and emotional support more than men in their friendships (Fehr, 2004; Oswald et al., 2004).

What is it about gender socialization that leads to less intimate self-disclosure among men? Research suggests that males in North American culture appear to be governed by a more rigid set of gender rules than females, especially regarding emotional expression (Bank & Hansford, 2000; Timmers et al., 1998). As a result, a man is likely to have more difficult a time acting vulnerable and dependent. This restriction on male emotional expressiveness was demonstrated in a study in which male and female participants read a story about a man or a woman who appeared to be extremely upset while flying in a plane (Derlega & Chaikin, 1976). The reason this individual was so upset was that his or her mother had just suffered a nervous breakdown. Noticing this agitation, the person sitting next to the individual inquired as to whether he or she was anxious about flying. In one condition, participants read that the individual concealed the problem by replying, "Yes, I guess I am. I haven't flown that much before." In another condition, the character in the story revealed the actual problem. After reading the story, participants were asked to estimate the character's degree of psychological adjustment. Results indicated that if the character was depicted as a man, he was considered to be more unstable if he disclosed his mother's real problem than if he concealed it. For a female character, the results were exactly opposite—not disclosing was judged more indicative of maladjustment. Male and female participants did not differ in their assessments. Both men and women considered the emotionally expressive male and the inexpressive female to be maladjusted. These results, and similar findings from other studies, suggest that one important reason men disclose less than women is that for them to reveal tender and vulnerable feelings—to let down their emotional guard—is to run the risk of inviting negative evaluations from both men and women (Chelune, 1976; Felmlee, 1999).

Before reading further, take a few minutes and complete the self-disclosure questionnaire in *Self/Social Connection 10.2*. If possible, ask some of your male and female

Self/Social Connections Exercise 10.2

Do You Self-Disclose Differently to Your Male and Female Friends?

Instructions

Think of a close male friend and a close female friend. Indicate for the topics listed below the degree to which you have disclosed to each person using the following scale:

Discussed not at all   1   2   3   4   Discussed fully and completely

Male Friend		Female Friend
_____	1. My personal habits	_____
_____	2. Things I have done that I feel guilty about	_____
_____	3. Things I wouldn't do in public	_____
_____	4. My deepest feelings	_____
_____	5. What I like and dislike about myself	_____
_____	6. What is important to me in life	_____
_____	7. What makes me the person I am	_____
_____	8. My worst fears	_____
_____	9. Things I have done that I am proud of	_____
_____	10. My close relationships with other people	_____

_____ Male Friend Total score   Female Friend Total score _____

Scoring Directions

You can determine your overall self-disclosure score for each of your friends by adding up the scores in the column. The higher the score, the greater the self-disclosure to the person. Is there an appreciable difference between these two scores? If there is a difference, does it correspond to what has been found in more systematic investigations of self-disclosure in intimate relationships?

friends to complete it as well, so that you can informally test for some of the gender differences we have discussed concerning friendship self-disclosure.

Physical Touching

Beyond verbal communication, men and women also differ in the degree to which they engage in physical contact with a same-sex friend (Felmlee, 1999). In North American culture, both heterosexual men and women view hugging and other forms of physical intimacy among men as less appropriate than among male-female and female-female pairings (Derlega et al., 2001). Generally, men are encouraged to hug one another only when they are involved in sporting events where expressions of physical intimacy are consistent with the masculine gender role (Mormon & Floyd, 1998). This injunction against male physical intimacy is not the norm in many European, Latin, African, and Middle Eastern cultures (Axtell, 1993; DiBaise & Gunnoe, 2004).

In one study investigating this physical touching taboo in the United States, Val Derlega and his colleagues (1989) asked friends and heterosexual dating partners to act out an imaginary scene where one person was greeting the other at the airport after returning from a trip. The greetings were photographed and later evaluated by judges for the intimacy of physical contact, ranging from no touch at all to combinations of hugging and kissing. As Figure 10.4 shows, dating partners exhibited the highest levels of physical intimacy; all of them engaged in a combination of hugging and kissing. When friendship touching was analyzed, male friends employed significantly less touching than did either female friends or mixed-sex friends. Further investigation of participants' perceptions of physical touch indicated that men were more likely than women to interpret touching as an indication of sexual desire.

Why are male friendships less intimate than female friendships, and why is there this social injunction against men being emotionally and physically expressive? A number of social scientists contend that avoidance of emotional and physical expressiveness is due

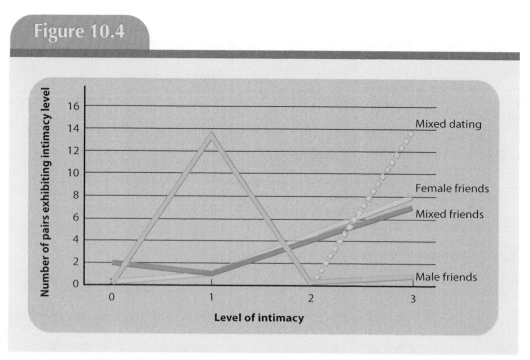

Figure 10.4

Gender Differences in Touching During Social Interaction

How do men and women differ with respect to touching when greeting a friend or dating partner? In North American cultures, physical intimacy is highest among dating partners, second highest among female friends and mixed-sex friends, and lowest among male friends. Have you observed and/or experienced such gender differences in your own life?

to males being socialized to conform to _heterosexual masculinity_, which entails valuing masculine traits related to power and control, while devaluing feminine traits related to the expression of tenderness and vulnerability (Brendan, 2002). As previously noted, men are most likely to conform to gender stereotypes and the norms surrounding heterosexual masculinity when in the company of other men. One important aspect of heterosexual masculinity involves the denigration of male homosexuality because it is perceived to be the antithesis of masculinity (Herek, 2000). For a man to express warmth, nurturance, or caring toward another man is often interpreted as an indication of homosexuality (Derlega et al., 2001). Thus, being masculine requires men to avoid acting in ways that might signal homosexual desires to other men (Theodore & Basow, 2000).

The contemporary conception of masculinity as not encompassing tenderness and affection in male friendships is a fairly recent historical development in North American culture (Williams, 1992). According to historians, until the late nineteenth century, a man could express tender affection for an intimate male friend without fearing the disapproval of others (Rotundo, 1989). This all changed around the 1880s, when _homosexuality_ and _heterosexuality_ came to be defined as clearly distinct and nonoverlapping social roles. Masculinity was redefined to exclude "manly love" (Nardi, 1992a). As we move through the twenty-first century, the changes in gender roles may eventually lead men to feel less constrained in their expression of tenderness and affection toward other men. Until that time, however, male heterosexual friendships in the United States and Canada will generally lack the emotional intensity and gratification of the average female friendship.

Mate Rivalry

Research on emerging and young adults find that heterosexual women think there are both plusses and minuses in their same-sex friendships (Bleske & Buss 2000). On the plus side, young women frequently report that their female friends provide companionship and emotional support, give them mating advice, and help them meet possible romantic partners. On the minus side, heterosexual women also report that their female friends sometimes make them feel bad about themselves and compete with them for attention from desirable potential romantic partners. The women who are most likely to perceive this mate rivalry in their female friendships are those who perceive themselves—and who are judged by others—as less physically attractive than their friends (Bleske-Rechek & Lighthall, 2010). This finding is consistent with Tesser's self-evaluation maintenance model (see Chapter 3, pp. 100–102), which states that individuals are threatened by a close other outperforming them on a trait they value highly because it threatens their sense of self-worth. One common reaction to such feelings of threat is to evaluate the source of that threat—their friends—more negatively.

Competition and mate rivalry also occur in men's friendships. However, given the looks-for-status exchange that has historically characterized men's and women's mating judgments, the rivalry between male friends might hinge less on physical attractiveness and more on men's perceptions of their own and their friends' levels of social dominance and physical prowess (Buss 2004).

CROSS-SEX HETEROSEXUAL FRIENDSHIPS GRAVITATE TO AN "INTIMACY MEAN".

From our review of past research, we can conclude that women's friendships are typically more intimate and openly expressive than those of men. Yet what happens when men and women are friends? Research suggests that in these friendships there is a gravitation to the "intimacy mean." Men tend to be more emotionally open and self-disclosing than they are with their male friends, while women disclose less and are not as intimate as they are with their women friends (Monsour, 1997). Generally, heterosexual men believe their female friends provide more emotional support and security than their male friends, but not as much as women with whom they have romantic relationships. Women, on the other hand, do not perceive their cross-sex friendships as being that intimate, and they are likely to turn to female friends for highly personalized interaction (Wright & Scanlon, 1991).

Although cross-sex friendships are quite common, as in all friendships, similarity attracts. Heidi Reeder (2003) found that young adults who have a nontraditional gender-role orientation (masculine women and feminine men) have a higher proportion of cross-sex friendships than those with a traditional orientation (feminine women and masculine men). In other words, consistent with the matching hypothesis (Chapter 9, p. 373), men and women are more likely to form and maintain friendships with the other sex when they have interests and personality traits that are traditionally associated with the other sex.

The biggest problem or challenge in cross-sex friendships is sexual tension (Werking, 1997). One-fourth of cross-sex friendship failures are due to problems caused by romantic and/or sexual desires, with men being more likely than women to experience such desires (Bleske-Rechek & Buss, 2001; Schneider & Kenny, 2000). This gender difference may occur because men not only tend to view sex as the primary means of achieving intimacy with women, but they also tend to misinterpret certain signs of affection (for example, physical touching) as indicating sexual desire (Haselton & Buss, 2000). In the workplace, concerns about coworkers misinterpreting their friendliness as romantic or sexual interest is often a barrier to establishing cross-sex friendships (Elsesser & Peplau, 2006).

Although most cross-sex friendships do not have these problems, survey research suggests that half of all college students have engaged in sexual activity with an other-sex friend on at least one occasion, and one-third have engaged in sexual activity on multiple occasions (Afifi & Faulkner, 2000). When sex occurs, it does not necessarily change the friendship into a romantic relationship, nor does it necessarily end the friendship. If the two parties freely discuss the sexual contact and can agree on what it means to their relationship, the experience is likely to build trust and confidence in the friend's intentions and feelings.

Additional research indicates that sexual contact is much more common among cross-sex friendships that are relatively new than among those that are of longer duration (Reeder, 2000). One possible explanation for this finding is that it reflects the natural decline in sexual passion that occurs over time in most sexually based relationships (see pp. 414–423 for a discussion of passionate love). A second possible reason why sexual contact is less common in longer-term friendships is that partners recognize that for them to preserve the friendship, sexual urges must decrease, or at least be safely regulated. Related to this explanation is a third explanation contending that the lower levels of sexual contact in longer-term friendships mainly reflect the fact that cross-sex friends who don't redirect their sexual attraction eventually define themselves as romantic partners and, thus, are no longer included in studies of friendship.

> **"**Friendship is love without wings.**"**
>
> George Gordon (Lord Byron), English poet, 1788–1824

"FRIENDS-WITH-BENEFITS" RELATIONSHIPS POSE UNIQUE CHALLENGES AND DANGERS.

Our examination of cross-sex friendships would be incomplete if we did not also examine those instances where friends intentionally engage in sexual activity on occasion, but otherwise have a basic friendship (Bisson & Levine, 2009). On the surface, these "friends with benefits" relationships appear to carry some of the defining features of a true romantic relationship, such as intimacy and sexual passion, but the difference is that the two individuals do not consider their involvement to be romantic in nature. Based on recent surveys, "friends with benefits" relationships are not rare among young adults. For example, on American college campuses it is estimated that about half of all students have been involved in one or more such relationships, with men reporting both being involved in more simultaneous and more past sexual friendships than women. (Johnson et al., 2007; McGinty et al., 2007). This gender difference is consistent with research indicating that men typically express greater interest in casual sex, tend to have more sexual partners in general, and also have more social freedom to engage in sexually permissive behaviors than women (Oliver & Hyde, 1993).

"Friends with benefits" relationships incorporate sexual activity into a friendship. In the movie with the same title, the two main characters, played by Mila Kunis and Justin Timberlake, struggle with the biggest disadvantage of sexual friendships for the partners. What might that be?

Not surprisingly, individuals involved in "friends with benefits" relationships consider sex with a trusted friend to be the biggest advantage in these relationships, with men mentioning this as a big advantage somewhat more often than women, who mention emotional involvement somewhat more often than men. The biggest potential disadvantage that women and men both report is fear of potential harm to the friendship or someone getting their feelings hurt as a result of the sexual intimacy (Bisson & Levine, 2009). While hurt feelings are certainly a potential risk in sexual friendships, the more serious danger is sexually transmitted diseases. This is so because the friendship component may lead people to mistakenly believe that their partner is not a risk to their health, and thus, forego using condoms despite the fact that they are engaging in a casual sexual relationship that is not necessarily exclusive (Lehmiller et al., 2011).

For both women and men, friendship is more important than sex in sexual friendships. Individuals who enter such relationships tend to have a less romanticized view of love, believing that there are multiple people with whom they could fall in love and also that they can have sex without being in love (Puentes et al., 2008). Regarding expectations for the future, it appears that men and women hope that their sexual friendships will evolve differently. Men are more likely to express satisfaction with their sexual friendships staying the same, while women are more likely to hope that these relationships change into either a conventional romantic relationship or a conventional friendship (Lehmiller et al., 2011). Friends who want their sexual friendship to blossom into a romantic relationship have the highest emotional commitment to the relationship, followed by those who want their relationship to remain as is, with those who want the relationship to transition into a friendship being the least committed (Vanderdrift et al., 2010). Women's greater interest in having a "friends with benefits" relationship transition into a more conventional intimate relationship—either romance or friendship—may be due to cultural norms that evaluate women more negatively than men for engaging in sex outside of an exclusive relationship and also because sex is potentially more costly for women than men due to the possibility of pregnancy (Crawford & Popp, 2003).

As we can see from this overview, cross-sex friendships—both the platonic and sexual variety—provide an important source of intimacy for both men and women. Yet in order for these friendships to survive over time, women and men often must manage and negotiate some delicate issues, especially when sexual and/or romantic issues are raised.

GENDER DIFFERENCES DISAPPEAR IN SAME-SEX HOMOSEXUAL FRIENDSHIPS.

Sexual orientation appears to play an important role in shaping the same-sex friendship patterns of men. Survey studies by Peter Nardi and Drury Sherrod (1994) find that, in contrast to heterosexual persons, the same-sex friendships of gay men are as intimate as those of lesbians. This different same-sex friendship pattern among homosexuals and heterosexuals is partly due to heterosexual men avoiding intimacy in same-sex friendships out of fear of being labeled homosexual. Although many gay men are justifiably wary of expressing affection toward one another in heterosexual surroundings because of fear of ridicule and assault, no such anxiety exists in the gay community. Another reason greater intimacy occurs in gay male friendships is that for both gay men and lesbians, gay friends are frequently viewed as family (Nardi, 1992c). This is so because their biological families often reject them or do not fully accept them as family members (Oswald, 2000). Faced with these intimacy road-blocks, many gay people turn to friendships for their emotional well-being. As a gay man explained:

> Friends become part of my extended family. A lot of us are estranged from our families because we're gay and our parents don't understand or don't want to understand. … I can't talk to them about my relationships. I don't go to them; I've finally learned my lesson: Family is out. Now I've got a close circle of friends that I can sit and talk to about anything, I learned to do without the family.

(Kurdek & Schmitt, 1987, p. 65)

Another difference between homosexual and heterosexual same-sex friendships is that sexual intimacy is much more likely in homosexual friendships. Just as sexual desires often become salient in heterosexual cross-sex friendships, they are a common issue in homosexual same-sex friendships. In both cases, the sexual orientation of the two people can conceivably lead to sexual activity and, thus, pose problems or challenges to the friendship. Nardi and Sherrod's (1994) survey research suggests that about two-thirds of gay men and about one-half of lesbians have had sexual contact with their same-sex "close" or "best" friend, which is comparable to the sexual contact level found in heterosexual cross-sex friendships. As in these heterosexual friendships, sex among homosexual same-sex friends is much more likely early in the relationship than later (Nardi, 1992b, 1992c), undoubtedly due to the same previously discussed psychological and/or physiological forces. It is also true that "friends with benefits" relationships are as common among homosexual same-sex friends as they are among cross-sex heterosexual friends. Although more research is needed to better understand the social psychological dynamics underlying homosexual same-sex friendship, clearly it provides gay men and lesbians with a vital source of intimacy—and often a surrogate "family"—in a social environment that is often hostile toward their lifestyle.

IMPORTANT BARRIERS TO LONG-DISTANCE FRIENDSHIPS ARE FALLING.

When people think of friendships, they typically imagine relationships based on face-to-face interactions; yet an increasing number of friendships no longer primarily take place in face-to-face contexts but instead involve interaction on the Internet. Young adults are the best examples of this trend in friendship dynamics because they are more likely than other age groups to maintain contact with friends who are geographically distant to them through the Internet. In fact, nine out of ten college students have at least one long-distance friend, and the way they primarily nurture and maintain these relationships is through Internet avenues such as Facebook and email (Johnson, 2001).

Because young adults are more likely than older adults to use the Internet in communicating with friends who are not currently located in their geographic area, young people tend to have a greater number of social ties than their parents (Pew Internet, 2002). Survey studies of college students find that the use of the Internet for communication purposes among friends provides young adults with a useful extension of face-to-face interaction that benefits their friendships (Kujath, 2011). However, despite these Internet benefits, one factor that still distinguishes geographically-close friendships from long-distance friendships is that long-distance friends are much less likely to state that they rely upon one another to provide help when one of them are in trouble (Johnson et al., 2009). In this regard, proximity is still one important advantage that face-to-face friendships have over distant relationships.

SECTION SUMMARY

- Social penetration theory describes the development of relationships in terms of movement from superficial to more intimate levels of self-disclosure.

- People from individualist cultures may self-disclose more than those from collectivist societies.

- Women self-disclose more than men.

- Same-sex heterosexual female friendships are more emotionally intimate than same-sex heterosexual male friendships.

- The biggest problem in cross-sex friendships is sexual tension.

- In "friends-with-benefits" relationships, the friendship is more important than sex.

- Same-sex friendships of gay men are as intimate as those of lesbians.

- The Internet allows young adults to better maintain long-distance friendships compared to previous generations.

ROMANTIC RELATIONSHIPS

When my friends and I entered the fifth grade, we began thinking of girls as potential romantic partners. Being boys and having a history of doing things as a "pack," we often approached romance as a group activity. Gathered in the basement of one of our houses, we would first discuss which girl in our class we would call on the phone, and then, which of us would be the group's offering to her. It was a simple game. Look up the phone number, make the call, ask the question, and then congratulate or tease the member of the group who had been either rejected or embraced (at this age, only in a social sense) by the girl on the other end of the line.

> "Hello, is this Marsha?"
> (Pause)
> "Never mind who this is. Listen, do you want to go with John Despins?"
> (Another pause, the length of which was positively correlated with impending rejection.)
> "What?! No?!!" (Then in a hurried attempt to save face for John, the caller turned the rejection on its head.) "Yeah, well he doesn't want to go with you either!"

❝*I believe myself that romantic love is the source of the most intense delight that life has to offer.***❞**

Bertrand Russell, British philosopher, 1872–1970

The psychological drama and tension generated in these early attempts at discovering where one stood in the minds of those who were confusingly and romantically coveted were played out in increasing degrees of sophistication in the coming years. The uncertainty in seeking romance does not diminish in adulthood. In the remaining sections of this chapter we examine the psychological nature of romantic love and the factors that foster and inhibit it. However, let's first examine how ideas about romance have changed over time and how they differ across cultures.

CULTURE SHAPES HOW WE THINK ABOUT ROMANTIC LOVE.

Romantic love can be found in all recorded time periods, but it has undergone numerous social transformations (Hatfield & Rapson, 2002). The ancient Greeks considered romantic love a form of madness that "wounds" you, and the Greek god of love (Eros) was armed with a bow and a quiver of arrows. For the Greeks, romantic love was experienced almost exclusively outside of marriage and was more likely homosexual rather than heterosexual in nature (Bullough, 1976). During the Roman era, homosexual love—considered a "Greek vice"—gave way to heterosexual love. Yet the freeborn Roman male's self-concept as a world conqueror led him to view romance as a game played outside of marriage. Perhaps in keeping with this playful view of love, the Romans were one of the first Western societies to institutionalize divorce (Gathorne-Hardy, 1981). Later, as Christianity became more established

Romantic love is usually associated with when people are allowed to choose their partners.

"Whoever indulges in love without sense or moderation recklessly endangers his life; such is the nature of love that no one involved with it can keep his head."

Marie de France, French/English noble, 1160–1215

"Marriage is a noose."

Miguel de Cervantes Saavedra, Spanish novelist, 1547–1616

"The minute I heard my first love story I started looking for you, not knowing how blind that was. Lovers don't finally meet somewhere. They're in each other all along."

Jalal ad-Din Rumi thirteenth century Persian poet and Sufi mystic

within Roman society, sex was perceived as a corrupting influence, tolerated only in marriage. Romantic love was not highly valued. During the Middle Ages (AD 1000–1300), European aristocrats practiced courtly love. Romance was no longer a game, even though it still occurred outside of marriage. Courtly love was considered majestic and spiritual and, in theory, was never consummated (Murstein, 1974). It struck at first sight, conquered all, accepted no substitutes, and was a consuming passion of both agony and ecstasy.

Cross-cultural research indicates that associating romantic love with marriage typically occurs when people are free to choose their own partners (Rosenblatt & Cozby, 1972), although for centuries before and after courtly love, marriage was arranged by parents and based almost exclusively on political and property considerations. Beginning in the seventeenth and eighteenth centuries, as these more traditional considerations declined in importance, romantic love began to make some limited headway into marital arrangements (Stone, 1977). This new association of love and marriage first appeared in England but spread faster in the New World of North America, where social class considerations were not so rigidly defined. Although love was now considered possible—and perhaps even desirable—within marriage, early-twentieth-century marriage educators in America still counseled against basing marital choice on this "romantic impulse" (Burgess, 1926). The irrational nature of romantic love was believed to dangerously undermine what should be a very serious, prudent, and rational decision. However, as marriages became more egalitarian and more focused on mutual satisfaction, romance became even more attractive. With this increased desire for romance within marriage came a greater willingness to end marriages that had lost their romantic spark (Scanzoni, 1979).

Today, our Western conception of romantic love represents a combination of past ideas. It is generally no longer considered a form of madness, but it is something many of us believe we "fall into" and cannot control. Love leads to happiness, but we can also be hurt in love. Love is possible both within and outside of marriage, and as we explore more fully in the next section, it can be either heterosexual or homosexual in nature.

Heterosexist Views of Romantic Love

Despite the fact that between 2 and 5 percent of the world's adult population is primarily or exclusively attracted to their own sex, until fairly recently virtually all research on romantic relationships focused on heterosexual dating and marriage. The lack of research on homosexual romantic relationships, coupled with heterosexist beliefs that denigrated homosexuality, allowed cultural stereotypes to shape social perceptions by creating myths about the gay lifestyle (Herek, 1991).

> "*Love is like a virus. It can happen to anybody at any time.*"

— — — — — — — —

Maya Angelou, African-American writer, b. 1928

> "*Many years ago I chased a woman for almost two years, only to discover that her tastes were exactly like mine: We both were crazy about girls.*"

— — — — — — — —

Groucho Marx, American comedian, 1895–1977

One of the main myths is that people who are gay drift from one sexual liaison to another and are unsuccessful in developing enduring, committed romantic relationships (De Cecco, 1988). Yet actual surveys indicate that between 40 and 60 percent of gay men and between 45 and 80 percent of lesbians are currently in a steady relationship (Peplau et al., 1997). Gay and lesbian couples do break up more frequently than married couples, but this is also true of heterosexual couples who also don't have the formal legal institution of marriage to legitimize and stabilize their relationships or are involved in romantic relationships disapproved of by mainstream society (Adams & Jones, 1997).

As you can see in Figure 10.5, lesbians, gay men, and heterosexuals involved in monogamous romantic relationships all tend to score high on scales that evaluate liking and love for one's partner, and all tend to be equally well adjusted and satisfied (Kurdek, 2006; Kurdek & Schmitt, 1986). Based on our previous discussion of heterosexual men being less emotionally expressive, it isn't surprising to find that homosexual romantic love—especially lesbian love—tends to be *more* emotionally intimate than heterosexual love (Kurdek, 2003; Schreurs & Buunk, 1994). These findings indicate that, counter to cultural stereotypes, many lesbians and gay men establish lifelong partnerships, and the psychological dynamics in these relationships are more similar to than different from married heterosexual partnerships. Regardless of whether we are heterosexual or homosexual, our romantic relationships follow a similar psychological course and are influenced by many of the same personal, situational, and cultural factors.

Individualist Versus Collectivist Views

In general, people from Western cultures view love as a positive experience. However, in a cross-cultural study of love, Philip Shaver and his coworkers (1991) found that not all contemporary cultures share this perspective. In fact, people of China have a more pessimistic outlook on romantic love than most Western cultures (Rothbaum & Tsang, 1998).

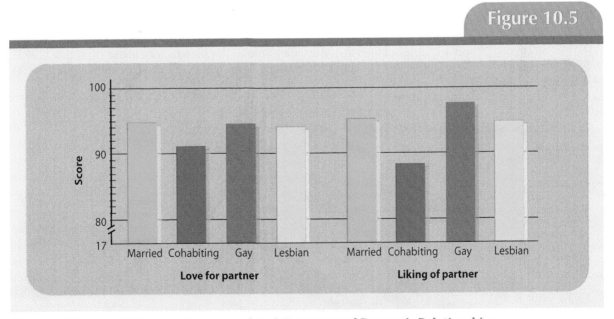

Figure 10.5

Expressed Love and Liking in Homosexual and Heterosexual Romantic Relationships

In a study of married, heterosexual cohabiting, gay, and lesbian monogamous couples, Kurdek and Schmitt (1986) obtained a liking and a loving score from each partner, which could range from a low of 17 to a high of 117. Higher scores indicated greater liking/loving. Results indicated that there were no differences in expressed love for one's partner between any of the different types of romantic relationships. In addition, the married, gay, and lesbian relationships expressed equally high amounts of liking of their partners. In contrast, heterosexual cohabiting couples had lower liking scores than the other couples. This study and others of its kind have dispelled the myth that gay couples are less capable of developing satisfying romantic relationships than are heterosexual couples.

Critical THINKING

Is there an inherent conflict between individualist values and the interdependence necessary to maintain romantic love?

❝*There is only one happiness in life, to love and be loved.***❞**

George Sand (pen name of Amandine Dupin), French novelist, 1804–1876

Consistent with ancient traditions, most contemporary Chinese associate romance with sorrow, pain, and unfulfilled affection. What do they think of the Western view of love? They regard it as unrealistically optimistic. In a very real sense, how we experience love speaks volumes about who we are as individuals and what we are as a culture (Dion & Dion, 1991).

A study by Robert Levine and his colleagues (1995) examined the importance of love as a basis for marriage in both individualist and collectivist cultures. Results indicated that there are cross-cultural differences in the perceived importance of romantic love. Individualist countries such as the United States, England, and Australia placed great importance on love in marriage, while collectivist countries such as India, Pakistan, Thailand, and the Philippines rated it as much less important. These beliefs appear to have behavioral consequences. Those countries placing great importance on love had higher marriage rates, lower fertility rates, and higher divorce rates. Other studies indicate that while collectivists tend to select mates who will best "fit in" to the extended family, individualists are more likely to select mates who are physically attractive or have "exciting" personalities. This does not mean, however, that love is not a part of a collectivist marriage. Instead, it means that, compared with individualist cultures, in collectivist cultures it is more common for people to marry, and then fall in love.

ONLINE ROMANCE AND SPEED DATING FOLLOW SIMILAR RULES AS FACE-TO-FACE ROMANCE.

Regardless of your culture or sexual orientation, finding suitable romantic partners is often perceived as a daunting task. For example, 44 percent of adult Americans are single, and of these, only 9 percent of women and 2 percent of men say they have found a meaningful romantic relationship at a bar or club (Mahay & Laumann, 2004). Given the perceived difficulty of finding desirable romantic partners, an increasing number of people throughout the world are seeking romance through the Internet. Indeed, recent national studies indicate that about 3 to 6 percent of current marriages or long-term partnerships began online (Madden & Lenhart, 2006; Mazzarella, 2007). Relationships that have their origin in cyberspace can begin in a variety of ways, including social network sites, interest groups or blogs, and matching services. However, as with traditional offline romantic relationships, online romantic relationships typically begin with friends and acquaintances playing a deciding role in the introductory phase (Sprecher, 2009). For example, by clicking on a friend's Facebook page, people can be linked to the friend's network.

Recent studies have shown that marriages and long term relationships that have started on the Internet are on the rise.

When people use online dating services to meet potential romantic partners, they can "virtually meet" and become acquainted by various means, including text messaging with cell phones and using web cameras connected to personal computers. Users typically provide information about themselves in a short profile and browse the profiles of others for possible matches. As in face-to-face encounters, users who post physically attractive photos receive more interest than those who post less attractive photos (Whitty & Carr, 2006). Although individuals who use computer-mediated dating services report that it does provide opportunities for some degree of intimacy, these same individuals also report less intimacy in their face-to-face relationships compared to people who do not use online dating services (Scott et al., 2006). These findings provide support for the hypothesis that people resort to virtual dating after not finding sufficient intimacy in their face-to-face personal relationships. One advantage that online dating services and other Internet media sites have over face-to-face encounters is that they provide new options for daters to reject others, mainly by one-click automated rejection or by remaining unresponsive to dating requests. Facebook users, for example, can simply ignore "friend" requests from unwanted romantic suitors. Online daters often resort to these options because it simplifies and streamlines what can often be a difficult, painful, and stressful process of romantic refusal (Tong & Walther, 2011).

Interviews with young adults who actively use online dating sites indicate that they have the same self-presentation concerns and follow similar rules of social interaction as are found in face-to-face meetings. For example, in presenting themselves to possible romantic partners, online daters try to manage initial impressions by creating a profile that is somewhere between their "actual self" and their "ideal self" (Ellison et al., 2006). Further, consistent with social penetration theory, self-disclosure moves gradually from superficial topics to more intimate exchanges (Gibbs et al., 2006). Although the deindividuation often induced by Internet anonymity sometimes results in earlier intimate self-disclosure than in face-to-face encounters, online daters typically follow reciprocal self-disclosure rules (Chiou, 2006; Whitty & Carr, 2006).

Another relatively new technique for finding romance is *speed dating*, in which people attend an event where they experience brief "dates" lasting between three and eight minutes with a series of potential romantic partners. After the event, participants indicate whether they would like to see each of their brief dating partners again. During the past ten years, millions of people in countries around the world have participated in speed dating events (Eastwick & Finkel, 2008; Finkel et al., 2007). In a study of 10,526 heterosexual speed daters, Robert Kurzban and Jason Weeden (2005) found that the criteria participants use in deciding whether to say "yes" or "no" to a second, longer date are similar to the criteria people use in normal romantic encounters. First, women are more selective than are men, saying "yes" to fewer dates. Second, individuals who believe they have high "romantic appeal" are more selective in choosing second dates than are those who rate themselves as less appealing. Physical attractiveness is the most important criteria for being a desirable date, but men place higher importance on appearance than do women in evaluating the other sex. Individuals high in attachment anxiety (preoccupied and fearful-avoidant) are those most likely to have problems in speed dating situations. This is so because their anxiety about being rejected causes them to not be choosy in both pursuing and accepting potential partners (McClure et al., 2010). More than those who are low in attachment anxiety, highly anxious speed daters make more attempts at matching themselves with others and their anxious eagerness often drives potential matches away.

PASSIONATE LOVE CAN BE TRIGGERED BY EXCITATION TRANSFER.

Beyond the difficulties of finding suitable partners, how do we typically experience romantic intimacy? In the 1970s, social scientists began developing multidimensional theories that identified various forms or styles of love. For example, John Lee's (1977) *typology of love styles* identified three primary styles of love (*eros*: passionate love, *ludus*: game-playing love, and *storge*: friendship love) and three secondary love styles (*pragma*:

pragmatic love, *mania*: possessive love, and *agape*: altruistic love). Similarly, in the 1980s Robert Sternberg (1986, 1997) proposed a *triangular theory of love* in which seven different types of love consisted of different degrees of passion, intimacy, and commitment. Although these theories were helpful in providing a framework for examining romantic love, subsequent research suggested that the two most fundamental types of love are *passionate love* and *companionate love* (Hendrick & Hendrick, 2003; Overbeek et al., 2007).

According to Elaine Hatfield (1988), **passionate love** is "a state of intense longing for union with another" (p. 193). It is a type of love that we feel with our bodies—a warm, tingling, body rush, stomach-in-a-knot kind of love. Indeed, neuroscientists have found evidence that passionate love produces changes in brain chemistry, which causes focused attention, concentrated motivation to attain a reward, and a sense of giddiness that is primarily fueled by one of nature's most powerful stimulants, dopamine (Barber, 2002; Kurup & Kurup, 2003). Spend a few minutes completing the items in *Self/Social Connection Exercise 10.3* to learn more about your own feelings of passionate love.

When neuroscientists conduct brain scans of romantically involved individuals who report high levels of passionate love for their partner, they find that many brain areas become active when these individuals view photos of their beloved (Bartels & Zeki, 2000; Fisher, 2004). Compared with the brain activity produced when they view photos of friends, love-struck individuals experience increased activity in the *caudate nucleus*, a large, C-shaped region that sits near the center of the brain (see Figure 10.6). This very primitive brain area not only directs bodily movement, it also plays a key role in the brain's "reward and pleasure system." In addition to activation of the caudate nucleus, passionate lovers also experience increased activity in other regions of the reward system, including areas of the septum and a brain region that is activated when people eat chocolate. Additional studies indicate that when we believe that our passionate love may be reciprocated, regions of the prefrontal cortex responsible for higher-order thinking join in the pursuit, planning tactics, exercising proper restraint, and monitoring our progress toward the goal of romantic bliss (Fisher, 1998, 2004). Passionate love is experienced most intensely during the early stages of a romantic relationship. According to Ellen Berscheid and Hatfield (1974), this type of romantic love is produced, or at least enhanced, during early romantic encounters due to a rather interesting transference of arousal from one stimulus to another. As a way to introduce you to this phenomenon, let me tell you how I met my wife.

One evening while I was a visiting assistant professor at Indiana University, I attended a modern dance concert. When purchasing my ticket, the ticketer ripped it in two and gave me half, instructing me to remember the number on my ticket stub because it would later be used in the performance. Indeed. The dance company was very avant-garde, and just before beginning the last performance piece, they brought a hat on stage filled with ticket stubs. If your ticket number was called, you were supposed to walk on stage and become part of the performance. Upon hearing this, I instinctively sunk lower in my seat. Ever since my sister had tried to teach me to dance the "twist" and the "pony" during my teenaged years—while laughing uncontrollably—I have always felt self-conscious on the dance floor (an excellent example of classical conditioning). As luck would have it, my number was called by one of the performers, a tall attractive woman, with long blonde hair. Maybe this wouldn't be so bad after all, I thought as I walked onstage. But

passionate love

A state of intense longing for union with another

" *When love is not madness, it is not love.* "

Spanish proverb

" *It's so easy to fall in love.* "

Buddy Holly, U.S. rock & roll singer, 1936–1959

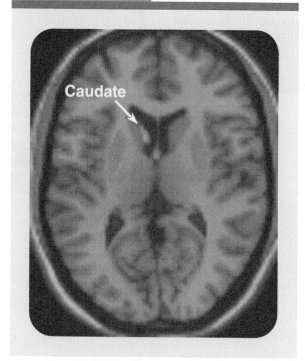

Figure 10.6

Love Activated in the Brain

When neuroscientists study the brain activity of people experiencing passionate love as they gaze at photos of their loved ones they find increased activity in the caudate nucleus. This primitive part of the brain processes dopamine and plays a key role in the "reward and pleasure system."

To What Degree Do You Experience Passionate Love for Someone?

Most young adults have experienced both the joy and despair of passionate love. The following items describe how you might feel when experiencing this type of romantic love. In responding to these statements, think of the person with whom you are currently romantically involved or at least attracted to romantically. If you are not currently in love, think of your most recent romantic partner with whom you experienced some degree of passion. If you have never experienced romantic love, think of the person who came closest to sparking passion in you. Using the following 9-point scale, respond to these statements while recalling how you felt when your romantic feelings were the strongest.

Not at all true   1   2   3   4   5   6   7   8   9   Definitely true

1. I would feel deep despair if _____ left me.
2. Sometimes I feel I can't control my thoughts; they are obsessively on _____.
3. I feel happy when I am doing something to make _____ happy.
4. I would rather be with _____ than with anyone else.
5. I'd get jealous if I thought _____ were falling in love with someone else.
6. I yearn to know all about _____.
7. I want _____ physically, emotionally, and mentally.
8. I have an endless appetite for affection from _____.
9. For me, _____ is the perfect romantic partner.
10. I sense my body responding when _____ touches me.
11. _____ always seems to be on my mind.
12. I want _____ to know me, my thoughts, my fears, and my hopes.
13. I eagerly look for signs indicating _____'s desire for _____.
14. I possess a powerful attraction for _____.
15. I get extremely depressed when things don't go right in my relationship with _____.

Scoring Instructions

To calculate your passionate love score, add up your responses to the 15 items. Your score can range from 15 to 135, with a higher score indicating greater passionate feelings for your romantic partner. "Very low passion" is in the 12–44 point range, "moderately low passion" is in the 45–74 point range, "moderately high passion" is in the 75–104 point range, and "very high passion" is in the 105–135 point range.

Hatfield, E., & Sprecher, S. (1986). Measuring passionate love in intimate relationships. *Journal of Adolescence, 9*, 383–410.

what did she want me to do? You guessed it, learn a complicated dance step in front of the entire audience. My heart began to beat rapidly and my face became flushed, but I concentrated as best I could as she led me through the steps. Halfway through the routine, in the middle of a big leg swing, my brand-new reversible belt buckle popped completely off my belt and shot across the dance floor! The dancer laughed, the audience roared. I was mortified. Somehow I finished the dance routine and sat down. Later, whenever I would see this dancer around town, my heart would race and my face would become flushed as I relived "the incident." She never noticed me during these near encounters, but now I certainly had her number. What were my feelings toward her? Attraction coupled with anxiety. Eight months later, I finally introduced myself when our paths crossed again, and we began dating. A year and a half later we were married.

In explaining the initial encounter with my future wife, social psychological research suggests that my acute embarrassment may have actually sparked a romantic attraction toward her. How? As discussed in Chapter 9 (pp. 357–359), Stanley Schachter's anxiety-affiliation research indicates that when unsure about our own emotional reactions, we often compare them with the reactions of similar others. Schachter (1964) took this insight and expanded on it in his **two-factor theory of emotions**. According to Schachter, our emotions are based on two components: physiological arousal and cognitions about what that arousal means. He proposed that if you are aroused but are not sure what you are feeling, you will look for cues in your surroundings. If everyone is acting happy, their smiles and laughter are likely to shape the emotional label you attach to your own state of arousal. The implication of the two-factor theory is that our emotions are subjective and highly vulnerable to being interpreted based on situational cues.

How might this theory explain passionate love? Drawing on Schachter's theory, Berscheid and Hatfield (1974) contend that the spark of passionate love is likely to occur when (1) you meet someone who fits your preconceived beliefs of an appropriate lover, and (2), while in this person's presence, you experience a state of physiological arousal. Returning to my "belt buckle" predicament, what sort of emotional label did I attach to my elevated heart rate and flushed face? Did I simply explain it as being due to the emotion of embarrassment? If I weren't standing next to someone whom I found attractive, this most certainly would have been the emotional label I attached to my arousal. End of story. However, life isn't usually that simple, is it? When arousal occurs in the presence of an appropriate love object, you may well interpret this arousal as romantic and sexual attraction. Dolf Zillmann (1984) has called this psychological process—in which arousal caused by one stimulus is transferred and added to arousal elicited by a second stimulus—**excitation transfer**. In such instances, our increased romantic interest can be traced to the transfer of arousal from one source to the object of our newfound affections.

Donald Dutton and Arthur Aron (1974) tested this romantic attribution of arousal hypothesis on two bridges at a popular tourist site in North Vancouver, British Columbia. One of the bridges, the Capilano Canyon Suspension Bridge, is 5 feet wide, 450 feet long, and constructed of wooden boards attached to wire cables that span the Capilano River at a height of 230 feet. This bridge is not for those with a fear of heights—it wob-

two-factor theory of emotions
A theory that emotional experience is based on two factors: physiological arousal and cognitive labeling of the cause of that arousal

excitation transfer
A psychological process in which arousal caused by one stimulus is transferred and added to arousal elicited by a second stimulus

Capilano Canyon Suspension Bridge, Vancouver, British Columbia. Dutton and Aron (1974) tested the romantic attribution of arousal hypothesis on this bridge, 230 feet above the Capilano River.

bles as you walk on it, and it sways in the wind. Nearby, there is another bridge that does not set your heart aflutter. It is solidly built out of heavy wood and stands only ten feet above a small, peaceful stream.

In their experiment, whenever an unaccompanied male began to walk across either bridge, he was approached by a male or female research assistant and asked to write an imaginative story in response to a picture while standing on the bridge. The assistant also told the man that if he wanted to receive information about the study's results he could give her (or him) a phone call. Dutton and Aron found that the men who were approached by a woman on the suspension bridge told stories with the highest sexual imagery of all the experimental groups. As you can see in Figure 10.7, these men were also more likely than any of the other groups to call the assistant. Apparently, they had attributed their arousal, which was undoubtedly principally caused by the swaying bridge, to the female assistant.

Although this is one interpretation of the results, can you think of another possibility? Perhaps the men who chose to walk across the dangerous-looking suspension bridge were more adventurous, both sexually and physically, than the men who chose the safer bridge. If this were the case, then it was their more adventurous personalities that caused both the bridge choice and the phoning of the female assistant. Dutton and Aron ruled out this possibility by repeating the experiment, but this time using only the suspension bridge. Half of the men were asked to write their stories as they stood on the bridge, while the others were approached after they had completed their walk and had calmed down. As expected, increased sexual imagery and phone calls were associated only with the condition in which men were approached as they crossed the bridge. Excitation transfer, not adventurous personalities, explained the men's actions.

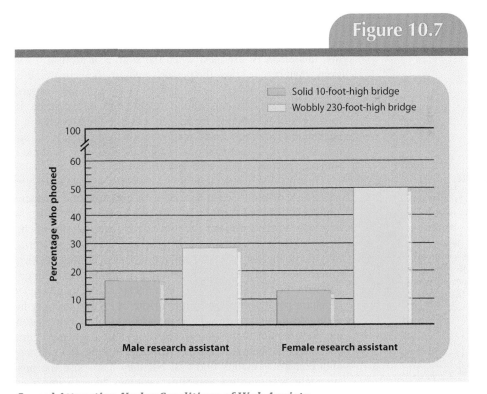

Figure 10.7

Sexual Attraction Under Conditions of High Anxiety

A male or female research assistant asked men to write an imaginative story in response to a picture while either standing on a solid 10-foot-high bridge or a wobbly 230-foot-high bridge. Men who were approached by the female assistant on the wobbly bridge were much more likely to later call her, supposedly to learn more about the study's findings. These men's imaginative stories also contained the highest sexual imagery of all the groups. How do these findings support the misattribution of arousal hypothesis?

The two-factor theory of emotion emphasizes the role our thoughts and beliefs play in accounting for our states of arousal. Yet other social psychologists suggest that a different mechanism may explain why fear and anxiety intensify romantic feelings (Kenrick & Cialdini, 1977; Riordan & Tedeschi, 1983). Referring to the anxiety-affiliation studies discussed in Chapter 9, Douglas Kenrick and Robert Cialdini (1977) proposed that in some circumstances the presence of others tends to calm anxious people. They argued that the reason the men on the suspension bridge were attracted to the female assistant was not because they thought she aroused them but because she in fact calmed them down. The men associated her with a reduction of anxiety, and that led to greater liking for her. Therefore, it is not transferred arousal that increases romantic feelings, but it is the emotional comfort people provide that increases their attractiveness.

This explanation of romantic attraction, although providing an alternative interpretation of the Dutton and Aron findings, soon ran into trouble based on the findings of another series of arousal studies. In one experiment, male participants' arousal was manipulated by having them run in place for either two minutes or fifteen seconds (White et al., 1981). As soon as the men completed this exercise, they watched a videotape of a woman they expected to meet sometime later. In one condition, the woman was made to look and sound attractive, while in another condition she appeared unattractive. After watching the videotape, the men rated the woman's attractiveness.

One thing to keep in mind about this experiment is that the men who participated did not experience any anxiety or fear, and thus Kenrick and Cialdini's arousal reduction explanation would predict no differences due to this exercise-induced arousal. Yet this arousal did heighten the men's emotional responses toward the target woman. Men who had exercised for two minutes evaluated the physically attractive woman as more attractive and the physically unattractive woman as less attractive than those who had exercised for only fifteen seconds. These findings suggest that arousal from a nonsexual stimulus can intensify a person's initial emotional reaction to a potential romantic partner, be it either positive or negative.

In a meta-analysis of thirty-three experiments, Craig Foster and his coworkers (1998) confirmed that excitation transfer does influence attractiveness. They also found that this effect is strongest when the source of arousal is ambiguous, but it can occur even when people know the person to whom they are attending does not primarily cause their arousal. In other words, simply being aroused—regardless of its source—facilitates whatever is the most natural response in that situation. If the target person is good-looking and reasonably meets our criteria for a romantic partner, we automatically become more attracted, and the attraction is stronger if the source of arousal is ambiguous. However, if the person is not good-looking or in some other way is an unsuitable romantic partner, we become less attracted.

Finally, one recent study found that amorous excitation transfer toward a stranger is less likely to occur when we are with our romantic partner. In this study, researchers approached people at amusement parks as they were either waiting to begin or as they had just finished a roller-coaster ride (Meston & Frohlich, 2003). Participants were shown a photo of a person of the other sex who was of average attractiveness and asked to evaluate the individual on attractiveness and dating desirability. They were also asked to rate the attractiveness of the person sitting next to them on the roller coaster. Consistent with the excitation transfer hypothesis, women and men who were not riding with a romantic partner rated the photo of the other sex stranger higher in attractiveness and dating desirability immediately after finishing the ride as compared to just prior to taking the ride. For those who were riding with a romantic partner, there were no significant rating differences between persons entering and exiting the ride. These results not only confirm previous findings, but they also raise the possibility that the relatively automatic arousal-attraction effect becomes "deactivated"—or perhaps we are less conscious of its effect—when we are with a current romantic partner.

Does this research also provide useful information on how you might spark passionate feelings in a desired romantic partner? Perhaps a scary movie, an exciting amusement park ride, or a shared exercise activity would provide the necessary arousal. For your own romantic feelings, the lesson to be learned from all these studies is that when your ticket is pulled out of the hat of romance, it may not matter whether your romantic feelings are initially triggered by excitation transfer or "the real thing." However, you'd bet-

> " We don't believe in rheumatism and true love until after the first attack. "
>
> Marie von Ebner-Eschenbach, Austrian author, 1830–1916

> " I am your clay. You are my clay. In life we share a single quilt. In death we will share our coffin. "
>
> Kuan Tao-sheng, Chinese poet and painter, 1262–1319

> " Will he always love me? I cannot read his heart. This morning my thoughts are as disordered as my black hair. "
>
> Harikawa, Japanese poet, 1135–1165

ter hope that your potential romantic partner's initial reaction toward you is one of attraction rather than repulsion, for excitation transfer may heighten either to equal degrees.

COMPANIONATE LOVE IS MORE STABLE AND ENDURING THAN PASSIONATE LOVE.

> **"** *If there is such a thing as a good marriage, it is because it resembles friendship rather than love.* **"**
>
> Michel de Montaigne, 1533-1592, French writer

If you have ever experienced passionate love you have most likely also experienced the hot flames of passion cooling to warm embers. Having grown up watching movie stars convulse with passion whenever they embrace on the silver screen, you may have been disillusioned to discover that the intensity of your feelings no longer matched Hollywood's depiction of love. You may well feel very close to your romantic partner, like best buddies, but the passion ebbs and flows. In this state of mind, you may wonder, "Is this what love becomes?" Social psychologists investigating the course of romantic relationships might reply, "Yes, in most cases, this is what becomes of romantic love … if you're lucky." Why is this so?

One reason the emotional roller-coaster ride of early love slows over time to a more smooth and steady experience is the fact that passion generally burns itself out. Passionate love is considered to be a relatively short-lived type of love, more typical of the early stages of a romantic relationship when one's partner's love is less certain (Hatfield et al., 2007). Indeed, passionate love thrives on the thrill and uncertainty of winning over another's affections. As we settle into a romantic relationship, the emotional freshness and uncertainty of passionate love is replaced by a more certain and dependable type of love—if love survives at all (Knobloch, 2007).

companionate love

The affection we feel for those with whom our lives are deeply entwined

In defining this less impassioned, more enduring **companionate love**, Hatfield (1988) states that it is "the affection we feel for those with whom our lives are deeply entwined" (p. 205). Companionate love exists between close friends as well as between lovers. It develops out of a sense of certainty in each other's love and respect, and a feeling of genuine mutual understanding (Acevedo & Aron, 2009; Sprecher, 1999).

Another difference between passionate love and companionate love is the beliefs that one has about one's partner. In the early stages of romantic relationships, when passions run high, lovers tend to see their partners through rose-colored glasses (Brehm, 1988). Their partners are "perfect," the "ideal man or woman," their "dream come true." As passion fades and couples develop companionate love based on mutual understanding, this idealization of one's beloved often gives way to a more realistic view. Yet, as we will discuss more fully later in the chapter (p. 427), although companionate love is a more reality-based love, successful and happy romantic partners are those who tend to see each other's imperfections in the best possible light.

As a romantic relationship grows, the emotional highs and lows of passionate love subside. What then predicts relationship satisfaction and longevity is the couple's degree of companionate love.

Evolutionary psychologists propose that sex-driven passionate love and commitment-driven companionate love evolved to meet different human needs (Diamond, 2003; Gonzaga & Haselton, 2008). According to this theory, sexual desire is governed by the *sexual mating system*, in which the goal is to sexually reproduce and thereby pass one's genes on to the next generation. In contrast, companionate love is governed by the *attachment system*, in which the goal is to establish and maintain a strong emotional bond between two people. As discussed earlier, attachment is a part of our evolutionary heritage that developed to foster childrearing and maximize the newborn's survival. Likewise, the attachment bond that develops between two parents in companionate love also ensures the survival of offspring (Fraley et al., 2005). Parents who love each other are more likely to stay together to raise their children, and there is strength in numbers. According to this evolutionary perspective, then, the sexual desire typical of passionate love fuels the sexual mating system, ensuring that a new generation is born into this world. In turn, the sharing and commitment typical of companionate love fuels the attachment system, ensuring that enough members of the new generation will survive childhood.

WOMEN AND MEN MAY DIFFER IN THEIR EXPERIENCE OF LOVE.

Although I have described the sexual desire associated with passionate love as preceding the strong emotional bonding associated with companionate love, there is evidence that women and men differ in the degree to which their experience of romantic love adheres to this pattern (Rose & Zand, 2000). Would it surprise you to learn that women appear more likely than men to feel sexually attracted toward others only after feeling romantically attracted to them? Or to pose this question somewhat differently, would it surprise you to learn that, in regard to love, men may be more driven by their passions and women may be more driven by their affections?

When college students were asked what they thought caused sexual desire, both sexes strongly agreed that the causes were often different for women and men (Peplau & Garnets, 2000; Regan et al., 2000). The most widely endorsed causes of female sexual desire were interpersonal experiences related to companionate love, whereas the most widely endorsed causes of male desire were biological processes and a physical "need" for sex. Thus, it appears that women tend to emphasize emotional intimacy as more of a necessity for sexuality than men. The same gender difference exists among homosexual adults. Like heterosexual women, lesbians are less likely than gay and heterosexual men to desire or engage in casual sex (Peplau & Fingerhut, 2007; Peplau et al., 2004). This may explain why men are much less "picky" than women in choosing possible romantic partners at speed dating events (Todd et al., 2007).

In thinking about these gender differences within the contexts of the sexual mating system and the attachment system, men appear more focused than women on the sexual mating aspect of this process that we identify as passionate love, whereas women are more focused than men on the attachment aspect that we identify as companionate love. For women more than men, the goal of sex is intimacy, and the best context for pleasurable sex is a committed relationship. For men, this is less true (Peplau, 2003). Of course, this does not mean that women are not interested in casual sex and men do not seek committed romantic relationships. It simply means that gender differences in motivational tendencies regarding sex and intimacy appear to exist. However, these are only tendencies, and many women and men do not fit these general patterns.

But wait a second. Over the years, a number of studies suggest that in some ways heterosexual men have a more romantic view of love than heterosexual women (Hobart, 1958; Spaulding, 1970; Sprecher & Toro-Morn, 2002). That is, men are more likely to believe in love at first sight, in love as the basis for marriage and for overcoming obstacles, and to believe that their romantic partners and their relationships will be perfect (Hendrick et al., 1984). True to these beliefs, other studies indicate that men tend to fall in love faster and fall out of love more slowly than women (Dion & Dion, 1985; Galperin & Haselton, 2010). They also are less likely than women to break up a premarital romance (Fletcher, 2002; Hill et al., 1979). This does not mean that women are unromantic. Women are typically at least as emotionally involved as their partners once they fall in love. In fact, they are more likely than men to report feeling intense romantic

> ❝*To be in love is merely to be in a state of perpetual anesthesia—to mistake an ordinary young woman for a goddess.*❞
>
> ————————
> H. L. Mencken, U.S. social critic, 1880–1956

sensations such as euphoria and giddiness for their partner, and to have more vivid memories of past romantic relationships (Dion & Dion, 1973; Harvey et al., 1986). In assessing these findings, it appears that men are more eager to fall in love than women, but once a man and a woman take the plunge, the woman's emotional expressiveness is at least equal to that of her partner's. If this indeed is the way men and women typically approach romance, the next question comes begging. Why is it that men appear very willing to fall in love, while women initially take a more cautious approach? Further, how do these differences relate to the already discussed gender differences in the experience of passionate and companionate love?

In keeping with our previous analysis, evolutionary theorists contend that the different approaches to love that men and women exhibit are principally due to the different investment the two sexes have in the results of sexual bonding, namely, the children that are born (Buss, 1995; Simpson & Gangestad, 2001). To maximize the probability that his genes will live on in future generations, it is to a man's advantage to establish sexual intimacy as quickly as possible in a relationship and to have frequent sexual encounters with many different women. Sparking passionate love is the means to this end. If a man can establish sexual intimacy early in a relationship, he could theoretically court one woman after another and therefore be a big winner in reproductive fitness. For a woman, a more discriminating approach is needed in choosing a mate because she has a limited number of eggs that can be fertilized during her time of reproduction. This biological limitation means the best strategy for women is to forestall passionate feelings, and instead, carefully judge their potential partners' strengths and weaknesses so they can identify men with the best genes and personality. Thus, according to evolutionary theorists, it is adaptive for men to emphasize passion and fall in love quickly, while the female evolutionary injunction is to move slowly in matters of love and emphasize commitment.

Although the evolutionary approach provides a plausible explanation for why men fall in love quickly while women are more cautious, how might it explain the fact that men are more reluctant than women to end a romantic relationship? From an evolutionary perspective, it might seem to make more sense for men to fall in and out of love quickly because such a strategy of numerous, short romantic relationships will maximize their chances of passing their genes on to future generations. One possible explanation offered by evolutionary theorists about why men fall out of love more slowly than women is that they have less to lose in a romantic relationship. Because they don't have to worry about a ticking biological clock and the risks of pregnancy, they can waste more time than women in a relationship that is going nowhere.

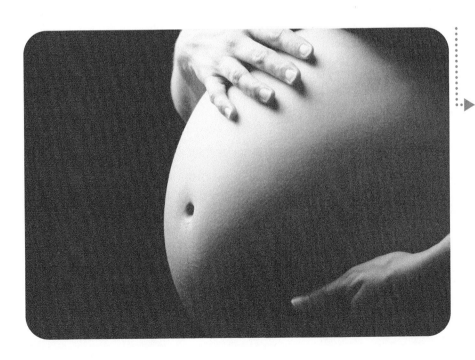

According to evolutionary theorists, how does sex-driven passionate love and commitment-driven companionate love influence women's and men's experience of romantic love?

In contrast to this evolutionary explanation's focus on genetic predispositions, the sociocultural perspective highlights cultural practices and the social distribution of power. According to sociocultural theorists, in most cultures around the world men and women are traditionally born with different social statuses, with men's *ascribed* status being considerably higher than that of women (Howard et al., 1987). Due to this cultural practice, young men tend to have greater expectations about their social and economic security than young women. Men may therefore feel they can afford to let their emotions and passions rule their mate selection; their status will be determined by them alone, and not by their partner's status. On the other hand, being aware of the sexual inequality in their culture, women might be more likely to believe that their future status will be determined more by their mates' status than their own. Women may therefore believe they cannot afford the luxury of following only their emotions and may adopt a more pragmatic approach to love. This sociocultural explanation is consistent with the data presented in Chapter 9 indicating that men place more importance on physical attractiveness in choosing a partner, while women emphasize social status.

Similarly, the sociocultural perspective further suggests that heterosexual men may fall in love quickly and out of love slowly because they are starved for intimacy due to their inability to express love and tenderness to their male friends. As discussed earlier, because males are socialized to value heterosexual masculinity, their same-sex friendships tend to lack intimacy. Therefore, often the only outlet they have to express warmth, tenderness, and deep affection is in a romantic relationship with a woman. This greater dependence on romantic relationships for emotional support is true for both married and unmarried heterosexual men (Haltzman et al., 2007). Thus, it may be that heterosexual men tend to fall in love more quickly and be less willing to end a romantic relationship because they place all their emotional "eggs" in this romantic basket. In contrast, women are more likely to spread their emotional eggs around, placing a number of them in their same-sex friendships.

Although I have been contrasting the evolutionary and cultural viewpoints, a growing number of social scientists believe that these two perspectives may often complement—rather than compete with—each other (Schaller, 1997). Cultural explanations of why women and men differ in their approach to and experience of love emphasize the different social roles and positions of power that the two sexes traditionally hold in society. In other words, they focus on how existing social conditions differentially influence the thinking and decision making of women and men regarding love. Yet what are the origins of these gender roles and cultural status systems? Evolutionary explanations focus on how these differences might have initially arisen due to evolutionary selection pressures. Perhaps the ultimate "best" explanation for gender differences in love may describe how selection pressures that operated in our prehuman ancestors shaped certain patterns of social behavior, leaving modern women and men with *certain* capacities to possibly react differently to love. Yet the degree to which women and men actually manifest these inherited capacities may well be decided by current social and environmental forces (Malach, 2001). In other words, culture and social learning may either enhance or override these inherited capacities.

SECTION SUMMARY

- Cultural and historical views of romance vary.

- Two types of romantic love consistently found in all studies are passionate love and companionate love.

- Passionate love is a relatively short-lived type of romantic love, more typical of the early stages of romance when one's partner's love is less certain.

- Companionate love is a slower developing and more enduring type of romantic love that develops out of a sense of certainty in each other's love and respect.

- Sex-driven passionate love and commitment-driven companionate love may have evolved to meet different human needs.

- Cultural and/or evolutionary forces may explain why women and men often differ in their experience of love.

WILL LOVE ENDURE?

More than one million divorces occur each year in the United States, and more than half of all marriages end in divorce (U.S. Bureau of the Census, 1998). Outside of marriage, the mortality rate of romantic relationships is even higher. Although the odds that love will endure are not good, we all know people who have built loving and satisfying relationships lasting many years. In this section we examine some of the factors that contribute to satisfaction and conflict in romance.

SOCIAL DISAPPROVAL OF ONE'S PARTNER HARMS RELATIONSHIP STABILITY.

As we have seen in other chapters, individuals' attitudes and beliefs are significantly shaped by other people's opinions (see Chapter 5, p. 162 and Chapter 7, p. 271). Given this influence, how is the health of a romantic relationship affected when partners perceive that their friends and families—and even society at large—disapprove of it? For example, national opinion polls suggest that the American public largely disapproves of interracial and same-sex romance, as well as expressing dissatisfaction toward relationships in which one partner is significantly older than the other (Golebiowska, 2007; Smith, 2007).

In a combined Internet and conventional survey study, Justin Lehmiller and Christopher Agnew (2006) found that individuals who were partners in these three types of *marginalized romantic relationships* were well aware of the societal disapproval and expected others to stigmatize them. This perceived disapproval and expectation of discrimination often had a negative impact on partners' satisfaction with and commitment to the relationship. In a seven-month follow-up study, Lehmiller and Agnew (2007) recontacted many of their original participants and discovered that about one-fourth of the couples had broken up. As predicted, individuals who had previously perceived higher levels of disapproval from friends, family, and society at large were more likely to have a failed relationship. Further, this failure was preceded by the individuals lowering their commitment to the relationship. The findings from these two studies provide compelling evidence that societal opinions about romantic relationships often play an important role in determining whether these relationships survive, by either lowering or raising the commitment of partners.

PEOPLE ARE HAPPIEST WITH ROMANTIC EQUITY.

As stated in Chapter 9 (p. 351), social exchange theory is based on the assumption that all relationships are like economic bargains in which each party tries to maximize their rewards while minimizing their costs. Although people in intimate relationships often attend to their partner's needs rather than their own, it would be naive to believe that once people fall in love they cease to consider their relationship rewards and costs. Indeed, one important factor determining whether a romantic relationship will endure is the perception the partners have about what they give to and receive from each other (Weigel et al., 2006). *Relationship maintenance behaviors* that couples provide to and receive from each other that figure into costs and rewards are activities such as sharing tasks, self-disclosing, providing or receiving advice, showing or receiving

Certain romantic relationships, such as same-sex relationships, are marginalized within American society. How does this disapproval affect relationship stability?

equity theory
....
The theory that people are
most satisfied in a
relationship when the ratio
between rewards and costs is
similar for both partners.

affection, and conceding to partner's requests (Stafford & Canary, 2006). Yet how are these rewards and costs tabulated?

In contrast to the selfish outlook proposed by social exchange theory, **equity theory** introduces the notion of fairness, or equity, for how rewards and costs are analyzed in an intimate relationship (Adams, 1965). This theory contends that people don't try to maximize their rewards and minimize their costs but, instead, are most satisfied when the *ratio* between the rewards and costs is similar for both partners. If one partner receives more rewards from the relationship but also makes greater contributions to it, the relationship is still equitable.

For the sake of illustration, consider an imaginary couple, Joyce and Louis, who are married and have a young baby. Joyce has put her career on hold to stay home, and despite the drudgery of household duties, she derives great pleasure in witnessing her child's development. Regarding Louis's perceptions, his career is advancing nicely, but it keeps him from his family for extended periods. Yet overall, he too is still pleased with their marriage. Employing some arbitrary numbers to describe these costs and rewards, let's say that Joyce's rewards equal 40, and Louis's benefits amount to 25. Even though Joyce receives more relationship rewards than Louis, the relationship is equitable because her costs are higher: 32 to Louis's 20. As you can see, the basic equation suggests a balanced or equitable relationship:

$$\frac{40}{32} \quad = \quad \frac{25}{20} \quad = \quad \frac{5}{4}$$

Joyce's ratio   Louis' ratio   Relationship ratio

If these two ratios were not equal, equity theory would predict that both partners would become distressed and would try to restore balance. How would this distress manifest itself? The partner who is *overbenefited* should feel guilty about the inequity, while the one who is *underbenefited* should experience anger and depression. Research indicates that inequity does indeed produce these negative emotions in both dating and married couples (Gleason et al., 2003). However, although people who are overbenefited tend to feel guilty, they generally are very satisfied and contented with the relationship. This is not the case for the underbenefited. Their anger and depression cause a great deal of dissatisfaction with the relationship (Sprecher, 1992). Given the stress that this inequity produces, it is not surprising that inequitable relationships are less likely to endure (Walster et al., 1978).

Although perceived inequity is damaging to romantic relationships, recent studies suggest that we tend to project our own care and supportiveness for our partners onto our perceptions of their caring and supportiveness (Lemay et al., 2007). In other words, if you take pleasure in satisfying your partner's needs without expecting anything in return, you tend to assume—sometimes incorrectly—that your partner also has this communal orientation. Likewise, if you generally try to maximize your rewards and minimize your costs in a romantic relationship, you tend to assume—sometimes incorrectly—that your partner also has this exchange orientation. This tendency to project your own level of responsiveness and caring for your partner onto your partner's motives and actions results in you perceiving that the relationship is equitable, perhaps even when it is not.

SELF-ESTEEM CAN BOTH FACILITATE AND UNDERMINE ROMANTIC LOVE.

Beyond perceptions of equity, how is romantic success affected by our feelings of self-worth? A commonly held belief is that self-love is a necessary precondition for loving others. For example, Nathaniel Branden, a writer of popular self-esteem books, specifically states, "If you do not love yourself, yo will be unable to love others" (Branden, 1994, pp. 7–8). Is this true?

Based on our discussion of attachment styles, this claim appears misleading. There is little evidence that people with high self-esteem are more capable of loving others than those with low self-esteem (Campbell & Baumeister, 2001). Indeed, some studies find that people with low self-esteem have more intense experiences of passionate love than those with high self-esteem (Dion & Dion, 1975; Hendrick & Hendrick, 1986). However, this passion is often fed by insecurity, such as that found among people with a preoccupied attachment style.

Self-esteem may not be related to the capacity to love, but it is related to loving in a way that maintains intimacy over time. Low self-esteem persons appear perfectly capable of experiencing high levels of passionate love, but they have a much more difficult time experiencing the emotional security found in companionate love. As you have already learned, passionate love is often fueled by a sense of uncertainty about winning over another's affections. People with low self-esteem often doubt the strength of their partners' love and tend to constantly seek reassurance (Joiner et al., 1992; Murray et al., 2001). While this emotional neediness can be appealing to romantic partners during the early stages of romance, it often becomes burdensome as the relationship matures.

A series of studies of dating couples conducted by Sandra Murray and her coworkers (2005) found that the insecurity experienced by low self-esteem individuals stems in part from them perceiving that their romantic partners are "too good for them." Just as low self-esteem people have difficulty generally accepting positive feedback from others as being valid (see Chapter 3, pp. 97–98), they also have difficulty believing that they deserve other people's love. Instead of feeling secure in their partners' expressions of affection, low self-esteem persons often misinterpret their partners' sometimes negative moods and actions as signals for impending rejection (Bellavia & Murray, 2003). Burdened with these concerns, low self-esteem persons begin finding fault in their partners, which helps them psychologically disengage from the anticipated rejection (Murray et al., 2002). Consistent with the self-fulfilling prophecy discussed in Chapter 1 (pp. 5–9), this increased negativity causes their once-admiring partners to feel less satisfied in the relationship, making a breakup much more likely. When the breakup occurs, low self-esteem individuals' feelings of unworthiness are confirmed (Downey et al., 1998).

Although low self-esteem provides hurdles to relationship success, additional research suggests that some forms of high self-esteem can also harm romantic relationships (Schuetz, 1998). For instance, individuals with unstable high self-esteem (see Chapter 3, p. 100) tend to respond to relationship problems with jealousy and even violence, especially when their self-esteem is threatened (Baumeister et al., 1996). On the other hand, people identified as *narcissists*—meaning those with grandiose self-concepts, feelings of superiority, and a strong need for power and acclaim—view love as a game and are fickle, selfish, and insensitive lovers (Campbell et al., 2002). Together, these studies suggest that there is no simple relationship between self-esteem and the durability of romantic relationships. Relationship intimacy can be threatened both by the type of low self-esteem that requires constant emotional reassurance, and by certain types of high self-esteem that induce either hostility when challenged or selfish gamesmanship. In the final analysis, the type of self-esteem that is best suited for enduring romance is that possessed by people with secure attachment styles: self-love that is stable and sufficiently strong to allow for the expression and acceptance of emotional intimacy while also being capable of handling relationship conflict in a constructive manner (Morrison et al., 1997).

ROMANTIC HAPPINESS IS BASED ON BOTH POSITIVE ILLUSIONS AND ACCURATE JUDGMENTS.

For many years, most psychologists asserted that lasting satisfaction in romantic relationships depends on people understanding their partners' real strengths and weaknesses (Brickman, 1987; Swann et al., 1994). Although it is hard to argue against the benefits of an occasional good dose of reality, a number of studies suggest that we have a need to perceive our romantic relationships as being better than others' (Gagné & Lydon, 2001; Sanderson & Evans, 2001). Yet how can we satisfy this need if we insist on scrutinizing our partner's flaws? One possible answer to this question is that, if we want happiness in love, we should allow our desire to feel good about our romantic relationships to dominate our desire to critically analyze relationship imperfections (Rusbult et al., 2000; Sedikides et al., 1998). Just as there is a *self-serving bias* that leads people with high self-esteem to see themselves in the best possible light (see Chapter 1, pp. 16–17), people in happy romantic relationships tend to attribute their partners' positive behaviors to dispositional causes ("their wonderful personality") and their negative behaviors to

Critical THINKING

Earlier in the chapter you learned that passionate love is associated with perceiving one's partner through rose-colored glasses. This idealization, however, often gives way to a more realistic view with the development of companionate love. Yet, if companionate love is more enduring than passionate love, how can the present findings—that perceiving one's partner in somewhat ideal terms leads to greater romantic happiness than perceiving her/him realistically—be explained?

situational factors ("a bad day"). This *partner-enhancing bias* not only makes lovers feel better and increases relationship trust (Miller et al., 2006; Miller & Rempel, 2004), it can also create a self-fulfilling prophecy (Drigotas et al., 1999).

In a series of studies, Sandra Murray and her colleagues discovered that an important component of a satisfying, stable romantic relationship is the ability to mix positive illusion with sober reality when perceiving one's partner. That is, those who can see virtues in their partners that their partners cannot even see in themselves tend to be happier with the relationship than those who perhaps have a more realistic view (Murray & Holmes, 1999). For instance, in one longitudinal study, dating couples who idealized each other more during the initial stages of their romance reported greater increases in satisfaction and decreases in conflicts and doubts over the course of a year than couples who saw each other in a more realistic light (Murray et al., 1996). In addition, during the year, the targets of these positive illusions actually incorporated these idealized images into their own self-concepts. Similar findings were also obtained with married couples (Murray & Holmes, 1997). These studies suggest that partners who idealize each other often create a self-fulfilling prophecy. By taking a "leap of faith" and seeing imperfect relationships in somewhat idealized ways, people not only satisfy their need to feel that their relationships are better than most other relationships but also create the conditions necessary for their positive illusions to be realized (Murray et al., 2006).

Despite research indicating that positive illusions facilitate the belief that one has found their "perfect match," couldn't there also be benefits to accurately reading your partner and the romantic relationship? In one representative study examining this possibility, Geoff Thomas and his colleagues (1997) investigated the ability of relationship partners to read each other's thoughts and feelings, an interpersonal skill they call *mind reading* (also known as *empathic accuracy*). In this study, either married or dating couples were videotaped while they discussed two serious problems in their relationship. Couples were instructed to try to resolve the problems during this ten-minute discussion. After completing this task, couples were separated and partners independently reviewed a videotape of the discussion, stopping the tape whenever they recalled experiencing a thought or emotion, and wrote it down. Next, the researchers gave each partner the time points the other partner had noted and asked each person to review the tape a second time, but now give their best guess as to what their partner was thinking and feeling at the indicated time points. Raters later assessed the similarity between the pairs of statements from the two partners to determine each one's accuracy in reading the other's thoughts and feelings. For comparison purposes, friends of the couple and strangers also reviewed these tapes and guessed what each person was thinking and feeling at the selected time points. Results indicated that couples averaged close to a 50 percent accuracy rate in assessing what their partners were thinking and feeling, which is significantly more accurate than friends of the dating partners (41 percent accuracy) or strangers (39 percent).

So what determines whether the beliefs we have about our partners are more shaped by the desire for accuracy or the desire for partner enhancement? It appears that the key ingredient in differentiating between our accurate judgments and our positive illusions is the degree to which the beliefs focus on us or on our partner (Fletcher & Kerr, 2010). Accuracy is likely to be more important for us when it involves behavior from our partners that provides information about how we are being perceived by them. Thus, when judging the extent to which our partner forgives us, loves us, or is angry and aggressive toward us, we may be very concerned with making accurate judgments, compared with when we judge the extent to which our partner is attractive, intelligent, creative, or funny. Failing to notice and react appropriately to our partner's actions that relate directly to us is likely to have harmful effects on our relationship. However, evaluating our partner more positively than others evaluate our partner on personal qualities not directly related to us serves to increase our satisfaction with our romantic relationship.

Although it is beneficial for us to be both cheerleaders and truth seekers in our romantic relationships, a number of studies suggest that women are more accurate than men in making partner and relationship judgments (Fletcher, 2002; Thomas & Fletcher, 2003) This gender difference may relate to the fact that women tend to be more concerned than men with managing and monitoring intimate relationships and are also more focused on maintaining relationship satisfaction. Due to these concerns and focus, women may be more keyed into the rewards and costs of adopting partner-enhancing biases in their romantic relationships. As you will soon discover, this gender difference in being concerned about managing and monitoring relationship issues has consequences that extend beyond evaluating partners and the relationship.

SOCIAL SUPPORT PREDICTS RELATIONSHIP SATISFACTION.

In the majority of Western cultures, most people involved in long-term romantic relationships consider their partners to be their best friends and the persons they would most likely turn to for support in times of need (Heffner et al., 2004; Pasch et al., 1997). Seeking and receiving such support has important benefits, including a decrease in stress and an increase in physical health and happiness, while simultaneously increasing satisfaction and commitment to the relationship (Taylor, 2007b). For example, a longitudinal study of married couples found that lower levels of depression were associated with both women and men receiving a good deal of *emotional support* (tenderness and understanding) and *information support* (advice and guidance) from their partners during the previous six months (Cutrona & Suhr, 1994). Similar to the findings of parental bonding with newborns and mind reading ability among intimate partners, additional research suggests that partners with higher oxytocin levels are more likely to provide social support during times of stress than partners with lower levels of this hormone (Taylor & Gonzaga, 2007). Further, receiving such support increases oxytocin levels in the recipient, which, in turn, fosters lower arousal and improved mood (Coan et al., 2006; Grewen et al., 2005).

Despite such benefits, research indicates that Asian Americans, who come from a collectivist cultural heritage, are less likely to actively seek social support than are European Americans, who come from an individualist heritage (Kim et al., 2006; Taylor et al., 2007). This finding mirrors the previously discussed research (p. 402) indicating that collectivists are reluctant to self-disclose their desires or fears to others. Apparently, this cultural difference is due to Asian Americans believing that seeking such support will not only burden their partners, it will also cause them to "lose face" (Taylor et al., 2004). The implication of these findings is not that Asian Americans do not benefit from social support; it is the active seeking of such support that is distressing to them. It is possible that Asian Americans—and people from collectivist cultures in general—are more likely to benefit from social support when it is offered without asking, or when they simply know that their partners care for and cherish them (Bolger & Amarel, 2007).

Beyond these cultural considerations, social support is also influenced by gender socialization. In North American culture, girls are raised to think, act, and define themselves in ways that emphasize their emotional connectedness to others more than boys (see Chapter 9, p. 353). These differences in gender learning result in women developing *relationship-enhancing* behaviors, while men develop more *individual-enhancing* behaviors, such as independence and control (Fritz et al., 2003; Underwood & Rosen, 2009). This gender difference may explain why women are better mind readers than men in heterosexual romantic relationships and also why women who provide greater social support than they receive in intimate relationships tend to be more self-confident and healthier (Väänänen et al., 2005). For these women, providing this social support enhances their standing and value among others because their behavior embodies the feminine gender role.

Of course, this does not mean that men are incapable of providing social support in romantic relationships. In fact, longitudinal research of married couples conducted by Lisa Neff and Benjamin Karney (2005) indicate that both women and men possess the basic skills necessary to provide support to their romantic partners. Where they appear to differ is in their tendency to actually provide positive support when their partners are experiencing more severe problems. Neff and Karney found that although men and women did not differ in the amount of support they generally provided their partners, they differed in providing adequate support when their partners were undergoing a great deal of stress. Unlike women who provided more positive support when their spouses were under great stress, men were much less capable of providing such support without also behaving negatively. Such negative behaviors included arguing with or criticizing their partners and breaking a promise. Given that women are generally more relation-

Seeking and receiving social support from one's partner has important benefits. How does gender and culture influence seeking and providing such support?

ship oriented than men, these results suggest that men may less likely notice and respond to subtle and indirect requests for support from their spouses than do women. It is also possible that because men are less relationship oriented they may be more likely than women to resent their role as support provider. When their spouse is expecting extra-special support during times of high stress, men's resentment may be more likely expressed in terms of these negative behaviors. Together, these studies suggest that men in heterosexual romantic relationships have partners who tend to not only have a good deal of experience in providing care and nurturance to others; they actually enjoy offering such support. In contrast, women in these romantic relationships have partners who, on average, have spent a lot of time learning how to be independent of others and often don't receive nearly as much personal satisfaction in engaging in the type of relationship-enhancing behaviors associated with offering social support.

WE ARE MEANER TO THOSE WE LOVE THAN WE ARE TO STRANGERS.

Despite the many emotional joys we derive from long-term intimate relationships, this closeness can also be the source of frequent frustrations and annoyances. A common reaction to these "aggravations of the heart" is to emotionally lash out at those we profess to love (Miller, 1997). For example, studies of married people interacting with either their spouses or strangers during casual conversation and while working on a problem-solving task found that they were much more polite, agreeable, and attentive to the strangers than to their spouses (Birchler et al., 1975). They not only interrupted their spouses, but they also often openly criticized and belittled them. The hard feelings and communication problems that result from this social insensitivity can gradually weaken lovers' emotional bonds (Finkel & Eastwick, 2007).

How do those who transgress against their partners perceive their actions? In an investigation of hurtful behavior in romantic relationships, Jessica Cameron and her coworkers (2002) asked heterosexual college student couples to describe a past transgression in which one of them had been the victim and the other had been the perpetrator in a negative relationship event. Realizing that almost everybody involved in a romantic relationship at some point causes harm to their partner, the researchers randomly assigned participants to either the "perpetrator" or "victim" role. Perpetrators were told to suggest possible negative episodes from their relationship in which they had upset their partner, while victims were instructed to assist their partner in settling upon the most appropriate transgression. Cameron and her colleagues found that during the subsequent retelling of the chosen negative event, the partner who was the

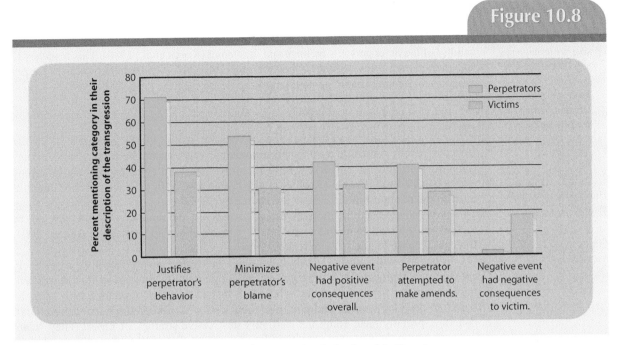

Figure 10.8

Perpetrators' and Victims' Perceptions of a Negative Relationship Event

When romantic couples were randomly assigned to describe a past transgression in which one of them had been the victim and the other had been the perpetrator in a negative relationship event, Jessica Cameron and her coworkers (2002) found that perpetrators and victims had decidedly different perceptions of the event and its aftermath. Compared with their partner victim, perpetrators minimized their blame, justified their actions, and downplayed the event's negative consequences. Perpetrators also were more likely than victims to state that they had attempted to make amends for the negative event and that the event ultimately had positive consequences for the relationship. Because participants were randomly assigned to the perpetrator and victim roles, what do the findings suggest about our capacity to delude ourselves when we act badly in romantic relationships?

perpetrator had a very different perception of the event and its aftermath from the partner who was the victim. In contrast to victims' descriptions of the transgression, perpetrators were more likely to minimize their own blameworthiness, justify their actions, ignore the negative consequences to their partners, and perceive greater improvement in themselves and in the relationship since the transgression (see Figure 10.8).

These findings suggest that when people behave badly in an intimate relationship, they are motivated to dissociate themselves from their undesirable actions. One way to accomplish this goal is for perpetrators to convince themselves that their actions were not really that bad, and further, their "bad" behavior was in many ways an ultimately "good thing" for them and the relationship. In interpreting these results, keep in mind that participants were randomly assigned to the perpetrator and victim roles. If the assignment had gone the other way, then the persons chosen for the victim role would have been the perpetrators. Presumably, they also would then have changed their assessments of both the event and how it had affected their relationship. In other words, this tendency to engage in such self-serving remembrances of harmful relationship behavior is something that all of us are potentially capable of doing.

When a relationship becomes troubled, harmful transgressions increase in frequency. People who feel emotionally snubbed respond by behaving badly toward their partner (Murray et al., 2003). In fact, couples headed for a breakup tend to be unable or unwilling to terminate the expression of negative emotions (Halford et al., 1990). For example, in a four-year longitudinal study of married couples, John Gottman and Robert Levenson (1992) discovered that those relationships that end in divorce tend to involve people who nag and whine a great deal and don't listen very well to their partner's concerns. When troubled couples interact, they often fall into what Gottman (1979) calls a *negative reciprocity cycle*, where positive behaviors tend to be ignored and negative behaviors are reciprocated. Although troubled couples may realize the damage they are inflicting on their relationship with each glare, harsh word, and slammed door, they nevertheless persist in these destructive actions. Happy couples, on the other hand, argue in a more constructive fashion (Blais et al., 1990). When they complain to each other, they also recognize the validity of the other person's feelings and viewpoint (Koren et al., 1980). This tendency to take their partner's point of view when arguing (a psychological state known as *perspective taking*) is important in maintaining relationship health (Arriaga & Rusbult, 1998).

PEOPLE USE DIFFERENT STRATEGIES TO COPE WITH A TROUBLED RELATIONSHIP.

How do people typically react when a romantic relationship becomes dissatisfying? Caryl Rusbult and her coworkers have identified four strategies people use in coping with a troubled relationship (Rusbult et al., 1986a, 1987, 2001). Their level of commitment to the relationship influences the strategies they choose, or find themselves using. The more satisfied and the more invested partners are, the more committed they will be to work on solutions to maintain and improve the relationship (Arriaga & Agnew, 2001; Bui et al., 1996). Figure 10.9 illustrates the primary qualities of these four strategies.

In dealing with conflict, Rusbult contends that some people may take a passively constructive approach by exhibiting *loyalty*. They simply wait, hoping that things will improve on their own. Individuals who adopt this strategy are often afraid to "rock the boat," so they say nothing and pray that their loyalty will keep the relationship afloat. Others, especially men, adopt the passively destructive strategy of *neglect*. They "clam up" and ignore their partners or spend less time with them. When together, neglectful persons often treat their partners poorly by constantly criticizing them for things unrelated to the real problem. Those who don't know how to deal with their negative emotions, or aren't motivated to improve the relationship but also aren't ready to end it, tend to employ this strategy. When people do conclude that the relationship is not worth saving, they *exit*, which is an active, yet destructive, strategy. A much more constructive and active strategy is *voice*. People discuss their problems, seek compromises, consult therapists, and attempt to salvage a relationship they still highly value.

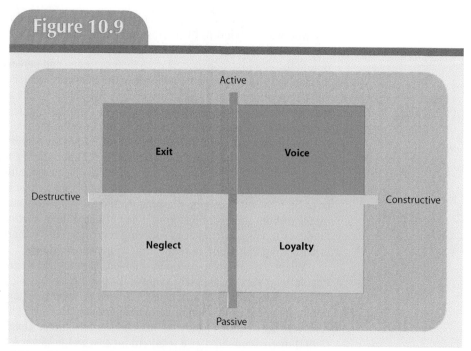

Figure 10.9

A Typology of Basic Coping Strategies

In dealing with relationship conflict people employ different strategies, which differ in terms of the dimensions of active-passive and constructive-destructive. In dealing with dissatisfactions in romantic relationships in your own life, which of these four basic strategies have you used?

Two destructive strategies people employ in dealing with relationship conflict are "exit" and "neglect." What are the two constructive strategies?

Rusbult and her colleagues (1986b) have found that one determinant of the strategies that people choose to employ in dealing with their dissatisfaction is their level of psychological masculinity and femininity. In survey studies involving lesbian, gay male, and heterosexual women and men, individuals with many feminine personality traits were much more likely to react constructively to relationship problems. They either actively searched for an acceptable resolution, or, if a solution did not seem possible, they remained quietly loyal to the relationship. In contrast, those who had many masculine traits and few feminine traits tended to respond destructively when trouble developed in their relationships. They passively neglected the problems and allowed things to deteriorate further, or they actively threatened to exit. These patterns were true for both men and women, regardless of sexual orientation. More generally, other studies indicate that high levels of femininity in one or both partners are associated with higher levels of relationship satisfaction and commitment (Lamke et al., 1994; Stets & Burke, 1996). In addition, longitudinal studies of married couples indicate that masculinity's negative impact on relationship satisfaction is due to the influence of the undesirable masculine personality traits in men (but not in women) related to arrogance and aggressiveness, and not due to the more desirable masculine traits related to independence and assertiveness (Bradbury et al., 1995).

Overall, these findings suggest that through the acquisition of feminine personality traits, people learn to react to relationship problems in a constructive manner (Ickes, 1985). On the other hand, acquiring undesirable masculine traits is downright destructive to relationship survival. Why might this be the case? As already mentioned, feminine traits are characterized by a communal orientation of warmth, intimacy, and a concern with interpersonal relations. On the other hand, masculine traits are characterized by a more individualistic orientation of power, dominance, and a concern with achieving instrumental (that is, work) goals. People with many feminine personality characteristics are more interested in resolving conflict through emotional sharing and compromise, whereas those with mostly masculine characteristics, especially those that are undesirable, prefer reaching decisions on their own and imposing their will on others. When described in this manner, it isn't surprising that these two gender orientations often achieve different results when conflicts arise in romance.

> "Love doesn't just sit there, like a stone, it has to be made, like bread; remade all the time, made new."
>
> Ursula K. LeGuin, U.S. science fiction writer, b. 1929

ROMANTIC BREAKUPS OFTEN CAUSE EMOTIONAL DISTRESS.

Ending a romantic relationship often causes increased emotional insecurity and even decreased physical health (Sbarra & Ferrer, 2006). The two most common emotions fol-

When rejected in love, why might heterosexual women suffer less emotionally than heterosexual men?

lowing a breakup are sadness and anger, with anger dampening rather quickly and sadness lingering over a longer period of time (Sbarra & Emery, 2005). Not surprisingly, persons who are still in love with their former partner have the most difficulty not getting stuck on sadness (Sbarra, 2006). In both heterosexual dating relationships and marriages, women tend to initiate the breakup more often than men (Hagestad & Smyer, 1982; Rubin et al., 1981). One possible reason for this gender difference is that women appear to be more attentive to and sensitive about relationship problems (Ptacek & Dodge, 1995).

In both heterosexual and homosexual relationships, the partner who initiates the breakup experiences less distress, but this effect is much more apparent for men than women in heterosexual romance (Frazier & Cook, 1993; Helgeson, 1994). Men also tend to suffer more than women when they are romantically rejected. A possible explanation for this effect involves the traditional gender roles taught to men and women. First, because power and control are central aspects of the traditional male gender role (Garfinkel, 1985), men may experience greater self-esteem threat and emotional distress when their partner takes relationship control away from them by ending the romance. Second, because heterosexual men tend to place all their emotional eggs in their romantic baskets, they may suffer more emotional pain when the bottom falls out of the relationship and those eggs are smashed (Barbee et al., 1990).

A similar effect is found regarding the ideologies of individualism and collectivism. In a study of romantic breakups in both the United States and Puerto Rico, Harry Triandis and his colleagues (1988) found that people with a more individualist orientation were the loneliest following a breakup. As discussed in Chapter 9 (p. 353), individualists' greater loneliness is most likely due to their less extensive social support network. When romantic relationships fall apart, individualists have fewer people to soothe their emotional pain than collectivists.

In coping with the loss of love, men and women are equally likely to spend considerable time talking to themselves about the relationship ("I'm lucky to have dumped that jerk!" "I've learned a valuable lesson"), distracting themselves by engaging in physical activities or doing things to improve their looks and sex appeal. However, women are more likely than men to cry, talk things over with their friends, read self-help books, and consult a therapist to better understand their feelings (Orimoto et al., 1993). These results suggest that women, more than men, tend to spend time following a breakup attending to their emotional needs in ways that may promote increased understanding so future relationships can be more satisfying.

Although our analysis thus far has focused on the sadness and distress that people often experience following romantic breakups, aren't there positive outcomes that often occur after leaving a low-quality relationship? Couldn't a breakup provide the opportunity to meet new challenges and discover new abilities? The psychological literature clearly indicates that negative—and even traumatic—events have the potential to promote personal growth (Calhoun et al., 2000; Frazier et al., 2004). Consistent with this hypothesis, one study of college students who had experienced romantic breakups found that they reported an average of five positive changes following the experience, with "positive changes in the self" being reported most frequently (Tashiro & Frazier, 2003). Additional research with college students and divorced couples further support the hypothesis that a rediscovery of neglected or previously unknown aspects of the self is a commonly reported positive outcome of romantic breakups (Lewandowski & Bizzoco, 2007). Thus, although sadness and anger are common emotions when romantic relationships end, these negative events are often the catalysts for personal growth.

SECTION SUMMARY

- A number of factors determine whether love will endure or fade:

  Social disapproval of a romantic relationship lowers partners' commitment.

  Romantic relationships are happiest when the ratio between the rewards and costs is similar for both partners.

  The positive self-esteem typical of securely attached individuals fosters romantic satisfaction.

  Couples who idealize each other tend to have happier relationships than those who have more accurate views, but accuracy is important when it provides a partner with information on how s/he is being perceived by the other.

  Receiving social support from one's partner increases satisfaction and commitment to the relationship.

  Troubled couples often are unable or unwilling to terminate the expression of negative emotions toward each other.

- In dealing with relationship dissatisfaction, we typically employ four distinct strategies: loyalty, neglect, voice, and exit.

- Losers in love experience sadness and anger, but breakups also provide the opportunity for personal growth.

APPLICATIONS

WHAT CAUSES JEALOUSY AND HOW CAN YOU COPE WITH IT?

jealousy
....
The negative emotional reaction experienced when a relationship that is important to a person's self-concept is threatened by a real or an imagined rival

Besides the many other problems that can besiege an intimate relationship, **jealousy** can also contribute to relationship failure. Jealousy is the negative emotional reaction experienced when a relationship that is important to a person's self-concept is threatened by a real or an imagined rival (Harris, 2004; Parrott & Smith, 1993). In most cases, the threat is another person, but people can also feel jealous about their partner's time involvement with work, hobbies, and family obligations (Buunk & Bringle, 1987). Some people mistakenly believe that jealousy indicates the depths of a partner's love and, thus, is a healthy sign in romantic relationships. In actuality, research demonstrates that it indicates the degree of a lover's dependence and, thus, is a sign of relationship insecurity (Marelich et al., 2003; Salovey & Rodin, 1991). It also triggers a host of negative feelings and behaviors and tends to lower self-esteem (Buunk & Dijkstra, 2001; Mathes et al., 1985).

Despite the negative and unpleasant effects brought on by jealousy, some people consciously try to manipulate situations to make their partners jealous. For example, a survey of college students found that one-third of young women and one-fifth of young men flirt with others or talk about former lovers in an attempt to gain their current lover's attention and to strengthen the relationship (White, 1980). Those who tried to induce jealousy stated they were more involved in the relationship than were their partners. In most cases, however, the actual consequences of these tactics were that they hurt, not helped, the relationship.

ARE THERE GENDER DIFFERENCES IN ROMANTIC JEALOUSY?

Jealousy can develop in friendships and family relationships, but romantic jealousy appears to be the strongest and most destructive form (Felson, 1997; Puente & Cohen, 2003). Both women and men experience the "green-eyed monster," but several evolutionary psychologists propose that the two sexes are aroused by different triggering events (Buss et al., 2000; Symons, 1979; Daly & Wilson, 1996). According to these theorists, due to natural selection pressures, men are genetically predisposed to become upset over a mate's *sexual* infidelity, while women are predisposed to become upset over a mate's *emotional* infidelity. For a man, his mate's sexual philandering increases the risk that the children he supports are not his own. This is a serious male problem from a fitness point of view because it sharply reduces a man's ability to pass his genes on to the next generation. In contrast, a woman cannot be tricked into bringing up an offspring not her own. Therefore, from a fitness perspective, she should be less concerned over the simple act of sexual infidelity in her mate. What should concern her about these sexual dalliances is the loss of her mate's emotional involvement in the relationship because that could result in him withdrawing his resources for her and her offspring. This is why women should be particularly upset over a mate's emotional infidelity. In contrast, men should be more upset than women by the consequences of short-term infidelities of their mates, while women should be more upset than men by the consequences of long-term infidelities.

Is there empirical support for this theory that jealousy has different evolutionary-based triggers in women and men? Yes and no. Studies that typically support this theory have used a forced-choice hypothetical scenario in which research participants are asked to imagine a romantic relationship where their partner is either having sex with someone else or is falling in love with someone else. Participants were then asked to choose which of the two types of infidelity would be more upsetting to them. In the United States, this scenario typically produces a significant gender effect: Between 40 and 60 percent of the men report they would be more upset by sexual infidelity, whereas around 75 percent of the women report that emotional infidelity would be worse. Similar gender differences have also been found in some European and Asian countries, but in China, Korea, Germany, New Zealand, and Holland the percentage of men choosing sexual infidelity as worse drops to as little as 25 to 30 percent (Brase et al., 2004; Buss et al., 2000; Buunk et al., 1996; Geary et al., 1995; Mullen & Martin, 1994). Taking these studies together, it appears that the evolutionary-based theory of gender differences in jealousy has mixed support (Sabini & Green, 2004; Sagarin, 2005).

In reviewing these findings, some social cognitive theorists have argued that the gender differences that have been found may not reflect inherited sex-based tendencies. Instead, they may simply indicate that women and men draw different conclusions about what infidelity means about their partner's love for them (Harris, 2003a, 2003b). According to this view, men tend to think sexual infidelity is more distressing because they believe that if a woman is having sex with another man she is probably also in love with him. In other words, sexual infidelity implies emotional infidelity. In contrast, because women tend to believe that men can have sex without being in love, a man's sexual infidelity does not necessarily imply emotional infidelity. So, for women, emotional infidelity is much worse than sexual infidelity. This theory of gender differences in jealousy has found support in two American studies and one Dutch study (DeSteno & Salovey, 1996; Dijkstra et al., 2001; Harris & Christenfeld, 1996). However, when Christine Harris (2002, 2003b) studied young adults and older adults who reported having actual experience with a mate's infidelity, no gender differences in jealous responses were found; both women and men reported focusing slightly more on emotional aspects of their partner's infidelity.

So where are we in our understanding of jealousy in women and men? Regardless of whether gender differences in jealousy are primarily caused by evolutionary-based natural selection pressures or relatively complex cognitive analysis, substantial gender differences probably do not exist (DeSteno et al., 2002; Harris, 2005). Further, instead of natural selection pressures shaping different inborn responses in men and women, it is at least equally likely that natural selection shaped fairly general jealousy mechanisms that evolved outside the mating context as a response to competition between siblings in a family (Harris, 2004). In nonhuman species, sibling rivalry is not uncommon. For example, among black eagles, the older sibling in the nest routinely kills the younger one. In humans, infants as young as six months express the type of emotional displeasure typically associated with jealousy when their mothers interact with a lifesize doll or a similar-aged peer in their presence (Hart et al., 1998). Although more research is needed, it is possible that romantic jealousy has its genetic roots in sibling rivalry and not in the sex-linked human mating system.

COPING WITH JEALOUSY

Regardless of the ultimate origins of jealousy in humans, what types of coping strategies, both of the constructive and destructive variety, could you employ in contending with this destructive emotion? A number of social psychologists suggest that all jealousy-coping strategies boil down to two major goal-oriented behaviors (Bryson, 1977, 1991; Marelich & Holt, 2006):

1. Attempts to maintain the relationship
2. Attempts to maintain one's own self-esteem

As can be seen in Table 10.2, if jealous individuals desire to maintain both the relationship and their self-esteem, they will try to negotiate a mutually satisfying solution with their partners. This constructive and active strategy corresponds to Rusbult's notion of relationship *voice.* However, if jealous individuals desire to maintain their romantic relationships regardless of the loss of self-esteem, they may swallow their pride and put up with the jealousy-inducing behavior. This passive approach corresponds to Rusbult's notion of relationship *loyalty.* In contrast to these relationship-maintaining strategies, those who are more concerned with self-esteem maintenance often use verbal and physical attacks against their partner or rival. Likewise, jealous people who are not principally attempting to either maintain the relationship or bolster their self-esteem often employ self-destructive behavior.

In commenting on these different coping strategies, Sharon Brehm (1992) brings up a good point: The jealous should think about both the short-term and long-term consequences of their coping responses *before* acting. For example, verbally or physically attacking your partner may temporarily intimidate him or her into staying in the relationship while it also shores up your own sagging self-esteem; however, in the long run, it will push your partner away and lower your self-worth. Similarly, begging and pleading with your partner to end another romance may succeed in the short run, but it will threaten your self-esteem as it reduces your partner's attraction to you.

A survey of young adults conducted by Peter Salovey and Judith Rodin (1988) found that the strategy of *self-reliance* was the most effective in reducing jealousy. This strategy involved jealous individuals *containing emotional outbursts, maintaining daily routines,* and *reevaluating the importance of the relationship.* Another strategy that reduced depression and anger among the jealous was *self-bolstering,* which involved thinking positively about oneself and doing nice things for oneself. Similarly, Elaine Hatfield and Richard Rapson (1993) found that encouraging people to make new friends, or to get a job, or to go back to school helped them to think better of themselves, which in turn reduced their jealousy.

The general recommendations coming from all this jealousy work is that the best antidotes to the "green-eyed monster" are to (1) avoid emotional outbursts that are destructive to you and others, and (2) develop a feeling of self-confidence about your ability to act and survive independent of the relationship. In the final analysis, even though intimacy involves an inclusion of the other in our self-concept, our own health and the health of the relationship depends on our ability to develop a sense of self that is independent of our partners.

Table 10.2

Different Ways of Coping with Jealousy

		RELATIONSHIP MAINTAINING BEHAVIORS	
		Yes	No
SELF-ESTEEM MAINTAINING BEHAVIORS	Yes	Negotiating a mutually acceptable solution	Verbal/physical attacks against the partner or rival
	No	Clinging to the relationship	Self-destructive behaviors

THE BIG PICTURE

So what have you learned about intimacy? Do you recognize a connection between the type of attachment style that you developed with your parents and your expectations about friendships and romantic relationships? What about the different types of romantic love? In contrast to the common Hollywood depiction of passion being the cornerstone of romance, research clearly indicates that companionship is what best supports an enduring romantic relationship. Of course, passion is important, but its primary function is not to preserve your romantic relationship as much as it is to spark the initial attraction. As the relationship progresses and is sustained by your mutual companionship, passion will likely diminish; yet it will probably also sporadically reignite, reminding each of you about your sensual chemistry. Hopefully, this knowledge will inoculate you against habitually entering and leaving relationships in search of the fantasy lover whose passion never fades.

Although "true love" usually does not match the idealized Hollywood version, an important component of a satisfying, stable romantic relationship is the ability to mix positive illusion with sober reality when perceiving your partner. As with your own self-perceptions, overlooking faults and exaggerating virtues in your partner will not only satisfy the need to feel that your relationship is better than most others but can actually create the conditions necessary for your positive illusions to become realized. Here again is an example of how you can shape your social reality and create self-fulfilling prophecies.

Although you have the power to substantially shape the course of your intimate relationships, you can run into problems if you believe that they are invulnerable to outside influences. Despite the folk saying, "No third party can break up a happy relationship," research suggests that friends' and family members' approval or disapproval of your romantic relationships will significantly determine whether they survive or fail (Sprecher & Felmlee, 1992). In addition, although you might believe that "love conquers all," numerous studies indicate that outside influences such as money problems and job stress not only promote hostility in romantic relationships, but they also make partners less emotionally supportive of each other, all of which contribute to breakups (Lynch et al., 1997).

As you have learned from the attachment studies reviewed in this chapter, the important people in the early years of your life significantly shaped what you expect from intimate relationships and how you behave with those you love. In the coming years, your success in developing and nurturing your intimate relationships will not only determine the quality of your own life, it will also largely shape the next generation's views of intimacy issues.

WEB SITES

ACCESSED THROUGH www.BVTLab.com/sop6
Web sites for this chapter focus on research and theory on adult attachment dynamics and the psychology of personal relationships.

ADULT ATTACHMENT LAB
This web page for the Adult Attachment Lab, which is directed by Dr. Phillip Shaver at the University of California at Davis, advances understanding of adult attachment dynamics. Here you will find an overview of self-report measures of adult attachment security, as well as recent studies conducted from the lab.

INTERNATIONAL ASSOCIATION FOR RELATIONSHIP RESEARCH
This web site is devoted to stimulating and supporting scholarship and research on personal relationships.

SOCIAL COGNITION AND PERSONAL RELATIONSHIPS
At this web site you can learn about the formation, evolution, maintenance, and dissolution of intimate relationships.

▶ Check out our web site
www.BVTLab.com
for chapter-by-chapter flashcards, summaries, and practice quizzes.

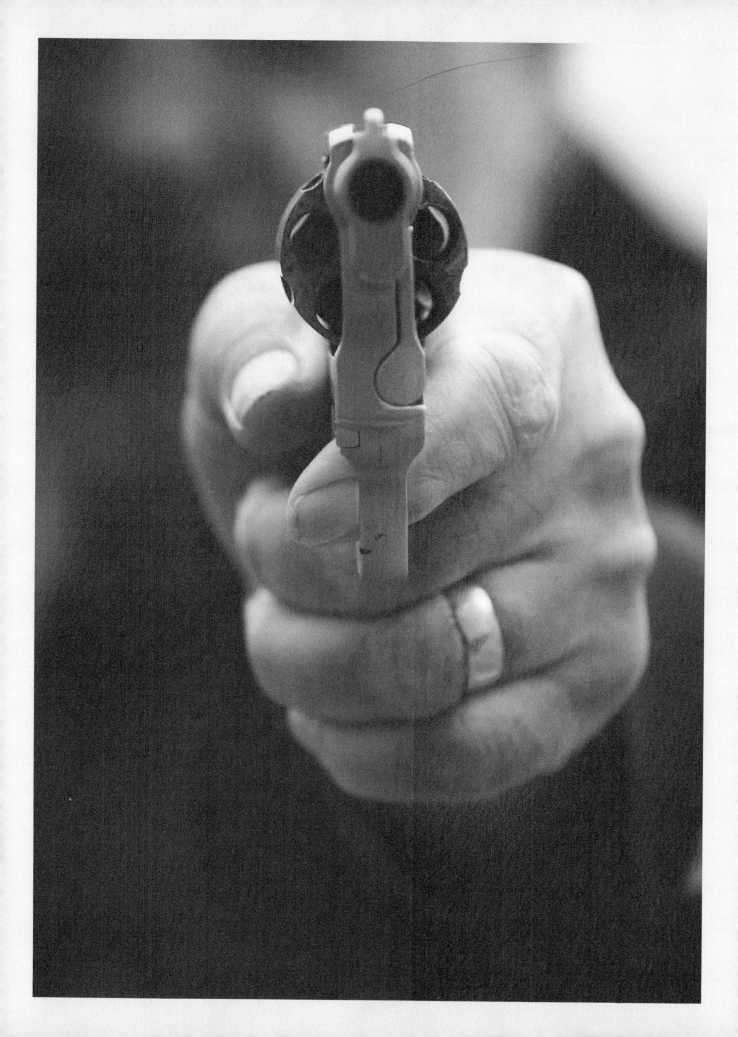

11 Chapter 11
Aggression

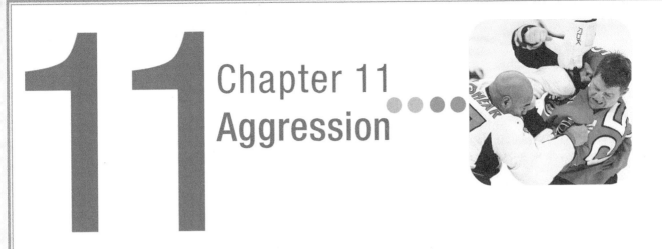

CHAPTER OUTLINE

INTRODUCTION

What Is Aggression?
Aggression is intentional harm.
Instrumental and hostile aggression have different goals.
Gender and personality moderate the expression of aggression.
Intergroup aggression is often more extreme than interpersonal aggression.

The Biology of Aggression
Evolution shaped our aggressive behavior patterns.
Biological factors influence aggressive behavior.

Aggression as a Reaction to Negative Affect
The frustration-aggression hypothesis asserts that frustration triggers aggression.
Unpleasant situations can activate aggressive thoughts and associations.
Alcohol consumption increases the likelihood of aggression.
Excitation transfer can intensify hostility-based aggression.

Learning Aggressive Behavior
Social learning theory emphasizes the shaping of aggressive behavior.
Media and video violence fosters aggressive behavior.
The "Culture of Honor" encourages male violence.

Sexual Aggression
Pornography promotes the "rape myth" and may increase violence against women.
Culture-based sexual scripts make acquaintance rape more likely.

Reducing Aggression
Punishment can both decrease and increase aggression
Inducing incompatible responses can inhibit aggression.
Teaching nonaggressive responses to provocation can control aggression.

INTRODUCTION

Twenty-year-old Tyler Peterson was the type of guy who was picked on by students when he was in high school. Yet now, two years removed from graduation, Tyler was a deputy sheriff in his small northern Wisconsin town of Crandon. In the early hours of October 7, 2007, during the high school's homecoming weekend, the young deputy sheriff drove to a house where a group of students and recent graduates were gathered for pizza and movies. Inside were his former longtime girlfriend, Jordanne Murray, and two of his best childhood buddies, Aaron Smith and Bradley Schultz. Tyler wanted to try to patch things up with Jordanne, but they instead began arguing. As their shouting intensified, others at the party began taunting Tyler, calling him a "worthless pig." Angry and rejected, the deputy stormed out of the house and then returned with his department-issued automatic rifle. In less than three minutes Tyler fired thirty rounds at those inside, killing Jordanne, his two best friends, and three other teenagers. One person survived with multiple wounds. Twelve hours later, the remorseful deputy shot and killed himself.

By all accounts, Tyler Peterson was "a normal kid" who liked to hunt and fish and loved the outdoors. So what can explain his actions on that fateful night? "I'm waiting for somebody to wake me up right now. This is a bad, bad dream," said Jenny Stahl, whose daughter, Lindsey, was the youngest victim. Rose Gerow, an aunt of one of the victims, voiced the shock and bewilderment of all the residents of this small town when she stated, "This is senseless because they were friends. These guys weren't after his girlfriend, they were just getting together." Holding hands with three other residents of the community, local pastor Bill Farr began crying as he told reporters, "This is going to take a long time for a community like this to get over. We just really need everyone's prayers right now."

WHAT IS AGGRESSION?

Before we try to understand aggression, we first need to define the concept. What is aggression, and how can we distinguish between different types? Also, what is the nature of gender and self-esteem differences in aggressive responding?

aggression

Any form of behavior that is intended to harm or injure some person, oneself, or an object

AGGRESSION IS INTENTIONAL HARM.

Although there is no universally agreed upon definition of **aggression**, one of the more common ones social psychologists use is that it is any form of behavior that is intended to harm or injure some person, oneself, or an object (Björkqvist & Niemelä, 1992).

Using this definition, we can clearly conclude that Tyler Peterson committed an aggressive act. In firing his rifle, he *intended* to harm the people at the party.

To test whether you can identify other aggressive actions based on this definition, read the following vignette and try to identify five acts of aggression.

> A thief fires a gun at a man he is trying to rob, but the bullet misses the mark and the man is uninjured. Panicked, the man accidentally knocks down a young girl as he flees the scene, and she badly cuts her knee on the pavement. Later, the girl screams in pain as a doctor puts five stitches in her knee to stop the bleeding. Upon finishing, the doctor asks the girl how badly it hurts. Still crying and now very angry, she grabs his moustache and yanks with all her might and sneers, "That's how much it hurts!" The next day, the thief is arrested and his cellmate verbally berates him for being such an inept burglar. Depressed and angry, the thief smashes his fist into the concrete cell wall, fracturing three fingers. While in the infirmary being treated for his injury, the thief angrily kicks and dents a waste container. In response, the attending medical assistant angrily shouts at the thief that if he does not calm down immediately he will face solitary confinement.

Can you correctly identify the five aggressive acts in this injury-filled story? What about the thief shooting but missing his intended victim? No harm, no aggression? Even though the bullet missed its mark, this is still an aggressive action because it was the intention of the thief to harm the man. In the second action, although the robbery victim's behavior caused injury to the girl, this is not an example of aggression because the man had no intention of hurting the child or anyone else. Neither is the behavior of the doctor treating the girl's wound an aggressive action. Although his actions caused pain and he performed those actions intentionally, the goal was to help the girl recover from her previous injury. Although the man and the doctor did not perform any aggressive actions, the little girl did. In pulling the doctor's moustache, she intentionally tried to seek retribution for the hurt she believed he caused. What about the thief's cellmate? The psychological harm intended in such verbal abuse qualifies this as an aggressive action. The fourth instance of aggression involved the prisoner's self-inflicted injury; intentional actions that cause harm to oneself are considered aggressive, even if they are impulsive. Finally, aggression can be directed against inanimate objects, as was the case when the thief kicked the waste container. The medical assistant's angry response to this outburst is not an example of aggression, but rather, illustrates assertiveness. *Assertiveness* is the ability to express yourself and your rights without violating the rights of others. People sometimes mistakenly label assertiveness as aggression. However, unlike aggression, assertiveness is designed not to hurt others.

Do you think you can identify aggression when it occurs? The reality is that some forms of aggression are more easily identified than are others.

INSTRUMENTAL AND HOSTILE AGGRESSION HAVE DIFFERENT GOALS.

instrumental aggression
· ·
The intentional use of harmful behavior so that one can achieve some other goal

❝*The wish to hurt, the momentary intoxication with pain, is the loophole through which the pervert climbs into the minds of ordinary men.*❞
- - - - - - - - - - - - - -
Jacob Bronowski, British mathematician, 1908–1974

hostile aggression
· ·
The intentional use of harmful behavior in which the goal is simply to cause injury or death to the victim

❝*A joke's a very serious thing.*❞
- - - - - - - - - - - - - -
Charles Churchill, British poet and satirist, 1731–1764

❝*Anger is a short madness.*❞
- - - - - - - - - - - - - -
Quintus Horatius Flaccus, Roman poet, 65–8 BC

There is a long history in social psychology distinguishing between two types of aggression, namely, instrumental and hostile (Geen, 1998). The aggression the thief used in his robbery attempt is an example of instrumental aggression. **Instrumental aggression**, which is also referred to as *proactive aggression*, is the intentional use of harmful behavior to achieve some other goal. In the robbery attempt, the thief used aggression as an instrument to achieve his real goal, which was obtaining the victim's money. The aggression that occurs in a military context is also often instrumental in nature. Here, the principal goal may be either to defend one's own territory or to confiscate the enemy's land. As a general rule, aggressive acts carried out with the objective of gaining material, psychological, or social benefits all fit our instrumental definition. In addition, aggression carried out to avoid punishment would also be classified as instrumental aggression. Research indicates that observers perceive acts of instrumental aggression differently, depending on their perceptions of the aggressor's motives. People who are perceived to engage in instrumental aggression fed by a desire to obtain rewards are evaluated more negatively and are thought to be less moral than those who appear to be motivated by a desire to avoid punishment (Reeder et al., 2002).

In contrast to this type of aggression, the Crandon shootings and most of the other aggressive instances in the imaginary vignette were examples of hostile aggression. **Hostile aggression**, which is also referred to as *reactive aggression*, is triggered by anger; and the goal of the intentionally harmful behavior is simply to cause injury or death to the victim. Tyler Peterson's goal was to kill those who had angered him. Similarly, the girl attacking the doctor, the thief smashing his hand against the wall, and the thief then destroying a medicine cabinet were all instances in which the aggressor's principal goal was to cause injury to another person or thing.

In thinking about instrumental and hostile aggression, it is important to keep in mind how they differ. Instrumental aggression is motivated by the anticipation of rewards or the avoidance of punishment. In that sense, it can be thought of as being relatively deliberate and rational. On the other hand, hostile aggression is not really motivated by the anticipation of rewards or the avoidance of punishments, even though these may indeed be ultimate consequences of the aggressive act. Instead, this type of aggression is often impulsive and irrational. There is a goal, but it is simply the desire to cause harm to the victim (Wann et al., 2003). Humor that is sarcastic and disparaging is a form of hostile aggression, and studies find that people who are angry rate hostile humor as funnier than those who are not angry (Kuiper et al., 2004; Ryan & Kanjorski, 1998). Hostile humor is also popular because it is a way to aggress against others without violating social norms (Ford & Ferguson, 2004; Zillmann & Bryant, 1980). Sigmund Freud (1905/2002) was the first to propose that hostile aggression is the motivation underlying a great deal of humor, describing hostile jokes as veiled attacks that allow a person to harm and triumph over another while maintaining respectability and goodness.

Research suggests that highly aggressive individuals can be distinguished by the degree to which they engage in instrumental and hostile aggression (Berkowitz, 1994). *Instrumental aggressors* tend to use "proactive" force in a cool and collected manner to attain their objectives (Atkins et al., 2001). Many robbers and schoolyard bullies fall into this category. In contrast, *hostile aggressors* tend to use "reactive" force in a highly emotional and impulsive manner. Their crimes often entail excessive use of violence due to their tempers getting out of hand. Hostile aggressors are especially likely to perceive danger in their world and to respond to ambiguous stimuli with aggression (Bushman, 1996).

Although the distinction between instrumental and hostile aggression has been useful in helping researchers grasp the complex problem of human violence, some social psychologists have criticized it as being too simplistic (Bushman & Anderson, 2001; Weinshenker & Siegel, 2002). The simple fact is that many aggressive actions cannot be neatly placed into only one of the categories. For example, a child may angrily hit another child who has taken her favorite toy, and then she may retrieve the toy while the victim cries. The motives

The sarcastic and anger-based humor of Lewis Black is an example of hostile aggression. What type of mood is associated with funnier evaluations of hostile humor?

underlying this aggression are both the infliction of pain (hostile aggression) and the recovery of the favored toy (instrumental aggression). In such instances, no clear distinctions can be made between hostile and instrumental aggression. In other instances, aggression might start out instrumentally, and then turn hostile. For example, a soldier's cool and methodical firing of a weapon at a hidden enemy may turn into impulsive rage when one of his comrades is killed. Despite this problem of multiple motives driving many aggressive actions, an extensive review of existing research suggests that there is a sound scientific basis for retaining the distinction between hostile and instrumental aggression (Vitaro & Brendgen, 2005).

GENDER AND PERSONALITY MODERATE THE EXPRESSION OF AGGRESSION.

Research has found considerable evidence that individual differences in aggression are relatively stable, meaning that some people are more prone to aggressive outbursts than others (Farrington, 1994). Attempts to better understand these individual differences have resulted in studies examining gender and personality as variables likely to moderate the expression of aggression.

Gender

A widespread belief in our culture is that men are more aggressive than women. Does research support this cultural belief? The answer is yes and no. Meta-analytic studies indicate that males and females do differ in one important kind of aggression: physical aggression. That is, males are more likely than females to engage in aggression that produces pain or physical injury (Archer, 2004; Eagly & Steffen, 1986a). This gender difference in willingness to cause physical injury is more pronounced (1) among children than adults, and (2) for unprovoked aggression than for provoked aggression (Bettencourt & Miller, 1996; Pellegrini & Bartini, 2001). In contrast, men and women are similar to one another in their verbal aggression and in expressing feelings of anger toward members of the other sex, but men are slightly more likely than women to express verbal aggression toward same-sex persons (Archer & Côté, 2005).

Although gender differences are considerably smaller than what gender stereotypes suggest, women and men do appear to have different social representations of their physical aggression. A number of studies have found that women tend to view their aggression as being stress-induced and precipitated by a loss of self-control that erupts into an antisocial act (Campbell et al., 1996, 1997b). As such, they perceive their aggression as a negative experience. Men, in contrast, are more likely to perceive their aggression as a means of exerting control over others and reclaiming social power and self-esteem (Bosson et al., 2009). Retaining social power and receiving proper respect is more important for men than it is for women, and thus, male aggression is more likely than female aggression to be fueled by perceptions of disrespect (Blincoe & Harris, 2011). Due to their different social perceptions, men often believe that resorting to physical violence is a positive experience. Further, they often mistakenly assume that others will not only approve of them acting aggressively but that their physical aggression will make them more attractive to women (Vandello et al., 2009). These gender differences in the experience of physical aggression may mean that the more spontaneous and unplanned behaviors typical of hostile aggression are more descriptive of the antisocial actions of women, while the more planned and calculated actions of instrumental aggression are more descriptive of male aggression.

One form of aggression that researchers largely ignored for many years is **indirect aggression**, a form of social manipulation in which the aggressor attempts to harm another person without a face-to-face encounter (Archer & Coyne, 2005; Vaillancourt, 2005).

Critical THINKING

Why might people who come from a collectivist cultural background be less likely to react negatively to teasing and not perceive it as a form of aggression compared to people who have a strong individualist background?

indirect aggression
. . . .
A form of aggressive manipulation involving attempts to harm another person without a face-to-face encounter (also known as relational aggression).

Research suggests that women of all ages engage in more indirect aggression, such as spreading bad or false stories about others or revealing someone's secrets, than men. Why might these gender differences exist?

Gossiping, spreading bad or false stories about someone, telling others not to associate with a person, and revealing someone's secrets are all examples of indirect aggression. The field studies by Finnish social psychologists Kaj Björkqvist and Kirsti Lagerspetz (see Figure 11.1) found that among adolescents in Finland, girls were more likely than boys to use indirect aggression (Björkqvist et al., 1992; Lagerspetz et al., 1988). Their research further indicated that while male physical aggression decreased significantly during adolescence, teenage girls continued to exhibit higher levels of indirect aggression

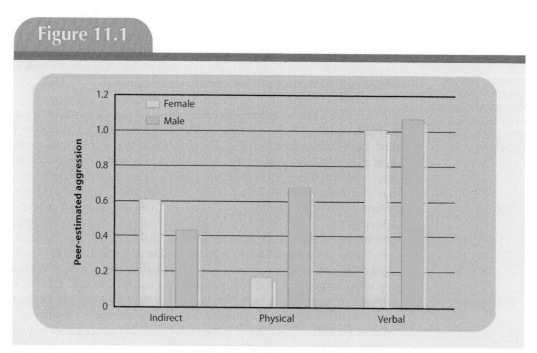

Figure 11.1

Gender Comparisons in Aggressive Strategies

In a study of the aggressive styles used by adolescents in Finland, Björkqvist and his colleagues (1992) found that verbal aggression (for example, yelling, insulting, name-calling) is the most used by both boys and girls. Boys display more physical aggression (hitting, kicking, shoving), whereas girls utilize more indirect forms of aggression (gossiping, writing nasty notes about another, telling bad or false stories).

at all age levels. Subsequent studies in other countries found similar preferences for indirect aggression among girls and women (Campbell, 1999; Fujihara et al., 1999; Theron et al., 2000; Vaillancourt, 2005). One of the insights gained by this research is that, by discovering that aggression is not always direct and physical, we more clearly see the need to reexamine the "peaceful female" stereotype.

One important question emerging from these studies is: Why might girls and women be more likely to choose indirect rather than direct aggressive means? Björkqvist and Lagerspetz suggest four possible reasons. One explanation is that girls are discouraged more than boys from engaging in direct acts of aggression. Because of this different gender socialization pattern, females may use more indirect aggression simply because it is more socially acceptable (Campbell, 1999). Another possibility involves the social structure of same-sex peer groups during childhood and adolescence. Girls typically form small, intimate play groups, while boys' groups tend to be bigger and less defined (Maccoby, 1990). Björkqvist and Lagerspetz suggest that indirect aggression may be more effective in the intimate social settings girls usually inhabit because such surroundings create greater opportunities to discover and pass on personal information about others. A third possibility has to do with the relative physical strengths of the two sexes. Women, typically being smaller than men, may have learned that indirect forms of aggression are more effective and less costly than direct personal attack. Finally, because research indicates that indirect retaliation to aggression is more common in older than in younger children, Lagerspetz and Björkqvist (1994) suggest that the greater use of indirect means by females during adolescence may reflect their earlier social maturation.

In our examination of gender differences in aggression, we must also consider the impact that culture has on people's willingness to act in an aggressive manner. Although a good deal of cross-cultural research indicates that women are less physically aggressive than men and less likely to commit homicide (Daly & Wilson, 1988), a number of societies encourage and teach women to be physically aggressive. For example, in her study of aggression among the islanders of Margarita, Venezuela, anthropologist H. B. Kimberley Cook (1992) discovered that aggression was an integral aspect of being a woman in Margarita. As one elderly woman told her:

> Women in Margarita are "guapa" (physically strong). When we fight, we punch and tear each other's hair. A long time ago, I had a fight with a woman. I chased her all around the ranchería. When I caught her, I grabbed her by the hair and pushed her face into the mud. She was screaming, but I wouldn't let go. I was stronger and I laughed. She didn't talk to me for years afterwards, but later we became friends again. (Cook, 1992, p. 156)

Unlike many women in North America, Margariteño women do not relate their aggression to a loss of self-control. Instead, their antisocial actions are an exercise of control, usually employed against other women in disputes over authority or jealousy concerning a man. When combined with the findings from other cross-cultural aggression studies (Burbank, 1987), Cook's observations illustrate that although women are less lethal and generally less physically aggressive than men, they are by no means the "gentle sex." As a species, we all share the capacity to cause harm to one another.

Personality

A major program of research conducted by Italian social psychologist Gian Vittorio Caprara and his associates (1994, 1996) indicates that three personality traits consistently related to aggression are *irritability* (the tendency to explode at the slightest provocation), *rumination* (the tendency to retain feelings of anger following provocation), and *emotional susceptibility* (the tendency to experience feelings of discomfort and inadequacy). Additional research indicates that adolescents who score low on the personality trait of *agreeableness*—with low scores associated with irritability, ruthlessness, and rudeness—tend to have high levels of both direct and indirect aggression (Gleason et al., 2004). A meta-analysis of sixty-three studies involving both children and adults found that irritability was positively associated with both provoked and unprovoked aggression, but rumination and emotional susceptibility were associated with greater aggression only after provocation (Bettencourt et al., 2006). Together, these findings suggest that highly aggressive people have a hard time controlling their emotions; they not only have quick tempers but also "stew in their own angry juices" following a confrontation (Denson et al., 2011).

The fact that aggressive-prone individuals tend to experience feelings of inadequacy is relevant to research discussed in Chapter 3 (p. 99) suggesting that aggression is one way some people seek to maintain or restore their self-esteem. For many years, it was thought that only low self-esteem individuals were susceptible to these types of aggressive outbursts, but there actually is little evidence to support this claim. For example, depressed people are less aggressive than nondepressed people, and individuals who are shy and self-deprecating are underrepresented among populations of violent criminals (Baumeister & Boden, 1998). A comprehensive review of the research literature suggests that aggression is more commonly a result of threats to highly favorable views of the self and is most likely to occur when a person's high self-esteem is fragile and unstable (Baumeister et al., 1996; Kernis & Goldman, 2006). Apparently, in these instances, aggression is a defensive reaction to avoid having to make any downward revision of self-esteem (Kirkpatrick et al., 2002; Tangney et al., 1992).

One puzzling aspect of habitual, hot-tempered aggression is that it occurs despite the aggressor often experiencing long-term negative consequences, such as losing friends or being arrested and jailed. Why don't these aggressive-prone individuals learn from their mistakes? A series of studies suggest that a possible reason for these aggressive individuals often not taking long-term consequences into account is that they tend to be habitually impulsive (Joireman et al., 2003). Instead of thinking of future consequences, many aggressive-prone individuals focus on the immediate consequences of their aggressive behavior, which they perceive as beneficial (for example, winning an argument or preserving their self-esteem).

INTERGROUP AGGRESSION IS OFTEN MORE EXTREME THAN INTERPERSONAL AGGRESSION.

> " *War nourishes war.* "
> ――――――――――
> Johann Schiller, German writer and philosopher, 1759–1805

Our analysis in this chapter primarily focuses on interpersonal acts of aggression, but violence also occurs on the group level. Indeed, it has been estimated that approximately 36 million people have died in wars fought over the past one hundred years and at least 119 million more have been killed by government genocide, massacres, and other mass killings (Bond, 2004; Rosenberg & Mercy, 1991). In comparing interpersonal versus intergroup acts of aggression, research indicates that group-initiated aggression is often more intense and harmful (Meier & Hinsz, 2004). What are some of the psychological factors that make collective aggression more likely and also more deadly?

As discussed in Chapter 6, *realistic group conflict theory* contends that when groups are in conflict, two important changes occur in each group. The first change involves increased hostility toward the opposing outgroup, while the second change involves an intensification of ingroup loyalty (Staub, 2004). This pattern of behavior is referred to as *ethnocentrism.* Both of these changes took place in the United States following the terrorist attacks of September 11, 2001; hatred of Islamic terrorist Osama bin Laden and his followers grew, as did patriotism. Similar changes had already taken place among the terrorists and their supporters long before the attack (Cooper, 2001; Crenshaw, 2000). In fact, the terrorists' hostility was carried to such an extreme that they cognitively placed the United States—the target outgroup—into an extremely negative social category that excluded us from acceptable norms and values (Bar-Tal, 1990; Demoulin et al., 2004). This process of **delegitimization** effectively removes the target outgroup from the perceived world of humanity, and thus, ingroup members do not feel inhibited about mistreating and aggressing against them (Castano & Giner-Sorolla, 2006; Leidner et al., 2010). *They* are not like us. *They* are trying to destroy our way of life. *They* deserve our aggression. Social neuroscience research indicates that the brain's medial prefrontal cortex—an area important for higher-order cognitive processing and decision making—is not as active when people are focused on delegitimized targets (Harris & Fiske, 2011).

delegitimization
. . . .
The process of cognitively placing an outgroup into an extremely negative social category that excludes them from acceptable norms and values, thereby eliminating inhibitions against harming them

Delegitimization often follows incidents of harm to one's ingroup by members of an outgroup (Freyd, 2002; Gerstenfeld, 2002). For example, shortly after the United States' invasion of Iraq, most Americans viewed Iraqi citizens with sympathy and compassion, considering them victims of Saddam Hussein's repressive regime. However, one year later, many Americans' attitudes toward Iraqi citizens had become hostile due to daily reports of U.S. soldiers being killed by Iraqis who opposed the foreign occupation. Likewise, many Iraqi citizens were initially grateful for the removal of their dictator by American troops. Yet, when these same troops were perceived as causing the deaths of many innocent Iraqis, Iraqis' attitudes toward American soldiers became increasingly hostile. Throughout both countries, political leaders, social commentators, and ordinary citizens increasingly defined the opposing country or faction within the country as an "evil" group that must be hunted down and destroyed.

Another reason collective aggression is more intense and harmful than individual aggression is due to the effects of group polarization. As discussed in Chapter 8 (pp. 328–330), *group polarization* refers to group-produced enhancement or exaggeration of members' initial attitudes following discussion. Due to group polarization effects, when planning collective aggression, group members' initial individual attitudes about an outgroup become more hostile after discussing how they should harm and punish their enemies.

Collective aggression not only has negative consequences for those who are delegitimized; it also hurts the aggressor group. In a cross-national study of 110 countries, Dane Archer and Rosemary Gartner (1984) found a strong tendency for violent crime to increase after major wars, in both defeated and victorious nations. This increase in aggression was found among civilians as well as war veterans, which suggests that there is a generalized behavioral shift across society concerning how to resolve disputes. These results were confirmed in a subsequent study of 186 societies (Ember & Ember, 1994), with additional research indicating that societies with more war tend to have more warlike sports and practice more severe punishments for all kinds of crimes (see Bond, 2004). The likely reason for this behavioral shift is that war legitimizes violence as an acceptable remedy for conflict. The social norms of cultures that go to war indirectly endorse aggression as "the correct way to behave." Based on these findings, Carol and Melvin Ember (1994) offer the following recommendation:

> If we want to reduce the likelihood of interpersonal violence in our society, we may mostly need to reduce the likelihood of war, which would minimize the need to socialize for aggression and possibly reduce the likelihood of all violence. (p. 643)

"Let me make very clear the position of my government and our country: We do not condone torture. I have never ordered torture. I will never order torture. The values of this country are such that torture is not a part of our soul and our being."

George W. Bush, U.S. president, June 25, 2004

SECTION SUMMARY

- Aggression involves any form of behavior that is intended to harm or injure some person, oneself, or an object.

- Instrumental aggression is the use of harmful behavior to achieve some other goal.

- In hostile aggression, harming another is the goal of the attack.

- Men are more physically aggressive, but women engage in more indirect aggression.

- Personality traits found in aggressive-prone persons include the following:

  irritability   rumination

  emotional   susceptibility

- Intergroup aggression is more extreme than interpersonal aggression because it often leads to delegitimization, which eliminates aggressive inhibitions against outgroup members.

THE BIOLOGY OF AGGRESSION

Besides deaths resulting from collective aggression, each year in the United States, about seventeen thousand people are killed in violent assaults (Centers for Disease Control, 2006). Worldwide, more than 563,000 homicides occur each year, representing a global rate of roughly 10.7 for every 100,000 individuals (Mercy & Hammond, 1999). Even when people do not directly participate in aggressive acts themselves, many enjoy watching others do so in action adventure films or sporting events (Mustonen, 1997). Aggression even manifests itself in the play guns and toy soldiers we produce and purchase for our children's enjoyment. Judging from their faces as they play with these toys, enjoyment is what it often brings them. Based on these observations, is it reasonable to conclude that the human race has an inborn tendency for aggression?

EVOLUTION SHAPED OUR AGGRESSIVE BEHAVIOR PATTERNS.

A number of social scientists concur with the judgment that we are an innately aggressive species. In fact, for more than one hundred years, many biologically oriented scientists have argued that aggression in humans—as well as aggression in other species—can be understood as an adaptive response to the environment. Evolutionary psychologists believe that males of many species, including our own, are more aggressive and have a stronger social dominance orientation than females, because aggression and dominance seeking have been the primary ways males have gained sexual access to females (Buss & Duntley, 2003). That is, by physically intimidating—and sometimes even killing—less aggressive males, the more aggressive males became socially dominant and thus were more likely to sexually reproduce. Unlike males, females' reproductive success did not depend on their level of aggression. Over many generations, this difference in the importance of aggression and dominance seeking in male and female reproductive success led to genetically based differences in male and female aggression.

One important point to keep in mind about evolutionary theory is that it assumes that aggression is not in itself a "bad" or "destructive" behavior; it is a way to secure resources, survive, and successfully reproduce (Tremblay & Nagin, 2005). However, unlike earlier instinct theories that emphasized individual survival (Lorenz, 1966), modern evolutionary theories stress genetic survival (Buss & Shackelford, 1997). From this perspective, genetic survival necessitates that aggression should be selective because relatives share many more of the same genes than strangers. In other words, relatives should not be attacked, for this reduces the likelihood that one's gene pool will be passed on to future generations. In general, research supports this hypothesis; aggression is much more likely to be directed against nonrelatives, and when relatives are attacked, they tend to be "relatives by marriage." For example, stepchildren, who by definition do not have genetic ties to one of their parents, are much more likely to be abused and killed than are other children (Daly & Wilson, 1991, 1996; Harris et al., 2007). A similar pattern is found in other animal species (Lore & Schultz, 1993).

> ❝The impulse to mar and to destroy is as ancient and almost nearly as universal as the impulse to create. The one is an easier way than the other of demonstrating power.❞
>
> Joseph Wood Krutch, U.S. author and critic, 1893–1970

Each year in the United States about 17,000 people are killed in violent assaults, which is a substantially higher assault rate than fifty years ago. On October 12, 2011, a man went into the Salon Meritage and fatally shot his ex-wife and seven more people, killing six of the eight victims.

One problem with solely relying on an evolutionary-based explanation for aggression in humans is that—as Figure 11.2 illustrates—levels of aggression vary so widely across cultures. A related problem is that wide differences in aggression occur within cultures over time. For example, three hundred years ago, Sweden had one of the highest documented rates of interpersonal violence in the Western world, and today it has one of the lowest (Lagerspetz, 1985). Genetic changes in human groups over such a short (in terms of evolution) time period are simply not possible. Instead, social and cultural factors are the more likely causes. Of course, this does not mean that evolutionary factors do not influence human aggression. It simply means that evolutionary forces, by themselves, cannot adequately explain human aggression.

BIOLOGICAL FACTORS INFLUENCE AGGRESSIVE BEHAVIOR.

Beyond focusing on how aggressive tendencies may have been shaped over hundreds of thousands of generations, scientists also study whether individual aggressive tendencies

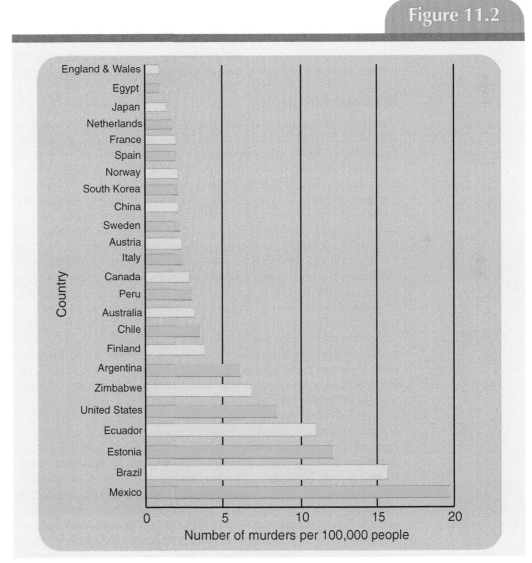

Figure 11.2

Murder Rates Around the Globe

A United Nations study reported that not only does the murder rate vary widely from country to country, but also that the murder rates within many countries change substantially from year to year. Do these data suggest that evolutionary-based explanations of aggression are false? How might you explain the data by considering both evolutionary and cultural factors in your analysis?

are inherited and whether hormonal fluctuations influence later aggressive responses. Unlike early instinct theories, contemporary biologists and evolutionary theorists do not argue that aggressive behavior is determined by some inborn fixed tendency. Instead, they propose that these biological background variables influence how we respond to situational provocations.

Behavior Genetics

Research on identical and fraternal twins in the field of behavior genetics suggests that our individual aggressiveness is most likely partly due to inheritance (Baker et al., 2007; Miles & Carey, 1997). That is, twins who share exactly the same genetic material (identical twins) tend to have more similar aggressive tendencies than twins who share only 50 percent of the same genes (fraternal twins). One problem with this research, however, is that parents tend to treat identical twins more similarly than fraternal twins, and thus, it is difficult for twin studies to clearly distinguish between genetic and environmental determinants of aggression (McCord, 1994). Despite this difficulty, research indicates that genetic and environmental factors often interact in shaping aggression. For example, a recent Swedish longitudinal study of more than 1,300 twin pairs found that parents' often harsh punishment of their children's early genetically influenced aggressive tendencies actually increases their later aggressive behavior (Narusyte et al., 2007). Thus, while it is clear that heritability plays a role in shaping human aggression, its degree of influence is still unknown (DiLalla, 2002; Pérusse & Gendreau, 2005).

Hormonal Activity

Chemical messengers in the bloodstream, known as hormones, clearly influence human aggression, but the exact nature of this relationship is still not clear (Johnson et al., 2007; Susman et al., 2007). The hormone that has been the focus of most research is *testosterone*, the most important male sex hormone (Liening & Joseph, 2010; Victoroff et al., 2011). Many experts believe that heightened testosterone levels make aggression more likely, and that aggression—or even nonaggressive competition—causes increases in testosterone levels. Consistent with this thinking, a number of studies have found higher than normal levels of testosterone in individuals of both sexes who exhibit high levels of social dominance, competitiveness, and aggression (Adelson, 2004; Carlson, 2004).

Recent studies examining the testosterone-aggression link find that this hormone appears to affect both conscious and unconscious thinking in ways that provoke anger and inhibit empathy and fear (van Honk & Schutter, 2007). When encountering angry faces, most people immediately detect a possible threat, consciously experience some degree of fear, and quickly respond in a nonthreatening way that reduces the likelihood of aggression in the situation. Similarly, when encountering fearful faces, most individuals consciously experience empathy and thereby are less likely to attack these fearful people (Toates, 2006). Interestingly, these typical responses are not found among individuals with high levels of testosterone. Research indicates that at implicit levels of processing, testosterone increases people's emotional sensitivity to angry faces, resulting in increased neural activity in brain regions critically involved in impulsive aggressive behavior (Hermans et al., 2008; van Honk & Schutter, 2007). Simultaneously, at conscious levels of processing, testosterone reduces the recognition of both angry and fearful faces, which causes individuals with high levels of testosterone to experience less fear when encountering an angry person and also less empathy when encountering a fearful person (Hermans et al., 2006a & b). Together, this research suggests that testosterone disrupts and redirects neural activity that normally inhibits aggressive behavior. In contrast to most people, when confronted by an angry person, individuals with high levels of testosterone are more prone to behave aggressively because they experience more implicit anger and less explicit fear. Similarly, when in the presence of a fearful person, individuals with high levels of testosterone behave more aggressively because they consciously feel less empathy.

Besides testosterone, the neurotransmitter *serotonin* also plays a role in aggressive behavior (Takahashi et al., 2011). Neurotransmitters are the brain's chemical messengers and serotonin is important in regulating aggression by operating like a braking mechanism on the type of impulsive actions often associated with hostile aggression. Low levels of serotonin in the brain fail to provide adequate control over such impulsive aggression (Almeida et al., 2011). Drugs that increase serotonin levels in the brain are effective in reducing aggression, along with other impulsive anti-social behaviors. For example, such drugs are often used to treat individuals who experience "road rage" while driving (Sansone & Sansone, 2010).

SECTION SUMMARY

- Evolutionary theorists contend that aggressive tendencies are selective and based on the principle of genetic survival.

- Biological research suggests that individual differences in aggressiveness are partly due to inheritance and hormonal changes.

AGGRESSION AS A REACTION TO NEGATIVE AFFECT

Japanese are world-famous for their politeness. One notable exception to this courteous behavior is a two-hundred-year-old event that takes place just before midnight on New Year's Eve in Ashikaga, a city fifty miles north of Tokyo. In what outsiders might consider to be a very strange festival, people walk in a procession up a dark mountain road to the Saishoji Temple, screaming curses at those who have frustrated them during the previous twelve months. "You idiot!" "Give me a raise!" "My teacher is stupid!" Although these words of blame, hostility, and anger would almost never be directed at the real sources of the Japanese's frustration, participants believe the screaming is beneficial. Is such behavior really beneficial to people? Does it reduce aggressive tendencies?

THE FRUSTRATION-AGGRESSION HYPOTHESIS ASSERTS THAT FRUSTRATION TRIGGERS AGGRESSION.

frustration-aggression hypothesis
. . . .
The theory that frustration causes aggression

catharsis
. . . .
The reduction in the aggressive drive following an aggressive act

If you had asked a group of social psychologists these questions in 1939, they most likely would have replied that releasing pent-up frustrations in this manner was a very good idea. At that time, John Dollard, Neal Miller, Leonard Doob, O. H. Mowrer, and Robert Sears had just published their now classic monograph, *Frustration and Aggression*, which outlined what came to be the most popular theory of aggression in the social sciences, namely the **frustration-aggression hypothesis**. They defined frustration as any external condition that prevents you from obtaining the pleasures you had expected to enjoy. In other words, if you are prevented from doing something that you want to do, you become frustrated. The original theory had three main propositions. The first proposition was that frustration always elicits the drive to attack others. The second proposition was that every act of aggression could be traced to some previous frustration (this essentially meant that all aggression is of the hostile variety). The third proposition was that engaging in aggression causes **catharsis**, which is the reduction in the aggressive drive following an aggressive act.

Research supports the general proposition that frustration can cause aggression. For example, archival studies have found a negative correlation between economic conditions and lynchings of African Americans in the pre-1930s South (Hepworth & West, 1988; Hovland & Sears, 1940; Tolnay & Beck, 1995). When Southern states experienced economic depression due to a drop in cotton prices, White southerners appeared to vent their frustration by lynching Blacks. In other words, African Americans became the scapegoats of White displaced aggression. Other studies have found a correlation between the loss of jobs in communities and an increase in child abuse and other violent behavior (Catalano et al., 1993; Steinberg et al., 1981).

Although this research has established a link between frustration and aggression, additional studies indicate that this link is subject to a rapid rate of decay (Green et al., 1998). If frustration is not acted upon quickly (often less than an hour), people are unlikely to aggress (Buvinic & Berkowitz, 1976). Frustration is most likely to produce an inclination to aggress when the person believes the hindrance was unfair and deliberate (Krieglmeyer et al., 2009). Thus, if someone catches your heel and sends you tumbling to the ground, you are less likely to hold it against him if you believe it was an accident rather than deliberate. Another basis for criticizing the theory was its contention that frustration was the root cause of all aggression. Subsequent research has clearly shown that frustration is simply one among many causes of aggression.

Finally, the claim that aggressive tendencies are reduced following the expression of aggression has been subjected to a great deal of scientific scrutiny. Although this notion of catharsis reflects a common belief that people can purge themselves of powerful emotions by "letting off steam" or "getting it off their chests," little empirical evidence supports this proposition.

In one representative study, Shahbaz Mallick and Boyd McCandless (1966) had third-grade girls and boys work on a block-construction task in pairs. What the young participants did not realize, however, was that the child working with them was a confederate who had been instructed to either allow participants to complete the block-construction task or to act very clumsy and impede completion. Immediately following this frustrating or non-frustrating experience, participants performed an intervening activity for about eight minutes. This activity either involved shooting a toy gun at a target or talking with the experimenter. Half of the children who talked with the experimenter were told during the course of the conversation that their partner had been tired and upset, while the rest merely engaged in neutral talk with the experimenter. At the end of this intervening activity, the young confederate was brought into another room, supposedly to work on another block-construction task. Each of the naive participants then was given an opportunity to hinder the confederate's progress by pushing a "hurt" button that would disrupt the confederate's work. Aggression was measured by the number of times the child pushed the button.

As Figure 11.3 shows, frustration generally increased aggression, except when participants were told that fatigue and emotional strain caused the confederate's clumsiness. This finding replicates previously discussed research indicating that aggression is much more likely following intentional rather than unintentional frustration. More important for our discussion of catharsis, however, is the fact that children's aggressive play did not result in any reduction in the number of attacks on the frustrator. Put simply, there is no evidence in these findings for catharsis. Engaging in make-believe violence does not purge aggressive drives (Bushman, 2002).

Direct acts of aggression also do not cause catharsis. In fact, a number of experiments indicate that people who are given the opportunity to aggress directly against someone who has frustrated them often become more aggressive, not less so (Buss, 1966; Geen, 1968). Sociologist Murray Straus's research indicates that this sort of escalation of aggression is a common pattern in domestic violence. Family conflicts often begin with verbal quarreling, which then escalates to screaming and yelling, and finally to physical aggression (Houry et al., 2004; Straus & Gelles, 1990). In contrast, households that engage in little or no verbal aggression rarely ever experience physical violence (less than half of 1 percent). Despite the lack of research support for catharsis, the popular media and many mental health professionals continue to advocate its use. For example, a common belief among many marriage counselors is that "couples who fight [verbally] together, stay together"—as long as they do not engage in vindictive verbal attacks. As Straus points out, however, the research literature indicates that once verbal aggression begins, it is difficult to keep it within manageable bounds. In such instances, advocating the venting of anger through aggressive means may be worse than useless—it may cause a general increase in aggressive behavior. This does not mean you should keep your frustrations and anger bottled up inside yourself. However, instead of yelling at others—or even punching a pillow when angry—the best strategy is to convey your feelings calmly and clearly, without being intentionally hurtful.

UNPLEASANT SITUATIONS CAN ACTIVATE AGGRESSIVE THOUGHTS AND ASSOCIATIONS.

Realizing that the association between frustration and aggression had been overstated, in the late 1960s Leonard Berkowitz (1969, 1989) developed a new theory to explain

Figure 11.3

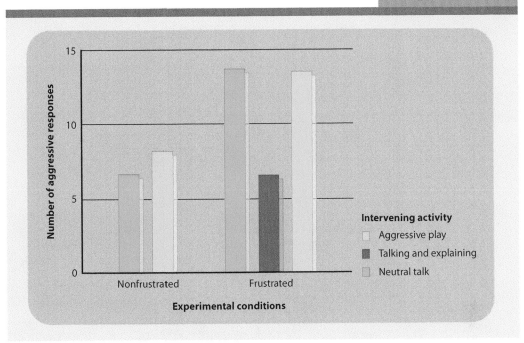

Does Children's Aggressive Play Have a Cathartic Effect?

In contradiction to the catharsis hypothesis, Mallick and McCandless (1966) found that children who had been frustrated by a "clumsy" child confederate showed no reduction in their aggressive responses after engaging in imaginary aggression. What did reduce aggression in the frustrated children was being told that the confederate's clumsiness had been caused by fatigue and strain (talking and explaining condition). What do these findings suggest about recommendations that aggression can be decreased by having people engage in make-believe violence?

how hostile aggression is often triggered by circumstances that arouse negative feelings. He asserted that frustration is just one of many factors that can stimulate negative affect. Besides frustration, other aversive factors such as pain, extreme temperatures, and encountering disliked people can also cause negative affect. It is this negative affect, and not frustration itself, that stimulates the inclination to aggress. The stronger the negative affect, whether it is caused by frustration or by some other aversive experience, the greater the aggressive inclination.

Cognitive-Associative Networks

cognitive-neoassociationist model
· ·
A theory of impulsive aggression that aversive events produce negative affect, which stimulates the inclination to aggress

Berkowitz named his theory the **cognitive-neoassociationist model** because he believes that when we experience negative affect due to some unpleasant condition, this affect is encoded into memory and becomes cognitively associated with specific types of negative thoughts, emotions, physiological responses, and reflexive behaviors (see Figure 11.4). Although these cognitive-associative networks are initially weak, the more they are activated, the stronger they become (Ratcliff & McKoon, 1994). When these associations are sufficiently strong, activating any one of them will likely activate the others, a process known as *priming* (see Chapter 4, p. 114). Thus, when we recall a past occasion in which we were extremely angry, this memory may prime hostile thoughts, angry feelings, and even anger/aggression-related reflexive actions, such as clenched fists and gritted teeth. One important implication of this theory is that even when our surroundings do not elicit negative affect, simply thinking about aggression can set us on the path to its activation (Dodge, 2011).

Initial "Fight" or "Flight" Tendencies

In addition to describing how cognitive-associative networks are formed, the cognitive-neoassociationist model further proposes that an aversive event initially activates not

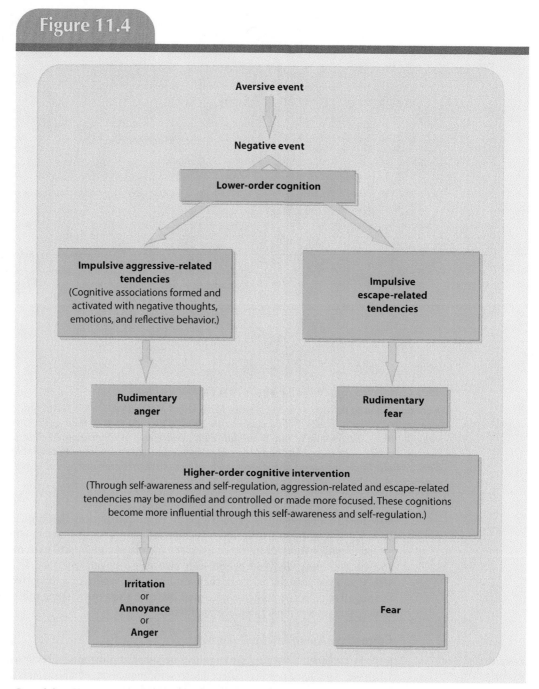

Cognitive-Neoassociationist Model of Hostile Aggression

Leonard Berkowitz's theory of impulsive aggression states that aversive events produce negative affect. This negative affect, in turn, stimulates the inclination to aggress. How can this aggressive inclination be "short-circuited"?

one, but two different networks at the same time. One network is related to the impulsive aggression-related tendencies already described (the fight response), while the other is related to impulsive escape-related tendencies (the flight response). Whether we react to negative affect with "fight" or "flight" depends on our (1) genetic predispositions, (2) prior conditioning and learning, and (3) attention to aspects of the situation that facilitate or inhibit aggression (Berkowitz, 1993). Because our present objective is to understand how aversive events lead to aggression, we will concentrate on the fight-response side of this model (the left side of Figure 11.4).

"Unthinking" Aggressive Responses

One thing to keep in mind is that the cognitive processes discussed thus far are simply impulsive reactions to negative affect, and thus, they represent only the potential first stage in aggression. The negative thoughts, emotions, and reflexive actions evoked in the cognitive-associative networks at this stage are primitive, or rudimentary, and have yet to be shaped and developed by higher-order cognitive processes of the brain's medial prefrontal cortex (Harris & Fiske, 2011). If this more-sophisticated thinking does not come into play, we may simply lash out with anger or aggression, and our targets may not even be those who triggered our anger (Bushman et al., 2005).

Higher-Order Cognitive Intervention

Although aggression is likely if we reflexively respond to negative affect, a very different outcome often occurs if higher-order cognitive processes are activated and we begin self-regulating. This represents stage two in the aggressive response. The cognitive-neoassociationist model contends that if these aggression-related tendencies are subjected to self-regulation, they are often modified and controlled. What causes the aggression-related tendencies in stage one to come under the control of the more complex cognitive processes of stage two? As previously discussed in Chapter 3 (p. 74), these cognitive control mechanisms are activated when we become self-aware and attend to what we are thinking, feeling, and doing (Mischel et al., 1996). Thus, when frustrated, we may try to make sense of—and control—our negative feelings before acting. Research indicates that individuals who are slow to anger when provoked do indeed experience hostile feelings, but they are much more likely than those with hot tempers to spontaneously harness self-regulatory resources and "cool" their anger (Wilkowski & Robinson, 2007). This type of higher-order thinking does not guarantee a nonaggressive response, but it does make it more likely (Kuppens et al., 2004).

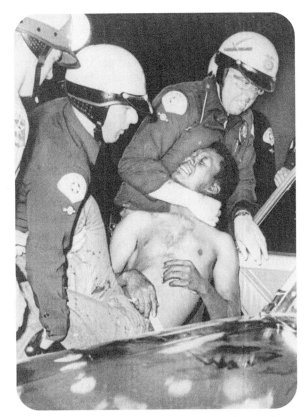

How does the heat hypothesis partly account for the increased levels of aggression in urban areas during the 1960s summer months?

The "Heat Hypothesis"

Beyond providing a better explanation for the association between frustration and aggression, the primary importance of the cognitive-neoassociationist model is in its explanation of our impulsive and affect-driven reactions to aggression. The model proposes that events resulting in particularly intense levels of negative affect generate strong activation of aggression-related cognitions and emotions, which produce powerful feelings of anger and inclinations to aggress.

One very common unpleasant situation that has often been associated with such aggressive responses is hot weather. Consistent with the cognitive-neoassociationist model, laboratory experiments demonstrate that hot temperatures increase hostile thoughts and feelings (Anderson et al., 1995). Also consistent with the model is the finding of an upward spiral effect, in which the discomfort caused by high temperatures is related to increased levels of aggression (Anderson et al., 1997). For example, archival studies suggest that the urban riots that erupted in many American cities in the 1960s were most likely to occur on hot days and then to diminish in intensity as the weather cooled (Carlsmith & Anderson, 1979). This effect also occurs for such aggressive behaviors as murder, assault, rape, and spousal abuse (Anderson & Anderson, 1984, 1996; Bushman et al., 2005). Although there is evidence that extremely high temperatures can actually lower aggression-related crimes due to people being less socially active (Cohn & Rotton, 2005; Rotton & Cohn, 2000), in general, there is a positive relationship between hot weather and hot tempers.

The heat hypothesis also explains why an analysis of more than fifty-seven thousand Major League baseball games finds that pitchers who play in hot weather are much more likely than those who play in cooler weather to retaliate and hit opposing batters after one of their teammates has been hit by a pitch (Larrick et al., 2011). It appears that high temperatures increase retaliation by pitchers because the pitchers are more likely to become angry and make hostile attributions about why their own teammates were hit by a pitch, and also because the high temperatures lower their inhibitions against retaliation.

The fact that hot temperatures appear to increase impulsive, hostile aggression has some interesting practical implications. First, it suggests that the frequency of hostile outbursts could be reduced in temperature-controlled environments. For example, using air conditioning in prisons might reduce the problems of inmate violence. Similar reductions of hostile aggression might also be achieved by controlling the temperatures in schools and work environments. Of course, air conditioning will not create harmony in these settings, but it may make it easier for people to curb their impulse to lash out when annoyed or provoked. Second, the heat hypothesis has obvious implications for global warming. By the middle of the twenty-first century, we can expect global temperatures to increase by two to eight degrees, which means there will be many more hot days in the summer months (Niemeyer et al., 2005). Craig Anderson (2001) estimates that such temperature increases could increase annual serious and deadly assaults by more than twenty-four thousand incidents in the United States. Unless we discover some way to "air condition" the planet, future generations may become all too familiar with the negative effects of the heat hypothesis.

Aggressive Cues As "Triggers" of Aggression

One question many people were asking following the Crandon shootings was whether Tyler Peterson would have acted on his anger if he were not carrying weapons. In other words, did the presence of his rifle and service revolver actually somehow trigger his aggression? Leonard Berkowitz would certainly consider this a distinct possibility. In addition to anger eliciting aggression, Berkowitz believes that the presence of aggression-associated cues in the environment can act as triggers for hostile outbursts by making aggressive thoughts more accessible. An aggression-associated cue is anything that is associated with either violence or unpleasantness. The most obvious aggressive cues are weapons, such as guns, knives, and clubs, while less obvious cues are negative attitudes and unpleasant physical characteristics. Numerous studies indicate that the presence of aggression-associated cues does indeed trigger aggression (Anderson et al., 1998; Lindsay & Anderson, 2000).

Aggression-associated cues can also heighten aggression. In a meta-analysis of twenty-three studies, Michael Carlson and his coworkers (1990) found strong support for the hypothesis that aggression-associated cues enhance aggressiveness among people who are already angry. This finding may go a long way in explaining the fact that a handgun kept in the home for self-protection is forty-three times more likely to kill a friend or family member than to be used in killing intruders (refer to Table 11.1). When domestic disputes erupt, the presence of firearms may enhance the aggressiveness of the angry parties, resulting in tragic consequences. As Berkowitz explains this effect, "Guns not only permit violence, they can stimulate it as well. The finger pulls the trigger, but the trigger may also be pulling the finger" (Berkowitz, 1968, p. 22).

An important caveat to Berkowitz's statement is that the weapons effect depends on the meaning people attach to guns and other weapons. For many people, guns are associated in memory to concepts related to aggression and hostility because they are viewed as instruments designed and used to hurt and kill people. Yet what about people who view guns less as objects of aggression against other people and more as objects

> *"Anger blows out the lamp of the mind."*
>
> Robert Ingersoll, American politician, 1833–1899

> *"There are so many conflicting emotions when your batter gets hit. Because how do you sort it out? How do you know for sure that the pitcher acted intentionally?"*
>
> St. Louis Cardinals manager Tony La Russa, born 1944

> *"Man only becomes dangerous when he is equipped with weapons."*
>
> Sir Edmund Leach, British social anthropologist, 1910–1989

Table 11.1

Facts Concerning Firearm Violence in the U.S.: Aggression-Eliciting Cues

1. Over 35 percent of U.S. households contain at least one firearm, and in half of those households the guns are loaded and/or easily accessible to children.
2. Guns kept in the home for self-protection are 43 times more likely to kill someone you know than to kill in self-defense.
3. The death rate of American children from guns is 12 times higher than in 25 other industrialized countries combined.
4. By the teen years, most homicides and suicides occur with firearms.
5. The risk of homicide in the home is three times greater and the risk of suicide in the home is five times greater for those households with guns.
6. Almost half of all deaths among African-American male teenagers involve firearms.
7. Handguns are increasingly being marketed as tools of self-defense for women. However, crime statistics indicate that for every one instance that a woman uses a handgun to kill a stranger in self-defense, 239 women are murdered with handguns. Often, the handguns used in these murders came from the woman's own household.

they use only for sport? If these people associate guns with having fun outdoors on weekends when they hunt for wild game, are they unlikely to have aggressive thoughts when in the presence of hunting guns? A series of studies conducted by Bruce Bartholow and his colleagues (2005) indicate that this appears to be the case. They found that although both hunting rifles and assault weapons served as cues to aggression for people with no prior hunting experience, only assault weapons served as an aggressive cue for hunters. Instead of priming negative thoughts and emotions, guns associated with animal hunting tended to activate nonaggressive responses among hunters. These findings suggest that an object serves as a cue to aggression only if it is closely linked with aggression-related concepts in memory.

What are the possible implications of these findings for social debates concerning gun ownership? One implication is that guns used for hunting are less likely to prime the sort of negative emotions and thoughts that lead to crimes of passion than guns used for protection. Consistent with this reasoning, a survey of over six thousand middle school students found that owning a pistol or handgun in order to gain respect or to frighten others was associated with extremely high levels of antisocial behavior, such as bullying, physical aggression, and delinquency (Cunningham et al., 2000). In contrast, students who owned hunting rifles and shotguns engaged in only slightly greater antisocial behavior than students who did not own guns of any kind. Returning to Berkowitz's previous statement of the "trigger pulling the finger," it appears that handguns and assault weapons are likely to "itch" more fingers than hunting rifles.

ALCOHOL CONSUMPTION INCREASES THE LIKELIHOOD OF AGGRESSION.

Although weapons may trigger aggressive outbursts in those who are already angry, alcohol is involved in about 50 percent of all violent crimes, including domestic abuse, assault, rape, and homicide (Bachman & Peralta, 2002; Busch & Rosenberg, 2004; Leonard & Quigley, 1999). Experimental studies find that when people drink beverages containing enough alcohol to make them legally intoxicated, they behave more aggressively or respond more strongly to provocation than do persons who consume nonalcoholic drinks (Giancola & Zeichner, 1997; MacDonald et al., 2000).

> ❝ … O thou invisible spirit wine, if thou hast no name to be known by,
> let us call thee devil! … O God, that men should put an enemy
> in their mouths to steal away their brains!
> That we should, with joy, pleasure, revel
> and applause, transform into beasts! ❞

William Shakespeare,
Othello (II, iii)

Studies have shown that alcohol is involved in about 50 percent of all violent crimes.

Why does the consumption of alcohol increase aggression? Few researchers contend that alcohol provides a direct biochemical stimulus to aggression. Instead, the general view is that alcohol weakens people's restraints against aggression by adversely affecting more controlled, effortful thinking while simultaneously leaving more automatic, impulsive responses relatively unaffected (Bartholow et al., 2003a; Ito et al., 1996). Some researchers believe that this weakening of restraints, or *disinhibition*, is partly caused by an interruption of one's ability to process and respond to the meaning of complex and subtle situational cues (Hull & Bond, 1986; Johnson et al., 2000). In other words, when provoked, people who are drunk are much less attentive than those who are sober to such inhibiting cues as the provocateur's intent and the possible negative consequences of violence. For example, in a shock-competition experiment, Kenneth Leonard (1989) found that alcohol did not influence participants' reactions to their competitors' explicit aggressive or nonaggressive signals, but it did interfere with their understanding of subtle aggressive signals. That is, following an aggressive exchange, intoxicated participants were more likely than those who were sober to misinterpret their competitors' subtly announced intentions of nonaggression as being aggression-as-usual.

Inattention to personal and social standards of nonviolence can also cause disinhibition. As discussed in Chapter 3 (p. 70), we are more attentive to personal and social standards of behavior when self-aware. However, alcohol consumption reduces self-awareness (Hull, 1981; Hull et al., 1986), and this can lead to impulsive, nonnormative actions, such as aggression. Thus, intoxicated people not only have problems attending to external cues that might defuse their inclinations to aggress but also have problems attending to internalized behavioral standards that might also inhibit aggression.

A third way this disinhibition effect may occur is through people's expectations of how alcohol will affect behavior (Begue et al., 2009). Perhaps you have heard people excuse a drunken individual's verbal aggression by saying, "It's the liquor talking." Such statements imply that it is not the drunken person misbehaving, but rather, it is the alcohol that is to blame. If people learn that normally inappropriate behavior is often excused when performed under the influence of alcohol, they may engage in those behaviors when drinking (Cameron & Stritzke, 2003; Gelles, 1993). From this perspective, alcohol's effect on aggression is due to a *learned disinhibition*. In support of this viewpoint, research indicates that people sometimes become more aggressive, not just when they have consumed alcohol, but also when they think they have consumed it (Lang et al., 1975). There is also evidence that some men who ordinarily disapprove of hitting a woman believe that being in an intoxicated state gives them a socially acceptable excuse to abuse their spouses (Straus & Gelles, 1990).

Critical
THINKING

How might alcohol impair judgment and, thus, lead to the aggressive outbursts found in domestic violence cases?

❝*Drunkeness ... is the highway to hell ....*❞

Elizabeth Joceline, English author, 1566–1622

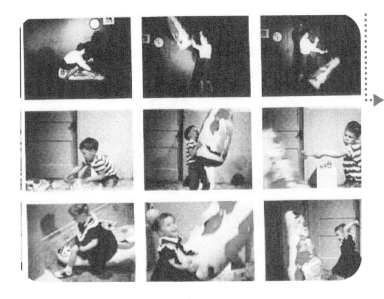

Bandura's Bobo doll studies clearly indicatie that children can learn aggressive actions through an adult.

a room to work on an art project. In another part of the room, an adult was playing quietly with TinkerToys. Near these toys were a mallet and a Bobo doll, which is a big, inflatable clown-like toy that is weighted at the bottom so that when it is pushed or punched down, it will quickly bounce back to an upright position. In the experimental condition, after playing with the TinkerToys for a minute, the adult stood up, walked over to the Bobo doll, and began to attack it. She punched the doll, kicked it, hit it with the mallet, and even sat on it. As she pummeled the clown doll, she yelled out, "Sock him in the nose! … Kick him! … Knock him down!" In the control condition, the adult simply played quietly and nonaggressively with her toys for ten minutes. After witnessing either the aggressive or nonaggressive adult model, the child was led into another room filled with many wonderful toys. However, before the child could play with these treasures, the experimenter aroused frustration by saying that these were her best toys and she must "save them for the other children." The child was then led to a third room, containing both aggressive and nonaggressive toys, including a Bobo doll.

What did children typically do in this third room? If they had witnessed the nonaggressive adult model, they played calmly. However, if they had been exposed to the aggressive adult, they were likely to beat up the Bobo doll, often shouting the same things at the clown during their attack as the previous adult model. Similar results were obtained when the child had no direct exposure to the adult but merely saw a film of the adult attacking the doll. Other experimental variations demonstrated that children were more likely to imitate same-sex models (boys imitating men and girls imitating women) than those of the opposite sex. Taken as a whole, these studies indicate that observing adult aggression can not only lower children's aggressive inhibitions, it can also teach them how to aggress.

As with direct aggression, the observational learning experiments demonstrated that children are likely to imitate others' aggressive acts if social models are rewarded for their behavior. For example, Mary Rosekrans and Willard Hartup (1967) had preschool children watch an adult model aggress against a Bobo doll. These aggressive actions were either praised ("Good for you! I guess you really fixed him that time") or scolded ("Now look what you've done; you've ruined it") by another adult. After watching this interaction, the children were allowed to play with the same toys. Another group of children who had not been exposed to the aggressive model also played with the toys. Results indicated that the children who had watched the aggressive model being rewarded were significantly more aggressive in their play behavior than the children in the other two groups (refer to Figure 11.5). This study and others reveal that children do not unthinkingly imitate a model's actions. Rather, they copy the actions of others who have been rewarded, not punished.

Although these findings might leave you with the impression that aggressive models who are punished have little negative impact on children's later behavior, this is not necessarily the case. The research demonstrates that children are less likely to imitate the

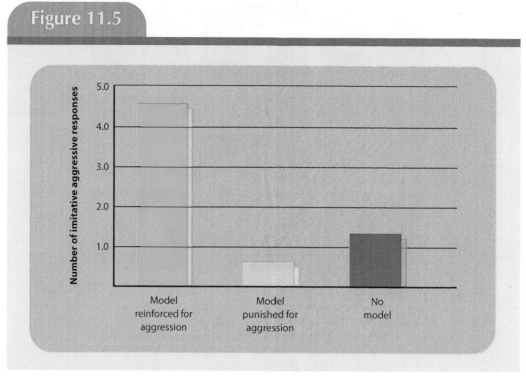

Modeling Aggression as a Function of Reinforcement and Punishment

Children were much more likely to imitate the aggressive behavior of an adult model if the adult had been rewarded rather than punished. Can you imagine how these social learning principles might exert their influence among children playing on a grade-school playground?

actions of punished aggressors. Does this mean these children fail to learn the aggressive behavior, or does it mean they simply inhibit the expression of these behaviors? In a study similar to Rosekrans and Hartup's experiment, Bandura (1965) offered all the children in the study a reward if they could imitate the aggressive behavior of the model that they had previously observed. Every single one of the participants could mimic the model's aggressive actions, even those who had seen the punished model. Thus, observing someone being punished for aggression does not prevent the learning of aggression—it simply inhibits its expression in certain circumstances. When children believe aggressive expression will lead to rewards, their inhibitions generally evaporate.

The Formation of Aggressive Scripts

Borrowing a concept from cognitive psychology, Rowell Huesmann (1986b, 1988) proposed that aggression—like other social behavior—is controlled by scripts. As first outlined in Chapter 4, a *script* is a preconception about how a series of events is likely to occur, which is developed and stored in memory and used as a guide for behavior and problem solving. Based on many social learning experiments (for example, Bandura's Bobo doll studies), Huesmann contends that children develop **aggressive scripts** by observing other people's aggressive actions. For instance, if children learn from their parents or friends that the proper way to respond to insults or other social slights is to physically or verbally assault their protagonists, when they are later actually insulted by someone, an aggressive script will be recalled from memory. This script not only provides the child with a prediction about what is likely to happen in this situation, but it also prescribes the proper way to act. Huesmann believes that the more exposure children have to aggressive role models, the greater the number of detailed aggressive scripts they will encode into memory. Those with strongly developed aggressive scripts are likely to choose an aggressive solution to social conflict because it will seem to them to be the best and most natural way to respond to such circumstances.

aggressive scripts
....
Guides for behavior and problem solving that are developed and stored in memory and are characterized by aggression

MEDIA AND VIDEO VIOLENCE FOSTERS AGGRESSIVE BEHAVIOR.

American children spend more than five hours a day engaged in some form of media entertainment, including television, films, and video games. Children in Europe and Asia engage in similar levels of video entertainment. Most of this entertainment involves considerable amounts of violence (Anderson et al., 2003a). Is this exposure to media violence something that parents and other adults should be concerned about?

Violence on Television and Film

Research indicates that although aggressive scripts most commonly form by observing people with whom we regularly interact, these scripts also can develop by viewing media violence (Anderson et al., 2003a, 2003b). Experimental studies indicate that immediately after watching violent television shows or movies, children act more aggressively in their play behavior and are more likely to choose aggressive solutions to social problems than those not exposed to such violence (Bushman & Huesmann, 2001). Further, three separate meta-analyses of laboratory and field experiments conducted over the past half-century demonstrate that exposure to media violence enhances children's and adolescents' aggression in interactions with strangers, classmates, and friends (Hearold, 1986; Paik & Comstock, 1994; Wood et al., 1991).

Longitudinal studies have also found a link between media violence and aggression. In perhaps the best of these studies—previously discussed in Chapter 2—Leonard Eron and Huesmann collected data on 856 people in the state of New York when they were about eight years old, then again when they were nineteen, and finally when they were about thirty years of age (Eron & Huesmann, 1984; Huesmann, 1986a). Their results: Early exposure to TV violence was related to later aggression—but only among the males. Boys who preferred to watch violent television shows when they were eight years of age were significantly more aggressive ten years later, even after controlling for their initial level of aggressiveness. In addition, as Figure 11.6 illustrates, the eight-year-old boys who

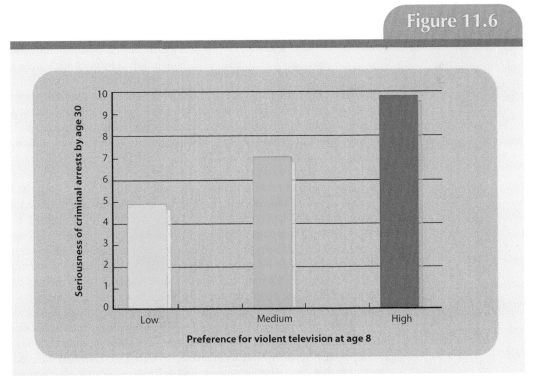

Figure 11.6

Childhood Preference for Violent Television and Later Aggressive Behavior

Boys who show a high preference for violent television shows at age 8 have been found to exhibit greater aggressive behavior later in life, as indicated by the number of criminal convictions by age 30. Does this mean that TV violence caused their later aggression?

Many studies over the past fifty years provide compelling evidence that media violence contributes to aggressive behavior in viewers. How does viewer identification with aggressive characters impact viewer aggression?

had the strongest preference for violent shows were much more likely to have been convicted of a serious crime by the time they reached the age of thirty. These findings suggest that the frequent viewing of televised violence contributes to later aggressive behavior beyond what you would expect due to stable aggressive traits (Huesmann et al., 2003).

Similar findings have been obtained in Europe, except that the European studies found no gender differences in the negative effects of TV violence (Huesmann & Eron, 1986). What appears to influence children's later aggressiveness is their *identification* with aggressive TV characters. Children who watch a lot of TV violence when they are young and identify with aggressive TV characters are most likely to become highly aggressive in late childhood, adolescence, and even young adulthood (Anderson & Bushman, 2002). Based on these lab, field, and longitudinal studies, solid evidence indicates that repeated exposure to violence on television can encourage children to develop aggressive scripts that make later antisocial conduct more likely (Huesmann & Miller, 1994; Johnson et al., 2002).

Violence in Music Videos and Lyrics

What about the violence often depicted in music videos and in music lyrics? Music executives and some pop psychologists assert that watching violent music videos and listening to violent music lyrics provide teenagers and young adults the opportunity to harmlessly "vent" their aggressive emotions and thoughts. However, our previous analysis of the catharsis hypothesis refutes this assertion (see p. 452). Yet is there any scientific evidence that this specific sort of media violence increases aggressive tendencies and behavior?

Several studies have examined how music videos affect adolescents' aggressive thinking and attitudes. In one such study involving young African-American men, exposure to violent rap music videos increased endorsement of violent behavior in response to a hypothetical conflict situation (Johnson et al., 1995). Similarly, college students shown rock music videos containing violence subsequently reported a greater acceptance of antisocial behavior compared with students in a control group (Hansen & Hansen, 1990). Regarding the effects of music lyrics, numerous studies have found consistent evidence that songs with violent lyrics increase aggression-related thoughts and feelings of hostility in listeners (Anderson et al., 2003b; Brummert-Lennings & Warburton, 2011). Overall, the implication of these findings is that watching and/or listening to violent music causes people to not only be more accepting of antisocial behavior, it also creates an emotional mindset that makes aggressive responses more likely.

Is there any evidence that listening to violent music lyrics actually increases aggressive behavior? Peter Fischer and Tobias Greitemeyer (2006) recently addressed this question in a series of studies where male and female participants in Germany listened to popular songs containing men-hating lyrics, women-hating lyrics, or neutral song lyrics. After listening to the selected songs, participants completed various psychological tasks, including some that measured aggressive attitudes and cognitions. When the study was supposedly completed, participants were asked to briefly help assign instructions to people in an unrelated study. The experimenter explained that this other study required people to stick their left hand in freezing cold ice water while they completed intellectual tasks, and they were further told that keeping the hand in ice water could be very painful, especially when this procedure lasted longer than twenty-five seconds. The participants' task was to decide how long two specific individuals—one female and one male—would hold their hand in the ice water. The assigned times given to the female and male were the dependent measures of aggression in the study.

Results indicated that male participants who listened to women-hating song lyrics not only reported more aggressive cognitions, but they also later behaved more aggressively to the female target person by assigning her significantly longer times of ice water treatment than did men who listened to neutral or men-hating lyrics. Similarly, women who listened to men-hating song lyrics reported more aggressive cognitions and later assigned significantly longer times of ice water treatment to the male target person than did women who listened to neutral or women-hating lyrics. Overall, these findings provide some evidence that exposure to violent music provokes aggressive thoughts in listeners and increases their aggressive responses toward people who are similar to the targeted victims in the music lyrics.

Violence in Video Games

In addition to the negative effects of watching or listening to violent media, research also indicates that playing violent video games has similar detrimental effects (Gentile et al., 2004; Krahé & Moller, 2004). However, unlike television and films, video games are interactive. Video-game players actually engage in virtual aggression, actively rehearse aggressive scripts, receive rewards for their aggression, and closely identify with the characters they control. Despite the denials from the video-game industry, at least two separate meta-analyses of existing video-game studies involving over three thousand participants found that exposure to high video-game violence is associated with heightened aggression in the real world among young adults and children (Anderson, 2004; Anderson & Bushman, 2001). There were no gender differences in these effects. Additional research indicates that even brief exposure to violent video games significantly increases aggressive thoughts, aggressive emotions, physiological arousal, and—most important—aggressive behavior (Anderson et al., 2007; Uhlmann & Swanson, 2004).

Beyond the learning of aggressive scripts and the priming of aggressive thoughts and emotions, another negative effect of exposure to media and video violence is emotional blunting or *desensitization*, which means simply becoming indifferent to aggressive outbursts. For example, in a series of experiments conducted by Ronald Drabman and Margaret Thomas, children who had just watched a violent movie were less concerned when they observed other youngsters fighting and were slower to stop the fight than a control group of children who had not seen the movie. This desensitization to violence was also observed in college students who watched a lot of violent TV programs and among those with a history of high exposure to violent video games. When their physiological responses were monitored, the heavy consumers exhibited the weakest levels of arousal when observing both fictional and realistic aggression (Bartholow et al., 2006; Thomas et al., 1977). These and other studies suggest that people who watch a lot of media-generated violence or play a

Video-game players are engaged in virtual aggression while playing.

lot of violent video games become habituated to violence in other aspects of their lives (Carnagey et al., 2007; Krahé et al., 2011). Because they are less anxious and bothered by aggressive behavior, they may be less inclined to regulate their aggressive urges when angry and more inclined to use the aggressive scripts they have learned as a means to solve social confrontations.

Another way in which media and video violence may increase aggression is through cognitive priming. According to Berkowitz (1984), the aggression-associated cues in television programs and films can cognitively prime a host of aggressive ideas and violent emotions, which in turn may trigger aggressive actions. Brad Bushman and Russell Geen (1990) found support for the priming hypothesis in experiments investigating the effects of media violence on viewers' thoughts and emotional responses. In these studies, college students wrote down the thoughts they had while watching excerpts from such violent movies as *48 Hours* and *The French Connection*. A control group watched a nonviolent scene from the TV series *Dallas*. Results indicated that viewers who watched the most aggressive episodes had the most aggressive thoughts, experienced the strongest increase in anger-related feelings, and had the greatest physiological arousal. The same effects have been found when people play violent video games (Anderson & Bushman, 2001; Anderson & Dill, 2000). In fact, recent studies find that when video gamers design and personalize their own in-game characters, they tend to experience even higher levels of arousal than when they play non-personalized games. More importantly, this personalization of in-game characters increases gamers' aggressive tendencies (Fischer et al., 2010).

Of course, this does not mean that all or even most children and young adults who regularly view or listen to media violence or play violent video games will begin terrorizing their schools and neighborhoods. However, while exposure to such staged violence is not the primary cause of aggression among the young, it may be the one factor that is easiest to control and reduce (Hamilton, 1998; Wilson et al., 1998).

THE "CULTURE OF HONOR" ENCOURAGES MALE VIOLENCE.

culture of honor
· · · · · · · · · · · · · · · · · · · ·
A belief system in which males are socialized to protect their reputation by resorting to violence

Cross-cultural research suggests that societies in which the economy is based on the herding of animals have more male violence than farming societies. For example, among the Native American cultures of North America, the herding Navajos were famous for their warring tendencies, while the farming Zunis tended to be nonviolent (Farb, 1978). Within given societies, researchers have also observed this contrast in aggression. In East African cultures, for instance, herders are easily provoked to violence, while farmers go out of their way to get along with their neighbors (Edgerton, 1971). Social psychologists Richard Nisbett and Dov Cohen (1996) believe that the greater violence exhibited by herding people is due to their **culture of honor**, which is a belief system that prepares men to protect their reputation by resorting to violence. In such cultures, honor is a man's most valued personal quality, and a man who claims honor but is not paid honor does not in fact have honor. Cultures of honor tend to develop in "lawless" settings, where a weak state cannot enforce laws or contracts, protect individuals from wrongdoing, or punish criminals. Instead, men on their own must be trustworthy, demand respect and fairness, and be prepared to pay back wrongs done to them. In honor cultures, men learn from childhood that it is important to project a willingness to fight to the death against insults and to vigorously protect their property—specifically, their animals—from theft. Insults have special importance in honor cultures because they are tests of who can do what to whom. Men who will not tolerate disrespect on even small issues send a signal to others that they will not be pushed around on big issues either (IJzerman et al., 2007). Nisbett and Cohen hypothesize that this culture of honor is more necessary in herding than in farming societies because herders' assets (animals) are more vulnerable to theft—and thus, more in need of aggressive protection—than are the assets of farmers (land).

How does this culture of honor theory relate to contemporary violence in the United States? First, in an archival analysis of crime statistics in this country, Nisbett and Cohen found that the southern and western states, which were settled by people whose economy was originally based on herding, have higher levels of current violence related to honor than the northern states, which were originally settled by farmers (Cohen, 1996; Cohen & Nisbett, 1994). Honor-related violence involves arguments, brawls, and lovers' triangles where a person's public prestige and honor have been challenged. Second, the cultures of the South and West are also more likely to approve of violence as indicated by viewership of violent TV programs, subscriptions to violent magazines, hunting license applications, and National Guard enrollments (Baron & Straus, 1989; Lee, 1995). Third, in a series of experimental studies, Cohen and Nisbett also found that, when insulted, young White men from the South not only became more stressed and angry than young White men from the North, but they also were more prepared to respond to insults with aggression (Cohen et al., 1996).

What these multimethod studies suggest is that southern and western White men tend to be more physically aggressive than northern White men in certain situations because they have been socialized to live by a code of honor that calls for quick and violent responses to threats to their property or personal integrity. Although the vast majority of these men no longer depend on herding for their livelihood, they still live by the culture of honor of their ancestors; and this code of conduct continues to be legitimated by cultural institutions (Cohen, 1998; Cohen & Vandello, 1998). Fueling such aggression is the belief that aggressive responses to honor-based threats are not only necessary but also socially sanctioned. Consistent with this idea is the finding that White male college students from the South are significantly more likely than White male college students from the North to overestimate the aggressiveness of their peers and to interpret other people's advice about how to respond to conflict as sanctioning physical aggression (Vandello et al., 2008).

Ironically, "honor" cultures tend to have very strong norms of politeness and hospitality. This emphasis on elaborate politeness may have developed as a way to reduce the likelihood that honor-bound men would be insulted during daily interactions. However, the anger suppression resulting from such politeness norms has the unfortunate effect of making it difficult to accurately perceive other people's anger until it has reached the boiling point, triggering aggression on their part.

Interestingly, similar regional differences in violence are not found among young African-American males; Black southern men are not more violent than Black northern men. Thus, this hypothesized culture of honor in the South and West is unique to White males. Having stated this, however, both psychologists and sociologists note that the higher incidence of violence among inner-city African-American males than among African-American males in rural or suburban areas may be partly related to a similar honor code (Cohen et al., 1998; Lee & Ousey, 2011). Thus, just as a culture of honor may exist among southern and western White men, in the inner city street culture there may also be a culture of honor that makes violent outbursts more likely. That is, in the inner city, where it is extremely difficult to pull oneself out of poverty by legal means, and where police provide little protection from crime and physical attack, young Black males may strive to gain and maintain respect by responding violently to any perceived insults. Of course, within this cultural analysis of violence it is always important to keep in mind that there is a great deal of individual difference in how people respond to such cultural influences (Leung & Cohen, 2011).

SECTION SUMMARY

- In social learning theory, aggression occurs because it has been rewarded in the past.

- Observational learning can foster the development of aggressive scripts.

- Exposure to media violence promotes antisocial conduct.

- The culture of honor is a belief system that prepares men to protect their reputation by resorting to violence.

SEXUAL AGGRESSION

Would it surprise you to know that in the past quarter century forcible rape has increased by 21 percent, making it the largest increase among all major crimes (Magid et al., 2004; Von et al., 1991)? What about the fact that more than one hundred thousand women in the United States report being raped each year—about one every six minutes (Federal Bureau of Investigation, 2001)? Does this fact surprise you? Are you shocked to learn that 28 percent of women using the Veterans Administration health care system experienced at least one sexual assault during their military service (Hillard, 2007)? These statistics are grim reminders concerning the dangers women face in American society. Yet rape is certainly not confined to the U.S. borders. It is a worldwide phenomenon, most common in societies characterized by male violence and a social ideology of male dominance (Jewkes & Abrahams, 2002; Muir & Macleod, 2003; Sanday, 1981). Although less common, men are also the victims of sexual assault, but they are much less likely to report a rape by a male perpetrator than are women (Pino & Meier, 1999). In this section we analyze three possible determinants of sexual aggression, namely pornography, sexual scripts, and jealousy.

PORNOGRAPHY PROMOTES THE "RAPE MYTH" AND MAY INCREASE VIOLENCE AGAINST WOMEN.

pornography

The combination of sexual material with abuse or degredation in a manner that appears to endorse, condone, or encourage such behavior

Erotica is typically defined as sexually suggestive or arousing material that is nonviolent and respectful of all persons portrayed. In contrast, **pornography** is the combination of sexual material with abuse or degradation in a manner that appears to endorse, condone, or encourage such behavior (Brown, 2003; Russell, 1993). Pornography is objectionable not for its sexual content, but rather, its abusive and degrading portrayal of another person, usually a female. Experimental studies demonstrate that exposure to erotic material generally elicits a pleasant emotional response and increased sexual arousal in both men and women, which usually results in them being less aggressive (Davis & Bauserman, 1993; Donnerstein et al., 1987). A different pattern appears to hold for people's response to pornography, as you will soon discover.

The Rape Myth

In a content analysis of 428 pornographic paperback books, sociologist Donald Smith (1976) found that physical abuse was a common theme in sexual encounters between men and women. Twenty percent of all sex episodes depicted in these books involved

Pornography is objectionable not because of its sexual content, but for its abusive and degrading portrayal of another person, usually a female.

rape. The story line focused on the victim's initial fear and terror at being attacked, followed by an awakening of her sexual desire as it proceeded. In more than 97 percent of these rape depictions, the victims experienced an orgasm during the sexual assault. Similar story themes are found in sexually oriented home videos and DVDs (Emmers-Sommer et al., 2005).

rape myth
....
The false belief that, deep down, women enjoy forcible sex and find it sexually exciting

This false belief that deep down, women enjoy forcible sex and find it sexually exciting, is known as the **rape myth**. People who believe in the rape myth are less likely to empathize with rape victims and are more likely to blame victims for causing the assault (Frese et al., 2004; Jimenez & Abreu, 2003). A number of studies indicate that heterosexual men are much more likely than heterosexual women to believe in the rape myth and to support and strengthen their peers' rape-myth beliefs (Bohner et al., 2006; Talbot et al., 2010). Although the definition of the rape myth is framed to include only women as targets, recent studies suggest that a similar myth exists for men; that is, some people falsely believe that if a man is sexually assaulted he must have had an unconscious desire to be raped. As with the traditional rape myth, heterosexual men are most likely to endorse male rape myths, especially when the victim is a gay man; gay men are least likely to endorse such beliefs (Chapleau et al., 2007; Davies & McCartney, 2003). Together, these findings suggest that the people who are most likely to strongly endorse false beliefs about sexual assault are males who have hostile attitudes toward the victim group (either women or gay men).

> **"**Everyone knows that murder is wrong, but a strange myth has grown up, and been seized on by filmmakers, that rape is really not so bad, that it may even be a form of liberation for the victim, who may be acting out what she secretly desires—and perhaps needs—with no harm done.**"**
>
> Lord Harlech, British Film Board

Not surprisingly, convicted rapists generally hold strong beliefs regarding the rape myth (Scully, 1985), but more disturbingly, there is evidence that exposure to pornography also increases ordinary men's rape-myth beliefs. In one such study, Neil Malamuth and James Check (1981) arranged for Canadian college students to attend commercial movies at campus theaters. Half of the students saw two nonviolent romantic movies, *A Man and a Woman and Hooper*. The other students saw two sexually aggressive films, *Swept Away* and *The Getaway*, in which women characters in both films become sexually aroused by a sexual assault and are romantically attracted to their assailant. Several days later, these same students were asked to complete a class questionnaire about their attitudes toward rape and other forms of aggression against women (refer to *Self/Social Connection Box 11.1*). None of the students realized that the questionnaire and the movies were connected in any way.

Results indicated that exposure to the two films portraying sexual aggression increased male viewers' acceptance of interpersonal aggression against women and tended to increase their acceptance of rape myths (see Figure 11.7 on p. 472). In contrast, females' acceptance of interpersonal aggression against women and of rape myths decreased after watching these sexually aggressive films. These data, which have been replicated in subsequent studies (Oddone-Paolucci et al., 2000), indicate that exposure to films that seem to condone sexual violence against women can cause men to become more accepting of such violence. Another disturbing fact about these findings is that they were not obtained by exposing men to pornographic material typically found in dult X-rated movies but, rather, were obtained from exposure to commercially successful R-rated films that contained pornographic elements in their story lines. Hollywood produces such films because there is a profitable market for them; and their target audience is men, who prefer films that mix sex and violence to those that mix sex and tenderness (Emmers-Sommer et al., 2006).

Does Pornography Provoke Male Aggression Against Women?

Thus far, we have learned that exposure to sexually violent films can cause men to become more accepting of false beliefs about rape and to have greater tolerance for violence against women. However, does this translate into men actually becoming more aggressive toward women? In an attempt to answer this question, social psychologists have conducted two separate lines of research: (1) lab experiments in which exposure to violent pornography is manipulated to see how it affects laboratory aggression, and (2) survey research on whether the prevalence of pornography in a particular geographic region is related to sexual assault.

Regarding lab experiments, a series of studies conducted by Edward Donnerstein and his colleagues suggest that although male-to-male aggression is no greater after exposure

Self/Social Connections Exercise 11.1

What Are Your Beliefs About Rape and Interpersonal Violence?

Rape Myth Acceptance Scale

Directions

There are nineteen items on this scale. For items 1 to 11, use the following 7-point scale to indicate your degree of agreement or disagreement:

Strongly Disagree   1   2   3   4   5   6   7   Strongly Agree

1. A woman who goes to the home or apartment of a man on their first date implies that she is willing to have sex.
2. Any female can get raped.
3. One reason that women falsely report a rape is that they frequently have a need to call attention to themselves.
4. Any healthy woman can successfully resist a rapist if she really wants to.
5. When women go around braless or wearing short skirts and tight tops, they are just asking for trouble.
6. In the majority of rapes, the victim is promiscuous or has a bad reputation.
7. If a girl engages in necking or petting and she lets things get out of hand, it is her own fault if her partner forces sex on her.
8. Women who get raped while hitchhiking get what they deserve.
9. A woman who is stuck up and thinks she is too good to talk to guys on the street deserves to be taught a lesson.
10. Many women have an unconscious wish to be raped, and may then unconsciously set up a situation in which they are likely to be attacked.
11. If a woman gets drunk at a party and has intercourse with a man she's just met there, she should be considered "fair game" to other males at the party who want to have sex with her too, whether she wants to or not.

Note: For items 12 and 13, use the following scale to answer the questions:

1 = About 0%   2 = About 25%   3 = About 50%   4 = About 75%   5 = About 100%

12. What percentage of women who report a rape would you say are lying because they are angry and want to get back at the man they accuse?
13. What percentage of reported rapes would you guess were merely invented by women who discovered they were pregnant and wanted to protect their own reputation?

Note: For items 14 to 19, use the following scale to indicate your response:

1 = Always   2 = Frequently   3 = Sometimes   4 = Rarely   5 = Never

A person comes to you and claims s/he was raped. How likely would you be to believe her/his statement if the person was

14. your best friend?
15. an Indian woman?
16. a neighborhood woman?
17. a young boy?

Exercise 11.1 *Continued*

18. a Black woman?
19. a White woman?

Scoring Instructions

Once you indicate your response to each item, reverse the scoring for item 2 (1 = 7, 2 = 6, 3 = 5, 5 = 3, 6 = 2, 7 = 1). Then add up your total score. The higher your total score, the greater your belief in the rape myth. The mean total score in Burt's (1980) original sample of 598 American adults (average age of 42 years) was 86.6, with a standard deviation of 11.9. How does your total score compare with Burt's original sample? Are you more or less likely to believe in the rape myth than these American adults? Have your friends complete this scale as well. How do your beliefs about the rape myth compare with their beliefs? Total score: _____

to violent pornography, male-to-female aggression is significantly increased (Donnerstein & Malamuth, 1997). In one representative study, Donnerstein and Leonard Berkowitz (1981) demonstrated that how rape is depicted in films is crucial in determining male viewers' later aggression. First, male participants were either angered or not by either a male or a female confederate and then were either shown a neutral, erotic, or one of two violent pornographic films. In both the sexually violent films, two men raped a woman,

Figure 11.7

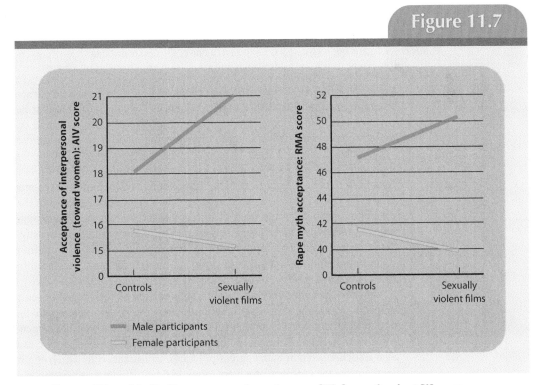

The Effects of Mass Media Exposure on Acceptance of Violence Against Women

Malamuth and Check (1981) found that men who had watched sexually violent commercial films were more accepting of interpersonal violence against women and were more accepting of the rape myth than men who were not exposed to such violent entertainment. What effect did such exposure have on women viewers?

Figure 11.8

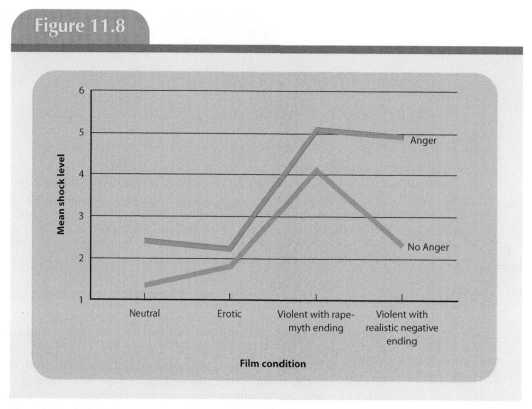

How Does the Film Victim's Reaction to Rape Affect Male Viewers' Subsequent Level of Aggression Toward Women?

Men who had been angered by a female confederate and who had then watched a sexually violent film administered more intense shocks to the female confederate, regardless of the film victim's own emotional reaction to being raped. How were these men's reactions different from males who were not angered by the female confederate, but who also were exposed to one of the two rape films?

but each film had a different ending. In one ending shown to some participants, the victim is smiling and not resisting as she experiences sexual gratification at being raped (rape-myth ending). In the other ending, the victim is in obvious pain and emotional turmoil, and she conveys disgust and humiliation at being raped (realistic negative ending).

As can be seen in Figure 11.8, males who had been angered by the female confederate and who had watched a sexually violent film administered more intense shocks to the female confederate, regardless of the film victim's own emotional reaction to being raped. However, when they were not angry, males who had been exposed to the rape film delivered intense shocks to the female confederate only when the film depicted the woman as enjoying the experience. These results are consistent with other investigations of aggression of a nonsexual nature, in which for nonangered individuals, victim pain cues tend to reduce aggression by inducing empathy. However, for highly angered individuals, a victim's pain can actually provoke increased aggression (Geen, 1978). Why this is the case is a matter of speculation. One possible explanation is that anger raises the threshold for empathy toward the victim's plight (Hartmann, 1969). Another explanation is Berkowitz's notion of aggression-associated cues (p. 457). For males who have been angered, watching a woman become the victim of sexual aggression may not only cause arousal, it may also associate women with aggression. Later, in a situation in which aggression is a behavioral option, the presence of a woman might be a sufficient aggression-eliciting cue for the already aroused male.

Although Donnerstein's overall findings and those of other experiments (Hui, 1986) suggest that men who watch violent pornography are more likely to engage in aggressive behaviors toward women, survey studies of actual sex crimes do not generally support this conclusion. For example, Danish social psychologist Berl Kutchinsky

(1971, 1985) reasoned that if pornography increases male sexual aggression against women, then sexual crimes should rise when pornography laws are relaxed. In an early test of this hypothesis, he gathered crime statistics for the time periods prior to and following the legalization of hard-core pornography in Denmark in the late 1960s. What he found was exactly opposite of what would be expected based on the experimental literature; the increased availability of pornography coincided with a decrease in sex offenses against children, while the number of reported rapes remained unchanged. Kutchinsky (1991) later extended his research by looking at rates of rape and nonsexual assault from 1964 to 1984 in Denmark, Sweden, Germany, and the United States. In all four countries, new laws made pornography much more available during the late 1960s and early 1970s. Did this increased availability of pornography coincide with an increase in sexual assault? Crime statistics indicate that rape rates increased only in the United States, but this change coincided with a similar increase in nonsexual violent crimes. Kutchinsky argued that this simultaneous increase in rapes and assaults is consistent with the belief that rape is primarily an act of violence rather than of sexual arousal. These results seem to suggest that the increased availability of pornography does not seem to directly contribute to increased sexual offenses (Bauserman, 1996).

So where are we in our understanding of the effects of pornography on men's sexual beliefs and aggressive actions toward women? There appears to be generally good support for the hypothesis that exposure to violent pornography increases men's acceptance of the rape myth. However, the contradictory findings in the experimental and survey literature regarding a possible pornography-aggression link suggest that additional research is necessary before we can reach any firm conclusions (Bensimon, 2007). In the meantime, research by Murray Straus and his colleagues has led them to suggest that rape rates are shaped by two sets of social forces (Baron & Straus, 1987, 1989). The first is *social disorganization*, which is brought about as a society experiences increases in poverty, urbanization, and divorce—the very social ills that the United States has increasingly experienced since the 1960s. The second is *hypermasculinity*, which is the desire to exercise power and dominance over women. The rape myth is a product of this hypermasculinity. The role that hypermasculinity plays in acquaintance rape is one of the primary topics of the next chapter section.

CULTURE-BASED SEXUAL SCRIPTS MAKE ACQUAINTANCE RAPE MORE LIKELY.

acquaintance rape
....
Forced sexual intercourse that occurs either on a date or between people who are acquainted or romantically involved (also known as date rape)

Forced sexual intercourse that occurs either on a date or between people who are acquainted or romantically involved is known as **acquaintance rape** (or *date rape*). On American college campuses, acquaintance rapes account for 85 percent of all rapes, and one-fourth of college women are victims of rape or attempted rape (Koss et al., 1987; Yancey & Hummer, 2003). Although surveys indicate that the vast majority of both men and women agree that sexual advances should stop when a woman says no, nearly half of young adults believe that when a woman says no she does not always mean it (Adams-Curtis & Forbes, 2004; Krahé et al., 2000).

One explanation for this belief that no does not always mean no comes from the sexual scripts that adolescents learn as they mature. As discussed earlier in the chapter, scripts provide guidance for people in their social behavior, enabling them to anticipate the goals, behaviors, and outcomes likely to occur in a particular setting. Much like the way children can learn aggressive scripts by watching violent television programs, adolescents and adults can also learn societal *sexual scripts* that make sexual aggression more likely in a dating relationship. The *resistant female role* and the *predator male role* highlight our culture's double standard for sexual activity between women and men. Put simply, frequent sexual activity outside of marriage has always been more socially acceptable for men than for women. Although it is socially acceptable for women to appear "sexy," they run the risk of being negatively labeled "promiscuous" or "loose" if they appear to be too sexually eager. Faced with this double standard, some women may see engaging in token resistance as a rational behavior to deflect this sort of negative social attribution (Muehlenhard & Hollabaugh, 1988; Shotland & Hunter, 1995).

The danger in employing this sexual script, however, is that it not only discourages honest communication between men and women but also perpetuates restrictive gender roles and encourages men to ignore women's refusals. Having encountered a woman who employed token resistance to sex might reinforce a man's belief in the rape myth—that is, he may believe that all a woman needs is a little encouragement or even force to overcome her inhibitions. This belief, in turn, may precipitate later acquaintance rapes. Thus, the small minority of women who use token resistance not only put themselves in danger, but they also endanger the majority of women who mean no when they say no.

Even though some women send mixed signals regarding their own sexual desires, this in no way justifies forced sex. It cannot be stressed enough that acquaintance rape occurs when a man refuses to stop his sexual aggression. Surveys on college campuses indicate that roughly 12 to 15 percent of male respondents admit having used force or violence to try to obtain sex against another's will (Sigelman et al., 1984). In an even more alarming series of survey findings, when asked to rate their likelihood of raping a woman if they could be absolutely assured that they would not be arrested or punished, between 35 and 51 percent of college male respondents state that there is at least "some possibility" of them doing so (Malamuth, 1981).

Although sexual gratification is clearly a motive in rape, studies of convicted rapists have found that they view rape as an aggressive conquest that validates their sense of hypermasculinity (Groth, 1979). Based on this work, social scientists have identified the desire to exercise power and dominance over women as key factors in sexual aggression (Locke & Mahalik, 2005; Malamuth & Thornhill, 1994). Similarly, in studies using college and community samples, men who either had a history of sexual aggression or were more accepting of violence against and dominance over women were also more likely to be sexually aroused by depictions of rape and to be insensitive to others' feelings (Dean & Malamuth, 1997; Yost & Zurbriggen, 2006). Together, this research suggests that enjoyment of sexual dominance is a more important motive than sexual gratification in sexual assault (Chiroro et al., 2004).

Researchers have identified characteristics of both the victimizer and the victim that closely correspond to the sexual scripts already discussed (Osman, 2003; Willan & Pollard, 2003). A victim often does not clearly communicate the limits of acceptable behavior to someone who persists after initial sexual advances have been discouraged. Instead of employing the highly effective tactic of declaring to her attacker, "This is rape and I'm calling the cops," a victim of acquaintance rape tends to be nonassertive or in the habit of giving mixed messages. The victim of acquaintance rape often has problems with forcefully conveying a clear message of no, and the victimizer often misperceives the actions of the victim, interpreting passivity as permission. He tends to be more sexually active than other men and treats women as if they were his property. An acquaintance rapist also generally has a history of antisocial behavior and displays a lot of anger and hostility toward women (Abrams et al., 2003; Allison & Wrightsman, 1993). Because he believes that women often need a little force to enjoy sex, the victimizer does not believe that acquaintance rape is rape, even after he has committed this crime.

SECTION SUMMARY

- Exposure to violent pornography increases men's acceptance of rape myths.

- Experimental studies suggest that violent pornography increases men's aggression toward women, but survey re-search does not generally support this conclusion.

- Sexual aggression may also be fostered through cultural sexual scripts where:

1. women are expected to act resistant to sex;

2. men are expected to persist in their sexual advances regardless of women's protests.

REDUCING AGGRESSION

As you see from our review, many different causes underlie human aggression. The resulting psychological and physical injury has naturally led social psychologists to try to determine how aggressive responses can be minimized. In this final section, we examine some relatively effective strategies.

PUNISHMENT CAN BOTH DECREASE AND INCREASE AGGRESSION.

Punishment is the most common treatment societies have employed to control aggression. Following such timeworn prescriptions as "an eye for an eye and a tooth for a tooth," legal systems throughout the world often use aggression to punish violent criminals, sometimes resorting to the ultimate punishment—death. Exercising this extreme form of punishment will certainly "relieve" convicted criminals of their aggressive tendencies, but short of killing aggressors, is punishment a truly effective technique?

> "*Violence and injury enclose in their net all that do such things, and generally return upon him who began.*"
>
> ---------------
>
> Lucretius Carus, Ancient Roman philosopher-poet, 99–55 BC

Three conditions are necessary for punishment to have a chance of being effective (Bower & Hilgard, 1981). First, the punishment must be *prompt*, administered quickly after the aggressive action. Second, it must be *relatively strong*, so that the aggressor duly notes its aversive qualities. Third, it must be *consistently applied* so that the aggressor knows that punishment will likely follow future aggressive actions. Even if these conditions are met, however, reduced aggression is not guaranteed. If potential aggressors are extremely angry, threats of punishment preceding an attack are unlikely to inhibit aggression (Baron, 1973). Here, the strength of the anger supersedes any concerns about the negative consequences of aggression. Likewise, the cognitive-neoassociationist model would suggest that punishment following aggression might actually provoke counteraggression in the aggressor-turned-victim because such punishment might provoke even more intense anger.

In further considering the effectiveness of using punishment to reduce aggression, one should be even more wary of using aggression in doling out punishment. Based on the research inspired by social learning theory, it is entirely possible that employing violent punishment as a treatment for aggression may simply teach and encourage observers to copy these violent actions. That is, the aggressive punisher may serve as an aggressive model. This is exactly the process underlying the continuing cycle of family violence—observing adult aggression appears to encourage rather than discourage aggression in children (Cast et al., 2006; Fosco et al., 2007; Mathurin et al., 2006).

Taking these factors into account, even though punishment may reduce aggressive behavior under certain circumstances, it does not teach the aggressor new prosocial forms of behavior. The aggressive behaviors are not being replaced by more productive kinds of actions but are, most likely, being only temporarily suppressed. For this reason, punishment by itself is unlikely to result in long-term changes in behavior.

INDUCING INCOMPATIBLE RESPONSES CAN INHIBIT AGGRESSION.

Have you ever been in a situation in which you were about to hit or verbally lash out at someone, when suddenly someone breaks the tension and dissipates your anger by making you laugh? As a youngster, my father often used this strategy whenever I became angry at all the "injustices" that he and my mother imposed upon me. As I stood there red-faced and fuming, he might make a funny gesture or suggest that my face looked as though it was about to explode like a firecracker. Suddenly my anger was transformed into giggles, and my parents were no longer the enemy who needed to be vanquished.

Critical THINKING

"Road rage" has unfortunately become an all-too-familiar term we read and hear about to describe violent outbursts by people driving cars. How could you use social psychological knowledge to reduce the likelihood of road rage on city streets and highways?

Using a well-established principle in psychology that states that all organisms are incapable of engaging in two incompatible responses, or of experiencing two incompatible emotions at the same time, Robert Baron (1983) has argued that inducing responses or emotions incompatible with anger or overt aggression may effectively deter such actions. In one field experiment that encapsulates the basic findings of many other studies investigating this *incompatible response strategy*, Baron (1976) instructed a research confederate driving a car near campus to frustrate other male motorists. The confederate accomplished this task by stopping at a traffic light and then hesitating for fifteen seconds before driving on when the light turned from red to green. Because motorists honk their horns frequently to express irritation (Turner et al., 1975), two observers sitting in a parked car nearby recorded whether the frustrated drivers honked their horns. This was the dependent measure of aggression.

Three different stimuli were introduced when the light was still red in order to determine whether incompatible responses would reduce the motorists' tendencies to aggress (honk). In one experimental condition, the induced incompatible response was empathy—a female confederate wearing a bandage on her leg hobbled across the street on crutches. In the se-cond condition, this same confederate induced humor by crossing the street wearing an outlandish clown mask. Finally, in the third experimental condition, mild sexual arousal was induced—the female confederate wore a very brief and revealing outfit while crossing the street. In addition to these experimental conditions, Baron also included two control conditions. In one (dis-traction), the confederate crossed the street dressed in conservative clothing, while in the other (control), she was absent en-tirely from the scene. Consistent with the incompatible response hypothesis, inducing empathy, humor, and mild sexual arousal resulted in less horn honking and a greater delay in horn honking than in either of the control conditions. These findings suggest that inducing incompatible responses in potential aggressors can inhibit overt aggressive behavior. Besides empathy, humor, and sexual arousal, additional research finds that prosocial music—such as Michael Jackson's "Heal the World" or the Beatles' "Help"—can also short-circuit aggressive responses (Greitemeyer, 2011).

TEACHING NONAGGRESSIVE RESPONSES TO PROVOCATION CAN CONTROL AGGRESSION.

Beyond the rather simple strategies of punishment and induction of incompatible emotions, social psychologists have also relied on the considerable cognitive abilities of human beings in constructing more elaborate techniques for controlling aggression (Dunn, 2001).

Social Modeling: Teaching by Example

Just as destructive models can teach people how to act aggressively, social learning theorists contend that nonaggressive models can urge observers to exercise restraint in the face of provocation. In an experiment supporting this claim, research participants who watched a nonaggressive model exhibit restraint in administering shocks to a "vic-tim" in a learning experiment were subsequently less aggressive than those who observed an aggressive model (Baron & Kepner, 1970).

Besides reducing aggression by modeling nonaggressive behavior, aggression can also be controlled by having an authority figure condemn the behavior of aggressive individuals. For example, research demonstrates that if a child watches violence on television in the presence of an adult who condemns the violence, the child is less likely to later imitate this aggression (Hicks, 1968; Horton & Santogrossi, 1978). This bit of knowledge was not lost on my wife and me in raising our children. On numer-ous occasions while watching television with our daughters, the screen would suddenly erupt with violent images so quickly that we did not have time to change the channel. Each time this happened we condemned the violence. These efforts had an impact. When Lillian was four years old, we were watching a Looney Toons cartoon and Elmer Fudd suddenly pulled out a shotgun and blew off Daffy Duck's head. With-out missing a beat Lillian turned to us and said, "Boy, that wasn't very nice was it? People shouldn't be so mean."

Internalizing Antiaggression Beliefs

As we have discussed throughout the text, when people internalize certain beliefs and attitudes into their self-concept, they are more likely to act in ways consistent with those beliefs and attitudes. Recognizing the important role that the self plays in behavior change, social scientists have devised a cognitive strategy to facilitate the internaliza-tion of antiviolent beliefs by simply having people think of reasons why aggression is a bad idea. For example, in one study, when children were prompted to generate reasons why it was bad to imitate TV violence, this intervention was effective in later reducing the impact that TV violence had on their attitudes and behavior regarding aggression (Huesmann et al., 1983). Generating these antiviolent be-liefs apparently caused the children to incorporate them into their self-concepts and overall worldview. The subsequent re-duction in aggression through this "belief ownership" was still measurable two years after the initial intervention.

Apologies as Aggression Controllers

The fact that people can reason and develop explanations for their actions and those of others also explains why apologies can effectively reduce anger and aggression (Eaton & Struthers, 2006). An experiment by Kenichi Ohbuchi and his coworkers (1989) demonstrated this aggression-reducing effect of apologies. In the experiment, Japanese college students were embarrassed by their poor performance while working on a complex experimental task. The reason they did so poorly was that the experimenter's assistant committed a series of errors in presenting the experimental materials to them. When the experimenter learned of each participant's poor performance, he roundly criticized the assistant, who then either apologized for causing the participants to fail, or said nothing. After this, participants were asked to rate the assistant on several dimensions and were told that these ratings would be used as a basis for the assistant's grade. A public apology in the experimenter's presence significantly reduced the participants' hostility in these ratings. This study is important because it suggests that merely offering an apology can defuse another's hostile aggression.

There is a gender difference in willingness to apologize, with women being more willing than men to take responsibility for a perceived social transgression (Gonzales et al., 1990). In fact, women tend to become more apologetic when severely reproached for a social transgression, while men respond more defensively to severe reproaches (Hodgins & Liebeskind, 2003). Underlying this greater unwillingness of men to offer apologies is a fear of "losing face" or social status in such confrontations (Hodgins et al., 1996). These gender differences may partly explain why men are more likely than women to be involved in physical altercations.

Social Skills Training

The art of apologizing is just one skill in a larger repertoire of interpersonal skills learned through the process of socialization. As children mature, their impulsive aggressive reactions to anger and conflict are often replaced by more socially acceptable responses, such as negotiation, compromise, and cooperative problem solving. However, children with low intelligence are less likely to learn these prosocial skills and, therefore, are more likely to retain a combative interpersonal style that invites aggression and further interferes with their intellectual development (Huesmann et al., 1987). For these antisocial children, and for adults who have trouble managing their own aggression, deliberately and consciously teaching them alternative non-aggressive strategies can be extremely beneficial.

Social skills training can take many forms, including the role playing of nonaggressive behaviors, modeling the prosocial actions of others, or generating nonaggressive alternative solutions to conflict (Greenberg & Kusche, 2006). In one twelve-session intervention program employing some of these cognitive strategies, Nancy Guerra and Ronald Slaby (1990) found that male and female juvenile delinquents not only showed increased skills in solving social problems, but they also exhibited a significant decrease in their aggressive beliefs and actions. This study, and others like it (McCarthy-Tucker et al., 1999), indicate that aggressive behavior can be changed by teaching people to replace maladaptive thoughts and behaviors with ones that foster social harmony and conflict resolution.

Reducing Exposure to Violence

An essential ingredient in reducing aggressive responses is to diminish people's exposure to violence. Recent studies indicate that aggressive behavior in children is significantly reduced when they spend less time watching violent television shows and playing violent video games (Rosenkoetter et al., 2004). One such study examined third- and fourth-grade students at two comparable schools over a six-month period (Robinson et al., 2001). In one of the schools, TV and video-game exposure was reduced by one-third by encouraging students and parents to engage in alternative forms of home entertainment, while in the other school no effort was made to reduce exposure. The researchers found that children at the intervention school were subsequently less aggressive on the playground than students at the control school, especially those students who were initially rated as most aggressive by their classmates.

SECTION SUMMARY

- Punishment can both increase and decrease aggression.

- Inducing incompatible responses can inhibit aggression.

- Nonaggressive responding can occur through the following:

    social modeling

    internalizing anti-aggression beliefs

    offering apologies

    social skills training

    reducing exposure to violence

APPLICATIONS

HOW CAN ACQUAINTANCE RAPE BE PREVENTED?

Given that sexual assault is all too commonly found within dating relationships, an increasing number of rape prevention pro-grams are being developed to not only train women how to protect themselves, but also to change the attitudes, beliefs, and behaviors of potential rapists, namely, ordinary men. Listed here are some of the common elements in these acquaintance rape prevention programs (Garrity, 2011):

Targeting the rape myth: Discrediting the rape myth is one of the most widely used—and effective—techniques in rape education pro-grams (Johansson-Love & Geer, 2003; Kress et al., 2006). Generally, participants first read or view fictional depictions of women becoming sexually aroused while being raped, followed by the presentation of the scientific and medical facts of rape trauma. One problem with most rape prevention programs is that they target rape myths only for female victims, despite the fact that 10 percent of rape victims are men.

Sexual communication training: As previously discussed, men are more likely than women to misinterpret friendliness from another person as sexual interest. Educating people about how such sexual misunderstandings come about has been shown to have a positive influence on beliefs and attitudes about rape and violence (Milhausen et al., 2006).

Discussing negative sexual scripts: Many programs accompany sexual communication training with discussions of the contrasting sexual scripts learned by most women and men that contribute to acquaintance rape (Pacifici et al., 2001).

Inducing empathy: Empathy is a feeling of compassion and tenderness for people who experience pain, loss, or other unfortunate circumstances in their lives. Because people who experience empathy are less likely to believe that victims caused their own plight, rape prevention programs that deliberately structure their presentation to induce empathy for sexual assault victims are more effective than programs that do not focus on empathy arousal (Foubert & Newberry, 2006; O'Donohue et al., 2003).

Role playing: After learning about the rape myth, negative sexual scripts, and sexual miscommunication, participants often engage in role-playing exercises. These role-playing activities involve practicing caring ways to refuse and respond to sexual advances, as well as responsibly handling sexual rejection (Pacifici et al., 2001).

Nonconfrontational approaches: When discussing rape myths, male misperceptions, and male "predators," trainers must be careful not to cast male participants into the "enemy" camp. Inducing defensiveness and alienation in male participants is one of the surest ways to guarantee that desirable changes will not take place (Dallager & Rosen, 1993). Instead, effective trainers adopt a nonconfrontational approach. When discussing cultural ideologies that promote rape, they emphasize the point that men are also victims of these ideologies because they are taught to behave according to a very restrictive hypermasculine role.

These are some of the basic elements in many acquaintance rape prevention programs. Yet, an effective program has more than just these elements—*time duration* of the training is also important. Rape education researchers contend that training programs that meet only once or twice are insufficient in effectively challenging rape-supportive ideology (Schaeffer & Nelson, 1993). Instead, they strongly recommend that classes meet weekly over several months. Such a format is ideally suited for a college course.

Kimberly Lonsway and her colleagues (1998) evaluated one such semester-long college program (Campus Acquaintance Rape Education, or CARE) that incorporates the course elements just listed. Their findings indicate that it is effective in changing beliefs and behaviors regarding sexual communication and sexual assault. For example, students who participated in the CARE program were subsequently less accepting of cultural rape myths and adversarial sexual beliefs than students who took a human sexuality course. The CARE students also became more willing and able to directly express themselves and assert their needs in ways that facilitated increased sexual communication in a dating relationship. In a two-year follow-up survey, Lonsway and her colleagues found that the CARE participants remained less accepting of cultural rape myths than students who were enrolled in the human sexuality course, but there were no group differences in endorsement of adversarial sexual beliefs. Although more research is needed in how to best design and implement rape prevention training programs, this study suggests that the changes that take place in such venues can have a lasting, positive impact.

THE BIG PICTURE

Nonviolence is the answer to the crucial political and moral questions of our time; the need for man to overcome oppression and violence without resorting to oppression and violence. Man must evolve for all human conflict a method which rejects revenge, aggression and retaliation. The foundation of such a method is love.

Rev. Martin Luther King, Jr., 1964

If we could point to one single strategy to effectively control aggression in a wide range of settings, it would simply be the adoption of the of the nonviolent philosophy practiced by civil rights leader Martin Luther King. Indeed, research suggests that forgiving others' aggressive acts against us can actually enhance our own health by lowering stress and increasing a sense of personal control (Witvliet, et al. 2001). Unfortunately, because the widespread adoption of a nonviolent philosophy will not take place anytime soon, we are left with a number of imperfect intervention strategies, each of which has a reasonable chance of reducing aggression when certain conditions are met.

The cognitive-neoassociationist model tells us that impulsive aggression is most likely to occur when we are engaged in highly routine activities and thus are not consciously monitoring our thoughts, feelings, or actions. However, if these aggression-related tendencies are subjected to higher-level thinking, we can often modify and control them. What causes these aggression-related tendencies to come under the control of more complex cognitive processes? Self-awareness, one of our great human gifts. Use this gift to control your own aggression. When you become angry, try to make sense of your negative feelings before reacting. Analyze the implications of your actions and consider alternative nonaggressive responses. By bringing into play these cognitive control mechanisms, the link between negative affect and aggression can be short-circuited.

In summary, although our present ability to control aggression may seem meager at best, keep in mind that our analysis of aggression reveals that this is a highly complex phenomenon. It not only springs from a number of psychological sources (for example, anger, fear of punishment, desire for rewards), it also appears to be shaped by a variety of environmental factors. For me, in some respects, the various forms of aggression in society today seem like a modern-day Hydra. In Greek mythology, the Hydra was a terribly dangerous nine-headed serpent that was exceedingly difficult to kill. Whenever one head was chopped off, two grew back. Fortunately for the ancient Greeks, the Hydra was finally destroyed by their superhero, Hercules. There are no superheroes in contemporary social psychology, nor in the larger society. Yet if we ever hope to slay our Hydra, it will entail a Herculean task by all elements of society.

WEB SITES

> Check out our web site
> www.BVTLab.com
> for chapter-by-chapter flashcards, summaries, and practice quizzes.

ACCESSED THROUGH www.BVTLab.com/sop6
Web sites for this chapter focus on research and theory on family violence, acquaintance rape, violence on television, and recommendations on how to control anger before it leads to aggression.

MINNESOTA CENTER AGAINST VIOLENCE AND ABUSE
This is the web site for the Minnesota Center Against Violence and Abuse listing links to education and training resources, papers and reports on aggression, and resource materials for teaching about family violence.

AMERICAN PSYCHOLOGICAL ASSOCIATION
The American Psychological Association web site has a number of relevant web pages, including one that examines research on the psychological effects of television violence and another on how to control anger before it leads to aggression.

"FRIENDS" RAPING FRIENDS: COULD IT HAPPEN TO YOU?
This is a web site devoted to the facts about acquaintance rape, including its causes and consequences, and how to avoid situations that might lead to acquaintance rape.

CENTER FOR THE STUDY AND PREVENTION OF VIOLENCE
This is the web site for the Center for the Study and Prevention of Violence, which has fact sheets on violence, research summaries, and a list of papers you can request.

NATIONAL CONSORTIUM ON VIOLENCE RESEARCH
This is the web site for the National Consortium on Violence Research, which is a research and training center specializing in violence research. The mission of the consortium is to advance basic scientific knowledge about the causes or factors contributing to interpersonal violence.

INTERNATIONAL SOCIETY FOR RESEARCH ON AGGRESSION
This web site is devoted to the scientific study of aggression and violence around the world.

Donations For Tsunami Survivors

12

Chapter 12
Prosocial Behavior: Helping Others

CHAPTER OUTLINE

PREVIEW   The presence of others can reduce people's tendencies to relieve others' suffering by helping. Does learning about the barriers to helping insulate us from their effects?

THE BIG PICTURE

WEB SITES

INTRODUCTION

In Chapter 2, you learned how social psychological research is sometimes motivated by the researcher's desire to explain some real-life incident that has received wide news coverage. One of the most powerful and memorable examples of a real-life event spurring social psychological research was the Kitty Genovese murder, which occurred on March 13, 1964, in the New York City borough of Queens. Although you may have previously read or heard about this infamous act of violence, almost all accounts in psychology textbooks have unknowingly misrepresented the facts in this case. Here now is the story based on a reanalysis of archived material (Manning et al., 2007; Rasenberger, 2006).

At 3:20 AM Kitty Genovese was returning home from work as a bar manager when a man attacked her with a hunting knife near her apartment building. Kitty screamed, "Oh, my God! He stabbed me. Please help me! Please help me!" After her cry rang out in the night, about three to six of her neighbors (not thirty-eight onlookers, as is often reported) went to their windows to see what was going on. These first eyewitnesses certainly heard Kitty's voice, but they may not have understood her words. One alarmed woman looked out her window, saw Kitty and her assailant "standing close together, not fighting or anything," and decided this was not an emergency. This onlooker went back to bed. A second eyewitness saw the assailant bending over and beating Kitty, who was already on the ground. This onlooker did nothing to intervene. A third eyewitness hollered at the assailant from his seventh-story window, "Hey, get out of there! Let that girl alone!" Probably because of this shouted command, the assailant got into his car and drove away. By then, a large number of neighbors were looking out their apartment windows. They saw Kitty pick herself up off the ground, reach for her purse, look around, and begin walking unsteadily away. She was no longer screaming but seemed to be walking in a slow "dreamlike" state. A couple of eyewitnesses later told police that Kitty's gait made them think that "she was either drunk, or had been beaten up."

Ten minutes passed in relative silence as Kitty staggered around a corner to a small hallway in a nearby building. She was now out of sight of almost all her neighbors. During that ten-minute time period, there is evidence that a few neighbors

On the night of March 31, 1964, Kitty Genovese was repeatedly stabbed outside her apartment building.

phoned the police but may have hung up before providing full details of the assault. Then witnesses saw the assailant return and begin casually walking down the sidewalk, looking side to side. One eyewitness ran from one window of her apartment to the next to keep the attacker in her sight. At the same time, another neighbor reached for the phone to call the police, but his wife told him, "Don't; thirty people have probably called by now." Within seconds, the killer found Kitty in the hallway where he sexually assaulted her and then stabbed her in the throat. Only one person saw part of that second attack. Instead of phoning the police, this man phoned a female neighbor, who immediately contacted the police and then rushed to Kitty's side. The police arrived on the scene within minutes, but Kitty died soon after.

It is now clear that most of the neighbors who were present during this tragic murder were not apathetic bystanders as has been so widely reported for so many years. Yet it is also clear that Kitty Genovese did not receive the timely help that may have saved her life that night. If you heard Kitty Genovese's cries for help do you think you would have come to her rescue? If you had instead only seen this victim walking unsteadily but did not see the first attack, do you think you would have understood what was happening? This murder and the events surrounding it—both real and misreported—were instrumental in prompting numerous studies on the social psychology of helping. In this chapter, we address and try to answer five basic questions about helping. First, why do we help? Second, who is most likely to help? Third, when do we help?, Fourth, whom do we help? And fifth, are there hidden costs for those who receive help?

WHY DO WE HELP?

prosocial behavior

Voluntary behavior that is carried out to benefit another person

Before tackling these five helping questions, let's begin by defining our topic. **Prosocial behavior** is voluntary behavior that is carried out to benefit another person (Batson & Powell, 2003; Dovidio et al., 2006). This definition excludes beneficial actions that are not performed voluntarily or are not performed with the intention of helping another. Thus, if a store manager forces employees to donate part of their salaries to charity, their actions would not be considered prosocial because they really would have had no *choice* in rendering assistance. Likewise, if a terrified person fleeing from a charging bull accidentally pushes someone out of the path of the animal, this action also would not be prosocial because the pushing was unintentional and was not meant to benefit another. On the other hand, the actions of the female neighbor who called the police and then ran to Kitty Genovese's side perfectly fit our definition because she freely chose those actions and her intention was to benefit another. Volunteering your time at a community food pantry, donating money to a local charity, or mowing the lawn of a sick neighbor would also be examples of prosocial behavior. All these behaviors each have unique characteristics, but they all involve intentional actions that benefit others.

> **"***Nothing makes you happier than when you reach out in mercy to someone who is badly hurt.***"**
>
> Mother Teresa, born Agnes Gonxha Bojaxhiu, Albanian Catholic nun and humanitarian, 1910–1997)

THERE ARE TWO BASIC FORMS OF HELPING.

Beyond the basic definition, philosophers and a number of social scientists have traditionally described two forms of helpful behavior that are based on very different motives. For example, nineteenth-century philosopher Auguste Comte (1875) contended that **egoistic helping**—in which the person wants something in return—is based on *egoism*, because the ultimate goal of the helper is to increase his or her own welfare. In contrast, Comte stated that **altruistic helping**, in which the person expects nothing in return, is based on *altruism*, because the ultimate goal is to increase another's welfare.

egoistic helping

A form of helping in which the ultimate goal of the helper is to increase his or her own welfare

altruistic helping

A form of helping in which the ultimate goal of the helper is to increase another's welfare without expecting anything in return

As we discuss later in the chapter, social scientists disagree on whether any useful distinctions can be made between egoistic and altruistic helping, and some argue that all helping is ultimately egoistic in nature. As already noted, many social scientists believe that people sometimes help solely to benefit another, while at other times they help in order to achieve some personal gain. In addition, it has also been suggested that because of inborn characteristics, people may be predisposed to pro-social behavior. Before reading further, spend a few minutes answering the items in *Self/Social Connection Exercise 12.1*.

Self/Social Connections Exercise 12.1

Is Your Helping Orientation Altruistic, Egoistic, or Unhelpful?

Helping-Orientation Questionnaire

Directions

While reading these descriptions of hypothetical situations, imagine yourself in each of them and pick the action that best describes what you would do:

1. You have come across a lost wallet with a large sum of money in it, as well as identification of the owner. You _____
    A. return the wallet without letting the owner know who you are.
    B. return the wallet in hopes of receiving a reward.
    C. keep the wallet and the money.
    D. leave the wallet where you found it.

2. A person in one of your classes is having trouble at home and with school work. You _____
    A. help the person as much as you can.
    B. tell the person not to bother you.
    C. leave the person alone to work out his or her own problems.
    D. agree to tutor the person for a reasonable fee.

3. When it comes to cooperation when you would rather not, you usually _____
    A. cooperate if it is helpful to others.
    B. cooperate if it is helpful to yourself.
    C. refuse to get involved.
    D. avoid situations where you might be asked to cooperate.

4. A neighbor calls you and asks for a ride to a store that is six blocks away. You _____
    A. refuse, thinking you will never need a favor from him (or her).
    B. explain that you are too busy at the moment.
    C. immediately give the ride and wait while the neighbor shops.
    D. consent if the neighbor is a good friend.

5. You are approached by someone asking for a contribution to a well-known charity. You _____
    A. give if there is something received in return.
    B. refuse to contribute.
    C. give whatever amount you can.
    D. pretend you are in a hurry.

6. You are in a waiting room with another person. If you heard a scream in the adjoining room and the other person failed to respond, you would _____
    A. help the screaming person whether the other person helps or not.
    B. help the screaming person only if the other person does too.
    C. wait to see if the screaming continues.
    D. leave the room.

7. When asked to volunteer for a task in which you will receive no pay, you _____
    A. avoid or put off answering.
    B. explain that you don't agree with the objectives to be accomplished and therefore couldn't volunteer.
    C. compromise and help if you will receive some recognition.
    D. volunteer without question.

Exercise 12.1 *Continued*

Scoring

The information below shows which answers on the Helping-Orientation Questionnaire indicate altruistic helping, egoistic helping, and unhelpful behavior. It also shows the percentage of people who gave each answer in a recent survey. Do your responses indicate that your helping-orientation is predominantly altruistic, egoistic, or unhelpful?

Item	Altruistic helping	Egoistic helping	Unhelpful behavior
1.	A (38 percent)	B (47 percent)	C,D (15 percent)
2.	A (86 percent)	D (4 percent)	B,C (10 percent)
3.	A (61 percent)	B (20 percent)	C,D (19 percent)
4.	C (33 percent)	D (56 percent)	A,B (11 percent)
5.	C (70 percent)	A (4 percent)	B,D (26 percent)
6.	A (50 percent)	B (10 percent)	C,D (40 percent)
7.	D (35 percent)	C (27 percent)	A,B (39 percent)

From D. Romer, et al., "A Person-Situation Approach to Altruistic Behavior" in *Journal of Personality and Social Psychology*, 51:1001–1012. Copyright 1986 by the American Psychological Association. Reprinted by permission. Why Do We Help?

HELPING IS CONSISTENT WITH EVOLUTIONARY THEORY.

As discussed in previous chapters, one principle of evolutionary theory is that any social behaviors that enhance reproductive success (the conception, birth, and survival of offspring) will continue to be passed on from one generation to the next. However, to reproduce, an animal must first survive. Often, an animal's survival depends on how well it can compete with other members of its own species for limited resources. This evolutionary fact would seem to dictate that animals should be selfish, looking out first and foremost for themselves. Yet what of the seemingly selfless act of helping?

Evolutionary psychologists have documented countless instances in which animals have put their own lives at risk to protect other members of their own species from danger (Fouts, 1997; Wilson, 1996). For example, a chimpanzee foraging for food with its troop will often emit a warning call to alert the others about a nearby predator. By calling out, this chimp is the one most likely to be caught by the predator. As this example illustrates, helping others can be downright deadly. When you are dead, your reproductive days are over. Thus, from an evolutionary perspective, how could helping be advantageous to reproduction?

Kin Selection

As previously outlined in the Chapter 11 discussion of aggression, evolutionary theorists contend that it is not individual survival that is important, but rather, it is *gene* survival that promotes reproductive fitness (Archer, 1991). Because your blood relatives share many of your same genes, by promoting their survival you can also preserve your genes even if you don't survive the helpful act. This principle of **kin selection** states that you will exhibit preferences for helping blood relatives because this will increase the odds that your genes will be transmitted to subsequent generations (Madsen et al., 2007; Stewart-Williams, 2007).

Although the principle of kin selection explains why we are more likely to help those who are related to us by blood, it does not explain the countless incidents of people helping total strangers. Stranger helping is found not only among humans but among other species as well. For example, female chimpanzees, lions, mule deer, dolphins, and bluebirds have been observed protecting and taking care of nonrelated newborns deserted by or separated from their mothers (Goodall, 1986; Lingle et al., 2007). Given

kin selection
....
A theory that people will exhibit preferences for helping blood relatives because this will increase the odds that their genes will be transmitted to subsequent generations

this fact, how can evolutionary theorists explain prosocial behavior that extends beyond one's family?

Reciprocal Helping

Robert Trivers (1971) has described a way in which helping strangers could have arisen through natural selection. This principle, which he called *reciprocal altruism*, involves mutual helping, usually separated in time. However, because "altruism" refers to motives and Trivers was merely referring to behavior, we will use the more accurate term **reciprocal helping** when referring to this mutual helping. According to this principle, people are likely to help strangers if it is understood that the recipient is expected to return the favor at some time in the future. In such a world of reciprocal helping, the cost of aiding another is more than offset by the later returned help (Hames & McCabe, 2007; Kurzban, 2003). For reciprocal helping to evolve, the benefit to the recipient must be high and the cost to the helper must be relatively low. In addition, the likelihood of their positions being reversed in the future must also be high, and there must be a way to identify "cheaters"—those who do not reciprocate (Brown & Moore, 2000).

A good example of reciprocal helping is *social grooming*. In many species, one individual cleans the other's fur or feathers; later, the "groomee" returns the favor (Matheson & Bernstein, 2000; Schino et al., 2007). Grooming is a low-cost activity (only time lost) that returns high benefits to the recipient (removing disease-carrying parasites). Trivers (1983) believes that reciprocal helping is most likely to evolve in a species when certain conditions exist. Three of these conditions are (1) *social group living*, so that individuals have ample opportunity to give and receive help; (2) *mutual dependence*, in which species survival depends on cooperation; and (3) the *lack of rigid dominance hierarchies*, so that reciprocal helping will enhance each animal's power.

Considerable research supports both kin selection and reciprocal helping among humans and other animals. For example, when threatened by predators, squirrels are much more likely to warn genetically related squirrels and squirrels with which they live than unrelated squirrels or those from other areas (Sherman, 1985). Similarly, across a wide variety of human cultures, relatives receive more help than nonrelatives, especially if the help involves considerable costs, such as being a kidney donor (Borgida et al., 1992). Reciprocal helping is also common in humans, and, consistent with evolutionary-based mechanisms to prevent cheating, when people are unable to reciprocate, they tend to experience guilt and shame (Fehr & Gaechter, 2002; Nahum-Shani et al., 2011; Wonderly, 1996). However, it is also true that people's perceptions of helpers' motives can weaken

reciprocal helping

An evolutionary principle stating that people expect that anyone helping another will have that favor returned at some future time, also known as reciprocal altruism

Social grooming among gorillas is an example of reciprocal helping. How does the evolutionary perspective explain such behavior?

feelings of obligation to reciprocate. Helpers who appear to render assistance only after weighing their costs and benefits are perceived as less worthy of reciprocal helping than those who appear to help out of empathy for the victim (Ames et al., 2004).

Taken together, this research suggests that there may be mechanisms for the genetic transmission of helpful inclinations from generation to generation. Yet unlike many species where altruistic behavior is closely tied to genetic heritage, human genes influence behavior in a more indirect manner (Kruger, 2003). As I have stated throughout this text, although ancient evolutionary forces may have left us with *capacities* (such as the capacity to behave altruistically), current social and environmental forces encourage or discourage the actual development and use of those capacities.

SOCIAL NORMS DEFINE THE RULES OF HELPING OTHERS.

Although prosocial behavior may have a genetic basis, it makes sense that social mechanisms would develop to enforce these evolutionarily adaptive helping strategies (Nesse, 2000; Simon, 1990). Chapter 7 discussed how general rules of conduct, known as *social norms*, prescribe how people should generally behave. These shared expectations are backed up by the proverbial carrot and stick: the threat of group punishment if the norms are not obeyed and the promise of rewards for conforming. Prosocial norms are expectations to behave selflessly in bestowing benefits on others. Three social norms that serve as guidelines for prosocial behavior deal with *reciprocity, responsibility,* and *justice*.

The first of these prosocial norms, the *norm of reciprocity*, is based on maintaining fairness in social relationships. As discussed in Chapters 7 and 10, this norm prescribes that people should be paid back for whatever they give us. Regarding prosocial behavior, this means helping those who help us (Brown & Moore, 2000; Gouldner, 1960). As mentioned in the previous section, this norm also explains the discomfort that people typically experience when they receive help but cannot give something back in return.

In comparison to the reciprocity norm, the other two prosocial norms dictate that people should help due to a greater awareness of what is right. For example, interviews with non-Jewish rescuers of Jews in Nazi-occupied territories during World War II found that the rescuers' willingness to risk their lives to save others was significantly shaped by a sense of social responsibility (Fagin-Jones & Midlarsky, 2007). According to the **norm of social responsibility,** we should help when others are in need and dependent on us (Bierhoff, 2002). Acting on this norm, adults feel responsible for the health and safety of children, teachers have a sense of duty and obligation to their students, and police and firefighters believe they must help even at the risk of their own lives. (Frey et al., 2010) This social responsibility norm requires help givers to render assistance regardless of the recipient's worthiness and without an expectation of being rewarded.

Unfortunately for the needy of the world, even though most people endorse the social responsibility norm, they often do not act in accordance with it. One reason for this nonadherence is that people also often believe in social justice (Darley, 2001). In contrast to the dependent-driven social responsibility norm, the **norm of social justice** stipulates that people should help only when they believe that others *deserve* assistance (Marjanovic et al., 2009). How does one become a "deserving" person? Melvin Lerner (1980, 1997) contends that at least in North American society, people become entitled to the deserving label by either possessing socially desirable personality characteristics or by engaging in socially desirable behaviors. Thus, according to the social justice norm, if "good" people encounter unfortunate circumstances, they deserve our help and we have a duty to render assistance. The norm of social justice appears to be stronger in individualist cultures—where people are held more personally responsible for their actions—than in collectivist cultures (Mullen & Skitka, 2009).

POLITICAL AND SOCIAL CLASS DIFFERENCES SHAPE WILLINGNESS TO HELP.

During national political campaigns, the Republican Party regularly attempts to dispel public perceptions that their candidates are unsympathetic to the needy by portraying themselves as "compassionate conservatives." Republicans often define *compassionate*

norm of social responsibility
• • • • • • • • • • • • • • • • • • •
A social norm stating that we should help when others are in need and are dependent on us

norm of social justice
• • • • • • • • • • • • • • • • • • •
A social norm stating that we should help only when we believe that others deserve our assistance

conservatism as the belief that conservatism and compassion complement each other, but the poor and others in need must also accept personal responsibility and self-reliance. In other words, those who seek help need to know that they can't blame "the system" for their own misfortunes. Is there any truth in associating compassion with liberal versus conservative political ideologies?

As previously discussed in Chapter 6 (pp. 219–221), American democracy was founded on the sometimes conflicting belief systems of *individualism* (or self-reliance) and *egalitarianism* (equal treatment of groups and sympathy for the disadvantaged). Because conservatives emphasize individualism and liberals emphasize egalitarianism in their respective political ideologies, they often develop different positions regarding the moral obligations society should have toward the disadvantaged (Graham et al., 2009). In essence, willingness to help depends on how conservatives and liberals judge the morality of those in need. For example, in explaining poverty, conservatives tend to make dispositional attributions, blaming poverty on self-indulgence, laziness, or low intelligence; and they respond with anger and neglect. In contrast, liberals tend to make situational attributions, perceiving the poor as victims of social injustice; and they respond with empathy and help giving (Biernat et al., 1996; Weiner et al., 2011).

Research also finds that conservatives are less willing to help victims of natural disasters than liberals. In a national sample of over one thousand adults following floods in the Mississippi and Ohio River valleys, Linda Skitka (1999) found that people with a conservative political orientation consistently held flood victims more responsible for their plight and for resolving it than did those with a liberal orientation. Invoking the social justice norm, conservatives were even reluctant to provide public support for immediate humanitarian aid (clean water, food, shelter) to those who had not taken actions to protect themselves against flood risks. Although liberals were significantly more compassionate in their willingness to provide immediate help, like conservatives, they were unenthusiastic about using federal disaster assistance to financially bail out victims. Overall, these studies suggest that, when faced with those who need help in situations not immediately life-threatening, liberals are more likely to adhere to the norm of social responsibility, while conservatives adhere more closely to the norm of social justice. In other words, "compassionate conservativism" is a more discriminating approach to helping others than that practiced by liberals, who have been accused by conservatives as having "bleeding hearts" when it comes to assisting those who are disadvantaged.

Closely related to questions regarding conservative and liberal differences in willingness to help is the question of whether helping might also be associated with socioeconomic status. In the United States, wealth has increasingly become concentrated in the hands of a select few. For example, households in the top 1 percent of the wealth distribution own 30 percent of the total wealth in the country, and individuals in this elite 1 percent economic bracket are more than 800 times wealthier than individuals in the bottom 40 percent economic bracket (Díaz-Giménez et al., 1997). Compared to the wealthy, individuals in the lower social classes have fewer economic resources and educational opportunities, while being exposed to greater everyday violence and hardships (Oakes & Rossi, 2003; Staggs et al., 2007). Due to these tough life circumstances, lower class individuals might be expected to focus on their own welfare because helping others drains a larger proportion of their resources compared to the wealthy. An alternative view is that individuals in the lower social classes should help others more because behaving generously is likely to promote trust and cooperation from others, thus ensuring that in times of hardship, their needs will also be met.

In a recent series of studies, Paul Piff and his coworkers (2010) analyzed the relationship between Americans' socioeconomic status and their willingness to engage in prosocial actions. Across four studies, the researchers found that, unlike upper-class individuals who tended to report social values that placed high priority on satisfying their own needs, lower class individuals expressed more concern for the welfare of others. Further, this difference in social values not only influenced individuals' emotional responses to others' misfortunes, it also influenced their willingness to help. Members of the lower class were more generous, charitable, trusting, and helpful compared with their upper class counterparts. These findings are consistent with nationwide surveys which report that lower income Americans give proportionally more of their incomes to charity than do higher income Americans (Greve, 2009; James & Sharpe, 2007). Piff and his colleagues contend that this research supports their theory that social class shapes people's prosocial tendencies so that those who have less give more, while those who have a great deal hold on to their wealth and are more likely to use it for their own purposes. The researchers further suggest that this different pattern of giving versus holding on to resources among lower and upper class people may also contribute to the increasing economic inequality in American society.

INDIVIDUALISTS AND COLLECTIVISTS DIFFER IN THEIR HELPING TENDENCIES.

If a free society cannot help the many who are poor, it cannot save the few who are rich.

John F. Kennedy, 35th U.S. president, 1917–1963

Help the weak ones that cry for help, help the prosecuted and the victim ... they are the comrades that fight and fall.

Nicola Sacco, Italian-born anarchist, 1891–1927

Research conducted in both individualist and collectivist cultures indicates that the norm of reciprocity may be universal (Gergen et al., 1975). Regarding the norm of social responsibility, a number of cross-cultural studies have found that adult members of collectivist cultures are not only more likely to help others of their ingroup than are members of individualist cultures but also to express greater enjoyment in meeting these social obligations than do individualists (Bontempo et al., 1990). Similar cross-cultural differences have also been obtained when studying children's prosocial actions. For example, children from the collectivist cultures of Kenya, Mexico, and the Philippines were found to be much more helpful than children from the United States (Whiting & Edwards, 1988). A likely reason for this difference is that collectivists are much more likely than individualists to stress ingroup cooperation and individual sacrifice. In such a context, people may feel greater moral obligation to help than if they grew up in a less group-oriented environment.

Joan Miller and her colleagues (1990) found support for this perspective in a study of the moral reasoning of South Asian Indians and of Americans. Participants read a series of hypothetical situations in which the main character in the story failed to help someone experiencing a life-threatening, a moderately serious, or a minor need. The needy person either was the main character's child, best friend, or a stranger. Results indicated that Indian respondents tended to perceive helping as the main character's social responsibility in all conditions, even when the need was minor. This means they believed that in all situations, giving help should be dictated by social norms and not by the personal norms of the potential helper. In comparison, American respondents believed that the norm of social responsibility should only be dictated in life-threatening cases or when parents were faced with moderately serious needs of their children. In all other instances, Americans believed that the main character's decision to help should be based on his or her own personal norms of help giving and should not be subject to social regulation.

Charitable organizations depend on people's generosity to receive the necessary funds to provide disadvantaged individuals with the help they need. Who is more likely to feel empathy for unfortunate others and donate a higher proportion of their income to the needy, the wealthy or the poor?

Critical
THINKING

What sort of cultural role models might influence the "helping habits" of boys and girls? How might greater gender role flexibility influence male and female helping tendencies?

Overall, it appears that collectivist Indian culture holds to a broader and more stringent view of social responsibility than does the individualist American culture (Miller, 1994; Miller et al., 2011). For life-threatening needs of both strangers and loved ones and for moderately serious needs of one's family members, both Indians and Americans are likely to subscribe to the social responsibility norm. However, for needs of friends and strangers that are not life threatening, Americans are generally less likely than Indians to subscribe to the social responsibility norm.

What about Americans with an ethnic heritage rooted in collectivism? Are they more helpful than Americans with more of an individualist heritage? Ronnie Janoff-Bulman and Hallie Leggatt (2002) tested this hypothesis by having Latino-American and Anglo-American college students complete a questionnaire assessing the extent to which they felt obligated to help and wanted to help across a variety of social situations. Results mirrored the cross-cultural findings for people with collectivist versus individualist orientations. Although respondents from both ethnic groups reported a strong sense of obligation to help close friends and family members in need, the more collectivist Latinos expressed a greater desire to engage in these expected behaviors than the more individualist Anglos. In addition, Latino students also felt a stronger sense of social obligation and desire to help more distant family members and friends than did Anglo students. The two ethnic groups did not differ in their motivation to help strangers. Additional research suggests that underlying Latino Americans' greater desire to help more distant family members and friends is a core aspect of traditional Latino American culture, namely *familism*, which refers to a set of norms related to family solidarity and emotional and economic interdependence within an extended family network (Armenta et al., 2011).

So does this mean that people with greater collectivist tendencies are more helpful than those with greater individualist tendencies? Not necessarily. The individualist-collectivist cultural differences discussed thus far apply only to ingroup helping. When ingroup members need help, people from collectivist cultures and collectivist-oriented Americans perceive help giving as both more obligatory ("I must help") and more personally desirable ("I want to help") than people from individualist cultures and Americans with a more individualist orientation. However, when those needing help are clearly members of an out-group, research suggests that people with greater collectivist tendencies are often less helpful than people with greater individualist tendencies (Conway et al., 2001; Kemmelmeier et al., 2006; L'Armand & Pepitone, 1975). Thus, when it comes to providing help, "compassionate collectivism" does not necessarily extend to those who are seen as "them" rather than "us."

GENDER AND PERSONALITY
INFLUENCE HELPING RESPONSES.

Do you think your willingness to help is influenced by your personality and whether you are a woman or a man? Alice Eagly and Maureen Crowley's (1986) meta-analytic review of 172 helping behavior studies indicates that men and women differ in their willingness to engage in certain prosocial actions; men generally help more than women, and they are more likely than women to help strangers. These gender differences are greatest when there is an audience, when there is potential danger involved in helping, and when the person in need is female. Although these differences appear real, they apply most to nonroutine prosocial acts such as offering help to strangers in distress. When other forms of prosocial behavior—such as helping a friend or caring for children—are studied, women generally prove to be more helpful than men. For example, women are more likely than men to provide social and emotional support to others (Shumaker & Hill, 1991), and they also are more willing to serve as caretakers for children and the elderly (Trudeau & Devlin, 1996). In addition, among children, there are few gender differences in helping, and the few differences that have been found indicate that girls tend to be a bit more helpful than boys (Eisenberg et al., 1996).

Based on these findings, we can make two tentative conclusions. First, women and men appear to be helpful in different ways. Second, these differences become stronger from childhood to adulthood and are most apparent when gender roles are salient. Consistent with the culturally valued male role of heroic rescuer, men are more likely than women to

Women tend to take on the role of caretaker more than men.

place themselves in danger when rendering assistance. In contrast, women are more likely than men to provide longer-term help involving empathy and caretaking, qualities consistent with the feminine gender role.

In addition to exploring the role that gender socialization plays in prosocial behavior, researchers have also identified two distinct emotional reactions associated with helping that are related to personality differences (Decety, 2011; Graziano et al., 2007). One emotional response is **empathy**, which is the feeling of compassion and tenderness you feel when viewing a victim's plight. The second emotional response is **personal distress**, which is an unpleasant state of arousal in which you become preoccupied with your own anxiety when seeing others in distress. There is some research indicating that parents who encourage the expression of emotion in their families tend to have children who experience empathic rather than distress reactions when witnessing others in need of help (Eisenberg et al., 1988). Additional longitudinal research indicates that as children emotionally mature their feelings of empathy generally increase, while their feelings of personal distress generally decrease (Davis & Franzoi, 1991).

Despite these developmental trends, individual adults differ in the degree to which they habitually experience both empathy and personal distress. Studies of fraternal and identical twins indicate that individual differences in empathy and personal distress may be partly due to genetic factors (Davis et al., 1994; Zahn-Wexler et al., 1992). That is, high empathy and high personal distress people appear to have an inherited sensitivity to emotional experiences that causes them to react more strongly to the observed experiences of others. Before reading further, spend a few minutes answering the items in *Self/Social Connection Exercise 12.2*. Based on your responses, are you high or low on empathic concern and personal distress?

Research indicates that individuals high in empathy not only are more willing to put themselves in situations in which the experience of sympathy for another is likely but also are generally more willing to help people in trouble than are those low in empathy (Unger & Thumuluri, 1997). For example, in an analysis of people's responses to the annual Jerry Lewis muscular dystrophy telethon, Davis (1983) found that people with high empathic concern were more likely to watch the telethon and to contribute their time, effort, and money as a result. In contrast, people high in personal distress showed no such tendency. We can conclude from this research that people who typically feel compassion for unfortunate others tend to be drawn toward situations in which their feelings of sympathy will be aroused. When exposed to others' misfortunes, they don't remain passive bystanders; rather, they tend to take action to try to relieve the suffering. In this regard, the experience of caring for others

empathy

A feeling of compassion and tenderness upon viewing a victim's plight

personal distress

An unpleasant state of arousal in which people are preoccupied with their own emotions of anxiety, fear, or helplessness upon viewing a victim's plight

Self/Social Connections Exercise 12.2

What Is Your Degree of Empathic Concern and Personal Distress?

Instructions:

To discover your level of empathic concern and personal distress, read each item below and then, using the following response scale, indicate how well each statement describes you.

> 0 = extremely uncharacteristic (not at all like me)
> 1 = uncharacteristic (somewhat unlike me)
> 2 = neither characteristic nor uncharacteristic
> 3 = characteristic (somewhat like me)
> 4 = extremely characteristic (very much like me)

Empathic Concern Scale
_____1. When I see someone being taken advantage of, I feel kind of protective toward him/her.
_____2. When I see someone being treated unfairly, I sometimes don't feel very much pity for him/her.*
_____3. I often have tender, concerned feelings for people less fortunate than me.
_____4. I would describe myself as a pretty soft-hearted person.
_____5. Sometimes I don't feel very sorry for other people when they are having problems.*
_____6. Other people's misfortunes do not usually disturb me a great deal.*
_____7. I am often quite touched by things that I see happen.

Personal Distress Scale
_____1. When I see someone who badly needs help in an emergency, I go to pieces.
_____2. I sometimes feel helpless when I am in the middle of a very emotional situation.
_____3. In emergency situations, I feel apprehensive and ill-at-ease.
_____4. I am usually pretty effective in dealing with emergencies.*
_____5. Being in a tense emotional situation scares me.
_____6. When I see someone hurt, I tend to remain calm.*
_____7. I tend to lose control during emergencies.

Scoring

Several of the items on these two scales are reverse-scored; that is, for these items a lower rating actually indicates a higher level of empathic concern or personal distress. Before summing the items, recode those with an asterisk (*) so that 0 = 4, 1 = 3, 3 = 1, 4 = 0.

Gender Differences in Empathic Concern and Personal Distress

Davis (1980) has found the following gender differences in levels of empathic concern and personal distress:

Empathic concern: Personal distress:

Male mean = 19.04   Male mean = 9.46
Female mean = 21.67   Female mean = 12.28

Are your scores above or below the mean for your sex?

From Mark H. Davis, "Interpersonal Reactivity Index" in *Empathy: A Social Psychological Approach.* Copyright /cW/1996. Boulder, CO: Westview Press.

represents a central self-concept value for those high in empathic concern (Emmons & Diener, 1986). Later in this chapter we will more closely examine how empathy and personal distress shape bystanders' responses to others' needs.

LEARNING TO BE A HELPER INVOLVES BOTH OBSERVATION AND DIRECT REINFORCEMENT.

Many people subscribe to the same helping norms, but they differ in their tendencies to act consistently with these norms. The internalization of prosocial values begins in the preschool years, and parents and other adults play a significant role in this developmental process (Grusec et al., 2002). Just as Chapter 11 outlined how aggression can be learned through modeling and direct reinforcement, we now examine how prosocial behavior is similarly learned.

Observational Learning in Children

Parenting plays an important role in fostering and inhibiting children's prosocial behavior (Knafo & Plomin, 2006). According to social learning theorists, observational learning or modeling can influence the development of helping in at least two ways (Rosenkoetter, 1999; Rushton, 1980). First, it can initially teach children how to engage in helpful actions. Second, it can show children what is likely to happen when they actually engage in helpful (or selfish) behavior. In this learning process, what models *say* and what they *do* both shape the observers' prosocial behaviors.

For example, in one study, sixth-grade girls played a game to win chips that could be traded for candy and toys (Midlarsky et al., 1973). Prior to actually playing, each of the girls watched a woman play the game. In the *charitable* condition, the adult put some of the chips she won into a jar labeled "money for poor children" and then urged the girl to think about the poor children who would "love to receive the prizes these chips can buy." In the *selfish* condition, the adult model also urged the child to donate chips to the poor children, but she did so after putting all her chips into a jar labeled "my money." Results indicated a clear effect of prosocial modeling. Girls who had observed the charitable model donated more chips to the poor than those who had seen the selfish model.

Although this study demonstrates that what one does has more effect on children than what one says, subsequent studies have shown that *preaching* can have a delayed effect in influencing prosocial behavior. In one of these studies, J. Philippe Rushton (1975) had children observe a same-sex adult model being either generous or selfish with her or his winning tokens from a game. Regardless of their actual behavior, some of the models told the watching child that one should be generous ("We should share our tokens …"), while others preached that one should be selfish ("We should not share our tokens …"). As in the previous study, the models' behavior had clear effects on the children's immediate helping, but what the models said had little immediate impact (see Figure 12.1). However, two months later, in a retest of their willingness to help, something interesting happened. Although the children who had observed the charitable models were still more helpful than those who had watched the selfish models, children exposed to the models who preached generosity now donated more of their winnings to charity than those children who heard models preach selfishness. By far the most generous were those children previously exposed to models who had acted consistently with their prosocial preachings. In addition, the models preaching generosity but behaving selfishly produced the most giving in the selfish model condition.

This study, along with others (Moore & Eisenberg, 1984), suggests that although children are more likely to be influenced by adults' deeds rather than their words, over the course of time, preaching generosity can have some positive effect on children's prosocial tendencies, even if it comes from people who do not practice what they preach. The finding that selfish people can, over time, promote prosocial behavior by preaching generosity is interesting, but why might this be the case? Wouldn't listeners simply discount a hypocrite's words?

In the short run, a hypocrite's preachings do appear to be discounted. However, in Chapter 5 we learned that although people with low credibility (like a hypocrite) are not very persuasive immediately after they present their message, over time listeners forget

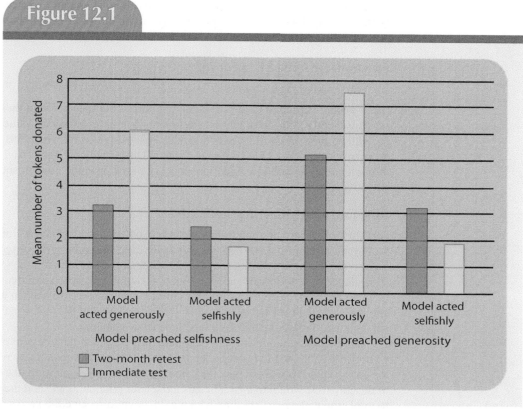

Figure 12.1

Immediate and Long-Term Effects of Modeling and Preaching on Children's Generosity

Children observed an adult model acting either generous or selfish and also listened to them preach either generosity or selfishness. How did the model's behavior and preaching influence the children's immediate willingness to donate tokens? What about their willingness to donate two months later?

where they heard it and then are influenced by the message content alone. This delayed effectiveness of a persuasive message from a noncredible source is known as the *sleeper effect* (see p. 188). In Rushton's study, although the children initially seemed to dismiss the selfish models' preachings of generosity, over time they were somewhat persuaded by the message content because they forgot where it originated.

Prosocial Modeling in Adults

Modeling prosocial behavior is not confined to children. In one study conducted in a natural setting, motorists who simply saw someone helping a woman change a flat tire were more likely to later stop and assist a second woman who was in a similar predicament (Bryan & Test, 1967). In another experiment (Rushton & Campbell, 1977), female college students interacted with a friendly woman as part of a study on social interaction (this was not the true purpose, and the woman was a confederate of the researchers). When the fabricated study was completed, the two women left the lab together and passed a table staffed by people asking for blood donations. When participants were asked first, only 25 percent agreed, and none actually followed through on their pledge six weeks later. However, when the confederate was asked first and signed up to donate blood, 67 percent of the participants also agreed to give blood, and 33 percent actually fulfilled their commitment. Additional research suggests that adults who may most likely be positively influenced by observing others' helpful actions are those who define themselves as highly moral or helpful individuals. In a set of studies, Karl Aquino and his colleagues (2011) found that people whose moral identity is highly self-defining were more likely than others to not only feel more intense positive emotions after witnessing acts of uncommon goodness, but to also profess a greater desire to become a better person by being more helpful to others.

The Lasting Consequences of Modeling

A number of studies have revealed the critical importance that prosocial parental model-ing plays in the lives of extraordinary helpers. For example, a study of civil rights activists in the late 1950s and 1960s found that previous parental modeling of pro-social behavior distinguished those who made many personal sacrifices from those who partic-ipated in only one or two freedom rides or marches. The fully committed activists had parents who had been excellent prosocial models when the activists were children, while the parents of the partially committed tended to be inconsistent models, often preaching prosocial action but not actually practicing it (Rosenhan, 1970). These find-ings mesh nicely with the previously discussed experiment by Rushton (1975). Com-bined with other studies, they indicate that adults' modeling of altruism can have a powerful effect on the altruistic tendencies of children that can last well into adulthood (Fogelman, 1996; Oliner & Oliner, 1988). Over time, helping others not only becomes one of the defining features of these individuals' self-concepts but also contributes to heightened self-esteem (Hitlin, 2007; Piliavin et al., 2002).

Based on this knowledge, social scientists believe they can make a clear recommen-dation to parents on how to raise children who will help those in need. Put simply, parents who try to instill prosocial values only by preaching and not by modeling altruism will likely raise children who are only weakly altruistic. Parents who not only preach altruism, but also let their prosocial actions serve as guidelines for their children's behavior, are much more likely to foster altruism in the next generation. In a very real sense, to be effec-tive altruistic teachers, one must not only "talk the talk," but also "walk the walk."

Rewarding Prosocial Behavior

Although observing the prosocial actions of others can shape children's and adults' own helping, the *consequences* of their actions will often determine whether they continue to engage in prosocial behavior. Social rewards, such as praise, are generally more effec-tive reinforcers than material rewards, such as money (Grusec, 1991). In one such "praise" experiment conducted by Rushton and Goody Teachman (1978), children were first induced to behave generously by having generosity modeled to them as in the pre-viously described game-token studies. When the children donated some of their win-nings to an orphan named Bobby, the model either praised the child for his or her imitative generosity (*reward condition*) by saying "Good for you, that's really nice of you," or scolded the child (*punishment condition*) by saying "That's kind of silly for you to give to Bobby. Now you will have fewer tokens for yourself." There was also a no-reinforcement condition in which the adult said nothing. As you can see in Figure 12.2, children who were praised gave more to Bobby on later trials than did children who were scolded. The effects of being either rewarded or punished for prosocial behavior were so strong that they still influenced how much the children gave to Bobby two weeks later. This study demonstrates that verbal praise or scolding by an adult model can either strengthen or weaken children's level of generosity.

Reinforcement also influences adult helping. For example, imagine yourself walk-ing along the main street in your hometown and being approached by a woman who asks how to get to a local department store. After giving her directions you continue along your way. Shortly, you pass by another woman who accidentally drops a small bag and continues walking, unaware that she has lost this possession. Would you return the bag to her? Do you think your decision to help the second woman would be influ-enced by how the first woman responded to your attempt to help her?

This was the question that researchers asked in a naturalistic study conducted on the streets of Dayton, Ohio, using just this scenario (Moss & Page, 1972). In the *reward* condition, the woman asking for directions rewarded her helper by saying, "Thank you very much, I really appreciate this." In contrast, in the *punishment* condi-tion the woman responded to help by saying, "I can't understand what you're saying; never mind, I'll ask someone else." Researchers found that when the first woman rewarded people, 90 percent of them helped the second woman. However, when pun-ished by the first woman, only 40 percent helped in the later situation. As in the study with children, this adult study suggests that people's future decisions to help are often

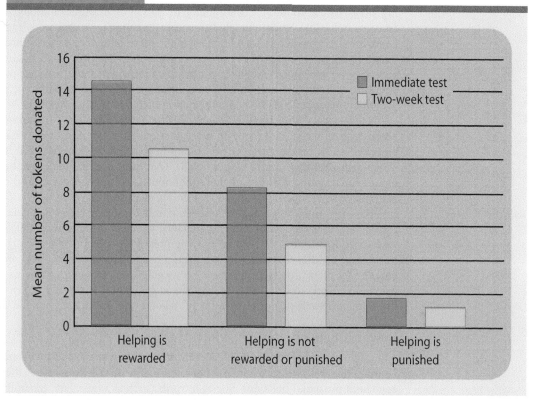

**The Effects of Positive Reinforcement and Punishment
on Model-Induced Generosity in Children**

*Do rewards and punishment affect children's willingness to help others? Rushton and Teachman (1978)
either praised, criticized, or said nothing to children who donated tokens to an orphan named Bobby. How
did these different consequences influence the children's subsequent willingness to donate tokens?*

influenced by the degree to which current helpful efforts are met by praise or rebuke.
Additional research suggests that when helpers are thanked for their efforts, they
experience stronger feelings of self-efficacy and social worth, which motivates them
to help others in the future (Grant & Gino, 2010). The take-away message here is that
even small expressions of gratitude can motivate prosocial behaviors by leading
helpers to feel socially valued.

SECTION SUMMARY

- In kin selection, we exhibit preferences for help-ing blood relatives because this increases the odds that our genes will be transmitted to subse-quent generations.

- In reciprocal helping, aiding strangers can be adaptive because any helpful act or favor is expected to be returned.

- Following are relevant social norms that promote helping:

reciprocity norm: Help those who help you.

social responsibility norm: Help those in need or those dependent on you.

social justice norm: Help those who deserve assistance.

- Liberals tend to follow the social responsibility norm while conservatives tend to follow the social justice norm.

- Lower class individuals express more concern and are more willing to help unfortunate others than upper class individuals.

- Collectivist cultures hold to a broader and more stringent view of social responsibility than individualist cultures.

- Women and men appear to be helpful in different ways.

  Men are more likely to help in dangerous situations.

  Women are more likely to provide longterm help.

- These gender differences increase from childhood to adulthood and when gender roles are salient.

- Individual differences in empathy and personal distress have opposite effects on helping responses.

- Prosocial behavior that is rewarded will become stronger.

- Parents who model prosocial behavior raise children who become helpful adults.

WHEN DO WE HELP?

As already mentioned, the chapter-opening story is a more accurate retelling of the Kitty Genovese murder than what has been commonly told over the past forty-some years in psychology textbooks. Rachel Manning and her colleagues (2007) contend that the original story of the thirty-eight unresponsive witnesses became a kind of modern parable of group apathy. Although a good portion of the original story is now discredited, the social psychological insights that indirectly resulted from the widespread media coverage are still relevant—and largely valid—today. Let us now examine some of these classic studies and the theories that emerged from this research.

BYSTANDER INTERVENTION INVOLVES A SERIES OF DECISIONS.

The supposed apathy of Kitty Genovese's neighbors was the topic of news stories, commentaries, religious sermons, and dinner conversation for some time after the murder. Two people who discussed the murder at length were social psychologists John Darley and Bibb Latané. Years later, Darley recalled the content of their discussion:

> Latané and I, shocked as anybody else, met over dinner a few days after this terrible incident had occurred and began to analyze this process in social psychological terms. … First, social psychologists ask not how are people different or why are the people who failed to respond monsters, but how are all people the same and how might anybody in that situation be influenced not to respond. Second, we asked: What influences reach the person from the group? We argued for a several-step model in which a person first had to define the situation. Emergencies don't come wearing signs saying "I am an emergency." In defining an event as an emergency, one looks at other people to see their reactions to the situation and interpret the meaning that lies behind their actions. Third, when multiple people are present, the responsibility to intervene does not focus clearly on any one person. … You feel a diffusion of responsibility in that situation and you're less likely to take responsibility. We argued that these two processes, definition and diffusion, working together, might well account for a good deal of what happened. (Evans, 1980, pp. 216–217)

bystander intervention model
• •
A theory that whether bystanders intervene in an emergency is a function of a five-step decision-making process.

According to the **bystander intervention model**, which eventually emerged as a result of this dinner discussion, the presence of other bystanders during an emergency inhibits helping. This model further contends that being helpful during an emergency involves not just one decision but, rather, a series of five decisions. As you can see from Figure 12.3, at each point in this five-step process, one decision results in no help being given, while the other decision takes the bystander one step closer to intervention.

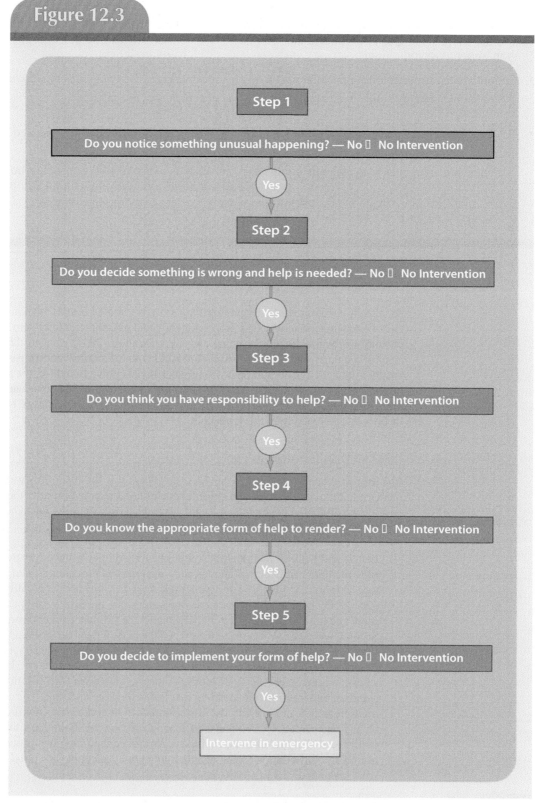

The Model of Bystander Intervention: A Five-Step Decision Process

As outlined by Latané and Darley (1970), the decision to help someone involves a five-step process. At any step, a bystander's decision could lead to either further analysis of the situation or to nonintervention.

Many emergency situations are not as clearly defined as others. How does the presence of other people affect bystanders' decision making when an emergency unfolds?

The first thing that you, as a potential helper, must do is *notice that something unusual is happening.* Unfortunately, in many social settings, countless sights and sounds flood our senses. Because it is impossible to attend to all these stimuli, and because we may be pre-occupied with something else, a cry for help could conceivably go completely unnoticed. This *stimulus overload effect* is more likely to occur in densely populated urban environments than in rural settings (Milgram, 1970). Indeed, it is one of the likely reasons why there is a negative correlation between population density and helping (Levine, 2003). That is, throughout the world, people who live in more crowded cities are less likely to help strangers in need of assistance than those who live in less densely populated urban centers (Levine et al., 1994; Yousif & Korte, 1995). Another reason it is sometimes difficult to notice things out of the ordinary is that what is unusual in one setting may be a normal occurrence in another. For example, in some neighborhoods, a person lying unconscious on the sidewalk may be extremely unusual and cause passersby to take notice. Yet, in other neighborhoods, this same person may be one of many street people who live and sleep outdoors much of the year—an all too common sight that passersby generally would take little, if any, notice of.

As a bystander to an emergency, if you do indeed notice that something unusual is happening, you move to the second step in the decision-making process: *deciding whether something is wrong and help is needed.* Returning to the previous example, if you pass by an unconscious man on the sidewalk you may ask yourself, "Did he suffer a heart attack or is he merely sleeping?" This is an extremely important decision, because if you decide he is merely sleeping you will continue on your way. But what if you are mistaken? Consider again the Kitty Genovese murder. After hearing Kitty's scream, one woman in the apartment building jumped out of bed and ran to her window because it was unusual to hear screams at this time of night (the first decision step). However, when she looked out her window and saw Kitty and her assailant "standing close together, not fighting or anything," she decided this was not an emergency (the second decision step). Only later did she learn that she was actually watching a sexual assault and murder. Incorrectly defining the situation led to her nonintervention.

When you define the situation as an emergency, the bystander intervention model states that the third decision you must make is *determining the extent to which you have responsibility to help.* According to Latané and Darley, one factor that may play a role in your decision to help or not is whether an appropriate authority figure is nearby. For instance, imagine sitting in your car at a busy intersection and noticing that in the car ahead of you, two people are arguing heatedly. Suddenly, one of these quarrelers begins hitting the other with a club. This is definitely unusual and it is clearly an emergency. The pertinent question now is, do you have responsibility to come to the victim's aid? Further, imagine that to your immediate right is a police car with two officers sitting inside. If you decide that it is their responsibility to render assistance, you will likely assume the role of an unresponsive bystander.

Let's continue this hypothetical emergency situation, but now imagine that there is no police car in sight. Faced with the reality of a clear emergency, you still may not help if you convince yourself that all the other motorists watching this incident could help just as well as you. The presence of these other potential helpers, like the presence of authority figures, may cause you to feel less personally responsible for intervening. This is how some—but clearly not all—bystanders in the Kitty Genovese case responded.

If you assume responsibility for helping, a fourth decision you must make is *the appropriate form of assistance to render*. In the heat of the moment, however, what if you are not sure what to do? You may become paralyzed with uncertainty about exactly how to render assistance. Unable to decide, you may not offer any help at all. Children are particularly likely not to have the appropriate skills or confidence to make a decision at this stage in the helping process.

Finally, if you notice something unusual, interpret it as an emergency, assume responsibility, and decide how best to help, you still must decide whether to *implement your course of prosocial action*. If you have decided to run to the car where the person is being beaten and intervene, you must now act on this intention. However, due to fear of injury or concern about testifying at a future trial, you may decide not to implement your previous decision and remain a passive bystander. In the Kitty Genovese case, the only person who directly intervened was the woman who came to her aid, although others did indirectly intervene by either shouting at the assailant or phoning the police.

As you can see from the outline of this model, Latané and Darley believe that the decision to intervene in a possible emergency involves a rather complex set of decisions. As a bystander, if you make an incorrect choice at any point in this process, you will not intervene. Two social psychological processes that often operate in emergency situations are the *audience inhibition effect* and the *diffusion of responsibility*. The inhibition effect can short-circuit helping at step 2 in the bystander intervention model, and diffusion of responsibility occurs in step 3.

OUTCOME AND INFORMATION DEPENDENCE PRODUCE THE AUDIENCE INHIBITION EFFECT.

Many emergency situations are not clearly defined as such, but rather, have some degree of ambiguity. You may realize that something unusual is happening (step 1 in the model), but you are not sure that it's an emergency (step 2). In one study designed to investigate bystander uncertainty, Latané and Darley (1968) recruited male college students for a study on problems of urban life. When a research participant arrived at the laboratory, he was ushered into a room, given a questionnaire, and then was left alone to complete it. Soon, what looked like white smoke (but wasn't) began to enter the room through a small wall vent. Within six minutes, the smoke was so thick it was difficult to see. The dependent variable was whether or not the participant would leave the room to report the problem before the six minutes had elapsed. What do you think happened?

When working alone, most participants usually hesitated a moment upon first seeing the smoke, but then walked over to the vent to investigate. In 75 percent of the trials, the participant finally left the room to report the emergency. In a second experimental condition, groups of three naive participants were seated in the room when smoke began to pour from the vent. In all trials, participants looked to one another to help them decide if there was an emergency, but in only 38 percent of these three-person groups did even a single person report the incident before the six-minute mark. Although 55 percent of the participants in the *alone* condition reported the smoke within the first two minutes, only 12 percent of the three-person groups did so. Finally, in a third condition, two confederates, acting like research participants, joined the one real participant in the room. As it began to fill with smoke, the confederates acted unconcerned. If the real participant asked them any questions, they replied, "I dunno" and continued working

Figure 12.4

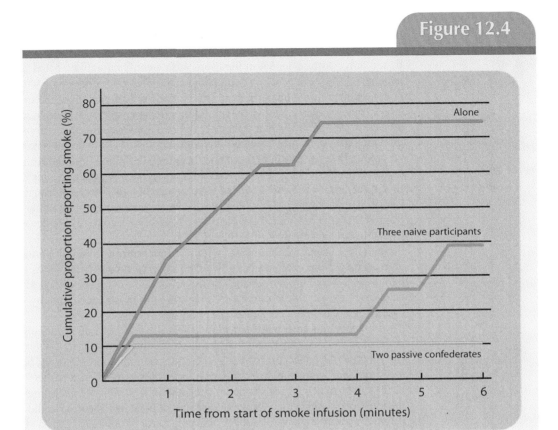

The Audience Inhibition Effect

When a room began filling with white smoke, people were much less likely to report the incident— and did so more slowly—when they were with others rather than alone. What two types of social dependence are interacting here to create the audience inhibition effect?

on the questionnaire. In the presence of these unconcerned confederates, only 10 percent of the participants reported the smoke. The other 90 percent coughed, rubbed their eyes, and opened the window, but they did not leave the room. These findings, summarized in Figure 12.4, indicate that when others are present, people are less likely to define a potentially dangerous situation as an emergency, but they also respond more slowly to the possible emergency. This **audience inhibition effect**, which is driven by *pluralistic ignorance* (see Chapter 7, p. 266), is particularly likely when other people are acting calmly.

In another investigation of the inhibition effect, Latané and Judith Rodin (1969) set up a situation in which some other person, besides the research participant, was in possible danger. First, a female researcher set participants to work on a questionnaire and then left through a collapsible curtained doorway to work in an adjoining office. From their room, participants could hear her shuffling papers and opening and closing drawers. After four minutes, the researcher turned on a tape recorder that broadcast the sound of her climbing on a chair to reach a stack of papers on a bookcase. Participants then heard the researcher's scream, quickly followed by a loud crash. "Oh, my God, my foot. … I … I … can't move … it," she moaned. "Oh … my ankle. … I … can't get this … thing … off me." After about two minutes of moaning, the woman could be heard dragging herself out of her office.

Seventy percent of the participants who were alone in the room tried to help by pulling open the curtain or running out the other door to find help. Consistent with the audience inhibition effect, when two strangers were sitting in the room, only 40 percent of the time did either of them help. When the two people sitting in the room were friends, at least one of them helped in 70 percent of the trials. Even though this is the same percentage of helping as in the alone condition, it still indicates an inhibition

audience inhibition effect
· · · · · · · · · · · · · · · · · · · ·
People are inhibited from helping for fear that other bystanders will evaluate them negatively if they intervene and the situation is not an emergency.

effect because two people were present. If these two friends did not inhibit each other's response, then helping should have occurred in 91 percent of the trials (70 percent $_{friend\ 1}$ + (70 percent × remaining 30 percent $_{friend\ 2}$) = 91 percent). Finally, in the last condition, a naive participant sat in the room with a confederate who acted unconcerned and nonchalant about the ruckus behind the curtain. Again, consistent with the inhibition effect, in this setting the participant tried to help only 7 percent of the time.

To better understand why the inhibition effect occurs, let's return to two concepts previously discussed in Chapter 7, namely *information dependence* and *outcome dependence*. As discussed in that chapter, when we are not clear about how to define a particular situation, we are likely to become dependent on others for a definition of social reality. Thus, when a group of people witnesses a possible emergency, each person bases his or her interpretation of the event partly or exclusively on the reaction of others (information dependence). The problem with this information seeking in an emergency is that in our culture we have learned that it is not socially acceptable to "lose your cool." If we become agitated and excitable during a crisis, we run the risk of being negatively evaluated by others (outcome dependence). Due to this concern, we will often pretend to be calm while witnessing an emergency. Acting cool and calm, we then observe others' behavior as a clue as how to define what we all are witnessing. However, because everyone else is also assuming this calm exterior, what we observe is a group of calm by-standers who, by their nonplussed demeanor, are defining the situation as a nonemergency.

In ambiguous emergency situations, then, the fear of being negatively evaluated (outcome dependence), combined with the tendency to look to others for further information (information dependence), results in the audience inhibition effect. In both the "smoke" study and the "woman in distress" study, the presence of others and their behavior significantly inhibited helping. Postexperimental debriefings indicated that some of those who did not intervene claimed they were either unsure of what had occurred or did not think the situation was very serious. Russell Clark and Larry Word (1972), in a replication of the Latané and Rodin study, made the situation even less ambiguous by allowing participants in the adjoining room to not only hear the crash of the person (this time a man) falling and his subsequent moaning, but now they could also feel the floor shake with the force of the crash. With this reduction in ambiguity, every single participant helped, regardless of the number of bystanders. However, when the situation was made more ambiguous (the victim did not cry out in pain), helping occurred only 30 percent of the time. In addition, as with the previous studies, participants in groups were less likely to help than those who were alone. This study clearly indicates that the audience inhibition effect is driven by our fear of being negatively evaluated. Indeed, those of us who are especially sensitive to embarrassment are the most likely to experience inhibition in emergencies (Tice & Baumeister, 1985). Thus, in an ambiguous emergency situation, we seem to be thinking, "What if I cause a big fuss by intervening and there is no emergency? I'll look like a fool and be mortified." However, if that fear of committing a social faux pas is reduced due to clear emergency signals, our inhibitions are greatly reduced and we are more likely to help.

DIFFUSION OF RESPONSIBILITY INCREASES WITH THE NUMBER OF BYSTANDERS.

Fear of embarrassment is one reason we do not intervene in some emergencies, but what about those situations in which someone clearly needs help and no one raises a finger to come to the victim's aid? Surely some other social psychological factor is operating. For example, at least some of the neighbors of Kitty Genovese, sitting in their own separate apartments, correctly guessed what was happening before the second fatal attack occurred. However, they knew—or assumed—that others were also watching this drama unfold below them. Darley and Latané believed that this realization that others could also help diffused these neighbors' own feelings of individual responsibility (step 3 in the model). They called this response to others' presence the *diffusion of responsibility*— the belief that the presence of other people in a situation makes one less personally responsible for events that occur in that situation (see Chapter 8, p. 320).

In an attempt to simulate the social psychological factors that they believed were present in the Genovese case, Darley and Latané (1968) designed an experiment in which they placed people in separate areas from which they then heard a victim cry for help. In this study, New York University students thought they were participating in a discussion about the kinds of personal problems undergraduates typically face in a large urban environment. They were also told that to avoid embarrassment, they each would be placed in a separate booth and would talk to one another through an intercom system. To further ensure they wouldn't be inhibited, the experimenter said he would not eavesdrop on their conversation. The way the intercom system worked was that only one person could speak at a time, and the others had to merely listen.

The study included three different conditions. Some participants were told the discussion would be with just one other student, while others were told they were either part of a three-person or a six-person group. In reality, all the other discussion participants were merely tape recordings. Discussion began with the first speaker stating that he was an epileptic who was prone to seizures when studying hard or when taking exams. When everyone else had spoken, the first speaker began to talk again, but now he was speaking in a loud and increasingly incoherent voice:

> I-er-um-I think I-I need-er-if-if could-er-er-somebody er-er-er-er-er-er-er give me a little-er-give me a little help here because-er-I-er-I'm-er-er-h-h-having a-a-a real problem-er-right now and I-er-if somebody could help me out it would-it would-er-er s-s-sure be-sure be good … because-er-there-er-er-a cause I-er-I-uh-I've got a-a one of the-er-seizure-er-things coming on and-and-and I could really-er-use some help so if somebody would-er-give me a little h-help-uh-er-er-er-er-er c-could somebody-er-er-help-er-uh-uh-uh (choking sounds). … I'm gonna die-er-er-I'm … gonna die-er-help-er-er-seizure-er-[chokes, then quiet].
> (Darley & Latané, 1968, p. 379)

How did participants respond to this concocted, yet convincing, emergency? It depended on the number of bystanders they thought were also aware of the epileptic's seizure. When participants thought they were the only ones listening to the emergency unfold, 85 percent of them left their booths to help before the victim's pleas for help were choked off. When they thought they were one of five bystanders, only 31 percent reacted in a similar prosocial manner. When participants thought there was one other bystander aware of the emergency, helping was intermediate, with 62 percent helping. Not only was helping less likely as the number of bystanders increased, but the *speed* of rendering assistance was significantly slower as well. As you can see from Figure 12.5, when participants thought there were four other bystanders, it took them three times longer to take any action (if they helped at all) than it did in the alone condition.

More than fifty subsequent laboratory and naturalistic studies have confirmed this diffusion of responsibility effect (Latané & Nida, 1981). On average, when participants believed they were the only bystander to an emergency, 75 percent of them helped, compared with only 53 percent who were in the presence of others. Diffusion of responsibility also occurs when people need help on the Internet (Barron & Yechiam, 2002; Blair et al., 2005). For example, in one study, more than forty-eight hundred people were monitored in four hundred different Internet chat groups over a month's time to determine the amount of time it took a bystander to render assistance to someone who asked for help (Markey, 2000). Results indicated that it took longer for people to receive help as the number of people present in a computer-mediated chat group increased. However, this diffusion of responsibility was virtually eliminated and help was received more quickly when help was asked for by specifying a bystander's name.

A recent meta-analysis of more than one hundred studies, involving over seventy-seven hundred participants from the 1960s to 2010, found strong support for the finding that bystanders inhibit helping responses and strong support for the idea that this effect becomes stronger with an increasing number of bystanders (Fischer et al., 2011). This meta-analysis also indicated that the audience inhibition effect is less pronounced in dangerous situations than in non-dangerous situations. Why might this be so? One likely possibility is that in dangerous situations, bystanders are more likely than in non-dangerous situations to label what they are witnessing as a clear-cut emergency because dangerous situations more closely fit the emergency prototype. In other words, the uncertainty and fear of embarrassment that drives the audience inhibition effect is greatly reduced when there is danger present.

"Where are they who claim kindred with the unfortunate?"

– – – – – – – – – –

Caroline Lamb, English novelist, 1785–1828

Critical THINKING

Do you think you would find these same bystander effects among people whose jobs regularly deal with helping others? How might you test whether the situational context or the salience of their "helping" social roles would influence their tendency to intervene?

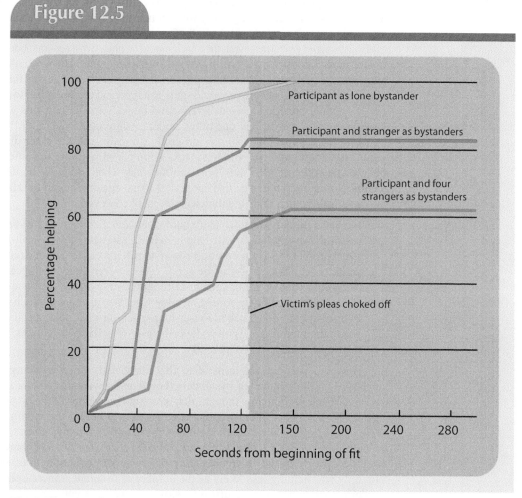

Figure 12.5

The Diffusion of Responsibility Effect

When participants heard over an intercom system someone having a seizure, how did the number of perceived bystanders influence their speed and willingness to help the victim?

Despite clear evidence that the presence of others influences people's decision to help, in postexperimental interviews participants in all of Latané and Darley's experiments tended to deny that others' assumed presence had any effect on their actions (or inactions). As discussed in Chapter 9, underestimating the effect that others have on your behavior makes it more likely that you will fall prey to their influence. After all, how can you guard against not falling into the nonhelpful mode when you don't recognize how the simple presence of others can change your feelings of personal responsibility?

Besides bystanders influencing helping responses in the traditional ways described thus far, Stephen Garcia and his colleagues (2002) wondered whether the presence of actual people is necessary to induce the bystander effect. Is it possible that simply imagining others is sufficient to induce a similar mental state of diffused responsibility, regardless of whether those others are available to respond? Research on *priming* suggests that merely activating knowledge structures from memory can influence people's social perceptions and behavior (see p. 114).

Garcia hypothesized that merely activating the construct of *group* in the minds of people would result in diffusion of responsibility. To test this hypothesis, he and his colleagues approached students who were sitting alone at a campus student center and asked them to complete a questionnaire. For participants in the *group condition*, the questionnaire included a group prime, which read as follows: "Imagine you won a dinner for yourself and ten of your friends at your favorite restaurant." For participants in the *one-person condition*, the inserted statement was similar but focused on only one friend: "Imagine you won a dinner for yourself and a friend at your favorite restaurant." Next, all participants answered the filler question: "What time of day would you most likely make your reservation?" The choices were 5 p.m., 6 p.m., 7 p.m., 8 p.m., 9 p.m., or 10 p.m. In the *neutral control condition*, participants read only the filler question, which was slightly modified to "What time of day would you make a dinner reservation?" For all participants, helping behavior was measured by their willingness to volunteer to help out with an experiment. Thus, on the last page of the questionnaire all participants read the following: "In addition to this survey, we are conducting a brief experiment in another room. How much time are you willing to spend on this other experiment?"

As hypothesized, participants who were prompted to imagined a group of ten people offered less helping assistance than did participants in either the one-person condition or the neutral control condition. Even though participants in the group condition imagined their friends, these imagined friends were not in the immediate vicinity to offer helping behavior assistance. Hence, these results suggest that others need not be physically present for diffusion of responsibility to occur; merely imagining a group can lead to lower levels of responsibility for helping others.

BYSTANDER INTERVENTION IS ALSO SHAPED BY EMOTIONAL AROUSAL AND COST-REWARD ASSESSMENTS.

Latané and Darley's bystander intervention model is best at explaining why people in a group of bystanders often don't interpret an event as an emergency, as well as why they often don't help even when it's clearly defined. Although this model provides a number of important pieces to the bystander puzzle, its focus is on the social problem of *nonintervention*. Yet why do we often decide to actually intervene in an emergency?

Jane Piliavin and her colleagues (1981) attempted to answer this question by developing a theory of bystander intervention that extends and complements Latané and Darley's model. These researchers added to the decision-making equation a consideration of bystanders' emotional arousal during an emergency and their assessment of the costs of helping and not helping. Essentially, their work focuses on the second half of Latané and Darley's model, namely, deciding on personal responsibility (step 3), deciding what to do (step 4), and implementing action (step 5).

This **arousal: cost-reward model** of helping contends that witnessing an emergency is emotionally arousing and is generally experienced as an uncomfortable tension that we, as bystanders, seek to decrease (Gaertner & Dovidio, 1977). This tension can be

arousal:cost-reward model

. . . .

A theory that helping or not helping is a function of emotional arousal and analysis of the costs and rewards of helping

According to the Arousal:Cost-Reward Model, what factors do we likely consider when trying to decide whether to help homeless people we encounter on city streets?

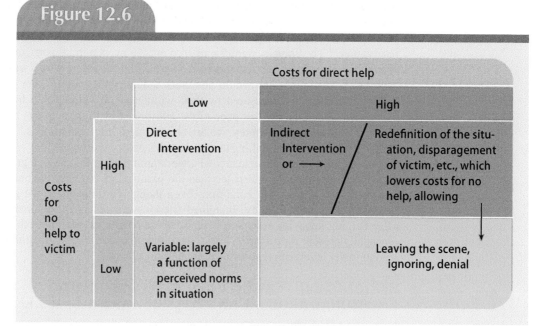

Figure 12.6

		Costs for direct help	
		Low	**High**
Costs for no help to victim	**High**	Direct Intervention	Indirect Intervention or ⟶ / Redefinition of the situation, disparagement of victim, etc., which lowers costs for no help, allowing
	Low	Variable: largely a function of perceived norms in situation	Leaving the scene, ignoring, denial

The Influence of Costs and Rewards on Direct Helping

According to Piliavin and Piliavin (1972), the type of response a moderately aroused observer will have to someone's need for help will be influenced by his or her assessment of the combination of personal costs for direct help and costs for no help to the victim. According to this model, when are bystanders most and least likely to help?

reduced in several different ways. We could intervene and thereby decrease our arousal, but we could also reduce arousal by either ignoring danger signs or benignly interpreting them as nothing to worry about. In addition to these avenues of action, we could reduce arousal by simply fleeing the scene. Which behavior we choose will be a function of our analysis of the costs and rewards for helping and for not helping. What are the costs to the bystander for helping? This could involve a host of expenditures—including loss of time, energy, resources, health (even life), as well as the risk of social disapproval and embarrassment if the help is not needed or is ineffective. Counterbalancing the costs of helping are the costs of not helping. These might include serious harm to the ignored victim and subsequent public scorn of the nonhelpful bystander. Realizing that one did not render assistance could also lead bystanders to engage in self-blame and experience loss of self-esteem.

According to Piliavin and her colleagues, if the costs of helping are low and the costs of not helping are high, bystanders will likely intervene (refer to Figure 12.6). In contrast, if these costs are reversed (high helping costs and low not-helping costs), bystanders are unlikely to render assistance. If both types of costs are low, intervention will depend on the perceived social norms in the situation. The most difficult situation for bystanders is one in which the costs for helping and for not helping are both high. Here, the arousal:cost-reward model suggests two likely courses of action. One is for bystanders to intervene indirectly by calling the police, an ambulance, or some other professional helping source. Another course of action is for bystanders to redefine the situation in a way that results in them not helping. Here, they could decide there really is no emergency after all, or that someone else will help, or that the victim deserves to suffer. For instance, imagine that you are walking down the street when you hear a child screaming in pain. Directing your gaze toward the screams, you see a lone young girl who has slammed a car door on her hand. In this situation, you will likely directly intervene because (1) the costs of not helping are high—the girl may seriously injure her hand if it is not removed from the door's grip soon, and you will experience terrible guilt if you don't help; and (2) the costs of helping are low—opening the car door will require little effort or loss of time, and helping will not put you in any danger.

Now, imagine that the child is not screaming in pain because her hand is caught in a door, but rather because an adult is beating her with a stick. Now, what will you do? Here, the costs of both not helping and helping are high—the girl may be seriously hurt, and you will experience guilt if you don't stop the beating; but the adult could seriously injure you if you intervene. Faced with these high costs, you may help indirectly by calling the police or by yelling from a safe distance for the adult to stop. Sadly, you might also convince yourself that the child must deserve the beating she is getting and continue on your way.

Now, imagine that the child is screaming in pain because an adult is spanking her bottom with moderate force. In this situation, both the costs of not helping and helping are probably low. Not intervening will probably not cause serious physical injury to the child, and intervening may only result in the adult telling you to mind your own business. If your perception of cultural norms is that spanking children is an unacceptable response to misbehavior, you may try to stop the punishment. Otherwise, you are unlikely to intervene.

Finally, imagine the same scene as in the previous paragraph, but now let's add that you are rushing to an important job interview. If you try to stop the spanking, you run the very real risk of arriving late. Here, your costs for helping are high and the costs for not helping are low. Weighing these factors, you are likely to continue on your way, perhaps muttering about the misguided actions of the adult but justifying your nonintervention to yourself ("If I didn't have this appointment, I'd give that adult a piece of my mind!").

A number of studies support the arousal:cost-reward model's hypothesis that people often weigh the costs of helping and not helping prior to rendering assistance (Dovidio et al., 1991; Fritzsche et al., 2000). For example, Lance Shotland and Margaret Straw (1976) staged a realistic fight between a man and a woman on an elevator. In one condition, 65 percent of the time bystanders intervened when the woman shouted, "Get away from me! I don't know you!" However, in another condition bystanders helped only 19 percent of the time when the woman shouted, "Get away from me! I don't know why I ever married you!" These differences in helping were apparently due to perceived costs. People who watched videotapes of the fights perceived the woman as being in greater danger when with the stranger than when with the husband. They also believed that the combatants would be more likely to turn on them if they tried to intervene in the "domestic" fight rather than the "stranger" fight. Thus, the "stranger" condition was perceived to involve higher costs for not helping and lower costs for helping than the "husband" condition.

Another study investigating the costs for helping and the costs for not helping was conducted on the Philadelphia subway system when a male confederate carrying a cane collapsed (Piliavin & Piliavin, 1972). In one condition, the victim had a thin trickle of fake blood slip from his mouth as he fell, while in a second condition he did not. The researchers assumed that the presence of blood would increase the costs of intervening because contact with blood for most people is repulsive. It was further assumed that bystanders would interpret the presence of blood to mean that the victim was in more danger than if no blood was visible. Thus, the "blood" condition was hypothesized to cause conflicting thoughts that would impede intervention ("The man needs help, but yikes! Look at that blood!"). True to these predictions, the unbloodied victim was directly helped more often (95 percent of the time) and more quickly than the bloody victim (helped 65 percent of the time). In one trial of the study, two teenagers witnessed the man collapse and rose to help but then saw the blood. "Oh, he's bleeding!" gasped one of them. Both promptly sat down.

POSITIVE AND NEGATIVE MOODS CAN EITHER INCREASE OR DECREASE HELPING.

Beyond the influence that fellow bystanders and perceived costs can have on prosocial behavior, research also demonstrates that people's willingness to help is affected by the mood they happen to be in when assistance is needed.

Good Moods and Generosity

Imagine this scene. Ralph bounds out of his psychology class feeling on top of the world because he has achieved one of the highest scores on his midterm exam. As he happily walks back to his apartment, he notices a woman carrying a tall stack of papers. Suddenly, the stack slips from her grasp and begins flying in all directions across campus. Without hesitation, Ralph springs into action and helps retrieve the errant papers.

Would Ralph have been so willing to help if he was in a less positive mood? Perhaps not. Research consistently indicates that good moods lead to more prosocial behavior. For example, in one study, Alice Isen (1970) administered a series of tests to college students and teachers, later telling them they had either performed very well or very poorly. Still others were told nothing at all about their performance. In addition to these three experimental conditions, a control group was not administered any tests at all. The participants who had "succeeded" at the tests were later more likely to help a woman struggling with an armful of books than any of the other participants. This *good mood effect* following success has been replicated in other studies (Klein, 2003), and additional research indicates that people are more likely to help others on sunny days than on cloudy ones (Cunningham, 1979), after finding money or being offered a tasty treat (Isen & Levin, 1972), and even after listening to uplifting music or a comedian deliver a funny routine (North et al., 2004; Wilson, 1981).

Other people's nonverbal behavior can also induce the good mood effect. In one field experiment, Nicolas Gueguen and Marie-Agnes De Gail (2003) had a confederate smile or not smile at a passerby a few seconds before another confederate dropped computer diskettes on the ground. Results indicated that the passersby were more likely to help pick up the diskettes if they had just received a smile. This finding is consistent with the more general finding that help seekers are much more successful in receiving aid if they smile while making their requests (Gueguen & Fischer-Lokou, 2004).

Why do positive moods lead to greater helping? Several possibilities have been offered. One is that when we are in a positive mood, we are more likely to perceive other people as "nice," "honest," and "decent," and thus deserving of our help (Isen, 1987). Another possibility is that we help others to enhance or prolong our good mood (Wegener & Petty, 1994). A third reason might be that, when happy, we are less likely to be absorbed in our own thoughts ("stewing in our own juices"), and thus, we are more attentive to others' needs (McMillen et al., 1977). A fourth possibility is that good moods increase the likelihood that we think about the rewarding nature of social activities in general. With the rewarding properties of helping being salient, our helping becomes more likely (Cunningham et al., 1990b). This enhanced attentiveness to the rewarding properties of helping may explain why good moods increase helpfulness only when the helpful task is expected to be pleasant. If helping is expected to entail unpleasant and aversive experiences, happy people are no more helpful than others (Isen & Simmonds, 1978; Rosenhan et al., 1981).

Bad Moods and Seeking Relief

What about negative moods and helping? Rewind your thoughts to Ralph and his psychology midterm. As the "string-puller" of all fictional characters in this text, I will now change Ralph's exam grade from "A" to "F." Now, instead of bounding out of class, he trudges. Given his present somber mood, will he still dart around campus retrieving wayward sheets of paper? Surprisingly, he might. Isen and her coworkers (1973) found that people who believed they had failed at an experimental task were more likely to help another person than those who did not experience failure. Although this response certainly seems to contradict the good mood effect just described, one possible link between the two is the rewarding properties of helping. Because helping others often makes us feel good about ourselves, when feeling bad we may help as a way of *escaping* our mood—just as we help when we are in a good mood to maintain that mood.

Feeling guilty can also increase helping (Basil et al., 2008). Michael Cunningham and his colleagues (1980) conducted a field study in which individuals were approached on the street by a young man who asked them to use his camera to take his picture for a class project. The problem for the would-be helpers was that the camera had been rigged to malfunction. When the helpers realized the camera was not working, the young man examined it closely and asked the helpers if they touched any of the dials. He then informed them that it would have to be repaired. The researchers assumed that such an encounter would induce a certain degree of guilt in these individuals. As they continued on their way, these now guilty people passed a young woman who suddenly dropped a file folder containing some papers. How do you think they responded to this needy situation? Eighty percent of those who were led to believe that they had broken the young man's camera helped the female stranger pick up her papers. Only 40 percent of the passersby who had no broken-camera experience paused to help. Another field study found that Roman Catholics were more likely to donate money to a charity just prior to making their confession of sins to a priest—when their guilt level should have been high—rather than immediately after being absolved of those sins (Harris et al., 1975).

Although these studies demonstrate that negative moods can lead to prosocial behavior, other studies suggest that when we experience extremely negative moods, such as grief or depression, we may be so focused on our own emotional state that we simply don't notice others' needs and concerns (Carlson & Miller, 1987). Still other studies suggest that even when experiencing less severe negative moods, we are less likely to help than those who are in good moods (Isen, 1984). Robert Cialdini and Douglas Kenrick (1976) attempted to explain why this is the case by proposing that when we are in a bad mood, our decision to help is often based on a simple self-serving question: Will helping make us feel better? This **negative state relief model** asserts that when we are in a bad mood, if the perceived benefits for helping are high and the costs are low, the expected *reward value* for helping will be high, and thus, we will likely help to lift our own spirits. However, if the perceived benefits and costs are reversed so that the reward value is low, we are unlikely to help. Essentially, this model predicts that bad moods are more likely to lead to helping than neutral moods when helping is easy and highly rewarding.

Despite the fact that the negative state relief model has generated considerable scientific debate over whether it accurately depicts foul mood effects, even its proponents have pointed out the limits of its application (Glomb et al., 2011). First, research indicates that increased helping due to bad moods is much more common among adults than children (Kenrick et al., 1979). One probable explanation for this age difference is that children are less likely to have learned the self-rewarding properties of helping—that it can pull one out of a bad mood. A second limitation is that the model specifies that only mildly negative feelings such as sadness, guilt, and temporary depression will increase helping. More intense negative emotions, such as hostile anger and resentment, result in decreased helping. Finally, because the helping exhibited by adults in a bad mood is of a self-serving nature, if sad or guilty people get their spirits raised from some other source (such as being complimented or hearing a funny joke), they will no longer have a need to help others (Cunningham et al., 1980). Figure 12.7 summarizes the effects that both bad moods and good moods have on helping.

THE EMPATHY-ALTRUISM HYPOTHESIS CONTENDS THAT EMPATHY PRODUCES ALTRUISTIC MOTIVATION.

The three previously discussed explanations of the conditions under which people are most likely to help others—arousal:cost-reward model, good mood effect, and negative state relief model—all assume there is an egoistic motive underlying prosocial behavior. All three explanations contend that helpful bystanders are ultimately trying to improve their own well-being by helping. Yet is egoism all that underlies prosocial action?

Although not denying that helping is often motivated by a desire to fulfill egoistic needs, Daniel Batson (1991, 2011) contends that sometimes our prosocial actions are truly *altruistic*, motivated solely by the desire to increase the welfare of another. In Batson's **empathy-altruism hypothesis**, he proposes that we typically experience either personal distress or empathy upon witnessing someone else suffer (refer back to p. 494). Batson contends that these two contrasting emotional reactions to a victim's plight—one focused on our own well-being (personal distress) and the other focused on the victim's (empathy)—result in very different motivations.

negative state relief model
· · · · · · · · · · · · · · · · · · · ·
A theory suggesting that for those in a bad mood, helping others may be a way to lift their own spirits if the perceived benefits for helping are high and the costs are low

empathy-altruism hypothesis
· · · · · · · · · · · · · · · · · · · ·
A theory proposing that experiencing empathy for someone in need produces an altruistic motive for helping.

Figure 12.7

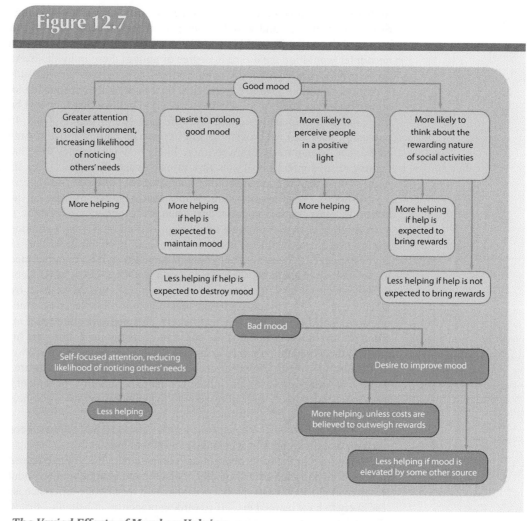

The Varied Effects of Mood on Helping

Depending on the circumstances, positive and negative moods can either increase or decrease helping.

Regarding the negative arousal state of personal distress, the greater our personal distress as a bystander, the more we will be motivated to have it reduced. Batson believes that Piliavin's arousal:cost-reward model does a good job of explaining how we respond to personal distress. Because reduction of this unpleasant arousal state is the primary motivation underlying personal distress, we will likely flee the stress-producing situation if at all possible. However, if we cannot easily escape, we will likely lend assistance in order to reduce our own unpleasant arousal. Described in this manner, one can clearly see that helping caused by personal distress is egoistic in nature.

Like personal distress, empathy for someone who is suffering will likely be an unpleasant emotion. However, unlike personal distress, empathy will not be satisfied by flight. Instead, Batson's empathy-altruism hypothesis contends that when we experience empathy, the stronger the feelings of compassion for the victim, the greater our motivation to help. Thus, when we feel great empathy, we are motivated more by our desire to improve the victim's welfare than attend to our own.

Support for the empathy-altruism hypothesis has been found in a number of studies in which bystanders' empathy or personal distress has been manipulated. In one of these studies, Batson and his coworkers (1981) had pairs of female college students participate in a task seemingly investigating how people work under aversive conditions. One participant was the "worker" who received electric shocks at random intervals during two trial periods; the other student observed the worker on a closed-circuit television as she performed the task. In actuality, the worker was a confederate. When the first aversive work trial began, the worker's facial expressions and body movements indicated that she found the shocks to be extremely uncomfortable. At the end of this trial, the worker explained that electric shocks in an accident as a child had traumatized her, and now, even mild shocks were often very painful. Responding to this "dilemma," the researcher asked the observer—who was naturally disturbed by this story—whether she would be willing to help the woman by trading places with her on the last trial. Batson and his colleagues predicted two factors would determine how participants responded to this dilemma: (1) whether or not they felt personal distress or empathy, and (2) whether or not they could flee this aversive situation.

Regarding the first factor, the experimenters assumed that everyone would experience arousal when witnessing the victim's plight, and that they would naturally attribute this arousal both to sympathy for the victim (empathy) and to personal discomfort (personal distress). To more clearly direct participants' interpretation of their arousal, the experimenters gave them a fictional drug, "Millentana" (a cornstarch placebo), as part of another study just prior to observing their partner being shocked. All participants were told that Millentana had a side effect. In the *empathy* condition, Batson and his coworkers wanted the participants to misattribute any feelings of personal distress to the drug and not to the victim's plight. To achieve this result, they said that the drug "produces a clear feeling of uneasiness and discomfort, a feeling similar to that you might experience while reading a particularly distressing novel." Due to this misattribution of personal distress to Millentana, the researchers assumed that participants in the empathy condition would perceive their emotional response to the victim to be primarily empathy. In contrast, those in the *personal distress condition* were told that the drug "produces a clear feeling of warmth and sensitivity, a feeling similar to that you might experience while reading a particularly touching novel." Following a similar logic, the experimenters assumed that these people would misattribute feelings of empathy to Millentana and perceive their emotional response to the victim to be primarily personal distress. Participants' subsequent self-reports indicated that the experimenters were successful in manipulating the women's emotional responses in the desired directions.

Regarding the second factor, ease of escape was manipulated by the instructions participants had previously received concerning their role as observer. In the *easy-escape* condition, they were told they would observe only the first trial, while in the *difficult-escape* condition, participants were told they would observe both trials.

How do you think these different emotional reactions affected willingness to help the victim? Results found that regardless of whether escape was difficult or easy, empathic observers tended to help by deciding to trade places with the confederate. On the other hand, the personally distressed observers chose to flee when fleeing was easy; they helped only if that was the only way to relieve their own discomfort. These findings are perfectly consistent with the empathy-altruism hypothesis.

In a replication of this experiment, instead of manipulating empathy and personal-distress arousal by giving people a placebo drug, Batson and his coworkers (1983) asked participants to describe their emotions after watching the confederate suffer. Based on these responses, participants were categorized as being either personally distressed or empathic. As in the previous experiment, the empathic observers chose to help regardless of how easy or difficult it was to escape. Likewise, those who experienced personal distress tended to flee if they could, and helped only if fleeing was not an option. Overall, the pattern that emerged in five separate studies is that, regardless of ease or difficulty of escape, empathic individuals provided help about 75 percent of the time. Likewise, those who experienced personal distress and could not escape easily tended to help at approximately the same level, about 79 percent. In contrast, when escape was easy for the personally distressed, their level of helping dropped dramatically, to only about 30 percent.

Based on these and other findings that are consistent with the empathy-altruism hypothesis (Sibicky et al., 1995), can we conclude that people who help due to empathy are motivated by true altruism? Certainly, Batson and most social scientists think there is compelling scientific evidence for this view (Batson, 2011; Fetchenhauer et al., 2007). Yet while empathy may indeed induce altruistic helping, additional research suggests that an important factor in actually triggering empathic feelings toward those in need is whether we highly value their welfare in the first place (Batson et al., 2007; Stürmer et al., 2006). When the welfare of those in need is highly valued, we often experience

Critical THINKING

How could you design a donation pitch to members of a local community center to help starving people in a foreign country, knowing that some message receivers will react with empathy, while others will react with personal distress?

empathy and are more likely to respond with altruistic helping (Davis et al., 2004). However, if we perceive victims' welfare as being of relatively low value, we are unlikely to empathize with their plight (Stürmer et al., 2005). Consistent with evolutionary theory, this link between helping and empathic concern is much more pronounced in the context of kinship relationships than among strangers (Maner & Gailliot, 2007).

Given the importance of empathy as a motivator for helping, it is noteworthy that there is new evidence that the ability to experience empathy is at least partly determined by the ability to accurately read people's faces for emotions signaling danger and distress. In a series of studies, Marsh and Ambady (2007) found that participants who were exposed to fear facial expressions experienced more empathy and a greater willingness to help than participants who were exposed to neutral facial expressions. They further found that participants who showed the greatest prosocial responding were those who recognized facial expressions of fear most accurately. Overall, these findings are consistent with the survival value hypothesis discussed in Chapter 4 (p. 125). Marsh and Ambady contend that the facial expression of fear serves as a *distress cue* to bystanders, triggering increased perceptual attention and empathic arousal. These findings are also consistent with one of the main insights from Darley and Latané's bystander intervention model: people are most likely to behave prosocially when they accurately interpret situational cues signaling that something is wrong and help is needed.

Because the experience of empathy often induces a helping response, is it possible that sometimes we are wary of feeling empathy out of concern for the costs of helping? This *empathy-avoidance hypothesis* assumes that we have an implicit knowledge of the empathy-helping relationship, and this knowledge sometimes causes us to actively avoid feeling empathy when we believe the cost of helping will be high. This collapse of compassion is most often motivated by self-interest, and research suggests that it accounts for many instances of nonintervention. For example, in a series of experiments, when people believed that helping a homeless man would entail considerable time and effort, they actively avoided situations in which their empathy for this man would be aroused (Shaw et al., 1994). Because helping large numbers of people is more costly than helping single individuals, empathy avoidance is especially likely when the number of people in need of help increases (Daryl & Keith, 2011). In essence, people often "turn off" their empathy in the face of mass suffering or when they otherwise conclude that helping will entail heavy costs (Slovic, 2007). These findings suggest that even normally soft-hearted people can steel themselves to the suffering of others if they avoid an empathic connection. Consider this the next time you pass a homeless person on the street or learn of a disaster affecting large numbers of people. Are you actively avoiding an empathic response because the perceived costs of helping are too great?

> **"***One death is a tragedy; one million is a statistic.***"**
>
> ----------
>
> Joseph Stalin, 1878–1953, Soviet Union Premier

SECTION SUMMARY

- The model of bystander intervention focuses on the influence that bystanders have on prosocial behavior.

    audience inhibition effect: Bystanders inhibit people from defining dangerous situations as emergencies.

    diffusion of responsibility: Bystanders make people feel less personally responsible for helping.

- The arousal:cost-reward model focuses attention on the perceived costs of prosocial behavior.

- Greater helping often follows good moods, but we may sometimes try to eliminate negative moods by helping others.

- The empathy-altruism hypothesis contends that

    bystanders who experience empathy will help to provide comfort for victims and

    bystanders who experience personal distress will help victims only to reduce their own negative arousal state.

- Because empathy motivates helping, people sometimes actively avoid experiencing empathy when the cost of helping is high.

WHOM DO WE HELP?

Thus far we have examined the *why, when,* and *who* of helping. Now it is time to ask the question, *whom* do we help? Are some people more likely to receive help than others?

WE TEND TO HELP SIMILAR OTHERS.

Perceiving a needy person as similar to us tends to increase our willingness to lend assistance (Stürmer et al., 2005). For example, gay men were more willing than heterosexuals to volunteer at an AIDS service organization, and their willingness to help was strongest when their social identity as "gay men" was most salient (Simon et al., 2000). In general, studies indicate that we are most willing to help ingroup members who need assistance. As already discussed (p. 493), this preference for providing ingroup help over outgroup help is more pronounced among people with a collectivist orientation than among those with greater individualist tendencies.

We often rely on physical cues in guessing people's ingroup-outgroup status. One salient physical cue often used in categorizing needy people into ingroups and outgroups is the clothes they wear. In a series of studies conducted at Lancaster University in England, individual students on campus observed a young man fall while jogging down a grassy hill and proceed to hold onto his ankle while shouting out in pain (Levine et al., 2005). The injured man was either wearing a Lancaster team soccer shirt, a rival Liverpool soccer shirt, or an unbranded nonsoccer sport shirt. Consistent with the similarity hypothesis, when onlookers had been previously primed to think of themselves as Lancaster soccer fans the injured man was more likely to be helped when wearing the ingroup shirt than when wearing the outgroup or nonbranded shirt. However, when onlookers had been previously primed to think of themselves simply as soccer fans they were as likely to help the injured man wearing a Liverpool soccer shirt as one wearing a Lancaster shirt, while offering less help to the nonsoccer-related victim. Together, these findings indicate that not only are we more likely to help people who are similar to us, but perceptions of dissimilarity can be submerged by inducing or encouraging potential helpers to expand their ingroup social categorization.

Given the widespread cultural prejudice that exists concerning sexual orientation issues, it is not surprising to find an antigay bias among heterosexual adults in their willingness to offer help to those in need. In one study examining this effect, Jason Ellis and Pauline Fox (2001) used an adaptation of the *wrong-number technique* in measuring

Even in natural disasters, we are more likely to donate funds to help victims if we perceive that they are similar rather than dissimilar to us.

We tend to help similar others. For example, gay men are more willing than heterosexuals to volunteer at an AIDS service organization, especially when their gay social identity has been primed.

helping behavior. In this research technique, a confederate places a telephone call to a randomly chosen phone number and informs the respondent that he or she had misdialed while calling from a cell phone. The confederate then asks the respondent to phone an important message to the confederate's romantic partner, as the confederate's cell phone battery was running out. The phone number given to the respondent is that of the experimenters who record whether or not the call is made and the gender of the caller. In this field experiment, the two independent variables were the gender of the caller (male or female) and the sexual orientation of the caller. The caller's sexual orientation was indirectly identified during the phone call. In the lesbian condition, the female caller, who identified herself as Jane, stated that she was trying to reach her partner, Karen. In the gay condition, the male caller, who identified himself as Barry, stated that he was trying to reach his partner, John. In the two heterosexual conditions, the female caller mentioned her partner Barry and the male caller mentioned his partner Karen. The dependent variable was whether or not the participant placed the call within five minutes of the request for help.

As expected, when the caller was self-identified as gay or lesbian, respondents were much less likely to help than when the caller was self-identified as heterosexual (31 percent versus 50 percent). Consistent with the greater prejudice expressed by heterosexual men to gay men compared to lesbians, male respondents were significantly less likely to give help to gay men than to lesbians (14 percent versus 48 percent). In contrast, female respondents did not significantly differ in their helping toward gay men and lesbians. These results suggest that although lesbians and gay men are discriminated against in helping, such discrimination does not appear to be equally applied to both groups by heterosexual men. This finding is consistent with previous research indicating that heterosexual men feel more negatively toward gay men than toward lesbians (Kite, & Whitely 1996).

Unlike sexual orientation issues, the influence that a victim's race has on helping behavior is far more complex. In a meta-analysis of thirty-one studies published from 1887 to 2002 that examined discrimination against Blacks in helping situations, Donald Saucier and his coworkers (2005) did not find evidence of blanket discrimination. However, consistent with the prediction of aversive racism (see Chapter 6, pp. 219–221), Blacks were least likely to be helped when White bystanders could rationalize decisions not to help with reasons having nothing to do with race. Specifically, when helping required lengthier, riskier, more difficult, and more effortful actions by potential helpers, Whites were less likely to help Black victims compared to White victims. These findings suggest that potential helpers perceive higher costs for helping when the person who needs help is of a different race. This meta-analysis also found that when White bystanders were further away from victims, victim race predicted whether help was offered: Black victims were offered help less often than White victims. Finally, the researchers found evidence that discrimination against Blacks was more likely for higher-level emergencies requiring quick helping decisions compared to lower-level emergencies allowing for more decision time. In other words, race discrimination in helping is most likely to occur when the ability to control prejudicial responding is inhibited by having to make fast decisions.

Although similarity may generally lead to greater helping, even a casual observer of the cultural scene can tell you that this is not the case when we consider whom male helpers prefer to assist. In a review of twenty-five studies that compared help received by male and female victims, Alice Eagly and Maureen Crowley (1986) found there was an overall tendency for men to provide more frequent help to women, not men. Women helpers, in contrast, did not show any gender bias. Although male helpers are acting out of line with the similarity effect, they are behaving perfectly in accord with the male gender role, which nurtures helping that is heroic and chivalrous—and is generally directed toward the benefit of female victims. In many cases, the help that men offer to women is clearly egoistic in nature; they more frequently help attractive than unattractive women (West & Brown, 1975).

Finally, while it is most often the case that people are more helpful to their friends than they are to strangers, there may be times when this is not so. As discussed in Chapter 3 (pp. 100–102), the *self-evaluation maintenance model* contends that when our friends succeed at a task, we may respond with either pride or jealousy. If their success is not in an area where we seek similar success, we are likely to bask in their reflected glory and feel proud of them. However, if their success involves a task or skill with which we strongly identify, we may be envious of them and also experience a loss of self-esteem due to social comparison. Is it possible that this self-evaluation maintenance process might influence our degree of helpfulness to friends? That is, if our friends are trying to succeed at a task that is highly relevant to our own feelings of self-worth, are we likely to go "all out" in helping them succeed?

To examine this possibility, Abraham Tesser and Jonathan Smith (1980) recruited pairs of friends to participate with strangers in a "work identification task" described either as a measure of important skills (high relevance condition) or as a trivial game (low relevance condition). After finishing work on this task and being informed that they had performed "a little below average," participants were told to choose clues for both their friend and the stranger as they worked on the same task. Some of the clues were easy and would likely boost performance, while other clues were so difficult that they would likely hinder performance. Which type of clues did participants choose for friends versus strangers?

Consistent with the self-evaluation maintenance model, participants in the low-relevance condition helped their friend more than they helped the stranger by giving their friend easier clues. However, when the task was important to the participants' feelings of self-worth (high-relevance condition), their degree of helpfulness reversed. Now, they gave harder clues to their friend than they did to the stranger. These results suggest that when there is a conflict between protecting our self-esteem and protecting the welfare of a friend, we may be less interested in our friend's welfare than our own feelings of self-worth.

WE HELP DESERVING OTHERS, BUT WE ALSO BLAME VICTIMS.

As discussed earlier in the Chapter (p. 490), whether people receive help in times of need will partly depend on others' inferences about the causes of their troubles. Following the principles of attribution theory discussed in chapter 4, we are more likely to help someone if we attribute the cause of their problems to external or uncontrollable factors rather than internal ones. For example, college students state that they would be more willing to lend an acquaintance money or give them their lecture notes if the need arose due to an uncontrollable cause, such as illness, rather than an internal, controllable cause, such as laziness (Weiner, 1980). Similarly, people's willingness to help the poor and other disadvantaged people is substantially shaped by what they believe caused these unfortunate events in the first place (Dionne, 1991). Put simply, if we believe people could not have prevented their predicament, we are more likely to help.

The reason we are more likely to help deserving others is due to the *norm of social justice* discussed earlier in the chapter. However, the problem in making inferences about the cause of a victim's troubles, and thereby deciding if she or he deserves our help, is that most of us believe in a just world (Bierhoff, 2002; Callan et al., 2006). The **just-world belief** is a belief that the world is a fair and equitable place, with people getting what they deserve (Lerner, 1997; Lucas et al., 2009). According to Melvin Lerner (1980), this social belief system is a defensive reaction to the sometimes cruel twists of fate encountered in life, but it is comforting because most of us conceive ourselves to be good and decent people. By believing in a just world, we have the illusion that we have more control over our lives than we actually do.

Although just-world believers often psychologically benefit from their positive illusions about how the world operates (Lipkus et al., 1996), this social belief can lead to some unfortunate social judgments, as illustrated by people's tendency to blame rape victims for their sexual assaults (Bell et al., 1994). Strong believers in a just world tend to make *defensive attributions* when explaining the plight of victims. In other words, they are prone to blame people for their misfortunes. Research demonstrates that this tendency to blame victims is strongest when people feel personally threatened by an apparent injustice (Hafer, 2000a&b). Thus, accident victims are more likely blamed for their fate if they are similar to us on some relevant characteristic, or if their injuries are severe rather than mild (Burger, 1981). By disparaging the victim, we reassure ourselves that the world is not only just, but also that we are not likely to fall victim to similar circumstances ("Because I'm really not like *them*").

Although many people believe in a just world, individual differences exist in the extent to which this belief is held. Because those with a strong just-world belief are more likely to be unsympathetic to victims, it's not surprising to find that they generally are also less likely to help those in need. Before reading further, spend a few minutes answering the items in *Self/Social Connection Exercise 12.3.*

Does this mean that people who are strong believers in a just world are always unhelpful bystanders? No. When a victim's suffering can be easily and promptly corrected, strong believers in a just world are much more likely to help than when the problems are of a widespread and enduring nature (Bierhoff et al., 1991). The likely reason for this effect is that helping someone who needs just a little bit of assistance to get back on

just-world belief

A belief that the world is a fair and equitable place, with people getting what they deserve in life.

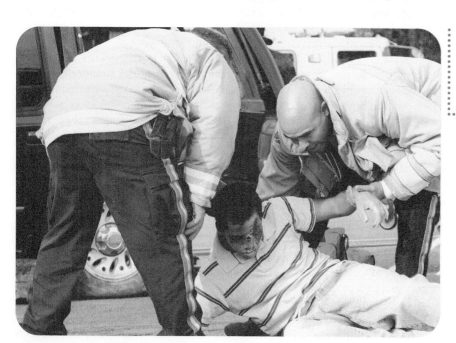

Do you believe that the world is a fair and equitable place, with people getting what they deserve? If so, how does assigning blame to accident victims reinforce your just-world beliefs?

Self/Social Connections Exercise 12.3

Do You Believe in a Just World?

Instructions:

Read the statements below and decide which of these you tend to agree with and with which you disagree.

_____1. Good deeds often go unnoticed.
_____2. When parents punish their children, it is almost always for good reason.
_____3. Many people suffer through absolutely no fault of their own.
_____4. By and large, people deserve what they get.
_____5. The political candidate who sticks up for his principles rarely gets elected.
_____6. Although evil men may hold political power for a while, in the general course of history good wins out.

Scoring Your Responses

The more of the even numbered statements you agreed with and the more of the odd numbered statements you disagreed with, the stronger is your belief in a just world. How does the belief in a just world influence both psychosocial well-being and willingness to help victims of unfortunate circumstances?

track confirms the just-world believer's perception that the truly deserving will not be unfairly punished. Thus, firm believers in a just world are much more likely to be onetime contributors to little Billy's heart operation fund than they are to be continuing contributors to a fund in search of a cure for AIDS or a program to promote affordable housing for the poor.

SECTION SUMMARY

- We are most likely to help similar others.

- We also are most likely to help deserving others.

- One unfortunate consequence of believing in a just world is that we tend to blame people for their misfortunes.

ARE THERE HIDDEN COSTS FOR HELP RECIPIENTS?

Throughout the chapter we have examined some of the factors that inhibit bystanders to provide assistance to others, but what if help is given? How do recipients typically respond? And what might prevent a person in need from asking for help?

BEING UNABLE TO RECIPROCATE HELP CAN CREATE STRESS.

People recognize that receiving help is a mixed blessing. Those who receive help often respond with feelings of relief and gratitude, but they also often feel embarrassed, indebted, and even inferior (Nadler, 1991). The contradictory feelings that often flow from prosocial actions help to explain why victims are sometimes less than gracious recipients of a helping hand. The potential that help giving has for producing resentment and hostility is aptly recognized in an Indian proverb that states, "Why do you hate me? I never even helped you" (Nadler & Fisher, 1986, p. 82).

In attempting to explain why receiving help may at times evoke unpleasant emotions, social psychologists have turned their attention to the fact that in exchange relationships (refer to Chapter 10, p. 392), people are especially attentive to *reciprocity*—a mutual exchange of resources. *Equity theory* (Chapter 10, p. 425) contends that people seek to maintain equity in their social relationships by keeping the exchange ratio of resources balanced, and they feel distressed when inequity exists (Hatfield et al., 1978). When people receive help, they commonly experience a feeling of inequity, because by definition, they realize they have a more favorable ratio of rewards to contributions than does the helper. Under such circumstances, recipients of help are motivated to restore actual equity by trying to return the favor (Greenberg & Frisch, 1972). But what happens if they cannot reciprocate?

Research indicates that recipients not only find nonreciprocal helping distressful but also are less likely to ask for assistance in the first place if they don't think they can repay the person in some way (Riley & Eckenrode, 1986). If they aren't in a position to refuse the help, they also might sometimes deal with their inability to restore equity by resenting the helper (Gross & Latané, 1974). In essence, help-givers may be resented if they don't allow recipients to restore equity in some way and thereby allow those who have been helped to live up to the reciprocity norm.

> **"** *... It is natural to avoid those to whom we have been too much obliged.* **"**
>
> Héloise, French abbess, 1098–1164

RECEIVING HELP CAN THREATEN SELF-ESTEEM.

The notion that receiving help may produce inequity and feelings of distress in a relationship suggests that it may also pose a threat to the recipient's self-esteem. For instance, in our individualist culture we place a high premium on self-reliance, and this value often is a key defining feature of our self-concept. Receiving help from someone puts us into a dependent role that is contrary to this individualistic value. According to Jeffrey Fisher and Arie Nadler's **threat-to-self-esteem model**, if receiving help contains such negative self-messages, we are likely to feel threatened and respond negatively (Nadler & Fisher, 1986). More specifically, this model states that when receiving help, we can perceive it as either *self-supporting* or *self-threatening*. Aid will be supportive to the extent that it (1) conveys caring for the recipient and (2) provides real benefits (Dakof & Taylor, 1990). It will be threatening to the extent that it (1) implies an inferiority-superiority relationship between recipient and helper and (2) conflicts with important cultural values of self-reliance and independence (Dunkel-Schetter et al., 1992).

threat-to-self-esteem model
· · · · · · · · · · · · · · · · · · ·
A theory stating that if receiving help contains negative self-messages, recipients are likely to feel threatened and respond negatively

In Israel, Nadler and Samer Halabi (2006) tested the threat-to-self-esteem model among Arab-Israelis, an ethnic group within the country that has lower social status than the more mainstream Jewish-Israelis. The researchers predicted that Arab-Israelis would be especially likely to react negatively to help from Jewish-Israelis when they perceived such help as threatening their desire for equality by implying that they are dependent on the higher status Jewish-Israelis. They also predicted that Arab-Israelis who strongly identified with other Arab-Israelis would be much more likely to reject such help because they would experience a stronger self-esteem threat than those who self-identify less with their ethnic group. In a series of both lab and field experiments, the researchers' hypotheses were supported: Arab-Israelis were much more likely to not seek and also reject help from Jewish-Israelis and evaluate the would-be helpers more negatively when the help was perceived to imply dependency. This negative reaction was especially likely among high ingroup identifiers.

> **"** *A charitable deed must be done as a duty which man owes to man, so that it conveys no idea of the superiority of the giver or the inferiority of the receiver.* **"**
>
> The Koran 2:262, Sacred Scripture of Islam

Characteristics of the helper and the recipient's own level of self-esteem will also determine whether aid is seen as supportive or threatening. Being helped by a friend, sibling, or a *similar* person is more likely to prompt social comparison, which in turn may call into question the recipient's level of competence (Searcy & Eisenberg, 1992). This is especially true when the helpful task involves something important to the recipient's self-concept. For example, if you are an aspiring psychologist who does not understand the subtleties of a particularly complex theory, asking a fellow student probably would be more threatening to your self-esteem than to ask your psychology professor. Why? The threat-to-self-esteem model would hypothesize that asking a fellow student for help would be more likely to reflect negatively on your own level of competence in this area than seeking help from the professor, a person who is clearly dissimilar to you in psychological training and knowledge (Nadler et al., 1983).

In one experiment testing this hypothesis, Nadler (1987) asked Israeli high school students to solve a series of anagrams when working alongside a same-sex partner. While describing the anagrams task the researchers told half of the students that their performance would provide accurate information on their intelligence and creativity. The rest were told that the task had no association with any important intellectual qualities. All the students were also told that during the task, they could ask their partner for help if they wished. Just before they began the anagrams, they were shown an attitude questionnaire their partner had supposedly completed a few minutes earlier. Half of these questionnaires were constructed to be similar to the participants' own attitude questionnaire responses, while the others were dissimilar in content. The question of interest was under what conditions the students would be most likely to avoid help seeking.

Consistent with the threat-to-self-esteem model, students were less likely to seek help from their partners when they believed they were similar to them, especially when the task was defined as requiring skills important to self-esteem, namely, intelligence and creativity. This reluctance to ask for help from similar others was greatest among adolescents high in self-esteem, who supposedly had the most self-regard to lose on these important personal qualities. One positive consequence of this self-esteem threat is that people who feel threatened in this manner become motivated to develop the necessary skills so that in the future, they will not have to seek help.

Given our previous discussion of gender differences in providing aid (with men tending to assume the role of the chivalrous helper of women), it is not surprising to find that men are more reluctant than women to ask for help (Barbee et al., 1993; Corney, 1990). After all, how often do you see Bruce Willis– or Sylvester Stallone–type characters asking for help in the movies? Such help seeking is more frowned upon for men than women and therefore poses a more serious threat to their self-esteem (Smith & DeWine, 1991). Evidence also shows that when heterosexual individuals seek help from someone of the other sex, men are more likely to prefer that it come from an unattractive woman, and women are more likely to prefer help from an attractive man (Nadler et al., 1982). This different pattern of help seeking can be explained as a function of traditional gender roles and self-esteem threat. For a traditional (masculine) heterosexual man, acting dependent toward an attractive woman would be perceived as imperiling his "macho" image in her eyes, but for a traditional (feminine) heterosexual woman, acting dependent toward an attractive man would be thought of as increasing, not decreasing, her appeal. In summary, then, our assessments of what effect such help seeking will have on our self-esteem will largely determine whether and from whom we will seek help.

> "*The gods help them that help themselves.*"
>
> ----------
>
> Aesop, Greek folk hero and teller of fables, sixth century BC

Most men consider asking for help to be a sign of weakness. This is even portrayed by macho movie characters.

SECTION SUMMARY

- The threat-to-self-esteem model hypothesizes that if receiving help poses a threat to self-esteem, the recipient may respond negatively, disparaging the help and the helper.

- Help recipients may resent help-givers if they are not given the opportunity to return the favor in some way.

CAN SOCIAL PSYCHOLOGICAL KNOWLEDGE ENHANCE PROSOCIAL BEHAVIOR?

Shortly after 6 p.m. on September 5, 1993, a nude man was seen running through Cornell University's campus. Suddenly, he stopped at the College Avenue Bridge and began climbing over the railing so that he could jump into the deep gorge below. Yet before he could commit suicide, some students grabbed and held him to the ground until police arrived. Although hundreds of people saw him run past and head toward the bridge, only a handful chose to intervene. These Good Samaritans later admitted that they might not have helped if not for the quick thinking of Cornell undergraduate Gretchen Goldfarb. "Something just clicked," Goldfarb said, in explaining how she realized that this was an emergency and not simply a prank. What was it that "clicked" in her mind? Social psychological knowledge. A few days earlier, she had learned in her psychology class about Darley and Latané's bystander intervention research, which demonstrated that people often do not help in emergencies unless someone first takes action. Armed with this knowledge, she admonished fellow bystanders to grab the man. In that moment, her application of social psychological knowledge played a pivotal role in saving a life.

LEARNING ABOUT THE BARRIERS TO HELPING

It is very likely that during the course of your life you will find yourself in an emergency situation like the one Gretchen Goldfarb experienced. Perhaps the most disturbing set of findings discussed in this chapter is the tendency of bystanders to fail to act when someone needs help. Because emergencies are often not clearly defined as such, and because of the potential for embarrassment if one intervenes and there is no actual emergency, the presence of others inhibits prosocial responding. However, as Goldfarb's story demonstrates, social psychological knowledge truly can release you from such inhibition.

In an empirical demonstration of the empowering effects of such knowledge, Arthur Beaman and his coworkers (1978) randomly assigned students to listen to either a lecture on Latané and Darley's bystander intervention research or to a topic irrelevant to helping. Two weeks later, while participating in a seemingly unrelated study, these same students walked past a person lying on the ground. A confederate who accompanied the student acted unconcerned at this possible emergency. How did the students react? Only 25 percent of those not previously exposed to the bystander intervention lecture stopped to offer assistance. This low prosocial response rate is consistent with Latané and Darley's own findings. Undoubtedly, these students took their cue from their unconcerned companion and defined the situation as a nonemergency. In contrast, students who had previously learned about the paralyzing effects of fellow bystanders on the intervention process acted very differently. Forty-three percent stopped to help the person. These findings suggest that simply knowing about the social barriers to helping can free one from their antisocial effects.

Jane Piliavin, codeveloper of the arousal:cost-reward model, believes that in addition to this knowledge-created awareness of the social dynamics of emergency situations, we must also understand that in our individualistic society we have been socialized to leave people alone and to mind our own business. Such training can effectively inhibit intervention:

> In our society, we are trained from an early age to see the problems of other people as "none of our business," to close our feelings off from others' experiences. We have only recently "discovered" child abuse, spouse abuse, incest, and other family "traditions" because of the sanctity of the home and respect for others' privacy. This tendency saves all of us a great deal of emotional distress, but it contributes to the bureaucratization of helping in our society and, we believe, to the increasing alienation and self-absorption of which we all are currently being accused. We may need more training as busybodies; respect for privacy prevents empathic arousal, and directs one's attention to the costs of intervention, specifically the cost of being thought "intrusive." (Piliavin et al., 1981, p. 254)

Piliavin and her colleagues state that in classes in which they have discussed the social psychological research and theories of helping, students repeatedly report an increased attentiveness and responsiveness to emergencies. In a very real and important sense, then, making people aware of the social dynamics of emergencies and the inhibiting effects of socialization may be an important key to unlocking people's prosocial tendencies.

THE BIG PICTURE

In this chapter, we addressed five basic questions about helping: Why do we help? When do we help? Who is most likely to help? Whom do we help? And, are there hidden costs for those who receive help? Now, let's turn the tables a bit: What if *you* are the one who needs help? How can you use your social psychological knowledge to increase the likelihood that others will assist you?

The *bystander intervention model* provides valuable insights in this regard, for it tells you that deciding to intervene in a possible emergency involves a rather complex set of decisions. If bystanders make an incorrect decision at any point in this process, they will not help you. Faced with these facts, as the victim, you must attack and neutralize the psychological factors that cause nonintervention. Essentially, you need to capitalize on the self's ability to construct social reality. You can do so by actively and forcefully altering people's social perceptions so that they adopt helping social roles.

The first psychological hurdle is the *audience inhibition effect*, in which the fear of being negatively evaluated, combined with the tendency to look to others for further information, leads bystanders to identify emergencies as nonemergencies. As the victim, you can eliminate this inhibition by clearly letting everyone know that this is an emergency and you need help.

After clearing this hurdle, you must next attack the *diffusion of responsibility*, which is bystanders' tendency to believe they are less personally responsible for helping when others are present. Here, you should implore specific people to help you, because it's hard to deny assistance when singled out of the crowd.

Finally, because some people may want to help but are unsure what to do, you can overcome this last hurdle by specifically giving them instructions ("You! Call an ambulance!" "You! Gather my belongings and bring them to me!"). Using your most authoritative voice will further increase obedience. And obedience is exactly what you are seeking here. In all likelihood, you probably won't need to direct everyone who is assisting you. Once you get the ball rolling, others are likely to spring into action on their own. However, the more quickly you consciously transform the social dynamics to facilitate helping, the better off you will be. Gretchen Goldfarb can attest to this social fact.

► Check out our web site
www.BVTLab.com
for chapter-by-chapter flashcards, summaries, and practice quizzes.

WEB SITES

ACCESSED THROUGH www.BVTLab.com/sop6
Web sites for this chapter focus on research and theory on helping, including how to raise children to be more altruistic and personal life stories of people who help others.

AMERICAN PSYCHOLOGICAL ASSOCIATION
The American Psychological Association has a web page that offers suggestions on how to raise children to be more altruistic, and supports the suggestion with relevant theories.

GIRAFFE PROJECT HEROES PROGRAM
This web site highlights the personal life stories of people who stick their necks out for the common good.

THE ALTRUISTIC PERSONALITY AND PROSOCIAL BEHAVIOR INSTITUTE
This web site is devoted to the institute founded in 1982 by Dr. Samuel Oliner and Dr. Pearl Oliner, who recognized the need for more research into the areas of altruism and prosocial behavior.

APPendIX

POSSIBLE ANSWERS FOR THE CRITICAL THINKING EXERCISES

A NOTE FROM THE AUTHOR

This appendix contains possible answers to the critical thinking sidebars in Chapters 1 to 12. In reading and comparing them with your own responses, analyze each answer's strengths and weaknesses. If you would like to help me improve my responses for the next edition, please drop me a line with your suggestions (or questions) using my e-mail address (Stephen.Franzoi@marquette.edu). For those critical thinking sidebar questions that asked you to provide personal recollections from your own experiences, I have understandably not provided a possible answer.

CHAPTER 1: INTRODUCING SOCIAL PSYCHOLOGY

Question: *Do you think that a judge's beliefs about the guilt or innocence of a defendant in a criminal trial could create a self-fulfilling prophecy among the jury, even if the judge does not voice her opinions?*

Possible Answer: Actually, several studies have investigated this very question. What they have found is that although judges may not directly convey to the jury their beliefs about the defendant's guilt or innocence, their nonverbal behavior and instructions to the jury prior to them beginning deliberations can influence jurors' decisions (Halverson et al., 1997). For example, scowling or smiling in the general direction of a defendant by a judge can signal to jurors some important information about the judge's beliefs, and this information can steer the evaluative direction of subsequent deliberations. It has been estimated that the effect of such subtle influence is sufficient to potentially increase the rate of guilty findings by 14 percent for a jury instructed by a judge who believes a defendant to be guilty (Rosenthal, 2003).

CHAPTER 2: RESEARCH METHODS IN SOCIAL PSYCHOLOGY

Question: *If you were a member of your college's institutional review board and a research proposal similar to the Milgram obedience study was submitted for approval, what questions would you ask to determine its risk/benefit ratio? Based on your assessment, would you approve the study?*

Possible Answer: Using the risk/benefit ratio, you would weigh the potential risks to the participants against the study's potential benefits to society, with greater weight given to the participants' welfare. While assessing a Milgram-type study proposal, you might ask whether there was any other way the researchers could conduct the study to minimize participant stress. In essence, because of the deception being used, full informed consent could not be obtained. As such, you might ask the researchers whether they were going to let the participants know up front that they could not reveal all the details of the purpose and procedures to be used in the study. You might also ask the researchers how they would respond to a participant who asked them to stop the study. Would they stop the study after the first request? Because of the deception and the destructive obedience that is being studied, you would probably also ask the researchers to specifically detail their debriefing procedures because these would need to be as sensitive and detailed as possible. You might also require follow-up interviews with participants to determine whether there were any delayed stress responses and further require that free counseling opportunities with a mental health professional be made available to participants if they wanted to discuss their research experience.

Would you approve a Milgram-type study? You might decide to do so only if it were seeking to shed light on an aspect of obedience that had not already been investigated. Given the fact that there already have been a number of Milgram obedience replications, you might find it difficult to justify approving another replication of the original study given the possible harm to participants. However, in considering your own answer to this question, keep in mind the following thought: the decision not to grant a request to conduct research on a particular topic also has ethical implications. If you do not allow certain research to be conducted because the behavior in question is socially undesirable or destructive when it naturally occurs in the "real world," the social sciences are likely to have crucial gaps in their knowledge base, and these gaps may prevent scientists from developing useful intervention strategies to lessen people's future suffering. What will be potentially lost by not allowing this study to go forward? These are just a few of the tough questions that you would grapple with as a member of an institutional review board.

Question: *Prior to conducting research, what precautions do you think social psychologists should take to ensure* *that the people who participate in their research will not be harmed? Should they be allowed to study people without their consent?*

Possible Answer: Just as you can never guarantee that someone won't be hurt taking a walk around the block, you cannot guarantee that participants in a social scientific study will never be harmed. However, what you can do is examine all aspects of your study so that all reasonable precautions are taken to minimize participant risk. Whenever the choice is between securing the welfare of the study or the welfare of the participant, you must always place the participant's welfare first. This means that some studies will simply not be conducted.

In most cases, social scientists should study people only with their "informed consent," meaning that they are provided with enough information about the research to be able to make a conscious choice to participate or not. In some cases, however, it may be necessary to study people without their informed consent. For instance, when researchers study helping behavior, they may stage a fake emergency in a public setting—for example, a person collapsing on the street—and then observe the responses of bystanders. In such a natural setting, you cannot ask people for permission to include them in the study beforehand.

Question: *What are some similarities and some differences between "random assignment" and "random selection"?*

Possible Answer: One similarity is that both of these research procedures are meant to serve as a safeguard against researchers unconsciously allowing their opinions and preferences to influence subject participation. Further, as their names imply, both random selection and random assignment involve the reliance upon a chance selection procedure. The difference is that while random selection has to do with giving everyone in the population being studied an equal chance of being included in the study, random assignment involves giving everyone who is already in the study an equal chance of being exposed to every level of the study's treatment conditions. Random assignment is associated with experimental designs in which there are different treatment conditions, whereas random selection is more often associated with survey research (although it is sometimes used in experiments).

Question: *Imagine that you are the leader of a team of researchers studying social psychological topics at a university. Under your tutelage, students are learning about the research process while working on your team. Besides instructing them on the proper scientific methods, statistical procedures, and ethical standards to adopt when conducting research, what advice would you give them concerning how they should approach scientific problems in their work?*

Possible Answer: In 1973, social psychologist William McGuire wrote an important article on how social psychologists should approach scientific problems. This article, "The Yin and Yang of Progress in Social Psychology," suggested that researchers adopt an Eastern philosophical approach to problem solving that defies conventional notions of logic by simultaneously entertaining contradictory and opposing explanations of reality. This approach to "doing" social psychology McGuire called *perspectivism*, and it requires that scientists engage in oppositional thinking when developing theories and hypotheses. When a scientist develops a hypothesis from a theory, she must also consider how other theories might also account for this hypothesis, and she must also develop an opposing hypothesis that is also derived from multiple theories. This approach to thinking about scientific problems frees the scientist's mind from being bound by the logic of only one explanation of events. Social psychologist Mahzarin Banaji (2004), a former graduate student of McGuire's, asserts that the student members of a research team with this perspectivist philosophy would feel safe and even elated when research findings run counter to their hypotheses. Instead of feeling that they somehow "failed" the leader of their research team, these students would view these findings as providing them with an opportunity to entertain alternative explanations that are closer to providing an accurate accounting of the social behavior under study. To learn more about perspectivism, check out the book *Perspectivism in Social Psychology*, edited by John T. Jost, Mahzarin R. Banaji, and Deborah A. Prentice and published in 2004 by the American Psychological Association.

CHAPTER 3: THE SELF

Question: *According to the strength model of self-regulation, when would a parent or a spouse be most likely to engage in domestic violence due to losing control of their emotions?*

Possible Answer: According to this theory, each act of self-regulation depletes the limited energy available for this purpose. Thus, immediately after exercising self-regulation in one activity, people will find it harder to regulate their behavior in an unrelated activity. From this perspective, domestic violence is most likely to occur when self-regulatory resources have been recently depleted. Thus, when abusers have just finished controlling or regulating their behavior—for example, working hard to prepare a meal when they would rather be relaxing, or holding their temper in check when talking to their employer on the phone—they are more susceptible to not being able to control their aggressive tendencies toward family members.

Question: *If you were to tell someone to "just be yourself," what would that mean to them depending on whether they were from an individualist or a collectivist culture?*

Possible Answer: When Chie Kanagawa and her colleagues (2001) asked that question of U.S. and Japanese college students, they received decidedly different responses. For the Americans, the statement implied a self comprised of personal attributes that were not influenced by the situation they happened to be in at the time. Further, these attributes reflected the Americans' unique qualities, and these qualities were mostly positive. In contrast, for the Japanese, the statement implied a self that was defined by the relationships inherent in the situation. Here, "being yourself" meant constructing a self-presentation that was fairly self-critical and would help one fit into the situation. This research suggests that, for individualists, being yourself assumes a relatively fixed and stable self-concept made up of generally positive personal attributes. For collectivists, being yourself assumes a self that changes according to the situation to better fit in with the group.

Question: *If your ethnic heritage is relevant to whom you think you are, what stage are you at in Phinney's model? Is this model an accurate portrayal of your own ethnic identity development?*

This answer will be unique to your personal experiences.

Question: *If low self-esteem people are likely to reject your attempts to increase their feelings of self-worth, what strategy might you use to feed their self-enhancement needs without triggering their need for self-verification?*

Possible Answer: Self-verification needs are most likely to override self-enhancement needs when low self-esteem people are presented with positive feedback that, if accepted, would require a major change in their self-concepts. Research suggests that low self-esteem persons can engage in direct forms of self-enhancement when the positive feedback is not related to a highly important aspect of their self-concepts (Seta et al., 1999). Thus, you could offer low self-esteem people subtle praise and other positive feedback that will make them feel good and hopefully boost their feelings of self-worth, without being so strong as to make them uncomfortable.

Question: *People with low implicit self-esteem don't like themselves but are not typically consciously aware of this negative self-regard. If you were a therapist, how might you use classical conditioning techniques to unconsciously increase a person's low implicit self-esteem?*

Possible Answer: Classical conditioning is a type of learning first identified by Russian physiologist Ivan Pavlov, in which a neutral stimulus acquires the capacity to elicit a response after being repeatedly paired with another stimulus that naturally elicits that response. In this nonconscious learning, the two stimuli are repeatedly paired until the presence of one evokes the expectation of the other. In a recent study, Jodene Baccus and her coworkers (2004) used classical conditioning techniques to increase implicit self-esteem. How did they accomplish this task? Sitting at a computer, research participants were told that a word would appear randomly in some area of the computer screen and their task was to click on the word with the mouse as quickly as possible. They were also told that doing so would cause an image to be displayed briefly (for 400 milliseconds) in that same area. Whenever a word appeared on the screen that the participants had previously noted was self-descriptive, it was paired with an image of a smiling face. The participants completed 240 trials, with 80 of those trials involving self-relevant words. Results indicated that those participants who were repeatedly exposed to pairings of self-relevant words with smiling faces showed enhanced implicit self-esteem compared with participants in a control condition. Although more research is needed to further understand this learning process, the finding in this study suggests that feelings of low self-esteem are not set in stone in childhood, but might be raised at a later time using basic learning principles.

Question: *Our self-esteem will often be threatened when we compare ourselves with those superior to us on some task. However, a review of the literature indicates that upward comparison can sometimes lead to higher self-esteem (Collins, 1996). How do you think this particular self-enhancement effect might occur?*

Possible Answer: Upward social comparison is generally regarded as a threat to self-esteem, but people often compare themselves with others who have better abilities and attributes than their own. Such upward comparison provides useful information, and it doesn't always lead to more negative self-evaluations. Rebecca Collins' (1996) meta-analysis of studies testing upward comparison effects found that people sometimes make upward comparisons in hopes of enhancing their self-esteem by discovering ways to improve themselves and by identifying attributes they share with their "betters."

Question: *Do you think that people raised in collectivist cultures might sometimes have different self-presentation concerns than persons raised in individualist cultures?*

Possible Answer: As discussed in Chapter 3 (p. 97), people in collectivist cultures tend to have a more interdependent view of themselves than those in individualist cultures. As a result, collectivists may often be more concerned than individualists about presenting the appropriate public self to their group. In Asian collectivist cultures, "saving face" or avoiding public embarrassment is more important than in individualist cultures. For example, in Japan, there are "convenience agencies" (benriya) that supply customers with rented "friends" who become additional guests at their weddings, mourners at family funerals, or romantic partners at important parties. Such extreme measures to manage others' impressions also occur in individualist cultures, but they may be more common in a social environment in which interdependent selves are more salient.

Question: *Of the different self-presentation strategies that you employed today, under what circumstances and with whom were they used? Which ones achieved the desired effect? Was there one strategy that you frequently employed? If you didn't use any, why was this the case?*

This answer will be unique to your personal experiences.

CHAPTER 4:
SOCIAL COGNITION
AND PERSON PERCEPTION

Question: *How is the spontaneously activated self-concept discussed in Chapter 3 related to schemas and priming effects?*

Possible Answer: As defined in Chapter 3, a spontaneous self-concept is that aspect of the self-concept that becomes salient and activated in a particular setting. In essence, a spontaneous self-concept is a self-schema or a set of self-schemas that have been situationally activated. Priming is the process by which recent exposure to certain stimuli or events increases the accessibility of certain schemas. Thus, for example, if you notice a parent comforting a crying child just as you walk into a store, your self-schema of empathy might be activated. Upon entering the store, this spontaneous empathic self-concept may cause you to take notice of the donation box for "Needy Children" at the service desk, prompting you to donate money to the cause.

Question: *If the representativeness heuristic is stereotyping operating in reverse, does that mean that stereotyping is also a heuristic?*

Possible Answer: Yes, stereotyping is definitely a heuristic. Like other heuristics, stereotyping provides a "shortcut in thinking" by supplying us with rich and distinctive information—but not necessarily accurate information—about individuals we do not personally know. Stereotypes provide us with a fast basis for social judgments, and they also "free up" cognition for other tasks. Stereotyping will be discussed more fully in Chapter 8.

Question: *In the days and weeks following the suicide attacks at the Pentagon and the World Trade Center by Arab terrorists, FBI offices around the country were flooded with calls from citizens reporting possible leads and suspects. Virtually every person who was perceived as being suspicious was of Arab descent. What cognitive heuristic was being used in making these social judgments? Why do you think people were relying on this heuristic?*

Possible Answer: People were relying on the representativeness heuristic, which involves the tendency to judge the category membership of things based on how closely they match the typical or average member of that category. Anyone who had physical characteristics, clothing, or a surname perceived to be associated with people from Middle Eastern cultures was much more likely to be judged as a possible terrorist. Further, Americans were primed to place people into the "terrorist" category because of the wide news coverage of the September 11th attacks. In this atmosphere of terrorist-saturated news coverage and discussion, Americans perceived future terrorist attacks to be quite likely, and many people believed they were possible targets. This tendency to judge the frequency or probability of an event in terms of how easy it is to think of examples of that event is known as the availability heuristic. The availability heuristic contributed to people relying on the representativeness heuristic. As previously discussed, evolutionary theory contends that the ability to recognize emotion from the observation of facial expressions is part of our evolutionary heritage.

Question: *Why might a neuroscientist argue that the hindsight bias is triggered by some of the same neurological activity that creates the storyline of dreams?*

Possible Answer: Social psychologists explain the hindsight bias as an attempt to make sense out of a surprising outcome; in essence, inserting missing causal connections so that our story of the event makes sense given the outcome. The part of our brains that does this cognitive work is the left hemisphere of the central cortex, what neuroscientist Mike Gazzaniga (2000) describes as the brain's "interpreter." The left hemisphere always strives to assign some rational meaning to behavior, even when there is none. According to the activation-synthesis theory of dreaming, a dream is the left hemisphere's attempt to interpret the random neural activity initiated in the midbrain during sleep (Hobson & McCarley, 1977; Hobson et al., 1998). Thus, the neurological activity that triggers the hindsight bias may involve some of the same neural activity that triggers dreams, with the right hemisphere helping construct most of the dream's visual features.

Question: *How might an evolutionary theorist explain the gender differences in decoding nonverbal communication?*

That is, from an evolutionary perspective, why would it be more beneficial for females than males to have good nonverbal skills?

Possible Answer: According to the evolutionary perspective, human beings, along with all other species on the planet, have evolved in ways that maximize the chances of their genes being passed on to their offspring so that these gene traits survive from generation to generation. Because only women could bear and breast-feed infants, evolutionary theorists contend that they evolved to take on the more nurturing and empathic role of domestic caretaker. To be a good nurturer of infants who cannot yet convey their desires through spoken language, being very attentive to nonverbal signals of sickness or distress would be very beneficial. Thus, women who were nonverbally skilled would be most likely to have offspring who survived through this vulnerable age period. Over thousands of generations, a sex difference may have emerged based on this natural selection pressure on women.

Question: *Health experts have grown increasingly alarmed about AIDS among young adults because most of this population are not practicing safe sex by using condoms (Langer et al., 2001). How might young adults' implicit personality theories about safe-sex partners be shaping their decisions not to use condoms?*

Possible Answer: A survey conducted by Diane Kimble and her colleagues (1992) found that young adults tend to have a well-developed and generally accepted set of ideas regarding who are safe sexual partners. Who are these sexually "safe" individuals? People who one knows and likes are perceived not to be a risk. As one respondent summed up this view, "When you get to know the person … as soon as you begin trusting the person … you don't really have to use a condom" (p. 926). Risky people, on the other hand, are those one does not know well, who are older, and who are overanxious for sex. Kimble and her coworkers interpreted the young adults' tendencies not to practice safe sex with partners they knew and liked as being due to their reluctance to link the risk of disease with loving or caring relationships. Unfortunately, the criteria these people use to judge AIDS risk is totally unrelated to a person's HIV status. Individuals who operate from such a belief system run the very real risk of exposure to AIDS and possibly death.

Question: *Why might someone argue that correspondent inference theory would not have been developed in a collectivist culture? Put another way, what individualist assumption is at the core of this theory?*

Possible Answer: A correspondent inference is an inference that the action of an actor corresponds to, or is indicative of, a stable personal characteristic. In developing correspondent inference theory, Jones and Davis assumed that people have a preference for explaining people's behavior in terms of their personalities, and that external attributions are merely default options, made only when internal causes cannot be found. This assumption makes perfect sense in an individualist culture, in which people are socialized to think of themselves and others as personally controlling their own actions, and that their rights and desires are at least as important as those of the group. Yet in a collectivist culture, where people are socialized to think first about the rights and desires of the group, it's likely that much greater attention would be paid to external causes of behavior than in an individualist culture. Because of these differences in cultural orientation, it's likely that correspondent inference theory would not have been developed in a collectivist culture.

Question: *Based on your understanding of correspondent inference theory, why do you think the fundamental attribution error is also known as the correspondence bias?*

Possible Answer: A correspondent inference is an inference that the actor's action corresponds to, or is indicative of, a stable personal characteristic. According to correspondent inference theory, people are motivated to make correspondent inferences because doing so increases their confidence that they can predict other actors' behavior in the future. The fundamental attribution error is the tendency to overestimate the impact of dispositional causes and underestimate the impact of situational causes when explaining actors' behavior. In other words, it reflects an overzealous desire to make a correspondent inference. Thus it could be called a correspondence bias.

CHAPTER 5:
ATTITUDES AND PERSUASION

Question: *Is there any wisdom in parents admonishing their children to straighten their posture and to avoid slouching? How might the manner in which parents try to correct slouching destroy these possible benefits?*

Possible Answer: Yes there is, because studies suggest that upright postures cannot only cause you to feel happier, but they can also cause you to have a more favorable attitude toward things in general. Yet these are subtle effects and could be easily destroyed by parents forcing their children to engage in this behavior. In such instances, the feeling of children that their parents are trying to control their behavior may well be sufficient to create the exact opposite mood. Thus, to capitalize on these positive posture effects, parents should steer clear of orders and threats.

Question: *Can you think of instances in your own life in which you convinced yourself that a bad experience was really a good and worthwhile one?*

Possible Answer: This answer will be unique to your personal experiences.

Question: *How do implicit and explicit attitudes relate to the self-perception process?*

Possible Answer: Bem's self-perception theory proposes that we often do not know our attitudes but simply infer them from our behavior. However, implicit attitude research demonstrates how implicit attitudes can unknowingly shape behavior. One possibility is that self-perception theory actually explains how implicit attitudes sometimes become explicit attitudes. Of course, this explanation is a reinterpretation of Bem's original theory of self-perception. In step 1, an implicit attitude prompts a person to behave a certain way, and then in step 2, self-reflection prompts the person to form an explicit attitude that is consistent with the already-existing implicit attitude.

In my example of teaching the research methods course, prior to reflecting on my past actions and developing an explicit positive attitude toward teaching this course, my behavior in the course was guided by my implicit positive attitude. Thus, self-reflection did not create a new attitude where none existed before, but instead, reflecting on my past behavior helped me consciously recognize that I already had an unconscious positive attitude. If this explanation is correct, self-reflection can be thought of as facilitating the formation of explicit attitudes due to the behavioral effects of preexisting implicit attitudes. For additional reading on topics related to this one, check out Timothy Wilson's (2002) book *Strangers to Ourselves: Discovering the Adaptive Unconscious.*

Question: *Observe the content of TV commercials in the morning, evening, and during weekend sports shows. When are female and male characters with traditional or nontraditional gender roles most or least likely to appear in these commercials? How do these characters enhance the persuasive power of these advertisements?*

Possible Answer: Even with the more balanced portrayal of the two sexes in TV commercials today, they are still constructed in ways that reinforce the image of gender most familiar to and comfortable for their target audience at a particular time of the day. R. Stephen Craig (1992) found that daytime ads, which are typically aimed at the female homemaker, focus on images of the traditional American household, with the wife taking care of the domestic family needs and the husband holding a position of authority at home and at the office. In contrast, weekend commercials targeted at the male sports viewer frequently exclude women and children altogether. These ads—dominated by alcohol and automo-

tive products—stress traditional stereotypes of masculinity, such as the importance of being strong, daring, rugged, independent, and competitive. When women do appear in weekend commercials, they are generally portrayed in either subservient roles to men (for example, secretary or flight attendant) or as sexual objects. The traditional gender stereotyping in daytime and weekend commercials stands in sharp contrast to those shown during the evening and geared toward dual-career couples and single working women. Here, women are more likely to be portrayed in positions of authority and in settings away from home than they are in daytime ads. Men, in contrast, are more likely to be portrayed as a parent or spouse, and more in settings at home than they are on weekend TV. Thus, Craig's analysis suggests that how men and women are portrayed in North American TV ads today depends on who is watching. Evening commercials represent a more sophisticated and balanced portrayal of gender roles, but daytime and weekend ads reflect more traditional orientations.

Question: *Why is it that when radio lottery advertisers are trying to persuade you to spend your money, they speak at a normal rate of speed, yet when they convey the odds of winning, their speech rate dramatically increases? Are they simply trying to save money by cutting down on the length of the commercial, or is there an equally important reason for this shift to fast-paced speech?*

Possible Answer: Although research indicates that fast talkers are generally more persuasive than slow talkers due to listeners' impressions that they are more credible, this is not why fast talking is used when announcing the odds of winning. Instead, a message that is presented very quickly is difficult to process and critically analyze, and this is exactly what the advertisers are counting on. They don't want listeners to elaborate on the message that their chances of winning the lottery are about equal to the likelihood that they will be struck by lightning while sitting in their living rooms!

Question: *In addition to using humor, the anti-binge drinking SMU ad also provides information on how much alcohol the typical SMU student consumes. Why might this information be effective in reducing binge drinking at SMU? When would reporting such normative information possibly promote—rather than reduce—binge drinking?*

Possible Answer: Providing information to fellow students on how much alcohol the typical SMU student consumes may be effective in reducing binge drinking if the campus drinking average is fairly low. Social norms campaigns that inform students that most students don't drink excessively can effectively reduce binge drinking. However these same social norms campaigns may actually promote binge drinking on campuses where student drinking is very high. Thus, this persuasive approach should be used cautiously, because it can backfire.

CHAPTER 6: PREJUDICE AND DISCRIMINATION

Question: *Test your knowledge of racial and ethnic group stereotypes by writing down what you think are some of the positive and negative characteristics typically associated with the following social groups in North American culture: Anglo-Whites, Asians, Blacks, Jews, and Latinos. Once you have listed characteristics for each group, compare them with the research findings summarized in the Appendix. Does your knowledge of group stereotypes tell us anything about your degree of prejudice toward these racial and ethnic groups?*

Possible Answer: Common stereotypes of these groups are listed below. Sometimes, people will deny knowledge of negative stereotypes of other groups out of fear that admitting to such knowledge is a sign of their own personal prejudice toward these groups. However, by itself, knowledge of these stereotypes tells us nothing about a person's degree of prejudice toward these racial and ethnic groups. Indeed, due to its personal relevance, you may have more extensive knowledge about the negative stereotypes associated with your own group than any other groups.

Question: *One of the important functions of stereotyping is that it saves cognitive effort. Thus, when we are tired, we may be more likely to base our impressions of others on stereotypes. If this is true, during what times of the day are people likely to rely on stereotypes when judging others?*

Possible Answer: Have you ever heard of "morning" and "night" people? Morning people wake up early, with a good deal of energy and alertness, but are ready to retire before 10:00 p.m. Night people, on the other hand, stay up much later in the evening, and have a hard time getting up early in the morning (Thoman, 1999). About 25 percent of us are "night persons," 25 percent are "morning persons," and the remaining 50 percent fall somewhere between these two extremes. This different sleep pattern appears to be related to differences in circadian body temperatures. Not surprisingly, in one study, college students who were identified as morning persons obtained better grades in early-morning classes than in evening classes. The exact opposite effect was found for students classified as night persons (Guthrie et al., 1995).

Question: *Recently in the United States media commentators have increasingly used the terms "red" and "blue" to refer to perceived cultural differences in America and American politics. Why might the increased use of these terms increase prejudice and conflict between political groups in America?*

RACIAL AND ETHNIC STEREOTYPES

Anglo-Whites	Asians	Blacks	Jews	Latinos
ambitious	hardworking	lazy	ambitious	lazy
intelligent	intelligent	ignorant	intelligent	ignorant
conceited	quiet	loud	pushy	loud
prejudiced	law-abiding	athletic	dishonest	proud
selfish	stupid	greedy	emotional	
cruel	rhythmic	clannish	rude	
industrious	funny	aggressive		
nervous	criminal	inefficient		
sly	hostile	unreliable		
corrupt	corrupt	family-oriented		
rich	poor	poor		
greedy	friendly	messy		

Sources: Allen, 1996; Fiske, 1998; Krueger, 1996; Mackie et al., 1996; Wuthrow, 1982.

Possible Answer: The reason the increased use of the "red" and "blue" terms is likely to increase the conflict between political groups in America is that these categories create a cognitive "us" versus "them" dichotomy (Seyle & Newman, 2006). Research on minimal groups suggests that simply placing people into a social category different from your own is often sufficient to create an ingroup bias. The Robbers Cave Study suggests that when two groups perceive that they are competing for scarce resources, this provides fertile psychological ground for the development of prejudice and discrimination. The "red" versus "blue" designations place people into two distinct political factions and they also fuel the perception that one faction's success is the other faction's failure. This is very likely to trigger hostile feelings and increased ethnocentrism.

Question: *Try the following exercise. Listen to some of your favorite songs with lyrics involving romance. Do you tend to automatically imagine the person singing the song is expressing his or her love for a person of the other sex? How do these reactions relate to heterosexism? Now, actively imagine that the song is about same-sex love. How do you react to these lyrics and any visual images that come to mind?*

Possible Answer: Whether or not you automatically imagine the lyrics of romantic songs are about heterosexual love tells us little, if anything, about your level of heterosexism. Instead, regardless of your sexual orientation, such imagining simply illustrates how our culture is dominated by heterosexual assumptions about romantic relationships. Yet, it's likely that how you react to imagining homosexual romance in these same lyrics does provides some indication of your level of heterosexism. Given the fact that heterosexual romantic love is our cultural norm, if you regularly imagine that popular songs involve same-sex love, this probably takes more cognitive effort, or at least it may have in the past.

Question: *Can you think of a negative stereotype about Whites relative to Blacks that might cause White individuals to experience stereotype threat in a particular area of pursuit, thereby motivating them to disidentify with this activity?*

Possible Answer: A common negative stereotype about Whites is that they do not have the physical skills to compete against Blacks in most sports. This was the primary theme in the basketball movie *White Men Can't Jump.* When competing against Black basketball players, White players may become aware of this negative stereotype, experience stereotype threat, and underperform.

In an experimental demonstration of this effect, Jeff Stone and his colleagues (1999) described a golf task to White and Black college students as either diagnostic of "natural athletic ability" or "sports intelligence." White students performed worse than a control group when the task was thought to be associated with natural ability, while Black students performed worse than a control group when the task was framed as measuring intelligence. In a second experiment involving only White students, the researchers found that when the golf task was described as measuring natural athletic ability, those who performed worst were students who had previously stated that their self-esteem was significantly associated with success in athletic endeavors.

One likely consequence of regularly experiencing stereotype threat in athletic competition is that Whites may disidentify with sports achievement and choose to identify with other endeavors, such as academic achievement. In other words, they change their self-concept so that sports achievement is no longer very important to their self-esteem. Of course, this disidentification process does not have the negative impact on Whites' future career prospects as does Blacks' disidentification with academic achievement. Why? Because athletic performance, unlike academic performance, is seldom associated with career success in adulthood.

Question: *How would social identity theory explain the relationship between "pride" and "prejudice"?*

Possible Answer: There is a positive correlation between pride and prejudice. To indirectly increase or protect our own self-esteem, we try to bask in the reflected glory of our own group's esteem. To increase this group esteem, we may disparage and discriminate against other groups whose successes might reflect negatively on our own group's accomplishments. This intergroup process is psychologically identical to what we do in our interpersonal relationships when our friends are competing against other people for material and social rewards. In judging the competition, we tend to highlight our friends' good points and their competitors' bad points, while downplaying or forgetting our friends' bad points and their competitors' good points. In both cases, the result is that we actively construct a negative bias against other groups and individuals whose successes might indirectly threaten our own self-esteem.

Question: *The terrorist attacks in the United States in 2001 greatly increased Americans' perceived social threat. Based on authoritarianism research, what type of social consequences might we see in this country due to this heightened threat? Further, how might this same research explain the mind-set and behavior of the terrorists?*

Possible Answer: Authoritarianism research suggests that people with mild authoritarian tendencies may become more dogmatic and rigid in their social attitudes following such attacks. Thus, what we might expect from these people is a call for civil rights laws to be temporarily (or permanently) set aside to allow the government to identify and punish possible terrorists. President Bush implemented such a policy two months after the attacks when he announced that suspected foreign terrorists would be prosecuted in secret military tribunals rather than in civilian courts.

Authoritarian personalities will also generalize their outgroup prejudices toward groups within American culture that they perceive as "not real Americans." Due to their submission to established, legitimate authority figures, authoritarians are likely to severely criticize anyone who does not support the government's military or civil actions. When there is armed conflict with foreign countries, people with authoritarian tendencies are more likely to excuse atrocities committed by the United States.

Regarding the mind-set and actions of the terrorists, from news accounts it appears that they have a very rigid and dogmatic worldview. The popularity of this authoritarian mindset in the Middle East may be substantially driven by the severe economic and physical hardships that the Arab people have endured for so many years. The prevalence of this authoritarian thinking does not bode well for any kind of negotiated settlement.

CHAPTER 7: SOCIAL INFLUENCE

Question: *How might an individual's personality and behavior change as they gain or lose social power?*

Possible Answer: If social power increases people's tendencies to take action, then as people gain power they should exhibit a decreased sensitivity to threats (Croizet & Claire, 1998). Their increased power should cause them to develop a more decisive behavioral style, marked by increased confidence. Their personalities may become more extroverted and they may engage in a wider range of behaviors. They may now approach social situations looking more toward acquiring rewards rather than avoiding losses. What about those who lose power? If powerlessness activates a general tendency to inhibit action, then as people lose power they should show an increased sensitivity to threats. Their behavioral style should become indecisive, marked by decreased confidence. Likewise, their personalities may become more introverted; they may engage in a narrower range of behaviors; and they may approach situations looking to avoid losses rather than acquiring rewards.

Question: *Imagine that you are conducting an Asch-type conformity experiment, yet you also want to test whether you can increase nonconformity by inducing public self-presentation concerns in your participants. What variable could you introduce to the standard Asch research design to test the possibility that inducing public self-presentation concerns in your participants would increase nonconformity?*

Possible Answer: Because nonconformity may increase when others not involved in the influence attempt are present, you could have an experimental condition in which non-participants observe the line judgment tasks. If public self-presentation concerns significantly influence conformity, then this condition should result in greater nonconformity than in the standard Asch condition. This effect should occur when the line judgments are clear and easy, but probably won't occur when judgments are ambiguous and difficult. Instead, because the presence of an audience also induces public self-awareness—which leads to greater conformity to social standards—it's possible that ambiguous and difficult judgmental tasks will lead to greater conformity than in the standard Asch condition.

Question: *How might the foot-in-the-door compliance strategy be combined with the effects of post-decision dissonance to partly explain how some people initially become involved and then committed to religious or political cults?*

Possible Answer: In the foot-in-the-door strategy, a person who complies with a small request is more likely to later comply to a larger, less desirable request from the same person. Converts to cults are initially drawn to them by agreeing to read the cult's literature or agreeing to attend one meeting. The compliance with these small requests is used by cult members to secure even greater degrees of compliance later on. Of course, cult members also tend to act very warm and accepting toward possible recruits, thus making it more likely that they will want to seek greater ties to this group.

When the recruits do commit themselves to the cult, postdecision dissonance may exert its influence. Now, the attractive aspects of not joining and the unattractive aspects of joining are inconsistent with the decision to join the cult. Because this is viewed by new recruits as an important life decision, they will likely experience quite a bit of postdecision dissonance. According to cognitive dissonance theory, the new members will try to reduce the dissonance by focusing only on the positive aspects of the cult, while simultaneously focusing only on the negative aspects of their previous life. Other cult members, both new and old will eagerly reinforce this sort of thinking—often because they too need to justify their own decision to join—and the new members' allegiance to the cult is immensely strengthened.

CHAPTER 8: GROUP BEHAVIOR

Question: *In Chapter 6 you learned how ingroup biases can lead to prejudice and discrimination. How might this knowledge help you better understand the process by which the diffuse status characteristics of group members significantly determine their power in the group?*

Possible Answer: When observing an ingroup member and an outgroup member performing the same task, performance evaluations will tend to be biased in favor of the ingroup member. This ingroup bias may manifest itself by people selectively remembering ingroup members' good behavior and outgroup members' bad behavior, or by selectively forgetting or trivializing ingroup members' bad behavior and outgroup members' good behavior. In a group, the ingroup biasing that will usually have the biggest consequences for how much power and status members individually attain is the biasing exhibited by those members who hold "gatekeeping" roles. Gatekeepers are usually high-status members who give other members access to similar high-status positions. Gatekeepers will tend to single out those members in the group whom they perceive to be "one of them." Often this means they will prefer members who are similar to them on such diffuse status characteristics as race, sex, age, and wealth.

Question: *Imagine that you have been hired to design a training course to teach company employees how to efficiently use a complex computer program. How can you use the findings of social loafing research to design a training course that not only facilitates quick learning, but also encourages high productivity following learning?*

Possible Answer: Research indicates that people can learn complex tasks more quickly when they believe their individual efforts are not being evaluated, such as when they are performing as part of a larger group. This is the type of situation that also often leads to social loafing on well-learned tasks. In both situations, group performance allows task outcome responsibility to be diffused among fellow co-performers. To facilitate employees learning a complex computer program, you could design the training so that their individual efforts are not evaluated. This could be accomplished by training employees in a group setting. Group coperformance should reduce their evaluation apprehension—and presumably their arousal—and allow them to more carefully concentrate on the task at hand.

Once the employees have mastered the computer program, you could then either monitor their individual performance to reduce social loafing, or—if you didn't want to be so Orwellian—you could simply allow them to monitor their own performance by providing them with individual performance feedback. Both strategies have been found to be effective in reducing social loafing.

Question: *How could you use your knowledge of deindividuation when designing social environments to reduce crime?*

Possible Answer: If it is true that anonymity serves as an accountability cue causing people to believe that they will not be held accountable for their actions, then environments should be designed to reduce feelings of anonymity. Large mirrors, bright lighting, and even the presence of surveillance cameras (even if they are nonfunctional) will make it much less likely that people will feel anonymous. Large mirrors and surveillance cameras

will also induce public self-awareness, making it more likely that people will be attentive to social standards.

Question: *Based on social influence research, what type of individuals might be more susceptible to group polarization effects when working on judgmental tasks?*

Possible Answer: When the task is judgmental, people who are more concerned with how others will evaluate them will be more influenced by others' opinions. If they sense that the "socially acceptable" judgment is in a particular direction, they are likely to leapfrog over others to arrive at the most group-praiseworthy position. It's also possible that people with a high need for individuation—a desire to feel unique—may try to grab the most extreme position in the socially acceptable direction to "stand out from the crowd."

CHAPTER 9: INTERPERSONAL ATTRACTION

Question: *Immediately following the New York and Washington terrorist attacks on 9/11, people around the country were highly anxious and uncertain about what was happening. How do you think information dependence and outcome dependence shaped their thoughts, feelings, and behavior during this time?*

Possible Answer: Information dependence caused confused and anxious people to seek out one another so that they could gain an understanding of what was taking place. With this information, they could properly define and then respond to the unfolding events. Such information was most critical to individuals in the buildings attacked by the terrorists, because their lives depended on their correctly defining the situation as an emergency. Outcome dependence involves being dependent on others for rewards. While watching the horrendous events on television in the company of others, people may have monitored the expression of certain emotions (public displays of crying or prejudicial comments about Arab Americans) out of concern over how others might react. I know one person who watched news reports at work all day with coworkers despite not wanting to do so. Her explanation about why she did not walk away was that she was concerned that her colleagues would think of her as heartless if she left.

Question: *Consider again the findings from the Snyder et al. (1977) experiment and the Anderson and Bem (1981) study. When people thought that the individuals they were interacting with were physically attractive, they acted more outgoing and sociable toward them, which, in turn, resulted in those individuals acting more warm, confident, animated, and attractive. How do these findings relate to one of the basic messages of social psychology? Further, how can you generalize these findings beyond physical attractiveness effects to create a more pleasant and rewarding social world for yourself?*

Possible Answer: One of the basic messages of social psychology is that we actively create and re-create our social reality. The better you understand the psychological dynamics of this social constructive process, the better equipped you will be to shape your reality in the manner you desire. In a larger sense, the findings from these two studies point out that if you treat other people as if they are attractive and a joy to be around, they not only will appreciate and seek out your company, but—if they weren't before—they will now more likely become people who really are attractive and a joy to be around! This topic also relates to the "We like those who like us" discussion later in the chapter.

Question: *How has the similarity effect influenced your own personal relationships? Consider your best friends and your more casual friends. With whom do you share more similarities? Do these similarities fall into a particular category, such as shared values versus shared preferences?*

This answer will be unique to your personal experiences.

CHAPTER 10: INTIMATE RELATIONSHIPS

Question: *The self-sufficient cowboy who keeps to himself and doesn't engage in idle chitchat is one of the great icons of the American West. Hollywood actors John Wayne, Gary Cooper, and Clint Eastwood personified this extreme form of individualism in many of their film roles. Today, Hollywood uses this same rugged, individualist personality in creating the lead male role in action adventure films (Matt Damon, George Clooney, Will Smith). What attachment style would you say these film characters most often represent? Is this an attachment style we should be placing in our male cultural role models?*

Possible Answer: Securely attached adults easily become close to others, expect intimate relationships to endure, perceive others as generally trustworthy, and handle relationship conflict constructively. This type of an adult would be a very positive role model as a Hollywood movie figure. Unfortunately, this is definitely not how male cowboy/action film characters are typically portrayed. Thus, you already know that these characters are not the best role models for children and adults regarding intimate relationships. Yet it gets even worse. These male film characters represent the absolute worst attachment style for intimacy, namely, an avoidant one. Avoidant adults are uncomfortable with intimacy, have a hard time trusting others, and often express hostility during relationship conflicts. I guess that last difficulty would explain all the dead bodies that they leave in their wake. These cowboy/action characters sometimes tug at the audience's heartstrings by disclosing that "true love" is very hard to find and hold onto. Usually, there is a woman in their past who emotionally scarred them by either dying or rejecting them. Adults who watch these movies with children would be well advised to point out to the children afterward why Mr. Cowboy/Action Figure has such a hard time finding true love, and why imitation is not recommended.

Question: *Is there an inherent conflict between individualist values and the interdependence necessary to maintain romantic love?*

Possible Answer: Because individualists are raised to be autonomous and independent, perhaps they would have greater difficulty than collectivists maintaining an intimate relationship that is defined by partners depending on each other. The curious irony is that although individualists are more likely to marry due to romantic love, the way they've been socialized may make it less likely that their marriages will survive and their love will be nurtured. This is especially true for individualist males, who are most likely to be the ones socialized to be independent and relatively emotionally distant from others. However, because women are more likely socialized to be interdependent in their relations with other people, they may be best equipped to foster relationship success.

Question: *Earlier in the chapter you learned that passionate love is associated with perceiving one's partner through rose-colored glasses. This idealization, however, often gives way to a more realistic view with the development of companionate love. Yet, if companionate love is more enduring than passionate love, how can the present findings—that perceiving one's partner in somewhat ideal terms leads to greater romantic happiness than perceiving her/him realistically—be explained?*

Possible Answer: The giddy, roller-coaster emotional ride associated with passionate love doesn't usually endure in a romantic relationship but, rather, gives way to a more emotionally balanced form of romantic love, namely, companionate love. Passionate love can still exert its influence, but companionate love is the most influential. Yet, even with these romantic facts generally recognized, one manifestation of the importance of passion in an intimate relationship is revealed in the findings we are presently discussing. Put simply, those romantic relationships that have this "partner idealization" tendency appear to be the extra special romantic relationships, the ones that are perhaps closest to the enduring and happy relationships depicted in Hollywood movies (not necessarily including all the heavy breathing). They also would fall into the category that Sternberg calls "consummate love" and that Lee calls "agape" (altruistic love).

CHAPTER 11: AGGRESSION

Question: *Why might people who come from a collectivist cultural background be less likely to react negatively to teasing* *and not perceive it as a form of aggression compared to people who have a strong individualist background?*

Possible Answer: People with a strong individualist cultural background think and act in ways that maximize personal desire and positive self-regard, while people with a collectivist cultural background think and act in ways that maximize group goals and group cohesion. Due to these different motives, collectivists should be more likely than individualists to accept criticism from others and value self-critical emotions such as embarrassment. Consistent with this thinking, Belinda Campos and her colleagues (2007) found that Asian-American children were more likely than European-American children to attribute positive intentions to those who teased them.

Question: *How might alcohol impair judgment and, thus, lead to the aggressive outbursts found in domestic violence cases?*

Possible Answer: When people are intoxicated with alcohol, they are less likely to engage in self-awareness. Because self-awareness is necessary for self-regulation, and because self-regulation is part of the higher-level thinking necessary to control aggressive impulses, intoxication will make aggressive outbursts more likely.

Question: *In addition to excitation transfer, how else might violence erupt among rival sports fans?*

Possible Answer: One obvious factor is the negative affect sports fans experience following a bad turn of events for their team or an outright defeat. The aggressive tendencies sparked by this negative affect are less likely to be modified by higher-level thinking due to the fans' high arousal level. In addition, sporting events often take place outdoors in hot weather or indoors in hot, cramped facilities. Both arenas could heighten aggression due to the heat effect. Finally, avid sports fans strongly identify with their teams, and this social identity can lead to strong prejudices against the fans of rival teams, which can erupt into discriminatory violence.

Question: *"Road rage" has unfortunately become an all-too-familiar term we read and hear about to describe violent outbursts by people driving cars. How could you use social psychological knowledge to reduce the likelihood of road rage on city streets and highways?*

Possible Answer: You could employ Robert Baron's incompatible response strategy, in which you induce some emotional response in drivers that is likely to be incompatible with anger-induced aggression. Brooklyn, New York, employed this strategy by posting signs along the highway containing "knock-knock" jokes. You could also encourage radio stations with "happy" programming formats to advertise their dial numbers on billboards that drivers could see. Another way to use billboards would be to use the insights of social learning

theory to remind adults that they are role models for children and how they behave while driving will be observed and learned by younger passengers and drivers. This strategy might engage higher-order cognitive processes in angry drivers—as proposed by Berkowitz's cognitive-neoassociationist model—so that their anger doesn't precipitate aggression.

CHAPTER 12: PROSOCIAL BEHAVIOR: HELPING OTHERS

Question: *What sort of cultural role models might influence the "helping habits" of boys and girls? How might greater gender role flexibility influence male and female helping tendencies?*

Possible Answer: Social modeling studies suggest that children are most likely to imitate the behavior of people with whom they strongly identify, and for most children, this means same-sex adults. Thus, to foster good helping habits in children, existing cultural role models for boys and girls could be enlisted to convey this message to children in public service announcements.

In Hollywood movies, most leading-male actors play the traditional masculine role of helping people in dangerous situations, while being rather unwilling or ineffective in providing more mundane, long-term help, such as caring for children and the elderly. The underlying message in many of these movies is that this kind of assistance is unmanly and less important. Yet, in everyday living, this form of help is needed far more frequently than dangerous helping.

In contrast, most leading-female actors play characters with less gender-stereotyped roles. As such, they are often depicted as being willing to intervene in both dangerous situations and in those requiring nurturance and long-term care to needy others. This greater flexibility in helping responses reflects the greater gender flexibility available to women in contemporary culture. For instance, girls are generally allowed to engage in more nontraditional gender behavior than boys. As a result, you might expect that girls will learn to help in a wider variety of situations than boys.

Question: *Do you think you would find these same bystander effects among people whose jobs regularly deal with helping others? How might you test whether the situational context or the salience of their "helping" social roles would influence their tendency to intervene?*

Possible Answer: You probably would not find the same degree of bystander effects among nurses, doctors, and police officers because their experience and skill at handling emergencies would make it less likely that they would (1) worry about over-reacting in possible emergency situations and (2) assume that other bystanders have as much responsibility to help as them. It's likely that their tendency to diffuse responsibility would be further reduced if their "helping" social roles were currently salient to them because they would be even more aware of the social norms regarding helping for their occupations. It's also likely that doctors' and nurses' willingness to help will be greater in those situations in which their occupations best prepare them, namely, emergencies involving medical attention. However, because police officers are trained to intervene in both physically dangerous and medical emergencies, it's likely that there would be few differences in their willingness to respond. You might test these hypotheses in an experiment by having doctors, nurses, and police officers participate in a typical bystander intervention study, but (1) vary the degree to which their occupations are socially salient, and (2) vary the type of emergency (medical or physical endangerment) that they witness.

Question: *How could you design a donation pitch to members of a local community center to help starving people in a foreign country, knowing that some message receivers will react with empathy, while others will react with personal distress?*

Possible Answer: First, you want to convey an emotionally arousing message concerning how desperately these people need the audience's help. For those individuals who experience empathy, you can simply ask for their donations. However, for those who experience personal distress, you have to deal with the fact that they will try to escape the situation to reduce their distress. Thus, you need to make it difficult for them to escape the distress without donating money. You might set up your talk so that it precedes a dinner or event that everyone in attendance generally enjoys. Then, inform the audience that the enjoyable event will commence as soon as the donations reach a specified amount. This scenario is admittedly heavy-handed, but it should induce those who are experiencing personal distress to help in order to facilitate their own escape from this unpleasantly arousing situation.

GlOSSARY

A

Acquaintance Rape
Forced sexual intercourse that occurs either on a date or between people who are acquainted or romantically involved (also known as date rape).

Actor-Observer Effect
The tendency for people to attribute their own behavior to external causes but that of others to internal factors.

Aggression
Any form of behavior that is intended to harm or injure some person, oneself, or an object.

Aggressive Scripts
Guides for behavior and problem solving that are developed and stored in memory and are characterized by aggression.

Altruistic Helping
A form of helping in which the ultimate goal of the helper is to increase another's welfare without expecting anything in return.

Ambivalent Sexism
Sexism directed against women based on both positive and negative attitudes (hostility and benevolence), rather than uniform dislike.

Anchoring and Adjustment Heuristic
A tendency to be biased toward the starting value or anchor in making quantitative judgments.

Anticonformity
Opposition to social influence on all occasions, often caused by psychological reactance.

Applied Research
Research designed to increase the understanding of and solutions to real-world problems by using current social psychological knowledge.

Archival Research
A descriptive scientific method in which already-existing records are examined.

Arousal:Cost-Reward Model
A theory that helping or not helping is a function of emotional arousal and analysis of the costs and rewards of helping.

Attachment
The strong emotional bond between an infant and a caregiver.

Attitude
A positive or negative evaluation of an object.

Attitude Accessibility
The strength of the association between an object and an evaluation of it, typically measured by the speed with which people can access the evaluation from memory

Attribution
The process by which people use information to make inferences about the causes of behavior or events.

Audience Inhibition Effect
People are inhibited from helping for fear that other bystanders will evaluate them negatively if they intervene and the situation is not an emergency.

Authoritarian Personality
A personality trait characterized by submissiveness to authority, rigid adherence to conventional values, and prejudice toward outgroups.

Availability Heuristic
The tendency to judge the frequency or probability of an event in terms of how easy it is to think of examples of that event.

Aversive Racism
Attitudes toward members of a racial group that incorporate both egalitarian social values and negative emotions, causing one to avoid interaction with members of the group.

B

Balance Theory
A theory that people desire cognitive consistency or balance in their thoughts, feelings, and social relationships.

Basic Research
Research designed to increase knowledge about social behavior.

Belief
An estimate of the probability that something is true.

Body Esteem
A person's attitudes toward his or her body.

Bystander Intervention Model
A theory that whether bystanders intervene in an emergency is a function of a five-step decision-making process.

C

Catharsis
The reduction in the aggressive drive following an aggressive act.

Central Route to Persuasion
Persuasion that occurs when people think carefully about a communication and are influenced by the strength of its arguments.

Central Traits
Traits that exert a disproportionate influence on people's overall impressions, causing them to assume the presence of other traits.

Cerebral Cortex
The wrinkled-looking outer layer of the brain that coordinates and integrates all other brain areas into a fully functioning unit, that is the brain's "thinking" center, and that is much larger in humans than in other animals.

Characterization-Correction Model
A dual-process model that contends we initially automatically characterize people's behavior as being caused by dispositional factors and then later correct attribution to better account for situational factors.

Classical Conditioning
Learning through association, when a neutral stimulus (conditioned stimulus) is paired with a stimulus (unconditioned stimulus) that naturally produces an emotional response.

Cognitive Consistency
The tendency to seek consistency in one's cognitions.

Cognitive Dissonance
A feeling of discomfort caused by performing an action that is inconsistent with one's attitudes.

Cognitive-Neoassociationist Model
A theory of impulsive aggression that aversive events produce negative affect, which stimulates the inclination to aggress.

Collectivism

A philosophy of life stressing the priority of group needs over individual needs, a preference for tightly knit social relationships, and a willingness to submit to the influence of one's group.

Companionate Love

The affection we feel for those with whom our lives are deeply entwined.

Compliance

Publicly acting in accord with a direct request.

Confederate

A trained member of the research team who follows a script designed to create a specific impression on the research participant.

Confirmation Bias

The tendency to seek information that supports our beliefs while ignoring disconfirming information.

Conformity

A yielding to perceived group pressure by copying the behavior and beliefs of others.

Contact Hypothesis

The theory that under certain conditions, direct contact between antagonistic groups will reduce prejudice.

Contingency Model of Leadership

The theory that leadership effectiveness depends both on whether leaders are task oriented or relationship oriented and on the degree to which they have situational control.

Control Theory of Self-Regulation

A theory contending that, through self-awareness, people compare their behavior to a standard, and if there is a discrepancy, they work to reduce it.

Correlation Coefficient

A statistical measure of the direction and strength of the linear relationship between two variables, which can range from −1.00 to +1.00.

Correlational Research

Research designed to examine the nature of the relationship between two or more naturally occurring variables.

Correspondent Inference

An inference that the action of an actor corresponds to, or is indicative of, a stable personal characteristic.

Counterfactual Thinking

The tendency to evaluate events by imagining alternative versions or outcomes to what actually happened.

Courtesy Stigma

The tendency for individuals who are associated with stigmatized people to face negative evaluations from others.

Covariation Principle

A principle of attribution theory stating that for something to be the cause of a particular behavior, it must be present when the behavior occurs and absent when it does not occur.

Cultural Frame Switching

The process by which biculturalists switch between different culturally appropriate behaviors depending on the context.

Culture

The total lifestyle of a people, including all the ideas, symbols, preferences, and material objects that they share.

Culture of Honor

A belief system in which males are socialized to protect their reputation by resorting to violence.

D

Debriefing

A procedure at the conclusion of a research session in which participants are given full information about the nature and hypotheses of the study.

Deception

A methodological technique in which the researcher misinforms participants about the true nature of what they are experiencing in a study.

Deindividuation

The loss of a sense of individual identity and a loosening of normal inhibitions against engaging in behavior that is inconsistent with internal standards.

Delegitimization

The process of cognitively placing an outgroup into an extremely negative social category that excludes them from acceptable norms and values, thereby eliminating inhibitions against harming them.

Dependent Variable

The experimental variable that is measured because it is believed to depend on the manipulated changes in the independent variable.

Diffusion of Responsibility

The belief that the presence of other people in a situation makes one less personally responsible for the events that occur in that situation.

Discounting Principle

A principle of attribution theory stating that whenever there are several possible causal explanations for a particular event, people tend to be much less likely to attribute the effect to any particular cause.

Discrimination

A negative and/or patronizing action toward members of specific groups.

Dismissing-Avoidant Attachment Style

An expectation about social relationships characterized by low trust and avoidance of intimacy, combined with high self-esteem and compulsive self-reliance.

Door-in-the-Face Technique

A two-step compliance technique in which, after having a large request refused, the influencer counteroffers with a much smaller request.

Dual Attitudes

The simultaneous possession of contradictory implicit and explicit attitudes toward the same object.

Dual-Process Models of Attribution

Theories of attribution that propose that people initially engage in a relatively automatic and simple attributional assessment but then later consciously correct this attribution with more deliberate and effortful thinking

Dual-Process Theories

Theories of social cognition that describe two basic ways of thinking about social stimuli, one involving automatic, effortless thinking and the other involving more deliberate, effortful thinking.

E

Egoistic Helping

A form of helping in which the ultimate goal of the helper is to increase his or her own welfare.

Elaboration Likelihood Model

A theory that persuasive messages can cause attitude change in two ways, each differing in the amount of cognitive effort or elaboration it requires.

Embarrassment

An unpleasant emotion experienced when we believe that others have good reason to think a flaw has been revealed in us.

Empathy
A feeling of compassion and tenderness upon viewing a victim's plight.

Empathy-Altruism Hypothesis
A theory proposing that experiencing empathy for someone in need produces an altruistic motive for helping.

Equity Theory
The theory that people are most satisfied in a relationship when the ratio between rewards and costs is similar for both partners.

Ethnic Identity
An individual's sense of personal identification with a particular ethnic group.

Ethnocentrism
A pattern of increased hostility toward outgroups accompanied by increased loyalty to one's ingroup.

Evolution
The genetic changes that occur in a species over generations due to natural selecting.

Evolutionary Psychology
An approach to psychology based on the principle of natural selection.

Excitation Transfer
A psychological process in which arousal caused by one stimulus is transferred and added to arousal elicited by a second stimulus.

Expectation States Theory
A theory that states that the development of group status is based on members' expectations of others' probable contributions to the achievement of group goals. These expectations are shaped not only by members' task-relevant characteristics but also by diffuse-status characteristics, such as race, sex, age, and wealth.

Experimental Method
Research designed to test cause-effect relationships between variables.

Explicit Attitude
A consciously held attitude.

Explicit Cognition
Deliberate judgments or decisions of which we are consciously aware.

Explicit Prejudice
Prejudicial attitudes that are consciously held, even if they are not publicly expressed.

Explicit Self-Esteem
A person's conscious and deliberate evaluation of his or her self-concept.

External Attribution
An attribution that locates the cause of an event to factors external to the person, such as luck, or other people, or the situation.

External Validity
The extent to which a study's findings can be generalized to people beyond those in the study itself.

F

False Consensus Effect
The tendency to overestimate how common one's own attitudes, opinions, and beliefs are in the general population.

False Uniqueness Effect
The tendency to underestimate how common one's own desirable traits and abilities are in the general population.

Fearful-Avoidant Attachment Style
An expectation about social relationships characterized by low trust and avoidance of intimacy, combined with a feeling of being unworthy of others' love and a fear of rejection.

Foot-in-the-Door Technique
A two-step compliance technique in which the influencer secures compliance to a small request, and then later follows this with a larger, less desirable request.

Frontal Lobe
The region of the cerebral cortex situated just behind the forehead that is involved in the coordination of movement and higher mental processes, such as planning, social skills, and abstract thinking. This is the area of the brain that is the originator of self processes.

Frustration-Aggression Hypothesis
The theory that frustration causes aggression.

Fundamental Attribution Error
The tendency to overestimate the impact of dispositional causes and underestimate the impact of situational causes on other people's behavior.

G

Gender
The meanings that societies and individuals attach to being female and male.

Gender Identity
The identification of oneself as a male or a female.

Gender Schema
A cognitive structure for processing information based on its perceived male or female qualities.

Genes
The biochemical units of inheritance for all living organisms.

Group
Several interdependent people who have emotional ties and interact on a regular basis.

Group Polarization
Group-produced enhancement or exaggeration of members' initial attitudes through discussion.

Groupthink
A deterioration of mental efficiency, reality testing, and moral judgment in a group that results from an excessive desire to reach consensus.

H

Heterosexism
A system of cultural beliefs, values, and customs that exalts heterosexuality and denies, denigrates, and stigmatizes any nonheterosexual form of behavior or identity.

Heuristics
Timesaving mental shortcuts that reduce complex judgments to simple rules.

Hindsight Bias
The tendency, once an event has occurred, to overestimate our ability to have foreseen the outcome.

Hostile Aggression
The intentional use of harmful behavior in which the goal is simply to cause injury or death to the victim.

Hypothesis
An educated guess or prediction about the nature of things based upon a theory.

I

Ideology
A set of beliefs and values held by the members of a social group, which explains its culture both to itself and to other groups.

Illusory Correlation
The belief that two variables are associated with each other when in fact there is little or no actual association.

Implicit Association Test (IAT)

A technique for measuring implicit attitudes and beliefs based on the idea that people will give faster responses to presented concepts that are more strongly associated in memory.

Implicit Attitude

An attitude that is activated automatically from memory, often without the person's awareness that she or he possesses it.

Implicit Cognition

Judgments or decisions that are under the control of automatically activated evaluations occurring without our awareness.

Implicit Personality Theories

A type of schema people use to organize and make sense of which personality traits and behaviors go together.

Implicit Prejudice

Unconsciously held prejudicial attitudes.

Implicit Self-Esteem

A person's unintentional and perhaps unconscious evaluation of his or her self-concept.

Independence

Not being subject to control by others.

Independent Self

A way of conceiving the self in terms of unique, personal attributes and as a being that is separate and autonomous from the group.

Independent Variable

The experimental variable that the researcher manipulates.

Indirect Aggression

A form of aggressive manipulation involving attempts to harm another person without a face-to-face encounter (also known as relational aggression).

Individualism

A philosophy of life stressing the priority of individual needs over group needs, a preference for loosely knit social relationships, and a desire to be relatively autonomous of others' influence.

Informational Influence

Conformity based on the belief that others may have more accurate information.

Informed Consent

A procedure by which people freely choose to participate in a study only after they are told about the activities they will perform.

Ingroup

A group to which we belong and that forms a part of our social identity.

Ingroup Bias

The tendency to give more favorable evaluations and greater rewards to ingroup members than to outgroup members.

Institutional Review Boards (IRBs)

A panel of scientists and nonscientists who ensure the protection and welfare of research participants by formally reviewing researchers' methodologies and procedures prior to data collection.

Instrumental Aggression

The intentional use of harmful behavior so that one can achieve some other goal.

Interaction Effect

An experimental result that occurs when two independent variables in combination have different effects on the dependent variable than when alone.

Interactionism

An important perspective in social psychology that emphasizes the combined effects of both the person and the situation on human behavior.

Interdependent Self

A way of conceiving the self in terms of social roles and as a being that is embedded in and dependent on the group.

Intergroup Anxiety

Anxiety due to anticipating negative consequences when interacting with an outgroup member.

Internal Attribution

An attribution that locates the cause of an event to factors internal to the person, such as personality traits, moods, attitudes, abilities, or effort.

Internal Validity

The extent to which cause-and-effect conclusions can validly be made in a study.

Interpersonal Attraction

The desire to approach other people.

Intimacy

Sharing that which is inmost with others.

J

Jealousy

The negative emotional reaction experienced when a relationship that is important to a person's self-concept is threatened by a real or imagined rival.

Jigsaw Classroom

A cooperative group-learning technique designed to reduce prejudice and raise self-esteem.

Just-World Belief

A belief that the world is a fair and equitable place, with people getting what they deserve in life.

K

Kin Selection

A theory that people will exhibit preferences for helping blood relatives because this will increase the odds that their genes will be transmitted to subsequent generations.

L

Leader

The person who exerts the most influence and provides direction and energy to the group.

Learned Helplessness

The passive resignation produced by repeated exposure to negative events that are perceived to be unavoidable.

Loneliness

Having a smaller or less satisfactory network of social and intimate relationships than one desires.

Low-Ball Technique

A two-step compliance strategy in which the influencer secures agreement with a request by understating its true cost.

M

Matching Hypothesis

The proposition that people are attracted to others who are similar to them in particular characteristics.

Mere Exposure Effect

The tendency to develop more positive feelings toward objects and individuals the more we are exposed to them.

Meta-Analysis

The use of statistical techniques to summarize results from similar studies on a specific topic to estimate the reliability and overall size of the effect.

Minority Influence

The process by which dissenters produce change within a group.

Minority Slowness Effect

The tendency of those who hold a minority opinion to express that opinion less quickly than people who hold the majority opinion.

Misattribution of Arousal
A situation in which the explanation of the physiological symptoms of arousal is switched from the real source to another one.

Motivated-Tactician Model
An approach to social cognition that conceives of people as being flexible social thinkers who choose among multiple cognitive strategies based on their current goals, motives, and needs.

Multiple Self-aspects Framework
A theory that describes self-concept as a collection of multiple self-aspects that organize and guide a person's behavior when they are activated in specific situations.

N

Natural Selection
The process by which organisms with inherited traits best suited to the environment reproduce more successfully than less well-adapted organisms over a number of generations, and a process which leads to evolutionary changes.

Naturalistic Observation
A descriptive scientific method that investigates behavior in its natural environment.

Need for Cognition
An individual preference for and tendency to engage in effortful cognitive activities.

Negative State Relief Model
A theory suggesting that for those in a bad mood, helping others may be a way to lift their own spirits if the perceived benefits for helping are high and the costs are low.

Negativity Effect
The tendency for negative traits to be weighted more heavily than positive traits in impression formation.

Nonconscious Mimicry
The tendency to adopt the behaviors, postures, or mannerisms of interaction partners without conscious awareness or intention.

Nonverbal Communication
Communicating feelings and intentions without words.

Norm of Social Justice
A social norm stating that we should help only when we believe that others deserve our assistance.

Norm of Social Responsibility
A social norm stating that we should help when others are in need and dependent on us.

Normative Social Influence
Conformity, compliance, or obedience based on a desire to gain rewards or avoid punishments (outcome dependence).

O

Obedience
The performance of an action in response to a direct order.

Observational Research
A scientific method involving systematic qualitative and/or quantitative descriptions of behavior.

Observer Bias
Occurs when preconceived ideas held by the researcher affect the nature of the observations made.

Operant Conditioning
A type of learning in which behavior is strengthened if followed by reinforcement and weakened if followed by punishment.

Operational Definition
A very clear description of how a variable in a study has been measured.

Optimistic Explanatory Style
A habitual tendency to attribute negative events to external, unstable, and specific causes, and positive events to internal, stable, and global causes.

Outgroup
Any group with which we do not share membership.

Outgroup Homogeneity Effect
Perception of outgroup members as being more similar to one another than are members of one's ingroup.

P

Participant Observation
A descriptive scientific method where a group is studied from within by a researcher who records behavior as it occurs in its usual natural environment.

Passionate Love
A state of intense longing for union with another.

Peripheral Route to Persuasion
Persuasion that occurs when people do not think carefully about a communication and instead are influenced by cues that are irrelevant to the content or quality of the communication.

Person Perception
The process by which we try to detect other people's temporary states and enduring dispositions (also called social perception).

Personal Distress
An unpleasant state of arousal in which people are preoccupied with their own emotions of anxiety, fear, or helplessness upon viewing a victim's plight.

Personal-Group Discrimination Discrepancy
The tendency for members of disadvantaged groups to minimize personal discrimination in their own lives.

Persuasion
The process of consciously attempting to change attitudes through the transmission of some message.

Pessimistic Explanatory Style
A habitual tendency to attribute negative events to internal, stable, and global causes, and positive events to external, unstable, and specific causes.

Physical Attractiveness Stereotype
The belief that physically attractive individuals possess socially desirable personality traits and lead happier lives than less attractive persons.

Pluralistic Ignorance
The tendency to think that everyone else is interpreting a situation in a certain way, when in fact they are not.

Population
All the members of an identifiable group from which a sample is drawn.

Pornography
The combination of sexual material with abuse or degradation in a manner that appears to endorse, condone, or encourage such behavior.

Positive Psychology
An approach to psychology that studies ways to enrich human experience and maximize human functioning.

Positivity Bias
The tendency for people to evaluate individual human beings more positively than groups or impersonal objects.

Prejudice
Attitudes toward members of specific groups that directly or indirectly suggest they deserve an inferior social status.

Preoccupied Attachment Style
An expectation about social relationships characterized by trust but combined with

a feeling of being unworthy of others' love and a fear of abandonment.

Primacy Effect
The tendency for the first information received to carry more weight than later information on one's overall impression.

Priming
The process by which recent exposure to certain stimuli or events increases the accessibility of certain memories, categories, or schemas.

Prosocial Behavior
Voluntary behavior that is carried out to benefit another person.

Protection-Motivation Theory
A theory proposing that fear induces both a self-protective response and an appraisal of whether the fear-arousing threat can be avoided.

Prototype
The most representative member of a category.

R

Racism
Prejudice and discrimination based on a person's racial background.

Random Assignment
Placement of research participants into experimental conditions in a manner that guarantees that all have an equal chance of being exposed to each level of the independent variable.

Random Selection
A procedure for selecting a sample of people to study in which everyone in the population has an equal chance of being chosen.

Rape Myth
The false belief that, deep down, women enjoy forcible sex and find it sexually exciting.

Realistic Group Conflict Theory
The theory that intergroup conflict develops from competition for limited resources.

Recency Effect
The tendency for the last information received to carry greater weight than earlier information.

Reciprocal Helping
An evolutionary principle stating that people expect that anyone helping another will have that favor returned at some future time. Also known as reciprocal altruism.

Reciprocity Norm
The expectation that one should return a favor or a good deed.

Reference Group
A group to which people orient themselves, using its standards to judge themselves and the world.

Replication
Repeating a study's scientific procedures using different participants in an attempt to duplicate the findings.

Representativeness Heuristic
The tendency to judge the category membership of things based on how closely they match the "typical" or "average" member of that category.

S

Sample
A group of people who are selected to participate in a research study.

Schema
A schema is an organized structure of knowledge about a stimulus that is built up from experience and that contains causal relations; it is a theory about how the social world operates.

Scientific Method
A set of procedures used to gather, analyze, and interpret information in a way that reduces error and leads to dependable generalizations.

Script
A schema that describes how a series of events is likely to occur in a well-known situation, and which is used as a guide for behavior and problem solving.

Secure Attachment Style
An expectation about social relationships characterized by trust, a lack of concern with being abandoned, and a feeling of being valued and well liked.

Self
A symbol-using social being who can reflect on his or her own behavior.

Self-Affirmation Theory
A theory predicting that people will often cope with specific threats to their self-esteem by reminding themselves of other unrelated but cherished aspects of their self-concept.

Self-Awareness
A psychological state in which you take yourself as an object of attention.

Self-Concept
The sum total of a person's thoughts and feelings that defines the self as an object.

Self-Consciousness
The habitual tendency to engage in self-awareness.

Self-Disclosure
The revealing of personal information about oneself to other people.

Self-Discrepancies
Discrepancies between our self-concept and how we would ideally like to be (ideal self) or believe others think we should be (ought self).

Self-Enhancement
The process of seeking out and interpreting situations so as to attain a positive view of oneself.

Self-Esteem
A person's evaluation of his or her self-concept.

Self-Evaluation Maintenance Model
A theory predicting under what conditions people are likely to react to the success of others with either pride or jealousy.

Self-Fulfilling Prophecy
The process by which someone's expectations about a person or group leads to the fulfillment of those expectations.

Self-Handicapping
Actions that people take to sabotage their performance and enhance their opportunity to excuse anticipated failure.

Self-Monitoring
The tendency to use cues from other people's self-presentations in controlling one's own self-presentations.

Self-Perception Theory
The theory that we often infer our internal states, such as our attitudes, by observing our behavior.

Self-Regulation
The ways in which people control and direct their own actions.

Self-Serving Bias
The tendency to take credit for positive outcomes but deny responsibility for negative outcomes in our lives.

Self-Verification
The process of seeking out and interpreting situations so as to confirm one's self-concept.

Sex
The biological status of being female or male

Sexism
Any attitude, action, or institutional structure that subordinates a person because of her or his sex.

Sexual Prejudice
Negative attitudes based on sexual orientation, whether the target is homosexual, bisexual, or heterosexual.

Sleeper Effect
The delayed effectiveness of a persuasive message from a noncredible source.

Social Anxiety
The unpleasant emotion people experience due to their concern with interpersonal evaluation and the loss of social status.

Social Categorization
The process of forming categories of people based on their common attributes.

Social Cognition
The way in which we interpret, analyze, remember, and use information about the social world.

Social Comparison Theory
The theory that proposes that we evaluate our thoughts and actions by comparing them to those of others.

Social Desirability Bias
A type of response bias in surveys in which people respond to a question by trying to portray themselves in a favorable light rather than responding in an accurate and truthful manner.

Social Dilemma
Any situation in which the most rewarding short-term choice for an individual will ultimately cause negative consequences for the group as a whole.

Social Dominance Theory
A theory contending that societal groups can be organized in a power hierarchy in which the dominant groups enjoy a disproportionate share of the society's assets and the subordinate groups receive most of its liabilities.

Social Exchange Theory
The theory that proposes that we seek out and maintain those relationships in which the rewards exceed the costs.

Social Facilitation
The enhancement of dominant responses due to the presence of others.

Social Identities
Aspects of a person's self-concept based on his or her group memberships.

Social Identity Theory
A theory suggesting that people seek to enhance their self-esteem by identifying with specific social groups and perceiving these groups as being better than other groups.

Social Impact Theory
The theory that the amount of social influence others have depends on their number, strength, and immediacy to those they are trying to influence.

Social Influence
The exercise of social power by a person or group to change the attitudes or behavior of others in a particular direction.

Social Learning Theory
A theory that social behavior is primarily learned by observing and imitating the actions of others, and secondarily by being directly rewarded and punished for our own actions.

Social Loafing
Group-induced reduction in individual output when performers' efforts are pooled and, thus, cannot be individually judged.

Social Neuroscience
The study of the relationship between neural processes of the brain and social processes.

Social Norm
An expected standard of behavior and belief established and enforced by a group.

Social Penetration Theory
A theory that describes the development of close relationships in terms of increasing self-disclosure.

Social Power
The force available to the influencer to motivate attitude or behavior change.

Social Psychology
The scientific discipline that attempts to understand and explain how the thought, feeling, and behavior of individuals are influenced by the actual, imagined, or implied presence of others.

Social Role
A cluster of socially defined expectations that individuals in a given situation are expected to fulfill.

Social Role Theory
The theory that virtually all of the documented behavioral differences between males and females can be accounted for in terms of cultural stereotypes about gender and the resulting social roles that are taught to the young.

Social Skills Training
A behavioral training program designed to improve interpersonal skills through observation, modeling, role playing, and behavioral rehearsal.

Stereotype
Beliefs about the personalities, abilities, and motives of a social group that doesn't allow for individual variation.

Stereotype Threat
The apprehension people feel when performing a task in which their group is stereotyped to lack ability.

Stigma
An attribute that serves to discredit a person in the eyes of others.

Strategic Self-Presentation
Conscious and deliberate efforts to shape other people's impressions in order to gain power, influence, sympathy, or approval.

Subliminal Conditioning
Classical conditioning that occurs in the absence of conscious awareness of the stimuli involved.

Subliminal Perception
The processing of information that is below one's threshold of conscious awareness.

Superordinate Goal
A mutually shared goal that can be achieved only through intergroup cooperation.

Surveys
Structured sets of questions or statements given to a group of people to measure their attitudes, beliefs, values, or behavioral tendencies.

Symbolic Interactionism
A contemporary sociological theory, inspired by Mead's insights and based on the premise that the self and social reality emerge due to the meaningful communication among people.

System Justification Theory
A theory proposing that members of disadvantaged groups often adopt beliefs endorsing the legitimacy and fairness of the unequal group status hierarchy in society.

T

Temporal Model of Group Membership
A theory of group membership describing the changes that occur over time in members and in the group due to their mutual influence and interdependence.

That's-Not-All Technique
A two-step compliance technique in which the influencer makes a large request, then immediately offers a discount or bonus before the initial request is refused.

Theory
An organized system of ideas that seeks to explain how two or more events are related.

Theory of Planned Behavior
The theory that people's conscious decisions to engage in specific actions are determined by their attitudes toward the behavior in question, the relevant subjective norms, and their perceived behavioral control.

Theory of Psychological Reactance
The theory that people believe they possess specific behavioral freedoms, and that they will react against and resist attempts to limit this sense of freedom.

Thought Suppression
The attempt to prevent certain thoughts from entering consciousness.

Threat-to-Self-Esteem Model
A theory stating that if receiving help contains negative self-messages, recipients are likely to feel threatened and respond negatively.

Transformational Leader
Leader who change (transform) the outlook and behavior of followers so that they move beyond their self-interests for the good of the group or society.

Two-Factor Theory of Emotions
A theory that emotional experience is based on two factors: physiological arousal and cognitive labeling of the cause of that arousal.

V

Values
Enduring beliefs about important life goals that transcend specific situations.

Variables
Factors in scientific research that can be measured and that are capable of changing (or varying).

References ••••••

Aarts, H., & Dijksterhuis, A. (2000). Habits as knowledge structures: Automaticity in goal-directed behavior. *Journal of Personality and Social Psychology, 78,* 53–63.

Aarts, H., & Dijksterhuis, A. (2003). The silence of the library: Environment, situational norm, and social behavior. *Journal of Personality and Social Psychology, 84,* 18–28.

Abelson, R. P. (1972). Are attitudes necessary? In B. T. King & E. McGinnies (Eds.), *Attitudes, conflicts, and social change.* New York: Academic Press.

Abelson, R. P. (1982). Three modes of attitude-behavior consistency. In M. P. Zanna, E. T. Higgins, & C. P. Herman (Eds.), *Consistency in social behavior: The Ontario symposium* (Vol. 2, pp. 131–147). Hillsdale, NJ: Erlbaum.

Aboud, F. E., & Levy, S. R. (2000). Interventions to reduce prejudice and discrimination in children and adolescents. In S. Oskamp (Ed.), *Reducing prejudice and discrimination* (pp. 269–293). Mahwah, NJ: Erlbaum.

Abrams, D., Ando, K., & Hinkle, S. (1998). Psychological attachment to the group: Cross-cultural differences in organizational identification and subjective norms as predictors of workers' turnover intentions. *Personality and Social Psychology Bulletin, 24,* 1027–1039.

Abrams, D., & Hogg, M. A. (2004). Metatheory: Lessons from social identity research. *Personality and Social Psychology Review, 8,* 98–106.

Abrams, D., Viki, G. T., Masser, B., & Böhner, G. (2003). Perceptions of benevolent and hostile sexism in victim blame and rape proclivity. *Journal of Personality and Social Psychology, 84,* 111–125.

Abramson, L. Y., Bardone-Cone, A. M., Vohs, K. D., Joiner, T. E. Jr., & Heatherton, T. F. (2006). Cognitive vulnerability to bulimia. In L. B. Alloy & J. H. Riskind (Eds.), *Cognitive vulnerability to emotional disorders* (pp. 329–364). Mahwah, NJ: Erlbaum.

Abramson, L. Y., Seligman, M. E. P., & Teasdale, J. (1978). Learned helplessness in humans: Critique and reformulation. *Journal of Abnormal Psychology, 87,* 358–372.

Acevedo, B. P., & Aron, A. (2009). Does a long-term relationship kill romantic love? *Review of General Psychology, 13,* 59–65.

Ackerman, J. M., Kenrick, D. T., & Schaller, M. (2007). Is friendship akin to kinship? *Evolution and Human Behavior, 28,* 365–374.

Adamopoulos, J. (1999). The emergence of cultural patterns of interpersonal behavior. In J. Adamopoulos & Y. Kashima (Eds.), *Social psychology and cultural context* (pp. 63–76). Thousand Oaks, CA: Sage.

Adams, G., & Anderson, S. L. (2004). The cultural grounding of closeness and intimacy. In D. Mashek & A. Aron (Eds.), *Handbook of closeness and intimacy* (pp. 321–339). Mahwah, NJ: Erlbaum.

Adams, G., Biernat, M., Branscombe, N. R., Crandall, C. S., & Wrightsman, L. S. (2008). Beyond prejudice: Toward a sociocultural psychology of racism and oppression. In G. Adams, M. Biernat, N. R. Branscombe, C. S. Crandall, & L. S. Wrightsman (Eds.), *Commemorating Brown: The special psychology of racism and discrimination* (pp. 215–246). Washington, DC: American Psychological Association.

Adams, G., Tormala, T. T., & O'Brien, L. T. (2006). The effect of self-affirmation on perception of racism. *Journal of Experimental Social Psychology, 42,* 616–626.

Adams, J. M., & Jones, W. H. (1997). The conceptualization of marital commitment: An integrative analysis. *Journal of Personality and Social Psychology, 73,* 1177–1196.

Adams, J. S. (1965). Inequity in social exchange. In L. Berkowitz (Ed.), *Advances in experimental social psychology* (Vol. 2, pp. 267–299). New York: Academic Press.

Adams-Curtis, L. E., & Forbes, G. B. (2004). College women's experiences of sexual coercion: A review of cultural, perpetrator, victim, and situational variables. *Trauma, Violence, and Abuse, 5,* 91–122.

Adelson, R. (2004). Hormones, stress and aggression: A vicious cycle. *Monitor on Psychology, 35,* 18–19.

Adorno, T. W., Frenkel-Brunswik, E., Levinson, D., & Sanford, R. (1950). *The authoritarian personality.* New York: Harper.

Afifi, W. A., & Faulkner, S. L. (2000). On being "just friends": The frequency and impact of sexual activity in cross-sex friendships. *Journal of Social and Personal Relationships, 17,* 205–222.

Ahlering, R. F. (1987). Need for cognition, attitudes, and the 1984 presidential election. *Journal of Research in Personality, 21,* 100–102.

Aiello, J. R., & Douthitt, E. A. (2001). Social facilitation from Triplett to electronic performance monitoring. *Group Dynamics, 5,* 163–180.

Ailes, R. (1988). *You are the message.* New York: Doubleday.

Ainsworth, M. D. S. (1989). Attachments beyond infancy. *American Psychologist, 44,* 709–716.

Ajzen, I. (1985). From intentions to actions: A theory of planned behavior. In J. Kuhl & J. Beckmann (Eds.), *Action control: From cognition to behavior* (pp. 11–39). New York: Springer-Verlag.

Ajzen, I. (1988). *Attitudes, personality, and behavior.* Chicago: Dorsey.

Ajzen, I. (1991). The theory of planned behavior. *Organizational Behavior and Human Decision Processes, 50,* 179–204.

Ajzen, I. (1996). The social psychology of decision making. In E. T. Higgins & R. M. Sorrentino (Eds.), *Handbook of motivation and cognition: Foundations of social behavior* (Vol. 2, pp. 297–325). New York: Guilford.

Ajzen, I. (2001). Nature and operation of attitudes. *Annual Review of Psychology, 52,* 27–58.

Ajzen, I., Brown, T. C., & Carvajal, F. (2004). Explaining the discrepancy between intentions and actions: The case of hypothetical bias in contingent valuation. *Personality and Social Psychology Bulletin, 30,* 1108–1121.

Ajzen, I., & Holmes, W. H. (1976). Uniqueness of behavioral effects in causal attribution. *Journal of Personality, 44,* 98–108.

Albarracín, D., & Vargas, P. (2010). Attitudes and persuasion: From biology to social responses to persuasive intent. In S. T. Fiske, D. T. Gilbert, & G. Lindzey (Eds.). *Handbook of social psychology, Vol 1* (5th ed.) (pp. 394–427). Hoboken, NJ: John Wiley.

Alexander, M. G., Brewer, M. B., & Livingston, R. W. (2005). Putting stereotype content in context: Image theory and interethnic stereotypes. *Personality and Social Psychology Bulletin, 31,* 781–794.

Alicke, M. D., LoSchiavo, F. M., Zerbst, J., & Zhang, S. (1997). The person who outperforms me is a genius: Maintaining perceived competence in upward social comparison. *Journal of Personality and Social Psychology, 73,* 781–789.

Alicke, M. D., Yurak, T. J., & Vredenburg, D. S. (1996). Using personal attitudes to judge others: The roles of outcomes and consensus. *Journal of Research in Personality, 30,* 103–119.

Alksnis, C., Desmarais, S., & Wood, E. (1996). Gender differences in scripts for types of dates. *Sex Roles, 34,* 321–336.

Allen, V. L., & Levine, J. M. (1969). Consensus and conformity. *Journal of Experimental Social Psychology, 5,* 389–399.

Allen, V. L., & Levine, J. M. (1971). Social support and conformity: The role of independent assessment of reality. *Journal of Experimental Social Psychology, 7,* 48–58.

Alley, T. R., & Cunningham, M. R. (1991). Averaged faces are attractive, but very attractive faces are not average. *Psychological Science, 2,* 123–125.

Allison, J. A., & Wrightsman, L. S. (1993). *Rape: The misunderstood crime.* Newbury Park, CA: Sage.

Allison, S. T., & Messick, D. M. (1985). Effects of experience on performance in a replenishable resource trap. *Journal of Personality and Social Psychology, 49,* 943–948.

Allman, J. M., & Hasenstaub, A. (1999). Brains, maturation times, and parenting. *Neurobiology of Aging, 20,* 447–454.

Allport, F. H. (1920). The influence of the group upon association and thought. *Journal of Experimental Psychology, 3,* 159–182.

Allport, F. H. (1924). *Social psychology.* Boston: Houghton Mifflin.

Allport, G. W. (1935). Attitudes. In C. Murchison (Ed.), *A Handbook of Social Psychology* (pp. 798–844). Worcester, MA: Clark University Press.

Allport, G. W. (1943). The ego in contemporary psychology. *Psychological Review, 50,* 451–478.

Allport, G. W. (1954). *The nature of prejudice.* Cambridge, MA: Addison-Wesley.

Allport, G. W. (1985). The historical background of social psychology. In G. Lindzey & E. Aronson (Eds.), *The Handbook of Social Psychology* (Vol. I, 3rd ed., pp. 1–46). New York: Random House.

Alluisi, E. A., & Warm, J. S. (1990). Things that go together: A review of stimulus-response compatibility and related effects. In R. W. Proctor & T. G. Reeve (Eds.), *Stimulus-response compatibility: An integrated perspective* (pp. 3–30). Amsterdam: North Holland.

Almeida, M., Lee, R., & Coccaro, E. F. (2011). Cortisol responses to ipsapirone challenge correlate with aggression, while basal cortisol levels correlate with impulsivity, in personality disorder and healthy volunteer subjects. *Journal of Psychiatric Research, 44,* 874–880.

Altemeyer, B. (1981). *Right-wing authoritarianism.* Winnipeg: University of Manitoba Press.

Altemeyer, B. (1988). *Enemies of freedom: Understanding right-wing authoritarianism.* San Francisco: Jossey-Bass.

Altemeyer, B. (2004). Highly dominating, highly authoritarian personalities. *Journal of Social Psychology, 144,* 421–447.

Altheide, D. L. (2000). Identity and the definition of the situation in a mass-mediated context. *Symbolic Interaction, 23,* 1–27.

Altman, I. (1973). Reciprocity of interpersonal exchange. *Journal of Theory of Social Behavior, 3,* 249–261.

Altman, I., & Taylor, D. A. (1973). *Social penetration theory: The development of interpersonal relationships.* New York: Holt, Rinehart.

Álvarez, R. (2001). The social problem as an enterprise: Values as a defining factor.

Social Problems, 48, 3–10.

Alvaro, E. M., & Crano, W. D. (1997). Indirect minority influence: Evidence for leniency in source evaluation and counterargumentation. *Journal of Personality and Social Psychology, 72,* 949–964.

Alwin, D. F., Cohen, R. L., & Newcomb, T. M. (1991). *Political attitudes over the life span: The Bennington women after fifty years.* Madison: University of Wisconsin Press.

Ambady, N., & Adams, R. B., Jr. (2011). Us versus them: The social neuroscience of perceiving out-groups. In A. Todorov, S. T. Fiske, & D. A. Prentice (Eds.). *Social neuroscience: Toward understanding the underpinnings of the social mind* (pp. 135–143). New York: Oxford University Press.

Ambady, N., Shih, M., Kim, A., & Pittinsky, T. L. (2001). Stereotype susceptibility in children: Effects of identity activation on quantitative performance. *Psychological Science, 12,* 385–390.

Ambady, N., & Weisbuch, M. (2010). Nonverbal behavior. In S. T. Fiske, D. T. Gilbert, & G. Lindzey (Eds.). *Handbook of Social Psychology, Vol. 1* (5th ed.) (pp. 464–497). Hoboken, NJ: John Wiley.

American Psychological Association. (1982). *Ethical principles in the conduct of research with human participants.* Washington, DC: Author.

Ames, D. R. (2004). Inside the mind reader's tool kit: Projection and stereotyping in mental state inference. *Journal of Personality and Social Psychology, 87,* 340–353.

Ames, D. R., Flynn, F. J., & Weber, E. U. (2004). It's the thought that counts: On perceiving how helpers decide to lend a hand. *Personality and Social Psychology Bulletin, 30,* 461–474.

Amiot, C. E., & Sansfacon, S. (2011). Motivations to identify with social groups: A look at their positive and negative consequences. *Group Dynamics: Theory, Research, and Practice, 15,* 105–127.

Amir, Y. (1969). Contact hypothesis in ethnic relations. *Psychological Bulletin, 71,* 319–342.

Amodio, D. M. (2011). Self-regulation in intergroup relations: A social neuroscience framework. In A. Todorov, S. T. Fiske, & D. A. Prentice (Eds.). *Social neuroscience: Toward understanding the underpinnings of the social mind* (pp. 101–122). New York: Oxford University Press.

Amodio, D. M., Harmon-Jones, E., Devine, P. G., Curtin, J. J., Hartley, S. L., & Covert, A. E. (2004a). Neural signals for the detection of unintentional race bias. *Psychological Science, 15,* 88–93.

Amodio, D. M., & Lieberman, M. D. (2009). Pictures in our heads: Contributions of fMRI to the study of prejudice and stereotyping. In T. D. Nelson (Ed.). *Handbook of prejudice, stereotyping, and discrimination* (pp. 347–365). New York: Psychology Press.

Amodio, D. M., Shah, J. Y., Sigelman, J., Brazy, P. C., & Harmon-Jones, E. (2004b). Implicit regulatory focus associated with asymmetrical frontal cortical activity. *Journal of Experimental Social Psychology, 40,* 225–232.

Amsterdam, B. (1972). Mirror self-image reactions before age two. *Developmental Psychobiology, 5,* 297–305.

Andersen, S. M., & Glassman, N. S. (1996). Responding to significant others when they are not there: Effects on interpersonal inference, motivation, and affect. In R. M. Sorrentino & E. T. Higgins (Eds.), *Handbook of motivation and cognition* (pp. 262–321). New York: Guilford.

Anderson, C., & Berdahl, J. L. (2002). The experience of power: Examining the effects of power on approach and inhibition tendencies. *Journal of Personality and Social Psychology, 83,* 1362–1377.

Anderson, C., & Cromwell, R. L. (1977). "Black is beautiful" and the color preferences of Afro-American youth. *Journal of Negro Education, 46,* 76–88.

Anderson, C., John, O. P., Keltner, D., & Kring, A. M. (2001). Who attains social status? Effects of

personality and physical attractiveness in social groups. *Journal of Personality and Social Psychology, 81,* 116–132.

Anderson, C. A. (1997). Effects of violent movies and trait hostility on hostile feelings and aggressive thoughts. *Aggressive Behavior, 23,* 161–178.

Anderson, C. A. (2001). Heat and violence. *Current Directions in Psychological Science, 10,* 33–38.

Anderson, C. A. (2004). An update on the effects of playing violent video games. *Journal of Adolescence, 27,* 113–122.

Anderson, C. A., & Anderson, D. C. (1984). Ambient temperature and violent crime: Tests of the linear and curvilinear hypotheses. *Journal of Personality and Social Psychology, 46,* 91–97.

Anderson, C. A., & Anderson, K. B. (1996). Violent crime rate studies in philosophical context: A destructive testing approach to heat and Southern culture of violence effects. *Journal of Personality and Social Psychology, 70,* 740–756.

Anderson, C. A., Benjamin, A., & Bartholow, B. D. (1998). Does the gun pull the trigger? Automatic priming effects of weapon pictures and weapon names. *Psychological Science, 9,* 308–314.

Anderson, C. A., Berkowitz, L., Donnerstein, E., Huesmann, L. R., Johnson, J. D., Linz, D., Malamuth, N. M., & Wartella, E. (2003a). The influence of media violence on youth. *Psychological Science in the Public Interest, 4,* 81–110.

Anderson, C. A., & Bushman, B. J. (1997). External validity of "trivial" experiments: The case of laboratory aggression. *Review of General Psychology, 1,* 19–41.

Anderson, C. A., & Bushman, B. J. (2001). Effects of violent video games on aggressive behavior, aggressive cognition, aggressive affect, physiological arousal, and prosocial behavior: A meta-analytic review of the scientific literature. *Psychological Science, 12,* 353–359.

Anderson, C. A., & Bushman, B. J. (2002). Media violence and the American public revisited. *American Psychologist, 57,* 448–450.

Anderson, C. A., Bushman, B. J., & Groom, R. W. (1997). Hot years and serious and deadly assault: Empirical tests of the heat hypothesis. *Journal of Personality and Social Psychology, 73,* 1213–1223.

Anderson, C. A., Carnagey, N. L., & Eubanks, J. (2003b). Exposure to violent media: The effects of songs with violent lyrics on aggressive thoughts and feelings. *Journal of Personality and Social Psychology, 84,* 960–971.

Anderson, C. A., & Dill, K. E. (2000). Video games and aggressive thoughts, feelings, and behavior in the laboratory and in life. *Journal of Personality and Social Psychology, 78,* 772–790.

Anderson, C. A., Deuser, W. E., & DeNeve, K. M. (1995). Hot temperatures, hostile affect, hostile cognition, and arousal: Tests of a general model of affective aggression. *Personality and Social Psychology Bulletin, 21,* 434–448.

Anderson, C. A., Gentile, D. A., & Buckley, K. E. (2007). *Violent video game effects on children and adolescents: Theory, research, and public policy.* New York: Oxford University Press.

Anderson, C. A., Miller, R. S., Riger, A. L., Dill, J. C., & Sedikides, C. (1994). Behavioral and characterological attributional styles as predictors of depression and loneliness: Review, refinement, and test. *Journal of Personality and Social Psychology, 66,* 549–558.

Anderson, D. E., DePaulo, B. M., & Anfield, M. E. (2002). The development of deception detection skill: A longitudinal study of same-sex friends. *Personality and Social Psychology Bulletin, 28,* 536–545.

Anderson, D. E., DePaulo, B. M., Anfield, M. E., Tickle, J. J., & Green, E. (1999). Beliefs about cues to deception: Mindless stereotypes or untapped wisdom? *Journal of Nonverbal Behavior, 23,* 67–88.

Anderson, E., Siegel, E. H., Bliss-Moreau, E., & Barrett, L. F. (2011). The visual impact of gossip, *Science, 332.*

Anderson, J. L., Crawford, C. B., Nadeau, J., & Lindberg, T. (1992). Was the Duchess of Windsor right? A cross-cultural review of the socioecology of ideals of female body shape. *Ethology and Sociobiology, 13,* 197–227.

Anderson, N. H. (1968). A simple model for information integration. In R. B. Abelson, E. Aronson, W. J. McGuire, T. M. Newcomb, M. J. Rosenberg, & P. H. Tannenbaum (Eds.), *Theories of cognitive consistency: A sourcebook* (pp. 731–743). Chicago: Rand McNally.

Anderson, N. H. (1981). *Foundations of information integration theory.* New York: Academic Press.

Anderson, S. M., & Bem, S. L. (1981). Sex typing and androgyny in dyadic interaction: Individual differences in responsiveness to physical attractiveness. *Journal of Personality and Social Psychology, 41,* 74–86.

Andersson, J., & Rönnberg, J. (1997). Cued memory collaboration: Effects of friendship and type of retrieval cue. *European Journal of Cognitive Psychology, 9,* 273–287.

Andreoletti, C., Zebrowitz, L. A., & Lachman, M. E. (2001). Physical appearance and control beliefs in young, middle-aged, and older adults. *Personality and Social Psychology Bulletin, 27,* 969–981.

Anseel, F., & Duyck, W. (2008). Unconscious Applicants: A Systematic Test of the Name-Letter Effect. *Psychological Science, 19*(10), 1059–1061. Anthony, D. B., Wood, J. V., & Holmes, J. G. (2006). Testing sociometer theory: Self-esteem and the importance of acceptance for social decision-making. *Journal of Experimental Social Psychology, 43,* 425–432.

Aquino, K., Freeman, D., Reed, A. I., Lim, V. K. G., & Felps, W. (2009). Testing a social-cognitive model of moral behavior.: The interactive influence of situations and moral identity centrality. *Journal of Personality and Social Psychology, 97.* 123–141.

Aquino, K., & Reed, A. (2002). The self-importance of moral identity. *Journal of Personality and Social Psychology, 83,* 1423–1440.

Aquino, K., McFerran, B., & Laven, M. (2011). Moral identity and the experience of moral elevation in response to acts of uncommon goodness. *Journal of Personality and Social Psychology, 100.* 703–718.

Arce, C. H., Murguia, E., & Frisbie, W. P. (1987). Phenotype and life chances among Chicanos. *Hispanic Journal of Behavioral Sciences, 9,* 19–32.

Archer, D., & Gartner, R. (1984). *Violence and crime in cross-national perspective.* New Haven, CT: Yale University Press.

Archer, J. (1991). Human sociobiology: Basic concepts and limitations. *Journal of Social Issues, 47,* 11–26.

Archer, J. (2004). Sex differences in aggression in real-world settings: A meta-analytic review. *Review of General Psychology, 8,* 291–322.

Archer, J., & Côté, S. (2005). Sex differences in aggressive behavior: A developmental and evolutionary perspective. In R. E. Tremblay, W. W. Hartup, & J. Archer (Eds.). *Developmental origins of aggression* (pp. 425–443). New York: Guilford Press.

Archer, J., & Coyne, S. M. (2005). An integrated review of indirect, relational, and social aggression. *Personality and Social Psychology Review, 9,* 212–230.

Archer, R. L. (1979). Role of personality and the social situation. In G. J. Chelune (Ed.), *Self-disclosure* (pp. 28–58). San Francisco: Jossey-Bass.

Archibald, F. S., Bartholomew, K., & Marx, R. (1995). Loneliness in early adolescence: A test of the cognitive discrepancy model of loneliness. *Personality and Social Psychology Bulletin, 21,* 296–301.

Arendt, F. (2010). Cultivation effects of a newspaper

on reality estimates and explicit and implicit attitudes. *Journal of Media Psychology: Theories, Methods and Applications, 22,* 147–159.

Armenta, B. E., Knight, G. P., Carlo, G., & Jacobson, R. P. (2011). The relation between ethnic group attachment and prosocial tendencies: The mediating role of cultural values. *European Journal of Social Psychology, 41,* 107–115.

Armitage, C. J., & Conner, M. (1999). The theory of planned behaviour: Assessment of predictive validity and "perceived control." *British Journal of Social Psychology, 38,* 35–54.

Armitage, C. J., & Conner, M. (2000). Attitudinal ambivalence: A test of three key hypotheses. *Personality and Social Psychology Bulletin, 26,* 1421–1432.

Aron, A., & Aron, E. N. (1986). *Love as the expansion of self: Understanding attraction and satisfaction.* New York: Hemisphere.

Aron, A., & Aron, E. N. (1997). Self-expansion motivation and including other in the self. In S. Duck (Ed.), *Handbook of personal relationships: Theory, research and interventions* (2nd ed., pp. 251–270). Chichester, England: Wiley.

Aron, A., Aron, E. N., & Norman, C. (2001). Self-expansion model of motivation and cognition in close relationships and beyond. In G. J. O. Fletcher & M. S. Clark (Eds.), *Blackwell handbook of social psychology: Interpersonal processes.* Malden, MA: Blackwell.

Aron, A., Aron, E. N., Tudor, M., & Nelson, G. (1991). Close relationships as including other in the self. *Journal of Personality and Social Psychology, 60,* 241–253.

Aronoff, Joel. (2006). How we recognize angry and happy emotion in people, places, and things. *Cross-Cultural Research: The Journal of Comparative Social Science, 40,* 83–105.

Aronoff, J., Woike, B. A., & Hyman, L. M. (1992). Which are the stimuli in facial displays of anger and happiness? Configurational bases of emotion recognition. *Journal of Personality and Social Psychology, 62,* 1050–1066.

Aronson, E. (1969). The theory of cognitive dissonance: A current perspective. In L. Berkowitz (Ed.), *Advances in experimental social psychology* (Vol. 4, pp. 1–34). New York: Academic Press.

Aronson, E., & Carlsmith, J. M. (1963). Effect of the severity of threat on the devaluation of a forbidden behavior. *Journal of Abnormal and Social Psychology, 66,* 584–588.

Aronson, E., & Mills, J. (1959). The effect of severity of initiation on liking for a group. *Journal of Abnormal and Social Psychology, 59,* 177–181.

Aronson, E., Stephan, C., Sikes, J., Blaney, N., & Snapp, M. (1978). *The jigsaw classroom.* Beverly Hills, CA: Sage.

Aronson, E., & Thibodeau, R. (1992). The jigsaw classroom: A cooperative strategy for reducing prejudice. In J. Lynch, C. Modgil, & S. Modgil (Eds.), *Cultural diversity in the schools.* London: Falmer Press.

Aronson, J., Blanton, H., & Cooper, J. (1995). From dissonance to disidentification: Selectivity in the self-affirmation process. *Journal of Personality and Social Psychology, 68,* 986–996.

Aronson, J., Fried, C. B., & Good, C. (2002). Reducing the effects of stereotype threat on African American college students by shaping theories of intelligence. *Journal of Experimental Social Psychology, 38,* 113–125.

Aronson, J., Lustina, M. J., Good, C., Keough, K., Steele, C. M., & Brown, J. (1999). When White men can't do math: Necessary and sufficient factors in stereotype threat. *Journal of Experimental Social Psychology, 35,* 29–46.

Arriaga, X. B., & Agnew, C. R. (2001). Being committed: Affective, cognitive, and conative components of relationship commitment. *Personality and Social Psychology Bulletin, 27,* 1190–1203.

Arriaga, X. B., & Rusbult, C. E. (1998). Standing in my partner's shoes: Partner perspective taking and reactions to accommodative dilemmas. *Personality and Social Psychology Bulletin, 24,* 927–948.

Arrow, H., Henry, K. B., Poole, M. S., Wheelan, S., & Moreland, R. (2005). Traces, trajectories, and timing: The temporal perspective on groups. In M. S. Poole, S. Marshall, & A. B. Hollingshead (Eds), *Theories of small groups: Interdisciplinary perspectives* (pp. 313–367). Thousand Oaks, CA: Sage.

Asch, S. E. (1946). Forming impressions of personality. *Journal of Abnormal and Social Psychology, 41,* 258–290.

Asch, S. E. (1951). Effects of group pressure upon the modification and distortion of judgments. In H. Guetzkow (Ed.), *Groups, leadership, and men.* Pittsburgh, PA: Carnegie Press.

Asch, S. E. (1952). *Social psychology.* Englewood Cliffs, NJ: Prentice-Hall.

Asch, S. E. (November 1955). Opinions and social pressure. *Scientific American,* 31–35.

Asch, S. E. (1956). Studies of independence and conformity: A minority of one against a unanimous majority. *Psychological Monographs, 70* (Whole No. 416).

Asch, S. E., & Zukier, H. (1984). Thinking about persons. *Journal of Personality and Social Psychology, 46,* 1230–1240.

Ash, M. G. (1992). Cultural contexts and scientific change in psychology: Kurt Lewin in Iowa. *American Psychologist, 47,* 198–207.

Ashburn-Nardo, L., & Smith, J. S. (2008). Black college students' extropunitive and intropunitive responses to prejudice: Implications for concrete attitudes toward school in a predominantly white institution. *Journal of Black Psychology, 34,* 479–493.

Ashby, F. G., Isen, A. M., & Turken, A. U. (1999). A neuropsychological theory of positive affect and its influence on cognition. *Psychological Review, 106,* 529–550.

Ashton, M. C., & Esses, V. M. (1999). Stereotype accuracy: Estimating the academic performance of ethnic groups. *Personality and Social Psychology Bulletin, 25,* 225–236.

Atkins, M. S., Osborne, M. L., Bennett, D. S., Hess, L. E., & Halperin, J. M. (2001). Children's competitive peer aggression during reward and punishment. *Aggressive Behavior, 27,* 1–13.

Averhart, C. J., & Bigler, R. S. (1997). Shades of meaning: Skin tone, racial attitudes, and constructive memory in African American children. *Journal of Experimental Child Psychology, 67,* 363–388.

Axsom, D. (1989). Cognitive dissonance and behavior change in psychotherapy. *Journal of Experimental Social Psychology, 21,* 149–160.

Axtell, R. E. (1993). *Gestures: The Do's and Taboos of Body Language Around the World* (3rd ed.). New York: Wiley.

Aydin, N., Fischer, P., & Frey, D. (2010). Turning to God in the face of ostracism: Effects of social exclusion on religiousness. *Personality and Social Psychology Bulletin, 36,* 742–753.

Ayman, R. (2004). Situational and contingency approaches to leadership. In J. Antonakis, A. T. Cianciolo, & R. J. Sternberg (Eds.), *The nature of leadership* (pp. 148–170). Thousand Oaks, CA: Sage.

Ayyash-Abdo, H. (2001). Individualism and collectivism: The case of Lebanon. *Social Behavior and Personality, 29,* 503–518.

Baccus, J. R., Baldwin, M. W., & Packer, D. J. (2004). Increasing implicit self-esteem through classical conditioning. *Psychological Science, 15,* 498–502.

Bachman, R., & Peralta, R. (2002). The relationship between drinking and violence in an adolescent population: Does gender matter? *Deviant Behavior, 23,* 1–19.

Bachnik, J. M. (1992). The two "faces" of self and society in Japan. *Ethos, 20,* 3–32.

Back, M. D., Stopfer, J. M., Vazire, S., Gaddis, S., Schmukle, S. C., Egloff, B. & Gosling, S. D. (2010). Facebook profiles reflect actual personality, not self-idealization. *Psychological Science, 21,* 372–374.

Back, M. D., Schmukle, S. C., & Egloff, B. (2008). Becoming friends by chance. *Psychological Science, 19,* 439–440.

Backman, C. W. (1983). Toward an interdisciplinary social psychology. In L. Berkowitz (Ed.), *Advances in Experimental Social Psychology* (Vol. 14, pp. 219–261). New York: Academic Press.

Bagozzi, R. P. (1981). Attitudes, intentions, and behavior: A test of some key hypotheses. *Journal of Personality and Social Psychology, 41,* 607–627.

Bailey, D. F., & Bradbury-Bailey, M. (2010). Promoting the self-esteem of adolescent African American males. In M. H. Guindon (Ed.). *Self-esteem across the lifespan* (pp. 159–172). New York: Routledge.

Bahns, A. J., & Branscombe, N. R. (2011). Effects of legitimizing discrimination against homosexuals on gay bashing. *European Journal of Social Psychology, 41,* 388–396.

Baker, L. A., Jacobson, K. C., Raine, A., Lozano, D. I., & Bezdjian, S. (2007). Genetic and environmental bases of childhood antisocial behavior: A multi-informant twin study. *Journal of Abnormal Psychology, 116,* 219–235.

Baker, L. R., & Oswald, D. L. (2010). Shyness and online social networking services. *Journal of Social and Personal Relationships, 27,* 873–889.

Baker, S. M., & Petty, R. E. (1994). Majority and minority influence: Source-position imbalance as a determinant of message scrutiny. *Journal of Personality and Social Psychology, 67,* 5–19.

Bales, R. F. (1970). *Personality and interpersonal behavior.* Fort Worth, TX: Holt, Rinehart.

Bales, R. F., & Slater, P. E. (1955). Role differentiation. In T. Parsons & R. F. Bales (Eds.), *Family, socialization, and interaction processes* (pp. 259–306). Glencoe, IL: Free Press.

Balliet, D., Mulder, L. B., Van Lange, P. A. M. (2011). Reward, punishment, and cooperation: A meta-analysis. *Psychological Bulletin, 137,* 594–615.

Ball-Rokeach, S. J., Rokeach, M., & Grube, J. W. (1984). *The great American values test: Influencing behavior and belief through television.* New York: Free Press.

Banaji, M. R. (2004). The opposite of a great truth is also true: Homage to koan #7. In J. T. Jost, M. R. Banaji, & D. A. Prentice (Eds.), *Perspectivism in social psychology: The yin and yang of scientific progress* (pp. 127–140). Washington, DC: American Psychological Association.

Banaji, M. R. (2002). Social psychology of stereotypes. In N. J. Smelser & P. B. Baltes (Eds.), *International encyclopedia of the social and behavioral sciences.* New York: Elsevier/North Holland.

Banaji, M. R., Bazerman, M. H., & Chugh, D. (2003, December). How (un)ethical are you? *Harvard Business Review, 5526, 1–11.*

Banaji, M. R., & Heiphetz, L. (2010). Attitudes. In S. T. Fiske, D. T. Gilbert, & G. Lindzey (Eds.). *Handbook of social psychology, Vol. 1* (5th ed.) (pp. 353–393). Hoboken, NJ: John Wiley.

Bandura, A. (1965). Influences of models' reinforcement contingencies on the acquisition of initiative responses. *Journal of Personality and Social Psychology, 1,* 589–593.

Bandura, A. (1979). The social learning perspective: Mechanism of aggression. In H. Toch (Ed.), *Psychology of crime and criminal justice.* New York: Holt, Rinehart.

Bandura, A. (1986). *Social foundations of thought and action: A social-cognitive theory.* Englewood Cliffs, NJ: Prentice-Hall.

Bandura, A. (2005). Toward a psychology of human agency. *Perspectives on Psychological Science,*

1, 164–180.

Bandura, A., & Huston, A. C. (1961). Identification as a process of incidental learning. *Journal of Abnormal and Social Psychology, 63,* 575–582.

Bandura, A., Ross, D., & Ross, S. A. (1961). Transmission of aggression through imitation of aggressive models. *Journal of Abnormal and Social Psychology, 63,* 575–582.

Bandura, A., & Walters, R. H. (1963). *Social learning and personality development.* New York: Holt, Rinehart.

Bank, B. J., & Hansford, S. L. (2000). Gender and friendship: Why are men's best same-sex friendships less intimate and supportive? *Personal Relationships, 7,* 1–23.

Bankston, C. L. III, & Caldas, S. J. (1997). The American school dilemma: Race and scholastic performance. *The Sociological Quarterly, 38,* 423–429.

Bar-Tal, D. (1990). Causes and consequences of delegitimization: Models of conflict and ethnocentrism. *Journal of Social Issues, 46,* 65–81.

Bar-Tal, D. (2000). *Shared beliefs in a society: Social psychological analysis.* Thousand Oaks, CA: Sage.

Barbee, A. P., Cunningham, M. R., Winstead, B. A., Derlega, V. J., Gulley, M. R., Yankeelov, P. A., & Druen, P. B. (1993). Effects of gender role expectations on the social support process. *Journal of Social Issues, 49,* 175–190. .

Barbee, A. P., Gulley, M. R., & Cunningham, M. R. (1990). Support seeking in personal relationships. *Journal of Social and Personal Relationships, 7,* 531–540.

Barber, N. (2002). *The science of romance: Secrets of the sexual brain.* Amherst, NY: Prometheus Books.

Barbuto, J. E., Jr. (1997). Taking the charisma out of transformational leadership. *Journal of Social Behavior and Personality, 12,* 689–697.

Barbuto, J. E., Jr. (2000). Influence triggers: A framework for understanding follower compliance. *Leadership Quarterly, 11,* 365–387.

Bardi, A., & Schwartz, S. H. (2003). Values and behavior: Strength and structure of relations. *Personality and Social Psychology Bulletin, 29,* 1207–1220.

Bargh, J. A., & Chartrand, T. L. (1999). The unbearable automaticity of being. *American Psychologist, 54,* 462–479.

Bargh, J. A., Chen, M., & Burrows, L. (1996). Automaticity of social behavior: Direct effects of trait construct and stereotype activation on action. *Journal of Personality and Social Psychology, 71,* 230–244.

Bargh, J. A., & McKenna, K. Y. A. (2004). The Internet and social life. *Annual Review of Psychology, 55,* 573–590.

Bargh, J. A., & Pietromonaco, P. (1982). Automatic information processing and social perception: The influence of trait information presented outside of conscious awareness on impression formation. *Journal of Personality and Social Psychology, 43,* 437–449.

Barley, S. R., & Bechky, B. A. (1994). In the backrooms of science: The work of technicians in science labs. *Work and Occupations, 21,* 85–126.

Barnlund, D. C. (1989). *Communicative styles of Japanese and Americans.* Belmont, CA: Wadsworth.

Baron, L., & Straus, M. A. (1987). Four theories of rape: A macrosociological analysis. *Social Problems, 34,* 467–489.

Baron, L., & Straus, M. A. (1989). *Four theories of rape in American society: A state-level analysis.* New Haven, CT: Yale University Press.

Baron, R. A. (1973). Threatened retaliation from the victim as an inhibitor of physical aggression. *Journal of Research in Personality, 7,* 103–115.

Baron, R. A. (1976). The reduction of human aggression: A field study of the influence of incompatible reactions. *Journal of Applied Social Psychology, 6,* 260–274.

Baron, R. A. (1983). The control of human aggression: A strategy based on incompatible responses. In R. G. Geen & E. I. Donnerstein (Eds.), *Aggression: Theoretical and empirical reviews* (Vol. 2, pp. 173–190). New York: Academic Press.

Baron, R. A. (1986). Self-presentation in job interviews: When there can be "too much of a good thing." *Journal of Applied Social Psychology, 16,* 16–28.

Baron, R. A., & Kepner, C. R. (1970). Model's behavior and attraction toward the model as determinants of adult aggressive behavior. *Journal of Personality and Social Psychology, 14,* 335–344.

Baron, R. S. (1986). Distraction-conflict theory: Progress and problems. In L. Berkowitz (Ed.), *Advances in experimental social psychology* (Vol. 19, pp. 1–40). New York: Academic Press.

Baron, R. S. (2005). So right it's wrong: Groupthink and the ubiquitous nature of polarized group decision making. (2005). In M. P. Zanna (Ed.), *Advances in experimental social psychology* (Vol. 37, pp. 219–253). San Diego, CA: Elsevier Academic Press.

Baron, R. S., Vandello, J. A., & Brunsman, B. (1996). The forgotten variable in conformity research: Impact of task importance on social influence. *Journal of Personality and Social Psychology, 71,* 915–927.

Barrett, L., Dunbar, R., & Lycett, J. (2002). *Human evolutionary psychology.* Princeton, NJ: Princeton University Press.

Barrett, L., Henzi, P., & Dunbar, R. (2003). Primate cognition: From "what now?" to "what if?" *Trends in Cognitive Sciences, 7,* 494–497.

Barrett, L. F., & Bliss-Moreau, E. (2009). She's emotional. He's having a bad day: Attributional explanations for emotion stereotypes. *Emotion, 9,* 649–658.

Barron, G., & Yechiam, E. (2002). Private e-mail requests and the diffusion of responsibility. *Computers in Human Behavior, 18,* 507–520.

Barsalou, L. W. (1991). Deriving categories to achieve goals. In M. I. Posner, (Ed.), *The psychology of learning and motivation* (Vol. 27, pp. 1–64). New York: Academic Press.

Bartels, A., & Zeki, S. (2000). The neural basis of romantic love. *Neuroreport, 11,* 3829–3834.

Bartels, M., Cacioppo, J. T., Hudziak, J. J., & Boomsma, D. I. (2008). Genetic and environmental contributions to stability in loneliness throughout childhood. *American Journal of Medical Genetics Part B (Neuropsychiatric Genetics), 147,* 385–391.

Bartholow, B. D., Anderson, C. A., & Carnagey, N. L. (2005). Interactive effects of life experience and situational cues on aggression: The weapons priming effect in hunters and nonhunters. *Journal of Experimental Social Psychology, 41,* 48–60.

Bartholow, B. D., Bushman, B. J., & Sestir, M. A. (2006). Chronic violent video game exposure and desensitization to violence: Behavioral and event-related brain potential data. *Journal of Experimental Social Psychology, 42,* 532–529.

Bartholow, B. D., Pearson, M. A., Gratton, G., & Fabiani, M. (2003a). Effects of alcohol on person perception: A social cognitive neuroscience approach. *Journal of Personality and Social Psychology, 85,* 627–638.

Bartholow, B. D., Sher, K. J., & Krull, J. L. (2003b). Changes in heavy drinking over the third decade of life as a function of collegiate fraternity and sorority involvement: A prospective, multilevel analysis. *Health Psychology, 22,* 616–626.

Bartholomew, K. (1990). Avoidance of intimacy: An attachment perspective. *Journal of Social and Personal Relationships, 7,* 147–178.

Bartholomew, K., Kwong, M. J., & Hart, S. D. (2001). Attachment. In W. J. Livesley (Ed.). *Handbook of personality disorders: Theory, research, and treatment* (pp. 196–230). New York: Guilford.

Bartlett, F. C. (1932). *Remembering: A study in experimental and social psychology.* London: Cambridge University Press.

Barton, J., Stephens, J., & Haslett, T. (2009). Action research: Its foundations in open systems thinking and relationship to the scientific method. *Systemic Practice and Action Research, 22,* 475–488.

Bartone, P. T., Snook, S. A., & Tremble, T. R., Jr. (2002). Cognitive and personality predictors of leader performance in West Point cadets. *Military Psychology, 14,* 321–338.

Bartz, J. A., & Lydon, J. E. (2004). Close relationships and the working self-concept: Implicit and explicit effects of priming attachment on agency and communion. *Personality and Social Psychology Bulletin, 30,* 1389–1401.

Basil, D. Z., Ridgway, N. M., & Basil, M. D. (2008). Guilt and giving: A process model of empathy and efficacy. *Psychology & Marketing, 25,* 1–23.

Basow, S. A. (1986). *Gender stereotypes: Traditions and alternatives* (2nd ed.). Monterey, CA: Brooks/Cole.

Bass, B. M. (2008). *The Bass handbook of leadership: Theory, research, and managerial applications.* New York, NY: Free Press.

Bassett, J. F. (2010). The effects of mortality salience and social dominance orientation on attitudes toward illegal immigrants. *Social Psychology, 41,* 52–55.

Bassett, J. F., Cate, K. L., & Dabbs, J. M., Jr. (2002). Individual differences in self-presentation style: Driving an automobile and meeting a stranger. *Self & Identity, 1,* 281–288.

Bassili, J. N. (2003). The minority slowness effect: Subtle inhibitions in the expression of views not shared by others. *Journal of Personality and Social Psychology, 84,* 261–276.

Bassili, J. N., & Provencal, A. (1988). Perceiving minorities: A factor-analytic approach. *Personality and Social Psychology Bulletin, 14,* 5–15.

Batson, C. D. (1991). *The altruism question: Toward a social psychological answer.* Hillsdale, NJ: Erlbaum.

Batson, C. D. (2011). *Altruism in humans.* New York: Oxford University Press.

Batson, C. D., Ajmad, N., Lishner, D. A., & Tsang, J. (2002a). Empathy and altruism. In C. R. Snyder, & S. J. Lopez. (Eds.), *Handbook of positive psychology* (pp. 485–498). London: Oxford University Press.

Batson, C. D., Chang, J., Orr, R., & Rowland, J. (2002b). Empathy, attitudes and action: Can feeling for a member of a stigmatized group motivate one to help the group? *Personality and Social Psychology Bulletin, 28,* 1656–1666.

Batson, C. D., Coke, J. S., Chard, F., Smith, D., & Taliaferro, A. (1979). Generality of the "glow of goodwill": Effects of mood on helping and information acquisition. *Social Psychology Quarterly, 42,* 176–179.

Batson, C. D., Duncan, B. D., Ackerman, P., Buckley, T., & Birch, K. (1981). Is empathic emotion a source of altruistic motivation? *Journal of Personality and Social Psychology, 40,* 290–302.

Batson, C. D., Eklund, J. H., Chermok, V. L., Hoyth, J. L., & Ortiz, B. G. (2007). An additional antecedent of empathic concern: Valuing the welfare of the person in need. *Journal of Personality and Social Psychology, 93,* 65–74.

Batson, C. D., O'Quinn, K., Fultz, J., Vanderplas, N., & Isen, A. M. (1983). Influence of self-reported distress and empathy on egoistic versus altruistic motivation to help. *Journal of Personality and Social Psychology, 45,* 706–718.

Batson, C. D., & Powell, A. A. (2003). Altruism and prosocial behavior. In T. Millon, & M. J. Lerner (Eds.), *Handbook of psychology: Personality and social psychology* (Vol. 5, pp. 463–484). New York: Wiley.

Batson, C. D., Sager, K., Garst, E., Kang, M., Rubchinsky, K., & Dawson, K. (1997). Is empathy-induced helping due to self-other merging? *Journal of Personality and Social Psychology, 73,* 495–509.

Batson, C. D., Sympson, S. C., Hindman, J. L., Decruz,

P., Todd, R. M., Weeks, J. L., Jennings, G., & Burris, C. T. (1996). "I've been there, too": Effect on empathy of prior experience with a need. *Personality and Social Psychology Bulletin, 22,* 474–482.

Battaglia, D. M., Richard, F. D., Datteri, D. L., & Lord, C. G. (1998). Breaking up is (relatively) easy to do: A script for the dissolution of close relationships. *Journal of Social and Personal Relationships, 15,* 829–845.

Baudouina, J. Y., & Tiberghienb, G. (2004). Symmetry, averageness, and feature size in the facial attractiveness of women. *Acta Psychologica, 117,* 313–332.

Baum, N. (2010). After a terror attack: Israeli-Arab professionals' feelings and experiences. *Journal of Social and Personal Relationships, 27,* 685–704.

Baumeister, R. F. (1982). A self-presentational view of social phenomena. *Psychological Bulletin, 91,* 3–26.

Baumeister, R. F. (1991). *Escaping the self: Alcoholism, spirituality, masochism, and other flights from the burden of selfhood.* New York: Basic Books.

Baumeister, R. F. (1998). The self. In D. T. Gilbert, S. T. Fiske, & G. Lindzey (Eds.), *The handbook of social psychology* (4th ed., Vol. 1, pp. 680–740). New York: McGraw-Hill.

Baumeister, R. F., & Alquist, J. L. (2009). Is there a downside to good self-control? *Self and Identity, 8, 115-130.*

Baumeister, R. F., & Boden, J. M. (1998). Aggression and the self: High self-esteem, low self-control, and ego threat. In R. Geen & E. Donnerstein (Eds.), *Human aggression: Theories, research, and implications for social policy* (pp. 111–138). San Diego, CA: Academic Press.

Baumeister, R. F., DeWall, C. N., Ciarocco, N. J., & Twenge, J. M. (2005). Social exclusion impairs self-regulation. *Journal of Personality and Social Psychology, 88,* 589–604.

Baumeister, R. F., & Heatherton, T. F. (1996). Self-regulation failure: An overview. *Psychological Inquiry, 7,* 1–15.

Baumeister, R. F., Heatherton, T. F., & Tice, D. M. (1994). *Losing control: How and why people fail at self-regulation.* San Diego: Academic Press.

Baumeister, R. F., & Ilko, S. A. (1995). Shallow gratitude: Public and private acknowledgment of external help in accounts of success. *Basic and Applied Social Psychology, 16,* 191–209.

Baumeister, R. F., & Jones, E. E. (1978). When self-presentation is constrained by the target's knowledge: Consistency and compensation. *Journal of Personality and Social Psychology, 36,* 608–618.

Baumeister, R. F., & Leary, M. R. (1995). The need to belong: Desire for interpersonal attachments as a fundamental human motivation. *Psychological Bulletin, 117,* 497–529.

Baumeister, R. F., Smart, L., & Boden, J. M. (1996). Relation of threatened egotism to violence and aggression: The dark side of high self-esteem. *Psychological Review, 103,* 5–33.

Baumeister, R. F., Twenge, J. M., & Nuss, C. K. (2002). Effects of social exclusion on cognitive processes: Anticipated aloneness reduces intelligent thought. *Journal of Personality and Social Psychology, 83,* 817–827.

Baumeister, R. F., & Vohs, K. D. (2002). Self-regulation and the executive function of the self. In M. R. Leary & J. P. Tangney (Eds.), *Handbook of self and identity* (pp. 197–217). New York: Guilford Press.

Baumeister, R. F., & Vohs, K. D. (Eds.) (2004). *Handbook of self-regulation: Research, theory, and applications.* New York: Guilford.

Baumeister, R. F., Vohs, K. D., DeWall, C. N., & Zhang, L. (2007). How emotion shapes behavior: Feedback, anticipation, and reflection, rather than direct causation. *Personality and Social Psychology Review, 11,* 167–203.

Baumeister, R. F., Vohs, K. D., & Funder, D. C. (2007). Psychology as the science of self-reports and finger movements: Or whatever happened to

actual behavior? *Perspectives on Psychological Science, 4,* 396–403.

Baumrind, D. (1964). Some thoughts on ethics of research: After reading Milgram's "Behavioral Study of Obedience." *American Psychologist, 19,* 421–423.

Bauserman, R. (1996). Sexual aggression and pornography: A review of correlational research. *Basic and Applied Social Psychology, 18,* 405–427.

Baxter, L. A. (1987). Self-disclosure and relationship disengagement. In V. Derlega & J. H. Berg (Eds.), *Self-disclosure: Theory, research, and therapy* (pp. 155–174). New York: Plenum.

Bazzini, D., Curtin, L., Joslin, S., Regan, S., & Martz, D. (2010). Do animated Disney characters portray and promote the beauty-goodness stereotype? *Journal of Applied Social Psychology, 40,* 2687–2709.

Beach, S. R. H., & Tesser, A. (2000). Self-evaluation maintenance and evolution: Some speculative notes. In J. Suls & L. Wheeler (Eds.), *Handbook of social comparison: Theory and research,* (pp. 123–140). New York: Kluwer Academic/Plenum.

Beaman, A. L., Barnes, P. J., Klentz, B., & McQuirk, B. (1978). Increasing helping rates through information dissemination: Teaching pays. *Personality and Social Psychology Bulletin, 9,* 181–196.

Beaman, A. L., Cole, M., Preston, M., Klentz, B., & Steblay, N. M. (1983). Fifteen years of the foot-in-the-door research: A meta-analysis. *Personality and Social Psychology Bulletin, 9,* 181–186.

Beaman, A. L., Klentz, B., Diener, E., & Svanum, S. (1979). Self-awareness and transgression in children: Two field studies. *Journal of Personality and Social Psychology, 37,* 1835–1846.

Beauducel, A., Brocke, B., & Leue, A. (2006). Energetical bases of extraversion: Effort, arousal, EEG, and performance. *International Journal of Psychophysiology, 62,* 212–223.

Becker, B. J. (1986). Influence again: Another look at studies of gender differences in social influence. In J. S. Hyde & M. C. Linn (Eds.), *The psychology of gender: Advances through meta-analysis.* Baltimore: Johns Hopkins University Press.

Becker, B. J. (1986). Influence again: Another look at studies of gender differences in social influence. In J. S. Hyde & M. C. Linn (Eds.), *The psychology of gender: Advances through meta-analysis.* Baltimore: Johns Hopkins University Press.

Becker, J., Ayman, R., & Korabik, K. (2002). Discrepancies in self/subordinates' perceptions of leadership behavior: Leader's gender, organizational context and leader's self-monitoring. *Group and Organization Management, 27,* 226–244.

Becker, J. C., Tausch, N., Spears, R., & Christ, O. (2011). Committed Dis(s)idents: Participation in radical collective action fosters disindentification with the broader in-group but enhances political identification. *Personality and Social Psychology Bulletin, 37.*

Becker, J. C., & Wright, S. C. (2011). Yet another dark side of chivalry: Benevolent sexism undermines and hostile sexism motivates collective action for social change. *Journal of Personality and Social Psychology, 37.*

Beets, M. W., Flay, B. R., Vuchinich, S., Li, K., Acock, A., & Snyder, F. J. (2009). Longitudinal patterns of binge drinking among first year college students with a history of tobacco use. *Drug and Alcohol Dependence, 103,* 1–8.

Begue, L., Subra, B., Arvers, P., Muller, D., Bricout, V., & Zorman, M. (2009). A message in a bottle: Extrapharmacological effects of alcohol on aggression. *Journal of Experimental Social Psychology, 45,* 137–142.

Beilock, S. L., Jellison, W. A., Rydell, R. J., McConnell, A. R., & Carr, T. H. (2006). On the causal

mechanisms of stereotype threat: Can skills that don't rely heavily on working memory still be threatened? *Personality and Social Psychology Bulletin, 32,* 1059–1071.

Bell, K. L., & DePaulo, B. M. (1996). Liking and lying. *Basic and Applied Social Psychology, 18,* 243–266.

Bell, S. T., Kuriloff, P. J., & Lottes, I. (1994). Understanding attributions of blame in stranger-rape and date-rape situations: An examination of gender, race, identification, and students' social perception of rape victims. *Journal of Applied Social Psychology, 24,* 1719–1734.

Bellah, R., Madsen, R., Sullivan, W., Swindler, A., & Tipton, S. (1985). *Habits of the heart: Individualism and commitment in American life.* Berkeley: University of California Press.

Bellavia, G., & Murray, S. L. (2003). Did I do that? Self-esteem related differences in reactions to romantic partners' moods. *Personal Relationships, 10,* 77–96.

Bem, D. J. (1965). An experimental analysis of self-persuasion. *Journal of Experimental Social Psychology, 1,* 199–218.

Bem, D. J. (1967). Self-perception: An alternative interpretation of cognitive dissonance phenomena. *Psychological Review, 74,* 183–200.

Bem, D. J. (1972). Self-perception theory. In L. Berkowitz (Ed.), *Advances in experimental social psychology* (Vol. 6). New York: Academic Press.

Bem, S. L. (1993). *The lenses of gender: Transforming the debate on sexual inequality.* New Haven: Yale University Press.

Benet-Martínez, V., & Haritatos, J. (2005). Bicultural identity integration (BII): Components and socio-personality antecedents. *Journal of Personality, 73,* 53–67.

Benet-Martínez, V., & Karakitapoglu-Aygun, Z. (2003). The interplay of cultural values and personality in predicting life satisfaction: Comparing Asian-and European-Americans. *Journal of Cross-Cultural Psychology, 34,* 38–61.

Benet-Martínez, V., Lee, F., & Leu, J. (2006). Biculturalism and cognitive complexity: Expertise in cultural representations. *Journal of Cross-Cultural Psychology, 37,* 1–23.

Benner, A. D. (2011). Latino adolescents' loneliness, academic performance, and the buffering nature of friendships. *Journal of Youth and Adolescence, 40,* 556–567.

Bennett, K. K., & Elliott, M. (2005). Pessimistic explanatory style and cardiac health: What is the relation and the mechanism that links them? *Basic and Applied Social Psychology, 27,* 239–248.

Bensimon, P. (2007). The role of pornography in sexual offending. *Sexual Addiction & Compulsivity, 14,* 95–117.

Ben-Zeev, T., Fein, S., & Inzlicht, M. (2005). Arousal and stereotype threat. *Journal of Experimental Social Psychology, 41,* 174–181.

Beren, S. E., Hayden, H. A., Wilfley, D. E., & Striegel-Moore, R. H. (1997). Body dissatisfaction among lesbian college students. *Psychology of Women Quarterly, 21,* 431–445.

Berg, J. H. (1984). The development of friendships between roommates. *Journal of Personality and Social Psychology, 46,* 346–356.

Berg, J. H., & Clark, M. S. (1986). Differences in social exchange between intimate and other relationships: Gradually evolving or quickly apparent? In V. J. Derlega & B. A. Winstead (Eds.), *Friendship and social interaction* (pp. 101–128). New York: Springer-Verlag.

Berger, J., & Webster, M., Jr. (2006). Expectations, status, and behavior. In P. J. Burke (Ed.), *Contemporary social psychological theories* (pp. 268–300). Stanford, CA: Stanford University Press.

Berkowitz, L. (September 1968). Impulse, aggression and the gun. *Psychology Today,* pp. 18–22.

Berkowitz, L. (1969). The frustration-aggression

hypothesis revisited. In L. Berkowitz (Ed.), *Roots of aggression* (pp. 1–28). New York: Atherton.

Berkowitz, L. (1984). Some effects of thoughts on anti- and prosocial influences of media events: A cognitive-neoassociation analysis. *Psychological Bulletin, 95,* 410–427.

Berkowitz, L. (1989). Frustration-aggression hypothesis: Examination and reformulation. *Psychological Bulletin, 106,* 59–73.

Berkowitz, L. (1993). *Aggression: Its causes, consequences, and control.* New York: McGraw-Hill.

Berkowitz, L. (1994). On the escalation of aggression. In M. Potegal & J. F. Knutson (Eds.), *The dynamics of aggression: Biological and social processes in dyads and groups* (pp. 33–41). Hillsdale, NJ: Erlbaum.

Bernache-Assollant, I., Laurin, R., Bouchet, P., Bodet, G., & Lacassagne, M. F.(2010). Refining the relationship between ingroup identification and identity management strategies in the sport context: The moderating role of gender and the mediating role of negative mood. *Group Processes & Intergroup Relations, 13,* 639–652.

Bernard, J. (1981). The good-provider role: Its rise and fall. *American Psychologist, 36,* 1–12.

Bernard, M. M., Maio, G. R., & Olson, J. M. (2003). The vulnerability of values to attack: Inoculation of values and value-relevant attitudes. *Personality and Social Psychology Bulletin, 29,* 63–75.

Berndsen, M., Spears, R., Pligt, J., & McGarty, C. (2002). Illusory correlation and stereotype formation: Making sense of group differences and cognitive biases. In C. McGarty, V. Y. Yzerbyt, & R. Spears (Eds.). *Stereotypes as explanations: The formation of meaningful beliefs about social groups* (pp. 90–110). New York: Cambridge University Press.

Bernstein, D. M., Erdfelder, E., Meltzoff, A. N., Peria, W., & Loftus, G. R. (2011). Hindsight bias from 3 to 95 years of age. *Journal of Experimental Psychology: Learning, Memory and Cognition, 37,* 378–391.

Berscheid, E., & Hatfield, E. (1969). *Interpersonal attraction.* Reading, MA: Addison-Wesley.

Berscheid, E., & Hatfield (Walster), E. (1974). A little bit about love. In T. Huston (Ed.), *Foundations of interpersonal attraction* (pp. 355–381). New York: Academic Press.

Bessenoff, G. R., & Del Priore, R. E. (2007). Women, weight, and age: Social comparison to magazine images across the lifespan. *Sex Roles, 56,* 215–222.

Betsch, T., Plessner, H., Schwieren, C. (2001). I like it but I don't know why: A value-account approach to implicit attitude formation. *Personality and Social Psychology Bulletin, 27,* 242–253.

Bettencourt, B. A., & Miller, N. (1996). Gender differences in aggression as a function of provocation: A meta-analysis. *Psychological Bulletin, 119,* 422–447.

Bettencourt, B. A., Talley, A., Benjamin, A. J., & Valentine, J. (2006). Personality and aggressive behavior under provoking and neutral conditions: A meta-analytic review. *Psychological Bulletin, 132,* 751–777.

Bhargava, R. (1992). *Individualism in social science: Forms and limits of a methodology.* Oxford: Clarendon Press.

Bicchieri, C., & Lev-On, A. (2007). Computer-mediated communication and cooperation in social dilemmas: An experimental analysis. *Politics, Philosophy & Economics, 6,* 139–168.

Bierbauer, G. (1979). Why did he do it? Attribution of obedience and the phenomenon of dispositional bias. *European Journal of Social Psychology, 9,* 67–84.

Bierhoff, H. W. (2002). Just world, social responsibility, and helping behavior. In M. Ross & D. T. Miller (Eds.), *The justice motive in everyday life* (pp. 189–203). New York: Cambridge University Press.

Bierhoff, H. W., Klein, R., & Kramp, P. (1991). Evidence for the altruistic personality from data on accident research. *Journal of Personality, 59,* 263–280.

Biernat, M., Vescio, T. K., & Theno, S. A. (1996). Violating American values: A "value congruence" approach to understanding outgroup attitudes. *Journal of Experimental Social Psychology, 32,* 387–410.

Billig, M. (1985). Prejudice, categorization and particularization: From a perceptual to a rhetorical approach. *European Journal of Social Psychology, 15,* 79–104.

Birchler, G. R., Weiss, R. L., & Vincent, J. P. (1975). Multimethod analysis of social reinforcement exchange between maritally distressed and nondistressed spouse and stranger dyads. *Journal of Personality and Social Psychology, 31,* 349–360.

Birnbaum, M. H. (2004). Methodological and ethical issues in conducting social psychology research via the Internet. In C. Sansone, C. C. Morf, & A. T. Panter (Eds.), *Handbook of methods in social psychology* (pp. 359–382). Thousand Oaks, CA: Sage.

Bisson, M. A., & Levine, T. R. (2009). Negotiating a friends with benefits relationship. *Archives of Sexual Behavior, 38,* 66–73.

Björkqvist, K., Lagerspetz, K. M. J., & Kaukiainen, A. (1992). Do girls manipulate and boys fight? Developmental trends regarding direct and indirect aggression. *Aggressive Behavior, 18.*

Björkqvist, K., & Niemelä, P. (1992). New trends in the study of female aggression. In K. Björkqvist & P. Niemelä (Eds.), *Of mice and women: Aspects of female aggression* (pp. 3–16). San Diego, CA: Harcourt Brace Jovanovich.

Blagrove, M. (1996). Effects of length of sleep deprivation on interrogative suggestibility. *Journal of Experimental Psychology: Applied, 2,* 48–59.

Blaine, B. E., DiBlasi, D. M., & Connor, J. M. (2002). The effect of weight loss on perceptions of weight controllability: Implications for prejudice against overweight people. *Journal of Applied Biobehavioral Research, 7,* 44–56.

Blair, C. A., Thompson, L. F., & Wuensch, K. L. (2005). Electronic helping behavior: The virtual presence of others makes a difference. *Basic and Applied Social Psychology, 27,* 171–178.

Blair, I. V., Judd, C. M., & Chapleau, K. M. (2004). The influence of Afrocentric facial features in criminal sentencing. *Psychological Science, 15,* 674–679.

Blair, I. V., Judd, C. M., Sadler, M. S., & Jenkins, C. (2002). The role of Afrocentric features in person perception: Judging by features and categories. *Journal of Personality and Social Psychology, 83,* 5–25.

Blair, I. V., Park, B., & Bachelor, J. (2003). Understanding intergroup anxiety: Are some people more anxious than others? *Group Processes and Intergroup Relations, 6,* 151–169.

Blair, J. P., Levine, T. R. & Shaw, A. S. (2010). Content in context improves deception detection accuracy. *Human Communication Research, 30,* 423–442.

Blais, M. R., Sabourin, S., Boucher, C., & Vallerand, R. J. (1990). Toward a motivational model of couple happiness. *Journal of Personality and Social Psychology, 59,* 1021–1031.

Blakely, G. L., Andrews, M. C., & Fuller, J. (2003). Are chameleons good citizens? A longitudinal study of the relationship between self-monitoring and organizational citizenship behavior. *Journal of Business & Psychology, 18,* 131–144.

Blaney, P. H. (1986). Affect and memory: A review. *Psychological Bulletin, 99,* 229–246.

Blanchard, F., Crandall, C., Brigham, J., & Vaughn, L. (1994). Condemning and condoning racism: A social context approach to interracial settings. *The Journal of Applied Psychology, 79,* 993–997.

Blandon-Gitlin, I., Sperry, K., & Leo, R. (2011). Jurors believe interrogation tactics are not likely to elicit false confessions: Will expert witness testimony inform them otherwise?. *Psychology, Crime & Law, 17,* 239–260.

Blank, H., Fischer, V., & Erdfelder, E. (2003). Hindsight bias in political elections. *Memory, 11,* 491–504.

Blascovich, J. (2002). Social influence within immersive virtual environments. In R. Schroeder (Ed.), *The social life of avatars* (pp. 127–145). New York: Springer-Verlag.

Blascovich, J. (2003). The virtual social animal. Sage Presidential Address to the 4th Annual Meeting of the Society of Personality and Social Psychology. February 6, Los Angeles, CA.

Blascovich, J., Mendes, W. B., Hunter, S. B., Lickel, B., & Kowai-Bell, N. (2001a). Perceiver threat in social interactions with stigmatized others. *Journal of Personality and Social Psychology, 80,* 253–267.

Blascovich, J., Spencer, S. J., Quinn, D., & Steele, C. (2001b). African Americans and high blood pressure: The role of stereotype threat. *Psychological Science, 12,* 225–229.

Blass, T. (1984). Social psychology and personality: Toward a convergence. *Journal of Personality and Social Psychology, 47,* 1013–1027.

Blass, T. (1996). Attribution of responsibility and trust in the Milgram obedience experiment. *Journal of Applied Social Psychology, 26,* 1529–1535.

Blass, T. (1999). The Milgram paradigm after 35 years: Some things we now know about obedience to authority. *Journal of Applied Social Psychology, 29,* 955–978.

Blass, T. (Ed.). (2000). *Obedience to authority: Current perspectives on the Milgram paradigm.* Mahwah, NJ: Erlbaum.

Bleske, A. L., & Buss, D. B. (2000). Can men and women be just friends? *Personal Relationships, 21,* 131–151.

Bleske-Rechek, A. L., & Buss, D. M. (2001). Opposite-sex friendship: Sex differences and similarities in initiation selection and dissolution. *Personality and Social Psychology Bulletin, 27,* 1310–1323.

Bleske-Rechek, A., & Lighthall, M. (2010). Attractiveness and rivalry in women's friendships with women. *Human Nature, 21,* 82–97.

Bless, H., Clore, G. L., Schwarz, N., Golisano, V., Rabe, C., & Wölk, M. (1996). Mood and the use of scripts: Does a happy mood really lead to mindlessness? *Journal of Personality and Social Psychology, 71,* 665–679.

Blincoe, S., & Harris, M. J. (2011). Status and inclusion, anger and sadness: Gendered responses to disrespect. *European Journal of Social Psychology, 41,* 508–517.

Block, L. G., & Keller, P. A. (1997). Effects of self-efficacy and vividness on the persuasiveness of health communication. *Journal of Consumer Psychology, 6,* 31–54.

Blumer, H., & Morrione, T. J. [Ed]. (2006). *George Herbert Mead and human conduct.* Lanham, MD: Rowman & Littlefield.

Bodenhausen, G. V. (1990). Stereotypes as judgmental heuristics: Evidence of circadian variations in discrimination. *Psychological Science, 1,* 319–322.

Boen, F., Vanbeselaere, N., Pandelaere, M., Dewitte, S., Duriez, B., Snauwaert, B., Feys, J., Dierckx, V., & Van Avermaet, E. (2002). Politics and basking in reflected-glory: A field study in Flanders. *Basic and Applied Social Psychology, 24,* 205–214.

Bohm, R., Funke, F., & Harth, N. S. (2010). Same-race and same-gender voting preferences and the role of perceived realistic threat in the democratic primaries and caucuses 2008. *Analyses of Social Issues and Public Policy, 10,* 248–261.

Bohner, G., Crow, K., Erb, H., & Schwarz, N. (1992). Affect and persuasion: Mood effects on the processing of message content and context cues and on subsequent behaviour. *European Journal of Social Psychology, 22,* 511–530.

Bohner, G., Einwiller, S., Erb, H. P., & Siebler, F. (2003). When small means comfortable: Relations between product attributes in two-sided advertising. *Journal of Consumer Psychology, 29.*

Bohner, G., Siebler, F., & Schmelcher, J. (2006). Social norms and the likelihood of raping: Perceived rape myth acceptance of others affects men's rape proclivity. *Personality and Social Psychology Bulletin, 32,* 286–297.

Boldero, J., & Francis, J. (2000). The relation between self-discrepancies and emotion: The moderating roles of self-guide importance, location relevance, and social self-domain centrality. *Journal of Personality and Social Psychology, 78,* 38–52.

Boldry, J. G., Gaertner, L., & Quinn, J. (2007). Measuring the measures: A meta-analytic investigation of the measures of outgroup homogeneity. *Group Processes & Intergroup Relations, 10,* 157–178.

Bolger, N., & Amarel, D. (2007). Effects of social support visibility on adjustment to stress: Experimental evidence. *Journal of Personality and Social Psychology, 92,* 458–475.

Bolino, M. C., & Turnley, W. H. (2003). More than one way to make an impression: Exploring profiles of impression management. *Journal of Management, 29,* 141–160.

Bonanno, G. A., Rennicke, C., & Dekel, S. (2005). Self-enhancement among high-exposure survivors of the September 11th terrorist attack: Resilience or social maladjustment? *Journal of Personality and Social Psychology, 88,* 984–998.

Bond, C. F., Jr., & DePaulo, B. M. (2006). Accuracy of Deception Judgments. *Personality and Social Psychology Review, 10,* 214–234.

Bond, C. F., Jr., Thomas, B. J., & Paulson, R. M. (2004). Maintaining lies: The multiple-audience problem. *Journal of Experimental Social Psychology, 40,* 29–40.

Bond, C. F., Jr., & Titus, L. J. (1983). Social facilitation: A meta-analysis of 241 studies. *Psychological Bulletin, 94,* 265–292.

Bond, M. H. (2004). Culture and aggression—From context to coercion. *Personality and Social Psychology Review, 8,* 62–78.

Bond, R., & Smith, P. B. (1996). Culture and conformity: A meta-analysis of studies using Asch's (1952b, 1956) line judgment task. *Psychological Bulletin, 119,* 111–137.

Bonnot, V., & Croizet, J-C. (2007). Stereotype internalization and women's math performance: The role of interference in working memory. *Journal of Experimental Social Psychology, 43,* 857–866.

Bontempo, R., Lobel, S., & Triandis, H. (1990). Compliance and value internalization in Brazil and the U.S. *Journal of Cross-Cultural Psychology, 21,* 201–213.

Borgida, E., Conner, C., & Manteufel, L. (1992). Understanding living kidney donation: A behavioral decision-making perspective. In S. Spacapan & S. Oskamp (Eds.), *Helping and being helped* (pp. 183–212). Newbury Park, CA: Sage.

Bornstein, G., Kugler, T., & Ziegelmeyer, A. (2004). Individual and group decisions in the centipede game: Are groups more "rational" players? *Journal of Experimental Social Psychology, 40,* 599–605.

Bornstein, R. F. (1989). Exposure and affect: Overview and meta-analysis of research, 1968–1987. *Psychological Bulletin, 106,* 265–289.

Bornstein, R. F., Leone, D. R., & Galley, D. J. (1987). The generalizability of subliminal mere exposure effects: Influence of stimuli perceived without awareness on social behavior. *Journal of Personality and Social Psychology, 53,* 1070–1079.

Bossard, J. (1932). Residential propinquity as a factor in marriage selection. *American Journal of Sociology, 38,* 219–224.

Bosson, J. K., Haymovitz, E. L., & Pinel, E. C. (2004). When saying and doing diverge: The effects of stereotype threat on self-reported versus non-verbal anxiety. *Journal of Experimental Social*

Psychology, 40, 247–255.

Bosson, J. K., Vandello, J. A., Burnaford, R. M., Weaver, J. R., & Wasti, S. A. (2009). Precarious manhood and displays of physical aggression. *Personality and Social Psychology Bulletin, 35,* 623–634.

Bourgeois, M. J., & Bowen, A. (2001). Self-organization of alcohol-related attitudes and beliefs in a campus housing complex: An initial investigation. *Health Psychology, 20,* 434–437.

Boven, L. V., White, K., Kamida, A., & Gilovich, T. (2003). Intuitions about situational correction in self and others. *Journal of Personality and Social Psychology, 85,* 249–258.

Bower, G. H., & Hilgard, E. R. (1981). *Theories of learning* (5th ed.). Englewood Cliffs, NJ: Prentice Hall.

Bowlby, J. (1969). *Attachment and loss.* (Vol. I. *Attachment).* New York: Wiley.

Boysen, S. T., & Himes, G. T. (1999). Current issues and emerging theories in animal cognition. *Annual Review of Psychology, 50,* 683–705.

Brackett, M. A., Alster, B., Wolfe, C. J., Katulak, N. A., & Fale, E. (2007). Creating an emotionally intelligent school district: A skills-based approach. In R. Bar-On, J. G. Maree, & M. J. Elias (Eds.). *Educating people to be emotionally intelligent* (pp. 123–137). Westport, CT: Praeger.

Brackett, M. A., Lopes, P. N., Ivcevic, Z., Mayer, J. D., & Salovey, P. (2004). Integrating emotion and cognition: The role of emotional intelligence. In D. Dai & R. J. Sternberg (Eds.), *Motivation, emotion, and cognition: Integrating perspectives on intellectual functioning* (pp. 175–194). Mahwah, NJ: Lawrence Erlbaum.

Bradbury, T. N., Campbell, S. M., & Fincham, F. D. (1995). Longitudinal and behavioral analysis of masculinity and femininity in marriage. *Journal of Personality and Social Psychology, 68,* 328–341.

Brage, D., Meredith, W., & Woodward, J. (1993). Correlates of loneliness among midwestern adolescents. *Adolescence, 28,* 685–693.

Brainerd, C. J., Reyna, V. F., & Brandse, E. (1995). Are children's false memories more persistent than their true memories? *Psychological Science, 6,* 359–364.

Branden, N. (1994). *The six pillars of self-esteem.* New York: Bantam Books.

Brandstätter, V., Lengfelder, A., & Gollwitzer, P. M. (2001). Implementation intentions and efficient action initiation. *Journal of Personality and Social Psychology, 81,* 946–960.

Branscombe, N. R., Schmidtt, M. T., & Harvey, R. D. (1999). Perceiving pervasive discrimination among African-Americans: Implications for group identification and well-being. *Journal of Personality and Social Psychology, 77,* 135–149.

Branscombe, N. R., Spears, R., Ellemers, N., & Doosje, B. (2002). Intragroup and intergroup evaluations on group behavior. *Personality and Social Psychology Bulletin, 28,* 744–753.

Branscombe, N. R., & Wann, D. L. (1994). Collective self-esteem consequences of outgroup derogation when a valued social identity is on trial. *European Journal of Social Psychology, 24,* 641–651.

Brase, G. L., Caprar, D., & Voracek, M. (2004). Sex differences in responses to relationship threats in England and Romania. *Journal of Social and Personal Relationships.*

Brauer, M., Judd, C. M., & Gliner, M. D. (1995). The effects of repeated expressions on attitude polarization during group discussions. *Journal of Personality and Social Psychology, 68,* 1014–1029.

Breckler, S. J. (1984). Empirical validation of affect, behavior, and cognition as distinct components of attitude. *Journal of Personality and Social Psychology, 52,* 384–389.

Brehm, J. W. (1966). *A theory of psychological reactance.* New York: Academic Press.

Brehm, S. S. (1988). Passionate love. In R. J. Sternberg & M. L. Barnes (Eds.), *The psychology of love* (pp. 232–263). New Haven,

CT: Yale University Press.

Brehm, S. S. (1992). *Intimate relationships.* New York: McGraw-Hill.

Brehm, S. S., & Brehm, J. W. (1981). *Psychological reactance: A theory of freedom and control.* New York: Academic Press.

Brendan, G. (2002). "I've always tolerated it but . . .": Heterosexual masculinity and the discursive reproduction of homophobia. In A. Coyle & C. Kitzinger, Celia (Eds.), *Lesbian and gay psychology: New perspectives* (pp. 219–238). Malden, MA: Blackwell.

Brendl, C. M., Chattopadhyay, A., Pelham, B. W., & Carvallo, M. (2005). Name letter branding: Valence transfers when product specific needs are active. *Journal of Consumer Research, 32,* 405–415.

Brendl, C. M., Markman, A. B., & Messner, C. (2001). How do indirect measures of evaluation work? Evaluating the inference of prejudice in the Implicit Association Test. *Journal of Personality and Social Psychology, 81,* 760–773.

Brennan, K. A., Clark, C. L., & Shaver, P. R. (1998). Self-report measurement of adult attachment: An integrative overview. In J. A. Simpson & W. S. Rholes (Eds.), *Attachment theory and close relationships* (pp. 46–76). New York: Guilford.

Brewer, G., & Riley, C. (2009). Height, relationship satisfaction, jealousy, and mate retention. *Evolutionary Psychology, 7,* 477–489.

Brewer, M. B. (2004). Taking the social origins of human nature seriously: Toward a more imperialist social psychology. *Personality and Social Psychology Review, 8,* 107–113.

Brewer, M. B., & Kramer, R. K. (1986). Choice behavior in social dilemmas: Effects of social identity, group size, and decision framing. *Journal of Personality and Social Psychology, 50,* 543–549.

Brewer, M. B., & Lui, L. (1984). Categorization of the elderly by the elderly: Effects of perceiver's category membership. *Personality and Social Psychology Bulletin, 10,* 585–595.

Brickman, P. (1987). *Commitment, conflict, and caring.* Englewood Cliffs, NJ: Prentice-Hall.

Brigham, J. C. (2006). The jury system in the United States of America. In M. F. Kaplan & A. M. Martin (Eds.), *Understanding world jury systems: Through social psychological research* (pp. 11–29). New York: Psychology Press.

Brigham, J. C., Bennett, L. B., Meissner, C. A., & Mitchell, T. L. (2007). The influence of race on eyewitness memory. In R. Lindsay, D. Ross, J. Read, & M. Toglia (Eds.), *Handbook of eyewitness psychology: Memory for people* (pp. 257–281). Mahwah, NJ: Lawrence Erlbaum Associates.

Briley, D. A., Shrum, L. J., & Wyer, Jr., R. S. (2007). Subjective impressions of minority group representation in the media: A comparison of majority and minority viewers' judgments and underlying processes. *Journal of Consumer Psychology, 17,* 36–48.

Briñol, P., Gandarillas, B., Horcajo, J., & Becerra, A. (2010). Emotion and meta-cognition: Implications for attitude change. *Revista de Psicologia Social, 25,* 157–183.

Briñol, P., & Petty, R. E. (2003). Overt head movements and persuasion: A self-validation analysis. *Journal of Personality and Social Psychology, 84,* 1123–1139.

Bristow, D. N., & Sebastian, R. J. (2001). Holy cow! Wait til next year! A closer look at the brand loyalty of Chicago Cubs baseball fans. *Journal of Consumer Marketing, 18,* 256–275.

Brody, L. R. (1999). *Gender, emotion, and the family.* Cambridge, MA: Harvard University Press.

Brody, L. R., & Hall, J. A. (1993). Gender and emotion. In M. Lewis & J. M. Haviland (Eds.), *Handbook of emotions* (pp. 447–460). New York: Guilford.

Brooks, M. L., Swann, W. B. Jr., & Mehta, P. H. (2011). Reasserting the self: Blocking self-verifying behavior triggers compensatory self-verification. *Self and Identity, 10,* 77–84.

Brown, C. M., & McConnell, A. R. (2009). When

chronic isn't chronic: The moderating role of active self-aspects. *Personality and Social Psychology Bulletin, 35,* 3–15.

Brown, D. (2003). Pornography and erotica. In J. Bryant & D. Roskos-Ewoldsen (Eds.), *Communication and emotion: Essays in honor of Dolf Zillmann. LEA's communication series* (pp. 221–253). Mahwah, NJ: Lawrence Erlbaum.

Brown, J. D. (1993). Motivational conflict and the self: The double-bind of low self-esteem. In R. F. Baumeister (Ed.), *Self-esteem: The puzzle of low self-regard* (pp. 117–130). New York: Plenum.

Brown, J. D., & Dutton, K. A. (1995). The thrill of victory, the complexity of defeat: Self-esteem and people's emotional reactions to success and failure. *Journal of Personality and Social Psychology, 68,* 712–722.

Brown, J. D., Novick, N. J., Lord, K. A., & Richards, J. M. (1992). When Gulliver travels: Social context, psychological closeness, and self-appraisals. *Journal of Personality and Social Psychology, 62,* 717–727.

Brown, K. T., Brown, T. N., Jackson, J. S., Sellers, R. M., & Manuel, W. J. (2003). Teammates on and off the field? White student athletes. *Journal of Applied Social Psychology, 33,* 1379–1403.

Brown, L. H., Silvia, P. J., Myin-Germeys, I., & Kwapil, T. R. (2007). When the need to belong goes wrong: The expression of social anhedonia and social anxiety in daily life. *Psychological Science, 18,* 778–782.

Brown, R., Eller, A., Leeds, S., & Stace, K. (2007). Intergroup contact and intergroup attitudes: A longitudinal study. *European Journal of Social Psychology, 37,* 692–703.

Brown, R., Maras, P., Masser, B., Vivian, J., & Hewstone, M. (2001). Life on the ocean wave: Testing some intergroup hypotheses in a naturalistic setting. *Group Processes and Intergroup Relations, 4,* 81–97.

Brown, W. M., & Moore, C. (2000). Is prospective altruist-detection an evolved solution to the adaptive problem of subtle cheating in cooperative ventures? Supportive evidence using the Wason selection task. *Evolution and Human Behavior, 21,* 25–37.

Brownstein, A. L., Read, S. J., & Simon, D. (2004). Bias at the racetrack: Effects of individual expertise and task importance on predecision reevaluation of alternatives. *Personality and Social Psychology Bulletin, 30,* 891–904.

Bruins, J. J., Liebrand, W. P., & Wilke, H. A. (1989). About the saliency of fear and greed in social dilemmas. *European Journal of Social Psychology, 19,* 155–162.

Brumbaugh, C. C., Fraley, R. C. (2010). Adult attachment and dating strategies: How do insecure people attract mates? *Personal Relationships, 17,* 599–614.

Brummert-Lennings, H. I., & Warburton, W. A. (2011). The effect of auditory versus violent media exposure on aggressive behavior: The role of song lyrics, video clips and musical tone. *Journal of Experimental Social Psychology, 47,* 794–799.

Brunell, A. B., Pilkington, C. J., & Webster, G. D. (2007). Perceptions of risk in intimacy in dating couples: Conversation and relationship quality. *Journal of Social & Clinical Psychology, 26,* 92–119.

Bruner, J. S., Goodnow, J. J., & Austin, G. A. (1956). *A study of thinking.* New York: Wiley.

Bruner, J. S., & Taguiri, R. (1954). Person perception. In G. Lindzey (Ed.), *Handbook of social psychology* (Vol. 2, pp. 634–654). Reading, MA: Addison-Wesley.

Brunet, P. M., & Schmidt, L. A. (2007). Is shyness context specific? Relation between shyness and online self-disclosure with and without a live webcam in young adults. *Journal of Research in Personality, 41,* 938–945.

Brus, M. (May 21, 1998). My friend Steve Glass, the conartist. *The Daily Pennsylvanian.* http://www.dailypennsylvanian.com

Bryan, A. D., Webster, G. D., & Manaffiey, A. L. (2011). The big, the rich and the powerful: Physical, financial, and social dimensions of dominance in mating and attraction. *Personality and Social Psychology Bulletin, 37,* 363–382.

Bryan, J. H., & Test, N. A. (1967). Models and helping: Naturalistic studies in aiding behavior. *Journal of Personality and Social Psychology, 6,* 400–407.

Bryant, F. B., & Guilbault, R. L. (2002). "I knew it all along" eventually: The development of hindsight in reaction to the Clinton impeachment verdict. *Basic & Applied Social Psychology, 24,* 27–41.

Bryson, J. B. (1977). Situational determinants of the expression of jealousy. In H. Sigall (Chair), *Sexual jealousy.* Symposium presented at the annual meeting of the American Psychological Association, San Francisco.

Bryson, J. B. (1991). Modes of response to jealousy-evoking situations. In P. Salovey (Ed.), *The psychology of jealousy and envy* (pp. 178–207). New York: Guilford Press.

Buck, R. (1977). Nonverbal communication of affect in preschool children: Relationships with personality and skin conductance. *Journal of Personality and Social Psychology, 35,* 225–236.

Buckley, K. E., Winkel, R. E., & Leary, M. R. (2004). Reactions to acceptance and rejection: Effects of level and sequence of relational evaluation. *Journal of Experimental Social Psychology, 40,* 14–28.

Buehler, R., & Griffin, D. (1994). Change of meaning effects in conformity and dissent: Observing construal processes over time. *Journal of Personality and Psychology, 67,* 984–996.

Bugental, D. (2000). Acquisition of the algorithms of social life: A domain-based approach. *Psychological Bulletin, 126,* 187–219.

Buhrmester, Michael D; Blanton, Hart; Swann, William B Jr. (2011). Implicit self-esteem: Nature, measurement, and a new way forward. *Journal of Personality and Social Psychology, 100,* 365–385.

Bui, K.-V. T., Peplau, L. A., & Hill, C. T. (1996). Testing the Rusbult model of relationship commitment and stability in a 15-year study of heterosexual couples. *Personality and Social Psychology Bulletin, 22,* 1244–1257.

Bullough, V. L. (1976). *Sexual variance in society and history.* Chicago: University of Chicago Press.

Burbank, V. K. (1987). Female aggression in cross-cultural perspective. *Behavior Science Research, 21,* 70–100.

Burger, J. M. (1981). Motivational biases in the attribution of responsibility for an accident: A meta-analysis of the defensive-attribution hypothesis. *Psychological Bulletin, 90,* 496–512.

Burger, J. M. (1986). Increasing compliance by improving the deal: The that's-not-all technique. *Journal of Personality and Social Psychology, 51,* 277–283.

Burger, J. M. (1987). Desire for control and conformity to a perceived norm. *Journal of Personality and Social Psychology, 53,* 355–360.

Burger, J. M. (1999). The foot-in-the-door compliance procedure: A multiple-process analysis and review. *Personality and Social Psychology Bulletin, 3,* 303–325.

Burger, J. M. (2009). Replicating Milgram: Would people still obey today? *American Psychologist, 64, 1–11.*

Burger, J. M., & Caldwell, D. F. (2003). The effects of monetary incentives and labeling on the foot-in-the-door effect: Evidence for a self-perception process. *Basic and Applied Social Psychology, 25,* 235–241.

Burgess, E. W. (1926). The romantic impulse and family disorganization. *Survey, 57,* 290–294.

Burke, P. J., Stets, J. E., & Cerven, C. (2007). Gender, legitimation, and identity verification in groups. *Social Psychology Quarterly, 70,* 27–42.

Burnstein, R. (2005). Texas becomes newest "majority-minority" state, Census Bureau announces. Retrieved from http://www.census.gov/newsroom/releases/archives/population/cb05-118.html

Burris, C. T., & Rempel, J. K. (2004). "It's the end of the world as we know it": Threat and the spatial-symbolic self. *Journal of Personality and Social Psychology, 86,* 19–42.

Burriss, R. P., Roberts, S. C., Welling, L. L. M., Puts, D. A., & Little, A. C. (2011). Heterosexual romantic couple mate assortatively for facial symmetry, but not masculinity. *Personality and Social Psychology Bulletin, 37,* 601–013.

Burt, M. (1980). Cultural myths and supports for rape. *Journal of Personality and Social Psychology, 38,* 217–230.

Busch, A. L., & Rosenberg, M. S. (2004). Comparing women and men arrested for domestic violence: A preliminary report. *Journal of Family Violence, 19,* 49–57.

Bushman, B. J. (1996). Individual differences in the extent and development of aggressive cognitive-associative networks. *Personality and Social Psychology Bulletin, 22,* 811–819.

Bushman, B. J. (2002). Does venting anger feed or extinguish the flame? Catharsis, rumination, distraction, anger, and aggressive responding. *Personality and Social Psychology Bulletin, 28,* 724–731.

Bushman, B. J., & Anderson, C. A. (2001). Is it time to pull the plug on the hostile versus instrumental aggression dichotomy? *Psychological Review, 108,* 273–279.

Bushman, B. J., & Baumeister, R. F., (2002). Does self-love or self-hate lead to violence? *Journal of Research in Personality, 36,* 543–545.

Bushman, B. J., Bonacci, A. M., Pedersen, W. C., Vasquez, E. A., & Miller, N. (2005). Chewing on it can chew you up: Effects of rumination on triggered displaced aggression. *Journal of Personality and Social Psychology, 88,* 969–983.

Bushman, B. J., & Geen, R. G. (1990). Role of cognitive-emotional mediators and individual differences in the effects of media violence on aggression. *Journal of Personality and Social Psychology, 58,* 156–163.

Bushman, B. J., & Huesmann, L. R. (2001). Effects of televised violence on aggression. In D. Singer & J. Singer (Eds.), *Handbook of children and the media* (pp. 223–254). Thousand Oaks, CA: Sage.

Bushman, B. J., Wang, M. C., & Anderson, C. A. (2005). Is the curve relating temperature to aggression linear or curvilinear? Assaults and temperature in Minneapolis reexamined. *Journal of Personality and Social Psychology, 89,* 62–66.

Buss, A. H. (1966). Instrumentality of aggression, feedback, and frustration as determinants of physical aggression. *Journal of Personality and Social Psychology, 3,* 153–162.

Buss, A. H. (1980). *Self-consciousness and social anxiety.* San Francisco: W. H. Freeman.

Buss, D. M. (1989). Sex differences in human mate preferences: Evolutionary hypotheses tested in 37 cultures. *Behavioral and Brain Sciences, 12,* 1–49.

Buss, D. M. (1995). Evolutionary psychology: A new paradigm for psychological science. *Psychological Inquiry, 6,* 1–30.

Buss, D. M. (2004). *Evolutionary psychology: The new science of the mind* (2nd ed.). Boston: Allyn and Bacon.

Buss, D. M., & Duntley, J. D. (2003). Homicide: An evolutionary psychological perspective and implications for public policy. In R. W. Bloom & N. Dess (Eds.), *Evolutionary psychology and violence: A primer for policymakers and public policy advocates* (pp. 115–128). Westport, CT: Praeger.

Buss, D. M., & Kenrick, D. T. (1998). Evolutionary social psychology. In D. T. Gilbert, S. T. Fiske, & G. Lindzey (Eds.), *The handbook of social psychology* (Vol. II, pp. 982–1026). Boston, MA: McGraw-Hill.

Buss, D. M., & Shackelford, T. K. (1997). Human aggression in evolutionary psychological perspective. *Clinical Psychology Review,* *17,* 605–619.

Buss, D. M., & Shackelford, T. K., Choe, J., Buunk, B. P., & Dijkstra, P. (2000). Distress about mating rivals. *Personal Relationships, 7,* 235–243.

Butterworth, G. (1992). Origins of self-perception in infancy. *Psychological Inquiry, 3,* 103–111.

Buunk, A. P., Groothof, H. A. K., & Siero, F. W. (2007). Social comparison and satisfaction with one's social life. *Journal of Social and Personal Relationships, 24,* 197–205.

Buunk, B. J., Angleitner, A., Oubaid, V., & Buss, D. M. (1996). Sex differences in jealousy in evolutionary and cultural perspective: Tests from the Netherlands, Germany, and the United States. *Psychological Science, 7,* 359–363.

Buunk, B. J., & Bringle, R. G. (1987). Jealousy in love relationships. In D. Perlman & S. Duck (Eds.), *Intimate relationships: Development, dynamics, and deterioration* (pp. 123–147). Newbury Park, CA: Sage.

Buunk, B. J., & van der Laan, V. (2002). Do women need female role models? Subjective social status and the effects of same-sex and opposite-sex comparisons. *Revue Internationale de Psychologie Sociale, 15,* 129–155.

Buunk, B. P., & Dijkstra, P. (2001). Evidence from a homosexual sample for a sex-specific rival-oriented mechanism: Jealousy as a function of a rival's physical attractiveness and dominance. *Personal Relationships, 8,* 391–406.

Buvinic, M. L., & Berkowitz, L. (1976). Delayed effects of practiced versus unpracticed responses after observation of movie violence. *Journal of Experimental Social Psychology, 12,* 283–293.

Byrne, D. (1997). An overview (and underview) of research and theory within the attraction paradigm. *Journal of Social and Personal Relationships, 14,* 417–431.

Byrne, D., Gouaux, C., Griffitt, W., Lamberth, J., Murakawa, N., Prasad, M. B., & Ramirez, M. III. (1971). The ubiquitous relationship: Attitude similarity and attraction. A cross-cultural study. *Human Relations, 24,* 201–207.

Byrne, D., & Nelson, D. (1965). Attraction as a linear function of proportion of positive reinforcements. *Journal of Personality and Social Psychology, 1,* 659–663.

Cacioppo, J. T. (2004). Common sense, intuition, and theory in personality and social psychology. *Personality and Social Psychology Review, 8,* 114–122.

Cacioppo, J. T., Amaral, D. G., Blanchard, J. J., Cameron, J. L., Carter, C. S., Crews, D., Fiske, S., Heatherton, T., Johnson, M. K., Kozak, M. J., Levenson, R. W., Lord, C., Miller, E. K., Ochsner, K., Raichle, M. E., Shea, M. T., Taylor, S. E., Young, L. J., & Quinn, K. J. (2007). Social neuroscience: Progress and implications for mental health. *Perspectives on Psychological Science, 2,* 99–123.

Cacioppo, J. T., & Berntson, G. C. (2001). The affect system and racial prejudice. In J. A. Bargh & D. K. Apsley (Eds.), *Unraveling the complexities of social life: A festschrift in honor of Robert B. Zajonc* (pp. 95–110). Washington, DC: American Psychological Association.

Cacioppo, J. T., Fowler, J. H., & Christakis, N. A. (2009). Alone in the crowd: The structure and spread of loneliness in a large social network. *Journal of Personality and Social Psychology, 97,* 977–991.

Cacioppo, J. T., Hawkley, L. C., & Bernston, G. G. (2003). The anatomy of loneliness. *Current Directions in Psychological Science, 12,* 71–74.

Cacioppo, J. T., Lorig, T. S., Nusbaum, H. C., & Bernston, G. G. (2004). Social neuroscience: Bridging social and biological systems. In C. Sansone, C. C. Morf, & A. T. Panter (Eds.), *Handbook of methods in social psychology* (pp. 383–404). Thousand Oaks, CA: Sage.

Cacioppo, J. T., Marshall-Goodell, B. S., Tassinary, L. G., & Petty, R. E. (1992). Rudimentary determinants of attitudes: Classical conditioning is more

effective when prior knowledge about the attitude stimulus is low than high. *Journal of Experimental Social Psychology, 28,* 207–233.

Cacioppo, J. T., & Petty, R. E. (1982). The need for cognition. *Journal of Personality and Social Psychology, 42,* 116–131.

Cacioppo, J. T., & Petty, R. E. (1989). Effects of message repetition on argument processing, recall, and persuasion. *Basic and Applied Social Psychology, 10,* 3–12.

Cacioppo, J. T., Petty, R. E., Feinstein, J. A., & Jarvis, W. B. G. (1996). Dispositional differences in cognitive motivation: The life and times of individuals varying in need for cognition. *Psychological Bulletin, 119,* 197–253.

Cacioppo, J. T., Petty, R. E., Kao, C. F., & Rodriguez, R. (1986). Central and peripheral routes to persuasion: An individual differences perspective. *Journal of Personality and Social Psychology, 51,* 1032–1043.

Cacioppo, J. T., Priester, J. R., & Berntson, G. G. (1993). Rudimentary determinants of attitudes II: Arm flexion and extension have differential effects on attitudes. *Journal of Personality and Social Psychology, 65,* 5–17.

Calhoun, L. G., Cann, A., Tedeschi, R. G., & McMillan, J. (2000). A correlational test of the relationship between posttraumatic growth, religion, and cognitive processing. *Journal of Traumatic Stress, 13,* 521–527.

Callan, M. J., Ellard, J. H., & Nicol, J. E. (2006). The belief in a just world and immanent justice reasoning in adults. *Personality and Social Psychology Bulletin, 32,* 1645–1658.

Cameron, C. A., & Stritzke, W. G. K. (2003). Alcohol and acquaintance rape in Australia: Testing the presupposition model of attributions about responsibility and blame. *Journal of Applied Social Psychology, 33,* 983–1008.

Cameron, J. J., Ross, M., & Holmes, J. G. (2002). Loving the one you hurt: Positive effects of recounting a transgression against an intimate partner. *Journal of Experimental Social Psychology, 38,* 307–314.

Campbell, A. (1999). Staying alive: Evolution, culture, and women's intrasexual aggression. *Behavioral and Brain Sciences, 22,* 203–252.

Campbell, A., Muncer, S., Guy, A., & Banim, M. (1996). Social representations of aggression: Crossing the sex barrier. *European Journal of Social Psychology, 26,* 135–147.

Campbell, A., Muncer, S., & Odber, J. (1997a). Aggression and testosterone: Testing a bio-social model. *Aggressive Behavior, 23,* 229–238.

Campbell, A., Sapochnik, M., & Muncer, S. (1997b). Sex differences in aggression: Does social representation mediate form of aggression? *British Journal of Social Psychology, 36,* 161–171.

Campbell, J. B., & Hawley, C. W. (1982). Study habits and Eysenck's theory of extraversion-introversion. *Journal of Research in Personality, 16,* 139–146.

Campbell, J. D., & Fairey, P. J. (1989). Informational and normative routes to conformity: The effect of faction size as a function of norm extremity and attention to the stimulus. *Journal of Personality and Social Psychology, 57,* 457–468.

Campbell, W. K., & Baumeister, R. F. (2001). Is loving the self necessary for loving another? An examination of identity and intimacy? In M. Clark & G. Fletcher (Eds.), *The Blackwell handbook of social psychology: Vol. 2. Interpersonal processes* (pp. 437–456). London: Blackwell.

Campbell, W. K., Bonacci, A. M., Shelton, J., Exline, J. J., & Bushman, B. J. (2004). Psychological entitlement: Interpersonal consequences and validation of a new self-report measure. *Journal of Personality Assessment, 83,* 29–45.

Campbell, W. K., Bosson, J. K., Goheen, T. W., Lakey, C. E., & Kernis, M. H. (2007). Do narcissists dislike themselves "deep down inside?" *Psychological Science, 18,* 227–229.

Campbell, W. K., Foster, C. A., & Finkel, E. J. (2002). Does self-love lead to love for others? A story of

narcissistic game playing. *Journal of Personality and Social Psychology, 83,* 340–354.

Campbell, W. K., & Sedikides, C. (1999). Self-threat magnifies the self-serving bias: A meta-analytic integration. *Review of General Psychology, 3,* 23–43.

Campos, B., Keltner, D., Beck, J. M., Gonzaga, G. C., & John, O. P. (2007). Culture and teasing: The relational benefits of reduced desire for positive self-differentiation. *Personality and Social Psychology Bulletin, 33,* 3–16.

Canli, T., Zhao, Z., Desmond, J. E., Kang, E., Gross, J., & Gabrieli, J. D. E. (2001). An fMRI study of personality influences on brain reactivity to emotional stimuli. *Behavioral neuroscience, 115,* 33–42.

Cantor, J. R., & Venus, P. (1983). The effect of humor on recall of a radio advertisement. *Journal of Broadcasting, 24,* 13–22.

Caporael, L. R. (2001). Parts and whole: The evolutionary importance of groups. In C. Sedikides & M. B. Brewer (Eds.), *Individual self, relational self, collective self* (pp. 241–258). Philadelphia: Psychology Press.

Cappe, R. F., & Alden, L. E. (1986). A comparison of treatment strategies for clients functionally impaired by extreme shyness and social avoidance. *Journal of Consulting and Clinical Psychology, 54,* 796–801.

Caprara, G. V., Barbaranelli, C., & Zimbardo, P. G. (1996). Understanding the complexity of human aggression: Affective, cognitive, and social dimensions of individual differences in propensity toward aggression. *European Journal of Personality, 10,* 133–155.

Caprara, G. V., Perugini, M., & Barbaranelli, C. (1994). Studies of individual differences in aggression. In M. Potegal & J. F. Knutson (Eds.), *The dynamics of aggression: Biological and social processes in dyads and groups* (pp. 123–153). Hillsdale, NJ: Erlbaum.

Carey, K. B, Borsari, B., Carey, M. P., & Maisto, S. A. (2006). Patterns and importance of self-other differences in college drinking norms. *Psychology of Addictive Behaviors, 20,* 385–393.

Carli, L. L. (1990). Gender, language, and influence. *Journal of Personality and Social Psychology, 59,* 941–951.

Carli, L. L. (1999). Cognitive reconstruction, hindsight, and reactions to victims and perpetrators. *Personality and Social Psychology Bulletin, 25,* 966–979.

Carli, L. L., Ganley, R., & Pierce-Otay, A. (1991). Similarity and satisfaction in roommate relationships. *Personality and Social Psychology Bulletin, 17,* 419–426.

Carli, L. L., LaFleur, S. J., & Loeber, C. C. (1995). Nonverbal behavior, gender, and influence. *Journal of Personality and Social Psychology, 68,* 1030–1041.

Carlsmith, J. M., & Anderson, C. A. (1979). Ambient temperature and the occurrence of collective violence: A new analysis. *Journal of Personality and Social Psychology, 37,* 337–344.

Carlson, M., Charlin, V., & Miller, N. (1988). Positive mood and helping behavior: A test of six hypotheses. *Journal of Personality and Social Psychology, 55,* 211–299.

Carlson, M., Marcus-Newhall, A., & Miller, N. (1990). The effects of situational aggressive cues: A quantitative review. *Journal of Personality and Social Psychology, 58,* 622–633.

Carlson, M., & Miller, N. (1987). Explanation of the relation between negative mood and helping. *Psychological Bulletin, 102,* 91–108.

Carlson, N. R. (2004). *Physiology of behavior.* Boston: Allyn & Bacon.

Carnagey, N. L., Anderson, C. A., & Bushman, B. J. (2007). The effect of video game violence on physiological desensitization to real-life violence. *Journal of Experimental Social Psychology, 43,* 489–496.

Carretie, L., Hinojosa, J. A., & Mercado, F. (2003). Cerebral patterns of attentional habituation to emotional visual stimuli. *Psychophysiology, 40,* 381–388.

Carstensen, L. L. (1998). A life-span approach to social motivation. In J. Heckhausen & C. Dweck (Eds.), *Motivation and self-regulation across the life span* (pp. 341–364). New York: Cambridge University Press.

Carstensen, L. L., Isaacowitz, D., & Charles, S. T. (1999). Taking time seriously: A theory of socioemotional selectivity. *American Psychologist, 54,* 165–181.

Carter, P. L. (2003). "Black" cultural capital, status positioning, and schooling conflicts for low-income African American youth. *Social Problems, 50,* 136–155.

Cartwright, D. (1971). Risk taking by individuals and groups: An assessment of research employing choice dilemmas. *Journal of Personality and Social Psychology, 20,* 245–261.

Caruso, E., Epley, N., & Bazerman, M. (2004). *Leader of the packed: The costs and benefits of perspective taking in group endeavors.* Unpublished manuscript.

Carvallo, M., & Gabriel, S. (2006). No man is an island: The need to belong and dismissing avoidant attachment style. *Personality and Social Psychology Bulletin, 32,* 697–709.

Carver, C. S., & Scheier, M. F. (1981). *Attention and self-regulation: A control-theory approach to human behavior.* New York: Springer-Verlag.

Carver, C. S., & Scheier, M. F. (1998). *On the self-regulation of behavior.* Cambridge, UK: Cambridge University Press.

Case, K. A., Fishbein, H. D., Ritchey, P. N. (2008). Personality, prejudice and discrimination against women and homosexuals. *Current Research in Social Psychology, 14,* article ID 2.

Casey, R. J., & Ritter, J. M. (1996). How infant appearance informs: Child care providers' responses to babies varying in appearance of age and attractiveness. *Journal of Applied Developmental Psychology, 17,* 495–518.

Caspi, A., Harrington, H., Moffitt, T. E., Milne, B. J., & Poulton, R. (2006). Socially isolated children 20 years later: Risk of cardiovascular disease. *Archives of Pediatric and Adolescent Medicine, 160,* 805–811.

Casselden, P. A., & Hampson, S. E. (1990). Forming impressions from incongruent traits. *Journal of Personality and Social Psychology, 59,* 253–262.

Cast, A. D., Schweingruber, D., & Berns, N. (2006). Childhood physical punishment and problem solving in marriage. *Journal of Interpersonal Violence, 21,* 244–261.

Cast, A. D., Stets, J. E., & Burke, P. J. (1999). Does the self conform to the views of others? *Social Psychology Quarterly, 62,* 68–82.

Castano, E., & Giner-Sorolla, R. (2006). Not quite human: Infrahumanization in response to collective responsibility for intergroup killing. *Journal of Personality and Social Psychology, 90,* 804–818.

Castano, E., & Yzerbyt, V. Y. (1998). The highs and lows of group homogeneity. *Behavioural Processes, 42,* 219–238.

Castelli, L., & Carraro, L. (2010). Striving for difference: On the spontaneous preference for ingroup members who maximize ingroup positive distinctiveness. *European Journal of Social Psychology, 40,* 881–890.

Castelli, L., Tomelleri, S., & Zogmaister, C. (2008). Implicit ingroup metafavoritism: Subtle preference for ingroup members displaying ingroup bias. *Personality and Social Psychology Bulletin, 34,* 807–818.

Castro, V. S. (2003). *Acculturation and psychological adaptation.* Westport, CT: Greenwood Press.

Catalano, R., Dooley, D., Novaco, R. W., Wilson, G., & Hough, R. (1993). Using ECA survey data to examine the effect of job layoffs on violent behavior. *Hospital and Community Psychiatry, 44,* 874–879.

Ceci, S. J., & Bruck, M. (1993). Suggestibility of the child witness: A historical review and synthesis.

Psychological Bulletin, 113, 403–439.

Cecil, H., Evans, R. I., & Stanley, M. A. (1996). Perceived believability among adolescents of health warning labels on cigarette packs. *Journal of Applied Social Psychology, 26,* 502–519.

Celuch, K., & Slama, M. (1995). "Getting along" and "getting ahead" as motives for self-presentation: Their impact on advertising effectiveness. *Journal of Applied Social Psychology, 25,* 1700–1713.

Centers for Disease Control and Prevention, National Center for Injury Prevention and Control. Web-based Injury Statistics Query and Reporting System (WISQARS) [online]. (2006) [cited 2006 Feb 8]. Available from: URL: www.cdc.gov/ncipc/wisqars.

Cesario, J., Plaks, J. E., & Higgins, E. T. (2006). Automatic social behavior as motivated preparation to interact. *Journal of Personality and Social Psychology, 90,* 893–910.

Chaiken, S. (1979). Communicator physical attractiveness and persuasion. *Journal of Personality and Social Psychology, 37,* 1387–1397.

Chaiken, S. (1980). Heuristic versus systematic information processing and the use of source versus message cues in persuasion. *Journal of Personality and Social Psychology, 39,* 752–766.

Chaiken, S. (1987). The heuristic model of persuasion. In M. P. Zanna, J. M. Olson, & C. P. Herman (Eds.), *Social influence: The Ontario symposium* (Vol. 5, pp. 3–39). Hillsdale, NJ: Erlbaum.

Chaiken, S., & Baldwin, M. W. (1981). Affective-cognitive consistency and the effect of salient behavioral information on the self-perception of attitudes. *Journal of Personality and Social Psychology, 41,* 1–12.

Chaiken, S., Pomerantz, E. M., & Giner-Sorolla, R. (1995). Structural consistency and attitude strength. In R. E. Petty & J. A. Krosnick (Eds.), *Attitude strength: Antecedents and consequences* (pp. 387–412). Mahwah, NJ: Erlbaum.

Chaiken, S., & Trope, Y. (Eds.) (1999). *Dual-process theories in social psychology.* New York: Guilford.

Chambon, M., Droit-Volet, S., & Niedenthal, P. M. (2008). The effect of embodying the elderly on time perception. *Journal of Experimental Social Psychology, 44,* 672–678.

Chang, L., Hau, K. T., & Guo, A. M. (2001). The effect of self-consciousness on the expression of gender views. *Journal of Applied Social Psychology, 31,* 340–351.

Chapdelaine, A., Kenny, D. A., & LaFontana, K. M. (1994). Matchmaker, matchmaker, can you make me a match? Predicting liking between two unacquainted persons. *Journal of Personality and Social Psychology, 67,* 83–91.

Chapleau, K. M., Oswald, D. L., & Russell, B. L. (2007). How ambivalent sexism toward women and men support rape myth acceptance. *Sex Roles, 57,* 131–136.

Chapleau, K. M., Oswald, D. L., & Russell, B. L. (2008). Male Rape Myths: The role of gender, violence, and sexism. *Journal of Interpersonal Violence, 23*(5), 600–615.

Chapman, G. B., & Johnson, E. J. (1999). Anchoring, activation and the construction of value. *Organizational Behavior and Human Decision Processes, 79,* 120–138.

Chapman, G. B., & Johnson, E. J. (2002). Incorporating the irrelevant: Anchors in judgments of belief and value. In T. Gilovich, D. Griffin, & D. Kahneman (Eds.), *Heuristic and biases: The psychology of intuitive judgment* (pp. 617–624). New York: Cambridge University Press.

Chapman, J. (2006). Anxiety and defective decision making: An elaboration of the groupthink model. *Management Decision, 44,* 1391–1404.

Chappell, K. D., & Davis, K. E., (1998). Attachment partner choice and partner perception: An experimental test of the attachment-security hypothesis. *Personal Relationships, 5,* 327–342.

Chartrand, T. L., & Bargh, J. A. (1999). The chameleon

effect: The perception-behavior link and social interaction. *Journal of Personality and Social Psychology, 76,* 893–910.

Chartrand, T. L., Cheng, C. M., & Jefferis, V. E. (2002). You're just a chameleon: The automatic nature and social significance of mimicry. In M. Jarymowicz & R. K. Ohme (Eds.), *Natura automatyzmow (Nature of automaticity)* (pp. 19–24). Warszawa: IPPAN & SWPS.

Chartrand, T. L., Maddux, W. W. & Lakin, J. L. (2005). Beyond the Perception-Behavior Link: The Ubiquitous Utility and Motivational Moderators of Nonconscious Mimicry. In R. R. Hassin, J. S. Uleman, & J. A. Bargh (Eds.). (2005). *The new unconscious* (pp. 334–361). New York: Oxford University Press.

Chartrand, T. L., Pinckert, S., & Burger, J. M. (1999). When manipulation backfires: The effects of time delay and requester on the foot-in-the-door technique. *Journal of Applied Social Psychology, 29,* 211–221.

Chatzisarantis, N. L. D., & Hagger, M. S. (2007). Mindfulness and the intention-behavior relationship within the theory of planned behavior. *Personality and Social Psychology Bulletin, 33,* 663–676.

Chelune, G. J. (1976). Reactions to male and female disclosure at two levels. *Journal of Personality and Social Psychology, 34,* 1000–1003.

Chen, C-K., Gustafson, D. H., & Lee, Y-D. (2002). The effect of a quantitative decision aid—Analytic Hierarchy Process—on group polarization. *Group Decision and Negotiation, 11,* 329–344.

Chen, F. F., & Kenrick, D. T. (2002). Repulsion or attraction? Group membership and assumed attitude similarity. *Journal of Personality and Social Psychology, 83,* 111–125.

Chen, G. (1995). Differences in self-disclosure patterns among Americans versus Chinese. *Journal of Cross-Cultural Psychology, 26,* 84–91.

Chen, H., Yates, B. T., & McGinnies, E. (1988). Effects of involvement on observers' estimates of consensus, distinctiveness, and consistency. *Personality and Social Psychology Bulletin, 14,* 468–478.

Chen, N. Y., Shaffer, D. R., & Wu, C. (1997). On physical attractiveness stereotyping in Taiwan: A revised sociocultural perspective. *Journal of Social Psychology, 137,* 117–124.

Chen, S. (2001). The role of theories in mental representations and their use in social perception: A theory-based approach to significant-other representations and transference. In G. B. Moskowitz (Ed), *Cognitive social psychology: The Princeton symposium on the legacy and future of social cognition* (pp. 125–142). Mahwah, NJ: Erlbaum.

Chen, S., Boucher, H. C., & Tapias, M. P. (2006). The relational self revealed: Integrative conceptualization and implications for interpersonal life. *Psychological Bulletin, 132,* 151–179.

Chen, S. C. (1937). Social modification of the activity of ants in nest-building. *Physiological Zoology, 10,* 420–436.

Chen, X. P., Wasti, S. A., & Triandis, H. C. (2007). When does group norm or group identity predict cooperation in a public goods dilemma? The moderating effects of idiocentrism and allocentrism. *International Journal of Intercultural Relations, 31,* 259–276.

Chen, Y., Wang, Q., & Xie, J. (2011). Online social interactions: A natural experiment on word of mouth versus observational learning. *Journal of Marketing Research, 48,* 238–254.

Cheung, B. Y., Chudek, M., & Heine, S. J. (2011). Evidence for a sensitive period for acculturation: Younger immigrants report acculturating at a faster rate. *Psychological Science, 22,* 147–152.

Chiou, W. B. (2006). Adolescents' sexual self-disclosure on the Internet: Deindividuation and impression management. *Adolescence, 41,* 547–561.

Chiroro, P., Bohner, G., Viki, G. T., & Jarvis, C. I. (2004). Rape myth acceptance and rape proclivity: Expected dominance versus expected arousal as mediators in acquaintance-rape situations. *Journal of Interpersonal Violence, 19.*

Chiu, C., Hong, Y., & Dweck, C. S. (1997). Lay dispositionism and implicit theories of personality. *Journal of Personality and Social Psychology, 73,* 19–30.

Chiu, C. Morris, M. W., Hong, Y., & Menon, T. (2000). Motivated cultural cognition: The impact of implicit cultural theories on disposition attribution varies as a function of need for closure. *Journal of Personality and Social Psychology, 78,* 247–259.

Chiu, C. & Hong, Y. (2005). Cultural competence: Dynamic processes. In A. Elliot & C. S. Dweck (eds.), *Handbook of motivation and competence* (pp. 489–505). New York: Guilford.

Chiu, R. K., & Babcock, R. D. (2002). The relative importance of facial attractiveness and gender in Hong Kong selection decisions. *The International Journal of Human Resources Management, 13,* 141–155.

Choi, I., & Nisbett, R. E. (1998). Situational salience and cultural differences in the correspondence bias and in the actor-observer bias. *Personality and Social Psychology Bulletin, 24,* 949–960.

Choi, I., & Nisbett, R. E. (2000). Cultural psychology of surprise: Holistic theories and recognition of contradiction. *Journal of Personality and Social Psychology, 79,* 890–905.

Choi, I., Nisbett, R. E., & Norenzayan, A. (1999). Causal attribution across cultures: Variation and universality. *Psychological Bulletin, 125,* 47–63.

Chrisler, J. C. (2003). Ageism: The equal opportunity oppression. *Psychology of Women Quarterly, 27,* 187–188.

Christ, O., Hewstone, M., Tausch, N., Wagner, U., Voci, A., Hughes, J., & Cairns, E. (2010). Contact effects: Cross-sectional and longitudinal impact on outgroup attitudes, behavioral intentions, and attitude certainty. *Personality and Social Psychology Bulletin, 36,* 1662–1674.

Christensen, L. (1988). Deception in psychological research: When is its use justified? *Personality and Social Psychology Bulletin, 14,* 664–675.

Christensen, P. N., & Kashy, D. A. (1998). Perceptions of and by lonely people in initial social interaction. *Personality and Social Psychology Bulletin, 24,* 322–329.

Christensen, P. N., Rothberger, H., Wood, W., & Matz, D. C. (2004). Social norms and identity relevance: A motivational approach to normative behavior. *Personality and Social Psychology Bulletin, 30,* 1295–1309.

Christopher, A. N., Morgan, R. D., Marek, P., Keller, M., & Drummond, K. (2005). Materialism and self-presentational styles. *Personality and Individual Differences, 38,* 137–149.

Chua, H. F., Leu, J., & Nisbett, R. E. (2005). Culture and Diverging Views of Social Events. *Personality and Social Psychology Bulletin, 31,* 925–934.

Church, A. T., Ortiz, F. A., Katigbak, M. S., Avdeyeva, T. V., Emerson, A. M., Flores, J., & Reyes, J. I. (2003). Measuring individual and cultural differences in implicit trait theories. *Journal of Personality and Social Psychology, 85,* 332–347.

Cialdini, R. B., Borden, R. J., Thorne, A., Walker, M. R., Freeman, S., & Sloan, L. R. (1976). Basking in reflected glory: Three (football) field studies. *Journal of Personality and Social Psychology, 34,* 366–375.

Cialdini, R. B., Braver, S. L., & Lewis, S. K. (1974). Attributional bias and the easily persuaded other. *Journal of Personality and Social Psychology, 30,* 631–637.

Cialdini, R. B., Cacioppo, J. T., Bassett, R., & Miller, J. A. (1978). Low-ball procedure for producing compliance: Commitment then cost. *Journal of Personality and Social Psychology, 36,* 463–476.

Cialdini, R. B., & Goldstein, N. J. (2004). Social influence: Compliance and conformity. *Annual Review of Psychology, 55,* 591–621.

Cialdini, R. B., & Kenrick, D. T. (1976). Altruism as hedonism: A social development perspective on the relationship of negative mood state and helping. *Journal of Personality and Social Psychology, 34,* 907–914.

Cialdini, R. B., & Trost, M. R. (1998). Social influence: Social norms, conformity, and compliance. In D. T. Gilbert, S. T. Fiske, & G. Lindzey (Eds.), *The handbook of social psychology* (4th ed., Vol. 2, pp. 151–192). New York: McGraw-Hill.

Cialdini, R. B., Trost, M., & Newsom, J. (1995). Preference for consistency: The development of a valid measure and the discovery of surprising behavioral implications. *Journal of Personality and Social Psychology, 69,* 318–328.

Cialdini, R. B., Vincent, J. E., Lewis, S. K., Catalan, J., Wheeler, D., & Darby, B. L. (1975). Reciprocal concessions procedure for inducing compliance: The door-in-the-face technique. *Journal of Personality and Social Psychology, 31,* 206–215.

Cialdini, R. B., Wosinska, W., Barrett, D. W., Butner, J., & Gornik-Durose, M. (2001). The differential impact of two social influence principles on individual and collectivists in Poland and the United States. In W. Wosinska, R. B. Cialdini, D. W. Barrett, & J. Reykowski (Eds), *The practice of social influence in multiple cultures* (pp. 33–50). Mahwah, NJ: Erlbaum.

Ciarocco, N. J., Sommer, K. L., & Baumeister, R. F. (2001). Ostracism and ego depletion: The strains of silence. *Personality and Social Psychology Bulletin, 27,* 1156–1163.

Ciesla, J. A., Dickson, K. S., Anderson, N. L., & Neal, D. J. (2011). Negative repetitive thought and college drinking: Angry rumination, depressive rumination, co-rumination, and worry. *Cognitive Therapy and Research, 35,* 142–150.

Cini, M. A., Moreland, R. L., & Levine, J. M. (1993). Group staffing levels and responses to prospective and new group members. *Journal of Personality and Social Psychology, 65,* 723–734.

Clark, K. B., & Clark, M. (1947). Racial identification and preferences in Negro children. In T. M. Newcomb & T. L. Hartley (Eds.), *Readings in social psychology* (pp. 167–178). New York: Holt.

Clark, K. B., & Clark, M. P. (1939). The development of self and the emergence of racial identifications in Negro preschool children. *Journal of Social Psychology, 10,* 591–599.

Clark, M. S., & Mills, J. (2004). In H. T. Reis & C. E. Rusbult (Eds.), *Close relationships: Key readings (p*p. 245–256). Philadelphia, PA: Taylor & Francis.

Clark, R. D., III, & Word, L. E. (1972). Why don't bystanders help? Because of ambiguity? *Journal of Personality and Social Psychology, 24,* 392–400.

Clary, E. G., Snyder, M., Ridge, R. D., Miene, P. K., & Haugen, J. A. (1994). Matching messages to motives in persuasion: A functional approach to promoting volunteerism. *Journal of Applied Social Psychology, 24,* 1129–1149.

Clement-Guillotin, C., & Fontayne, P. (2011). Situational malleability of gender schema: The case of the competitive sport context. *Sex Roles, 64,* 426–439.

Clore, G. L., & Baldridge, B. (1968). Interpersonal attraction: The role of agreement and topic interest. *Journal of Personality and Social Psychology, 9,* 340–346.

Coan, J. A., Schaefer, H. S., & Davidson, R. J. (2006). Lending a hand: Social regulation of the neural response to threat. *Psychological Science, 17,* 1032–1039.

Cohen, D. (1996). Law, social policy, and violence: The impact of regional cultures. *Journal of Personality and Social Psychology, 70,* 961–978.

Cohen, D. (1998). Culture, social organization, and patterns of violence. *Journal of Personality and Social Psychology, 75,* 408–419.

Cohen, D., & Nisbett, R. E. (1994). Self-protection and the culture of honor: Explaining southern violence. *Personality and Social Psychology Bulletin, 20,* 551–567.

Cohen, D., Nisbett, R. E., Bowdle, B., & Schwarz, N. (1996). Insult, aggression, and the southern culture of honor: An "experimental ethnography." *Journal of Personality and Social Psychology, 70,* 945–960.

Cohen, D., & Vandello, J. A. (1998). Meanings of violence. *Journal of Legal Studies, 27,* 501–518.

Cohen, D., Vandello, J. A., & Rantilla, A. K. (1998). The sacred and the social: Cultures of honor and violence. In P. Gilbert & B. Andrews (Eds.), *Shame: Interpersonal behavior, psychopathology, and culture* (pp. 261–282). Oxford: Oxford University Press.

Cohen, G. L., Steele, C. M., & Ross, L. D. (1999). The mentor's dilemma: Providing critical feedback across the racial divide. *Personality and Social Psychology Bulletin, 25,* 1302–1318.

Cohen, R. L., & Alwin, D. F. (1993). Bennington women of the 1930s: Political attitudes over the life course. In K. D. Hulberet, & D. T. Schuster (Eds.), *Women's lives through time: Educated American women of the twentieth century* (pp. 117–139). San Francisco, CA: Jossey-Bass.

Cohen, T. R., Montoya, R. M., & Insko, C. A. (2006). Group morality and intergroup relations: Cross-cultural and experimental evidence. *Personality and Social Psychology Bulletin, 32,* 1559–1572.

Cohn, E. G., & Rotton, J. (2005). The curve is still out there: A reply to Bushman, Wang, and Anderson's (2005) "Is the curve relating temperature to aggression linear or curvilinear?" *Journal of Personality and Social Psychology, 89,* 67–70.

Cohn, M. A., Mehl, M. R., & Pennebaker, J. W. (2004). Linguistic markers of psychological change surrounding September 11, 2001. *Psychological Science, 15,* 687–693.

Coker, D. R. (1984). The relationships among gender concepts and cognitive maturity. *Sex Roles, 10,* 19–31.

Cole, D. A., Ciesla, J.A., Dallaire, D. H., Jacquez, F. M., Pineda, A. Q., LaGrange, B., Truss, A. E., Folmer, A. S., Tilghman-Osborne, C., & Felton, J. W. (2008). Emergence of attributional style and its relation to depressive symptoms. *Journal of Abnormal Psychology, 117,* 16–31.

Collins, A. M., & Loftus, E. F. (1975). A spreading-activation theory of semantic processing. *Psychological Review, 82,* 407–428.

Collins, B. E., & Brief, D. E. (1995). Using person-perception vignette methodologies to uncover the symbolic meanings of teacher behaviors in the Milgram paradigm. *Journal of Social Issues, 51,* 89–106.

Collins, M. A., & Ziebrowitz, L. A. (1995). The contributions of appearance to occupational outcomes in civilian and military settings. *Journal of Applied Social Psychology, 25,* 129–163.

Collins, N. L., & Miller, L. C. (1994). Self-disclosure and liking: A meta-analytic review. *Psychological Bulletin, 116,* 457–475.

Collins, R. L. (1996). For better or worse: The impact of upward social comparison on self-evaluations. *Psychological Bulletin, 119,* 51–69.

Comer, D. R. (1995). A model of social loafing in real work groups. *Human Relations, 48,* 647–667.

Compton, R. J., Williamson, S., Murphy, S. G., & Heller, W. (2002). Hemispheric differences in affective response: Effects of mere exposure. *Social Cognition, 20,* 1–16.

Comte, I. A. (1875). *Systems of positive polity* (Vol. 1). London: Longmans, Green. (First published 1851.)

Conger, J. A., Kanungo, R. N., & Menon, S. T. (2000). Charismatic leadership and follower effects. *Journal of Organizational Behavior, 21,* 747–767.

Conner, R. C., & Norriss, K. S. (1982). Are dolphins reciprocal altruists? *American Naturalist, 119,* 358–374.

Conrath, D. W. (1973). Communication patterns, organizational structure, and man: Some relationships. *Human Factors, 15,* 459–470.

Conway, L. G. III, Ryder, A. G., Tweed, R. G., & Sokol, B. W. (2001). Intranational cultural variation: Exploring further implications of collectivism within the United States. *Journal of Cross-Cultural Psychology, 32,* 681–697.

Conway, L. G., & Schaller, M. (2002). On the verifiability of evolutionary psychological theories: An analysis of the psychology of scientific persuasion. *Personality and Social Psychology Review, 6,* 152–160.

Conway, M., & Dubé, L. (2002). Humor in persuasion on threatening topics: Effectiveness is a function of audience sex role orientation. *Personality & Social Psychology Bulletin, 28,* 863–873.

Cook, G. I., Marsh, R. L., & Hicks, J. L. (2003). Halo and devil effects demonstrate valenced-based influences on source-monitoring decisions. *Consciousness and Cognition, 12,* 257–278.

Cook, H. B. K. (1992). Matrilocality and female aggression in Margariteño society. In K. Björkqvist & P. Niemelä (Eds.), *Of mice and women: Aspects of female aggression* (pp. 149–162). San Diego, CA: Harcourt Brace Jovanovich.

Cook, J. E., Arrow, H., & Malle, B. F. (2011). The effect of feeling stereotyped on social power and inhibition. *Personality and Social Psychology Bulletin, 37,* 165–180.

Cook, K. S., Cheshire, C., & Gerbasi, A. (2006). Power, dependence, and social exchange. In P. Burke (Ed.), *Contemporary social psychological theories* (pp. 194–216). Stanford, CA: Stanford University Press.

Cook, S. W. (1964). Desegregation: A psychological analysis. In W. W. Charters, Jr., & N. L. Gage (Eds.), *Readings in the social psychology of education.* Boston: Allyn & Bacon.

Cook, T. D., & Shadish, W. R. (1994). Social experiments: Some developments over the past fifteen years. *Annual Review of Psychology, 45,* 545–580.

Cooley, C. H. (1902). *Human nature and the social order.* New York: Scribner's Press.

Cooper, H. H. A. (2001). Terrorism: The problem of definition revisited. *American Behavioral Scientist, 44,* 881–893.

Cooper, J. (2007). *Cognitive dissonance: Fifty years of a classic theory.* Thousand Oaks, CA: Sage.

Cooper, J., & Fazio, R. (1984). A new look at dissonance theory. In l. Berkowitz (Ed.). *Advances in experimental social psychology* (Vol. 17, pp. 229–267). New York: Academic Press.

Cooper, J., Mirabile, R., & Scher, S. J. (2005). *Actions and attitudes: The theory of cognitive dissonance.* In T. C. Brock & M. C. Green (Eds.). *Persuasion: Psychological insights and perspectives,* 2nd ed. (pp. 63–79). Thousand Oaks, CA: Sage.

Corby, N. H., Jamner, M. S., & Wolitski, R. J. (1996). Using the theory of planned behavior to predict intention to use condoms among male and female injecting drug users. *Journal of Applied Social Psychology, 26,* 52–75.

Cordero, E. D. (2011). Self-esteem, social support, collectivism, and the thin-ideal in Latina undergraduates. *Body Image, 8,* 82–85.

Corney, R. (1990). Sex differences in general practice attendance and help seeking for minor illness. *Journal of Psychosomatic Research, 34,* 525–534.

Correll, J., Park, B., Judd, C. M., & Wittenbrink, B. (2002). The police officer's dilemma: Using ethnicity to disambiguate potentially threatening individuals. *Journal of Personality and Social Psychology, 83,* 1314–1329.

Correll, J., Park, B., Judd, C. M., Wittenbrink, B., Sadler, M. S., & Keese, T. (2007). Across the thin blue line: Police officers and racial bias in the decision to shoot. *Journal of Personality and Social Psychology, 92,* 1006–1023.

Correll, J., Urland, G. R., & Ito, T. A. (2006). Event-related potentials and the decision to shoot: The role of threat perception and cognitive control. *Journal of Experimental Social Psychology, 42,* 120–128.

Correll, S. J., & Ridgeway, C. L. (2003). Expectation states theory. In J. Delamater (Ed.), *Handbook of social psychology and social research* (pp. 29–51). New York: Kluwer Academic/Plenum.

Costello, K., & Hodson, G. (2011). Social dominance-based threat reactions to immigrants in need of assistance. *European Journal of Social Psychology, 41,* 220–231.

Cottrell, C. A., & Neuberg, S. L. (2005). Different emotional reactions to different groups: A sociofunctional threat-based approach to "prejudice." *Journal of Personality and Social Psychology, 88,* 770–789.

Cottrell, N. B., Wack, D. L., Sekerak, G. J., & Rittle, R. H. (1968). Social facilitation of dominant responses by the presence of an audience and the mere presence of others. *Journal of Personality and Social Psychology, 9,* 245–250.

Cowan, P. A., & Walters, R. H. (1963). Studies of reinforcement of aggression: I. Effects of scheduling. *Child Development, 34,* 543–551.

Craig, R. S. (1992). The effect of television day part on gender portrayals in television commercials: A content analysis. *Sex Roles, 26,* 197–211.

Crandall, C. S. (1988). Social contagion of binge eating. *Journal of Personality and Social Psychology, 55,* 588–598.

Crandall, C. S. (1994). Do parents discriminate against their overweight daughters? *Personality and Social Psychology Bulletin, 21,* 724–735.

Crandall, C. S., D'Anello, S., Sakalli, N., Lazarus, E., Wieczorkowska, G., & Feather, N. T. (2001). An attribution-value model of prejudice: Anti-fat attitudes in six nations. *Personality and Social Psychology Bulletin, 27,* 30–37.

Crandall, C. S., Eshleman, A. E., & O'Brien, L. (2002). Social norms and the expression and suppression of prejudice: The struggle for internalization. *Journal of Personality and Social Psychology, 82,* 359–378.

Crandall, C. S., Nierman, A., & Hebl, M. (2009). Anti-fat prejudice. In T. D. Nelson (Ed.). *Handbook of prejudice, stereotyping, and discrimination* (pp. 469–487). New York: Psychology Press.

Crandall, C. S., Silvia, P. J, N'Gbala, A. N., Tsang, J. A., & Dawson, K. (2007). Balance theory, unit relations, and attribution: The underlying integrity of Heiderian theory. *Review of General Psychology, 11,* 12–30.

Crano, W. D. (1995). Attitude strength and vested interest. In R. E. Petty & J. A. Krosnick (Eds.), *Attitude strength: Antecedents and consequences* (pp. 131–157). Mahwah, NJ: Erlbaum.

Crary D. (June 26, 2011). Gay marriage gets a boost. *Journal Sentinel,* p. 13A. Crawford, M., & Popp, D. (2003). Sexual double standards: A review and methodological critique of two decades of research. *Journal of Sex Research, 40,* 13–26.

Creasey, G., & Ladd, A. (2005). Generalized and specific attachment representations: Unique and interactive roles in predicting conflict behaviors in close relationships. *Personality and Social Psychology Bulletin, 31,* 1026–1038.

Crenshaw, M. (2000). The psychology of terrorism: An agenda for the 21st century. *Political Psychology, 21,* 405–420.

Crisp, R. J., Heuston, S., Farr, M. J., & Turner, R. N. (2007). Seeing red or feeling blue: differentiated emotions and ingroup identification in soccer fans. *Group Processes, Intergroup Relations, 10,* 9–26.

Crisp, R. J., Hewstone, M., & Rubin, M. (2001). Does multiple categorization reduce intergroup bias? *Personality and Social Psychology Bulletin, 27,* 76–89.

Crites, S. L., Cacioppo, J. T., Gardner, W. L., & Berntson, G. G. (1995). Bioelectrical echoes from evaluative categorization: II. A late positive brain potential that varies as a function of attitude registration rather than attitude report.

Journal of Personality and Social Psychology, 68, 997–1013.

Crocker, J., Karpinski, A., Quinn, D. M., & Chase, S. K. (2003). When grades determine self-worth: Consequences of contingent self-worth for male and female engineering and psychology majors. *Journal of Personality and Social Psychology, 85,* 507–516.

Crocker, J., & Luhtanen, R. K. (2003). Level of self-esteem and contingencies of self-worth: Unique effects on academic, social, and financial problems in college students. *Personality and Social Psychology Bulletin, 29,* 701–712.

Crocker J., Luhtanen, R.K., Blaine, B., and Brodnax, S. (1994). Collective self-esteem and collective well-being among White, Black, and Asian college students, *Psychology Bulletin 20,* 503–513.

Crocker, J., & Major, B. (1989). Social stigma and self-esteem: The self-protective properties of stigma. *Psychological Review, 96,* 608–630.

Crocker, J., Major, B., & Steele, C. (1998). Social stigma. In D. T. Gilbert, S. T. Fiske, & G. Lindzey (Eds.), *The handbook of social psychology* (4th ed.). New York: McGraw-Hill.

Crocker, J., & Park, L. E. (2004). The costly pursuit of self-esteem. *Psychological Bulletin, 130,* 392–414.

Crocker, J., & Quinn, D. M. (2000). Social stigma and the self: Meanings, situations, and self-esteem. In T. F. Heatherton, R. E. Kleck, M. R. Hebl, & J. G. Hull (Eds.), *The social psychology of stigma* (pp. 153–183). New York: Guilford.

Croizet, J. C., & Claire, T. (1998). Extending the concept of stereotype threat to social class: The intellectual underperformance of students from low socioeconomic backgrounds. *Personality and Social Psychology Bulletin, 24,* 588–594.

Crosby, F. J., Iyer, A., & Sincharoen, S. (2006). Understanding affirmative action. *Annual Review of Psychology, 57,* 585–611.

Crosby, F. J., & Nyquist, L. (1977). The female register: An empirical study of Lakoff's hypothesis. *Language in Society, 6,* 313–322.

Cross, S. E., Bacon, P. L., & Morris, M. L. (2000). The relational-interdependent self-construal and relationships. *Journal of Personality and Social Psychology, 78,* 791–808.

Cross, S. E., & Gore, J. (2002). Cultural models of the self. In M. Leary & J. Tangney (Eds.), *Handbook of self and identity* (pp. 536–564). New York: Guilford.

Cross, S. E., & Gore, J. S. (2004). The relational self-construal and the construction of closeness. In A. Aron & D. Mashek (Eds.), *The handbook of closeness and intimacy* (pp. 229–245) Mahwah, NJ : Lawrence Erlbaum.

Cross, S. E., Hardin, E. E., & Gercek-Swing, (2011). The what, how, why, and where of self-construal. *Personality and Social Psychology Review, 15,* 142–179.

Cross, S. E., & Madson, L. (1997). Models of the self: Self-construals and gender. *Psychological Bulletin, 122,* 5–37.

Cross, S. E., & Morris, M. L. (2003). Getting to know you: The relational self-construal, relational cognition, and well-being. *Personality and Social Psychology Bulletin, 29,* 512–523.

Cross, S. E., Morris, M. L., & Gore, J. S. (2002). Thinking about oneself and others: The relational-interdependent self-construal and social cognition. *Journal of Personality and Social Psychology, 82,* 399–418.

Cross, W. E. (1991). *Shades of black: Diversity in African-American identity.* Philadelphia: Temple University Press.

Crowley, A. E., & Hoyer, W. D. (1994). An integrative framework for understanding two-sided persuasion. *Journal of Consumer Research, 20,* 561–574.

Culos-Reed, S. N., Brawley, L. R., Martin, K. A., & Leary, M. R. (2002). Self-presentation concerns and health behaviors among cosmetic surgery patients. *Journal of Applied Social Psychology, 32,* 560–569.

Cummings, E. M., & Cummings, J. S. (2002). Parenting and attachment. In M. H. Bornstein (Ed.), *Handbook of parenting: Vol. 3. Being and becoming a parent* (2nd ed., pp. 35–58). Mahwah, NJ: Erlbaum.

Cunningham, M. R. (1979). Weather, mood, and helping behavior: Quasi-experiments with the sunshine Samaritan. *Journal of Personality and Social Psychology, 37,* 1947–1956.

Cunningham, M. R. (1986). Measuring the physical in physical attractiveness: Quasi-experiments on the sociobiology of female facial beauty. *Journal of Personality and Social Psychology, 50,* 925–935.

Cunningham, M. R., Barbee, A. P., & Pike, C. L. (1990a). What do women want: Facialmetric assessment of multiple motives in the perception of male physical attractiveness. *Journal of Personality and Social Psychology, 59,* 61–72.

Cunningham, M. R., Shaffer, D. R., Barbee, A. P., Wolff, P. L., & Kelley, D. J. (1990b). Separate processes in the relation of elation and depression to helping: Social versus personal concerns. *Journal of Experimental Social Psychology, 26,* 13–33.

Cunningham, M. R., Steinberg, J., & Grev, R. (1980). Wanting to and having to help: Separate motivation for positive mood and guilt-induced helping. *Journal of Personality and Social Psychology, 38,* 181–192.

Cunningham, P. B., Henggeler, S. W., Limber, S. P., Melton, G. B., & Nation, M. A. (2000). Patterns and correlates of gun ownership among nonmetropolitan and rural middle school students. *Journal of Clinical Child Psychology, 29,* 432–442.

Cunningham, W. A., Nelzek, J. B., & Banaji, M. R. (2004). Implicit and explicit ethnocentrism: Revisiting the ideologies of prejudice. *Personality and Social Psychology Bulletin, 30,* 1332–1346.

Cunningham, W. A., Preacher, K. J., & Bonaji, M. R. (2001). Implicit attitude measures: Consistency, stability, and convergent validity. *Psychological Science, 12,* 163–170.

Curran, J. P. (1977). Skills training as an approach to the treatment of heterosexual-social anxiety: A review. *Psychological Bulletin, 84,* 140–157. .

Curtis, R. C., & Miller, K. (1986). Believing another likes or dislikes you: Behaviors making the beliefs come true. *Journal of Personality and Social Psychology, 51,* 284–290.

Custers, R., & Aarts, H. (2007). Goal-discrepant situations prime goal-directed actions if goals are temporarily or chronically accessible. *Personality and Social Psychology Review, 33,* 623–633.

Cutrona, C. (1982). Transition to college: Loneliness and the process of social adjustment. In L. A. Peplau & D. Perlman (Eds.), *Loneliness: A sourcebook of current theory, research and therapy* (pp. 291–309). New York: Wiley.

Cutrona, C. E., & Suhr, J. A. (1994). Social support communication in the context of marriage: An analysis of couples' supportive interactions. In B. B. Burleson, T. L. Albrecht, & I. G. Sarason (Eds.), *Communication of social support: Messages, relationships, and community* (pp. 113–135). Thousand Oaks, CA: Sage.

Cvencek, D., Greenwald, A. G., & Meltzoff, A. N. (2011). Measuring implicit attitudes of 4-year-olds: The preschool implicit association test. *Journal of Experimental Child Psychology, 109,* 187–200.

Dakof, G. A., & Taylor, S. E. (1990). Victims' perceptions of social support: What is helpful from whom? *Journal of Personality and Social Psychology, 58,* 80–89.

Dal Cin, S., Gibson, B., Zanna, M. P., Shumate, R. & Fong, G. T. (2007). Smoking in movies, implicit associations of smoking with the self, and intentions to smoke. *Psychological Science, 18,* 559–563.

Dalakas, V., Madrigal, R., & Anderson, K. L. (2004). "We are number one!" The phenomenon of basking-in-reflected-glory and its implications for sports marketing. In L. R. Kahle, & C. Riley (Eds.). *Sports marketing and the psychology of marketing communication* (pp. 67–79). Mahwah, NJ: Lawrence Erlbaum.

Dallager, C., & Rosen, L. A. (1993). Effects of a human sexuality course on attitudes toward rape and violence. *Journal of Sex Education & Therapy, 19,* 193–199.

Dalton, M. A., Sargent, J. D., Dalton, M. A., Sargent, J. D., Beach, M. L., Titus-Ernstoff, L., Gibson, J. J., Ahrens, M. B., Tickle, J. J., & Heatherton, T. F. (2003). Effect of viewing smoking in movies on adolescent smoking initiation: A cohort study. *The Lancet 362* (9380):281–285.

Daly, J. A., Caughlin, J. P., & Stafford, L. (1997). Correlates and consequences of social-communicative anxiety. In J. A. Daly, J. C. McCroskey, J. Ayres, T. Hopf, & D. M. Ayres (Eds.), *Avoiding communication: Shyness, reticence, and communication apprehension* (2nd ed., pp. 21–71). Creskill, NJ: Hampton Press.

Daly, M., & Wilson, M. (1988). *Homicide.* New York: Aldine De Gruyer.

Daly, M., & Wilson, M. (1991). A reply to Gelles: Stepchildren are disproportionately abused, and diverse forms of violence can share causal factors. *Human Nature, 2,* 419–426.

Daly, M., & Wilson, M. I. (1996). Violence against stepchildren. *Current Directions in Psychological Science, 5,* 77–81.

Damasio, A.R., Anderson, S. W. (2003). The frontal lobes. In K. M. Heilman and E. Valenstein (Eds.), *Clinical neuropsychology,* (4th Ed). New York: Oxford University Press.

Dambrun, M., Guimond, S., & Duarte, S. (2002). The impact of hierarchy-enhancing vs. attenuating academic major on stereotyping: The mediating role of perceived social norm. *Current Research in Social Psychology, 7,* 114–136.

Dambrun, M., & Valentine, E. (2010). Reopening the study of extreme social behaviors: Obedience to authority within an immersive video environment. *European Journal of Social Psychology, 40,* 760–773.

Dana, E. R., Lalwani, N., & Duval, S. (1997). Objective self-awareness and focus of attention following awareness of self-standard discrepancies: Changing self or changing standards of correctness. *Journal of Social and Clinical Psychology, 16,* 359–380.

Danel, D., & Pawlowski, B. (2007). Eye-mouth-eye angle as a good indicator of face masculinization, asymmetry, and attractiveness (Homo sapiens). *Journal of Comparative Psychology, 121,* 221–225.

Dardenne, B., Dumont, M., & Bollier, T. (2007). Insidious dangers of benevolent sexism: Consequences for women's performance. *Journal of Personality and Social Psychology, 93,* 764–779.

Dardenne, B., & Leyens, J.-P. (1995). Confirmation bias as a social skill. *Personality and Social Psychology Bulletin, 21,* 1229–1239.

Darke, P. R., & Chaiken, S. (2005). The pursuit of self-interest: Self-interest bias in attitude judgment and persuasion. *Journal of Personality and Social Psychology, 89,* 864–883.

Darley, J. M. (1995). Constructive and destructive obedience: A taxonomy of principal-agent relationships. *Journal of Social Issues, 51,* 125–154.

Darley, J. M. (2001). Citizens' sense of justice and the legal system. *Current Directions in Psychological Science, 10,* 10–13.

Darley, J. M., & Latané, B. (1968). Bystander intervention in emergencies: Diffusion of responsibility. *Journal of Personality and Social Psychology, 8,* 377–383.

Darwin, C. (1859). *On the origin of species by natural selection.* New York: New York University Press, 1988.

Darwin, C. (1871). *The descent of man.* London: John Murray.

Darwin, C. (1872). *Expression of emotion in man and animals.* London: Murray.

Daryl, C.C., & Keith, P.B. (2011). Escaping affect: How motivated emotion regulation creates insensitivity to mass suffering. *Journal of Personality and Social Psychology, 100.* 1–15.

Das, E. H. H. J., & de Wit, J. B. F. (2003). Fear appeals motivate acceptance of action recommendations: Evidence for a positive bias in the processing of persuasive messages. *Personality and Social Psychology Bulletin, 29,* 650–664.

Dasgupta, N., & Greenwald, A. G. (2001). On the malleability of automatic attitudes: Combating automatic prejudice with images of admired and disliked individuals. *Journal of Personality and Social Psychology, 81,* 800–814.

Davies, M. F. (1994). Private self-consciousness and the perceived accuracy of true and false personality feedback. *Personality and Individual Differences, 17,* 697–701.

Davies, M., & McCartney, S. (2003). Effects of gender and sexuality on judgements of victim blame and rape myth acceptance in a depicted male rape. *Journal of Community and Applied Social Psychology, 13,* 391–398.

Davies, P. G., Spencer, S. J., & Steele, C. M. (2005). Clearing the air: Identity safety moderates the effects of stereotype threat on women's leadership aspirations. *Journal of Personality and Social Psychology, 88,* 276–287.

Davila, J., & Sargent, E. (2003). The meaning of life (events) predicts changes in attachment security. *Personality and Social Psychology Bulletin, 29,* 1383–1395.

Davis, C. G., Lehman, D. R., Silver, R. C., Wortman, C. B., & Ellard, J. H. (1996). Self-blame following a traumatic life event: The role of perceived avoidability. *Personality and Social Psychology Bulletin, 22,* 557–567.

Davis, C. G., Lehman, D. R., Wortman, C. B., Silver, R. C., & Thompson, S. C. (1995). The undoing of traumatic life events. *Personality and Social Psychology Bulletin, 21,* 109–124.

Davis, C. G., & Macdonald, S. L. (2004). Threat appraisals, distress, and the development of positive life changes following 9/11 in a Canadian sample. *Cognitive Behavioural Therapy 33(2)* 68–78.

Davis, C. G., & Nolen-Hoeksema, S. (2001). Loss and meaning: How do people make sense of loss? *American Behavioral Scientist, 44,* 726–741.

Davis, C. M., & Bauserman, R. (1993). Exposure to sexually explicit materials: An attitude change perspective. In J. Bancroft (Ed.), *Annual Review of Sex Research* (Vol. 4, pp. 121–209). Mt. Vernon, IA: Society for the Scientific Study of Sex.

Davis, D., Shaver, P. R., & Vernon, M. L. (2004). Attachment style and subjective motivations for sex. *Personality and Social Psychology Bulletin, 30.* 1076–1090.

Davis, J. H., Au, T., Hulbert, L., Chen, X., & Zarnoth, P. (1997). Effects of group size and procedural influence on consensual judgments of quantity: The example of damage awards and mock civil juries. *Journal of Personality and Social Psychology, 73,* 703–718.

Davis, J. L., & Rusbult, C. E. (2001). Attitude alignment in close relationships. *Journal of Personality and Social Psychology, 81,* 65–84.

Davis, M. H. (1980). A multidimensional approach to individual differences in empathy. *Psychological Documents, 10,* 85.

Davis, M. H. (1983). Empathic concern and the muscular dystrophy telethon: Empathy as a multidimensional construct. *Personality and Social Psychology Bulletin, 9,* 223–229.

Davis, M. H., & Franzoi, S. L. (1986). Adolescent loneliness, self-disclosure, and private self-consciousness: A longitudinal investigation. *Journal of Personality and Social Psychology, 51,* 595–608.

Davis, M. H., & Franzoi, S. L. (1991). Stability and change

in adolescent self-consciousness and empathy. *Journal of Research in Personality, 25,* 70–87.

Davis, M. H., & Kraus, L. A. (1989). Social contact, loneliness, and mass media use: A test of two hypotheses. *Journal of Applied Social Psychology, 19,* 1100–1124.

Davis, M. H., Luce, C., & Kraus, S. J. (1994). The heritability of characteristics associated with dispositional empathy. *Journal of Personality, 62,* 369–391.

Davis, M. H., Soderlund, T., Cole, J., Gadol, E., Kute, M., Myers, M., & Weihing, J. (2004). Cognitions associated with attempts to empathize: How do we imagine the perspective of another? *Personality and Social Psychology Bulletin, 30,* 1625–1635.

Davis, T. L. (1995). Gender differences in masking negative emotions: Ability or motivation? *Developmental Psychology, 31,* 660–667.

Dawson, E., Gilovich, T., & Regan, D. T. (2002). Motivated reasoning and performance on the Wason Selection Task. *Personality and Social Psychology Bulletin, 28,* 1379–1387.

Dawson, R. E., & Prewitt, K. (1969). *Political socialization.* Boston: Little, Brown.

Day, D. V., Shleicher, D. J., Unckless, A. L., & Hiller, N. J. (2002). Self-monitoring personality at work: A meta-analytic investigation of construct validity. *Journal of Applied Psychology, 87,* 390–401.

De Cecco, J. P. (1988). *Gay relationships.* Binghamton, NY: Haworth.

Decety, J. (2011). Promises and challenges of the neurobiological approach to empathy. *Emotion Review, 3,* 115–116.

De Dreu, C. K. W., & McCusker, C. (1997). Loss frames and cooperation in two-person social dilemmas: A transformational analysis. *Journal of Personality and Social Psychology, 72,* 1093–1106.

De Jaegher, H., Di Paolo, E., & Gallagher, S. (2010). Can social interaction constitute social cognition? *Trends in Cognitive Sciences, 14,* 441–447.

Dean, K. E., & Malamuth, N. M. (1997). Characteristics of men who aggress sexually and of men who imagine aggressing: Risk and moderating variables. *Journal of Personality and Social Psychology, 72,* 449–455.

Deaux, K. (1996). Social identification. In E. T. Higgins & A. W. Kruglanski (Eds.), *Social psychology: Handbook of basic principles* (pp. 777–798). New York: Guilford.

Debono, K., & Packer, M. (1991). The effects of advertising appeal on perceptions of product quality. *Personality and Social Psychology Bulletin, 17,* 194–200.

de Bruijn, G. J., Kremers, S. P. J., De Vet, E., De Nooijer, J., Van Mechelen, W., & Brug, J. (2007). Does habit strength moderate the intention-behaviour relationship in the theory of planned behaviour? The case of fruit consumption. *Psychology & Health, 22,* 899–916.

Dechene, A., Stahl, C., Hansen J., & Wanke, M. (2009). Mix me a list: Context moderates the truth effect and the mere-exposure effect. *Journal of Experimental Social Psychology, 45,* 1117–1122.

DeFleur, M. L., & Petranoff, R. M. (1959). A televised test of subliminal persuasion. *Public Opinion Quarterly, 23,* 168–180.

de Hoog, N., Stroebe, W., & de Wit, J. B. F. (2005). The impact of fear appeals on processing and acceptance of action recommendations. *Personality and Social Psychology Bulletin, 31,* 24–33.

de Hoog, N., Stroebe, W., & de Wit, J. B. F. (2007). The impact of vulnerability to and severity of a health risk on processing and acceptance of fear-arousing communications: A meta-analysis. *Review of General Psychology, 11,* 258–285.

de Kwaadsteniet, E. W., van Dijk, E., Wit, A., De Cremer, D. (2010). Anger and retribution after collective overuse: The role of blaming and environmental uncertainty in social dilemmas. *Personality and Social Psychology Bulletin,*

36, 59–70.

Delgado-Gaitan, C. (1994). Socializing young children in Mexican-American families: An intergenerational perspective. In P. M. Greenfield & R. R. Cocking (Eds.), *Cross-cultural roots of minority child development* (pp. 55–86). Hillsdale, NJ: Erlbaum.

Dembroski, T. M., Lasater, T. M., & Ramirez, A. (1978). Communicator similarity, fear arousing communications, and compliance with health care recommendations. *Journal of Applied Social Psychology, 8,* 254–269.

Demetriou, C., & Silke, A. (2003). A criminological Internet "sting": Experimental evidence of illegal and deviant visits to a website trap. *British Journal of Criminology, 43,* 213–222.

Demoulin, S., Rodriguez, R. T., Rodriguez, A. P., Vaes, J., Paladino, M. P., Gaunt, R., Cortes, B. P., & Leyens, J. P. H. (2004). Emotional prejudice can lead to infra-humanization. In W. Stroebe & M. Hewstone (Eds.), *European Review of Social Psychology* (Vol. 15, pp. 259–296). Chichester, England: Wiley.

DeNeve, K. M., & Cooper, H. (1998). The happy personality: A meta-analysis of 137 personality traits and subjective well-being. *Psychological Bulletin, 124,* 197–229.

Denny, D., & Pittman, C. (2007). Gender identity: From dualism to diversity. In M. S. Tepper & A. F. Owens (Eds.), *Sexual Health Vol 1: Psychological Foundations* (pp. 205–229). Westport, CT: Praeger.

Denson, T. F., Pedersen, W. C., Friese, M., Hahm, A., & Roberts, L. (2011). Understanding Impulsive aggression: Angry rumination and reduced self-control capacity are mechanisms underlying the provocation-aggression relationship. *Personality and Social Psychology Bulletin, 37,* 850–862.

DePaulo, B. M. (1992). Nonverbal behavior and self-presentation. *Psychological Bulletin, 111,* 230–243.

DePaulo, B. M., & Bell, K. L. (1996). Truth and investment: Lies are told to those who care. *Journal of Personality and Social Psychology, 71,* 703–716.

DePaulo, B. M., & Friedman, H. S. (1998). Nonverbal communication. In D. T. Gilbert, S. T. Fiskle, & G. K. Lindsey (Eds.), *The handbook of social psychology* (4th ed., Vol. 2, pp. 3–40). New York: McGraw-Hill.

DePaulo, B. M., Kashy, D. A., Kirkendol, S. E., Wyer, M. M., & Epstein, J. A. (1996). Lying in everyday life. *Journal of Personality and Social Psychology, 70,* 979–995.

DePaulo, B. M., Lindsay, J. J., Malone, B. E., Muhlenbruck, L., Charlton, K., & Cooper, H. (2003). Cues to deception. *Psychological Bulletin, 129,* 74–112.

DePaulo, B. M., & Morris, W. L. (2004). Discerning lies from truths: Behavioural cues to deception and the indirect pathway of intuition. In P-A. Granhag & L. Stromwall (Eds.), *The detection of deception in forensic contexts* (pp. 15–40). New York: Cambridge University Press.

DePaulo, B. M., & Pfeifer, R. L. (1986). On-the-job experience and skill at detecting deception. *Journal of Applied Social Psychology, 16,* 249–267.

Depue, R. A., & Collins, P. F. (1999). Neurobiology of the structure of personality: Dopamine, facilitation of incentive motivation, and extraversion. *Behavioral and Brain Sciences, 22,* 491–569.

Depue, R. A., Luciana, M., Arbisi, P., Collins, P., & Leon, A. (1994). Dopamine and the structure of personality: Relation to agonist-induced dopamine activity to positive emotionality. *Journal of Personality and Social Psychology, 67,* 485–498.

Derlega, V. J., Anderson, S., Winstead, B. A., & Greene, K. (2011). Positive disclosure among college students: What do they talk about, to whom, and why? *The Journal of Positive*

Psychology, 6, 119–130.

Derlega, V. J., Catanzaro, D., & Lewis, R. J. (2001). Perceptions about tactile intimacy in same-sex and opposite-sex pairs based on research participants' sexual orientation. *Psychology of Men and Masculinity, 2,* 124–132.

Derlega, V., & Chaikin, A. L. (1976). Norms affecting self-disclosure in men and women. *Journal of Consulting and Clinical Psychology, 44,* 376–380.

Derlega, V. J., Lewis, R. J., Harrison, S., Winstead, B. A., & Costanza, R. (1989). Gender differences in the initiation and attribution of tactile intimacy. *Journal of Nonverbal Behavior, 13,* 83–96.

Desforges, D. M., Lord, C. G., Pugh, M. A., Sia, T. L., Scarberry, N. C., & Ratcliff, C. D. (1997). Role of group representativeness in the generalization part of the contact hypothesis. *Journal of Applied Social Psychology, 19,* 183–204.

DeSteno, D., Bartlett, M. Y., Braverman, J., & Salovey, P. (2002). Sex differences in jealousy: Evolutionary mechanism or artifact of measurement? *Journal of Personality and Social Psychology, 83,* 1103–1116.

DeSteno, D. A., & Salovey, P. (1996). Evolutionary origins of sex difference in jealousy: Questioning the fitness of the model. *Psychological Science, 7,* 367–372.

de Tocqueville, A. (1969). *Democracy in America* (13th ed.; J. P. Mayer, Ed., & G. Lawrence, Trans.). New York: Doubleday. (Original work published 1862)

Deutsch, M., & Gerard, H. B. (1955). A study of normative and informational social influence upon individual judgment. *Journal of Abnormal and Social Psychology, 51,* 629–636.

Deutsch, R., Gawronski, B., & Strack, F. (2006). At the boundaries of automaticity: Negation as reflective operation. *Journal of Personality and Social Psychology, 91,* 385–405.

Devine, P. G. (1989). Stereotypes and prejudice: Their automatic and controlled components. *Journal of Personality and Social Psychology, 56,* 5–18.

Devine, P. G., Evett, S. R., & Vasquez-Suson, K. A. (1996). Exploring the interpersonal dynamics of intergroup contact. In R. M. Sorrentino & E. T. Higgins (Eds.), *Handbook of motivation and cognition: The interpersonal context* (Vol. 3, pp. 423–464). New York: Guilford.

Devine, P. G., & Sharp, L. B. (2009). Automaticity and control in stereotyping and prejudice. (2009). In T. Nelson (Ed.), *Handbook of prejudice, stereotyping, and discrimination* (pp. 61–88). New York: Psychology Press.

Devlin, P. K., & Cowan, G. A. (1985). Homophobia, perceived fathering, and male intimate relationships. *Journal of Personality Assessment, 49,* 467–473.

DeVos, G. (1985). Dimensions of the self in Japanese culture. In A. Marsella, G. DeVos, & F. L. K. Hsu (Eds.), *Culture and self* (pp. 149–184). London: Tavistock.

Devue, C., & Bredart, S. (2011). The neural correlates of visual self-recognition. *Consciousness and Cognition: An International Journal. 20,* 40–51.

de Waal, F. (2002). *The ape and the sushi master: Cultural reflections of a primatologist.* New York: Basic Books.

DeWall, C. N., Maner, J. K., & Rouby, D. A. (2009). Social exclusion and early-stage interpersonal perception: Selective attention to signs of acceptance. *Journal of Personality and Social Psychology, 96,* 729–741.

DeWall, C. N., & Baumeister, R. F. (2006). Alone but feeling no pain: Effects of social exclusion on physical pain tolerance and pain threshold, affective forecasting, and interpersonal empathy. *Journal of Personality and Social Psychology, 91,* 1–15.

DeWall, C. N., Pond, R. S., Jr., Campbell, W. K., & Twenge, J. M. (2011). Tuning in to psychological change: Linguistic markers of psychological traits and emotions over time in popular U.S. song lyrics. *Psychology of Aesthetics, Creativity, and the Arts.*

Diamond, L. M. (2003). What does sexual orientation orient? A biobehavioral model distinguishing romantic love and sexual desire. *Psychological Review, 110,* 173–192.

Diaz, T. (1999). *Making a killing: The business of guns in America.* New York: Free Press.

Díaz-Giménez, J., Quadrini, V., & Rios-Rull, J. V. (1997). Dimensions of inequality: Facts on the U.S. distributions of earnings, income, and wealth. *Federal Reserve Bank of Minneapolis Quarterly Review, 21,* 3–21.

DiBaise, R., & Gunnoe, J. (2004). Gender and culture differences in touching behavior. *Journal of Social Psychology, 144,* 49–62.

Di Conza, A., Gnisci, A., Perugini, M., & Senese, V. P. (2010). Implicit and explicit attitudes and voting behavior. 2004 European election in Italy and 2005 general election in England. *Psicologia Sociale, 5,* 305–333.

Diekmann, K., Tenbrunsel, A. E., & Galinsky, A. D. (2003). From self-prediction to self-defeat: Behavioral forecasting, self-fulfilling prophecies, and the effect of competititve expectations. *Journal of Personality and Social Psychology, 85,* 672–683.

Diener, E. (1980). Deindividuation: The absence of self-awareness and self-regulation in group members. In P. B. Paulus (Ed.), *Psychology of group influence* (pp. 209–242). Hillsdale, NJ: Erlbaum.

Diener, E., Fraser, S. C., Beaman, A. L., & Kelem, R. T. (1976). Effects of deindividuation variables on stealing among Halloween trick-or-treaters. *Journal of Personality and Social Psychology, 33,* 178–183.

Diener, E., Suh, E. M., Lucas, R. E., & Smith, H. L. (1999). Subjective well-being: Three decades of progress. *Psychological Bulletin, 125,* 276–302.

Diener, E., & Wallbom, M. (1976). Effects of self-awareness on antinormative behavior. *Journal of Research in Personality, 10,* 107–111.

Diener, E., Wolsie, B., & Fujita, F. (1995). Physical attractiveness and subjective well-being. *Journal of Personality and Social Psychology, 69,* 120–129.

Dijker, A. J., & Koomen, W. (1996). Stereotyping and attitudinal effects under time pressure. *European Journal of Social Psychology, 26,* 61–74.

Dijksterhuis, A. (2010). Automaticity and the unconscious. In S. T. Fiske, D. T. Gilbert, & G. Lindzey (Eds.). *Handbook of social psychology, Vol. 1* (5th ed.) (pp. 228–267). Hoboken, NJ: John Wiley.

Dijksterhuis, A., & Bargh, J. A. (2001). The perception-behavior expressway: The automatic effects of social perception on social behavior. In M. P. Zanna (Ed.), *Advances in experimental social psychology* (Vol. 33, pp. 1–40). San Diego, CA: Academic Press.

Dijksterhuis, A., & Knippenberg, A. V. (1996). The knife that cuts both ways: Facilitated and inhibited access to traits as a result of stereotype activation. *Journal of Experimental Social Psychology, 32,* 271–288.

Dijkstra, J. K., Gillessen, A. H. N., Lindenberg, S., & Veenstra, R. (2010) Same-gender and cross-gender likeability: Associations with popularity and status enhancement. *The Journal of Early Adolescence, 30,* 773–802.

Dijkstra, P., & Barelds, D. P. H. (2011). Women's meta-perceptions of attractiveness and their relations to body image. *Body Image, 8,* 74–77.

Dijkstra, P., Groothof, H. A. K., Poel, G. A., Laverman, T. T. G., Schrier, M., & Buunk, B. P. (2001). Sex differences in the events that elicit jealousy among homosexuals. *Personal Relationships, 8,* 41–54.

DiLalla, L. F. (2002). Behavior genetics of aggression in children: Review and future directions. *Developmental Review, 22,* 593–622.

Dimberg, U., & Soderkvist, S. (2011). The voluntary facial action technique: A method to test the facial feedback hypothesis. *Journal of Nonverbal Behavior, 35,* 17–33.

Dimberg, U., Thunberg, M., & Elmehed, K. (2000). Unconscious facial reactions to emotional facial expressions. *Psychological Science, 11,* 86–89.

Dindia, K., & Allen, M. (1992). Sex differences in self-disclosure: A meta-analysis. *Psychological Bulletin, 112,* 106–124.

Dion, K. K. (1972). Physical attractiveness and evaluations of children's transgressions. *Journal of Personality and Social Psychology, 24,* 285–290.

Dion, K. K., Berscheid, E., & [Walster] Hatfield, E. (1972). What is beautiful is good. *Journal of Personality and Social Psychology, 24,* 285–290.

Dion, K. L., & Dion, K. K. (1973). Correlates of romantic love. *Journal of Consulting and Clinical Psychology, 41,* 51–56.

Dion, K. K., & Dion, K. (1975). Self-esteem and romantic love. *Journal of Personality, 43,* 39–57.

Dion, K. K., & Dion, K. L. (1985). Personality, gender, and the phenomenology of romantic love. In P. R. Shaver (Ed.), *Self, situations and behavior: Review of personality and social psychology* (Vol. 6, pp. 209–239). Beverly Hills, CA: Sage.

Dion, K. K., & Dion, K. L. (1991). Psychological individualism and romantic love. *Journal of Social Behavior and Personality, 6,* 17–33.

Dionne, E. J., Jr. (1991). *Why Americans hate politics.* New York: Simon & Schuster.

Ditto, P. H., Scepansky, J. A., Munro, G. D., Apanovich, A. M., & Lockhart, L. K. (1998). Motivated sensitivity to preference-inconsistent information. *Journal of Personality and Social Psychology, 75,* 53–69.

Dodd, E., Giuliano, T., Boutell, J., & Moran, B. (2001). Respected or rejected: Perceptions of women who confront sexist remarks. *Sex Roles, 45,* 567–577.

Dodge, K. A. (2011). Social information processing patterns as mediators of the interaction between genetic factors and life experiences in the development of aggressive behavior. In P. R. Shaver & M. Mikulincer (Eds.). *Human aggression and violence: Causes, manifestations, and consequences (p*p. 165–185). Washington, DC: American Psychological Association.

Dodgson, P. G., & Wood, J. V. (1998). Self-esteem and the cognitive accessibility of strengths and weaknesses after failure. *Journal of Personality and Social Psychology, 75,* 178–197.

Dodwell, P. (2002). *Brave new mind: A thoughtful inquiry into the nature and meaning of mental life.* New York: Oxford University Press.

Domes, G., Heinrichs, M., Michel, A., Berger, C., & Herpertz, S. C. (2007). Oxytocin improves "mind-reading" in humans. *Biological Psychiatry, 61,* 731–733.

Donahue, M. J. (1985). Intrinsic and extrinsic religiousness: Review and meta-analysis. *Journal of Personality and Social Psychology, 48,* 400–419.

Donnerstein, E., & Berkowitz, L. (1981). Victim reactions in aggressive erotic films as a factor in violence against women. *Journal of Personality and Social Psychology, 41,* 710–724.

Donnerstein, E., Linz, D., & Penrod, S. (1987). *The question of pornography.* New York: Free Press.

Donnerstein, E., & Malamuth, N. (1997). Pornography: Its consequences on the observer. In L. B. Schlesinger, & E. Revitch (Eds.), *Sexual dynamics of anti-social behavior* (2nd ed., pp. 30–49). Springfield, IL: Thomas.

Dordick, G. A. (1997). *Something left to lose: Personal relations and survival among New York's homeless.* Philadelphia: Temple University Press.

Dorfman, J., Shames, V. A., & Kihlstrom, J. F. (1996). Intuition, incubation, and insight: Implicit cognition in problem solving. In G. Underwood (Ed.), *Implicit cognition* (pp. 257–296). Oxford: Oxford University Press.

Doty, R. M., Peterson, B. E., & Winter, D. G. (1991). Threat and authoritarianism in the United States, 1978–1987. *Journal of Personality and Social Psychology, 61,* 629–640.

Doty, R. M., Winter, D. G., Peterson, B. E., & Kemmelmeier, M. (1997). Authoritarianism and American students' attitudes about the Gulf War, 1990–1996. *Personality and Social Psychology Bulletin, 23,* 1133–1143.

Douglas, K. M., Sutton, R. M., & Stathi, S. (2010). Why I am less persuaded than you: People's intuitive understanding of the psychology of persuasion. *Social Influence, 5,* 133–148.

Dovidio, J. F. (2001). On the nature of contemporary prejudice: The third wave. *Journal of Social Issues, 57,* 829–849.

Dovidio, J. F., & Gaertner, S. L. (2010). Intergroup bias. In S. T. Fiske, D. T. Gilbert, & G. Lindzey (Eds.). *Handbook of social psychology, Vol. 1* (5th ed.) (pp. 1084–1121). Hoboken, NJ: John Wiley.

Dovidio, J. F., Kawakami, K., & Beach, K. R. (2001). Implicit and explicit attitudes: Examination of the relationship between measures of intergroup bias. In R. Brown & S. L. Gaertner (Eds.), *Blackwell handbook of social psychology: Vol. 4. Intergroup relation* (pp. 175–197). Oxford, UK: Blackwell.

Dovidio, J. F., Kawakami, K., & Gaertner, S. L. (2002b). Implicit and explicit prejudice and interracial interaction. *Journal of Personality and Social Psychology, 82,* 62–68.

Dovidio, J. F., Piliavin, J. A., & Clark, R. D., III (1991). The arousal:cost reward model and the process of intervention: A review of the evidence. In M. S. Clark (Ed.), *Review of personality and social psychology: Vol. 12. Prosocial behavior* (pp. 86–118). Newbury Park, CA: Sage.

Dovidio, J. F., Piliavin, J. A., Schroeder, D. A., & Penner, L. (2006). *The social psychology of prosocial behavior.* Mahwah, NJ: Lawrence Erlbaum.

Downey, G., Freitas, A. L., Michaelis, B., & Khouri, H. (1998). The self-fulfilling prophecy in close relationships: Rejection sensitivity and rejection by romantic partners. *Journal of Personality and Social Psychology, 75,* 545–560.

Downey, G., Mougios, V., Ayduk, O., London, B. E., & Shoda, Y. (2004). Rejection sensitivity and the defensive motivational system, *Psychological Science, 15,* 668–673.

Drachman, D., DeCarufel, A., & Insko, C. A. (1978). The extra credit effect in interpersonal attraction. *Journal of Experimental Social Psychology, 14,* 458–467.

Draelants, H., & Darchy-Koechlin, B. (2011)Flaunting one's academic pedigree? Self-presentation of students from elite French schools. *British Journal of Sociology of Education, 32,* 17–34.

Drigotas, S. M., Rusbult, C. E., Wieselquist, J., & Whitton, S. W. (1999). Close partner as sculptor of the ideal self: Behavioral affirmation and the Michelangelo phenomenon. *Journal of Personality and Social Psychology, 77,* 293–323.

Dru, V. (2007). Authoritarianism, social dominance orientation and prejudice: Effects of various self-categorization conditions. *Journal of Experimental Social Psychology, 43,* 877–883.

Dryer, D. C., & Horowitz, L. M. (1997). When do opposites attract? Interpersonal complementarity versus similarity. *Journal of Personality and Social Psychology, 72,* 592–603.

Duan, C. (2000). Being empathic. The role of motivation to empathize and the nature of target emotions. *Motivation & Emotion, 24,* 29–50.

DuBois, D. L. (in press). Promoting the self-esteem of children. In T. P. Gullotta & M. Bloom (Eds.) & L. Bond (Section Ed.), *Encyclopedia of primary prevention and health promotion: Childhood.* New York: Kluwer Academic/Plenum.

Duck, S., Pond, K., & Leatham, G. (1994). Loneliness and the evaluation of relational events. *Journal of Social and Personal Relationships, 11,* 253–276.

Duck, S., & Wright, P. H. (1993). Reexamining gender differences in same-gender friendships: A close look at two kinds of data. *Sex Roles, 28,* 709–727.

Duckitt, J. (2001). A dual-process cognitive-motivational theory of ideology and prejudice. In M. P. Zanna (Ed.). *Advances in experimental social psychology,* Vol. 33 (pp. 41–113). San Diego, CA: Academic Press.

Duckitt, J. (2005). Personality and prejudice. In J. F. Dovidio, P. Glick, & L. Rudman (Ed.), *On the nature of prejudice: Fifty years after Allport* (pp. 395–412). Malden, MA: Blackwell Publishing

Duckitt, J., & Fisher, K. (2003). The impact of social threat on worldview and ideological attitudes. *Political Psychology, 24,* 199–222.

Duckitt, J., & Mphuting, T. (1998). Group identification and intergroup attitudes: A longitudinal analysis in South Africa. *Journal of Personality and Social Psychology, 74,* 80–85.

Duckitt, J., & Sibley, C. G. (2007). Right wing authoritarianism, social dominance orientation and the dimensions of generalized prejudice. *European Journal of Personality, 21,* 113–130.

Duclos, S. E., Laird, J. D., Schneider, E., Sexter, M., Stern, L., & Van Lighten, O. (1989). Emotion-specific effects of facial expressions and postures on emotional experience. *Journal of Personality and Social Psychology, 57,* 100–108.

Dunbar, R. (2002). Brains on two legs: Group size and the evolution of intelligence. In F. B. M. de Waal (Ed.), *Tree of origin: What primate behavior can tell us about human social evolution* (pp. 173–191). Cambridge, MA: Harvard University Press.

Dunbar, R. (2003). Solution of the social brain. *Science, 302,* 1160–1161.

Dunbar, R. I. M. (1993). Coevolution of neocortical size, group size and language in humans. *Behavioral and Brain Sciences, 16,* 681–735.

Dunbar, R. I. M. (1996). *Grooming, gossip, and the evolution of language.* Cambridge: Harvard University Press.

Dunbar, R. I. M. (2000). Causal reasoning, mental rehearsal and the evolution of primate cognition. In C. Heyes & L. Huber (Eds.), *Evolution of cognition* (pp. 205–221). Cambridge, MA: MIT Press.

Duncan, C. P., & Nelson, J. E. (1985). Effects of humor in a radio advertising experiment. *Journal of Advertising, 14,* 33–40.

Dunkel-Schetter, C., Blasband, D. E., Feinstein, L. G., & Herbert, T. B. (1992). Elements of supportive interactions: When are attempts to help effective? In S. Spacapan & S. Oskamp (Eds.), *Helping and being helped: Naturalistic studies* (pp. 83–114). Newbury Park, CA: Sage.

Dunn, E. W., Biesanz, J. C., & Human, L. J. (2007). Misunderstanding the affective consequences of everyday interactions: The hidden benefits of putting one's best face forward. *Journal of Personality and Social Psychology, 92,* 990–1005.

Dunn, J. (2001). The development of children's conflict and prosocial behaviour: Lessons from research on social understanding and gender. In J. Hill & B. Maughan (Eds.), *Conduct disorders in childhood and adolescence: Cambridge child and adolescent psychiatry* (pp. 49–66). New York: Cambridge University Press.

Dunning, D. (1999). A newer look: Motivated social cognition and the schematic representation of social concepts. *Psychological Inquiry, 10,* 1–11.

Dunning, D. (2004). But what would a balanced approach look like? *Behavioral and Brain Sciences, 27.*

Dunning, D., Leuenberger, A., & Sherman, D. A. (1995). A new look at motivated inference: Are self-serving theories of success a product of motivational forces? *Journal of Personality and Social Psychology, 69,* 58–68.

Dutton, D. G. (2007). *The psychology of genocide, massacres, and extreme violence: Why "normal" people come to commit atrocities.* Westport, CT: Praeger Security International.

Dutton, D. G., & Aron, A. P. (1974). Some evidence for heightened sexual attraction under conditions of high anxiety. *Journal of Personality and Social Psychology, 30,* 510–517.

Dutton, D. G., & Tetreault, C. (2009). Who will act badly in toxic situations? *Journal of Aggression,*

Conflict, and Peace Research, 1, 45–57.

Duval, S., & Wicklund, R. A. (1972). *A theory of objective self-awareness.* New York: Academic Press.

Dykas, M. J., & Cassidy, J. (2011). Attachment and the processing of social information across the life span: Theory and evidence. *Psychological Bulletin, 137,* 19–46.

Eagly, A. H. (1987). *Sex differences in social behavior: A social-role interpretation.* Hillsdale, NJ: Erlbaum.

Eagly, A. H. (1992). Uneven progress: Social psychology and the study of attitudes. *Journal of Personality and Social Psychology, 63,* 693–710.

Eagly, A. H. (1996). Differences between women and men: Their magnitude, practical importance, and political meaning. *American Psychologist, 50,* 158–159.

Eagly, A. H. (2007). Female leadership advantage and disadvantage: Resolving the contradictions. *Psychology of Women Quarterly, 31,* 1–12.

Eagly, A. H., Ashmore, R. D., Makhijani, M. G., & Longo, L. C. (1991). What is beautiful is good, but . . .: A meta-analytic review of research on the physical attractiveness stereotype. *Psychological Bulletin, 110,* 107–128.

Eagly, A. H., & Chaiken, S. (1993). *The psychology of attitudes.* Fort Worth, TX: Harcourt Brace Jovanovich.

Eagly, A. H., & Chravala, C. (1986). Sex differences in conformity: Status and gender-role interpretations. *Psychology of Women Quarterly, 10,* 203–220.

Eagly, A. H., & Crowley, M. (1986). Gender and helping behavior: A meta-analytic review of the social psychological literature. *Psychological Bulletin, 100,* 283–308.

Eagly, A. H., & Johannesen-Schmidt, M. C. (2001). The leadership styles of women and men. *Journal of Social Issues, 57,* 781–797.

Eagly, A. H., Johannesen-Schmidt, M. C., & van Engen, M. L. (2003). Transformational, transactional, and laissez-faire leadership styles: A meta-analysis comparing women and men. *Psychological Bulletin, 129,* 569–591.

Eagly, A. H., & Johnson, B. T. (1990). Gender and leadership style: A meta-analysis. *Psychological Bulletin, 108,* 233–256.

Eagly, A. H., & Karau, S. J. (2002). Role congruity theory of prejudice toward female leaders. *Psychological Review, 109,* 573–598.

Eagly, A. H., Karau, S. J., & Makhijani, M. G. (1995). Gender and the effectiveness of leaders: A meta-analysis. *Psychological Bulletin, 117,* 125–145.

Eagly, A. H., Makhijani, M. G., & Klonsky, B. G. (1992). Gender and the evaluation of leaders: A meta-analysis. *Psychological Bulletin, 111,* 3–22.

Eagly, A. H., & Steffen, V. J. (1986). Gender and aggressive behavior: A meta-analytic review of the social psychological literature. *Psychological Bulletin, 100,* 309–330.

Eagly, A. H., & Wood, W. (1999). The origins of sex differences in human behavior. *American Psychologist, 54,* 408–423.

Eaton, J., & Struthers, C. W. (2006). The reduction of psychological aggression across varied interpersonal contexts through repentance and forgiveness. *Aggressive Behavior, 32,* 195–206.

Ebbesen, E. B., Kjos, G. L., & Konecni, V. J. (1976). Spatial ecology: Its effects on the choice of friends and enemies. *Journal of Experimental Social Psychology, 12,* 505–518.

Echabe, A. E. & Garate, J. F. V. (1994). Private self-consciousness as moderator of the importance of attitude and subjective norm: The prediction of voting. *European Journal of Social Psychology, 24,* 285–293.

Echabe, A. E., Rovira, D. P., & Garate, J. F. V. (1988). Testing Ajzen and Fishbein's attitudes model: The prediction of voting. *European Journal of Social Psychology, 18,* 181–189.

Edgerton, R. (1971). *The individual in cultural adaptation.* Berkeley: University of California Press.

Edney, J. J. (1979). The nuts game: A concise commons dilemma analog. *Environmental Psychology and*

Nonverbal Behavior, 3, 252–254.

Edson, R. (1976). *The intuitive journey and other works.* New York: Harper & Row.

Edwards, K., & Smith, E. E. (1996). A disconfirmation bias in the evaluation of arguments. *Journal of Personality and Social Psychology, 71,* 5–24.

Eimer, M., & Schlaghecken, F. (2002). Links between conscious awareness and response inhibition: Evidence from masked priming. *Psychonomic Bulletin and Review, 9,* 514–520.

Eisenberg, N., Martin, C. L., & Fabes, R. A. (1996). Gender development and gender effects. In D. C. Berliner & R. C. Calfee (Eds.), *Handbook of educational psychology* (pp. 358–396). New York: Prentice-Hall.

Eisenberger, N. I. (2011). Social pain: Experiential, neurocognitive, and genetic correlates. In A. Todorov, S. T. Fiske, & D. A. Prentice (Eds.). *Social neuroscience: Toward understanding the underpinnings of the social mind (pp.* 229–248). New York: Oxford University Press.

Eisenberger, N. I., Lieberman, M. D., & Williams, K. D. (2003). Does rejection hurt? An fMRI study of social exclusion. *Science, 302,* 290–292.

Eisenberger, R., Cotterell, N., & Marvel, J. (1987). Reciprocation ideology. *Journal of Personality and Social Psychology, 53,* 743–750.

Ekman, P. (1994). Strong evidence for universals in facial expressions: A reply to Russell's mistaken critique. *Psychological Bulletin, 115,* 268–287.

Ekman, P., Friesen, W. V., & O'Sullivan, M. (1988). Smiles when lying. *Journal of Personality and Social Psychology, 54,* 414–420.

Ekman, P., & O'Sullivan, M. (1991). Who can catch a liar? *American Psychologist, 46,* 913–920.

Elfenbein, H. A., & Ambady, N. (2002). On the universality and cultural specificity of emotion recognition: A meta-analysis. *Psychological Bulletin, 128,* 205–235.

Elias, S. M., & Mace, B. L. (2005). Social power in the classroom: Student attributions for compliance. *Journal of Applied Social Psychology, 35*(8), 1738–1754.

Ellemers, N., Rijswijk, W. V., Roefs, M., & Simons, C. (1997). Bias in intergroup perceptions: Balancing group identity with social reality. *Personality and Social Psychology Bulletin, 23,* 186–198.

Ellemers, N., Spears, R., & Doosje, B. (2002). Self and social identity. *Annual Review of Psychology, 53,* 161–186.

Eller, A., & Abrams, D. (2004). Come together: Longitudinal comparisons of Pettigrew's reformulated intergroup contact model and the common ingroup identity model in Anglo-French and Mexican-American contexts. *European Journal of Social Psychology, 34*(3), 229–256.

Elliot, A. J., & Reis, H. T. (2003). Attachment and exploration in adulthood. *Journal of Personality and Social Psychology, 85,* 317–331.

Elliott, G. C. (2001). The self as social product and social force: Morris Rosenberg and the elaboration of a deceptively simple effect. In T. J. Owens, S. Stryker, & N. Goodman (Eds.), *Extending self-esteem theory and research: Sociological and psychological currents* (pp. 10–28). Cambridge: Cambridge University Press.

Ellis, A. P. J., West, B. J., Ryan, A. M., & DeShon, R. P. (2002). The use of impression management tactics in structured interviews: A function of question type? *Journal of Applied Psychology, 87,* 1200–1208.

Ellis, J., & Fox, P. (2001). The effect of self-identified sexual orientation on helping behavior in a British sample: Are lesbians and gay men treated differently? *Journal of Applied Social Psychology, 31,* 1238–1247.

Ellison, N., Heino, R., & Gibbs, J. (2006). Managing impressions online: Self-presentation processes in the online dating environment. *Journal of Computer-Mediated Communication, 11,* 415–441.

Ellsworth, P. C., & Mauro, R. (1998). Psychology and

law. In D. T. Gilbert, S. T. Fiske, & G. Lindzey (Eds.), *The handbook of social psychology* (4th ed., Vol. 2, pp. 684–732). New York: McGraw-Hill.

Elms, A. C. (1975). The crisis of confidence in social psychology. *American Psychologist, 30,* 967–976.

Elms, A. C. (1994). Keeping deception honest: Justifying conditions for social scientific research stratagems. In E. Erwin, S. Gendin, & L. Kleiman (Eds.), *Ethical issues in scientific research: An anthology* (pp. 121–140). New York: Garland.

Elms, A. C. (1995). Obedience in retrospect. *Journal of Social Issues, 51,* 21–31.

Elms, A. C., & Milgram, S. (1966). Personality characteristics associated with obedience and defiance toward authoritative command. *Journal of Experimental Research in Personality, 1,* 282–289.

Elsesser, K., & Peplau, L. A. (2006). The glass partition: Obstacles to cross-sex friendships at work. *Human Relations, 59,* 1077–1100.

Ely, R. J., & Thomas, D. A. (2001). Cultural diversity at work: The effects of diversity perspectives on work group processes and outcomes. *Administrative Science Quarterly, 46,* 229–273.

Ember, C. R., & Ember, M. (1994). War, socialization, and interpersonal violence: A cross-cultural study. *Journal of Conflict Resolution, 38,* 620–646.

Emmers-Sommer, T. M., Pauley, P., Hanzal, A., & Triplett, L. (2006). Love suspense, sex, and violence: Men's and women's film predilections, exposure to sexually violent media, and their relationship to rape myth acceptance. *Sex Roles, 55,* 311–320.

Emmers-Sommer, T. M., Triplett, L., Pauley, P., Hanzal, A., & Rhea, D. (2005). The impact of film manipulation on men's and women's attitudes toward women and film editing. *Sex Roles, 52,* 683–695.

Emmons, R. A., & Diener, E. (1986). A goal-affect analysis of everyday situational choices. *Journal of Research in Personality, 20,* 309–326.

End, C. M., Kretschmar, J. M., & Dietz-Uhler, B. (2004). College students' perceptions of sports fandom as a social status determinant. *International Sports Journal, 8,* 114–123.

Engestrom, Y., Brown, K., Engestrom, R., & Koistinen, K. (1990). Organizational forgetting: An activity-theoretical perspective. In D. Middleton & D. Edwards (Eds.), *Collective remembering* (pp. 137–168). Newbury Park, CA: Sage.

Epley, N., Akalis, S., Waytz, A, & Cacioppo, J. T. (2008). Creating social connection through inferential reproduction: Loneliness and perceived agency in gadgets, gods, and greyhounds. *Psychological Science, 19,* 114–120.

Epley, N., & Gilovich, T. (1999). Just going along: Nonconscious priming and conformity to social pressure. *Journal of Experimental Social Psychology, 35,* 578–589.

Epley, N., & Gilovich, T. (2001). Putting adjustment back in the anchoring and adjustment heuristic: Differential processing of self-generated and experimenter-provided anchors. *Psychological Science, 12,* 391–396.

Epley, N., & Huff, C. (1998). Suspicion, affective response, and educational benefit as a result of deception in psychology research. *Personality and Social Psychology Bulletin, 24,* 759–768.

Epley, N., Van Boven, L., & Caruso, E. M. (2004). Balance where it really counts. *Behavioral and Brain Sciences, 27.*

Epstein, J. L. (1985). After the bus arrives: Resegregation in desegregation schools. *Journal of Social Issues, 41,* 23–43.

Epstein, S. (1973). The self-concept revisited, or a theory of a theory. *American Psychologist, 28,* 404–416.

Erber, R., Wegner, D. M., & Therriault, N. (1996). On being cool and collected: Mood regulation in anticipation of social interaction. *Journal of Personality and Social Psychology, 70,* 757–766.

Erdfelder, E., Brandt, M., & Broder, A. (2007).

Recollection biases in hindsight judgments. *Social Cognition, 25,* 114–131.

Erdogan, B., & Enders, J. (2007). Support from the top: Supervisors' perceived organizational support as a moderator of leader-member exchange to satisfaction and performance relationships. *Journal of Applied Psychology, 92,* 321–330.

Erickson, B., Lind, E. A., Johnson, B. C., & O'Barr, W. M. (1978). Speech style and impression formation in a court setting: The effects of "powerful" and "powerless" speech. *Journal of Experimental Social Psychology, 14,* 266–279.

Eron, L. D. (1963). Relationship of TV viewing habits and aggressive behavior in children. *Journal of Abnormal and Social Psychology, 67,* 193–196.

Eron, L. D., & Huesmann, L. R. (1984). The control of aggressive behavior by changes in attitudes, values, and the conditions of learning. In R. J. Blanchard & D. C. Blanchard (Eds.), *Advances in the study of aggression* (Vol. 1, pp. 139–171). New York: Academic Press.

Eron, L. D., Huesmann, L. R., Lefkowitz, M. M., & Walder, L. O. (1972). Does television violence cause aggression? *American Psychologist, 27,* 253–263.

Esses, V. M., Jackson, L. M., & Armstrong, T. L. (1998). Intergroup competition and attitudes toward immigrants and immigration: An instrumental model of group conflict. *Journal of Social Issues, 54,* 699–724.

Estow, S., Jamieson, J. P., & Yates, J. R. (2007). Self-monitoring and mimicry of positive and negative social behaviors. *Journal of Research in Personality, 41,* 425–433.

Evans, A. D., Xu, F., & Lee, K. (2011). When all signs point to you: Lies told in the face of evidence. *Developmental Psychology, 47,* 39–49.

Evans, P. C. (2003). "If only I were thin like her, maybe I could be happy like her": The self implications of associating a thin female ideal with life success. *Psychology of Women Quarterly, 27,* 209–214.

Evans, R. I. (1980). *The making of social psychology: Discussions with creative contributors.* New York: Gardner Press.

Eysenck, H. J. (1990). Biological dimensions of personality. In L. A. Pervin (Ed.), *Handbook of personality theory and research* (pp. 244–276). New York: Guilford.

Fagin-Jones, S., & Midlarsky, E. (2007). Courageous altruism: Personal and situational correlates of rescue during the Holocaust. *The Journal of Positive Psychology, 2,* 136–147.

Fagot, B. I. (1985). Changes in thinking about early sex role development. *Developmental Review, 5,* 83–98.

Falk, C. F., Heine, S. J., Yuki, M., & Takemura, K. (2009). Why do Westerners self-enhance more than East Asians? *European Journal of Personality, 23,* 183–203.

Farb, P. (1978). *Man's rise to civilization: The cultural ascent of the Indians of North America.* New York: Penguin.

Farley, S. D. (2011). Is gossip power? The inverse relationships between gossip, power, and likability. *European Journal of Social Psychology, 41.*

Farr, R. M. (1996). *The roots of modern social psychology.* Cambridge, MA: Blackwell.

Farrington, D. P. (1994). Childhood, adolescent, and adult features of violent males. In L. R. Huesmann (Ed.), *Aggressive behavior: Current perspectives* (pp. 215–240). New York: Plenum.

Fawkner, H. J., & McMurray, N. (2002). Body image in men: Self-reported thoughts, feelings, and behaviors in response to media images. *International Journal of Men's Health, 1,* 137–162.

Fazio, R. H. (1990). Multiple processes by which attitudes guide behavior: The MODE model as an integrative framework. In M. P. Zanna (Ed.), *Advances in experimental social psychology* (Vol. 23, pp. 75–109). New York: Academic Press.

Fazio, R. H. (1995). Attitudes as object-evaluation

associations: Determinants, consequences, and correlates of attitude accessibility. In R. E. Petty & J. A. Krosnick (Eds.), *Attitude strength: Antecedents and consequences* (pp. 247–282). Mahwah, NJ: Erlbaum.

Fazio, R. H. (2001). On the automatic activation of associated evaluations. An overview. *Cognition and emotion, 14,* 1–27.

Fazio, R. H., & Williams, C. J. (1986). Attitude accessibility as a moderator of the attitude-perception and attitude-behavior relations. *Journal of Personality and Social Psychology, 51,* 505–514.

Fazio, R. H., Zanna, M. P., & Cooper, J. (1977). Dissonance and self-perception: An integrative view of each theory's proper domain of application. *Journal of Experimental Social Psychology, 13,* 464–479.

Feagin, F. R., & Sikes, M. P. (1994). *Living with racism: The Black middle class experience.* Boston: Beacon.

Feather, N. T. (2004). Value correlates of ambivalent attitudes toward gender relations. *Personality and Social Psychology Bulletin, 30,* 3–12.

Federal Bureau of Investigation (Oct. 22, 2001). *Crime in the United States.* http://www.fbi.gov/pressrel/pressrel01/cius2000.htm

Federico, C. M. (2004) Predicting attitude extremity: The interactive effects of schema development and the need to evaluate and their mediation by evaluative integration. *Personality and Psychology Bulletin, 30,* 1281–1294.

Federman, J. (1998). (Ed.) *National television violence study, Vol. 3.* (1998). Thousand Oaks, CA: Sage.

Feeney, J. A. (2003). The systemic nature of couple relationships: An attachment perspective. In P. Erdman & T. Caffery (Eds.). *Attachment and family systems: Conceptual, empirical, and therapeutic relatedness* (pp. 139–163). New York: Brunner/Mazel.

Fehr, B. (2004). Intimacy expectations in same-sex friendships: A prototype interaction-pattern model. *Journal of Personality and Social Psychology, 86,* 265–284.

Fehr, E., & Gaechter, S. (2002). Altruistic punishment in humans. *Nature, 415,* 137–140.

Feinberg, J. M., & Aiello, J. R. (2006). Social facilitation: A test of competing theories. *Journal of Applied Social Psychology, 36,* 1087–1109.

Feingold, A. (1988). Matching for attractiveness in romantic partners and same-sex friends: A meta-analysis and theoretical critique. *Psychological Bulletin, 104,* 226–235.

Feingold, A. (1992a). Gender differences in mate selection preferences: A test of the parental investment model. *Psychological Bulletin, 112,* 125–139.

Feingold, A. (1992b). Good-looking people are not what we think. *Psychological Bulletin, 111,* 304–341.

Feingold, A., & Mazzella, R. (1998). Gender differences in body image are increasing. *Psychological Science, 9,* 190–195.

Fejfar, M. C., & Hoyle, R. H. (2000). Effect of private self-awareness on negative affect and self-referent attribution: A qualitative review. *Personality and Social Psychology Review, 4,* 132–142.

Feldman, S., & Stenner, K. (1997). Perceived threat and authoritarianism. *Political Psychology, 18,* 741–770.

Felmlee, D. H. (1999). Social norms in same- and cross-gender friendships. *Social Psychology Quarterly, 62,* 53–67.

Felson, R. B. (1997). Anger, aggression, and violence in love triangles. *Violence and victims, 12,* 345–362.

Fenigstein, A., Scheier, M. F., & Buss, A. H. (1975). Public and private self-consciousness: Assessment and theory. *Journal of Consulting and Clinical Psychology, 43,* 522–527.

Fenigstein, A., & Vanable, P. A. (1992). Paranoia and self-consciousness. *Journal of Personality and Social Psychology, 62,* 129–138.

Ferguson, G. (1955). Legal research on trial.

Judicature, 39, 78–82.

Ferguson, M. J. (2007). On the automatic evaluation of end-states. *Journal of Personality and Social Psychology, 92*, 596–611.

Ferguson, M. J., & Bargh, J. A. (2004). Liking is for doing: The effects of goal pursuit on automatic evaluation. *Journal of Personality and Social Psychology, 87*, 557–572.

Fernald, J. L. (1995). Interpersonal heterosexism. In B. Lott, & D. Maluso (Eds.), *The social psychology of interpersonal discrimination* (pp. 80–117). New York: Guilford.

Ferrari, J. R., & Tice, D. M. (2000). Procrastination as a self-handicap for men and women: A task-avoidance strategy in a laboratory setting. *Journal of Research in Personality, 34*, 73–83.

Festinger, L. (1954). A theory of social comparison processes. *Human Relations, 7*, 117–140.

Festinger, L. (1957). *A theory of cognitive dissonance.* Stanford, CA: Stanford University Press.

Festinger, L., & Carlsmith, J. M. (1959). Cognitive consequences of forced compliance. *Journal of Abnormal and Social Psychology, 47*, 382–389.

Festinger, L., Pepitone, A., & Newcomb, T. (1952). Some consequences of deindividuation in a group. *Journal of Abnormal and Social Psychology, 47*, 382–389.

Festinger, L., Reicken, H. W., & Schachter, S. (1956). *When prophecy fails.* Minneapolis: University of Minnesota Press.

Festinger, L., Schachter, S., & Back, K. (1950). *Social pressures in informal groups: A study of a housing community.* New York: Harper.

Fetchenhauer, D., Flache, A., Buunk, A. P., & Lindenberg, S. (Eds.) (2007). *Solidarity and prosocial behavior: An integration of sociological and psychological perspectives.* New York: Springer.

Fiedler, F. E. (1967). *A theory of leadership effectiveness.* New York: McGraw-Hill.

Fiedler, F. E. (1987, September). When to lead, when to stand back. *Psychology Today*, pp. 26–27.

Fiedler, F. E. (1993). The leadership situation and the black box in contingency theories. In M. M. Chemers & R. Ayman (Eds.), *Leadership theory and research: Perspectives and directions* (pp. 1–28). San Diego, CA: Academic Press.

Fiedler, F. E., & Garcia, J. E. (1987). *New approaches to effective leadership.* New York: Wiley.

Fiedler, K. (2004). Tools, toys, truisms, and theories: Some thoughts on the creative cycle of theory formation. *Personality and Social Psychology Review, 8*, 123–131.

Fiedler, K., Walther, E., & Nickel, S. (1999). Covariation-based attribution: On the ability to assess multiple covariates of an effect. *Personality and Social Psychology Bulletin, 25*, 607–622.

Figueredo, A. J., Landau, M. J., & Sefcek, J. A. (2004). Apes and angels: Adaptionism versus panglossianism. *Behavioral and Brain Sciences, 27.*

Fine, G. A. (2006). Impression management, and preadolescent behavior. In G. Handel (Ed.), *Childhood socialization (2nd ed.,* pp. 213–236). New Brunswick, NJ: AldineTransaction.

Fine, G. A., & Elsbach, K. D. (2000). Ethnography and experiment in social psychological theory building: Tactics for integrating qualitative field data with quantitative lab data. *Journal of Experimental Social Psychology, 36*, 51–76.

Finkel, E. J., & Eastwick, P. W. (2007). Speed-dating: A powerful and flexible paradigm for studying romantic relationship initiation. In S. Sprecher, A. Wenzel, & J. Harvey (Eds.), *The handbook of relationship initiation.* Mahwah, NJ: Erlbaum.

Finkel, E. J., Eastwick, P. W., & Matthews, J. (2007). Speed dating as an invaluable tool for studying romantic attraction: A methodological primer. *Personal Relationships, 14*, 149–166.

Firestone, I. J., Kaplan, K. J., & Russell, J. C. (1973). Anxiety, fear, and affiliation with similar state versus dissimilar state others: Misery sometimes loves miserable company. *Journal of Personality and Social Psychology, 26*, 409–414.

Fischer, P., Kastenmuller, A., & Grietemeyer, T. (2010).

Media violence and the self: The impact of personalized gaming characters in aggressive video games on aggressive behavior. *Journal of Experimental Social Psychology, 46*, 192–195.

Fischer, P., Krueger, J. I., Greitemeyer, T., Vogrincic, C., Kastenmuller, A., Frey, D., Heene, M., Wicher, M., & Kainbacher, M. (2011). The bystander-effect: A meta-analytic review on bystander intervention in dangerous and non-dangerous emergencies. *Psychological Bulletin.*

Fishbein, M., & Ajzen, I. (1975). *Beliefs, attitude, intention, and behavior: An introduction to theory and research.* Reading, MA: Addison-Wesley.

Fishbein, M., & Ajzen, I. (2009). *Predicting and changing behavior: The reasoned action approach.* New York: Taylor & Francis.

Fishbein, M., & Coombs, F. S. (1974). Basis for decision: An attitudinal analysis of voting behavior. *Journal of Applied Social Psychology, 4*, 95–124.

Fisher, P. & Greitemeyer, T. (2006). Music and Aggression: The Impact of sexual-aggressive song lyrics on aggression-related Thoughts, Emotions, and behavior toward the same and the opposite sex. *Personality and Social Psychology Bulletin, 32*, 1165–1176.

Fiske, A. P., & Haslam, N. (1996). Social cognition is thinking about relationships. *Current Directions in Psychological Science, 5*, 143–148.

Fiske, A. P., Kitayama, S., Markus, H. R., & Nisbett, R. E. (1998). The cultural matrix of social psychology. In D. T. Gilbert, S. T. Fiske, & G. Lindzey (Eds.), *The handbook of social psychology* (Vol. II, pp. 915–981). Boston, MA: McGraw-Hill.

Fiske, S. T. (1993). Controlling other people: The impact of power on stereotyping. *American Psychologist, 48*, 621–628.

Fiske, S. T. (2004). Developing a program of research. In C. Sansone, C. C. Morf, & A. T. Panter (Eds.), *Handbook of methods in social psychology* (pp. 71–90). Thousand Oaks, CA: Sage.

Fiske, S. T., & Cox, M. G. (1979). Person concepts: The effect of target familiarity and descriptive purpose on the process of describing others. *Journal of Personality, 47*, 136–161.

Fiske, S. T., & Molm, L. D. (2010). Bridging inequality from both sides now. *Social Psychology Quarterly, 73*, 341–346.

Fiske, S. T., & Neuberg, S. L. (1990). A continuum model of impression formation, from category-based to individuating processes: Influence of information and motivation on attention and interpretation. In M. P. Zanna (Ed.), *Advances in experimental social psychology* (Vol. 23). New York: Academic Press.

Fleischhauer, M., Enge, S., Brocke, B., Ullrich, J., Strobel, A., & Strobel, A. (2010). Same or different? Clarifying the relationship of need for cognition to personality and intelligence. *Personality and Social Psychology Bulletin, 36*, 82–96.

Fletcher, G. (2002). *The new science of intimate relationships.* Malden, MA: Blackwell.

Fletcher, G. J. O., & Kerr, P. S. G. (2010). Through the eyes of love: Reality and illusion in intimate relationships. *Psychological Bulletin, 136*, 627–658.

Fletcher, G. J. O., Tither, J. M., O'Loughlin, C., Friesen, M., & Overall, N. (2004). Warm and homely or cold and beautiful? Sex differences in trading off traits in mate selection. *Personality and Social Psychology Bulletin, 30*, 659–672.

Fletcher, J. K., & Käufer, K. (2003). Shared leadership. In C. L. Pearce & J. A. Conger (Eds.), *Shared leadership. Reframing the hows and whys of leadership* (pp. 21–47). Thousand Oaks, CA: Sage.

Florack, A., Scarabis, M., & Bless, H. (2001). When do associations matter? The use of automatic associations toward ethnic groups in person judgments. *Journal of Experimental Social Psychology, 37*, 518–524.

Flynn, F. J. (2005). Having an open mind: The impact of openness to experience on interracial attitudes

and impression formation. *Journal of Personality and Social Psychology, 88*, 816–826.

Foddy, M., & Smithson, M. (1996). Relative ability, paths of relevance, and influence in task-oriented groups. *Social Psychology Quarterly, 59*, 140–153.

Foels, R., & Pappas, C. J. (2004). Learning and unlearning the myths we are taught: Gender and social dominance orientation. *Sex Roles, 50*, 743–757.

Fogelman, E. (1996). Victims, perpetrators, bystanders, and rescuers in the face of genocide and its aftermath. In C. B. Strozier & M. Flynn (Eds.), *Genocide, war, and human survival* (pp. 87–97). Lanham, MD: Rowman & Littlefield.

Fointiat, V. (2006). "You're helpful" versus "that's clear": Social versus functional label in the foot-in-the-door paradigm. *Social and Behavior and Personality, 34*, 461–466.

Follenfant, A., & Ric, R. (2010). Behavioral rebound following stereotype suppression. *European Journal of Social Psychology, 40*, 774–782.

Follette, W. C., Davis, D., & Kemmelmeier, M. (2003). Ideals and realities in the development and practice of informed consent. In W. O'Donohue & K. Ferguson (Eds.), *Handbook of professional ethics for psychologists: Issues, questions, and controversies* (pp. 195–226). Thousand Oaks, CA: Sage.

Forbes, C. E., & Schamder, T. (2010). Retraining attitudes and stereotypes to affect motivation and cognitive capacity under stereotype threat. *Journal of Personality and Social Psychology, 99*, 740–754.

Ford, C. S., & Beach, F. A. (1951). *Patterns of sexual behavior.* New York: Harper & Row.

Ford, T. E., & Ferguson, M. A. (2004). Social consequences of disparagement humor: A prejudice norm theory. *Personality and Social Psychology Review, 8*, 79–94.

Fordham, S. (1985). *Black student school success as related to fictive kinship: Final report.* The National Institute of Education, Washington, DC.

Forgas, J. P. (1998). Asking nicely? The effects of mood on responding to more or less polite requests. *Personality and Social Psychology Bulletin, 24*, 173–185.

Forrest, J. A., & Feldman, R. S. (2000). Detecting deception and judge's involvement: Lower task involvement leads to better lie detection. *Personality and Social Psychology Bulletin, 26*, 118–125.

Förster, J., & Strack, F. (1996). Influence of overt head movements on memory for valenced words: A case of conceptual-motor compatibility. *Journal of Personality and Social Psychology, 71*, 421–430.

Forsyth, D. R. (1990). *Group dynamics* (2nd ed.). Pacific Grove, CA: Brooks/Cole.

Foshee, V. A., Bauman, K. F., Arriaga, X. B., Koch, G. G., & Linder, G. F. (1998). An evaluation of safe dates, an adolescent dating violence prevention program. *American Journal of Public Health, 88*, 45–50.

Fosco, G.M., DeBoard, R.L., & Grych, J.H. (2007). Making sense of family violence: Implications of children's appraisals of interparental aggression for their short- and long-term functioning. *European Psychologist, 12*, 6–16.

Foster, C. A., Witcher, B. S., Campbell, W. K., & Green, J. D. (1998). Arousal and attraction: Evidence for automatic and controlled processes. *Journal of Personality and Social Psychology, 74*, 86–101.

Foster, E. K., & Rosnow, R. L. (2006). Gossip and network relationships. In D. C. Kirkpatrick, S. W. Duck, & M. K. Foley (Eds.). *Relating difficulty: The processes of constructing and managing difficult interaction* (pp. 161–180). Mahwah, NJ: Erlbaum.

Foster, M. D. (1999). Acting out against gender discrimination: The effects of different social identities. *Sex Roles, 40*, 167–186.

Foubert, J. D., & Newberry, J. T. (2006). Effects of two versions of an empathy-based rape prevention program on fraternity men's survivor empathy, attitudes, and behavioral intent to commit rape or sexual assault. *Journal of College Student Development, 47,* 133–148.

Fournier, M. A., Moskowitz, D. S., & Zuroff, D. C. (2002). Social rank strategies in hierarchical relationships. *Journal of Personality and Social Psychology, 83,* 425–433.

Fouts, R. (1997). *Next of kin: What chimpanzees have taught me about who we are.* New York: William Morrow.

Fox, D. R. (1985). Psychology, ideology, utopia, and the commons. *American Psychologist, 40,* 48–58.

Fraley, R. C. (2002). Attachment stability from infancy to adulthood: Meta-analysis and dynamic modeling of developmental mechanisms. *Personality and Social Psychology Review, 6,* 123–151.

Fraley, R. C., Brumbaugh, C. C., & Marks, M. J. (2005). The evolution and function of adult attachment: A comparative and phylogenetic analysis. *Journal of Personality and Social Psychology, 89,* 731–746.

Fraley, R. C., & Spieker, S. J. (2003). Are infant attachment patterns continuously or categorically distributed? A taxometric analysis of strange situation behavior. *Developmental Psychology, 39,* 387–404.

Frank, M. G., Ekman, P., & Friesen, W. V. (2005). Behavioral markers and recognizability of the smile of enjoyment. In P. Ekman & E. L. Rosenberg (Eds.), *What the face reveals: Basic and applied studies of spontaneous expression using the facial action coding system (FACS),* pp. 217–238. Oxford: Oxford University Press.

Frank, M. G., & Gilovich, T. (1989). Effect of memory perspective on retrospective causal attributions. *Journal of Personality and Social Psychology, 57,* 399–403.

Franklin, K. (2000). Antigay behaviors among young adults: Prevalence, patterns and motivators in a noncriminal population. *Journal of Interpersonal Violence, 15,* 339–362.

Franzoi, S. L. (1995). The body-as-object versus the body-as-process: Gender differences and gender considerations. *Sex Roles, 33,* 417–437.

Franzoi, S. L. (2007). History of social psychology. In R. Baumeister & K. Vohs (Eds.), *Encyclopedia of Social Psychology.* pp. 431–439. Thousand Oaks, CA: Sage.

Franzoi, S. L., & Chang, Z. (2002). The body esteem of Hmong and Caucasian young adults. *Psychology of Women Quarterly, 26,* 89–91.

Franzoi, S. L., & Davis, M. H. (2005). Self-awareness and self-consciousness. In V. Derlega, B. Winstead, & W. Jones (Eds.), *Personality: Contemporary theory and research* (pp. 281–308) (3rd ed.). Belmont, CA: Thomson Wadsworth.

Franzoi, S. L., & Klaiber, J. R. (2007). Body use and reference group impact: With whom do we compare our bodies? *Sex Roles, 56,* 205–214.

Franzoi, S. L., & Shields, S. A. (1984). The body esteem scale: Multidimensional structure and sex differences in a college population. *Journal of Personality Assessment, 48,* 173–178.

Franzoi, S. L., Vasquez, K., Sparapani, E., Frost, K., Martin, J., & Aebly, M. (2012). Exploring body comparison tendencies: Women are self-critical whereas men are self-hopeful. *Psychology of Women Quarterly.*

Fraser, C., Gouge, C., & Billig, M. (1971). Risky shifts, cautious shifts, and group polarization. *European Journal of Social Psychology, 1,* 7–30.

Frazier, P., Steward, J., & Mortensen, H. (2004). Perceived control and adjustment to trauma: A comparison across events. *Journal of Social and Clinical Psychology, 23,* 303–324.

Frazier, P. A., & Cook, S. W. (1993). Correlates of distress following heterosexual relationship dissolution. *Journal of Social and Personal Relationships, 10,* 55–67.

Frederick, D.A., Buchanan, G. M., Sadeghi-Azar, L., Peplau, L. A., Haselton, M.G., Berezovskaya, A., & Lipinski, R. E. (2007). Desiring the muscular ideal: Men's body satisfaction in the United States, Ukraine, and Ghana. *Psychology of Men & Masculinity, 8,* 103–117.

Frederick, D. A., Peplau, L. A., & Lever, J. (2006). The swimsuit issue: Correlates of body image in a sample of 52,677 heterosexual adults. *Body Image, 3,* 413–419.

Fredricks, A. J., & Dossett, D. L. (1983). Attitude-behavior relations: A comparison of the Fishbein-Ajzen and the Bentler-Speckart models. *Journal of Personality and Social Psychology, 45,* 501–512.

Fredrickson, B. L., & Carstensen, L. L. (1990). Choosing social partners: How age and anticipated endings make people more selective. *Psychology and Aging, 5,* 335–347.

Frederico, C. M., & Sidanius, J. (2002). Racism, ideology, and affirmative action revisited: The antecedents and consequences of "principled objections" to affirmative action. *Journal of Personality and Social Psychology, 82,* 488–502.

Freeman, J. B., & Ambady, N. (2011). A dynamic interactive theory of person construal. *Psychological Review, 118,* 247–279.

Freedman, J. L. (1965). Long-term behavioral effects of cognitive dissonance. *Journal of Experimental Social Psychology, 1,* 145–155.

Freedman, J. L. (1984). Effect of television violence on aggressiveness. *Psychological Bulletin, 96,* 227–246.

Frenkl, O. J., & Doob, A. N. (1976). Post-decision dissonance at the polling booth. *Canadian Journal of Behavioral Science, 8,* 347–350.

Frese, B., Moya, M. L., & Megias, J. L. (2004). Social perception of rape: How rape myth acceptance modulates the influence of situational factors. *Journal of Interpersonal Violence, 19,* 143–161.

Frey, B. S., Savage, D. A., & Torgler, B. (2010). Noblesse oblige? Determinants of survival in a life-and-death situation. *Journal of Economic Behavior & Organization, 74,* 1–11.

Frey, D., & Schulz-Hardt, S. (2001). Confirmation bias in group information seeking and its implications for decision making in administration, business and politics. In F. Butera, & G. Mugny (Eds.), *Social influence in social reality: Promoting individual and social change* (pp. 53–73). Ashland, OH: Hogrefe & Huber.

Frey, K. P., & Eagly, A. H. (1993). Vividness can undermine the persuasiveness of messages. *Journal of Personality and Social Psychology, 65,* 32–44.

Freyd, J. J. (2002). In the wake of terrorist attack, hatred may mask fear. *Analyses of Social Issues and Public Policy, 2,* 5–8.

Friedkin, N. E. (2010). The attitude-behavior linkage in behavioral cascades. *Social Psychology Quarterly, 73,* 96–213.

Friese, M., Bluemke, M., & Wanke, M. (2007). Predicting voting behavior with implicit attitude measures: The 2002 German parliamentary election. *Experimental Psychology, 54,* 247–255.

Frieze, I. H., Olson, J. E., & Russell, J. (1991). Attractiveness and income for men and women in management. *Journal of Applied Social Psychology, 21,* 1039–1057.

Fritsch, J. (2000, February 26). The Diallo verdict: The overview; 4 officers in Diallo shooting are acquitted of all charges. *The New York Times,* p. A1.

Fritz, H. L., Nagurney, A. J., & Helgeson, V. S. (2003). Social interactions and cardiovascular reactivity during problem disclosure among friends. *Personality and Social Psychology Bulletin, 29,* 713–725.

Fritzsche, B. A., Finkelstein, M. A., & Penner, L. A. (2000). To help or not to help: Capturing individuals' decision policies. *Social Behavior and Personality, 28,* 561–578.

Froming, W. J., Corley, E. B., & Rinker, L. (1990). The influence of public self-consciousness and the audience's characteristics on withdrawal from embarrassing situations. *Journal of Personality, 58,* 603–622.

Froming, W. J., Nasby, W., & McManus, J. (1998).

Prosocial self-schemas, self-awareness, and children's prosocial behavior. *Journal of Personality and Social Psychology, 75,* 766–777.

Froming, W. J., Walker, G. R., & Lopyan, K. J. (1982). Public and private self-awareness: When personal attitudes conflict with societal expectations. *Journal of Experimental Social Psychology, 18,* 476–487.

Fujihara, T., Kohyama, T., Andreu, J. M., & Ramirez, J. M. (1999). Justification of interpersonal aggression in Japanese, American and Spanish students. *Aggressive Behavior, 25,* 185–195.

Fujita, K., Trope, Y., Liberman, N., & Levin-Sagi, M. (2006). Construal levels and self-control. *Journal of Personality and Social Psychology, 90,* 351–367.

Fung, H. H., & Carstensen, L. L. (2003). Sending memorable messages to the old: Age differences in preferences and memory for advertising. *Journal of Personality and Social Psychology, 85,* 163–178.

Fung, H. H., Carstensen, L. L., & Lang, F. R. (2001). Age-related patterns in social networks among European-Americans and African-Americans: Implications for socioemotional selectivity across the life span. *International Journal of Aging and Human Development, 52,* 185–206.

Fung, H. H., Carstensen, L. L., & Lutz, M. A. (1999). Influence of time on social preferences: Implications for life-span development. *Psychology and Aging, 14,* 595–604.

Fung, H. H., Stoeber, F. S., Yeung, D. Y., & Lang, F. R. (2008). Cultural specificity of socioemotional selectivity: Age differences in social network composition among Germans and Hong Kong Chinese. *Journal of Gerontology: Psychological Sciences, 63B,* 156–164.

Furnham, A., McClelland, A., & Omer, L. (2003). A cross-cultural comparison of ratings of perceived fecundity and sexual attractiveness as a function of body weight and waist-to-hip ratio. *Psychology Health and Medicine, 8,* 219–230.

Furnham, A., Moutafi, J., & Baguma, P. (2002). A cross-cultural study on the role of weight and waist-to-hip ratio on female attractiveness. *Personality and Individual Differences, 32,* 729–745.

Gabrenya, W. K., Jr., Wang, Y. E., & Latané, B. (1985). Social loafing on an optimizing task: Cross-cultural differences among Chinese and Americans. *Journal of Cross-Cultural Psychology, 16,* 223–242.

Gabriel, S., Renaud, J. M., & Tippin, B. (2007). When I think of you, I feel more confident about me: The relational self and self-confidence. *Journal of Experimental Social Psychology, 43,* 772–779.

Gabrieli, J. D. E. (1999). The architecture of human memory. In J. K. Foster & M. Jelicic (Eds.), *Memory: Systems, process, or function* (pp. 205–231). Oxford, England: Oxford University Press.

Gaertner, S. L., & Dovidio, J. F. (1977). The subtlety of white racism, arousal, and helping behavior. *Journal of Personality and Social Psychology, 35,* 691–707.

Gaertner, S. L., & Dovidio, J. F. (2000). *Reducing intergroup bias: The common ingroup identity model.* Philadelphia, PA: Psychology Press.

Gaertner, S. L., & Dovidio, J. F. (2009). A common ingroup identity: A categorization-based approach for *reducing intergroup bias.* In T. Nelson (Ed.), *Handbook of prejudice, stereotyping, and discrimination* (pp. 489–505). New York: Psychology Press.

Gagné, F. M., & Lydon, J. E. (2001). Mindset and relationship illusions: The moderating effects of domain specificity and relationship commitment. *Personality and Social Psychology Bulletin, 27,* 1144–1155.

Gailliot, M. T., & Baumeister, R. F. (2007). The physiology of willpower: Linking blood glucose to self-control. *Personality and Social Psychology Review, 11,* 303–327.

Gailliot, M. T., Baumeister, R. F., DeWall, C. N., Maner, J. K., Plant, E. A., Tice, D. M., Brewer, L. E., &

Schmeichel, B. J. (2007). Self-control relies on glucose as a limited energy source: Willpower is more than a metaphor. *Journal of Personality and Social Psychology, 92,* 325–336.

Gaines, S. O., Jr. (1995). Relationships between members of cultural minorities. In J. T. Wood & S. Duck (Eds.), *Understudied relationships: Off the beaten track* (pp. 51–88). Thousand Oaks, CA: Sage.

Galinsky, A. D., Gruenfeld, D. H., & Magee, J. C. (2003). From power to action. *Journal of Personality and Social Psychology, 85,* 453–466.

Galinsky, A. D., & Moskowitz, G. B. (2000). Counterfactuals as behavioral primes: Priming the simulation heuristic and consideration of alternatives. *Journal of Experimental Social Psychology, 36,* 384–409.

Gallese, V., Eagle, M. N., & Migone, P. (2007). Intentional attunement: Mirror neurons and the neural underpinnings of interpersonal relations. *Journal of the American Psychoanalytic Association, 55,* 131–176.

Gallup, G. G., Jr. (1977). Self-recognition in primates: A comparative approach to the bidirectional properties of consciousness. *American Psychologist, 32,* 329–338.

Galperin, A., & Haselton, M. (2010). Predictors of how often and when people fall in love. *Evolutionary Psychology, 8,* 5–28.

Gammage, K. L., Carron, A. V., & Estabrooks, P. A. (2001). Team cohesion and individual productivity: The influence of the norm of reciprocity and the identifiability of individual effort. *Small Group Research, 32,* 3–18.

Gamson, W. A., Fireman, B., & Rytina, S. (1982). *Encounters with unjust authority.* Homewood, IL: Dorsey Press.

Gana. K., Lourel, M., Trouillet, R., Fort, I., Mezred. D., Blaison, C., Boudjemadi, V., K'Delant, P., & Ledrich, J. (2011). Judgment of riskiness: Impact of personality, naïve thinking, and heuristic thinking among female students. *Psychology & Health, 25,* 131–147.

Gangestad, S. W., & Simpson, J. A.(Eds.). (2007). *The evolution of mind: Fundamental questions and controversies.* New York: Guilford Press.

Gangestad, S. W., & Snyder, M. (2000). Self-monitoring: Appraisal and reappraisal. *Psychological Bulletin, 126,* 530–555.

Garcia, S. M., Weaver, K., Moskowitz, G. B., & Darley, J. M. (2002). Crowded minds: The implicit bystander effect. *Journal of Personality and Social Psychology, 83,* 843–853.

Garcia-Retamero, R., & Lopez-Zafra, E. (2006). Prejudice against women in male-congenial environments: Perceptions of gender role congruity in leadership. *Sex Roles, 55,* 51–61.

Gardner, W. L., Gabriel, S. & Hochschild, L. (2002). When you and I are "we," you are not threatening: The role of self-expansion in social comparison. *Journal of Personality and Social Psychology, 82,* 239–251.

Gardner, W. L., Gabriel, S., & Lee, A. Y. (1999). "I" value freedom, but "we" value relationships: Self-construal priming mirrors cultural differences in judgment. *Psychological Science, 15,* 321–326.

Gardner, W. L., Pickett, C., Jefferis, V., & Knowles, M. L. (2005). On the outside looking in: Loneliness and social monitoring. *Personality and Social Psychology Bulletin, 31,* 1549–1560.

Garfinkel, P. (1985). *In a man's world.* New York: New American Library.

Garrity, S. E. (2011). Sexual assault prevention programs for college-aged men: A critical evaluation. *Journal of Forensic Nursing, 7,* 40–48.

Gastil, J., Burkhalter, S., & Black, L. W. (2007). Do juries deliberate? A study of deliberation, individual difference, and group member satisfaction at a municipal courthouse. *Small Group Research, 38,* 337–359.

Gates, M. F., & Allee, W. C. (1933). Conditioned behavior of isolated and grouped cockroaches on a simple maze. *Journal of Comparative Psychology, 15,* 331–358.

Gathorne-Hardy, J. (1981). *Marriage, love, sex and divorce.* New York: Summit Books.

Gawronski, B. (2003). On difficult questions and evident answers: Dispositional inference from role-constrained behavior. *Personality and Social Psychology Bulletin, 29,* 1459–1475.

Gawronski, B., & Bodenhausen, G. V. (2006). Associative and propositional processes in evaluation: An integrative review of implicit and explicit attitude change. *Psychological Bulletin, 132,* 692–731.

Gawronski, B., LeBel, E. P., & Peters, K. R. (2007). What do implicit measures tell us? Scrutinizing the validity of three common assumptions. *Perspectives in Psychological Science, 2,* 181–193.

Gawronski, B., & Strack, F. (2004). On the prepositional nature of cognitive consistency: Dissonance changes explicit, but not implicit attitudes. *Journal of Experimental Social Psychology, 40,* 535–542.

Gazzaniga, M. S. (Ed.). (2000). *The new cognitive neuroscience* (2nd ed.). Cambridge, MA: The MIT Press.

Geary, D. C., Rumsey, M., Bow-Thomas, C. C., & Hoard, M. K. (1995). Sexual jealousy as a facultative trait: Evidence from the pattern of sex differences in adults from China and the United States. *Ethology and Sociobiology, 16,* 355–383.

Geary, J., & DePaulo, B. M. (2007). Can People Accurately Detect Lies? In J. A. Nier (Ed.), *Taking sides: Clashing views in social psychology* (2nd ed., pp. 138–151). New York: McGraw-Hill.

Geen, R. G. (1968). Effects of frustration, attack, and prior training on aggressiveness upon aggressive behavior. *Journal of Personality and Social Psychology, 9,* 316–321.

Geen, R. G. (1978). Some effects of observing violence upon the behavior of the observer. In B. Maher (Ed.), *Progress in experimental personality research* (Vol. 8). New York: Academic Press.

Geen, R. G. (1990). *Human aggression.* Stony Stratford: Open University Press.

Geen, R. G. (1996). Preferred stimulation levels in introverts and extraverts: Effects on arousal and performance. *Journal of Personality and Social Psychology, 46,* 1303–1312.

Geen, R. G. (1998). Aggression and antisocial behavior. In D. T. Gilbert, S. T. Fiske, & G. Lindzey (Eds.), *The handbook of social psychology* (4th ed.). New York: McGraw-Hill.

Gere, J., & MacDonald, G. (2010). An update of the empirical case for the need to belong. *The Journal of Individual Psychology, 66,* 93–115.

Geiselman, R. E., Haight, N. A., & Kimata, L. G. (1984). Context effects in the perceived physical attractiveness of faces. *Journal of Experimental Social Psychology, 20,* 409–424.

Gelfand, M. J., Fitzgerald, L. F., & Drasgow, F. (1995). The structure of sexual harassment: A confirmatory analysis across cultures and setting. *Journal of Vocational Behavior, 47,* 164–177.

Gelles, R. J. (1993). Alcohol and other drugs are associated with violence: They are not its cause. In R. J. Gelles & D. R. Loseke (Eds.), *Current controversies on family violence* (pp. 182–196). Newbury Park, CA: Sage.

Gentile, D. A., Lynch, P. J., Linder, J. R., & Walsh, D. A. (2004). The effects of violent video game habits on adolescent hostility: Aggressive behaviors and school performance. *Journal of Adolescence, 27,* 5–22.

Georgesen, J. C., & Harris, M. J. (2000). The balance of power: Interpersonal consequences of differential power and expectancies. *Personality and Social Psychology Bulletin, 26,* 1239–1257.

Gerard, H. B., & Mathewson, G. C. (1966). The effects of severity of initiation on liking for a group: A replication. *Journal of Experimental Social Psychology, 2,* 278–287.

Gergen, K. J., Ellsworth, P., Maslach, C., & Seipel, M. (1975). Obligation, donor resources, and

reactions to aid in 3 cultures. *Journal of Personality and Social Psychology, 43,* 462–474.

Gerlach, A. L., Wilhelm, F. H., & Roth, W. T. (2003). Embarrassment and social phobia: The role of parasympathetic activation. *Journal of Anxiety Disorders, 17,* 197–210.

Gerstenfeld, P. B. (2002). A time to hate: Situational antecedents of intergroup bias. *Analyses of Social Issues and Public Policy, 2,* 61–67.

Gervey, B. M., Chiu, C., Hong, Y., & Dweck, C. S. (1999). Differential use of person information in decisions about guilt versus innocence: The role of implicit theories. *Personality and Social Psychology Bulletin, 25,* 17–27.

Giancola, P. R., & Zeichner, A. (1997). The biphasic effects of alcohol on human physical aggression. *Journal of Abnormal Psychology, 106,* 598–607.

Gibbons, F. X., & McCoy, S. B. (1991). Self-esteem, similarity, and reactions to active versus passive downward comparison. *Journal of Personality and Social Psychology, 60,* 414–424.

Gibbons, F. X., Carver, C. S., Scheier, M. F., & Hormuth, S. E. (1979). Self-focused attention and the placebo effect: Fooling some of the people some of the time. *Journal of Experimental Social Psychology, 15,* 263–274.

Gibbs, J. L., Ellison, N. B., & Heino, R. D. (2006). Self-presentation in online personals: The role of anticipated future interaction, self-disclosure, and perceived success in internet dating. *Communication Research, 33,* 152–177.

Gibson, B., & Maurer, J. (2000). Cigarette smoking in the movies: The influence of product placement on attitudes toward smoking and smokers. *Journal of Applied Social Psychology, 30,* 1457–1473.

Giddens, A. (1981). *Profiles and critiques of social theory.* London: Macmillan.

Gil-Burmann, C., Pelaez, F., & Sanchez, S. (2002). Mate choice differences according to sex and age: An analysis of personal advertisements in Spanish newspapers. *Human Nature, 13,* 493–508.

Gilbert, D. T. (1989). Thinking lightly about others: Automatic components of the social inference process. In J. Uleman & J. Bargh (Eds.), *Unwanted thought: Limits of awareness, intention, and control* (pp. 189–211). New York: Guilford.

Gilbert, D. T. (1998). Ordinary personalogy. In D. T. Gilbert, S. T. Fiske, & G. Lindzey (Eds.), *The handbook of social psychology* (4th ed., Vol. 2, pp. 89–150). New York: McGraw-Hill.

Gilbert, D. T., & Hixon, J. G. (1991). The trouble of thinking: Activation and application of stereotypic beliefs. *Journal of Personality and Social Psychology, 60,* 509–517.

Gilbert, D. T., Pelham, B. W., & Krull, D. S. (1988). On cognitive busyness: When person perceivers meet persons perceived. *Journal of Personality and Social Psychology, 54,* 733–740.

Gilbert, P., McEwan, K., Mitra, R., Franks, L., Richter, A., & Rockliff, H. (2008). Feeling safe and content: A specific affect regulation system? Relationship to depression, anxiety, stress and self-criticism. *Journal of Positive Psychology, 3,* 182–191.

Gill, M. J., & Swann, W. B., Jr. (2004). On what it means to know someone: A matter of pragmatics. *Journal of Personality and Social Psychology, 86,* 405–418.

Gillespie, A. (2005). G.H. Mead: Theorist of the Social Act. *Journal for the Theory of Social Behaviour, 35,* 19–39.

Gillihan, S. J., & Farah, M. J. (2005). Is self special? A critical review of evidence from experimental psychology and cognitive neuroscience. *Psychological Bulletin, 131,* 76–97.

Gilovich, T., Medvec, V. H., & Chen, S. (1995). Commission, omission, and dissonance reduction: Coping with regret in the "Monty Hall" problem. *Personality and Social Psychology Bulletin, 21,* 182–190.

Gilovich, T., & Savitsky, K. (2002). Like goes with like: The role of representativeness in erroneous and pseudo-scientific beliefs.

In T. Gilovich, D. Griffin, & D. Kahneman (Eds.), *Heuristic and biases: The psychology of intuitive judgment* (pp. 617–624). New York: Cambridge University Press.

Gjerde, P. F., Onishi, M., & Carlson, K. S. (2004). Personality characteristics associated with romantic attachment: A comparison of interview and self-report methodologies. *Personality and Social Psychology Bulletin, 30,* 1402–1415.

Gleason, K. A., Jensen-Campbell, L. A., & Richardson, D. S. (2004). Agreeableness as a predictor of aggression in adolescence. *Aggressive Behavior, 30,* 43–61.

Gleason, M. E. J., Iida, M., Bolger, N., & Shrout, P. E. (2003). Daily supportive equity in close relationships. *Personality and Social Psychology Bulletin, 29,* 1036–1045.

Glenn, E. S. (1966). *Mind, culture and politics.* Cited in Stewart, E. C., & Bennett, M. J. (1991). *American cultural patterns: A cross-cultural perspective* (p. 102). Yarmouth, ME: Intercultural Press.

Glick, P., & 15 coauthors. (2004). Bad but bold: Ambivalent attitudes toward men predict gender inequality in 16 nations. *Journal of Personality and Social Psychology, 86,* 713–728.

Glick, P., Diebold, J., Bailey-Werner, B., & Zhu, L. (1997). The two faces of Adam: Ambivalent sexism and polarized attitudes toward women. *Personality and Social Psychology Bulletin, 23,* 1323–1334.

Glick, P., & Fiske, S. T. (1996). *The ambivalent sexism inventory: Differentiating hostile and benevolent sexism. Journal of Personality and Social Psychology, 70,* 491–512.

Glick, P., & Fiske, S. T. (1999). The ambivalence toward men inventory: Differentiating hostile and benevolent beliefs about men. *Psychology of Women Quarterly, 23,* 519–536.

Glick, P., & Fiske, S. T. (2001). Ambivalent stereotypes as legitimizing ideologies: Differentiating paternalistic and resentful prejudice. In J. T. Jost & B. Major (Eds.), *The psychology of legitimacy: Emerging perspectives on ideology, justice, and intergroup relations.* New York: Cambridge University Press.

Glick, P., & Hilt, L. (2000). From combative children to ambivalent adults: The development of gender prejudice. In T. Eckes & M. Trautner (Eds.), *Developmental social psychology of gender.* Hillsdale, NJ: Erlbaum.

Glick, P., Sakalli-Ugurlu, N., Ferreira, M. C., & de Souza, M. A. (2002). Ambivalent sexism and attitudes toward wife abuse in Turkey and Brazil. *Psychology of Women Quarterly, 26,* 292–297.

Glomb, T. M., Bhave, D. P., Miner, A. G., & Wall, M. (2011). Doing good, feeling good: Examining the role of organizational citizenship behaviors in changing mood. *Personnel Psychology, 64,* 191–223.

Godfrey, D. K., Jones, E. E., & Lord, C. G. (1986). Self-promotion is not ingratiating. *Journal of Personality and Social Psychology, 50,* 106–115.

Goethals, G. R. (2005). Presidential leadership. *Annual Review of Psychology, 56,* 545–570.

Goethals, G. R., Messick, D. M., & Allison, S. T. (1991). The uniqueness bias: Studies of constructive social comparison. In J. Suls & T. A. Wills (Eds.), *Social comparison: Contemporary theory and research.* Hillsdale, NJ: Erlbaum.

Goethals, G. R., & Zanna, M. P. (1979). The role of social comparison in choice shifts. *Journal of Personality and Social Psychology, 37,* 1469–1476.

Goffman, E. (1959). *The presentation of self in everyday life.* Garden City, NY: Doubleday.

Goffman, E. (1963). *Stigma: Notes on the management of spoiled identity.* Englewood Cliffs, NJ: Prentice-Hall.

Goldberg, C. (May 18, 2003). *Privacy an issue in brain imaging: Machines can track unconscious preferences, fear. Boston Globe.*

Goldberg, I., Harel, M., & Malach, R. (2006). When the brain loses its self: Prefrontal inactivation during sensorimotor processing. *Neuron, 50,* 329–339.

Golebiowska, E. A. (2007). The contours and etiology of Whites' attitudes toward Black-White interracial marriage. *Journal of Black Studies, 38,* 268–287.

Gollwitzer, P. M., & Schaal, B. (1998). Meta-cognition in action: The importance of implementation intentions. *Personality and Social Psychology Review, 2,* 124–136.

Goldwurm, G. F., Bielli, D., Corsale, B., & Marchi, S. (2006). Optimism training: Methodology and results. *Homeostasis in Health and Disease, 44,* 27–33.

Gomez, A., Brooks, M. L., Buhrmester, M. C., Vazquez, A., Jetten, J., & Swann, W. B. Jr. (2011). On the nature of identity fusion: Insights into the construct and a new measure. *Journal of Personality and Social Psychology, 100,* 918–933.

Goncalo, J. A., Polman, E., & Maslach, C. (2010). Can confidence come too soon? Collective efficacy, conflict and group performance over time. *Organizational Behavior and Human Decision Processes, 113,* 13–24.

Gonzaga, G. C., Campos, B., & Bradbury, T. (2007). Similarity, convergence, and relationship satisfaction in dating and married couples. *Journal of Personality and Social Psychology, 93,* 34–48.

Gonzaga, G. C., & Haselton, M. G. (2008). The evolution of love and long-term bonds. In J. P. Forgas & J. Fitness (Eds.), *Social relationships: Cognitive, affective, and motivational processes* (pp. 39–54). Hove, England: Psychology Press.

Gonzales, M. H., Aronson, E., & Costanzo, M. (1988). Increasing the effectiveness of energy auditors: A field experiment. *Journal of Applied Social Psychology, 18,* 1049–1066.

Gonzales, M. H., Pederson, J. H., Manning, D. J., & Wetter, D. W. (1990). Pardon my gaffe: Effects of sex, status, and consequence severity on accounts. *Journal of Personality and Social Psychology, 58,* 610–621.

Gonzalez, R., Sirlopu, D., & Kessler, T. (2010). Prejudice among Peruvians and Chileans as a function of identity, intergroup contact, acculturation preferences, and intergroup emotions. *Journal of Social Issues, 66,* 803–824.

Good, C., Aronson, J., & Inzlicht, M. (2003). Improving adolescents' standardized test performance: An intervention to reduce the effects of stereotype threat. *Applied Developmental Psychology, 24,* 645–662.

Goodall, J. (1986). *The chimpanzees of Gombe.* Cambridge, MA: Harvard University Press.

Gorassini, D. R., & Olson, J. M. (1995). Does self-perception change explain the foot-in-the-door effect? *Journal of Personality and Social Psychology, 69,* 91–105.

Gordijn, E. H., Hindriks, I., Koomen, W., Dijksterhuis, A., & Knippenberg, A. V. (2004). Consequences of stereotype suppression and internal suppression motivation: A self-regulation approach. *Personality and Social Psychology Bulletin, 30,* 212–224.

Gordon, R. A. (1996). Impact of ingratiation on judgments and evaluations: A meta-analytic investigation. *Journal of Personality and Social Psychology, 71,* 54–70.

Gore, J. S., & Cross, S. E. (2006). Pursuing goals for us: Relationally autonomous reasons in long-term goal pursuit. *Journal of Personality and Social Psychology, 90,* 848–861.

Gore, J. S., Cross, S. E., & Morris, M. L. (2006). Let's be friends: Relational self-construal and the development of intimacy. *Personal Relationships, 13,* 83–102.

Göregenli, M. (1997). Individualist-collectivist tendencies in a Turkish sample. *Journal of Cross-Cultural Psychology, 28,* 787–794.

Gosling, S. D. (2004). Another route to broadening the scope of social psychology: Ecologically valid research. *Behavioral and Brain Sciences, 27.*

Gosnell, C. L., Britt, T. W., & Mckibben, E. S. (2011). Self-presentation in everyday life: Effort, closeness, and satisfaction. *Self and Identity, 10,* 18–31.

Gottman, J. M. (1979). *Marital interaction.* New York: Academic Press.

Gottman, J. M., & Levenson, R. W. (1992). Marital processes predictive of later dissolution: Behavior, physiology, and health. *Journal of Personality and Social Psychology, 63,* 221–233.

Goukens, C., Dewitte, S., & Warlop, L. (2009). Me, myself, and my choices: The influence of private self-awareness on choice. *Journal of Marketing Research, 46,* 682–692.

Gouldner, A. W. (1960). The norm of reciprocity: A preliminary statement. *American Sociological Review, 25,* 161–178.

Grabe, S., & Hyde, J. S. (2006). Ethnicity and body dissatisfaction among women in the United States: A meta-analysis. *Psychological Bulletin, 132,* 622–640.

Graen, G. B., & Hui, C. (2001). Approaches to leadership: Toward a complete contingency model of face-to-face leadership. In M. Erez & U. Kleinbeck (Eds), *Work motivation in the context of a globalizing economy* (pp. 211–225). Mahwah, NJ: Erlbaum.

Graham, J., Haidt, J., & Nosek, B. A. (2009). Liberals and conservatives rely on different set of moral foundations. *Journal of Personality and Social Psychology, 96,* 1029–1046.

Graham, S. R. (1992). What does a man want? *American Psychologist, 47,* 837–841.

Gramzow, R. H., & Gaertner, L. (2005). Self-esteem and favoritism towards novel in-groups: The self as an evaluative base. *Journal of Personality and Social Psychology, 88,* 801–815.

Graves, F. C., & Hennessy, M. B. (2000). Comparison of the effects of the mother and an unfamiliar adult female on cortisol and behavioral responses of pre- and postweaning guinea pigs. *Developmental Psychobiology, 36,* 91–100.

Graziano, W. G., Habashi, M. M., Sheese, & Tobin, R. M. (2007). Agreeableness, empathy, and helping: A person X situation perspective. *Journal of Personality and Social Psychology, 93,* 583–599.

Grealy, L. (1994). *Autobiography of a face.* Boston: Houghton Mifflin.

Greaves, L. (1996). *Smoke screen: Women's smoking and social control.* Halifax, Canada: Fernwood.

Green, C. W. (1998). Normative influence on the acceptance of information technology: Measurement and effects. *Small Group Research, 29,* 85–123.

Green, D. P., Glaser, J., & Rich, A. (1998). From lynching to gay bashing: The elusive connection between economic conditions and hate crime. *Journal of Personality and Social Psychology, 75,* 82–92.

Green, J. D., & Sedikides, C. (1999). Affect and self-focused attention revisited: The role of affect orientation. *Personality and Social Psychology Bulletin, 25,* 104–119.

Green, M. C., & Brock, T. C. (2000). Transportation in the persuasiveness of public narratives. *Journal of Personality and Social Psychology, 79,* 701–721.

Greenberg, M. S., & Frisch, D. M. (1972). Effects of intentionality on willingness to reciprocate a favor. *Journal of Experimental Social Psychology, 8,* 99–111.

Greenberg, M. T, & Kusche, C. A. (2006). Building social and emotional competence: The PATHS curriculum. In S. R. Jimerson & M. Furlong (Eds), *Handbook of school violence and school safety: From research to practice* (pp. 395–412). Mahwah, NJ: Lawrence Erlbaum.

Greenland, K., & Brown, R. (1999). Categorization and intergroup anxiety in contact between British and Japanese nationals. *European Journal of Social Psychology, 29,* 503–521.

Greenspan, D. H., Keltner, D. J., & Anderson, C. (2003). The effects of power on those who possess it: How social structure can affect social cognition. In G. A. Bodenhausen & A. J. Lambert (Eds.), *Foundations of social cognition: A festschrift in honor of Robert S. Wyer, Jr.* (pp. 237–261). Washington, DC: American Psychological Association.

Greenwald, A. G. (1980). The totalitarian ego:

Fabrication and revision of personal history. *American Psychologist, 35,* 603–618.

Greenwald, A. G., Oakes, M. A., & Hoffman, H. G. (2003). Targets of discrimination: Effects of race on responses to weapons holders. *Journal of Experimental Social Psychology, 39,* 399–405.

Greenwald, A. G., & Pratkanis, A. R. (1984). The self. In R. S. Weyer & T. K. Srull (Eds.), *The handbook of social cognition* (Vol. 3). Hillsdale, NJ: Erlbaum.

Greenwald, A. G., & Ronis, D. L. (1978). Twenty years of cognitive dissonance: Case study of the evolution of a theory. *Psychological Review, 85,* 53–57.

Greenwood, D. N., & Long, C. R. (2011). Attachment, belongingness needs, and relationship status predict imagined intimacy with media figures. *Communication Research, 38,* 278–297.

Gregory, W. L., Cialdini, R. B., & Carpenter, K. M. (1982). Self-relevant scenarios as mediators of likelihood estimates and compliance: Does imagining make it so? *Journal of Personality and Social Psychology, 43,* 89–99.

Greitemeyer, T. (2011). Exposure to music with prosocial lyrics reduces aggression: First evidence and test of the underlying mechanism. *Journal of Experimental Social Psychology, 47,* 28–36.

Greve, F. (2009, May 23). America's poor are its most generous. *The Seattle Times.*

Grewen, K. M., Girdler, S. S., Amico, J., & Light, K. C. (2005). Effects of partner support on resting oxytocin, cortisol, norepinephrine, and blood pressure before and after warm partner contact. *Psychosomatic Medicine, 67,* 531–538.

Griffith, R. L. Chmielowski, T., & Yoshita, Y. (2007). Do applicants fake? An examination of the frequency of applicant faking behavior. *Personnel Review, 36,* 341–355.

Griskevicius, V., Goldstein, N. J., Mortensen, C. R., Cialdini, R. B., & Kenrick, D. T. (2006). Going along versus going alone: When fundamental motives facilitate strategic (non)conformity. *Journal of Personality and Social Psychology, 91,* 281–294.

Gross, A. E., & Latané, J. G. (1974). Receiving help, reciprocation, and interpersonal attraction. *Journal of Applied Social Psychology, 4,* 210–223.

Gross, S. R., & Miller, N. (1997). The "golden section" and bias in perceptions of social consensus. *Personality and Social Psychology Review, 1,* 241–271.

Groth, A. N. (1979). *Men who rape: The psychology of the offender.* New York: Plenum.

Gruenfeld, D. H., & Preston, J. (2000). Upending the status quo: Cognitive complexity in U.S. Supreme Court justices who overturn legal precedent. *Personality and Social Psychology Bulletin, 26,* 1013–1022.

Gruner, C. R. (1985). Advice to the beginning speaker on using humor: What the research tells us. *Communication Education, 34,* 142–147.

Grusec, J. E. (1991). The socialization of empathy. In M. S. Clark (Ed.), *Review of personality and social psychology: Vol. Prosocial behavior* (pp. 9–33). Newbury Park, CA: Sage.

Grusec, J. E., Davidov, M., & Lundell, L. (2002). In P. K. Smith, & C. H. Hart (Eds.), *Blackwell handbook of childhood social development. Blackwell handbooks of developmental psychology* (pp. 457–474). Malden, MA: Blackwell.

Gudjonsson, G. H. (1991). Suggestibility and compliance among alleged false confessors and resisters in criminal trials. *Medicine, Science, and the Law, 31,* 147–151.

Gudjonsson, G. H. (2001). False confession. *Psychologist, 14,* 588–591.

Gudjonsson, G. H. (2003). *The psychology of interrogations and confessions: A handbook.* New York: Wiley.

Gueguen, N., & De Gail, M. A. (2003). The effect of smiling on helping behavior: Smiling and good samaritan behavior. *Communication Reports, 16,* 133–140.

Gueguen, N., & Fischer-Lokou, J. (2004). Hitchhikers'

smiles and receipt of help. *Psychological Reports, 94,* 756–760.

Gueguen, N., & Jacob, C. (2001). Fund-raising on the Web: The effect of an electronic foot-in-the-door on donation. *Cyberpsychology and Behavior, 4,* 705–709.

Gueguen, N., Pascual, A., & Dagot, L. (2002). Low-ball and compliance to a request: An application in a field setting. *Psychological Reports, 91,* 81–84.

Guerin, B. (1986). Mere presence effects in humans: A review. *Journal of Personality and Social Psychology, 22,* 38–77.

Guerra, N. G., & Slaby, R. G. (1990). Cognitive mediators of aggression in adolescent offenders: 2. Intervention. *Developmental Psychology, 26,* 269–277.

Guille, L. (2004). Men who batter and their children: An integrated review. *Aggression and Violent Behavior, 9,* 129–163.

Guimond, S., Chatard, A., Martinot, D., Crisp, R. J., & Redersdorff, S. (2006). Social comparison, self-stereotyping, and gender differences in self-construals. *Journal of Personality and Social Psychology, 90,* 221–242.

Guimond, S., Dambrun, M., Michinov, M., & Duarte, S. (2003). Does social dominance generate prejudice? Integrating individual and contextual determinants of intergroup cognitions. *Journal of Personality and Social Psychology, 84,* 697–721.

Guinote, A., Mauro, C., Pereira, M. H., & Monteiro, M. B. (2007). Children's perceptions of group variability as a function of status. *International Journal of Behavioral Development, 31,* 97–104.

Guinote, A., Willis, G. B., & Martellotta, C. (2010). Social power increases implicit prejudice. *Journal of Experimental Social Psychology, 46,* 299–307.

Gunderson, E. A., Ramirez, G., Levine, S. C., & Beilock, S. L. (2011). The role of parents and teachers in the development of gender-related math attitudes. *Sex Roles, 64.*

Gutek, B. A., & Koss, M. P. (1993). Changed women and changed organizations: Consequences of coping with sexual harassment. *Journal of Vocational Behavior, 42,* 28–48.

Guthrie, J. P., Ash, R. A., & Bendapudi, V. (1995). Additional validity evidence for a measure of morningness. *Journal of Applied Psychology, 80,* 186–190.

Guyll, M., Madon, S., Prieto, L., & Scherr, K. C. (2010). *Journal of Social Issues, 66,* 113–130.

Hadaway, C. K., Marler, P. L., & Chaves, M. (1993). What the polls don't show: A closer look at U.S. church attendance. *American Sociological Review, 58,* 741–752.

Hagestad, G. O., & Smyer, M. A. (1982). Dissolving long-term relationships: Patterns of divorcing in middle age. In S. Duck (Ed.), *Personal relationships, 4: Dissolving relationships* (pp. 155–188). New York: Academic Press.

Haidt, J., & Kesebir, S. (2010). Morality. In S. T. Fiske, D. T. Gilbert, & G. Lindzey (Eds.). *Handbook of social psychology, Vol. 1* (5th ed.) (pp. 797–832). Hoboken, NJ: John Wiley.

Halberstadt, J., & Rhodes, G. (2003). It's not just average faces that are attractive: Computer-manipulated averageness makes birds, fish, and automobiles attractive. *Psychonomic Bulletin and Review, 10,* 149–156.

Halford, W. K., Hahlweg, K., & Dunne, M. (1990). The cross-cultural consistency of marital communication associated with marital distress. *Journal of Marriage and the Family, 52,* 487–500.

Hall, J. A. (1978). Gender effects in decoding nonverbal cues. *Psychological Bulletin, 85,* 845–875.

Hall, J. A. (1984). *Nonverbal sex differences: Communication accuracy and expressive style.* Baltimore: Johns Hopkins University Press.

Hall, J. A., & Mast, M. S. (2008). Are women always more interpersonally sensitive than men? Impact of goals and content domain. *Personality and Social Psychology Bulletin,*

34, 144–155.

Hall, S., & Brannick, M. T. (2002). Comparison of two random-effects methods of meta-analysis. *Journal of Applied Psychology, 87,* 377–389.

Haltzman, S., Holstein, N., & Moss, S. B. (2007). Men, marriage, and divorce. In J. E. Grant & M. N. Potenza (Eds.), *Textbook of men's mental health* (pp. 283–305). Washington, DC: American Psychiatric Publishing.

Halverson, A. M., Hallahan, M., Hart, A. J., & Rosenthal, R. (1997). Reducing the biasing effects of judges' nonverbal behavior with simplified jury instruction. *Journal of Applied Psychology, 82,* 590–598.

Halevy, N., Berson, Y., & Galinsky, A. D. (2011). The mainstream is not electable: When vision triumphs over representativeness in leader emergence and effectiveness. *Personality and Social Psychology Bulletin, 37,* 893–904.

Ham, J., & Vonk, R. (2003). Smart and easy: Co-occurring activation of spontaneous trait inferences and spontaneous situational inferences. *Journal of Experimental Social Psychology, 39,* 434–447.

Hamamura, T., & Heine, S. J. (2008). The role of self-criticism in self-improvement and face maintenance among Japanese. In E. C. Chang (Ed). *Self-criticism and self-enhancement: Theory, research, and clinical implications* (pp. 105–122). Washington, DC: American Psychological Association.

Hames, R., & McCabe, C. (2007). Meal sharing among the Ye'Kwana. *Human Nature, 18,* 1–21.

Hamilton, D. L., & Gifford, R. K. (1976). Illusory correlation in interpersonal judgments. *Journal of Experimental Social Psychology, 12,* 392–407.

Hamilton, J. T. (1998). *Channeling violence: The economic market for violent television programming.* Princeton, NJ: Princeton University Press.

Hammond, K. R. (2004). The wrong standard: Science, not politics, needed. *Behavioral and Brain Sciences, 27*(3), 341.

Hampson, S. E. (1988). The dynamics of categorization and impression formation. In T. K. Srull & R. S. Wyer, Jr. (Eds.), *Advances in social cognition: Vol. 1. A dual process model of impression formation* (pp. 77–82). Hillsdale, NJ: Erlbaum.

Haney, C., & Zimbardo, P. G. (2009). Persistent dispositionalism in interactionist clothing: Fundamental attribution error in explaining prison abuse. *Personality and Social Psychology Bulletin, 35,* 807–814.

Haney, P., & Durlak, J. A. (1998). Changing self-esteem in children and adolescents: A meta-analytic review. *Journal of Clinical Child Psychology, 27,* 423–433.

Hansen, C. H., & Hansen, R. D. (1988). Finding the face in the crowd: An anger superiority effect. *Journal of Personality and Social Psychology, 54,* 917–924.

Hansen, C. H., & Hansen, R. D. (1990). Rock music videos and antisocial behavior. *Basic and Applied Social Psychology, 11,* 357–369.

Hansen, J., & Wanke, M. (2009). Liking what's familiar: The importance of unconscious familiarity in the mere-exposure effect. *Social Cognition, 27,* 161–182.

Harari, H., Mohr, D., & Hosey, K. (1980). Faculty helpfulness to students: A comparison of compliance techniques. *Personality and Social Psychology Bulletin, 6,* 373–377.

Harbus, A. (2002). The medieval concept of the self in Anglo-Saxon England. *Self & Identity, 1,* 77–97.

Hardin, C. D. (2004). (Self-)conceptions as social actions. In J. T. Jost, M. R. Banaji, & D. A. Prentice (Eds.), *Perspectivism in social psychology: The yin and yang of scientific progress* (pp. 161–172). Washington, DC: American Psychological Association.

Hardin, G. (1968). The tragedy of the commons. *Science, 162,* 1243–1248.

Hare, A. P., & Kent, M. V. (1994). Leadership. In A. P. Hare, H. H. Blumberg, M. F. Davies, & M. V.

Kent (Eds.), *Small group research: A handbook* (pp. 155–166). Norwood, NJ: Ablex.

Haritatos, J., & Benet-Martinez, V. (2002). Bicultural identities: The interface of cultural, personality, and socio-cognitive processes. *Journal of Research in Personality, 6,* 598–606.

Harkins, S. G., & Symanski, K. (1989). Social loafing and group evaluation. *Journal of Personality and Social Psychology, 56,* 934–941.

Harlow, H. F., & Harlow, M. K. (1962). Social deprivation in monkeys. *Scientific American, 200,* 68–74.

Harré, R. (1999). Discourse and the embodied person. In D. J. Nightingale & J. Cromby (Eds.), *Social constructionist psychology: A critical analysis of theory and practice* (pp. 97–112). Buckingham: Open University Press.

Harris, C. R. (2002). Sexual and romantic jealousy in heterosexual and homosexual adults. *Psychological Science, 13,* 7–12.

Harris, C. R. (2003a). A review of sex differences in sexual jealousy, including self-report data, psychophysiological responses, interpersonal violence, and morbid jealousy. *Personality and Social Psychology Review, 7,* 102–128.

Harris, C. R. (2003b). Factors associated with jealousy over real and imagined infidelity: An examination of the social-cognitive and evolutionary psychology perspectives. *Psychology of Women Quarterly, 27,* 319–329.

Harris, C. R. (2004). The evolution of jealousy. *American Scientist, 92,* 62–71.

Harris, C. R. (2005). Male and female jealousy, still more similar than different: Reply to Sagarin (2005). *Personality and Social Psychology Review, 9,* 76–86.

Harris, C. R., & Christenfeld, N. (1996). Gender, jealousy, and reason. *Psychological Science, 7,* 364–366.

Harris, G. T., Hilton, N. Z., Rice, M. E., & Eke, A. W. (2007). Children killed by genetic parents versus stepparents. *Evolution and Human Behavior, 28,* 85–95.

Harris, K. J., Kacmar, K. M., Zivnuska, S., & Shaw, J. D. (2007). The impact of political skill on impression management effectiveness. *Journal of Applied Psychology, 92,* 278–285.

Harris, L. T, & Fiske, S. T. (2011). Perceiving humanity or not: A social neuroscience approach to dehumanized perception. In A. Todorov, S. T. Fiske, & D. A. Prentice (Eds.). *Social neuroscience: Toward understanding the underpinnings of the social mind* (pp. 123–134). New York: Oxford University Press.

Harris, M. (1999). *Theories of culture in postmodern times.* Walnut Creek, CA: Alta Mira Press.

Harris, M. B., Benson, S. M., & Hall, C. L. (1975). The effects of confession on altruism. *Journal of Social Psychology, 96,* 187–192.

Harris, M. J., Milich, R., Corbitt, E. M., Hoover, D. W., & Brady, M. (1992). Self-fulfilling effects of stigmatizing information on children's social interactions. *Journal of Personality and Social Psychology, 63,* 41–50.

Harris, S. M. (1995). Family, self, and sociocultural contributions to body-image attitudes of African-American women. *Psychology of Women Quarterly, 19,* 129–145.

Harrison, A., & Saeed, L. (1977). Let's make a deal: An analysis of revelations and stipulations in lonely hearts advertisements. *Journal of Personality and Social Psychology, 35,* 257–264.

Harrison, L. A., & Lynch, A. B. (2005). Social role theory and the perceived gender role orientation of athletes. *Sex Roles, 52,* 229–236.

Hart, A. J., Whalen, P. J., Shin, L. M., McInerney, S. C., Fischer, H., & Rauch, S. L. (2000). Differential response in the human amygdala to racial outgroup vs. ingroup face stimuli. *Neuroreport, 11,* 2351–2355.

Hart, D., & Whitlow, J. W., Jr. (1995). The experience of self in the bottlenose dolphin. *Consciousness and Cognition, 4,* 244–247.

Hart, J. W., Bridgett, D. J., & Karau, S. J. (2001). Coworker ability and effort as determinants of individual effort on a collective task. *Group Dynamics: Theory, Research, and Practice, 5,* 181–190.

Hart, S., Field, T., del Valle, C., & Letourneau, M. (1998). Infants protest their mothers' attending to an infant-size doll. *Social Development, 7,* 54–61.

Hart, W., Albarracin, D., Eagly, A. H., Brechan, I., Lindberg, M. J., & Merrill, L. (2009). Feeling validated versus being correct: A meta-analysis of selective exposure to information. *Psychological Bulletin, 135,* 555–588.

Harter, S. (2006). The self. In W. Damon & R. Lerner (Eds.), *Handbook of Child Psychology, Vol. 3: Social, emotional, and personality development* (pp. 505–570). New York: Wiley.

Hartley, T. R., Ginsburg, G. P., Heffner, K. (1999). Self-presentation and cardiovascular reactivity. *International Journal of Psychophysiology, 32,* 75–88.

Hartley, W. S. (1970). *Manual for the twenty statements problem.* Kansas City, MO: Department of Research, Greater Kansas City Mental Health Foundation.

Hartmann, D. P. (1969). Influence of symbolically modeled instrumental aggression and pain cues on aggressive behavior. *Journal of Personality and Social Psychology, 11,* 280–288.

Hartung, F. M., & Renner, B. (2011). Social curiosity and interpersonal perception: A judge X trait interaction. *Personality and Social Psychology Bulletin, 37,* 796-814.

Harvey, E. L., & Hill, A. J. (2001). Health professionals' views of overweight people and smokers. *International Journal of Obesity, 25,* 1253–1261.

Harvey, J. H., Flanary, R., & Morgan, M. (1986). Vivid memories of vivid loves gone by. *Journal of Social and Personal Relationships, 3,* 359–373.

Haselton, M. G., & Buss, D. M. (2000). Error management theory: A new perspective on biases in cross-sex mind reading. *Journal of Personality and Social Psychology, 78,* 81–91.

Haselton, M. G., & Nettle, D. (2006). The paranoid optimist: An integrative evolutionary model of cognitive biases. *Personality and Social Psychology Review, 10,* 47–66.

Hashimoto, H. (2011). Interdependence as a self-sustaining set of beliefs. *Japanese Journal of Experimental Social Psychology, 50,* 182-193.

Haslam, S. A., Jetten, J., Postmes, T., & Haslam, C. (2009). Social identity, health and well-being: An emerging agenda for applied psychology. *Applied Psychology: An International Review, 58,* 1–23.

Haslam, S. A., Reicher, S. D., & Platow, M. J. (2011). *The new psychology of leadership: Identity, influence, and power.* New York: Psychology Press.

Hass, R. G., Katz, I., Rizzo, N., Bailey, J., & Eisenstadt, D. (1991). Cross-racial appraisal as related to attitude ambivalence and cognitive complexity. *Personality and Social Psychology Bulletin, 17,* 83–92.

Hastie, R., Penrod, S., & Pennington, N. (1983). *Inside the jury.* Cambridge, MA: Harvard University Press.

Hastorf, A., & Cantril, H. (1954). They saw a game: A case study. *Journal of Abnormal and Social Psychology, 49,* 129–134.

Hatfield, E. (1988). Passionate and companionate love. In R. J. Sternberg & M. L. Barnes (Eds.), *The psychology of love* (pp. 191–217). New Haven, CT: Yale University Press.

Hatfield, E., Aronson, E., Abrahams, D., & Rottman, L. (1966). The importance of physical attractiveness in dating behavior. *Journal of Personality and Social Psychology, 4,* 508–516.

Hatfield, E., & Rapson, R. L. (1993). *Love, sex, and intimacy: Their psychology, biology, and history.* New York: HarperCollins.

Hatfield, E., & Rapson, R. L. (2002). Passionate love and sexual desire: Cultural and historical perspectives. In A. L. Vangelisti & H. T. Reis (Eds.), *Stability and change in relationships. Advances in personal relationships* (pp. 306–324). New York: Cambridge University Press.

Hatfield, E., Rapson, R. L., & Martel, L. D. (2007). Passionate love and sexual desire. In S. Kitayama, Shinobu & D. Cohen (Eds.). *Handbook of cultural psychology.* (pp. 760–779). New York: Guilford Press.

Hatfield, E., Walster, G. W., & Piliavin, J. (1978). Equity theory and helping relationships. In L. Wispé (Ed.), *Altruism, sympathy and helping* (pp. 115–139). New York: Academic Press.

Hau, K. T., & Salili, F. (1991). Structure and semantic differential placement of specific causes: Academic causal attributions by Chinese students in Hong Kong. *International Journal of Psychology, 26,* 175–193.

Haugtvedt, C. P., & Petty, R. E. (1992). Personality and persuasion: Need for cognition moderates the persistence and resistance of attitude changes. *Journal of Personality and Social Psychology, 63,* 308–319.

Haugtvedt, C. P., Schumann, D. W., Schneier, W. L., & Warren, W. L. (1994). Advertising repetition and variation strategies: Implications for understanding attitude strength. *Journal of Consumer Research, 21,* 176–189.

Hawkins, S. A., & Hastie, R. (1990). Hindsight: Biased judgments of past events after the outcomes are known. *Psychological Bulletin, 107,* 311–327.

Haxby, J. V. (2011). Social neuroscience and the representation of others: Commentary. In A., Todorov, S. T. Fiske, & D. A. Prentice (Eds.). *Social neuroscience: Toward understanding the underpinnings of the social mind* (pp. 77–81). New York: Oxford University Press.

Hazan, C., & Shaver, P. (1987). Romantic love conceptualized as an attachment process. *Journal of Personality and Social Psychology, 52,* 511–524.

Hearold, S. (1986). A synthesis of 1043 effects of television on social behavior. In G. Comstock (Ed.), *Public communication and behavior* (Vol. 1, pp. 66–133). New York: Academic Press.

Heath, L., Acklin, M., & Wiley, K. (1991). Cognitive heuristics and AIDS risk assessment among physicians. *Journal of Applied Social Psychology, 21,* 1859–1867.

Heatherton, T. F. (2011). Building a social brain. In A. Todorov, S. T. Fiske, & D. A. Prentice (Eds.). *Social neuroscience: Toward understanding the underpinnings of the social mind* (pp. 274–283). New York: Oxford University Press.

Heatherton, T. F., & Baumeister, R. F. (1991). Binge eating as escape from self-awareness. *Psychological Bulletin, 110,* 86–108.

Hebl, M. R., & Dovidio, J. F. (2005). Promoting the "social" in the examination of social stigmas. *Personality and Social Psychology Review, 9,* 156–182.

Hebl, M. R., Foster, J. B., Mannix, L. M., & Dovidio, J. F. (2002). Formal and interpersonal discrimination: A field study of bias toward homosexual applicants. *Personality and Social Psychology Bulletin, 28,* 815–825.

Hebl, M. R., King, E. B., Glick, P., Singletary, S. L., & Kazama, S. (2007). Hostile and benevolent reactions toward pregnant women: Complementary interpersonal punishments and rewards that maintain traditional roles. *Journal of Applied Psychology, 92,* 1499–1511.

Hebl, M. R., & Mannix, L. M. (2003). The weight of obesity in evaluating others: A mere proximity effect. *Personality & Social Psychology Bulletin, 29,* 28–38.

Hebl, M. R., & Turchin, J. M. (2005). The stigma of obesity: What about men? *Basic and Applied Social Psychology, 27,* 267–275.

Hebl, M. R., Xu, J., & Mason, M. F. (2003). Weighing the care: Patients' perceptions of physician care as a function of gender and weight. *International Journal of Obesity, 27,* 269–275.

Hecht, M. A., & LaFrance, M. (1998). License or obligation to smile: The effect of power and sex on amount and type of smiling. *Personality and Social Psychology Bulletin, 24,* 1332–1342.

Heffner, K. L., Ginsburg, G. P., & Hartley, T. R. (2002).

Appraisals and impression management opportunities: Person and situation influences on cardiovascular reactivity. *International Journal of Psychophysiology, 44,* 165–175.

Heffner, K. L., Kiecolt-Glaser, J. K., Loving, T. J., Glaser, R., & Malarkey, W. B. (2004). Spousal support satisfaction as a modifier of physiological responses to marital conflict in younger and older couples. *Journal of Behavioral Medicine, 11.*

Heider, F. (1946). Attitudes and cognitive organization. *Journal of Psychology, 21,* 107–112.

Heider, F. (1958). *The psychology of interpersonal relations.* New York: Wiley.

Heiervang, E., & Goodman, R. (2011). Advantages and limitations of web-based surveys: Evidence from a child mental health survey. *Social Psychiatry and Psychiatric Epidemiology, 46,* 69–76.

Heimpel, S. A., Wood, J. V., Marshall, M. A., & Brown, J. D. (2002). Do people with low self-esteem want to feel better? Self-esteem differences in motivation to repair negative moods. *Journal of Personality and Social Psychology, 82,* 128–147.

Heine, S. J. (2011). Evolutionary explanations need to account for cultural variation. *Behavioral and Brain Sciences, 34,* 26–27.

Heine, S. J., & Hamamura, T. (2007). In search of East Asian self-enhancement. *Personality and Social Psychology Review, 11,* 4–27.

Heine, S. J., & Lehman, D. R. (1997). Culture, dissonance, and self-affirmation. *Personality and Social Psychology Bulletin, 23,* 389–400.

Heine, S. J., & Lehman, D. R. (1999). Culture, self-discrepancies, and self-satisfaction. *Personality and Social Psychology Bulletin, 25,* 915–925.

Heine, S. J., & Raineri, A. (2009). Self-improving motivations and collectivism: The case of Chileans. *Journal of Cross-Cultural Psychology, 40,* 158–163.

Heine, S. J., Takemoto, T., Moskalenko, S., Lasaleta, J., & Henrich, J. (2008). Mirrors in the head: Cultural variation in objective self-awareness. *Personality and Social Psychology Bulletin, 34,* 879–887.

Helgesen, S. (1990). *The female advantage: Women's ways of leadership.* New York: Doubleday.

Helgeson, V. S. (1994). Long-distance romantic relationships: Sex differences in adjustment and breakup. *Personality and Social Psychology Bulletin, 20,* 254–265.

Helmbrecht, J. (2002). Grammar and function of we. In A. Duszak (Ed.), *Us and others: Social identities across languages, discourses and cultures* (pp. 31–49). Amsterdam: John Benjamins.

Henderson-King, D., & Stewart, A. J. (1999). Educational experiences and shifts in group consciousness: Studying women. *Personality and Social Psychology Bulletin, 25,* 390–399.

Henderson, J. A., & Anglin, J. M. (2003). Facial attractiveness predicts longevity. *Evolution and Human Behavior, 24,* 351–356.

Hendrick, C., & Hendrick, S. (1986). A theory and method of love. *Journal of Personality and Social Psychology, 50,* 392–402.

Hendrick, C., & Hendrick, S. S. (2003). Romantic love: Measuring cupid's arrow. In S. J. Lopez & C. R. Snyder (Eds.), *Positive psychological assessment: A handbook of models and measures* (pp. 235–249). Washington, DC: American Psychological Association.

Hendrick, C., Hendrick, S., Foote, F. H., & Slapion-Foote, M. J. (1984). Do men and women love differently? *Journal of Social and Personal Relationships, 1,* 177–195.

Hennessey, B. A. (2007). Promoting social competence in school-aged children: The effects of the Open Circle Program. *Journal of School Psychology, 45,* 349–360.

Henningsen, D. D., Henningsen, M. L. M., Eden, J., & Cruz, M. G. (2006). Examining the symptoms of groupthink and retrospective sensemaking. *Small Group Research, 37,* 36–64.

Henry, P. J., & Hardin, C. D. (2006). The contact hypothesis revisited: Status bias in the reduction of implicit prejudice in the United States and Lebanon. *Psychological Science, 17,* 862–868.

Hepper, E. G., & Carnelley, K. (in press). Attachment and romantic relationships: The roles of working models of self and other. To appear in M. Paludi (Ed.), *The psychology of love: Vol. 3: Emotion and romance.* Praeger.

Hepworth, J. T., & West, S. G. (1988). Lynchings and the economy: A time-series reanalsis of Hovland and Sears (1940). *Journal of Personality and Social Psychology, 55,* 239–247.

Herek, G. M. (1987). Religious orientation and prejudice: A comparison of racial and sexual attitudes. *Personality and Social Psychology Bulletin, 13,* 34–44.

Herek, G. M. (1988). Heterosexuals' attitudes toward lesbians and gay men: Correlates and gender differences. *Journal of Sex Research, 25,* 451–477.

Herek, G. M. (1991). Myths about sexual orientation: A lawyer's guide to social science research. *Law and Sexuality: A Review of Lesbian and Gay Legal Issues, 1,* 133–172.

Herek, G. M. (2000). The psychology of sexual prejudice. *Current Directions in Psychological Science, 9,* 19–22.

Herek, G. M. (2002). Gender gaps in public opinion about lesbians and gay men. *Public Opinion Quarterly, 66,* 40–46.

Herek, G. M. (2003). Why tell if you're not asked? Self-disclosure, intergroup contact, and heterosexuals' attitude toward lesbians and gay men. In L. D. Garnets & D. C. Kimmel (Eds.), *Psychological perspectives on lesbian, gay, and bisexual experiences* (2nd ed., pp. 188–200). New York: Columbia University Press.

Herek, G. M. (2004). Beyond "homophobia": Thinking about sexual prejudice and stigma in the twenty-first century. *Sexuality Research and Social Policy, 1,* 6–24.

Herek, G. M. (2009). Sexual prejudice. In T. D. Nelson (ed.). *Handbook of prejudice, stereotyping, and discrimination (p*p. 441–467). New York: Psychology Press.

Herek, G. M., & Capitanio, J. P. (1996). "Some of my best friends": Intergroup contact, concealable stigma, and heterosexuals attitudes toward gay men and lesbians. *Personality and Social Psychology Bulletin, 22,* 412–424.

Herek, G. M., & Garnets, L. D. (2007). Sexual orientation and mental health. *Annual Review of Clinical Psychology, 3,* 353–375.

Herek, G. M., & Gonzalez, M. (2006). Attitudes toward homosexuality among U.S. residents of Mexican descent. *Journal of Sex Research, 43*(2), 122–135.

Herek, G. M., Widaman, K. F., & Capitanio, J. P. (2005). When sex equals AIDS: Symbolic stigma and inaccurate beliefs about sexual transmission of AIDS among U.S. adults. *Social Problems, 52,* 15–37.

Hergovich, A., & Olbrich, A. (2003). The impact of the Northern Ireland conflict on social identity, Groupthink and integrative complexity in Great Britain. *Review of Psychology, 10,* 95–106.

Hermans, D., De Houwer, J., & Eelen, P. (2001). A time course analysis of the affective priming effect. *Cognition and Emotion, 15,* 143–165.

Hermans, E. J., Putnam, P., Baas, J., Koppeschaar, H. P., & van Honk, J. (2006a). Testosterone acutely reduces the fear potentiated startle. *Biological Psychiatry, 59,* 872–874.

Hermans, E. J., Putnam, P., & van Honk, J. (2006b). Testosterone reduces empathic mimicking in healthy young women. *Bioloneuroendocrinology, 31,* 859–866.

Hermans, E. J., Ramsey, N. F., & van Honk, J. (2008). Exogenous testosterone potentiates the neural circuitry of reactive aggression in humans. *Biological Psychiatry, 63,* 263–270.

Hertel, G., Kerr, N. L., & Messé, L. A. (2000). Motivation gains in groups: Paradigmatic and theoretical advances on the Köhler effect. *Journal of Personality and Social Psychology, 79,* 580–601.

Hewstone, M. (1996). Contact and categorization: Social psychological interventions to change intergroup relations. In C. N. Macrae, C. Stangor, & M. Hewstone (Eds.), *Stereotypes and stereotyping* (pp. 323–368). New York: Guilford.

Hewstone, M., & Brown, R. J. (1986). Contact is not enough: An intergroup perspective on the "contact hypothesis." In M. Hewstone & R. Brown (Eds.), *Contact and conflict in intergroup encounters* (pp. 1–44). Oxford: Basil Blackwell.

Heyman, J., & Ariely, D. (2004). Effort for payment: A tale of two markets. *Psychological Science, 15,* 787–793.

Hicks, D. (1968). Short- and long-term retention of affectively varied modeled behavior. *Psychonomic Science, 11,* 369–370.

Hiel, A. V., Pandelaere, M., & Duriez, B. (2004). The impact of need for closure on conservative beliefs and racism: Differential mediation by authoritarian submission and authoritarian dominance. *Personality and Social Psychology Bulletin, 30,* 824–837.

Higgins, E. T. (1987). Self-discrepancy: A theory relating self and affect. *Psychological Review, 94,* 319–340.

Higgins, E. T. (1996). The "self digest": Self-knowledge serving self-regulatory functions. *Journal of Personality and Social Psychology, 71,* 1062–1083.

Higgins, E. T. (2000). Social cognition: Learning about what matters in the social world. *European Journal of Social Psychology, 30,* 3–39.

Higgins, E. T. (2004). Making a theory useful: Lessons handed down. *Personality and Social Psychology Review, 8,* 138–145.

Higgins, E. T., Bond, R. N., Klein, R., & Strauman, T. (1986). Self-discrepancies and emotional vulnerability: How magnitude, accessibility, and type of discrepancy influence affect. *Journal of Personality and Social Psychology, 51,* 5–15.

Higgins, E. T., Rholes, W. S., & Jones, C. R. (1977). Category accessibility and impression formation. *Journal of Experimental Social Psychology, 13,* 141–154.

Higgins, R. L., & Harris, R. N. (1988). Strategic "alcohol" use: Drinking to self-handicap. *Journal of Social and Clinical Psychology, 6,* 191–202.

Hill, C. T., Rubin, Z., & Peplau, L. A. (1979). Breakups before marriage: The end of 103 affairs. In G. Levinger & O. C. Moles (Eds.), *Divorce and separation* (pp. 64–82). New York: Basic Books.

Hill, R. A., & Dunbar, R. (2003). Social network size in humans. *Human Nature, 14,* 53–72.

Hillard, G. (Oct. 3, 2007). Scars of war run deep for many female vets. *National Public Radio.* http://www.npr.org/

Hinck, S. S., & Thomas, R. W. (1999). Rape myth acceptance in college students: How far have we come? *Sex Roles, 40,* 815–832.

Hing, L. S. S., Li, W., & Zanna, M. P. (2002). Inducing hypocrisy to reduce prejudicial responses among aversive racists. *Journal of Experimental Social Psychology, 38,* 71–78.

Hirt, E. R. (1990). Do I see only what I expect? Evidence for an expectancy-guided retrieval model. *Journal of Personality and Social Psychology, 58,* 937–951.

Hirt, E. R., Deppe, R. K., & Gordon, L. J. (1991). Self-reported versus behavioral self-handicapping: Empirical evidence for a theoretical distinction. *Journal of Personality and Social Psychology, 61,* 981–991.

Hirt, E. R., McCrea, S. M., & Boris, H. I. (2003). "I know you self-handicapped last exam": Gender differences in reactions to self-handicapping. *Journal of Personality and Social Psychology, 84,* 177–193.

Hirt, E. R., McCrea, S. M., & Kimble, C. E. (2000). Public self-focus and sex differences in behavioral self-handicapping: Does increasing self-threat still make it "just a man's game"? *Personality and Social Psychology Bulletin, 26,* 1131–1141.

Hirt, E. R., Zillmann, D., Erickson, G. A., & Kennedy, C. (1992). Costs and benefits of allegiance: Changes in fans' self-ascribed competencies after team victory versus defeat. *Journal of Personality and Social Psychology, 63*, 724–738.

Hitlin, S. (2007). Doing good, feeling good: Values and the self's moral center. *Journal of Positive Psychology. 2*, 249–259.

Ho, D. Y. F., & Chiu, C. Y. (1994). Component ideas of individualism, collectivism, and social organization: An application in the study of Chinese culture. In U. Kim, H. C. Triandis, C. Kagitcibasi, S. C. Choi, & G. Yoon (Eds.), *Individualism and collectivism: Theory, method, and applications* (pp. 137–156). Thousand Oaks, CA: Sage.

Hobart, C. W. (1958). The incidence of romanticism during courtship. *Social Forces, 36*, 364–367.

Hobson, J. A., & McCarley, R. W. (1977). The brain as a dream state generator: An activation-synthesis hypothesis of the dream process. *The American Journal of Psychiatry, 134*, 1335–1348.

Hobson, J. A., Stickgold, R., & Pace-Schott, E. F. (1998). The neuropsychology of REM sleep dreaming. *NeuroReport, 9*(3), R1–R14.

Hodges, S. D., Klaaren, K. J., & Wheatley, T. (2000). Talking about safe sex: The role of expectations and experience. *Journal of Applied Social Psychology, 2*, 330–349.

Hodgins, H. S., & Liebeskind, E. (2003). Apology versus defense: Antecedents and consequences. *Journal of Experimental Social Psychology, 39*, 297–316.

Hodgins, H. S., Liebeskind, E., & Schwartz, W. (1996). Getting out of hot water: Facework in social predicaments. *Journal of Personality and Social Psychology, 71*, 300–314.

Hodson, G., & Esses, V. M. (2002). Distancing oneself from negative attributes and the personal-group discrimination discrepancy. *Journal of Experimental Social Psychology, 38*, 500–507.

Hoelzl, E., Kirchler, E., & Rodler, C. (2002). Hindsight bias in economic expectations: I knew all along what I want to hear. *Journal of Applied Psychology, 87*, 437–443.

Hof, P. R., & Van der Gucht, E. (November 27, 2006). The structure of the cerebral cortex of the humpback whale, Megaptera novaeangliae (Cetacea, Mysticeti, Balaenopteridae). *The Anatomical Record*, published online. http://www3.interscience.wiley.com/cgi-bin

Hoffman, J. (2001). *Gender and sovereignty: Feminism, the state and international relations.* New York: Palgrave.

Hoffman, L. E. (1992). American psychologists and wartime research on Germany, 1941–1945. *American Psychologist, 47*, 264–273.

Hofmann, S. G. (2006). The emotional consequences of social pragmatism: The psychophysiological correlates of self-monitoring. *Biological Psychology, 73*, 169–174.

Hofstede, C. (1980). *Culture's consequences: International differences in work related values.* Beverly Hills, CA: Sage.

Hogg, M. A. (1992). *The social psychology of group cohesiveness: From attraction to social identity.* London: Harvester-Wheatsheaf.

Hogg, M. A. (2010). Influence and Leadership. In S. T. Fiske, D. T. Gilbert, & L. Gardner (Eds.), *Handbook of social psychology* (5th ed., pp. 1167–1207). Hoboken, NJ: John Wiley.

Hogg, M. A., & Abrams, D. (1988). *Social identifications: A social psychology of intergroup relations and group processes.* London: Routledge.

Holland, R. W., Meertens, R. M., & Van Vugt, M. (2002). Dissonance on the road: Self-esteem as a moderator of internal and external self-justification strategies. *Personality and Social Psychology Bulletin, 28*, 1713–1724.

Holland, R. W., Verplanken, B., & van Knippenberg, A. (2003). From repetition to conviction: Attitude accessibility as a determinant of attitude certainty. *Journal of Experimental Social Psychology, 39*, 594–601.

Hollingshead, A. B. (2001). Cognitive interdependence and convergent expectations in transactive memory. *Journal of Personality and Social Psychology, 81*, 1080–1089.

Holmes, B. M., & Johnson, K. R. (2009). Adult attachment and romantic partner preference: A review. *Journal of Social and Personal Relationships, 26*, 833–852.

Holstein, J. A., & Miller, G. (Eds.). (2000). *Perspectives on social problems, (Vol. 12).* Stamford, CT: JAI Press.

Holtgraves, T. (2004). Social desirability and self-reports: Testing models of socially desirable responding. *Personality and Social Psychology Bulletin, 30*, 161–172.

Holzl, E., & Kirchler, E. (2005). Causal attribution and hindsight bias for economic developments. *Journal of Applied Psychology, 90*, 167–174.

Homans, G. C. (1958). Social behavior as exchange. *American Journal of Sociology, 63*, 597–606.

Honeycutt, J. M. (2003). *Imagined interactions: Daydreaming about communication.* Cresskill, NJ: Hampton Press.

Hong, L. K., & Duff, R. W. (2002). Modulated participant-observation: Managing the dilemma of distance in field research. *Field Methods, 14*, 190–196.

Hong, Y. Y., Benet-Martinez, Chiu, C. Y., & Morris, M. W. (2003). Boundaries of cultural influence: Construct activation as a mechanism for cultural differences in social perception. *Journal of Cross-Cultural Psychology, 34*, 453–464.

Hong, Y. Y., Ip, G., Chiu, C. Y., Morris, M., & Menon, T. (2001). Cultural identity and dynamic construction of the self: Collective duties and individual rights in Chinese and American cultures. *Social Cognition, 19*, 251–268.

Hong, Y. Y., Morris, M. W., Chiu, C.Y., & Benet-Martínez, V. (2000). Multicultural minds: A dynamic constructivist approach to culture and cognition. *American Psychologist, 55*, 709–720.

Hooper, N., Saunders, J., & McHugh, L. (2010). The derived generalization of thought suppression. *Learning & Behavior, 38*, 160–168.

Hoorens, V., & Nuttin, J. M. (1993). Overevaluation of own attributes: Mere ownership or subjective frequency? *Social Cognition, 11*, 177–200.

Hornsey, M. J., & Imani, A. (2004). Criticizing groups from the inside and the outside: An identity perspective on the intergroup sensitivity effect. *Personality and Social Psychology Bulletin, 4*, 365–383.

Hornsey, M. J., & Jetten, J. (2004). The individual within the group: Balancing the need to belong with the need to be different. *Personality and Social Psychology Review, 8*, 248–264.

Horton, R. W., & Santogrossi, D. A. (1978). The effect of adult commentary on reducing the influence of televised violence. *Personality and Social Psychology Bulletin, 4*, 337–340.

Hoshino-Browne, E., Zanna, A. S., Spencer, S. J., Zanna, M. P., Kitayama, S., & Lackenbauer, S. (2005). On the cultural guises of cognitive dissonance: The case of Easterners and Westerners. *Journal of Personality and Social Psychology, 89*, 294–310.

Hosoda, M., Stone-Romero, E. F., & Coats, G. (2003). The effects of physical attractiveness on job-related outcomes: A meta-analysis of experimental studies. *Personnel Psychology, 56*, 431–462.

Hoss, R. A., Ramsey, J. L., Griffin, A. M., & Langlois, J. H. (2005). The role of facial attractiveness and facial masculinity/femininity in sex classification of faces. *Perception, 34*, 1459–1474.

Houry, D., Feldhaus, K., Peery, B., Abbott, J., Lowenstein, S. R., Al-Bataa-De-Montero, S., & Levine, S. (2004). A positive domestic violence screen predicts future domestic violence. *Journal of Interpersonal Violence, 19*, 955–966.

Hovland, C. I., & Sears, R. R. (1940). Minor studies in aggression: VI. Correlation of lynchings with economic indices. *Journal of Personality, 9*, 301–310.

Hovland, C. I., & Weiss, W. (1951). The influence of source credibility on communication effectiveness. *Public Opinion Quarterly, 15*, 635–650.

Hovland, C. I., Janis, I. L., & Kelley, H. H. (1953). *Communication and persuasion.* New Haven, CT: Yale University Press.

Hovland, C. I., Lumsdaine, A. A., & Sheffield, F. D. (1949). *Experiments on mass communication.* Princeton, NJ: Princeton University Press.

Howard, D. J. (1995). "Chaining" the use of influence strategies for producing compliance behavior. *Journal of Social Behavior and Personality, 10*, 169–185.

Howard, J. A., Blumstein, P., & Schwartz, P. (1987). Social evolutionary theories? Some observations on preferences in human mate selection. *Journal of Personality and Social Psychology, 53*, 194–200.

Hoyle, R. H. (2005). Design and analysis of experimental research on groups. In S. A. Wheelan (Ed.), *Handbook of group research and practice* (pp. 223–239). Thousand Oaks, CA: Sage.

Hoyt, C. T., & Blascovich, J. (2007). Leadership efficacy and women leaders' responses to stereotype activation. *Group Processes and Intergroup Relations, 10*, 595–616.

Hoyt, W. T. (2000). Rater bias in psychological research: When is it a problem and what can we do about it? *Psychological Methods, 5*, 64–86.

Huczynski, A., & Buchanan, D. (1996). Can leaders change their styles? In J. Billsberry (Ed.), *The effective manager: Perspectives and illustrations* (pp. 42–46). Thousand Oaks, CA: Sage.

Huesmann, L. R. (1986a). The effects of film and television violence among children. In S. J. Katz & P. Vesin (Eds.), *Children and the media* (pp. 101–128). Paris: Centre International de l'Enfance.

Huesmann, L. R. (1986b). Psychological processes promoting the relation between exposure to media violence and aggressive behavior by the viewer. *Journal of Social Issues, 42*, 125–140.

Huesmann, L. R. (1988). An information processing model for the development of aggression. *Aggressive Behavior, 14*, 125–139.

Huesmann, L. R., Moise-Titus, J., Podolski, C. L., 7 Eron, L. D. (2003). Longitudinal relations between children's exposure to TV violence and their aggressive and violent behavior in young adulthood: 1977–1992. *Developmental Psychology, 39*, 201–221.

Huesmann, L. R., & Eron, L. D. (Eds.). (1986). *Television and the aggressive child: A cross-national comparison.* Hillsdale, NJ: Erlbaum.

Huesmann, L. R., Eron, L. D., Klein, R., Brice, P., & Fischer, P. (1983). Mitigating the imitation of aggressive behaviors by changing children's attitudes about media violence. *Journal of Personality and Social Psychology, 44*, 899–910.

Huesmann, L. R., Eron, L. D., & Yarmel, P. W. (1987). Intellectual functioning and aggression. *Journal of Personality and Social Psychology, 52*, 232–240.

Huesmann, L. R., & Miller, L. S. (1994). Long-term effects of repeated exposure to media violence in childhood. In L. R. Huesmann (Ed.), *Aggressive behavior: Current perspectives* (pp. 153–186). New York: Plenum.

Hugenberg, K., & Bodenhausen, G. V. (2004). Category membership moderates the inhibition of social identities. *Journal of Experimental Social Psychology, 40*, 233–238.

Hughes, M., & Hertel, B. R. (1990). The significance of color remains: A study of life chances, mate and ethnic consciousness among black Americans. *Social Forces, 68*, 1105–1120.

Huguet, P., Latané, B., & Bourgeois, M. (1998). The emergence of a social representation of human rights via interpersonal communication: Empirical evidence for the convergence of two theories. *European Journal of Social Psychology, 28*, 831–846.

Hui, C. H., & Triandis, H. C. (1986). Individualism-collectivism, a study of cross-cultural researchers. *Journal of Cross-Cultural Psychology, 17*, 225–248.

Hull, C. L. (1943). *Principles of behavior: An*

introduction to behavior theory. New York: Appleton-Century-Crofts.

Hull, J. G. (1981). A self-awareness model of the causes and effects of alcohol consumption. *Journal of Abnormal Psychology, 90,* 586–600.

Hull, J. G., & Bond, C. F., Jr. (1986). Social and behavioral consequences of alcohol consumption and expectancy: A meta-analysis. *Psychological Bulletin, 99,* 347–360.

Hull, J. G., & Young, R. D. (1983). Self-consciousness, self-esteem, and success-failure as determinants of alcohol consumption in male social drinkers. *Journal of Personality and Social Psychology, 44,* 1097–1109.

Hull, J. G., Young, R. D., & Jouriles, E. (1986). Applications of the self-awareness model of alcohol consumption: Predicting patterns of use and abuse. *Journal of Personality and Social Psychology, 51,* 790–796.

Hunsberger, B. (1995). Religion and prejudice: The role of religious fundamentalism, quest, and right-wing authoritarianism. *Journal of Social Issues, 51,* 113–129.

Hunter, M. (1998). Colorstruck: Skin color stratification in the lives of African American women. *Sociological Inquiry, 68,* 517–535.

Huntington, S. P. (2004). *Who Are We? The Challenges to America's National Identity.* New York: Simon & Schuster.

Huskinson, T. L. H., & Haddock, G. (2004). Individual differences in attitude structure: Variance in the chronic reliance on affective and cognitive information. *Journal of Experimental Social Psychology, 40,* 82–90.

Huth-Bocks, A. C., Levendosky, A. A., Bogat, G. A., & von Eye, A. (2004). The impact of maternal characteristics and contextual variables on infant-mother attachment. *Child Development, 75,* 480–496.

Huynh, Q. L., Devos, T., & Smalarz, L. (2011). Perpetual foreigner in one's own land: Potential implications for identity and psychological adjustment. *Journal of Social and Clinical Psychology, 30,* 133–162.

Hyatt, C. W., & Hopkins, W. D. (1994). Self-awareness in bonobos and chimpanzees: A comparative perspective. In S. T. Parker, R. W. Mitchell, & M. L. Boccia (Eds.), *Self-awareness in animals and humans: Developmental perspectives* (pp. 248–253). Cambridge, UK: Cambridge University Press.

Hyde, J. S. (2005). The gender similarities hypothesis. *American Psychologist, 60,* 581–592.

Hyers, L. L. (2007). Resisting prejudice every day: Exploring women's assertive responses to anti-Black racism, anti-Semitism, heterosexism, and sexism. *Sex Roles, 56,* 1–12.

Iacoboni, M. (2007). Face to face: The neural basis of social mirroring and empathy. *Psychiatric Annals, 37,* 236–241.

Iacoboni, M., Lieberman, M. D., Knowlton, B. J., Molnar-Szakacs, I., Moritz, M., Throop, C. J., & Fiske, A. P. (2004). Watching social interactions produces dorsomedial prefrontal and medial parietal BOLD ƒMRI signal increases compared to a resting baseline. *NeuroImage 21, 1167–1173.*

Ichheiser, G. (1934). Über zurechnungstäuschungen. [About misattributions]. *Monatsschrift für Kriminalpsycholgie und Strafrechtsreform, 25,* 129–142.

Ichheiser, G. (1943). Misinterpretations of personality in everyday life and the psychologist's frame of reference. *Character and Personality, 12,* 145–160.

Ickes, W. (1985). Sex-role influences in dyadic interaction: A theoretical model. In C. Mayo & N. Henley (Eds.), *Compatible and incompatible relationships* (pp. 187–208). New York: Springer-Verlag.

Igou, E. R., & Bless, H. (2003). Inferring the importance of arguments: Order effects and conversational rules. *Journal of Experimental Social Psychology, 39,* 91–99.

IJzerman, H., van Dijk, W., & Gallucci, M. (2007). A bumpy train ride: A field experiment on insult, honor, and emotional reactions. *Emotion, 7,* 869–875.

Illes, J., & Raffin, T. A. (2002). Neuroethics: An emerging new discipline in the study of brain and cognition. *Brain and Cognition, 50,* 341–344.

Inglehart, R., & Baker, W. (2000). Modernization, cultural change and the persistence of traditional values. *American Sociological Review, 65,* 19–51.

Inglehart, R., & Oyserman, D. (2004). Individualism, autonomy and self-expression: The human development syndrome. In H. Vinken, J. Soeters, & P. Ester (Eds.), *Comparing cultures: Dimensions of culture in a comparative perspective.* Leiden, The Netherlands: Brill.

Ingram, R. E. (1990). Self-focused attention in clinical disorders: Reviews and a conceptual model. *Psychological Bulletin, 107,* 156–176.

Inman, M. L., McDonald, N., & Ruch, A. (2004: 26, 59–75). Boasting and firsthand and secondhand impressions: A new explanation for the positive teller-listener extremity effect. *Basic and Applied Social Psychology.*

Inman, M. L., Reichl, A. J., & Baron, R. S. (1993). Do we tell less than we know or hear less than we are told? Exploring the teller-listener extremity effect. *Journal of Experimental Social Psychology, 29,* 528–550.

Insko, C. A., Schopler, H. J., Gaertner, G., Wildschutt, T., Kozar, R., Pinter, B., Finkel, E. J., Brazil, D. M., Cecil, C. L., & Montoya, M. R. (2001). Interindividual-intergroup discontinuity reduction through the anticipation of future interaction. *Journal of Personality and Social Psychology, 80,* 95–111.

Insko, C. A., Smith, R. H., Alicke, M. D., Wade, J., & Taylor, S. (1985). Conformity and group size: The concern with being right and the concern with being liked. *Personality and Social Psychology Bulletin, 11,* 41–50.

Inzlicht, M., & Ben-Zeev, T. (2000). A threatening intellectual environment: Why females are susceptible to experiencing problem-solving deficits in the presence of males. *Psychological Science, 11,* 365–371.

Inzlicht, M., & Ben-Zeev, T. (2003). Do high-achieving female students underperform in private? The implications of threatening environments on intellectual processing. *Journal of Educational Psychology, 95,* 796–805.

Inzlicht, M., & Gutsell, J. N. (2007). Running on empty: Neural signals for self-control failure. *Psychological Science, 18,* 933–937.

Inzlicht, M., & Kang, S. K. (2010). Stereotype threat spillover: How coping with threats to social identity affects aggression, eating, decision making, and attention. *Journal of Personality and Social Psychology, 99,* 467–481.

Isbell, L. M. (2004). Not all happy people are lazy or stupid: Evidence of systematic processing in happy moods. *Journal of Experimental Social Psychology, 40,* 341–349.

Isbell, L. M., & Wyer, R. S. (1999). Correcting for mood-induced bias in the evaluation of political candidates: The roles of intrinsic and extrinsic motivation. *Personality and Social Psychology Bulletin, 25,* 237–249.

Isen, A. M. (1970). Success, failure, attention, and reactions to others: The warm glow of success. *Journal of Personality and Social Psychology, 15,* 294–301.

Isen, A. M. (1984). Toward understanding the role of affect in cognition. In S. R. Wyer & T. K. Srull (Eds.), *Handbook of social cognition* (Vol. 3, pp. 179–236). New York: Academic Press.

Isen, A. M. (1987). Positive affect, cognitive processes, and social behavior. In L. Berkowitz (Ed.), *Advances in experimental social psychology* (Vol. 20, pp. 203–253). New York: Academic Press.

Isen, A. M., Horn, N., & Rosenhan, D. L. (1973). Effects of success and failure on children's generosity. *Journal of Personality and Social Psychology, 27,* 239–247.

Isen, A. M., & Levin, P. A. (1972). Effect of feeling good on helping: Cookies and kindness. *Journal of Personality and Social Psychology, 21,* 384–388.

Isen, A. M., & Simmonds, S. F. (1978). The effect of feeling good on a helping task that is incompatible with good mood. *Social Psychology Quarterly, 41,* 346–349.

Isenberg, D. (1986). Group polarization: A critical review and meta-analysis. *Journal of Personality and Social Psychology, 50,* 1141–1151.

Ishii-Kuntz, M. (1989). Collectivism or individualism? Changing patterns of Japanese attitudes. *Social Science Review, 73,* 174–179.

Ito, T. A. (2011). Perceiving social category information from faces: Using ERPs to study person perception. In A. Todorov, S. T. Fiske, & D. A. Prentice (Eds.). *Social neuroscience: Toward understanding the underpinnings of the social mind (*pp. 85–100). New York: Oxford University Press.

Ito, T. A., Miller, N., & Pollock, V. E. (1996). Alcohol and aggression: A meta-analysis on the moderating effects of inhibitory cues, triggering effects, and self-focused attention. *Psychological Bulletin, 120,* 60–82.

Ito, T. A., & Urland, G. R. (2003). Race and gender on the brain: Electrocortical measures of attention to the race and gender of multiply categorizable individuals. *Journal of Personality and Social Psychology, 85,* 616–626.

Ito, T. A., Urland, G. R., Willadsen-Jensen, E., & Correll, J. (2006). The social neuroscience of stereotyping and prejudice: Using event-related brain potentials to study social perception. In J. T. Cacioppo, P. S. Visser, & C. L. Pickett (Eds.), *Social Neuroscience: People thinking about thinking people* (pp. 189–212). Cambridge, MA: MIT Press.

Iwao, S. (1989). Social psychology's models of social behavior: Is it not time for West to meet East? Unpublished manuscript. Keio University, Institute for Communications Research, Tokyo, Japan.

Izard, C. E. (1994). Innate and universal facial expressions: Evidence from developmental and cross-cultural research. *Psychological Bulletin, 115,* 288–299.

Izard, C. E., Fantauzzo, C. A., Castle, J. M., Haynes, O. M., Rayias, M. F., & Putnam, P. H. (1995). The ontogeny and significance of infants' facial expressions in the first 9 months of life. *Developmental Psychology, 31,* 997–1013.

Jackman, M. R. (1994). *The velvet glove: Paternalism and conflict in gender class and race relations.* Berkeley, CA: University of California Press.

Jackson, J. W. (1993). Realistic group conflict theory: A review and evaluation of the theoretical and empirical literature. *Psychological Record, 43,* 395–413.

Jackson, L. M. (2011). *The psychology of prejudice: From attitudes to social action.* Washington, DC: American Psychological Association.

Jackson, L. M., Esses, V. M., & Burris, C. T. (2001). Contemporary sexism and discrimination: The importance of respect for men and women. *Personality and Social Psychology Bulletin, 27,* 48–61.

Jackson, S. E., Brett, J. F., Sessa, V. I., Cooper, D. M., Julin, J. A., & Peyronnin, K. (1991). Some differences make a difference: Individual dissimilarity and group heterogeneity as correlates of recruitment, promotions, and turnover. *Journal of Applied Psychology, 76,* 675–689.

Jacobs, R. C., & Campbell, D. T. (1961). The perpetuation of an arbitrary tradition through several generations of a laboratory microculture. *Journal of Abnormal and Social Psychology, 62,* 649–658.

James, L. M., & Olson, J. M. (2000). Jeer pressure: The behavioral effects of observing ridicule of others. *Personality and Social Psychology Bulletin, 26,* 474–485.

James, R. N., III, & Sharpe, D. L. (2007). The nature

and causes of the U-shaped charitable giving profile. *Nonprofit and Voluntary Sector Quarterly, 36,* 218–238.

James, W. (1890). *The principles of psychology* (2 vols.). New York: Henry Holt.

Jamieson, D. W., Lydon, J. E., & Zanna, M. P. (1987). Attitude and activity preference similarity: Differential bases of interpersonal attraction for low and high self-monitors. *Journal of Personality and Social Psychology, 53,* 1052–1060.

Janis, I. L. (1967). Effects of fear arousal on attitude change: Recent developments in theory and experimental research. In L. Berkowitz (Ed.), *Advances in experimental social psychology* (Vol. 3, pp. 166–224). New York: Academic Press.

Janis, I. L. (1982). *Groupthink* (2nd ed.). Boston: Houghton Mifflin.

Janis, I. L. (1996). Groupthink. In J. Billsberry (Ed.), *The effective manager: Perspectives and illustrations* (pp. 166–178). Thousand Oaks, CA: Open University Press.

Janis, I. L., & Feshbach, S. (1953). Effects of fear-arousing communications. *Journal of Abnormal and Social Psychology, 48,* 78–92.

Janis, I. L., Kaye, D., & Kirschner, P. (1965). Facilitating effects of "eating while reading" on responsiveness to persuasive communications. *Journal of Personality and Social Psychology, 1,* 17–27.

Janoff-Bulman, R., & Leggatt, H. K. (2002). Culture and social obligation: When "shoulds" are perceived as "wants." *Journal of Research in Personality, 36,* 260–270.

Jarvis, W. B. G., & Petty, R. E. (1996). The need to evaluate. *Journal of Personality and Social Psychology, 70,* 172–194.

Jaskowski, P., Skalska, B., & Verleger, R. (2003). How the self controls its "automatic pilot" when processing subliminal information. *Journal of Cognitive Neuroscience, 15,* 911–920.

Jefferis, V. E., van Baaren, R., & Chartrand, T. L. (2003). *The functional purpose of mimicry for creating interpersonal closeness.* Manuscript under review, Ohio State University.

Jeffrey, L. R., Miller, D., & Linn, M. (2001). Middle school bullying as a context for the development of passive observers to the victimization of others. In R. A. Geffner & M. Loring (Eds.), *Bullying behavior: Current issues, research, and interventions* (pp. 143–156). Binghamton, NY: Haworth Maltreatment and Trauma Press/The Haworth Press.

Jellison, W. A., McConnell, A. R., & Gabriel, S. (2004). Implicit and explicit measures of sexual orientation attitudes: Ingroup preferences and related behaviors and beliefs among gay and straight men. *Personality and Social Psychology Bulletin, 30,* 629–642.

Jenson, R. E., & Moore, S. G. (1977). The effect of attribute statements on cooperativeness and competitiveness in school-age boys. *Child Development, 48,* 305–307.

Jepson, C., & Chaiken, S. (1990). Chronic issue-specific fear inhibits systematic processing of persuasive communications. *Journal of Social Behavior and Personality, 5,* 61–84.

Jetten, J., Hornsey, M. J., & Adarves-Yorno, I. (2006). When group members admit to being conformist: The role of relative intragroup status in conformity self-reports. *Personality and Social Psychology Bulletin, 32,* 162–173.

Jewkes, R., & Abrahams, N. (2002). The epidemiology of rape and sexual coercion in South Africa: An overview. *Social Science and Medicine, 55,* 1231–1244.

Jimenez, J. A., & Abreu, J. M. (2003). Race and sex effects on attitudinal perceptions of acquaintance rape. *Journal of Counseling Psychology, 50,* 252–256.

Johansson-Love, J., & Geer, J. H. (2003). Investigation of attitude change in a rape prevention program. *Journal of Interpersonal Violence, 18,* 84–99.

John, O. P., Cheek, J. M., & Klohnen, E. C. (1996). On the nature of self-monitoring: Construct explication

with Q-sort ratings. *Journal of Personality and Social Psychology, 71,* 763–776.

Johnson, A. J. (2001). Examining the maintenance of friendships: Are there differences between geographically close and long distance friends? *Communication Quarterly, 49,* 425–436.

Johnson, A. J., Haigh, M. M., Craig, E. A., & Becker, J. A. H. (2009). Relational closeness: Comparing undergraduate college students' geographically close and long-distance friendships. *Personal Relationships, 16,* 631–646.

Johnson, A. L., Crawford, M. T., Sherman, S. J., Rutchick, A. M., Hamilton, D. L., Ferreira, M. B., & Petrocelli, J. V. (2006). A functional perspective on group memberships: Differential need fulfillment in a group typology. *Journal of Experimental Social Psychology, 42,* 707–719.

Johnson, C., Clay-Warner, J., & Funk, S. J. (1996). Effects of authority structures and gender on interaction in same-sex task groups. *Social Psychology Quarterly, 59,* 221–236.

Johnson, D. L., Wiebe, J. S., Gold, S. M., Andreasen, N. C., Hichwa, R. D., Watkins, G. L., et al. (1999). Cerebral blood flow and personality: A positron emission tomography study. *American Journal of Psychiatry, 156,* 252–257.

Johnson, H. D., Brady, E., McNair, R., Congdon, D., Niznik, J., & Anderson, S. (2007). Identity as a moderator of gender differences in the emotional closeness of emerging adults' same- and cross-sex friendships. *Adolescence, 42,* 1–23.

Johnson, J. D., Jackson, L. A., & Gatto, L. (1995). Violent attitudes and deferred academic aspirations: Deleterious effects of exposure to rap music. *Basic and Applied Social Psychology, 16,* 27–41.

Johnson, J. D., Noel, N. E., & Sutter-Hernandez, J. (2000). Alcohol and male acceptance of sexual aggression: The role of perceptual ambiguity. *Journal of Applied Social Psychology, 30,* 1186–1200.

Johnson, J. G., Cohen, P., Smailes, E. M., Kasen, S., & Brook, J. S. (2002). Television violence and aggressive behavior during adolescence and adulthood. *Science, 295,* 2468–2471.

Johnson, M. B., & Drucker, J. (2009). Two recently confirmed false confessions: Bryon A Halsey and Jeffrey M Deskovic. *Journal of Psychiatry & Law, 37,* 51–72.

Johnson, R. T., Burk, J. A., Kirkpatrick, L. A. (2007). Dominance and prestige as differential predictors of aggression and testosterone levels in men. *Evolution and Human Behavior, 28,* 345–351.

Johnston, K. L., & White, K. M. (2003). Binge-drinking: A test of the role of group norms in the theory of planned behaviour. *Psychology and Health, 18,* 63–77.

Johnston, L. D., O'Malley, P. M., & Bachman, J. G. (2003). *Monitoring the Future national survey results on drug use, 1975–2002. Volume II: College students and adults ages 19–40* (NIH Publication No. 03–5376). Bethesda, MD: National Institute on Drug Abuse.

Johnston, V. S., & Franklin, M. (1993). Is beauty in the eye of the beholder? *Ethology and Sociobiology, 14,* 183–199.

Joiner, T. E., Alfano, M. S., & Metalsky, G. I. (1992). When depression breeds contempt: Reassurance seeking, self-esteem and rejection of depressed college students and their roommates. *Journal of Abnormal Psychology, 12,* 112–134.

Joireman, J., Anderson, J., & Strathman, H. (2003). The aggression paradox: Understanding links among aggression, sensation seeking, and the consideration of future consequences. *Journal of Personality and Social Psychology, 84,* 1287–302.

Joireman, J. A., Lasane, T. P., Bennett, J., Richards, D., & Solaimani, S. (2001). Integrating social value orientation and the consideration of future consequences within the extended form activation model of proenvironmental

behavior. *British Journal of Social Psychology, 40,* 133–145.

Jonas, E., Graupmann, V., Kayser, D. N., Zanna, M., Traut-Mattausch, E., & Frey, D. (2009). Culture, self, and the emergence of reactance: Is there a "universal" freedom? *Journal of Experimental Social Psychology, 45,* 1068–1080.

Jonas, E., Schulz-Hardt, S., Frey, D., & Thelan, N. (2001). Confirmation bias in sequential information search after preliminary decisions: An expansion of dissonance theoretical research on selective exposure to information. *Journal of Personality and Social Psychology, 80,* 557–571.

Jones, D., & Hill, K. (1993). Criteria of facial attractiveness in five populations. *Human Nature, 4,* 271–296.

Jones, E. E. (1964). *Ingratiation.* New York: Appleton-Century-Crofts.

Jones, E. E. (1990). *Interpersonal perception.* New York: W. H. Freeman.

Jones, E. E. (1998). Major developments in five decades of social psychology. In D. T. Gilbert, S. T. Fiske, & G. Lindzey (Eds.), *The handbook of social psychology* (4th ed., Vol. 1, pp. 3–57). New York: McGraw-Hill.

Jones, E. E., & Davis, K. E. (1965). A theory of correspondent inferences: From acts to dispositions. In L. Berkowitz (Ed.), *Advances in experimental social psychology* (Vol. 2, pp. 219–266). New York: Academic Press.

Jones, E. E., Davis, K. E., & Gergen, K. J. (1961). Role playing variations and their informational value for person perception. *Journal of Abnormal and Social Psychology, 63,* 302–310.

Jones, E. E., & Harris, V. A. (1967). The attribution of attitudes. *Journal of Experimental Social Psychology, 3,* 1–24.

Jones, E. E., & Nisbett, R. E. (1972). The actor and the observer: Divergent perceptions of the causes of behavior. In E. E. Jones, D. E. Kanouse, H. H. Kelley, R. E. Nisbett, S. Valins, & B. Weiner (Eds.), *Attribution: Perceiving the causes of behavior* (pp. 79–94). Morristown, NJ: General Learning Press.

Jones, E. E., & Pittman, T. S. (1982). Toward a general theory of strategic self-presentation. In J. Suls (Ed.), *Psychological perspectives on the self.* Hillsdale, NJ: Erlbaum.

Jones, L. W., Sinclair, R. C., & Courneya, K. A. (2003). The effects of source credibility and message framing on exercise intentions, behaviors and attitudes: An integration of the elaboration likelihood model and prospect theory. *Journal of Applied Social Psychology, 33,* 179–196.

Jones, S. S. (2007). Imitation in infancy: The development of mimicry. *Psychological Science, 18,* 593–599.

Jones, W. H., Carpenter, B. N., & Quintana, D. (1985). Personality and interpersonal predictors of loneliness in two cultures. *Journal of Personality and Social Psychology, 48,* 1503–1511.

Jones, W. H., Hobbs, S. A., & Hockenbury, D. (1982). Loneliness and social skills deficits. *Journal of Personality and Social Psychology, 42,* 682–689.

Jones, W. H., Sansone, C., & Helm, B. (1983). Loneliness and interpersonal judgments. *Personality and Social Psychology Bulletin, 9,* 437–441.

Jordan, C. H., Spencer, S. J., & Zanna, M. P. (2003). "I love me ... I love me not": Implicit self-esteem, explicit self-esteem, and defensiveness. In S. J. Spencer, S. Fein, M. P. Zanna, & J. M. Olson (Eds.), *Motivated social perception: The Ontario symposium* (Vol. 9, pp. 117–145). Mahwah, NJ: Erlbaum.

Jordan, C. H., Spencer, S. J., & Zanna, M. P. (2005). Types of high self-esteem and prejudice: How implicit self-esteem relates to ethnic discrimination among high explicit self-esteem individuals. *Personality and Social Psychology Bulletin, 31,* 693–702.

Jordan, J., Mullen, E., & Murnighan, J. K. (2011).

Striving for the moral self: The effects of recalling past moral actions on future moral behavior. *Personality and Social Psychology Bulletin, 37,* 701–713.

Joseph, N., & Hunter, C. D. (2011) Ethnic-racial socialization messages in the identity development of second-generation Haitians. *Journal of Adolescent Research, 26,* 344–380.

Jost, J. T., Banaji, M. R., & Prentice, D. A. (Eds.). (2004). *Perspectivism in social psychology: The yin and yang of scientific progress.* Washington, DC: American Psychological Association.

Jost, J., Glaser, J., Kruglanski, A., & Sulloway, F. (2003). Political conservatism as motivated social cognition. *Psychological Bulletin, 129,* 339–375.

Jost, J. T., Kivetz, Y., Rubini, M., Guermandi, G., & Mosso, C. (2005). System-justifying functions of complementary regional and ethnic stereotypes: Cross-national evidence. *Social Justice Research, 18,* 305–333.

Jost, J. T., Pietrzak, J., Liviatan, I., Mandisodza, A., & Napier, J. (2007). System justification as conscious and nonconscious goal pursuit. In J. Shah & W. Gardner (Eds.), *Handbook of motivation science.* New York: Guilford.

Judd, C. M., Blair, I. V., & Chapleau, K. M. (2004). Automatic stereotypes vs. automatic prejudice: Sorting out the possibilities in the Payne (2001) weapon paradigm. *Journal of Experimental Social Psychology, 40,* 75–81.

Judd, C. M., James-Hawkins, L., Yzerbyt, V., & Kashima, Y. (2005). Fundamental dimensions of social judgment: Understanding the relations between judgments of competence and warmth. *Journal of Personality and Social Psychology, 89,* 899–913.

Judd, C. M., Park, B., Ryan, C., Brauer, M., & Kraus, S. (1995). Stereotypes and ethnocentrism: Diverging interethnic perceptions of African American and White American youth. *Journal of Personality and Social Psychology, 69,* 460–481.

Judd, C. M., Ryan, C. S., & Park, B. (1991). Accuracy in the judgment of in-group and out-group variability. *Journal of Personality and Social Psychology, 61,* 366–379.

Judd, M., & Brauer, M. (1995). Repetition and evaluative extremity. In R. E. Petty & J. A. Krosnick (Eds.), *Attitude strength: Antecedents and consequences* (pp. 43–71). Mahwah, NJ: Erlbaum.

Judge, T. A., & Bono, J. E. (2001). Relationship of core self-evaluations traits—self-esteem, generalized self-efficacy, locus of control, and emotional stability—with job satisfaction and job performance: A meta-analysis. *Journal of Applied Psychology, 86,* 80–92.

Jussim, L., Cain, T. R., Crawford, J. T., Harber, K., & Cohen, F. (2009). The unbearable accuracy of stereotypes. In T. D. Nelson (Ed.). *Handbook of prejudice, stereotyping, and discrimination* (pp. 199–227). New York: Psychology Press.

Jussim, L., Robustelli, S. L., & Cain, T. R. (2009). Teacher expectations and self-fulfilling prophecies. In K. R. Wenzel & A. Wigfield (Eds.). *Handbook of motivation at school (pp.* 349–380). New York: Routledge/Taylor & Francis Group.

Jussim, L., Yen, H., & Aiello, J. R. (1995). Self-consistency, self-enhancement, and accuracy in reactions to feedback. *Journal of Experimental Social Psychology, 31,* 322–356.

Kacmar, K. M., Delery, J. E., & Ferris, G. R. (1992). Differential effectiveness of applicant impression management tactics on employment interview decisions. *Journal of Applied Social Psychology, 22,* 1250–1272.

Kagitcibasi, C. (1994). A critical appraisal of individualism and collectivism: Toward a new formulation. In U. Kim, H. C. Triandis, C. Kagitcibasi, S. Choi, & G. Yoon (Eds.), *Individualism and collectivism: Theory, method, and applications* (pp. 52–65). Thousand Oaks, CA: Sage.

Kahneman, D. (1995). Varieties of counterfactual thinking. In N. J. Roese & J. M. Olson (Eds.),

What might have been: The social psychology of counterfactual thinking (pp. 375–396). Hillsdale, NJ: Erlbaum.

Kahneman, D., & Frederick, S. (2002). Representativeness revisited: Attribute substitution in intuitive judgment. In T. Gilovich, D. Griffin, & D. Kahneman (Eds.), *Heuristic and biases: The psychology of intuitive judgment* (pp. 49–81). New York: Cambridge University Press.

Kahneman, D., & Tversky, A. (1973). On the psychology of prediction. *Psychological Review, 80,* 237–251.

Kahneman, D., & Tversky, A. (1982). The simulation heuristic. In D. Kahneman, P. Slovic, & A. Tversky (Eds.), *Judgment under uncertainty: Heuristics and biases.* New York: Cambridge University Press.

Kaiser, C. R., & Major, B. (2004). Judgments of deserving and the emotional consequences of stigmatization. In L. Tiedens & C. W. Leach (Eds.), *The social life of emotions* (pp. 270–291). New York: Cambridge University Press.

Kaiser, C. R., Vick, S. B., & Major, B. (2004). A prospective investigation of the relationship between just-world beliefs and the desire for revenge after September 11, 2001. *Psychological Science, 15,* 503–506.

Kaiser, F. G., Byrka, K., & Hartig, T. (2010). Reviving Campbell's paradigm for attitude research. *Personality and Social Psychology Review, 14,* 351–367.

Kalkhoff, W., & Thye, S. R. (2006). Expectation states theory and research: New observations from meta-analysis. *Sociological Methods & Research, 35,* 219–249.

Kallgren, C. A., Reno, R. R., & Cialdini, R. B. (2000). A focus theory of normative conduct: When norms do and do not affect behavior. *Personality and Social Psychology Bulletin, 26,* 1002–1012.

Kallgren, C. A., & Wood, W. (1986). Access to attitude-relevant information in memory as a determinant of attitude-behavior consistency. *Journal of Experimental Social Psychology, 22,* 328–338.

Kalven, H., Jr., & Zeisel, H. (1966). *The American jury.* Boston: Little, Brown.

Kamide, H., & Daibo, I. (2009). Application of a self-evaluation maintenance model to psychological health in interpersonal contexts. *The Journal of Positive Psychology, 4,* 557–565.

Kanagawa, C., Cross, S. E., & Markus, H. R. (2001). "Who am I?" The cultural psychology of the conceptual self. *Personality and Social Psychology Bulletin, 27,* 90–103.

Kanazawa, S. (1992). Outcome or expectancy? Antecedent of spontaneous causal attribution. *Personality and Social Psychology Bulletin, 18,* 659–668.

Kanemasa, Y. (2007). The relationship between early adult attachment styles and adjustment in friendships. *Japanese Journal of Social Psychology, 22,* 274–284.

Kaplan, K. J., Firestone, I. J., Degnore, R., & Morre, M. (1974). Gradients of attraction as a function of disclosure probe intimacy and setting formality: On distinguishing attitude oscillation from attitude change—Study one. *Journal of Personality and Social Psychology, 30,* 638–646.

Kaplan, M. F. (1987). The influencing process in group decision making. In C. Hendrick (Ed.), *Review of personality and social psychology: Group processes* (Vol. 8, pp. 189–212). Beverly Hills, CA: Sage.

Kaplan, M. F., & Martin, A. M. (1999). Effects of differential status of group members on process and outcome of deliberation. *Group Processes and Intergroup Relations, 2,* 347–364.

Kaplan, M. F., & Miller, C. E. (1983). Group discussion and judgment. In P. B. Paulus (Ed.), *Basic group processes* (pp. 65–94). New York: Springer-Verlag.

Kaplan, M. F., & Miller, C. E. (1987). Group decision making and normative versus informational

influence: Effects of type of issue and assigned decision rule. *Journal of Personality and Social Psychology, 53,* 306–313.

Karasawa, K. (1995). An attributional analysis of reactions to negative emotions. *Personality and Social Psychology Bulletin, 21,* 456–467.

Karasawa, M. (2003). Projecting group liking and ethnocentrism on ingroup members: False consensus effect of attitude strength. *Asian Journal of Social Psychology, 6,* 103–116.

Karau, S. J., & Kelly, J. R. (1992). The effects of time scarcity and time abundance on group performance quality and interaction process. *Journal of Experimental Social Psychology, 28,* 542–571.

Karau, S. J., & Williams, K. D. (1993). Social loafing: A meta-analytic review and theoretical integration. *Journal of Personality and Social Psychology, 65,* 681–706.

Karau, S. J., & Williams, K. D. (1995). Social loafing, research findings, implications, and future directions. *Current Directions in Psychological Science, 4,* 134–140.

Karpinski, A. (2004). Measuring self-esteem using the implicit association test: The role of the other. *Personality and Social Psychology Bulletin, 30,* 22–34.

Karraker, K. H., & Stern, M. (1990). Infant physical attractiveness and facial expression: Effects on adult perceptions. *Basic and Applied Social Psychology, 11,* 371–385.

Karremans, J. C., Stroebe, W., & Claus, J. (2006). Beyond Viary's fantasies: The impact of subliminal priming and brand choice. *Journal of Experimental Social Psychology, 42,* 792–798.

Kashdan, T. B., & Roberts, J. E. (2006). Affective outcomes in superficial and intimate interactions: Roles of social anxiety and curiosity. *Journal of Research in Personality, 40,* 140–167.

Kashdan,, T. B., & Steger, M. F. (2006). Expanding the topography of social anxiety: An experience-sampling assessment of positive emotions, positive events, and emotion suppression. *Psychological Science, 17,* 120–128.

Kashima, Y. (1987). Conceptions of person: Implications in individualism/collectivism research. In C. Kagitcibisi (Ed.), *Growth and progress in cross-cultural psychology* (pp. 104–112). Lisse, The Netherlands: Swets & Zeitlinger.

Kashima, Y. (2009). Culture comparison and culture priming: A critical analysis. In R. S. Wyer, C. Chiu, & Y. Hong (Eds.), *Understanding culture: Theory, research, and application* (pp. 53–77). New York: Psychology Press.

Kashima, Y., & Foddy, M. (2002). Time and self: The historical construction of the self. In Y. Kashima, M. Foddy, & M. Platow (Eds.), *Self and identity: Personal, social and symbolic* (pp. 181–206). Mahwah, NJ: Erlbaum.

Kashima, Y., & Kerekes, A. R. Z. (1994). A distributed memory model of averaging phenomena in person impression formation. *Journal of Experimental Social Psychology, 30,* 407–455.

Kashima, Y., Kokubo, T., Kashima E. S., Boxall, D., Yamaguchi, S., & Macrae, K. (2004). Culture and self: Are there within-culture differences in self between metropolitan areas and regional cities? *Personality and Social Psychology Bulletin, 30,* 816–823.

Kashima, Y., Siegel, M., Tanaka, K., & Kashima, E. S. (1992). Do people believe behaviours are consistent with attitudes? Towards a cultural psychology of attribution processes. *British Journal of Social Psychology, 31,* 111–124.

Kashima, Y., Yamaguchi, S., Kim, U., Choi, S. C., Gelfand, M. J., & Yuki, M. (1995). Culture, gender, and self: A perspective from individualism-collectivism research. *Journal of Personality and Social Psychology, 69,* 925–937.

Kashy, D. A., & DePaulo, B. M. (1996). Who lies? *Journal of Personality and Social Psychology, 70,* 1037–1051.

Kassin, S. M. (1997). The psychology of confession

evidence. *American Psychologist, 52,* 221–233.

Kassin, S. M., & Kiechel, K. L. (1996). The social psychology of false confessions: Compliance, internalization, and confabulation. *Psychological Science, 7,* 125–128.

Katkin, E. S., Wiens, S., & Ohman, A. (2001). Nonconscious fear conditioning, visceral perception, and the development of gut feeling. *Psychological Science, 12,* 366–370.

Kastrin, A. (2008). Meta-analysis: Its role in psychological methodology. *Psiboloska Obzorja/Horizons of Psychology, 17,* 25–42.

Katz, I., & Hass, R. G. (1988). Racial ambivalence and American value conflict: Correlational and prime studies of dual cognitive structures. *Journal of Personality and Social Psychology, 55,* 893–905.

Katz, I., Wackenhut, J., & Hass, R. G. (1986). Racial ambivalence, value duality, and behavior. In J. F. Dovidio & S. L. Gaertner (Eds.), *Prejudice, discrimination, and racism* (pp. 35–60). New York: Academic Press.

Katz, P. (1986). Gender identity: Development and consequences. In R. Ashmore & F. Del Boca (Eds.), *The social psychology of female-male relations* (pp. 21–67). Orlando, FL: Academic Press.

Kawakami, K., Dovidio, J. F., Moll, J., Hermsen, S., & Russin, A. (2000). Just say no (to stereotyping): Effects of training in the negation of stereotypic associations on stereotype activation. *Journal of Personality and Social Psychology, 78,* 871–888.

Kawakami, N., & Yoshida, F. (2010). Effects of subliminal mere exposure to group members on intergroup evaluation: Category evaluation measured in the Implicit Association Test. *Japanese Journal of Psychology, 81,* 364–372.

Kawakami, K., Young, H., & Dovidio, J. F. (2002). Automatic stereotyping: Category, trait, and behavioral activations. *Personality and Social Psychology Bulletin, 28,* 3–15.

Kay, A. C., & Jost, J. T. (2003). Complementary justice: Effects of "poor but happy" and "poor but honest" stereotype exemplars on system justification and implicit activation of the justice motive. *Journal of Personality and Social Psychology, 85,* 823–837.

Kay, A. C., Jost, J. T., Mandisodza, A. N., Sherman, S. J., Petrocelli, J. V., & Johnson, A. L. (2007). Panglossian ideology in the service of system justification: How complementary stereotypes help us to rationalize inequality. In M. Zanna (Ed.), *Advances in Experimental Social Psychology, Vol. 39* (pp. 305–358). San Diego: Academic Press.

Keating, C. F. (2006). Why and how the silent self speaks volumes: Functional approaches to nonverbal impression management. In V. Manusov & M. L. Patterson (Eds.), *The Sage handbook of nonverbal communication* (pp. 321–339). Thousand Oaks, CA: Sage.

Keating, C. F. (1985). Gender and the physiognomy of dominance and attractiveness. *Social Psychology Quarterly, 48,* 61–70.

Keating, C. F., Pomerantz, J., Pommer, S. D., Ritt, S. J. H., Miller, L. M., & McCormick, J. (2005). Going to college and unpacking hazing: A functional approach to decrypting initiation practices among undergraduates. *Group Dynamics: Theory, Research, and Practice, 9,* 104–126.

Keller, S., Maddock, J. E., Laforge, R. G., Velicer, W. F., & Basler, H.-D. (2007). Binge drinking and health behavior in medical students. *Addictive Behaviors, 32,* 505–515.

Kelley, H. H. (1950). The warm-cold variable in first impressions of persons. *Journal of Personality, 18,* 431–439.

Kelley, H. H. (1967). Attribution theory in social psychology. In D. L. Vine (Ed.), *Nebraska symposium on motivation.* Lincoln: University of Nebraska Press.

Kelley, H. H. (1972). Causal schemata and the attribution process. In E. Jones, D. Kanouse, H.

Kelley, R. Nisbett, S. Valms, & B. Weiner (Eds.), *Attribution: Perceiving the causes of behavior.* Morristown, NJ: General Learning Press.

Kelly, J. R., Jackson, J. W., & Hutson-Comeaux, S. L. (1997). The effects of time pressure and task differences on influence modes and accuracy in decision-making groups. *Personality and Social Psychology, 23,* 10–22.

Kelman, H. C. (1958). Compliance, identification and internalization: Three processes of attitude change. *Journal of Conflict Resolution, 2,* 51–60.

Kelman, H. C. (2006). Interests, relationships, identities: Three central issues for individuals and groups in negotiating their social environment. *Annual Review of Psychology, 57,* 1–26.

Kelman, H. C., & Hovland, C. I. (1953). "Reinstatement" of the communicator in delayed measurement of opinion change. *Journal of Abnormal and Social Psychology, 48,* 327–335.

Keltner, D., & Beer, J. S. (2005). Self-conscious emotion and self-regulation. In A. Tesser, J. V. Wood, & D. A. Stapel (Eds.), *On building, defending and regulating the self: A psychological perspective* (pp. 197–215). New York: Psychology Press.

Keltner, D., Gruenfeld, D. H., & Anderson, C. (2003). Power, approach, and inhibition. *Psychological Review, 110,* 265–284.

Keltner, D., & Lerner, J. S. (2010). In S. T. Fiske, D. T. Gilbert, & G. Lindzey (Eds.). *Handbook of social psychology, Vol. 1* (5th ed.) (pp. 317–352). Hoboken, NJ: John Wiley.

Kemmelmeier, M. (2001). Private self-consciousness as a moderator of the relationship between value orientations and attitudes. *Journal of Social Psychology, 141,* 61–74.

Kemmelmeier, M., Davis, D., & Follette, W. C. (2003). Seven "sins" of misdirection? Ethical controversies surrounding the use of deception in research. In W. O'Donohue & K. Ferguson (Eds.), *Handbook of professional ethics for psychologists: Issues, questions, and controversies* (pp. 227–256). Thousand Oaks, CA: Sage.

Kemmelmeier, M., Jambor, E. E., & Letner, J. (2006). Individualism and good works: Cultural variation in giving and volunteering across the United States. *Journal of Cross-Cultural Psychology, 37,* 327–344.

Kemper, V. (2004, July 10). "Groupthink" led to decision to attack Iraq. *Los Angeles Times.*

Kennedy, Q., Fung, H. H., & Carstensen, L. L. (2001). Aging, time estimation and emotion. In S. H. McFadden & R. C. Atchley (Eds.), *Aging and the meaning of time* (pp. 51–74). New York: Springer.

Kenny, D. A. (2004). PERSON: A general model of interpersonal perception. *Personality and Social Psychology Review, 8,* 265–280.

Kenrick, D. T., Baumann, D. J., & Cialdini, R. B. (1979). A step in the socialization of altruism as hedonism: Effects of negative mood on children's generosity under public and private conditions. *Journal of Personality and Social Psychology, 37,* 747–755.

Kenrick, D. T., & Cialdini, R. B. (1977). Romantic attraction: Misattribution versus reinforcement explanations. *Journal of Personality and Social Psychology, 35,* 381–391.

Kenrick, D. T., Gabrielidis, C., Keefe, R. C., & Cornelius, J. S. (1996). Adolescents' age preferences for dating partners: Support for an evolutionary model of life-history strategies. *Child Development, 67,* 1499–1511.

Kenrick, D. T., Gutierres, S. E., & Goldberg, L. L. (1989). Influence of popular erotica on judgments of strangers and mates. *Journal of Experimental Social Psychology, 25,* 159–167.

Kenrick, D. T., & Luce, C. L. (2000). An evolutionary life-history model of gender differences and similarities. In T. Eckes & H. M. Trautner (Eds.), *The developmental social psychology of gender* (pp. 35–63). Mahwah, NJ: Erlbaum.

Kenrick, D. T., & Maner, J. K. (2004). One path to balance and order in social psychology: An evolutionary perspective. *Behavioral and Brain Sciences, 27.*

Kenrick, D. T., & Trost, M. R. (1987). A biosocial theory of heterosexual relationships. In K. Kelly (Ed.), *Families, males, and sexuality.* Albany: State University of New York Press.

Kerckhoff, A. C., & Davis, K. E. (1962). Value consensus and need complementarity in mate selection. *American Sociological Review, 27,* 295–303.

Kernis, M. H. (2003). Toward a conceptualization of optimal self-esteem. *Psychological Inquiry, 14,* 1–26.

Kernis, M. H., & Goldman, B. M. (2006). Assessing stability of self-esteem and contingent self-esteem. In M. H. Kernis (Ed.), *Self-esteem issues and answers: A sourcebook of current perspective* (pp. 77–85). New York: Psychology Press.

Kim, H. Y., & Chung, J. E. (2011). Consumer purchase intention for organic personal care products. *Journal of Consumer Marketing, 28,* 40–47.

Kernis, M. H., & Lakey, C. E. (2010). Fragile versus secure high self-esteem: Implications for defensiveness and insecurity. In R. M. Arkin, K. C. Oleson, & P. J. Carroll (Eds.). *Handbook of the uncertain self* (pp. 360-378). New York: Psychology Press.

Kernis, M. H., Paradise, A. W., Whitaker, D. J., Wheatman, S. R., & Goldman, B. N. (2000). Master of one's psychological domain? Not likely if one's self-esteem is unstable. *Personality and Social Psychology Bulletin, 26,* 1297–1305.

Kerr, N. L. (1983). Motivation losses in small groups: A social dilemma. *Journal of Personality and Social Psychology, 45,* 819–828.

Kerr, N. L. (1992). Issue importance and group decision making. In S. Worchel, W. Wood, & J. A. Simpson (Eds.), *Group process and productivity* (pp. 68–88). Newbury Park, CA: Sage.

Kerr, N. L., & MacCoun, R. J. (1985). The effects of jury size and polling method on the process and product of jury deliberation. *Journal of Personality and Social Psychology, 48,* 349–363.

Kerr, N. L., Messé, L. A., Seok, D., Sambolec, E. J., Lount, Jr., R. B., & Park, E. S. (2007). Psychological mechanisms underlying the Köhler motivation gain. *Personality and Social Psychology Bulletin, 33,* 828–841.

Kerr, N. L., Seok, D. H., Poulsen, J. R., Harris, D. W., & Messe, L. A. (2008). Social ostracism and group motivation gain. *European Journal of Social Psychology, 38,* 736–746.

Kerr, N. L., & Tindale, R. S. (2004). Group performance and decision making. *Annual Review of Psychology, 55,* 623–655.

Kessler, K., & Hollbach, S. (2005). Group-based emotions as determinants of ingroup identification. *Journal of Experimental Social Psychology, 41,* 677–685.

Kessler, R. C., Mickelson, K. D., & Williams, D. R. (1999). The prevalence, distribution, and mental health correlates of perceived discrimination in the United States. *Journal of Health and Social Behavior, 40,* 208–230.

Key, W. B. (1989). *The age of manipulation.* New York: Holt.

Kiefer, A. K., & Sekaquaptewa, D. (2007). Implicit stereotypes, gender identification, and math-related outcomes. *Psychological Science, 18,* 13–18.

Kierstead, M. D. (April 6, 1981) The Shetland pony. *The New Yorker,* pp. 40–48.

Kiesler, C. A., & Pallak, M. S. (1975). Minority influence: The effect of majority reactionaries and defectors, and minority and majority compromisers, upon majority opinion and attraction. *European Journal of Social Psychology, 5,* 237–256.

Kiesler, S., Sproull, L., & Waters, K. (1996). A prisoner's dilemma experiment on cooperation with people and human-like computers. *Journal of*

Personality and Social Psychology, 70, 47–65.

Kihlstrom, J. F. (2004). Is there a "people are stupid" school in social psychology? *Behavioral and Brain Sciences, 27*, 348.

Kilham, W., & Mann, L. (1974). Level of destructive obedience as a function of transmitter and executant roles in the Milgram obedience paradigm. *Journal of Personality and Social Psychology, 29*, 696–702.

Kim, D-Y. (2003). After the South and North Korea summit: Malleability of explicit and implicit national attitudes of South Koreans. *Peace and Conflict: Journal of Peace Psychology, 9*, 159–170.

Kim, H., & Markus, H. R. (1999). Deviance of uniqueness, harmony or conformity? A cultural analysis. *Journal of Personality and Social Psychology, 77*, 785–800.

Kim, H. S., & Sherman, D. K. (2007). "Express yourself": Culture and the effect of self-expression on choice. *Journal of Personality and Social Psychology, 92*, 1–11.

Kim, H. S., Sherman, D. K., Ko, D., & Taylor, S. E. (2006). Pursuit of comfort and pursuit of harmony: Culture, relationships, and social support seeking. *Personality and Social Psychology Bulletin, 32*, 1595–1607.

Kim, U. (1994). Individualism and collectivism: Conceptual clarification and elaboration. In U. Kim, H. C. Triandis, C. Kagitcibsi, S. Choi, & G. Yoon (Eds.), *Individualism and collectivism: Theory, method, and applications* (pp. 19–40). Thousand Oaks, CA: Sage.

Kim, U., & Choi, S. H. (1994). Individualism, collectivism, and child development: A Korean perspective. In P. M. Greenfield & R. R. Cocking (Eds.), *Cross-cultural roots of minority child development* (pp. 227–257). Hillsdale, NJ: Erlbaum.

Kimble, D. L., Covell, N. H., Weiss, L. H., Newton, K. J., & Fisher, J. D. (1992). College students use implicit personality theory instead of safer sex. *Journal of Applied Social Psychology, 22*, 921–933.

Kimmel, A. J. (2004). Ethical issues in social psychology research. In C. Sansone, C. C. Morf, & A. T. Panter (Eds.), *Handbook of methods in social psychology* (pp. 45–70). Thousand Oaks, CA: Sage.

Kinder, D. R. (1998). Opinion and action in the realm of politics. In D. T. Gilbert, S. T. Fiske, & G. Lindzey (Eds.), *The handbook of social psychology* (4th ed., Vol. 2, pp. 778–867). New York: McGraw-Hill.

Kirkpatrick, L. A., Waugh, C. E., Valencia, A., & Webster, G. D. (2002). The functional domain specificity of self-esteem and the differential prediction of aggression. *Journal of Personality and Social Psychology, 82*, 756–767.

Kirkpatrick, S. A., & Locke, E. A. (1991). Leadership: Do traits matter? *Academy of Management Executives, 5(2)*, 48–60.

Kirkpatrick, S. A., & Locke, E. A. (1996). Direct and indirect effects of three core charismatic leadership components on performance and attitudes. *Journal of Applied Psychology, 81*, 36–51.

Kitayama, S. (May 25, 2007). *Voluntary settlement and the spirit of independence: Some more evidence from Japan's "northern frontier."* Paper presented at the American Psychological Science 19th Annual Convention. Washington, DC.

Kitayama, S., Ishii, K., Imada, T., Takemura, K., & Ramaswamy, J. (2006). Voluntary settlement and the spirit of independence: Evidence from Japan's "northern frontier". *Journal of Personality and Social Psychology, 91*, 369–384.

Kitayama, S., Park, H., Sevincer, A. T., Karasawa, M., & Uskul, A. K. (2009). A cultural task analysis of implicit independence: Comparing North America, Western Europe, and East Asia. *Journal of Personality and Social Psychology, 97*, 236–255.

Kitayama, S., Snibbe, A. C., Markus, H. R., & Suzuki, T.

(2004). Is there any "free" choice?: Self and dissonance in two cultures. *Psychological Science, 15*, 527–533.

Kite, M. E., & Whitley, B. E., Jr. (1996). Sex differences in attitudes toward homosexual persons, behaviors, and civil rights: A meta-analysis. *Personality and Social Psychology Bulletin, 22*, 336–353.

Kito, M. (2005). Self-disclosure in romantic relationships and friendships among American and Japanese college students. *Journal of Social Psychology, 145*, 127–140.

Kitty, Tsui, Chinese-American poet, b. 1952. From Tsui, K. (1989). Chinatown talking story. In Asian Women United of California (Ed.), *Making waves: An Anthology of Writings by and about Asian American women* (p. 132). Boston: Beacon Press.

Klahr, D., & Simon, H. A. (1999). Studies of scientific discovery: Complementary approaches and convergent findings. *Psychological Bulletin, 125*, 524–543.

Klauer, C. K., Ehrenberg, K., & Wegener, I. (2003). Crossed categorization and stereotyping: Structural analyses, effect patterns, and dissociative effects of context relevance. *Journal of Experimental Social Psychology, 39*, 332–354.

Klein, O., Spears, R., & Reicher, S. (2007). Social identity performance: Extending the strategic side of SIDE. *Personality and Social Psychology Review, 11*, 28–45.

Klein, W. M. P. (2003). Effects of objective feedback and "single other" or "average other" social comparison feedback on performance judgments and helping behavior. *Personality and Social Psychology Bulletin, 29*, 418–429.

Klein, W. M., & Weinstein, N. D. (1997). Social comparison and unrealistic optimism about personal risk. In B. P. Buunk & F. X. Gibbons (Eds.), *Health, coping and well-being* (pp. 25–61). London, UK: Erlbaum.

Kling, K. C., Hyde, J. S., Showers, C. J., & Buswell, B. N. (1999). Gender differences in self-esteem: A meta-analysis. *Psychological Bulletin, 125*, 470–500.

Klinger, L. J., Hamilton, J. A., & Cantrell, P. J. (2001). Children's perceptions of aggressive and gender-specific content in toy commercials. *Social Behavior and Personality, 29*, 11–20.

Klohnen, E. C., & Bera, S. (1998). Behavioral and experiential patterns of avoidantly and securely attached women across adulthood: A 31-year longitudinal perspective. *Journal of Personality and Social Psychology, 74*, 211–223.

Knafo, A., & Plomin, R. (2006). Parental discipline and affection and children's prosocial behavior: Genetic and environmental links. *Journal of Personality and Social Psychology, 90*, 147–164.

Knapp, M. L., Stafford, L., & Daly, J. A. (1986). Regrettable messages: Things people wish they hadn't said. *Journal of Communication, 36*, 40–58.

Knee, C. R., & Canevello, A. (2006). Implicit theories of relationships and coping in romantic relationships. In K. D. Vohs & E. J. Finkel (Eds.), *Self and relationships: Connecting intrapersonal and interpersonal processes* (pp. 160–176). New York: Guilford Press.

Kniffin, K. M., & Wilson, D. S. (2005). Utilities of gossip across organizational levels: Multilevel selection, free-riders, and teams. *Human Nature, 16*, 278–292.

Knight, R. T., & Grabowecky, M. (1995). Escape from linear time: Prefrontal cortex and conscious experience. In M. S. Gazzaniga (Ed.), *The cognitive neurosciences* (pp. 1357–1371). Cambridge, MA: MIT Press.

Knobloch, L.K. (2007). Perceptions of turmoil within courtship: Associations with intimacy, relational uncertainty, and interference from partners. *Journal of Social and Personal Relationships, 24*, 363–384.

Knox, R. E., & Inkster, J. A. (1968). Postdecision

dissonance at posttime. *Journal of Personality and Social Psychology, 8*, 319–323.

Knox, R. E., & Safford, R. K. (1976). Group caution at the race track. *Journal of Experimental Social Psychology, 12*, 317–324.

Koch, S. (1981). Psychology and its human clientele: Beneficiaries or victims? In R. A. Kasschau & F. S. Kessel (Eds.), *Psychology and society: In search of symbiosis* (pp. 24–47). New York: Holt, Rinehart.

Koffka, K. (1935). *Principles of gestalt psychology.* London: Routledge.

Köhler, W. (1929). *Gestalt psychology.* New York: Liveright.

Komatsu, L. K. (1992). Recent reviews of conceptual structure. *Psychological Bulletin, 112*, 500–526.

Konrath, S., Bushman, B. J., & Campbell, W. K. (2006). Attentuating the link between threatened egotism and aggression. *Psychological Science, 17*, 995–1001.

Koole, S. L., Jager, W., van den Berg, A. E., Vlek, C. A. J., & Hofstee, W. K. B. (2001). On the social nature of personality: Effects of extraversion, agreeableness, and feedback about collective resource use on cooperation in a resource dilemma. *Personality and Social Psychology Bulletin, 27*, 289–301.

Koren, P., Carlton, K., & Shaw, D. (1980). Marital conflict: Relations among behaviors, outcomes, and distress. *Journal of Consulting and Clinical Psychology, 48*, 460–468.

Kortenkamp, K. V., & Moore, C. F. (2006). Time, uncertainty, and individual differences in decisions to cooperate in resource dilemmas. *Personality and Social Psychology Bulletin, 32*, 603–615.

Kosfeld, M., Heinrichs, M., Zak, P. J., Fischbacher, U., & Fehr, E. (2005). Oxytocin increases trust in humans. *Nature, 435*, 673–676.

Kosic, A., Pierro, A., & Mannetti, L. (2002). Curve north and curve south: Perception of ingroup and outgroup homogeneity and heterogeneity in Lazio and Roma fans. *Rassegna di Psicologia, 19*, 91–102.

Koss, M. P., Gidycz, C. A., & Wisniewski, N. (1987). The scope of rape: Incidence and prevalence of sexual aggression and victimization in a national sample of higher education students. *Journal of Consulting and Clinical Psychology, 55*, 162–170.

Kowert, P. A. (2002). *Groupthink or deadlock: When do leaders learn from their advisors?* Albany, NY: State University of New York Press.

Kozlowski, S. W. J., & Bell, B. S. (2003). Work groups and teams in organizations. In W. C. Borman, D. R. Ilgen, & R. J. Klimoski (Eds.), *Comprehensive handbook of psychology: Industrial and organizational psychology* (Vol. 12). New York: John Wiley.

Krahé, B., & Moller, I. (2004). Playing violent electronic games, hostile attributional style, and aggression-related norms in German adolescents. *Journal of Adolescence, 27*, 53–69.

Krahé, B., Moller, I., Heusmann, L. R., Kirwil, L., Felber, J., & Berger, A. (2011). Desensitization to media violence: Links with habitual media violence exposure, aggressive cognitions, and aggressive behavior. *Journal of Personality and Social Psychology, 100*, 630–646.

Krahé B., Scheinberger-Olwig, R., & Koplin, S. (2000). Ambiguous communication of sexual intentions as a risk marker of sexual aggression. *Sex roles, 1*, 313–337.

Kraus, M. W., & Chen, S. (2009). Striving to be known by significant others: Automatic activation of self-verification goals in relationship contexts. *Journal of Personality and Social Psychology, 97*, 58–73.

Kraut, R. E. (1973). Effects of social labeling on giving to charity. *Journal of Experimental Social Psychology, 9*, 551–562.

Kraut, R., Olson, J., Banaji, M., Bruckman, A., Cohen, J., & Couper, M. (2003). Psychological research online: Opportunities and challenges. *American Psychologist.*

Krefting, L. A. (2003). Intertwined discourses of merit and gender: Evidence from academic employment in the USA. *Gender, Work and Organization, 10,* 260–278.

Kress, V. E., Shepherd, J. B., Anderson, R. I., Petuch, A. J., Nolan, J. M., & Thiemeke, D. (2006). Evaluation of the impact of a coeducational sexual assault prevention program on college students' rape myth attitudes. *Journal of College Counseling, 9,* 148–157.

Krieglmeyer, R., Wittstadt, D., & Strack, F. (2009). How attribution influences aggression: Answers to an old question by using an implicit measure of anger. *Journal of Experimental Social Psychology, 45,* 379–385.

Kristiansen, C. M., & Hotte, A. M. (1996). Morality and the self: Implications for the when and how of value-attitude behavior relations. In C. Seligman, J. Olson, & M. P. Zanna (Eds.), *The psychology of values: The Ontario symposium* (Vol. 8). Mahwah, NJ: Erlbaum.

Krisztian, I. (2009). The psychology of relationship harmony in the East-Asian collectivistic societies. *Magyar Pszichológiai Szemle, 64,* 179–202.

Krosnick, J. A. (1999). Survey research. *Annual Review of Psychology, 50,* 537–567.

Krosnick, J. A., & Alwin, D. F. (1989). Aging and susceptibility to attitude change. *Journal of Personality and Social Psychology, 59,* 1140–1152.

Krosnick, J. A., Betz, A. L., Jussim, L. J., & Lynn, A. R. (1992). Subliminal conditioning of attitudes. *Personality and Social Psychology Bulletin, 18,* 152–162.

Krueger, J. (1998). Enhancement bias in descriptions of self and others. *Personality and Social Psychology Bulletin, 24,* 505–516.

Krueger, J. I., & Funder, D. C. (2004). Towards a balanced social psychology: Causes, consequences and cures for the problem-seeking approach to social behavior and cognition. *Behavioral and Brain Sciences, 27.*

Krueger, J. I., Ham, J. J., & Linford, K. M. (1996). Perceptions of behavioral consistency: Are people aware of the actor-observer effect? *Psychological Science, 7,* 259–264.

Krueger, J. I., Hasman, J. F., Acevedo, M., & Villano, P. (2003). Perceptions of trait typicality in gender stereotypes: Explaining the role of attribution and categorization processes. *Personality and Social Psychology Bulletin, 29,* 108–116.

Kruger, D. J. (2003). Evolution and altruism: Combining psychological mediators with naturally selected tendencies. *Evolution and Human Behavior, 24,* 118–125.

Kruger, J., & Dunning, D. (1999). Unskilled and unaware of it: How difficulties in recognizing one's own incompetence lead to inflated self-assessments. *Journal of Personality and Social Psychology, 77,* 1121–1134.

Kruglanski, A. W., & Orehek, E. (2007). Partitioning the domain of social inference: Dual mode and systems models and their alternatives. *Annual Review of Psychology, 58,* 291–316.

Kruglanski, A. W., & Webster, D. M. (1996). Motivated closing of the mind: "Seizing" and "freezing." *Psychological Review, 103,* 263–283.

Krull, D. S. (2001). On partitioning the fundamental attribution error: Dispositionalism and the correspondence bias. In G. B. Moskowitz (Ed.), *Cognitive social psychology: The Princeton symposium on the legacy and future of social cognition* (pp. 211–227). Mahwah, NJ: Erlbaum.

Krull, D. S., & Dill, J. C. (1996). On thinking first and responding fast: Flexibility in social inference processes. *Personality and Social Psychology Bulletin, 22,* 949–959.

Krull, D. S., & Erickson, D. J. (1995). Inferential hopscotch: How people draw social inferences from behavior. *Current Directions in Psychological Science, 13,* 35–38.

Krull, D. S., Loy, M. H. M., Lin, J., Wang, C. F., Chen, S., & Zhao, X. (1999). The fundamental attribution error: Correspondence bias in individualist and collectivist cultures. *Personality and Social Psychology Bulletin, 25,* 1208–1219.

Kugihara, N. (2001). Effects of aggressive behaviour and group size on collective escape in an emergency: A test between a social identity model and deindividuation theory. *British Journal of Social Psychology, 40,* 575–598.

Kuhn, M. H., & McPartland, T. S. (1954). An empirical investigation of self-attitudes. *American Sociological Review, 19,* 68–76.

Kühnen, U., Hannover, B., & Schubert, B. (2001). The semantic-procedural interface model of the self: The role of self-knowledge for context-dependent versus context-independent modes of thinking. *Journal of Personality and Social Psychology, 80,* 397–409.

Kühnen, U., & Oyserman, D. (2002). Thinking about the self influences thinking in general: Cognitive consequences of salient self-concept. *Journal of Experimental Social Psychology, 38,* 492–499.

Kuiper, N., Grimshaw, M., Leite, C., & Kirsh, G. (2004). Humor is not always the best medicine: Specific components of sense of humor and psychological well-being. *Humor: International Journal of Humor Research, 17,* 135–168. doi:10.1515/humr.2004.002

Kujath, C. L. (2011). Facebook and MySpace: Complement or substitute for face-to-face interaction? *Cyberpsychology, Behavior, and Social Networking, 14,* 75–78.

Kulig, J. W. (2000). Effects of forced exposure to a hypothetical population on false consensus. *Personality and Social Psychology Bulletin, 26,* 629–636.

Kulik, J. A., & Mahler, H. I. M. (1989). Stress and affiliation in a hospital setting: Preoperative roommate preferences. *Personality and Social Psychology Bulletin, 15,* 183–193.

Kulik, J. A., Mahler, H. I. M., & Earnest, A. (1994). Social comparison and affiliation under threat: Going beyond the affiliate-choice paradigm. *Journal of Personality and Social Psychology, 66,* 301–309.

Kulik, J. A., Mahler, H. I. M., & Moore, P. J. (1996). Social comparison and affiliation under threat: Effects on recovery from major surgery. *Journal of Personality and Social Psychology, 71,* 967–979.

Kulynych, J. (2002). Legal and ethical issues in neuroimaging research: Human subjects protection, medical privacy and the public communication of research results. *Brain and Cognition, 50,* 345–357.

Kumkale, G. T., & Albarracín, D. (2004). The sleeper effect in persuasion: A meta-analytic review. *Psychological Bulletin, 130,* 143–172.

Kunda, Z. (1999). *Social cognition: Making sense of people.* Cambridge, MA: MIT Press.

Kunda, Z. (Ed.). (2000). *Social cognition: Making sense of people.* Cambridge, MA: The MIT Press.

Kunda, Z., Davies, P. G., Adams, B. D., & Spencer, S. J. (2002). The dynamic time course of stereotype activation: Activation, dissipation, and resurrection. *Journal of Personality and Social Psychology, 82,* 283–299.

Kunovich, R. M., & Deitelbaum, C. (2004). Ethnic conflict, group polarization, and gender attitudes in Croatia. *Journal of Marriage and Family, 66,* 1089–1107.

Kupke, T., Hobbs, S. A., & Cheney, T. H. (1979). Selection of heterosocial skills: I. Criterion-related validity. *Behavior Therapy, 10,* 327–335.

Kuppens, P., Van Mechelen, I., & Meulders, M. (2004). Every cloud has a silver lining: Interpersonal and individual differences determinants of anger-related behaviors. *Personality and Social Psychology Bulletin, 30,* 1550–1564.

Kurdek, L. A. (2003). Differences between gay and lesbian cohabiting couples. *Journal of Social and Personal Relationships, 20,* 411–436.

Kurdek, L. A. (2006). Differences between partners from heterosexual, gay, and lesbian cohabiting couples. *Journal of Marriage and Family, 68,* 509–528.

Kurdek, L. A., & Schmitt, J. P. (1986). Relationship quality of partners in heterosexual married, heterosexual cohabiting, and gay and lesbian relationships. *Journal of Personality and Social Psychology, 51,* 711–720.

Kurdek, L. A., & Schmitt, J. P. (1987). Perceived emotional support from families and friends in members of homosexual, married, and heterosexual cohabiting couples. *Journal of Homosexuality, 14,* 57–68.

Kurup, R. K., & Kurup, P. A. (2003). Hypothalamic digoxin, hemispheric dominance, and neurobiology of love and affection. *International Journal of Neuroscience, 113,* 721–729.

Kurzban, R. (2003). Biological foundations of reciprocity. In E. Ostrom, J. Walker (Eds.), *Trust and reciprocity: Interdisciplinary lessons from experimental research. A volume in the Russell Sage Foundation series on trust* (pp. 105–127). New York: Sage.

Kurzban, R., & Weeden, J. (2005). HurryDate: Mate preferences in action. *Evolution and Human Behavior, 26,* 227–244.

Kutchinsky, B. (1971). Towards an explanation of the decrease in registered sex crimes in Copenhagen. *Technical report of the Commission on Obscenity and Pornography* (Vol. 7, pp. 263–310). Washington, DC: U.S. Government Printing Office.

Kutchinsky, B. (1985). Pornography and its effects in Denmark and the United States: A rejoinder and beyond. *Comparative Social Research, 8,* 301–330.

Kutchinsky, B. (1991). Pornography and rape: Theory and practice? *International Journal of Law and Psychiatry, 14,* 47–64.

L'Armand, K., & Pepitone, A. (1975). Helping to reward another person: A cross-cultural analysis. *Journal of Personality and Social Psychology, 31,* 189–198.

LaBarbera, P., & MacLachlan, J. (1979). Time-compressed speech in radio advertising. *Journal of Marketing, 43,* 30–36.

LaFrance, M., Hecht, M. A., & Paluck, E. L. (2003). The contingent smile: A meta-analysis of sex differences in smiling. *Psychological Bulletin, 129,* 305–334.

Lagerspetz, K. (1985). Are wars caused by aggression? In F. L. Denmark (Ed.), *Social/ecological psychology and the psychology of women.* New York: Elsevier (North-Holland).

Lagerspetz, K. M. J., & Björkqvist, K. (1994). Indirect aggression in boys and girls. In L. R. Huesmann (Ed.), *Aggressive behavior: Current perspectives* (pp. 131–150). New York: Plenum.

Lagerspetz, K. M. J., Björkqvist, K., & Peltonen, T. (1988). Is indirect aggression typical of females? Gender differences in aggressiveness in 11– to 12–year-old children. *Aggressive Behavior, 14,* 403–414.

Lakin, J. L., & Chartrand, T. L. (2003). Using nonconscious behavioral mimicry to create affiliation and rapport. *Psychological Science, 14,* 334–339.

Lakkis, J., Ricciardelli, L. A., & Williams, R. J. (1999). Role of sexual orientation and gender-related traits in disordered eating. *Sex Roles, 31,* 1–16.

Lakoff, G. (1996). *Moral politics: What conservatives know that liberals don't.* Chicago: University of Chicago Press.

Lakoff, R. T. (1975). *Language and woman's place.* New York: Harper & Row.

Lambert, A. J., Payne, B. K., Jacoby, L. L., Shaffer, L. M., Chasteen, A. L., & Khan, S. R. (2003). Stereotypes as dominant responses: On the "social facilitation" of prejudice in anticipated public contexts. *Journal of Personality and Social Psychology, 84,* 277–295.

Lambird, K. H., & Mann, T. (2006). When do ego threats lead to self-regulation failure? Negative consequences of defensive high self-esteem. *Personality and Social Psychology Bulletin, 32,*

1177–1187.

Lamke, L. K., Sollie, D. L., Durbin, R. G., & Fitzpatrick, J. A. (1994). Masculinity, femininity and relationship satisfaction: The mediating role of interpersonal competence. *Journal of Social and Personal Relationships, 11,* 535–554.

Lampel, J., & Bhalla, A. (2007). The role of status seeking in online communities: Giving the gift of experience. *Journal of Computer-Mediated Communication, 12,* 434–455.

Lan, P. C. (2003). Negotiating social boundaries and private zones: The micropolitics of employing migrant domestic workers. *Social Problems, 50,* 525–549.

Landau, M. J., Solomon, S., Greenberg, J., Cohen, F., Pyszczyhski, T., Arndt, J., Miller, C. H., Ogilvie, D. M., & Cook, A. (2004). Deliver us from evil: The effects of mortality salience and reminders of 9/11 on support for President George W. Bush. *Personality and Social Psychology Bulletin 30,* 1136–1150.

Lang, A. R., Goeckner, D. J., Adesso, V. J., & Marlatt, G. A. (1975). Effects of alcohol on aggression in male social drinkers. *Journal of Abnormal Psychology, 84,* 508–518.

Langer, E. J. (1978). Rethinking the role of thought in social interaction. In J. H. Harvey, W. Ickes, & R. F. Kidd (Eds.), *New directions in attribution research* (Vol. 2, pp. 35–58). Hillsdale, NJ: Erlbaum.

Langer, E. J. (1989). Minding matters: The consequences of mindlessness-mindfulness. In L. Berkowitz (Ed.), *Advances in experimental social psychology* (Vol. 22, 137–173). San Diego: Academic Press.

Langer, L. M., Warheit, G. J., & McDonald, L. P. (2001). Correlates and predictors of risky sexual practices among a multi-racial/ethnic sample of university students. *Social Behavior and Personality, 29,* 133–144.

Langfred, C. W. (1998). Is group cohesiveness a double-edged sword? An investigation of the effects of cohesiveness on performance. *Small Group Research, 29,* 124–143.

Langlois, J. H., & Downs, A. C. (1980). Mothers, fathers, and peers as socialization agents of sex-typed behaviors in young children. *Child Development, 51,* 1237–1247.

Langlois, J. H., Kalakanis, L., Rubenstein, A. J., Larson, A., Hallam, M., & Smoot, M. (2000). Maxims or myths of beauty? A meta-analytic and theoretical review. *Psychological Bulletin, 126,* 390–423.

Langlois, J. H., Roggman, L. A., & Musselman, L. (1994). What is average and what is not average about attractive faces? *Psychological Science, 5,* 214–220.

Lanning, K. (2002). Reflections on September 11: Lessons from four psychological perspectives. *Analysis of Social Issues and Public Policy, 2,* 27–34.

LaPiere, R. T. (1932). Attitudes vs. actions. *Social Forces, 13,* 230–237.

Larrick, R. P., Timmerman, T. A., Carton, A. M., & Abrevaya, J. (2011). Temper, temperature, and temptation: Heat-related retaliation in baseball. *Psychological Science, 22,* 423–428.

Larsen, R. J. (2000). Toward a science of mood regulation. *Psychological Inquiry, 11,* 129–141.

Lassiter, G. D., Geers, A. L., Handley, I. M., Weiland, P. E., & Munhall, P. J. (2002). Videotaped interrogations and confessions: A simple change in camera perspective alters verdicts in simulated trials. *Journal of Applied Psychology, 87,* 867–874.

Latané, B. (1981). The psychology of social impact. *American Psychologist, 36,* 343–356.

Latané, B. (1997). Dynamic social impact: The social consequences of human interaction. In C. McGarty & S. A. Haslam (Eds.), *The message of social psychology: Perspectives on mind in society* (pp. 200–220). Cambridge, MA: Blackwell.

Latané, B. (2000). Pressures to uniformity and the evolution of cultural norms: Modeling dynamic social impact. In D. R. Ilgen & C. L. Hulin (Eds.), *Computational modeling of behavior in organizations: The third scientific discipline* (pp. 189–220). Washington, DC: American Psychological Association.

Latané, B., & Bourgeois, M. J. (1996). Experimental evidence for dynamic social impact: The emergence of subcultures in electronic groups. *Journal of Communication, 46,* 35–47.

Latané, B., & Darley, J. M. (1968). Group inhibition of bystander intervention in emergencies. *Journal of Personality and Social Psychology, 10,* 215–221.

Latané, B., & Darley, J. M. (1970). *The unresponsive bystander: Why doesn't he help?* Englewood Cliffs, NJ: Prentice-Hall.

Latané, B., & L'Herrou, T. (1996). Spatial clustering in the conformity game: Dynamic social impact in electronic groups. *Journal of Personality and Social Psychology, 70,* 1218–1230.

Latané, B., Liu, J. H., Nowak, A., Bonevento, M., & Zheng, L. (1995). Distance matters: Physical space and social impact. *Personality and Social Psychology Bulletin, 21,* 795–805.

Latané, B., & Nida, S. (1981). Ten years of research on group size and helping. *Psychological Bulletin, 89,* 308–324.

Latané, B., & Rodin, J. (1969). A lady in distress: Inhibiting effects of friends and strangers on bystander intervention. *Journal of Experimental Social Psychology, 5,* 189–202.

Latané, B., Williams, K., & Harkins, S. (1979). Many hands make light the work: The causes and consequences of social loafing. *Journal of Personality and Social Psychology, 37,* 822–832.

Latting, J. K. (1993). Soliciting individual change in an interpersonal setting: The case of racially or sexually offensive language. *Journal of Applied Behavioral Science, 29,* 464–484.

Laughlin, P. R. (1996). Group decision making and collective induction. In E. Witte & J. Davis (Eds.), *Understanding group behavior: Vol. 1. Small group processes and interpersonal relations* (pp. 61–80). Hillsdale, NJ: Erlbaum.

Laughlin, S. B. (2004). The implications of metabolic energy requirements for the representation of information in neurons. In M. S. Gazzaniga (Ed.), *The cognitive neurosciences* (3rd ed., pp. 187–196). Cambridge, MA: MIT Press.

Laurenceau, J. P., Barrett, L. F., & Pietromonaco, P. R. (1998). Intimacy as an interpersonal process: The importance of self-disclosure, partner disclosure, and perceived partner responsiveness in interpersonal exchanges. *Journal of Personality and Social Psychology, 74,* 1238–1251.

Lavin, T. J. (1987). Divergence and convergence in the causal attributions of married couples. *Journal of Marriage and the Family, 49,* 71–80.

Lavrakas, P. J. (1993). *Telephone survey methods: Sampling, selection, and supervision* (2nd ed.), Newbury Park, CA: Sage.

Lawler, E. J. (1992). Affective attachments to nested groups: A choice-process theory. *American Sociological Review, 57,* 327–339.

Lawler-Row, K. A., Hyatt-Edwards, L, Wuensch, K. L., & Karremans, J. C. (2011). Forgiveness and health: The role of attachment. *Personal Relationships, 18,* 170–183.

Lawrence, R. A. (2004). Review of the oxytocin factor: Tapping the hormone of calm, love, and healing. *Birth: Issues in Perinatal Care, 31,* 157.

Lazarus, R. S. (1984). On the primacy of cognition. *American Psychologist, 39,* 124–129.

Leary, M. R. (1996). *Self-presentation: Impression management and interpersonal behavior.* Boulder, CO: Westview Press.

Leary, M. R. (2005). Sociometer theory and the pursuit of relational value: Getting to the root of self-esteem. *European Review of Social Psychology, 16,* 75–111.

Leary, M. R., & Guadagno, J. (2011). The sociometer, self-esteem, and the regulation of interpersonal behavior. In K. D. Vohs & R. F. Baumeister (Eds.). *Handbook of self-regulation: Research, theory, and applications* (2nd ed.) (pp. 339–354). New York: Guilford Press.

Leary, M. R., Nezlek, J. B., Downs, D., Radford-Davenport, J., Martin, J., & McMullen, A. (1994). Self-presentation in everyday interactions: Effects of target familiarity and gender composition. *Journal of Personality and Social Psychology, 67,* 664–673.

Leary, M. R., Tambor, E. S., Terdal, S. K., & Downs, D. L. (1995). Self-esteem as an interpersonal motive: The sociometer hypothesis. *Journal of Personality and Social Psychology, 68,* 518–530.

LeBon, G. (1903). *Psychologie des foules [The psychology of the crowd].* Paris: Alcan.

Leck, K., & Simpson, J. (1999). Feigning romantic interest: The role of self-monitoring. *Journal of Research in Personality, 33,* 69–91.

LeDoux, J. (1998). *The emotional brain.* New York: Simon & Schuster.

Lee, A. R. (2003). Stability and change in Korean values. *Social Indicators Research, 62–63,* 93–117.

Lee, J. A. (1977). A typology of styles of loving. *Personality and Social Psychology Bulletin, 3,* 173–182.

Lee, K., Ashton, M. C., Pozzebon, J. A., Visser, B. A., Bourdage, J. S., & Oguntowora, B. (2009). Similarity and assumed similarity in personality reports of well-acquainted persons. *Journal of Personality and Social Psychology, 96,* 460–472.

Lee, M. R., & Ousey, G. C. (2011). Reconsidering the culture and violence connection: Strategies of action in the rural south. *Journal of Interpersonal Violence, 26,* 899–929.

Lee, R. S. (1995). Regional subcultures as revealed by magazine circulation patterns. *Cross-Cultural Research, 29,* 91–120.

Lee, S. T., & Cheng, I. H. (2010). Assessing the TARES as an ethical model for antismoking ads. *Journal of Health Communication, 15,* 55–75.

Lee, T. M. C., Liu, H. L., Tan, L. H., Chan, C. C. H., Mahankali, S., Feng, C. M., Hou, J., Fox, P. T., & Gao, J. H. (2002). Lie detection by functional magnetic resonance imaging. *Human Brain Mapping, 15,* 157–164.

Leffler, A., Gillespie, D. L., & Conaty, J. C. (1982). The effects of status differentiation on nonverbal behavior. *Social Psychology Quarterly, 45,* 153–161.

Legault, L., Green-Demers, I., Grant, P., & Chung, J. (2007). On the self-regulation of implicit and explicit prejudice: A self-determination theory perspective. *Personality and Social Psychology Bulletin, 33,* 732–749.

Lehmiller, J. J., & Agnew, C. R.. (2006). Marginalized relationships: The impact of social disapproval on romantic relationship commitment. *Personality and Social Psychology Bulletin, 32,* 40–51.

Lehmiller, J. J., & Agnew, C. R. (2007). Perceived marginalization and the prediction of romantic relationship stability. *Journal of Marriage and Family, 69,* 1036–1049.

Lehmiller, J. J., Law, A. T., & Tormala, T. T. (2010). The effect of self-affirmation on sexual prejudice. *Journal of Experimental Social Psychology, 46,* 276–285.

Lehmiller, J. J., VanderDrift, L. E., & Kelly, J. R. (2011). Sex differences in approaching friends with benefits relationships. *Journal of Sex Research, 48,* 275–284.

Leibold, J. M., & McConnell, A. R. (2004). Women, sex, hostility, power, and suspicion: Sexually aggressive men's cognitive associations. *Journal of Experimental Social Psychology, 40,* 256–263.

Leidner, B., Castano, E., Zaiser, E., & Giner-Sorolla, R. (2010). Ingroup glorification, moral disengagement, and justice in the context of collective violence. *Personality and Social Psychology Bulletin, 36,* 1115–1129.

Leippe, M. R., & Eisenstadt, D. (1994). The generalization of dissonance reduction: Decreasing prejudice through induced compliance. *Journal of Personality and Social Psychology, 67,* 395–413.

Leippe, M. R., & Elkin, R. A. (1987). When motives clash: Issue involvement and response involvement as determinants of persuasion. *Journal of Personality and Social Psychology, 52,* 269–278.

Leit, R. A., Pope, H. G., & Gray, J. J. (2001). Cultural expectations of muscularity in men: The evolution of *Playgirl* centerfolds. *International Journal of Eating Disorders, 29,* 90–93.

Le Maner-Idrissi, G., & Renault, L. (2006). Are there sex differences in the acquisition of a gender schema? *Enfance, 58,* 251–265.

Lemay, E. P., Jr, & Ashmore, R. D. (2006). The relationship of social approval contingency to trait self-esteem: Cause, consequence, or moderator? *Journal of Research in Personality, 40,* 121–139.

Lemay, E. P. Jr, Clark, M. S., & Feeney, B. C. (2007). Projection of responsiveness to needs and the construction of satisfying communal relationships. *Journal of Personality and Social Psychology, 92,* 834–853.

Lent, R. W., & Fouad, N. A. (2011). The self as agent in social cognitive career theory. In P. J. Hartung & L. M. Subich (Eds.). *Developing self in work and career: Concepts, cases, and contexts* (pp. 71–87). Washington, DC: American Psychological Association.

Leonard, K. (1989). The impact of explicit aggressive and implicit nonaggressive cues on aggression in intoxicated and sober males. *Personality and Social Psychology Bulletin, 15,* 390–400.

Leonard, K. E., & Quigley, B. M. (1999). Drinking and marital aggression in newlyweds: An event-based analysis of drinking and the occurrence of husband marital aggression. *Journal of Studies on Alcohol, 60.*

Lerner, M. J. (1980). *The belief in a just world: A fundamental delusion.* New York: Plenum.

Lerner, M. J. (1997). What does the belief in a just world protect us from: The dread of death or the fear of undeserved suffering? *Psychological Inquiry, 8,* 29–32.

Leung, A. K. Y., & Cohen, D. (2011). Within and between-culture variation: Individual differences and the cultural logistics of honor, face and dignity cultures. *Journal of Personality and Social Psychology, 100,* 507–526.

Leung, K., & Chan, D. K. S. (1999). Conflict management across cultures. In J. Adamopoulos & Y. Kashima (Eds.), *Social psychology and cultural context* (pp. 177–188). Thousand Oaks, CA: Sage.

Lev-Ari, S., & Keysar, B. (2010). Why don't we believe non-native speakers? The influence of accent on credibility. *Journal of Experimental Social Psychology, 46,* 867–1158.

Leventhal, H. (1970). Findings and theory in the study of fear communications. In L. Berkowitz (Ed.), *Advances in experimental social psychology* (Vol. 5, pp. 119–186). New York: Academic Press.

Levin, S. (2004). Perceived group status differences and the effects of gender, ethnicity, and religion on social dominance orientation. *Political Psychology, 25,* 31–48.

Levine, J. M., & Moreland, R. L. (1998). Small groups. In D. Gilbert, S. T. Fiske, & G. Lindzey (Eds.), *Handbook of social psychology* (4th ed.). New York: McGraw-Hill.

Levine, J. M., & Moreland, R. L. (2002). Group reactions to loyalty and disloyalty. In S. R. Thye & E. J. Lawler (Eds.), *Group cohesion, trust and solidarity: Advances in group processes* (Vol. 19, pp. 203–228). New York: Elsevier Science/JAI Press.

Levine, J. M., Moreland, R. L., & Hausmann, L. R. M. (2005). Managing group composition: Inclusive and exclusive role transitions. In D. Abrams, M. A. Hogg, & J. M. Marques (Eds.). *The social psychology of inclusion and exclusion* (pp. 137–160). New York: Psychology Press.

Levine, M., Prosser, A., Evans, D., & Reicher, S. (2005). Identity and emergency intervention: How social group membership and inclusiveness of group boundaries shape helping behavior. *Personality*

and Social Psychology Bulletin, 31, 443–453.

Levine, R., & Norenzayan, A. (1999). The pace of life in 31 countries. *Journal of Cross-Cultural Psychology, 26,* 554–571.

Levine, R. A., & Campbell, D. T. (1972). *Ethnocentrism.* New York: Wiley.

Levine, R. V. (2003). The kindness of strangers. *American Scientist, 91,* 226–233.

Levine, R. V., Martinez, T. S., Brase, G., & Sorenson, K. (1994). Helping in 36 U.S. cities. *Journal of Personality and Social Psychology, 67,* 69–82.

Levine, R., Sata, S., Hashimoto, T., & Verma, J. (1995). Love and marriage in eleven cultures. *Journal of Cross-Cultural Psychology, 26,* 554–571.

Levine, T. R., Shaw, A., & Shulman, H. C. (2010). Increasing deception detection accuracy with strategic questioning. *Human Communication Research, 36,* 216–231.

Levy, B. R., & Banaji, M. R. (2002). Implicit ageism. In T. D. Nelson (Ed.), *Ageism: Stereotyping and prejudice against older persons* (pp. 49–75). Cambridge, MA: MIT Press.

Lewandowski, G. G., Jr., Aron, A., Bassis, S., & Kunak, J. (2006). Losing a self-expanding relationship: Implications for the self-concept. *Personal Relationships, 13,* 317–331.

Lewandowski, G. W., & Bizzoco, N. M. (2007). Addition through subtraction: Growth following the dissolution of a low quality relationship. *The Journal of Positive Psychology, 2,* 40–54.

Lewandowski, G. M., Nardone, N., & Raines, A. J. (2010). The role of self-concept clarity in relationship quality. *Self & Identity, 9,* 416–433.

Lewin, K. (1936). *Principles of topological psychology.* New York: McGraw-Hill.

Lewin, K. (1943). Forces behind food habits and methods of change. *Bulletin of the National Research Council, 8,* 35–65.

Lewin, K. (1947). Group decision and social change. In T. M. Newcomb & E. L. Hartley (Eds.), *Readings in social psychology* (pp. 330–344). New York: Holt.

Lewin, K. (1951). Problems of research in social psychology. In D. Cartwright (Ed.), *Field theory in social science* (pp. 155–169). New York: Harper & Row.

Lewin, K., Lippitt, R., & White, R. K. (1939). Patterns of aggressive behavior in experimentally created "social climates." *Journal of Social Psychology, 10,* 271–299.

Lewis, M. (2011). The origins and uses of self-awareness or the mental representation of me. *Consciousness and Cognition: An International Journal, 20,* 120–129.

Lewis, M., & Brooks, J. (1978). Self-knowledge in emotional development. In M. Lewis & L. Rosenblum (Eds.), *The development of affect* (pp. 205–226). New York: Plenum.

Lewis, M. A., & Neighbors, C. (2004). Gender-specific misperceptions of college student drinking norms. *Psychology of Addictive Behaviors 18(4) 334–339.*

Leyens, J. P. (1990). Intuitive personality testing: A social approach. In J. Extra, A. van Knippenberg, J. van der Pligt, & M. Poppe (Eds.), *Fundamentele sociale psychologie* [Basic social psychology] (Vol. 4, pp. 3–20). Tilburg, The Netherlands: Tilburg University Press.

Leyens, J. P. (Ed.). (1991). Prolegomena for the concept of implicit theories of personality. *European Bulletin of Cognitive Psychology, 11,* 131–136.

Leyens, J. P., Camino, L., Parke, R. D., & Berkowitz, L. (1975). Effects of movie violence on aggression in a field setting as a function of group dynamics and cohesiveness. *Journal of Personality and Social Psychology, 32,* 346–360.

Leyens, J. P., & Dardenne, B. (1994). La perception et connaissance d'autrui [People perception]. In M. Richelle, J. Requin, & M. Robert (Eds.), *Traité de psychologie expérimentale [Handbook of experimental psychology]* (Vol. 2, pp. 81–132). Paris: Presses Universitaires de France.

Li, N. P., Valentine, K. A., & Patel, L. (2011). Mate preferences in the US and Singapore: A cross-cultural test of the mate preference priority model. *Personality and Individual Differences, 50,* 291–294.

Liberman, A., & Chaiken, S. (1996). The direct effect of personal relevance on attitudes. *Personality and Social Psychology Bulletin, 22,* 269–279.

Liberman, V., Samuels, S. M., & Ross, L. (2004). The name of the game: Predictive power of reputations versus structural labels in determining prisoner's dilemma game moves. *Personality and Social Psychology Bulletin, 30,* 1175–1185.

Liden, R. C., & Mitchell, T. R. (1988). Ingratiatory behaviors in organizational settings. *Academy of Management Review, 13,* 572–587.

Lieberman, M. D. (2003). Reflective and reflexive judgment processes: A social cognitive neuro-science approach. In J. P. Forgas, K. Williams, & W. V. Hippel (Eds.), *Social judgments: Implicit and explicit processes* (pp. 44–67). New York: Cambridge University Press.

Lieberman, M. D., & Eisenberger, N. I. (2005). Conflict and habit: A social cognitive neuroscience to the self. In A. Tesser, J. V. Wood, & D. A. Stapel (Eds.), *On building, defending and regulating the self: A psychological perspective (p*p. 77–102). New York: Psychology Press.

Lieberman, M. D., & Pfeifer, J. H. (2005). The self and social perception: Three kinds of questions in social cognitive neuroscience. In A. Easton & N. Emery (Eds.), *Cognitive neuroscience of emotional and social behavior* (pp. 195–235). Philadelphia: Psychology Press.

Liening, S. H., & Jospeh, R. A. (2010). It is not just about testosterone: Physiological mediators and moderators of testosterone's behavioral effects. *Social and Personality Psychology Compass, 4,* 982–994.

Likert, R. (1932). A technique for the measurement of attitudes. *Archives of Psychology, 140,* 5–53.

Lilienfeld, S. O. (2011). Public skepticism of psychology: Why many people perceive the study of human behavior as unscientific. *American Psychologist.* Advance online publication. doi: 10.1037/a0023963

Lin, C. L., Lee, S. H., & Horng, D. J. (2011). The effects of online reviews on purchasing intention: The moderating role of need for cognition. *Social Behavior and Personality, 39,* 71–82.

Lin, M. H., Kwan, V. S. Y., Cheung, A., & Fiske, S. (2005). Stereotype content model explains prejudice for an envied outgroup: Scale of anti-Asian American stereotypes. *Personality and Social Psychology Bulletin, 31,* 34–47.

Linder, D. E., Cooper, J., & Jones, E. E. (1967). Decision freedom as a determinant of the role of incentive magnitude in attitude change. *Journal of Personality and Social Psychology, 6,* 245–254.

Lindsay, J. J., & Anderson, C. A. (2000). From antecedent conditions to violent actions: A general affective aggression model. *Personality and Social Psychology Bulletin, 26,* 533–547.

Lingle, S., Rendall, D., Wilson, W. F., Deyoung, R. W., & Pellis, S. M. (2007). Altruism and recognition in the antipredator defence of deer: 2. Why mule deer help nonoffspring fawns. *Animal Behaviour, 73,* 907–916.

Lipkus, I. M. (1991). The construction and preliminary validation of a global belief in a just world scale and the exploratory analysis of the multidimensional belief in a just world scale. *Personality and Individual Differences, 12,* 1171–1178.

Lipkus, I. M., & Bissonnette, V. L. (1996). Relationships among belief in a just world, willingness to accommodate, and marital well-being. *Personality and Social Psychology Bulletin, 22,* 1043–1056.

Lipkus, I. M., Dalbert, C., & Siegler, I. C. (1996). The importance of distinguishing the belief in a just world for self versus for others: Implications for psychological well-being. *Personality and Social Psychology Bulletin, 22,* 666–677.

Lippa, R. A. (2005). Sex and gender. In V. J. Derlega, B.

A. Winstead, & W. H. Jones (Eds.), *Personality: Contemporary theory and research* (3rd ed., pp. 332–365). Belmont, CA: Thomson Wadsworth.

Lippa, R., & Arad, S. (1999). Gender, personality, and prejudice: The display of authoritarianism and social dominance in interviews with college men and women. *Journal of Research in Personality, 33,* 463–493.

Lips-Wiersma, M., & Mills, C. (2002). Coming out of the closet: Negotiating spiritual expression in the workplace. *Journal of Managerial Psychology, 17,* 183–202.

Little, A. C., & Mannion, H. (2006). Viewing attractive or unattractive same-sex individuals changes self-rated attractiveness and face preferences in women. *Animal Behaviour, 72,* 981–987.

Littleford, L. N., Wright, M. O., & Sayoc-Parial, M. (2005). White students' intergroup anxiety during same-race and interracial interactions: A multimethod approach. *Basic and Applied Social Psychology, 27,* 85–94.

Liu, C. J., & Li, S. (2009). Contextualized self: When the self runs into social dilemmas. *International Journal of Psychology, 44,* 451–458.

Livingston, R. W. (2002). The role of perceived negativity in the moderation of African Americans' implicit and explicit racial attitudes. *Journal of Experimental Social Psychology, 38,* 405–413.

Livingston, R. W., & Brewer, M. B (2002). What are we really priming? Cue-based versus category-based processing of facial stimuli. *Journal of Personality and Social Psychology, 82,* 5–18.

Locke, K. D. (2007). Personalized and generalized comparisons: Causes and consequences of variations in the foci of social comparisons. *Personality and Social Psychology Bulletin, 33,* 213–225.

Locke, B.D., & Mahalik, J. R. (2005). Examining masculinity norms, problem drinking, and athletic involvement as predictors of sexual aggression in college men. *Journal of Counseling Psychology, 52,* 279–283.

Loden, M. (1985). *Feminine leadership or how to succeed in business without being one of the boys.* New York: Times Books.

Loewenstein, G., & Small, D. A. (2007). The scarecrow and the tin man: The vicissitudes of human sympathy and caring. *Review of General Psychology, 11,* 112–126.

Lofland, J., & Lofland, L. (1995). *Analyzing social settings: A guide to qualitative observation and analysis* (3rd ed.). Belmont, CA: Wadsworth.

Loftus, E. F., & Coan, D. (1995). The construction of childhood memories. In D. Peters (Ed.), *The child witness in context: Cognitive, social and legal perspectives.* New York: Kluwer.

Lohrke, F. T., & Frownfelter-Lohrke, C. (2011). Review of Handbook of research on electronic surveys and measurements. *Organizational Research Methods, 14,* 389–393.

Lonsway, K. A., Klaw, E. L., Berg, D. R., Waldo, C. R., Kothari, C., Mazurek, C. J., & Hegeman, K. E. (1998). Beyond "no means no": Outcomes of an intensive program to train peer facilitators for campus acquaintance rape education. *Journal of Interpersonal Violence, 13,* 73–92.

Lopes, P. N., Brackett, M. A., Nezlek, J. B., Schütz, A., Sellin, I., & Salovey, P. (2004). Emotional intelligence and social interaction. *Personality and Social Psychology Bulletin, 30,* 1018–1034.

Lore, R., & Schultz, L. A. (1993). Control of human aggression: A comparative perspective. *American Psychologist, 48,* 16–25.

Lorenz, K. (1966). *On aggression.* New York: Harcourt, Brace & World.

Lotar, M., & Kamenov, Z. (2006). Relation between self-handicapping and positive and negative perfectionism. *Socijalna Psihijatrija, 34,* 117–123.

Lottes, I. L., & Kuriloff, P. J. (1994). The impact of college experience on political and social attitudes. *Sex Roles, 31,* 31–54.

Loukopoulos, P., Eek, D., Garling, T., & Fujii, S. (2006). Palatable punishment in real-world social dilemmas? Punishing others to increase cooperation among the unpunished. *Journal of Applied Social Psychology, 36,* 1274–1290.

Lovaglia, J. J., & Houser, J. A. (1996). Emotional reactions and status in groups. *American Sociological Review, 61,* 867–883.

Lowe, K. B., Kroeck, K. G., & Sivasubramaniam, N. (1996). Effectiveness correlates of transformational and transactional leadership: A meta-analytic review. *Leadership Quarterly, 7,* 385–391.

Lucas, R. E., Diener, E., Grob, A., Suh, E., & Shao, L. (2000). Cross-cultural evidence for the fundamental features of extraversion. *Journal of Personality and Social Psychology, 79,* 452–468.

Lucas, T., Alexander, S., Firestone, I., & Lebreton, J. M (2009). Belief in a just world, social influence and illness attributions: Evidence of a just world boomerang effect. *Journal of Health Psychology, 14,* 258–266.

Luce, R. D., & Raiffa, H. (1957). *Games and decisions.* New York: Wiley.

Luginbuhl, J., & Palmer, R. (1991). Impression management aspects of self-handicapping: Positive and negative effects. *Personality and Social Psychology Bulletin, 17,* 655–662.

Luhan, W. J., Kocher, M. G., & Sutter, M. (2009). Group polarization in the team dictator game reconsidered. *Experimental Economics, 12,* 26–41.

Lumsdaine, A., & Janis, I. (1953). Resistance to counterpropaganda produced by a one-sided versus a two-sided propaganda presentation. *Public Opinion Quarterly, 17,* 311–318.

Luo, S., & Klohnen, E. C. (2005). Assortative mating and marital quality in newlyweds: A couple-centered approach. *Journal of Personality and Social Psychology, 88,* 304–326.

Luo, S., & Zhang, G. (2009). What leads to romantic attraction: Similarity, reciprocity, security, or beauty? Evidence from a speed-dating study. *Journal of Personality, 77,* 933–964.

Luong, G., Charles, S. T., & Fingerman, K. L. (2010). Better with age: Social relationships across adulthood. *Journal of Social and Personal Relationships, 28,* 9–23.

Lupfer, M. B., Weeks, M., & Dupuis, S. (2000). How pervasive is the negativity bias in judgments based on character appraisal? *Personality and Social Psychology Bulletin, 26,* 1353–1366.

Lwin, M. O., Stanaland, A. J. S., & Williams, J. D. (2010). American symbolism in intercultural communication: An animosity/ethnocentrism perspective on intergroup relations and consumer attitudes. *Journal of Communication, 60,* 491–514.

Lynch, J. W., Kaplan, G. A., & Shema, S. J. (1997). Cumulative impact of sustained economic hardship on physical, cognitive, psychological, and social functioning. *New England Journal of Medicine, 337,* 1889–1895.

Lyubomirsky, S., Caldwell, N. D., & Nolen-Hoeksema, S. (1998). Effects of ruminative and distracting responses to depressed mood on retrieval of autobiographical memories. *Journal of Personality and Social Psychology, 75,* 166–177.

Ma, V., & Schoeneman, T. J. (1997). Individualism versus collectivism: A comparison of Kenyan and American self-concepts. *Basic and Applied Social Psychology, 19,* 261–273.

Maass, A., Clark, R. D., III, & Haberkorn, G. (1982). The effects of differential ascribed category membership and norms on minority influence. *European Journal of Social Psychology, 12,* 89–104.

Maccoby, E. E. (1990). Gender and relationships: A developmental account. *American Psychologist, 45,* 513–520.

Maccoby, E. E. (1998). *The two sexes: Growing up apart, coming together.* Stanford, CA: Stanford University Press.

MacDonald, G., & Borsook, T. K. (2010). Attachment avoidance and feelings of connection in social interaction. *Journal of Experimental Social Psychology, 46,* 1122–1125.

MacDonald, G., Kingsbury, R., & Shaw, S. (2005). Adding insult to injury: Social pain theory and response to social exclusion. In K. D. Williams, J. P. Forgas, & W. von Hippel (Eds.), *The social outcast: Ostracism, social exclusion, rejection, and bullying* (pp. 77–90). New York: Psychology Press.

MacDonald, G., & Leary, M. R. (2005). Why does social exclusion hurt? The relationship between social and physical pain. *Psychological Bulletin, 131,* 202–223.

MacDonald, G., & Nail, P. R. (2005). Attitude change and the public-private attitude distinction. *British Journal of Social Psychology, 44(1),* 15–28.

MacDonald, G., Zanna, M. P., & Holmes, J. G. (2000). An experimental test of the role of alcohol in relationship conflict. *Journal of Experimental Social Psychology, 36,* 182–193.

Mackay, N. (January 11, 2004). Former Bush aide: U.S. plotted Iraq invasion long before 9/11. *Sunday Herald.*

Macrae, C. N., Hewstone, M., & Griffiths, R. J. (1993). Processing load and memory for stereotype-based information. *European Journal of Social Psychology, 23,* 77–87.

Macrae, C. N., Milne, A. B., & Bodenhausen, G. V. (1994). Stereotypes as energy-saving devices: A peek inside the cognitive toolbox. *Journal of Personality and Social Psychology, 66,* 37–47.

Macrae, C. N., & Quadflieg, S. (2010). Perceiving people. . In S. T. Fiske, D. T. Gilbert, & G. Lindzey (Eds.). *Handbook of social psychology, Vol. 1* (5th ed.) (pp. 428–463). Hoboken, NJ: John Wiley.

Macrae, C. N., Quinn, K. A., Mason, M. F., & Quadflieg, S. (2005). Understanding others: The face and person construal. *Journal of Personality and Social Psychology, 89,* 686–695.

Madden, M., & Lenhart, A. (2006). Online dating. Washington, DC: *Report for the Pew Internet & American Life Project.* Retrieved June 15, 2007 from http://www.pewinternet.org

Maddison, R., & Prapavessis, H. (2007). Self-handicapping in sport: A self-presentation strategy. In S. Jowette, & D. Lavallee (Eds.), *Social psychology in sport* (pp. 209–220). Champaign, IL: Human Kinetics.

Maddox, K. B. (2004). Perspectives on racial phenotypicality bias. *Personality and Social Psychology Bulletin, 8,* 383–401.

Maddux, J. E., & DuCharme, K. A. (1997). Behavioral intentions in theories of health behavior. In D. S. Gochman (Ed.), *Handbook of health behavior research I: Personal and social determinants* (pp. 133–151). New York: Plenum.

Maddux, J. E., & Rogers, R. W. (1983). Protection motivation and self-efficacy: A revised theory of fear appeals and attitude change. *Journal of Experimental Social Psychology, 19,* 469–479.

Madsen, E. A., Tunney, R. J., Fieldman, G., Plotkin, H. C., Dunbar, R. I. M, Richardson, J-M., & McFarland, D. (2007). Kinship and altruism: A cross-cultural experimental study. *British Journal of Psychology, 98,* 339–359.

Maestripieri, D. (2001). Biological bases of maternal attachment. *Current Directions in Psychological Science, 10,* 79–82.

Magid, D. J., Houry, D., Koepsell, T. D., Ziller, A., Soules, M. R., & Jenny, C. (2004). The epidemiology of female rape victims who seek immediate medical care: Temporal trends in the incidence of sexual assault and acquaintance rape. *Journal of Interpersonal Violence, 19,* 3–12.

Mahaffey, A. L., Bryan, A., & Hutchison, K. E. (2005). Using startle eye blink to measure the affective component of antigay bias. *Basic and Applied Social Psychology, 27,* 37–45.

Mahay, J., & Laumann, E. O. (2004). Meeting and mating over the life course. In E. O. Laumann, S. Ellingson, J. Mahay, A. Paik, & Y.

Youm (Eds), *The sexual organization of the city* (pp. 127–164). Chicago, IL: University of Chicago Press.

Majied, K. F. (2010). The impact of sexual orientation and gender expression bias on African American students. *Journal of Negro Education, 79,* 151–165.

Major, B., Kaiser, C. R., & McCoy, S. K. (2003). It's not my fault: When and why attributions to prejudice protect well-being. *Personality and Social Psychology Bulletin, 29,* 772–781.

Major, B., Kaiser, C. R., O'Brien, L. T., & McCoy, S. K. (2007). Perceived discrimination as worldview threat or worldview confirmation: Implications for self-esteem. *Journal of Personality and Social Psychology, 92,* 1068–1086.

Major, B., & O'Brien, L. T. (2005). The social psychology of stigma. *Annual Review of Psychology, 56,* 393–421.

Major, B., Spencer, S., Schmader, T., Wolfe, C., & Crocker, J. (1998). Coping with negative stereotypes about intellectual performance: The role of psychological disengagement. *Personality and Social Psychology Bulletin, 24,* 34–50.

Malach, P. A. (2001). The role of gender and culture in romantic attraction. *European Psychologist, 6,* 96–102.

Malamuth, N. M. (1981). Rape fantasies as a function of exposure to violent sexual stimuli. *Archives of Sexual Behavior, 10,* 33–47.

Malamuth, N. M. (2003). Criminal and noncriminal sexual aggressors: Integrating psychopathy in a hierarchical–mediational conference model. *Annual New York Academy of Science, 989,* 33–58.

Malamuth, N. M., & Check, J. V. P. (1981). The effects of mass media exposure on acceptance of violence against women: A field experiment. *Journal of Research in Personality, 15,* 436–446.

Malamuth, N. M., Linz, D., Heavey, C. L. Barnes, G. & Acker M, (1995). Using the confluence model of sexual aggression to predict men's conflict with women: A 10-year follow-up study. *Journal of Personality and Social Psychology, 69,* 353–369.

Malamuth, N. M., & Thornhill, N. W. (1994). Hostile masculinity, sexual aggression, and gender-based domineeringness in conversations. *Aggressive Behavior, 20,* 185–193.

Mallick, S. K., & McCandless, B. R. (1966). A study of catharsis of aggression. *Journal of Personality and Social Psychology, 4,* 591–596.

Manago, A.M., Graham, M.B., Greenfield, P.M., & Salimkhan, G. (2008). Self-presentation and gender on MySpace. *Journal of Applied Developmental Psychology, 29,* 446–458.

Mandel, D. R. (2003). Counterfactuals, emotions, and context. *Cognition and Emotion, 17,* 139–159.

Mandel, D. R., & Lehman, D. R. (1996). Counterfactual thinking and ascriptions of cause and preventability. *Journal of Personality and Social Psychology, 71,* 450–463.

Maner, J. K., & Gailliot, M. T. (2007). Altruism and egoism: Prosocial motivations for helping depend on relationship context. *European Journal of Social Psychology, 37,* 347–358.

Mann, L. (1981). The baiting crowd in episodes of threatened suicide. *Journal of Personality and Social Psychology, 41,* 703–709.

Manning, R., Levine, M., & Collins, A. (2007). The Kitty Genovese murder and the social psychology of helping; The parable of the 38 witnesses. *American Psychology, 62,* 555–562.

Mantell, D. M. (1971). The potential for violence in Germany. *Journal of Social Issues, 27,* 101–112.

Maranto, C. L., & Stenoien, A. F. (2000). Weight discrimination: A multidisciplinary analysis. *Employee Responsibilities and Rights Journal, 12,* 9–24.

Marcus, D. K., & Miller, R. S. (2003). Sex differences in judgments of physical attractiveness: A social relations analysis. *Personality and Social Psychology Bulletin, 29,* 325–335.

Marcus, D. K., Wilson, J. R., & Miller, R. S. (1996). Are perceptions of emotion in the eye of the beholder? A social relations analysis of judgments of embarrassment. *Personality and Social Psychology Bulletin, 22,* 1220–1228.

Marelich, W. D., Gaines, S. O. Jr., & Branzet M. R. (2003). Commitment, insecurity and arousability: Testing a transactional model of jealousy. *Representative Research in Social Psychology, 27,* 23–31.

Marelich, W. D., & Holt, T. (2006). Salvaging the self and romantic jealousy response. In A. P. Prescott (Ed.), *The concept of self in psychology* (pp. 167–181). Hauppauge, NY: Nova Science Publishers.

Margie, O. (2006).Training in communication skills: Research, theory and practice. In O. Margie (Ed), *The handbook of communication skills* (3rd ed., pp. 553–565). New York: Routledge.

Marjanovic, Z., Greenglass, E. R., Struthers, C. W., & Faye, C. (2009). Helping following natural disasters: A social-motivational analysis. *Journal of Applied Psychology, 39,* 2604–2625.

Mark, M. M., Boburka, R. R., Eyssell, K. M., Cohen, L. L., & Mellor, S. (2003). "I couldn't have seen it coming": The impact of negative self-relevant outcomes on retrospections about foreseeability. *Memory, 11,* 443–454.

Mark, M. M., & Mellor, S. (1991). Effect of self-relevance of an event on hindsight bias: The foreseeability of a layoff. *Journal of Applied Psychology, 76,* 569–577.

Markey, P. M. (2000). Bystander intervention in computer-mediated communication. *Computers in Human Behavior, 16,* 183–188.

Markman, A. B. (1999). *Knowledge representation.* Mahwah, NJ: Erlbaum.

Markus, H. R. (1977). Self-schemata and processing information about the self. *Journal of Personality and Social Psychology, 35,* 63–78.

Markus, H. R., & Kitayama, S. (1991). Culture and the self: Implications for cognition, emotion, and motivation. *Psychological Review, 98,* 224–253.

Markus, H. R., & Kitayama, S. (1994). A collective fear of the collective: Implications for selves and theories of selves. *Personality and Social Psychology Bulletin, 20,* 568–579.

Markus, H. R., Smith, J., & Moreland, R. L. (1985). Role of the self-concept in the perception of others. *Journal of Personality and Social Psychology, 49,* 1494–1512.

Marlowe, C. M., Schneider, S. L., & Nelson, C. E. (1996). Gender and attractiveness biases in hiring decisions: Are more experienced managers less biased? *Journal of Applied Psychology, 81,* 11–21.

Marlowe, F., & Wetsman, A. (2001). Preferred waist-to-hip ratio and ecology. *Personality and Individual Differences, 30,* 481–489.

Marrow, A. J. (1969). *The practical theorist: The life and work of Kurt Lewin.* New York: Basic Books.

Marsh, A. A., & Ambady, N. (2007). The influence of the fear facial expression on prosocial responding. *Cognition & Emotion, 21,* 225–247.

Marsh, K. L., & Julka, D. L. (2000). A motivational approach to experimental tests of attitude functions theory. In G. R. Maio & J. M. Olson (Eds.), *Why we evaluate: Functions of attitudes* (pp. 271–294). Mahwah, NJ: Erlbaum.

Martin, C. J. H., & Bull, P. (2010). The situational argument: Do midwives agree or acquiesce with senior staff? *Journal of Reproductive and Infant Psychology, 28,* 180–190.

Martin, R. (1988). Ingroup and outgroup minorities: Differential impact upon public and private responses. *European Journal of Social Psychology, 18,* 39–52.

Martin, R., Hewstone, M., & Martin, P. Y. (2003). Resistance to persuasive messages as a function of majority and minority source status. *Journal of Experimental Social Psychology, 39,* 585–593.

Martin, R., Hewstone, M., & Martin, P. Y. (2007). Systematic and heuristic processing of majority- and minority-endorsed messages: The effects of varying outcome relevance and levels of orientation on attitude and message processing. *Personality Social Psychology Bulletin, 33,* 43–56.

Martin, R., Hewstone, M., & Martin, P. Y. (2008). Majority versus minority influence: the role of message processing in determining resistance to counter-persuasion. *European Journal of Social Psychology, 38,* 16–34.

Martinek, T. J. (1981). Physical attractiveness: Effects on teacher expectations and dyadic interactions in elementary school children. *Journal of Sport Psychology, 3,* 196–205.

Martins, Y., Tiggemann, M., & Kirkbride, A. (2007). Those Speedos become them: The role of self-objectification in gay and heterosexual men's body image. *Personality Social Psychology Bulletin, 33,* 634–647.

Maruyama, G. (2004). Program evaluation, action research, and social psychology: A powerful blend for addressing applied problems. In C. Sansone, C. C. Morf, & A. T. Panter (Eds.), *Handbook of methods in social psychology* (pp. 429–442). Thousand Oaks, CA: Sage.

Marwell, G., Aiken, M. T., & Demerath, N. J., III. (1987). The persistence of political attitudes among 1960s civil rights activists. *Public Opinion Quarterly, 51,* 383–399.

Mashek, D. J., Aron, A., & Boncimino, M. (2003). Confusion of self with close others. *Personality and Social Psychology Bulletin, 29,* 382–392.

Maslow, A. H. (1970). *Motivation and personality.* New York: Harper & Row.

Mason, W. A. (1997). Discovering behavior. *American Psychologist, 52,* 713–720.

Mast, M. S., & Hall, J. A. (2004). When is dominance related to smiling? Assigned dominance, dominance preference, trait dominance, and gender as moderators. *Sex Roles, 50,* 387–399.

Masters, K. S. (2009). Milgram, stress research, and the Institutional Review Board. *American Psychologist, 64,* 621–622.

Masuda, M. (2003). Meta-analyses of love scales: Do various love scales measure the same psychological constructs? *Japanese Psychological Research, 45,* 25–37.

Mathes, E. W., Adams, H. E., & Davies, R. M. (1985). Jealousy: Loss of relationship rewards, loss of self-esteem, depression, anxiety, and anger. *Journal of Personality and Social Psychology, 48,* 1552–1561.

Matheson, K., Cole, B., & Majka, K. (2003). Dissidence from within: Examining the effects of intergroup context on group members' reactions to attitudinal opposition. *Journal of Experimental Social Psychology, 39,* 161–169.

Matheson, M. D., & Bernstein, I. S. (2000). Grooming, social bonding, and agonistic aiding in rhesus monkeys. *American Journal of Primatology, 51,* 177–186.

Mathie, N. L., & Wakeling, H. C. (2011). Assessing socially desirable responding and its impact on self-report measures among sexual offenders. *Psychology, Crime & Law, 17,* 215–237.

Mathurin, M. N., Gielen, U. P., & Lancaster, J. (2006). Corporal punishment and personality traits in the children of St. Croix, U.S. Virgin Islands. *Cross-Cultural Research: The Journal of Comparative Social Science, 40,* 306–324.

Matsumoto, D., Consolacion, T., Yamada, H., Suzuki, R., Franklin, B., Paul, S., Ray, R., & Uchida, H. (2002). American-Japanese cultural differences in judgments of emotional expressions of different intensities. *Cognition & Emotion, 16,* 721–747.

Matsumoto, D., & Willingham, B. (2006). The thrill of victory and the agony of defeat: Spontaneous expressions of medal winners on the 2004 Athens Olympic games. *Journal of Personality and Social Psychology, 91,* 568–581.

Mauss, I. B., Shallcross, A. J., Troy, A. S., John, O. P., Ferrer, E., Wilhelm, F. H., & Gross, J. (2011). Don't hide your happiness! Positive emotion dissociation, social connectedness, and psychological functioning. *Journal of Personality and Social Psychology, 100,* 738–748.

Mazur, A., & Booth, A. (1998). Testosterone and dominance in men. *Behavioral and Brain Sciences, 21,* 353–397.

Mazzarella, S. R. (2007). Cyberdating success stories and the mythic narrative of living "happily-ever-after with the one." In M.L. Galician & D. L. Merskin (Eds.), *Critical thinking about sex, love, and romance in the mass media* (pp. 23–37). Mahwah, NJ: Lawrence Erlbaum.

McAdams, D. P. (1988). Personal needs and personal relationships. In S. Duck (Ed.), *Handbook of personal relationships: Theory, research, and interventions* (pp. 7–22). New York: Wiley.

McArthur (Zebrowitz), L. Z. (1982). Judging a book by its cover: A cognitive analysis of the relationship between physical appearance and stereotyping. In A. H. Hastorf & A. M. Isen (Eds.), *Cognitive social psychology* (pp. 149–211). New York: Elsevier/North Holland.

McAuliffe, S. P., & Knowlton, B. J. (2001). Hemispheric differences in object identification. *Brain and Cognition, 45,* 119–128.

McCall, M., & Nattrass, K. (2001). Carding for the purchase of alcohol: I'm tougher than other clerks are! *Journal of Applied Social Psychology, 31,* 2184–2194

McCall, M., Reno, R. R., Jalbert, N., & West, S. G. (2000). Communal orientation and attributions between the self and other. *Basic and Applied Social Psychology, 22,* 301–308.

McCann, S. J. H. (1999). Threatening times and fluctuations in American church memberships. *Personality and Social Psychology Bulletin, 25,* 325–336.

McCarthy-Tucker, S., Gold, A., & Garcia, E., III. (1999). Effects of anger management training on aggressive behavior in adolescent boys. *Journal of Offender Rehabilitation, 29,* 129–141.

McCauley, C. R. (2004). Psychological issues in understanding terrorism and the response to terrorism. In C. E. Stout (ed.). *Psychology of terrorism: Coping with the continuing threat, condensed edition* (pp. 33–65). Westport, CT: Praeger/Greenwood.

McCauley, C. R., & Segal, M. E. (1987). Social psychology of terrorist groups. In C. Hendrick (Ed.), *Group processes and intergroup relations: Review of personality and social psychology* (Vol. 9, pp. 231–256). Newbury Park, CA: Sage.

McClure, M. J., Lydon, J. E., Baccus, J. R., & Baldwin, M. W. (2010). A signal detection analysis of chronic attachment anxiety at speed dating: Being unpopular is only the first part of the problem. *Personality and Social Psychology Bulletin, 36,* 1024–1036.

McConahay, J. B. (1986). Modern racism, ambivalence, and the modern racism scale. In S. L. Gaertner & J. Dovidio (Eds.), *Prejudice, discrimination, and racism: Theory and research.* New York: Academic Press.

McConnell, A. R., Rydell, R. J., & Brown, C. M. (2009). On the experience of self-relevant feedback: How self-concept organization influences affective responses and self-evaluations. *Journal of Experimental Social Psychology, 45,* 695–707.

McConnell, A. R., Rydell, R. J., Strain, L. M., & Mackie, D. M. (2008). Forming implicit and explicit attitudes toward individuals: Social group association cues. *Journal of Personality and Social Psychology, 94,* 792–807.

McConville, M. (1993). *Corroboration and confession: The impact of a ride requiring that no conviction can be sustained on the basis of confession evidence alone.* London: HMSO. (Royal Commission on Criminal Justice Research Study No. 13).

McCord, J. (1994). Aggression in two generations. In L. R. Huesmann (Ed.), *Aggressive behavior: Current perspectives* (pp. 241–251). New York: Plenum.

McCrea, S., Hirt, E., & Milner, B. (2008). She works hard for the money: Valuing effort underlies

gender differences in behavioral self-handicapping. *Journal of Experimental Social Psychology, 44,* 292–311.

McCroskey, J. C. (1997). Willingness to communicate, communication apprehension, and self-perceived communication competence: Conceptualizations and perspectives. In J. A. Daly, J. C. McCroskey, J. Ayres, T. Hopf, & D. M. Ayres (Eds.), *Avoiding communication: Shyness, reticence, and communication apprehension* (2nd ed., pp. 75–108). Creskill, NJ: Hampton Press.

McCullough, M. E., Bellah, C. G., Kilpatrick, S. D., & Johnson, J. L. (2001). Vengefulness: Relationships with forgiveness, rumination, well-being, and the Big Five. *Personality and Social Psychology Bulletin, 27,* 601–610.

McDougall, W. (1908). *An introduction to social psychology.* London: Methuen.

McElroy, T., Seta, J. J., & Waring, D. A. (2006). Reflections of the self: How self-esteem determines decision framing and increases risk taking. *Journal of Behavioral Decision Making, 19,* 1–19.

McFarland, S. G. (2005). On the eve of war: Authoritarianism, social dominance, and American students' attitudes toward attacking Iraq. *Personality and Social Psychology Bulletin, 31,* 360–367.

McGarty, Craig. (2004). Forming stereotypes of entitative groups. In V. Yzerbyt, C. M. Judd, & O. Olivier (Eds.), *The psychology of group perception: Perceived variability, entitativity, and essentialism (pp. 161–178).* New York: Psychology Press.

McGarty, C., & Haslam, S. A. (1997). Introduction and a short history of social psychology. In C. McGarty & S. A. Haslam (Eds.), *The message of social psychology: Perspectives on mind in society* (pp. 1–19). Cambridge, MA: Blackwell.

McGarty, C., Turner, J. C., Hogg, M. A., David, B., & Wetherell, M. S. (1992). Group polarization as conformity to the prototypical group member. *British Journal of Social Psychology, 31,* 1–19.

McGarty, C., Yzerbyt, V. Y., & Spears, R. (Eds.). (2002). *Stereotypes as explanations: The formation of meaningful beliefs about social groups.* New York: Cambridge University Press.

McGinty, K., Knox, D., & Zusman, M. E. (2007). Friends with benefits: Women want "friends," men want "benefits." *College Student Journal, 41,* 1128–1131.

McGowan, S. (2002). Mental representations in stressful situations: The calming and distressing effects of significant others. *Journal of Experimental Social Psychology, 38,* 152–161.

McGrath, J. E., Arrow, H., & Berdahl, J. L. (2000). The study of groups: Past, present, and future. *Personality and Social Psychology Review, 4,* 95–105.

McGrath, R. E. (2011). *Quantitative models in psychology.* Washington, DC: American Psychological Association.

McGregor, I., Nail, P. R., Marigold, D. C., & Kang, S. J. (2005). Defensive pride and consensus: Strength in imaginary numbers. *Journal of Personality and Social Psychology, 89,* 978–996.

McGuire, W. J. (1968). Personality and susceptibility to social influence. In E. F. Borgatta & W. W. Lambert (Eds.), *Handbook of personality theory and research.* Chicago: Rand McNally.

McGuire, W. J. (1973). The yin and yang of progress in social psychology: Seven koan. *Journal of Personality and Social Psychology, 26,* 446–456.

McGuire, W. J. (1999). *Constructing social psychology: Creative and critical processes.* Cambridge: Cambridge University Press.

McGuire, W. J. (2004). A perspectivist approach to theory construction. *Personality and Social Psychology Review, 8,* 173–182.

McGuire, W. J., McGuire, C. V., Child, P., & Fujioka, T. (1978). Salience of ethnicity in the spontaneous self-concept as a function of one's ethnic distinctiveness in the social environment.

Journal of Personality and Social Psychology, 36, 511–520.

McGuire, W. J., & Papageorgis, D. (1961). The relative efficacy of various types of prior belief-defense in producing immunity against persuasion. *Journal of Abnormal and Social Psychology, 62,* 327–337.

McKenna, F. P., Stanier, R. A., & Lewis, C. (1991). Factors underlying illusory self-assessments of driving skill in males and females. *Accident Analysis and Prevention, 23,* 45–52.

McLachlan, S., & Hagger, M. S. (2011). The influence of chronically accessible autonomous and controlling motives on physical activity within an extended theory of planned behavior. *Journal of Applied Social Psychology, 41,* 445–470.

McMillan, W., Stice, E. & Rohde, P. (2011). High- and low-level dissonance-based eating disorder prevention programs with young women with body image concerns: An experimental trial. *Journal of Consulting and Clinical Psychology, 79,* 129–134.

McMillen, D. L., Sander, D. V., & Solomon, G. S. (1977). Self-esteem, attentiveness, and helping behavior. *Personality and Social Psychology Bulletin, 3,* 257–261.

McMullen, M. N., & Markman, K. D. (2000). Downward counterfactuals and motivation: The wake-up call and the Pangloss effect. *Personality and Social Psychology Bulletin, 26,* 575–584.

McNally, A. M., Palfai, T. P., Levine, R. V., & Moore, B. M. (2003). Attachment dimensions and drinking-related problems among young adults: The mediational role of coping motives. *Addictive Behaviors, 28,* 1115–1127.

Mead, G. H. (1934). *Mind, self, and society.* Chicago: University of Chicago Press.

Medvene, L. J., Teal, C. R., & Slavich, S. (2000). Including the other in self: Implications for judgments of equity and satisfaction in close relationships. *Journal of Social and Clinical Psychology, 19,* 396–419.

Meeker, B. F., & Weitzel-O'Neill, P. A. (1977). Sex roles and interpersonal behavior in task-oriented groups. *American Sociological Review, 42,* 91–105.

Meeus, W. H. J., & Raaijmakers, Q. A. W. (1986). Administrative obedience: Carrying out orders to use psychological administrative violence. *European Journal of Social Psychology, 16,* 311–324.

Meeus, W. H. J., & Raaijmakers, Q. A. W. (1987). Administrative obedience as a social phenomenon. In W. Doise & S. Moscovici (Eds.), *Current issues in European social psychology* (Vol. 2, pp. 183–230). Cambridge, England: Cambridge University Press.

Meeus, W. H. J., & Raaijmakers, Q. A. W. (1995). Obedience in modern society: The Utrecht studies. *Journal of Social Issues, 51,* 155–175.

Meevissen, Y. M. C., Peters, M. L., & Alberts, H. J. E. M. (2011). Become more optimistic by imagining a best possible self: Effects of a two week intervention. *Journal of Behavior Therapy and Experimental Psychiatry, 42,* 371–378.

Mehl, M. R., & Pennebaker, J. W. (2003). The social dynamics of a cultural upheaval: Social interactions surrounding September 11, 2001. *Psychological Science, 14,* 579–585.

Mehlman, R. C., & Snyder, C. R. (1985). Excuse theory: A test of the self-protective role of attributions. *Journal of Personality and Social Psychology, 49,* 994–1001.

Meier, B. P., & Hinsz, V. B. (2004). A comparison of human aggression committed by groups and individuals: An interindividual-intergroup discontinuity. *Journal of Experimental Social Psychology, 40,* 551–559.

Meier, B. P., Robinson, M. D., Carter, M. S., & Hinsz, V. B. (2010). Are sociable people more beautiful? A zero-acquaintance analysis of agreeableness, extraversion, and attractiveness. *Journal of Research in Personality, 44,* 293–296.

Meins, E. (1999). Sensitivity, security, and internal

working models: Bridging the transmission gap. *Attachment and Human Development, 1,* 325–342.

Mellars, P. A. (1996). *The Neanderthal legacy.* Princeton, NJ: Princeton University Press.

Mellers, B., Hertwig, R., & Kahneman, D. (2001). Do frequency representations eliminate conjunction effects? An exercise in adversarial collaboration. *Psychological Science, 12,* 269–275.

Meltzoff, A. N., & Moore, M. K. (1989). Imitation in newborn infants: Exploring the range of gestures imitated and the underlying mechanisms. *Developmental Psychology, 25,* 954–962.

Mendoza-Denton, N. (2008). *Homegirls: Language and cultural practice among Latina youth gangs.* Malden, MA: Blackwell.

Mendoza-Denton, R., Downey, G., Purdie, V. J., Davis, A., & Pietrzak, J. (2002). Sensitivity to status-based rejection: Implications for African American students' college experience. *Journal of Personality and Social Psychology, 83,* 896–918.

Mercy, J. A., & Hammond, W. R. (1999). Combining action and analysis to prevent homicide. In M. D. Smith & M. A. Zahn (Eds.), *Homicide: A sourcebook of social research* (pp. 297–310). Thousand Oaks, CA: Sage.

Merikle, P. M., & Skanes, H. E. (1992). Subliminal self-help audiotapes: A search for placebo effects. *Journal of Applied Psychology, 77,* 772–776.

Merton, R. (1948). The self-fulfilling prophecy. *Antioch Review, 8,* 193–210.

Mesagno, C., Marchant, D., & Morris, T. (2009). Alleviating choking: The sounds of distraction. *Journal of Applied Sport Psychology, 21,* 131–147.

Mesquita, B., & Frijda, N. (1992). Cultural variations in emotions: A review. *Psychological Bulletin, 112,* 179–204.

Meston, C. M., & Frohlich, P. F. (2003). Love at first fright: Partner salience moderates roller-coaster-induced excitation transfer. *Archives of Sexual Behavior, 32,* 537–544.

Meyer, J. P., & Koebl, S. L. M. (1982). Dimensionality of students' causal attributions for test performance. *Personality and Social Psychology Bulletin, 8,* 31–36.

Michel, M., Corneille, O., & Rossion, B. (2009). Holistic face encoding is modulated by perceived face race: Evidence form perceptual adaptation. *Visual Cognition, 18,* 434–455.

Midlarsky, E., Bryan, J. H., & Brickman, P. (1973). Aversive approval: Interactive effects of modeling and reinforcement on altruistic behavior. *Child Development, 44,* 321–328.

Mikulincer, M., & Shaver, P. R. (2003). The attachment behavioral system in adulthood: Activation, psychodynamics, and interpersonal processes. *Advances in Experimental Social Psychology, 35,* 53–152.

Mikulincer, M., & Shaver P. R. (2006). *Attachment in adulthood structure, dynamics, and change.* New York: Guilford Press.

Miles, D. R., & Carey, G. (1997). Genetic and environmental architecture of human aggression. *Journal of Personality and Social Psychology, 72,* 207–217.

Milgram, S. (1963). Behavioral study of obedience. *Journal of Abnormal and Social Psychology, 67,* 371–378.

Milgram, S. (1965). Some conditions of obedience and disobedience to authority. *Human Relations, 18,* 57–76.

Milgram, S. (1970). The experience of living in cities. *Science, 167,* 1461–1468.

Milgram, S. (1974). *Obedience to authority: An experimental view.* New York: Harper & Row.

Milgram, S. (1992). *The individual in a social world: Essays and experiments.* Reading, MA: Addison-Wesley.

Milhausen, R. R., McBride, K. R., Jun, M. K. (2006). Evaluating a peer-led, theatrical sexual assault prevention program: How do we measure success? *College Student Journal, 40,* 316–328.

Millar, M. G., & Millar, K. U. (1996). The effects of direct and indirect experience on affective and cognitive responses and the attitude-behavior relation. *Journal of Experimental Social Psychology, 32,* 561–579.

Miller, A. G., Gillen, B., Schenker, C., & Radlove, S. (1973). Perception of obedience to authority. *Proceedings of the 81st Annual Convention of the American Psychological Association, 8,* 127–128.

Miller, C. E. (1989). The social psychological effects of group decision rules. In P. B. Paulus (Ed.), *Psychology of group influence* (2nd ed., pp. 327–355). Hillsdale, NJ: Erlbaum.

Miller, C. T., & Downey, K. T. (1999). A meta-analysis of heavyweight and self-esteem. *Personality and Social Psychology Review, 3,* 68–84.

Miller, D. T., & Prentice, D. A. (1994). The self and the collective. *Personality and Social Psychology Bulletin, 20,* 451–453.

Miller, D. T., & Prentice, D. A. (1996). The construction of norms and standards. In E. T. Higgins & A. W. Kruglanski (Eds.), *Social psychology: Handbook of basic principles* (pp. 799–829). New York: Guilford.

Miller, D. T., & Turnbull, W. (1990). The counterfactual fallacy: Confusing what might have been with what ought to have been. *Social Justice Research, 4,* 1–19.

Miller, J. G. (1984). Culture and the development of everyday social explanation. *Journal of Personality and Social Psychology, 46,* 961–978.

Miller, J. G. (1988). Bridging the content-structure dichotomy: Culture and the self. In M. H. Bond (Ed.), *The cross-cultural challenge to social psychology* (pp. 266–281). Beverly Hills, CA: Sage.

Miller, J. G. (1994). Cultural diversity in the morality of caring: Individually oriented versus duty-based interpersonal moral codes. *Cross-Cultural Research, 28,* 3–39.

Miller, J. G., Bersoff, D. M., & Harwood, R. L. (1990). Perceptions of social responsibilities in India and in the United States: Moral imperatives or personal decisions? *Journal of Personality and Social Psychology, 58,* 33–47.

Miller, J. G., Das, R., & Chakravarthy, S. (2011). Culture and the role of choice in agency. *Journal of Personality and Social Psychology, 101,* 45–61.

Miller, L. C., Cooke, L. L., Tsang, J., & Morgan, F. (1992). Should I brag? Nature and impact of positive and boastful disclosures for women and men. *Human Communication Research, 18,* 364–399.

Miller, M. L., & Thayer, J. F. (1989). On the existence of discrete classes in personality: Is self-monitoring the current joint to carve? *Journal of Personality and Social Psychology, 57,* 143–155.

Miller, N., & Davidson-Podgorny, G. (1987). Theoretical models of intergroup relations and the use of cooperative teams as an intervention for desegregated settings. In C. Hendrick (Ed.), *Group processes and intergroup relations: Review of personality and social psychology* (Vol. 9, pp. 41–67). Beverly Hills, CA: Sage.

Miller, N., Maruyama, G., Beaber, R. J., & Valone, K. (1976). Speed of speech and persuasion. *Journal of Personality and Social Psychology, 34,* 615–624.

Miller, P. J. E., Niehuis, S., & Huston, T. L. (2006). Positive illusions in marital relationships: A 13-year longitudinal. study. *Personality and Social Psychology Bulletin, 32,* 1579–1594.

Miller, P. J. E., & Rempel, J. K. (2004). Trust and partner-enhancing attributions in close relationships. *Personality and Social Psychology Bulletin, 30,* 695–705.

Miller, R. L., Brickman P., & Bolen, D. (1975). Attribution versus persuasion as a means of modifying behavior. *Journal of Personality and Social Psychology, 31,* 430–441.

Miller, R. S. (1987). Empathic embarrassment: Situational and personal determinants of reactions to the embarrassment of another. *Journal of Personality and Social Psychology, 53,* 1061–1069.

Miller, R. S. (1995). Embarrassment and social behavior. In J. P. Tangney & K. W. Fischer (Eds.), *Self-conscious emotions: The psychology of shame, guilt, embarrassment, and pride* (pp. 322–339). New York: Guilford.

Miller, R. S. (1997). We always hurt the ones we love: Aversive interactions in close relationships. In R. M. Kowalski (Ed.), *Aversive interpersonal behaviors* (pp. 11–29). New York: Plenum.

Miller, R. S., & Schlenker, B. R. (1985). Egotism in group members: Public and private attributions of responsibility for group performance. *Social Psychology Quarterly, 48,* 85–89.

Miller, S. A. (1995). Parents' attributions for their children's behavior. *Child Development, 66,* 1557–1584.

Milliman, R. E. (1986). The influence of background music on the behavior of restaurant patrons. *Journal of Consumer Research, 13,* 286–289.

Mills, J. (1958). Changes in moral attitudes following temptation. *Journal of Personality, 26,* 517–531.

Mills, J., & Clark, M. S. (2001). Viewing close romantic relationships as communal relationships: Implications for maintenance and enhancement. In J. Harvey & A. Wenzel (Eds.), *Close romantic relationships: Maintenance and enhancement* (pp. 13–25). Mahwah, NJ: Lawrence Erlbaum.

Minton, H. L. (2002). *Departing from deviance: A history of homosexual rights and emancipatory science in America.* Chicago: University of Chicago Press.

Mintz, L. B., & Kashubeck, S. (1999). Body image and disordered eating among Asian American and Caucasian college students: An examination of race and gender differences. *Psychology of Women Quarterly, 23,* 781–796.

Mischel, W., Cantor, N., & Feldman, S. (1996). Principles of self-regulation: The nature of willpower and self-control. In E. T. Higgins & A. W. Kruglanski (Eds.), *Social psychology: Handbook of basic principles* (pp. 329–360). New York: Guilford Press.

Mita, T. H., Dermer, M., & Knight, J. (1977). Reversed facial images and the mere-exposure hypothesis. *Journal of Personality and Social Psychology, 35,* 597–601.

Mitchell, J. P., Heatherton, T. F., Kelley, W. M., Wyland, C. L., Wegner, D. M., & Macrae, C. N. (2007). Separating sustained from transient aspects of cognitive control during thought suppression. *Psychological Science, 18,* 292–297.

Miyamoto, Y., & Kitayama, S. (2002). Cultural variation in correspondence bias: The critical role of attitude diagnosticity of socially constrained behavior. *Journal of Personality and Social Psychology, 83,* 1239–1248.

Moghaddam, F. M. (2005). The staircase to terrorism: A psychological exploration. *American Psychologist, 60,* 161–169.

Mohr, J. J., & Fassinger, R. E. (2006). Sexual orientation identity and romantic relationship quality in same-sex couples. *Personality and Social Psychology Bulletin, 32,* 1085–1099.

Mok, A., & Morris, M. W. (2011). An upside to bicultural identity conflict: Resisting groupthink in cultural ingroups. *Journal of Experimental Social Psychology, 46,* 1114–1117.

Molla, M., Astrom, A. N., & Brehane, Y. (2007). Applicability of the theory of planned behavior to intended and self-reported condom use in a rural Ethiopian population. *AIDS Care, 19,* 425–431.

Moller, A. C., Deci, E. L., & Ryan, R. M. (2006). Choice and ego-depletion: The moderating role of autonomy. *Personality and Social Psychology Bulletin, 32,* 1024–1036.

Money, J., & Ehrhardt, A. A. (1972). *Man and woman, boy and girl.* Baltimore: Johns Hopkins University Press.

Monsour, M. (1997). Communication and cross-sex friendship across the lifecycle: A review of the literature. *Communication Yearbook, 20,* 375–414.

Monteith, M. J. (1993). Self-regulation of prejudiced responses: Implications for progress in prejudice-reduction efforts. *Journal of Personality and Social Psychology, 65,* 469–485.

Monteith, M. J. (1996). Affective reactions to prejudice-related discrepant responses: The impact of standard salience. *Personality and Social Psychology Bulletin, 22,* 48–59.

Monteith, M. J., & Mark, A. (2009). The self-regulation of prejudice. In T. Nelson (Ed.), *Handbook of prejudice, stereotyping, and discrimination* (pp. 507–524). New York: Psychology Press.

Monteith, M. J., Ashburn-Nardo, L., Voils, C. I., & Czopp, A. M. (2002). Putting the brakes on prejudice: On the development and operation of cues for control. *Journal of Personality and Social Psychology, 83,* 1029–1050.

Monteith, M. J., Deneen, N. E., & Tooman, G. D. (1996). The effect of social norm activation on the expression of opinions concerning gay men and blacks. *Basic and Applied Social Psychology, 18,* 267–288.

Monteith, M. J., Sherman, J. W., & Devine, P. G. (1998). Suppression as a stereotype control strategy. *Personality and Social Psychology Review, 2,* 63–82.

Monteith, M. J., & Spicer, C. V. (2000). Contents and correlates of Whites' and Blacks' racial attitudes. *Journal of Experimental Social Psychology, 36,* 125–154.

Montepare, J. M., & Zebrowitz-McArthur, L. (1988). Impressions of people created by age-related qualities of their gaits. *Journal of Personality and Social Psychology, 55,* 547–556.

Montoya, R. M., & Horton, R. S. (2004). On the importance of cognitive evaluation as a determinant of interpersonal attraction. *Journal of Personality and Social Psychology, 86,* 696–712.

Moore, B. S., & Eisenberg, N. (1984). The development of altruism. *Annals of Child Development, 1,* 107–174.

Moore, D. A., & Small, D. A. (2007). Error and bias in comparative judgment: On being both better and worse than we think we are. *Journal of Personality and Social Psychology, 92,* 972–989.

Moore, T. E. (1995). Subliminal self-help auditory tapes: An empirical test of perceptual consequences. *Canadian Journal of Behavioural Science, 27,* 9–20.

Moorhead, G., Ference, R., & Neck, C. P. (1991). Group decision fiascoes continue: Space shuttle *Challenger* and a revised groupthink framework. *Human Relations, 44,* 539–550.

Moors, A., & De Houwer, J. (2006). Automaticity: A theoretical and conceptual analysis. *Psychological Bulletin, 132,* 297–326.

Moradi, B., & Huang, Y. P. (2008). Objectification theory and psychology of women: A decade of advances and future directions. *Psychology of Women Quarterly, 32,* 377–398.

Moreland, R. L., & Levine, J. M. (1988). Group dynamics over time: Development and socialization in small groups. In J. E. McGrath (Ed.), *The social psychology of time* (pp. 151–181). Newbury Park, CA: Sage.

Moreland, R. L., & Levine, J. M. (2001). Socialization in organizations and work groups. In M. E. Turner (Ed.), *Groups at work: Theory and research: Applied social research* (pp. 69–112). Mahwah, NJ: Erlbaum.

Moreland, R. L., & Levine, J. M. (2002). Socialization and trust in work groups. *Group Processes and Intergroup Relations, 5,* 185–201.

Morf, C. C., & Rhodewalt, R. (1993). Narcissism and self-evaluation maintenance: Explorations in object relations. *Personality and Social Psychology Bulletin, 19,* 668–676.

Morling, B., & Kitayama, S. (2008). Culture and motivation. In J. Y. Shah & W. L. Gardner (Eds.), *Handbook of motivation science* (pp. 417–433). New York: Guilford Press.

Mormon, M. T., & Floyd, K. (1998). "I love you, man": Overt expressions of affection in male-male interaction. *Sex Roles, 38,* 871–881.

Morrill, C., & Fine, G. A. (1997). Ethnographic contributions to organizational sociology. *Sociological Methods and Research, 25,* 424–451.

Morris, M. W., & Larrick, R. P. (1995). When one cause casts doubt on another: A normative analysis of discounting in causal attribution. *Psychological Review, 102,* 331–355.

Morris, W. N., Miller, R. S., & Spangenberg, S. (1977). The effects of dissenter position and task difficulty on conformity and response to conflict. *Journal of Personality, 45,* 251–266.

Morrison, K. (2005). Motivating women and men to take protective action against rape: Examining direct and indirect persuasive fear appeals. *Health Communication, 18,* 237–256.

Morrison, K. R., Plaut, V. C., & Ybarra, O. (2010). Predicting whether multiculturalism positively or negatively influences white Americans' intergroup attitudes: the role of ethnic identification. *Personality and Social Psychology Bulletin, 36,* 1648–1661.

Moscovici, S. (1980). Toward a theory of conversion behavior. In L. Berkowitz (Ed.), *Advances in experimental social psychology* (Vol. 13, pp. 2209–2239). New York: Academic Press.

Moscovici, S., & Mugny, G. (1983). Minority influence. In P. B. Paulus (Ed.), *Basic group processes* (pp. 41–64). New York: Springer-Verlag.

Moscovici, S., & Nemeth, C. (1974). Social influence II: Minority influence. In C. Nemeth (Ed.), *Social psychology: Classic and contemporary integrations* (pp. 217–249). Chicago: Rand McNally.

Moscovici, S., & Zavalloni, M. (1969). The group as a polarizer of attitudes. *Journal of Personality and Social Psychology, 12,* 125–135.

Moskalenko, S., & Heine, S. J. (2003). Watching your troubles away: Television viewing as a stimulus for subjective self-awareness. *Personality and Social Psychology Bulletin, 29,* 76–85.

Moss, E., Bureau, J. F, Cyr, C., Mongeau, C., & St. Laurent, D. (2004). Correlates of attachment at age 3: Construct validity of the preschool attachment classification system. *Developmental Psychology, 40,* 323–334.

Moss, M. K., & Page, R. A. (1972). Reinforcement and helping behavior. *Journal of Applied Social Psychology, 2,* 360–371.

Mruk, C. J. (2006). *Self-esteem research, theory, and practice: Toward a positive psychology of self-esteem.* New York: Springer.

Muehlenhard, C. L., & Hollabaugh, L. C. (1988). Do women sometimes say no when they mean yes? The prevalence and correlates of women's token resistance to sex. *Journal of Personality and Social Psychology, 54,* 872–879.

Muennig, P. 2008. The body politic: The relationship between stigma and obesity-associated disease. *BMC Public Health, 8,* 128–38.

Mugny, G., & Perez, J. A. (1991). *The social psychology of minority influence.* Cambridge, England: Cambridge University Press.

Muir, G., & Macleod, M. D. (2003). The demographic and spatial patterns of recorded rape in a large UK metropolitan area. *Psychology, Crime & Law, 9,* 345–355.

Mulac, A., & Lundell, T. L. (1986). Linguistic contributors to the gender-linked language effect. *Journal of Language and Social Psychology, 5,* 81–101.

Mulilis, J. P., Duval, T. S., & Rombach, D. (2001). Personal responsibility for tornado preparedness: Commitment or choice? *Journal of Applied Social Psychology, 31,* 1659–1688.

Mullen, B., & Copper, C. (1994). The relation between group cohesiveness and performance: An integration. *Psychological Bulletin, 115,* 210–227.

Mullen, B., & Hu, L. (1989). Perceptions of ingroup and outgroup variability: A meta-analytic integration. *Basic and Applied Social Psychology, 10,* 233–252.

Mullen, B., & Johnson, C. (1995). Cognitive representation in ethnophaulisms and illusory correlation in stereotyping. *Personality and Social Psychology Bulletin, 21,* 420–433.

Mullen, B., Migdal, M. J., & Rozell, D. (2003). Self-awareness, deindividuation, and social identity: Unraveling theoretical paradoxes by filling empirical lacunae. *Personality and Social Psychology Bulletin, 29,* 1071–1081.

Mullen, B., & Riordan, C. A. (1988). Self-serving attributions for performance in naturalistic settings: A meta-analytic review. *Journal of Applied Social Psychology, 18,* 3–22.

Mullen, E., & Skitka, L. J. (2009). Comparing Americans' and Ukranians' allocations of public assistance: The role of affective reactions in helping behavior. *Journal of Cross-Cultural Psychology, 40,* 301–318.

Mullen, P. E., & Martin, J. (1994). Jealousy: A community study. *British Journal of Psychiatry, 164,* 35–43.

Muller, P. A., & Stahlberg, D. (2007). The role of surprise in hindsight bias: A metacognitive model of reduced and reversed hindsight bias. *Social Cognition, 25,* 165–184.

Muller, S. L., Williamson, D. A., & Martin, C. K. (2002). False consensus effect for attitudes related to body shape in normal weight women concerned with body shape. *Eating and Weight Disorders, 7,* 124–130.

Munoz, Y., Chebat, J. C., & Suissa, J. A. (2010). Using fear appeals in warning labels to promote responsible gambling among VLT players: The key role of Depth of Information Processing. *Journal of Gambling Studies, 26,* 593–609.

Munsch, R. (1986). *Love you forever.* Ontario, Canada: Firefly Books, Limited.

Muraven, M., Tice, D. M., & Baumeister, R. F. (1998). Self-control as limited resource: Regulatory depletion patterns. *Journal of Personality and Social Psychology, 74,* 774–789.

Murdoch, D., Pihl, R., & Ross, D. (1990). Alcohol and crimes of violence: Present issues. *International Journal of Addictions, 25,* 1065–1081.

Murphy, P. L., & Miller, C. T. (1997). Postdecisional dissonance and the commodified self-concept: A cross-cultural examination. *Personality and Social Psychology Bulletin, 23,* 50–62.

Murphy, S. T. (2001). Feeling without thinking: Affective primacy and the nonconscious processing of emotion. In J. A. Bargh & D. K. Apsley (Eds.), *Unraveling the complexities of social life: A festschrift in honor of Robert B. Zajonc* (pp. 39–53). Washington, DC: American Psychological Association.

Murray, S. L., Bellavia, G., Rose, P., & Griffin, D. W., (2003). Once hurt, twice hurtful: How perceived regard regulates daily marital interactions. *Journal of Personality and Social Psychology, 84,* 126–147.

Murray, S. L., & Holmes, J. G. (1997). A leap of faith? Positive illusions in romantic relationships. *Personality and Social Psychology Bulletin, 23,* 586–604.

Murray, S. L., & Holmes, J. G. (1999). The (mental) ties that bind: Cognitive structures that predict relationship resilience. *Journal of Personality and Social Psychology, 77,* 1228–1244.

Murray, S. L., Holmes, J. G., Bellavia, G., Griffin, D. W., & Dolderman, D. (2002a). Kindred spirits? The benefits of egocentrism in close relationships. *Journal of Personality and Social Psychology, 82,* 563–581.

Murray, S. L., Holmes, J. G., & Collins, N. L. (2006). Optimizing assurance: The risk regulation system in relationships. *Psychological Bulletin, 132,* 641–666.

Murray, S. L., Holmes, J. G., & Griffin, D. W. (1996). The benefits of positive illusions: Idealization and the construction of satisfaction in close relationships. *Journal of Personality and Social Psychology, 70,* 79–98.

Murray, S. L., Holmes, J. G., Griffin, D. W., Bellavia, G., & Rose, P. (2001). The mismeasure of love:

How self-doubt contaminates relationship beliefs. *Personality and Social Psychology Bulletin, 27,* 423–436.

Murray, S. L., Rose, P., Bellavia, G., Holmes, & Kusche, A. (2002b). When rejection stings: How self-esteem constrains relationship-enhancement processes. *Journal of Personality and Social Psychology, 83,* 556–573.

Murray, S. L., Rose, P., Holmes, J. G., Derrick, J., Podchaski, E. J., Bellavia, G., & Griffin, D. W. (2005). Putting the partner within reach: A dyadic perspective on felt security in close relationships. *Journal of Personality and Social Psychology, 88,* 327–347.

Murstein, B. I. (1974). *Love, sex, and marriage through the ages.* New York: Springer.

Musch, J., & Reips, U. D. (2000). A brief history of Web experimenting. In M. H. Birnbaum (Ed.), *Psychological experiments on the Internet* (pp. 61–87). San Diego, CA: Academic Press.

Mussweiler, T., & Bodenhausen, G. V. (2002). I know you are, but what am I? Self-evaluative consequence of judging in-group and out-group members. *Journal of Personality and Social Psychology, 82,* 19–32.

Mussweiler, T., & Rüter, K. (2003). What friends are for! The use of routine standards in social comparison. *Journal of Personality and Social Psychology, 85,* 467–481.

Mussweiler, T., & Strack, F. (2000). The use of category and exemplar knowledge in the solution of anchoring tasks. *Journal of Personality and Social Psychology, 78,* 1038–1052.

Mustonen, A. (1997). Nature of screen violence and its relation to program popularity. *Aggressive Behavior, 23,* 281–292.

Myers, D. G., & Bishop, G. D. (1970). Discussion effects on racial attitudes. *Science, 169,* 778–789.

Myers, D. G., & Kaplan, G. D. (1976). Group-induced polarization in simulated juries. *Personality and Social Psychology Bulletin, 2,* 63–66.

Myers, D. G., & Lamm, H. (1976). The group polarization phenomenon. *Psychological Bulletin, 83,* 602–627.

Nabi, R. L., Moyer-Guse, E., & Byrne, S. (2007). All joking aside: A serious investigation into the persuasive effect of funny social issue messages. *Communication Monographs, 74,* 29–54.

Nadler, A. (1987). Determinants of help seeking behaviour: The effects of helper's similarity, task centrality and recipient's self-esteem. *European Journal of Social Psychology, 17,* 57–67.

Nadler, A. (1991). Help-seeking behavior: Psychological costs and instrumental benefits. In M. S. Clark (Ed.), *Prosocial behavior: Review of personality and social psychology* (Vol. 12, pp. 290–311). Newbury Park, CA: Sage.

Nadler, A., & Fisher, J. D. (1986). The role of threat to self-esteem and perceived control in recipient reactions to help: Theory development and empirical validation. In L. Berkowitz (Ed.), *Advances in experimental social psychology* (Vol. 19, pp. 81–122). New York: Academic Press.

Nadler, A., Fisher, J. D., & Ben-Itzhak, S. (1983). With a little help from my friend: Effects of single or multiple act aid as a function of donor and task characteristics. *Journal of Personality and Social Psychology, 44,* 310–321.

Nadler, A., & Halabi, S. (2006). Intergroup helping as status relations: Effects of status stability, identification, and type of help on receptivity to high-status group's help. *Journal of Personality and Social Psychology, 91,* 97–110.

Nadler, A., Shapiro, R., & Ben-Itzhak, S. (1982). Good looks may help: Effects of helper's physical attractiveness and sex of helper on males' and females' help-seeking behavior. *Journal of Personality and Social Psychology, 42,* 90–99.

Nadler, J. T., & Clark, M. H. (2011). Stereotype threat: A meta-analysis comparing African Americans to Hispanic Americans. *Journal of Applied Social Psychology, 41,* 872–890.

Nagy, T. F. (2011). *Essential ethics for psychologists: A primer for understanding and mastering core issues.* Washington, DC: American Psychological Association.

Nahemow, L., & Lawton, M. P. (1975). Similarity and propinquity in friendship formation. *Journal of Personality and Social Psychology, 32,* 205–213.

Nahum-Shani, I., Bamberger, P. A., & Bacharach, S. B. (2011). Social support and employee well-being: The conditioning effect of perceived patterns of supportive exchange. *Journal of Health and Social Behavior, 52,* 123–129.

Nail, P. R., Harton, H. C., & Decker, B. P. (2003). Political orientation and modern versus aversive racism: Tests of Dovidio and Gaertner's integrated model. *Journal of Personality and Social Psychology, 84,* 754–770.

Nail, P. R., MacDonald, G., & Levy, D. A. (2000). Proposal of a four-dimensional model of social response. *Psychological Bulletin, 126,* 106–116.

Nakanishi, D. T., & Nishida, T. Y. (Eds.). (1995). *The Asian American educational experience.* New York: Routledge.

Nardi, P. M. (1992a). Seamless souls: An introduction to men's friendships. In P. M. Nardi (Ed.), *Men's friendships* (pp. 1–14). Newbury Park, CA: Sage.

Nardi, P. M. (1992b). Sex, friendship, and gender roles among gay men. In P. M. Nardi (Ed.), *Men's friendships* (pp. 173–185). Newbury Park, CA: Sage.

Nardi, P. M. (1992c). That's what friends are for: Friends as family in the gay and lesbian community. In K. Plummer (Ed.), *Modern homosexualities* (pp. 108–120). New York: Routledge.

Nardi, P. M., & Sherrod, D. (1994). Friendship in the lives of gay men and lesbians. *Journal of Social and Personal Relationships, 11,* 185–199.

Narusyte, J., Andershed, A. K., Neiderhiser, J. M., & Lichtenstein, P. (2007). Aggression as a mediator of genetic contributions to the association between negative parent-child relationships and adolescent antisocial behavior. *European Child & Adolescent Psychiatry, 16,* 128–137.

National Institute on Alcohol Abuse and Alcoholism. (2002). *Task Force of the National Advisory Council on Alcohol Abuse and Alcoholism. A call to action: changing the culture of drinking at U.S. colleges.* Washington, DC: National Institutes of Health.

Nayar, B. (2002). Ideological binarism in the identities of native and non-native English speakers. In A. Duszak (Ed.), *Us and others: Social identities across languages, discourses and cultures* (pp. 463–480).

Neely, C. L. (2008). Reviews of Indian feminisms: Law, patriarchies, and violence in India and body evidence: Intimate violence against South Asian women in America. *Violence Against Women, 14,* 496–501.

Neff, L. A., & Karney, B. R. (2005). Gender differences in social support: A question of skill or responsiveness? *Journal of Personality and Social Psychology, 88,* 79–90.

Neighbors, C., Larimer, M. E., Geisner, I. M., & Knee, C. R. (2004). Feeling controlled and drinking motives among college students: Contingent self-esteem as a mediator. *Self and Identity, 3,* 207–224.

Neisser, U., Boodoo, G., Bouchard, T. J., Jr., Boykin, A. W., Brody, N., Ceci, S. J., Halpern, D. F., Loehlin, J. C., Perloff, R., Sternberg, R. J., & Urbina, S. (1996). Intelligence: Knowns and unknowns. *American Psychologist, 51,* 77–101.

Nelson, K. (1986). *Event knowledge: Structure and function in development.* Mahwah, NJ: Erlbaum.

Nemanich, L. A., & Keller, R. T. (2007). Transformational leadership in an acquisition: A field study of employees. *Leadership Quarterly, 18,* 49–68.

Nemeth, C. (1977). Interactions between jurors as a function of majority vs. unanimity decision rules. *Journal of Applied Social Psychology, 7,* 38–56.

Nemeth, C. J., Connell, J. B., Rogers, J. D., & Brown, K. S. (2001). Improving decision making by means of dissent. *Journal of Applied Social Psychology, 31,* 48–58.

Nemeth, C. J., Swedlund, M., & Kanki, B. (1974). Patterning of the minority's responses and their influence on the majority. *European Journal of Social Psychology, 4,* 53–64.

Nesdale, D., & Dalton, D. (2011) Children's social groups and intergroup prejudice: Assessing the influence and inhibition of social group norms. *British Journal of Developmental Psychology.*

Nesse, R. M. (2000). How selfish genes shape moral passions. *Journal of Consciousness Studies, 7,* 227–231.

Neumann, R., Hess, M., Schulz, S. M. & Alpers, G. W. (2005). Automatic behavioural responses to valence: Evidence that facial action is facilitated by evaluative processing. *Cognition & Emotion, 19,* 499–513.

Neumann, R., Hülsenbeck, K., & Seibt, B. (2004). Attitudes towards people with AIDS and avoidance behavior: Automatic and reflective bases of behavior. *Journal of Experimental Social Psychology, 40,* 543–550.

Neumark-Sztainer, D., Story, M., Falkner, N. H., Beuhring, T., & Resnick, M. D. (1999). Sociodemographic and personal characteristics of adolescents engaged in weight loss and weight/muscle gain behaviors: Who is doing what? *Preventative Medicine, 28,* 40–50.

Newby-Clark, I. R., McGregor, I., & Zanna, M. P. (2002). Thinking and caring about cognitive inconsistency: When and for whom does attitudinal ambivalence feel uncomfortable? *Journal of Personality and Social Psychology, 82,* 157–166.

Newby-Clark, I. R., & Ross, M. (2003). Conceiving the past and future. *Personality and Social Psychology Bulletin, 29,* 807–818.

Newcomb, M. D., Rabow, J., & Hernandez, A. C. R. (1992). A cross-national study of nuclear attitudes, normative support, and activist behavior: Addictive and interactive effects. *Journal of Applied Social Psychology, 22,* 780–800.

Newcomb, T. M. (1943). *Personality and social change: Attitude formation in a student community.* New York: Dryden.

Newcomb, T. M. (1951). Social psychological theory: Integrating individual and social approaches. In J. Rohrer & M. Sherif (Eds.), *Social psychology at the crossroads.* New York: Harper.

Newcomb, T. M. (1958). Attitude development as a function of reference groups. In E. E. Maccoby, T. M. Newcomb, & E. L. Hartley (Eds.), *Readings in social psychology* (3rd ed., pp. 265–275). New York: Holt, Rinehart.

Newcomb, T. M. (1961). *The acquaintance process.* New York: Holt, Rinehart.

Newcomb, T. M., Koenig, K. E., Flacks, R., & Warwick, D. P. (1967). *Persistence and change: Bennington College and its students after twenty-five years.* New York: Wiley.

Newcomb, T. M., Komarovsky, M. W. P., Lewis, O., & Maas, H. S. (1953). Social role. In J. M. Seidman (Ed.), *The adolescent: A book of readings* (pp. 414–464). Ft. Worth, TX: Dryden Press.

Newcombe, N., & Arnkoff, D. B. (1979). Effect of speech style and sex of speaker on person perception. *Journal of Personality and Social Psychology, 37,* 1293–1303.

Newman, L. S. (2001). A cornerstone for the science of interpersonal behavior? Person perception and person memory, past, present, and future. In G. B. Moskowitz (Ed.), *Cognitive social psychology: The Princeton symposium on the legacy and future of social cognition* (pp. 191–207). Mahwah, NJ: Erlbaum.

Newman, M. L., Berry, D. S., & Richards, J. M. (2003). Lying words: Predicting deception from linguistic styles. *Personality and Social Psychology Bulletin, 29,* 665–675.

Nezlek, J. B., & Leary, M. R. (2002). Individual differences in self-presentational motives in daily social interaction. *Personality and Social Psychology Bulletin, 28,* 211–223.

Nezlek, J. B., & Plesko, R. M. (2003). Affect- and self-based models of relationships between daily events and daily well-being. *Personality and Social Psychology Bulletin, 29,* 584–596.

Nezlek, J. B., Schütz, A., & Sellin, I. (2007). Self-presentational success in daily social interaction. *Self and Identity, 6,* 361–379.

Niedenthal, P. M., Brauer, M., Robin, L., & Innes-Ker, A. (2003). Adult attachment and the perception of facial expression of emotion. *Journal of Personality and Social Psychology, 82,* 419–433.

Niemeyer, S., Petts, J., & Hobson, K. (2005). Rapid climate change and society: Assessing responses and thresholds. *Risk Analysis, 25,* 1443–1456.

Nienhuis, A. E., Manstead, A. S. R., & Spears, R. (2001). Multiple motives and persuasive communication: Creative elaboration as a result of impression motivation and accuracy motivation. *Personality and Social Psychology Bulletin, 27,* 118–132.

Nisbett, R. E., Caputo, C., Legant, P., & Marecek, J. (1973). Behavior as seen by the actor and as seen by the observer. *Journal of Personality and Social Psychology, 27,* 154–164.

Nisbett, R. E., & Cohen, D. (1996). *Culture of honor: The psychology of violence in the south.* Boulder, CO: Westview Press.

Nix, G., Watson, C., Pyszcznski, T., & Greenberg, J. (1995). Reducing depressive affect through external focus of attention. *Journal of Social and Clinical Psychology, 14,* 36–52.

Nolan, S. A., Flynn, C., & Garber, J. (2003). Prospective relations between rejection and depression in young adolescents. *Journal of Personality and Social Psychology, 85,* 745–755.

Nolen-Hoeksma, S., Girgus, J. S., & Seligman, M. E. P. (1992). Predictors and consequences of childhood depressive symptoms: Five year longitudinal study. *Journal of Abnormal Psychology, 101,* 405–422.

Norenzayan, A., Choi, I., & Nisbett, R. E. (2002). Cultural similarities and differences in social inference: Evidence from behavioral predictions and lay theories of behavior. *Personality and Social Psychology Bulletin, 28,* 109–120.

Norenzayan, A., & Nisbett, R. E. (2000). Culture and causal cognition. *Current Directions in Psychological Science, 9,* 132–135.

North, A. C., Tarrant, M., & Hargreaves, D. J. (2004). The effects of music on helping behavior: A field study. *Environment and Behavior, 36,* 266–275.

Northouse, P. G. (2001). *Leadership: Theory and practice* (2nd ed.). Thousand Oaks, CA: Sage.

Norton, M. I., Sommers, S. R., Apfelbaum, E. P., Pura, N., & Ariely, D. (2006). Color blindness and interracial interaction. *Psychological Science, 17,* 949–953.

Nosek, B. A., Banaji, M., & Greenwald, A. G. (2002). Harvesting implicit group attitudes and beliefs from a demonstration web site. *Group Dynamics, 6,* 101–115.

Noveck, J., & Tompson, T. (August 20, 2007). Young people name family as key happiness factor. *Journal Sentinel,* p. 1B.

Nowak, A. (2004). Dynamical minimalism: Why less is more in psychology. *Personality and Social Psychology Review, 8,* 183–192.

Nowak, M., & Sigmund, K. (1993). A strategy of win-stay, lose-shift that outperforms tit-for-tat in the Prisoner's Dilemma game. *Nature, 364,* 56–58.

Nuttin, J. M. (1985). Narcissism beyond Gestalt and awareness—the Name Letter Effect. *European Journal of Social Psychology, 15,* 353–361.

Nyberg, L., Forkstam, C., Petersson, K. M., Cabeza, R., & Ingvar, M. (2002). Brain imaging of human memory systems: Between-systems similarities and within-system differences. *Cognitive Brain Research, 13,* 281–292.

Nye, J. L., & Brower, A. M. (Eds.). (1996). *What's social about social cognition? Research on socially shared cognition in small groups.* Thousand Oaks, CA: Sage.

Oakes, J. M., & Rossi, R. H. (2003). The measurement of SES in health research: Current practice and steps toward a new approach. *Social Science and Medicine, 56,* 769–784.

Oberman, L. M., Pineda, J. A., & Ramachandran, V. S. (2007). The human mirror neuron system: A link between action observation and social skills. *Social Cognitive and Affective Neuroscience, 2,* 62–66.

O'Donnell, C. R. (1995). Firearm deaths among children and youth. *American Psychologist, 50,* 771–776.

O'Donohue, W., Yeater, E. A., & Fanetti, M. (2003). Rape prevention with college males: The roles of rape myth acceptance, victim empathy, and outcome expectancies. *Journal of Interpersonal Violence, 18,* 513–531.

O'Farrell, T., & Murphy, C. M. (1995). Marital violence before and after alcoholism treatment. *Journal of Consulting and Clinical Psychology, 63,* 256–262.

Ochsner, K. N., & Lieberman, M. D. (2001). The emergence of social cognitive neuroscience. *American Psychologist, 56,* 717–734.

Oda, Ryo. (2001). Lemur vocal communication and the origin of human language. In T. Matsuzawa (Ed.), *Primate origins of human cognition and behavior* (pp. 115–134). New York: Springer-Verlag.

Oddone-Paolucci, E., Genuis, M., & Violato, C. (2000). A meta-analysis of the published research on the effects of pornography. In C. Violato & E. Oddone-Paolucci (Eds.), *The changing family and child development* (pp. 48–59). Aldershot, England: Ashgate.

Ogbu, J. U. (1993). Differences in cultural frame of reference. *International Journal of Behavioral Development, 16,* 483–506.

Onoda, K. (2010). Why mind feels pain: Current status of studies on ostracism from social neuroscience. *Japanese Journal of Physiological Psychology and Psychophysiology, 28,* 29–44.

Ohbuchi, K., Kamdea, M., & Agarie, N. (1989). Apology as aggression control: Its role in mediating appraisal of and response to harm. *Journal of Personality and Social Psychology, 56,* 219–227.

Öhman, A., Lundqvist, D., & Esteves, F. (2001). The face in the crowd revisited: A threat advantage with schematic stimuli. *Journal of Personality and Social Psychology, 80,* 381–396.

Ohtsubo, Y., Miller, C. E., Hayashi, N., & Masuchi, A. (2004). Effects of group decision rules on decisions involving continuous alternatives: The unanimity rule and extreme decisions in mock civil juries. *Journal of Experimental Social Psychology, 40,* 320–331.

Oishi, S., Diener, E. F., Lucas, R. E., & Suh, E. M. (1999). Cross-cultural variations in predictors of life satisfaction: Perspectives from needs and values. *Personality and Social Psychology Bulletin, 25,* 980–990.

Oishi, S., Lun, J., & Sherman, G. D. (2007). Residential mobility, self-concept, and positive affect in social interactions. *Journal of Personality and Social Psychology, 93,* 131–141.

Okimoto, T. G., & Brescoll, V. L. (2010). The price of power: Power seeking and backlash against female politicians. *Personality and Social Psychology Bulletin, 36,* 923–935.

Oliner, S. P., & Oliner, P. M. (1988). *The altruistic personality: Rescuers of Jews in Nazi Europe.* London: Free Press.

Oliver, M. B., & Hyde, J. S. (1993). Gender differences in sexuality: A meta-analysis. *Psychological Bulletin, 114,* 29–51.

Olson, J. M., & Roese, N. J. (1995). The perceived funniness of humorous stimuli. *Personality and Social Psychology Bulletin, 21,* 908–913.

Olson, K. R., Lambert, A. J., & Zacks, J. M. (2004). Graded structure and the speed of category verification: On the moderating effects of anticipatory control for social vs. non-social categories. *Journal of Experimental Social Psychology, 40,* 239–246.

O'Mahen, H. A., Beach, S. R. H., & Tesser, A. (2000). Relationship ecology and negative communication in romantic relationships: A self-evaluative maintenance perspective. *Personality and Social Psychology Bulletin, 26,* 1343–1352.

Omarzu, J. (2000). A disclosure decision model: Determining how and when individuals will self-disclose. *Personality and Social Psychology Review, 4,* 174–185.

Orbell, J. M., van de Kragt, A. J. C., & Dawes, R. M. (1988). Explaining discussion-induced cooperation. *Journal of Personality and Social Psychology, 54,* 811–819.

Orimoto, L., Hatfield, E., Yamakawa, R., & Denney, C. (1993). Gender differences in emotional reactions and coping strategies following a break-up. Reported in E. Hatfield & R. Rapson (1996), *Love, sex, and intimacy: Their psychology, biology, and history* (p. 231). Needham Heights, MA: Allyn & Bacon.

Orina, M. M., Collins, W. A., Simpson, J. A., Salvatore, J. E., Haydon, K. C., & Kim, J. S. (2011). Developmental and dyadic perspectives on commitment in adult romantic relationships. *Psychological Science.*

Ormel, J., & Schaufeli, W. B. (1991). Stability and change in psychological distress and their relationship with self-esteem and locus of control: A dynamic equilibrium model. *Journal of Personality and Social Psychology, 60,* 288–299.

Orne, M. T. (1962). On the social psychology of the psychological experiment: With particular reference to demand characteristics and their implications. *American Psychologist, 17,* 776–783.

Orpen, C. (1996). The effects of ingratiation and self promotion tactics on employee career success. *Social Behavior and Personality, 24,* 213–214.

Ortman, J. M., & Guarneri, C. E. (2009). *United States Population Projections: 2000 to 2050.* Retrieved from http://www.census.gov/population/www/projections/analytical-document09.pdf

Ortmann, A., & Hertwig, R. (1997). Is deception acceptable? *American Psychologist, 52,* 746–747.

Osborne, J. W. (1995). Academics, self-esteem, and race: A look at the underlying assumptions of the disidentification hypothesis. *Personality and Social Psychology Bulletin, 21,* 449–455.

Osborne, R. E. (2002). "I may be homeless, but I'm not helpless": The costs and benefits of identifying with homelessness. *Self and Identity, 1,* 43–52.

Osman, S. L. (2003). Predicting men's rape perceptions based on the belief that "no" really means "yes." *Journal of Applied Social Psychology, 33,* 683–692.

Ost, J., Costall, A., & Bull, R. (2001). False confessions and false memories: A model for understanding retractors' experiences. *Journal of Forensic Psychiatry, 12,* 549–579.

Oswald, D. L. (2005). Understanding anti-Arab reactions post-9/11: The role of threats, social categories, and personal ideologies. *Journal of Applied Social Psychology, 35,* 1775–1799.

Oswald, D. L. (2007). "Don't ask, don't tell": The influence of stigma concealing and perceived threat on perceiver's reactions to a gay target. *Journal of Applied Social Psychology, 37,* 928–947.

Oswald, D. L., Clark, E. M., & Kelly, C. M. (2004). Friendship maintenance behaviors: An analysis of individual and dyad behaviors. *Journal of Social and Clinical Psychology, 23,* 413–441.

Oswald, D. L., & Harvey, R. D. (2003). A Q-methodological study of women's subjective perspectives on mathematics. *Sex Roles, 49,* 133–142.

Oswald, R. F. (2000). A member of the wedding? Heterosexism and family ritual. *Journal of Social and Personal Relationships, 17,* 349–368.

Ottati, V. C., & Deiger, M. (2002). Visual cues and the candidate evaluation process. In V. C. Ottati, R. S. Tindale, J. Edwards, F. B. Bryant, L. Heath, D. C. O'Connell, Y. Suarez-Balcazar, & E. J. Posavac (Eds.), *The social psychology of politics. Social psychological applications to social issues* (pp. 75–87). New York: Kluwer Academic/Plenum.

Ottati, V. C., & Isbell, L. M. (1996). Effects of mood during exposure to target information and subsequently reported judgments: An on-line model of misattribution and correction. *Journal of Personality and Social Psychology, 71,* 39–53.

Oved, Y. (1988). *Two hundred years of American communes.* New Brunswick, NJ: Transaction Press.

Overall, N. C., & Fletcher, G. J. O. (in press). Perceiving regulation from intimate partners: Reflected appraisal and self-regulation processes in close relationships. *Personal Relationships.*

Overbeek, G., Ha, T., Scholte, R., de Kemp, R., & Engels, R. C. M. E. (2007). Intimacy, passion, and commitment in romantic relationships: Validation of a "triangular love scale" for adolescents. *Journal of Adolescence, 30,* 523–528.

Overstreet, N. M., Quinn, D. M., & Agocha, V. B. (2010). Beyond thinness: The influence of a curvaceous body ideal on body dissatisfaction in Black and White women. *Sex Roles, 63,* 91–103.

Oyserman, D., Bybee, D., Terry, K., & Hart-Johnson, T. (2004). Possible selves as roadmaps. *Journal of Research in Personality, 38,* 130–149.

Oyserman, D., Coon, H. M., & Kemmelmeier, M. (2002). Rethinking individualism and collectivism: Evaluation of theoretical assumptions and meta-analysis. *Psychological Bulletin, 128,* 3–72.

Oyserman, D., & Packer, M. J. (1996). Social cognition and self-concept: A socially contextualized model of identity. In J. L. Nye & A. M. Brower (Eds.), *What's social about social cognition: Research on socially shared cognition in small groups* (pp. 175–201). Thousand Oaks, CA: Sage.

Oyserman, D., Sakamoto, I., & Lauffer, A. (1998). Cultural accommodation: Hybridity and the framing of social obligation. *Journal of Personality and Social Psychology, 74,* 1606–1618.

Ozener, B., & Fink, B. (2010). Facial symmetry in young girls and boys from a slum and a control area of Ankara Turkey. *Evolution and Human Behavior, 31,* 436–441.

Pacifici, C., Stoolmitler, M., & Miller, C. (2001). Evaluating a prevention program for teenagers on sexual coercion: A differential effectiveness approach. *Journal of Consulting and Clinical Psychology, 69,* 552–559.

Packer, D. J. (2008). Identifying systematic disobedience in Milgram's obedience experiments: A meta-analytic review. *Association for Psychological Science, 3*(4), 301–304.

Packer, D. J. (2009). Avoiding groupthink: Whereas weakly identified members remain silent, strongly identified members dissent about collective problems. *Psychological Science, 20,* 546–548.

Page, R. M. (1991). Loneliness as a risk factor in adolescent hopelessness. *Journal of Research in Personality, 25,* 189–195.

Paik, H., & Comstock, G. (1994). The effects of television violence on anti-social behavior: A meta-analysis. *Communication Research, 21,* 516–546.

Paletz, S. B. F., Peng, K., Erez, M., & Maslach, C. (2003). Ethnic composition and its differential impact on group processes in diverse teams. *Small Group Research, 20,* 1–31.

Paletz, S. B. F., & Schunn, C. D. (2010). A social-cognitive framework of multidisciplinary team innovation. *Topics in Cognitive Science, 2,* 73–95.

Pallak, S. R. (1983). Salience of a communicator's physical attractiveness and persuasion: A heuristic versus systematic processing interpretation. *Social Cognition, 2,* 158–170.

Paluck, E. L. (2011). Peer pressure against prejudice: A high school field experiment examining social network change. *Journal of Experimental Social Psychology, 47,* 350–358.

Park, B. (1986). A method for studying the development of impressions of real people. *Journal of Personality and Social Psychology, 51,* 907–917.

Palmer, C., & Thompson, K. (2011). Everyday risks and professional dilemmas: Fieldwork with alcohol-based (sporting) subcultures: Corrigendum. *Qualitative Research, 11,* 112.

Parent, M. C., & Moradi, B. (2011). His biceps become him: A test of objectification theory's application to drive for muscularity and propensity for steroid use in college men. *Journal of Counseling Psychology, 58,* 246–256.

Park, B., & Rothbart, M. (1982). Perception of out-group homogeneity and levels of social categorization: Memory for the subordinate attributes of ingroup and outgroup members. *Journal of Personality and Social Psychology, 42,* 1051–1068.

Park, J., Malachi, E., Sternin, O., & Tevet, R. (2009). Subtle bias against Muslim job applicants in personnel decisions'. *Journal of Applied Social Psychology, 39,* 2174-2190.

Park, L. E. (2007). Appearance-based rejection sensitivity: Implications for mental and physical health, affect, and motivation. *Personality and Social Psychology Bulletin 33,* 490–504.

Park, L. E., Crocker, J., & Mickelson, K. D. (2004). Attachment styles and contingencies of self-worth. *Personality and Social Psychology Bulletin, 30,* 1243–1254.

Park, L. E., Crocker, J., & Vohs, K. D. (2006) In K. D. Vohs & E. J. Ei (Eds.), *Self and relationships: Connecting intrapersonal and interpersonal processes* (pp. 84–103). New York: Guilford Press.

Park, S., & Catrambone, R. (2007). Social facilitation effects of virtual humans. *Human Factors, 49,* 1054–1060.

Park, Y., Killen, M., Crystal, D. S., & Watanabe, K. (2003). Korean, Japanese, and U.S. students' judgments about peer exclusion: Evidence for diversity. *International Journal of Behavioral Development, 27,* 555–565.

Parks, C. D., Sanna, L. J., & Posey, D. C. (2003). Retrospection in social dilemmas: How thinking about the past affects future cooperation. *Journal of Personality and Social Psychology, 84,* 988–996.

Parnell, R. J., & Buchanan-Smith, H. M. (2001). Animal behaviour: An unusual social display by gorillas. *Nature, 412,* 294.

Parrott, W. G., & Smith, R. H. (1993). Distinguishing the experiences of envy and jealousy. *Journal of Personality and Social Psychology, 64,* 906–920.

Pasch, L. A., Bradbury, T. N., & Sullivan, K. T. (1997). Social support in marriage: An analysis of intraindividual and interpersonal components. In G. R. Pierce, B. Lakey, I. G. Sarason, & B. R. Sarason (Eds.), *Sourcebook of social support and personality* (pp. 229–256). New York: Plenum.

Patrick, H., Neighbors, C., & Knee, C. R. (2004). Appearance-related social comparisons: The role of contingent self-esteem and self-perceptions of attractiveness. *Personality and Social Psychology Bulletin, 30,* 501–514.

Patterson, F. G. P., & Cohen, R. H. (1994). Self-recognition and self-awareness in lowland gorillas. In S. T. Parker, R. W. Mitchell, & M. L. Boccia (Eds.), *Self-awareness in animals and humans: Developmental perspectives* (pp. 273–290). Cambridge, UK: Cambridge University Press.

Patterson, M. L. (2008). Back to social behavior: Mining the mundane. *Basic and Applied Social Psychology, 30,* 93–101.

Patterson, M. L. (in press). The decline of behavioral research? Examining language and communication journals. *Journal of Language and Social Psychology.*

Paulhus, D. L., & Levitt, K. (1987). Desirable responding triggered by affect: Automatic egotism? *Journal of Personality and Social Psychology, 52,* 245–259.

Payne, B. K. (2001). Prejudice and perception: The role of automatic and controlled processes in misperceiving a weapon. *Journal of Personality and Social Psychology, 81,* 181–192.

Payne, B. K., Jacoby, L. L., & Lambert, A. J. (2004). Memory monitoring and the control of stereotype distortion. *Journal of Experimental Social Psychology, 40,* 52–64.

Pearson, A. R., Dovidio, J. F., & Gaertner, S. L. (2009). The nature of contemporary prejudice: Insights from aversive racism. *Social and Personality Compass, 3,* 314–338.

Pederson, E. R., LaBrie, J. W., & Lac, A. (2008). Assessment of perceived and actual norm in varying contexts: Exploring Social Impact Theory among college students. *Addictive Behaviors, 33,* 525–564.

Peeters, G. (2003). Positive-negative asymmetry in the human information search and decision-making: Five basic and applied studies on voting behavior. In S. P. Shohov (Ed.), *Advances in psychology research, Vol. 19,* (pp. 61–92). Hauppauge, NY: Nova Science Publishers.

Pek, J. C. X., & Leong, F. T. L. (2003). Sex-related self-concepts, cognitive styles and cultural values of traditionality-modernity as predictors of general and domain-specific sexism. *Asian Journal of Social Psychology, 6,* 31–49.

Pelham, B. W., Carvallo, A., & Jones, J. T. (2005). Implicit egotism. *Current Directions in Psychological Science, 14,* 106–110.

Pelham, B. W., Mirenberg, M. C., & Jones, J. T. (2002). Why Susie sells seashells by the seashore: Implicit egotism and major life decisions. *Journal of Personality and Social Psychology, 82,* 469–487.

Pellegrini, A. D., & Bartini, M. (2001). Dominance in early adolescent boys: Affiliative and aggressive dimensions and possible functions. *Merrill-Palmer Quarterly, 47,* 142–163.

Peluchette, J. V., Karl, K., & Rust, K. (2006). Dressing to impress: Beliefs and attitudes regarding workplace attire. *Journal of Business and Psychology, 21,* 45–63.

Pendleton, M. G., & Batson, C. D. (1979). Self-presentation and the door-in-the-face technique for inducing compliance. *Personality and Social Psychology Bulletin, 5,* 77–81.

Pendry, L. F., & Macrae, C. N. (1994). Stereotypes and mental life: The case of the motivated but thwarted tactician. *Journal of Experimental Social Psychology, 30,* 303–325.

Penner, L. A., Dovidio, J. F., West, T. V., Gaertner, S. L., Albrecht, T. L., Dailey, R. K., & Markova, T. (2010). Aversive racism and medical interactions with Black patients: A field study. *Journal of Experimental Social Psychology, 46,* 436–440.

Pennington, N., & Hastie, R. (1988). Explanation-based decision making: Effects of memory structure on judgment. *Journal of Experimental Psychology: Learning, Memory, and Cognition, 14,* 521–533.

Pennington, N., & Hastie, R. (1990). Practical implications of psychological research on juror and jury decision making. *Personality and Social Psychology Bulletin, 16,* 90–105.

Pennington, N., & Hastie, R. (1992). Explaining the evidence: Tests of the story model for juror decision making. *Journal of Personality and Social Psychology, 62,* 189–206.

Penny, H., & Haddock, G. (2007). Anti-fat prejudice among children: The "mere proximity" effect in 5–10 year olds. *Journal of Experimental Social Psychology, 43,* 678–683

Pepitone, A. (1968). An experimental analysis of self dynamics. In C. Gordon & K. Gergen (Eds.), *The self in social interaction.* New York: Wiley.

Peplau, L. A. (2003). Human sexuality: How do men and women differ? *Current Directions in Psychological Science, 12,* 37–40.

Peplau, L. A., Bikson, T. K., Rook, K. S., & Goodchilds, J. D. (1982). Being old and living alone. In L. A. Peplau & D. Perlman (Eds.), *Loneliness: A sourcebook of current theory, research and therapy* (pp. 327–347). New York: Wiley.

Peplau, L. A., Cochran, S. D., & Mays, V. M. (1997). A national survey of the intimate relationships of African American lesbians and gay men: A look at commitment, satisfaction, sexual behavior and HIV disease. In B. Greene & G. Herek (Eds.), *Psychological perspectives on lesbian and gay issues: Ethnic and cultural diversity among lesbians and gay men.* Newbury Park, CA: Sage.

Peplau, L. A., Fingerhut, A. W. (2007). The close relationships of lesbian and gay men. *Annual Review of Psychology, 58,* 405–424.

Peplau, L. A., Fingerhut, A., & Beals, K. (2004). Sexuality in the relationships of lesbians and gay men. In J. Harvey, A. Wenzel, & S. Sprecher (Eds.), *Handbook of sexuality in close relationships* (pp. 349–369). Mahwah, NJ: Erlbaum.

Peplau, L. A., & Garnets, L. D. (2000). A new paradigm for understanding women's sexuality and sexual orientation. *Journal of Social Issues, 56,* 329–350.

Perdue, C. W., Dovidio, J. F., Gurtman, M. B., & Tyler, R. B. (1990). Us and them: Social categorization and the process of intergroup bias. *Journal of Personality and Social Psychology, 59,* 475–486.

Perez, E. O. (2010). Explicit evidence on the import of implicit attitudes: The IAT and immigration policy judgments. *Political Behavior, 32,* 517–545.

Perlman, D. (2007). The best of times, the worst of times: The place of close relationships in psychology and our daily lives. *Canadian Psychology, 48,* 19–23.

Peruche, B. M., & Plant, E. A. (2006). The correlates of law enforcement officers' automatic and controlled race-based responses to criminal suspects. *Basic and Applied Social Psychology, 28,* 193–199.

Pérusse, D., & Gendreau, P. L. (2005). Genetics and the development of aggression. In R. E. Tremblay, W. W. Hartup, & J. Archer (Eds.), *Developmental origins of aggression (*pp. 223–241). New York: Guilford Press.

Pessin, J. (1933). The comparative effects of social and mechanical stimulation on memorizing. *American Journal of Psychology, 45,* 263–270.

Peters, L. H., Hartke, D. D., & Pohlmann, J. T. (1985). Fiedler's contingency theory of leadership: An application of the meta-analytic procedures of Schmidt and Hunter. *Psychological Bulletin, 97,* 274–285.

Peterson, B. E. (2003). Authoritarianism and methodological innovation. *Analyses of Social Issues and Public Policy, 3,* 185–187.

Peterson, C., Maier, S. F., & Seligman, M. E. P. (1993). *Learned helplessness: A theory for the age of personal control.* New York: Oxford University Press.

Peterson, C., & Park, N. (2007). Explanatory style and emotion regulation. In J. Gross & J. James (Eds.), *Handbook of emotion regulation* (pp. 159–179). New York: Guilford Press.

Peterson, C., & Seligman, M. E. P. (1987). Explanatory style and illness. *Journal of Personality, 55,* 237–265.

Peterson, C., Seligman, M. E. P., & Vaillant, G. E. (1988). Pessimistic explanatory style is a risk factor for physical illness: A thirty-five-year longitudinal study. *Journal of Personality and Social Psychology, 55,* 23–27.

Peterson, C., Seligman, M. E. P., Yurko, K. H., Martin, L. R., & Friedman, H. S. (1998). Catastrophizing and untimely death. *Psychological Science, 9,* 127–130.

Peterson, R. S., & Nemeth, C. J. (1996). Focus versus flexibility: Majority and minority influence can both improve performance. *Personality and Social Psychology Bulletin, 22,* 14–23.

Petrie, K. J., Booth, R. J., & Pennebaker, J. W. (1998). The immunological effects of thought suppression. *Journal of Personality and Social Psychology, 75,* 1264–1272.

Petrocelli, J. V., Percy, E. J., Sherman, S. J., & Tormala, Z. L. (2011) Counterfactual potency. *Journal of Personality and Social Psychology, 100,* 30–46.

Petrova, P. K., Cialdini, R. B., & Sills, S. J. (2007). Consistency-based compliance across cultures. *Journal of Experimental Social Psychology, 43,* 104–111.

Pettigrew, T. F. (1969). Racially separate or together? *Journal of Social Issues, 25,* 43–69.

Pettigrew, T. F. (1998). Intergroup contact theory. *Annual Review of Psychology, 49,* 65–85.

Pettigrew, T. F. (2010). The ultimate Lewinian. In M. H. Gonzales, C. Tavris, & J. Aronson (Eds.). *The scientist and the humanist: A festschrift in honor of Elliot Aronson (*pp. 21–29). New York: Psychology Press.

Pettigrew, T. F., & Tropp, L. R. (2006). A meta-analytic test of intergroup contact theory. *Journal of Personality and Social Psychology, 90,* 751–783.

Pettijohn II, T. F., & Jungeberg, B. J. (2004). *Playboy* playmate curves: Changes in facial and body feature preferences across social and economic conditions. *Personality and Social Psychology Bulletin, 30,* 1186–1197.

Pettit, G. S. (2004). Violent children in developmental perspective. Risk and protective factors and the mechanisms through which they (may) operate. *Current Directions in Psychological Science, 13,* 194–197.

Petty, R. E. (2004). Multi-process models in social psychology provide a more balanced view of social thought and action. *Behavioral and Brain Sciences, 27.*

Petty, R. E., Briñol, P., Loersch, C., & McCaslin, M. J. (2009). The need for cognition. In M. R. Leary & R. H. Hoyle (Eds.), *Handbook of individual differences in social behavior* (pp. 318–329). New York: Guilford.

Petty, R. E., Briñol, P., & Tormala, Z. L. (2002). Thought confidence as a determinant for persuasion: The self-validation hypothesis. *Journal of Personality and Social Psychology, 82,* 722–741.

Petty, R. E., & Cacioppo, J. T. (1979). Issue involvement can increase or decrease persuasion by enhancing message-relevant cognitive responses. *Journal of Personality and Social Psychology, 37,* 1915–1926.

Petty, R. E., & Cacioppo, J. T. (1984). Source factors and the elaboration likelihood model of persuasion. *Advances in Consumer Research, 11,* 668–672.

Petty, R. E., & Cacioppo, J. T. (1986). *Communication and persuasion: Central and peripheral routes to attitude change.* New York: Springer-Verlag.

Petty, R. E., & Cacioppo, J. T. (1990). Involvement and persuasion: Tradition versus integration. *Psychological Bulletin, 107,* 367–374.

Petty, R. E., Barden, J., & Wheeler, S. C. (2009). The Elaboration Likelihood Model of persuasion: Developing health promotions for sustained behavioral change. In R. J. DiClemente, R. A. Crosby & M. C. Kegler (Eds.). *Emerging theories in health promotion practice and research* (2nd ed.) (pp. 185–214). San Francisco, CA: Jossey-Bass.

Petty, R. E., DeStono, D., & Rucker, D. D. (2001). The role of affect in attitude change. In J. P. Forgas (Ed.), *Handbook of affect and social cognition* (pp. 212–233). Mahwah, NJ: Erlbaum.

Petty, R. E., Haugtvedt, C. P., & Smith, S. M. (1995). Elaboration as a determinant of attitude strength: Creating attitudes that are persistent, resistant, and predictive of behavior. In R. E. Petty & J. A. Krosnick (Eds.), *Attitude strength: Antecedents and consequences.* Hillsdale, NJ: Erlbaum.

Petty, R. E., Rucker, D., Bizer, G., & Cacioppo, J. T. (2004a). The elaboration likelihood model of persuasion. In J. S. Seiter & G. H. Gass (Eds.), *Perspectives on persuasion, social influence and compliance gaining* (pp. 65–89). Boston: Allyn & Bacon.

Petty, R. E., Tormala, Z. L., & Rucker, D. D. (2004b). Resisting persuasion by counterarguing: An attitude strength perspective. In J. T. Jost, M. R. Banaji, & D. A. Prentice (Eds.), *Perspectivism in social psychology: The yin and yang of scientific progress* (pp. 37–51). Washington, DC: American Psychological Association.

Petty, R. E., & Wegener, D. T. (1998). Attitude change: Multiple roles for persuasion variables. In D. Gilbert, S. Fiske, & G. Lindzey (Eds.), *The handbook of social psychology* (4th ed., pp. 323–390). New York: McGraw-Hill.

Petty, R. E., Wegener, D. T., & Fabrigar, L. R. (1997). Attitudes and attitude change. *Annual Review of Psychology, 48,* 609–647.

Pew Internet & American Life Project. (2002). The Internet goes to college: How students are living in the future with today's technology. Retrieved July 18, 2005, from http://www.pewinternet.org/pdfs/PIPCollege Report.pdf

Pew Research Center. (2007). *How young people view their lives, future, and politics: A portrait of Generation Next.* http://people-press.org/reports/pdf/300.pdf

Pezzo, M. V. (2003). Surprise, defence, or making sense: What removes hindsight bias? *Memory, 11,* 421–441.

Pezzo, M. V., & Pezzo, S. P. (2007). Making sense of failure: A motivated model of hindsight bias. *Social Cognition, 25,* 147–164.

Pfeffer, J., Fong, C. T., Cialdini, R. B., & Portnoy, R. R. (2006). Overcoming the self-promotion dilemma: Interpersonal attraction and extra help as a consequence of who sings one's praises. *Personality and Social Psychology Bulletin, 32,* 1362–1374.

Pharo, H., Gross, J., Richardson, R. & Hayne, H. (2011). Age-related changes in the effect of ostracism. *Social Influence, 6,* 22–38.

Phelps, E. A., O'Connor, K. J., Cunningham, W. A., Funayama, E. S., Gatenby, J. C., & Gore, J. C., (2000). Performance on indirect measures of race evaluation predicts amygdala activation. *Journal of Cognitive Neuroscience, 12,* 729–738.

Phillips, A. G., & Silvia, P. J. (2005). Self-awareness and the emotional consequences of self-discrepancies. *Personality and Social Psychology Bulletin, 31,* 703–713.

Phills, C. E., Kawakami, K., Tabi, E., Nadolny, D., & Inzlicht, M. (2011). Mind the gap: Increasing associations between the self and blacks with approach behaviors. *Journal of Personality and Social Psychology, 100,* 197–210.

Phinney, J. S. (1991). Ethnic identity and self-esteem: A review and integration. *Hispanic Journal of Behavioral Sciences, 13,* 193–208.

Phinney, J. S. (1993). A three-stage model of ethnic identity development. In M. Bernal & G. Knight (Eds.), *Ethnic identity: Formation and transmission among Hispanics and other minorities* (pp. 61–79). Albany: State University of New York Press.

Phinney, J. S., Cantu, C. L., & Kurtz, D. A. (1997). Ethnic and American identity and self-esteem. *Journal of Youth and Adolescence, 26,* 165–185.

Phinney, J. S., & Kohatsu, E. (1997). Ethnic and racial identity and mental health. In J. Schulenberg, J. Maggs, & K. Hurrelmann (Eds.), *Health risks and developmental transitions during adolescence,* pp. 420–443. New York: Cambridge University Press.

Pickett, C. L., Gardner, W. L., & Knowles, M. (2004). Getting a cue: The need to belong and enhanced sensitivity to social cues. *Personality and Social Psychology Bulletin, 30,* 1095–1107.

Pietromonaco, P. R., & Carnelley, K. B. (1994). Gender and working models of attachment: Consequences for perception of self and romantic relationships. *Personal Relationships, 1,* 3–26.

Piff, P.K., Kraus, M.W., Cote, S., Cheng, B.H., & Keltner, D. (2010) Having less, giving more: The influence of social class on prosocial behavior. *Journal of Personality and Social Psychology, 99.* 771–784.

Piliavin, J. A., Dovidio, J. F., Gaertner, S. L., & Clark, R. D., III. (1981). *Emergency intervention.* New

York: Academic Press.

Piliavin, J. A., Grube, J. A., & Callero, P. L. (2002). Role as resource for action in public service. *Journal of Social Issues, 58,* 469–485.

Piliavin, J. A., & Piliavin, I. M. (1972). The effect of blood on reactions to a victim. *Journal of Personality and Social Psychology, 23,* 253–261.

Pilkington, C. J., & Smith, K. A. (2000). Self-evaluation maintenance in a larger social context. *British Journal of Social Psychology, 39,* 213–227.

Pino, N. W., & Meier, R. F. (1999). Gender differences in rape reporting. *Sex Roles, 40,* 979–990.

Pion, G. M., Mednick, M. T., Astin, H. S., Hall, C. C. I., Kenkel, M. B., Keita, G. P., Kohut, J. L., & Kelleher, J. C. (1996). The shifting gender composition of psychology: Trends and implications for the discipline. *American Psychologist, 51,* 509–528.

Pishyar, R., Harris, L. M., & Menzies, R. G. (2004). Attentional bias for words and faces in social anxiety. *Anxiety, Stress, and Coping, 17,* 23–36.

Plaks, J. E., Grant, H., & Dweck, C. S. (2005). Violations of implicit theories and the sense of prediction and control: Implications for motivated person perception. *Journal of Personality and Social Psychology, 88,* 245–262.

Plant, E. A., & Butz, D. A. (2006). The causes and consequences of an avoidance-focus for interracial interactions. *Personality and Social Psychology Bulletin, 32,* 833–846.

Platek, S. M., & Singh, D. (2010). Optimal waist-to-hip ratios in women activate neural reward centers in men. *PLoS ONE, 5.*

Plaut, V. C., Thomas, K. M., & Goren, M. J. (2009). Is multiculturalism or colorblindness better for minorities? *Psychological Science, 20,* 444–446.

Pleban, R., & Tesser, A. (1981). The effects of relevance and quality of another's performance on interpersonal closeness. *Social Psychology Quarterly, 44,* 278–285.

Plomin, R., Nitz, K., & Rowe, D. C. (1990). Behavior genetics and aggressive behavior in childhood. In M. Lewis & S. Miller (Eds.), *Handbook of developmental psychopathology* (pp. 119–133). New York: Plenum.

Plotnik, J. M., de Waal, F. B. M, & Reiss, D. (2006). Self-recognition in an Asian elephant. *Proceedings of the National Academy of Sciences, 103,* 17053–17057.

Plous, S. (1989). Thinking the unthinkable: The effects of anchoring on likelihood estimates of nuclear war. *Journal of Applied Social Psychology, 19,* 67–91.

Pohl, R. F., Bender, M., & Lachman, G. (2002). Hindsight bias around the world. *Experimental Psychology, 49,* 270–282.

Poldrack, R. A., & Wagner, A. D. (2004). What can neuroimaging tell us about the mind? Insights from prefrontal cortex. *Current Directions in Psychological Science, 13,* 177–181.

Pollard, J. S. (1995). Attractiveness of composite faces: A comparative study. *International Journal of Comparative Psychology, 8*(2), 77–83.

Pollock, C. L., Smith, S. D., Knowles, E. S., & Bruce, H. J. (1998). Mindfulness limits compliance with the that's-not-all technique. *Personality and Social Psychology, 24,* 1153–1157.

Pomerantz, E. M., Ruble, D. N., & Bolger, N. (2004). Supplementing the snapshots with video footage: Taking a developmental approach to understanding social psychological phenomena. In C. Sansone, C. C. Morf, & A. T. Panter (Eds.), *Handbook of methods in social psychology* (pp. 405–425). Thousand Oaks, CA: Sage.

Pontari, B. A. (2009). Appearing socially competent: The effects of a friend's presence on the socially anxious. *Personality and Social Psychology Bulletin, 35,* 283–294.

Pontari, B. A., & Schlenker, B. R. (2000). The influence of cognitive load on self-presentation: Can cognitive busyness help as well as harm social performance? *Journal of Personality and Social Psychology, 78,* 1092–1108.

Poole, M. S., Hollingshead, A. B., McGrath, J. E., &

Moreland, R. L. (2004). Interdisciplinary perspectives on small groups. *Small Group Research, 35,* 3–16.

Pope, H. G., Jr., Olivardan, R., Borowiecki, J., & Cohane, G. H. (2001). The growing commercial value of the male body: A longitudinal survey of advertising in women's magazines. *Psychotherapy and Psychosomatics, 70,* 189–192.

Pope, H. G., Olivardia, R., Gruber, A., & Borowiecki, J. (1999). Evolving ideals of male body image as seen through action toys. *International Journal of Eating Disorders, 26,* 65–72.

Porter, J. F., & Critelli, J. W. (1994). Self-talk and sexual arousal in sexual aggression. *Journal of Social and Clinical Psychology, 13,* 223–239.

Posavac, H. D., & Posavac, S. S. (1998). Exposure to media images of female attractiveness and concern with body weight among young women. *Sex Roles, 38,* 187–201.

Post, J. M., Panis, L. K. (2011). Crime of obedience: "Groupthink" at Abu Ghraib. *International Journal of Group Psychotherapy. 61,* 49–66.

Postmes, T., & Spears, R. (1998). Deindividuation and antinormative behavior: A meta-analysis. *Psychological Bulletin, 123,* 238–259.

Poteat, V. P., Espelage, D. L., & Green, H. D., Jr. (2007). The socialization of dominance: Peer group contextual effects on homophobic and dominance attitudes. *Journal of Personality and Social Psychology, 92,* 1040–1050.

Pouliasi, K., & Verkuyten, M. (2007). Networks of meaning and the bicultural mind: A structural equation modeling approach. *Journal of Experimental Social Psychology, 43,* 955–963.

Poutvaara, P., Jordahl, H., & Berggren, N. (2009). Faces of politicians: Babyfacedness predicts inferred competence but not electoral success. *Journal of Experimental Social Psychology, 45,* 1132–1135.

Powers, S. I., Pietromonaco, P. R., Gunlicks, M., & Sayer, A. (2006). Dating couples' attachment styles and patterns of cortisol reactivity and recovery in response to a relationship conflict. *Journal of Personality and Social Psychology. 90,* 613–628.

Powers, T. A., & Zuroff, D. C. (1988). Interpersonal consequences of overt self-criticism: Comparison with neutral and self-enhancing presentations of self. *Journal of Personality and Social Psychology, 54,* 1054–1062.

Pozo, C., Carver, C. S., Wellens, A. R., & Scheier, M. F. (1991). Social anxiety and social perception: Construing others' reactions to the self. *Personality and Social Psychology Bulletin, 17,* 355–362.

Pratkanis, A. R., & Aronson, E. (1992). *Age of propaganda: The everyday use and abuse of persuasion.* New York: W. H. Freeman.

Pratkanis, A. R., Eskenazi, J., & Greenwald, A. G. (1994). What you expect is what you believe (but not necessarily what you get): A test of the effectiveness of subliminal self-help audio-tapes. *Basic and Applied Social Psychology, 15,* 251–276.

Pratkanis, A. R., Greenwald, A. G., Leippe, M. R., & Baumgardner, M. H. (1988). In search of reliable persuasion effects: III. The sleeper effect is dead. Long live the sleeper effect. *Journal of Personality and Social Psychology, 54,* 203–218.

Pratt, D. D. (1991). Conceptions of self within China and the United States: Contrasting foundations for adult education. *International Journal of Intercultural Relations, 15,* 285–310.

Pratto, F. (1996). Sexual politics: The gender gap in the bedroom, the cupboard, and the cabinet. In D. Buss & N. Malamuth (Eds.), *Sex, power, and conflict: Evolutionary and feminist perspectives* (pp. 179–230). New York: Oxford University Press.

Prentice, D. A. (1987). Psychological correspondence of possessions, attitudes, and values. *Journal of Personality and Social Psychology, 53,* 993–1003.

Prentice, D. A. (2004). Values and evaluations. In J. T. Jost, M. R. Banaji, & D. A. Prentice (Eds.), *Perspectivism in Social Psychology: The yin and yang of scientific progress* (pp. 69–81). Washington, DC: American Psychological Association.

Prentice, D. A., Trail, T. E., & Cantor, N. (2001). *Making choices and living with the consequences: Values, activities, and well-being among college students.* Unpublished manuscript, Princeton University.

Prentice-Dunn, S., & Rogers. R. W. (1980). Effects of deindividuating situational cues and aggressive models on subjective deindividuation and aggression. *Journal of Personality and Social Psychology, 39,* 104–113.

Prentice-Dunn, S., & Rogers, R. W. (1982). Effects of public and private self-awareness on deindividuation and aggression. *Journal of Personality and Social Psychology, 43,* 503–513.

Price, K. H., Harrison, D. A., & Gavin, J. H. (2006). Withholding inputs in team contexts: Member composition, interaction processes, evaluation structure, and social loafing. *Journal of Applied Psychology, 91,* 1375–1384.

Priest, R. F., & Sawyer, J. (1967). Proximity and peership: Bases of balance in interpersonal attraction. *American Journal of Sociology, 72,* 633–649.

Priester, J. R., Cacioppo, J. T., & Petty, R. E. (1996). The influence of motor processes on attitudes toward novel versus familiar semantic stimuli. *Personality and Social Psychology Bulletin, 22,* 442–447.

Priester, J. R., & Petty, R. E. (1995). Source attributions and persuasion: Perceived honesty as a determinant of message scrutiny. *Personality and Social Psychology Bulletin, 21,* 637–654.

Priester, J. R., & Petty, R. E. (2001). Extending the bases of subjective attitudinal ambivalence: Interpersonal and intrapersonal antecedents of evaluative tension. *Journal of Personality and Social Psychology, 80,* 19–34.

Principe, C. P., & Langlois, J. H. (2011). Faces differing in attractiveness elicit corresponding affective responses. *Cognition and Emotion, 25,* 140–148.

Prislin, R., & Christensen, P. N. (2005). The effects of social change within a group on membership preferences: To leave or not to leave? *Personality and Social Psychology Bulletin, 31,* 595–609.

Pronin, E., Berger, J., & Molouki, S. (2007). Alone in a crowd of sheep: Asymmetric perceptions of conformity and their roots in an introspective illusion. *Journal of Personality and Social Psychology, 92,* 585–595.

Pronin, E., & Ross, L. (2006). Temporal differences in trait self-ascription: When the self is seen as an other. *Journal of Personality and Social Psychology, 90,* 197–209.

Pronin, E., Steele, C. M., & Ross, L. (2004). Identity bifurcation in response to stereotype threat: Women and mathematics. *Journal of Experimental Social Psychology, 40,* 152–168.

Pruitt, D. G. (1971). Choice shifts in group discussion: An introductory review. *Journal of Personality and Social Psychology, 20,* 339–360.

Pryor, J. B., Reeder, G. D., Yeadon, C., & Hesson-McInnis, M. (2004). A dual-process model of reactions to perceived stigma. *Personality and Social Psychology, 87,* 436–452.

Ptacek, J. T., & Dodge, K. L. (1995). Coping strategies and relationship satisfaction in couples. *Personality and Social Psychology Bulletin, 21,* 76–84.

Puente, S., & Cohen, D. (2003). Jealousy and the meaning (or nonmeaning) of violence. *Personality and Social Psychology Bulletin, 29,* 449–460.

Puentes, J., Knox, D., & Zusman, M. E. (2008). Participants in "friends with benefits" relationships. *College Student Journal, 42,* 176–180.

Purdon, C., Rowa, K., & Antony, M. M. (2007). Diary records of thought suppression by individuals with obsessive-compulsive disorder. *Behavioural and Cognitive Psychotherapy, 35,* 47–59.

Pugh, S. D., Groth, M., & Hennig-Thurau, T. (2011). Willing and able to fake emotions: A closer examination of the link between emotional dissonance and employee well-being. *Journal of Applied Psychology, 96,* 377–390.

Puhl, R. M., T. Andreyeva, and K. D. Brownell. (2008a). Perceptions of weight discrimination: Prevalence and comparison to race and gender discrimination in America. *International Journal of Obesity 32,* 992–1000.

Puhl, R. M., & Brownell, K. D. (2006). Confronting and coping with weight stigma: An investigation of overweight and obese adults. *Obesity, 14,* 1802–1815.

Puhl, R. M., Moss-Racusin, C. A., Schwartz, M. B., & Brownell, K. D. (2008b). Weight stigmatization and bias reduction: Perspectives of overweight and obese adults. *Health Education Research, 23,* 347–358.

Pyszczynski, T., & Greenberg, J. (1992). *Hanging on and letting go: Understanding the onset, maintenance, and remission of depression.* New York: Springer-Verlag.

Pyykkö, R. (2002). Who is "us" in Russian political discourse? In A. Duszak (Ed.), *Us and others: Social identities across languages, discourses and cultures* (pp. 233–264). Amsterdam: John Benjamins.

Quillian, L. (1995). Prejudice as a response to perceived group threat: Population composition and anti-immigrant and racial prejudice in Europe. *American Sociological Review, 60,* 586–611.

Quinn, D. M. (2006). Concealable versus conspicuous stigmatized identities. In S. Levin & C. van Laar (Eds.), *Stigma and group inequality: Social psychological perspectives* (pp. 45–64). Mahwah, NJ: Erlbaum.

Quinn, K. A., & Macrae, C. N. (2005). Categorizing others: The dynamics of person construal. *Journal of Personality and Social Psychology, 88,* 467–479.

Quiñones-Vidal, E., López-Garcia, J. J., Peñaranda-Ortega, M., & Tortosa-Gil, F. (2004). The nature of social and personality psychology as reflected in *JPSP*, 1965–2000. *Journal of Personality and Social Psychology, 86,* 435–452.

Quist, R. M., & Resendez, M. G. (2002). Social dominance threat: Examining social dominance theory's explanation of prejudice as legitimizing myths. *Basic and Applied Social Psychology, 24,* 287–293.

Radelet, M. L., Bedau, H. A., & Putnam, C. E. (1992). *In spite of innocence: Erroneous convictions in capital cases.* Boston: Northeastern University Press.

Räikkönen, K., Matthews, K. A., Flory, J. D., Owens, J. F., & Gump, B. B. (1999). Effects of optimism, pessimism, and trait anxiety on ambulatory blood pressure and mood during everyday life. *Journal of Personality and Social Psychology, 76,* 104–113.

Ramirez, J. M., & Latané, B. (2001). Dynamic social impact theory predicts regional variation in, and the development of social representations of, aggression. In J. M. Ramirez & D. S. Richardson (Eds.), *Cross-cultural approaches to research on aggression and reconciliation* (pp. 9–21). Huntington, NY: Nova Science.

Ramsoy, N. R. (1966). Assortive mating and the structure of cities. *American Journal of Sociology, 31,* 773–786.

Rasenberger, J. (2006). "Nightmare on Austin Street." *American Heritage Magazine, 57*(5), 65–67.

Rasmussen, J. L., Rajecki, D. W., Ebert, A. A., Lagler, K., Brewer, C., & Cochran, E. (1998). Age preferences in personal advertisements: Two life history strategies or one matching tactic? *Journal of Social and Personal Relationships, 15,* 77–89.

Ratcliff, J. J., Lassiter, G. D., Markman, K. D., & Snyder, C. J. (2006). Gender differences in attitudes toward gay men and lesbians: The role of motivation to respond without prejudice. *Personality and Social Psychology Bulletin, 32,* 1325–1338.

Ratcliff, R., & McKoon, G. (1994). Retrieving information from memory: Spreading-activation theories versus compound-cue theories. *Psychological Review, 101,* 177–184.

Rattan, S. N. S. (2011). Self, culture, and anxious experiences. *Journal of Adult Development, 18,* 28–36.

Raven, B. H. (2001). Power/interaction and interpersonal influence: Experimental investigations and case studies. In A. Lee-Chai & J. Bargh (Eds.), *The use and abuse of power: Multiple perspectives on the causes of corruption* (pp. 217–240). Philadelphia, PA: Psychology Press.

Read, J. D. (1996). From a passing thought to a false memory in 2 minutes: Confusing real and illusory events. *Psychonomic Science and Review, 3,* 105–111.

Redding, R. E. (2001). Sociopolitical diversity in psychology. *American Psychologist, 56,* 205–215.

Reeder, G. D., Kumar, S., Hesson-McInnis, M. S., & Trafimow, D. (2002). Inferences about the morality of an aggressor: The role of perceived motive. *Journal of Personality and Social Psychology, 83,* 789–803.

Reeder, H. M. (2000). "I like you … as a friend": The role of attraction in cross-sex friendship. *Journal of Social and Personal Relationships, 17,* 329–348.

Reeder, H. M. (2003). The effect of gender role orientation on same- and cross-sex friendship formation. *Sex Roles, 49,* 143–152.

Regan, D. T. (1971). Effects of a favor and liking on compliance. *Journal of Experimental Social Psychology, 7,* 627–639.

Regan, D. T., & Gilovich, T. (2004). Social psychological research isn't negative, and its message fosters compassion. *Behavioral and Brain Sciences, 27.*

Regan, D. T., & Kilduff, M. (1988). Optimism about elections: Dissonance reduction at the ballot box. *Political Psychology, 9,* 101–107.

Regan, P. C., Levin, L., Sprecher, S., Christopher, F. S., & Cate, R. (2000). Partner preferences: What characteristics do men and women desire in their short-term sexual and long-term romantic partners? *Journal of Psychology & Human Sexuality, 12,* 1–21.

Reich, A. A. (2004). What you expect is not always what you get: The roles of extremity, optimism, and pessimism in the behavioral confirmation process. *Journal of Experimental Social Psychology, 40,* 199–215.

Reifman, A., Watson, W. K., & McCourt, A. (2006). Social networks and college drinking: Probing processes of social influence and selection. *Personality and Social Psychology Bulletin, 32,* 820–832.

Reinard, J. C. (1988). The empirical study of the persuasive effects of evidence: The status after fifty years of research. *Human Communications Research, 15,* 3–59.

Reinecke, J., Schmidt, P., & Ajzen, I. (1996). Application of the theory of planned behavior to adolescents' condom use: A panel study. *Journal of Applied Social Psychology, 26,* 749–772.

Reis, H. T., & Gable, S. L. (2003). Toward a positive psychology of relationships. In C. L. M. Keyes & J. Haidt (Eds.), *Flourishing: Positive psychology and the life well-lived* (pp. 129–159).

Reis, H. T., & Gosling, S. D. (2010). Social psychological methods outside the laboratory. In S. T. Fiske, D. T. Gilbert, & G. Lindzey (Eds.). *Handbook of social psychology, Vol. 1* (5th ed.) (pp. 82–114). Hoboken, NJ: John Wiley.

Reis, H. T., Maniaci, M. R., Caprariello, P. A., Eastwick, P. W., & Finkel, E. J. (2011). Familiarity does indeed promote attraction in live interaction. *Journal of Personality and Social Psychology, 7.*

Reisenzein, R. (1983). The Schachter theory of emotion: Two decades later. *Psychological Bulletin, 94,* 239–264.

Reisman, J. M. (1984). Friendliness and its correlates. *Journal of Social and Clinical Psychology, 2,* 143–155.

Rempel, J. K., & Burris, C. T. (2006). Push-you-pull-you: The boundaried self in close relationships. *Personality and Social Psychology Bulletin, 32,* 256–269.Rendell, L., Fogarty, L., Hoppitt, W. J. E., Morgan, T. J. H., Webster, M. M., & Laland, K. N. (2011). Cognitive culture: Theoretical and empirical insights into social learning strategies. *Trends in Cognitive Sciences, 15,* 68–76.

Reynolds, K. J., Turner, J. C., & Haslam, S. A. (2000). When are we better than them and they worse than us? A closer look at social discrimination in positive and negative domains. *Journal of Personality and Social Psychology, 78,* 64–80.

Rhodewalt, F., & Davison, J., Jr. (1983). Reactance and the coronary-prone behavior pattern: The role of self-attribution in response to reduced behavioral freedom. *Journal of Personality and Social Psychology, 44,* 220–228.

Richeson, J. A., & Nussbaum, R. J. (2004). The impact of multiculturalism versus color-blindness on racial bias. *Journal of Experimental Social Psychology, 40,* 417–423.

Richter, A., & Ridout, N. (2011). Self-esteem moderates affective reactions to briefly presented emotional faces. *Journal of Research in Personality.*

Ridgeway, C. L. (1982). Status in groups: The importance of motivation. *American Sociological Review, 47,* 76–88.

Ridgeway, C. L. (1991). The social construction of status value: Gender and other nominal characteristics. *Social Forces, 70,* 367–386.

Ridgeway, C. L. (2001). Gender, status, and leadership. *Journal of Social Issues, 57,* 637–655.

Ridley, M., & Dawkins, R. (1981). The natural selection of altruism. In J. P. Rushton & R. M. Sorrentino (Eds.), *Altruism and helping behavior: Social, personality, and developmental perspectives.* Hillsdale, NJ: Erlbaum.

Riggio, R. E., & Conger, J. A. (2007). Getting it right: The practice of leadership. In J. A. Conger & R. E. Riggio (Eds.), *The practice of leadership: Developing the next generation of leaders* (pp. 331–344). San Francisco, CA: Jossey-Bass.

Riggs, J. M., & Gumbrecht, L. B. (2005). Correspondence bias and American sentiment in the wake of September 11, 2001. *Journal of Applied Social Psychology, 35,* 15–28.

Riley, D., & Eckenrode, J. (1986). Social ties: Subgroup differences in costs and benefits. *Journal of Personality and Social Psychology, 51,* 770–778.

Rilling, J. K. (2011). The social brain in interactive games. In A. Todorov, S. T. Fiske, & D. A. Prentice (Eds.). *Social neuroscience: Toward understanding the underpinnings of the social mind* (pp. 217–228). New York: Oxford University Press.

Ringelmann, M. (1913). Research on animate sources of power: The work of man. *Annales de l'Institut National Agronomique, 2e serietome XII,* 1–40.

Riordan, C. A., & Tedeschi, J. T. (1983). Attraction in aversive environments: Some evidence for classical conditioning and negative reinforcement. *Journal of Personality and Social Psychology, 44,* 683–692.

Roberts, B. W., & Helson, R. (1997). Changes in culture, changes in personality: The influence of individualism in a longitudinal study of women. *Journal of Personality and Social Psychology, 72,* 641–651.

Roberts, W. R. (1954). *Aristotle.* New York: Modern Library.

Robins, R. W., & Beer, J. S. (2001). Positive illusions about the self: Short-term benefits and long-term costs. *Journal of Personality and Social Psychology, 80,* 340–352.

Robins, R. W., Spranca, M. D., & Mendelsohn, G. A. (1996). The actor-observer effect revisited: Effects of individual differences and repeated social interactions on actor and observer attributions. *Journal of Personality and Social Psychology, 71,* 375–389.

Robinson, D. T., & Balkwell, J. W. (1995). Density, transitivity, and diffuse status in task-oriented groups. *Social Psychology Quarterly, 58,* 241–254.

Robinson, T. N., Wilde, M. L., Navracruz, L. C., Haydel, K. F., & Varady, A. (2001). Effects of reducing children's television and video game use on aggressive behavior: A randomized controlled trial. *Archives of Pediatrics and Adolescent Medicine, 155,* 17–23.

Roccas, S., & Brewer, M. B. (2002). Social identity complexity. *Personality and Social Psychology Review, 6,* 88–106.

Roccato, M., & Ricolfi, L. (2005). On the correlation between right-wing authoritarianism and social dominance orientation. *Basic and Applied Social Psychology, 27,* 187–200.

Rochat, P. (2011). The self as phenotype. *Consciousness and Cognition: An International Journal, 20,* 109–119.

Rochot, F., Maggioni, O., & Modigliani, A. (2000). The dynamics of obeying and opposing authority: A mathematical model. In T. Blass (Ed.), *Obedience to authority: Current perspectives on the Milgram paradigm* (pp. 161–192). Mahwah, NJ: Erlbaum.

Rodafinos, A., Vucevic, A., & Sideridis, G. D. (2005). The effectiveness of compliance techniques: Foot in the door versus door in the face. *Journal of Social Psychology, 145,* 237–239.

Rodrigues, A., Assmar, E. M. L, & Jablonski, B. (2005). Social psychology and the invasion of Iraq. *Revista de Psicología Social, 20,* 387–398.

Rodriguez-Bailon, R., Moya, M., & Yzerbyt, V. (2000). Why do superiors attend to negative stereotypic information about their subordinates? Effects of power legitimacy on social perception. *European Journal of Social Psychology, 30,* 651–671.

Roese, N. J. (1997). Counterfactual thinking. *Psychological Bulletin, 121,* 133–148.

Roese, N. J., Hur, T., & Pennington, G. L. (1999). Counterfactual thinking and regulatory focus: Implications for action versus inaction and sufficiency versus necessity. *Journal of Personality and Social Psychology, 77,* 1109–1120.

Rofé, Y. (1984). Stress and illness: A utility theory. *Psychological Review, 91,* 235–250.

Rogers, C. R. (1947). Some observations on the organization of personality. *American Psychologist, 2,* 358–368.

Rogers, R. W., & Prentice-Dunn, S. (1997). Protection motivation theory. In D. S. Gochman (Ed.), *Handbook of health behavior research I: Personal and social determinants* (Vol. 1, pp. 113–132). New York: Plenum.

Rogoff, B., Paradise, R., Arauz, R. M., Correa-Chávez, M., & Angelillo, C. (2003). Firsthand learning through intent participation. *Annual Review of Psychology, 54,* 175–203.

Rohan, M. J. (2000). A rose by any name? The values construct. *Personality and Social Psychology Review, 4,* 255–277.

Roisman, G. I., Holland, A., Fortuna, K, Fraley, R. C., Clausell, E., & Clarke, A. (2007). The adult attachment interview and self-reports of attachment style: An empirical rapprochement. *Journal of Personality and Social Psychology, 92,* 678–697.

Rokach, A. (2007). The effect of age and culture on the causes of loneliness. *Social Behavior and Personality, 35,* 169–186.

Rokach, A., & Bacanli, H. (2001). Perceived causes of loneliness: A cross-cultural comparison. *Social Behavior and Personality, 29,* 169–182.

Rokeach, M. (1973). *The nature of human values.* New York: Free Press.

Romer, D., Gruder, C. L., & Lizzadro, T. (1986). A person-situation approach to altruistic behavior. *Journal of Personality and Social Psychology, 51,* 1001–1012.

Rosch, E. H. (1978). Principles of categorization. In E. Rosch & B. L. Lloyd (Eds.), *Cognition and categorization.* Hillsdale, NJ: Erlbaum.

Rosch, E., & Mervis, C. B. (1975). Family resemblances: Studies in the internal structure of categories. *Cognitive Psychology, 7,* 573–605.

Rose, J. (1994). Communication challenges and role functions of performing groups. *Small Group Research, 25,* 411–432.

Rose, S., & Zand, D. (2000). Lesbian dating and courtship from young adulthood to midlife. *Journal of Gay and Lesbian Social Services, 11,* 77–104.

Rosekrans, M., & Hartup, W. (1967). Imitative influences of consistent and inconsistent response consequences to a model on aggressive behavior in children. *Journal of Personality and Social Psychology, 7,* 429–434.

Rosenberg, M. (1965). *Society and the adolescent child.* Princeton, NJ: Princeton University Press.

Rosenberg, M., Schooler, C., & Schoenbach, C. (1989). Self-esteem and adolescent problems: Modeling reciprocal effects. *American Sociological Review, 54,* 1004–1018.

Rosenberg, M. L., & Mercy, J. A. (1991). Assaultive violence. In M. L. Rosenberg & M. A. Fenley (Eds.), *Violence in America: A public health approach* (pp. 14–50). New York: Oxford University Press.

Rosenberg, Morris.1989. *Society and the alolescent self-image.* Revised edition. Middletown, CT: Wesleyan University Press.

Rosenblatt, P. C., & Cozby, P. C. (1972). Courtship patterns associated with freedom of choice of spouse. *Journal of Marriage and the Family, 34,* 689–695.

Rosenhan, D. L. (1970). The natural socialization of altruistic autonomy. In J. Macaulay & L. Berkowitz (Eds.), *Altruism and helping behavior.* New York: Academic Press.

Rosenhan, D. L., Salovey, P., & Hargis, K. (1981). The joys of helping: Focus of attention mediates the impact of positive affect on altruism. *Journal of Personality and Social Psychology, 40,* 899–905.

Rosenkoetter, L. I. (1999). The television situation comedy and children's prosocial behavior. *Journal of Applied Social Psychology, 29,* 979–993.

Rosenkoetter, L. I., Rosenkoetter, S. E., Ozretich, R. A., & Acock, A. C. (2004). Mitigating the harmful effects of violent television. *Journal of Applied Developmental Psychology, 25,* 25–47.

Rosenthal. L., & Levy, S. R. (2010). Understanding women's risk for HIV infection using social dominance theory and the four bases of gendered power. *Psychology of Women's Quarterly, 34,* 21–35.

Rosenthal, R. (1991). Teacher expectancy effects: A brief update 25 years after the Pygmalion experiment. *Journal of Research in Education, 1,* 3–12.

Rosenthal, R. (2002). Covert communication in classrooms, clinics, courtrooms, and cubicles. *American Psychologist, 57,* 839–849.

Rosenthal, R. (2003). Covert communication in laboratories, classrooms, and the truly real world. *Current Directions in Psychological Science, 12,* 151–154.

Rosenthal, R., & Jacobson, L. (1968). *Pygmalion in the classroom: Teacher expectation and pupils' intellectual development.* New York: Holt.

Rosenthal, R., & Rubin, D. B. (1982). Further meta-analytic procedures for assessing cognitive gender differences. *Journal of Educational Psychology, 74,* 708–712.

Ross, E. A. (1908). *Social psychology: An outline and sourcebook.* New York: Macmillan.

Ross, L. (1977). The intuitive psychologist and his shortcomings: Distortions in the attribution process. In L. Berkowitz (Ed.), *Advances in experimental social psychology* (Vol. 10, pp. 174–221). New York: Academic Press.

Ross, L., Amabile, T. M., & Steinmetz, J. L. (1977a). Social roles, social control, and biases in social perception processes. *Journal of Personality and Social Psychology, 35,* 485–494.

Ross, L., Greene, D., & House, P. (1977b). The "false consensus effect": An egocentric bias in social perception and attribution processes. *Journal of Experimental Social Psychology, 13,* 279–301.

Ross, M. A., & Holmberg, D. (1993). Are wives' memories for events in relationships more vivid than their husbands' memories? *Journal of Social and Personal Relationships, 9,* 585–604.

Ross, L., Lepper, M., & Ward, A. (2010). History of social psychology: Insights, challenges, and contributions to theory and application. In S. T. Fiske, D. T. Gilbert, & G. Lindzey (Eds.). *Handbook of social psychology, Vol. 1* (5th ed.) (pp. 3–50). Hoboken, NJ: John Wiley.

Ross, M., & Miller, D. T. (Eds.). (2002). *The justice motive in everyday life.* New York: Cambridge University Press.

Rossano, M. J. (2003). *Evolutionary psychology: The science of human behavior and evolution.* Hoboken, NJ: John Wiley.

Rotenberg, K. J., & Kmill, J. (1992). Perception of lonely and nonlonely persons as a function of individual differences in loneliness. *Journal of Social and Personal Relationships, 9,* 325–330.

Rotenberg, K. J., Bartley, J. L., & Toivonen, D. M. (1997). Children's stigmatization of chronic loneliness in peers. *Journal of Social Behavior and Personality, 12,* 577–584.

Rotenburg, K. J., Addis, N., Betts, L. R., Corrigan, A., Fox, C., Hobson, Z., Rennison, s., Trueman, M., & Boulton, M. J. (2010). The relation between trust beliefs and loneliness during early childhood, middle childhood and adulthood. *Personality and Social Psychology Bulletin, 36,* 1086–1100.

Rothbaum, F., & Tsang, B. Y. P. (1998). Lovesongs in the United States and China: On the nature of romantic love. *Journal of Cross-Cultural Psychology, 29,* 306–319.

Rothberger, H. (1997). External intergroup threat as an antecedent to perceptions of in-group and out-group homogeneity. *Journal of Personality and Social Psychology, 73,* 1206–1212.

Rothstein, H. R., McDaniel, M. A., & Borenstein, M. (2002). Meta-analysis: A review of quantitative cumulation methods. In F. Drasgow & N. Schmitt (Eds.), *Measuring and analyzing behavior in organizations: Advances in measurement and data analysis. The Jossey-Bass business & management series.* San Francisco: Jossey-Bass.

Rotton, J., & Cohn, E. G. (2000). Violence is a curvilinear function of temperature in Dallas: A replication. *Journal of Personality and Social Psychology, 78,* 1074–1081.

Rotundo, A. (1989). Romantic friendships: Male intimacy and middle-class youth in the northern United States, 1800–1900. *Journal of Social History, 23,* 1–25.

Rowatt, W. C., Cunningham, M. R., & Druen, P. B. (1998). Deception to get a date. *Personality and Social Psychology Bulletin, 24,* 1228–1242.

Rowatt, W. C., Franklin, L. M., & Cotton, M. (2005). Patterns and personality correlates of implicit and explicit attitudes toward Christians and Muslims. *Journal for the Scientific Study of Religion, 44,* 29–43.

Rowe, D. J. (November 14, 2003). "Fabulist" Stephen Glass calls biopic of his life my own personal horror film. *Suburban Chicago Newspapers.* http://www.suburbanchicagonews.com/entertainment/e14glass.htm

Rowold, J., & Heinitz, K. (2007). Transformational and charismatic leadership: Assessing the convergent, divergent and criterion validity of the MLQ and the CKS. *Leadership Quarterly, 18,* 121–133.

Rozell, E. J., & Gundersen, D. E. (2003). The effects of leadership impression management on group perceptions of cohesion, consensus, and communication. *Small Group Research, 34,* 197–222.

Rozin, P. (2001). Social psychology and science: Some lessons from Solomon Asch. *Personality and Social Psychology Review, 5,* 2–14.

Rozin, P., & Roysman, E. B. (2001). Negativity bias, negativity dominance, and contagion. *Personality and Social Psychology Review, 5,* 296–320.

Rubin, M., & Hewstone, M. (1998). Social identity theory's self-esteem hypothesis: A review and some suggestions for clarification. *Personality and Social Psychology Review, 2,* 40–62.

Rubin, Z., Peplau, L. A., & Hill, C. T. (1981). Loving and leaving: Sex differences in romantic attachments. *Sex Roles, 7,* 821–835.

Rucker, D. D., & Petty, R. E. (2004). When resistance is futile: Consequences of failed counterarguing for attitude certainty. *Journal of Personality and Social Psychology, 86,* 219–235.

Rudasill, K. M. (2011). Review of Self and social regulation: Social interaction and the development of social understanding and executive functions. *Developmental Neuropsychology, 36,* 403–404.

Ruder, M., & Bless, H. (2003). Mood and the reliance on the ease of retrieval heuristic. *Journal of Personality and Social Psychology, 85,* 20–32.

Rudman, L. A. (2005). Rejection of women? Beyond prejudice as antipathy. In J. F. Dovidio, P. Glick, & L. Rudman (Eds.), *On the nature of prejudice: Fifty years after Allport* (pp. 106–120). Malden, MA: Blackwell Publishing.

Rudman, L. A., & Glick, P. (2008). *The social psychology of gender: How power and intimacy shape gender relations.* New York: Guilford Press.

Rudman, L. A., & Goodwin, S. A. (2004). Gender differences in automatic ingroup bias: Why do women like women more than men like men? *Journal of Personality and Social Psychology, 87,* 494–509.

Rudman, L. A., Phelan, J. E., & Heppen, J. B. (2007). Developmental Sources of Implicit attitudes. *Personality and Social Psychology Bulletin, 33,* 1700–1713.

Rudmin, F. (1999). Gustav Ichheiser. In J. A. Garraty (Ed.), *American national biography.* New York: Oxford University Press.

Rusbult, C. E., Johnson, D. J., & Morrow, G. D. (1986a). Impact of couple patterns of problem solving on distress and nondistress in dating relationships. *Journal of Personality and Social Psychology, 50,* 744–753.

Rusbult, C. E., & Martz, J. M. (1995). Remaining in an abusive relationship: An investment model analysis of nonvoluntary dependence. *Personality and Social Psychology Bulletin, 21,* 558–571.

Rusbult, C. E., Morrow, G. D., & Johnson, D. J. (1987). Self-esteem and problem-solving behaviour in close relationships. *British Journal of Social Psychology, 26,* 293–303.

Rusbult, C. E., Olsen, N., Davis, J. L., & Hannon, P. A. (2001). Commitment and relationship maintenance mechanisms. In J. Harvey & A. Wenzel (Eds.), *Close romantic relationships: Maintenance and enhancement* (pp. 87–113). Mahwah, NJ: Erlbaum.

Rusbult, C. E., Van Lange, P. A. M., Wildschut, T., Yovetich, N. A., & Verette, J. (2000). Perceived superiority in close relationships: Why it exists and persists. *Journal of Personality and Social Psychology, 79,* 521–545.

Rusbult, C. E., Zembrodt, I., & Iwaniszek, J. (1986b). The impact of gender and sex-role orientation on responses to dissatisfaction in close relationships. *Sex Roles, 15,* 1–20.

Ruscher, J. B., Fiske, S. T., & Schnake, S. B. (2000). The motivated tactician's juggling act: Compatible vs. incompatible impression goals. *British Journal of Social Psychology, 39,* 241–256.

Rushton, J. P. (1975). Generosity in children: Immediate and long term effects of modeling, preaching, and moral judgment. *Journal of Personality and Social Psychology, 31,* 459–466.

Rushton, J. P. (1980). *Altruism, socialization, and society.* Englewood Cliffs, NJ: Prentice-Hall.

Rushton, J. P. (1989). Genetic similarity in male friendships. *Ethology and Sociobiology, 10,* 361–373.

Rushton, J. P., & Campbell, A. C. (1977). Modeling, vicarious reinforcement and extraversion on blood donating in adults: Immediate and long term effects. *European Journal of Social Psychology, 7,* 297–306.

Rushton, J. P., & Teachman, G. (1978). The effects of positive reinforcement, attributions, and punishment on model-induced altruism in children. *Personality and Social Psychology Bulletin, 4,* 322–325.

Russell, D., Peplau, L. A., & Cutrona, C. E. (1980). The revised UCLA Loneliness Scale: Concurrent and discriminant validity evidence. *Journal of Personality and Social Psychology, 39,* 472–480.

Russell, D. E. H. (1993). *Making violence sexy: Feminist views on pornography.* New York: Teachers College Press.

Russell, J. A., & Yik, S. M. (1996). Emotion among the Chinese. In M. H. Bond (Ed.), *The handbook of Chinese psychology.* Hong Kong, China: Oxford University Press.

Rutherford, A, Unger, R., & Cherry, F. (2011). Reclaiming SPSSI's sociological past: Marie Jahoda and the immersion tradition in social psychology. *Journal of Social Issues, 67,* 42–58.

Rutland, A., Cameron, L., Jugert, P., Nigbur, D., Brown, R., Watters, C., Hossain, R., Landau, A., & Le Touze, D. (2011). Group identity and peer relations: A longitudinal study of group identity, perceived peer acceptance, and friendships amongst ethnic minority English children. *British Journal of Developmental Psychology.*

Ryan, C. S. (2003). Stereotype accuracy. In W. Stroebe & M. Hewstone (Eds.), *European review of social psychology* (Vol. 13, pp. 75–109). Chichester, UK: John Wiley.

Ryan, C. S., Hunt, J. S., Weible, J. A., Peterson, C. R., & Casas, J. F. (2007). Multicultural and colorblind ideology, stereotypes, and ethnocentrism among Black and White Americans. *Group Processes and Intergroup Relations, 10,* 617–637.

Ryan, C. S., Robinson, D. R., & Hausmann, R. M. (2004). Group socialization, uncertainty reduction and the development of new members' perceptions of group variability. In V. Yzerbyt, C. M. Judd, & O'Corneille (Eds.), *The psychology of group perception: Contributions to the study of homogeneity, entitativity, and essentialism.* Philadelphia: Psychology Press.

Ryckman, R. M., Robbins, M. A., Thornton, B., Kaczor, L. M., Gayton, S. L., & Anderson, C. V. (1991). Public self-consciousness and physique stereotyping. *Personality and Social Psychology Bulletin, 17,* 400–405.

Rydell, R. J., & Boucher, K. L. (2010) Capitalizing on multiple social identities to prevent stereotype threat: The moderating role of self-esteem. *Personality and Social Psychology Bulletin, 36,* 239–250.

Saarni, C. (1999). *The development of emotional competence.* New York: Guilford.

Sabini, J., Garvey, B., & Hall, A. L. (2001). Shame and embarrassment revisited. *Personality and Social Psychology Bulletin, 27,* 104–117.

Sabini, J., & Green, M. C. (2004). Emotional responses to sexual and emotional infidelity. Constants and differences across genders, samples, and methods. *Personality and Social Psychology Bulletin, 30,* 1375–1388.

Sachdev, I., & Bourhis, R. Y. (1987). Status differentials and intergroup behaviour. *European Journal of Social Psychology, 17,* 277–293.

Sachdev, I., & Bourhis, R. Y. (1991). Power and status differentials in minority and majority group relations. *European Journal of Social Psychology, 21,* 1–24.

Sagarin, B. J. (2005). Reconsidering evolved sex differences in jealousy: Comment on Harris (2003). *Personality and Social Psychology Review, 9,* 62–75.

Sage, G. H., & Loudermilk, S. (1979). The female athlete and role conflict. *Research Quarterly, 50,* 88–96.

Sagiv, L., Sverdlik, N., & Schwarz, N. (2011). To compete or to cooperate? Values' impact on perception and action in social dilemma games. *European Journal of Social Psychology, 41,* 64–77.

Saguy, A. C., & Ward, A. (2011). Coming out as fat: Rethinking stigma, *Social Psychology Quarterly, 74,* 53–75.

Sakalli-Ugurlu, N. (2002). The relationship between sexism and attitudes toward homosexuality in a sample of Turkish college students. *Journal of Homosexuality, 42,* 53–64.

Sakalli-Ugurlu, N., & Glick, P. (2003). Ambivalent sexism and attitudes toward women who engage in premarital sex in Turkey. *Journal of Sex Research, 40,* 296–302.

Saks, M. J., & Marti, M. W. (1997). A meta-analysis of the effects of jury size. *Law and Human Behavior, 21,* 451–468.

Salovey, P., & Rodin, J. (1988). Coping with envy and jealousy. *Journal of Social and Clinical Psychology, 7,* 15–33.

Salovey, P., & Rodin, J. (1991). Provoking jealousy and envy: Domain relevance and self-esteem threat. *Journal of Social and Clinical Psychology, 10,* 395–413.

Salovey, P., Rothman, A. J., & Rodin, J. (1998). Health behavior. In D. T. Gilbert, S. T. Fiske, & G. Lindzey (Eds.), *The handbook of social psychology* (4th ed., Vol. 2, pp. 633–683). New York: McGraw-Hill.

Salvy, S. J., Bowker, J. C., Nitecki, L. A., Kluczynsi, M. A., Germeroth, L. J., & Roemmich, J. N. (2011). Impact of simulated ostracism on overweight and normal-weight youths' motivation to eat and food intake. *Appetite, 56,* 39–45.

Saltzman, S. (November 27, 2002). Ad majors raise alcohol awareness. *SMU Daily Campus.* http://www.smudailycampus.com

Sampson, E. E. (1988). The debate on individualism: Indigenous psychologies of the individual and their role in personal and societal functioning. *American Psychologist, 43,* 15–22.

Sanchez-Burks, J., Nisbett, R. E., & Ybarra, O. (2000). Cultural styles, relational schemas, and prejudice against outgroups. *Journal of Personality and Social Psychology, 79,* 174–189.

Sanday, P. (1981). The socio-cultural context of rape: A cross-cultural study. *Journal of Social Issues, 37,* 5–27.

Sanders, G. S., & Baron, R. S. (1975). The motivating effects of distraction on task performance. *Journal of Personality and Social Psychology, 32,* 956–963.

Sanders Thompson, V. L. (1991). Perceptions of race and race relations which affect African-American identification. *Journal of Applied Social Psychology, 21,* 1502–1516.

Sanderson, C. A., & Evans, S. M. (2001). Seeing one's partner through intimacy-colored glasses: An examination of the processes underlying the intimacy goals-relationship satisfaction link. *Personality and Social Psychology Bulletin, 27,* 463–473.

Sandys, M., & Dillehay, R. C. (1995). First-ballot votes, predeliberation dispositions, and final verdicts in jury trials. *Law and Human Behavior, 19,* 175–195.

Sani, F. (2005). When subgroups secede: Extending and refining the social psychological model of schism in groups. *Personality and Social Psychology Bulletin, 31,* 1074–1086.

Sani, F., & Reicher, S. (2000). Contested identities and schisms in groups: Opposing the ordination of women as priests in the Church of England. *British Journal of Social Psychology, 39,* 95–112.

Sani, F., & Todman, J. (2002). Should we stay or should we go? A social psychological model of schisms in groups. *Personality and Social Psychology Bulletin, 28,* 1647–1655.

Sani, F., Todman, J., & Lunn, J. (2005). The fundamentality of group principles and perceived group entitativity. *Journal of Experimental Social Psychology, 41,* 567–573.

San Martin, S., Camarero, C., & San Jose, R. (2011). Does involvement matter in online shopping satisfaction and trust? *Psychology & Marketing, 28,* 145–167.

Sanna, L. J., Chang, E. C., & Meier, S. (2001). Counterfactual thinking and self-motives. *Personality and Social Psychology Bulletin, 27,* 1023–1034.

Sanna, L. J., & Mark, M. M. (1995). Self-handicapping, expected evaluation, and performance: Accentuating the positive and attenuating the negative. *Organizational Behavior and Human Decision Processes, 64,* 84–102.

Sanna, L. J., & Turley, K. J. (1996). Antecedents to spontaneous counterfactual thinking: Effects of expectancy violation and outcome valence. *Personality and Social Psychology Bulletin, 22,* 906–919.

Sansone, C., Morf, C. C., & Panter, A. T. (2004). The research process: Of big pictures, little details, and the social psychological road in between. In C. Sansone, C. C. Morf, & A. T. Panter (Eds.), *Handbook of methods in social psychology* (pp. 3–16). Thousand Oaks, CA: Sage.

Sansone, R. A., & Sansone, L. A. (2010). Road rage: What's driving it? *Psychiatry, 7,* 14–18.

Santee, R. T., & Maslach, C. (1982). To agree or not to agree: Personal dissent amid social pressure to conform. *Journal of Personality and Social Psychology, 42,* 690–700.

Sargent, M. J., & Bradfield, A. L. (2004). Race and information processing in criminal trials: Does the defendant's race affect how the facts are evaluated? *Personality and Social Psychology Bulletin, 30,* 985–994.

Sarnoff, I., & Zimbardo, P. G. (1961). Anxiety, fear, and social affiliation. *Journal of Abnormal and Social Psychology, 62,* 356–363.

Saucier, D. A., Miller, C. T., & Doucet, N. (2005). Differences in helping Whites and Blacks: A meta-analysis. *Personality and Social Psychology Review, 9,* 2–16.

Savin, H. B. (1973). Professors and psychological researchers: Conflicting values in conflicting roles. *Cognition, 2,* 147–149.

Savitsky, K., Epley, N., & Gilovich, T. (2001). Do others judge us as harshly as we think? Overestimating the impact of our failures, shortcomings, and mishaps. *Journal of Personality and Social Psychology, 81,* 44–56.

Savitsky, K., & Gilovich, T. (2003). The illusion of transparency and the alleviation of speech anxiety. *Journal of Experimental Social Psychology, 39,* 618–625.

Savitsky, K., Van Boven, L., Epley, N., & Wight, W. M. (2005). The unpacking effect in allocations of responsibility for group tasks. *Journal of Experimental Social Psychology, 41,* 447–457.

Sbarra, D. A. (2006). Predicting the onset of emotional recovery following nonmarital relationship dissolution: Survival analyses of sadness and anger. *Personality and Social Psychology Bulletin, 32,* 298–312.

Sbarra, D. A., & Emery, R. E. (2005). The emotional sequelae of nonmarital relationship dissolution: Analysis of change and intraindividual variability over time. *Personal Relationships, 12,* 213–232.

Sbarra, D. A., & Ferrer, E. (2006). The structure and process of emotional experience following nonmarital relationship dissolution: Dynamic factor analyses of love, anger, and sadness. *Emotion, 6,* 224–238.

Scanzoni, J. (1979). Social exchange and behavioral interdependence. In R. L. Burgess & T. L. Huston (Eds.), *Social exchange in developing relationships.* New York: Academic Press.

Schachner, D. A., & Shaver, P. R. (2004). Attachment dimensions and sexual motives. *Personal Relationships, 11,* 179–195.

Schachter, S. (1951). Deviation, rejection and communication. *Journal of Abnormal and Social Psychology, 46,* 190–207.

Schachter, S. (1959). *The psychology of affiliation.*

Stanford, CA: Stanford University Press.

Schachter, S. (1964). The interaction of cognitive and physiological determinants of emotional state. In L. Berkowitz (Ed.), *Advances in experimental social psychology* (Vol. 1, pp. 49–80). New York: Academic Press.

Schack, C. M. (2010). Identity construction on Facebook—A qualitative study of young people's use of the social online network Facebook. *Psyke & Logos, 31,* 174–192.

Schacter, D. L., & Buckner, R. L. (1998). On the relations among priming, conscious recollection, and intentional retrieval: Evidence from neuroimaging research. *Neurobiology of Learning and Memory, 70,* 284–303.

Schaeffer, A. M., & Nelson, E. S. (1993). Rape-supportive attitudes: Effects of on-campus residence and education. *Journal of College Student Development, 34,* 175–179.

Schafer, M., & Crichlow, S. (1996). Antecedents of groupthink: A quantitative study. *Journal of Conflict Resolution, 40,* 415–435.

Schafer, M. H., & Ferraro, K. F. (2011). The stigma of obesity: Does perceived weight discrimination affect identity and physical health? *Social Psychology Quarterly, 74,* 76–97.

Schaller, M. (1997). Beyond "competing," beyond "compatible." *American Psychologist, 52,* 1379–1380.

Scharf, M., Mayseless, O., & Kivenson-Baron, I. (2004). Adolescents' attachment representations and developmental tasks in emerging adulthood. *Developmental Psychology, 40,* 430–444.

Schaufeli, W. B. (1988). Perceiving the causes of unemployment: An evaluation of the causal dimensions scale in a real-life situation. *Journal of Personality and Social Psychology, 54,* 347–356.

Scheier, M. F. (1980). Effects of public and private self-consciousness on the public expression of personal beliefs. *Journal of Personality and Social Psychology, 39,* 514–521.

Scheier, M. F., & Carver, C. S. (1977). Self-focused attention and the experience of emotion: Attraction, repulsion, elation, and depression. *Journal of Personality and Social Psychology, 35,* 625–636.

Scheier, M. F., & Carver, C. S. (1980). Private and public self-attention, resistance to change, and dissonance reduction. *Journal of Personality and Social Psychology, 39,* 390–405.

Scher, S. J., & Rauscher, F. (Eds.). (2003). *Evolutionary psychology: Alternative approaches.* New York: Kluwer Press.

Schimmack, U., Oishi, S., Furr, R. M., & Funder, D. C. (2004). Personality and life satisfaction: A facet-level analysis. *Personality and Social Psychology Bulletin, 30,* 1062–1075.

Schindler, I., Fagundes, C. P., & Murdock, K. W. (2010). Predictors of romantic relationship formation: Attachment style, prior relationships, and dating goals. *Personal Relationships, 17,* 97–105.

Schino, G., di Sorrentino, E. P., & Tiddi, B. (2007). Grooming and coalitions in Japanese macaques (Macaca fuscata): Partner choice and the time frame reciprocation. *Journal of Comparative Psychology, 121,* 181–188.

Schlegel, R. J., Hicks, J. A., King, L. A., & Arndt, J. (2011). Feeling like you know who you are: Perceived true self-knowledge and meaning in life. *Personality and Social Psychology Bulletin, 37,* 745–756.

Schlenker, B. R. (1980). *Impression management: The self-concept, social identity, and interpersonal relations.* Monterey, CA: Brooks/Cole.

Schlenker, B. R., & Wowra, S. A. (2003). Carryover effects of feeling socially transparent or impenetrable on strategic self-presentation. *Journal of Personality and Social Psychology, 85,* 871–880.

Schliemann, A. D., Carraher, D. W., & Ceci, S. (1997). Everyday cognition. In J. W. Berry, P. R. Dasen, & T. S. Saraswathi (Eds.), *Handbook of cross-cultural psychology: Vol. 2. Basic processes and human development* (pp. 177–216). Boston: Allyn & Bacon.

Schmader, T., & Major, B. (1999). The impact of ingroup vs. outgroup performance on personal values. *Journal of Experimental Social Psychology, 35,* 47–67.

Schmeichel, B. J., Demaree, H. A., Robinson, J. L., & Pu, J. (2006). Ego depletion by response exaggeration. *Journal of Experimental Social Psychology, 42,* 95–102.

Schmeichel, B. J., Vohs, K. D., & Baumeister, R. F. (2003). Intellectual performance and ego depletion: Role of the self in logical reasoning and other information processing. *Journal of Personality and Social Psychology, 85,* 33–46.

Schmid Mast, M. S., & Hall, J. A. (2006). Women's advantage at remembering others' appearance: A systematic look at the why and when of a gender difference. *Personality and Social Psychology Bulletin, 32,* 353–364.

Schmid Mast, M. S., & Hall, J. A. (2004). When is dominance related to smiling? Assigned dominance, dominance preference, trait dominance, and gender as moderators. *Sex Roles, 50,* 387–399.

Schmidt, G., & Weiner, B. (1988). An attributional-affect-action theory of behavior: Replications of judgments of helping. *Personality and Social Psychology Bulletin, 14,* 610–621.

Schmitt, D. P., & Allik, J. (2005). Simultaneous administration of the Rosenberg Self-Esteem Scale in 53 nations: Exploring the universal and culture-specific features of global self-esteem. *Journal of Personality and Social Psychology, 89,* 623–642.

Schmitt, M. T., Branscombe, N. R., & Kapen, D. M. (2003). Attitudes toward group-based inequality: Social dominance or social identity? *British Journal of Social Psychology, 42,* 161–186.

Schnall, S., Abrahamson, A., & Laird, J. D. (2002). Premenstrual syndrome and misattribution: A self-perception, individual differences perspective. *Basic and Applied Social Psychology, 24,* 215–228.

Schneider, C. S., & Kenny, D. A. (2000). Cross-sex friends who were once romantic partners: Are they platonic friends now? *Journal of Social and Personal Relationships, 17,* 451–466.

Schneider, D. J. (2004). *The psychology of stereotyping.* New York: Guilford Press.

Schoenmakers, T., Wiers, R. W., Jones, B. T., Bruce, G., & Jansen, A. T. M. (2007). Attentional re-training decreases attentional bias in heavy drinkers without generalization. *Addiction, 102,* 399–405.

Schoneman, P. H., Byrne, D., & Bell, P. A. (1977). Statistical aspects of a model for interpersonal attraction. *Bulletin of the Psychonomic Society, 9,* 243–246.

Schreurs, K. M. G., & Buunk, B. P. (1994). Intimacy, autonomy, and relationship satisfaction in Dutch lesbian couples and heterosexual couples. *Journal of Psychology and Human Sexuality, 7,* 41–57.

Schriesheim, C. A., Tepper, B. J., & Tetrault, L. A. (1994). Least preferred coworker score, situational control, and leadership effectiveness: A meta-analysis of contingency model performance predictions. *Journal of Applied Psychology, 79,* 561–573.

Schubert, T. W., & Häfner, M. (2003). Contrast from social stereotypes in automatic behavior. *Journal of Experimental Social Psychology, 39,* 577–584.

Schuetz, A. (1998). Self-esteem and interpersonal strategies. In J. P. Forgas, K. D. Williams, & L. Wheeler (Eds.), *The social mind: Cognitive and motivational aspects of interpersonal behavior.* New York: Cambridge University Press.

Schulman, S., Elicker, J., & Sroufe, A. (1994). Stages of friendship growth in preadolescents as related to attachment history. *Journal of Social and Personal Relationships, 11,* 341–361.

Schuman, H. (1995). Attitudes, beliefs, and behavior.

In K. S. Cook, G. A. Fine, & J. S. House (Eds.), *Sociological perspectives on social psychology* (pp. 68–89). Boston: Allyn & Bacon.

Schuman, H. (2002). Sense and nonsense about surveys. *Contexts, 1,* 40–47.

Schuman, H., & Scott, J. (1987). Problems in the use of survey questions to measure public opinion. *Science, 236,* 957–959.

Schuman, H., & Scott, J. (1989). Generations and collective memories. *American Sociological Review, 54,* 359–381.

Schumann, D. W., Petty, R. E., & Clemons, D. S. (1990). Predicting the effectiveness of different strategies of advertising variation: A test of the repetition-variation hypotheses. *Journal of Consumer Research, 17,* 192–202.

Schuster, B., Forsterling, F., & Weiner, B. (1989). Perceiving the causes of success and failure: A cross-cultural examination of attributional concepts. *Journal of Cross-Cultural Psychology, 20,* 191–213.

Scott, V. M., Mottarella, K. E., & Lavooy, M. J. (2006). Does virtual intimacy exist? A brief exploration into reported levels of intimacy in online relationships. *CyberPsychology & Behavior, 9,* 759–761.

Schwartz, M. B., Vartanian, L. R., Nosek, B. A., & Brownell, K. D. (2006). The influence of one's own body weight on implicit and explicit anti-fat bias. *Obesity, 14,* 440–447.

Schwartz, S. H. (1994). Are there universal aspects in the content and structure of values? *Journal of Social Issues, 50,* 19–45.

Schwartz, S. H. (1997). Values and culture. In D. Munro, S. Carr, & J. Schumaker (Eds.), *Motivation and culture* (pp. 69–84). New York: Routledge.

Schwartz, S. H. (2003). Mapping and interpreting cultural differences around the world. In H. Vinken, J. Soeters, & P. Ester (Eds.), *Comparing cultures: Dimensions of culture in a comparative perspective.* Leiden, The Netherlands: Brill.

Schwartz, S. H., & Bardi, A. (2001). Value hierarchies across cultures: Taking a similarities perspective. *Journal of Cross-Cultural Psychology, 32,* 268–290.

Schwartz, S. H., & Boehnke, K. (2002). *Evaluating the structure of human values with confirmatory factor analysis.* Manuscript submitted for publication.

Schwartz, S. H., & Sagiv, L. (1995). Identifying culture specifics in the content and structure of values. *Journal of Cross-Cultural Psychology, 26,* 92–116.

Schwarz, N. (1990). Feelings as information: Informational and motivational functions of affective states. In E. T. Higgins & R. M. Sorrentino (Eds.), *Handbook of motivation and cognition: Foundations of social behavior* (Vol. 2, pp. 527–561). New York: Guilford.

Schwarz, N. (1998). Warmer and more social: Recent developments in cognitive social psychology. *Annual Review of Sociology, 24,* 239–264.

Schwarz, N. (2003). Self-reports in consumer research: The challenge of comparing cohorts and cultures. *Journal of Consumer Research, 29,* 588–594.

Schwarz, N., Bless, H., Strack, F., Klumpp, G., Rittenauer-Schatka, & Simons, A. (1991). Ease of retrieval as information: Another look at the availability heuristic. *Journal of Personality and Social Psychology, 61,* 195–202.

Schwarz, N., & Vaughn, L. A. (2002). The availability heuristic revisited: Ease of recall and content of recall as distinct sources of information. In T. Gilovich, D. Griffin, & D. Kahneman (Eds.), *Heuristics and biases: The psychology of intuitive judgment* (pp. 103–119). New York: Cambridge University Press.

Schwarzwald, J., Bizman, A., & Raz, M. (1983). The foot-in-the-door paradigm: Effects of second request size on donation probability and donor generosity. *Personality and Social Psychology Bulletin, 9,* 443–450.

Schwarzwald, J., Koslowsky, M., & Ochana-Levin, T. (2004). Usage of and compliance with power tactics in routine versus nonroutine work settings. *Journal of Business and Psychology, 18,* 385–395.

Scully, D. (1985). *The role of violent pornography in justifying rape.* Paper prepared for the Attorney General's Commission on Pornography Hearings, Houston, TX.

Searcy, E., & Eisenberg, N. (1992). Defensiveness in response to aid from a sibling. *Journal of Personality and Social Psychology, 62,* 422–433.

Searle, J. R. (1995). Ontology is the question. In P. Baumgartner & S. Payr (Eds.), *Speaking minds: Interviews with twenty eminent cognitive scientists* (p. 202–213). Princeton, NJ: Princeton University Press.

Sears, D. O., & Funk, C. L. (1991). The role of self-interest in social and political attitudes. In M. Zanna (Ed.), *Advances in experimental social psychology* (pp. 2–91). San Diego: Academic Press.

Sears, D. O., & Henry, P. J. (2003). The origins of symbolic racism. *Journal of Personality and Social Psychology, 85,* 259–275.

Sechrist, G. B., Swim, J. K., & Stangor, C. (2004). When do the stigmatized make attributions to discrimination occurring to the self and others? The roles of self-presentation and need for control. *Journal of Personality and Social Psychology, 87,* 111–122.

Sedikides, C., Campbell, W. K., Reeder, G. D., & Elliot, A. J. (1998). The self-serving bias in relational context. *Journal of Personality and Social Psychology, 74,* 378–386.

Sedikides, C., & Skowronski, J. J. (1997). The symbolic self in evolutionary context. *Personality and Social Psychology Review, 1,* 80–102.

Sedikides, C., & Strube, M. J. (1997). Self-evaluation: To thine own self be good, to thine own self be sure, to thine own self be true, and to thine own self be better. In M. P. Zanna (Ed.), *Advances in experimental social psychology* (Vol. 29, pp. 209–269). San Diego: Academic Press.

Seeman, M. (1997). The elusive situation in social psychology. *Social Psychology Quarterly, 60,* 4–13.

Segal, M. W. (1974). Alphabet and attraction: An unobtrusive measure of the effect of propinquity in a field setting. *Journal of Personality and Social Psychology, 30,* 654–657.

Segerstrom, S. C., & Nes, L. S. (2007). Heart rate variability reflects self-regulatory strength, effort, and fatigue. *Psychological Science, 18,* 275–281.

Segerstrom, S. C., Taylor, S. E., Kemeny, M. E., & Fahey, J. L. (1998). Optimism is associated with mood, coping, and immune change in response to stress. *Journal of Personality and Social Psychology, 74,* 1646–1655.

Segura, S., & McCloy, R. (2003). Counterfactual thinking in everyday life situations: Temporal order effects and social norms. *Psicológica, 24,* 1–15.

Seiter, John S. (2007). Ingratiation and gratuity: The effect of complimenting customers on tipping behavior in restaurants. *Journal of Applied Social Psychology, 37,* 478–485.

Selfhout, M., Denissen, J., Branje, S., & Meeus, W. (2009). In the eye of the beholder: Perceived, actual, and peer-related similarity in personality, communication, and friendship intensity during the acquaintanceship process. *Journal of Personality and Social Psychology, 96,* 1152–1165.

Seligman, M. E. P. (1991). *Learned optimism.* New York: Alfred A. Knopf.

Seligman, M. E. P. (2011). Flourish: A visionary new understanding of happiness and well-being. *Flourish: A visionary new understanding of happiness and well-being.* xii, New York: Free Press.

Seligman, M. E. P., & Maier, S. F. (1967). Failure to escape traumatic shock. *Journal of Experimental Psychology, 74,* 1–9.

Sellers, R. M., & Shelton, J. N. (2003). The role of racial identity in perceived racial discrimination. *Journal of Personality and Social Psychology, 84,* 1079–1092.

Sengrupta, J., & Johar, G. V. (2001). Contingent effects of anxiety on message elaboration and persuasion. *Personality and Social Psychology Bulletin, 27,* 139–150.

Senior, C., Ward, J., & David, A. S. (2002). Representational momentum and the brain: An investigation into the functional necessity of V5/MT. *Visual Cognition, 9,* 81–92.

Seta, C. E., & Garren, W. C., Jr. (2011). Judging the severity of sexually harassing events. *Basic and Applied Social Psychology, 33,* 81–87.

Seta, J. J., Donaldson, S., & Seta, C. E. (1999). Self-relevance as a moderator of self-enhancement and self-verification. *Journal of Research in Personality, 33,* 442–462.

Seyle, D. C., & Newman, M. L. (2006). A house divided? The psychology of red and blue America. *American Psychologist, 61,* 571–580.

Shaffer, L. S. (2005). From mirror self-recognition to the looking-glass self: Exploring the justification hypothesis. *Journal of Clinical Psychology, 61,* 47–65.

Shana, L., & van Laar, C. (Eds.). (2006). *Stigma and group inequality: Social psychological perspectives.* Mahwah, NJ: Lawrence Erlbaum.

Shanab, M. E., & Yahya, K. A. (1977). A behavioral study of obedience in children. *Journal of Personality and Social Psychology, 35,* 530–536.

Shapiro, J. R. (2011). Different groups, different threats: A multi-threat approach to the experience of stereotype threats. *Personality and Social Psychology Bulletin, 37,* 464–480.

Shapiro, J. R., & Neuberg, S. L. (2007). From stereotype threat to stereotype threats: Implications of a multi-threat framework for causes, moderators, mediators, consequences, and interventions. *Personality and Social Psychology Review, 11,* 107–130.

Share, T. L., & Mintz, L. B. (2002). Differences between lesbians and heterosexual women in disordered eating and related attitudes. *Journal of Homosexuality, 42,* 89–106.

Shaver, P., & Klinnert, M. (1982). Schachter's theories of affiliation and emotion: Implications of developmental research. In L. Wheeler (Ed.), *Review of personality and social psychology* (Vol. 3). Beverly Hills, CA: Sage.

Shaver, P. R., Wu, S., & Schwartz, J. C. (1991). Cross-cultural similarities and differences in emotion and its representation: A prototype approach. In M. S. Clark (Ed.), *Review of personality and social psychology* (Vol. 13, pp. 175–212). Beverly Hills, CA: Sage.

Shavitt, S., Swan, S., Lowery, T. M., & Wänke, M. (1994). The interaction of endorser attractiveness and involvement in persuasion depends on the goal that guides message processing. *Journal of Consumer Psychology, 3,* 137–162.

Shaw, J. (2003). Automatic for the people: How representations of significant others implicitly affect goal pursuit. *Journal of Personality and Social Psychology, 84,* 661–681.

Shaw, L. L., Batson, C. D., & Todd, R. M. (1994). Empathy avoidance: Forestalling feeling for another in order to escape the motivational consequences. *Journal of Personality and Social Psychology, 67,* 879–887.

Sheeran, P. (2002). Intention-behavior relations: A conceptual and empirical review. In M. Hewstone & W. Stroebe (Eds.), *European review of social psychology* (Vol. 12, pp. 1–36). Chichester, England: Wiley.

Sheeran, P., Orbell, S., & Trafimow, D. (1999). Does the temporal stability of behavioral intentions moderate intention-behavior and past behavior-future behavior relations? *Personality and Social Psychology Bulletin, 25,* 721–730.

Sheldon, K. M. (1999). Learning the lessons of tit-for-tat: Even competitors can get the message. *Journal of Personality and Social Psychology, 77,* 1245–1253.

Sheldon, K. M., & Ryan, R. M. (2011). Positive psychology and self-determination theory: A natural interface. In V. I. Chirkov, R. M. Ryan, & K. M. Sheldon (Ed). *Human autonomy in cross-cultural context: Perspectives on the psychology of agency, freedom, and well-being* (pp. 33–44). New York: Springer.

Shelton, J. N. (2000). A reconceptualization of how we study issues of racial prejudice. *Personality and Social Psychology Review, 4,* 374–390.

Shelton, J. N., & Richeson, J. A. (2005). Intergroup contact and pluralistic ignorance. *Journal of Personality and Social Psychology, 23,* 91–107.

Shelton, J. N., Richeson, J. A., & Salvatore, J. (2005). Expecting to be the target of prejudice: Implications for interethnic interactions. *Personality and Social Psychology Bulletin, 31,* 1189–1202.

Sheppard, J. A., Ouellette, J. A., & Fernandez, J. K. (1996). Abandoning unrealistic optimism: Performance estimates and the temporal proximity of self-relevant feedback. *Journal of Personality and Social Psychology, 70,* 844–855.

Sherif, M. (1935). A study of some social factors in perception. *Archives of Psychology, 27* (187), 1–60.

Sherif, M. (1936). *The psychology of social norms.* New York: Harper.

Sherif, M. (1966). *In common predicament: Social psychology of intergroup conflict and cooperation.* Boston: Houghton Mifflin.

Sherif, M., & Cantril, H. (1947). *The psychology of ego-involvements: Social attitudes and identifications.* New York: Wiley.

Sherif, M., Harvey, O. J., White, B. J., Hood, W. R., & Sherif, C. (1961). *Intergroup conflict and cooperation: The Robbers' Cave experiment.* Norman, OK: Oklahoma Book Exchange.

Sherif, M., & Sherif, C. W. (1956). *An outline of social psychology.* New York: Harper & Brothers.

Sherman, J. W., & Klein, S. B. (1994). Development and representation of personality impressions. *Journal of Personality and Social Psychology, 67,* 972–983.

Sherman, P. W. (1985). Alarm calls of Belding's ground squirrels to aerial predators: Nepotism or self-preservation? *Behavioral Ecology and Sociobiology, 17,* 313–323.

Sherman, R. C., Buddie, A. M., Dragan, K. L., End, C. M., & Finney, L. J. (1999). Twenty years of *PSPB:* Trends in content, design, and analysis. *Personality and Social Psychology Bulletin, 25,* 177–187.

Sherman, S. (2011). Changing the world: The science of transformative action. In R. Biswas-Diener (Ed). *Positive psychology as social change* (pp. 329–345). New York: Springer.

Sherman, S. J., Castelli, L., & Hamilton, D. L. (2002). The spontaneous use of a group typology as an organizing principle in memory. *Journal of Personality and Social Psychology, 82,* 328–342.

Sherman, S. J., & Johnson, A. L. (2003). Perceiving groups: How, what, and why? In G. A. Bodenhausen & A. J. Lambert (Eds.), *Foundations of social cognition: A festschrift in honor of Robert S. Wyer, Jr.* (pp. 155–180). Washington, DC: American Psychological Association.

Sherman, S. J., Mackie, D. M., & Driscoll, D. M. (1990). Priming and the differential use of dimensions in evaluation. *Personality and Social Psychology Bulletin, 16,* 405–418.

Shestowsky, D., Wegener, D. T., & Fabrigar, L. R. (1998). Need for cognition and interpersonal influence: Individual differences in impact on dyadic decisions. *Journal of Personality and Social Psychology, 74,* 1317–1328.

Shields, C. A., Brawley, L. R., & Ginis, K. A. M. (2007). Interactive effects of exercise status and observer gender on the impressions formed of men. *Sex Roles, 56,* 231–237.

Shields, S. A. (2002). *Speaking from the heart: Gender and the social meaning of emotion.* Cambridge: Cambridge University Press.

Shields, S. A. (2007). Passionate men, emotional women: Psychology constructs gender difference in the late 19th century. *History of Psychology, 10,* 92–110.

Shinha, J. B. P. (2003). Trends toward indigenization of psychology in India. In K. S. Yang, K. K. Hwang, P. B. Pedersen, & I. Daibo (Eds.), *Progress in Asian social psychology: Conceptual and empirical contributions* (pp. 11–27). Westport, CT: Praeger.

Shoda, Y., Mischel, W., & Peake, P. K. (1990). Predicting adolescent cognitive and self-regulatory competencies from preschool delay of gratification: Identifying diagnostic conditions. *Developmental Psychology, 26,* 978–986.

Shotland, R. L., & Hunter, B. A. (1995). Women's "token resistant" and compliant sexual behaviors are related to uncertain sexual intentions and rape. *Personality and Social Psychology Bulletin, 21,* 226–236.

Shotland, R. L., & Straw, M. K. (1976). Bystander response to an assault: When a man attacks a woman. *Journal of Personality and Social Psychology, 34,* 990–999.

Shoyama, S., Tochihara, Y., & Kim, J. (2003). Japanese and Korean ideas about clothing colors for elderly people: Intercountry and intergenerational differences. *Color Research and Application, 28,* 139–150.

Shrauger, J. S. (1975). Responses to evaluation as a function of initial self-perceptions. *Psychological Bulletin, 82,* 581–596.

Shu, L. L., Gino, F., & Bazerman, M. H. (2011). Dishonest deed, clear conscience: When cheating leads to moral disengagement and motivated forgetting. *Personality and Social Psychology Bulletin, 37,* 330–349.

Shumaker, S. A., & Hill, D. R. (1991). Gender differences in social support and physical health. *Health Psychology, 10,* 102–111.

Sibicky, M. E., Schroeder, D. A., & Dovidio, J. F. (1995). Empathy and helping: Considering the consequences of intervention. *Basic and Applied Social Psychology, 16,* 435–453.

Sibley, C. G., Wilson, M. S., & Duckitt, J. (2007). Antecedents of men's hostile and benevolent sexism: The dual roles of social dominance orientation and right-wing authoritarianism. *Personality and Social Psychology Bulletin, 33,* 160–172.

Sidanius, J., Pratto, F., & Brief, D. (1995). Group dominance and the political psychology of gender: A cross-cultural comparison. *Political Psychology, 16,* 381–396.

Sieck, W. R., Smith, J. L., Grome, A., & Rababy, D. A. (2011). Expert cultural sensemaking in the management of Middle Eastern crowds. In K. L. Mosier & U. M. Fischer (Eds.). *Informed by knowledge: Expert performance in complex situations* (pp. 105–121). New York: Psychology Press; US.

Sigelman, C. K., Berry, C. J., & Wiles, K. A. (1984). Violence in college students' dating relationships. *Journal of Applied Social Psychology, 5,* 530–548.

Sigurdsson, J. F., & Gudjonsson, G. H. (1996). Psychological characteristics of "false confessors": A study among Icelandic prison inmates and juvenile offenders. *Personality and Individual Differences, 20,* 321–329.

Silvia, P. J., & Duval, T. S. (2001a). Objective self-awareness theory: Recent progress and enduring problems. *Personality and Social Psychology Review, 5,* 230–241.

Silvia, P. J., & Duval, T. S. (2001b). Predicting the interpersonal targets of self-serving attributions. *Journal of Experimental Social Psychology, 37,* 333–340.

Silvia, P. J., & O'Brien, M. E. (2004). Self-awareness and constructive functioning: Revisiting "The

Human Dilemma". *Journal of Social and Clinical Psychology, 23,* 475–489.

Simon, B., Pantaleo, G., & Mummendey, A. (1995). Unique individual or interchangeable group member? The accentuation of intragroup differences versus similarities as an indicator of the individual self versus the collective self. *Journal of Personality and Social Psychology, 69,* 106–119.

Simon, B., Stürmer, S., & Steffens, K. (2000). Helping individuals or group members? The role of individual and collective identification in AIDS volunteerism. *Personality and Social Psychology Bulletin, 26,* 497–506.

Simon, H. (1990). A mechanism for social selection and successful altruism. *Science, 250,* 1665–1668.

Simons, H. W. (1971). Persuasion and attitude change. In L. L. Barker & R. J. Kibler (Eds.), *Speech communication behavior: Perspectives and principles* (pp. 227–248). Englewood Cliffs, NJ: Prentice-Hall.

Simons, H. W., Berkowitz, N. N., & Moyer, R. J. (1970). Similarity, credibility, and attitude change: A review and a theory. *Psychological Bulletin, 73,* 1–16.

Simonsohn, U. (2011). Spurious? Name similarity effects (implicit egotism) in marriage, job, and moving decisions. *Journal of Personality and Social Psychology.*

Simonsohn, U. (in press). Spurious also? Name-similarity-effects (implicit egotism) in employment decisions. *Psychological Science.*

Simonton, D. K. (1994). *Greatness: Who makes history and why.* New York: Guilford.

Simonton, D. K. (1998). Historiometric methods in social psychology. *European Review of Social Psychology, 9,* 267–293.

Simpson, B. (2006). Social identity and cooperation in social dilemmas. *Rationality and Society, 18,* 443–470.

Simpson, J. A., & Gangestad, S. W. (2001). Evolution and relationships: A call for integration. *Personal Relationships, 8,* 341–355.

Simpson, J. A., Rholes, W. S., Campbell, L., & Wilson, C. L. (2003). Changes in attachment orientations across the transition to parenthood. *Journal of Experimental Social Psychology, 39,* 317–331.

Singelis, T. M., Triandis, H. C., Bhawuk, D. S., & Gelfand, M. (1995). Horizontal and vertical dimensions of individualism and collectivism: A theoretical and measurement refinement. *Cross-Cultural Research, 29,* 240–275.

Singh, D. (1993). Adaptive significance of female physical attractiveness: Role of waist-to-hip ratio. *Journal of Personality and Social Psychology, 65,* 293–307.

Singh, R., & Teoh, J. B. P. (2000). Impression formation from intellectual and social traits: Evidence for behavioral adaptation and cognitive processing. *British Journal of Social Psychology, 39,* 537–554.

Singh, V., & Vinnicombe, S. (2006). Opening the boardroom doors to women directors. In D. McTavish & K. Miller (Eds.), *Women in leadership and management* (pp. 127–147). Northampton, MA: Edward Elgar Publishing.

Sivacek, J., & Crano, W. D. (1982). Vested interest as a moderator of attitude-behavior consistency. *Journal of Personality and Social Psychology, 43,* 210–221.

Skinner, B. F. (1938). *The behavior of organisms.* New York: Appleton-Century-Crofts.

Skitka, L. J. (1999). Ideological and attributional boundaries on public compassion: Reactions to individuals and communities affected by a natural disaster. *Personality and Social Psychology Bulletin, 25,* 793–808.

Skitka, L. J. (2006). Patriotism or nationalism? Understanding post-September 11, 2001 flag display behavior. *Journal of Applied Social Psychology.*

Slecbos, E., Ellemers, N., & de Gilder, D. (2006). The carrot and the stick: Affective commitment and acceptance anxiety for discretionary group efforts by respected and disrespected group members. *Personality and Social Psychology Bulletin, 32,* 244–255.

Sloman, S. A. (2002). Two systems of reasoning. In T. Gilovich, D. Griffin, & D. Kahneman (Eds.), *Heuristics and biases: The psychology of intuitive judgment* (pp. 379–396). Cambridge, England: Cambridge University Press.

Slotter, E. B., & Gardner, W. L. (2009). Where do you end and I begin? Evidence for anticipatory, motivated self-other integration between relationship partners. *Journal of Personality and Social Psychology, 96,* 1137–1151.

Slotter, E. B., Gardner, W. L., & Finkel, E. J. (2010). Who am I without you? The influence of romantic breakup on the self-concept. *Personality and Social Psychology Bulletin, 36,* 147–160.

Slovic, P. (2007). "If I look at the mass I will never act": Psychic numbing and genocide. *Judgment and Decision Making, 2,* 79–95.

Smith, A., & Berard, S. P. (1982). Why are human subjects less concerned about ethically problematic research than human subjects committees? *Journal of Applied Social Psychology, 12,* 209–221.

Smith, A. E., Jussim, L., & Eccles, J. (1999). Do self-fulfilling prophecies accumulate, dissipate, or remain stable over time? *Journal of Personality and Social Psychology, 77,* 548–565.

Smith, A. M. (2007). Same-sex marriages: Legal issues. In A. E. Bennett (Ed.), *Family structure and support issue (p*p. 111–134). Hauppauge, NY: Nova Science.

Smith, D. (August 1976). *Sexual aggression in American pornography: The stereotype of rape.* Paper presented at the American Sociological Association meetings, New York.

Smith, E. R., Coats, S., & Walling, D. (1999). Overlapping mental representations of self, ingroup, and partner: Further response time evidence for a connectionist model. *Personality and Social Psychology Bulletin, 25,* 873–882.

Smith, E. R., & Henry, S. (1996). An ingroup becomes part of the self: Response time evidence. *Personality and Social Psychology Bulletin, 22,* 635–642.

Smith, G. F., & Dorfman, D. D. (1975). The effect of stimulus uncertainty on the relationship between frequency of exposure and liking. *Journal of Personality and Social Psychology, 31,* 150–155.

Smith, G. L., & DeWine, S. (1991). Perceptions of subordinates and requests for support: Are males and females perceived differently when seeking help? *Organizational Studies, 16,* 408–427.

Smith, G. T., Hohlstein, L. A., & Atlas, J. G. (1989, August). *Race differences in eating disordered behavior and eating-related experiences.* Paper presented at the 97th annual convention of the American Psychological Association, New Orleans, LA.

Smith, J. M., & Szathmáry, E. (1995). *The major transitions in evolution.* Oxford, England: W. H. Freeman.

Smith, M. B. (2002). Self and identity in historical/sociocultural context: "Perspectives on selfhood" revisited. Y. Kashima, M. Foddy, & M. Platow (Eds.), *Self and identity: Personal, social and symbolic* (pp. 229–243). Mahwah, NJ: Erlbaum.

Smith, P. B., Peterson, M. F., Bond, M., & Misumi, J. (1990). Leadership style and leader behaviour in individualistic and collectivist cultures. In S. Iwawaki, Y. Kashima, & K. Leung (Eds.), *Innovations in cross-cultural psychology* (pp. 76–85). Amsterdam: Swets & Zeitlinger.

Smith, N. K., Cacioppo, J. T., Larsen, J. T., & Chartrand, T. L. (2003). May I have your attention please: Electrocortical responses to positive and negative stimuli.

Neuropsychologia, 41, 171–183.

Smith, P. K., & Trope, Y. (2006). You focus on the forest when you're in charge of the trees: Power priming and abstract information processing. *Journal of Personality and Social Psychology, 90,* 578–596.

Smith, R. J. (July 23, 2004). Operational relationship with Al Qaeda discounted. *Washington Post* (p. A01).

Smith, S. M., Haugtvedt, C. P., & Petty, R. E. (1994). Humor can either enhance or disrupt message processing: The moderating role of humor relevance. Unpublished manuscript.

Smith, S. M., McIntosh, W. D., & Bazzani, D. G. (1999). Are the beautiful good in Hollywood? An investigation of the beauty-and-goodness stereotype on film. *Basic and Applied Social Psychology, 21,* 69–80.

Smith, S. M., & Shaffer, D. R. (1991). Celerity and cajolery: Rapid speech may promote or inhibit persuasion through its impact on message elaboration. *Personality and Social Psychology Bulletin, 17,* 663–669.

Smith, S. M., & Shaffer, D. R. (2000). Vividness can undermine or enhance message processing: The moderating role of vividness congruency. *Personality and Social Psychology Bulletin, 26,* 769–779.

Smith, S. S., & Moore, M. R. (2000). Intraracial diversity and relations among African Americans: Closeness among Black students at a dominantly White university. *American Journal of Sociology, 106,* 1–39.

Smith-Lovin, L., & Winkielman, P. (2010). The social psychologies of emotion: A bridge that is not too far. *Social Psychology Quarterly, 73,* 327–332.

Snodgrass, J. G., & Thompson, R. L. (1997). *The self across psychology: Self-recognition, self-awareness, and the self-concept.* New York: New York Academy of Sciences.

Snyder, M. (1974). The self-monitoring of expressive behavior. *Journal of Personality and Social Psychology, 30,* 526–537.

Snyder, M. (1987). *Public appearances/private realities: The psychology of self-monitoring.* New York: Freeman.

Snyder, C. R. (2000). The past and possible futures of hope. *Journal of Social and Clinical Psychology, 19,* 11–28.

Snyder, M., & Cunningham, M. R. (1975). To comply or not to comply: Testing the self-perception explanation of the foot-in-the-door phenomenon. *Journal of Personality and Social Psychology, 31,* 64–67.

Snyder, M., & DeBono, K. G. (1985). Appeals to image and claims about quality: Understanding the psychology of advertising. *Journal of Personality and Social Psychology, 49,* 586–597.

Snyder, M., & Simpson, J. A. (1984). Self-monitoring and dating relationships. *Journal of Personality and Social Psychology, 47,* 1281–1291.

Snyder, M., & Swann, W. B. (1978). Hypothesis-testing processes in social interaction. *Journal of Personality and Social Psychology, 36,* 1202–1212.

Snyder, M., Tanke, E. D., & Berscheid, E. (1977). Social perception and interpersonal behavior: On the self-fulfilling nature of social stereotypes. *Journal of Personality and Social Psychology, 35,* 656–666.

Sohlberg, S., & Birgegard, A. (2003). Persistent complex subliminal activation effects: First experimental observations. *Journal of Personality and Social Psychology, 85,* 302–316.

Solano, C. H., & Koester, N. H. (1989). Loneliness and communication problems: Subjective anxiety or objective skills? *Personality and Social Psychology Bulletin, 15,* 126–133.

Sommers, S. R. (2006). On racial diversity and group decision making: Identifying multiple effects of racial composition on jury deliberations. *Journal of Personality and Social Psychology, 85,* 597–612.

Son Hing, L. S., Li, W., & Zanna, M. P. (2002). Inducing hypocrisy to reduce prejudicial responses

among aversive racists. *Journal of Experimental Social Psychology, 38,* 71–78.

Sorrentino, R. M. (2003). Motivated perception and the warm look: Current perspectives and future directions. In S. J. Spencer, S. Fein, M. P. Zanna, & J. M. Olson (Eds.), *Motivated social perception: The Ontario symposium,* Vol. 9, pp. 299–316. Mahwah, NJ: Erlbaum.

Sorrentino, R. M., & Higgins, E. T. (1986). Motivation and cognition: Warming to synergism. In R. M. Sorrentino & E. T. Higgins (Eds.), *The handbook of motivation and cognition: Foundations of social behavior* (pp. 3–19). New York: Guilford.

Spaulding, C. (1970). The romantic love complex in American culture. *Sociology and Social Research, 55,* 82–100.

Spencer-Rodgers, J., Peng, K., Wang, L., & Hou, Y. (2004). Dialectical self-esteem and East-West differences in psychological well-being. *Personality and Social Psychological Bulletin, 30,* 1416–1432.

Spencer, S. J., Steele, C. M., & Quinn, D. M. (1999). Stereotype threat and women's math performance. *Journal of Experimental Social Psychology, 35,* 4–28.

Spitzer, B. L., Henderson, K. A., & Zivian, M. T. (1999). Gender differences in population versus media body sizes: A comparison over four decades. *Sex Roles, 40,* 545–565.

Sprecher, S. (1992). How men and women expect to feel and behave in response to inequity in close relationships. *Social Psychology Quarterly, 55,* 57–69.

Sprecher, S. (1999). "I love you more today than yesterday": Romantic partners' perceptions of changes in love and related affect over time. *Journal of Personality and Social Psychology, 76,* 46–53.

Sprecher, S. (2009). Relationship initiation and formation on the Internet. *Marriage & Family Review, 45,* 761–782.

Sprecher, S., & Felmlee, D. (1992). The influence of parents and friends on the quality and stability of romantic relationships: A three wave longitudinal investigation. *Journal of Marriage and the Family, 54,* 888–900.

Sprecher, S., Metts, S., Burleson, B., Hatfield, E., & Thompson, A. (1995). Domains of expressive interaction in intimate relationships: Associations with satisfaction and commitment. *Family Relations, 44,* 1–8.

Sprecher, S., Sullivan, Q., & Hatfield, E. (1994). Mate selection preferences: Gender differences examined in a national sample. *Journal of Personality and Social Psychology, 66,* 1074–1080.

Sprecher, S., & Toro-Morn, M. (2002). A study of men and women from different sides of earth to determine if men are from Mars and women are from Venus in their beliefs about love and romantic relationships. *Sex Roles, 46,* 131–147.

Staats, A. W., & Staats, C. K. (1958). Attitudes established by classical conditioning. *Journal of Abnormal and Social Psychology, 57,* 37–40.

Staats, A. W., Staats, C. K., & Crawford, H. L. (1962). First-order conditioning of meaning and the parallel conditioning of a GSR. *Journal of General Psychology, 67,* 159–167.

Stafford, L., & Canary, D. J. (2006). Equity and interdependence as predictors of relational maintenance strategies. *Journal of Family Communications, 6,* 227–254.

Stagner, R. (1986). Reminiscences about the founding of SPSSI. *Journal of Social Issues, 42,* 35–42.

Stangor, C., & McMillan, D. (1992). Memory for expectancy-congruent and expectancy-incongruent information: A review of the social and social developmental literatures. *Psychological Bulletin, 111,* 42–61.

Stanovich, K. E. (2004). Balance in psychological research: The dual process perspective. *Behavioral and Brain Sciences, 27.*

Stanovich, K. E., & West, R. F. (2002). Individual differences in reasoning: Implications for the rationality debate? In T. Gilovich, D. Griffin, & D. Kahneman (Eds.), *Heuristics and biases: The psychology of intuitive judgment* (pp. 421–440). Cambridge, England: Cambridge University Press.

Stanton, W. R., Currie, G. D., Oei, T. P. S., & Silva, P. A. (1996). A developmental approach to influences on adolescents' smoking and quitting. *Journal of Applied and Developmental Psychology, 17,* 307–319.

Staub, E. (2004). Understanding and responding to group violence: Genocide, mass killing, and terrorism. In F. M. Moghaddam & A. J. Marsella. (Eds.), *Understanding terrorism: Psychosocial roots, consequences, and interventions* (pp. 151–168). Washington, DC: American Psychological Association.

Staudinger, U. M., Freund, A. M., Linden, M., & Maas, I. (1999). Self, personality, and life regulation: Facets of psychological resilience in old age. In P. B. Baltes & K. U. Mayer (Eds), *The Berline Aging Study: Aging from 70 to 100* (pp. 302–328). New York: Cambridge University Press.

Steele, C. M. (1988). The psychology of self-affirmation: Sustaining the integrity of the self. In L. Berkowitz (Ed.), *Advances in experimental social psychology* (Vol. 21, pp. 261–302). New York: Academic Press.

Steele, C. M. (1997). A threat in the air: How stereotypes shape intellectual identity and performance. *American Psychologist, 52,* 613–629.

Steele, C. M. (2010). *Whistling Vivaldi: And other clues to how stereotypes affect us.* New York: W. W. Norton.

Steele, C. M., & Aronson, J. (1995). Stereotype threat and the intellectual test performance of African-Americans. *Journal of Personality and Social Psychology, 68,* 797–811.

Steele, C. M., & Josephs, R. A. (1990). Alcohol myopia: Its prized and dangerous effects. *American Psychologist, 45,* 921–933.

Steele, C. M., & Liu, T. J. (1981). Making the dissonant act unreflective of self: Dissonance avoidance and the expectancy of a value-affirming response. *Personality and Social Psychology Bulletin, 7,* 393–397.

Steele, C. M., Spencer, S. J., & Aronson, J. (2002). Contending with group image: The psychology of stereotype and social identity threat. In M. P. Zanna (Ed.), *Advances in experimental social psychology* (Vol. 34, pp. 379–440). San Diego: Academic Press.

Steele, C. M., Spencer, S. J., Hummel, M., Carter, K., Harber, K., Schoem, D., & Nisbett, R. (2004). African-American college achievement: A "wise" intervention. *Unpublished manuscript, Stanford University.*

Steele, C. M., Spencer, S. J., & Lynch, M. (1993). Self-image resilience and dissonance: The role of affirmational resources. *Journal of Personality and Social Psychology, 64,* 885–896.

Steffens, M. C., & Jelenec, P. (2010). Separating implicit gender stereotypes regarding math and language: Implicit ability stereotypes are self-serving for boys and men but not for girls and women. *Sex Roles, 64.* 324–335.

Steinberg, L. D., Catalano, R., & Dooley, D. (1981). Economic antecedents of child abuse and neglect. *Child Development, 52,* 975–985.

Stelmack, R. M., & Geen, R. G. (1992). The psychophysiology of extraversion. In A. Gale & M. W. Eysenck (Eds.), *Handbook of individual differences: Biological perspectives* (pp. 227–254). New York: Wiley.

Stelzl, M., Janes, L., & Seligman, C. (2008). Champ or chump: Strategic utilization of dual social identities of others. *European Journal of Social Psychology, 38,* 128–138.

Stephan, W. G. (1980). A brief historical overview of school desegregation. In W. G. Stephan & J. R. Feagin (Eds.), *School desegregation: Past, present, and future* (pp. 3–24). New York: Plenum.

Stephan, W. G., Boniecki, K. A., Ybarra, O., Bettencourt, A., Ervin, K. A., Jackson, L. A., et al.

(2002). The role of threats in the racial attitudes of Blacks and Whites. *Personality and Social Psychology Bulletin, 28,* 1242–1254.

Stephan, W. G., Stephan, C. W., & de Vargas, M. (1996). Emotional expression in Costa Rica and the United States. *Journal of Cross-Cultural Psychology, 27,* 147–160.

Stephens, D. P., & Few, A. L. (2007). The effects of images of African American women in hip hop on early adolescents' attitudes toward physical attractiveness and interpersonal relationships. *Sex Roles, 56,* 251–264.

Stepper, S., & Strack, F. (1993). Proprioceptive determinants of emotional and nonemotional feelings. *Journal of Personality and Social Psychology, 64,* 211–220.

Stern, I., & Westphal, J. D. (2010). Stealthy footsteps to the boardroom: Executives' backgrounds, sophisticated interpersonal influence behavior, and board appointments. *Administrative Science Quarterly, 55,* 278–319.

Sternberg, R. J. (1986). A triangular theory of love. *Psychological Review, 93,* 119–135.

Sternberg, R. J. (1997). Construct validation of a triangular love scale. *European Journal of Social Psychology, 27,* 313–335.

Stets, J. E., & Burke, P. J. (1996). Gender, control, and interaction. *Social Psychology Quarterly, 59,* 193–220.

Stevens, C. K., & Kristof, A. L. (1995). Making the right impression: A field study of applicant impression management during job interviews. *Journal of Applied Psychology, 80,* 587–606.

Stewart, E. C., & Bennett, M. J. (1991). *American cultural patterns: A cross-cultural perspective.* Yarmouth, ME: Intercultural Press.

Stewart-Knox, B. J., Sittlington, J., Rugkasa, J., Harrisson, S., Treacy, M., & Abaunza, P. S. (2011). Smoking and peer groups: Results from a longitudinal qualitative study of young people in Northern Ireland. *British Journal of Social Psychology, 44,* 397–414.

Stewart-Williams, S. (2007). Altruism among kin vs. nonkin: Effects of cost of help and reciprocal exchange. *Evolution and Human Behavior, 28,* 193–198.

Stinson, D. A., Logel, C., Holmes, J. G., Wood, J. V., Forest, A. L., Gaucher, D., Fitzsimons, G. M., & Kath, J. (2010). The regulatory function of self-esteem: Testing the epistemic and acceptance signaling systems. *Journal of Personality and Social Psychology, 99,* 993–1013.

Stokes, J. P. (1987). The relation of loneliness and self-disclosure. In V. J. Derlega & J. H. Berg (Eds.), *Self-disclosure: Theory, research, and therapy* (pp. 175–202). New York: Plenum.

Stokes, J., & Levin, I. (1986). Gender differences in predicting loneliness from social network characteristics. *Journal of Personality and Social Psychology, 51,* 1069–1074.

Stone, J., Lynch, C. I., Sjomeling, M., & Darley, J. M. (1999). Stereotype threat effects on Black and White athletic performance. *Journal of Personality and Social Psychology, 77,* 1213–1227.

Stone, J., Wiegand, A. W., Cooper, J., & Aronson, E. (1997). When exemplification fails: Hypocrisy and the motive for self-integrity. *Journal of Personality and Social Psychology, 72,* 54–65.

Stone, L. (1977). *The family, sex and marriage in England: 1500–1800.* New York: Harper & Row.

Stoner, J. A. F. (1961). *A comparison of individual and group decisions involving risk.* Unpublished master's thesis, MIT, Cambridge, MA.

Storms, M. D. (1973). Videotape and the attribution process: Reversing actors' and observers' points of view. *Journal of Personality and Social Psychology, 27,* 165–175.

Stouten, J., De Cremer, D., & van Dijk, E. (2006). Violating equality in social dilemmas: Emotional and retributive reactions as a function of trust, attribution, and honesty. *Personality and Social Psychology Bulletin, 32,* 894–906.

Strack, F., & Deutsch, R. (2004). Reflective and

impulsive determinants of social behavior. *Personality and Social Psychology Review, 8,* 220–247.

Strack, F., Martin, L. L., & Stepper, S. (1988). Inhibiting and facilitating conditions of facial expressions: A nonobtrusive test of the facial feedback hypothesis. *Journal of Personality and Social Psychology, 54,* 768–777.

Strahan, E. J., LaFrance, A., Wilson, A. E., Ethier, N., Spencer, S. J., & Zanna, M. P. (2008). Victoria's dirty secret: How sociocultural norms influence adolescent girls and women. *Personality and Social Psychology Bulletin, 34,* 288–301.

Strahan, E. J., Spencer, S. J., & Zanna, M. P. (2002). Subliminal priming and persuasion: Striking while the iron is hot. *Journal of Experimental Social Psychology, 38,* 556–568.

Strahan, E. J., Spencer, S. J., & Zanna, M. P. (2005). Subliminal priming and persuasion: How motivation affects the activation of goals and the persuasiveness of messages. In K. R. Kardes, P. M. Herr, & J. Nantel (Eds.), *Applying social cognition to consumer-focused strategy* (pp. 267–280). Mahwah, NJ: Lawrence Erlbaum.

Strassberg, D. S., & Holty, S. (2003). An experimental study of women's Internet personal ads. *Archives of Sexual Behavior, 32,* 253–260.

Stratham, A., & Rhoades, K. (2001). Gender and self-esteem: Narrative and efficacy in the negotiation of structural factors. In T. J. Owens, S. Stryker, & N. Goodman (Eds.), *Extending self-esteem theory and research: Sociological and psychological currents* (pp. 255–284). Cambridge: Cambridge University Press.

Straus, M. A., & Gelles, R. J. (1990). *Physical violence in American families: Risk factors and adaptations to violence in 8,145 families.* New Brunswick, NJ: Transaction.

Straus, M. A., Gelles, R. J., & Steinmetz, S. K. (1980). *Behind closed doors: Violence in the American family.* Garden City, NY: Doubleday/Anchor.

Straus, S. G., Parker, A. M., & Bruce, J. B. (2011). The group matters: A review of processes and outcomes in intelligence analysis. *Group Dynamics: Theory, Research, and Practice, 15,* 128–146.

Strauss, B. (2002). Social facilitation in motor tasks: A review of research and theory. *Psychology of Sport and Exercise, 3,* 237–256.

Street, R. L., Jr., & Brady, R. M. (1982). Speech rate acceptance ranges as a function of evaluative domain, listener speech rate, and communication context. *Communication Monographs, 49,* 290–308.

Streeter, S. A., & McBurney, D. H. (2003). Waist-to-hip ratio and attractiveness: New evidence and a critique of a "critical test." *Evolution and Human Behavior, 24,* 88–98.

Striegel-Moore, R. H., Silberstein, L. R., & Rodin, J. (1993). The social self in bulimia nervosa: Public self-consciousness, social anxiety, and perceived fraudulence. *Journal of Abnormal Psychology, 102,* 297–303.

.Stryker, S. (1997). "In the beginning there is society": Lessons from a sociological social psychology. In C. McGarty & S. A. Haslam (Eds.), *The message of social psychology: Perspectives on mind in society* (pp. 315–327). Cambridge, MA: Blackwell.

Stucke, T. S., & Sporer, S. L. (2002). When a grandiose self-image is threatened: Narcissism and self-concept clarity as predictors of negative emotions and aggression following ego-threat. *Journal of Personality, 70,* 509–532.

Stuphorn, I. S., Brown, J. W., & Schall, J. D. (2003). Performance monitoring by the anterior cingulated cortex during saccade countermanding. *Science, 302,* 120–122.

Stürmer, S., Snyder, M., Kropp, A., & Siem, B. (2006). Empathy-motivated helping: The moderating role of group membership. *Personality and Social Psychology Bulletin, 32,* 943–956.

Stürmer, S., Snyder, M., & Omoto, AS. M. (2005). Prosocial emotions and helping: The moderating role of group membership. (2005). *Journal of Personality and Social Psychology, 88,* 532–546.

Stuss, D. T., Gallup, G. G., & Alexander, M. P. (2001). The frontal lobes are necessary for "theory of mind." *Brain, 124,* 279–286.

Suh, E. J., Moskowitz, D. S., Fournier, M. A., & Zuroff, D. C. (2004). Gender relationships: Influences on agentic and communal behaviors. *Personal Relationships, 11,* 41–59.

Sui, J., Zhu, Y., & Chiu, C-y. (2007). Bicultural mind, self-construal, and self- and mother-reference effects: Consequences of cultural priming on recognition memory. *Journal of Experimental Social Psychology, 43,* 818–824.

Sumner, W. (1906). *Folkways.* New York: Ginn.

Susman, E. J., Dockray, S., Schiefelbein, V. L., Herwehe, S., Heaton, J. A., & Dorn, L. D. (2007). Morningness/eveningness, morning-to-afternoon cortisol ratio, and antisocial behavior problems during puberty. *Developmental Psychology, 43,* 811–822.

Sussman, N. M. (2000). The dynamic nature of cultural identity throughout cultural transitions: Why home is not so sweet. *Personality and Social Psychology Review, 4,* 355–373.

Swami, V., Frederick, D. A., Aavik, T., Alcalay, L., Allik, J., Anderson, D., Andrianto, S., Arora, A., Brannstrom, A., Cunningham, J., Danel, D., Doroszweicz, K., Forbes, G. B., Furnham, A., Greven, C. U., Halberstadt, J., Hao, S., Haubner, T., Hwang, C. S., Inman, M., Jaafar, J. L., Johansson, J., Jung, J., Keser, A., Kretzschmar, M., Lachenicht, L., Li, N. P., Locke, K., Lonnqvist, J. E., Lopez, C., Loutzenhiser, L., Maisel, N. C., McCabe, M. P., McCreary, D. R., McKibbin, W. F., Mussap, A., Neto, F., Nowell, C., Alampay, L. P., Pillai, S. K., Pokrajac-Bulian, A., Proyer, R. T., Quintelier, K., Ricciardelli, L. A., Rozmus-Wrzesinska, M., Ruch, W., Russo, T., Schutz, A., Shackelford, T. K., Shashidharan, S., Simonetti, F., Sinniah, D., Swami, M., Vandermassen, G., van Marijke, D., Verkasalo, M., Voracek, M., Yee, C. K., Zhang, E. X., Zhang, X., & Zivcic-Becirevic, I. (2010). The attractive female body weight and female body dissatisfaction in 26 countries across 10 world regions: Results of the International Body Project I. *Personality and Social Psychology Bulletin, 36,* 309–325.

Swann, W. B., Jr. (1984). Quest for accuracy in person perception: A matter of pragmatics. *Psychological Review, 91,* 457–477.

Swann, W. B., Jr. (1990). To be adored or to be known? The interplay of self-enhancement and self-verification. In E. T. Higgins & R. M. Sorrentino (Eds.), *Handbook of motivation and cognition: Foundations of social behavior* (Vol. 2, pp. 408–448). New York: Guilford.

Swann, W. B., Jr. (1997). The trouble with change: Self-verification and allegiance to the self. *Psychological Science, 8,* 177–183.

Swann, W. B., Jr., & Bosson, J. K. (2010). Self and identity. In S. T. Fiske, D. T. Gilbert, & G. Lindzey (Eds.), *Handbook of social psychology (5th ed.) (*pp. 589–628). Hoboken, NJ: Wiley.

Swann, W. B., Jr., Bosson, J. K., & Pelham, B. W. (2002a). Different partners, different selves: The verification of circumscribed identities. *Personality and Social Psychology Bulletin, 28,* 1215–1228.

Swann, W. B., Jr., Chang-Schneider, C., & McClarty, K. L. (2007). Do people's self-views matter? Self-concept and self-esteem in everyday life. *American Psychologist, 62,* 1–11.

Swann, W. B., Jr., De La Ronde, C., & Hixon, J. G. (1994). Authenticity and positive strivings in marriage and courtship. *Journal of Personality and Social Psychology, 66,* 857–869.

Swann, W. B., Jr., & Ely, R. J. (1984). A battle of wills: Self-verification versus behavioral confirmation. *Journal of Personality and Social Psychology, 46,* 1287–1302.

Swann, W. B. Jr., Gomez, A., Huici, C., Morales, J. F., & Hixon, J. G. (2010) Identity fusion and self-

sacrifice: Arousal as a catalyst of pro-group fighting, dying and helping behavior. *Journal of Personality and Social Psychology, 99,* 82–841.

Swann, W. B., Jr., Griffin, J. J., Predmore, S., & Gaines, B. (1987). The cognitive-affective crossfire: When self-consistency confronts self-enhancement. *Journal of Personality and Social Psychology, 52,* 881–889.

Swann, W. B., Jr., Kwan, V. S. Y., Polzer, J. T., & Milton, L. P. (2003). Fostering group identification and creativity in diverse groups: The role of individuation and self-verification. *Personality and Social Psychology Bulletin, 29,* 1396–1406.

Swann, W. B., Jr., Milton, L. P., & Polzer, J. T. (2000). Should we create a niche or fall in line? Identity negotiation and small group effectiveness. *Journal of Personality and Social Psychology, 79,* 238–250.

Swann, W. B., Jr., Polzer, J. T., Seyle, D. C., & Ko, S. J. (2004). Finding value in diversity: Verification of personal and social self-views in diverse groups. *Academy of Management Review, 29,* 9–27.

Swann, W. B., Jr., Rentfrow, P. J., & Guinn, J. S. (2002b). Self-verification: The search for coherence. In C. R. Snyder & S. J. Lopez (Eds.), *Handbook of positive psychology* (pp. 366–381). New York: Oxford University Press.

Swartz, S. (2011). 'Going deep' and 'giving back': Strategies for exceeding ethical expectations when researching amongst vulnerable youth. *Qualitative Research, 11,* 47–68.

Swim, J. K., Cohen, L. L., & Hyers, L. L. (1998). Experiencing everyday prejudice and discrimination. In J. K. Swim & C. Stangor (Eds.), *Prejudice: The targets' perspective* (pp.38–61). San Diego, CA: Academic Press.

Swim, J. K., Ferguson, M. J., & Hyers, L. L. (1999). Avoiding stigma by distancing. *Basic and Applied Social Psychology, 21,* 61–68.

Swim, J. K, & Hyers, L. L. (2009). Sexism. In T. D. Nelson (Ed.). *Handbook of prejudice, stereotyping, and discrimination* (pp. 407–430). New York: Psychology Press.

Swim, J. K., Hyers, L. L., Cohen, L. L., & Ferguson, M. J. (2001). *Everyday sexism: Evidence for its incidence, nature, and psychological impact from three daily diary studies.* Manuscript submitted for publication.

Swim, J. K., Hyers, L. L., Cohen, L. L., Fitzgerald, D. F., & Bylsma, W. H. (2003). African American college students' experiences with everyday racism: Characteristics of and responses to these incidents. *Journal of Black Psychology, 29,* 38–67.

Swinton, W. (1880). *A complete course in geography: Physical, industrial, and political.* New York: Ivison, Blakeman, Taylor, & Co.

Symons, D. (1979). *The evolution of human sexuality.* New York: Oxford University Press.

Szymanski, D. M., & Henning, S. L. (2007). The role of self-objectification in women's depression: A test of objectification theory. *Sex Roles, 56,* 45–53.

Tacikowski, P., Brechmann, A., Marchewka, A., Jednorog, K., Dobrowolny, M., & Nowicka, A. (2011). Is it about the self or the significance? An *f*MRI study of self-name recognition. *Social Neuroscience, 6,* 98–107.

Taggar, S., & Ellis, R. (2007). The role of leaders in shaping formal team norms. *Leadership Quarterly, 18,* 105–120.

Tajfel, H. (1982). *Social identity and intergroup relations.* Cambridge, England: Cambridge University Press.

Tajfel, H., Billig, M. G., Bundy, R. P., & Flament, C. (1971). Social categorization and intergroup behavior. *European Journal of Social Psychology, 1,* 149–178.

Tajfel, H., & Turner, J. (1979). An integrative theory of intergroup conflict. In W. G. Austin & S. Worchel (Eds.), *The social psychology of intergroup relations.* Monterey, CA: Brooks/Cole.

Takahashi, A., Quadros, I. M., de Almeida, R. M. M., & Miczek, K. A. (2011). Brain serotonin receptors and transporters: Initiation vs. termination of

escalated aggression. *Psychopharmacology, 213,* 83–212.

Takemura, K., & Arimoto, H. (2008). Independent self in Japan's "North Frontier": An experiment of cognitive dissonance in Hokkaido. *Japanese Journal of Experimental Social Psychology, 48,* 40–49.

Talbot, K. K., Neill, K. S., & Rankin, L. L. (2010). Rape-accepting attitudes of university undergraduate students. *Journal of Forensic Nursing, 6,* 170–179.

Tamir, M., & Mauss, I. B. (2011). Social cognitive factors in emotion regulation: Implications for well-being. In I. Nyklicek, A. Vingerhoets, & M. Zeelenberg (Eds.). *Emotion regulation and well-being* (pp. 31–47). New York: Springer.

Tanford, S., & Penrod, S. (1984). Social influence model: A formal integration of research on majority and minority influence. *Psychological Bulletin, 95,* 189–225.

Tangney, J. P., Wagner, P., Fletcher, C., & Gramzow, R. (1992). Shamed into anger? The relation of shame and guilt to anger and self-reported aggression. *Journal of Personality and Social Psychology, 62,* 669–675.

Tarde, G. (1903). *The laws of imitation.* (Elsie Clews Parson, Trans.). New York: Henry Holt. (Original work published in 1890).

Tashiro, T., & Frazier, P. (2003). "I'll never be in a relationship like that again": Personal growth following romantic relationship breakups. *Personal Relationships,10,* 113–128.

Tashiro, T., Frazier, P., & Berman, M. (2006). Stress-related growth following divorce and relationship dissolution. In M. A. Fine & J. H. Harvey (Eds.), *Handbook of divorce and relationship dissolution* (pp. 361–384). Mahwah, NJ: Lawrence Erlbaum.

Tata, J., Anthony, T., Lin, H., Newman, B., Tang, S., Millson, M., & Sivakumar, K. (1996). Proportionate group size and rejection of the deviate: A meta-analytic integration. *Journal of Social Behavior and Personality, 11,* 739–752.

Taylor, D. M., Wright, S. C., Moghaddam, F. M., & Lalonde, R. N. (1990). The personal-group discrimination discrepancy: Perceiving my group, but not myself, to be a target for discrimination. *Personality and Social Psychology Bulletin, 16,* 254–262.

Taylor, J., & Riess, M. (1989). "Self-serving" attributions to valenced causal factors: A field experiment. *Personality and Social Psychology Bulletin, 15,* 337–348.

Taylor, L. S., Fiore, A. T., Mendelsohn, G. A., & Cheshire, C. (2011). "Out of my league": A real-world test of the matching hypothesis. *Personality and Social Psychology Bulletin, 36,* 942–954.

Taylor, S. E. (1998). The social being in social psychology. In D. T. Gilbert, S. T. Fiske, & G. Lindzey (Eds.), *The handbook of social psychology* (4th ed., pp. 58–95). New York: McGraw-Hill.

Taylor, S. E. (2007a). Theory development as a family affair. *Journal of Experimental Social Psychology, 42,* 129–132.

Taylor, S. E. (2007b). Social support. In H. S. Friedman & R. C. Silver (Eds.), *Foundations of health psychology (*pp. 145–171). New York: Oxford University Press.

Taylor, S. E., & Brown, J. D. (1988). Illusion and well-being. A social psychological perspective on mental health. *Psychological Bulletin, 103,* 193–210.

Taylor, S. E., & Fiske, S. T. (1975). Point of view and perceptions of causality. *Journal of Personality and Social Psychology, 32,* 439–445.

Taylor, S. E., Klein, L. C., Gruenewald, T. L., Gurung, R. A. R., & Fernandes-Taylor, S. (2003a). In J. Suls & K. A. Wallston (Eds.), *Social psychological foundations of health and illness. Blackwell series in health psychology and behavioral medicine* (pp. 314–331). Malden, MA: Blackwell.

Taylor, S. E., Lerner, J. S., Herman, D. K., Sage, R. M., &

McDowell, N. K. (2003b). Portrait of the self-enhancer: Well adjusted and well liked or maladjusted and friendless? *Journal of Personality and Social Psychology, 84,* 165–176.

Taylor, S. E., Sherman, D. K., Kim, H. S., Jarcho, J., Takagi, K., & Dunagan, M. S. (2004). Culture and social support: Who seeks it and why? *Journal of Personality and Social Psychology, 87,* 354–362.

Taylor, S. E., Welch, W. T.., Kim, H. S., & Sherman, D. K. (2007). Cultural differences in the impact of social support on psychological and biological stress responses. *Psychological Science, 18,* 831–837.

Teachman, B. A., Gapinski, K. D., Brownell, K. D., Rawlins, M., & Jeyaram, S. (2003). Demonstrations of implicit anti-fat bias: The impact of providing causal information and evoking empathy. *Health Psychology, 22,* 68–78.

Teagarden, M. B. (2007). Best practices in cross-cultural leadership. In J. A. Conger & R. E. Riggio (Eds.), *The practice of leadership: Developing the next generation of leaders* (pp. 300–330). San Francisco, CA: Jossey-Bass.

Telles, E. E., & Marguia, E. (1990). Phenotype discrimination and income differences among Mexican Americans. *Social Science Quarterly, 71,* 682–696.

Tenbrunsel, A. E., & Messick, D. M. (2004). Ethical fading: The role of self-deception in unethical behavior. *Social Justice Research,17,* 223–236.

Tesser, A. (1988). Toward a self-evaluation maintenance model of social behavior. In L. Berkowitz (Ed.), *Advances in experimental social psychology* (Vol. 21, pp. 181–227). New York: Academic Press.

Tesser, A., & Bau, J. J. (2002). Social psychology: Who we are and what we do. *Personality and Social Psychology Review, 6,* 72–85.

Tesser, A., Campbell, J., & Smith, M. (1984). Friendship choice and performance: Self-evaluation maintenance in children. *Journal of Personality and Social Psychology, 46,* 561–574.

Tesser, A., & Smith, M. (1980). Some effects of task relevance and friendship on helping: You don't always help the one you like. *Journal of Experimental Social Psychology, 16,* 582–590.

Tetlock, P. E., Peterson, R. S., McGuire, C., Chang, S., & Feld, P. (1992). Assessing political group dynamics: A test of the groupthink model. *Journal of Personality and Social Psychology, 63,* 403–425.

Tharp, R. G. (1994). Intergroup differences among Native Americans in socialization and child cognition: An ethnogenetic analysis. In P. M. Greenfield & R. R. Cocking (Eds.), *Cross-cultural roots of minority child development* (pp. 87–105). Hillsdale, NJ: Erlbaum.

t'Hart, P., Rosenthal, U., & Kouzmin, A. (1993). Crisis decision making: The centralization thesis revisited. *Administration and Society, 25,* 12–45.

Theodore, P. S., & Basow, S. A. (2000). Heterosexual masculinity and homophobia: A reaction to the self. *Journal of Homosexuality, 40,* 31–48.

Theron, W. H., Matthee, D. D., Steel, H. R., & Ramirez, J. M. (2000). Direct and indirect aggression in women: A comparison between South African and Spanish university students. In J. M. Ramirez & D. S. Richardson (Eds.), *Cross-cultural approaches to research on aggression and reconciliation* (pp. 99–109). Huntington, NY: Nova.

Thibaut, J. W., & Kelley, H. H. (1959). *The social psychology of groups.* New York: Wiley.

Thomaes, S., & Bushman, B. J. (2011). Mirror, mirror, on the wall, who's the most aggressive of them all? Narcissism, self-esteem, and aggression. In P. R. Shaver & M. Mikulincer (Eds.). *Human aggression and violence: Causes, manifestations, and consequences* (pp. 203–219). Washington, DC: American Psychological Association.

Thoman, E. B. (1999). Morningness and eveningness: Issues for study of the early ontogeny of these circadian rhythms. *Human Development, 42,*

206–212.

Thomas, G., & Fletcher, G. J. O. (1997). Empathic accuracy in close relationships. In W. Ickes (Ed.), *Empathic accuracy* (pp. 194–218). New York: Guilford.

Thomas, G., & Fletcher, G. J. O. (2003). Mind-reading accuracy in intimate relationships: Assessing the roles of the relationship, the target, and the judge. *Journal of Personality and Social Psychology, 85,* 1079–1094.

Thomas, G. , Fletcher, G. J. O., & Lange, C. (1997). One-line empathic accuracy in marital interaction. *Journal of Personality and Social Psychology, 72,* 839–850.

Thomas, J. J., & Daubman, K. A. (2001). The relationship between friendship quality and self-esteem in adolescent girls and boys. *Sex Roles, 45,* 53–65.

Thomas, M. H., Horton, R. W., Lippincott, E. C., & Drabman, R. S. (1977). Desensitization to portrayals of real-life aggression as a function of exposure to television violence. *Journal of Personality and Social Psychology, 35,* 450–458.

Thompson, D. K. (2011). Functional magnetic resonance imaging: Critical analysis of techniques and interpretation. *Journal of the International Neuropsychological Society, 17,* 376–379.

Thorndike, E. L. (1911). *Animal intelligence: Experimental studies.* New York: Macmillan.

Thornton, K. C. (2003). When the source of embarrassment is a close other. *Individual Differences Research, 1,* 189–200.

Thurstone, L. L. (1928). Attitudes can be measured. *American Journal of Sociology, 33,* 529–554.

Tice, D. M. (1991). Esteem protection or enhancement? Self-handicapping motives and attributions differ by trait self-esteem. *Journal of Personality and Social Psychology, 60,* 711–725.

Tice, D. M., & Baumeister, R. F. (1985). Masculinity inhibits helping in emergencies: Personality does predict the bystander effect. *Journal of Personality and Social Psychology, 49,* 420–428.

Tice, D. M., Baumeister, R. F., Shmueli, D., & Muraven, M. (2007). Restoring the self: Positive affect helps improve self-regulation following ego depletion. *Journal of Experimental Social Psychology, 43,* 379–384.

Tice, D. M., Bratslavsky, E., & Baumeister, R. F. (2001). Emotional distress regulation takes precedence over impulse control: If you feel bad, do it! *Journal of Personality and Social Psychology, 80,* 53–67.

Tice, D. M., Butler, J. L., Muraven, M. B., & Stillwell, A. M. (1995). When modesty prevails: Differential favorability of self-presentation to friends and strangers. *Journal of Personality and Social Psychology, 69,* 1120–1138.

Tickle, J. J., Hull, J. G., Sargent, J. D., Dalton, M. A., & Heatherton, T. F. (2006). A structural equation model of social influences and exposure to media smoking on adolescent smoking. *Basic and Applied Social Psychology, 28,* 117–129.

Timmers, M., Fischer, A. H., & Manstead, A. S. R. (1998). Gender differences in motives for regulating emotions. *Personality and Social Psychology Bulletin, 24,* 974–985.

Tjaden, P., & Thoennes, N. (2000). *Extent, nature, and consequences of intimate partner violence.* Washington, DC: U.S. Department of Justice.

Toates, F. (2006). A model of the hierarchy of behaviour, cognition, and consciousness. *Consciousness and Cognition: An International Journal, 15,* 75–118.

Todd, A. R., Seok, D., Kerr, N. L., & Messé, L. A. (2006). Social compensation: Fact or social comparison artifact? *Group Processes and Intergroup Relations, 9,* 431–442.

Todd, P., Penke, L., Fasolo, B., & Lenton, A. P. (2007). *Different cognitive processes underlie human mate choices and mate preferences. Proceedings of the National Academy of Sciences.*

Todorov, A. (2011). Evaluating faces on social

dimensions. In A. Todorov, S. T. Fiske, & D. A. Prentice (Eds.). *Social neuroscience: Toward understanding the underpinnings of the social mind* (pp. 54–76). New York: Oxford University Press.

Tolnay, S. E., & Beck, E. M. (1995). *A festival of violence: An analysis of Southern lynchings, 1882-1930.* Urbana: University of Illinois Press.

Tolstedt, B. E., & Stokes, J. P. (1984). Self-disclosure, intimacy, and the depenetration process. *Journal of Personality and Social Psychology, 46,* 84–90.

Tomasello, M. (2011). Human culture in evolutionary perspective. In M. J. Gelfand, C. Chiu, & Y. Hong, Ying-yi. (Eds.) *Advances in culture and psychology (Vol 1)* (pp. 5-51). New York: Oxford University Press.

Tong, S. T., & Walther, J. B. (2011). Just say "no thanks": Romantic rejection in computer-mediated communication. *Journal of Social and Personal Relationships, 28,* 488–506.

Tormala, Z. L., & Petty, R. E. (2002). What doesn't kill me makes me stronger: The effects of resisting persuasion on attitude certainty. *Journal of Personality and Social Psychology, 83,* 1298–1313.

Tormala, Z. L., & Petty, R. E. (2007). Contextual contrast and perceived knowledge: Exploring the implications for persuasion. *Journal of Experimental Social Psychology, 43,* 17–30.

Tower, R. K., Kelly, C., & Richards, A. (1997). Individualism, collectivism and reward allocation: A cross-cultural study in Russia and Britain. *British Journal of Social Psychology, 36,* 331–345.

Townsend, J. M., & Levy, G. D. (1990). Effects of potential partners' physical attractiveness and socioeconomic status on sexuality and partner selection. *Archives of Sexual Behavior, 19,* 149–164.

Townsend, J. M., & Wasserman, T. (1997). The perception of sexual attractiveness: Sex differences in variability. *Archives of Sexual Behavior, 26,* 243–268.

Tracey, T. J. (1994). An examination of the complementarity of interpersonal behavior. *Journal of Personality and Social Psychology, 67,* 864–878.

Tracey, T. J. G. (2004). Levels of interpersonal complementarity: A simplex representation. *Personality and Social Psychology Bulletin, 30,* 1211–1225.

Trafimow, D., Triandis, H. C., & Goto, S. G. (1991). Some tests of the distinction between the private self and the collective self. *Journal of Personality and Social Psychology, 60,* 649–655.

Trapnell, P. D., & Campbell, J. D. (1999). Private self-consciousness and the five-factor model of personality: Distinguishing rumination from reflection. *Journal of Personality and Social Psychology, 76,* 284–304.

Trappey, C. (1996). A meta-analysis of consumer choice and subliminal advertising. *Psychology and Marketing, 13,* 517–530.

Travis, C. B., McKenzie, B., Wiley, D. L., & Kahn, A. S. (1988). Sex and achievement domain: Cognitive patterns of success and failure. *Sex Roles, 19,* 509–525.

Travis, L. E. (1925). The effect of a small audience upon eye-hand coordination. *Journal of Abnormal and Social Psychology, 20,* 142–146.

Treadway, D. C., Ferris, G. R., Duke, A. B., Adams, G. L., & Thatcher, J. B. (2007). The moderating role of subordinate political skill on supervisors' impressions of subordinate ingratiation and ratings of subordinate interpersonal facilitation. *Journal of Applied Psychology, 92,* 848–855.

Tremblay, R. E., & Nagin, D. S. (2005). The developmental origins of physical aggression in humans. In R. E. Tremblay, W. W. Hartup, & J. Archer (Eds.), *Developmental origins of aggression* (pp. 83–106). New York: Guilford Press.

Triandis, H. C. (1972). *The analysis of subjective culture.* New York: Wiley.

Triandis, H. C. (1989). The self and social behavior in

differing cultural contexts. *Psychological Review, 96,* 506–520.

Triandis, H. C., Botempo, R., Villareal, M. J., Asai, M., & Lucca, N. (1988). Individualism and collectivism: Cross-cultural perspectives on self-ingroup relationships. *Journal of Personality and Social Psychology, 54,* 323–338.

Triplett, N. (1897). The dynamogenic factors in pacemaking and competition. *American Journal of Psychology, 9,* 507–533.

Trivers, R. L. (1971). The evolution of reciprocal altruism. *Quarterly Review of Biology, 46,* 35–57.

Trivers, R. L. (1983). The evolution of cooperation. In D. L. Bridgeman (Ed.), *The nature of prosocial development.* New York: Academic Press.

Troisi, J. D., & Gabriel, S. (2011). Chicken soup really is good for the soul: "Comfort food" fulfills the need to belong. *Psychological Science, 20,* 1–7.

Trope, Y. (1998). Dispositional bias in person perception: A hypothesis-testing perspective. In J. M. Darley & J. Cooper (Eds.), *Attribution and social interaction: The legacy of Edward E. Jones* (pp. 67–97). Washington, DC: American Psychological Association.

Trudeau, K. J., & Devlin, S. (1996). College students and community service: Who, with whom, and why? *Journal of Applied Social Psychology, 26,* 1867–1888.

Tulving, E. (1997). Human memory. In M. S. Gazzaniga (Ed.), *Conversations in the cognitive neurosciences.* Cambridge, MA: MIT Press.

Turner, C. W., Layton, J. F., & Simons, L. S. (1975). Naturalistic studies of aggressive behavior: Aggressive stimuli, victim visibility, and horn honking. *Journal of Personality and Social Psychology, 31,* 1098–1107.

Turner, F. J. (1920). *The frontier in American history.* New York: Henry Holt.

Turner, J. C. (1985). Social categorization and the self-concept: A social cognitive theory of group behavior. In E. J. Lawler (Ed.), *Advances in group processes* (Vol. 2, pp. 77–122). Greenwich, CT: JAI Press.

Turner, J. C. (1987). *Rediscovering the social group: A self-categorization theory.* Oxford, England: Basil Blackwell.

Turner, M. E., Pratkanis, A. R., & Struckman, C. K. (2007). Groupthink as social identity maintenance. In A. R. Pratkanis (Ed.), *The science of social influence: Advances and future progress* (pp. 223–246). New York: Psychology Press.

Turnley, W. H., & Bolino, M. C. (2001). Achieving desired images while avoiding undesired images: Exploring the role of self-monitoring in impression management. *Journal of Applied Psychology, 86,* 351–360.

Tuten, T. L., & Bosnjak, M. (2002). Need to evaluate and the big-five factor model. In S. P. Shohov (Ed.), *Advances in psychology research* (Vol. 15, pp. 111–120). Hauppauge, NY: Nova Science.

Tversky, A., & Kahneman, D. (1973). Availability: A heuristic for judging frequency and probability. *Cognitive Psychology, 5,* 207–232.

Tversky, A., & Kahneman, D. (1974). Judgment under uncertainty: Heuristics and biases. *Science, 185,* 1124–1131.

Twenge, J. M. (1997). Changes in masculine and feminine traits over time: A meta-analysis. *Sex Roles, 36,* 305–325.

Twenge, J. M., & Campbell, W. K. (2001). Age and birth cohort differences in self-esteem: A cross-temporal meta-analysis. *Personality and Social Psychology Review, 5,* 321–344.

Twenge, J. M., & Campbell, W. K. (2008). Increases in positive self-views among high school students: Birth cohort changes in anticipated performance, self-satisfaction, self-liking, and self-competence. *Psychological Science, 19,* 1082–1086.

Twenge, J. M., & Campbell, W. K. (2009). *The narcissism epidemic: Living in the age of enlightenment.* New York: Free Press.

Twenge, J. M., Catanese, K. R., & Baumeister, R. F. (2003). Social exclusion and the deconstructed state: Time perception, meaninglessness, lethargy, lack of emotion, and self-awareness. *Journal of Personality and Social Psychology, 85,* 409–423.

Tyler, J. M., & Feldman, R. S. (2005). Deflecting threat to one's image: Dissembling personal information as a self-presentation strategy. *Basic and Applied Social Psychology, 27,* 371–378.

Tyler, J. M., Feldman, R. S., & Reichert, A. (2006). The price of deceptive behavior: Disliking and lying to people who lie to us. *Journal of Experimental Social Psychology, 42,* 69–77.

Tyler, T. R. (1997). The psychology of legitimacy: A relational perspective on voluntary deference to authorities. *Personality and Social Psychology Review, 1,* 323–345.

Tyler, T. R., & Jost, J. T. (2007). Psychology and the law: Reconciling normative and descriptive accounts of social justice and system legitimacy. In A. W. Kruglanski & E. T. Higgins (Eds.), *Social psychology: Handbook of basic principles* (2nd ed.). New York: Guilford.

U.S. Bureau of the Census. (1998). *Statistical abstract of the United States* (118th ed.). Washington, DC: U.S. Government Printing Office.

U.S. Department of Commerce. (2002). *A nation online: How Americans are expanding their use of the Internet.* Washington, DC: U.S. Government Printing Office.

Uehara, E. S. (1995). Reciprocity reconsidered: Goulder's "moral norm of reciprocity" and social support. *Journal of Social and Personal Relationships, 12,* 483–502.

Uhlmann, E., & Swanson, J. (2004). Exposure to violent video games increases automatic aggressiveness. *Journal of Adolescence, 27,* 41–52.

Uleman, J. S. (1999). Spontaneous versus intentional inferences in impression formation. In S. Chaiken & Y. Trope (Eds.), *Dual-process theories in social psychology* (pp. 141–160). New York: Guilford.

Ullah, A. A. K. M. (2011). HIV/AIDS-Related stigma and discrimination: A study of health care providers in Bangladesh. *Journal of International Association of Physicians in AIDS Care, 10,* 97–104.

Underwood, M. K., & Rosen, L. H. (2009). Gender, peer relations, and challenges for girlfriends and boyfriends coming together in adolescence. *Psychology of Women Quarterly, 33,* 16–20.

Unger, L. S. (1996). The potential for using humor in global advertising. *Humor: International Journal of Humor Research, 9,* 143–168.

Unger, L. S., & Thumuluri, L. K. (1997). Trait empathy and continuous helping: The case of voluntarism. *Journal of Social Behavior and Personality, 12,* 785–800.

Unger, R. K. (2002). Them and us: Hidden ideologies—Differences in degree or kind? *Analyses of Social Issues and Public Policy, 2,* 43–52.

Unger, R. (2011). SPSSI leaders: Collective biography and the dilemma of value-laden action and value-neutral research. *Journal of Social Issues, 67,* 73–91.

United Nations. (1991). Special topic: International migration studies. In *United Nations demographic year book.* New York: United Nations.

Ursu, S., Stenger, V. A., Shear, M. K., Jones, M. R., & Carter, C. S. (2003). Overactive action monitoring in obsessive-compulsive disorder: Evidence from functional magnetic resonance imaging. *Psychological Science, 14,* 347–353.

Uziel, L. (2007). Individual differences in the social facilitation effect: A review and meta-analysis. *Journal of Research in Personality, 41,* 579–601.

Väänänen, A., Buunk, B. P., Kivimäki, M., Pentti, J., & Vahtera, J. (2005). When it is better to give than to receive: Long-term health effects of perceived reciprocity in support exchange. *Journal of Personality and Social Psychology, 89,* 176–193.

Vaillancourt, T. (2005). Indirect aggression among humans: Social construct or evolutionary adaptation? In R. E. Tremblay, W. W. Hartup,

& J. Archer (Eds.), *Developmental origins of aggression* (pp. 158–177). New York: Guilford Press.

Vala, J., Lima, M. L., & Caetano, A. (1996). Mapping European social psychology: Co-word analysis of the communications at the 10th general meeting of the EAESP. *European Journal of Social Psychology, 26,* 845–850.

Valenzano, D. R., Mennucci, A., Tartarelli, G., & Cellerino, A. (2006). Shape analysis of female facial attractiveness. *Vision Research, 46,* 1282–1291.

Valkenburg, P. M., & Peter, J. (2007). Preadolescents' and adolescents' online communication and their closeness to friends. *Developmental Psychology, 43,* 267–277.

van Baaren, R. B., Fockenberg, D. A., Holland, R. W., Janssen, L., & van Knippenberg, A. (2006). The moody chameleon: The effect of mood on non-conscious mimicry. *Social Cognition, 24,* 426–437.

van Baaren, R. B., Holland, R. W., Kawakami, K., & van Knippenberg, A. (2004). Mimicry and prosocial behavior. *Psychological Science, 15,* 71–74.

van Baaren, R. B., Holland, R. W., Steenaert, B., & van Knippenberg, A. (2003a). Mimicry for money: Behavioral consequences of imitation. *Journal of Experimental Social Psychology, 39,* 393–398.

van Baaren, R. B., Maddux, W. W., Chartrand, T. L., de Bouter, C., & van Knippenberg, A. (2003b). It takes two to mimic: Behavioral consequences of self-construals. *Journal of Personality and Social Psychology, 84,* 1093–1102.

Van Bavel, J. J., Packer, D. J., & Cunningham, W. A. (2008). The neural substrates of in-group Bias: A functional magnetic resonance imaging investigation. *Psychological Science, 19,* 1130–1138.

van de Kragt, A. J. C., Dawes, R. M., Orbell, J. M., Braver, S. R., & Wilson, L. A. (1986). Doing well and doing good as ways of resolving social dilemmas. In H. A. M. Wilke, D. M. Messick, & C. G. Rutte (Eds.), *Experimental social dilemmas* (pp. 177–204). Frankfurt: Verlag Peter Lang.

vanDellen, M. R., Bradfield, E. K., & Hoyle, R. H. (2010a). Self-regulation of state self-esteem following threat: Moderation by trait self-esteem. In R. H. Hoyle (Ed.), *Handbook of personality and self-regulation* (pp. 430–473). Malden, MA: Blackwell.

vanDellen, M. R., Campbell, W. K., Hoyle, R. H., & Bradfield, E. K. (2010b). Compensating, resisting, and breaking: A meta-analytic examination of reactions to self-esteem threat. *Personality and Social Psychology Review. 15,* 51–74.

Vandello, J. A., & Cohen, D. (1999). Patterns of individualism and collectivism across the United States. *Journal of Personality and Social Psychology, 77,* 279–292.

Vandello, J. A., & Cohen, D. (2004). When believing is seeing: Sustaining norms of violence in cultures of honor. In M. Schaller & C. S. Crandall (Eds.), *The psychological foundations of culture* (pp. 281–304). Mahwah, NJ: Erlbaum.

Vandello, J. A., Cohen, D., & Ransom, S. (2008). U.S. Southern and Northern differences in perceptions of norms about aggression: Mechanisms for the perpetuation of a culture of honor. *Journal of Cross-Cultural Psychology, 39,* 162–177.

Vandello, J. A., Ransom, S., Hettinger, V. E., & Askew, K. (2009). Men's misperceptions about the acceptability and attractiveness of aggression. *Journal of Experimental Social Psychology, 45,* 1209–1219.

van de Rijt, A., & Macy, M. W. (2006). Power and dependence in intimate exchange. *Social Forces, 84,* 1455–1470.

van den Bos, W., van Dijk, E., Westenberg, M., Rombouts, S. A. R. B., & Crone, E. A. (2011). Changing brains, changing perspectives: The neurocognitive development of reciprocity.

Psychological Science, 22, 60–70.

VanderDrift, L. E., Lehmiller, J. J., & Kelly, J. R. (2010). Commitment in friends with benefits relationships: Implications for relational and safe-sex outcomes. *Personal Relationships.*

Van der Zee, K., Oldersma, F., Buunk, B. P., & Bos, D. (1998). Social comparison preferences among cancer patients as related to neuroticism and social comparison orientation. *Journal of Personality and Social Psychology, 75,* 801–810.

Van Goozen, S. H. M. (2005). Hormones and the developmental origins of aggression. In R. E. Tremblay, W. W. Hartup, & J. Archer (Eds.), *Developmental origins of aggression* (pp. 281–306). New York: Guilford Press.

Vanhaudenhuyse, A., Demertzi, A., Schabus, M., Noirhomme, Q., Bredart, S., Boly, M., Phillips, C., Soddu, A., Luxen, A., Moonen, G., & Laureys, S. (2011). Two distinct neuronal networks mediate the awareness of environment and of self. *Journal of Cognitive Neuroscience, 23,* 570–578.

Van Hiel, A., Vanneste, S., & De Cremer, D. (2008). Why did they claim too much? The role of causal attributions in explaining level of cooperation in commons and anticommons dilemmas. *Journal of Applied Social Psychology, 38,* 173–197.

van Honk, J., & Schutter, D. J. L. G. (2007). Testosterone reduces conscious detection of signals serving social correction. *Psychological Science, 18,* 663–667.

Van Hooff, M. H., Voorhorst, F. J., Kapteln, M. B., Hirasing, R. A., Koppenaal C., Schoemaker J. (2000). Insulin, androgen, and gonadotropin concentration, body mass index, and waist-to hip ratio in the first years after menarche in girls with regular menstrual cycle, irregular menstrual cycles, or oligomenorrhea. *Journal of Clinical Endocrinology and Metabolism, 85,* 1394–1400.

Vanhoomissen, T., & Overwalle, F. V. (2010). Me or not me as source of ingroup favoritism and outgroup derogation: A connectionist perspective. *Social Cognition, 28,* 84–110.

Van Lange, P. A. M. (1999). The pursuit of joint outcomes and equality in outcomes: An integrative model of social value orientation. *Journal of Personality and Social Psychology, 77,* 337–349.

Van Lange, P. A. M., Otten, W., De Bruin, E. M. N., & Joireman, J. A. (1997). Development of prosocial, individualistic, and competitive orientations: Theory and preliminary evidence. *Journal of Personality and Social Psychology, 73,* 733–746.

Van Overwalle, R., Drenth, T., & Marsman, G. (1999). Spontaneous trait inferences: Are they linked to the actor or to the action? *Personality and Social Psychology Bulletin, 25,* 450–462.

Van Overwalle, R., & Labiouse, C. (2004). A recurrent connectionist model of person impression formation. *Personality and Social Psychology Review, 8,* 28–61.

van Staden, W., & Coetzee, K. (2010). Conceptual relations between loneliness and culture. *Current Opinion in Psychiatry, 23,* 524–529.

Van Vugt, M., & De Cremer, D. (1999). Leadership in social dilemmas: The effects of group identification on collective actions to provide public goods. *Journal of Personality and Social Psychology, 76,* 587–599.

Van Vugt, M., & Hart, C. M. (2004). Social identity as social glue: The origins of group loyalty. *Journal of Experimental Social Psychology, 86,* 585–598.

Van Zalk, N., Van Zalk, M., Kerr, M., & Stattin, H. (2011). Social anxiety as a basis for friendship selection and socialization in adolescents' social networks. *Journal of Personality, 79,* 499–526.

Vandereycken, W. (1994). Emergence of bulimia nervosa as a separate diagnostic entity: Review of the literature from 1960 to 1979.

International Journal of Eating Disorders, 16, 105–116.

Vangelisti, A. L., Knapp, M. L., & Daly, J. A. (1990). Conversational narcissism. *Communication Monographs, 57,* 251–274.

Varma, A., Toh, S. M., & Pichler, S. (2006). Ingratiation in job applications: Impact on selection decisions. *Journal of Managerial Psychology, 21,* 200–210.

Vartanian, L. R., & Hopkinson, M. M. (2010). Social connectedness, conformity, and internalization of societal standards of attractiveness. *Body Image, 7,* 86–89.

Vassar, M. J., & Kizer, K. W. (1996). Hospitalizations for firearm-related injuries: A population-based study of 9,562 patients. *Journal of the American Medical Association, 275,* 1734–1739.

Vaughn, B. E., & Langlois, J. H. (1983). Physical attractiveness as a correlate of peer status and social competence in preschool children. *Developmental Psychology, 19,* 561–567.

Veltkamp, M., Custers, R., & Aarts, H. (2011). Motivating consumer behavior by subliminal conditioning in the absence of basic needs: Striking even while the iron is cold. *Journal of Consumer Psychology, 21,* 49–56.

Verkuyten, M., Drabbles, M., & van den Nieuwenhuijzen, K. (1999). Self-categorization and emotional reactions to ethnic minorities. *European Journal of Social Psychology, 29,* 605–619.

Verkuyten, M., & Hagendoorn, L. (1998). Prejudice and self-categorization: The variable role of authoritarianism and in-group stereotypes. *Personality and Social Psychology Bulletin, 24,* 99–110.

Verkuyten, M., & Yildiz, A. A. (2007). National (dis)identification and ethnic and religious identity: A study among Turkish-Dutch Muslims. *Personality and Social Psychology Bulletin, 33,* 1448–1462.

Verplanken, B., & Orbell, S. (2003). Reflections on past behavior: A self-report index of habit strength. *Journal of Applied Social Psychology, 33,* 1313–1330.

Vicary, A. M., & Fraley, R. C. (2007). Choose your own adventure: Attachment dynamics in a simulated relationship. *Personality and Social Psychology Bulletin, 33,* 1279–1291.

Victoroff, J., Quota, S., Adelman, J. R., Celinska, B., Stern, N., Wilcox, R., & Sapolsky, R. M. (2011). Support for religio-political aggression among teenaged boys in Gaza: Part II: Neuroendocrinological findings. *Aggressive Behavior, 37,* 121–132.

Viki, G. T., Abrams, D., & Hutchison, P. (2003). The "true" romantic: Benevolent sexism and paternalistic chivalry. *Sex Roles, 49,* 533–537.

Vince, G. (April 19, 2006). Watching the brain "switch off" self-awareness. *NewScientist.com news service, http://www.newscientist.com/article.ns?id=dn9019*

Vingilis, E., Wade, T. J., & Adlaf, E. (1998). What factors predict student self-rated physical health? *Journal of Adolescence, 21,* 83–97.

Visser, P. S., & Krosnick, J. A. (1998). The development of attitude strength over the life cycle: Surge and decline. *Journal of Personality and Social Psychology, 75,* 1389–1410.

Visser, P. S., Krosnick, J. A., & Simmons, J. P (2003). Distinguishing the cognitive and behavioral consequences of attitude importance and certainty: A new approach to testing the common-factor hypothesis. *Journal of Experimental Social Psychology, 39,* 118–141.

Vitaro, F., & Brendgen, M. (2005). Proactive and reactive aggression: A developmental perspective. In R. E. Tremblay, W. W. Hartup, & J. Archer (Eds.), *Developmental origins of aggression* (pp. 178–201). New York: Guilford Press.

Vohs, K. D., Baumeister, R. F., & Ciarocco, N. J. (2005). Self-regulation and self-presentation: Regulatory resource depletion impairs impression

management and effortful self-presentation depletes regulatory resources. *Journal of Personality and Social Psychology, 88,* 632–657.

Von, J. M., Kilpatrick, D. G., Burgess, A. W., & Hartman, C. R. (1991). Rape and sexual assault. In M. L. Rosenberg & M. A. Fenley (Eds.), *Violence in America: A public health approach* (pp. 95–122). New York: Oxford University Press.

von Hippel, C., Issa, M., Ma, R., & Stokes, A. (2011). Stereotype threat: Antecedents and consequences for working women. *European Journal of Social Psychology, 41,* 151–161.

von Hippel, W., Brener, L., & von Hippel, C. (2008). Implicit prejudice toward injecting drug users predicts intentions to change jobs among drug and alcohol nurses. *Psychological Science, 19,* 7–11.

von Hippel, W., Hawkins, C., & Schooler, J. W. (2001). Stereotype distinctiveness: How counterstereotypic behavior shapes the self-concept. *Journal of Personality and Social Psychology, 81,* 193–205.

Vonofakou, C., Hewstone, M., & Voci, A. (2007). Contact with out-group friends as a predictor of meta-attitudinal strength and accessibility of attitudes toward gay men. *Journal of Personality and Social Psychology, 92,* 804–820.

Vorauer, J. D., & Kumhyr, S. M. (2001). Is this about you or me? Self- versus other-directed judgments and feelings in response to intergroup interaction. *Personality and Social Psychology Bulletin, 27,* 706–719.

Vrij, A. (2000). *Detecting lies and deceit: The psychology of lying and the implications for professional practice.* Chichester, UK: Wiley.

Vrij, A., Edward, K., & Bull, R. (2001). Stereotypical verbal and nonverbal responses while deceiving others. *Personality and Social Psychology Bulletin, 27,* 899–909.

Wagner, J. A. (1995). Studies of individualism-collectivism: Effects on cooperation in groups. *Academy of Management Review, 38,* 152–172.

Wakslak, C., Jost, J.T., Tyler, T.R., & Chen, E. (2007). Moral outrage mediates the dampening effect of system justification on support for redistributive social policies. *Psychological Science, 18,* 267–274.

Wall, J. A. Jr., Beriker, N., & Wu, S. (2010). Turkish community mediation. *Journal of Applied Social Psychology, 40,* 2019–2042.

Waller, D., Loomis, J. M., Gollege, R. G., Beall, A. C. (2002). Place learning in humans: The role of distance and direction information. *Spatial Cognition and Computation, 2,* 333–354.

Walsh, R. (2011). Helping or hurting: are adolescent intervention programs minimizing racial inequality?. *Education and Urban Society, 43,* 370–395.

Walster [Hatfield], E., Walster, G. W., & Traupmann, J. (1978). Equity and premarital sex. *Journal of Personality, 36,* 82–92.

Walumbwa, F. O., Lawler, J. J., & Avolio, B. J. (2007). Leadership, individual differences, and work-related attitudes: A cross-culture investigation. *Applied Psychology: An International Review, 56,* 212–230.

Wang, Q. (2006). Culture and the development of self-knowledge. *Current Directions in Psychological Science, 15,* 182–187.

Wang, S. S., Brownell, K. D., & Wadden, T. A. (2004). The influence of the stigma of obesity on overweight individuals. *International Journal of Obesity, 28,* 1333–1337.

Wänke, M., Bless, H., & Biller, B. (1996). Subjective experience versus content of information in the construction of attitude judgments. *Personality and Social Psychology Bulletin, 22,* 1105–1113.

Wänke, M., Bless, H., & Igou, E. R. (2001). Next to a star: Paling, shining, or both? Turning interexemplar contrast into interexemplar assimilation. *Personality and Social Psychology Bulletin, 27,* 14–29.

Wann, D. L., & Branscombe, N. R. (1990). Die-hard and fair-weather fans: Effects of identification on

BIRGing and CORFing tendencies. *Journal of Sport and Social Issues, 14,* 103–117.

Wann, D. L., Haynes, G., McLean, B., & Pullen, P. (2003). Sport team identification and willingness to consider anonymous acts of hostile aggression. *Aggressive Behavior, 29,* 406–413.

Wanshaffe, K. R. (2002). Social facilitation in young toddlers. *Psychological Reports, 90,* 349–350.

Ward, A., Lyubomirsky, S., Sousa, L., & Nolen-Hoeksema, S. (2003). Can't quite commit: Rumination and uncertainty. *Personality and Social Psychology Bulletin, 29,* 96–107.

Wartella, E., & Reeves, B. (1985). Historical trends in research on children and the media: 1900–1960. *Journal of Communication, 35,* 118–133.

Wason, P. C. (1960). On the failure to eliminate hypotheses in a conceptual task. *Quarterly Journal of Experimental Psychology, 12,* 129–140.

Waters, E., Merrick, S., Treboux, D., Crowell, J., & Albersheim, L. (2000). Attachment security in infancy and early adulthood: A twenty-year longitudinal study. *Child Development, 71,* 684–689.

Watson, D., Suls, J., & Haig, J. (2002). Global self-esteem in relation to structural models of personality and affectivity. *Journal of Personality and Social Psychology, 83,* 185–197.

Weary, G., Vaughhn, L. A., Stewart, B. D., & Edwards, J. A. (2006). Adjusting for the correspondence bias: Effects of causal uncertainty, cognitive busyness, and causal strength of situational information. *Journal of Experimental Social Psychology, 42,* 87–94.,

Webb, T. T., Looby, E. J., & Fults-McMurtery, R. (2004). African American men's perceptions of body figure attractiveness: An acculturation study. *Journal of Black Studies, 34,* 370–385.

Webb, T. L., & Sheeran, P. (2003). Can implementation intentions help to overcome ego-depletion? *Journal of Experimental Social Psychology, 39,* 279–286.

Weber, E. U., Bockenholt, U., Hilton, D. J., & Wallace, B. (1993). Determinants of diagnostic hypothesis generation: Effects of information, base rates, and experience. *Journal of Experimental Psychology: Learning, Memory, and Cognition, 19,* 1151–1164.

Wechsler, H., & Kuo, M. (2000). College students define heavy episodic drinking and estimate its prevalence: Results of a national survey. *Journal of American College Health, 49,* 59–64.

Wechsler, H., Lee, J. E., Kuo, M., Seibring, M., Nelson, T. F., & Lee, H. (2002). Trends in college binge drinking during a period of increased prevention efforts: Findings from 4 Harvard School of Public Health college alcohol study surveys, 1993–2001. *Journal of American College Health, 50,* 203–217.

Wedell, D. H., Parducci, A., & Geiselman, R. E. (1987). A formal analysis of ratings of physical attractiveness: Successive contrast and simultaneous association. *Journal of Experimental Social Psychology, 23,* 230–249.

Weeks, J. W., Heimberg, R. G., & Heuer, R. (2011). Exploring the role of behavior submissiveness in social anxiety. *Journal of Social and clinical Psychology, 30,* 217–249.

Wegener, D. T., Clark, J. K., & Petty, R. E. (2006). Not all stereotyping is created equal: Differential consequences of thoughtful versus nonthoughtful stereotyping. *Journal of Personality and Social Psychology, 90,* 42–59.

Wegener, D. T., & Petty, R. E. (1994). Mood management across affective states: The hedonic contingency hypothesis. *Journal of Personality and Social Psychology, 66,* 1034–1048.

Wegener, D. T., & Petty, R. E. (1995). Effects of mood on persuasion processes: Enhancing, reducing, and biasing scrutiny of attitude-relevant information. In L. L. Martin & A. Tesser (Eds.), *Striving and feeling: Interactions between goals and affect.* Hillsdale, NJ: Erlbaum.

Wegener, D. T., Petty, R. E., Dove, N. L., & Fabrigar, L. R. (2004). Multiple routes to resisting attitude change. In E. S. Knowles & J. A. Linn (Eds.), *Resistance and persuasion* (pp. 13–38). Mahwah NJ: Erlbaum.

Wegener, D. T., Petty, R. E., & Smith, S. M. (1995). Positive mood can increase or decrease message scrutiny: The hedonic contingency view of mood and message processing. *Journal of Personality and Social Psychology, 69,* 5–15.

Wegge, J. R., Van Dick, R., Fischer, G. K., Wecking, C., & Moltzen, K. (2006). Work motivation, organizational identification, and well-being in call centre work. *Work & Stress, 20,* 60–83.

Wegner, D. M. (1994). Ironic processes of mental control. *Psychological Review, 101,* 34–52.

Wegner, D. M., Erber, R., & Raymond, P. (1991). Transactive memory in close relationships. *Journal of Personality and Social Psychology, 61,* 923–929.

Wegner, D. M., & Schneider, D. J. (2003). The white bear story. *Psychological Inquiry, 14,* 326–329.

Weick, K. E. (1985). Systematic observational methods. In G. Lindzey & E. Aronson (Eds.), *The handbook of social psychology* (3rd ed., Vol. 1, pp. 567–634). New York: Random House.

Weigel, D. J., Bennett, K. K., & Ballard-Reisch, D. S. (2006). Influence strategies in marriage: Self and partner links between equity, strategy use, and marital satisfaction and commitment. *Journal of Family Communication, 6,* 77–95.

Weigel, R. H., Vernon, D. T., & Tognacci, L. S. (1974). Increasing attitude-behavior correspondence by broadening the scope of the behavioral measure. *Journal of Personality and Social Psychology, 30,* 724–728.

Weinberger, M. G., & Campbell, L. (1991). The use and impact of humor in radio advertising. *Journal of Advertising Research, 30,* 44–52.

Weiner, B. (1980). A cognitive (attribution)-emotion-action model of motivated behavior: An analysis of judgments of help-giving. *Journal of Personality and Social Psychology, 39,* 186–200.

Weiner, B. (1982). The emotional consequences of causal attributions. In M. S. Clark & S. T. Fiske (Eds.), *Affect and cognition: The 17th annual Carnegie symposium on cognition* (pp. 185–210). Hillsdale, NJ: Erlbaum.

Weiner, B. (1986). *An attribution theory of motivation and emotion.* New York: Springer-Verlag.

Weiner, B., Frieze, I., Kukla, A., Reed, L., Rest, S., & Rosenbaum, R. M. (1972). Perceiving the causes of success and failure. In E. E. Jones, D. E. Kanouse, H. H. Kelley, R. E. Nisbett, S. Valins, & B. Weiner (Eds.), *Attribution: Perceiving the causes of behavior* (pp. 95–120). Morristown, NJ: General Learning Press.

Weiner, B., Osborne, D., & Rudolph, U. (2011). An attributional analysis of reactions to poverty: The political ideology of the giver and the perceived morality of the receiver. *Personality and Social Psychology Review, 15.* 199–213.

Weinfield, N. S., Sroufe, L. A., & Egeland, B. (2000). Attachment from infancy to early adulthood in a high-risk sample: Continuity, discontinuity, and their correlates. *Child Development, 71,* 695–702.

Weinshenker, N., & Siegel, A. (2002). Bimodal classification of aggression: Affective defense and predatory attack. *Aggression and Violent Behavior, 7,* 237–250.

Weisbuch, M., Mackie, D. M., & Garcia-Marques, T. (2003). Prior source exposure and persuasion: Further evidence for misattributional processes. *Personality and Social Psychology Bulletin, 29,* 691–700.

Weiss, B., & Feldman, R. S. (2006). Looking good and lying to do it: Deception as an impression management strategy in job interviews. *Journal of Applied Social Psychology, 36,* 1070–1086.

Weissman, D. H., Giesbrecht, B., Song, A. W., Mangun, G. R., & Woldorff, M. G. (2003). Conflict monitoring in the human anterior cingulated cortex during selective attention to global and local object features. *NeuroImage, 19,* 1361–1368.

Wells, G. L., & Petty, R. E. (1980). The effects of overt head movements on persuasion: Compatibility and incompatibility of responses. *Basic and Applied Social Psychology, 1,* 219–230.

Welzel, C., Inglehart, R., & Klingemann, H. D. (2003). The theory of human development: A cross-cultural analysis. *European Journal of Political Research, 42,* 341–379.

Wenzlaff, R. M., & Luxton, D. D. (2003). The role of thought suppression in depressive rumination. *Cognitive Therapy and Research, 27,* 293–308.

Werking, K. (1997). *We're just good friends.* New York: Guilford.

Werth, L., & Foerster, J. (2002). Implicit person theories influence memory judgments: The circumstances under which metacognitive knowledge is used. *European Journal of Social Psychology, 32,* 353–362.

Werth, L., Markel, P., & Forster, J. (2006). The role of subjective theories for leadership evaluation. *European Journal of Work and Organizational Psychology, 15,* 102–127.

West, J. O. (1988). *Mexican-American folklore.* Little Rock, AK: August House.

West, S. G., & Brown, T. J. (1975). Physical attractiveness, the severity of the emergency and helping: A field experiment and interpersonal simulation. *Journal of Experimental Social Psychology, 11,* 531–538.

Westen, D. (2007). *The political brain.* New York: Public Affairs.

Wheeler, L., & Kim, Y. (1997). What is beautiful is culturally good: The physical attractiveness stereotype has different content in collectivist cultures. *Personality and Social Psychology Bulletin, 23,* 795–800.

Wheeler, S. C., Morrison, K. R., DeMarree, K. G., & Petty, R. E. (2008). Does self-consciousness increase or decrease priming effects? It depends. *Journal of Experimental Social Psychology, 44,* 882–889.

Whitchurch, E. R., Wilson, T. D., & Gilbert, D. T. (2011). "He loves me, he loves me not…": Uncertainty can increase romantic attraction. *Psychological Science, 22,* 172–175.

White, G. L. (1980). Inducing jealousy: A power perspective. *Personality and Social Psychology Bulletin, 6,* 222–227.

White, G. L., Fishbein, S., & Rutstein, J. (1981). Passionate love: The misattribution of arousal. *Journal of Personality and Social Psychology, 41,* 56–62.

White, M., & LeVine, R. A. (1986). What is an *Ii ko* (good child)? In H. Stevenson, H. Azuma, & K Hakuta (Eds.), *Child development and education in Japan* (pp. 55–62). New York: Freeman.

Whiteside, U., Chen, E., Neighbors, C., Hunter, D., Lo, T., & Larimer, M. (2007). Difficulties regulating emotions: Do binge eaters have fewer strategies to modulate and tolerate negative affect? *Eating Behaviors, 8,* 162–169.

Wyland, C. L., & Forgas, J. P. (2010). Here's looking at you kid: Mood effects on processing eye gaze as a heuristic cue. *Social Cognition, 28,* 122–145.

Whiting, B. B., & Edwards, C. P. (1988). *Children of different worlds: The foundation of social behavior.* Cambridge, MA: Harvard University Press.

Whitty, M. T., & Carr, A. N. (2006). *Cyberspace romance: The psychology of online relationships.* New York: Palgrave Macmillan.

Wicherts, J. M., Dolan, C. V., & Hessen, D. J. (2005). Stereotype threat and group differences in test performance: A question of measurement invariance. *Journal of Personality and Social Psychology, 89,* 696–716.

Wicker, A. W. (1969). Attitude versus actions: The relationship of verbal and overt behavioral responses to attitude objects. *Journal of Social Issues, 25,* 41–78.

Widom, C. S. (1989). Does violence beget violence? A critical examination of the literature. *Psychological Bulletin, 106,* 3–28.

Wigboldus, D. H. J., Dijksterhuis, A., & Knippenberg, A. V. (2003). When stereotypes get in the way: Stereotypes obstruct stereotype-inconsistent trait inferences. *Journal of Personality and*

Social Psychology, 84, 470–484.

Wiggins, J. A., Dill, F., & Schwartz, R. D. (1965). On "status-liability." *Sociometry, 28,* 197–209.

Wilke, H. A. M. (1996). Status congruence in small groups. In E. Witte & J. Davis (Eds.), *Understanding group behavior: Vol. 2. Small group processes and interpersonal relations* (pp. 67–91). Hillsdale, NJ: Erlbaum.

Wilkowski, B. M., & Robinson, M. D. (2007). Keeping one's cool: Trait anger, hostile, thoughts, and the recruitment of limited capacity control. *Personality and Social Psychology Bulletin, 33,* 1201–1213.

Willan, V. J., & Pollard, P. (2003). Likelihood of acquaintance rape as a function of males' sexual expectations, disappointment, and adherence to rape-conducive attitudes. *Journal of Social and Personal Relationships, 20,* 637–661.

Williams, D. G. (1985). Gender, masculinity-femininity, and emotional intimacy in same-sex friendship. *Sex Roles, 12,* 587–600.

Wong, R. Y. M., & Hong, Y. Y. (2005). Dynamic influences on cooperation in the prisoner's dilemma. *Psychological Science, 16,* 429–434.

Williams, K. D. (2007). Ostracism. *Annual Review of Psychology, 58,* 425–452.

Williams, K. D., Cheung, D. K. T., & Choi, W. (2000). Cyberostracism: Effects of being ignored over the Internet. *Journal of Personality and Social Psychology, 79,* 748–762.

Williams, K. D., Harkins, S., & Latané, B. (1981). Identifiability as a deterrent to social loafing: Two cheering experiments. *Journal of Personality and Social Psychology, 40,* 303–311.

Williams, K. D., Jackson, J. M., & Karau, S. J. (1995). Collective hedonism: A social loafing analysis of social dilemmas. In D. A. Schroeder (Ed.), *Social dilemmas: Perspectives on individuals and groups* (pp. 116–141). Westport, CT: Praeger.

Williams, K. D., & Sommer, K. L. (1997). Social ostracism by coworkers: Does rejection lead to loafing or compensation? *Personality and Social Psychology Bulletin, 23,* 693–706.

Williams, K. D., & Zadro, L. (2001). Ostracism: On being ignored, excluded, and rejected. In M. Leary (Ed.), *Interpersonal rejection* (pp. 21–53). New York: Oxford Press.

Williams, W. L. (1992). The relationship between male-male friendship and male-female marriage. In P. M. Nardi (Ed.), *Men's friendships* (pp. 186–200). Newbury Park, CA: Sage.

Willingham, D. T., & Dunn, E. W. (2003). What neuroimaging and brain localization can do, cannot do, and should not do for social psychology. *Journal of Personality and Social Psychology, 85,* 662–671.

Wilson, B. J., Donnerstein, E., Linz, D., Kunkel, D., Potter, J., Smith, S. L., Blumenthal, E., & Gray, T. (1998). Content analysis of entertainment television: The importance of context. In J. T. Hamilton (Ed.), *Television violence and public policy* (pp. 13–53). Ann Arbor, MI: University of Michigan Press.

Wilson, D. W. (1981). Is helping a laughing matter? *Psychology, 18,* 6–9.

Wilson, E. O. (1996). *In search of nature.* Washington, DC: Island Press.

Wilson, M. S., & Liu, J. H. (2003). Social dominance orientation and gender: The moderating role of gender identity. *British Journal of Social Psychology, 42,* 187–198.

Wilson, R. S., Krueger, K. R., Arnold, S. E., Schneider, J. A., Kelly, J. F., Barnes, L. L., et al. (2007). Loneliness and risk of Alzheimer disease. *Archives of General Psychiatry, 64,* 234–240.

Wilson, T. D.(2002). *Strangers to ourselves: Discovering the adaptive unconscious.* Cambridge, MA: Harvard University Press.

Wilson, T. D., Aronson, E., & Carlsmith, K. (2010). The art of laboratory experimentation. In S. T. Fiske, D. T. Gilbert, & G. Lindzey (Eds.). *Handbook of social psychology, Vol 1* (5th ed.) (pp. 51–81). Hoboken, NJ: John Wiley.

Wilson, T. D., Lindsey, S., & Schooler, T. Y. (2000). A model of dual attitudes. *Psychological Review, 107,* 101–126.

Winchatz, M. R. (2010). Participant observation and the nonnative ethnographer: Implications of positioning on discourse-centered fieldwork. *Field Methods, 22,* 340–356.

Windschitl, P. D., & Wells, G. L. (1997). Behavioral consensus information affects people's inferences about population traits. *Personality and Social Psychology Bulletin, 23,* 148–156.

Wiseman, M. C., & Moradi, B. (2010). Body image and eating disorder symptoms in sexual minority men: A test and extension of the objectification theory. *Journal of Counseling Psychology, 57,* 154–166.

Wittenbaum, G. M. (1998). Information sampling in decision-making groups: The impact of members' task-relevant status. *Small Group Research, 29,* 57–84.

Wittenbaum, G. M., & Stasser, G. (1996). Management of information in small groups. In J. L. Nye & A. M. Brower (Eds.), *What's social about social cognition? Research on socially shared cognition in small groups* (pp. 3–28). Thousand Oaks, CA: Sage.

Wittenbaum, G. M., Hubbell, A. P., & Zuckerman, C. (1999). Mutual enhancement: Toward an understanding of the collective preference for shared information. *Journal of Personality and Social Psychology, 77,* 967–978.

Witvliet, C. V. O., Ludwig, T. E., & Vander Laan, K. L. (2001). Granting forgiveness or harboring grudges: Implications for emotion, physiology, and health. *Psychological Science, 12,* 117–123.

Wolf, L. E. (2010). The research ethics committee is not the enemy: Oversight of community-based participatory research. *Journal of Empirical Research on Human Research Ethics, 5,* 77–86.

Woll, S. (2002). *Everyday thinking: Memory, reasoning, and judgment in the real world.* Mahwah, NJ: Lawrence Erlbaum.

Wolsko, C., Park, B., & Judd, C. M. (2006). Considering the tower of Babel: Correlations of assimilation and multiculturalism among ethnic minority and majority groups in the United States. *Social Justice Research, 19,* 277–306.

Wood, J. V. (1996). What is social comparison and how should we study it? *Personality and Social Psychology Bulletin, 22,* 520–537.

Wood, J. V., Heimpel, S. A., & Michela, J. L. (2003). Savoring versus dampening: Self-esteem differences in regulating positive affect. *Journal of Personality and Social Psychology, 85,* 566–580.

Wood, J. V., Heimpel, S. A., Newby-Clark, I. R., & Ross, M. (2005). Snatching defeat from the jaws of victory: Self-esteem differences in the experience and anticipation of success. *Journal of Personality and Social Psychology, 89,* 764–780.

Wood, W., & Eagly, A. H. (2010). Gender. In S. T. Fiske, D. T. Gilbert, & G. Lindzey (Eds.). *Handbook of social psychology, Vol 1* (5th ed.) (pp. 629–667). Hoboken, NJ: John Wiley.

Wood, W., Lundgren, S., Ouellette, J. A., Busceme, S., & Blackstone, T. (1994). Minority influence: A meta-analytic review of social influence processes. *Psychological Bulletin, 115,* 323–345.

Wood, W., Wong, F. Y., & Chachere, J. G. (1991). Effects of media violence on viewers' aggression in unconstrained social interaction. *Psychological Bulletin, 109,* 371–383.

Wood, W. L., Rhodes, N., & Biek, M. (1995). Working knowledge and attitude strength: An information-processing analysis. In R. E. Petty & J. A. Krosnick (Eds.), *Attitude strength: Antecedents and consequences* (pp. 283–313). Mahwah, NJ: Erlbaum.

Worchel, S., & Andreoli, V. M. (1978). Facilitation of social interaction through deindividuation of the target. *Journal of Personality and Social Psychology, 36,* 549–556.

Worringham, C. F., & Messick, D. M. (1983). Social facilitation of running: An unobtrusive study. *Journal of Social Psychology, 121,* 23–29.

Wosinska, W., Cialdini, R. B., Barrett, D. W., &

Reykowski, J. (Eds.). (2001). *The practice of social influence in multiple cultures.* Mahwah, NJ: Erlbaum.

Wosinska, W., Dabul, A. J., Whetstone-Dion, R., & Cialdini, R. B. (1996). Self-presentational responses to success in the organization: The costs and benefits of modesty. *Basic and Applied Social Psychology, 18,* 229–242.

Wright, P. H., & Scanlon, M. B. (1991). Gender role orientations and friendship: Some attenuation, but gender differences abound. *Sex Roles, 24,* 551–566.

Wright, S. C., Aron, A., McLaughlin-Volpe, T., & Ropp, S. A. (1997). The extended contact effect: Knowledge of cross-group friendships and prejudice. *Journal of Personality and Social Psychology, 73,* 73–90.

Wright, S. C., Taylor, D. M., & Moghaddam, F. M. (1990). Responding to membership in a disadvantaged group: From acceptance to collective protest. *Journal of Personality and Social Psychology, 58,* 994–1003.

Wrosch, C., Scheier, M. F., Miller, G. E., Schulz, R., & Carver, C. S. (2003). Adaptive self-regulation of unattainable goals: Goal disengagement, goal reengagement, and subjective well-being. *Personality and Social Psychology Bulletin, 29,* 1494–1508.

Wu, S., & Keysar, B. (2007). The effect of culture on perspective. *Psychological Science, 18,* 600–606.

Wyer, N. A. (2007). Motivational influences on compliance with and consequences of instructions to suppress stereotypes. *Journal of Experimental Social Psychology, 43,* 417–424.

Wyland, C. L., & Forgas, J. (2007). On bad mood and white bears: The effects of mood state on ability to suppress unwanted thoughts. *Cognition and Emotion,* 1–12.

Yamagishi, T. (1986). The provision of a sanctioning system as a public good. *Journal of Personality and Social Psychology, 51,* 110–116.

Yamagishi, T. (1988). Seriousness of social dilemmas and the provision of a sanctioning system. *Social Psychology Quarterly, 51,* 32–42.

Yamagishi, T., Tanida, S., Mashima, R., Shimona, E., & Kanazawa, S. (2003). You can judge a book by its cover: Evidence that cheaters may look different from cooperators. *Evolution and Human Behavior, 24,* 290–301.

Yamawaki, N., Ostenson, J., & Brown, C. R. (2009). The functions of gender role traditionality, ambivalent sexism, injury and frequency of assault on domestic violence perception: A study between Japanese and American college students. *Violence Against Women, 15,* 1126–1142.

Yancey, M. P., & Hummer, R. A. (2003). Fraternities and rape on campus. In M. Silberman (Ed.), *Violence and society: A reader* (pp. 215–222). Upper Saddle River, NJ: Prentice-Hall.

Yip, T. (2005). Sources of situational variation in ethnic identity and psychological well-being: A palm pilot study of Chinese American students. *Personality and Social Psychology Bulletin, 31,* 1603–1616.

Yoo, H. C., Steger, M. F., & Lee, R. M. (2010). Validation of the subtle and blatant racism scale for Asian American college students. *Cultural Diversity and Ethnic Minority Psychology, 16,* 323–334.

Yoon, J. M. D., & Tennie, C. (2010). Contagious yawning: A reflection of empathy, mimicry, or contagion? *Animal Behaviour, 79,* e1–e3.

Yost, J. H., & Weary, G. (1996). Depression and the correspondent inference bias: Evidence for more effortful cognitive processing. *Personality and Social Psychology Bulletin, 22,* 192–200.

Yost, M. R., & Zurbriggen, E. L. (2006). Gender differences in the enactment of sociosexuality: An examination of implicit social motives, sexual fantasies, coercive sexual attitudes, and aggressive sexual behavior. *Journal of Sex Research, 43,* 163–173.

Yousif, Y., & Korte, C. (1995). Urbanization, culture, and helpfulness: Cross-cultural studies in England and the Sudan. *Journal of Cross-Cultural Psychology, 26,* 474–489.

Yu, D. L., & Seligman, M. E. P. (2002). Preventing depressive symptoms in Chinese children. *Prevention & Treatment, 5.*

Yun, S., Cox, J., & Sims, H. P. Jr. (2006). The forgotten follower: A contingency model of leadership and follower self-leadership. *Journal of Managerial Psychology, 21,* 374–388.

Yzerbyt, V. Y., Rocher, S., & Schadron, G. (1996). Stereotypes as explanations: A subjective essentialistic view of group perception. In R. Spears, P. J. Oakes, N. Ellemers, & S. A. Haslam (Eds.), *The social psychology of stereotyping and group life.* Cambridge: Blackwell.

Zadro, L., Williams, K. D., & Richardson, R. (2004). How low can you go? Ostracism by a computer is sufficient to lower self-reported levels of belonging, control, self-esteem, and meaningful existence. *Journal of Experimental Social Psychology, 40,* 560–567.

Zahn-Wexler, C., Robinson, J., & Emde, R. N. (1992). The development of empathy in twins. *Developmental Psychology, 28,* 1038–1047.

Zajonc, R. B. (1965). Social facilitation. *Science, 149,* 269–274.

Zajonc, R. B. (1968). Attitudinal effects of mere exposure. *Journal of Personality and Social Psychology Monograph Supplement, 9* (2, Part 2), 1–27.

Zajonc, R. B. (1984). On the primacy of affect. *American Psychologist, 39,* 117–123.

Zajonc, R. B. (1993). Brain temperature and subjective emotional experience. In M. Lewis & J. M. Haviland (Eds.), *Handbook of emotions* (pp. 209–220). New York: Guilford.

Zajonc, R. B., Murphy, S. T., & Inglehart, M. (1989). Feeling and facial efference: Implications of the vascular theory of emotion. *Psychological Review, 96,* 395–416.

Zaki, J. & Ochsner, K. (2011). You, me, and my brain: Self and other representations in social cognitive neuroscience. In A., Todorov, S. T. Fiske, & D. A. Prentice (Eds.). *Social neuroscience: Toward understanding the underpinnings of the social mind* (pp. 14–39). New York: Oxford University Press.

Zanna, M. P., Kiesler, C. A., & Pilkonis, P. A. (1970). Positive and negative attitudinal affect established by classical conditioning. *Journal of Personality and Social Psychology, 14,* 321–328.

Zanna, M. P., & Rempel, J. K. (1988). Attitudes: A new look at an old concept. In D. Bar-Tal & A. W. Kruglanski (Eds.), *The social psychology of knowledge* (pp. 315–334). New York: Cambridge University Press.

Zanot, E. J., Pincus, J. D., & Lamp, E. J. (1983). Public perceptions of subliminal advertising. *Journal of Advertising, 12,* 37–45.

Zaragoza, M. S., & Mitchell, K. J. (1996). Repeated exposure to suggestion and the creation of false memories. *Psychological Science, 7,* 294–300.

Zárate, M. A., Garcia, B., Garza, A. A., & Hitlan, R. T. (2004). Cultural threat and perceived realistic group conflict as dual predictors of prejudice. *Journal of Experimental Social Psychology, 40,* 99–105.

Zarbatany, L., Conley, R., & Pepper, S. (2007). Personality and gender differences in friendship needs and experiences in preadolescence and young adulthood. *International Journal of Behavioral Development, 28,* 299–310.

Zdaniuk, B., & Levine, J. M. (2001). Group loyalty: Impact of members' identification and contributions. *Journal of Experimental Social Psychology, 37,* 502–509.

Zebrowitz, L. A. (1997). *Reading faces.* Boulder, CO: Westview.

Zebrowitz, L. A., & Montepare, J. M. (1992). Impressions of babyfaced individuals across the life span. *Developmental Psychology, 28,* 1143–1152.

Zebrowitz, L. A., Tenenbaum, D. R., & Goldstein, L. H. (1991). The impact of job applicants' facial maturity, sex, and academic achievement on hiring recommendations. *Journal of Applied Social Psychology, 21,* 525–548.

Zebrowitz, L. A., Voinescu, L., & Collins, M. A. (1996). "Wide-eyed" and "crooked-faced": Determinants of perceived and real honesty across the life span. *Personality and Social Psychology Bulletin, 22,* 1258–1269.

Zhang, F., & Parmley, M. (2011). What your best friend sees that I don't see: Comparing female close friends and casual acquaintances on the perception of emotional facial expressions of varying intensities. *Personality and Social Psychology Bulletin, 37,* 28–39.

Zhang, X., Yeung, D. Y., Fung, H. H., & Lang, F. R. (2011). Changes in peripheral social partners and loneliness over time: The moderating role of interdependence. *Psychology and Aging.*

Zhou, M. (2002). Between *us* and *them* in Chinese: Use of *lai* (come) and *qu* (go) in the construction of social identities. In A. Duszak (Ed.), *Us and others: Social identities across languages, discourses and cultures* (pp. 52–67). Amsterdam: John Benjamins Publishing.

Zhu, D., Xie, X., & Gan, Y. (2010). Information source and valence: How information credibility influences earthquake risk perception. *Journal of Environmental Psychology.*

Zillmann, D. (1983). Arousal and aggression. In R. G. Geen & E. I. Donnerstein (Eds.), *Aggression: Theoretical and empirical reviews: Vol. 1. Theoretical and methodological issues* (pp. 75–101). New York: Academic Press.

Zillmann, D. (1984). *Connections between sex and aggression.* Hillsdale, NJ: Erlbaum.

Zillmann, D. (1994). Cognition-excitation interdependencies in the escalation of anger and angry aggression. In M. Potegal & J. F. Knutson (Eds.), *The dynamics of aggression: Biological and social processes in dyads and groups* (pp. 45–71). Hillsdale, NJ: Erlbaum.

Zillmann, D., Katcher, A. H., & Milavsky, B. (1972). Excitation transfer from physical exercise to subsequent aggressive behavior. *Journal of Experimental Social Psychology, 8,* 247–259.

Zimbardo, P. (1969). The human choice: Individuation, reason, and order versus deindividuation, impulse, and chaos. In W. J. Arnold & D. Levine (Eds.), *Nebraska Symposium on Motivation, Vol. 17.* Lincoln: University of Nebraska Press.

Zimbardo, P. G (producer). (1972). *The Stanford prison experiment.* Slide/tape presentation.

Zimbardo, P. (2007). *The Lucifer effect: Understanding how good people turn evil.* New York: Random House.

Zimmerman, F., & Sieverding, M. (2011). Young adults' images of abstaining and drinking: Prototype dimensions, correlates and assessment methods. *Journal of Health Psychology, 16,* 410–420.

Zitek, E. M., & Hebl, M. R. (2007). The role of social norm clarity in the influenced expression of prejudice over time. *Journal of Experimental Social Psychology, 43,* 867–876.

Zou, X., Tam, K., Morris, M. W., Lee, S., Lau, I. Y., & Chiu, C. (2009). Culture as common sense: Perceived consensus versus personal beliefs as mechanisms of cultural influence. *Journal of Personality and Social Psychology, 97,* 579–597.

Zuckerman, E. W., & Jost, J. T. (2001). What makes you think you're so popular? Self-evaluation maintenance and the subjective side of the "friendship paradox." *Social Psychology Quarterly, 64,* 207–223.

Zuckerman, M., DePaulo, B. M., & Rosenthal, R. (1981). Verbal and nonverbal communication of deception. In L. Berkowitz (Ed.), *Advances in experimental social psychology* (Vol. 14, pp. 1–59). New York: Academic Press.

Zuckerman, M., & Gerbasi, K. C. (1977). Belief in a just world and trust. *Journal of Research in Personality, 11,* 306–317.

Zuckerman, M., & O'Loughlin, R. E. (2006). Self-enhancement by social comparison: A prospective analysis. *Personality and Social Psychology Bulletin, 32,* 751–760.

Zurcher, L. A. (1977). *The mutable self.* Beverly Hills, CA: Sage.

Zuwerink, J. R., Devine, P. G., Monteith, M. J., & Cook, D. A. (1996). Prejudice toward Blacks: With and without compunction? *Basic and Applied Social Psychology, 18,* 131–150.

Text and Line Art Credits

CHAPTER 2:

Exercise 2.1, p. 42: Morris Rosenburg, © 1979. Used by permission of The Morris Rosenburg Foundation, The University of Maryland.

CHAPTER 3:

Exercise 3.1, pp. 72–73: Adapted, p. 524, from "Public and Private Self-Consciousnesss: Assessment and Theory." Fenigstein, Allan; Scheier, Michael F.; Buss, Arnold H. *Journal of Consulting and Clinical Psychology*, Vol 43(4), Aug 1975, 522–527. Copyright ©1975 by The American Psychological Association. Adapted with permission.
Exercise 3.2, p. 81: Adapted from W. S. Hartley (1970). *Manual for the Twenty Statements Problem*. Used with permission by Resource Development Institute (formerly Greater Kansas City Mental Health Foundation.)
Exercise 3.3, p. 94: Adapted, p. 531, from "Selfmonitoring of expressive behavior." Snyder, Mark. *Journal of Personality and Social Psychology*, Vol 30(4), Oct 1974, 526–537. Copyright © 1974 by The American Psychological Association. Adapted with permission.

CHAPTER 4:

Figure 4.6, p. 144: From L. Ross, T. M. Amabile, & J. L. Steinmetz, "Social Roles, Social Control, and Biases in Social Perception Process," *Journal of Personality and Social Psychology* 35, 485–494. Copyright © 1977 by the American Psychological Association.
Figure 4.7, p. 145: From M. D. Storms, "Videotape and the Attribution Process: Reversing Actors' and Observers' Points of View," *Journal of Personality and Social Psychology*, 27 165–175. Copyright © 1973 by the American Psychological Association.

CHAPTER 5:

Exercise 5.1, p. 160: Adapted, p. 176, from Jarvis, W. B. G., and Petty R. E.

(1996). "The Need to Evaluate," *Journal of Personality and Social Psychology*, 70(1), 172–194. Copyright © 1996 by the American Psycho logical Association. Adapted with permission.
Figure 5.5, p. 175: Adapted from Cialdini, R. B., Trost, M. R., & Newsom, J. T. (1995). Preference for consistency: The development of a valid measure and the discovery of surprising behavioral implications. *Journal of Personality and Social Psychology*, 69(2), 318–328. Copyright © 1995 by the American Psychological Association.
Figure 5.6, p. 176: E. Aronson & J. Mills, "The Effect of Severity of Initiation on Liking for a Group," *Journal of Abnormal and Social Psychology*, 59, 177–181, Copyright © 1959.
Exercise 5.2, p. 179: Adapted, p. 328, from Cialdini, R. B., Trost, M. R., and Newsom, J. T. "Preference for Consistency: The Development of a Valid Measure and the Discovery of Surprising Behaviorial Implications," *Journal of Personality and Social Psychology*, 69, 318–328. Copyright © 1995 by The American Psychological Association. Adapted with permission.
Exercise 5.3, p. 187: Adapted, pp. 120–121, " The Need for Cognition." Cacioppo, John T.; Petty, Richard E. *Journal of Personality and Social Psychology*, Vol. 42(1), Jan 1982, 116–131. Copyright ©1982 by the American Psychological Association. Adapted with permission.
Figure 5.12, p. 197: From R. E. Petty, Z. L. Tormala, & D. D. Rucker, "Resisting Persuasion by Counterarguing: An Attitude Strength Perspective," *Social Psychology: The Yin and Yang of Scientific Progress*, pp. 37–51. Copyright © 2004 by the American Psychological Association.
Figure 5.13, p. 201: Reprinted from E. J. Strahan, S. J. Spencer, & M. P. Zanna, "Subliminal Priming and Persuasion: Striking While the Iron is Hot," *Journal of Experimental Social Psychology*, 38, 556–568. Copyright 2002 with permission from Elservier.

CHAPTER 6:

Figure 6.1, p. 210: Reprinted from D. L. Hamilton, R. K. Clifford, "Illusory Correlation in Interpersonal Judgments," *Journal of Experimental Social Psychology*, 12, 392–407. Copyright © 1976 with permission from Elsevier.
Table 6.2, p. 220: "The Protestant Ethic" from H. L. Mirels and J. B. Garrett, *Journal of Consulting and Clinical Psychology*, 36, 40–44. American Psychological Association. Adapted with permission by H. L. Mirels. "HumanitarianismEgalitarianism" from I. Katz, R. G. Hass, "Racial Ambivalence and American Value Conflict: Correlation and Prime Studies of Dual Cognitive Structures," *Journal of Personality and Social Psychology*, 55, 893–905. Copyright © 1988 by the American Psychological Association. Adapted with permission.
Figure 6.6, p. 235: From C. W. Perdue, J. R. Dovidio, M. B. Gurtman, & R. B. Taylor, "Us and Them: Social Categorization and the Process of Intergroup Bias," *Journal of Personality and Social Psychology*, 59, 475–486. Copyright © 1990 by the American Psychological Association.
Exercise 6.1, pp. 225–226: "Inventory: Differentiating Hostile and Benevolent Sexism" *Journal of Personality and Social Psychology*, 70, 491–512. Copyright © 1995 by Peter Glick and Susan T. Fiske. Used by permission.
Song lyrics, p. 211: *Merry Little Minuet*. Words and Music by Sheldon Harnick. Copyright © 1958 (Renewed) Sheldon Mayer Harnick. Mayerling Productions Ltd. Owner of publishing and allied rights (administered by R&H Music); Alley Music Corp.; and Trio Music Company. International Copyright Secured. All Rights Reserved. Used by permission.

CHAPTER 7:

p. 293: Adapted excerpt of experiment—150 volts (pp. 73–74) from *Obedience to Authority: An Experimental View*.

CHAPTER 8:

Figure 8.2, p. 314: Reprinted form Moreland, Levine, "Socialization in Small Groups: Temporal Changes in Individual Group Relations," *Advances in Experimental Social Psychology*, Vol. 15, L. Berkowitz, ed. Copyright © 1982 with permission from Elsevier.

Figure 8.5, p. 323: From E. Diener, S. C. Fraser, A. L. Beaman, & R. T. Kelem, "Effects on Deindividuation Variables on Stealing Among Halloween TrickorTreaters," *Journal of Personality and Social Psychology*, 33, 178–183. Copyright © 1976 by the American Psychological Association.

CHAPTER 9:

Exercise 9.1, pp. 354–355: From S. E. Cross, P. L. Bacon, & M. L. Morris, "The RelationalInterdependent Self-construal and Relationships," *Journal of Personality and Social Psychology*, 78, 791–808. Copyright © 2000 by the American Psychological Association. Adapted with permission.

Figure 9.1, p. 357: Adapted from Leon Festinger, Stanley Schachter, and Kurt Back, *Social Pressures in Informal Groups: A Study of a Housing Community*. Copyright © 1950 by Leon Festinger, Stanley Schachter, and Kurt Back. All rights reserved. Used with the permission of Stanford University Press, www.sup.org.

Figure 9.7, p. 375: From D. Byrne & D. Nelson, "Attraction as a Linear Function of Proportion of Positive Reinforcements," *Journal of Personality and Social Psychology*, 1, 659–663. Copyright © 1965 by the American Psychological Association.

CHAPTER 10:

Figure 10.1, p. 391: From A. Aron, E. N. Aron, & D. Smollan, "Inclusion of Other in the Self Scale and the Structure of Interpersonal Closeness," *Journal of Personality and Social Psychology*, 63, 597. Copyright © 1992 by the American Psychological Association. Adapted with permission.

Exercise 10.1, p. 398: Adapted, p. 244 from Bartholomew, K., & Horowitz, L. M. (1991). "Attachment Styles Among Young Adults: A Test of a FourCategory Model." *Journal of Personality and Social Psychology*, 61(2), 226–244. Copyright © 1991 by the American Psychological Association. Adapted with permission.

Exercise 10.3, p. 416: From "Measuring Passionate Love in Intimate Relationships" by E. Hatfield and S. Sprecher in *Journal of Adolescence*, 9, 383–410. Copyright © 1986 with permission from Elsevier.

Figure 10.3, p. 401: From I. Altman, D. A. Taylor, "Social Penetration Theory: The Development of InterPersonal Relationships." Used by permission of the author.

Figure 10.4, p. 405: With kind permission from Springer Science+ Business Media, *Journal of Nonverbal Behavior*, 13, 1989, pp. 83–96, Valerian J. Derlega et al.

Text, pp. 389: From *Love You Forever*, Robert Munsch, © 1990. Used by permission of the author.

CHAPTER 11:

Figure 11.1, p. 445: Reprinted from K. Bjorkqvist, K. Osterman, & A. Kaukiainen, "The Development of Direct and Indirect Aggressive Strategies in Males and Females," in *Of Mice and Women: Aspects of Female Aggression* edited by K. Bjorkqvist and P. Niemele. Copyright © 1992 with permission from Elsevier.

Figure 11.3, p. 454: From S. K. Mallick, B. R. McCandless, "A Study of Catharsis of Aggression," *Journal of Personality and Social Psychology*, 4, 591–596. Copyright © 1966 by the American Psychological Association.

Figure 11.5, p. 463: From M. Rosekrans & W. Hartup, "Imitative Influences of Consistent and Inconsistent Response Sequences to a Model on Aggressive Behavior in Children," *Journal of Personality and Social Psychology*, 7, 429–434. Copyright © 1967 by the American Psychological Association.

Figure 11.6, p. 464: Based on Figure 3 from "Psychological Processes Promoting the Relation Between Exposure to Media Violence and Aggressive Behavior by the Viewer," *Journal of Social Issues*, 42, 125–140, Copyright © 1986. Used by permission of Blackwell Publishing. 436–446. Copyright © 2002 with permission from Elsevier.

Exercise 11.1, pp. 471–472: Adapted p. 223, from "Cultural Myths and Supports for Rape." Burt, Martha R. *Journal of Personality and Social Psychology*, Vol 38(2), Feb 1980, 217–230. Copyright © 1980 by the American Psychological Association. Adapted with permission.

CHAPTER 12:

Exercise 12.1, pp. 487–488: Adapted, pp. 1011–1012, from Romer, D., Gruder, C. L., & Lizzaro, T. (1986). "A PersonSituation Approach to Altruistic Behavior." *Journal of Personality and Social Psychology*, 51(5), 1001–1012. Copyright © 1986 by the American Psychological Association. Adapted with permission.

Exercise 12.2, pp. 495: From Mark Davis, "Interpersonal Reactivity Index" in *Empathy: A Social Psychological Approach*, copyright © 1996. Reprinted by permission of Westview Press, a member of Perseus Books Group.

Figure 12.4, p. 504: From B. Latané & J. M. Darley, "Group Inhibition of Bystander Intervention in Emergencies," *Journal of Personality and Social Psychology*, 10, 215–221. Copyright © 1968 by the American Psychological Association.

Figure 12.5, p. 507: From J. M. Darley & B. Latané, "Bystander Intervention in Emergencies: Diffusion of Responsibility," *Journal of Personality and Social Psychology*, 8, 377–383. Copyright © 1968 by the American Psychological Association.

PhOTo CreDiTs

CHAPTER 1:

iStockphoto, p. 1; iStockphoto, p. 2; AP Wide World Photos, p. 4; iStockphotos, p. 7; Wikipedia, p. 10; Syracuse University Archives p. 11; Wikipedia, p. 13; iStockphoto, p. 16; iStockphoto, p. 17; iStockphoto, p. 19; Dreamstime, p. 20; Wikipedia, p. 22; iStockphoto, p. 29; Shutterstock, p. 29; Wikipedia, p. 30; Wikipedia, p. 30; iStockphoto, p. 31

CHAPTER 2:

iStockphoto, p. 33; iStockphoto, p. 34; iStockphoto, p. 35; iStockphoto, p. 39; iStockphoto, p. 45; iStockphoto, p. 47; iStockphoto, p. 49; Wikipedia, p. 56; AP Wide World Photos, p. 59; iStockphoto, p. 61; Shutterstock, p. 63; iStockphoto, p. 63

CHAPTER 3:

iStockphoto, p. 65; iStockphoto, p. 66; iStockphoto, p. 67; Dreamstime p. 69; iStockphoto, p. 76; iStockphoto, p. 82; AP Wide World Photos, p. 83; iStockphoto, p. 85; iStockphoto, p.85; iStockphoto, p. 86; iStockphoto, p. 89; iStockphoto, p. 96; iStockphoto, p. 99; Shutterstock, p. 105; iStockphoto, p. 105

CHAPTER 4:

iStockphoto, p. 107; Professor Franzoi p. 108; iStockphoto, p. 110; iStockphoto, p. 112; iStockphoto, p. 116; iStockphoto, p. 122; iStockphoto, p. 125; iStockphoto, p. 129; iStockphoto, p. 130; iStockphoto, p. 131; AP Wide World Photos, p. 132; iStockphoto, p. 133; Shutterstock, p. 153; iStockphoto, p. 153

CHAPTER 5:

AP Wide World Photos, p.155; iStockphoto, p. 156; iStockphotos, p. 157; iStockphotos, p. 161; Professor Franzoi p. 169; Wikipedia, p. 171; iStockphotos, p. 172; iStockphotos, p. 180; AP Wide World Photos, p.185; iStockphotos, p. 190; Professor Franzoi, p. 192; iStockphotos, p. 192; Shutterstock, p. 202; iStockphotos, p. 202

CHAPTER 6:

AP Wide World Photos, p. 203; Wikipedia, p. 204; Wikipedia, p. 206; Wikipedia, p. 206; iStockphoto, p. 206; iStockphoto, p. 211; iStockphoto, p. 216; AP Wide World Photos, p. 217; iStockphoto, p. 223; iStockphoto, p. 223; Wikipedia, p. 224; iStockphoto, p. 224; iStockphoto, p. 228; Wesleyan University, p. 234; Wikipedia, p. 238; AP Wide World Photos, p. 238; Wikipedia, p. 240; iStockphoto, p. 244; iStockphoto, p. 251; Shutterstock, p. 255; iStockphoto, p. 255

CHAPTER 7:

AP Wide World Photos, p. 257; AP Wide World Photos, p. 258; Wikipedia, p. 259; Wikipedia, p. 260; iStockphoto, p. 267; AP Wide World Photos, p. 268; Solomon Asch Center for Study of Ethnopolitical Conflict, p. 270; iStockphoto, p. 276; iStockphoto, p. 276; Wikipedia, p. 278; AP Wide World Photos, p. 280; iStockphoto, p. 282; Milgram, p. 288; iStockphoto, p. 292; iStockphoto, p. 292; Shutterstock, p. 303; iStockphoto, p. 303

CHAPTER 8:

AP Wide World Photos, p. 305; AP Wide World Photos, p. 306; BrokenSphere/Wikimedia Commons, p. 308; iStockphoto, p. 311; iStockphoto, p. 313; iStockphoto, p. 322; iStockphoto, p. 326; Wikipedia, p. 331; Wikipedia, p. 331; iStockphoto, p. 335; Shutterstock, p. 346; iStockphoto, p. 346

CHAPTER 9:

AP Wide World Photos, p. 347; iStockphoto, p. 348; Wikipedia, p. 349; iStockphoto, p. 352; iStockphoto, p. 353; iStockphoto, p. 356; AP Wide World Photos, p. 357; iStockphoto, p. 360; AP Wide World Photos, p. 365; iStockphoto, p. 369; iStockphoto, p. 378; iStockphoto, p. 380; Shutterstock, p. 386; iStockphoto, p. 386

CHAPTER 10:

iStockphoto, p. 387; AP Wide World Photos, p. 388; iStockphoto, p. 392; iStockphoto, p. 394; iStockphoto, p. 400; iStockphoto, p. 402; AP Wide World Photos, p. 408; iStockphoto, p. 411; iStockphoto, p. 413; Wikipedia, p. 417; Professor Franzoi, 417; iStockphoto, p. 421; iStockphoto, p. 422; iStockphoto, p. 424; iStockphoto, p. 429; iStockphoto, p. 432; iStockphoto, p. 433; Shutterstock, p. 438; iStockphoto, p. 438

CHAPTER 11:

iStockphoto, p. 439; AP Wide World Photos, p. 440; iStockphoto, p. 614; Dreamstime, p. 422; iStockphoto, p. 444; Wikipedia, p. 445; Wikipedia, p. 449; Wikipedia, p. 456; iStockphoto, p. 459; Albert Bandura, p. 462; iStockphoto, p. 465; AP Wide World Photos, p. 465; iStockphoto, p. 466; iStockphoto, p. 669; Shutterstock, p. 481; iStockphoto, p. 481

CHAPTER 12:

Wikipedia, p. 483; iStockphoto, p. 484; AP Wide World Photos, p. 485; Wikipedia, p. 489; Wikipedia, p. 492; iStockphoto, p. 494; iStockphoto, p. 502; iStockphoto, p. 508; iStockphoto, p. 509; Wikipedia, p. 516; iStockphoto, p. 517; iStockphoto, p. 519; Dreamstime, p. 522; Shutterstock, p. 524; iStockphoto, p. 524

Name Index

Subject InDEx ●●●●●●